Fifth Edition

CHILD DEVELOPMENT AND EDUCATION

TERESA M. MCDEVITT

University of Northern Colorado

JEANNE ELLIS ORMROD

University of Northern Colorado (Emerita)

PEARSON

Boston Columbus Indianapolis New York San Francisco Upper Saddle River
Amsterdam Cape Town Dubai London Madrid Milan Munich Paris Montreal Toronto
Delhi Mexico City São Paulo Sydney Hong Kong Seoul Singapore Taipei Tokyo

Vice President and Editorial Director: Jeffery W. Johnston
Vice President and Publisher: Kevin Davis
Executive Development Editor: Linda Ashe Bishop
Editorial Assistant: Lauren Carlson
Vice President, Director of Marketing: Margaret Waples
Marketing Manager: Joanna Sabella
Senior Managing Editor: Pamela Bennett
Senior Project Manager: Mary M. Irvin
Senior Operations Supervisor: Matt Ottenweller
Senior Art Director: Diane Lorenzo
Cover Designer: Candace Rowley
Photo Researcher: Lori Whitley
Permissions Specialist: Becky Savage
Cover Art: Drew Meyers/Corbis Images
Project Coordination: Norine Strang, S4Carlisle Publishing Services
Composition: S4Carlisle Publishing Services
Printer/Binder: Courier/Kendalville
Cover Printer: Lehigh-Phoenix Color Corp.
Text Font: ITC Garamond Std 10/12

Credits and acknowledgments for material borrowed from other sources and reproduced, with permission, in this textbook appear on appropriate page within text.

Every effort has been made to provide accurate and current Internet information in this book. However, the Internet and information posted on it are constantly changing, so it is inevitable that some of the Internet addresses listed in this textbook will change.

Library of Congress Cataloging-in-Publication Data
McDevitt, Teresa M.
  Child development and education / Teresa M. McDevitt, Jeanne Ellis Ormrod. —5th ed.
    p. cm.
Includes bibliographical references and index.
ISBN-13: 978-0-13-248620-0
ISBN-10: 0-13-248620-2
1. Child development. 2. Adolescent psychology. 3. Educational psychology. I. Ormrod, Jeanne Ellis. II. Title.
  LB1115.M263 2013
  305.231—dc23   2011038300

10 9 8 7 6 5 4 3 2 1

ISBN 10:   0-13-248620-2
ISBN 13: 978-0-13-248620-0

To our families,

CONNOR, ALEXANDER, and EUGENE

CHRISTINA, ALEX, JEFFREY, RICHARD, BRIAN,

and (the newest member!) OLIVIA

TERESA M. MCDEVITT (left) is a psychologist with specializations in child development and educational psychology. She received a Ph.D. and M.A. in child development from Stanford University's Psychological Studies in Education program, an Ed.S. in educational evaluation from Stanford University, and a B.A. in psychology from the University of California, Santa Cruz. Since 1985 she has served the University of Northern Colorado in a variety of capacities—in teaching courses in child and adolescent psychology, human development, educational psychology, program evaluation, and research methods; in advisement of graduate students; in administration and university governance; and in research and grant writing. Her research focuses on child development, families, and teacher education. She has published articles in such journals as *Child Development, Learning and Individual Differences, Child Study Journal, Merrill-Palmer Quarterly, Youth and Society,* and *Science Education,* among others. She has gained extensive practical experiences with children, including raising two children with her husband and working in several positions with children—as an early childhood teacher of toddlers and preschool children, an early childhood special education teacher, and a volunteer in school and community settings. Teresa enjoys spending time with her children and husband and, when she has the chance, traveling internationally with her family.

JEANNE ELLIS ORMROD (right) is an educational psychologist with specializations in learning, cognition, and child development. She received a Ph.D. and M.S. in educational psychology at The Pennsylvania State University and an A.B. in psychology from Brown University; she also earned licensure in school psychology through postdoctoral work at Temple University and the University of Colorado, Boulder. She has worked as a middle school geography teacher and school psychologist and has conducted research in cognitive development, memory, problem solving, spelling, and giftedness. She is currently Professor Emerita of Psychological Sciences at the University of Northern Colorado; the "Emerita" means that she has officially retired from the university. However, she can't imagine ever *really* retiring from a field she enjoys so much. She is the author or coauthor of several other Merrill/Pearson Education books, including *Educational Psychology: Developing Learners; Essentials of Educational Psychology; Human Learning; Case Studies: Applying Educational Psychology; Practical Research,* and, most recently, *Our Minds, Our Memories: Enhancing Thinking and Learning at All Ages.* Jeanne has three grown children and has recently welcomed her first grandchild, Olivia, to her family.

Preface

As psychologists and teacher educators, we have been teaching child and adolescent development for many years. A primary goal in our classes has been to help students translate developmental theories into practical implications for teaching youngsters with unique characteristics and needs. In past years, the child development textbooks available to our students were typically quite thorough in their descriptions of theory and research, but they generally offered few concrete suggestions for working with infants, children, and adolescents.

With this book, now in its fifth edition, we bridge the gap between theory and practice. We draw from innumerable theoretical concepts; research studies conducted around the world; and our own experiences as parents, teachers, psychologists, and researchers to identify strategies for promoting young people's physical, cognitive, and social-emotional growth. As in the previous editions, this book focuses on childhood and the adolescent years and draws implications that are primarily educational in focus.

As we wrote the fifth edition, we took to heart requests from readers that we elaborate on the amazing positive developmental outcomes that children achieve in diverse cultural environments and bioecological circumstances. You will see several new features and read about a great deal of cutting-edge research that describes the wonders of childhood. We also responded to suggestions that we expand on our commitment to scientifically based, practical guidance by including additional exercises in observing children, discerning individual needs, and providing developmentally appropriate education.

We addressed other suggestions as well. We had received feedback that students needed additional assistance with study skills. We added learning objectives at the beginning of the chapters to help students identify core principles. Learning activities on MyEducationLab are catalogued according to these learning objectives, providing students with another important tool for keeping track of their progress in acquiring basic concepts. Margin notes alert students to concepts addressed on some teaching tests and also focus students' attention on important material.

Several features of the book make it different from other textbooks about child and adolescent development. In particular, the book

- Continually relates abstract theories to educational practices in schools
- Not only describes but also *demonstrates* developmental phenomena
- Guides observations of children and adolescents
- Facilitates analysis of what children and adolescents say, do, and create
- Offers concrete strategies for effective teaching of, and working with, children and adolescents
- Fosters a thorough understanding of children's growth from infancy to late adolescence within the domains of physical, social-emotional, and cognitive development.

In the next few pages, we provide examples of how the book accomplishes these goals.

More so than any other text, *Child Development and Education* spells out the practical implications of developmental research and theory for those who teach and work with children and adolescents. Taking a look at the following features will show you how this text differs from and is more appropriate for educators than other child and adolescent development texts.

Development and Practice

In addition to discussing applications throughout the text itself, we provide *Development and Practice* features that offer concrete strategies for facilitating children's development. To help readers move from research to practice, each strategy is followed by examples of a professional implementing the technique in a classroom or other setting. This popular feature has been expanded in the fifth edition with additional examples that now specify the age period, allowing readers to quickly find applications for age levels of greatest interest. You will find examples of the *Development and Practice* feature on pages 166, 211, and 359 of this text.

DEVELOPMENT AND PRACTICE
Providing Appropriate Stimulation for Infants and Young Children

Give children some choice in their sensory experiences.

- A home child care provider offers a variety of simple toys for infants to explore and play with. She often places several items within reach, and she respects infants' occasional rejection and apparent dislike of certain items. (Infancy)
- A preschool teacher makes available a variety of sensory materials that children can observe and manipulate. The teacher includes an array of smelling jars with various scents (e.g., herbs, vanilla, and orange slices), sound boxes with small objects (e.g., rice, beans, and coarse salt), and a water table with funnels, containers, and other pouring toys. (Early Childhood)

Allow children periods of quiet and calm.

- A teacher in an infant child care center realizes that the center is often busy and noisy. Knowing that too much stimulation can be unsettling, he monitors the sights, sounds, textures, and smells that are present at any one time. He tries to tone down the environment a bit when introducing a new child to the center. (Infancy)
- A preschool teacher includes a brief rest time after snack to allow children to recharge their batteries. Children who want or need a nap can lie down on mats while non-nappers complete puzzles or participate in other quiet activities. (Early Childhood)

Avoid the "better baby" trap.

- A child care provider attends a workshop on brain development, where several presenters make a strong pitch for certain new products that are supposedly essential for intellectual growth. Fortunately, she knows enough about cognitive development to realize that children benefit equally from a wide variety of toys and that an intensive "sensory stimulation" approach is not in children's best interest. (Infancy)
- A toddler teacher designs his curriculum carefully, exposing children to a wide range of developmentally appropriate objects, including blocks, sensory materials, dolls, trucks, durable books, and coloring materials. When parents ask about his plans to "multiply the intelligence" of children, the teacher explains that he does not use flash cards or structured academic lessons with toddlers. Instead, he cultivates their intelligence through a carefully selected curriculum that fosters children's natural curiosity and nurtures their budding sense of self, language development, and knowledge of the world. (Infancy)

Recognize that temperamental and cultural differences partly determine the optimal amount of stimulation for each child.

- A teacher in a child care center has noticed that some of the toddlers in her group seem to respond to a good deal of sensory input by getting excited and animated, whereas others fuss, go to sleep, or in some other

OBSERVATION GUIDELINES
Assessing Cognitive Processing and Metacognition

CHARACTERISTIC	LOOK FOR	EXAMPLE	IMPLICATION
Intersubjectivity	• Reciprocal interaction with caregivers • Attempts to coordinate one's own actions toward an object with the actions of another person • Social referencing (i.e., responding to an object or event based on how an adult responds to it)	A teacher at a child care center is obviously frightened when a large dog appears just outside the fenced-in play yard, and she yells at the dog to go away. Fifteen-month-old Owen observes her reaction and begins to cry.	Regularly engage infants in affectionate and playful interactions (smiles, coos, etc.). Remember that your own actions and reactions toward objects and events will communicate messages about the value, appeal, and safety of those objects and events.
Attention	• Sustained attention to human beings and inanimate objects • Ability to stay on task for an age-appropriate period • On-task behavior when distracting stimuli are present	During after-lunch story time, a second-grade teacher has been reading Roald Dahl's Charlie and the Chocolate Factory. Most of the children are quiet and attentive the entire time, but Ben fidgets and squirms, and soon he finds a new form of entertainment: making silly faces at nearby classmates.	Monitor children's ability to pay attention in an age-appropriate fashion. If children have exceptional difficulty staying on task, minimize distractions, teach them strategies for focusing their attention more effectively, and give them opportunities to release pent-up energy appropriately.
Automatization of Basic Skills	• Retrieval of simple facts in a rapid, effortless fashion • Ability to use simple problem-solving strategies quickly and efficiently	Elena easily solves the problem 4/12 5 x36 because she realizes almost immediately that 4/12 is the same as 1/3.	Give children numerous opportunities to use and practice essential facts and skills; do so within the context of interesting and motivating activities.
Learning Strategies	• Use of rehearsal in the elementary grades • Use of more integrative strategies (e.g., organization, elaboration) in the secondary grades • Flexible use of strategies for different	Terri studies each new concept in her high school physics class by repeating the textbook definition aloud three or four times. Later she can barely remember the definitions she has studied, and she is unable to apply the	Show struggling learners that their difficulties may be due to ineffective strategies, and teach them strategies that can help them learn more successfully.

Observation Guidelines

To work productively with children and adolescents, one must first be able to draw appropriate inferences from their behavior. Knowledge of developmental concepts and principles provides an essential lens through which professionals must look if they are to understand children. One of the foundational goals of this text is to help educators observe developmental nuances in the infants, children, and adolescents with whom they work. To this end, throughout the book we include *Observation Guidelines* tables. As you can see on pages 101, 143, and 324, these tables offer specific characteristics to look for, present illustrative examples, and provide specific recommendations for practitioners.

Improving Your Observation Skills

Another tool for helping readers to assess the needs and abilities of children is a new feature titled *Improving Your Observation Skills*. By carefully inspecting photographs of children and the artifacts they have created, readers gain experience in analyzing children's facial expressions, body language, activities, and artifacts for underlying information about their needs and abilities. Readers also have the opportunity to compare their judgments with interpretations from the authors at the end of each chapter. You can find examples on pages 55 and 63, 102 and 108, and 345 and 367.

Improving Your Observation Skills

Sense of Community. These children are constructing original pieces of art with encouragement from their teacher. What specifically is the teacher doing to establish a productive sense of community in her classroom? Compare your response with the explanation at the end of the chapter.

Developmental Trends Tables

Six-year-olds often think and act differently than 11-year-olds do, and 11-year-olds can, in turn, be quite different from 16-year-olds. Most chapters have one or more *Developmental Trends* tables that highlight the developmental differences that readers are apt to observe in infancy (birth–2 years), early childhood (2–6 years), middle childhood (6–10 years), early adolescence (10–14 years), and late adolescence (14–18 years). In the Developmental Trends tables, the diversity of potential characteristics is highlighted, and implications for practice are offered. See pages 25–26, 170, and 302–303 for examples.

Preparing for Your Licensure Examination

Preparing for Your Licensure Examination

Your teaching test may ask you to recognize developmental changes in sustained and purposeful attention.

Many prospective teachers are required to demonstrate their knowledge of child development on teaching tests. To prepare for these tests, readers can focus on key theorists and concepts that are especially significant in the field of child development. As they read through the book, readers will be alerted with margin notes to specific concepts that they might encounter on the *Praxis II*™ and other licensure tests.

Applying Concepts in Child Development

A chapter-ending section called *Applying Concepts in Child Development* (see, for example, pages 32–34, 282–283, and 366–367) has been entirely revamped with this edition to sharpen students' ability to apply knowledge of child development to realistic scenarios. Included in this section are three features, beginning with an *Improving Your Observation Skills* exercise in which readers compare their own inspections of photographs and artifacts, using concepts from the chapter, with explanations from the authors. In the *Practicing for Your Licensure Examination* section, several types of questions help future teachers prepare for the *Praxis II*™ tests and other licensure exams. Readers examine a brief case study and then consider chapter concepts as they answer a constructed-response question and two multiple-choice questions. Finally, readers complete an *Improving Your Ability to Interpret Children's Artifacts and Reflections* feature that give readers practice in evaluating and interpreting children's work and statements. Not only does this feature provide readers with additional authentic illustrations of chapter content, but it also offers them an opportunity to apply their knowledge of child development in assessing children's creations.

APPLYING CONCEPTS IN CHILD DEVELOPMENT

The exercises in this section will help you build your ability to apply your knowledge of child development in your work with children.

Improving Your Observation Skills

On page 250, you examined maps of Loveland, Colorado, and were asked, *"How do the maps drawn by a first grader (top), fifth grader (middle), and seventh grader (bottom) reflect different levels of knowledge about their local community?"* The first grader's map includes only a few features of her town that she knows well (her house and school, nearby mountains) and distorts spatial relationships among the features. The third grader's map shows many features of his immediate neighborhood and their proximity to one another. The seventh grader's map encompasses numerous town landmarks and their relative locations on major streets. It also makes greater use of symbols—for instance, single lines for roads, squares for buildings, and distinctive letter Ms to indicate McDonald's restaurants. This collection of maps reflects age-related increases in detailed knowledge about the community and accuracy in representing connections among roads, buildings, and lakes (see Forbes, Ormrod, Bernardi, Taylor, & Jackson, 1999).

 On page 280, you examined 7-year-old Nathan's writing sample and were asked, *"What patterns of errors do you notice in Nathan's word spellings?"* With the exception of the L in the first line, Nathan correctly captured some of the sounds in the words he was trying to spell. He acknowledged the *d* in *drew*, the *s* in *this*, and the *b* and *t* in *bat*. But he omitted several other consonants, as well as all of the vowel sounds except for the initial *i*. We might suspect that Nathan has difficulty hearing all the distinct sounds in spoken words and matching them with the letters he sees in written words. Such difficulties are common in young elementary school students who have significant reading disabilities.[23]

the students to become "experts" on their topic in their region. There are a lot of requirements to this assignment. I'm collecting things as we go along because I think a project this long will be difficult for them to organize . . . ?

So we spent all week in the library. I collected a minimum of two pages of notes yesterday, which will be a small part of their grade. The one thing that surprised me in our work in the library was their lack of skills. They had such difficulty researching, finding the information they needed, deciding what was important, and organizing and taking notes. As they worked, I walked around helping and was shocked. The librarian had already gotten out all of the appropriate resources. Even after they had the books in front of them, most did not know what to do. For instance, if they were assigned "economy," most looked in the index for that particular word. If they didn't find it, they gave up on the book. After realizing this, I had to start the next day with a brief lesson on researching and cross-referencing. I explained how they could look up *commerce*, *imports*, *exports*, and how these would all help them. I was also shocked at how poor their note-taking skills were. I saw a few kids copying paragraphs word for word. Almost none of them understood that notes don't need to be in full sentences. So, it was a long week at the library.

Next week is devoted to group work and time to help them work on their rough drafts. With the difficulty they had researching, I can imagine the problems that will arise out of turning their notes into papers. (Journal entry courtesy of Jessica Jensen)

Constructed-Response Question

1. Initially, the intern realizes that her students will need some structure to complete the project successfully. In what ways do she and the librarian structure the assignment for the students?

Multiple-Choice Questions

2. How does the students' prior knowledge (or lack thereof) influence the effectiveness of their strategies?

More than any other text, *Child Development and Education* situates children in the contexts of their upbringing and articulates the implications of these experiences for educators. Through numerous illustrations of distinct family, cultural, and socioeconomic backgrounds, readers gain a practical understanding of adjustments that effectively meet the needs of individual children. To get a sense of how the book situates development, see the features below.

Bioecology of Child Development

Effective teachers and practitioners appreciate that a child's growth is embedded within the contexts in which he or she grows. New to this edition, the *Bioecology of Child Development* feature shows that the child's well-being is the outcome of dynamically interacting factors, including personal characteristics, health, unique collection of genes, and individual initiative as well as the social settings in which the child spends time, including the family, peer group, school, culture, and institutions of society. Within every chapter, one or more illustrations of a breadth of bioecological factors are identified as influences on a particular aspect of children's growth. You can see examples of the bioecological notation on pages 133, 304, and 348.

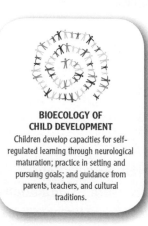

BIOECOLOGY OF CHILD DEVELOPMENT

Children develop capacities for self-regulated learning through neurological maturation; practice in setting and pursuing goals; and guidance from parents, teachers, and cultural traditions.

DEVELOPMENT IN CULTURE
Memory

Across a wide range of environmental circumstances, children develop some similar memory characteristics, including an increasingly efficient working memory capacity and an expanding array of schemas and scripts about people and events. Co-existing with these common trends are cultural variations in memory.

Obviously, cultural experiences affect the content of children's memory. At the kitchen table, on city streets, and in the classroom, children form specific memories about how institutions in their culture operate and how they themselves are expected to behave. Distinct methods of re-membering also are acquired during cultural exchanges. Repeated exposure to some information is sufficient to form memories when meaningful patterns are present in the material. Thus children easily learn and remember songs, stories, dances, woodcarvings, games, and configurations of objects in familiar environments (Gaunt, 2006; Kearins, 1981; Rogoff, 2003). In industrialized societies, children are generally taught to use memory strategies for learning and retrieving abstract information (Bjorklund, Dukes, & Brown, 2009).

Cultural experiences also influence children's autobiographical memory. As children remi-nisce with their parents and other adults, they learn customs related to telling life stories (Fivush, 2009). Children who are regularly asked to talk about personal experiences seem to retain espe-cially early images of their lives. The Māori, an indigenous people of New Zealand, speak in great detail with children about such significant early experiences as the occasion of their birth (E. Reese, Hayne, & MacDonald, 2008). Of course, children cannot recall their own births be-cause of memory limitations in infancy. Nevertheless, discussions about the past seem to help Māori children remember important occasions at later ages, and the earliest memories of Māori adults date back to 2 1/2 years on average (E. Reese et al., 2008). Other

Mother: You want to do whatever you want to do. I see." (dialogue is from Q. Wang, 2006, p. 186)

With each question and comment, the mother scaffolds an inter-pretation of the events—the boy hit, scratched, and yelled because he did not want to be with his parents at the fair. Parents from European American families tend to ask a lot of questions that evoke details from children, par-ticularly about children's personal feelings and motivations (Fivush, 2009; M. L. Howe et al., 2009; Q. Wang, 2006).

Do you remember when? As this young girl talks with her mother (par-ents) about an event they experienced together, she develops memorable images of her childhood.

Development in Culture

Every child acquires the values and traditions of one or more cultures, and these cultural frameworks give meaning to everything the child experiences. It is crucial for teachers and practitioners to gain a cultural perspective, in which they develop insights into their own backgrounds and learn how to identify, respect, and accommodate the practices of children and their families. Another new feature of this edition is the *Development in Culture* feature, in which a particular aspect of development is illustrated in one or more cultural settings. You can find examples of this feature on pages 135, 221, and 295.

Helping You See Development, Not Just Read About It

Learning about development is important for educators. More significant, however, is ensuring that educators can observe children, analyze what they observe, and apply what they have learned in decisions that meet children's needs. Several features present children and adolescents in real situations, provide samples of their work, and help readers use and apply the information they are learning in the book.

Case Studies

To care for children, adults need to focus on their general developmental levels but also on the unique characteristics of their lives. Case studies help readers apply their growing understanding of development and, at the same time, consider children's individual circumstances. Each chapter begins with a case study and related questions that illustrate and frame chapter content. A chapter-ending case provides readers with an additional opportunity to apply chapter content to children with distinctive needs. The questions that accompany each of these end-of-chapter cases help the reader in this application process; examples of answers to these questions appear in Appendix A. You will find examples of the introductory case studies on pages 241 and 325 and ending cases on pages 282 and 366.

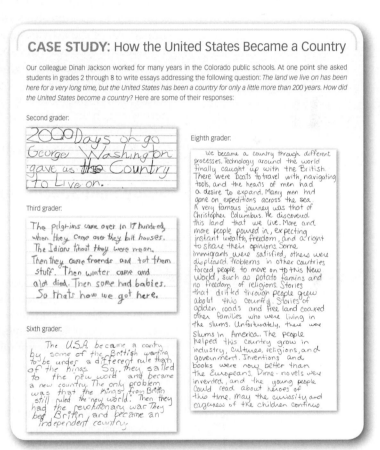

CASE STUDY: How the United States Became a Country

Our colleague Dinah Jackson worked for many years in the Colorado public schools. At one point she asked students in grades 2 through 8 to write essays addressing the following question: *The land we live on has been here for a very long time, but the United States has been a country for only a little more than 200 years. How did the United States become a country?* Here are some of their responses:

Second grader:

2000 Days oh go George Washington gave us the Country to Live on.

Third grader:

The pilgrims came over in 17 hundred, when they came over they built houses. The Idian tihoot they were mean. Then they came fraends and tot them stuff. Then winter came and alot died. Then some had babies. So thats how we got here.

Sixth grader:

The U.S.A. became a contry by some of the British wanting to be under a different rule than of the kings. So, they sailed to the new world and became a new country. The only problem was that the kings from Britin still ruled the "new world". Then they had the revolutionary war They beat Britin, and became an independent country

Eighth grader:

We became a country through different processes. Technology around the world finally caught up with the British. There were boats to travel with, navigating tools, and the hearts of men had a desire to expand. Many men had gone on expeditions across the sea. A very famous journey was that of Christopher Columbus. He discovered this land that we live. More and more people poured in, expecting instant wealth, freedom, and a right to share their opinions. Some immigrants were satisfied, others were displeased. Problems in other countries forced people to move up to this New World, such as potato famins and no freedom of religions. Stories that drifted through people grew about this country. Stories of golden roads and free land coaxed other families who were living in the slums. Unfortunately, there were slums in America. The people helped this country grow in industry, cultures, religions, and government. Inventions and books were now better than the Europeans. Dime-novels were invented, and the young people could read about heroes of this time. May the curiosity and eagerness of the children continue

Improving Your Ability to Interpret Children's Artifacts and Reflections

Consider what you've learned about schools as environments for child development as you analyze the following artifacts from several children.

Teachers at Work

A group of researchers asked students in elementary and middle schools to draw pictures of their teachers working in the classroom (Haney, Russell, & Bebell, 2004). We've selected five of the students' pictures and have given the artists fictitious names to help you identify them individually in your response. As you examine the pictures below and on the following page, consider these questions:

- What do each of the students seem to be suggesting about how teachers *socialize* children?
- What might the students be communicating about the *hidden curriculum* in their school?

Ladarius

Improving Your Ability to Interpret Children's Artifacts and Reflections

Improving Your Ability to Interpret Children's Artifacts and Reflections features give readers practice in evaluating and interpreting children's work. Reviewing authentic children's artifacts offers readers an opportunity to observe what children write and illustrate as a window into their development. Readers use chapter concepts in determining how a child is progressing within a particular domain of development. You will find examples of children's artifacts and reflections in the chapter-ending section called *Applying Concepts in Child Development*. See examples on pages 238, 323, and 531.

MyEducationLab™

Proven to **engage students**, provide **trusted content**, and **improve results**, Pearson MyLabs have helped over 8 million registered students reach true understanding in their courses. **MyEducationLab™** engages students with real-life teaching situations through dynamic videos, case studies, and student artifacts. Student progress is assessed, and a personalized study plan is created based on the student's unique results. Automatic grading and reporting keep educators informed to quickly address gaps and improve student performance. All of the activities and exercises in MyEducationLab are built around essential learning outcomes for teachers and are mapped to national standards.

In *Preparing Teachers for a Changing World,* Linda Darling-Hammond and her colleagues point out that grounding teacher education in real classrooms—among real teachers and students and among actual examples of students' and teachers' work—is an important, and perhaps even an essential, part of training teachers for the complexities of teaching in today's classrooms.

In the MyEducationLab for this course students will find the following features and resources.

Study Plan Specific to Your Text

MyEducationLab gives students the opportunity to test themselves on key concepts and skills, track their own progress through the course, and access personalized Study Plan activities. The customized Study Plan—with enriching activities—is generated based on the results of the pretest. Study Plans tag incorrect questions from the pretest to the appropriate textbook learning outcome, helping students focus on the topics they need help with. Personalized Study Plan activities may include eBook reading assignments, and review, practice and enrichment activities. They also include *Video Examples*—described in Margin Notes throughout the text and accessible via MyEducationLab—which allow students to explore topics such as memory, friendship, and families from the perspective of children from various age groups. The opportunity to see children and adolescents, even as they are at different levels of development, perform the same task or talk about the same topic (e.g., what it means to be a friend) is extremely powerful in demonstrating developmental differences.

After students complete the enrichment activities, they can take a posttest to identify the concepts they've mastered or the areas where they may need extra help. MyEducationLab then reports the Study Plan results to the instructor. Based on these reports, the instructor can adapt course material to suit individual learning needs or those of the entire class.

Connection to National Standards

MyEducationLab for Child Development is mapped to the newly revised (2011) InTASC standards. The InTASC standards are nationally recognized, model core teaching standards prepared by the Interstate Teacher Assessment and Support Consortium and dedicated to the reform of the preparation, licensure, and ongoing professional development of teachers. Each topic, activity, and exercise on MyEducationLab lists intended learning outcomes aligned to these national standards.

Assignments and Activities

Designed to enhance student understanding of concepts covered in class, these assignable exercises show concepts in action (through videos, cases, and/or student and teacher artifacts). They help students deepen content knowledge and synthesize and apply concepts and strategies they read about in the book. (Correct answers for these assignments are available to the instructor only under the "Instructor Resource" tab.) The MyEducationLab that accompanies this text has a wealth of application activities to advance student learning.

- **Application Exercises:** Provide students with the opportunity to apply the concepts and principles of child development in a variety of short scenarios.
- **Interpreting Children's Artifacts and Reflections:** Give students additional experience interpreting artifacts.
- **Practice Essay Questions:** Provide students practice answering essay questions similar to those they might find on a quiz or a test.
- **Artifact Analyses:** Ask students to apply developmental concepts in analyzing written work or oral responses to interview questions.
- **Video Analyses:** Present video clips of children and teachers in action, and ask students to apply developmental concepts in drawing conclusions.
- **Understanding Research Exercises:** Increase student understanding of how recent and classic investigations in child development contribute to knowledge about development and deepen student understanding of developmental research methods.
- **Supplementary Readings Exercises:** Offer students opportunities to build on developmental concepts with activities related to advanced readings.
- **Supplementary Readings:** Provide new information that extends student understanding of concepts developed in the text.

Building Teaching Skills and Dispositions

These unique learning units help students practice and strengthen skills that are essential to quality teaching. After presenting the steps involved in a core teaching process, students are given an opportunity to practice applying this skill via videos, student and teacher artifacts, and/or case studies of authentic classrooms. Providing multiple opportunities to practice a single teaching concept, each activity encourages a deeper understanding and application of concepts, as well as the use of critical thinking skills. After practice, students take a quiz, and then scores are reported to the instructor gradebook.

Lesson Plan Builder

The **Lesson Plan Builder** is an effective and easy-to-use tool students can use to create, update, and share quality lesson plans. The software also makes it easy to integrate state content standards into any lesson plan.

IRIS Center Resources

The IRIS Center at Vanderbilt University (http://iris.peabody.vanderbilt.edu), funded by the U.S. Department of Education's Office of Special Education Programs (OSEP), develops training enhancement materials for preservice and in-service teachers. The center works with experts from across the country to create challenge-based interactive modules, case study units, and podcasts that provide research-validated information about working with students in inclusive settings. In your MyEducationLab course we have integrated this content where appropriate.

Simulations in Classroom Management

One of the most difficult challenges facing teachers today is how to balance classroom instruction with classroom management. These interactive cases focus on the classroom management issues teachers most frequently encounter on a daily basis. Each simulation presents a scenario at the beginning and then offers a series of choices to solve each challenge. Along the way students receive mentor feedback on their choices and have the opportunity to make better choices if necessary. Upon exiting each simulation students will have a clear understanding of how to address these common classroom management issues and will be better equipped to handle them in the classroom.

Certification and Licensure

The Certification and Licensure section of MyEducationLab is set up to lead students to resources designed to help students pass their licensure exam by giving them access to state test requirements, overviews of what tests cover, and sample test items. The **"Certification and Licensure"** tab includes the following:

- **State Certification Test Requirements:** Here students can click on a state and will then be taken to a list of state certification tests to find the requirements they need to secure state certification.
- Students can click on the **Licensure Exams** they need to take to find:
  - Basic information about each test
  - Descriptions of what is covered on each test
  - Sample test questions with explanations of correct answers.
- **National Evaluation Series™** by Pearson: Here students can see the tests in the NES, learn what is covered on each exam, and access sample test items with descriptions and rationales of correct answers. They can also purchase interactive online tutorials developed by Pearson Evaluation Systems and the Pearson Teacher Education and Development group.
- **ETS Online Praxis Tutorials:** Here students can purchase interactive online tutorials developed by ETS and by the Pearson Teacher Education and Development group. Tutorials are available for the Praxis I exams and for select Praxis II exams.

Visit www.myeducationlab.com for a demonstration of this exciting new online teaching resource.

The same comprehensive attention to developmental concepts that guided educators in the fourth edition is also found in this fifth edition. However, there are several new features in this edition. The following list points out what is new in the fifth edition of *Child Development and Education*.

- Greater sensitivity to cultural and bioecological issues including two new features: *Development in Culture* and *Bioecology of Child Development*
- New ways to practice skills in observing and identifying children's developmental trends and milestones in *Improving Your Observation Skills*
- A rearrangement of some discussions related to social-emotional concepts
- Support for teacher licensure preparation in *Preparing for Your Licensure Examination* features, which alert teacher candidates to developmental concepts and theorists they may need to know to pass a teacher licensure exam
- Practice test examples, including both case studies with constructed-response questions and sample multiple-choice questions, which are located in the new end-of-chapter material called *Applying Concepts in Child Development*
- Thoroughly updated research including over a thousand new research citations

More information is available about how these changes are integrated into the text in the following paragraphs.

Sensitivity to Cultural and Bioecological Issues

Material on cultural and bioecological factors will help readers to increase their sensitivity to children from diverse backgrounds. This includes two new features, *Development in Culture* and *Bioecology of Child Development* and a number of new photographs that not only illustrate the diverse nature of development but also identify how the development of children and adolescents is influenced by social, environmental, and cultural contexts. Selected examples of cultural and bioecological issues addressed in this text include:

Chapter 1. Developmentally appropriate practice in Japan; Bronfenbrenner's bioecological theory.

Chapter 2. Using action research to learn about children from different cultures; relevance of research findings for children from different populations

Chapter 3. Bioecological model as a guiding framework; M. B. Spencer's bioeocological theory and its implications for addressing the assets and risk factors children experience; elaboration of children's experience in cultures; new recommendations for affirming the backgrounds of children from diverse backgrounds

Chapter 4. International themes in biological foundations; birth from a bioecological perspective

Chapter 5. Children's health being affected by the numerous environments they inhabit; maturation and initiation ceremonies in different cultures

Chapter 6. Role of social interaction in cognitive development from Piagetian and Vygotskian theories; play in a cultural setting

Chapter 7. Memory in a cultural context; personal initiative and ecological factors affecting self-regulated learning

Chapter 8. Bioecological contexts of intelligence; perspectives on multiple intelligences in China

Chapter 9. Acquiring sociolinguisitic patterns in a cultural setting; bioecology of language acquisition; learning second languages in Cameroon

Chapter 10. Bioecology of subject matter learning; literacy education in Bosnia

Chapter 11.   Bioecology of attachment security; bioecology of emotions; temperament in a cultural setting

Chapter 12.   Bioecology of self and social cognition; immigrant families in Ireland

Chapter 13.   Bioecology of motivation; bioecology of self-regulation; achievement orientation in Tanzania

Chapter 14.   Bioecology of moral development; bioecology of aggression and prosocial behavior; moral development in Columbia

Chapter 15.   Bioecology of social skills; children's peer culture

Rearrangement of Concepts in Social-Emotional Development

Readers had asked for a fuller analysis of peer relationships, and we addressed this suggestion by integrating a section on interpersonal relationships, previously in Chapter 14, into the section on peers in Chapter 15. The result is a more complete explanation of peer relationships that should help adults to better understand young people's social lives. With this change, we were also able to provide a more coherent focus on moral development in Chapter 14. This revision enables readers to see more clearly how they can foster children's understanding of their moral responsibilities.

Preparing for Your Licensure Examination

Many prospective teachers are required to demonstrate their knowledge of child development on teaching tests. As they read through the book, readers will be alerted to specific concepts that they might encounter on the *Praxis II*™ and other teaching tests. These margin notes (see pages 100 and 372) also serve the related purpose of reminding readers of key theorists and concepts that are especially significant in the field of child development. Additional support for licensure tests is given in the ending case studies and associated questions in the end-of-chapter section, *Applying Concepts in Child Development*.

Thoroughly Updated Research on Children's Development

More than a thousand new citations are included with this edition, reflecting the many important discoveries that have been made in recent years. Every chapter includes updates that collectively offer a cutting-edge perspective on children's growth. With this thoroughly up-to-date perspective on child development, readers will be better prepared to meet the needs of children from many walks of life. Selected examples are as follows.

Chapter 1.   Mechanisms by which the developmental process constrains the operations of nature and nurture.

Chapter 2.   New illustrations of several research designs, for example, a quasi-experimental design into effectiveness of treatments for reducing high levels of aggression in elementary and junior high students

Chapter 3.   Updates on children's experiences in low-income families and implications for their support

Chapter 4.   Concepts of multifactorial traits and niche construction; alternative and non-medical practices in birth and care of the newborn baby

Chapter 5.   Astrocytes and other glial cells; Allison Gopnik's research on infant development; neurological development in adolescents; food pyramid; obesity; recess and physical activity; Title IX regulations; sleep and schools; prevention and intervention programs related to alcohol and drug use

Chapter 6.   Illustration of a Vygotskian task; applications of Piagetian and Vygotskian theories; updates on neo-Piagetian and neo-Vygotskian contributions

Chapter 7.   Neurological underpinnings of attention and memory; implicit memory processes; goals in self-regulated learning; epistemic beliefs (formerly known as epistemological beliefs); recommendations for addressing exceptionalities in information processing

Chapter 8.   Fostering intelligence; neurological basis of intelligence; creativity; nurturing intelligence in children with gifts and talents

Supplementary Materials

The following online supplements to the textbook are available for downloading at www.pearsonhighered.com. Simply click on "Educators," enter the author, title, or ISBN, and select this textbook. Click on the "Resources" tab to view and download the available supplements.

Online Instructor's Manual

This manual (ISBN: 0-13-290252-4) contains an outline of the primary chapter headings and sections, with a corresponding list of instructional materials to be used in each section; and suggestions and resources for learning activities, supplemental lectures, group activities, and handouts. Each element has been carefully crafted to provide opportunities that support, enrich, and expand on what students read in the text.

Online Test Bank and MyTest

The Online Test Bank (ISBN: 0-13-290251-6) and MyTest each contain an average of 60 items per chapter. These test items are categorized and marked as either lower-level items that ask students to identify or explain concepts they have learned or higher-level items that require students to apply their knowledge of developmental concepts and research to specific classroom situations. A new secure option for creating and customizing exams can be made with MyTest, accessible through MyEducationLab. MyTest can be accessed with a MyEducationLab access code (ISBN: 0-13-290249-4).

Online PowerPoint® Slides

The Online PowerPoint slides (ISBN: 0-13-290250-8) include key concept summaries, outlines, and other graphic aids to enhance learning. They are designed to help students understand, organize, and remember concepts and developmental theories.

MyEducationLab™

As described above, a new online learning tool, MyEducationLab, is available at www.myeducationlab.com. **MyEducationLab™** offers quizzes to test mastery of chapter objectives; *Review, Practice, and Enrichment* exercises to deepen understanding; *Activities and Applications* to foster usage of chapter concepts; *Video Examples* of children in action; and *Building Teaching Skills and Dispositions* exercises to provide interactive practice in applying the core principles of child development.

Acknowledgments

Although we are listed as the sole authors of this textbook, in fact many individuals have contributed in significant ways to its content and form. Our editor, Kevin Davis, recognized the need for an applied child development book and nudged us to write one. Kevin has been the captain of our ship throughout all five editions, charting our journey and alerting us when we drifted off course. We thank Kevin for his continuing encouragement, support, insights, task focus, and high standards.

We have been equally fortunate to work with a series of expert development editors: Julie Peters (on the first and second editions), Autumn Benson (on the third edition), Christie Robb (on the fourth edition), and Linda Bishop (on the fifth edition). It was a special treat to work with Linda again on the current edition of the book because she had supported our initial planning many years ago when we were only beginning to dream about how we might bring child development to life for teachers. Julie, Autumn, Christie, and Linda have seen us through the day-to-day challenges of writing the book—for instance, offering creative ideas for improving the manuscript, locating artifacts to illustrate key concepts, pushing us to condense when we were unnecessarily wordy, insisting that certain concepts be clarified, overseeing the quality of the book's increasingly sophisticated online website, being a willing ear whenever we needed to vent our frustrations, and, in general, coordinating our writing efforts until books went into production. We thank Julie, Autumn, Christie, and Linda for their advice, support, and good humor, and also for their willingness to drop whatever else they were doing to come to our assistance at critical times.

Others at both Pearson Education and S4Carlisle Publishing Services have been key players in bringing the book to fruition. Lorretta Palagi worked diligently to keep the manuscript focused, concise, and clear. Mary Irvin and Norine Strang guided the manuscript through the production process; without a complaint, they let us continue to tweak the book in innumerable small ways even as production deadlines loomed dangerously close. Becky Savage, with the help of Jenn Kennett, secured permissions for the excerpts and figures we borrowed from other sources and was flexible when we added to our list at the eleventh hour. Lori Whitley and Carol Sykes sifted through many piles of photos to identify those that could best capture key developmental principles in a visual form. Lauren Carlson assisted us with innumerable administrative details that made our lives easier throughout the project. Marketing whizzes Joanna Sabella and Maggie Waples helped us get out the word about the book. Pearson Education sales representatives across the country offered us encouragement and relayed invaluable recommendations they had heard from instructors using the book.

We are also deeply indebted to the creators of videos available on MyEducationLab. Jayne Downey, who coordinated production of many of the original videos, shared our desire to represent children and adolescents in a natural and positive light so that adults could understand them sympathetically. Among the many tasks she undertook were to recruit children and families, secure the services of interviewers, draft questions, film children in their homes, edit video clips, and interpret children's thoughts and actions. Stuart Garry brought his technological know-how, in-depth knowledge of developmental theory, artistic talents, and keen attention to producing Jayne's videos. Others were vital contributors as well. Jason Cole expertly programmed the software package. We extend our appreciation to Greg Pierson, Director of University Schools, and to Keli Cotner, Director of the Campus Child Care Center at the University of Northern Colorado, for granting permission and assistance to Jayne Downey in filming classrooms and facilities. Dana Snyder and Kelle Nolke, teachers at University Schools, kindly assisted with videotaping in their classroom; Dana Snyder also permitted her own lessons to be taped. We also acknowledge the excellent job done by interviewers Stacey Blank, Tara Kaysen, Addie Lopez, Laura Sether, and Lisa Blank. The children and families were especially generous in allowing Jayne and the interviewers to come into their homes and film the children. We are grateful that numerous other individuals affiliated with Pearson Education also permitted us to use their footage of children in our exercises.

Finally, we are indebted to several individuals for their exemplary work in the development, design, and revision of MyEducationLab. Autumn Benson and Gail Gottfried drew on their knowledge of technology, instruction, and child development as they designed materials for the inaugural run of MyEducationLab. Three additional colleagues offered expertise in updates to MyEducationLab and related materials: Lynn Dean prepared the Study Plan for this edition of the book, Deborah Scigliano wrote the Test Bank, Instructor's Manual, and PowerPoint slides, and Marilyn Welsh wrote items for the summative test for the book.

Children, Adolescents, Teachers, and Other Professionals Equally important contributors to the book were the many young people and practitioners who provided the work samples, written reflections, other artifacts, and verbal responses that appear throughout the 15 chapters and in MyEducationLab. The work of the following young people contributed immeasurably to the depth and richness of our discussions:

Davis Alcorn	Tina Ormrod Fox	Jessica Lumbrano	Corwin Sether
Jacob Alcorn	Eddie Garcia	Krista Marrufo	Alex Sheehan
Curtis Alexander	Palet Garcia	Steven Merrick	Connor Sheehan
Kyle Alexander	Veronica Garcia	Margaret Mohr	Aftyn Siemer
David Alkire	James Garrett III	Tchuen-Yi Murry	Karma Marie Smith
Geoff Alkire	Amaryth Gass	Mike Newcomb	Alex Snow
Brenda Bagazuma	Andrew Gass	Malanie Nunez	Sam Snow
Andrew Belcher	Tony Gass	Dustin O'Mara	Connor Stephens
Katie Belcher	Dana Gogolin	Alex Ormrod	Megan Lee Stephens
Kayla Blank	Ivy Gogolin	Jeff Ormrod	Joe Sweeney
Madison Blank	Kenton Groissaint	Shir-Lisa Owens	Emma Thompson
Brent Bonner	Acadia Gurney	Isiah Payan	Grace Tober
Diamond Bonner	Amanda Hackett	Isabelle Peters	Sarah Toon
Ricco Branch	Jared Hale	Michelle Pollman	David Torres
Marsalis Bush	Cody Havens	Laura Prieto-Velasco	Joseph Torres
Eric Campos	Tyler Hensley	Cooper Remignanti	Samuel Torres
Leif Carlson	Elisabet Deyanira	Ian Rhoades	Madison Tupper
Zoe Clifton	Hernandez	Talia Rockland	Danielle Welch
Wendy Cochran	Lauryn Hickman	Oscar Rodriguez	Brady Williamson
Jenna Dargy	Sam Hickman	Elizabeth Romero	John Wilson
Noah Davis	William Hill	Corey Ross	Joey Wolf
Shea Davis	Brandon Jackson	Katie Ross	Lindsey Woollard
Mayra de la Garza	Rachel Johnson	Trisha Ross	Anna Young
Brandon Doherty	Jordan Kemme	Amber Rossetti	
Daniel Erdman	Marianne Kies	Bianca Sanchez	
Rachel Foster	Sarah Luffel	Daniela Sanchez	

We also thank the children in the first- and second-grade classroom of Dana Snyder and Kelle Nolke at the Laboratory School, Greeley, Colorado (now University Schools).

To ensure that we included children's work from a wide variety of geographic locations and backgrounds, we contacted organizations north and south, east and west to obtain work samples that would reflect ethnic, cultural, and economic diversity. We want to thank these individuals for their assistance and coordination efforts: Don Burger at Pacific Resources for Education and Learning (PREL), Michelle Gabor of the Salesian Boys' and Girls' Club, Rita Hocog Inos of the Commonwealth of the Northern Mariana Islands Public School System, Bettie Lake of the Phoenix Elementary School District, Heidi Schork and members of the Boston Youth Clean-Up Corps (BYCC), and Ann Shump of the Oyster River School District. Furthermore we thank the many teachers, counselors, principals, and other professionals—a child welfare case worker, a neurologist, a public health educator—who were so helpful in our efforts to identify artifacts, anecdotes, dialogues, and professional strategies to illustrate developmental concepts; key among them were Janet Alcorn, Rosenna Bakari, Trish Belcher, Paula Case, Michael Gee, Jennifer Glynn, Evie Greene, Diana Haddad, Betsy Higginbotham, Betsy Hopkins, Dinah Jackson, Jesse Jensen, Mike McDevitt, Erin Miguel, Michele Minichiello, Andrew Moore, Dan Moulis, Tina Ormrod Fox, Annemarie Palincsar, Kellee Patterson, Elizabeth Peña, Jrene Rahm, Nancy Rapport, Gwen Ross, Karen Scates, Cindy Schutter, Karen Setterlin, Jean Slater, Julie Spencer, Nan Stein, Peggy Torres, Sally Tossey, Pat Vreeland, and Cathy Zocchi.

Colleagues and Reviewers In addition, we received considerable encouragement, assistance, and support from our professional colleagues. Developmentalists and educational psychologists at numerous institutions around the country have offered insightful reviews of one or more chapters. We are especially indebted to the following reviewers for this edition:

Daisuke Akiba, Queens College

Brigid Beaubien, Eastern Michigan University

Jennifer Betters-Bubon, University of Wisconsin–Madison

Jean Clark, University of South Alabama

Michael Cunningham, Tulane University

Heather Davis, North Carolina State University

Suzanne Fegley, University of Pennsylvania

Hema Ganapathy-Coleman, Indiana State University

Connie Gassner, Ivy Tech Community College

Jennie Lee-Kim, University of Maryland

Debra S. Pierce, Ivy Tech Community College

Candy Skelton, Texas A&M University–Corpus Christi

We continue to appreciate the guidance of reviewers for earlier editions of the book. These individuals helped guide our early efforts:

Karen Abrams, Keene State College

Jan Allen, University of Tennessee

Lynley Anderman, University of Kentucky

Patricia Ashton, University of Florida

David E. Balk, Kansas State University

Thomas M. Batsis, Loyola Marymount University

Doris Bergen, Miami University

Irene Bersola-Nguyen, California State University–Sacramento

Donna M. Burns, The College of St. Rose

Heather Davis, University of Florida

Teresa K. DeBacker, University of Oklahoma

Deborah K. Deemer, University of Northern Iowa

Karen Drill, University of Illinois at Chicago

Eric Durbrow, The Pennsylvania State University

William Fabricius, Arizona State University

Daniel Fasko, Morehead State University

Kathleen Fite, Texas State University

Sherryl Browne Graves, Hunter College

William Gray, University of Toledo

Michael Green, University of North Carolina–Charlotte

Glenda Griffin, Texas A&M University

Deborah Grubb, Morehead State University

Linda L. Haynes, University of South Alabama

Melissa Heston, University of Northern Iowa

James E. Johnson, The Pennsylvania State University

Joyce Juntune, Texas A&M University

Michael Keefer, University of Missouri–St. Louis

Judith Kieff, University of New Orleans

Nancy Knapp, University of Georgia

Carol A. Marchel, Winthrop University

Mary McLellan, Northern Arizona University

Sharon McNeely, Northeastern Illinois University

Kenneth Merrell, University of Iowa

Marilyn K. Moore, Illinois State University

Tamera Murdock, University of Missouri–Kansas City

Bridget Murray, Indiana State University

Kathy Nakagawa, Arizona State University

Virginia Navarro, University of Missouri–St. Louis

Terry Nourie, Illinois State University

Larry Nucci, University of Illinois–Chicago

Jennifer Parkhurst, Duke University

Sherrill Richarz, Washington State University

Kent Rittschof, Georgia Southern University

Linda Rogers, Kent State University

Richard Ryan, University of Rochester

Sue Spitzer, California State University, San Bernardino

Benjamin Stephens, Clemson University
Bruce Tuckman, The Ohio State University
Rob Weisskirch, California State University–
Monterey Bay
Kathryn Wentzel, University of Maryland–
College Park

Andrew R. Whitehead, East Stroudsburg
University of Pennsylvania
Allan Wigfield, University of Maryland–
College Park
Thomas D. Yawkey, The Pennsylvania State
University

Increasingly, we have heard from colleagues at other institutions who have taken the time to let us know what they think about the book and how it might be improved. We are grateful for such very helpful feedback. In addition, staff and administrators at the University of Northern Colorado—especially staff at the Michener Library and Mark Alcorn, Carolyn Edwards, Helen Reed, Eugene Sheehan, and Robbyn Wacker—unselfishly provided advice, resources, and time.

Our Families Finally, our families have been supportive and patient over the extended period we have been preoccupied with reading, researching, writing, and editing. Our children gave of themselves in anecdotes, artwork, and diversions from our work. Our husbands picked up the slack around the house and gave us frequent emotional boosts and comic relief. Much love and many thanks to Eugene, Connor, and Alex (from Teresa) and to Richard, Tina, Alex, and Jeff (from Jeanne).

T.M.M.
J.E.O.

Brief Contents

Contents

Part 4 • Social and Emotional Development

Chapter 11 Emotional Development 416

Chapter 12 Development of Self and Social Understandings 456

Chapter 13 Development of Motivation and Self-Regulation 494

Special Features

Basic Developmental Issues

Developmental Trends

Preparing for Your Licensure Examination

Situating Development in Bioecological Contexts

Bioecology of Child Development

Development in Culture

Helping You See Development, Not Just Read About It

Case Studies

New Integrative Learning Features

Video Examples

Chapter One

Making a Difference in the Lives of Children and Adolescents

CASE STUDY: Tonya

At any given moment, in almost every classroom, at least one child is having difficulty adjusting. The struggling child may be delayed in academic skills, careless in following classroom rules, or rejected by peers. In Mary Renck Jalongo's first-grade classroom, Tonya had such problems (Jalongo, Isenberg, & Gerbracht, 1995).

Fortunately for Tonya, Mary was knowledgeable about child development. Mary realized that Tonya, like every child, had positive qualities and, with the right support, would be able to overcome her difficulties.

To determine how best to help Tonya, Mary considered the little girl's full circumstances. Academically, Tonya was delayed. She had been retained in kindergarten and was not catching up as quickly as Mary would have liked. Physically, Tonya received inadequate nutrition and was chronically hungry at school. Socially, Tonya had few friends, having previously insisted that classmates give her their snacks and prized possessions and, when they refused, pilfered these items from their desks.

To compound her problems, Tonya lacked the support of her principal, who thought that a harsh punishment—no recess for a month—was an appropriate response to Tonya's thefts. Moreover, Tonya's mother was sick, at a debilitating stage with lupus, and not able to work outside the home or attend school functions.

In spite of these challenging conditions, Tonya was eager to develop productive skills and solve some of her own problems. When Mary asked Tonya why she took other children's snacks, she answered simply that she was hungry. When asked if she ate breakfast, Tonya replied that she did not because she had to take care of her younger brother. After Mary invited her to think about possible solutions, Tonya volunteered that she and her brother might be able to get breakfast at their aunt's house. Tonya followed through with this solution, walking daily with her brother to her aunt's house for an early morning meal.

Mary also realized that Tonya had the capacity to repair her relationships with peers. After securing Tonya's promise that she would stop taking other children's things, Mary stood by Tonya's side in front of the class and announced that Tonya had agreed not to take anyone's belongings and could now be trusted. As a result, Tonya was gradually accepted by the other children, began to concentrate on her schoolwork, and ultimately blossomed into a healthy, well-adjusted young woman (M. R. Jalongo, personal communication, June 12, 2007).

- What kind of impact did Mary Jalongo have on Tonya's life?
- How did Mary draw on her understanding of child development as she worked with Tonya?

Mary Jalongo made a difference in Tonya's life. By drawing on her knowledge of child development, Mary realized that Tonya could grow and change if given sensitive, loving care. By encouraging Tonya and her brother to eat breakfast with their aunt, Mary helped meet Tonya's physical needs and paved the way for closer ties to extended family. By repairing Tonya's damaged reputation with the other children, Mary helped Tonya earn their acceptance. Feeling comfortable physically and secure emotionally, Tonya was better prepared to tackle academic challenges and develop a healthy sense of who she was and how she fit into the world around her. Thanks, in part, to Mary Jalongo's thoughtful intercession, Tonya would ultimately thrive.

OBJECTIVES

1.1: Describe the three basic issues that characterize developmental change.

1.2: Differentiate among seven theoretical perspectives on development.

1.3: Identify educational implications of the major theories of child development.

1.4: Identify the characteristics of five developmental periods from infancy through late adolescence.

1.5: Offer recommendations for working effectively with youngsters of various ages.

1.6: Formulate developmentally appropriate practices that teachers and other professionals can use.

THE FIELD OF CHILD DEVELOPMENT

The study of human development helps us understand how human beings change from the time of conception, through maturation into adulthood, and on into old age and death. This book covers the early part of the human journey—beginning at conception and including prenatal growth, birth, infancy, childhood, and adolescence. The field of **child development** seeks to identify and explain persistent, cumulative, and progressive changes in the physical, cognitive, and social-emotional development of children and adolescents.

As you will learn throughout this book, a child's developmental journey is guided by four factors:

- *Nature*—the genetic inheritance affecting the child's growth
- *Nurture*—the influences of the social and physical environment in which the child lives
- *Existing conditions for the child*—the physiological and psychological foundations upon which new advancements can be built
- *The child's own activity*—the child's choices, mental processes, emotional responses, and behaviors

As you will also discover in your reading, development includes changes that are common to most children and adolescents as well as those that are specific to particular individuals. At times, we will talk about developments that nearly everyone undergoes, such as acquiring complex language skills and developing consideration for other people's feelings. At other times, we will discuss developments that differ considerably among youngsters. For example, some children respond to difficulties at school by seeking support from peers, teachers, and family members, whereas others begin to withdraw from school and participate in risky behaviors (M. B. Spencer, 2006).

To describe the many factors that contribute to children's growth, scholars of child development draw from many academic disciplines. In this book, our descriptions of children's development pull from research primarily in psychology but also in biology, sociology, anthropology, and the applied fields of early intervention, education, child and family studies, juvenile justice, counseling, social work, and medicine. We emphasize research that is relevant to children's education and experiences in schools.

Our primary goal in this book is to help you support healthy, optimal development in all children and adolescents. We pursue this goal by focusing on two specific objectives. First, we want you to learn how children and adolescents think, feel, and act at various ages. This information can help you understand the individual children and adolescents with whom you work. Second, we want you to be able to apply what you learn in your classroom, school, and community. You can use practical ideas from the field of child development in your instruction, classroom routines, and ongoing relationships with children and adolescents.

Three Developmental Domains

The study of child development is organized into three domains, or broad areas of study: physical development, cognitive development, and social-emotional development. **Physical development** is concerned with the biological changes of the body. It includes genetics, a fetus's growth in the mother's womb, the birth process, brain development, and the acquisition of such motor skills as throwing a ball and using scissors. It also encompasses behaviors that promote and impede health and environmental factors that influence physical growth. **Cognitive development** refers to the age-related transformations that occur in children's reasoning, concepts, memory, and language—changes that are cultivated by children's experiences in families, schools, and communities. **Social-emotional development** includes the many modifications that occur in emotions, self-concept, motivation, social relationships, and moral reasoning and behavior—advancements that also depend in large part on children's interactions with other people.

child development
Study of the persistent, cumulative, and progressive changes in the physical, cognitive, and social-emotional development of children and adolescents.

physical development
Systematic changes of the body and brain and age-related changes in motor skills and health behaviors.

cognitive development
Systematic changes in reasoning, concepts, memory, and language.

social-emotional development
Systematic changes in emotions, self-concept, motivation, social relationships, and moral reasoning and behavior.

Although the three domains may appear to be independent areas, they are in fact closely interrelated. For example, an increase in the ability to look at situations from multiple perspectives enhances social skills. Similarly, growth in the brain permits improvements in planning for the future. Thus, in their everyday work with children, educators often address more than one domain at a time. An elementary teacher might plan a period of quiet reading after a physically active social studies lesson, and a high school chemistry teacher could raise questions about both scientific matters and moral issues when discussing a company's disposal of toxins into the community's groundwater.

Effects of Context on Development

All areas of development depend on the **context** of children's lives—their experiences in families, schools, neighborhoods, community organizations, cultural and ethnic groups, and society at large. Child development research has shown that some sort of "family" or other cluster of close, caring relationships is a critical condition for optimal development. Schools, too, play a significant role in development, not only by fostering cognitive skills but also by communicating messages about children's potential for achievement and by providing an arena in which children can practice social skills. As a member of one or more ethnic groups and **cultures**—long-standing social groups with defined values, traditions, and symbol systems—children form interpersonal relationships and enter into daily activities with a sense of purpose. Furthermore, in their local communities and broader societies, children gain access to peers, other adult role models, recreation, the media, and such institutions as social services, banks, and medical clinics.

In preparing to teach or in some other way care for children, you are about to become a vital part of the developmental context of young people. Your productive role in that context will be strengthened by a thorough foundation in child development. As you can see in Figure 1-1, this book provides this foundation in its coverage of the three areas of development (physical, cognitive, and social-emotional domains), the settings in which children and adolescents grow, and the research methods that reveal youngsters' developmental journeys.

Improving Your Observation Skills

Being in the choir. How are these children's physical, cognitive, and social-emotional needs being met by their experiences in the choir? Compare your response with the explanation at the end of the chapter.

context
The broad social environments, including family, schools, neighborhoods, community organizations, culture, ethnicity, and society at large, that influence children's development.

culture
The values, traditions, and symbol systems of a long-standing social group that give purpose and meaning to children's daily activities and interpersonal relationships.

nature
Inherited characteristics and tendencies that affect development.

nurture
Environmental conditions that affect development.

BASIC ISSUES IN DEVELOPMENT

In their attempts to explain the changes that take place during childhood, child development theorists have grappled with, but not yet resolved, three key issues. First, they wonder how genetic factors and the environment combine to influence development. Second, they speculate about which developmental paths are true for everyone and which others are unique to individuals. Third, they debate about the developmental changes that can be characterized as major transformations or, alternatively, as a series of gradual trends. Let's now look more closely at these three issues, which are referred to as questions of (a) nature and nurture, (b) universality and diversity, and (c) qualitative and quantitative change.

Nature and Nurture

In the study of development, **nature** refers to the inherited characteristics and tendencies that influence development. **Nurture** consists of the environmental conditions that influence development. Nature and nurture are partners in a child's growth and well-being.

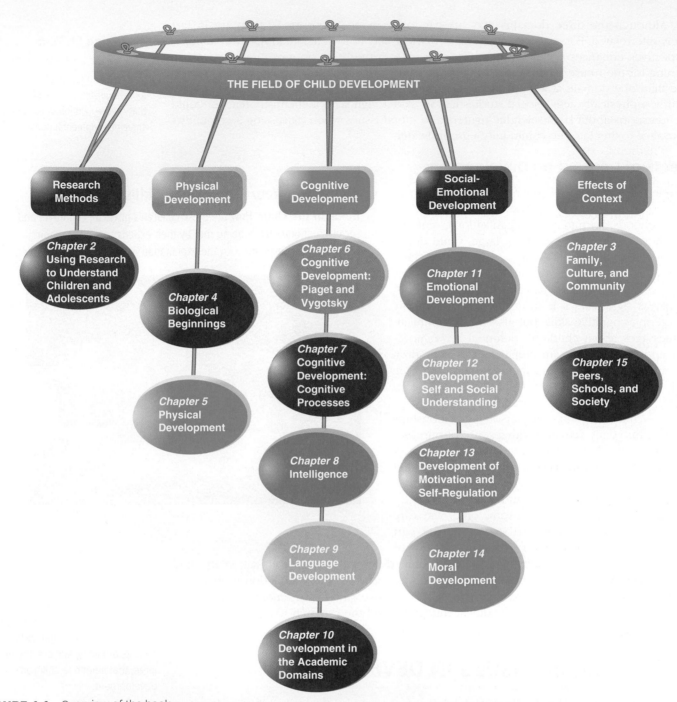

FIGURE 1-1 Overview of the book.

Nature contributes to both common human traits and individual differences among children. Some characteristics have a powerful genetic basis and appear in virtually everyone. Almost all children have the capacity to learn to walk, understand language, imitate others, use simple tools, and draw inferences about how other people view the world. Other characteristics, including stature, eye color, and facial appearance, vary among children and are also strongly determined by heredity. Similarly, children's **temperaments**—their characteristic ways of responding to emotional events, novel stimuli, and their own impulses—are affected by their individual genetic makeup (Rothbart & Bates, 2006; Schmidt, Fox, Perez-Edgar, & Hamer, 2009). Likewise, being slow or quick to learn from everyday experiences has some genetic basis (Petrill et al., 2004).

temperament

A child's characteristic ways of responding to emotional events, novel stimuli, and personal impulses.

Heredity is powerful, but it has limits. The effects of heredity depend very much on the child's developmental level, health, activity, and exposure to environmental substances. Whereas some hereditary instructions, such as the chromosomes that determine sex, exert an influence from the beginning, other instructions emerge only gradually through the process of **maturation**, the genetically guided changes that occur over the course of development. For example, the changes of puberty begin after the pituitary gland in the brain senses it is time to release certain hormones and initiate the process of sexual maturation.

Children's experiences affect all aspects of their being, from the health of their bodies to the curiosity of their minds. *Nurture* affects children's development through multiple channels: physically through nutrition, activities, and stress; intellectually through informal experiences and formal instruction; and socially through exposure to adult role models and participation in peer relationships. However, nurture faces definite limits. Even the best environments cannot overpower every possible defective gene. And, unfortunately, the conditions of nurture are *not* always *nurturing*. For example, children who have abusive parents must rely on people outside the immediate family for stable, affectionate care.

Historically, many theorists saw nature and nurture as separate and rival factors. Some theorists believed that biological factors are ultimately responsible for growth. Other theorists assumed that children become whatever the environment shapes them to be. In recent decades, developmental theorists have learned that nature and nurture intermesh dynamically in the lives of developing children (J. P. Spencer et al., 2009). Particular genes (the basic units of heredity) get selected for expression according to the body's maturational state and exposure to nutrition, light, toxins, viruses, and stressful experiences. Furthermore, the child is an active partner in his or her own development, choosing friends and activities that in turn affect the expression of genes (Sameroff, 2009). Consider the following specific principles of how nature and nurture exert their effects in the developing child:

Nature and nurture are constrained by the developmental process. Genes and environment alone are not sufficient to explain the complex sequences of events that occur in the changing brain and body. The *developmental process* itself is a factor in growth. In other words, current structures in the child's brain and body limit the emerging handiwork of nature and nurture (Champagne, 2009; Stiles, 2008). During a child's prenatal growth in the womb, new cells specialize in particular ways and move to appropriate locations depending on instructions from nearby cells. The result is a miraculous sequence of changes. Thus, the globular hands that first emerge during prenatal development do not form fingers overnight. Instead, a cascade of reactions allows fingers to sprout, project from the palm, and gradually elongate into the elegant digits that will ultimately permit the child to draw with crayons and zip up a jacket. Each tiny step forward extends its predecessor state.

The relative effects of heredity and environment vary for different areas of development. Some abilities are strongly influenced by genetically controlled systems in the brain. The abilities to distinguish among various speech sounds and use appropriate grammatical structures develop without formal training under a wide range of environmental conditions (Gallistel, Brown, Carey, Gelman, & Keil, 1991; R. A. Hayes & Slater, 2008; Keen, 2009). In contrast, abilities in traditional school subject areas (e.g., reading, geography) and advanced artistic and physical skills (e.g., playing the piano, playing competitive soccer) rely heavily on instruction and practice (Bruer, 1999; R. K. Olson, 2008; Schraw, 2006).

Inherited tendencies make individual children more or less responsive to particular environmental influences. Because of their genetic makeup, some children are easily affected by certain conditions in the environment, whereas others are less affected (Bugental, 2009; Rutter, 1997). Children who are, by nature, inhibited may be quite shy around other people if they have few social contacts. However, if their parents and teachers arrange for them to make friends, these otherwise shy children may become more socially outgoing (Arcus, 1991; Kagan & Fox, 2006). In contrast, children who have more extroverted

maturation
Genetically guided changes that occur over the course of development.

temperaments may be sociable regardless of their specific environment, persistently seeking out peers with whom they can talk, laugh, and play.

Some genes exert their effects only in certain environments. Children are sometimes born with particular genes that put them at risk for developing psychological problems. For example, a certain chemical, serotonin, is produced in the brain and influences a person's mood. Some people have a short form of a gene (known as 5HTT) that makes it difficult for their brains to recycle serotonin, such that insufficient amounts of the chemical are available for maintaining emotional processes. As a result, these individuals are at risk for becoming chronically sad and irritable. Yet the short form of this gene does not cause emotional depression unless these individuals are also maltreated as children or grow up in a stressful environment (Caspi et al., 2003). Conversely, being raised in a potentially traumatizing environment is associated with later depression only in individuals who have this short gene.

Individual differences in heredity may exert stronger effects when environments are favorable than when environments are impoverished. When youngsters have decent experiences in their culture, community, and age-group, heredity often plays a strong role in their individual characteristics. Thus, when children grow up with adequate nutrition, a warm and stable home environment, and appropriate educational experiences, heredity affects how quickly and thoroughly they acquire new skills. But when they have experiences that are quite unusual—for instance, when they experience extreme deprivation—the influence of environment outweighs that of heredity (D. C. Rowe, Almeida, & Jacobson, 1999; Sameroff, 2009). For example, when children grow up deprived of adequate nutrition and stimulation, they may fail to develop advanced intellectual skills, even though they were born with such potential (Plomin & Petrill, 1997; D. C. Rowe, Jacobson, & Van den Oord, 1999).

Timing of environmental exposure matters. When children are changing rapidly in any area, they are especially prone to influence by the environment. Early in a mother's pregnancy, her use of certain drugs may damage her future offspring's quickly growing organs and limbs. Just prior to birth, exposure to the same drugs may adversely affect the baby's brain, which at that point is forming neurological connections that will be needed for survival and learning in the outside world. In a few cases a certain stimulation *must* occur during a brief period if a prospective ability is to become functional (C. Blakemore, 1976; Hubel & Wiesel, 1965; Stiles, 2008). In such cases there is a *critical period* for stimulation. At birth, certain areas of the brain are tentatively reserved for processing visual patterns—lines, shapes, contours, depth, and so forth. In virtually all cases, infants encounter adequate stimulation to preserve these brain circuits. However, when cataracts are present at birth and not removed for a few years, a child's vision is obstructed, and areas of the brain that otherwise would be devoted to these visual functions are redirected for other purposes and lose some of their original capacity.

In many and probably most other developmental areas, however, children may be most receptive to a certain type of stimulation at one point in their lives but remain able to benefit from it to some degree later as well. Many theorists use the term **sensitive period** when referring to such a long time frame of heightened receptivity to particular environmental experiences. Sensitive periods appear to be more common than critical periods, reflecting nature's fortunate practice of giving children second chances to learn important skills. During early childhood, children are naturally predisposed to tune in to the sounds, structure, and meaning of language, suggesting a sensitive period for learning language. Educators can realistically expect to make meaningful progress with children who are delayed in language and literacy as long as the children receive instruction in missing experiences and encounter high expectations for their success.

Children's natural tendencies affect their environment. In addition to being affected by nature and nurture, children's growth is influenced by their own developmental levels and behaviors. Youngsters make many choices, seek out information and, over time, refine their knowledge and beliefs (Flavell, 1994; Piaget, 1985). Children often request information

sensitive period
A period in development when certain environmental experiences have a more pronounced influence than is true at other times.

("What does *cooperate* mean, Mommy?") and experiences ("Uncle Ignacio, can I play on your computer?"). Children even help create environments that intensify their genetic tendencies. For example, children with irritable dispositions might pick fights, thereby creating a more aggressive climate in which to interact.

As children get older, they become increasingly able to seek stimulation that suits their tendencies. Imagine that Marissa has an inherited talent for such verbal skills as acquiring new vocabulary words and comprehending stories. As a young child, Marissa depends on her parents to read to her. As she grows older, Marissa chooses her own books and begins to read to herself. Marissa's experience would suggest that genetic tendencies become more powerful as children grow older—an expectation that is consistent with genetic research (Plomin & Spinath, 2004; Scarr & McCartney, 1983).

Universality and Diversity

Developmental changes that occur in just about everyone are said to reflect a certain degree of **universality**. Unless significant disabilities are present, all young children learn to sit, walk, and run, almost invariably in that order. Other developmental changes are highly individual, reflecting **diversity**. The first words of some children are social gestures such as "bye-bye," and only later do these children add words for objects and actions. Other children initially learn words for objects and physical properties and later add social expressions.

Theorists differ in their beliefs regarding the extent to which developmental accomplishments are universal among all human beings or unique to particular individuals. Some propose that maturation and shared genes contribute to universality in development (e.g., Gesell, 1928). They point out that despite widely varying environments, virtually all human beings acquire fundamental motor skills, proficiency in language, and the ability to inhibit immediate impulses. Certain consistencies in children's environments provide an additional route to universality. In all corners of the world, children observe that objects always fall down rather than up and that people often get angry when someone intentionally hurts them. In the same manner, children universally participate in everyday cultural activities, for example, completion of household chores and involvement in community festivities.

universality
In a particular aspect of human development, the commonalities seen in the way virtually all individuals progress.

diversity
In a particular aspect of human development, the varied ways in which individuals progress.

Yet other theorists have been impressed by diversity in child development. They point out that nature permits variations in genes affecting facial features and physical and intellectual abilities. Other theorists view the environment (nurture) as weighing heavily in diversity. They propose that factors as global as the historical period of one's upbringing and as personal as one's family relationships help to shape a child's individuality (Baltes, Lindenberger, & Staudinger, 2006; Bornstein & Lansford, 2010). Some of these theorists also see culture as a significant source of diversity: Children differ in the competencies they acquire based on the particular tools, communication systems, and values that they regularly encounter (Griedler & Shields, 2008; Rogoff, 2003).

Earlier we mentioned that the relative influences of nature and nurture vary from one area of development to another. The same pattern is true for universality and diversity. Development tends to be more universal in some aspects of physical development, such as the sequences in which puberty unfolds. In other areas, including many aspects of cognitive and social-emotional development, diversity tends to be more prevalent. Nevertheless, there is always *some* diversity, even in physical development. Obviously, children vary in height, weight, and skin color, and some are born with physical disabilities or become injured. Throughout the book you will find instances of developmental universality, but just as often, you will see divergence among developmental pathways.

SIMILAR IN SOME WAYS, DIFFERENT IN OTHERS. Teachers can design classroom routines that accommodate common age-related abilities as well as allow for individual experiences in children.

Qualitative and Quantitative Change

Sometimes development reflects dramatic changes in the essence or underlying structure of a characteristic. Such major reorganizations are called **qualitative changes**. When children learn to run, they propel their bodies forward in a way that is distinctly different from walking—they are not simply moving faster. When they begin to talk in two-word sentences rather than with single words, they are, for the first time, using rudimentary forms of grammar. But not all development involves dramatic change. In fact, development frequently occurs as a gradual progression, or *trend,* with many small additions and modifications to behaviors and thought processes. These progressions are called **quantitative changes**. For example, children gradually grow taller and learn about such diverse realms as the animal kingdom and society's rules for showing courtesy.

Stage Theories

Theorists who emphasize qualitative changes often use the term **stage** to refer to a period of development characterized by a particular way of behaving or thinking. According to a **stage theory** of development, individuals progress through a series of stages that are qualitatively different from one another.[1]

Some stage theories have proposed *hierarchical* levels. In hierarchical models, each stage is seen as providing the essential foundation for stages that follow. After observing children in a wide variety of logical tasks and thought-provoking situations, the eminent psychologist **Jean Piaget** (1896–1980) proposed a stage theory to describe transformations in children's logical thinking and reasoning. His observations led him to conclude that as infants, children interact with the world primarily through trial-and-error behavior, discovering the properties of a rubber ball as they mouth it and roll it on the floor. As children mature, they begin to represent, symbolically "manipulate," and make mental predictions about objects and actions in the world around them. They know, for example, that the ball will bounce when they drop it on a wooden floor. Later they begin to derive logical deductions about concrete, real-world objects and situations, perhaps inferring that both the rubber in the ball and the planks on the wooden floor have some similar properties because of their shared origins in trees. And once they reach adolescence, they become capable of thinking systematically about abstract ideas—for instance, by thinking about the unseen physical factors (e.g., *momentum, gravity*) influencing the ball's bounce.

Another famous stage theorist, **Erik Erikson** (1902–1994), focused on a set of primary developmental challenges that individuals face at different points in their lives. During their infancy and early childhood years, youngsters learn first to trust others and then to act self-sufficiently. As adolescents, youngsters reflect on their *identities* as boys or girls; members of particular ethnic groups; and individuals with defined interests and goals for the future. In Erikson's theory, stages are "soft": People do not fully replace earlier developments with new modes of thinking (Kohlberg, Levine, & Hewer, 1983). Instead, earlier struggles persist—and sometimes intrude—into new challenges. For example, a young adult who has failed to develop a clear identity may be confused about the kind of role to play in romantic relationships (J. Kroger, 2003).

Historically, a few stage theories described *universal* progressions: All children were thought to go through the same sequence of changes, although the ages at which individual children pass through each level were believed to vary according to the environment. Piaget was a strong believer in universal progressions in children's thinking. In contrast, Erikson assumed that people deal with and resolve the social-emotional dilemmas in their lives in distinctly individual ways.

qualitative change
Relatively dramatic developmental change that reflects considerable reorganization or modification of functioning.

quantitative change
Developmental change that involves a series of minor, trendlike modifications.

stage
A period of development characterized by a qualitatively distinct way of behaving or thinking.

stage theory
Theory that describes development as involving a series of qualitatively distinct changes.

---

[1]Note that developmentalists have a more precise meaning for the term *stage* than is communicated by the same word in everyday speech. Parents often make comments like "He's at the terrible twos stage." Such comments reflect the idea that children are behaving typically for their age-group. When developmental scholars say a child is in a certain stage, they additionally assume that the child is undergoing a series of age-related qualitative transformations.

However, research has *not* entirely confirmed the idea that young people proceed through stages one at a time or that they always move in the same direction (e.g., Ceci & Roazzi, 1994; K. W. Fischer & Bidell, 2006; Kurtines & Gewirtz, 1991; Metz, 1995). A 9-year-old girl may easily plan ahead while playing chess (her hobby) but have difficulty planning ahead while writing a complex essay (an unfamiliar activity). Nor do stage progressions always appear to be universal across cultures and educational contexts (e.g., Glick, 1975; S.-C. Li, 2007). Youngsters raised in vastly different cultures often learn to think in significantly different ways (M. Cole & Cagigas, 2010; M. Cole & Packer, 2011). Given these and other research findings, few contemporary developmental theorists support strict versions of stage theories (Parke, Ornstein, Rieser, & Zahn-Waxler, 1994).

Many theorists now believe that qualitative changes do exist—not as inevitable, universal, and hierarchical patterns, but rather as dynamic states of thinking and acting that evolve as children mature and try new things. It is obvious that the actions of adolescents differ from those of 2-year-old children. Fifteen-year-olds are not simply taller and more knowledgeable about the world; they go about their day-to-day living in qualitatively different ways. Maturation-based developments, such as the brain's increases in memory capacity, plus ever-expanding knowledge and experience, permit both gradual and occasionally dramatic changes in thinking and behaving (Barrouillet, Gavens, Vergauwe, Gaillard, & Camos, 2009; Flavell, 1994; Morra, Gobbo, Marini, & Sheese, 2008). Thus, contemporary developmental theorists tend to see both qualitative and quantitative changes in children's development.

Applying Basic Lessons from Child Development

As you read this book, you will find that the three basic developmental issues of nature and nurture, universality and diversity, and qualitative and quantitative change surface periodically within individual chapters. They are also presented in Basic Developmental Issues tables in each chapter. The first of these tables, "Illustrations in the Three Domains," provides examples of how the basic developmental issues are reflected in the domains of physical, cognitive, and social-emotional development. These big ideas also have several general implications for your work with children:

• **Accept the powerful influences of both nature and nurture on growth.** A child's fate is never sealed—it always depends on care from adults and the child's own efforts. Again and again, nurture matters. But so does nature. How children respond to instruction and guidance depends, in part, on their genetic inheritance. An important implication is that when children show unusual talents, you can offer extra challenges. And when children's natural inclinations become stumbling blocks to positive growth, you can provide additional support.

• **Become familiar with general developmental trends and common variations.** General trends at a particular age level guide the daily work of educators. For example, an elementary teacher familiar with Piaget's theory knows that young children have difficulty with abstract ideas and so arranges many concrete, hands-on experiences. At the same time, many variations in developmental pathways—the timing, appearance, and nature of changes—also must be accommodated. By growing familiar with the developmental diversity among children, you can learn to give individual youngsters the specific support they need.

• **Look for both quantitative and qualitative changes in children's characteristics.** As you teach children academic concepts, the benefits of physical activity, ways to get along with peers, and so on, you might find that children often learn information in a quantitative fashion. That is, they soak up facts and skills rapidly and incrementally. You can support such learning by providing children with rich and varied resources. On other occasions children might need to revamp their basic ways of thinking before they can progress. Much of the momentum for qualitative change comes from the child, but teachers and other professionals can support new ways of thinking by exposing children to sophisticated reasoning. For example, a class discussion about school rules can prompt children to learn that breaking rules not only leads to punishment (an understanding that typically comes early in life) but also upsets other people (a later acquisition). With this new insight, many children become more considerate of others.

BASIC DEVELOPMENTAL ISSUES
Illustrations in the Three Domains

ISSUE	PHYSICAL DEVELOPMENT	COGNITIVE DEVELOPMENT	SOCIAL-EMOTIONAL DEVELOPMENT
Nature and Nurture	Nature guides the order and timing in which specific parts of the brain are formed. Genetic factors also determine certain individual dispositions, such as a tendency toward thinness or a susceptibility to diabetes. All growth depends on nurture. Nutrition, exercise, and athletic training influence health and motor skills (Chapters 4 and 5).	Some aspects of intelligence, learning, and language seem to be guided by genes. However, many contemporary theorists emphasize the environmental influences, including informal learning experiences, adult modeling and mentoring, family relationships, and formal schooling (Chapters 3, 5, 6, 7, 8, 9, and 10).	Individual differences in temperament are partly controlled by heredity. Environmental influences are evident in the development of self-esteem and motivation. Becoming aggressive, on the one hand, or helpful and empathic on the other, occurs due to the combined influences of nature and nurture (Chapters 11, 12, 13, and 14).
Universality and Diversity	The emergence of key physical features (e.g., gender-specific characteristics during puberty) is basically universal. Diversity is evident in the ages at which children and adolescents accomplish motor milestones (e.g., becoming able to sit, stand, and walk), as well as in their general state of physical health (Chapter 5).	The basic components of human language (e.g., an ability to combine words using grammatical rules) and learning (e.g., the mechanisms that allow new information to be compared to previous experiences) are nearly universal. Diversity is evident in the effectiveness with which children learn and remember academic information (Chapters 6, 7, 8, and 9).	The need for peer affiliation represents a universal aspect of development in children and adolescents. However, there are considerable individual differences in the kinds of social groups that young people join and the degree to which they are popular with peers (Chapter 15).
Qualitative and Quantitative Change	Some aspects of physical development (e.g., transformations during prenatal development and puberty) reflect dramatic qualitative change. Most of the time, however, physical development occurs gradually as a result of many small changes (e.g., young children slowly grow taller) (Chapters 4 and 5).	Children's logical reasoning skills show some qualitative change; for instance, children acquire new, more sophisticated ways of solving problems. Quantitative change occurs as children gradually gain knowledge in various academic disciplines (Chapters 6, 7, and 10).	Some evidence suggests that with appropriate social experience, children's understanding of morality undergoes qualitative change, often in conjunction with changes in logical reasoning. In a quantitative manner, children gradually come to understand how other people's minds work and discover that others' knowledge, beliefs, and desires may be different from their own (Chapters 12 and 14).

THEORIES OF CHILD DEVELOPMENT

To guide their research questions, methods, and interpretations of data, developmental scholars construct **theories**, integrated collections of principles and explanations regarding particular phenomena. Seven theoretical approaches have dominated academic discussions of child development and practical concerns about children since the field emerged. We examine the theories and their practical implications here, one by one, and then refer to them selectively in later chapters as they become relevant to particular topics.

Biological Theories

The adaptive ability of children's bodies to support their survival, growth, and learning is the focus of **biological theories**. When heredity increases children's chances for survival, they live into their adult years, have children of their own, and pass on their genes to the next generation. As children, our ancestors had to be prepared to form bonds with protective caregivers; without such bonds, they would not have survived their early years. Thus children are now biologically predisposed to form attachments with primary caregivers.

theory
Integrated collection of principles and explanations regarding a particular phenomenon.

biological theory
Theoretical perspective that focuses on inherited physiological structures of the body and brain that support survival, growth, and learning.

Historically, biological theories emphasized the *maturation* of children's bodies and motor abilities (Gesell, 1928). Early theorists compiled detailed charts of the average ages at which children learn to sit, crawl, reach for objects, and so forth. According to this view, children walk when they are physiologically ready, and puberty begins when a biological clock triggers the appropriate hormones. In some instances maturation establishes sensitive periods for learning in particular domains. Italian physician and educator **Maria Montessori** (1870–1952) noticed that infants are perceptive of order and details in the physical world and that toddlers and preschool-aged children eagerly soak up details about language (Montessori, 1936, 1949). In the many Montessori schools now in existence in North America and Western Europe, teachers are urged to become careful observers of children's natural tendencies and to provide stimulating materials that entice children to engage in educational activities suited to their up-and-coming abilities.

A limitation of many early biological perspectives was that they largely overlooked the effects of children's experiences on development. In comparison, contemporary biological theorists emphasize that genes are flexible instructions that blend with environmental experiences to affect the child. Thus biological perspectives are now more balanced in their regard for nature and nurture (Bjorklund, 2003; Gottlieb, Wahlsten, & Lickliter, 2006; J. P. Spencer et al., 2009).

Two key principles that a practitioner can take away from biological theories are that (a) children's maturational levels impose limits on their interests and (b) children's physical abilities serve valuable functions for them, such as permitting age-appropriate exploration. For example, if you accept the idea that preschool children are predisposed to be physically active, you will understand that they need regularly scheduled time in safely equipped playgrounds.

Behaviorism and Social Learning Theories

Whereas biological theorists see heredity (nature) as a principal driving force behind development, advocates of behaviorism and social learning theories propose that developmental change is largely due to environmental influences (nurture). Conducting research with humans and other species (e.g., dogs, rats, pigeons), these theorists have shown that many behaviors can be modified through environmental stimuli. As a proponent of a perspective known as **behaviorism**, American psychologist **B. F. Skinner** (1904–1990) suggested that children actively "work" for rewards, such as food, praise, or physical contact, and tend to avoid behaviors that lead to punishment (Skinner, 1953, 1957). Other behavioral theorists have revealed how children learn emotional responses to certain stimuli (e.g., a fear of dogs) based on their experiences (e.g., receiving a painful dog bite).

A serious limitation of behaviorism is that it focuses exclusively on children's visible behaviors, with little consideration for how their internal thought processes might influence those actions. In contrast, contemporary **social learning theories** portray children's beliefs and goals as having crucial influences on their actions. Researchers in the social learning tradition have shown that behavior is not always a response to a reward or punishment in the immediate environment. Instead, children regularly anticipate the consequences of their actions and choose their behaviors accordingly, whether or not they have ever been rewarded or punished for these actions. Moreover, children learn a great deal by observing what other people do and what consequences (e.g., rewards and punishments) follow those behaviors, and they develop expectations for the kinds of tasks they are likely to achieve.[2]

Numerous practical applications have been derived from behaviorism and social learning theory, and you will encounter many of them as you read this book. For now, let's look at three overarching principles. First, environmental stimuli, such as rewards and punishments, clearly do influence children's actions and feelings. Mary Jalongo, in the opening case study, chose not to follow the advice of her principal in punishing Tonya harshly for stealing because she realized this response would do Tonya more harm than good. Second, children's

behaviorism
Theoretical perspective in which children's behavioral and emotional responses change as a direct result of particular environmental stimuli.

social learning theory
Theoretical perspective that focuses on how children's beliefs and goals influence their actions and how they often learn by observing others.

---

[2]In recent years social learning theory has increasingly incorporated thought processes into its explanations of learning; accordingly, it is sometimes called *social cognitive theory*.

actions are affected by what they see others doing. Children often imitate others' behaviors, whether those behaviors are desirable (e.g., the hoop shots of a famous basketball player) or disagreeable (e.g., a teacher's condescending actions toward the school custodian). Finally, children's confidence in their ability to achieve certain standards is based largely on their past experiences on similar tasks.

Psychodynamic Theories

Psychodynamic theories focus on the interaction between certain internal conflicts and the environment. These theories assert that early experiences play a critical role in later characteristics and behavior. They typically focus on social and personality development and, often, on abnormal development.

The earliest psychodynamic theorist, **Sigmund Freud** (1856–1939), was an Austrian physician who argued that young children continually find themselves torn by sexual and aggressive impulses, on the one hand, and desires to gain approval from parents and society, on the other (Freud, 1905, 1910, 1923). Freud proposed that as an outgrowth of their personal motives and social experiences in families, children progress through a series of qualitatively distinct stages, ideally learning to channel their impulses in socially appropriate ways. Another psychodynamic theorist, Erik Erikson, who was born in Germany and eventually moved to the United States, suggested that people grow as a result of resolving their own internal struggles. Compared to Freud, Erikson focused less on sexual and aggressive impulses and more on other parts of the developing personality, such as desires to feel competent and sure of one's own identity (Erikson, 1963).

Psychodynamic perspectives have made a lasting contribution by highlighting the significance of children's social-emotional needs. Several psychodynamic ideas remain influential today: Early social experiences can direct later development; concerted efforts may be needed to dislodge children from an unhealthy path; and children wrestle with a few specific issues during certain phases of life.

A significant weakness of psychodynamic theories has been the difficulty of supporting claims with research data. For one thing, it is difficult to verify what internal conflicts a particular person might have, in part because many of an individual's conflicts are presumed by psychodynamic theorists to be hidden to self-awareness. If we ourselves are not consciously aware of a conflict, we are unable to talk about that conflict with another person. In addition, generalizations cannot necessarily be made from the studies that the theorists themselves conducted. Freud developed his ideas from in-depth interviews with troubled adults—individuals whose childhoods do not necessarily reflect typical pathways. Critics additionally point out that desires to restrain sexual urges (Freud's theory) and define one's personal identity (Erikson's theory) may be principal motives for some people but not others. Finally, research has refuted several ideas central to psychoanalytical perspectives. Although Freud recommended that children perform mildly aggressive acts as a way to release inborn aggressive tendencies, research indicates that encouraging such acts can actually *increase* aggressive behavior (Mallick & McCandless, 1966; C. E. Smith, Fischer, & Watson, 2009).

Despite these serious problems, psychodynamic theories do remind educators that children often have mixed and confusing emotions. Adults can help children by teaching them to express their feelings in ways that both honestly reflect their experiences and are acceptable to other people.

Cognitive-Developmental Theories

Cognitive-developmental theories emphasize thinking processes and how they change, qualitatively, over time. According to these views, children play an active role in their own development: They seek out new and interesting experiences, try to understand what they see and hear, and work actively to reconcile any discrepancies between new information and what they previously believed to be true. Through these reflections, children's thinking becomes increasingly logical and abstract with age.

The earliest and best-known cognitive-developmental theorist was Swiss scientist Jean Piaget. With a career that spanned decades and spawned thousands of research studies

psychodynamic theory
Theoretical perspective that focuses on how early experiences and internal conflicts affect social and personality development.

cognitive-developmental theory
Theoretical perspective that focuses on major transformations to the underlying structures of thinking over the course of development.

around the world, Piaget focused primarily on children's cognitive development (Piaget, 1928, 1929, 1952a, 1952b). Using detailed observations, in-depth interviews, and ingenious experimental tasks, Piaget investigated the nature of children's logical thinking about such topics as numbers, physical causality, and psychological processes. Another prominent cognitive-developmental theorist, American psychologist **Lawrence Kohlberg** (1927–1987), is known for his extensive research on moral reasoning (Kohlberg, 1963, 1984).

Piaget, Kohlberg, and their colleagues have suggested that taking a developmental perspective means looking sympathetically at children and understanding the logic of their current level of thinking. Although adult-like reasoning may be the eventual, desired outcome for young people, cognitive-developmental theorists believe that it is a mistake to hurry children beyond their current capacities—that one cannot *make* a child think in ways beyond his or her current stage. They also believe that adults who try to push children beyond their present abilities create unnecessary stress and fail to nurture children's existing reasoning skills.

Many cognitive-developmental ideas are well regarded by the current generation of developmental scholars. Contemporary experts recognize that children's thinking often reflects a reasonable attempt to make sense of novel and puzzling information. However, cognitive-developmental theories have also undergone vigorous critiques. A central criticism is that researchers rarely find that children's development reflects clear-cut stages. Instead, children often move back and forth between more and less sophisticated ways of thinking. Critics point out, for example, that simply because children do not think abstractly about a particular topic does not mean that they are *incapable* of abstract reasoning, especially with the support of an adult. As we mentioned in our earlier discussion of stage theories, children are sometimes able to reason at a very high level in certain areas, while simultaneously being incapable of advanced reasoning in other areas.

Perhaps the most important principle that emerges from cognitive-developmental theories is that teachers need to understand children *as children*. To facilitate children's learning, educators must listen closely to children's conversations, permit children to actively explore their environment, observe their actions, and gently probe them about their ideas. Only when adults appreciate children's thinking can they hope to enhance it.

Cognitive Process Theories

Cognitive process theories focus on basic thinking processes. Of central concern is how people interpret and remember what they see and hear and how these processes change during childhood and adolescence.

Cognitive process researchers conduct detailed analyses of what children think and do. For instance, investigators have studied the eye movements of children scanning pictures, the length of time it takes them to read various kinds of text, and their strategies in completing puzzles. Such analyses are guided by clear models of how children attend to information, find it meaningful, and use it later.[3]

Recent research by American psychologist **Robert Siegler** illustrates the cognitive process approach. Siegler has found that children often spontaneously use a variety of different strategies when first learning to complete tasks in arithmetic. For instance, in solving the problem "2 + 4 = ?" children may count on their fingers, starting with the first number and then counting on from there ("two . . . then three, four, five, six—six altogether"), or simply recall the number fact "2 + 4 = 6" from memory. The same versatility is present as children begin to tackle such other tasks as telling time, spelling, and reading. Children's general tactic of trying out a range of solutions is often quite adaptive in helping them determine which methods work effectively with particular kinds of problems (Siegler, 2006; Siegler & Alibali, 2005).

Cognitive process theories now dominate much of the research in cognitive development. A key contribution of this perspective has been to describe children's thinking with painstaking detail, but critics suggest that there is a price to pay for taking such a focused

cognitive process theory
Theoretical perspective that focuses on the precise nature of human mental operations.

[3]Information processing theories, a family of theoretical perspectives that are examined in Chapter 7, offer influential frameworks for conducting precise analyses of children's thinking.

view on learning. Cognitive process researchers can easily overlook the larger issue of *why* children think as they do. For instance, cognitive process approaches often neglect the social-emotional factors and contexts of children's lives, factors that many other modern developmental theorists consider significant.

Another contribution of cognitive process theories has been the wealth of concrete, research-tested instructional strategies they have provided. Many teachers have found these applications to be quite useful. Cognitive process theories offer techniques for keeping children's attention, making the most of their limited memory capabilities, and challenging their misconceptions on particular topics.

Sociocultural Theories

Cognitive developmentalists and cognitive process theorists have focused squarely on how intellectual skills develop within an individual. By and large, both have paid little attention to the roles played by the broader social and cultural settings within which individuals live. **Sociocultural theories**, on the other hand, try to concentrate on the impact of *social systems* (e.g., families, teacher–child relationships, and community agencies) and *cultural* traditions (e.g., customs with print, types of household chores, and uses of memory aids). These theories see development as the process of children becoming full participants in the society into which they are born.

Russian psychologist and educator **Lev Vygotsky** (1896–1934) is the pioneering figure credited with advancing our knowledge of how children's minds are shaped by everyday experiences in social settings. Having studied the learning of both children and adults, Vygotsky concluded that people grow intellectually by taking part in everyday cultural activities and gradually assuming higher levels of responsibility (Vygotsky, 1962, 1978). Vygotsky believed that guidance with tools, especially advice on using such tangible materials as a protractor in mathematics or lined paper in writing, and such mental prompts as rules for how to dissect an angle, foster cognitive growth. Because different cultures impart distinct ways of thinking about and performing daily tasks, children's thoughts and behaviors develop in culturally specific ways.

sociocultural theory
Theoretical perspective that focuses on children's learning of tools, thinking processes, and communication systems through practice in meaningful tasks with other people.

The last two decades have seen a virtual explosion of research conducted within sociocultural perspectives (Griedler & Shields, 2008; Lillemyr, Søbstad, Marder, & Flowerday, 2011; Markus & Hamedani, 2007). This recent research is often well received by teachers because it focuses on real children in real settings and offers advice on steps teachers can take to support children's learning. Another strength of sociocultural theories is that they show concretely how specific cultural groups encourage children to use different modes of thinking.

As with any theoretical approach, however, sociocultural theories have limitations. Sociocultural theorists have described children's thinking with less precision than have investigators working within cognitive process perspectives. In some cases sociocultural theorists have taken for granted that children learn important skills simply by taking part in an activity; in reality, however, some children merely go through the motions and take little responsibility for completing a task.

Sociocultural theories offer important applications for educators and other adults. A key principle is that children learn valuable skills by being engaged in authentic adult tasks (Gauvain, 2001). Depending on their society, children may learn to weave, hunt, raise crops, care for livestock, look after younger children, worship in a religious community, barter and trade, read and write, or acquire some combination of these or other skills. In the classroom, it is important for adults to provide children with opportunities to tackle real-world tasks that were previously beyond their capabilities.

Sociocultural perspectives also offer implications as to how children's cultural practices at home influence their learning and

LIKE THIS. This South African girl is closely watching her mother grinding grain. From the perspective of sociocultural theories, children and adolescents learn a lot from participating in the routine, purposeful activities of their society.

behavior at school. Teachers can reach out to the range of cultures they serve by inviting families to share some aspects of their family traditions and encouraging children to make frequent choices in classroom tasks, for example selecting autobiographies of interest to them. Teachers can further incorporate some aspects of children's traditions in the classroom, perhaps their cultural greetings, and make their own cultural expectations transparent by clearly communicating rules and procedures for children's behavior.

Developmental Systems Theories

Developmental systems theories help clarify how multiple factors combine to promote child development. A child's body is an active, living *system,* an organized assembly of parts that work together to keep the child alive and growing. The child is also part of a physical environment and a member of multiple, interconnected social systems (Baltes et al., 2006; K. W. Fischer & Bidell, 2006; Lerner, 2002; Thelen & Smith, 2006). From this perspective, the child's own activity contributes to changes in and among these various systems.

Urie Bronfenbrenner (1917–2005), a native of Russia and immigrant to the United States at age 6, is undoubtedly the most widely known developmental systems theorist. In his *bioecological model* of human development, Bronfenbrenner described the influences that people, institutions, and prevailing cultural practices have on children. Of utmost importance are the immediate and extended families that children interact with every day (Bronfenbrenner & Morris, 2006). Parents and other primary caregivers form close bonds with children, meet children's emotional needs, arrange for children to take on increasingly responsible roles in society, and inspire children to become productive members of society. Yet children also clearly have influential relationships with people outside the family. In our introductory case Mary Jalongo played an important role in Tonya's life because she expressed her faith in Tonya and took a few practical steps to guide the little girl. Teachers, peers, and neighbors regularly support children and in some cases compensate for disadvantages at home or in the community (Criss, Pettit, Bates, Dodge, & Lapp, 1992; Crosnoe & Elder, 2004; Rhodes & Lowe, 2009).

Also important in the bioecological model are other elements of society. Institutions that parents participate in, such as the workplace and political systems, trickle down to influence children (Bronfenbrenner, 1979, 2005; Bronfenbrenner & Morris, 2006). Parents who receive decent wages and have close relationships with coworkers, friends, and family generally have adequate resources and energy to share with children. Those who don't receive sufficient support may find it difficult to remain engaged and patient with children.

As in the sociocultural framework, culture is seen as important in the bioecological model. Children's culture tells them whether they should be obedient and devoted or independent and self-assertive in their family, school, and society. Moreover, their culture tells them whether they are valued members of society or members of groups that must fight discrimination (Fegley, Spencer, Goss, Harpalani, & Charles, 2008; M. B. Spencer, 2006). The result of these many personal and cultural influences is that every child has protective factors—perhaps strong family relationships or warm relationships with neighbors—as well as risk factors—possibly economic poverty or racism in the community—that profoundly influence his or her outlook on life (Masten, Cutuli, Herbers, & Reed, 2009; M. B. Spencer, 2006).

Finally, the bioecological model suggests that children partly determine their own environment (see Figure 1-2). A boy who is quiet and reflective triggers a different style of instruction from his teacher than does another child who is disruptive and inattentive. Thus dynamic relationships exist between the child and the environment and among all systems in which the child develops. For example, if parents and teachers develop mutually respectful relationships, they are likely to magnify their support of a child. When parent–teacher relationships are weak, adults may blame one another for a struggling child's limitations, with the result that no one teaches the child needed skills. Because the child, parent, teachers, and other people in the environment are themselves maturing and responding to ongoing events, relationships affecting the child also change with time.

The power of developmental systems theories is that they capture it all—nature and nurture, and the child's own characteristics and activities. Ironically, the integrative character

> **Preparing for Your Licensure Examination**
> Your teaching test might ask you about the basic ideas of B. F. Skinner, Jean Piaget, Erik Erikson, Lev Vygotsky, Urie Bronfenbrenner, and other key developmental theorists.

developmental systems theory Theoretical perspective that focuses on the multiple factors, including systems inside and outside children, that combine to influence children's development.

FIGURE 1-2 The bioecological model examines the child's development within an interactive, multilayered, and changing environment. The family is crucially important, ideally loving the child and offering daily informal lessons on becoming a productive member of society. Others interacting with the child regularly, including teachers, peers, and neighbors, also play foundational roles in the child's life. Some social settings and individuals, such as employers and family friends, typically give the parents needed financial and emotional support and thus indirectly help the child. The child, in turn, actively influences family members and other people based on his or her physical appearance, developmental abilities, temperament, intellectual skills, and behavior. Cultural values and practices give meaning to the activities of the child, other people, and society's institutions. The child, the environment, and the interactions among these various systems exhibit constant change and adaptation.
Based on Bronfenbrenner, 2005; Bronfenbrenner & Morris, 2006; M. B. Spencer, 2006.

of these theories also creates their weaknesses. It is difficult to make predictions about any single factor in development because the effects of each factor are so intertwined with other elements of the developmental context.

Like the other theoretical perspectives, developmental systems theories offer valuable ideas for teachers and other practitioners. Contemporary ecological theorists suggest that educators can exert beneficial effects on children by considering children's own perceptions of experiences in their inter-related environments (M. B. Spencer, 2006). Thus, it is always important to listen to a child's ideas, as Mary did with Tonya in the introductory case, and to look at each child as facing strengths and limitations. Educators can also form their own close relationships with children, supplementing children's connections with family members and thoughtfully considering the skills and expectations that children have developed in other settings. Because youngsters can change dramatically after a transition (e.g., moving to a new school, encountering a bully in the school yard), educators must keep tabs on youngsters' evolving experiences and adjust services accordingly.

Taking a Strategic Approach to Theory

Table 1-1 summarizes the seven theoretical perspectives. With so many theories, it is tempting to ask, "Which one is right?" The answer is that, to some extent, they all are. Each perspective provides unique insights that no other approach currently offers. At the same time, no single theory can adequately explain all aspects of child development, and increasingly, theorists themselves find they must draw from more than one camp to do justice to all they

TABLE 1-1 Theories of Child Development

THEORETICAL PERSPECTIVES	POSITIONS	BASIC DEVELOPMENTAL ISSUES	REPRESENTATIVE THEORISTS[a]
Biological Theories	Investigators focus on genetic factors, physiological structures, and inborn dispositions that help the child adapt and survive in his or her environment. As an illustration, compared to young adolescents who slept well for relatively long periods at night, youngsters of the same age who slept less and reported interrupted sleep exhibited little activity in a part of their brain that is associated with positive emotions and sensations of being rewarded (Holm et al., 2009).	*Nature and Nurture*: Characteristics and behaviors that enhance an individual's chances for survival and reproduction are supported by genetic instructions. Adequate nutrients, supportive social relationships, and exploration in the physical environment are essential to normal growth. *Universality and Diversity*: Universally, children form bonds with caregivers, express themselves with language, infer other people's intentions and feelings, and use tools. Diversity in physical characteristics and abilities occurs through variations in genes and experience. *Qualitative and Quantitative Change*: Qualitative changes are seen in physical transformations at puberty and with sensitive periods in perceptual development and language learning. In other respects the child grows gradually, reflecting many quantitative transformations.	Charles Darwin Arnold Gesell Maria Montessori Konrad Lorenz John Bowlby Mary Ainsworth Sandra Scarr Robert Plomin David Bjorklund Susan Gelman Henry Wellman
Behaviorism and Social Learning Theories	Investigators focus on effects of environmental stimuli on behavioral change. In one investigation a group of girls with cystic fibrosis were more likely to engage in health-promoting exercise for 20-minute segments of time when they were given small immediate rewards (e.g., special snacks) and allowed to earn points that could be saved up and later exchanged for larger prizes (e.g., playing their favorite game with their parents) (Bernard, Cohen, & Moffet, 2009).	*Nature and Nurture*: Emphasis is on nurture. When children act, the environment responds with rewards or punishments or ignores the behavior. Children modify their actions based on their experiences, goals, and beliefs about whether an action will lead to desirable or undesirable consequences. *Universality and Diversity*: Children work for generally similar kinds of rewards (e.g., food, praise, physical contact). Yet preferences for particular incentives are somewhat individual, and because environments vary in how they respond to children's actions, diversity in behavior is expected. *Qualitative and Quantitative Change*: Development is quantitative: Children undergo countless incremental changes in behaviors.	B. F. Skinner John B. Watson Ivan Pavlov Sidney Bijou Donald Baer Albert Bandura
Psychodynamic Theories	Investigators focus on how early experiences and internal conflicts affect social and personality development. In an investigation in which divorced parents and their children were studied over a 10-year period, researchers detected the emergence of sibling rivalries that were based, in part, on unconsciously held allegiances to different parents (Wallerstein & Lewis, 2007).	*Nature and Nurture*: Sexual and aggressive urges are inborn. Family and society affect how children express instinctual urges, their basic trust in others, and their perceptions of themselves as individuals. *Universality and Diversity*: Universally, children struggle with strong feelings (e.g., aggression and sexuality, according to S. Freud) and personal challenges (e.g., the belief that they can or cannot make things happen, according to Erikson). Relationships with other people are highly varied and result in diversity in the ways in which children resolve life's challenges. *Qualitative and Quantitative Change*: Through a series of qualitatively distinct stages, children learn to resolve mixed feelings and gain a sense of their own identity.	Sigmund Freud Anna Freud Erik Erikson
Cognitive-Developmental Theories	Investigators focus on major transformations in children's thinking. One researcher found that young children focused on their own concrete views of an event, whereas older children and adolescents were able to consider how several individuals could see a single event from several valid points of view (Selman, 1980).	*Nature and Nurture*: Children are biological organisms strongly motivated to make sense of their personal worlds (nature). Access to a reasonably complex environment is vital to development (nurture). Young people also actively contribute to their own intellectual development. *Universality and Diversity*: Universality is emphasized. Variations among youngsters are most common at the highest stages of development, which require certain experiences (e.g., instruction in scientific reasoning). *Qualitative and Quantitative Change*: Children's thinking undergoes transformations in the essence of reasoning; new ways of classifying information build on previous systems but also involve reorganizations in thought processes. Quantitative additions to the knowledge base occur within stages.	Jean Piaget Bärbel Inhelder Lawrence Kohlberg David Elkind Robbie Case John Flavell

(continued)

TABLE 1-1   Theories of Child Development (continued)

THEORETICAL PERSPECTIVES	POSITIONS	BASIC DEVELOPMENTAL ISSUES	REPRESENTATIVE THEORISTS[a]
Cognitive Process Theories	Investigators focus on the precise nature of human cognitive operations. In one study adolescents who participated in debates with their peers and received instruction in how to make counterarguments acquired more sophisticated reasoning and argumentation skills (Kuhn & Udell, 2003).	*Nature and Nurture*: Both nature and nurture are important. Children are born with basic capacities to perceive, interpret, and remember information; these capacities change with brain maturation, experience, and reflection. *Universality and Diversity*: The desire to make sense of the world is universal. Diversity is present in the kinds of educational experiences children have and, to some degree, in their natural intellectual talents. *Qualitative and Quantitative Change*: The methods by which children perceive, interpret, and remember information gradually change both qualitatively (e.g., inventing new rules for solving arithmetic problems) and quantitatively (e.g., acquiring knowledge about plant species).	David Klahr Deanna Kuhn Robert Siegler Ann L. Brown Henry Wellman Susan Gelman John Flavell Robbie Case
Sociocultural Theories	Investigators focus on acquisition of tools, communication systems, intellectual abilities, and social-emotional skills through practice in meaningful tasks with other people. In one study children's ability to plan their informal activities (such as deciding what to do after school, what to eat for breakfast, and what to watch on television) improved over the elementary years and depended somewhat on their cultural background (Gauvain & Perez, 2005).	*Nature and Nurture*: Emphasis is on nurture. Children become familiar with tools used by their families as they take part in daily activities with them (nurture). The capacity to acquire the traditions and ideas of one or more cultures is inherited (nature). *Universality and Diversity*: All children learn language, beliefs espoused in their communities, and practical life skills. Variation is present in the particular tools, customs, and ideas that children in various societies acquire. *Qualitative and Quantitative Change*: Children shift qualitatively in how they carry out tasks. Initially, a child may look to a teacher for help when completing a puzzle and later independently follow the teacher's strategies (e.g., beginning by inserting pieces with a straight line). Quantitatively, children gradually take on responsibility in social groups.	Lev Vygotsky A. R. Luria James Wertsch Barbara Rogoff Patricia Greenfield Mary Gauvain Jerome Bruner Michael Cole
Developmental Systems Theories	Investigators focus on the multiple factors that interact in children's development. In one study a wide range of factors were associated with hours children slept at night, including children's own activities (e.g., excessive television viewing was associated with little sleep), family functioning (e.g., eating family meals together on weekdays was associated with relatively lengthy sleep), and demographic factors (e.g., older African American children slept fewer hours than did children from other groups) (Adam, Snell, & Pendry, 2007).	*Nature and Nurture*: Multiple factors in the child (nature) and outside the child (nurture) combine to influence developmental patterns. The child's own activity is also an essential factor in development. *Universality and Diversity*: Developmental changes occur in all individuals from conception to death. Some changes are common at a particular age, yet individual children face slightly different obstacles when acquiring new abilities depending on historical events and personal circumstances. *Qualitative and Quantitative Change*: Most change is quantitative, but shifts in action occur that result in entirely new ways of behaving. For example, a baby may use her arm to swat awkwardly at a toy and later learn to pick it up with a precise finger grip.	Urie Bronfenbrenner Arnold Sameroff Margaret Beale Spencer Richard Lerner Kurt Fischer Esther Thelen Gilbert Gottlieb Paul Baltes

[a]Several theorists have contributed to two or more theoretical perspectives. For example, John Flavell and Robbie Case have made important contributions to both cognitive-developmental and cognitive process theories, Albert Bandura has made contributions to social learning and cognitive process perspectives, and Henry Wellman and Susan Gelman have conducted research referring to biological functions and cognitive processes.

know about child development. In a sense, any theory is like a lens that brings certain phenomena into sharp focus but leaves other phenomena blurry or out of the picture.

As you proceed through the book, you will see that we frequently summarize specific theoretical perspectives on particular aspects of children's development—for example, theories about their cognitive development, moral development, and language acquisition. These specific frameworks offer precise analyses of children's learning in specific areas. Inevitably, however, any narrowly focused theory omits crucial information about the influences of children's own characteristics and the settings in which they live. We attempt to redress this limitation by periodically reminding you to take a bigger perspective, one that takes into account the dynamic ways in which children's own characteristics and multilayered environments influence their learning in particular domains. Whenever you notice the bioecological symbol in the margin (as you can see in the margin next to this paragraph), pay attention to how children are growing and changing based on a complex blend of factors, including their genetic makeup, relationships with others, and cultural practices and beliefs.

Bioecology of Child Development

DEVELOPMENTAL PERIODS

We can make our task of exploring child development more manageable by dividing the developmental journey into specific time periods. Age cutoffs are somewhat arbitrary, yet we know that children act in very different ways as they grow. In our discussions of changes in various abilities, we usually consider five periods: infancy (birth–2 years), early childhood (2–6 years), middle childhood (6–10 years), early adolescence (10–14 years), and late adolescence (14–18 years). Here we give an overview for each period, identifying the typical needs and accomplishments of youngsters and their implications for teachers and other practitioners. As we do, we refer you to some of the video clips in MyEducationLab.

Infancy (Birth–2 Years)

Infancy is a truly remarkable period. It is a time when basic human traits, such as emotional bonds with other people, nonverbal communication, language expression, and motor exploration of the physical environment, burst onto the scene.

A newborn baby is completely dependent on others. But the baby is equipped with an arsenal of skills—including a distinctive cry, physical reflexes, an interest in human faces, and a brain alert to novelty and sameness—that elicit comfort and stimulation from caregivers. In a matter of weeks, the baby smiles broadly during good-humored exchanges with a caregiver. As the caregiver responds warmly and consistently, attachment grows.

A sense of security nourishes infants' desire to learn. Babies want to know everything: what car keys taste like, what older family members do in the kitchen, and what happens when they drop a bowl of peas. Infants' growing facility with language builds on interests in concrete experiences, such as a parent's laughter and the sensation of warm water in the bathtub.

Intellectual curiosity fuels babies' drive to use physical skills. Babies reach, crawl, and climb to get objects they desire. The urge to explore coincides with a budding sense of mastery ("I *can* do it!") and independence ("*I* can do it!"). Emotional reactions, such as a legitimate fear of heights and uneasiness in the presence of strangers, limit physical exploration and occasionally prompt withdrawal.

Professional Viewpoints

Caregivers who work effectively with infants realize that each baby is unique, develops at his or her own rate, and is hungry for loving interaction. These caregivers emphasize *quality* of care, giving individualized, responsive, and affectionate attention to babies and their families (Chazan-Cohen, Jerald, & Stark, 2001; Petersen & Wittmer, 2008).

In addition, knowledgeable caregivers design the physical environment so that infants can explore objects and their surroundings freely. The "Environments: Infancy" video in MyEducationLab shows a setting where crawling infants can speed up and down cushioned ramps, and walking infants (*toddlers*) can swagger around open spaces.[4] When infants stumble, furniture poses little threat because

Go to the Video Examples section in Topic 1 of MyEducationLab to watch the "Environments: Infancy" video and see a setting that is safe and interesting for infants.

YUM. During infancy, children learn a great deal from mouthing objects and exploring things with their hands. This child is enjoying the taste and sensation of her birthday cake.

---

[4]Appreciation is extended to Greg Pierson, University Schools, and Keli Cotner, Campus Child Care Center, both of Greeley, Colorado, for granting permission to film their facilities.

it has been crafted with soft, rounded edges. Caregivers also consider infants' cognitive and social abilities in their design of the environment. In the video, notice a mirror that attracts attention; colorful toys with complex textures that beg to be touched; mobiles over cribs that encourage inspection; a tunnel that invites entering, exiting, and playing peekaboo games; and simple books to be examined while cuddling with a caregiver in a rocking chair.

High-quality care prepares an infant for the expanded learning opportunities of early childhood. The infant is ready to venture from the caregiver's lap.

Early Childhood (2–6 Years)

Early childhood is a period of incredible creativity, fantasy, and play. Preschool-aged children see life as a forum for imagination and drama: They reinvent the world, try on new roles, and work hard to play their parts in harmony.

Language and communication skills develop rapidly during early childhood. New vocabulary, sensitivity to communication rules, and facility with syntax (grammar) are noticeable advancements. Language builds on daily increases in knowledge about the world and, especially, the habits and patterns of daily life.

Physical changes are apparent as well. High levels of energy radiate from preschool-aged children's activities. The cautious movements of infancy give way to fluid rolling, tumbling, running, and skipping. Socially and emotionally, preschoolers are often endearing, trusting, and affectionate with adults. They become progressively more interested in peers, infuse fantasy into play, and contend with aggressive and self-centered impulses.

Professional Viewpoints

Effective teachers of young children channel children's natural energy with gentle guidance. They are respectful of young children's curiosity, spontaneity, and desire to try on new roles. They realize that children learn a great deal as they play and need unstructured free time as well as access to storybooks and other academic materials (Hirsh-Pasek, Golinkoff, Berk, & Singer, 2009).

Environments for young children are designed to encourage active and purposeful learning (National Association for the Education of Young Children [NAEYC], 1997, 2009). In the "Environments: Early Childhood" video in MyEducationLab, you can see a classroom where children draw and paint creatively. Play structures encourage children to climb, hide, and search for one another. Tables and chairs make it possible for children to sit and converse during mealtimes and group activities. A dramatic play area, furnished with kitchen appliances and dress-up clothes, encourages imagination. Elsewhere in the room children can sit and look at books and take turns on a computer. Mats let children recharge their batteries with rest; a separate bathroom area is available for toilet needs and hand washing. Outdoors, children can scoot on vehicles, ride bicycles, and play in the sand.

Given ample chances to explore the environment and interact with others, young children gain valuable knowledge about themselves and their world. They become ready to complete the realistic tasks of middle childhood.

Middle Childhood (6–10 Years)

Children continue to learn through play during the elementary years, but they also become capable of giving sustained attention to real-world activities (Bergen & Fromberg, 2009).[5] In fact, children now invest considerable effort in mastering the customs, tools, and accumulated

LET'S PLAY. Cooperative play is an important forum for learning during early childhood. These two boys are coordinating their fantasies as superheroes.

Go to the Video Examples section in Topic 1 to watch the "Environments: Early Childhood" video and observe a setting that encourages creative movement, pretend play, and hands-on learning in young children.

[5]Many children retain qualities typical of early childhood, including an interest in pretend play, until age 8 or older, which has led the NAEYC to classify children from birth until age 8 as "young children" (NAEYC, 1997). In this book we have used age 6 as the cutoff between early and middle childhood. Although age 6 is somewhat arbitrary, it marks the typical age for first grade, during which time schools introduce an academic curriculum. We also wanted to distinguish the middle childhood period from the early adolescent period, since some youngsters (girls in particular) begin the first phases of puberty as early as age 8 or 9.

knowledge of their community and culture. Children of this age often learn to read and write, apply rules in games and sports, care for younger brothers and sisters, and use computer technology.

Serious commitments to peers, especially to playmates of the same age and gender, also emerge during middle childhood. Friendships are important, and children learn much from spending time together and getting into—and out of—scuffles. Children also begin to compare their performance to that of others: Why do I have fewer friends than Maria does? Am I good enough to be picked for the baseball team? When they routinely end up on the losing side in such comparisons, children are more hesitant to take on new challenges.

In the elementary school years, children internalize many admonishments they've heard repeatedly (e.g., "Don't play near the river," "Keep an eye on your little brother"). They gain a sense of what is expected of them, and most are inclined to live up to these standards. Basic motor skills are polished, and many children become proficient in athletic skills.

GROWING IN THE GARDEN. Middle childhood is a time of sustained attention to realistic tasks. These children are learning how to care for plants in a community garden.

Professional Viewpoints

In middle childhood, children do their best thinking when they are familiar with a topic and have access to concrete objects for bolstering their reasoning. Teachers can nurture children's skills by observing them, learning about their skills and areas in which they are less knowledgeable, and implementing instructional methods that allow them to handle objects and make connections to their prior understandings (Association for Childhood Education International, 2009; National Board for Professional Teaching Standards, 2001).

You can see a classroom that provides noticeable support for children's academic learning in the "Environments: Middle Childhood" video in MyEducationLab. Maps are visible in several places, suggesting the importance of geography. Frequently used words are posted on cabinets for children to refer to while writing. Small objects can be manipulated, counted, and classified according to shape and other properties. Books, a computer, chalkboards, and other resources are available to extend children's learning. Tables and chairs permit group work, and sofas encourage relaxation while reading.

Having learned to think systematically, children are ready for some particularly challenging tasks: growing an adult body and speculating on what it means to hold a job, date, become intimate, and raise a family. This transition between childhood and adulthood takes time and effort, and there are growing pains along the way.

Early Adolescence (10–14 Years)

In early adolescence, a youngster embarks on the transition from having a childlike physique to having a reproductively mature body. Physical changes are accompanied by equally dramatic reorganizations in learning processes and relationships with parents and peers.

The physical changes of puberty are orderly and predictable, but many boys and girls alike experience them as puzzling, disconcerting events. Young adolescents sometimes look and feel awkward. Hormonal changes can lead to mood swings. Adolescents reflect on their changing selves and worry about how their peers perceive them. They wonder: What are they thinking of me? Am I one of the "cool" kids? Adults

MyEducationLab

Go to the Video Examples section in Topic 1 of MyEducationLab to watch the "Environments: Middle Childhood" video and view a setting that supports children's academic learning with concrete objects, displays of language rules, tables and chairs for group work, couches for relaxed reading, and other resources.

Improving Your Observation Skills

Who said that? Peer relationships are a high priority during adolescence. How are these adolescents showing their interest in one another? Compare your response with the explanation at the end of the chapter.

have accelerating expectations for teenagers, which are not always easy to meet. Peers become a sounding board through which adolescents seek assurance that their appearance and behaviors are acceptable.

Adolescents begin to think in a far-reaching, logical, and abstract manner. The interests of young adolescents broaden well beyond family and peer group. Feeling powerful and idealistic, adolescents challenge the existing order, wondering why schools, governments, and the earth's ecosystem cannot be improved overnight.

Diversity is present in every developmental phase, but individual differences are especially pronounced in early adolescence. The ages at which the sequences of puberty begin can vary considerably from one individual to the next. Thus not all young adolescents begin puberty during the 10- to 14-year age range. Some, girls especially, may begin puberty before age 10. Others, boys in particular, may not begin puberty until the end of this age span.

Professional Viewpoints

Middle school educators suggest that every student should be supported by one adult (an *adviser*) who keeps an eye on the student's academic and personal development, perhaps within the context of a "home base" period or other group meeting time (National Middle School Association, 2006). The adviser–student relationship, when stable and positive, can help young adolescents weather rapid developmental changes. In addition to being personal advocates, teachers can educate learners with varied instructional methods and offer extended time for learning during the regular school day and in after-school programs. Breadth in the curriculum accommodates adolescents' need for autonomy by allowing students to choose some of their classes in elective areas.

Several environments designed to meet the developmental needs of young adolescents are shown in the "Environments: Early Adolescence" video in MyEducationLab. Classrooms are equipped with a rich array of instructional resources, including clocks, an easel, chalkboards, maps, binders, and a computer. Adolescents' artwork, papers, and a diorama are displayed for all to admire. A code of conduct reminds adolescents to treat themselves, others, and the environment with kindness and respect. A small room with two desks is set aside for private conversations with familiar adults. Hallways are clean and uncluttered, school colors are prominent, and rows of lockers give adolescents places to store personal supplies and congregate between classes.

First steps toward maturity are often hesitant ones. With affection from parents and teachers, young adolescents gradually gain confidence that the adult world is within reach.

MyEducationLab

Go to the Video Examples section in Topic 1 of MyEducationLab to watch the "Environments: Early Adolescence" video and see a setting that encourages young adolescents to focus on academic learning, work together in groups, talk privately with advisors, and follow a code of conduct emphasizing kindness and respect.

Late Adolescence (14–18 Years)

As teenagers continue to mature, they lose some of the gawky, uneven features of early adolescence and blossom into attractive young adults. Resembling young adults, older adolescents often feel entitled to make decisions. Common refrains often include the word *my*: "It's *my* hair, *my* body, *my* clothes, *my* room, *my* education, *my life!*"

Late adolescence can be a confusing time to make decisions due to the abundance of mixed messages that society communicates. Teenagers may be encouraged to abstain from sexual activity, yet they continually encounter provocative sexual images in the media. Similarly, parents and teachers urge healthy eating habits, yet junk food is everywhere—in vending machines at school, at the refreshment stand at the movie theater, and often in kitchen cabinets at home.

Fortunately, many high school students make wise decisions. They try hard in school, gain job experience, and refrain from seriously risky behaviors. Some students are less judicious in their choices: They experiment with alcohol, drugs, sex, and violence and in general think more about here-and-now pleasures than long-term consequences.

Peer relationships remain a high priority in late adolescence. Affiliations with age-mates can have either a good or bad influence, depending on typical pastimes of the group. At the same time, most adolescents continue to savor their ties with trusted adults and preserve fundamental values championed by parents and teachers, such as the importance of a good education and the need to be honest and fair.

Individual differences in academic achievement are substantial during the high school years. Indeed, wide variations in students' abilities are among the biggest challenges faced by high schools today. Some low-achieving students drop out of high school altogether, perhaps looking for environments where they can be successful. Many of the low achievers who stay in school hang out with students who share their pessimistic views of education.

Professional Viewpoints

Older adolescents, who are beginning to take on grown-up responsibilities, need intelligent, behind-the-scenes support from adults. Schools that offer personalized services to adolescents—for example, those that ensure that the aspirations, strengths, and limitations of each student are known by a teacher or another school staff member—seem to be especially successful in meeting high school students' needs (National Association of Secondary School Principals, 2004).

School environments can help meet adolescents' needs for personalized attention by doing several things. As you can see in the "Environments: Late Adolescence" video in MyEducationLab, classrooms can be arranged so students face one another, making it hard for anyone to remain anonymous. Of course, physical arrangements must be adapted to instructional formats, and what matters more than layout is that teachers communicate affection, respect, and high expectations to *all* adolescents. In the science classrooms in this clip, numerous types of equipment, resources, and materials are present; these can be used flexibly to meet individual learning needs. Statements of responsibility and citizenship are posted on a wall. A mural contains images appealing to a range of interests, including music, drama, and athletics. The message seems to be that *everyone* belongs here.

The five periods of development just identified appear in Developmental Trends tables throughout the book. These tables summarize key developmental tasks, achievements, and variations at different age levels. In addition, they suggest implications for teachers and other practitioners who work with young people in each developmental period. The first of these tables, "Accomplishments and Diversity at Different Age Levels," gives an overview of the domains of physical, cognitive, and social-emotional development.

MyEducationLab

Go to the Video Examples section in Topic 1 of MyEducationLab to watch the "Environments: Late Adolescence" video and see a setting that encourages adolescents to become proficient in primary subjects, achieve deeper understandings in areas of personal interest, and follow a code of conduct emphasizing responsibility and citizenship.

FROM THEORY TO PRACTICE

The practical applications in this book build on a single basic principle: Children are nurtured most effectively when adults understand how children *generally* progress but also show sensitivity to children's *individual* needs. In other words, teachers engage in **developmentally appropriate practice**, instruction and caregiving adapted to the age, characteristics, and developmental progress of individual youngsters.

Developmentally appropriate practice enables growing children to be active learners, recognizes that adult-level functioning is not always either realistic or valuable for children to imitate, and encourages children to work together in an ethical and democratic fashion (Kohlberg & Mayer, 1972). Developmentally appropriate practice also represents an optimistic expectation that children *can* grow in positive directions.

By knowing the typical characteristics and thinking abilities of children at a particular age, adults set the groundwork for effective instruction and services. By further considering the uniqueness of children and the ways in which culture inevitably affects children's beliefs and skills, educators can refine their support for individual students (Mena & Eyer, 2007). Development and Practice features, which appear throughout the book, provide illustrations of educators guiding young people of various ages and responding to the unique needs of each youngster. The first of these, "Engaging in Developmentally Appropriate Practice with Infants, Children, and Adolescents," appears on the next page.

developmentally appropriate practice
Instruction and other services adapted to the age, characteristics, and developmental progress of individual children.

DEVELOPMENTAL TRENDS
Accomplishments and Diversity at Different Age Levels

AGE	WHAT YOU MIGHT OBSERVE	DIVERSITY	IMPLICATIONS
Infancy (Birth–2 Years) 	**Physical Development** • Motor skills that include rolling over, sitting, crawling, standing, walking • Growing ability to reach, grab, manipulate, and release objects • Rudimentary self-feeding by the end of infancy **Cognitive Development** • Ability to distinguish among different faces (beginning in the first months) • Rapid growth in communication, including crying, using gestures and facial expressions, synchronizing attention with caregivers, babbling, forming one-word sentences, and constructing multiple-word sentences • Ability to imitate simple gestures with a model present, progressing to complex imitation of actions and patterns from memory • Increasing ability to remember people and things out of sight **Social-Emotional Development** • Formation of close bonds with responsive and affectionate caregivers • Use of words to name needs and desires • Playing side by side with peers but also interacting at times • Increasing awareness of ownership and boundaries of self ("Me!" "Mine!") • Developing sense of power and will ("No!")	• Considerable diversity exists in age when, and in manner in which, babies develop motor skills. • Self-feeding and self-help skills emerge later in families that encourage children to rely on others for meeting basic needs. • Children's temperaments and physical abilities affect their exploration of the environment. • Infants receiving restricted nutrition may be less alert and energetic than those with adequate nutrition • Presence of dangers in the environment may lead families to limit children's exploration. • Some young children learn two or three languages, especially when proficiency in multiple languages is valued by caregivers. • Ability to pretend is displayed early by some children and later by others. • Nonverbal communication varies with culture. For instance, a child may be discouraged from making eye contact with an elder as a sign of respect. • Children who have few experiences with peers may appear tentative, detached, or aggressive. • Infants and toddlers who spend time in multiage settings interact differently than do those accustomed to same-age groups. • Some children are encouraged by families to share possessions, and others are encouraged to respect individual rights of property.	• Provide a safe, appropriate, sensory-rich environment so infants can move, explore surroundings, and handle objects. • Hold infants gently, and care for their physical needs in an attentive manner. • Learn and respond sensitively to each infant's distinctive manner of approaching or resisting new people, objects, and events. • Encourage but do not rush infants to learn motor skills, such as walking. • Learn what each family wants for its children, and try to provide culturally sensitive care. • Recognize that children's early images of themselves are influenced by unconscious messages from adults (e.g., "I enjoy holding you" or "I'm sad and unable to attend to your needs"). • Speak to infants regularly to enrich their language development. • Communicate regularly with families about infants' daily activities, including how much and what they eat and drink, how well they sleep, and what their moods are during the day.
Early Childhood (2–6 Years) 	**Physical Development** • Increasing abilities in such motor skills as running and skipping, throwing a ball, building block towers, and using scissors • Increasing competence in basic self-care and personal hygiene **Cognitive Development** • Dramatic play and fantasy with peers • Ability to draw simple figures • Some knowledge of colors, letters, and numbers • Recounting of familiar stories and events **Social-Emotional Development** • Developing understanding of gender and ethnicity • Emerging abilities to defer immediate gratification, share toys, and take turns • Modest appreciation that other people have their own desires, beliefs, and knowledge • Some demonstration of sympathy for people in distress	• Children master coordinated physical skills (e.g., skipping) at different ages. • Individual differences in fine motor proficiency and gross motor agility are substantial. • Some children enter kindergarten having had few social experiences with age-mates; others have been in child care with age-mates since infancy. • Family and cultural backgrounds influence the kinds of skills that children have mastered by the time they begin school. • Some children have had a lot of experience listening to storybooks, but others have been read to only rarely. • Many children at this age have difficulty following rules, standing quietly in line, and waiting for their turns.	• Provide sensory-rich materials that encourage exploration (e.g., water table, sandbox, textured toys). • Arrange a variety of activities (e.g., assembling puzzles, coloring, building with blocks, dancing) that permit children to exercise fine motor and gross motor skills. • Encourage children to engage in cooperative and fantasy play by providing props and open play areas. • Read to children regularly to promote vocabulary and literacy skills. • Give children frequent opportunities to play, interact with peers, and make choices. • Communicate expectations for behavior so that children learn to follow the rules of group settings. • Communicate regularly with families about children's academic and social progress.

DEVELOPMENTAL TRENDS (continued)

AGE	WHAT YOU MIGHT OBSERVE	DIVERSITY	IMPLICATIONS
Middle Childhood (6–10 Years) 	**Physical Development** • Successful imitation of complex physical movements • Ability to ride a bicycle • Participation in organized sports **Cognitive Development** • Development of basic skills in reading, writing, mathematics, and other academic subject areas • Ability to reason logically about concrete objects and events in the immediate environment **Social-Emotional Development** • Increasing awareness of how one's own abilities compare with those of peers • Desire for time with age-mates, especially friends of the same gender • Increasing responsibility for household chores • Adherence to rules of games • Understanding of basic moral principles (e.g., fairness and equity)	• Children begin to compare their academic and physical performance to that of others, and children who perceive they are doing poorly may have less motivation to achieve. • Some children have few chances to exercise with their families or friends. • Many children are unable to sit quietly for long periods. • Individual differences are evident in children's performance in academic areas. • Children differ in temperament and sociability; some are outgoing, whereas others are more reserved and shy. • A few children may show unacceptable levels of aggression toward others.	• Tailor instructional methods (e.g., cooperative groups, individualized assignments, choices in activities) and materials to meet diversity in children's talents, background knowledge, and interests. • Address deficiencies in basic skills (e.g., in reading, writing, and math) before they develop into serious delays. • Provide moderately challenging tasks that encourage children to learn new skills, perform well, and attempt increasingly difficult activities. • Provide the guidance necessary to help children interact more successfully with peers (e.g., by suggesting ways to resolve conflicts and finding a "buddy" for a newcomer to a school or club). • Prohibit bullying and enforce codes of conduct.
Early Adolescence (10–14 Years)	**Physical Development** • Onset of puberty • Significant growth spurt • Increased appetite **Cognitive Development** • Emerging capacity to think and reason about abstract ideas • Preliminary exposure to advanced academic content in specific subject areas **Social-Emotional Development** • Continued (and perhaps greater) interest in peer relationships • Self-consciousness about appearance • Emerging sexual interest in the opposite gender or same gender, depending on orientation • Challenges to parents, teachers, and other authorities regarding rules and boundaries • Occasional moodiness	• Young adolescents exhibit considerable variability in the age at which they begin puberty. • Academic problems often become more pronounced during adolescence; students who encounter frequent failure become less engaged in school activities. • Adolescents seek out peers whose values are compatible with their own and who will give them recognition and status. • Some young adolescents begin to engage in deviant and risky activities (e.g., unprotected sex, cigarette smoking, use of drugs and alcohol).	• Suggest and demonstrate effective study strategies as adolescents begin to tackle difficult subject matter. • Give struggling adolescents the extra academic support they need to be successful. • Provide a regular time and place where young adolescents can seek guidance and advice about academic or social matters (e.g., offer your classroom or office as a place where students can occasionally eat lunch). • Provide opportunities for adolescents to contribute to decision making in clubs and recreation centers. • Hold adolescents accountable for their actions, and impose appropriate consequences when they break rules.
Late Adolescence (14–18 Years)	**Physical Development** • Achievement of sexual maturity and adult height • For some teens, development of a regular exercise program • Development of specific eating habits (e.g., becoming a vegetarian, consuming junk food) **Cognitive Development** • In-depth study of certain academic subject areas • Consideration of career tracks and job prospects **Social-Emotional Development** • Dating • Increasing independence (e.g., driving a car, making choices for free time) • Frequent questioning of existing rules and societal norms • Increasing commitment to personal values, career prospects, ethnic affiliations, and other elements of an identity	• Older adolescents aspire to widely differing educational and career tracks (e.g., some aspire to college, others anticipate securing employment immediately after high school, and still others make no plans for life after high school). • Some teens participate in extracurricular activities; those who do are more likely to stay in school until graduation. • Some adolescents make poor choices regarding the peers with whom they associate. • Some teens become sexually active, and some become parents. • Teenagers' neighborhoods and communities offer differing opportunities and temptations. • Some adolescents are keenly aware of prejudice and discrimination to themselves and others who share their culture, ethnicity, gender, or sexual orientation.	• Communicate caring and respect for all adolescents. • Allow choices in academic subjects and assignments, but hold adolescents to high standards for performance. • Provide the guidance and assistance that low-achieving students may need to be more successful. • Help adolescents explore higher education opportunities and a variety of career paths. • Encourage involvement in extracurricular activities. • Arrange opportunities for adolescents to make a difference in their communities through volunteer work and service learning projects.

DEVELOPMENT AND PRACTICE

Engaging in Developmentally Appropriate Practice with Infants, Children, and Adolescents

Infancy

Set up a safe and stimulating environment for exploration.

- A caregiver in an infant center designs her environment so infants can safely crawl, walk, and climb both inside and on the playground. A quiet corner is reserved for small infants not yet able to move around. Various materials and toys are carefully arranged to be in reach and invite use. Duplicates of popular toys are available.

Arrange clean and quiet areas for meeting physical needs.

- A teacher in an early intervention program sets up his environment so that he can help toddlers meet their physical needs in a hygienic and quiet area. He talks to children while feeding, diapering, and toileting, explaining what's happening and praising children when they take small steps toward self-care.

Provide culturally sensitive care, and support families' home languages.

- A family child care provider who is bilingual in Spanish and English uses both languages with toddlers in her care. She has cloth and cardboard books in both languages (some of the books are homemade), as well as recordings of songs and stories.

Early Childhood

Provide reassurance to children who have difficulty separating from their families.

- A child care provider establishes a routine for the morning. After children say good-bye to their parents, the children stand at the window with their teacher, watch their parents walk to their cars, and then find an activity to join.

Create a classroom environment that permits children to explore their physical and cultural world.

- A preschool teacher makes several "stations" available to children during free-choice time. The stations include a water table and areas for playing with blocks, completing puzzles, doing arts and crafts, engaging in dramatic play, and listening to audio recordings of books.

Introduce children to the world of literature.

- A preschool teacher reads to children at least once each day. She chooses books with entertaining stories and vivid illustrations that readily capture everyone's attention, interest, and imagination.

Middle Childhood

Encourage family members to become active participants in their children's activities.

- A religious educator invites parents and other family members to contribute in some small way to one of the classes. Different parents assist with musical performances, bake cookies, and give hands-on help during lessons.

Ensure that all students acquire basic academic skills.

- A second-grade teacher individualizes reading instruction for her students based on their current knowledge and skills. With the help of a classroom aid, she works on mastery of letter identification and letter-sound correspondence with some, reading of simple stories with others, and selection of appropriate books with a few students who are already reading independently. She makes sure that all children have regular opportunities to listen to stories in small groups and on audiotape.

Give children the guidance they need to establish and maintain positive relationships with their peers.

- When two children are quarreling, their teacher asks them to generate a few suggestions from which they can eventually choose to settle the dispute.

Early Adolescence

Design a curriculum that is challenging and motivating and that incorporates knowledge and skills from several content areas.

- A middle school teacher designs a unit on "war and conflict," integrating writing skills and knowledge of social studies. He encourages students to bring in newspaper clippings about current events and to write about political debates.

Assign every young adolescent an adviser who looks after the adolescent's welfare.

- During homeroom with her advisees, a seventh-grade teacher personally makes sure that each student is keeping up with assignments. She also encourages her advisees to talk with her informally about their academic and social concerns.

Show sensitivity to youngsters who are undergoing the physical changes of puberty.

- A sports coach makes sure that adolescents have privacy when they dress and shower after team practice.

Late Adolescence

Expect students to meet high standards for achievement, but give them the support they need to meet those standards.

- An English composition teacher describes and then posts the various steps involved in writing—planning, drafting, writing, editing, and revising—and asks his students to use these steps in their essays. He then monitors his students' work, giving feedback and suggestions as necessary and making sure that students execute each step in a way that enhances the quality of their writing.

Encourage adolescents to give back to their communities.

- A high school requires all students to participate in 50 hours of volunteer work or service learning in their town.

Educate adolescents about the academic requirements of jobs and colleges.

- A high school guidance counselor posts vacant positions in the area, listing the work experience and educational requirements for each.

Applying Knowledge of Child Development in the Classroom and Community

In later chapters we pinpoint specific strategies that you can use in your work with children. Here we offer six general strategies that will help you get started in nurturing children's potential for positive growth:

- **Develop warm relationships with children.** Affectionate relationships with teachers and other caregivers promote children's emotional well-being, academic achievement, and acceptance by peers (Gagnon, Huelsman, Kidder-Ashley, & Ballard, 2009; Howes & Ritchie, 2002; Pianta, 1999). Adults can reach out to children by expressing affection, responding sensitively to children's individual needs, and continually advocating for children's welfare. The specific ways in which adults express their concern for children are somewhat culturally based, as you can see in the Development in Culture feature "Developmentally Appropriate Practice in Japan." A Development in Culture feature appears in every chapter to help you become increasingly conscious of how children's needs are closely intertwined with the values and customs of their particular culture.

- **Consider children's age-related abilities.** Children exhibit predictable sequences of growth, such as noticing that one pile of cookies has more than another during infancy, learning to count a small number of objects during early childhood, performing basic numerical calculations in elementary school, and understanding more abstract mathematical principles as adolescents (Berthold & Renkl, 2009; Bussi & Boni, 2009; Sophian, 2008). By addressing children's evolving abilities and interests, adults can select curricula and learning experiences that are well matched to children's learning needs (NAEYC, 2009).

- **Capitalize on each child's strengths.** Individual children have different strengths, depending on their genes, present environment, and past experiences. A child who is particularly curious about the physical world may, as an infant, carefully observe patterns of light, and at later ages proceed to become a determined explorer in the sand, an industrious builder of blocks, and, eventually, a bioengineer who designs life-saving medical equipment. Adults can support this child's curiosity by encouraging exploration and providing challenging educational experiences.

- **Recognize that children's immaturity serves a purpose.** When we compare children's abilities to our own, children inevitably come up short. Yet from a developmental perspective, the "immaturities" youngsters display often serve a purpose (Bjorklund, Periss, & Causey, 2009; Bruner, 1972). Children's play often appears to adults to be a waste of time but allows children to explore the properties of objects, coordinate their activities with those of other children, exercise physically, solve problems, and express themselves emotionally. Similarly, although adults sometimes describe preschoolers as being naively optimistic because of their tendency to overestimate what they can accomplish, children's self-assurance leads them to be persistent when faced with demanding learning tasks.

- **Nudge children toward advanced thinking and behaving.** To some extent, adults must meet children *where the children are,* at children's current level of functioning. But to promote development, adults must also introduce tasks of increasing complexity. Ideally, adults help children to set goals that can be reasonably achieved with hard work and modest levels of support. A school counselor, for instance, may work with an isolated child to set specific goals that will promote her effective interaction with peers. One

Improving Your Observation Skills

My teacher. How does 11-year-old Melanie show in her artwork that Mrs. Lorenzo's classroom is a warm and friendly place to be? Compare your response with the explanation at the end of the chapter.

DEVELOPMENT IN CULTURE
Developmentally Appropriate Practice in Japan

Around the world, sympathetic adults conscientiously meet children's physical, cognitive, social, and emotional needs in ways that are guided by their society's customs. Thus, *developmentally appropriate practices* are to some degree culturally defined.

In Japan, teachers exercise sensitivity by carefully observing and anticipating the needs of children. Teachers interpret subtle facial cues that children may exhibit and situational factors that hint at children's motivations (Rothbaum, Nagaoka, & Ponte, 2006). A Japanese preschool teacher who observes a worried young child staring intently at a juice box would not wait for the child to ask for help but would rather infer the child's difficulty and discretely demonstrate how to insert the

LET ME HELP. Many Japanese teachers anticipate the needs of children in their care.

straw into the box and take a sip of juice. Japanese teachers generally value empathy and emotional closeness and believe that they should help children *before* the children verbalize their concerns (Rothbaum et al., 2006).

Japanese teachers also demonstrate compassion while encouraging children to get along with peers. They ask children to respond empathically when classmates appear isolated and lonely (Hayashi, Karasawa, & Tobin, 2009). Teachers may unobtrusively ease a shy boy or girl into a group of children playing together, as in asking a shy child to join a pretend tea party in the housekeeping area of the classroom. Because preschool class sizes tend to be large in Japan, children have many occasions to solve conflicts on their own, teach one another rules of etiquette, and assist peers in distress (Hayashi et al., 2009). When children do require intervention from adults, teachers do not confront children directly about their misdeeds but rather tactfully demonstrate or explain proper behavior (Peak, 2001; Tobin, Wu, & Davidson, 1989).

Japanese teachers of older children express their concern for children by communicating high expectations and providing engaging learning activities. In Japan, all children are considered capable but not necessarily equally motivated to work diligently on academic tasks (Ansalone, 2006). As a result, teachers often remind children to work hard. When individual differences in achievement levels become obvious, exceptionally skilled students are invited to tutor their less proficient peers. Thus, mistakes are opportunities for learning and collaboration and not signs of weakness. By emphasizing effort, teachers communicate their optimism about children's prospects for high academic achievement while also preparing children to fit into a society that sees hard work as the primary means to achievement.

such goal might be to stand close to a small group of children and make a point of saying something complimentary or relevant to their conversation. Initially, children may need occasional reminders but eventually will initiate these behaviors on their own.

• **Integrate the cultural values and customs of children into lessons.** By learning about the cultures of children in your care, you gain an important route by which to make activities truly meaningful and motivating. One way to learn about their culture is to invite children to share their backgrounds, for example, information about their hobbies, chores, aspirations for the future, and origins of their ancestors. After learning about their backgrounds, you can incorporate these themes into the curriculum, for example, being a refugee or moving to a new land, and also allow children the freedom to select some of their own projects reflecting these cultural values.

• **Consider how you might accommodate bioecological factors in children's lives.** Many children follow similar developmental pathways, but exceptions are everywhere. Children have personal experiences—perhaps growing up in poverty, having a chronic illness, or losing a family member to death or incarceration—that present unique challenges. Likewise, children have individual profiles of advantages—maybe an exceptional talent in computer programming or advocacy from a concerned relative—that can leverage positive growth. Educators can consider children's risks and protective factors and tailor emotional support and instructional decisions accordingly.

Strengthening the Commitment

A commitment to developmentally appropriate practice isn't something that can be applied automatically or that necessarily lasts forever. Teachers and other practitioners must continually discern the group characteristics *and* individual needs of young people. Furthermore, researchers continue to advance the frontiers of knowledge about child development. Therefore, educators can—and must—continue to learn more about the advantages and disadvantages that children of various ages face growing up in their community. Following are three useful things you can do:

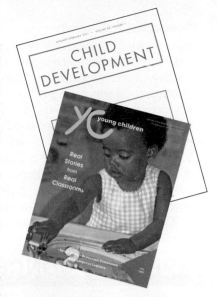

- **Continue to take courses in child development.** Additional course work is one sure way of keeping up to date on (a) the latest research results on child and adolescent development and (b) their practical implications for work with young people. Such course work has been shown to enhance professional effectiveness with children (Darling-Hammond, 1995; Darling-Hammond & Bransford, 2005).

- **Find colleagues who share your concerns about children.** New teachers sometimes feel overwhelmed with pressures to accomplish their many responsibilities and may temporarily lose sight of the developmental perspectives they had previously gained in college. Working together, teachers can remind one another to focus on children's needs by selecting age-appropriate curricular programs and designing physical settings suitable for the children with whom they work (Early et al., 2007).

- **Obtain new perspectives from colleagues.** Many professional organizations hold regular meetings at which you can hear researchers and practitioners exchange ideas. Such meetings enable everyone to learn about the latest research findings and discover new methods for supporting children. Professional organizations also publish journals and magazines with new research findings and standards for instruction, care, and guidance of young people.

Throughout this chapter we have maintained that children's developmental paths depend significantly on the guidance of teachers and other caring adults. As you will discover throughout this book, you can do a lot to help children navigate their individual developmental journeys. You can definitely make a difference in children's lives.

KEEPING INFORMED. Find guidance about working with children and adolescents through professional organizations such as the National Association for the Education of Young Children and academic journals such as *Child Development.*

Cover of *Young Children* reprinted with permission from the National Association for the Education of Young Children. Cover of *Child Development* reprinted with permission from Blackwell Publishing.

SUMMARY

The Field of Child Development

The field of child development examines how human beings change beginning at conception and throughout prenatal development, infancy, childhood, and adolescence. Each child's developmental journey is guided by four factors: nature, nurture, the child's existing structures in brain and body, and the child's own activity. Developmental theorists typically focus on the progression of children in three domains—physical, cognitive, and social-emotional—and look at how a variety of contexts affect children's overall adjustment.

Basic Issues in Development

Developmental theorists wrestle with three basic issues related to children's development. First, they wonder how much development is influenced by nature (heredity) and how much by nurture (environment). Second, they speculate about the extent to which developmental paths are universal (true for everyone) or diverse (unique to individuals). And third, they debate about whether developmental changes can be characterized as qualitative (involving major transformations) or quantitative (reflecting gradual trends). Clearly, development is influenced by nature *and* nurture; some aspects of development are universal and others reflect diversity; and the course of development is characterized by both qualitative and quantitative change.

Theories of Child Development

Developmentalists have proposed a wide variety of explanations as to how and why children and adolescents change over time. These explanations can be categorized into seven theoretical frameworks: biological, behaviorism and social learning, psychodynamic, cognitive-developmental, cognitive process, sociocultural, and developmental systems perspectives. These perspectives focus on different domains of development and place greater or lesser importance on nature versus nurture, universality versus diversity, and qualitative versus quantitative change. Teachers and other practitioners find theories relevant to their work because these frameworks help to guide their observations and decision making.

Developmental Periods

Infancy (birth to 2 years) is a remarkable time characterized by rapid growth and the emergence of basic human traits, including emotional bonds with other people, language, and motor mobility. Early childhood (2–6 years) is a time of imaginative play, rapid language development, advances in gross motor and fine motor skills, and expansion of social skills. During middle childhood (6–10 years), children tackle in earnest the tasks that they will need to participate effectively in adult society; they also develop friendships and internalize many of society's rules and prohibitions. In early adolescence (10–14 years), youngsters are preoccupied with the physical changes of puberty and sensitive about how they appear to others; at the same time, they are thinking in increasingly abstract and logical ways. Late adolescence (14–18 years) is a period of intensive interaction with peers and greater independence from adults. Although many older adolescents make wise choices, others engage in risky and potentially dangerous behaviors.

From Theory to Practice

Effective care of youngsters is based on an understanding of typical developmental pathways and respect for individual differences. As a future educator, you can identify and capitalize on individual children's strengths and nudge children toward increasing responsibility. Through ongoing education, conversations with colleagues, and participation in professional organizations, you can keep up to date on advancements in child development and maintain an optimistic outlook on your ability to help children.

APPLYING CONCEPTS IN CHILD DEVELOPMENT

The exercises in this section will help you build your ability to apply your knowledge of child development in your work with children.

Improving Your Observation Skills

On page 5, you examined a photograph of children in a choir and were asked, "*How are these children's physical, cognitive, and social-emotional needs being met by their experiences in the choir?*" The adults caring for these children appear to have addressed children's physical needs by allowing the children to clap their hands and move their bodies, cognitive needs by teaching children songs and dances of their culture, and social-emotional needs by encouraging children's self-expression and sense of belonging to a worthwhile group. Although adults often think about the domains separately, the reality is that these areas of life are closely interconnected. For instance, if a young girl is not allowed to move throughout the day (a physical experience), she is likely to become agitated or bored and unable to learn (a cognitive outcome).

On page 23, you examined a photograph of adolescents in a high school classroom and were asked, "*How are these adolescents showing their interest in one another?*" As other students carry on with their schoolwork, the boy and girl in the foreground are paying attention to one another, as can be seen by their mutual smiles and eye contact. Preoccupation with peers, including peers of the opposite gender, is an emblematic feature of the adolescent period.

On page 29, you examined a child's drawing of a classroom and were asked, "*How does 11-year-old Melanie show in her artwork that Mrs. Lorenzo's classroom is a warm and friendly place to be?*" Melanie drew Mrs. Lorenzo putting her arm around a child and also included a smiling face on the bulletin board. Mrs. Lorenzo may have made a difference for Melanie by expressing an interest in the little girl's life and adjusting to her particular strengths and challenges.

Practicing for Your Licensure Examination

Many teaching tests require students to apply what they have learned about child development to brief vignettes and multiple-choice questions. You can practice for your licensure examination by reading the following case study and answering a series of questions.

Latisha

Read the case and then answer the questions that follow it.

Latisha, who is 13 years old, lives in a housing project in an inner-city neighborhood in Chicago. An adult asks her to describe her life and family, her hopes and fears, and her plans for the future. She responds as follows:

My mother works at the hospital, serving food. She's worked there for 11 years, but she's been moved to different departments. I don't know what my dad does because he don't live with me. My mother's boyfriend lives with us. He's like my step father.

In my spare time I just like be at home, look at TV, or clean up, or do my homework, or play basketball, or talk on the phone. My three wishes would be to have a younger brother and sister, a car of my own, and not get killed before I'm 20 years old.

I be afraid of guns and rats. My mother she has a gun, her boyfriend has one for protection. I have shot one before and it's like a scary feeling. My uncle taught me. He took us in the country and he had targets we had to like shoot at. He showed us how to load and cock it and pull the trigger. When I pulled the trigger at first I feel happy because I learned how to shoot a gun, but afterward I didn't like it too much because I don't want to accidentally shoot nobody. I wouldn't want to shoot nobody. But it's good that I know how to shoot one just in case something happened and I have to use it.

Where I live it's a quiet neighborhood. If the gangs don't bother me or threaten me, or do anything to my family, I'm OK. If somebody say hi to me, I'll say hi to them as long as they don't threaten me. . . . I got two cousins who are in gangs. One is in jail because he killed somebody. My other cousin, he stayed cool. He ain't around. He don't be over there with the gang bangers. He mostly over on the west side with his grandfather, so I don't hardly see him. . . . I got friends in gangs. Some of them seven, eight years old that's too young to be in a gang. . . . They be gang banging because they have no one to turn to. . . . If a girl join a gang it's worser than if a boy join a gang because to be a girl you should have more sense. A boy they want to be hanging on to their friends. Their friends say gangs are cool, so they join.

The school I go to now is more funner than the school I just came from. We switch classes and we have 40 minutes for lunch. The

Board of Education say that we can't wear gym shoes no more. They say it distracts other people from learning, it's because of the shoe strings and gang colors.

My teachers are good except two. My music and art teacher she's old and it seems like she shouldn't be there teaching. It seem like she should be retired and be at home, or traveling or something like that. And my history teacher, yuk! He's a stubborn old goat. He's stubborn with everybody.

When I finish school I want to be a doctor. At first I wanted to be a lawyer, but after I went to the hospital I said now I want to help people, and cure people, so I decided to be a doctor. (J. Williams & Williamson, 1992, pp. 11–12)[a]

Constructed-Response Question

1. In what ways does the context in which Latisha is growing up affect her development? Describe at least three elements of Latisha's environment that may influence her.

[a] "Case Study: Latisha" by J. Williams and K. Williamson, from "I Wouldn't Want to Shoot Nobody: The Out-of-School Curriculum as Described by Urban Students" from ACTION IN TEACHER EDUCATION, Volume 14, No. 2, pp.11–12, 1992. Copyright © 1992 by J. Williams and K. Williamson. Reprinted with permission of Action in Teacher Education, published by the Association of Teacher Educators, Manassas Park, VA.

Multiple-Choice Questions

2. Which of the following theoretical accounts of Latisha's characteristics would most likely focus on the active role that Latisha plays in her own development and the stage-like changes that may periodically take place in her thinking?

   a. A biological theory
   b. A behaviorist or social learning theory
   c. A psychodynamic theory
   d. A cognitive-developmental theory

3. Which of the following theoretical accounts of Latisha's characteristics would most likely explain her characteristics as being the outcome of numerous factors interacting inside her and in her multilayered social environment?

   a. A cognitive-process theory
   b. A sociocultural theory
   c. A developmental systems theory
   d. A biological theory

Once you have answered these questions, compare your responses with those presented in Appendix A.

Improving Your Ability to Interpret Children's Artifacts and Reflections

Consider chapter concepts as you analyze the following artifact created by a child.

James's Changes, Big and Small

Twelve-year-old James wrote about the combination of gradual changes and more dramatic overhauls he experienced in his life as he adjusted to his seventh-grade year of middle school. His essay is shown at right and also retyped below, with punctuation and spelling errors intact. As you read his reflections, answer the following questions:

- Decide which of his changes reflect a series of incremental, *quantitative changes,* and which other changes seem to be entirely new experiences, or *qualitative changes,* for James.
- Offer recommendations for how an educator might support James.

Hi there, I am a kid who is 12 years old. In my life so far I have been through a lot of intresting things. I am in 7th grade, and in 7th grade you get to play sports for your school. Right now I am in football, and with sports you don't get home til around 6:00, it is hard too. You don't get a lot of time for Homework. It makes a big difference than last year because you can't play sports in 6th grade. Some of the small things that have changed from last year is that, I have gotten bigger, more athletic, more educated, and also got more homework in school. The girls have also changed, I am starting to do more stuff with them. Such as hang out and talk more with each other. Back to school, my relationship with teachers has changed a little. I talk to them more, about grades. I am a lot more concerned about my grades as the years pass. I actually have conversations with them, instead of just talking about school. Also my parents exspect me to be more responsible, with everything. They trust me a lot more, and I like that. Sometimes I feel like they never understand me though. Thats about all I have to say about my middle school year.

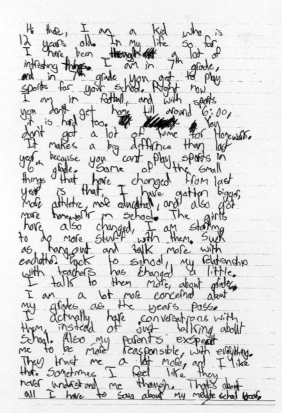

Once you have analyzed the artifact, compare your ideas with those presented in Appendix B. For further practice in analyzing children's artifacts and reflections, go to the Activities and Applications section in Chapter 1 of MyEducationLab.

Key Concepts

child development (p. 4)
physical development (p. 4)
cognitive development (p. 4)
social-emotional
   development (p. 4)
context (p. 5)
culture (p. 5)
nature (p. 5)

nurture (p. 5)
temperament (p. 6)
maturation (p. 7)
sensitive period (p. 8)
universality (p. 9)
diversity (p. 9)
qualitative change (p. 10)
quantitative change (p. 10)

stage (p. 10)
stage theory (p. 10)
theory (p. 12)
biological theory (p. 12)
behaviorism (p. 13)
social learning theory (p. 13)
psychodynamic
   theory (p. 14)

cognitive-developmental
   theory (p. 14)
cognitive process theory (p. 15)
sociocultural theory (p. 16)
developmental systems
   theory (p. 17)
developmentally appropriate
   practice (p. 25)

PEARSON
myeducationlab

Now go to www.myeducationlab.com to:
- Take a Quiz to test your mastery of chapter objectives.
- Study chapter content with an individualized Study Plan.
- Deepen your understanding of particular concepts and principles with Review, Remediation, and Enrichment Exercises.
- Apply what you have learned in the chapter to your work with children in Building Teaching Skills and Dispositions exercises.
- Observe children and their unique contexts in Video Examples.

Chapter Two

Using Research to Understand Children and Adolescents

CASE STUDY: Jack's Research

Elementary School Principal Jack Reston had recently joined a committee in his district charged with reducing student absenteeism. He realized that research could inform the work of his committee and guide new policies at his school. He carefully considered a productive direction for an investigation. He wrote:

I began by asking three questions:

1. What student characteristics are associated with student absenteeism?
2. What are some longitudinal effects of student absenteeism?
3. What are some effective strategies to prevent student absenteeism?

I reviewed current studies, literature, local and national profiles, written surveys, and interviews. I found that absenteeism was highly associated with dropping out of school, academic failure, and delinquency. I learned what students and parents in our school believed about the relationship between school and absenteeism. I concluded that I really did not understand the belief systems of families at risk for poor attendance in school. I conducted a massive survey of students and parents within a four-day period of time. Surveys gathered data concerning such things as respectfulness of students, safety in school, conflict management, discipline, school rules, self-esteem, and academics. In addition, the survey gathered data on mobility rates, volunteerism, and levels of education in parents. The identity of the families surveyed was kept unknown. . . .

Student teachers from a nearby university and local educators with experience in action research interviewed selected students and parents. The interviews were conducted over the telephone or face-to-face. (Reston, 2007, pp. 141–142)[a]

In analyzing the data, Jack learned that, by and large, students at his school were not motivated by such extrinsic rewards as drawings for prizes or certificates. He also learned that students did not perceive rules to be fair or effectively enforced by the school. In reflecting on these perceptions and the relatively low achievement of some students, Jack realized that he needed to change a few policies and his style of interacting with students:

This information led to major changes in our approach to improving attendance in our school. First, we stopped spending large sums of money for rewards and drawings. Although these are nice things for students, they are ineffective in dealing with the problem of poor attendance. Second, we recognized punitive measures were having little effect on attendance. This led us to the belief that students succeeding in school were more likely to attend school regularly.

We began a concentrated effort to improve the success of students at school both academically and emotionally. This included the use of student/parent/teacher/principal contracts, daily planners for students, individual conferences between the student and the principal every 14 days to review grades and behaviors, better assessments to locate students having academic problems, improved instructional techniques and alignment of curriculum, and more concentrated efforts to improve the self-esteem of students. . . .

Based on these findings, I worked with teachers and parents to develop quick responses that unite the student, parent, educator, and community in a preventive effort to minimize absenteeism. (Reston, 2007, p. 142)[a]

- What procedures did Jack follow to make sure his research was of high quality?
- What ethical practices did Jack use as he conducted his research?

[a]Excerpts from "Reflecting on Admission Criteria" by J. Reston. In *Action Research: A Guide for the Teacher Researcher* (3rd ed., pp. 141–142), by G. E. Mills, 2007, Upper Saddle River, NJ: Merrill/Prentice Hall. Reprinted with permission of the author.

OBJECTIVES

2.1: Explain basic ethical and scientific standards in research with children.

2.2: Identify the four main data collection techniques used in developmental research and explain the advantages and limitations of each.

2.3: Differentiate among the research designs most frequently used in developmental research.

2.4: Evaluate the quality of particular kinds of research investigations and their implications for your work with children.

2.5: Explain how teachers and other practitioners can obtain information from children in an instructive and ethical manner.

2.6: Distinguish appropriate and inappropriate inferences about children from developmental research data and from information collected by teachers in classrooms.

Jack Reston ensured that his data were of high quality by first examining other relevant investigations and then gathering comprehensive responses from children and parents. He also followed ethical practices, protecting the confidentiality of participants' individual responses and engaging all members of the community in a search for solutions. In the end Jack's research prompted him to improve his services for students. It directed him to express an intensified interest in children's welfare, check on their academic progress, and offer needed support for their emerging organizational skills.

PRINCIPLES OF RESEARCH

To contribute to knowledge of child development, researchers must follow three basic principles. First and foremost, they must obey a strict ethical code. Second, they must follow the steps of the scientific method. Finally, they must select children and adolescents who can provide the desired information. We examine each of these principles in turn.

Ethical Protection of Children

WHAT'S SO FUNNY? Researchers wanting to document what these boys find amusing would need to have obtained approval from authorities and consent from the boys and their parents before asking them questions.

A paramount concern for researchers is that they conduct research in an ethical manner, in particular, that they are honest and respectful of the rights of children (American Psychological Association, 2002; Koelch et al., 2009; Office for Human Research Protections, 2008; Society for Research in Child Development, 2007). To protect children's rights, researchers follow these specific ethical standards:

- *Do no harm.* Researchers prioritize the welfare of children over their own desires for information. They avoid procedures that cause children stress, embarrassment, or pain.
- *Get approval from authorities.* Before collecting data from children, researchers obtain approval for their proposed study from authorities in research ethics at their university, school district, or other organization. In their proposals, researchers report the kinds of data children will provide, any risks and benefits children might encounter, plans for reducing risks to minimal levels, and measures for advising children and families about the research.
- *Obtain consent from participants and their families.* Also before collecting data, researchers explain to parents and children what the study entails in time and involvement and ask for written permission for the children to take part in the research. Depending on their ages, children may also be asked to give their assent orally or in writing. If permission is unnecessary because researchers will not intrude on children's customary activities, for example, if researchers plan to observe children's spontaneous play at the park, appropriate institutional authorities would review the study but not require written consent.
- *Preserve children's privacy.* Investigators usually describe group trends in their results. When researchers single out a particular child, they identify the child with a fictitious name and withhold identifying information.
- *Be honest.* Children generally expect adults to be honest. Researchers do not exploit or undermine this assumption. Thus deception with children is almost always avoided.
- *Communicate openly.* After children provide the data that will be used in the investigation, researchers respond to any questions or concerns children or parents might have. When the investigators write up their results, they often send families a brief description of their findings. Investigators also share the results with other scholars and, if appropriate, with the public.

The Scientific Method

The **scientific method** is a powerful strategy for gaining and refining insights about children because it requires researchers to think critically about the data they collect and the conclusions they draw. For developmental scholars, the scientific method commonly includes these general steps:

1. *Pose a question.* Researchers clearly state the question they want to answer. When they can make predictions about the outcomes of their study, they also state hypotheses.
2. *Design an investigation.* Once the question is clear, researchers must figure out what kinds of information will help answer the question and, if applicable, test the hypotheses.
3. *Collect data.* Researchers recruit children and then gather information using carefully defined procedures.
4. *Analyze the data.* Researchers organize the data, categorize children's responses, look for themes, and, when appropriate, perform statistical tests. After making sense of the data, they draw conclusions relevant to the research question.
5. *Share the results.* Researchers write up the study's purpose, methods, results, and conclusions and present the paper at a conference, submit it to a journal, or both. Scientific peers evaluate the paper on its merits, identify any flawed arguments, and build on the ideas they find especially convincing. This give-and-take among scientists leads to scientific progress.

Research Participants

In most types of developmental research, investigators wish to make fairly broad claims about children of a certain age or background. To make their work manageable, they limit their interest to a reasonable number of children. Thus researchers first define a population and then select a subgroup, or **sample**, of that population. For example, imagine that a team of psychologists wants to know what adolescents in public high schools in San Francisco, California, think about desirable careers. With the help of administrators in San Francisco schools, the researchers obtain a list of homeroom teachers and randomly select 10 percent of these teachers. Next, the researchers ask the selected teachers to distribute letters, consent forms, and surveys to students and parents. If the return rate for these materials is fairly high, investigators can be reasonably confident that their *sample* of adolescents is representative of the larger *population* of adolescents in public schools in San Francisco. If instead many potential participants decide not to join the study, or they drop out before data collection is completed, the resulting sample may be so small that the results cannot be said to represent trends in the population.

In other kinds of studies, generalizing to a large population is not the goal. Developmental scholars may study one child or a small group of children intensively. These researchers hope to analyze children's experiences in enough depth that they can draw accurate conclusions about the experiences of *these children*—not about children overall. Investigators recruit children who have the characteristics of interest (for example, being from a single cultural group) and then follow these children closely. In their reports, the investigators would conscientiously describe the experiences of the children while protecting their confidentiality and not presuming that the children's experiences inevitably apply to others with similar circumstances.

Regardless of whether investigators want to obtain a large representative sample or a small number of children for in-depth analysis, they must consider the backgrounds of the children. Historically, children from middle-income, White European American backgrounds were overrepresented in developmental research, whereas children of color, language environments other than English-only families, and low-income communities were underrepresented (e.g., García Coll et al., 1996; McLoyd, Aikens, & Burton, 2006). Fortunately, many developmental researchers now recruit participants with varied characteristics, including those from such traditionally neglected populations as migrant and homeless families. These outreach efforts are currently enriching our knowledge of diversity in the daily challenges

scientific method
Multistep process of carefully defining and addressing a research question using critical thinking and analysis of the evidence.

sample
The specific participants in a research study; their performance is often assumed to indicate how a larger population of individuals would perform.

ARTIFACT 2-1 Grace's apple tree. It seems apparent from 7-year-old Grace's drawing that she understands that apples grow on the branches of trees. To inquire into other aspects of her understanding, for example, why apples grow on some trees and not others, an investigator could ask Grace a series of questions.

children face and the assets children in various families and communities have (Bornstein, 2010; Grigorenko & Takanishi, 2010; McLoyd et al., 2009; M. B. Spencer, 2006). In writing this book, we have made special efforts to include research with diverse samples of children, and we encourage you to watch for information about children's backgrounds when you read investigations yourself. When the backgrounds of participants differ significantly from those of children in your care, you will want to be especially cautious in following the researchers' recommendations for helping children.

ANALYZING DEVELOPMENTAL RESEARCH

Investigators convert general principles of research into specific features of a study that fit their research questions. Usually they make good choices, implementing sound methods that adequately answer their questions. Occasionally, though, researchers make poor decisions, collect data haphazardly, or draw unwarranted interpretations from their data. To interpret developmental research critically, you need to become familiar with common data collection techniques and research designs.

Data Collection Techniques

Researchers gather data using four kinds of techniques: self-reports, tests and other assessment tasks, physiological measures, and observations of behavior. Each of these methods offers a unique window into the minds and habits of children and adolescents.

Self-Reports

Researchers often ask children to explain their beliefs, attitudes, hopes, and frustrations. In fact, some of the most informative research data comes in the form of youngsters' own statements about themselves—that is, in the form of **self-reports**. Self-reports take two primary forms, interviews and questionnaires.

During **interviews**, researchers ask questions to explore the reasoning of children. Interviewers who succeed in making children feel safe and comfortable can learn a lot about how children think about things. In the "Research: Early Adolescence" video in MyEducationLab, you can listen as the interviewer gently but persistently asks 12-year-old Claudia questions about why she grouped seashells precisely as she did. The interviewer begins the discussion in this way:

Interviewer:	All right. Why did you make the groups that you did?
Claudia:	Mm, some, they were the ones that looked the most alike.
Interviewer:	How did you decide which shells to put where?
Claudia:	Um, I looked at them, like, and how they looked on every side. And I put them with the ones that looked closest like each other.
Interviewer:	Okay. So what were you looking for when you were grouping them?
Claudia:	Um, details.

Up until this point, Claudia describes her reasoning in a fairly general way. After several questions and requests for information from the interviewer, Claudia elaborates:

Interviewer:	Why are those in a group?
Claudia:	Um, they looked kind of the same. Feel like they both, they have the little thing there. And they fold over like that and have a tip.
Interviewer:	Okay. What makes them different from the other ones?
Claudia:	They're longer kind of. And they're smoother than the other ones.
Interviewer:	Oh, okay. And then those ones at the far corner over there. Now tell me about those ones.
Claudia:	They were smaller than these, so I put them together. And they both pretty much, or all of 'em pretty much, had the same kind of thing.
Interviewer:	Like what?
Claudia:	Like, they all had the cone at the top. The kind of pocket area.

MyEducationLab

Listen to an interviewer use several different types of requests to elicit information from Claudia in the "Research: Early Adolescence" video in the Video Examples section in Topic 2 of MyEducationLab.

self-report
Data collection technique whereby participants are asked to describe their own characteristics and performance.

interview
Data collection technique that obtains self-report data through face-to-face conversation.

Investigators typically conduct interviews in a face-to-face conversation, which allow them to establish rapport and read children's facial expressions. Researchers occasionally interview young people over the telephone, reducing costs of travel and recruiting participants who might avoid a face-to-face interview on the topic. One group of researchers interviewed 14- to 16-year-old adolescents by telephone and found that many of the youth willingly reported being able to purchase alcohol by showing fake driver's licenses or getting help from others; behaviors they might not have revealed in face-to-face interactions. (M.-J. Chen, Gruenewald, & Remer, 2009).

Developmental researchers use **questionnaires** when they need to gather responses from a large number of participants. When young people complete questionnaires, they typically read questions or statements and choose from defined options that express feelings, attitudes, or actions. In studies of adolescents' motivation, researchers have occasionally asked adolescents to indicate how much they agree that they want to learn as much as possible in class or, alternatively, just want to avoid failing in school. From such responses, researchers have learned that adolescents' motivational beliefs are related to the courses they select in high school and the levels of achievement they attain (Crosnoe & Huston, 2007; Witkow & Fuligni, 2007).

Many questionnaires are completed by youngsters in a paper-and-pencil format, but in some situations youngsters are asked to answer questions on the computer or listen to questions through earphones (Langhaug, Cheung, Pascoe, Hayes, & Cowan, 2009). Developmental researchers have tried other technologies as well, including beepers that emit signals at regular intervals throughout the day to remind adolescents to record their activities and feelings in notebooks (Larson & Richards, 1994).

Self-reports have advantages and disadvantages. Valuable insights emerge from interviews when researchers ask children about their views, probe children's understandings in a thorough yet sensitive fashion, and confirm what children say with other types of data. However, interviews are time-consuming and highly dependent on an interviewer's skills. Questionnaires are an efficient way to determine group trends in youngsters' experiences yet exceed many children's reading abilities, do not allow researchers to probe, and are not set up for children to express confusion or mixed feelings. In addition, when researchers are unaware of children's typical ways of thinking, they may unintentionally create response options that are out of sync with children's actual ideas. Computers and other technologies can lend efficiency to the research enterprise but are costly and depend on youngsters' familiarity with the equipment. Despite their limitations, self-reports of various kinds give us vivid glimpses into the thoughts and actions of growing youngsters.

Tests and Other Assessment Tasks

A **test** is an instrument designed to assess knowledge, abilities, or skills in a fairly consistent fashion from one individual to the next. Some tests involve paper and pencil, whereas others do not, but all typically yield a result in the form of a number (e.g., a score on an intelligence test) or category (e.g., "alert" or "proficient").

In research studies, tests are frequently used to gauge the effectiveness of educational programs. In an intervention for children from low-income families, participants regularly completed tests of cognitive ability from ages 3 months to 12 years and again at age 21 (F. A. Campbell, Ramey, Pungello, Sparling, & Miller-Johnson, 2002). Test scores indicated that individuals who participated in a full-time high-quality child care program beginning as infants not only exhibited larger cognitive gains in the first few years of life but also had higher reading and math scores at age 21 compared to individuals who did not participate in the program. A second intervention, beginning at age 5 and lasting for 3 years, was less effective. Thus these tests were valuable in revealing that interventions may be most effective when initiated at a very young age.

ARTIFACT 2-2 Connor's history notes. An investigator examining 14-year-old Connor's history notes might conclude that Connor has been exposed to key doctrines in U.S. history. To determine what Connor truly understands about these concepts, the investigator could ask Connor to explain "popular sovereignty" and "social contract" in his own words.

questionnaire
Data collection technique that obtains self-report data through a paper-and-pencil inventory.

test
Instrument designed to assess knowledge, abilities, or skills in a consistent fashion across individuals.

Developmental scholars also measure children's abilities in ways that we would not necessarily think of as "tests." Scholars make use of a variety of other **assessments**, tasks that require children to express their understandings or solve realistic problems. Researchers conducting separate investigations might record children's efficiency in navigating through a maze, their accuracy in detecting emotional expressions, or their understanding of commonly used verbal expressions. Some assessments involve spoken language—not the in-depth interviews described earlier but rather brief question-and-answer exchanges. In the "Cognitive Development: Late Adolescence" video in MyEducationLab, you can see an assessment that reveals 14-year-old Alicia's understanding of proverbs:

Interviewer:	What does it mean when someone says, "Better to light a candle than to curse the darkness"?
Alicia:	Well, it means, probably, that you're actually getting somewhere than just complaining about it and not doing anything about it.
Interviewer:	What does it mean when someone says, "An ant may well destroy a dam"?
Alicia:	I think it probably means that even though they're really small, they can still change things.

An advantage of tests and other assessments is that they provide clues to children's thinking. From her responses, we know that Alicia can look beyond common expressions to determine their essential, underlying meanings. Assessments tell us only so much, however—we cannot tell *how* Alicia was able to decipher the proverbs. Had she previously encountered them, or did she apply strong reasoning skills on the spot? By themselves, single assessments can rarely tell us how children acquired their ideas or how they might change their skills if given particular kinds of instruction. Accordingly, researchers sometimes administer several assessments repeatedly, perhaps before, during, and after instruction or some other intervention.

Physiological Measures

To learn about children's physical development, researchers often turn to **physiological measures**, indications of such bodily conditions as heart rate, hormone levels, bone growth, brain activity, eye movements, body weight, and lung capacity. Physiological measures provide valuable information about children's health, emotional states, and physical growth.

In addition, physiological measures have enabled significant advances in our knowledge of infants' cognitive development. Researchers have learned a great deal about infants' attention, perception, and memory by exploiting infants' tendency to respond differently to familiar and unfamiliar stimuli. When infants are shown the same object or pattern repeatedly, they grow accustomed to it and lose interest (Colombo & Mitchell, 2009; Hayden, Bhatt, Kangas, & Zieber, 2011). You can see an infant grow tired of a rattle in the "Habituation" video of MyEducationLab. This tendency, called **habituation**, can be assessed through changes in heart rate, sucking, and eye movements. Studies in habituation have shown that infants perceive depth from visual cues and can discriminate among various speech sounds (e.g., particular consonants and vowels) and movements (e.g., putting objects in or beside a container; Fais, Kajikawa, Shigeaki, & Werker, 2009; Granrud, 2006; Hespos, Saylor, & Grossman, 2009).

New medical technologies have also improved our understanding of brain development. We have learned of fascinating developmental patterns through animal research, analyses of brains of individuals who died during childhood, and new technologies that can be safely implemented with living children. An example of the last of these methods is magnetic resonance imaging (MRI), which measures the varying magnetic densities of different parts of the brain (Paus, 2005; see Figure 2-1 for an example of an MRI of a child's brain). One investigation examined MRIs of the brains of healthy individuals from age 7 to age 30 and found that compared to the children's brains, adults' brains showed fewer but stronger connections in areas of the brain that support judgment, restraint, and the ability to plan for the future (Sowell, Delis, Stiles, & Jernigan, 2001).

An advantage of physiological measures is that they give precise indications of how children's bodies and brains are functioning. A disadvantage is that the meaning of the data they yield is not always clear. For example, the fact that infants perceive differences among

MyEducationLab

Observe this interview in the "Cognitive Development: Late Adolescence" video, located in the Video Examples section in Topic 2 of MyEducationLab.

MyEducationLab

Watch an infant become accustomed to a toy in the "Habituation" video located in the Video Examples section in Topic 2 of MyEducationLab.

assessment
Task that children complete and researchers use to make judgments of children's understandings and skills.

physiological measure
Direct assessment of physical development or physiological functioning.

habituation
Changes in children's physiological responses to repeated displays of the same stimulus, reflecting loss of interest.

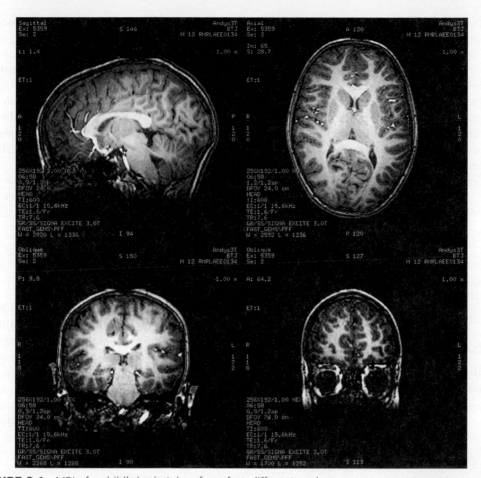

FIGURE 2-1   MRI of a child's brain taken from four different angles.

various perceptual stimuli does not necessarily indicate that they are consciously aware of these patterns or that they can act on them in any meaningful way. Another limitation is that many physiological tests cannot be administered very often because they cause discomfort (e.g., some brain-scan procedures can be quite noisy) or may be harmful if done too frequently (as is the case with X-rays).

Observations

Researchers conduct **observations** when they carefully watch the behavior of youngsters. Observations offer rich portraits of children's lives, particularly when they take place over an extended time and are supplemented with interviews, tests, and other data.

Researchers who conduct observations generally keep a detailed record of significant events that take place in a particular setting, such as a neighborhood playground or family home. The following observation reveals interactions between a father and his 5-year-old daughter, Anna:

11:05 a.m.   Anna looks at her father, who is sitting on the couch reading the newspaper: "Wanna play Legos, Dad?" Dad says, "Sure," and puts down the paper and gets on the floor. Anna pushes a pile of Legos toward Dad and says, "Here. You can build the factory with the volcanoes."

11:06 a.m.   Dad looks puzzled and says, "What factory?" Anna laughs and says, "The one where they make molten steel, silly!" Dad says, "Oh, I forgot," and picks up a gray Lego and fits a red one to it. (Pellegrini, 1996, p. 22)

Although observers hope to describe events as faithfully as possible, they must make decisions about what to record and what to ignore. The observer who writes about Anna and her father may focus on the pair's negotiations over what to play and what to pretend.

observation
Data collection technique whereby a researcher carefully observes and documents the behaviors of participants in a research study.

MyEducationLab

Go to the "Emotional Development: Infancy" video in the Video Examples section in Topic 2 of MyEducationLab and observe Madison's eye movements as she examines the visual properties of objects. What can you learn from Madison's eye movements?

Other events, such as Anna dropping toys or her father scratching his head, would receive less attention.

Researchers frequently use observations to document characteristics and behaviors (e.g., hairstyles, dress codes, bullying behaviors) that young people display in public settings. Observations are also helpful for studying actions that individuals may be unaware of or unable to articulate (e.g., the types of questions that teachers direct toward boys vs. girls) and behaviors that violate social rules (e.g., temper tantrums, petty thefts). Observations of what children look at and listen to likewise tell us a lot about children's interests. For example, by observing 7-month-old Madison in the "Emotional Development: Infancy" video in MyEducationLab, you can see Madison's interest in the visual properties of toys and books.

The strength of observations is their ability to tell us what children actually *do*—not what children *say* they do or what parents report about children's actions. Observations have their weaknesses, however. For one thing, the presence of an observer might change the behaviors under investigation. They may misbehave or, alternatively, stay on task more than usual. Some young people become self-conscious or even anxious in the company of a stranger. To minimize these reactions, researchers often spend considerable time in a setting before they observe formally. That way, children grow accustomed to the researchers and eventually carry on as they normally would.

Another weakness of observations is that researchers' expectations can influence their conclusions. An observer who perceives children as hostile may categorize an interaction between two boys as "hitting," whereas an observer who perceives children as friendly may see the same scuffle as "energetic play." Researchers handle this problem by spending as much time as possible in the setting, carefully defining the events and behaviors they observe, and discussing their observations with other observers.

Improving Your Observation Skills

Let's wrestle! How might researchers determine whether these two boys from the Canadian First Nation are playing or fighting? Compare your response with the explanation at the end of the chapter.

Integrity in Data Collection

Regardless of exactly how scholars collect their information, they continually ask themselves *how* they know their data collection methods are of high quality. The specific terms for quality vary somewhat with the kind of investigation. In studies with relatively large samples and statistical analyses, researchers typically are concerned with **validity**, the extent to which data collection methods actually assess what the researchers intend to assess. To address validity, investigators must show that they are examining the essential parts of a well-defined domain. For instance, researchers who see mathematical skill as being comprised of both computational proficiencies (adding, subtracting, multiplying, dividing) and problem-solving abilities (making sense of situations by determining underlying mathematical patterns) must make a point to include *both* types of competencies in their assessments.

Researchers must also rule out the influence of other, irrelevant traits. For instance, do scores on a test of mathematical ability reflect children's knowledge of a particular culture—for instance, are there too many questions about American sports? Or, are children expected by test developers to answer questions hurriedly when they have acquired a cultural disposition for patient introspection? Does a test of scientific reasoning assess children's desire to please the experimenter as much as it assesses finesse in thinking skills? Only when researchers can say no to such questions do they have some assurance that their methods are valid.

The validity of data is also enhanced when investigators reflect on the state of mind of research participants. Skilled researchers recognize that children must be reasonably rested and attentive during experimental tasks. Investigators also recognize that young people bring

validity
Extent to which a data collection technique actually assesses what the researcher intends for it to assess.

their own expectations and agendas to interactions with adults. Some participants (adolescents especially) may give responses to shock a researcher or in some other way undermine the research effort. Others may tell a researcher what they think the researcher wants to hear. Furthermore, youngsters may understand words and phrases differently than researchers do. Probing sensitively, searching for confirmation through a variety of sources, and reassuring children that they are not personally being evaluated are strategies investigators use to improve the validity of data.

As we suggested earlier, developmental researchers who conduct observations try to put children at ease by allowing the children to grow accustomed to their presence before collecting data. Observers also realize that they cannot record all aspects of children's behavior and must instead focus on a limited number of carefully defined actions. In addition, investigators know that they could be biased in their interpretations of children's behavior and therefore ask their colleagues to independently record children's actions and thereby provide a basis for comparison about conclusions.

Researchers must also ask whether their data collection techniques are yielding consistent, dependable results—in other words, whether their methods have **reliability**. Data are reliable when the same kind of result is obtained in a variety of circumstances. In general, reliability is lower when unwanted influences (usually temporary in nature) affect the results. Children and adolescents inevitably perform differently on some occasions than on others; they may be more or less rested, attentive, cooperative, honest, or articulate. Their performance can also be influenced by characteristics of the researcher (e.g., gender, educational background, ethnic origin, appearance) and conditions in the research setting (e.g., how quiet the room is, how instructions are worded, and what kinds of incentives are given for participation).

Sometimes the instrument itself influences the reliability of scores, as can occur when two different forms of a single assessment yield dissimilar conclusions about children. This could happen if one form is more difficult or if two researchers interpret the same data differently. When the researchers are making subjective judgments (e.g., about the sophistication of children's artistic skills), they must establish clear standards or run the risk of making undependable judgments.

In studies with small sample sizes and the goal of sensitively portraying the experiences of children, researchers tend to use different terms for the integrity of their data collection. These scholars might suggest that they have tried to produce *trustworthy* or *credible* results by spending a long time observing children, reflecting on their own possible biases, asking participating children for their interpretations of the events, getting input from colleagues, and corroborating the results with several distinct kinds of data.

Having carefully collected information from children, researchers must also consider the meaning of the data within the broader context of the study. To a large extent, the research design directs the interpretation of the data.

Research Designs

The *research design* translates the research question into the concrete details of a study. The design specifies the procedures and schedule of data collection and strategies for analyzing the data. In child development research the design typically focuses on one of four themes: (a) the effects of new interventions on children, (b) the elements of children's development that occur in association with one another, (c) the particular aspects of children's behavior that change with time and those others that stay the same, or (d) the nature of children's everyday experiences.

Studies that Identify Causal Effects of Interventions

In an **experimental study**, an investigator manipulates one aspect of the environment and measures its impact on children. Experiments typically involve an intervention, or *treatment*. Participants are divided into two or more groups, with separate groups receiving different treatments or perhaps with one group (a **control group**) receiving either no treatment or a presumably ineffective one. Following the treatment(s), the investigator looks at the groups for differences in the children's behavior.

Preparing for Your Licensure Examination
Your teaching test might ask you to identify the characteristics of assessments that are valid and reliable.

reliability
Extent to which a data collection technique yields consistent, dependable results—results that are only minimally affected by temporary and irrelevant influences.

experimental study
Research study in which a researcher manipulates one aspect of the environment (a treatment), controls other aspects of the environment, and assesses the treatment's effects on participants' behavior.

control group
Group of participants in a research study who do not receive the treatment under investigation; often used in an experimental study.

In a true experimental design, participants are assigned to groups on a *random* basis; they have essentially no choice in the treatment (or lack thereof) that they receive.[1] Random assignment increases the likelihood that any differences among individuals (perhaps dissimilarities in motivations or personalities of group members) are evenly distributed among the groups and due to chance alone. With the exception of administering a particular treatment, the experimenter makes all conditions of the research experience identical or very similar for all of the groups. The researcher thus tries to ensure that the only major difference among the groups is the experimental treatment. Therefore, any differences in children's subsequent behaviors are almost certainly the *result* of treatment differences.

In many situations experiments are impossible, impractical, or unethical. When random assignment is not a viable strategy, researchers may conduct a **quasi-experimental study**, in which they administer one or more experimental treatments to existing groups (e.g., classrooms or schools; D. T. Campbell & Stanley, 1963). Because researchers cannot make sure that the groups are similar in every respect, the possibility exists that some other variable (e.g., presence of gangs at one school but not the other) may account for any later difference in characteristics of participants in the different sites.

An illustration of a quasi-experimental design can be found in an investigation examining the effectiveness of different treatments for aggression with 904 elementary and junior high students in Israel (Shechtman & Ifargan, 2009). Three classrooms at a single grade level in each of 13 schools were randomly assigned to one of three 4-month-long treatments. A counseling group included activities that addressed circumstances that led children to act out aggressively and coached them in controlling aggressive urges. Students who participated in an in-class intervention read literature and took part in discussions and other activities emphasizing the inappropriateness of aggression and fostering empathy for classmates. Students who participated in a control group took part in their regular classes and completed the research instruments. This study is considered a quasi-experiment because the children were not randomly assigned to treatments as individuals—rather, they were members of a classroom and shared the same treatment (or no treatment) with their classmates. Before and after the 4-month period, students rated their own behavior on a seven-point scale in terms of how characteristic various aggressive behaviors were of them (with 1 being "is not characteristic of me at all" and 7 being "is very characteristic of me"). Among the key findings of the study were that children who had been previously identified by their teachers as being especially aggressive rated themselves as significantly less aggressive after participating in either the counseling or in-class intervention group, whereas children in the control group did not, as you can see in the following table:

Average Scores on Levels of Aggression Before and After Participation in Treatment Groups

Type of Aggression	Counseling Group		In-Class Intervention		Control Group	
	Before	After	Before	After	Before	After
Verbal aggression	4.49	4.06	4.45	3.90	4.23	4.37
Physical aggression	4.09	3.28	4.28	3.28	4.04	3.89

Experiments are unique among research designs in the degree to which outside influences are controlled and therefore eliminated as possible explanations for the results. For this reason, experiments are the method of choice when a researcher wants to identify cause-and-effect relationships. Another strength of experiments is that their rigorous procedures allow other researchers to replicate the conditions of the study. A common limitation, however, is that to ensure adequate control of procedures, researchers must sometimes conduct their interventions in artificial laboratory settings that are considerably different from conditions in the real world. Also, ethical and practical considerations make it impossible to

quasi-experimental study Research study in which one or more experimental treatments are administered but in which random assignment to groups is not possible.

[1]Ethical considerations may lead researchers to give members of the control group an alternative treatment—something of value that will not compromise the experimental comparison. In other circumstances researchers make the experimental treatment available to children in the control group *after* the study has been completed.

conduct true experiments related to some research questions, and when quasi-experiments are carried out instead, causal effects are not fully certain.

Studies that Identify Associations

Some studies uncover patterns already present in children's lives. In an investigation examining associations, a researcher collects information on one variable, such as the amount of time per week parents read to children, and sees if it is related to another variable, such as the size of children's vocabulary. Associations often are examined with a **correlation**, which measures the extent to which two variables are related to each other. If a correlation exists, one variable changes when the other variable does, in a somewhat predictable fashion.

In correlational studies, associations are often measured with a statistic known as the *correlation coefficient*, a number that is typically between –1 and +1. The sign of the coefficient (+ or –) tells us about the direction of the relationship. Among a group of children at a particular age level, height and weight tend to be positively correlated—taller children tend to weigh more than shorter children. In comparison, children's age and the number of hours they sleep at night tend to be negatively correlated; as children grow older, they tend to sleep somewhat less. The size of the coefficient tells us how strong the relationship is. A coefficient that is close to either +1 or –1 (e.g., +.89 or –.76) indicates a strong link between the variables, whereas coefficients that are close to zero (e.g., +.15 or –.22) indicate a weak connection between the variables. Coefficients in the middle range (e.g., those in the .40s and .50s, whether positive or negative) indicate moderate associations.

In a **correlational study**, investigators look for naturally occurring associations among existing characteristics, behaviors, or other variables. In a study with ninety 10- to 11-year-old girls in a rural community in the northwest part of the United States, the amount of time girls watched physically aggressive programs on television was positively associated with teachers' reports of the girls exhibiting certain kinds of aggression. Viewing a lot of aggressive content on television was associated with frequency of verbal aggression (e.g., calling children names, in a coefficient of +.38), with physical aggression (e.g., hitting or kicking peers, in a coefficient of +.25), and relational aggression (e.g., spreading rumors or gossiping about classmates, in a coefficient of +.21) (Linder & Gentile, 2009). Because these data are correlational and not experimental, they do not give definitive clues as to what factors might have led girls who had been exposed to high levels of violence to become aggressive themselves. Although televised aggression might have provoked aggression in the girls, other conditions, such as parents' difficulty in maintaining warm relationships with their daughters, may have led the girls to spend a lot of time watching television *and* become aggressive at school. Note also that the associations are rather weak, suggesting that additional factors account for the degree to which girls became antagonistic with classmates.

Correlational studies have the advantages of being relatively inexpensive to conduct and permitting the analysis of several relationships in a single investigation. One disadvantage, however, is that cause-and-effect relationships cannot be determined from correlational data alone. This is a serious limitation: Although correlational studies may demonstrate an association between two or more variables, they can never tell us the specific factors that explain *why* it exists. In other words, correlation *does not* necessarily indicate causation.

Studies that Show Developmental Change and Stability

Some investigations, known as *developmental studies*, examine how children grow, change, or stay the same as they become older and have more experiences. One approach is a **cross-sectional study**, in which a researcher compares individuals at two or more age levels at the same point in time. In a study with first- and third-grade boys, Coie, Dodge, Terry, and Wright (1991) found that first graders were more likely to be targets of aggression than were third graders.

Another option for studying developmental stability and change is the **longitudinal study**, in which a researcher studies one group of children or adolescents over a lengthy period of time, often for several years and sometimes even for decades. Longitudinal studies allow us to see any changes in a characteristic when the same measurement is taken on repeated occasions. Longitudinal designs also allow us to examine the factors in children's

correlation
Extent to which two variables are related to each other, such that when one variable increases, the other either increases or decreases in a somewhat predictable fashion.

correlational study
Research study that explores relationships among variables.

cross-sectional study
Research study in which the performance of individuals at different ages is compared at a single point in time.

longitudinal study
Research study in which the performance of a single group of people is tracked over a period of time.

early lives that forecast their later performance. An example of a longitudinal study is Eron's (1987) investigation into factors potentially related to aggressive behavior. Eron collected data at three points in time, first when the participants were in third grade, a second time 10 years later, and a third time 12 years after that. Factors evident when the participants were children, including a punitive style of discipline by their parents, the children's own preferences for watching violent television shows, and the children's lack of a guilty conscience about hurting others, were associated with their aggressiveness and criminal behavior 10 and 22 years later.

To strengthen inferences that can be made about change and stability in child development, some researchers have creatively modified developmental designs. A few have tried *microgenetic methods*, which you might think of as brief but thorough longitudinal designs. Researchers implementing microgenetic methods may study children's strategies while learning a new task over a few hours, days, or weeks (Siegler, 2006; Vygotsky, 1978). Other variations include a combination of cross-sectional and longitudinal designs. A *cohort-sequential design* replicates a longitudinal study with new *cohorts*—that is, with one or more additional groups of people born in certain subsequent years. To illustrate, Suhr (1999) conducted a cohort-sequential study to examine children's scores in mathematics, reading recognition, and reading comprehension. Scores were collected every 2 years for children who were born in 1980, 1981, 1982, and 1983. Suhr found that growth in skills was rapid between ages 5 and 10 but slowed down after age 10. Because the data included children from four different birth years, Suhr could be reasonably confident that the spurt of learning that occurred between 5 and 10 years was a reasonably accurate result and not an anomaly of one particular group.

The particular strengths and limitations of developmental studies are design-specific. Cross-sectional studies offer an efficient snapshot of how characteristics or behaviors probably change with age, but these age differences can be attributed to a variety of factors, including maturation, exposure to schooling experiences, and general changes in society. Longitudinal studies allow prediction of later characteristics based on earlier qualities but are expensive, time-consuming, and of questionable relevance to other populations of children. The hybrid designs that combine the features of cross-sectional and longitudinal designs have definite advantages, but they are extremely expensive to carry out and create demands for continued involvement in data collection that many potential research participants would rather avoid.

Studies that Describe Children's Everyday Experiences in Natural Contexts

In a *naturalistic study*, researchers examine children's experiences in their families, peer groups, schools, clubs, and elsewhere. In this kind of investigation, researchers try not to prejudge children's ideas and instead listen carefully to the views of the children themselves. In a recent study with adolescents from low-income families who were attending middle schools in an urban community, interviewers asked the students to talk about how they might respond to particular conflicts (Farrell et al., 2008). The adolescents mentioned such dimensions as their emotional responses (e.g., "If they just keep on coming and coming … I lose my temper," p. 402) and their personal goals (e.g., "I want to be able to stay on a good record like I got. I don't want to stay in fights and stuff. Because that's the way that you won't get in college and you won't get a good job," p. 403). The themes that are found in a naturalistic investigation are not necessarily those that are expected by the researchers, contributing to a sense of discovery in this kind of research.

In some naturalistic studies, known as **ethnographies**, scholars look at the everyday rules of behavior, beliefs, social structures, and other cultural patterns of an entire group of people—perhaps a community, classroom, or family. Researchers who conduct ethnographies typically spend many months and occasionally even a year or more collecting detailed notes in an ordinary setting, getting to know the people who congregate there and the meaning of their ways (Warming, 2011; Wolcott, 1999).

In another type of naturalistic investigation, a researcher conducts a **case study**, wherein a single person's or a small group's experiences are documented in depth over

ethnography
Naturalistic research study in which investigators spend an extensive period of time documenting the cultural patterns of a group of people in everyday settings.

case study
Naturalistic research study in which investigators document a single person's or a small group's experiences in depth over a period of time.

a period of time. (Research case studies are not to be confused with the case studies that begin and end the chapters in this book, which are more limited in scope.) Other naturalistic studies take the form of **grounded theory studies**, in which researchers typically collect in-depth data on a particular topic—often one related to young people's experiences with a particular phenomenon—and use those data to develop a theory about that phenomenon (Corbin & Strauss, 2008). For example, a researcher might ask young children to describe and draw pictures of enjoyable playgrounds in an attempt to capture the general experience of play in children (Hyvönen & Kangas, 2007).

The results of naturalistic studies tend to be verbally descriptive and less reliant on statistical tests than is the case with the three other designs we've examined.[2] As an example, two researchers conducted interviews with 17 adolescent boys living in either a residential treatment center or a halfway home and summarized the kinds of justifications the boys gave for their aggression (V. A. Lopez & Emmer, 2002). Using a grounded theory approach, the researchers asked the boys about their violent crimes and identified two motives. In "vigilante crimes," the boys used physical aggression to avenge another person's actual or perceived wrongful act. Sixteen-year-old Tax used a vigilante motivation in trying to protect his cousin:

> We had went over there to go use the phone and I went to go use the restroom. And when I came out, they had beat him [cousin] down, and hit him with a brick in his head, and cracked his skull open. So I got into a fight with one of them. I hit him with a lock and broke his jaw. He had to get three stitches in his head. (V. A. Lopez & Emmer, 2002, p. 35)

In "honor crimes," the boys used violence to protect themselves or their gang. Seventeen-year-old Muppet gave this explanation for his participation in a drive-by shooting:

> Around my birthday me and a bunch of my cousins [fellow gang members] found out about B [name of rival gang] named A who was talking shit and had jumped one of my cousins so we found out where he [rival gang member] lived and we went by and shot up his trailer house. We don't like Bs [members of rival gang] to begin with. (V. A. Lopez & Emmer, 2002, p. 37)

A key strength of naturalistic studies is their sensitivity to children's own views about their everyday events and relationships. In the study we just examined, the young people viewed their aggressive acts as reasonable ways to preserve their own identities and solve conflicts. Such studies also make it possible to capture the complexities and subtle nuances of children's experiences in complex environments, making naturalistic studies informative windows into the bioecology of children's development. Naturalistic studies have several limitations, however. They are difficult and time-consuming to carry out, usually require extensive data collection, and produce results that fail to disentangle causes and effects in children's lives.

In the description of investigations in this section, we included several studies focusing on one topic, children's aggression. We learned that conscientiously planned interventions can diminish aggression in children, that watching violence on television is associated with children's own fighting, that punitive child rearing by parents is associated with their children's aggressiveness later in life, and that violent youth see their aggressive acts as justified. More generally, each of the designs we've examined affords valuable insights into child development, and together they give us a more complete picture into the many dimensions of children's lives.

Becoming a Thoughtful Consumer of Research

As you examine research studies, you will want to get in the habit of reading the methods, results, and conclusions critically. If you ask a few simple questions of the investigations, you can begin to distinguish studies that are worthy of your consideration from those that are not.

---

[2]Naturalistic studies are sometimes called qualitative studies because their analyses draw heavily on verbal interpretations. Of course, many qualitative studies do report numerical results, including the number of children who articulate a particular theme.

Bioecology of Child Development
Investigators who ask children about their experiences in families, peer groups, schools, and communities contribute to our understanding of the bioecology of child development.

grounded theory study
Naturalistic research study in which investigators develop and elaborate new theories while comparing data (such as interview statements from participants) to the researchers' emerging interpretations.

As an illustration, imagine that a group of elementary teachers wants to improve children's ability to get along with peers and teachers. In their initial conversations, the teachers decide that what they most want to do is increase the frequency of kind, respectful, and cooperative behaviors that children exhibit to one another and to school staff. A committee is appointed to study the matter in greater depth, and in particular to look at what research has to say about existing programs. The committee addresses the following questions:

What Is the Purpose of the Research?

The committee wants to find research into effective educational programs that foster respectful and cooperative behaviors in children. With the help of a reference librarian at a nearby university, the committee identifies promising electronic databases and keywords (e.g., *character education, moral education, prosocial behavior*) to use in its search. It soon finds articles examining three widely used programs: an Ethics Curriculum for Children (Leming, 2000), the Positive Action program (Flay & Allred, 2003), and the Caring School Community (Solomon, Watson, Delucchi, Schaps, & Battistich, 1988), as well as an Internet site that compares the effectiveness of these and other similar programs (Institute of Education Sciences, 2006). The committee focuses on three articles that seem especially pertinent as shown in Table 2-1.

Who Participated in the Investigations?

The committee notes that all three investigations had fairly large samples. The studies drew from different parts of the country and recruited children from families with varying income levels and ethnic backgrounds. However, none of the samples is as diverse as the population at the committee's own school, which includes many children from immigrant families and different ethnic backgrounds.

What Are the Designs of the Studies?

Each of the studies used a quasi-experimental design. Because participants were not randomly assigned to treatment and control groups, the committee cannot know for sure whether any group differences in outcomes were due to the program content, preexisting differences between the groups, or some other factor.

What Information Is Presented About the Integrity of the Data?

The strength of the data varied across the three studies. The evaluation of the Ethics Curriculum for Children depended on participating teachers' ratings of students' behaviors; in making their ratings, the teachers may have been affected by observer bias, that is, they may have seen what they *expected* to see in various students. The evaluation of Positive Action involved school records related to disciplinary referrals, suspensions, and absentee rates. Absenteeism can be recorded accurately, but administrators' disciplinary actions could have been influenced by personal biases toward or against particular students. The investigators examining the Caring School Community program appeared to have been especially thoughtful about the quality of their data in that observers did not know which children were participants in the program.

Are the Studies Published in Reputable Journals?

Most journals use the process of sending manuscripts out to specialists in the field to comment on strengths, limitations, and suitability for publication. The committee determines that each of the three articles was published in a reputable journal that accepts only those articles that have been favorably reviewed by experts in the field.

Bioecology of Child Development

Some educational programs work effectively in particular settings but not others because of differences in children's cultural values, relationships, resources, and risk factors. When selecting educational programs, teachers need to attend to the match between the backgrounds of research participants and those of their own students.

DO THE RIGHT THING. A character education program may effectively inspire these young people to live up to a strong moral code yet be less successful with a different population of students.

TABLE 2-1 Analyzing Research on Program Effectiveness: The Case of "Character Education"

Purpose of the Analysis: *Finding a program that fosters kind, respectful, and cooperative behaviors in elementary school children*

QUESTIONS FOR THE ANALYSIS	SELECTED PROGRAMS FOR REVIEW		
	ETHICS CURRICULUM FOR CHILDREN (LEMING, 2000)	POSITIVE ACTION (FLAY & ALLRED, 2003)	CARING SCHOOL COMMUNITY (SOLOMON et al., 1988)
What are the objectives of the research?	The researchers evaluated the Ethics Curriculum for Children, a program that aims to promote elements of "good character" using a read-aloud multicultural literature-based program. The program is organized around traits of courage, loyalty, justice, respect, hope, honesty, and love.	The researchers evaluated Positive Action, a program that aims to promote character development and the social-emotional skills of children and adolescents and to reduce drug use, school suspension rates, and violence rates through classroom discussion, role playing, games, songs, and other structured activities.	The researchers evaluated the Caring School Community, a program that aims to foster productive social behaviors (e.g., cooperation) and a general sense of affection and respectfulness through structured classroom lessons, cross-age buddies, schoolwide initiatives, and activities at home.
Who participated in the investigation?	The Ethics Curriculum for Children has been used in more than 1,500 schools. In Leming's study, participants were 965 first- to sixth-grade students from predominantly European American and African American backgrounds in semirural areas of Pennsylvania and Illinois.	Positive Action has been used in more than 11,000 schools. In Flay and Allred's study, participants were students from European American, African American, and Hispanic American backgrounds in 36 elementary schools in a Southeastern school district.	The Caring School Community program has been implemented in more than 2,700 classrooms. In Solomon and colleagues' studies, participants were approximately 600 K–4 students from six elementary schools in a middle- to upper-middle income suburban community in San Ramon, California.
What is the design of the study?	A quasi-experimental design compared outcomes for children who participated in the ethics curriculum to outcomes of children in control-group classes that did not use this curriculum or another character education program.	A quasi-experimental design compared outcomes for children who participated in the Positive Action curriculum with children in schools in the same district that did not implement Positive Action. Positive Action and control-group schools served families with similar income levels.	A quasi-experimental design compared outcomes for children in three schools who participated in the Caring School Community program with children in three other schools in the same district. The treatment and control-group schools served families with similar income levels.
What information is presented about the integrity of the data?	Teachers completed a rating scale of each student's character-related behavior before and after the program. The items on the scale were internally consistent—that is, they all seemed to be assessing the same characteristic—which indicates high reliability and indirectly suggests adequate validity as well. However, teachers may have been biased in their observations of children, perhaps threatening the validity of the rating-scale scores.	The researchers obtained school records of disciplinary referrals, out-of-school suspensions, and extended absences. School officials typically follow strict guidelines in keeping records for disciplinary referrals and suspensions, but possibly school faculty members were biased in the students they did (and did not) refer for disciplinary action.	Outside observers were carefully trained in rating the children's behaviors and did not know which schools were and were not participating in the Caring School Community program. The researchers presented several forms of evidence to indicate good reliability and validity of the data. For example, observers' ratings of students' cooperative behaviors were positively correlated with teachers' ratings of students' behavior in small groups.
Is the study published in a reputable journal?	Yes. The study was published in *Journal of Moral Education*. The author and his colleagues have also published a few other reports on the curriculum.	Yes. The study was published in *American Journal of Health Behavior*. The authors have published extensively on this program.	Yes. The study was published in *American Educational Research Journal*. Numerous other investigations on the program have been published in reputable journals.
Do the analyses suggest significant results in areas of concern for your own purposes?	No. The results focusing on behavior change are difficult to interpret. In grades 1–3, participants in the Ethics Curriculum showed *less* desirable behavior than did children in the control-group classes. (As the researcher points out, teachers in the experimental-group classes may have had higher expectations for their students and been disappointed at not seeing dramatic changes.) In grades 4–6, participants in the program did exhibit better behavior than those in the control group.	Not primarily in the areas of concern for the committee. The focus of the study was on rates of violence and suspension (which decreased following the curriculum) and on absenteeism (which did not decrease). However, the authors did not specifically indicate improvements in behaviors of concern to this analysis (e.g., respectfulness, cooperation).	Yes. Compared to students without exposure to this program, students in the Caring School Community exhibited higher levels of spontaneous helping behaviors and supportive and friendly behaviors. No differences were found in an additional measure of helping behaviors.
Overall, does the program meet the needs of the school?	No. The program has merits, but the evidence is not strong for an increase in helpful and cooperative behaviors in children.	Maybe. The program appears to decrease students' violence but does not dramatically increase helpful and cooperative behaviors.	Yes. The program appears to increase students' helpful, cooperative behaviors in school settings.

NOTE: Given that the goal of the analysis is to find a program that fosters cooperative and helpful behaviors of elementary school children, instruments and results that targeted helping behaviors and productive conduct of children of this age are included in the table, and reports about other outcomes (e.g., knowledge, attitudes, values, and achievement) and data from other age-groups are not included.

Do the Analyses Suggest Significant Results in Areas of Concern?

As shown in Table 2-1, results were not consistently favorable in the Ethics Curriculum for Children study. Results were generally favorable for the Positive Action and Caring School Community programs. Furthermore, the committee finds additional support for the Positive Action and Caring School Community programs in the other resources it examines (Battistich, 2003; Institute of Education Sciences, 2006). After considerable discussion, the committee decides that the outcomes for the Positive Action program are only tangentially related to the goals of fostering cooperative and helping behaviors. The committee concludes that the Caring School Community yielded results that most closely align with its own goals for improvement in children's behavior.

After completing its analysis, the committee recommends the Caring School Community to the school faculty because of the program's favorable outcomes in fostering children's cooperative behaviors, the high validity and reliability of the data, and an extensive set of studies available on the program's effects (see the final row in Table 2-1). Committee members realize that they should cautiously examine how the program works for children at their school given that the populations of children in the research and their own setting are somewhat different.

As you read research articles and reports, you can ask yourself questions similar to the ones the committee addressed. You will find that it takes some practice to adapt your analysis to the particular data collection techniques and designs of individual investigations. With experience, you can gradually gain expertise in distinguishing dependable information about child development from sources you cannot trust.

GATHERING DATA AS AN EDUCATOR

As you have seen, academic researchers work diligently to collect information about children and adolescents in ways that are ethical, sensitive, valid, and reliable. Teachers and other school professionals do the same, although their strategies are somewhat different.

Inviting Children's Self-Reports

From a young age, children are motivated to tell adults what makes them happy, relieved, or satisfied, on the one hand, and distressed, angry, or sad, on the other. It is up to adults to set aside the time, put youngsters at ease, and let them speak their minds. Here's how you can gain access to children's perspectives:

• **Let children know you care.** The surest way into a child's heart is naturally to express affection sincerely and consistently. When you have earned a child's trust, the child is more likely to articulate what's on his or her mind.

• **Develop your interviewing skills.** Too often, conversations between adults and children are short, ask-a-question-and-get-an-answer exchanges. Lengthier dialogues, perhaps with an individual child or a small group of children, can be far more informative. Getting children to talk takes experience, but there are a few specific things you can do (D. Fisher & Frey, 2007; Graue & Walsh, 1998; Koekoek, Knoppers, & Stegeman, 2009). First of all, you can try a combination of open-ended questions ("How was your day?") and close-ended questions ("Did you watch TV when you went home from school?"). Also, include some general requests for information that are not in question form ("Tell me more about that"). Try not to ask a long series of questions, or your probing may seem like an inquisition. Make sure you pause after asking a question to give children plenty of time to formulate their thoughts, and communicate that you really care about what they have to say. Sometimes it is appropriate to ask children how *other children* view life; this can be an effective way to help them feel safe in speaking their minds. For example, rather than asking children how they feel about achievement tests, ask them how *other children* feel ("How did kids at your school feel last week when they took the state achievement test?").

• **Listen intently to children's experiences.** Unless adults truly listen to young people, they cannot fully understand young people's experiences. Sometimes children see the world in the same way as adults, but perhaps more often children have vastly different viewpoints. In a study with sixth graders in the Philadelphia public schools (B. L. Wilson & Corbett, 2001), young adolescents appeared to share many priorities and goals with adults. The students stated that they wanted teachers to push them to complete assignments (even when they resisted), to maintain order (even when they misbehaved), and to teach them difficult material (even when they struggled). Despite their apparent desire to succeed, these youngsters were unaware of what it took to do well when subjects became complicated, and they were naive about skills needed for success in college. From these results, we realize that teachers need to be persistent in explaining concepts, teaching study skills, and preparing adolescents for the reality of college.

• **Develop classroom routines that allow students to express their understandings.** Teachers can establish classroom procedures that allow children to share their interpretations (D. Fisher & Frey, 2007). Bringing in provocative materials, including works of art from different cultures, can create a forum for children's storytelling, conversation, and analysis (Mulcahey, 2009). Some teachers use the Think–Pair–Share discussion strategy, in which teachers stop midway through a lesson, ask children to think about a particular question or issue, have children form pairs to discuss their responses, and finally ask children to share their ideas with the rest of the class (Lyman, 1981). Other teachers use the Whip Around technique, a structured activity at the end of a lesson: They pose a question, ask children to write their responses on a piece of paper, and then "whip around" the group asking children to give their responses orally (D. Fisher & Frey, 2007). From such responses teachers can gain a sense of what children have learned and what information needs to be reviewed the following day. These techniques can foster self-expression in children, provided that teachers communicate that everyone is encouraged to participate and no one will be ridiculed for what he or she says.

Interpreting Tests, Other Assessments, and Artifacts

In addition to observing and listening to children, you can also examine their assignments and the many other products they create—artwork, scribbled notes to friends, test responses, and so forth. To learn from children's performance on tests and artifacts (work samples and other things they create), you might follow these recommendations:

• **When evaluating children's responses to your own assessments, use explicit scoring criteria.** You are most likely to be accurate in the judgments you make about children's performance when you use carefully designed evaluation criteria. Designing a **rubric**, a list of the ideal features of a completed task, is a common tactic used by teachers to increase the fairness of grading. If you have shared the criteria with children ahead of time (and we encourage you to do so), children will be able to guide their learning toward clear standards and will better understand your feedback after you have evaluated their performance (E. J. Lee & Lee, 2009; Stiggins, 2007).

• **Keep in mind both the advantages and limitations of paper-and-pencil tests.** Paper-and-pencil tests are often an efficient way of determining what children have and have not learned. Furthermore, a well-designed test can reveal a great deal about children's thinking processes. However, appraisals of children that rely exclusively on test scores often paint a lopsided picture of their abilities. For instance, children who have limited reading and writing skills (perhaps because they have a learning disability or have only recently begun to learn English) are likely to perform poorly in spite of their understandings. Furthermore, paper-and-pencil tests, by their very nature, can tell us little if anything about children's self-confidence, motor skills, ability to work well with others, or expertise at using equipment.

• **Interpret standardized tests cautiously.** No single assessment has perfect validity and reliability, and as a result, major decisions about children, such as whether they are promoted to the next grade or allowed to graduate from high school, should *never* be made on the basis of a single test score (American Educational Research Association, 2000).

Preparing for Your Licensure Examination
Your teaching test might include items about effective ways to ask questions and encourage children's participation in discussions.

Preparing for Your Licensure Examination
Your teaching test might ask you about how rubrics help students to complete learning tasks.

Preparing for Your Licensure Examination
Your teaching test might ask you whether it is advisable to make a decision about children based on the results of a single test score.

rubric
A list of the ideal features of an assessment, often used by students in completing a task and by teachers in evaluating students' performance.

• **Remember that validity and reliability apply to all assessments.** Never overinterpret any single product a child has created. For example, imagine that a 6-year-old draws a self-portrait with a frowning face, as one of Teresa's sons once did. The boy's teacher concluded that he was unhappy and had low self-esteem, but nothing could have been further from the truth: The child was (and continues to be) a generally happy, self-confident individual. Perhaps on that single occasion he was simply having a bad day or was annoyed with the teacher who asked him to draw the picture.

• **Watch for cultural bias in assessments.** Children often interpret test questions differently than do adult examiners, particularly when the children come from different cultural backgrounds. As an example, one team of researchers examined the science scores of a culturally and linguistically diverse group of elementary children (Luykx et al., 2007). Many of the children misinterpreted questions because of their cultural and language backgrounds. Several of the Spanish-speaking children confused the abbreviations of *F* and *C* (intended to stand for Fahrenheit and Celsius) with the Spanish words *frío* and *caliente*, and a few Haitian children misconstrued an item that asked how long they would be able to play between 4 p.m. and a 6 p.m. dinner, probably because they typically would have had their own main meal (which they called "dinner") earlier in the day. This assessment seems to have been unfairly biased against children who did not speak English or had different everyday experiences than did the test developers.

In general, an assessment is tainted with **cultural bias** when it offends or unfairly penalizes some individuals because of their ethnicity, gender, socioeconomic status, or cultural background. When examining children's responses yourself, you can consider how children's apparent errors may arise because of a language difference or distinct cultural perspective. If you suspect a cultural bias, you will need to obtain additional information from children before drawing any firm conclusions about their abilities.

• **Assess environments to determine the extent to which they support children's well-being.** Some assessment strategies identify the strengths, priorities, and limitations of families, classrooms, and other settings. In our opening case study, Jack Reston learned that his school was not initially meeting the needs of all children as well as he hoped. In addition, assessment strategies are vital to prevention programs and other community services. For instance, a community team planning a program to prevent substance abuse could examine conditions in the community that possibly encourage students to use and abuse illicit street drugs (U.S. Department of Health and Human Services, 2009).

Examining Physiological Data from Children

Other than counting sit-ups or making note of other simple athletic accomplishments, teachers generally do not collect physiological information from children. On rare occasions teachers might see a medical report brought in by a parent about a child's health condition, brain injury, or disability. In such a circumstance, teachers naturally refrain from making judgments for which they are not qualified. However, teachers who become aware of children's medical impairments sometimes gain helpful advice from school nurses, school psychologists, or parents about the educational implications of these conditions.

Observing Children

If you carefully watch children and adolescents in classrooms, after-school programs, and other settings, you can learn a lot about their interests, values, and abilities. Here are some suggestions to enhance your observation skills:

cultural bias
Extent to which an assessment offends or unfairly penalizes some individuals because of their ethnicity or cultural background, gender, or socioeconomic status.

• **Observe how children respond to the demands of particular settings.** Teachers and other practitioners often watch children move among various settings, such as the classroom, cafeteria, and playground. As you observe children and adolescents, ask yourself what they are doing, why they might be behaving as they are, how they might be interpreting events, and how the setting may be affecting their behavior. When you are able to gather observations across multiple settings, you can gain deeper insights into the needs of individual children.

For example, a child who appears uninhibited and happy on the playground but fearful and tense in the classroom may need tutoring or another kind of assistance in order to be academically successful.

• **Observe youngsters' nonverbal behaviors.** Careful observation of children's postures, actions, and emotional expressions can provide important information about their preferences and abilities. For example, an infant caregiver may learn that one 18-month-old toddler slows down, pulls at his ear, and seeks comfort when he's sleepy, whereas another child speeds up, squirms, and becomes irritable when ready for a nap. During an interview with a teenage boy, a school counselor might notice that he seems withdrawn and despondent. In response, the counselor inquires sympathetically about how things are going for him at home and school.

• **Consider children's developmental states.** When you sense an unmet need, analyze the situation using your knowledge of child development. Your emerging familiarity with typical characteristics of different age-groups can help you focus in on particular things in your observations. Observation Guidelines tables throughout the book can assist you in identifying particular developmental abilities in children and adolescents. The first of these, "Learning from Children and Adolescents," on page 56, suggests some general things to look for in your work with young people.

• **Separate direct observations from inferences.** To observe accurately, you need to begin to distinguish what you actually see from what you think it means. It is not possible to be entirely objective, but you can make some headway in tempering your own reactions to events. One strategy that may help you is to keep separate records of what you see and how you make sense of the experience. Here are some notes from a student teacher, Ana, who recorded her observations in a "Notetaking" column and her interpretations in a "Notemaking" one:

Improving Your Observation Skills

Read this! Teachers can learn a lot from watching children's facial expressions, postures, and other nonverbal behaviors. What might you infer from the nonverbal behavior displayed by these Ethiopian fifth-grade students? Compare your response with the explanation at the end of the chapter.

Preparing for Your Licensure Examination

Your teaching test might ask you what you can infer from children's hand gestures, eye contact, facial expressions, and tone of speech.

Notetaking	Notemaking
A child is working at the computer. There are fourteen students working at their desks. Six students are working with another teacher (aide) in the back of the room. It is an English reading/writing group she is working with—speaking only in English. I see a mother working with one child only and she is helping the student with something in English. There is a baby in a carriage nearby the mother. I hear classical music playing very lightly. I can only hear the music every once in a while when the classroom is really quiet. I stand up and move around the room to see what the children at their desks are working on. They are writing scary stories. The baby makes a funny noise with her lips and everyone in the class laughs and stares for a few seconds, even the teacher. . . .	The class seems to be really self-directed. . . . I am not used to seeing students split up into different groups for Spanish and English readers because in my class they are Spanish readers, but it is really good for me to see this because it happens in a lot of upper grade settings, and I will be working in an upper grade bilingual setting next placement. I really like the idea of putting on music during work times. I know that when I hear classical music it really helps me to relax and calm down, as well as focus. I think that it has the same effect on the students in this class. I'm noticing more and more that I really cherish the laughter in a classroom when it comes from a sincere topic or source. It is also nice to see the students *and* the *teacher* laughing. . . . (C. Frank, 1999, pp. 11–12)[3]

Trying to notice the nuances in children's activities without jumping to conclusions can help you become a more perceptive observer. By distinguishing what you see from what it might mean, you can also learn about your own expectations and priorities as a teacher, as Ana might have done when rereading her "Notemaking" comments.

[3]From *Ethnographic Eyes: A Teacher's Guide to Classroom Observation* (pp. 11–12), by Carolyn Frank, 1999, Portsmouth, NH: Heinemann. Copyright 1999 by Carolyn Frank. Reprinted with permission.

OBSERVATION GUIDELINES
Learning from Children and Adolescents

CHARACTERISTIC	LOOK FOR	EXAMPLE	IMPLICATION
What Children Say	• *Verbal expressions* of likes and dislikes • *Thoughtful and insightful questions* about the topic at hand (indicates high task engagement and motivation) • *Previously answered questions* (might indicate either inattentiveness or lack of understanding) • *Complaints* about the difficulty of an assignment (might indicate low motivation, lack of ability or confidence, or an overloaded schedule of academic and social obligations)	In a whining tone, Danielle asks, "Do we really have to include *three* arguments in our persuasive essays? I've been thinking really hard and can only come up with one!"	Read between the lines in the questions children ask and the comments they make. Consider what their statements might indicate about their existing knowledge, skills, motivation, and self-confidence.
What Children Produce in Assessments and Artifacts	• *Careful and thorough work* (indicates high motivation and conscientious style) • *Unusual and creative accomplishments* in the form of ideas, artwork, or constructions (indicates high motivation and a willingness to take risks) • *Numerous sloppy errors* (might indicate that a child did an assignment hurriedly, has poor proofreading skills, or has a learning disability)	When Martin's social studies teacher gives several options for how students might illustrate the idea of *democracy,* Martin creates a large poster of colorful, cartoon-like characters engaging in voting, expressing their views about government, and making new laws.	When looking at and evaluating children's work, don't focus exclusively on "right" and "wrong" answers. Examine a variety of artifacts when drawing inferences about children's abilities and interests.
What Children Do	• *Exploration of the environment* through manipulation of objects, focused attention, and attempts to make sense of events in conversations with other people (may indicate inquisitiveness for certain kinds of information) • *Preferred activities during free time* (may show children's foremost desires and interests) • *Interest in people*, including initiating interactions as well as responding to others' social gestures (may indicate comfort levels in social situations) • *Quiet periods of self-absorption* (may indicate either thoughtful self-reflection or sadness) • *Facial expressions* (reflecting enjoyment, excitement, sadness, confusion, anger, or frustration) • *Tenseness of limbs* (might indicate either intense concentration or excessive anxiety) • *Slouching in seat* (might indicate fatigue, boredom, or resistance to an activity)	Whenever his teacher engages the class in a discussion of controversial issues, James participates eagerly. When she goes over the previous night's homework, however, he crosses his arms, slouches low in his seat, pulls his hat low over his eyes, and says nothing.	Provide a safe environment with interesting and attractive objects for active exploration. Make changes to the environment based on the preferred activities of children who inhabit it. Use children's body language as a rough gauge of interest, and modify activities that do not appear to be eliciting children's attention. Speak individually and confidentially with children who often show signs of sadness or anger.

• **Try out different kinds of observations.** The kinds of observations you conduct will depend on what you hope to gain from watching and listening to children. *Running records* are narrative summaries of a child's activities during a single period of time (Nicolson & Shipstead, 2002). Running records provide teachers and other professionals with opportunities to focus on a particular child and draw conclusions about the child's emerging developmental abilities. In Figure 2-2 you can see an excerpt from a running record prepared by a language specialist who observed a child with a hearing impairment. After carefully scrutinizing the running record, the language specialist concluded that Taki understood some aspects of

Center/Age level: Center for Speech and Language/3- to 6-Year-Olds	
Date: 7/17	Time: 10:20–10:26 AM
Observer: Naoki	Child/Age: Taki/5;1
	Teacher: Camille

Taki is seated on the floor with Kyle (4;8) and Camille, the teacher, in a corner of the classroom; both children have their backs to the center of the room. Taki sits with her right leg tucked under her bottom and her left leg bent with her foot flat on the floor. The Listening Lotto card is in front of her on the floor, and she holds a bunch of red plastic markers in her right hand. Camille begins the tape.

Comments
10:20

No intro of game.
Hearing aid working.

   The first sound is of a baby crying. Taki looks up at Camille, who says, "What's that?" Taki looks at Kyle, who has already placed his marker on the crying baby. Camille says, "That's a baby crying," and points to the picture on Taki's card. Taki places the marker with her left hand as the next sound, beating drums, begins.

   Taki looks at Kyle as the drumming continues. Camille points to the picture of the drums on Taki's card, and Taki places her marker.

Understands process.

   The next sound is of a toilet flushing. Taki looks at Kyle and points to the drums. Kyle says, "Good, Taki. We heard drums banging." Taki smiles. Camille says, "Do you hear the toilet flushing?" as she points to the correct picture. Taki places her marker and repositions herself to sit cross-legged. She continues to hold the markers in her right hand and place them with her left. . . .

10:22
Kyle supportive of Taki.

Conclusions: Taki's receptive language was on display when she followed the teacher's directions in Listening Lotto (put markers on the appropriate spots), but she did not demonstrate success on her own. Her fine motor control was in evidence as she adeptly handled small markers.

FIGURE 2-2   Running record for Taki during Listening Lotto. Note that specialists in child development often list a child's age in years and additional months, separating the two numbers by a semicolon. Taki's age of 5 years and 1 month is indicated as "5;1." *From* Through the Looking Glass: Observations in the Early Childhood Classroom *(3rd ed., pp. 118–119), by S. Nicolson and S. G. Shipstead, 2002, Upper Saddle River, New Jersey: Merrill/Prentice Hall. Copyright 2002 by Pearson Education. Reprinted with permission.*

spoken language when she followed directions. However, Taki needed help when completing the Listening Lotto game. These kinds of conclusions can offer professionals good ideas about next steps. Possibly, the language specialist realized she needed to look further into Taki's hearing ability.

   Anecdotal records are descriptions of brief incidents observed by teachers and other professionals (Nicolson & Shipstead, 2002; Paley, 2007). An anecdotal record is typically made when an adult notices a child take an action or make a statement that is developmentally significant. Anecdotal records are sometimes made of children's accomplishments, physical milestones, social interaction patterns, ways of thinking, and concerns. Anecdotal records tend to be much briefer than running records, and they may be written up later in the day. Teachers may accumulate these notes about children, use the records to help identify individual needs, and share them with family members during conferences, informal conversations, and meetings. Figure 2-3 shows teacher-prepared anecdotal records for three young children.

   Teachers sometimes use *checklists* and *rating scales* when they wish to evaluate the degree to which children's behaviors reflect specific criteria. Checklists allow observers to note whether a child's actions or work products reflect specific standards. Figure 2-4 shows a checklist that a debate teacher might use to evaluate a student's oral presentation. Rating scales are similar to checklists, but rating scales ask observers not simply whether a child shows a particular behavior but rather how *often* or *consistently* the child shows the behavior. Figure 2-5 shows a rating scale of paying attention during class time.

   One means of recording observations is not necessarily better than another. Instead, each observational system has a distinct purpose. As you gain experience in observing youngsters, you are likely to see how your own understanding of individual children grows when you use several observational methods and supplement them by listening to what children say.

Preparing for Your Licensure Examination
Your teaching test might ask you about the purposes of anecdotal records.

10/5 Tatiana (2;0):	While sitting on the floor in the art area peeling the wrappers off crayons, she looked up as the caregiver grew near and said, "I making the crayons all naked."
1/15 Maggie (4;8):	I listened as Maggie chattered on and on while the two of us cleaned up the block area. Finally I winked and said, "It all sounds like baloney to me." Maggie quickly asked, "What's baloney?" I replied, "It's a word that means you made all that up!" She thought for a few seconds and said, "No, it's salami!"
2/24 Matthew (7;4):	While discussing *In a Dark, Dark Room and Other Scary Stories* by Alvin Schwartz, Matthew thoughtfully shared, "Do you know what kind of scary things I like best? Things that are halfway between real and imaginary." I started to ask, "I wonder what . . ." Matthew quickly replied, "Examples would be aliens, shadows, and dreams coming true." (Nicolson & Shipstead, 2002, p. 139)

FIGURE 2-3 Anecdotal records for young children. These anecdotes reveal creativity in language use by children.

From Through the Looking Glass: Observations in the Early Childhood Classroom *(3rd ed., p. 139), by S. Nicolson and S. G. Shipstead, 2002, Upper Saddle River, New Jersey: Merrill/Prentice Hall. Copyright 2002 by Pearson Education. Reprinted with permission.*

Directions: On the space in front of each item, place a plus sign (+) if performance is satisfactory; place a minus sign (–) if the performance is unsatisfactory.

_____ 1. States the topic at the beginning of the report.

_____ 2. Speaks clearly and loudly enough to be heard.

_____ 3. Uses language appropriate for the report.

_____ 4. Uses correct grammar.

_____ 5. Speaks at a satisfactory rate.

_____ 6. Looks at the class members when speaking.

_____ 7. Uses natural movements and appears relaxed.

_____ 8. Presents the material in an organized manner.

_____ 9. Holds the interest of the class.

FIGURE 2-4 Checklist for evaluating an oral presentation.

From Gronlund's Writing Instructional Objectives for Teaching and Assessment *(8th ed., pp. 86–87), by Norman E. Gronlund and Susan M. Brookhart, 2009, Upper Saddle River, NJ: Pearson Education. Copyright 2009 by Pearson Education. Reprinted with permission.*

Promising tactics for gathering data from children include compiling information from multiple sources, reflecting on the advantages and disadvantages of each piece of data, and drawing conclusions on the entire collection of information. As we now explain, you can also use other strategies for increasing the validity of your decisions.

Increasing the Accuracy of Conclusions About Children

As an educator or other professional working with children, you will have many demands on your time that compete with your ability to collect information from children. Your primary motivations, of course, will be effectively teaching and in other ways nurturing young people.

Because you will be busy and have limited data from children, you must take extra care to think critically about the information you collect. We recommend these tactics:

• **Confront your own biases.** Everyone has some preconceived notions about children. Individual teachers may occasionally underestimate or overestimate what children of a given age are able to accomplish. They might also expect that boys and girls are unequally capable in certain subjects, believe that children from different cultural groups see the world in ways that are completely different from or fully identical to their own points of view, or assume that the children themselves are responsible for any limitations in their learning. Obviously, such beliefs can be untrue. When looking at data from particular children, it is important to consider how you might be looking at the information more favorably or critically depending on your expectations.

• **Continually question the meaning of your data.** Validity and reliability are and must be ongoing concerns not only for researchers but also for teachers and other practitioners. Educators must be appropriately cautious when interpreting data they have gathered about children.

• **Form multiple hypotheses.** In your efforts to observe children and adolescents, never be content with a single interpretation, no matter how obvious that explanation might seem to you. Always consider multiple possible reasons for the behaviors you observe, and resist the temptation to settle on one of them as "correct" until you've had a chance to eliminate other possibilities. In this regard, teachers and some other practitioners actually have an advantage over professional researchers. Whereas researchers often see children for only brief periods, practitioners can deepen their understanding of children's needs over a relatively long time frame.

• **Use multiple sources of information.** Because no single source of data ever has "perfect" validity and reliability, teachers and other school personnel often patch together several different sources of information when drawing conclusions about children's needs. A high school teacher who observes his students with bored expressions might wish to look carefully at their responses on tests and see if students find the material too easy or difficult. The teacher could also ask students in class to describe their understandings of the subject. In this manner, the teacher would be combining observations, tests responses, and analyses of students' self-reports in an attempt to better understand his students' comprehension of the material.

Directions: For each statement, circle the appropriate description for how frequently the child shows the behavior.

1. Comes to the lesson with the necessary books, writing utensils, and notebooks.

| Never | Occasionally | Often | Very Often |

2. Watches the teacher during instructions.

| Never | Occasionally | Often | Very Often |

3. Gets to work right away.

| Never | Occasionally | Often | Very Often |

4. Avoids distractions in the classroom.

| Never | Occasionally | Often | Very Often |

5. Turns in completed assignments.

| Never | Occasionally | Often | Very Often |

FIGURE 2-5 Rating scale of paying attention during classroom lessons.

Conducting Action Research

To improve educational services for children, teachers can conduct systematic studies of children's experiences in school and then revise their strategies based on interpretations of the data. In our introductory case study, Jack Reston conducted research in order to evaluate and improve absenteeism policies at his school. Such locally focused research, known as **action research**, takes numerous forms. Examples include assessing the effectiveness of a new teaching technique, gathering information about adolescents' opinions on a schoolwide issue, and conducting an in-depth case study of a particular child (Cochran-Smith & Lytle, 1993; G. E. Mills, 2007; Ponder, Vander Veldt, & Lewis-Ferrell, 2011).

Action research employs the following steps:

1. *Identify an area of focus.* The teacher-researcher begins with a problem and gathers preliminary information that might shed light on the situation. Usually this involves perusing the research literature for investigations of related problems and perhaps also surfing the Internet or conducting informal interviews of colleagues or students. He or she then identifies one or more research questions and develops a research plan (data collection techniques, necessary resources, schedule, etc.) for answering those questions. At this point, the teacher seeks guidance from supervisors and experts in research ethics and considers how he or she might eventually improve the situation being addressed in the research.

2. *Collect data.* The teacher-researcher collects data relevant to the research questions. Such data might be obtained from questionnaires, interviews, observations, achievement tests, children's journals or portfolios, or existing records (e.g., school attendance patterns, rates of referral for discipline problems, hours spent by volunteers on school projects). Many times the teacher-researcher uses two or more of these sources in order to address research questions from various angles.

3. *Analyze and interpret the data.* The teacher-researcher looks for patterns in the data. Sometimes the analysis involves computing simple statistics (e.g., percentages, averages, correlation coefficients). At other times it involves a nonnumerical inspection of the data. In either case, the teacher-researcher relates the patterns observed to the original research questions.

action research
Systematic study of an issue or problem by a teacher or other practitioner, with the goal of bringing about more productive outcomes for children.

4. *Develop an action plan.* The final step distinguishes teachers' research from the more traditional research studies we described earlier: The teacher-researcher uses the information collected to identify a new practical strategy—for instance, to change instructional techniques, advising practices, home visiting schedules, or school policies.

A good example of action research is a case study conducted by Michele Sims (1993). Initially concerned with why middle school students of average intelligence struggle to comprehend classroom material, Sims began to focus on one of her students, a quiet boy named Ricardo. She talked with Ricardo, had conversations with other teachers and with university faculty, wrote her ideas in her journal, and made notes of Ricardo's work. The more she learned, the better she understood who Ricardo was as an individual and how she could foster his development. She also became increasingly aware of how often she and her fellow teachers overlooked the needs of quiet students:

> We made assumptions that the quiet students weren't in as much need. My colleague phrased it well when she said, "In our minds we'd say to ourselves—'that child will be all right until we get back to him.'" But we both wanted desperately for these children to do more than just survive. (Sims, 1993, p. 288)

Action research serves many positive functions. It can solve problems, broaden perspectives on adults' relationships with children, clarify children's understandings of and attitudes toward learning particular academic topics, foster a community spirit among adults who are jointly caring for children, and make schools and communities more humane (Chant, 2009; Noffke, 1997; Robins et al., 2009). It can also help teachers gain insights into the characteristics of children from unfamiliar cultures, as you can see in the Development in Culture feature "Using Action Research to Learn About the Culture of Children and Families." For individual teachers, conducting research is also a good way to improve their abilities to identify and meet the needs of youngsters generally. The Development and Practice feature "Getting a Flavor for Conducting Research as a Teacher" suggests some initial steps you can take.

Ethical Guidelines for Teacher-Researchers

Regardless of how you go about collecting data from children, you must protect their welfare. We recommend that you learn as much as possible at college about your legal and ethical responsibilities as a school professional. In addition, we offer the following guidelines:

• **Keep your supervisor informed of your research initiatives.** Guidance from principals and other supervisors helps teachers and counselors protect the rights of children and families. Supervisors can inform you of regulations in your district or community and procedures for getting your research plan approved. After you collect your data, school leaders can give you a fresh set of eyes when it comes to interpreting the results and considering their implications for any possible changes in practice.

• **Be tentative in your conclusions.** Sloppy research or observations of children can do more harm than good. For instance, a teacher might wrongly infer that children have poor comprehension skills by taking responses on one test too seriously and not realizing that the children had, in fact, been distracted after a fire drill. Acting on a false perception, the teacher might attempt to remediate children's alleged weaknesses in comprehension. Therefore, you should try not to put too much weight on any single piece of information. Instead, you can collect a range of data samples—such as written essays, test scores, projects, informal observations of behavior—and look for general trends. Even then, be cautious in the conclusions you draw, and consider multiple hypotheses to explain the patterns you see. Finally, when sharing your perceptions of children's talents and abilities with parents, acknowledge that these are your *interpretations*, based on the data you have available, rather than irrefutable facts.

• **Administer and interpret tests or research instruments only if you have adequate training.** Many instruments, especially psychological assessments, physiological measures, and standardized achievement tests, must be administered and interpreted by individuals trained

DEVELOPMENT IN CULTURE

Using Action Research to Learn About the Culture of Children and Families

Misunderstandings occasionally arise in people from different cultures, including in teachers and children from dissimilar backgrounds. For example, a number of teachers wonder why children from immigrant families do not learn English quickly, participate in lessons like other children, or achieve at advanced levels (Rothstein-Fisch, Trumbull, & Garcia, 2009). Conversely, some children who have been raised in traditions different from their teachers find their teachers to be strange and insensitive.

Such a clash of cultures is hardly inevitable. Teachers can gain an appreciation for children's traditions by observing children at school and encouraging them to talk and write about their cultural origins. However, everyday observation and social exchange are not always enough. When teachers' initial efforts prove insufficient, teachers can turn to action research as a way to delve into children's customs and frames of mind.

Action research can be especially effective in fostering teachers' cultural sensitivity when it includes three elements. First, teachers can acquire new understandings about children by remaining open to using entirely new ways of interpretation. Tiffany, an experienced elementary teacher, conducted research in her second-grade classroom of ethnically diverse children from low-income families, the majority of whom were Mexican American (Riemer & Blasi, 2008). Tiffany had previously mandated which classroom centers individual children could visit during the day but wondered how the children would respond if they were able to make some of their own decisions. The children surprised her with their maturity:

> I began to notice that they were taking control of their learning. They researched and learned what they wanted to learn about, they worked with other students that they or I would normally not group them with, and they even created their own organizational tool to keep track of the centers they visited. They gave themselves choices between working on research projects, preparing presentations of the research collected, and/or visiting centers. . . . I gave them more independence and therefore, they did not need me as much. They also relied more on one another. . . . I have had increased awareness as to what my students are truly capable of, owning their education. (Riemer & Blasi, 2008, p. 58)

Second, teachers may change their ideas when they reflect on their own values and biases. One kindergarten teacher joined a research team of university faculty and other teachers who were hoping to learn more about the needs of children and their immigrant Latino families (Rothstein-Fisch et al., 2009). As a result of her introspection and discussions with colleagues, she realized that these parents had a valid perspective that was different from her own:

> It was a revelation that the parents weren't wrong, just different, because it never felt right to me to think they were wrong. But deep down I thought they were wrong and I knew that was racist and that was eluding me (Rothstein-Fisch et al., 2009, p. 477).

After conducting her research, the teacher and her colleagues began to open up to families in new ways, talking informally with parents as they dropped off and picked up their children, taking photographs of families at open houses, experimenting with formats for conferences, and building on families' desires for a relaxed atmosphere during school meetings.

Finally, teachers can learn a lot by spending time with children and their families (Lahman, 2008). Bernie, a sophomore preparing to teach, conducted an in-depth observational study of Amish children in Ohio (Glasgow, 1994). Early in her research Bernie was judgmental, confessing that she thought of the Amish as "a simple, unsophisticated people with very naive ideas about the ways of our world" (Glasgow, 1994, p. 43). She noticed a sense of peacefulness in their lives but also believed that "the Amish culture stifles personal growth, intellectual advancement, and creativity" (p. 43). As she spent more time in the Amish community, Bernie became increasingly sensitive to cultural traditions and values, gaining permission from an Amish elder to visit a one-room schoolhouse and take careful field notes about what she saw. With increasing contact with people in the Amish culture, Bernie came to appreciate the integrity of their customs. At the end of her observations, she planned to explore new ways to reach Amish children in her future classroom.

By being open to new interpretations, reflecting on their own biases and values, and collecting data over an extended period of time, teachers and other practitioners can acquire a thoughtful understanding of children and families from different cultures. This heightened sensitivity can pay enormous dividends in relationships between teachers and children.

YOU MIGHT BE SURPRISED. Teachers and other practitioners can learn a great deal about children's cultural beliefs and traditions by reflecting on personal values and possible biases, remaining open to new interpretations of children's abilities, and spending time with them in their community.

DEVELOPMENT AND PRACTICE
Getting a Flavor for Conducting Research as a Teacher

Keep a journal of your observations and reflections.

- A second-grade teacher regularly makes notes of the centers that children visit when they have a free choice, using the information to make adjustments in unpopular areas. (Middle Childhood)
- A high school English teacher keeps a daily log of students' comments and insights about the novels they are reading. The teacher reassigns novels that provoke the most interest the following year and replaces novels that do not engage students. (Late Adolescence)

Talk with your colleagues about what you are observing and hypothesizing.

- A middle school teacher observes that a new student regularly comes to class late without a notebook or pen and appears distracted during class. The teacher wonders about the family's financial resources and speaks privately with the principal to see if the school can secure school supplies for the young man. (Early Adolescence)
- A school counselor notices that girls in a school club are excited about their participation. She asks colleagues for their ideas about how they might further encourage the girls' interests. (Late Adolescence)

Invite children and families to contribute to your inquiry.

- A teacher in an infant room hears parents complain that their employers do not grant them time off to care for their children when sick. She asks three parents who have been most vocal to help her look into family leave regulations. (Infancy)
- A high school principal notices that an exceptionally high number of students have been referred to her for physical aggression during the past year. She asks a school improvement team of teachers, school counselors, parents, and students to examine possible reasons for the increase in violence and discuss possible solutions. (Late Adolescence)

Inquire into the circumstances of children who appear sad, inattentive, or disengaged at school.

- A preschool teacher is concerned about a 3-year-old girl who has recently become unhappy at school. During free play, the young girl quietly and repeatedly puts a doll in a box and places the box under a toy crib. The teacher talks with the girl's mother at the end of the day and learns that the mother, who had been a full 5 months along in her pregnancy, recently had a miscarriage. Her 3-year-old daughter knew about the pregnancy and was upset about the family's loss. The teacher expresses her sympathy to the mother and suggests that the little girl seems to be coping with this loss through play. (Early Childhood)
- A middle school teacher observes that a few students sit in the back of the room and appear to be mentally "tuned out." She talks privately with the students, learns about their backgrounds and interests, and tries out new strategies that might capture the attention of these students. (Early Adolescence)

Enlist the assistance of children or families.

- An elementary teacher wonders what her children are learning during independent learning time. She asks the children to interview one another and take notes on their partner's answers. In analyzing the children's responses, the teacher realizes that only some of the children are using the time effectively due to different perceptions about the purpose of the period. (Middle Childhood)
- A career counselor examines his community's employment rates and enlists the help of adolescents to survey local businesses about possible needs that youngsters could meet in after-school jobs. (Late Adolescence)

---

in their use. In untrained hands they can yield results that are highly suspect and, in some cases, potentially detrimental to children. For example, a teacher who interprets an intelligence test as a perfect reflection of a child's ability would be wrongly concluding that the child's answers on a single day are convincing evidence of the child's potential for learning.

• **Be sensitive to children's perspectives.** Children are apt to notice any unusual attention you give them. When Michele Sims was collecting data about Ricardo, she made the following observation:

> I'm making a conscious effort to collect as much of Ricardo's work as possible. It's difficult. I think this shift in the kind of attention I'm paying to him has him somewhat rattled. I sense he has mixed feelings about this. He seems to enjoy the conversations we have, but when it comes to collecting his work, he may feel that he's being put under a microscope. Maybe he's become quite accustomed to a type of invisibility. (Sims, 1993, p. 285)

When data collection makes children feel so self-conscious that their performance is impaired, a teacher-researcher must seriously consider whether the value of the information collected outweighs possible detrimental effects. Otherwise, teachers' good intentions can actually put children at a disadvantage.

• **Maintain confidentiality.** When teachers have obtained the necessary permissions and clearances, they are permitted to share the general results of their research with colleagues.

Some teachers also make their findings known to an audience beyond the walls of their institution; for instance, they may make presentations at conferences or write journal articles describing what they have learned. However, you must never broadcast research findings in ways that violate the confidentiality of children's responses. Children would naturally feel betrayed if teachers were to disclose the responses that they as individuals have made. Teachers must likewise protect their data sources from examination by onlookers: It would be unwise to leave a notebook containing running records or completed checklists on a table where other children and adults would have access to them.

Knowledge about children comes from a variety of sources—not only from research but also from one's own intuition, conversations with other teachers, and children's performance in the classroom. None of these sources is adequate in and of itself. Each source becomes more powerful when complemented by other approaches.

SUMMARY

Principles of Research

Research with children needs to be guided by strong ethical standards, the scientific method, and access to children and adolescents who can supply needed information. The manner in which researchers integrate these principles into their investigations depends largely on the kinds of methods they use.

Analyzing Developmental Research

Developmental researchers use various methods for collecting data, including interviews and questionnaires, tests and other assessment tasks, physiological measures, and observations. Regardless of the method, the data should be accurate measures of the characteristics or behaviors being studied (a matter of *validity*) and minimally influenced by temporary, irrelevant factors (an element of *reliability*). Investigators also use research designs that match their questions.

Designs differ in the extent to which they allow conclusions about cause-and-effect relationships, find associations among two or more variables, trace age trends over time, and observe children and adolescents in natural environments. To make the most of developmental studies, you must judge whether the conclusions are warranted and applicable to your own work with young people.

Gathering Data as an Educator

Teachers and caregivers often gather data about children and adolescents. Educators can learn a great deal from their conversations with youngsters, assessments of the products they create, and everyday observations of their behavior. As with other kinds of investigations, research carried out by teachers and other practitioners must be conducted with concern for ethics and the integrity of the data.

APPLYING CONCEPTS IN CHILD DEVELOPMENT

The exercises in this section will help you build your ability to apply your knowledge of child development in your work with children.

Improving Your Observation Skills

On page 44, you examined a photograph of two boys and were asked, "*How might researchers determine whether these two boys from the Canadian First Nation are playing or fighting?*" These two boys appear to be enjoying their outdoor frolicking. To distinguish a playful ruckus from fighting, developmental investigators use such criteria as the boys' smiling or frowning facial expressions; any evidence of pushing, biting, or hitting; and existence of reciprocal behaviors such as chasing and tumbling. The researchers would need to define their criteria carefully and practice categorizing behaviors they observed separately to make sure that their eventual interpretations were reliable.

On page 55, you examined a photograph of four students and were asked, "*What might you infer from the Ethiopian fifth-grade students?*" The girls appear to be paying close attention to the lesson. Two of the girls have a faint smile. Several of the girls appear to be raising their hands volunteering to answer or participate in the discussion. It is not always possible to tell how involved children are in activity from their behavior, but the posture and gaze of these girls is consistent with a high level of engagement.

Practicing for Your Licensure Examination

Many teaching tests require students to apply what they have learned about child development to brief vignettes and multiple-choice questions. You can practice for your licensure examination by reading the following case study and answering a series of questions.

The Study Skills Class

Read the case and then answer the questions that follow it.

As a last-minute teaching assignment, Deborah South took on a study skills class of 20 low-achieving and seemingly unmotivated eighth graders. Later she described a problem she encountered and her attempt to understand the problem through action research (South, 2007):

> My task was to somehow take these students and miraculously make them motivated, achieving students. I was trained in a study skills program before the term started and thought that I was prepared. . . .
>
> Within a week, I sensed we were in trouble. My 20 students often showed up with no supplies. Their behavior was atrocious. They called each other names, threw various items around the room, and walked around the classroom when they felt like it. . . .
>
> Given this situation, I decided to do some reading about how other teachers motivate unmotivated students and to formulate some ideas about the variables that contribute to a student's success in school. Variables I investigated included adult approval, peer influence, and success in such subjects as math, science, language arts, and social studies, as well as self-esteem and students' views of their academic abilities.
>
> I collected the majority of the data through surveys, interviews, and report card/attendance records in an effort to answer the following questions:
>
> - How does attendance affect student performance?
> - How are students influenced by their friends in completing schoolwork?
> - How do adults (parents, teachers) affect the success of students?
> - What levels of self-esteem do these students have?
>
> As a result of this investigation, I learned many things. For example, for this group of students attendance does not appear to be a factor—with the exception of one student, their school attendance was regular. Not surprisingly, peer groups did affect student performance. Seventy-three percent of my students reported that their friends never encouraged doing homework or putting any effort into homework.
>
> Another surprising result was the lack of impact of a teacher's approval on student achievement. Ninety-four percent of my students indicated that they never or seldom do their homework to receive teacher approval. Alternatively, 57 percent indicated that they often or always do their homework so that their families will be proud of them.
>
> One of the most interesting findings of this study was the realization that most of my students misbehave out of frustration at their own lack of abilities. They are not being obnoxious to gain attention, but to divert attention from the fact that they do not know how to complete the assigned work.
>
> When I looked at report cards and compared grades over three quarters, I noticed a trend. Between the first and second quarter, student performance had increased. That is, most students were doing better than they had during the first quarter. Between the second and third quarters, however, grades dropped dramatically. I tried to determine why that drop would occur, and the only common experience shared by these 20 students was the fact that they had been moved into my class at the beginning of the third quarter.

> When I presented my project to the action research class during our end-of-term "celebration," I was convinced that the "cause" of the students' unmotivated behavior was my teaching. . . . This conclusion, however, was not readily accepted by my critical friends and colleagues . . . who urged me to consider other interpretations of the data. (pp. 1–2)[a]

Constructed-Response Question

1. What methods did Deborah use to collect her data? Describe one potential strength and limitation of each method.

Multiple-Choice Questions

2. What kind of research did Deborah conduct?

   a. Action research
   b. An experimental study
   c. A correlational study
   d. A cross-sectional study

3. Deborah tentatively concluded that her own teaching led to the dramatic drop in grades from the second quarter to the third. Is her conclusion justified?

   a. Yes, Deborah's conclusion is justified because she collected several different kinds of data.
   b. Yes, Deborah's conclusion is justified because she is in the position to understand her students best.
   c. No, Deborah's conclusion is not fully justified because without an experimental design, a variety of reasons for the change in students' behavior remain possible.
   d. No, Deborah's conclusion is not fully justified because teachers are never able to collect data with any merit.

Once you have answered these questions, compare your responses with those presented in Appendix A.

Improving Your Ability to Interpret Children's Artifacts and Reflections

Consider chapter concepts as you analyze the following artifact created by a child.

I Went to Davis's House

The note above was written by 9-year-old Alex. He left it on the kitchen counter for his parents when they were out for a walk. As you examine it, use your understanding of research in deciding whether a teacher could draw firm conclusions about Alex's knowledge of the mechanics of English from this single artifact from Alex.

Once you have analyzed the artifact, compare your ideas with those presented in Appendix B. For further practice in analyzing children's artifacts and reflections, go to the Activities and Applications section in Chapter 2 of MyEducationLab.

[a] From "What Motivates Unmotivated Students?" by D. South. In *Action Research: A Guide for the Teacher Researcher* (3rd ed., pp. 1–2), by G. E. Mills, 2007, Upper Saddle River, NJ: Merrill/Prentice Hall. Reprinted with permission of the author.

Key Concepts

scientific method (p. 39)
sample (p. 39)
self-report (p. 40)
interview (p. 40)
questionnaire (p. 41)
test (p. 41)
assessment (p. 42)

physiological measure (p. 42)
habituation (p.42)
observation (p. 43)
validity (p. 44)
reliability (p. 45)
experimental study (p. 45)
control group (p. 45)

quasi-experimental
   study (p. 46)
correlation (p. 47)
correlational study (p. 47)
cross-sectional study (p. 47)
longitudinal study (p. 47)
ethnography (p. 48)

case study (p. 48)
grounded theory
   study (p. 49)
rubric (p. 53)
cultural bias (p. 54)
action research (p. 59)

PEARSON
myeducationlab

Now go to www.myeducationlab.com to:

- Take a Quiz to test your mastery of chapter objectives.
- Study chapter content with an individualized Study Plan.
- Deepen your understanding of particular concepts and principles with Review, Remediation, and Enrichment Exercises.
- Apply what you have learned in the chapter to your work with children in Building Teaching Skills and Dispositions exercises.
- Observe children and their unique contexts in Video Examples.

Chapter Three

Family, Culture, and Community

Cedric Lavar Jennings and his mother Barbara are a close-knit family of two. One night in Cedric's senior year, they go to his high school to pick up his first-semester grade report. Knowing that he is one of the top students—perhaps *the* top student—in his physics class, Cedric is shocked to discover a B for his semester's work. He's furious, because, as he tells his mother, many students have been cheating on class exams, whereas he has been taking the exams the hard way—*honestly*. At first Barbara isn't overly concerned, but as Ron Suskind reports in *A Hope in the Unseen* (1998), when Cedric asks what they will do, she soon realizes that he needs her to be the vigilant protector she has always been.

The two of them immediately go in search of Cedric's physics teacher, Mr. Momen. After finding him, Cedric complains vigorously and points out that Mr. Momen often leaves the room when students are taking tests—hence, the rampant cheating. Although Mr. Momen tries to defend himself, Barbara stands firm, insisting that her son would not lie about something so important. Mr. Momen finally agrees to give Cedric a retest over the semester's material.

Afterward, Barbara advises her son that he *must* get an A. Cedric studies hard for the test, earns a perfect score, and ultimately receives an A for the semester. He brings home the test for her to examine, and as she looks at it, it dawns on her that their relationship is changing, and that she can no longer be at his side when he heads off to college. Cedric also realizes that he is now ready to advocate for himself. He points to the test score and suggests that the paper certifies Barbara's successful graduation as mother.

- Why could Cedric assume his mother would help him at school?
- What qualities did Cedric learn from his mother?

As a child, Cedric had found his mother to be a loving caregiver. Having grown accustomed to his mother's faithful care, Cedric could now safely assume she would back him up when he asked for her help. Like Cedric, most children can depend on their family for love and reassurance, food and shelter, and oversight and guidance. In this chapter, you will learn that the family's care has profound effects on children. From Barbara, Cedric had learned to work hard, act with integrity, and confront injustice. Having benefited from his mother's support, Cedric could now enter society as a productive young man.

CRADLES OF CHILD DEVELOPMENT

A happy and healthy childhood depends on a loving relationship with families, regular exposure to the traditions of a culture, and participation in a responsive community. The *bio-ecological model* and related developmental theories help us to identify the effects of these three interacting contexts.

Family

A **family** consists of two or more people who live together and are related by such enduring factors as birth, marriage, adoption, or long-term mutual commitment. Families with children usually have one or two adults (most often the parents) who serve as heads of the family and care for the children for many years. Heads of the family exercise authority over children and take responsibility for the children's welfare.

OBJECTIVES

3.1: Identify the primary contributions of family, culture, and community to a child's development.

3.2: Describe how different family structures offer unique benefits and challenges for children.

3.3: Differentiate family process from family structure, and explain how family members influence one another.

3.4: Describe and illustrate strategies for forming partnerships with families.

3.5: Describe the distinct experiences children of color and children from immigrant families sometimes have.

3.6: Identify specific methods teachers and other professionals can use to meet the needs of children from all backgrounds.

3.7: Demonstrate the ability to advocate for children from low-income families.

According to the bioecological model, every child needs at least one adult devoted to his or her health, education, and welfare (Bronfenbrenner, 2001). Typically, heads of family have the necessary dedication to meet the child's many needs. Caring for children ideally begins before birth, when prospective parents take protective measures to increase their chances of having a healthy pregnancy. After birth, sensitive hands-on care makes it possible for infants to form close bonds with parents, explore the world, and develop harmonious relationships with people outside the family (Ainsworth, 1963, 1973; Booth-LaForce & Kerns, 2009; Bowlby, 1969/1982; Morelli & Rothbaum, 2007; Whipple, Bernier, & Mageau, 2011).

Families continue to feed, clothe, and attend to growing children's basic needs. But just as importantly, family members are key figures in the **socialization** of children. That is, by encouraging certain behaviors and beliefs (and *dis*couraging others), parents and other heads of family help children act and think in ways their society deems appropriate. Heads of family teach and model proper ways of behaving in various situations, reward particular behaviors and punish others, and arrange for the children to gain certain kinds of experiences and avoid less productive ones (Bornstein, 2009; Gauvain & Parke, 2010).

Culture

In the bioecological model, the culture of a longstanding social group gives meaning to habits and relationships in the family and community. Thus, culture helps children to experience events as predictable and worthwhile. Culture also adds an intellectual dimension by exposing children to the accumulated wisdom, advanced discoveries, and creative works of a society.

MAKE A WISH, PAPA. Parents and other family members typically offer children the affection, direction, and cultural experiences necessary for becoming well-adjusted and productive members of society.

Children become familiar with the actions of important everyday routines as families maintain households, work and play, and relate to one another. Cultural behaviors also include a group's rituals, such as worshipping and celebrating holidays. The effects of culture can be observed by comparing the customs of people in distinct groups or separate regions. Cultural groups exhibit variations in meal practices (what, how, and with whom they eat), division of responsibility (who obtains food, prepares dinner, and disciplines the children), and social practices (how and with whom children play, how marital partners are selected). Cultural groups also encourage particular practices for supporting children's education. For instance, one parent volunteers at school by reading to children, helping out at a school carnival, and doing odd jobs for teachers, whereas another parent helps children at home with school assignments and shows respect to teachers by *not* interfering with their work (García Coll & Marks, 2009).

Cultural beliefs, although not as obvious as behaviors, are an equally important part of a group's heritage. Core beliefs vary among different societies. For example, **individualistic cultures** encourage independence, self-assertion, competition, and expression of personal needs (Ayçiçegi-Dinn & Caldwell-Harris, 2011; Kağitçibaşi, 2007; Markus & Hamedani, 2007; Oyserman & Lee, 2007; Triandis, 2007). Many families from the United States and Western Europe raise their children in an individualistic manner. Core ideas in **collectivistic cultures** are that people should be obedient to and dependent on authority figures, honorable and cooperative, and invested in accomplishments of groups rather than in personal achievements. Many families in Asia, Africa, and South America raise their children in a collectivistic manner.

The two bookends of culture—behaviors and beliefs—are closely related. Common behavioral practices are grounded in beliefs about what is true, healthy, appropriate, and rational (Kitayama, Duffy, & Uchida, 2007). Adults within a culture, therefore, justify their typical ways of raising children by asserting familiar values. As an example, consider how families defend their sleeping practices. Many European American parents have children sleep alone in their own rooms or beds, and they explain that this practice ensures nighttime privacy for adults and fosters independence in children. Other parents, particularly those in certain

family
Two or more people who live together and are related by such enduring factors as birth, marriage, adoption, or long-term mutual commitment.

socialization
Systematic efforts by other people and institutions to prepare youngsters to act in ways deemed by society to be appropriate and responsible.

Asian cultures, sleep beside children and say that co-sleeping arrangements foster intimacy and solidarity among family members (S. Li et al., 2009; Shweder et al., 1998).

Of course, *differences* between cultures in beliefs and behaviors are only half of the story (Akiba & García Coll, 2003). Many cultural groups share such fundamental principles as commitments to achieving academically and treating others respectfully. Hence, within a single classroom, children from distinct cultures may be more similar than different in their behavior. Furthermore, dissimilarities *between* groups are often eclipsed by prominent individual differences *within* groups. For example, within a classroom each child may adhere to individualistic principles in distinct ways, with some excelling academically, others achieving advanced levels in computer games, and still others raising an unprecedented amount of money for a local charity (Gauvain, 2009; Goodnow, 2010). Finally, a group's especially strong commitment to a particular worldview does not prevent its members from endorsing other beliefs as well. Plenty of Western parents encourage children to assert their personal rights (an individualistic orientation) but also to live by a code of honor (a collectivistic orientation). Likewise numerous non-Western parents augment a primarily collectivistic orientation with individualistic ideals, socializing children to be mindful of the family's needs while also asserting their private wishes.

Another important element of culture is that children are frequently involved with multiple groups. Increasingly, children become familiar with several different cultures due to such circumstances as their family having immigrated, two or more heritages being represented within the family, and frequent exchanges occurring among ethnic cultures within the community. When children become acquainted with more than one culture, they often acquire some of the beliefs and practices of each culture. In such a circumstance, a family may socialize children to develop an allegiance to one or more aspects of their upbringing, for instance, encouraging an immigrant child born in Riyadh, Saudi Arabia, and currently residing in Toronto, Canada, to identify as either a Saudia Arabian, a Saudi immigrant, a Canadian, a Muslim, or a Canadian Muslim. As they grow, children increasingly express their own preferences for particular customs and determine how they fit within various groups (García Coll & Marks, 2009; Suárez-Orozco, Suárez-Orozco, & Todorova, 2008).

Community

A child's **community** includes the local neighborhood and the surrounding area. It gives the child a bridge to the outside world. Particularly when they are young, children tend to make friends in their neighborhood, at the local school, in a hometown sports team, or as part of a nearby club or center. As they grow older, youngsters continue to spend spare time in activities that are reasonably close by and affordable but also venture farther from home. You can see how important recreational opportunities are to youngsters by listening to 14-year-old Brendan in the "Neighborhood: Early Adolescence" video in MyEducationLab. Here's how Brendan describes his neighborhood:

> There's a lot of people. Nice people. And there's fun stuff to do around here. . . . We play football or sports in the backyards, and we have playgrounds and a basketball court.

Community institutions vary in quality depending on the wealth and characteristics of local neighborhoods. Some neighborhoods are able to provide nicely furnished schools and safe spaces for children's play. Yet in many economically disadvantaged neighborhoods, youngsters must often attend run-down schools and encounter a number of peers who use illegal substances and participate in criminal acts (Leventhal, Dupéré, & Brooks-Gunn, 2009). Similarly, the activities in which local adults engage convey to youngsters what behaviors are expected. When neighbors partake in illegal activities, prey on youth, and allow youngsters to get into trouble, children are at increased risk for exhibiting such negative behaviors as bullying peers, destroying others' property, cheating and telling lies, and being disobedient at school (Eamon & Mulder, 2005). Fortunately, support from teachers, neighbors, parents, and other family members lessens the harm of impoverished environments (Gauvain & Parke, 2010).

The bioecological model indicates that the community, through the resources made available to parents, also influences children indirectly. Parents obtain salaries, employment benefits, and services from community agencies, all of which enhance their ability to meet

Bioecology of Child Development

In the bioecological model, families are at the heart of children's development.

Go to the Video Examples section in Topic 3 of MyEducationLab to watch the "Neighborhood: Early Adolescence" video and listen to Brendan talk about recreational opportunities.

individualistic culture
Cultural group that encourages independence, self-assertion, competition, and expression of personal needs.

collectivistic culture
Cultural group that encourages obedience to and dependence on authority figures and being honorable, cooperative, and invested in group accomplishments.

community
The neighborhood in which a child and his or her family live and the surrounding vicinity.

Improving Your Observation Skills

Our neighborhoods. What developmental differences are present in drawings of neighborhoods by Marsalis, age 7½; (top), and James, age 13 (bottom)? Compare your response with the explanation at the end of the chapter.

children's many needs. Of course, these resources are sometimes insufficient, with some parents needing to work excessively long hours and not receiving paid leave when children are sick, circumstances that can trigger stress and culminate in ineffective parenting (Repetti & Wang, 2010). The social environment also affects parents' ability to care for children. Parents generally have their own friends who occasionally step in to supervise children's activities, offer advice on parenting strategies, and provide emotional support to parents (Bronfenbrenner, 2005; Cochran & Niego, 2002; C. J. Patterson & Hastings, 2007).

Addressing the Contexts of Children's Lives

Children enter school having taken part in formative experiences in their family, culture, and community. In the best of circumstances, these contexts are fountains of nurture: The family has cared for children, the culture has given meaning to children's lives, and the community has supplied good social contacts and decent living conditions. With optimal support, children can typically reach their potential, becoming physically healthy, exercising their natural talents, and evolving into responsible citizens, as Cedric did in our chapter-opening case study. The Basic Developmental Issues table "Considering Family, Culture, and Community" describes the many favorable ways in which nature and nurture, universality and diversity, and qualitative and quantitative change are manifested in the family, culture, and community.

Yet children also face challenges in their environments. Too often children face economic poverty, prejudice, violence, neglect, and abuse.

Sympathetic teachers and practitioners can help children navigate through their multifaceted environment and overcome hardships therein. But to be able to offer constructive support, teachers and other practitioners must become aware of children's surroundings. Following are three fundamental ways to become proactive about children's experiences in families, cultures, and communities:

• **Build on children's assets and adversities in particular environments.** In a theoretical extension to the bioecological model, American psychologist **Margaret Beale Spencer** and her colleagues have examined *risk factors* in children's environments that increase children's vulnerability to problematic outcomes (e.g., dropping out of school, being incarcerated, becoming an adolescent parent) and the *protective factors* that offset these risks (M. B. Spencer, 2006; Swanson, Cunningham, Youngblood, & Spencer, 2009). Risk factors include economic poverty, unstable family conditions, restrictive gender stereotypes, racial discrimination, and underfunded schools. Protective factors include being intelligent, physically attractive, or a member of a high status social group, and having well-educated parents and a compassionate and involved extended family. A person's risks and protective factors are influential throughout life.

Teachers should look at *every* child as having a unique profile of assets that set the stage for new growth as well as risks that deter progress and necessitate specialized services, resources, or instruction. For example, a teacher may approach a girl who is generally

BASIC DEVELOPMENTAL ISSUES
Considering Family, Culture, and Community

ISSUE	FAMILY	CULTURE	COMMUNITY
Nature and Nurture	As agents of nature, parents give their children genes for basic human traits and for their own individual characteristics (such as dispositions to be physically healthy or frail). As agents of nurture, families typically care for children, serve as role models, involve children in affectionate relationships, and encourage children's participation in routine activities.	The general capacity for culture has evolved over millions of years and is inscribed in the human genetic code. In the daily lives of children and families, cultural traditions and beliefs nurture children by giving meaning, purpose, and predictability to interpersonal relationships, activities, tool use, and communication systems.	Human beings are a social species with a natural inclination to congregate in communities. When a community contains friendly neighbors, decent housing, accessible playmates, safe playgrounds, and reasonably stable and well-paying jobs, it exerts nurturing influences on children's development.
Universality and Diversity	Children universally need one or more adults to advocate enthusiastically and steadfastly for their welfare, and heads of family usually serve in this manner. Families differ considerably in their membership and their styles of expressing affection and authority.	Children need (and almost always have) opportunities to participate in meaningful cultural activities. Cultural diversity occurs in particular beliefs (such as whether or not children are perceived to be capable of reasoning at a young age) and behaviors (such as how men and women contribute to the household).	Communities universally create a link to the outside world for children and families. Communities vary in population density, other geographical features, and degree of support for children and families.
Qualitative and Quantitative Change	Some changes in family roles occur in a trendlike, quantitative fashion, as when children gradually become more responsible for their own behavior. Children may slowly learn the steps in preparing a meal (e.g., washing the vegetables, buttering the bread, and grilling the meat). Other changes facilitate entirely new ways of thinking and behaving, as when an 8-year-old boy is asked to look after his 4-year-old sister for the first time.	Some cultures view development in terms of abrupt qualitative changes; for instance, certain rituals signify passage from childhood to adulthood and may be accompanied by an immediate and major change in young people's roles in the community. Other cultures view development as a series of small, gradual steps; for instance, children are gradually given more independence.	Children's experiences in communities show a few qualitative changes. Getting a driver's license or part-time job can shift youngsters' behaviors in fairly dramatic ways in that they can make unprecedented choices about pastimes and purchases. Many changes are probably incremental in form, such as children gradually learning about a city's neighborhoods as they venture farther from home during walks and bicycle rides.

self-reflective but regularly rude to peers with the suggestion that together they brainstorm solutions for expressing anger productively. Having gotten to know the girl personally, the teacher realizes that the girl wants to interact constructively with friends and is well able to address her own social limitations if given a modicum of guidance.

• **Help children adjust to competing pressures.** Teachers and other practitioners can consider the distinct experiences children have in their family, peer group, classroom, and community. Usually children can move easily from one social group to the next, but occasionally children become distressed when key individuals in their lives fail to get along, place incompatible demands on them, or misunderstand them. Thus an adolescent girl whose parents dislike her friends may feel torn by conflicting loyalties (A. C. Fletcher, Hunter, & Eanes, 2006). Adults can also empathize with children who articulate such concerns and also watch for nonverbal signs of distress, such as being withdrawn or acting out, which may indicate children's difficulty in adapting to pressures in the environment. Finally, teachers can help children who are new to their classroom ease into the new setting by explaining expectations and introducing them to classmates (García Coll & Marks, 2009; Suárez-Orozco et al., 2008).

• **Appeal to children's initiative.** Rarely do children submit passively to pressures from other people or institutions. Instead, they invariably pursue their own goals, enlist cooperation from other people, learn new skills, and adapt the environment to better meet their needs (Bronfenbrenner & Morris, 2006; M. B. Spencer, 2006). This sense of initiative is a valuable resource that can be cultivated at school. An elementary teacher might ask children who complain about a dirty playground to recommend tactics that will discourage littering and foster everyone's pride in the school environment (Howard, 2007). Similarly, a high school teacher might respond to an adolescent's concerns about inequities in the school system by suggesting that she consider joining a local coalition of community members that has been effectively tackling educational reform.

FAMILY STRUCTURES

MY MOM, MY FAMILY. More than one in four children grow up in a family headed by a single parent.

family structure
In a family with children, the family's makeup; specifically, the children in a family home and the adults who live with and care for the children.

A child's **family structure** refers to the makeup of the family—the people who live with the child in the family home, including any other children residing there and the adult or adults who care for the child and any siblings. Consider these statistics compiled on the family structures of American children:

• 67 percent live with two married parents.
• 3 percent live with two unmarried parents.
• 23 percent live with their mother only.
• 3 percent live with their father only.
• 4 percent live without a parent in their household and instead reside in some other living arrangement, such as with grandparents, other relatives, or foster parents. (Federal Interagency Forum on Child and Family Statistics, 2009).

Keep in mind that some children's circumstances defy such cut-and-dried categories. Many children are in the process of adjusting to one or more family changes, perhaps the addition of a new stepparent, the marriage of their previously unmarried parents, or the coming or going of a parent's unmarried (*cohabiting*) partner in the family home. Other children live with one parent yet stay in contact with their second parent, in accordance with custody agreements or informal arrangements.

Some people assume that two-parent families are the only suitable arrangement for raising children. In reality, children eagerly soak up affection from responsive adults in a wide range of family units with little concern for how their family's makeup compares to society's stereotypes of ideal families. Although you would never want to pigeon-hole a child based on his or her family type, you can learn to be sensitive to the kinds of advantages and challenges that children are apt to have in various family structures.

Mothers and Fathers

When a mother and father are present in the home, children tend to form close bonds with both parents (M. E. Lamb, Chuang, & Cabrera, 2005; Veríssimo, Santos, Vaughn, Torres, Monteiro, & Santos, 2011; M. S. Wong, Mangelsdorf, Brown, Neff, & Schoppe-Sullivan, 2009). Having two adults in the home magnifies the affection children receive and allows one parent to compensate when the other parent is unavailable (Meteyer & Perry-Jenkins, 2009). In large part due to the emotional and financial resources generally present in two-parent families, children living with a mother and father tend to achieve at somewhat higher levels in school and show fewer behavior problems than children in other kinds of families (Magnuson & Berger, 2009).

Being in a two-parent family also exposes children to two distinct styles of parenting. Mothers generally tend to children's physical needs (e.g., feeding, bathing, scheduling doctors' appointments), watch over the children, and display affection (e.g., kisses, hugs, smiles) toward children (Belsky, Gilstrap, & Rovine, 1984; Craig, 2006; Parke & Buriel, 2006; Phares, Fields, & Kamboukos, 2009). As children grow, relationships with mothers tend to be more intimate than those with fathers, and mothers are more likely to encourage children to open up about personal matters (Harach & Kuczynski, 2005; Smetana, Metzger, Gettman, & Campione-Barr, 2006).

In contrast, fathers are more physically playful and instrumental in guiding children to get along with people outside the family (M. E. Lamb et al., 2005; Parke & Buriel, 2006; Phares et al., 2009). Nevertheless, fathers are not simply playmates; most fathers spend substantial amounts of time caring for their children and are quite competent in feeding, bathing, and in other ways nurturing children (M. E. Lamb, Frodi, Hwang, Frodi, & Steinberg, 1982; Mackey, 2001). In many societies fathers become more involved as children grow older, especially in disciplining, encouraging self-reliance, and modeling subtle masculine qualities, including being a dependable source of financial support for one's family (Munroe & Munroe, 1992; National Institute of Child Health and Human Development Early Child Care Research Network, 2008; Parke & Buriel, 2006; Pruett & Pruett, 2009).

MY FAMILY. A 5-year-old boy includes *(clockwise, from top)* his older brother, father, himself, and mother in his drawing. Also included are the family goldfish, house, and driveway.

In addition to providing children with two adult caregivers, two-parent families show children how to carry out adult relationships. A man and woman have much to work out on a daily basis as an intimate couple and as **coparents**, partners in raising their children (Feinberg, Kan, & Goslin, 2009). Many parents air their differences constructively and search for solutions that are mutually beneficial, giving children valuable lessons in cooperation and conflict resolution (Cummings & Merrilees, 2010; J. P. McHale & Rasmussen, 1998). Children benefit in another way as well. Emotionally close couples are inclined to shower affection on their children (Dube, Julien, Lebeau, & Gagnon, 2000; Ward & Spitze, 1998).

The lessons other children receive are less favorable. Some children frequently overhear parents' heated arguments. Such loud and bitter exchanges can frighten children and are poor models for dealing with conflict. Arguments also put parents in a foul mood, which can quickly spill over into harsh interactions with children (P. T. Davies, Sturge-Apple, Woitach, & Cummings, 2009; S. G. O'Leary & Vidair, 2005). Marital conflict is associated with assorted problems in youngsters, including physical aggression, depression, anxiety, and difficulties in personal relationships (Feinberg, Kan, & Hetherington, 2007; Finger, Hans, Bernstein, & Cox, 2009; Frosch, Mangelsdorf, & McHale, 2000; Meteyer & Perry-Jenkins, 2009).

Divorcing Parents

Once an infrequent occurrence, divorce is now commonplace. In the United States more than 4 in 10 first marriages end in divorce, and approximately half of American children are affected by their parents' divorce (Lansford, 2009).

For children, the divorce of parents is not a single event but instead a series of occurrences, each one requiring adjustment. News of a divorce can be a crushing blow for children, even though the children may have previously witnessed their parents' animated disagreements. Immediately after being told about the separation, children may receive less comfort than they need due to parents' own distress (Kaslow, 2000). Children may also find that the household becomes more chaotic than it was previously. Custodial parents—one or both parents who look after the children in their homes—often struggle to complete all the tasks involved in maintaining an organized household, including shopping, cooking, cleaning, paying bills, and monitoring children's activities and homework (Wallerstein & Kelly, 1980). As the divorce is being finalized, children learn where they will live. Financial setbacks can complicate everyone's adjustment. Parents who previously owned a house may have to sell it, and so, on top of everything else, children must move to new (and inevitably smaller) quarters and lose proximity to close friends and neighbors (J. B. Kelly, 2007).

As the coparents begin to establish separate households, children learn how their parents will get along (or not) and what role each parent will now play with them. One parent may withdraw from their children and eventually invest, both emotionally and financially, in a new life and perhaps a new family. Thus one unfortunate consequence of some divorces is

coparents
The two (or more) parents who share responsibility for rearing their children.

that children lose contact with one of their parents, more often their father (J. B. Kelly, 2007; Lansford, 2009). However, this trend is by no means universal. Many fathers actively seek joint custody arrangements after a divorce (R. A. Thompson, 1994b).

All of these changes can overwhelm children. Divorce is especially troubling for young children, who may erroneously believe that their own naughty behavior caused the family's breakup (Fausel, 1986; Lansford, 2009; Wallerstein, 1984). Older children and adolescents usually respond reasonably well, even though they may initially find their parents' divorce quite painful and subsequently perceive it as disruptive for a period of years and sometimes decades (Hetherington, Bridges, & Insabella, 1998; Kushner, 2009; Lansford, 2009; Wallerstein, Lewis, & Blakeslee, 2001). Given time and support, however, most youngsters ultimately learn to accept their parents' divorce and do *not* develop significant psychological problems (Lansford, 2009).

Children's adjustment to divorce is facilitated by several factors. Coparents and other adults can help children by maintaining affectionate relationships with them, holding firm and consistent expectations for their behavior, willingly listening to their concerns, and encouraging them to keep up contact with friends, nonresident parents, and other family members (Hetherington & Clingempeel, 1992; J. B. Kelly, 2007; Kushner, 2009). Children who have good coping skills, for example, those who are inclined to talk with a friend when upset rather than let their anxiety escalate, are more likely to adjust favorably to the breakup (Lansford, 2009; Pedro-Carroll, 2005). And, of course, children are likely to flourish when coparents establish reasonably productive relationships with one another, agree on expectations and disciplinary measures, and keep a lid on their own disputes (Hetherington, Cox, & Cox, 1978; J. B. Kelly, 2007; Kushner, 2009). In a few cases divorce is actually beneficial for children's development, for instance, when children are removed from high levels of parental conflict or abuse (Lansford, 2009; Sarrazin & Cyr, 2007).

Single Parents

All families are unique, but as a group families headed by one parent are especially diverse in their backgrounds. Most single parents are divorced or have never been married, but a few are widowed, separated, or have a spouse who is only temporarily absent (U.S. Census Bureau, 2009a). More than 8 in 10 single parents in the United States are women (U.S. Census Bureau, 2009a). Some single mothers, particularly older unmarried mothers who are well educated, are able to provide adequate food, shelter, and opportunities for their children, whereas other single mothers, especially those who are young and uneducated, tend to have limited financial resources and often live in undesirable housing arrangements (C. J. Patterson & Hastings, 2007; M. Wen, 2008).

Single parents carry out the tasks of parenting with the realization that much responsibility falls on their shoulders (Beckert, Strom, Strom, Darre, & Weed, 2008). This realization often leads single parents to see their children's needs as a top priority. Perhaps because of this clear focus, many single-parent families function well, particularly if they have a reasonable standard of living and the support of a stable network of family and friends (C. J. Patterson & Hastings, 2007). In fact, the simple structure of single-parent families provides some advantages: Children may be shielded from intense conflict between parents, observe strong coping skills in their custodial parent, and enjoy the intimacy of a small family.

Single-parent families do experience unique challenges, though. Single parents, mothers and fathers alike, often express reservations about their ability to "do it all"—juggle children, home, and work responsibilities (Beckert et al., 2008; R. A. Thompson, 1994b). Unless they have the support of extended family members, neighbors, and friends, single parents may have difficulty with several dimensions of caregiving: remaining affectionate and patient with children; offering children the rich range of roles, activities, and relationships that maximize positive developmental outcomes; and coping when they are tired, sick, or emotionally taxed (Garbarino & Abramowitz, 1992; Magnuson & Berger, 2009). Furthermore, some single parents lack time to supervise and help children with homework (Kendig & Bianchi, 2008). Fortunately, single parents tend to be well aware of their personal limitations and inclined to reach out to others for assistance.

Parents and Stepparents

Many divorced parents eventually remarry. When they do, they and their children become members of a **stepfamily**, a family in which an original parent-and-children family structure expands to include a new parent figure and any children in his or her custody.[1] Approximately 8 percent of children in two-parent families live with a biological or adoptive parent and a stepparent (Federal Interagency Forum on Child and Family Statistics, 2009).

As is true for all family structures, children in stepfamilies are exposed to benefits and challenges. A new adult may bring additional income to the family and can help with household duties. Children can forge relationships with a new parent figure and, sometimes, with new brothers and sisters as well. Yet children may feel that they must now share a parent's time and affection with the new spouse. They may believe, too, that the new stepparent is interfering with a possible reunion of the divorced parents and that by showing affection to the stepparent, they are betraying the nonresident parent (R. Berger, 2000; Bigner, 2006).

For a stepfamily to blend successfully, it must establish its own identity and traditions. Having entered the marriage with habits of their own, the man and woman must jointly decide how to spend money, divide household chores, prepare and serve meals, and celebrate holidays. The couple must also develop productive ways of expressing and resolving conflicts and determining rules and disciplinary techniques. And, whereas a couple without children can initially focus on one another, the newly married parent and stepparent must attend to the needs of the children as well as to their own relationship.

Most children in stepfamilies eventually adjust well to their new family situation (R. Berger, 2000; Hetherington et al., 1998). Relationships between stepparents and children are not always as affectionate as those between biological parents and children, and stepparents may have greater difficulty disciplining children (Gold, 2009). Yet in many (probably most) instances, stepparents soon become important parts of children's lives.

Extended Family

Many children have strong ties with relatives, especially with grandparents. In the United States, 9 percent of all children live with at least one grandparent (U.S. Census Bureau, 2009b). Grandparents often become primary guardians when a child's parents are young and economically poor, neglectful, imprisoned, or incapacitated by illness or substance abuse, or when a parent dies (Dolan, Casanueva, Smith, & Bradley, 2009; O. W. Edwards & Taub, 2009). Custodial grandparents sometimes worry that they do not have adequate energy and financial resources to raise a second generation of children, yet their mature outlook and extensive parenting skills often lead them to be more competent caregivers than the noncustodial parents (C. B. Cox, 2000; Cross, Day, & Byers, 2010; O. W. Edwards & Taub, 2009; Letiecq, Bailey, & Dahlen, 2008).

stepfamily
Family created when one parent–child(ren) group combines with another parent figure and any children in his or her custody.

Improving Your Observation Skills

Mom is Wow. In her fourth-grade class, 9½-year-old Shea wrote a Mother's Day poem for her stepmother, Ann, using the "Mom is Wow" structure Shea's teacher provided. How does Shea perceive Ann, who had been a family member for about 3 years at the time Shea wrote the poem? Compare your response with the explanation at the end of the chapter.

MOM is WOW

She is great at hide-and-seek
She takes me to look at an antique
I get to see her three times a week

MOM is WOW

She helped teach me multiplication
She encourages my imagination
She is involved when it comes to participation

MOM is WOW

She's a great stepmom, I guarantee
She lets us watch Disney TV
She is an important part of the family tree

MOM is WOW

No matter what, she is never late
If I have a question, she will demonstrate
When it comes to stepmoms, she's great

MOM is WOW

[1] Stepfamilies are also known as *reconstituted families or blended families*.

In some families, other extended family members assume central roles in the lives of children. Aunts, uncles, and cousins may step forward to raise children when they are the only viable parent figure for a child (Sear & Mace, 2008).

Adoptive Parents

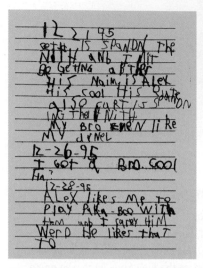

ARTIFACT 3-1 I got a brother, cool, hah? Adoption forms and expands families, sometimes overnight. In his journal, 7-year-old Connor communicates his excitement about becoming a big brother. Eight-month-old Alex is placed in Connor's family on December 20, and by December 28, Connor is aware of some of Alex's likes, such as playing peekaboo and being carried by him.

Two or 3 out of every 100 children in the United States are adopted (U.S. Census Bureau, 2004). Adoption is almost always a positive arrangement for children, especially when the new parents have thoughtfully chosen to expand their family and warmly accept their adopted children's individual qualities. Adoption can also be a blessing for adoptive parents and siblings, who find themselves with a new child to love.

The past few decades have seen several changes in adoption policies. One growing practice is *open adoption,* in which the birth mother (perhaps in consultation with the birth father) chooses the adopting family with help from an agency. Adoptive families often gain access to medical records through open adoption, and adopted children may have a chance someday to meet their birth parents. In *international adoption,* families in one country adopt children orphaned or relinquished in another country. In a third trend, many adoption agencies have become increasingly flexible in evaluating potential adoptive parents; the result is a growing number who are single, older, gay, lesbian, from lower-income groups, and from a different racial background than the adopted child (Bigner, 2006; Samuels, 2009b). A final trend is the adoption of increasing numbers of older children.

Although adopted children are at slightly greater risk for emotional, behavioral, and academic problems compared to children reared by biological parents, most adopted children thrive in the new family and grow up to be well-adjusted individuals (Freeark, 2006; Palacios & Sánchez-Sandoval, 2005). Adopted children seem to cope best when family members talk openly about the adoption yet provide the same love and nurturance that they would offer any biological offspring (Bigner, 2006; Brodzinsky, 2006).

Occasionally children adopted at an older age have physical or mental disabilities or may require special services due to preexisting conditions or poor care earlier in life (Rutter, 2005; Rycus, Freundlich, Hughes, Keefer, & Oakes, 2006; T. X. Tan, 2009). In extreme cases children may have been abused or neglected or have had several different placements before being adopted, and these children sometimes find it difficult to form secure relationships with new family members (Rycus et al., 2006; T. X. Tan, 2009). Professional intervention can be helpful (and is sometimes critical) for adoptive families when children's past circumstances now lead them to resist forming close bonds with new family members.

Foster Care

In *foster care,* children are placed with families through a legal but temporary arrangement, commonly due to their birth parents' neglect, maltreatment of children, or substance abuse (P. A. Fisher, Kim, & Pears, 2009). Children in foster care must adjust to several difficult circumstances—previous inadequate care from birth parents, the ordeal of being taken from their first families, and the need to form relationships with an entirely new family.

Foster parents also face challenges. They must build a trusting relationship with a child who might feel unloved, be a victim of abuse, or exhibit an emotional or behavioral difficulty (M. E. Cox, Orme, & Rhoades, 2003; Orme & Buehler, 2001). In addition, foster parents deal with numerous social service agencies but generally receive minimal financial support. Fortunately, many prospective caregivers are drawn to become foster parents because they themselves grew up in foster care or have a special interest in caring for children who have survived difficult conditions (Barber & Delfabbro, 2004).

Many children in foster care grow attached to their foster families but nevertheless long to return to their biological families (Samuels, 2009a). In fact, the majority of U.S. children in foster care are reunited with their birth families within a year (U.S. Department of Health and Human Services, 2007). Nevertheless, some birth parents are unable or unwilling to resume duties as parents, or they may have died, and their children are kept in foster care or are eventually adopted, on average at about 6 or 7 years of age, often by their foster parents and sometimes by other adults who are eager to adopt older children (U.S. Department of Health and Human Services, 2007). Unfortunately, because of heavy caseloads in agencies, crowded court dockets, and the general preferences of adoptive parents for newborn infants, foster children are sometimes shuffled among numerous temporary arrangements before being placed into permanent homes (McKenzie, 1993). Such a transitory existence is particularly detrimental when children have already faced challenges—perhaps neglect, abuse, abandonment, or early exposure to drugs or HIV.

Despite the odds, many children in foster care form healthy relationships with foster parents and peers and do well in school (Kufeldt, Simard, & Vachon, 2003; G. Schofield & Beek, 2009). Foster parents who have specialized training from social workers are especially likely to help children achieve good developmental outcomes (P. A. Fisher et al., 2009). Supported foster parents assist their children in gaining a sense of security, as 16-year-old Maria, placed in her foster family at age 8, reveals:

> My (foster) mum says to everyone that it's really hard for me, but I don't think it is. She says, well you've been through a lot, but well it doesn't seem a lot now, because it's over and done with. It just feels like a normal family now. I don't really look at them as anything different than a mum and dad really. They treat me the same as their normal family, take me on holiday, go shopping. (G. Schofield & Beek, 2009, p. 264)

Other Heads of Family

Our discussion of family structures has not been exhaustive; some children experience variations on these configurations or live in other family arrangements altogether. A growing number of children live with *gay* or *lesbian parents*. In the United States, approximately one in five male couples and one in three female couples are raising children (Gates & Ost, 2004; Goldberg, 2010). Children who have gay or lesbian parents are as intelligent and well adjusted as other children, and most grow up to be heterosexual adults (C. J. Patterson, 2009). Children of homosexual parents may notice peers occasionally teasing their parents, but these children nevertheless maintain healthy friendships and cope with this prejudice without too much problem (C. J. Patterson, 2009).

An increasing number of unmarried heterosexual couples have children together. Compared to married parents, *cohabiting parents* tend to be (on average) younger, less educated, and less financially stable; somewhat less satisfied with their relationships; and less warm and attentive to their children (Aronson & Huston, 2004; Klausi & Owen, 2009). Children of cohabiting couples tend to achieve lower grades in school and exhibit more behavior problems, but these disadvantages may disappear when cohabiting couples have good social support and access to adequate financial resources (C. J. Patterson & Hastings, 2007).

Adolescent parents often receive support from government and social agencies. Although many adolescent parents are sensitive and reliable caregivers, single adolescent mothers are apt to experience a lot of stress and frequently lack awareness about children's emotional, cognitive, and social needs (Borkowski et al., 2002). Teenage parents who are anxious and unrealistic about child development can become inattentive, inconsistent, and overly critical with their children. The unhappy result is that their children face risks for delayed language development and lower-than-average academic achievement (Borkowski et al., 2002; Lefever, Nicholson, & Noria, 2007). Nonetheless, many adolescent parents are competent caregivers, and practitioners can better the odds for young mothers by effectively educating them at school and advising them about developmentally appropriate care of small children (Robbers, 2008).

INTERNATIONAL ADOPTIONS HAVE BECOME INCREASINGLY COMMON. Adopted children acquire the customs of their adoptive families and occasionally also learn the traditions of their birth parents by being tutored, participating in community events with others from similar backgrounds, and traveling with adoptive families to their native lands.

Accommodating the Full Range of Family Structures

Most school professionals place a high value on being inclusive and respectful of children and their families. Following are some specific tactics educators can use to be supportive:

• **When organizing activities, make them flexible enough to be relevant to a wide range of family circumstances.** School assignments and extracurricular activities sometimes involve one or more family members. With a little creativity, teachers can easily broaden activities so that they accommodate diverse family structures. Recall the Mother's Day poem Shea wrote to her stepmother (p. 75). Shea's teacher gave her enough time to write two poems, one for her mother and one for her stepmother.

• **Encourage acceptance of diverse family structures.** Occasionally children tease classmates from nontraditional families. Some children of gay or lesbian parents may be ridiculed because of their parents' sexual orientation, and adopted children sometimes hear peers ask who their "real" parents are or why their birth parents gave them away (C. J. Patterson, 2009; Samuels, 2009b). At the preschool and elementary levels, teachers can counteract such attitudes by reading stories about children in a variety of family structures and expressing the view that loving families are formed in many ways. In the secondary grades adolescents tend to be more accepting about diverse family structures; nevertheless, teachers should keep an ear open for, and emphatically discourage, any derogatory comments about family circumstances.

TEACHERS CAN REACH OUT TO ALL HEADS OF FAMILY. These two fathers are actively involved in their sons' education and will both want to be included in conferences regarding their progress.

• **Include mothers, fathers, custodial grandparents, and other heads of family.** When children live in two-parent families, professionals outside the family often direct communication about children to mothers alone. Educators can try to equalize communications to mothers and fathers. By doing so, they can validate the incredibly influential roles that mothers and fathers alike play in children's lives. It is also important to acknowledge the presence of other heads of family, such as grandparents serving as guardians. And whenever possible, extended family members should be welcome at school open houses, plays, and concerts.

• **Be supportive when children undergo a major family transition.** Many events, including divorce, remarriage, departure of a parent's nonmarital partner, death of a family member, or movement from one foster family to another, can change a child's family life dramatically. In each case one or more caregivers may become unavailable, and other new relationships may begin (Adam, 2004). Adjustment to family transitions takes time, and practitioners should be prepared to offer long-term support. Teachers and counselors can help children identify and express their feelings, realize that they are not being abandoned and did not cause their parents' divorce, distinguish events in the family that they can and cannot control, accept that there are benefits to being in a stepfamily, and find strengths in themselves that have sustained them during family transitions (Pedro-Carroll, 2005; Recker, Clark, & Foote, 2008).

• **Remain patient while children are figuring out how to adjust to new family structures.** Many youngsters must adapt to moving back and forth between two houses and following two sets of rules. Consider 16-year-old Selina's articulation of the tensions that arise when she prepares to change households:

> It gets to about five o'clock on Sunday and I get like a really awful feeling and then . . . aah, packing up again . . . I don't complain about it. That's just the way it is. There's no *point* complaining about it, nothing's going to change. . . . [But] usually on a Sunday around that time . . . we're upset because we're having to move and everyone's tempers . . . you know, you get quite irritable. . . . (Smart, Neale, & Wade, 2001, p. 128)

In such circumstances teachers can express sympathy for the child's frustration but also encourage the child to come up with a plan for keeping track of belongings (including homework) during moves between houses.

• **Let children say what they want to say; don't pry.** Children often prefer to keep family matters to themselves. They may feel that teachers and counselors are inappropriately snooping into their personal lives. It is desirable, therefore, for adults to offer reassurance without being too inquisitive. When children do bring up family problems, you can help them consider options for dealing with the problems and protect their privacy.

• **Extend a hand to students who are living in foster care.** Children in foster care may be emotionally overburdened and have trouble asking for assistance. Furthermore, they may have profound academic and social needs and sometimes engage in behaviors that upset even experienced professionals. Nevertheless, children in foster care almost invariably benefit when adults articulate clear and consistent expectations and offer ongoing personal support. Teachers and other school personnel can also offer practical help with homework and assignments when children miss school because they are attending court hearings or moving between residences.

FAMILY PROCESSES

Family relationships affect the skills and dispositions that children develop. In fact, family *processes* overshadow family *structures* in the power of their effects on children (Lansford, 2009). In this section we examine the mutually influential interchanges that family members have. We also examine risk factors in families and offer suggestions for establishing productive working relationships with families.

Families' Influences on Children

As agents of socialization, parents and other heads of family combine affection with discipline. They also encourage children to participate in everyday routines and become involved in children's education.

Parenting Styles

The foundation of parenting is love. Parents communicate affection by responding sensitively to children's gestures, giving them emotional support, and celebrating their accomplishments.

A second vital element of parenting is discipline. Children have strong wills of their own but generally lack foresight and self-restraint. In response, parents teach children to curb impulses, anticipate the outcomes of actions, follow rules, and make amends for wrongdoings. Parents use a variety of techniques for disciplining children, including reasoning, scolding, temporarily withdrawing affection, removing privileges, imposing additional restrictions, and, occasionally, spanking children. A reasonable balance between love and appropriate discipline fosters children's cognitive skills and **self-regulation**, the ability to direct and control personal actions and emotions (Eisenberg, Chang, Ma, & Huang, 2009; Laible & Thompson, 2007; Maccoby, 2007).

Most parents around the world manage to find acceptable, balanced ways to show love and wield authority (R. H. Bradley, Corwyn, McAdoo, & Coll, 2001; Rohner & Rohner, 1981; Scarr, 1992). However, parents vary in the specific ways in which they express affection and implement discipline; that is, they develop characteristic **parenting styles**. Research on parenting styles was pioneered in the 1960s by American psychologist **Diana Baumrind** and has been subsequently refined by Baumrind and numerous other developmental scholars (Baumrind, 1967, 1971, 1980, 1989, 1991; Sorkhabi, 2005).

Considerable evidence with U.S. families indicates that a style of parenting that blends warmth with firm discipline is associated with children's mature, competent, independent, and considerate behavior and a commitment to achieving at school (Dornbusch, Ritter, Leiderman, Roberts, & Fraleigh, 1987; Gonzalez & Wolters, 2006; Lamborn, Mounts,

Bioecology of Child Development
Children thrive when they are in affectionate relationships with parents and other family members and are encouraged to take on responsibility for challenging tasks at home.

self-regulation
Process of directing and controlling one's personal actions and emotions.

parenting style
General pattern of behaviors that a parent uses to nurture and discipline his or her children.

Steinberg, & Dornbusch, 1991; Simons-Morton & Chen, 2009; Steinberg, Elmen, & Mounts, 1989). Parents who use this approach, called an **authoritative parenting style**, are affectionate and responsive, ask children to show age-appropriate behavior, give reasons for why certain standards of behavior are necessary, consider children's perspectives, and include children in decision making. Authoritative parenting seems to foster healthy development in children because it offers necessary structure and guidance but also nurtures children's sense of personal autonomy (Grolnick & Pomerantz, 2009; Pomerantz & Wang, 2009).

In a second, very different approach, known as the **authoritarian parenting style**, parents exert strong control and demand immediate compliance while offering little affection, few reasons for requests ("Clean your room because I told you to—and I mean *now!*"), and hardly any chance for negotiation. Like authoritative parenting, authoritarian parenting reflects efforts to direct children's behavior, but authori*tative* parents guide children with warmth and flexibility, whereas authori*tarian* parents are less affectionate and more rigid. Children of consistently authoritarian parents tend to be withdrawn, mistrusting, and unhappy; they are apt to have low self-esteem, little self-reliance, and poor social skills; and they have a greater-than-average tendency to act aggressively toward others (Coopersmith, 1967; Lamborn et al., 1991; Nguyen, 2008; Simons, Whitbeck, Conger, & Conger, 1991). Authoritarian parenting may be associated with some difficulties in adjustment in children because it offers structure but fails to support children's sense of autonomy (Grolnick & Pomerantz, 2009).

These patterns are not universal, however (Baumrind, 1982; Chao, 1994; Deater-Deckard, Dodge, Bates, & Pettit, 1996; Pomerantz & Wang, 2009; Steinberg, Lamborn, Darling, Mounts, & Dornbusch, 1994). Authoritative parenting is typically associated with good developmental outcomes, but authoritarian parenting is sometimes as well. One likely reason is that some parents productively combine elements of the two styles. In collectivistic cultures, including some East Asian and Middle Eastern societies, demands for full and immediate compliance are associated with parental warmth and acceptance—not rejection—and seem to help children adjust well in their society (Chao, 1994, 2000; Dwairy et al., 2006; Kağitçibaşi 2007; Rudy & Grusec, 2006).

Other aspects of families' lives may make the authori*tative* style ineffective or difficult to implement. When families live in dangerous neighborhoods, for example, parents may better serve children by being sternly directive, particularly if parents communicate the consequences of disregarding strict rules (Hale-Benson, 1986; McWayne, Owsianik, Green, & Fantuzzo, 2008). In other situations parents are strict not because they are consciously preparing children to survive in hazardous environments, but rather because economic hardship and other family stresses provoke them to be short tempered with children (Bronfenbrenner, Alvarez, & Henderson, 1984; L. F. Katz & Gottman, 1991; Ricketts & Anderson, 2008).

In another pattern, parents exert *little control* over children, and children generally suffer from this lack of direction. Parents who use a **permissive parenting style** appear to care about their children, but they relinquish important decisions to children (even fairly young ones)—allowing them to decide when to go to bed, what chores (if any) to do around the house, and what curfews to abide by ("Okay. Stay up later, but try to get some sleep tonight."). Children in such families are typically immature, impulsive, demanding, and dependent on parents, and, not surprisingly, disobedient when parents ask them to do something they do not want to do. These children also tend to have difficulty in school, to be aggressive with peers, and to engage in delinquent acts as adolescents (Lamborn et al., 1991; Pulkkinen, 1982; Tucker, Ellickson, & Klein, 2008). Apparently, these generally affectionate family environments do not adequately compensate for their lack of guidance.

A few parents are not only permissive but also indifferent to their children. When using an **uninvolved parenting style**, parents make few demands and respond to children in an uncaring and rejecting manner. Children of uninvolved parents frequently exhibit serious difficulties in many areas, including problems with school achievement, emotional control, tolerance for frustration, and delinquency (Lamborn et al., 1991; Rothrauff, Cooney, & An, 2009; Simons, Robertson, & Downs, 1989). These children receive neither adequate affection nor the guidance they need to develop essential skills.

authoritative parenting style
Parenting style characterized by emotional warmth, high expectations and standards for behavior, consistent enforcement of rules, explanations regarding the reasons behind these rules, and the inclusion of children in decision making.

authoritarian parenting style
Parenting style characterized by strict expectations for behavior and rigid rules that children are required to obey without question.

permissive parenting style
Parenting style characterized by emotional warmth but few expectations or standards for children's behavior.

uninvolved parenting style
Parenting style characterized by a lack of emotional support and a lack of standards regarding appropriate behavior.

As you might expect, the effects of these and other styles of parenting depend partly on children's interpretations of parents' intentions. Children see parents' discipline as being legitimate (if not always welcome) to the degree that parents have previously been involved, affectionate, and respectful caregivers (Grusec & Davidov, 2007; Maccoby, 2007; C. R. Martinez & Forgatch, 2001). Through a variety of tactics, which clearly differ among cultural groups, parents demonstrate their concern and usually convince children that they are imposing restrictions for children's own good. As a result, children usually accept parents' authority, even though they may sporadically (and sometimes recurrently) haggle with parents (Hoffman, 1994). In comparison, when parents use harsh discipline and come across as demeaning, cruel, or hostile, children may comply with parents' demands only when the parents are physically present. Later alone, children may feel resentful and choose to disregard parents' instructions.

The apparently significant impact of parenting styles raises the question of how parents develop particular strategies in the first place. A variety of factors seem important, including parents' own childrearing experiences, the cultural patterns they have observed over time, the training they have received about parenting, and the stressful conditions they are currently experiencing (Bornstein, 2006a; D. Gross et al., 2009; Kitamura et al., 2009). In addition, children's own characteristics influence parents' disciplinary techniques. Parents are more likely to reason with characteristically compliant children, whereas they regularly use harsh discipline with chronically irritable children (K. E. Anderson, Lytton, & Romney, 1986; Bornstein, 2006). Situational factors, especially parents' current goals and the kinds of misbehavior children exhibit, strongly influence parents' strategies with children (Grusec & Davidov, 2007). Thus a parent may reason with a 4-year-old boy about wearing a jacket on a cool day, allowing him to decide his clothing, but forcefully remove him when he ventures into a busy street because of the immediate hazard.

Daily Activities

Parents informally teach children essential skills during shared activities. **Guided participation**, in which a child engages in everyday adult tasks and routines, typically with considerable supervision, is an important way in which parents support children's learning. In a (typically) nurturing manner, parents allow children to take part in such activities as cooking, completing errands, worshipping, gardening, and volunteering in the community. With parental guidance, children are motivated to take on increasing levels of responsibility for planning and carrying out activities (Rogoff, 2003; Perez & Gauvain, 2009).

The activities parents arrange, both inside and outside the home, affect children's academic learning and expectations about school. Many parents informally teach children the purposes and patterns of language and expose children to books, art, music, computer technology, and scientific and mathematical thinking (Eccles, 2007; Hess & Holloway, 1984; LeFevre et al., 2009; Zeece & Wallace, 2009). Virtually all parents expose their children to important occupational skills, perhaps carpentry, construction, or roofing (González, Moll, & Amanti, 2005). When children enter school, their families comment on various aspects of schooling—how to behave, what goals to strive for, how hard to try, and so on.

Families play another important role through their involvement in children's schooling. At home, many heads of family discuss school activities with children, assist with homework, and praise children or give feedback about in-class projects. At school, heads of family may volunteer in the classroom, participate in parent advisory groups, join fund-raising initiatives, confer with teachers about children's classroom progress, and so forth. Students whose parents are involved in school activities generally achieve at high levels perhaps because these parents convey high value for education, communicate effectively with teachers, and gain insights into the kinds of help children need at home (Crosnoe, 2009; Eccles, 2007).

However, in some cases, parents become involved in unhelpful ways by intrusively directing a child's schoolwork or putting excessive

guided participation
Active engagement in adult activities, typically with considerable direction and structure from an adult or other more advanced individual; children are given increasing responsibility and independence as they gain experience and proficiency.

LAUNDRY TIME. Children learn a lot from participating in routine activities with parents. Everyone helps with laundry in this family, with the exception, perhaps, of the family dog.

levels of pressure on children to achieve (Levpušček & Zupančič, 2009; E. T. Tan & Goldberg, 2009). Furthermore, not every family finds it easy to become involved at school or sees their presence at school as appropriate. Parents in some cultures believe that parents should offer tangible assistance at home and *not* interfere at school (García Coll & Marks, 2009). These families often set aside a quiet place at home for homework, provide help with assignments, and monitor children's academic progress.

Children's Influences on Families

While children are under parents' guidance and control, they are also busily expressing their own wants and needs, often quite emphatically, as Cedric did in spurring his mother into action in our chapter-opening case study. Through their requests, demands, and actions, children influence parents and siblings.

Children's Effects on Parents

Socialization of children involves *reciprocal influences,* whereby children and their parents simultaneously affect one another's behaviors and together create the environment in which they all live. Parents largely set the tone, but children contribute immensely to family dynamics.

ARTIFACT 3-2   Thank you, Mom.
Children make gestures that affect their parents. Ten-year-old Samuel thanks his mother for all she has taught him. His mother is likely to respond with pride.

Reciprocal influences are evident in parent–child interactions from the very beginning (R. Q. Bell, 1988). Babies demand comfort by crying, but they also coo, chatter, lure their parents into contact in a most disarming manner, and in other ways communicate that parents are important people. A father intent on sweeping the kitchen floor will find it hard to resist the antics of his 6-month-old daughter who wriggles, chatters, and smiles at him.

Reciprocal influences continue as children grow. Preschoolers and parents frequently play games that require both parties to take turns and imitate one another (Kohlberg, 1969). Older children bring home their enthusiasm for new hobbies, interests, and technologies. A good example comes from the field of political socialization. In a series of studies, children whose classrooms participated in "Kids Voting USA," a program in citizenship education for students from kindergarten through grade 12, were compared with children whose classrooms did not participate (M. McDevitt, 2005; M. McDevitt & Kiousis, 2007). Not only did the children in the citizenship program learn more about political issues and practices, they also apparently brought their excitement about politics home. Parents of participating children began to pay more attention to the news, talked more often about politics, and formed stronger opinions themselves about candidates and political issues. By discussing political issues with their children, parents in turn helped the children clarify emerging political ideas (M. McDevitt & Caton-Rosser, 2009; M. McDevitt & Ostrowski, 2009).

Reciprocal influences are additionally evident in the family's emotional exchanges. When parents treat their children warmly, the children usually reciprocate with affectionate gestures. In contrast, when parents establish a negative climate, children may learn to accuse and ridicule their parents. Some family members intensify demands as they interact, as shown in this interchange:

Mother:	I told you to clean your room. This is a *disaster*.
Daughter:	Get outta *my* room!
Mother:	*(raises her voice)* You clean up that mess or you're grounded! *(stamps her foot)*
Daughter:	Hah! You can't make me!
Mother:	For a month! *(shouting now)*
Daughter:	You stink! *(stomps out of her room and marches to the front door)*
Mother:	For two months! *(shouting louder)*
Daughter:	As if you'd notice I was gone! *(slams door)*

During this exchange, things go from bad to worse: The daughter is blatantly disobedient, the mother intensifies her demands, and both mother and daughter become angrier. Such exchanges are common in some troubled families (Bugental, 2009; Cavell, Hymel, Malcolm, & Seay, 2007; G. R. Patterson & Reid, 1970). When patterns of negative interaction become habitual, it is difficult for family members to learn new ways of responding to one another. However, both parents and children can grow and change, often in response to intensive counseling and other interventions (Bugental, 2009).

Various aspects of children's temperaments and natural abilities are partly responsible for the routine exchanges that families develop. Children who are easily frustrated and apt to be noncompliant tend to provoke adults' severe and intrusive behavior (Bornstein, 2009; Calkins, Hungerford, & Dedmon, 2004). The same principle of children's effects seems to apply with their cognitive abilities (Lugo-Gil & Tamis-LeMonda, 2008; Scarr, 1992). A father with an extensive vocabulary and advanced verbal reasoning may genetically endow his daughter with similar talents. As her verbal skills blossom, the young girl may ask her parents to read to her, explain the meanings of challenging words, and discuss complex ideas. On the surface, the parents promote their daughter's verbal abilities through their actions. But the daughter also influences her parents, instigating and shaping her own opportunities for learning.

ARTIFACT 3-3 Taking care of Dad. Children take initiative when they see beloved family members in distress. Six-year-old Alex wrote this sympathy card to his father the day Alex's grandfather (his father's father) died.

Siblings' Responses to One Another

Children have an impact not only on their parents but also on any siblings present in the family. Approximately 80 percent of children in the United States and in Europe live in a household with at least one sibling (J. Dunn, 2007; Kreider & Fields, 2005).

Siblings serve many purposes for children. First and foremost, close sibling relationships can supplement parent–child bonds (Seibert & Kerns, 2009). Other functions of siblings depend on the relative ages of children. In mainstream Western society, older siblings often look after young children when parents do brief errands. In many other societies, older children are the primary caregivers for younger brothers and sisters for a significant part of the day (Parke & Buriel, 2006; Weisner & Gallimore, 1977; Zhang et al., 2009). Older siblings also serve as role models, tutors, and playmates for younger children.

Sibling relationships of all kinds are characterized by familiarity and emotion. During early and middle childhood, children spend more time with siblings than with parents or children outside the family (J. Dunn, 2007; S. M. McHale & Crouter, 1996). As they interact, siblings express emotions that range from full-bellied laughter to outright anger. The relationships that evolve among siblings are often quite close but occasionally become sources of conflict and stress (J. Dunn, 2007; Randell & Peterson, 2009). Children regularly compete for limited resources, including parents' attention, and occasionally become downright combative over seemingly trivial issues (such as who gets to select first from a full plate of freshly baked cookies: "*Lemme* go first!" "No, it's *my* turn!"). Competition among children in the family probably has some benefits, including creating motivations to figure out how siblings think (Recchia & Howe, 2009). However, resentment may brew if one child feels slighted by a parent who appears to favor another (G. H. Brody, Stoneman, & McCoy, 1994; J. Dunn, 2007).

Within a single family, individual children may encounter quite different childrearing strategies (I. Berger & Felsenthal-Berger, 2009; J. Dunn, 2007). The intellectual and social experiences of children depend partly on their *birth order*—that is, on whether children were born first, second, or somewhere later down the line. Older siblings tend to have a slight advantage academically, perhaps because of the exclusive time they had with their parents before any brothers or sisters came along, and also possibly because they themselves benefit from teaching younger siblings (Chiu, 2007; Zajonc & Mullally, 1997; J. Xu, 2008). Younger siblings show greater skill in interacting with peers, possibly as a result of negotiating with older siblings (J. Dunn, 1984; N. Miller & Maruyama, 1976).

Despite their importance for many children, siblings are by no means essential for healthy development. *Only children*—children without brothers or sisters—are often stereotyped as lonely, spoiled, and egotistical, but research findings on their adjustment are favorable (Miao & Wang, 2003; S. Newman, 2001). On average, only children perform well in school and enjoy particularly close relationships with their parents (Falbo, 1992; Falbo & Polit, 1986).

Risk Factors in Families

As you have seen, "good" families—those that foster children's physical, cognitive, and social-emotional development—come in a wide variety of packages, and they use many, probably countless, distinct styles. In sometimes strikingly different ways, a multitude of psychologically healthy families adequately meet children's basic needs.

Unfortunately, not all families provide optimal environments for children. **Child maltreatment** is the most serious outcome of an unhealthy family environment. Maltreatment takes four major forms (Centers for Disease Control and Prevention, 2009b; English, 1998). *Neglect* occurs when caregivers fail to provide food, clothing, shelter, health care, or affection and do not adequately supervise children's activities (the *uninvolved* parents we described earlier would be considered neglectful if they were truly disengaged from their children). Caregivers engage in *physical abuse* when they intentionally cause physical harm to children, perhaps by kicking, biting, shaking, or punching them. If spanking causes serious bruises or other injuries, it, too, is considered physical abuse. Caregivers engage in *sexual abuse* when they seek sexual gratification from children through such acts as genital contact or pornographic photography. Caregivers engage in *emotional abuse* when they consistently ignore, isolate, reject, denigrate, or terrorize children or when they corrupt children by encouraging them to engage in substance abuse or criminal activity. Sadly, some parents and other caregivers submit children to more than one form of abuse (Belenky, Clinchy, Goldberger, & Tarule, 1986).

Staggering numbers of children—about one in seven children in the United States—are maltreated by family members or other caregivers (Finkelhor, Ormrod, Turner, & Hamby, 2005; Wulczyn, 2009). The occurrence of child maltreatment seems to be related to characteristics of both the adult perpetrator and the child victim. Adults who maltreat children usually suffer from such serious psychological problems as depression, anxiety, and substance abuse problems (Ayoub, 2006; Barth, 2009; Egeland, 2009). Many have little contact with family or friends, are economically disadvantaged, move around a lot, were maltreated themselves as children, have large families to care for, and believe that physical punishment is appropriate and justified by religious or cultural beliefs. Some abusive parents are quite naive about children's development and become angry when children fail to fulfill unrealistic expectations. Children most likely to be maltreated are those who are very young (premature infants are especially at risk); have disabilities; or are irritable, not easily soothed, aggressive, or exceedingly noncompliant (Ayoub, 2006; Barth, 2009).

Tragically, children can suffer long-term consequences from being neglected or assaulted by family members (Wulczyn, 2009). Children who have been maltreated are at risk for becoming aggressive, withdrawn, and depressed, for viewing themselves negatively, and for developing maladaptive ways of coping and interacting with other people. These children are also at risk for physical problems and even death.

Educators and others working with children and adolescents must, by law, contact proper authorities (e.g., the school principal or Child Protective Services) when they suspect child abuse or neglect. Two helpful resources are the National Child Abuse Hotline (1-800-4-A-CHILD®, or 1-800-422-4453)[2] and the Internet website for Childhelp USA®

> Dear Diary,
> Father was home early from the bar. He was really drunk this time. I was just sitting down reading a book when he started hitting me. My mom tried to help me but it was no use. Finnaly went to a corner when he fainted. After that mom and I left for Aunt Mary. Maybe we'll be safe there.

ARTIFACT 3-4 **It was no use.** Like the father described in this child's diary entry, many family members who are abusive suffer from serious psychological problems.

child maltreatment
Adverse treatment of a child in the form of neglect, physical abuse, sexual abuse, or emotional abuse.

[2] The National Child Abuse Hotline receives calls from the United States, Canada, the U.S. Virgin Islands, Puerto Rico, and Guam. Many other countries have similar organizations.

at www.childhelpusa.org. When a concern is expressed to Child Protective Services, the authorities may be able to verify the maltreatment and provide the family with counseling, parent education, housing assistance, substance abuse treatment, home visits, and referrals for other services. Unfortunately, reports to Child Protective Services do not always lead to immediate services for maltreated children or their families. Sometimes authorities cannot find sufficient evidence to substantiate suspicions, and at other times high caseloads prevent authorities from giving prompt assistance (Larner, Stevenson, & Behrman, 1998; Wolock, Sherman, Feldman, & Metzger, 2001).

As they wait for intervention, maltreated children desperately need stable, caring relationships with adults outside the family. Sadly, many maltreated children have acquired negative social behaviors that elicit rejection from other adults, and possibly for this reason maltreated children are at risk for developing low-quality relationships with teachers (Pianta, Hamre, & Stuhlman, 2003). Teachers can try to avoid being provoked by misbehavior and instead make special efforts to address children's reactions to maltreatment (e.g., inattentiveness, disruptive behavior, or withdrawal from activities). When an investigation is under way, continued sensitivity from teachers is essential because children now must adjust to changes in family structure (e.g., a child might be placed with a foster family) or family climate (e.g., a mother might become depressed when she learns she could lose custody of her children). Furthermore, teachers can help by expressing their confidence in children's abilities and providing a sense of normalcy during periods of upheaval in the family (Phasha, 2008).

Forming Partnerships with Families

Parents and teachers have much in common. They both take on tough (but gratifying) responsibilities that demand long hours, an unwavering devotion to children, and flexible methods. Of course, parents and teachers occasionally find themselves on opposite sides of the table, as initially happened in our introductory case. When teachers and families ultimately communicate effectively (Barbara and Mr. Momen eventually did, with help from Cedric), they are likely to magnify their positive effects on children. Ideally, then, teachers and parents (and other heads of family) become partners who collaborate in support of children's learning. We offer the following recommendations on forming constructive partnerships with families:

• **Get to know who is in children's families.** As you have learned, families come in many forms. Thus an important first step is to determine who the guardians are and whether other family members care for children on a daily basis. The Observation Guidelines table "Identifying Family Conditions" lists characteristics of families that teachers can take into consideration.

• **Communicate with each of the children's primary caregivers.** When two parents are actively involved in a child's life—whether they live in the same household or not—teachers should try to get to know both parents and show respect for the role that each plays in the child's development.

• **Put parents and other heads of family at ease during conversations with them.** Most parents want to be heard rather than just "talked at," yet some are anxious, uncertain, distrustful, or reluctant to voice their perspectives without encouragement (Hoover-Dempsey & Sandler, 1997; Kersey & Masterson, 2009). Educators can look for signs of discomfort, use friendly body language, comment optimistically about children's abilities, display a sense of humor, treat parents as authorities who can help them learn about children's needs, ask specific questions (e.g., "What does Kira like to do in her free time?"), and assure parents that they should feel free to call whenever they have questions or concerns.

• **Recognize the important role of siblings.** Teachers can often take advantage of children's close-knit relationships with siblings, especially when children face a loss or challenge. For instance, in times of family crisis (e.g., the death of a grandparent or a parent's imprisonment), children may need contact with siblings, perhaps on the playground, in the lunchroom, or in the nurse's office. Educators can also welcome siblings during schoolwide

OBSERVATION GUIDELINES
Identifying Family Conditions

CHARACTERISTIC	LOOK FOR	EXAMPLE	IMPLICATION
Family Structure	• *Single versus multiple caregivers* • *Presence or absence of siblings* • *Extended family members* living in the home • *Nonrelatives* living in the home • *Children's relationships* with other family members	Alexis's chronic kidney disease causes periodic bouts of fatigue and irritability. During flare-ups, she finds comfort in being with her older sister at recess and lunch. Alexis's teachers have observed the girls' close relationship and provide opportunities for them to be together when Alexis is feeling poorly.	Accept all heads of family as valued, legitimate caregivers of children. Include extended family members (especially those who appear to be regular caregivers) at school functions. Give youngsters time to be with siblings in times of personal or family crisis.
Cultural Background	• *Language(s)* spoken at home • *Routines* in eating, bathing, sleeping, preparing household meals, and carrying out chores • *Loyalty* to and sense of responsibility for other family members • *Attitudes* toward cooperation and competition • *Communication styles* (whether they make eye contact, ask a lot of questions, verbally articulate their concerns, etc.)	Carlos is very reserved in class. He follows instructions and shows that he wants to do well in school. However, he rarely seeks his teacher's help. Instead, he often asks his cousin (a classmate) for assistance.	Remember that most children and parents value academic achievement, despite what their behaviors may make you think. Adapt instructional styles to children's preferred ways of interacting and communicating. Consider how families' cultural knowledge and skills might enrich the classroom.
Family Livelihood	• *Presence of a family business* (e.g., farm, cottage industry) that requires children's involvement • *Parental unemployment* • *Older children and adolescents with part-time jobs* (e.g., grocery store work, paper routes)	April completes several chores on the family farm before going to school each morning. She keeps records of the weight and health of three calves born last year. She constructs charts to show their progress as a project for her seventh-grade science class.	Take outside work commitments into account when assigning homework. For example, give students at least 2 days to complete short assignments and at least a week for longer ones.
Parenting Styles	• *Parents' warmth or coldness* toward their children • *Parents' expectations* for their children's behavior and performance • *Parents' willingness to discuss issues* and negotiate solutions with their children • *Parents' disciplinary techniques* • *Possible effects of children's temperaments* on parents' disciplinary styles • *Children's interpretations* of parents' motives in disciplinary practices • *Cultural values*, such as honoring one's elders, that give meaning to parents' disciplinary customs • *Dangers and opportunities* in the community that influence the use and effects of a given parenting style	At a parent–teacher conference, Julia's parents express their exasperation about trying to get Julia to do her homework: "We've tried everything—reasoning with her, giving ultimatums, offering extra privileges for good grades, punishing her for bad grades—but nothing seems to work. She'd rather hang out with her friends every night."	Realize that most parents have their children's best interests at heart and use disciplinary methods they have seen others use. Recognize that parents often adapt their parenting styles to children's temperaments. With all children, communicate high expectations, show sensitivity to children's needs, and give reasons for your requests.
Disruptive Influences	• *Changes in family membership* (e.g., as a result of death, divorce, remarriage, or cohabitation) • *Changes in residence* • *Physical or mental illness* in parents or other family members • *Parental alcoholism or substance abuse* • *Economic poverty* • *Long-term stress* in the family	Justin has had trouble concentrating since his parents' divorce, and he no longer shows much enthusiasm for class activities.	Show compassion for children undergoing a significant family transition. Listen patiently if children want to talk. Realize that some families may quickly return to healthy functioning, but others may be in turmoil for lengthy periods. Seek the assistance of a counselor when children have unusual difficulty.

(continued)

OBSERVATION GUIDELINES (continued)

CHARACTERISTIC	LOOK FOR	EXAMPLE	IMPLICATION
Maltreatment	• *Frequent injuries*, usually attributed to "accidents" • *Age-inappropriate sexual knowledge* or behavior • *Extreme negative emotions*, perhaps withdrawal, anxiety, or depression • *Excessive aggression and hostility* evident in behaviors (e.g., name calling, hitting, and pushing) • *Untreated medical or dental needs* • *Chronic hunger* • *Poor hygiene and grooming* • *Lack of warm clothing in cold weather*	Johnny often has bruises on his arms and legs, which his mother says are the result of a "blood problem." He recently broke his collarbone, and soon after that he had a black eye. "I fell down the stairs," he explained but refused to say more.	Immediately report possible signs of child maltreatment to a school counselor or principal. Contact Child Protective Services for advice about additional courses of action that should be followed.

events by reserving a room and making durable toys and child-friendly snacks available. During parent–teacher conferences, teachers can refrain from making comparisons between students and their siblings. And when making classroom placements, teachers and other school personnel can listen respectfully to families' perspectives on siblings' needs. Some parents of twins favor keeping them together in the classroom, especially in the early grades and if the children have had little experience being separated (Preedy, 1999; Segal & Russell, 1992; Tinglof, 2007). At the same time, teachers will have their own experiences with siblings and can share these with parents.

• **Ask parents and other heads of family about their goals, concerns, and strategies for supporting children.** During conversations with families, teachers can invite parents to talk about their philosophies of parenting and priorities for children. Some teachers invite parents to come to the classroom to talk about their ancestors and cultures; other teachers ask parents to complete questionnaires about their children's abilities and interests (Kersey & Masterson, 2009).

• **Advise parents about children's age-related challenges.** Based on their familiarity with children of a particular age level, teachers gain insights into the developmental tasks children are apt to tackle. Teachers realize that infants regularly protest when separated from parents at the child care center, young children exhibit oppositional behavior when frustrated, elementary school children worry when they don't learn to read as quickly as peers, and so on. Teachers can help parents see that these age-related characteristics are a natural way that children develop and can be constructively addressed. In Figure 3-1, a teacher helps parents understand their middle-school children's developmental qualities. You can find a list of typical concerns of parents and ways teachers might address them in the Developmental Trends table "The Family's Concerns for Children of Different Ages."

• **Walk in their shoes.** Families sometimes live very different lives than those of the professionals who work with them. By talking with community leaders, reading the research on local cultures, and listening sympathetically to parents, educators can learn a lot

Adolescent Development

Eleven . . . is a time of breaking up, of discord and discomfort. Gone is the bland complaisance of the typical ten-year-old. Eleven is a time of loosening up, of snapping old bonds, of trial and error as the young child tests the limits of what authority will and will not permit

Louise Bates Ames, Ph.D.
Your Ten- to Fourteen-Year-Old
Gesell Institute of Human Development

To understand your adolescent, you need to consider . . .
. . . the child's basic individuality.
. . . what is expected of anyone of his or her particular age level.
. . . what environment your child finds himself or herself in.

Eleven-year-olds can be . . .
egocentric,
energetic,
always "loving" or "hating";

as well as . . .
not as cooperative or accepting as in the past
more angry than in the past
inattentive
hungry all the time
more interested in the clothes they wear (but not in cleaning them!)
uncertain
more apt to cry
fearful
rebellious
very interested and involved in family activities

FIGURE 3-1 Understanding your adolescent. Teachers can be valuable sources of information about child and adolescent development. In this flier for parents, middle school teacher Erin Miguel describes several common characteristics of young adolescents.

"Handout on Adolescent Development" by Erin Miguel Keith. Copyright © September 2000 by Erin Miguel Keith. Reprinted with permission.

about families' lives. For example, by seeking information about homeless families who reside in temporary shelters, teachers would learn about the many efforts these parents make to protect their children from harmful people in their environment (Torquati, 2002). With such insights, teachers can advise parents about the school's procedures for ensuring a safe, stimulating environment for children.

• **Remember that most parents view their children's behavior as a reflection of their own competence.** Parents typically feel proud when their children are successful in school and get along well with friends. In contrast, parents may respond to their children's academic difficulties or behavior problems with embarrassment, shame, anger, or denial. Teachers are more likely to have productive discussions with parents if they avoid placing blame and instead propose that students, parents, and teachers work as a team to identify solutions. It always helps to have something positive to share during such conversations. Whenever possible, teachers and other practitioners can share one favorable comment about a child each time they contact his or her parent (Kersey & Masterson, 2009).

• **Ask for input.** Parents and other heads of family have important views on how well schools are serving children and how they might be improved. School leaders can solicit these ideas in a variety of venues. A number of parents can participate on a school management team, participate in hiring of teachers, and help to plan schoolwide events (J. Bryan & Henry, 2008; Halgunseth, 2009).

• **Ask for help.** Parents know their children intimately and are likely to have insights they can share with teachers and other practitioners. Parents of children with disabilities are especially likely to be able to share an informed perspective on their children's abilities, needs, and effective educational strategies (Ray, Pewitt-Kinder, & George, 2009). Furthermore, parents have a right to know about the significant challenges their child encounters and may also be able to offer suggestions or support the school's intervention with related activities at home.

• **Be alert to cultural differences.** When conferring with parents about children's problematic classroom behaviors, educators should keep in mind that people from different cultural groups usually have distinct ideas about how children should be disciplined. Some Chinese American parents believe that Western schools are too lenient in correcting inappropriate behavior (Hidalgo, Siu, Bright, Swap, & Epstein, 1995; Kağitçibaşi, 2007). In some Native American and Asian cultures, a child's misbehaviors may be seen as bringing shame on the family or community; thus a common disciplinary strategy is to ignore or ostracize the child for an extended period of time (Pang, 1995; Salend & Taylor, 1993). As educators talk with family members, they can listen with an open mind and try to find common ground they can use to support children.

• **Strive to build positive relationships with families of all ethnic backgrounds.** Children and parents from ethnic minority groups are less likely to enjoy supportive relationships with teachers than are children and parents from European American backgrounds (J. Hughes & Kwok, 2007). Weak relationships are likely to occur when teachers are unaware of families' cultural perspectives and uncomfortable with their communication styles (J. Hughes & Kwok, 2007). Knowing that good parent–teacher and teacher–child relationships are beneficial for *all* children, teachers can make extra efforts to reach out to families with backgrounds different from their own.

• **Accommodate language and literacy differences.** Many immigrant parents are not yet fluent in the dominant languages of their new land and may not be able to communicate with teachers or read correspondence from school. When a child's parents speak a language other than English, educators can try to include in conversations someone trusted by the parents who can converse fluently with them in their native tongue. Educators should also have newsletters and other written messages translated whenever it is reasonable to do so.

DEVELOPMENTAL TRENDS
The Family's Concerns for Children of Different Ages

AGE	TOPICS	DIVERSITY	IMPLICATIONS
Infancy (Birth–2 Years) 	**Physical Development** • Ensuring infants' basic safety by instituting precautions so they cannot put themselves in danger (e.g., by tumbling down stairs, swallowing cleaning supplies) • Meeting infants' physical needs (e.g., feeding on a baby's schedule, diapering, and easing baby into a sleep schedule that conforms to adults' patterns) • Giving proper nutrition to match physiological needs and pace of growth **Cognitive Development** • Talking with infants and responding enthusiastically to their smiling and babbling • Encouraging infants to take turns in conversations and simple games • Providing appropriate sensory stimulation **Social-Emotional Development** • Watching for infants' preferences and abiding by these (for example, after noticing that an infant likes trucks, selecting picture books with trucks to share with the child) • Arranging for responsive caregivers to whom children can become emotionally attached • Affirming infants' feelings so that they begin to understand emotions • Responding with reasonable promptness to infants' cries	• Some parents promote independence in infants by encouraging them to try self-help actions, such as picking up bits of food and feeding themselves; others prefer to do these things for infants. • Nap time may depend on parents' beliefs about desirable sleeping practices. • Parents may differ in how much they talk with infants. Some may verbalize frequently; others may soothe infants and focus on non-verbal gestures. • Families differ in beliefs about out-of-home care. Some parents resist commercial child care and will leave infants only for brief periods with familiar relatives. Other parents are comfortable with employed caregivers. • Concerns of parents depend partly on the temperament and health status of infants. When infants are difficult to soothe or are sick, parents may be quite concerned.	• Complete daily records of infants' physical care so parents are aware of how their infants' needs are met and the kind of day they have had. • Talk with parents about the developmental milestones you notice in infants. For example, tell parents when you see a new tooth breaking through the gums. • Post a chart of typical developmental milestones (e.g., rolling over, sitting up, uttering a first word) so that parents can think about what their infants might be presently learning. Select a chart that emphasizes the wide variation in ages at which infants normally attain developmental milestones. • Ask parents to share their concerns about their infants, and offer appropriate reassurance.
Early Childhood (2–6 Years)	**Physical Development** • Ensuring children's basic safety (e.g., protecting them from street traffic and household chemicals) • Helping children with self-care routines (e.g., dressing, brushing teeth, bathing) • Finding appropriate outlets for physical energy **Cognitive Development** • Answering children's seemingly incessant questions • Channeling curiosity into constructive activities • Reading stories and in other ways promoting a foundation for literacy • Preparing for transition to formal schooling **Social-Emotional Development** • Curbing temper tantrums • Promoting sharing among siblings and peers • Addressing conflicts and aggressive behavior • Forming relationships with new caregivers in child care and preschool	• Some parents, worrying about their children's safety, are exceptionally reluctant to leave them in the care of others. • Low-income families have little or no discretionary income with which to purchase books and other supplies for cognitive enrichment. • Some kindergartners and first graders have had little or no prior experiences with other children; for instance, they may be only children or may not have previously attended child care or preschool. • Some parents (especially those from higher-income, professional backgrounds) may give children too many intellectually challenging activities and too few chances to relax or play.	• Suggest possible approaches to teaching young children about self-care habits, social skills, and impulse control. • Keep parents regularly informed about their children's progress in both academic and social skills. • Provide books and other stimulating materials that parents can check out and use at home. • When highly educated parents seem overly concerned about accelerating their children's cognitive development, suggest literature that encourages a balance between stimulation and relaxation.

(continued)

DEVELOPMENTAL TRENDS (continued)

AGE	TOPICS	DIVERSITY	IMPLICATIONS
Middle Childhood (6–10 Years) 	**Physical Development** • Fostering healthy eating habits • Using safety equipment (e.g., seat belts in the car, helmets for cycling) • Establishing exercise routines and limiting television and electronic games **Cognitive Development** • Helping children acquire habits and expectations that will aid them in their academic work • Promoting mastery of basic academic skills • Enhancing children's education through family involvement and outings **Social-Emotional Development** • Giving children increasing independence and responsibility (e.g., for waking up on time, doing homework) • Monitoring interactions with siblings, playmates • Instilling moral values (e.g., honesty)	• Some parents are stressed from work responsibilities. • Some neighborhoods have few if any playgrounds or other places where children can safely play. • Children's special talents and interests influence their choices of activities outside the home. • Some children look after themselves for long periods after school, and they may or may not use this time wisely. • Some parents may worry that children are not receiving a sufficiently high-quality education. • Some parents whose children have disabilities may be concerned that their children's needs are not being effectively met at school or that their children are not accepted into peer groups.	• Obtain and distribute literature about safety measures from local police, fire departments, and pediatricians' offices. • Provide resource materials (perhaps through a parent library in the classroom) that parents can use to assist their children with academic subject matter. • Encourage parents' involvement in school activities and parent–teacher groups. • Suggest facilities and programs in the community (e.g., youth soccer leagues, scout organizations) that provide free or inexpensive opportunities for after-school recreation and skill development.
Early Adolescence (10–14 Years)	**Physical Development** • Recognizing and dealing with early stages of puberty • Encouraging physical fitness • Affording basic clothing during periods of rapid growth **Cognitive Development** • Supporting school-based changes in expectations for academic performance • Identifying appropriate mechanisms for developing young adolescents' talents and interests **Social-Emotional Development** • Showing sensitivity to self-consciousness about appearance • Accommodating requests for more leisure time with peers • Dealing with increased conflict as adolescents seek greater autonomy	• Adolescents differ in the age at which they begin puberty. • Some youngsters may have little access to recreational facilities. • Some parents may have considerable difficulty allowing their adolescents greater independence. • Overt parent–teenager conflicts are rare in some cultures, especially in those that cultivate respect for elders. • Various peer groups encourage behaviors that may or may not be productive. • Some parents may worry that their adolescents have hobbies (perhaps video games) that interfere with homework.	• Identify and inform parents about athletic and social programs in the community. • Collaborate with other teachers to establish a homework hotline through which students can get ongoing guidance for assignments. • Share with parents your impressions about reasonable expectations for independence and responsibility in young adolescents.
Late Adolescence (14–18 Years) 	**Physical Development** • Keeping track of teenagers' whereabouts • Encouraging students to maintain realistic schedules that allow adequate sleep • Worrying about risky driving • Concern about possible alcohol and drug use **Cognitive Development** • Encouraging youth to persist with increasingly challenging academic subject matter • Understanding adolescents' expanding capacity for logical, systematic thinking • Educating adolescents about employment prospects and college requirements **Social-Emotional Development** • Worrying about the loss of control over teenagers' social activities • Finding a reasonable balance between supervision and independence	• Alcohol and drugs are readily available in most communities, but their use is more frequent and socially acceptable in some neighborhoods and peer groups than in others. • Some parents refuse to believe that their children may be engaged in serious health-compromising behaviors, even when faced with the evidence. • Families differ in their knowledge of, and experiences with, higher education; some are unable to counsel their children about options in postsecondary education. • Parents differ in the extent to which they encourage teenagers' part-time employment.	• Suggest ways in which adolescents can maintain regular contact with families when away from home for lengthy periods (e.g., by making regular phone calls home). • Provide information about possible careers and educational opportunities after high school; include numerous options, including part-time and full-time vocational programs, community colleges, and 4-year colleges and universities.

Sources: W. A. Collins, 1990; Gallo, Hadley, Angst, Knafl, & Smith, 2008; A. Kirby, Edwards, & Hughes, 2008; Kutner, Olson, Warner, & Hertzog, 2008; Maccoby, 1984; Montemayor, 1982; Mortimer, Shanahan, & Ryu, 1994; Nesteruk, Marks, & Garrison, 2009; Paikoff & Brooks-Gunn, 1991; Pipher, 1994; Warton & Goodnow, 1991; Youniss, 1983.

• **Invite families to get involved at school**. Many family members have special abilities (such as woodworking, calligraphy, and storytelling) that they would happily demonstrate at school. Likewise, some parents are bilingual, and they might step forward to translate school materials for other parents who speak little English (Finders & Lewis, 1994). To benefit from these talents, you may wish to ask families at the beginning of the year about their interests in sharing particular kinds of expertise with the school. Teresa recalls that when her son Connor was in middle school, she and her husband received a booklet containing tearsheets with suggestions on how parents might contribute to school activities (such as driving on field trips, volunteering in the classroom, and bringing in treats for special events); it was easy to go through the booklet, choose a few activities, and send the sheets back to school.

• **Accommodate pressures on parents and other heads of family when asking for their help.** Encouraging parents to attend meetings or help at school is most likely to be effective when teachers recognize the obstacles in parents' way. Some parents have exhausting work schedules, lack adequate child care, or have difficulty communicating in English. One Chinese immigrant parent regretted not being able to attend meetings at school: "I cannot go to the teacher meetings. I work at a restaurant 6 days a week and we are too busy in the afternoon. My boss is harsh and he says I cannot leave . . . and I cannot lose this job" (Ji & Koblinsky, 2009, p. 701). Still others may be actively involved when their children are in elementary school but increasingly withdraw as their children move to middle and secondary levels (J. L. Epstein, 1996; Finders & Lewis, 1994; Roderick & Camburn, 1999). Thus, invitations must be sincere and offer a variety of things parents can do during the day, in the evening, or over the weekend.

• **Recognize the beneficial effects that parents have on children's learning at home.** Even though some parents do not attend school events, they may nevertheless work tirelessly at home to support their children's education. Some parents have moved from another country to ensure a good education and decent opportunities for their children. Other parents spend hours helping children with homework, limiting children's television, protecting quiet areas for homework, and urging children to study hard and show respect to teachers. In newsletters, meetings, and informal conversations with parents who are picking up or dropping off their children, teachers can let parents know the worthwhile ways in which their efforts at home are paying dividends for their children at school (S. W. Nelson & Guerra, 2009).

• **Reach out to parents and other heads of family who do not come to school.** Teachers can communicate proactively with family members who are not able or inclined to attend school meetings and events. Teachers might send home videotapes of children's work at school or photographs of children's participation in a special event such as a school play. Teachers may also prepare a class newsletter with highlights of school events (Kersey & Masterson, 2009).

• **When appropriate, visit families in their homes and in the community.** Home visits are a relatively common way of supporting parents' efforts at home, especially with young children (Gomby, Culross, & Behrman, 1999). Home visiting programs typically focus on educating parents about children's needs and preventing such problems as neglect or abuse. To make home visits maximally effective, educators can present themselves as friendly and nonjudgmental, make an effort to establish rapport with parents and other family members, and offer practical suggestions for helping children to learn. One educator considers home visits a vital first step in communicating with migrant families:

> At the beginning of the school year, [personnel from the school] went house by house in their whole zone.... Everybody—the counselors, the librarian, the clerks, the paraprofessionals— went to visit families. Everybody's home was visited at least once by somebody in the school in

a positive fashion. OK? They told [parents] *"Mire Señora, queremos que sepa que en la escuela nos importa su hija o hijo y queremos saber dónde vive y si le podemos ayudar en algo, estamos para servirle.* [Look, Miss, we want you to know that we care about your daughter or son and we want to know where you live and if we can help you in any way, we are here to serve you.]" And we began to get parents who said, "They care to come out here on an afternoon, when it's hot, you know, and visit? They really care about us!" (G. R. López, Scribner, & Mahitivanichcha, 2001, p. 264)

When home visits are not possible or appropriate, teachers can learn more about families by getting involved in their community. Educators can attend festivals, community events, and meetings of local groups, including those focused on educational reform (M. R. Brown, 2009). They can meet leaders from local cultural groups and invite them to speak to students and families about events in their community as well as to advise school staff about cultural expectations and traditions (Dotson-Blake, Foster, & Gressard, 2009).

• **Inform parents of services available to them.** Parents in distress are sometimes unaware of free and low-cost community services for which they are eligible. Teachers and other professionals can advise parents about potentially helpful services, such as parent education and outlets for family recreation (M. R. Brown, 2009; Staudt, 2001).

• **Use a variety of communication formats.** Families appreciate hearing about children's accomplishments, and they deserve to know about behaviors that consistently interfere with children's learning and adjustment. Likewise, teachers can learn a lot about a child's needs from talking with family members. Here are a few helpful forms of communication:

• *Meetings.* In most schools parent–teacher–student conferences are scheduled one or more times a year. These meetings are an excellent forum for celebrating children's successes and identifying areas that need additional attention. At one conference it may be mutually agreed that the teacher will find new assignments that better match the child's needs, the child will begin keeping track of due dates for homework, and the family will reserve a quiet place at home for the child to do homework uninterrupted.

• *Written communications.* Educators can use structured forms to let parents know what their children are doing. Prepared forms that specify activities and leave space for individual comments can be helpful. In Figure 3-2 a teacher describes 2½-year-old Sam's first day in the toddler room, including information about their program and how Sam fared. More formal newsletters communicate school- and community-wide events, resources, and policies.

• *Telephone conversations.* Telephone calls are useful when issues require immediate attention. Teachers might call parents to express concern when a student's behavior deteriorates unexpectedly, and they might also call to express their excitement about an important step forward. Parents, too, should feel free to call teachers. Keep in mind that many parents are at work during the school day; hence it is often helpful for teachers to take calls at home during the early evening hours.

• *E-mail and websites.* Increasingly, educators find that they can maintain regular contact with parents electronically—for instance, by sending e-mail messages and creating web pages that list events and assignments (S. Mitchell, Foulger, & Wetzel, 2009). In Figure 3-3 you can see an e-mail message sent by a school counselor to parents. Notice that the counselor not only advises parents of a problem but also asks for their help in encouraging proper behavior. Consider, also, that electronic communication

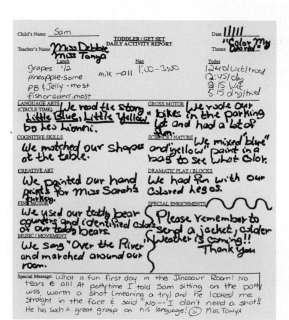

FIGURE 3-2 Sam's day. A structured daily activity form completed for 2½-year-old Sam. Parents often appreciate information about what their children did and learned during the day.

DEVELOPMENT AND PRACTICE
Making Schools Family Friendly

Learn about families.

- An elementary teacher hosts a Welcome Parents Meeting at the beginning of the school year and asks parents to complete a questionnaire (available in English and a few other languages for immigrant parents) about children's interests, abilities, and hobbies (Kersey & Masterson, 2009). (Middle Childhood)
- A high school adviser calls his advisees' parents at the beginning of the school year. The adviser asks the parents about their hopes for their son or daughter during the year and informs parents that he can be reached at a certain phone number and e-mail address and welcomes contact from them when they develop questions or concerns. (Late Adolescence)

Help children and their families feel that they are valued members of the school.

- A caregiver of toddlers provides storage boxes ("cubbies") for each child. On the outside of each box the child's name is posted, and photographs of the child and his or her family are displayed. Children regularly point to their parents and other family members throughout the day. (Early Childhood)
- A middle school principal sets up a school improvement team of teachers, the school counselor, a group of parents, and a couple of students. The principal treats the team with utmost respect and sends home letters of appreciation for their time and efforts. (Early Adolescence)

Recognize the significance of families in children's lives.

- A music teacher asks students to bring in the lyrics from their favorite family songs. She posts the words of the songs on a bulletin board labeled "My Family and Me." (Middle Childhood)
- A middle school social studies teacher invites parents and other family members to come to class and describe their jobs and the history of their ancestors. (Young Adolescence)

Acknowledge the strengths of families' varying backgrounds.

- An elementary teacher asks a community leader to come to class and talk about the cultural traditions of immigrant families. (Middle Childhood)
- When planning a lesson on the history of farming in Colorado, a middle school social studies teacher encourages families to bring in any photographs of farm tools that they use while planting and harvesting crops. (Early Adolescence)

Use a variety of formats to communicate with parents.

- A fourth-grade teacher works with the children in his class to produce a monthly newsletter for parents. Two versions of the newsletter are created, one in English and one in Spanish. (Middle Childhood)

- A high school drama teacher takes photographs of individual students during play practice and sends home the pictures as attachments to e-mail messages. (Late Adolescence)

Tell parents about children's strengths, even when communicating information about shortcomings.

- An elementary teacher is concerned about a child's disruptive behavior in class. In a phone call to the girl's parents, the teacher asks for the parents' insights, "Although I appreciate your daughter's energy and sociability, I'd like to work with you to find a way to increase her time on task" (Christenson, Palan, & Scullin, 2009, p. 11). (Middle Childhood)
- A high school counselor talks on the phone with the parents of a student. She describes several areas in which the student has made considerable progress but also asks for advice about strategies that might help him stay on task and be more agreeable with peers. (Late Adolescence)

Be sensitive to parents' concerns about their children.

- A 3-year-old girl's parents are concerned with her speech and mention to her teacher that she says "sool" for "school" and "hairpane" for "airplane." The teacher reassures the parents that such mispronunciations are common in young children, but also advises the parents that a speech therapist is available at the school district office should they want an expert opinion. (Early Childhood)
- A school counselor talks with worried parents of a 16-year-old girl who has begun smoking and possibly experimenting with drugs. Thinking about the girl's interest in photography, the counselor informs the parents about the school's after-school photography club, with hopes that the companionship of more academically oriented peers might get the student back on the right track. (Late Adolescence)

Encourage parents and guardians to get involved with school activities.

- An infant caregiver asks for volunteers to give their input into decisions about programs for children, such as how to staff a new room when enrollment grows or the kind of outdoor play space that makes the most sense given toddlers' needs and the limited budget of the center (J. Daniel, 2009). (Infancy)
- A high school principal sends home a book of "coupons" printed with assorted activities that parents and other family members might assist with at school (e.g., tutoring in the classroom, baking goodies for a school open house, serving on the parent advisory group). She supplements the book with a letter expressing her hope that all parents who have the time will return at least one coupon that commits them to a particular activity. (Late Adolescence)

Hello!

How much money would it take for you to agree to go back to your 7th grade year of school? You couldn't pay me enough!!!

Disrespect and thoughtless comments to peers seem to be on the upswing in the 7th grade at [our school]. Today we had a town meeting, and I had one of my serious chats with the class about the importance of treating others properly. I strongly encouraged students to step back and evaluate their own behavior. I asked them to think about whether their parents would be proud of how they treat others. I also asked if they personally were proud of how they treat others.

I think most of you know me well enough by now to know that I have a low tolerance for people who treat others poorly. If your child is having trouble with peers, please encourage him or her to talk with me. If s/he is struggling with taking that first step, I hope you would take the time to call me to discuss it. Unless I'm aware of concerns, I can't work on making things better.

It takes a village.

Nancy

FIGURE 3-3 Staying in touch. Professionals who work with families can sometimes stay in touch by electronic mail. In this e-mail message a counselor alerts parents to the social climate at school.

Courtesy of Nancy S. Rapport.

can be a two-way form of communication. Parents can be encouraged to send e-mails to teachers and to complete brief online forms. Such electronic communication, of course, can be used only when parents have easy access to computer technology and the Internet.

• *Parent discussion groups.* In some instances teachers, counselors, and principals may want to assemble a group of parents to discuss mutual concerns. School leaders might want to use a discussion group as a sounding board for evaluating possible school improvement plans. Or, a school counselor might convene a school involvement committee to plan such events as a career night for students and a Black History Month concert (J. Bryan & Henry, 2008).

None of the strategies just described will, in and of itself, guarantee a successful working relationship with parents and other heads of families. Meetings with parents occur somewhat infrequently. Written communication is ineffective with parents who have limited literacy skills. Some families do not want to be visited at home. And, of course, not everyone has a telephone, let alone e-mail. Despite difficulties with staying in touch, effective teachers and other practitioners do their best to form productive partnerships with families (e.g., see the Development and Practice feature "Making Schools Family Friendly" on page 93).

CHILDREN IN A DIVERSE SOCIETY

Increasingly diverse populations of children attend school, creating an opportunity—and a responsibility—for teachers to adjust their methods for the betterment of all children. In this section we focus on the range of experiences children have as members of defined social groups and as residents of particular kinds of communities.

Children's Experiences in Diverse Groups

The United States and many other nations have become highly diverse. About 22 percent of U.S. children live with at least one foreign-born parent (Federal Interagency Forum on Child and Family Statistics, 2009). Twenty-one percent of children speak a language other than English at home, and 5 percent have limited mastery of English (Federal Interagency Forum on Child and Family Statistics, 2009). Furthermore, as you can see in Table 3-1, the numbers of children of color—those in various "ethnic minority" groups, including children from Asian American, African American, Hispanic American, and Native American backgrounds—are collectively increasing at proportionally higher rates than the number of children from European American backgrounds.

Ethnicity

ethnicity
Membership in a group of people with a common cultural heritage and shared values, beliefs, and behaviors.

A person's **ethnicity** refers to the group of people with whom the individual shares values, beliefs, behaviors, and often a culture, heritage, geographical origin, racial background, or religious faith. However, ethnicity is not identical to such factors as culture or race. Although a single ethnic group is sometimes comprised of people from one cultural group, more often than not an ethnic group includes people from several different cultural groups. For example, people who are *Hispanic* tend to speak Spanish or Portuguese (or are descended

TABLE 3-1   Percentages of U.S. Children in Racial and Ethnic Groups

	ESTIMATES FOR YEAR			PROJECTIONS FOR YEAR	
ETHNICITY	**1980**	**1990**	**2000**	**2011**	**2021**
White	74	69	61	55	50
Black	15	15	16	15	14
Hispanic	9	12	17	23	27
Asian	2	3	4	4	5
American Indian/Alaska Native; multiple race; or any other race	1	1	4	5	6

NOTE: Figures are for U.S. children 17 years and under. Accumulated percentages may not equal 100 due to rounding error. Data from 2000 and after are not fully comparable to data from previous years due to changes in census categories. Hispanic children may be of any race but have parents who have identified them as being Hispanic.

Source: Federal Interagency Forum on Child and Family Statistics, 2009.

from individuals who spoke these languages) and originate from one of several very different regions (Spain, Portugal, Mexico, Central and South American countries, Spanish-speaking Caribbean nations); as a result, Hispanics share a few common values but have many distinct cultural practices (C. B. Fisher, Jackson, & Villarruel, 1998; García & Jensen, 2007). The implication of this heterogeneity is that knowing a child comes from a Hispanic American background gives only a rough idea as to what his or her cultural practices and beliefs might be.

In some ethnic groups, members may come from a single race, but this is not always the case. In general, *ethnicity* has a stronger association with cultural dimensions, and *race* connotes physical similarities such as skin color or eye shape (Coles, 2006). A child's race, often apparent to others, can be an especially strong factor in how he or she is treated and whether the child encounters discrimination or favoritism in society.

Today many children are *multiethnic* or *multiracial,* claiming ancestry from more than a single ethnic or racial group. For instance, a child whose mother has both African American and Native American heritages and whose father emigrated from England may be exposed to a variety of family traditions. Multiethnic children may affiliate with two or more ethnic groups and selectively carry out particular traditions depending on the context (e.g., eating contemporary American foods in restaurants and traditional Vietnamese dishes at family gatherings) (Hendriksen & Paladino, 2009). Multiethnic and multiracial children tend to become flexible and skillful in navigating through different cultural environments but occasionally confront pejorative comments about their appearance or backgrounds from others (Hendriksen & Paladino, 2009).

Immigration

Ethnicity is especially salient when people move from one environment to another—for instance, when they immigrate to a new country. When different cultural groups exist in the same region, the two groups interact and learn about one another. As people participate in the customs and take on the values of a new culture, **acculturation** occurs. Acculturation takes four different forms:

- **Assimilation.** Some people totally embrace the values and customs of the new culture, giving up their original cultural identity in the process. Assimilation is typically a gradual process that occurs over several generations and under conditions in which immigrants feel accepted by the host society.[3]

Bioecology of Child Development

A child's ethnicity, race, and culture sometimes afford distinct opportunities and occasionally noticeable hardships.

DON'T ASSUME. Membership in a particular racial or ethnic group is not always a good indication of a child's cultural beliefs and practices.

acculturation
Process of taking on the customs and values of a new culture.

assimilation
Form of acculturation in which a person totally embraces a culture, abandoning a previous culture in the process.

[3] The term *assimilation* is used in two separate ways by developmental scholars. In Piaget's theory cognitive assimilation refers to a process of learning. The terms *cultural assimilation* and *cognitive assimilation* are two distinct concepts.

- **Rejection**. Sometimes people move to a new culture without taking on any of their new community's cultural practices. Complete rejection of a new culture may occur when individuals have little need to interact with people in that culture or when the new society segregates immigrants to isolated regions.

- **Selective adoption**. Sometimes immigrants acquire some customs of the new culture while retaining other customs from their homeland. Families begin to celebrate some of the holidays of their new culture while continuing to observe other holidays from their country of origin. Children are likely to adopt new customs when parents encourage them to embrace their new society's customs and their community accepts them as valued participants.

- **Bicultural orientation**. Some people retain their original culture yet also acquire beliefs and master practices of their new culture, and they readily adjust behaviors to fit the particular contexts in which they find themselves. A bicultural orientation is promoted when the new society is tolerant of diversity. (Delgado-Gaitan, 1994; Kağitçibaşi, 2007; Mana, Orr, & Mana, 2009)

In previous decades total assimilation was considered by many people in the United States to be the optimal situation for immigrants. The route to success was presumed to entail blending into a "melting pot" in which people of different backgrounds become increasingly similar. More recently, however, researchers have discovered that when young immigrants give up their family's cultural traditions, they are at greater risk for developing serious conflicts with their parents and engaging in dangerous behaviors, including using alcohol and drugs, having unprotected sex, and engaging in criminal activities (Hwang, 2006; Roosa et al., 2009; Ying & Han, 2007).

Therefore, the idea that the United States and other nations with large immigrant populations are melting pots is giving way to the idea that the countries can be more productively thought of as a "mosaics" of cultural and ethnic pieces that all legitimately contribute to the greater good of society (C. B. Fisher et al., 1998). Consistent with this view, many immigrant children adjust most successfully when they learn certain aspects of their new culture while also retaining aspects of their original culture—that is, when they show a pattern of either *selective adoption* or *bicultural orientation*. You can learn more about the characteristics of children from different countries in the Development in Culture feature "Immigrant Children."

HONORING MULTIPLE HERITAGES. Children often adjust well when they remain knowledgeable about their ethnic heritage and also master customs of the dominant society.

Environmental Challenges and Coping Strategies

Children from immigrant families and those from ethnic minority backgrounds face unique risks and assets. One significant hardship is that teachers and other practitioners regularly misunderstand these children's abilities and motivations. Unless they come from a similar background, adults at school may not appreciate the skills and traditions children have learned at home (González et al., 2005; Riojas-Cortez, Huerta, Flores, Perez, & Clark, 2008; Olmedo, 2009).

All children possess what Puerto Rican American psychologist **Luis Moll** and his colleagues have called *funds of knowledge*, the intellectual and social information and traditions that are essential for completing activities in the household and local community (Moll, Amanti, Neff, & González, 2005). Examples include knowledge needed to plan and prepare the family's meals, celebrate traditions with the family, take part in hobbies, get along with others in the community, and so on. Such personal knowledge defines how children see the world and determines their expectations about the ideas that are important and the particular ways in which relationships are to be carried out. When children's funds of knowledge are unrecognized in the classroom, children may feel confused or disengaged from lessons.

Another challenge many ethnic minority children and families face is *discrimination,* inequitable treatment as a result of their group membership. Unfortunately, numerous children from ethnic and racial minority groups encounter racist insults from peers, rude

rejection
Form of acculturation in which a person fails to learn or accept any customs and values from a new cultural environment.

selective adoption
Form of acculturation in which a person assumes some customs of a new culture while also retaining some customs of a previous culture.

bicultural orientation
Form of acculturation in which a person is familiar with two cultures and selectively draws from the values and traditions of one or both cultures depending on the context.

DEVELOPMENT IN CULTURE
Immigrant Children

Children in immigrant families have some similar experiences. They go to school, make friends, learn about two or more cultures, and master increasingly difficult concepts and skills. Often they learn a second language and adjust to discrepant expectations between home and the dominant community. But children from immigrant families are by no means fully alike. They have quite different experiences depending on their personal characteristics and the circumstances of their family's immigration, their parents' jobs and income, and their culture's standing in the adopted society (Akiba & García Coll, 2003; Glick & Bates, 2010; Hernandez, Denton, & Macartney, 2010).

Such similarities and differences are evident in elementary school children from immigrant families in Providence, Rhode Island (García Coll & Marks, 2009). Many of the immigrant families there had moved from Cambodia, the Dominican Republic, and Portugal. Children from these three cultural groups had somewhat comparable experiences in that they grew up in low-income families, had parents with high expectations for their education, and achieved at relatively high levels at school. Yet the three groups also varied in their beliefs and customs. Cambodian, Dominican, and Portuguese American children ate the foods of their ancestors, celebrated holidays compatible with their separate heritages, and worshipped in their own churches or temples. Within each group, individual children developed unique habits and self-perceptions.

Families from Cambodia had moved to the United States to escape war, starvation, and persecution. Two parents with approximately 4 years of formal education typically headed Cambodian American families. Parents spoke Khmer to their children and were somewhat segregated from others in the new society. Teachers perceived Cambodian American parents to be uninvolved because the parents rarely came to school. However, from the parents' perspective, parents should defer to teachers' authority and not interfere with instruction. Teachers saw the children as attentive, conscientious, and socially skilled.

Families from the Dominican Republic had typically moved to the United States for economic opportunities and a safe environment for their children. Single-parent and two-parent families were both common among the Dominican immigrants. Families remained closely connected with extended family members back on the island. Families traveled back and forth between Providence and the Dominican Republic for birthdays, weddings, funerals, and family crises, and likewise Dominican relatives often came to visit families in Providence. A strong network of Dominicans in the United States eased the adaptation of new immigrants and enriched children with role models, festivals, and other cultural activities. With their typically dark skin, Dominican American youngsters were perceived to be Black by others, yet the Dominican American children generally identified with their

Dominican heritage and not as African Americans. The children tended to do well in school but frequently received lower grades as they grew older, and they had relatively high rates of absenteeism from school.

Families from Portugal tended to enter long-standing communities of Portuguese Americans. Recently emigrating Portuguese families had moved to the United States for economic opportunities. Most families had two parents in the home. Members of the Portuguese American community celebrated their cultural heritage but also moved in and out of the mainstream society with ease, in part because their White, European American facial features resembled the appearance of many local residents. Established Portuguese sports clubs and religious societies welcomed new immigrants, and numerous Portuguese Americans had penetrated positions of authority, including as police, political officials, and teachers. Two parents with little formal education were the typical heads of family.

Children in each of these three immigrant cultures generally coped well, drew on rich traditions from their family's culture, and took advantage of opportunities in the new land. In other respects the children were quite unique. They developed personally unique ways of expressing themselves and combining the various cultural practices in which they were immersed.

ALIKE, DIFFERENT, AND UNIQUE. Immigrant children face some similar developmental tasks but also differ according to their cultural experiences, family circumstances, and individual characteristics.

treatment from storeowners, and low academic expectations from teachers (G. H. Brody et al., 2006; T. R. Coker et al., 2009). Furthermore, their parents are apt to get less information about home mortgages (even when income and credit history are good) and may encounter discrimination in job interviews, performance reviews, and promotions, sometimes because of overt racist beliefs and at other times because of employers' subtle psychological biases (Roscigno, Karafin, & Tester, 2009; J. C. Ziegert & Hanges, 2005). Due in part to such discrimination, ethnic minority families are more likely than European American families to live in undesirable neighborhoods and to lack sufficient income to purchase books, magazines, and computers.

Children of color must develop coping strategies that allow them to adjust effectively under adverse circumstances (García Coll et al., 1996; McAdoo & Martin, 2005; Swanson et al., 2009; Varela et al., 2004). One coping strategy is to develop a strong **ethnic identity**, an awareness of being a member of a particular group and the commitment to adopting certain values and behaviors characteristic of the group. Youngsters develop their ethnic identity in response to the array of messages they receive from families, peers, community, and the media. They may hear tales of ancestors' struggles and victories in a discriminatory setting and see media portrayals of their ethnic group in particular roles—perhaps as leaders and trailblazers for humane causes or, alternatively, as violent and deviant troublemakers (C. B. Fisher et al., 1998; M. B. Spencer, 2006). Eventually, many youngsters form a coherent set of beliefs about their ethnic group, take pride in their cultural traditions, and reject demeaning messages from other people (Luster, 1992; Ogbu, 1994; Phinney, 1990; M. B. Spencer, Noll, Stoltzfus, & Harpalani, 2001).

A second important coping strategy is to take advantage of confidence-building strategies that are present in some form in every culture. For example, many African American families cultivate positive personal qualities, such as deep religious convictions and commitments to extended family members, which sustain children in difficult environmental conditions, including high unemployment and poverty (Coles, 2006; McCreary, Slavin, & Berry, 1996). Similarly, many children in Hispanic families benefit from their parents' strong work ethic and high educational aspirations for them (García & Jensen, 2007).

Creating Supportive Environments for All Children

With the growing diversity in our population, teachers can expect that, regardless of the community in which they work, they will have the opportunity to work with youngsters from diverse ethnic groups. You can see some illustrations of adults nurturing the strengths of youngsters in the Development and Practice feature "Supporting Children from Culturally and Linguistically Diverse Backgrounds." Here are some related strategies for helping children achieve academic and social success:

• **Reflect on how your own cultural experiences affect your responses to children and families from different cultures.** Like all human beings, teachers generally see their own customs as normal and sensible, particularly if they belong to a dominant culture (P. J. Miller & Goodnow, 1995). Having only superficial contact with another culture, teachers may find its traditions and beliefs as odd or unnatural. Reflecting on your upbringing, privileges, and experiences with other groups can sensitize you to any personal biases you might harbor against children from an unfamiliar culture (H. Wang & Olson, 2009). Also, immersing yourself in community events, reading historical biographies of prominent figures in other groups, and studying anthropologists' reports can enhance your knowledge and sensitivity to other groups.

• **Accept that what you do (and don't do) can perpetuate inequities.** Although very few professionals intentionally discriminate against young people based on their ethnicity or skin color, their actions sometimes perpetuate group differences (Howard, 2007; Sleeter & Grant, 1999). For instance, some teachers rarely modify instruction for students with diverse needs; instead, they present instruction in a take-it-or-leave-it manner. Clearly, teaching children from diverse backgrounds requires more than giving lip service to cultural diversity; it requires a genuine commitment to modifying interactions with children so they can achieve their full academic potential (Bakari, 2000).

• **Recognize the diversity that exists within social groups.** It is human nature to see cultural groups as simple, uniform entities. The reality is that any given group (e.g., children who are Native Americans or those whose families emigrated to the United States) is usually quite heterogeneous. For example, immigrant parents hold beliefs about education that vary depending on their country of origin and their own personal experiences—some might be seasonal migrant workers and others diplomats, foreign-born university students, or political asylum seekers (Kağitçibaşi, 2007). Similarly, the manner in which immigrant children

ethnic identity
Awareness of being a member of a particular ethnic or cultural group and willingness to adopt certain values and behaviors characteristic of that group.

Establish connections with local communities.

- An elementary school in a Mexican American community in Chicago reaches out to families by inviting children, parents, and teachers to take part in Mexican folkloric dance classes after school (Olmedo, 2009). The school includes both Mexican and American flags on an outdoor mural and celebrates the holidays of both nations at school. (Middle Childhood)
- A high school teacher encourages adolescents to take part in community service projects. The students may choose from a wide range of possibilities, including neighborhood cleanups, story time with preschoolers at the library, and volunteer work at a food bank or soup kitchen. (Late Adolescence)

Learn about the *funds of knowledge* children acquire at home.

- A preschool invites families to describe how they use plants in health remedies and meals (Riojas-Cortez et al., 2008). The family's strategies for using plants are integrated into science lessons, and the families are invited to take part in the lessons as well. (Early Childhood)
- A team of educators visits the family of Jacobo, a fourth grader who avoids reading and writing assignments (Genzuk, 1999). The team learns that Jacobo's father is a skilled hydraulics mechanic and that Jacobo himself is interested in mechanics. His teacher asks Jacobo to create an automotive journal that can be used as a resource in the classroom. Jacobo enthusiastically writes in his journal and shares it with others in the class. (Middle Childhood)

Bring children's background experiences into the classroom.

- An infant caregiver purchases compact disks with lullabies in Spanish and Mandarin Chinese, the two languages that are most often spoken by the immigrant families she serves. She regularly plays a song or two from each of the CDs and encourages the babies to clap their hands and sway with the music. (Infancy)
- A teacher asks her second-grade children to bring in lyrics from rap songs and help her select those that are nonoffensive. The children perform the selected songs and analyze them in terms of their literal and figurative meanings, rhyme scheme, and principles of alliteration (Ladson-Billings, 1995). (Middle Childhood)

Adapt to the cultural beliefs and practices of children.

- A Japanese family has recently placed their 8-month-old son in part-time child care. The baby is accustomed to his mother hand feeding him. His new caregiver holds him during mealtime and offers him small pieces of food. (Infancy)
- A third-grade teacher notices that few of the children are willing to answer her questions about common pets, even though it is clear from her individual conversations with them that they have pets and know the answers. She discovers that bringing attention to oneself is not appropriate in the children's culture and so modifies her style to allow for group responses. (Middle Childhood)

Use materials that represent all ethnic groups in a competent light.

- An elementary school librarian examines history books in the school's collection for the manner in which various cultural groups are represented. The librarian orders a few additional books to balance the treatment of groups that are excluded or misrepresented in the existing collection. (Middle Childhood)
- A middle school history teacher peruses a history textbook to make sure that it portrays all ethnic groups in a nonstereotypical manner. He supplements the text with readings that highlight important roles played by members of various ethnic groups throughout history. (Early Adolescence)

Provide opportunities for children of different backgrounds to get to know one another better.

- A teacher invites families to celebrate their children's birthdays at school on one Friday afternoon each month, with summer birthdays celebrated in August and May. The teacher also arranges for volunteers to bring in healthful treats on each Birthday Friday so that no children are inadvertently left out due to diet restrictions. The birthday celebrants are encouraged to bring in a photograph of their families and to tell the class who is in their family and where they are from. (Middle Childhood)
- To promote awareness of and involvement in community issues, a high school teacher engages his class in a large-scale public service project. He forms small groups that work on different phases of the project, for instance collecting data about public opinions, identifying relevant community agencies, and contacting local officials who might be willing to speak to the class. The teacher is careful to form groups that are comprised of children from various neighborhoods and ethnic groups. (Late Adolescence)

Expose youngsters to successful models from various ethnic backgrounds.

- A kindergarten teacher collaborates with a third-grade teacher to establish a reading buddy program. The older children come to kindergarten once a week to read to their buddies. Older children gain experience in reading aloud, and younger children admire their older buddies and learn from their stories. (Early Childhood)
- A middle school teacher invites several successful professionals from minority groups to tell her class about their careers. When some youngsters seem interested in particular career paths, she arranges for them to spend time with these professionals at their workplaces. (Early Adolescence)

Be neutral, inclusive, and respectful regarding children's religious practices.

- A preschool teacher encourages children in her class to bring in artifacts showing how they celebrate holidays during the winter months. Children bring in decorations related to Christmas, Ramadan, Kwanzaa, Hanukkah, and the winter solstice. The teacher passes around the materials and explains that children in her class celebrate many different holidays. (Early Childhood)
- A social studies middle school teacher asks students to select a historical figure who had struggled against religious persecution. After the students have conducted individual investigations, they take part in a class discussion and learn about the wide range of religious groups that have experienced persecution. (Early Adolescence)

Orient recent immigrants to the expectations and institutions of their new land.

- A middle school principal tries to meet with every new immigrant family. At the meeting, the principal hands out a simple welcome basket with a couple of pieces of fruit donated by a local company and a list of community resources in the area. (Early Adolescence)
- A high school offers a Newcomer Program for recent immigrants. The program introduces incoming students to practices in American society and advises students about the school's calendar, extracurricular activities, and sponsored social events (National Clearinghouse for English Language Acquisition, 2006). (Late Adolescence)

Preparing for Your Licensure Examination
Your teaching test might ask you to identify cultural differences in language, communication, and interpersonal relationships that can be accommodated in the classroom.

learn English in the United States varies according to ethnicity and cultural origin (Leventhal, Xue, & Brooks-Gunn, 2006). And, of course, children within a given group have varied interests, skills, and views that transcend their group's general patterns. Teachers can get to know children as individuals by asking them about their hopes for the future, preferences for spending free time, responsibilities at home, and prior experiences with academic subjects (Villegas & Lucas, 2007).

• **Allow children to follow practices from two or more cultures.** Earlier we introduced the idea that immigrant children often adjust well when they hold onto their family's cultural beliefs and practices rather than fully replace these beliefs and practices with those favored by the dominant society. The same principle holds for multiethnic children: Children raised by parents from different ethnic cultures are likely to value traditions from both sides of the family. Teachers and other practitioners can recognize that children who are exposed to more than one culture need tolerant settings in which they can safely explore separate parts of their multifaceted cultural heritage.

• **Make an effort to accommodate the practices and values of children's cultures.** Practitioners increase their effectiveness with youngsters by tailoring their services to children's cultural backgrounds (Council of National Psychological Associations for the Advancement of Ethnic Minority Interests, 2009; Howard, 2007; Villegas & Lucas, 2007). Being careful not to stereotype children, teachers can occasionally use instructional strategies that are sufficiently flexible that they allow children to use some of their cultural strengths and traditions. For example, a teacher may include some assignments that permit children to work either alone or with others. The Observation Guidelines table "Identifying Cultural Practices and Beliefs" on page 101 lists some values and styles of approaching tasks that teachers and other school personnel can accommodate.

culturally responsive teaching
A teacher's use of particular instructional strategies based on knowledge of children's cultural backgrounds and individual characteristics.

• **Include numerous cultural perspectives in curricula and instructional strategies.** As societies become the multicultural mosaic we spoke of earlier, it is essential that schools reflect this diversity. In **culturally responsive teaching**, teachers learn about children's cultural backgrounds and individual characteristics and use this information as they select curricula and instructional strategies (Brayboy & Castagno, 2009; Santamaria, 2009; Villegas & Lucas, 2007). Hence, a teacher might examine immigration during a social studies unit and invite parents to come to class and discuss their experiences in moving from one society to another. Teachers can also select multicultural curricula that include the contributions of people from more than one culture. Following are illustrations of what teachers might do:

ARTIFACT 3-5 Light. In the elementary years, children are able to understand basic differences in the way people of different cultures live. Nine-year-old Dana learned about how different people use natural and artificial light. Art by Dana.

• In history, look at wars and other major events from more than one perspective (e.g., the Spanish perspective of the Spanish-American War and Native American groups' views of pioneers' westward migration in North America).
• In social studies, examine discrimination and oppression.
• In mathematics, use numerical problems that refer to traditional legends and calendars.
• In literature, present the work of minority authors and poets.
• In art, consider creations and techniques by artists from around the world.
• In music, teach songs from many cultures and nations.
• In physical education, teach games or folk dances from other countries and cultures. (Asai, 1993; Averill et al., 2009; Boutte & McCormick, 1992; NCSS Task Force on Ethnic Studies Curriculum Guidelines, 1992; Pang, 1995; Sleeter & Grant, 1999)

Children of different ages have varying abilities to understand the symbolic meaning of another culture's customs. Thus teachers should adjust their culturally responsive strategies

OBSERVATION GUIDELINES
Identifying Cultural Practices and Beliefs

CHARACTERISTIC	LOOK FOR	EXAMPLE	IMPLICATION
Individualism	• *Independence*, assertiveness, and self-reliance • *Eagerness to pursue individual assignments* and tasks • *Willingness to compete* against others • *Pride in one's own accomplishments*	When given the choice of doing a project either by herself or with a partner, Melissa decides to work alone. She is thrilled when she earns a third-place ribbon in a statewide competition.	Provide time for independent work, and accommodate children's individual achievement levels. Give feedback about personal accomplishments in private rather than in front of peers.
Collectivism	• *Willingness to depend on others* • *Emphasis on group accomplishments* over individual achievements • *Preference for cooperative rather than competitive tasks* • *Concern about bringing honor* to one's family • *Strong sense of loyalty* to other family members	Tsusha is a talented and hard-working seventh grader. She is conscientious about bringing home her graded work assignments to show her parents but appears uncomfortable when praised in front of classmates.	Stress group progress and achievement more than individual successes. Make frequent use of cooperative learning activities.
Behavior Toward Authority Figures	• *Looking down* in the presence of an authority figure (common in some Native American, African American, Mexican American, and Puerto Rican children) vs. looking an authority figure in the eye (common in some children of European American descent) • *Observing an adult quietly* (an expectation in some Native American and some Hispanic groups) vs. asking questions when one doesn't understand (common in some European American groups)	A Native American child named Jimmy never says a word to his teacher. He appears frightened when his teacher looks him in the eye and greets him each morning. One day, the teacher looks in another direction and says, "Hello, Jimmy" as he enters the classroom. "Why hello Miss Jacobs," he responds enthusiastically (Gilliland, 1988, p. 26).	Recognize that different cultures show respect for authority figures in different ways; don't misinterpret lack of eye contact or nonresponse as an indication of disinterest or disrespect.
Valued Activities	• *Hopes for high achievement* in traditional academic areas (common in many cultural groups in Western countries) • *Personal values* for school achievement but lack of confidence in performing academically in some students • *Expectations for excellence* in culture-specific activities, such as art or dance (often seen in traditional Native American and Polynesian communities)	Clarence is obviously a very bright young man, but he reveals considerable ambivalence about showing his knowledge in front of peers. He often earns high marks in papers he write, but he rarely participates in class discussions and does not seem to show his knowledge on tests.	Show how academic subjects relate to children's lives. Acknowledge youngsters' achievement in nonacademic as well as academic pursuits. Continually communicate confidence in the potential achievement of youngsters and encourage hard work and good study habits. Be sensitive to children's feelings about being praised or displaying skills in front of others.
Conceptions of Time	• *Concern for punctuality* and acknowledgment of deadlines for assignments (common for some students of European descent) • *Relaxed feelings about specific times* and schedules (observed in some Hispanic and Native American communities)	Lucy and her parents are diligent about going to parent–teacher conferences but often arrive well after their scheduled time.	Encourage punctuality as a way of enhancing children's long-term success in mainstream Western society. At the same time, recognize that not all children are especially concerned about clock time. Be flexible when parents seem to disregard strict schedules.

Sources: Banks & Banks, 1995; Basso, 1984; Council of National Psychological Associations for the Advancement of Ethnic Minority Interests, 2009; García, 1994; Garrison, 1989; Gilliland, 1988; C. A. Grant & Gomez, 2001; Heath, 1983; Irujo, 1988; Kağitçibaşi, 2007; Kirschenbaum, 1989; Losey, 1995; Maschinot, 2008; McAlpine & Taylor, 1993; L. S. Miller, 1995; Ogbu, 1994; Oyserman & Lee, 2007; N. Reid, 1989; Shweder et al., 1998; M. B. Spencer, 2006; Tharp, 1994; Torres-Guzmán, 1998; Trawick-Smith, 2003; Triandis, 2007.

to the age range of their students. During middle childhood, children can learn about the tangible, concrete customs and livelihoods of different cultures. As children grow older, they become increasingly able to learn details, motivations, and underlying symbolism of different people's traditions.

Preparing for Your Licensure Examination

Your teaching test might ask you to identify ways to integrate children's cultural backgrounds into curricula.

• **Address gaps in children's understandings.** Some children who have missed a lot of school or previously studied in culturally *un*responsive schools lack basic skills. Teachers can help children by addressing the academic areas in which children have delays. Expressing a concern for children while teaching them basic skills are both key strategies, as a fifth-grade teacher at one school discovered when she considered the implications of culturally responsive teaching for a Hispanic student learning English:

> [The student] ". . . couldn't put two sentences together, let alone write the five-paragraph essay that is required to pass our 5th grade assessment." The teacher's first reaction was to ask, "How was this student allowed to slip by all these years without learning anything beyond 2nd grade writing skills?" When the teacher launched her [Culturally Responsive Teaching] project, however, her perspective became more proactive. She realized that she couldn't just deliver the 5th grade curriculum—she had to meet this student where he was. She built a personal connection with the student, learned about his family culture and interests (a fascination with monkeys was a major access point), and used this relationship to reinforce his academic development. The student responded to her high expectations and passed his 5th grade writing assessment. (Howard, 2007, p. 20)

Improving Your Observation Skills

The new arrivals. Thirteen-year-old Carol took these notes in her American history class. Throughout the unit, her teacher made a point of discussing the perspectives of different groups. What is Carol learning about the experiences of distinct groups who came to the New World in the 1600s? Compare your response with the explanation at the end of the chapter.

• **Foster respect for diverse cultures and ethnic groups.** When talking about cultural practices, teachers can emphasize the merits of particular traditions. Teachers can also select materials that represent cultural groups in a positive light—for instance, by choosing books and movies that portray people of varying ethnic backgrounds as legitimate participants in society rather than as exotic "curiosities" who live in a separate world. Educators should also avoid (or at least comment critically on) materials that portray members of minority groups in an overly simplistic, romanticized, exaggerated, or otherwise stereotypical fashion (Banks, 1994; Boutte & McCormick, 1992; Pang, 1995).

• **Create opportunities for children from different backgrounds to interact.** When youngsters have positive interactions with people from backgrounds other than their own, they gain further respect for different cultures. In schools in which children come from several distinct backgrounds, teachers and school counselors might promote friendships among students from different groups by using cooperative learning activities, teaching simple phrases in other students' native languages, and encouraging schoolwide participation in extracurricular activities. In culturally homogeneous schools, professionals might take youngsters beyond school boundaries—perhaps engaging them in community service projects or arranging a visit to a culturally inclusive center for the arts.

• **When cultural conflicts occur, find constructive ways to address them.** Occasionally, children and families follow cultural practices that are contradictory—at least on the surface—to those adhered to in the classroom. When this happens, it is a good idea to learn more about these practices. Investing in such an effort can better help practitioners understand why children act as they do and what accommodations might be made ("OK, avoiding certain foods shows their religious devotion; I can certainly offer other snack choices").

Showing respect for diverse cultural perspectives does not necessarily mean that "anything goes" or that there are no moral judgments to be made. No one, for example, needs to embrace a cultural practice in which some people's basic human rights are blatantly violated. Showing respect does mean, however, that adults and children must try to understand another cultural group's behaviors within the entirety of that culture's beliefs and traditions (M. N. Cohen, 1998).

• **Confront inequities.** As you have learned, children of color and those from immigrant groups often face discrimination. Educators can take the stand that inequities will *not* be tolerated at school. To profess its commitment to fairness and justice, one school district displays a statement of "Equity Vision":

> Roseville Area Schools is committed to ensuring an equitable and respectful educational experience for every student, family, and staff member, regardless of race, gender, sexual orientation, socioeconomic status, ability, home or first language, religion, national origin, or age. (Howard, 2007, p. 20)

Of course, children and families want to see good words backed up with good deeds. Teachers and principals must confront any policies that inadvertently favor one group or another (e.g., assigning inexperienced teachers to work with students who need the most help, having low expectations for students from ethnic minority backgrounds, and preferentially treating subgroups of students when selecting recipients for awards) (Villegas & Lucas, 2007).

Community Resources

Communities differ in a number of ways that influence children. Here we examine the impact of the community and family income on children's development and offer recommendations for working with children from low-income families.

Type of Community

Communities vary in their population density and geographical features, including climate, natural resources, and predominant cultures. These and other features of the community influence the opportunities and experiences of children.

Children in large cities live side by side with thousands and sometimes millions of others in a relatively confined region. These children often have ready access to ongoing events and resources related to music, art, drama, science, sports, and diverse cultures. Not every child in a big city can take advantage of its splendors, however. Some families can afford to live in nicely maintained houses, enroll their children in well-staffed schools, and take their children to museums, concerts, and sports events. Others cannot. Forced to live in unsafe neighborhoods, economically poor families and their children regularly encounter such problems as drugs, violence, crime, and racial segregation (D. S. Massey & Denton, 1993; Schaefer-McDaniel, 2007). Disadvantaged families often have little choice but to send their children to dilapidated schools with records of low student achievement and limited success in recruiting and retaining highly qualified teachers (Berliner, 2009; Dichele & Gordon, 2007; Jacob, 2007).

Families living in rural settings typically share their community with 2,500 or fewer citizens (B. K. Lawrence, 2009). Rural families, particularly those residing in farming communities, structure chores so that all family members contribute to the family's economic livelihood and periodically help neighbors with such seasonal projects as harvesting crops. As a result, rural families often foster a cooperative spirit and strong work ethic in children (García, 1994; B. K. Lawrence, 2009). A downside of rural environments is that many students must travel many miles to attend school each day and may not be able to participate in extracurricular activities (North Central Regional Educational Laboratory, 2008). Furthermore, some rural schools spend such a high proportion of available funds on transportation services that insufficient resources remain to invest in computers, Internet access, and professional development for teachers (Provasnik et al., 2007; Ullman, 2010b).

ARTIFACT 3-6 Day at the museum. Children learn a lot from visiting institutions in their community. After visiting an art museum, 6-year-old Lee drew this picture, representing themes of religion and warfare that he had perceived in the museum's paintings.

Families living in suburban communities reside in residential areas that are within commuting distance from a large city. On average, families in suburban communities have higher incomes than those who live in inner cities or rural areas, schools are often of higher quality, children are able to visit the cultural sights of the big city, nearly everyone has a bit of backyard and privacy, and children can play safely outdoors. As a result of these and other advantages, more high school students from suburban cities attend college than do students from big cities or rural areas (National Center for Education Statistics, 2007). However, economic resources are not equally distributed in suburban communities, not all young people have an optimistic outlook about their chances for future success, and students in suburban schools are as likely and sometimes more likely as their counterparts in large cities to engage in such risky behaviors as drinking alcohol and using illegal drugs (Greene & Forster, 2004; Luthar & Goldstein, 2008; Robbins, Dollard, Armstrong, Kutash, & Vergon, 2008).

Family Income

A child's experience in a community is strongly affected by the family's personal and financial resources. This idea is captured in the notion of the family's **socioeconomic status (SES)**, its standing in the community based on such variables as family income level, the prestige of parents' jobs, and parents' levels of education. A family's socioeconomic status—whether high-SES, middle-SES, or low-SES—gives us a sense of how much flexibility family members have with regard to where they live and what they buy, how much influence they have in political decision making, what educational opportunities they can offer children, and so on.

Children from high- and middle-SES families enjoy many material comforts and usually go to well-equipped schools with teachers who are experienced and amply trained in the subjects they teach. Children are generally encouraged by parents to learn productive skills in such after-school activities as soccer leagues and ballet classes. Families also socialize children to cooperate in structured team settings and negotiate with authority figures (Lareau, 2003). Parents speak often to children, expose them to sophisticated vocabulary, and foster their reasoning skills. Yet children in these families face disadvantages, including frequently being overcommitted and having little time to play. Despite attending good schools and living in safe neighborhoods, these children are at risk for emotional problems and substance abuse when parents put excessive pressure on them or do not become involved in their day-to-day activities (Luthar & Latendresse, 2005).

Children from low-income families have fewer material resources but nevertheless encounter definite advantages. In many low-income families, children receive substantial emotional support and are allowed discretion in how they spend their free time and consequently learn to manage their freedom creatively and effectively (Lareau, 2003). Even so, children from low-income families are not always prepared for the academic demands of school. Their parents do not regularly engage them in extended verbal give-and-take, nor do these parents encourage them to ask questions of, or assert themselves with, authority figures.

Children Living in Economic Poverty

Some families do not merely scrape by with limited means. They go without. Families in economic poverty have so little in financial resources that their ability to nurture children can be compromised (G. W. Evans & Kim, 2007; Hoover-Dempsey & Sandler, 1997; McLoyd, 1998b). Approximately 18 percent of U.S. children live in poverty (Federal Interagency Forum on Child and Family Statistics, 2009).

Children and adolescents living in poverty face serious challenges. Typical problems include these:

- *Poor nutrition and health care.* Some children are poorly fed and have little access to adequate health care; as a result, they may suffer from malnutrition and other chronic health problems.
- *Inadequate housing and material goods.* Many children live in tight quarters, perhaps sharing one or two rooms with several other family members. Some children have no place to live at all, except, perhaps, the family car or a homeless shelter. Children from

---

Preparing for Your Licensure Examination

Your teaching test might ask you about the kinds of risks experienced by children from low-income families.

socioeconomic status (SES) One's general standing in an economically stratified society, encompassing family income, type of job, and education level.

homeless families are sometimes reluctant to go to school because they lack bathing facilities and presentable clothing. Even the most basic school supplies may be beyond their reach.

- *Toxic environment.* Compared to their well-to-do peers, children in economically disadvantaged families are more likely to be exposed to factory pollution, toxic waste dumps, allergens that trigger asthma, and excessive noise.

- *Gaps in background knowledge.* Teachers typically assume that children have had certain kinds of experiences before they begin school—for instance, that they have been read to, have seen many kinds of animals at farms or zoos, and have had ample opportunities to explore their physical environment. However, some children who live in extreme poverty miss out on these foundational experiences. At home, poor children are, on average, less often spoken to and receive less overall cognitive stimulation than do children from economically advantaged families.

- *Increased probability of disabling conditions.* Children who live in poverty are more likely to have physical, mental, or social-emotional disabilities. Low-income families do not always have an adequate support network to address these disabilities.

- *Emotional stress.* Many poor children and their families live in chronically stressful conditions, constantly worrying about where their next meal is coming from or how long the landlord will wait before evicting them for not paying the rent. Experiencing chronic emotional stresses, low-income parents sometimes lose their patience with children and become punitive and insensitive. The many pressures of poverty also can undermine children's memory, attention, and coping skills.

- *Lower quality schools.* Schools in low-income neighborhoods and communities are often poorly funded and equipped, and they have high teacher turnover rates. Furthermore, some teachers at these schools have lower expectations for students— and offer a less demanding curriculum, assign less homework, and set lower standards for performance—than teachers of middle-SES students.

- *Public misconceptions.* People from economically advantaged backgrounds often have mixed feelings about low-SES families: They may feel pity yet simultaneously believe that poor people are responsible for their misfortunes, perhaps because of laziness, promiscuity, or overdependence on social welfare programs (L. M. Berger, Paxson, & Waldfogel, 2009; Berliner, 2006, 2009; G. W. Evans & Kim, 2007; G. W. Evans & Schamberg, 2009; Gershoff, Aber, & Raver, 2005; Linver, Brooks-Gunn, & Kohen, 2002; McLoyd, 1998a; McLoyd et al., 2009; Murnane, 2007; Payne, DeVol, & Smith, 2006; Sidel, 1996).

Some children and adolescents find the challenges of poverty so overwhelming that they engage in behaviors—dropping out of school, abusing drugs and alcohol, participating in criminal activities—that create further problems. However, many other children and adolescents from poor families do well despite the adversities they face: They are relatively hardy as they confront life's hardships (Abelev, 2009; Kim-Cohen, Moffitt, Caspi, & Taylor, 2004; Schilling, 2008). These youngsters show **resilience**, an ability to thrive despite adverse environmental conditions. For instance, almost half of low-income high school graduates subsequently enroll in college (National Center for Education Statistics, 2003). Let's examine strategies educators use to nurture this resilience in low-income youngsters.

RESILIENCE. Children and adolescents from low-income families show a strong ability to surmount life's challenges. These Columbian children live in poverty yet are socially skilled and mutually supportive.

Working with Children from Low-Income Families

Adults who want to make a difference in children's lives are especially likely to do so in schools and other institutions serving low-SES populations. But to be effective, teachers and other adults must be committed to their jobs, think creatively about how they can make the most of limited resources, and show a contagious enthusiasm for learning (L. W. Anderson & Pellicer, 1998;

resilience
Ability of some youngsters (often enhanced with environmental support) to thrive despite adverse environmental conditions.

E. H. Ogden & Germinario, 1988). Experts offer these recommendations for working with children from low-income families:

• **Invest in children's strengths.** Youngsters may become easily discouraged and resign themselves to the idea that their efforts are in vain when their teachers have concentrated on their weaknesses. In contrast, focusing on what's *right* with children can generate optimism, enthusiasm, and a definite commitment to learning in children. It doesn't take too long to figure out children's strengths when you are intentionally looking for them. Many children of poor immigrant families have two parents at home to support them; are physically healthy; and have extended families concerned with their welfare (Shields & Behrman, 2004). Adolescents who work part time to help their families make ends meet may have a sense of purpose for their lives and a good understanding of the working world (Schilling, 2008). Children of single, working parents may know far more than peers about cooking, cleaning, and taking care of younger siblings (Whiting & Edwards, 1988).

• **Foster a sense of community.** Children from low-income backgrounds may appreciate teachers' efforts to build a **sense of community**—a collection of shared beliefs that individuals in the group (e.g., a class or school) have common goals, respect one another's efforts, and believe that everyone makes an important contribution (L. W. Anderson & Pellicer, 1998; Watson & Battistich, 2006). Teachers can assign chores on a rotating basis, use cooperative learning activities, involve children and adolescents in cross-grade tutoring, and encourage everyone's participation in extracurricular activities (Downey, 2000). Because youngsters often feel more connected to their community when, in some small way, they give something back, educators can also sponsor community service projects. Children and their teachers might conduct a neighborhood cleanup, volunteer in a nursing home, serve as readers at the local library, or raise funds to benefit community causes (Ladson-Billings, 1994).

• **Convey clear and consistent expectations for children's behavior.** For all children, and especially for those who have had more than their share of life's challenges, knowing what's expected is important. Hence adults need to describe their expectations in clear, concrete terms (Downey, 2000). For instance, when finishing lunch in the cafeteria, children might be asked explicitly to "empty the napkins and leftovers into the trash bin, put the trays and dishes on the counter, and go quietly outside." When working in cooperative groups, young people might be reminded, "Everyone needs to participate in the discussions and contribute to the group project."

• **Show relevance of academic skills to children's lives and needs.** Finding personal relevance in classroom activities and subject matter is important for any child, but it may be especially critical for children from low-SES backgrounds (L. W. Anderson & Pellicer, 1998). Helping children see how they can use skills in their everyday lives makes learning meaningful as well as motivating.

• **Acquaint children with institutions in their community.** When children have not had the opportunity to see institutions in their society, they can often learn a lot from brief visits. Teachers sometimes take their classes on field trips to a zoo, museum, post office, fire station, and so forth, and thereby create new knowledge for children to build on in academic lessons. When field trips are too expensive or logistically impossible, an alternative is to bring the community to children—perhaps by having a representative of the local zoo bring some of the zoo's smaller residents to the children or by asking a police officer to describe the many public services that the police department provides.

• **Encourage children to get involved in extracurricular activities** Participation in sports and after-school activities can be instrumental in developing worthwhile skills and decreasing such risky behaviors as drug use, thefts, and violence (McLoyd et al., 2009). Teachers and other practitioners can encourage young people to get involved in fun and rewarding activities while helping them to take advantage of the community resources necessary to offset any expenses required for participation in the groups.

• **Communicate high expectations for children's success.** Some children from low-SES backgrounds do not expect much of their own academic skills. Yet teachers can communicate

sense of community
In a classroom or school, a collection of widely shared beliefs that students, teachers, and other staff have common goals, support one another's efforts, and make important contributions to everyone's success.

a can-do attitude, encourage students to challenge themselves, and provide support to help students reach their goals. Offering help sessions for challenging classroom material, finding low-cost academic enrichment programs available during the summer, helping adolescents fill out applications for college scholarships, and arranging for them to take college admission tests are just a few examples of such support (Kunjufu, 2006).

• **Give homeless children school supplies and help them ease into new communities.** Educators who work with children of homeless families can help them adjust to their new settings. For example, teachers, principals, and school counselors might pair homeless children with classmates who can explain school procedures and introduce them to peers; provide a notebook, clipboard, or other portable "desk" on which children can do their homework at the shelter; find adult or teenage volunteers to tutor them at the shelter; ask civic organizations to donate school supplies; meet with parents at the shelter rather than at school; and share copies of homework assignments, school calendars, and newsletters with shelter officials (Pawlas, 1994).

• **Be a mentor.** Young people from low-income families often benefit from the assistance of adults who befriend them and help them to navigate through challenges at school. A trusted teacher, counselor, or coach can show children how to express their needs and interests in educational environments. Particularly when youngsters encounter serious obstacles in their schooling, for example, failing subjects, missing school, or becoming a teenage parent, mentors can suggest practical ways to overcome difficulties and intensify the drive to make progress in school (Abelev, 2009; Schilling, 2008).

• **Advocate for the improvement of schools in economically disadvantaged areas.** Teachers and other practitioners can join community groups that are trying to improve schools. A variety of initiatives have been productive, including efforts to work within existing school systems and others that develop charter schools and alternative schools with clear objectives and strong family involvement (Fruchter, 2007; Kunjufu, 2006).

Virtually all children face challenges of one kind or another—perhaps stressful family dynamics, a mismatch between home and school cultures, or extremely limited economic resources. Yet virtually all children want to be successful in school and in the world at large. By attending to children's risks but also building on their strengths, teachers and other practitioners can, without doubt, help children make significant progress in their developmental journeys.

SUMMARY

Cradles of Child Development

Family, culture, and community provide essential foundations for child development. These three contexts teach children who they are as human beings, how they should relate to others, and what they can aspire to become as adults. Educators can help children by considering the interactive effects of the three contexts on children's behavior and well-being.

Family Structures

Families come in many forms, including two-parent families, single-parent families, stepfamilies, adoptive families, foster families, extended families, and numerous other types. Many youngsters experience one or more changes in family structure (e.g., as a result of divorce, remarriage, or death of a parent) at some point during their childhood. Individual family structures present unique benefits and challenges for children, but ultimately the quality of family relationships exceeds family structure in developmental significance. Teachers can be inclusive of families by recognizing the existence of many structures and encouraging families of all kinds to support their children's academic progress.

Family Processes

Parents influence children's development by building relationships, engaging children in activities, and showing affection and disciplining children. Children influence their families, in turn, by virtue of their temperaments, interests, and abilities. Children also influence one another as siblings, but having a sibling is not vital to normal, healthy development.

Most families provide safe and nurturing environments for children. However, some families maltreat children, either by neglecting them or by subjecting them to physical, sexual, or emotional abuse. Such maltreatment can have negative long-term effects on children's development.

Effective partnerships between educators and families rest on respect and communication. Teachers can validate the culture and contributions of families. They can also use several methods of communication (e.g., parent–teacher–student conferences, newsletters, the telephone), and they can encourage parents to become actively involved in their children's education.

Children in a Diverse Society

Children and families are profoundly affected by their experiences in ethnic, cultural, and immigrant groups. To a large extent, children's ethnicity affects their values, actions, and styles of communicating. Children also are influenced by their community's character and by the incomes of their families. Educators can build on children's experiences in the community and importantly, help economically disadvantaged children by providing support, resources, and acknowledgment of children's personal strengths.

APPLYING CONCEPTS IN CHILD DEVELOPMENT

The exercises in this section will help you build your ability to apply your knowledge of child development in your work with children.

Improving Your Observation Skills

On page 70, you examined two pictures of neighborhoods and were asked, "*What developmental differences are present in drawings of neighborhoods by Marsalis, age 7½ (top), and James, age 13 (bottom)?*" The younger child, Marsalis, drew a picture of his own house and yard. The older child, James, drew a picture of the broader community, a local river, and a bridge that he may be able to reach by bicycle. It is common for children to become increasingly involved in their community as they grow older and become more proficient in exploring surrounding areas.

On page 75, you examined a poem written by 9½-year-old Shea and were asked, "*How does Shea perceive Ann, who had been a family member for about 3 years at the time Shea wrote the poem?*" Shea's poem reveals the close relationship she had developed with her stepmother, Ann. Shea perceives her stepmother as a kind and reliable caregiver who enriches her life, helps her to learn productive skills, and shares enjoyable leisure time with her. Children in blended families face certain challenges, for example becoming adjusted to their new parents' habits and personalities and forming affectionate bonds with them, and Shea shows that she was well able to accomplish these ends.

On page 102, you examined the history notes recorded by 13-year-old Carol and were asked, "*What is Carol learning about the experiences of distinct groups who came to the New World in the 1600s?*" Carol's notes show that she learned about the hardships faced by men and women in the New World in the 1600s; she also learned about European settlers, African settlers, and enslaved Africans. Depending on their age, children acquire insights about different groups that vary in level of abstractness and comprehensiveness. Carol is exposed to numerous concepts about distinct groups of immigrants and may be developing an appreciation for how profoundly different their experiences were.

Practicing for Your Licensure Examination

Many teaching tests require students to use what they have learned about child development in responses to brief vignettes and multiple-choice questions. You can practice for your licensure examination by reading the following case study and answering a series of questions.

Four-Year-Old Sons

Read the case and then answer the questions that follow it.

A common behavior displayed by preschoolers is asking a lot of *why* questions. Consider how two mothers of 4-year-old boys interpret their sons' incessant questioning (Belenky, Bond, & Weinstock, 1997). Elizabeth describes her son Charles as being disrespectful in questioning her authority. For example, when Elizabeth tells Charles not to touch a dead bug, he questions her about why the insect is dead and why he shouldn't touch it. She believes his frequent questions reflect his intention to anger her by not listening respectfully or accepting her statements.

In contrast, Joyce describes her son Peter as having an insatiable curiosity. She believes that his frequent questions are a natural outgrowth of his need to analyze the world around him. She sees his responses to her requests as a natural outgrowth of his mental reflections. She admires and appreciates her son's questions because she believes that he sees implications of objects and events that she misses, and his questions help her to think through what they are doing together.

Constructed-Response Question

1. How do the two mothers interpret their sons' questions differently?

Multiple-Choice Questions

2. How might a teacher form partnerships with these mothers?

    a. A teacher could ask each of the mothers about their goals for children.

    b. A teacher could advise the mothers that young children are naturally curious and regularly ask a lot of questions to find out about the world.

    c. A teacher could use a variety of formats to inform parents of preschool events, for example, calling the mothers on the telephone and sending home newsletters about classroom activities.

    d. A teacher could try all of the strategies listed above.

3. Is there evidence from the description of Elizabeth that she is maltreating her son?

    a. No, because emotional abuse is not considered a type of maltreatment.

b. No, because although Elizabeth expresses her frustration with her son's frequent questioning, she refers to nothing that is a clear manifestation of maltreatment.
c. Yes, because Elizabeth clearly dislikes her son.
d. Yes, because impatience with a child's questioning is an indication of maltreatment.

Once you have answered these questions, compare your responses with those presented in Appendix A.

Improving Your Ability to Interpret Children's Artifacts and Reflections

Consider chapter concepts as you analyze the following responses from youngsters.

In My Neighborhood

Nicole Schaefer-McDaniel interviewed young adolescents living in New York City about their perceptions of their neighborhoods. As you read excerpts from the interviews, consider aspects of the neighborhoods that may have supported the adolescents' development and other aspects that may have presented challenges. Some of the youngsters are quoted more than once.

John, age 11: [The park] is always peaceful and not a lot of noise. It always quiet and no trouble happening here. (Schaefer-McDaniel, 2007, p. 422)[a]

Melanie, age 13: It's [the park] big and enough for everybody and they got card tables that what we do basically is play cards and it's right next to like if we were playing in the house, we walk right down the block [to the park] . . . there's a whole lot of stuff to do and it's like you don't have to walk far. (p. 423)

[a] "They Be Doing Illegal Things: Early Adolescents Talk About Their Inner-City Neighborhoods" by Nicole Schaefer-McDaniel, from JOURNAL OF ADOLESCENT RESEARCH, July 2007, Volume 22(4). Copyright © 2007 by Nicole Schaefer-McDaniel. Reprinted with permission of SAGE Publications.

Latisha, age 11: It [the neighborhood] is good 'cause there's good parts around there and there's restaurants and that's the best part about my neighborhood food . . . and [hair] salons. (p. 424)

Tyrone, age 11: The entire avenue . . . there's a lot of violence there especially when there's a block party . . . some people comes with guns. (p. 425)

Latisha, age 11: It's [the neighborhood] good 'cause the . . . cops are always around there just in case something happens. (p. 425)

Romel, age 12: We have real protection and cops . . . and like because like right next to our school is like three [police] stations and up there . . . there's nothing . . . so anything goes wrong you got police right here. (p. 426)

Mike, age 11: . . . 'cause my mother thinks it's too dangerous around there . . . so I either go to backyard in school or sometime I go [to another nearby school yard] . . . this block is dangerous . . . this one is dangerous . . . so I don't really like these blocks . . . I'd rather stay on my block. (p. 426)

Melanie, age 13: A lot of men out there and they always like fighting . . . and I don't like to walk past places in the night where there's a whole bunch of men. (p. 427)

John, age 11: You can see a lot of trash . . . a lot . . . people just throw them trash bags. (p. 427)

Latisha, age 11: What I hate the most is around here a lot of buildings get burned and some of the buildings they have a fire and the building burns down. (p. 428)

Once you have analyzed the artifact, compare your ideas with those presented in Appendix B. For further practice in analyzing children's artifacts and reflections, go to the Activities and Applications section in Chapter 3 of MyEducationLab.

Key Concepts

family (p. 68)
socialization (p. 68)
individualistic culture (p. 69)
collectivistic culture (p. 69)
community (p. 69)
family structure (p. 72)
coparents (p. 73)

stepfamily (p. 75)
self-regulation (p. 79)
parenting style (p. 79)
authoritative parenting style (p. 80)
authoritarian parenting style (p. 80)
permissive parenting style (p. 80)
uninvolved parenting style (p. 80)

guided participation (p. 81)
child maltreatment (p. 84)
ethnicity (p. 94)
acculturation (p. 95)
assimilation (p. 95)
rejection (p. 96)
selective adoption (p. 96)

bicultural orientation (p. 96)
ethnic identity (p. 98)
culturally responsive teaching (p. 100)
socioeconomic status (SES) (p. 104)
resilience (p. 105)
sense of community (p. 106)

myeducationlab

Now go to www.myeducationlab.com to:
- Take a Quiz to test your mastery of chapter objectives.
- Study chapter content with an individualized Study Plan.
- Deepen your understanding of particular concepts and principles with Review, Remediation, and Enrichment Exercises.
- Apply what you have learned in the chapter to your work with children in Building Teaching Skills and Dispositions exercises.
- Observe children and their unique contexts in Video Examples.

Chapter Four

Biological Beginnings

CASE STUDY: Birthing the Baby

Laurie and Tom had hoped for a natural childbirth with their first child, but during Laurie's labor, she had lost confidence and complied with her doctor's advice to take medications for strengthening contractions and diminishing pain (Bailes & Jackson, 2000). The outcome of her labor was joyous—a healthy son, Evan—but for a long time afterwards, the new parents regretted that Laurie had felt compelled to take somewhat risky and possibly unnecessary medications.

When Laurie and Tom learned they were expecting their second child, they planned once again for a natural childbirth, this time more deliberately. Laurie would deliver the baby at home with help from Tom and the midwife. The doctor would meet them at the hospital (a 5-minute drive from Laurie and Tom's house) if medical intervention proved necessary. Laurie's mother would look after Evan and support the laboring parents.

With a definite birth plan in place, Laurie relaxed. She saw a doctor, had regular checkups with her nurse-midwife, and ate well. Laurie and Tom prepared the nursery and helped Evan anticipate changes to his family. Baby-to-be grew quietly. And they all waited.

One evening close to her due date, Laurie went to sleep as usual but woke at 2 a.m. with clear fluid leaking from her body. Her membranes had broken. Labor was imminent. She called her midwife, who asked her to take her temperature and try to go back to sleep. Her temperature was normal, and Laurie slept a little. She woke at 6:30 a.m. and fed Evan. Two hours later, the midwife arrived and evaluated Laurie's condition and the baby's heart rate. Everyone was ready.

Productive contractions had not yet begun, however. The midwife reminded Laurie that her doctor wanted to become involved if labor had not started within 12 hours after her membranes had broken. Laurie became concerned. She, Tom, and the midwife put their heads together.

> The three of them jointly formulated a plan to encourage labor to start and to monitor maternal and fetal well-being. Laurie would walk, do nipple stimulation, rest, eat, and increase her fluid intake. She would also check her pulse and temperature every 3–4 hours.[a] (p. 541)

Yet Laurie had not experienced regular contractions when the midwife returned at 2 p.m. Tests performed by the midwife indicated that Laurie and the baby were fine. The midwife telephoned the doctor, who decided he would be willing to wait to intervene until the next morning as long as Laurie consented to take antibiotics to prevent infection. Laurie agreed.

Eventually, contractions began in earnest and then unexpectedly slowed down. Laurie worried that her labor would stall, as it had with her first baby. The midwife reassured Laurie but decided to give the couple their privacy and went home. During a later phone call, the midwife suggested that Laurie and Tom go for a brisk walk. When they returned, contractions intensified. The baby was coming!

By 3 a.m., Laurie's contractions were sharp. Laurie and Tom got into the shower to aid relaxation and then settled down to carry out the special things they had planned for labor. Laurie nibbled on an omelet Tom prepared with herbs he had grown in their garden. Tom read scriptures and then turned off the lights and massaged Laurie's back. The midwife checked the fetal heart tone (FHT) to ensure the well-being of the baby. Laurie labored away.

> By 5:30 AM, daylight began to come through the bedroom windows, renewing Laurie's energy. Grandma and Evan were still sleeping when Laurie told Tom and the midwife that it was time to push. Tom asked the midwife to invite Grandma in for the birth. Laurie's birth plan specified that she wanted to give birth in an upright position. The midwife and Tom assisted Laurie into a supported standing position. . . . During pushing, the FHTs were checked about every 5 minutes and Laurie smiled between contractions knowing that the home birth was proceeding as planned. At 6:03 AM, Laurie and Tom were thrilled when . . . their healthy 8 pound 4 ounce baby girl arrived.[a] (p. 542)

OBJECTIVES

4.1: Explain how genes and environmental experiences interact in a child's development.

4.2: Draw appropriate conclusions about strategies teachers and practitioners can use to address individual children's unique genetic profiles.

4.3: Characterize the phases of healthy prenatal growth and practices for nurturing and protecting the rapidly growing prenatal offspring.

4.4: Describe the multistage birth process and the period right after birth.

4.5: Offer recommendations for supporting mothers and infants during and immediately after birth.

Evan woke at his usual time to find a new baby sister in his parents' bed. He climbed into the bed, eager to hold the new baby.[a] (p. 542)

- What major changes would Laurie and Tom's baby have undergone during her prenatal development?
- What factors contributed to the health of the new baby?

[a]Excerpts from "Shared Responsibility in Home Birth Practice: Collaborating with Clients", by Alice Bailes and Marsha E. Jackson, 2000, *Journal of Midwifery and Women's Health, 45*(6), pp. 537–543.

While Laurie and Tom were planning their birth, baby-to-be was growing quietly and changing constantly. During the 9 months of prenatal development, their future child was transformed from a single cell, charged with a unique genetic makeup, into a fully formed baby, ready to live and learn, and, ultimately, to love. Laurie and Tom's baby had a healthy beginning because Laurie ate well, tried to relax, sought social support, and obtained medical care. Of course, natural biological processes were also an essential part of the baby's growth. In this chapter we show that prenatal growth and childbirth are extraordinary symphonies of developmental processes, each orchestrated by a harmonious blend of genetic and environmental factors. We find that there are many things prospective parents and caring professionals can do to give children healthy beginnings.

GENETIC FOUNDATIONS OF CHILD DEVELOPMENT

gene
Basic unit of heredity in a living cell; genes are made up of DNA and contained on chromosomes.

chromosome
Rodlike structure that resides in the nucleus of every cell of the body and contains genes that guide growth and development; each chromosome is made up of DNA and other biological instructions.

DNA
A spiral-staircase–shaped molecule that guides the production of proteins needed by the body for growth and development; short for *deoxyribonucleic acid.*

Like Laurie and Tom's children, every child has a unique profile of hereditary instructions that support his or her life, growth, human traits, and individuality. These guidelines are contained in a child's **genes**, the basic units of heredity.

Structure of Genes

Each gene tells the body either to create one or more proteins or to regulate other genes. Proteins produced by genes create life-sustaining reactions that, with adequate nutrition and a favorable environment, ultimately culminate in the physical characteristics of a growing child. Some proteins guide the production of new cells with particular properties (e.g., elastic skin cells or message-sending brain cells). Other proteins tell the body to increase in size, fight infection, repair damage, carry chemical signals throughout the body, and activate or inhibit other genes.

The 25,000 or so genes that exist in the human body are laid out in an orderly way on rod-like structures called **chromosomes** (U.S. Department of Energy Office of Science, 2008). Chromosomes are organized into 23 distinct pairs that are easily seen with a high-powered microscope (Figure 4-1). These 46 chromosomes reside in the center of virtually every cell in the body. One chromosome of each pair is inherited from the mother, the other from the father.

Genes are made up of deoxyribonucleic acid, or **DNA**. A DNA molecule is structured like a ladder that has been twisted many times into a spiral staircase (see Figure 4-2). Pairs of chemical substances comprise steps on the staircase, and a gene is comprised of a series of these steps. Location on the staircase helps scientists determine the identity of particular genes. Above and below genes on the DNA ladder are other instructions that tell genes when they should turn on and off and still other instructions whose functions remain a mystery. The hierarchical relationships among cells, chromosomes, genes, and DNA molecules are represented in Figure 4-3.

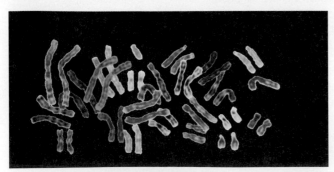

FIGURE 4-1 One person's chromosomes. Photograph of human chromosomes that have been extracted from a human cell, colored, and magnified.

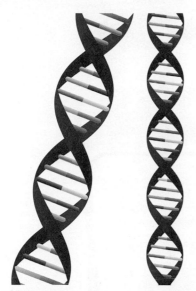

FIGURE 4-2 DNA. A DNA molecule is structured like a ladder that has been twisted into a spiral staircase.

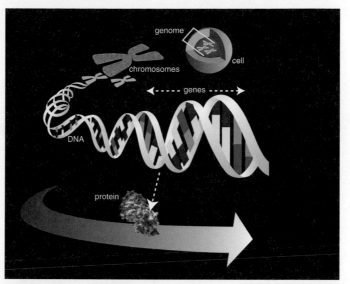

FIGURE 4-3 Hierarchy of genetic structures. Systems in the body are organized in orderly levels. The body contains billions of cells, most of which contain 46 chromosomes. Each chromosome contains thousands of genes. Genes are long sequences of DNA that assemble proteins.
Based on U.S. Department of Energy Office of Science, 2008.

Operation of Genes

The vast majority of genes are identical in all children (U.S. Department of Energy Office of Science, 2008; Venter et al., 2001). Among these universal genes are those that make it possible for children to develop basic human abilities, such as communicating with language, walking and running, and forming social relationships. The remaining (small) proportion of genes varies among children. Genes that vary predispose individual children to be relatively tall or short, heavy or thin, active or sedentary, eager to learn new things or content to rely on existing knowledge, emotionally agreeable or combative, and healthy or vulnerable to disease. Remarkably, universal and individual genes blend together in their effects, such that a given child develops a distinctive appearance, laughter, and running stride.

Both universal and individual genes initiate chains of events for the child (see Figure 4-4). Genes directly affect the operations of individual cells present in the child's organs, brain circuits, and other systems of the body. These systems in turn affect the child's behavior, relationships, and learning. Thus genes are powerful, but they are *not* simple recipes or blueprints for traits. Rather, the proteins that originate from genetic instructions are released into the child's cells, and their effects depend partly (largely, in some cases) on the child's health and activity. To illustrate, an 8-year-old boy genetically predisposed to asthma may rarely have respiratory flare-ups because his family gives him proper medical care and shields him from the hair of dogs and cats, his personal trigger for wheezing and coughing.

The causal chain also operates in reverse, with the child's experiences affecting genetic expression (look again at Figure 4-4). That is, the environment provides opportunities for learning and for exposure to nutrition and toxins; these experiences affect the body; and the health and operations of physical systems activate (or suppress) particular genes. For example, a 1-year-old boy who has been exposed to high levels of lead may not be able to fully express genes that would have otherwise permitted good motor skills and insatiable learning.

Notice in Figure 4-4 that *time* also affects genetic expression. In fact, only a subset of genes is active in a cell at any given moment. Responding to the body's health and maturational state, cells select particular genes for activation. Other genes remain dormant until it is their turn to be called into action. This fact helps explain the order of maturational changes

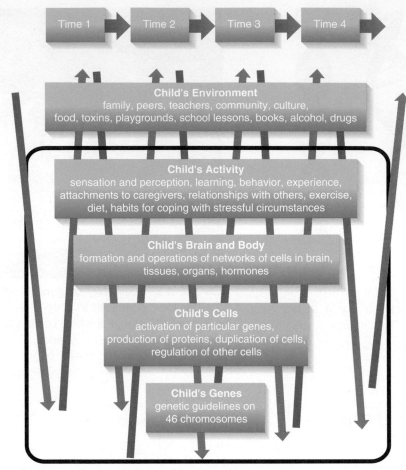

FIGURE 4-4 A cascade of dynamic reactions. Genes and environment initiate ripples of change throughout the child's body. Genes directly affect cells and indirectly influence other systems in the body and ultimately the child's experiences in a particular environment. The environment directly affects the body and indirectly affects the operation of cells and genetic expression. Particular direct and indirect effects are transformed over time, as new genes come into play and as the child's activity, experience, nutrition, relationships, and exposure to toxins also change. *Sources: Gottlieb, 1992; T. D. Johnston & Edwards, 2002.*

MyEducationLab

Go to the Video Examples section in Topic 4 of MyEducationLab to watch an animated video depicting the effects of hormones on children's growing bodies.

gamete
Reproductive cell that, in humans, contains 23 chromosomes rather than the 46 chromosomes present in other cells in the body; a male gamete (sperm) and a female gamete (ovum) join at conception.

meiosis
The process of cell division and reproduction by which gametes are formed.

in physical appearance and motor skills. To illustrate, a child is born with genes for sexual maturation but the body waits to trigger relevant hormones until the beginning of adolescence. (You can watch an animated video depicting the effects of hormones on children's growing bodies in MyEducationLab.) The delay in triggering certain genes also explains why some diseases and mental health conditions seem to appear out of nowhere: Genes that make people vulnerable to several conditions remain silent until maturational states and environmental circumstances elicit their effects.

Formation of Reproductive Cells

As we have said, normal human cells contain 46 chromosomes. There is an important exception: Male and female reproductive cells, called **gametes**, have only 23 chromosomes each—half of each chromosome pair. Gametes, which take the form of *sperm* in men and *ova* in women, are created in a process of cell division called **meiosis** (see Figure 4-5).

Meiosis

During meiosis, nature forms new reproductive cells so that a child has some genetic characteristics from both parents as well as some novel features. Meiosis begins when the 46 chromosomes within a male or female *germ cell* (a precursor to a gamete) pair up into 23 matched

General Process of Meiosis

Each germ cell has 46 chromosomes. Chromosomes begin to move together and pair up into 23 matched sets in the germ cells.

Each chromosome replicates (duplicates) itself. Notice that the single strands in the previous step have doubled in this step.

Crossing-over occurs: Pairs of duplicated chromosomes temporarily unite and exchange segments of chromosomes. This shuffling of genes between paired chromosomes—known as *crossing-over*—ensures unique combinations of genes that differ from those of both the mother and the father.

The pairs of doubled chromosomes separate and the cell divides, forming two new cells, each containing 23 double-structured chromosomes. Chromosomes randomly join with others in one of the two new cells. This process is called the *first meiotic division*. It further ensures genetic individuality.

The second meiotic division takes place. The cell divides in two and the double-structured chromosomes are separated. Chromosomes are now single-structured: the new cell now has one chromosome from each pair, and a total of 23 chromosomes. Resulting cells are now gametes that mature and become ready to unite at conception.

During conception, the sperm enters the ovum.

The two sets of 23 chromosomes, one from the father and one from the mother, unite to form a zygote.

Sperm in Men

Production of sperm begins for boys at puberty. During an initial phase, germ cells (precursors to sperm) are formed. *Only one pair from the 23 pairs of chromosomes is shown here.*

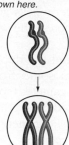

In the male, these first three steps have occurred sometime after puberty and continue to occur throughout the male's reproductive years.

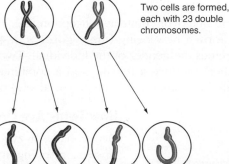

Two cells are formed, each with 23 double chromosomes.

There are now four male gametes (sperm).

Ova in Women

Production of ova begins for girls during prenatal development. During an initial phase, germ cells (precursors to ova) are formed. *Only one pair from the 23 pairs of chromosomes is shown here.*

In the female, these first three steps have occurred during prenatal development. At the completion of crossing-over, germ cells will rest until puberty.

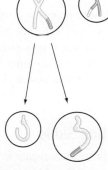

Meiosis resumes during puberty. With each ovulation, the germ cell will complete the first meiotic division producing two cells, each with 23 double chromosomes. One cell receives the majority of cell material and becomes viable. The other cell may reproduce but neither it nor its progeny will be a viable gamete.

Only one potentially viable ovum, which has 23 chromosomes, remains. This step of the second meiotic division occurs only if the ovum is fertilized with a sperm.

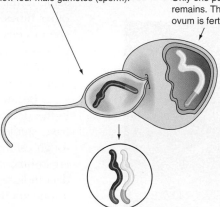

FIGURE 4-5   Reproductive cells. *Meiosis* is the multistep process of forming gametes, cells that join in reproduction to form a new organism.
Sources: K. L. Moore & Persaud, 2008; Sadler, 2010.

sets. The germ cell then duplicates each chromosome, and pairs of chromosomes line up side by side. Next, segments of genetic material are exchanged between each pair. This *crossing-over* of genetic material shuffles genes between paired chromosomes and produces new hereditary combinations that do not exist in either parent's chromosomes.

After crossing-over takes place, the pairs of duplicated chromosomes separate, and the cell divides into two new germ cells with half from each pair. Chance determines which of the duplicated chromosomes from each of the 23 pairs moves to one or the other of the two new cells. This phase thus provides a second route to genetic individuality. During this first cell division, one of the two new female germ cells gets the bulk of the cell matter and is strong and healthy—that is, it is viable—whereas the second, smaller cell disintegrates. Both new male germ cells are viable.

A second cell division takes place, and the duplicated chromosomes separate. Each new cell receives one of the duplicate chromosomes from each pair. The resulting male germ cells are ready to mature and become male gametes (sperm). The female germ cells undergo this second division only after being fertilized by sperm. When the female cell divides, once again, only one of the two new cells, a female gamete (an ovum), is viable. The process of meiosis thus produces one ovum and four sperm.[1]

The multiple steps of meiosis ensure that some traits are preserved across generations and other entirely new traits are created. Children share some features with both of their parents because they inherit half of their chromosomes from each parent. Children are unlike their parents (and siblings) in other respects because parts of chromosomes change slightly during meiosis; the chromosomal structures that children inherit are *not* exact duplicates of parents' chromosomes.[2] Furthermore, a single gene transmitted from parent to child (and shared by both) may operate differently in the two family members because other genes (not shared by both) may intensify or weaken that gene's effects.

Gender

When one sperm and one ovum unite at conception, the 23 chromosomes from each parent come together and form a new being (the **zygote**) with 46 chromosomes. The 23rd chromosome pair determines the gender of the individual: Two *X chromosomes* (one each from the mother and father) produce a female, and a combination of an *X chromosome* and a *Y chromosome* (from the mother and father, respectively) produces a male.

zygote
Cell formed when a male sperm joins with a female ovum; with reasonably healthy genes and nurturing conditions in the uterus, it may develop into a fetus and be born as a live infant.

monozygotic twins
Twins that began as a single zygote and so share the same genetic makeup.

dizygotic twins
Twins that began as two separate zygotes and so are as genetically similar as two siblings conceived and born at different times.

Improving Your Observation Skills

Twins. Are these two sisters from Brazil monozygotic or dizygotic twins? Compare your response with the explanation at the end of the chapter.

How Twins Are Created

Occasionally, a zygote splits into two separate cell clusters, resulting in two offspring instead of one. *Identical,* or **monozygotic twins**, come from the same fertilized egg and so have the same genes. At other times, two ova simultaneously unite with two sperm cells, again resulting in two offspring. These **dizygotic twins**, also known as *fraternal* twins, are as similar to one another as ordinary siblings. They share some genetic traits but not others.

Because monozygotic and dizygotic twins differ in the degree to which they share genes, researchers have studied them extensively. Twin studies permit rough estimates of the relative effects of heredity and environment on human characteristics. Considerable data indicate that monozygotic twins are more similar to one another than are dizygotic twins in their ability to learn new concepts and their tendency to be helpful and cooperative or irritable and aggressive (Ganiban, Ulbricht, Saudino, Reiss, & Neiderhiser, 2011; Knafo

[1] Sperm are produced continuously throughout a male's reproductive years. In girls, up to 2 million germ cells are present at birth. Many subsequently decay, and only about 40,000 remain at the beginning of adolescence. About 400 ova will be released during ovulation over the woman's lifetime.

[2] For any given parent, each event of meiosis begins with the exact same chromosomes from that parent. The process of meiosis tweaks the structure of chromosomes slightly; no two meiotic events change chromosomes in precisely the same way.

& Plomin, 2006; Natsuaki, Ge, Reiss, & Neiderhiser, 2009; Plomin & Spinath, 2004). Even so, "identical" twins are not identical in all psychological characteristics or even in their physical features—an indication that environment, experience, children's own choices, and even random factors also affect development throughout life.

Genetic Basis of Individual Traits

So far, you have learned that children have both uniform genes (that make them resemble one another in their human abilities) and variable genes (that contribute to their individuality). Uniform human genes, carried by all parents, are transmitted to every child. Genes that vary among children are transmitted through systematic patterns of inheritance as well as by less common mechanisms and biological errors during meiosis and later cell divisions. Let's look more closely at how children receive traits that contribute to their individuality.

Common Mechanisms of Genetic Transmission

When the two sets of 23 chromosomes combine into matched pairs during conception, the corresponding genes inherited from each parent pair up. Each gene pair includes two forms of the protein-coding instructions—two **alleles**—related to a particular physical characteristic. Sometimes the two genes in an allele pair give the same instructions ("Have dark hair!" "Have dark hair!"). At other times they give very different instructions ("Have dark hair!" "Have blond hair!"). When two genes give different instructions, one gene is often more influential than its counterpart. A **dominant gene** manifests its characteristic, in a sense overriding the instructions of a **recessive gene** with which it is paired. A recessive gene influences growth and development primarily when its partner is also recessive. For example, genes for dark hair are dominant and those for blond hair are recessive. Thus a child with a dark hair gene and a blond hair gene will have dark hair, as will a child with two dark hair genes. Only when two blond hair genes are paired together will a child have blond hair.

However, when two genes of an allele pair disagree, one gene doesn't always dominate completely. Sometimes one gene simply has a stronger influence than others, a phenomenon known as **codominance**. *Sickle cell disease,* a blood disorder, is an example. The disease develops in its full-blown form only when a person has two (recessive) alleles for it. Nevertheless, when an individual has one recessive allele for sickle cell disease and one healthy allele, he or she may experience temporary, mild symptoms when short of oxygen; occasionally develop more serious health problems; and have greater-than-average resistance to malaria (Barakat, Nicolaou, O'Hara, & Allen, 2009; Jorde, Carey, & Bamshad, 2010).

In reality, the influence of genes is often even more complex. Many physical traits and most psychological ones are dependent on multiple genes rather than on a single pair of alleles and are further influenced by specific factors in the environment. With a **multifactorial trait**, many separate genes work together with environmental factors in the expression of the characteristic. Height and vulnerability to certain illnesses, including some kinds of diabetes, epilepsy, and cancer, are determined by several genes acting together and interacting with such environmental influences as nutrition, activity, and toxins (J. W. Ball, Bindler, & Cowen, 2010; Dibbens, Heron, & Mulley, 2007; Marques, Oliveira, Pereira, & Outeiro, 2011).

Problems in Genetic Instructions

Sometimes problems occur in the genetic instructions that children receive (see Table 4-1). There are two primary types of genetic disorders, chromosomal abnormalities and single-gene defects. A child with a *chromosomal abnormality* may have an extra chromosome, a missing chromosome, or a wrongly formed chromosome. Because each chromosome holds thousands of genes, a child with a chromosomal abnormality tends to have many affected genes, and the result can be major physical and cognitive problems. Chromosomal abnormalities occur when chromosomes divide unevenly during meiosis. They can also occur after meiosis, when the zygote's cells divide unevenly, leaving the growing zygote with some cells with normal chromosomes and others with abnormal chromosomes. Chromosomal abnormalities may be caused by a variety of factors, including parents' exposure to viruses, radiation, and drugs.

alleles
Genes located at the same point on corresponding (paired) chromosomes and related to the same physical characteristic.

dominant gene
Gene that overrides any competing instructions in an allele pair.

recessive gene
Gene that influences growth and development primarily when the other gene in the allele pair is identical to it.

codominance
Situation in which the two genes of an allele pair, although not identical, both have some influence on a characteristic.

multifactorial trait
Particular characteristic determined by many separate genes combining in influence with environmental factors.

TABLE 4-1 Common Chromosomal and Genetic Disorders in Children

DISORDER	INCIDENCE	CHARACTERISTICS[a]	IMPLICATIONS FOR CARE
Chromosomal Abnormalities			
Children with chromosomal abnormalities are born with an irregular number of chromosomes (more than or fewer than 46) or with one or more chromosomes that have irregular structures (deletions from or duplications to large parts of an individual chromosome, or with a part of one chromosome moved to another location).			
Down syndrome	1 per 700–1,000 births	Children with Down syndrome have all or part of an extra 21st chromosome. Physical characteristics include distinctively shaped eyes, a protruding tongue, thick lips, a flat nose, short neck, wide gaps between toes, short fingers, specific health problems, and risks for heart problems and hearing loss. Intellectual disability can range from mild to severe. Children often have good visual discrimination skills and may be better at understanding verbal language than producing it.	Provide explicit instruction in any delayed skills (e.g., in language). Address health issues such as heart problems and potential feeding difficulties.
Klinefelter syndrome	1 per 500–1,000 boys	Only boys have Klinefelter syndrome; they have one Y chromosome and two or more X chromosomes. Diagnosis may not occur until adolescence, when testes fail to enlarge. Affected boys tend to have long legs, to grow modest breast tissue, and to remain sterile. They show lower than average verbal ability and some speech and language delays.	Offer an enriched verbal environment. Medical treatment may be given to support development of male sexual characteristics.
Turner syndrome	1 per 2,500–5,000 girls	Only girls have Turner syndrome; they have one X chromosome and are missing the second sex chromosome. Affected girls have broad chests, webbed necks, short stature, and specific health problems. They do not show normal sexual development and may have normal verbal ability but lower-than-average ability in processing visual and spatial information.	Provide instruction and support related to visual and spatial processing. Hormone therapy helps with bone growth and development of female characteristics.
Prader-Willi syndrome	1 per 10,000–25,000 births	A deletion of a segment of chromosome 15 is inherited from the father. Children with this syndrome tend to become obese and show an intellectual disability; they also have small hands and feet and are short in stature. They may develop maladaptive behaviors such as throwing frequent temper tantrums and picking at their own skin. Beginning at ages 1–6 years, children may eat excessively, hoard food, and consume unappealing substances (e.g., dirt).	Create developmentally appropriate plans to help children regulate eating, decrease inappropriate behaviors, and increase acceptable emotional expression. Seek medical care as necessary.
Angelman syndrome	1 per 10,000–30,000 births	A deletion of a segment on chromosome 15 is inherited from the mother. Children with this syndrome show an intellectual disability, a small head, seizures, and jerky movements. They have unusual, recurrent bouts of laughter not associated with happiness.	Provide appropriate educational support suited to children's skills and developmental levels. Seek medical care as necessary.
Single-Gene Defects			
Children with single-gene defects have a problem on a dominant gene (an error on one of the 22 paired chromosomes, that is, on any chromosome except X or Y), a recessive defect on both chromosomes in one of the 22 matched pairs, a problem in a recessive gene on the X chromosome (boys), or a problem in a gene on both X chromosomes (girls).[b]			
Neurofibromatosis	Mild form occurs in 1 per 2,500–4,000 births; severe form occurs in 1 per 40,000–50,000 births	Children with this dominant-gene defect develop benign and malignant tumors in the central nervous system. Learning disabilities are somewhat common and an intellectual disability occurs occasionally. Most individuals experience only minor symptoms, such as having colored and elevated spots on their skin.	Address learning disabilities; offer adaptive services to children with an intellectual disability. Tumors may need to be removed or treated. Surgery or braces may be needed if the spine becomes twisted.
Huntington disease (HD)	3–7 per 100,000 births	Children with this dominant-gene defect develop a progressive disorder of the central nervous system. Signs typically appear by age 35 to 45, though age of first symptoms has varied between 2 and 85 years. HD may be caused by the production of a protein that destroys brain cells. Early signs include irritability, clumsiness, depression, and forgetfulness. Eventually, loss of control over arms, legs, torso, or facial muscles occurs; speech becomes slurred; and severe mental disturbances arise.	Remove sharp edges from the physical environment. When memory deteriorates, provide visual instructions about daily tasks. Medication may be given to alleviate movement problems and depression.

DISORDER	INCIDENCE	CHARACTERISTICS[a]	IMPLICATIONS FOR CARE
Phenylketonuria (PKU)	1 per 15,000 births, with rates highest in people of Celtic origin (e.g., from Ireland and Scotland)	Children with this recessive-gene defect are at risk for developing an intellectual disability, eczema, seizures, and motor and behavioral problems such as aggression, self-mutilation, and impulsiveness. When children have both recessive genes for PKU, their livers cannot produce an enzyme that breaks down phenylalanine (an amino acid); this substance accumulates and becomes toxic to the brain.	Provide educational materials to enhance planning and memory skills and compensate for limitations. When phenylalanine is restricted from their diet, children develop much more normally, and an intellectual disability is avoided. Subtle problems may still result (e.g., awkward pencil grip and learning disabilities).
Sickle cell disease	1 per 500–600 children of African (black) descent; rates are also elevated in people of Mediterranean descent	Children with this disorder develop problems with blood circulation. The disease causes red blood cells to grow rigid, impeding their passage through small blood vessels and causing pain. Children may experience stroke, infection, tissue damage, and fatigue. Symptoms become obvious during the first or second year of life.	Be alert to medical crises, such as strokes. Offer comfort to children who are tired or in pain. Treatments include blood transfusions, medication for pain and infections, and other medicines to reduce frequency of medical crises.
Cystic fibrosis (CF)	1 per 3,300 children from European American backgrounds and 1 per 9,500 children from Hispanic American backgrounds	Children with this recessive-gene defect have glands that produce large amounts of abnormally thick, sticky mucus, which creates serious problems for breathing and digestion. CF is usually noticed in infancy due to persistent coughing, wheezing, pneumonia, and big appetite with little weight gain. Many individuals with CF now live well into their 40s.	Be aware of symptoms that require medical care. The condition is often treated with physical therapy, medication, and bronchial drainage.
Tay-Sachs disease	1 per 2,500–3,600 children among Ashkenazi Jews (of Eastern European ancestry)	Children with this recessive-gene defect develop a fatal, degenerative condition of the central nervous system. They lack an enzyme required to break down a fatty substance in brain cells. At about 6 months of age, children slow down in development, lose vision, display an abnormal startle response, and go into convulsions. Other functions are gradually lost, and children develop an intellectual disability, cannot move, and die by age 3 or 4.	Offer love and attention as you would to other children. Be alert to new accommodations that are needed in the environment, such as stabilizing and securing the surroundings when children lose sight. There is no known cure or treatment.
Thalassemia (Cooley's anemia)	1 in 800–2,500 individuals of Greek or Italian descent in the United States; rates are lower in other groups	Children with this recessive-gene develop a disease of blood cells in which oxygen is not transmitted effectively. They become pale, fatigued, and irritable within their first 2 years of life. Individuals with serious forms of the condition may develop feeding problems, diarrhea, and enlargement of the spleen and heart, infections, and unusual facial features and bone structures. Young people severely impaired by this condition sometimes die by early adulthood.	Help children cope with health problems. Treatment may include blood transfusions, antibiotics, and occasionally bone marrow transplants.
Duchenne muscular dystrophy	1 per 3,000–4,000 boys	Only boys acquire this X-linked recessive-gene defect, which causes a progressive muscular weakness because of a gene's failure to produce an essential protein needed by muscle cells. Between ages 2 and 5, affected boys begin to stumble and walk on their toes or with another unusual gait. They may lose the ability to walk between ages 8 and 14 and may later die from respiratory and cardiac problems.	Watch for respiratory infections and heart problems. Treatments include physical therapy, orthopedic devices, surgery, and medications to reduce muscle stiffness.

[a]This table describes typical symptoms for children with particular chromosomal and genetic problems. Children's actual level of functioning depends on the medical treatments they receive; their experiences with families, teachers, other caregivers, and other children; and their health and other genes they might possess. New medical treatments and educational interventions are constantly being tested, and many will increase quality of life for affected children.

[b]X-linked defects based on a single dominant gene also occur but are rare. For example, children who receive the gene for hypophosphatemia on the X chromosome produce low levels of phosphate and, as a result, have soft bones that are easily deformed.

Sources: J. W. Ball et al., 2010; Blachford, 2002; Burns, Brady, Dunn, & Starr, 2000; Cody & Kamphaus, 1999; Dykens & Cassidy, 1999; Hazlett, Gaspar De Alba, & Hooper, 2011; Jorde et al., 2010; Massimini, 2000; K. L. Moore & Persaud, 2008; Nilsson & Bradford, 1999; M. P. Powell & Schulte, 1999; J. T. Smith, 1999; Waisbren, 1999; Wynbrandt & Ludman, 2000.

MyEducationLab

Watch a video about the special medical needs of children with Down syndrome in the Video Examples section in Topic 4 of MyEducationLab.

Chromosomal abnormalities occur in about 1 in 150 births (March of Dimes, 2010). One such abnormality, an extra 21st chromosome or an extra piece of one, causes *Down syndrome*. Children with Down syndrome typically show delays in mental growth and are susceptible to heart defects and other health problems. Apparently, the extra 21st chromosome causes biochemical changes that redirect brain development. The severity of disabilities caused by Down syndrome and many other chromosomal abnormalities varies considerably from one affected child to the next. You can watch a video about the special medical needs of children with Down syndrome in MyEducationLab.

A second type of genetic disorder occurs when a child inherits a *single-gene defect* from one or both parents. Resulting physical problems tend to be more specific and subtle than those caused by chromosomal abnormalities. Nonetheless, some single-gene defects are quite serious. The usual pattern of inheritance is that children who inherit a dominant-gene defect show the problem. Those who inherit a recessive-gene defect show the problem only if both genes in the allele pair are defective (transmission is slightly different in X-chromosome-linked defects).

Some genetic problems do not fit neatly into the categories of chromosomal abnormality or single-gene defect. For instance, a few conditions are mild or severe depending on the particular sequence of chemical compounds on a gene. An example is *Fragile X syndrome*, which results from a genetic defect on the X chromosome. When this defect is small and limited, people who carry the problem gene are able to produce some of a particular protein needed by the body, and as a result they may show no symptoms or only mild learning disabilities. But the defect can intensify as it is passed from one generation to the next and lead to Fragile X syndrome (Narayanan & Warren, 2006). Children with Fragile X syndrome develop severe learning disabilities, emotional problems, and intellectual disabilities. Their physical characteristics include prominent ears, long faces, double-jointed thumbs, and flat feet, and they typically possess other health conditions, such as being prone to sinus and ear infections (J. W. Ball et al., 2010; Hagerman & Lampe, 1999). In addition, these children tend to be socially anxious, sensitive to touch and noise, and inclined to avoid eye contact and repeat certain activities over and over again (e.g., spinning objects, waving their arms, saying the same phrase). The problems of girls with Fragile X are generally less serious than those of boys because girls have a second X chromosome that is usually healthy enough to produce the missing protein.

SUCCESS. Positive attitudes of educators, advocacy by parents, and government regulations have resulted in improved educational services for many children with chromosomal abnormalities, genetic defects, and other disabilities.

Other physical problems are the result of multifactorial influences. *Spina bifida* (in which the spinal cord is malformed) and *cleft palate* (in which a split develops in the roof of the mouth) are examples of such conditions, which tend to run in some families but do not follow simple patterns of genetic transmission. Instead, affected children have genes that made them susceptible to particular environmental threats, such as their mother's vitamin deficiency or illness, as their body parts were being formed during prenatal development (J. W. Ball et al., 2010; K. L. Moore & Persaud, 2008). You can watch a video about a couple's experiences raising a child with spina bifida on MyEducationLab.

MyEducationLab

Watch a video about a couple's experience raising a child with spina bifida in the Video Examples section in Topic 4 of MyEducationLab.

All children require individualized care, but those with chromosomal abnormalities, single-gene defects, and other genetic conditions and birth defects may need interventions tailored to their specific conditions. In fact, children who have significant biologically based disabilities can, with systematic instruction tailored to their individual needs, make dramatic gains in their intellectual and social development.

Increasingly, parents and teachers have realized that these accommodations can usually be made in the regular classroom. In a practice called **inclusion**, children and adolescents with exceptional needs are educated within the general education classroom for all or part of the school day. Many teachers and specialists have found that when they keep an open mind about what their students can accomplish, and especially when they work together and think creatively about how they can adapt the curriculum, instruction, and activities to the needs of individual students, almost all students can participate in lessons in the regular classroom (Logan, Alberto, Kana, & Waylor-Bowen, 1994; Zigmond, Kloo, & Volonino, 2009).

The Awakening of Genes

Earlier we explained that only some genes are active within cells at any particular time. As a result, several genes have an almost immediate influence on the development of physical characteristics, but many others don't manifest themselves until later in *maturation,* when provoked to do so by hormones and other factors. For example, the infant's body length at birth is determined largely by exposure to prenatal conditions in the mother's uterus and is only minimally influenced by heredity. By 18 months of age, however, we see a definite correlation between children's heights and the heights of their parents, presumably because genetic factors have begun to exert their influence (Tanner, 1990).

Maturational influences in genetic expression are also seen in *sensitive periods.*[3] A sensitive period is an age range, dictated by heredity, during which highly specific environmental experiences are necessary for normal development. For the duration of a sensitive period, the child is biologically primed to develop a specific ability as long as these experiences are available. For example, children are especially sensitive to language input during infancy and early childhood. By regularly participating in conversations, young children easily learn one or more languages. Children deprived of language during early childhood require considerable intervention if they are to acquire a first language later in life.

In other areas, such as reading and engaging in productive social relationships, there is no single restricted time frame for learning. Children who have had inadequate experiences in these areas can frequently make up for time lost in the early years. However, educators should not simply wait for children who lag behind peers to catch up in fundamental academic and social skills. Such competencies build cumulatively over time, and without appropriate intervention, delayed children may easily fall further behind and come to see themselves as incapable.

A number of emerging characteristics are tightly controlled by genetic instructions, a phenomenon known as **canalization** (Waddington, 1957). Basic motor skills are highly canalized: Crawling, sitting, and walking appear under a wide range of circumstances and almost invariably without training or encouragement. Only extremely unusual environmental conditions can stifle them, such as when a young child exposed to heavy doses of a toxic substance (e.g., lead paint and pesticides) is seriously delayed in mastering basic motor and psychological skills (C. Cole & Winsler, 2010; Gottlieb, 1991). Spared from such toxic substances and allowed to move freely for even small amounts of time, children almost always develop such motor skills as handling objects and walking proficiently.

Many skills are *not* canalized, however. Most of the abilities that children acquire at school—reading, writing, mathematical problem solving, and so on—are modified by experiences both in and out of the classroom. Social skills also rely on environmental support. Deciphering other people's intentions, learning to anticipate others' actions, and taking turns during conversation are competencies that are refined with social experience. Thus, genes that support these particular abilities are flexible in the learning outcomes they permit.

Preparing for Your Licensure Examination
Your teaching test might ask you about legislation that governs the educational rights of students with exceptional learning needs.

inclusion
Practice of educating all students, including those with severe and multiple disabilities, in neighborhood schools and general education classrooms.

canalization
Tight genetic control of a particular aspect of development.

---

[3] Sensitive periods were introduced in Chapter 1.

The Blending of Heredity and Environment

In addition to responding to maturational states *inside* the child, genes attend to conditions that originate in the *outside* environment. Children who obtain nutritious meals, attention from loving caregivers, and exposure to challenging activities generally reach their full genetic potential (Brant et al., 2009; W. Johnson, Deary, & Iacono, 2009). Other environmental experiences, including encouragement of physical activity, exposure to light, protection from certain viruses, and in some cases, ingestion of medication, also influence children's development.

The tendency for a child's genes to be dynamically influenced by numerous internal and external factors means that few developmental outcomes can be anticipated with certainty. In other words, genes make particular characteristics likely but not guaranteed. The actual characteristics a child ends up with depend on the full complement of genes the child has *and* the child's ongoing experiences. A 6-year-old girl with a healthy diet and chances for regular physical activity will refine her motor skills, perhaps learning to ride a bicycle and play basketball. These new skills open the door for other developments, making new friends and becoming familiar with surrounding neighborhoods. Another 6-year-old girl who has a weak diet and leads a sedentary life will not find it as easy to acquire active physical skills or leverage athletic skills for social purposes.

Evidence from multifactorial traits indicates that environmental factors nudge certain genes into action at various times during development. People appear to have genetic predispositions to various temperaments—becoming particularly cheerful, outgoing, moody, anxious, or aggressive (Glahn & Burdick, 2011; Rothbart, Posner, & Kieras, 2006; A. C. Wood, Saudino, Rogers, Asherson, & Kuntsi, 2007; M. U. Zuckerman, 2007). Yet these traits are clearly also influenced by the environment, especially when children are young and gaining foundational skills in coping with emotions and relating to other people (Plomin, Owen, & McGuffin, 1994). We're not born wild or shy; instead, we're born with certain tendencies that our environments may or may not encourage.

As children grow, their environment continues to influence genetic expression but children themselves become progressively capable of altering their environments through their behaviors and choices, a phenomenon known as **niche construction** (Laland, Odling-Smee, & Feldman, 2000; E. Schultz, 2009; T. Ward & Durrant, 2011). Think about an athletic boy who joins a baseball team, organizes neighborhood games, requests sports equipment from parents, and in other ways creates occasions for practicing athletic skills. Consider another young man who is especially quick-witted and good humored, joins the drama club at school, entertains peers with his antics, and organizes a comedy night at his school. By altering certain aspects of their environment, both young men essentially arrange for the refinement of their own genetically based talents. As you might expect, there is a developmental trend in niche construction—with age, children become increasingly persistent in choosing their pastimes and therefore are progressively more proficient in expressing their unique characteristics.

It should now be clear to you that genes do not direct appearance, behavior, or even cell functioning in any simple, predetermined fashion. Genes operate in concert with one another; are affected by nutrition, stress, and other environmental agents; and are activated by hormones and physiological events. Furthermore, individual genes may be influential at particular points in development, suddenly bringing out characteristics that seem to come "from nowhere." In general, a child's genes present rough guidelines that may be either stretched or compressed, depending on the influence of other genes and the child's health, schooling, interpersonal relationships, environmental resources, and personal choices.

niche construction
A child's active shaping of the environment through behaviors, activities, and choices, often in accordance with personal genetically based tendencies.

Acknowledging Nature and Nurture in Children's Lives

Genetics may seem like a very abstract topic compared to a busy classroom full of children. Nevertheless, anyone working closely with children needs to understand the power of heredity. At the same time, evidence of strong environmental influences should inspire adults' optimism about their ability to exert beneficial effects on children. We offer the following recommendations:

• **Expect and make allowances for individual differences.** Teachers and other practitioners who value a multitude of physical characteristics, personality types, and talents are apt to put youngsters at ease. Children who are tall and short, chubby and thin, coordinated and clumsy, shy and outgoing, and calm and irritable all have a rightful place in the hearts of adults who teach and nurture them.

• **Remember that environmental factors influence virtually every aspect of development.** Children's development is *not* simply an outgrowth of biology. Even when children have inherited the potential for certain talents, temperaments, and deficits, their paths can be steered one way or another by environmental factors—physical experiences, social interactions, school instruction, and so on. For instance, children who are genetically predisposed to be irritable and distractible can, with guidance, learn more adaptive and socially productive ways of responding when frustrated (Beauchaine, Klein, Crowell, Derbridge, & Gatzke-Kopp, 2009; Reiss, 2005). In one study, the genes of a group of women were examined for the presence of a particular form of a gene whose function is to metabolize (break down into usable forms) a particular brain chemical, MAOA-uVNTR (Kinnally et al., 2009). With a deficient form of this gene, a person cannot metabolize this chemical and as a result is prone to act irritably, impulsively, and aggressively. Women who have the deficient gene but also had sensitive parents during their childhood years were less impulsive than women with the gene whose parents were insensitive. Other research indicates that men with this gene are especially likely to become aggressive and impulsive if they were previously maltreated as children (Caspi et al., 2002). Apparently, the disadvantages of this gene are primarily manifested when children are *not* nurtured responsively.

• **Intervene when children struggle.** There is an extended window of time for learning many things, but we cannot leave it to chance that delayed children will catch up on their own. Basic intellectual, social, and emotional skills affect many aspects of life, making it important to offer extra guidance when children's progress is unusually slow. Furthermore, without appropriate intervention, children who straggle far behind peers may come to doubt their capability for future learning, leading to even more serious problems, such as dropping out of school. In many schools, regular classroom teachers, special education teachers, counselors, and school psychologists work with students with exceptional learning needs and their families in designing instruction that will help the students make good progress.

• **Be mindful of your own reactions to challenging temperaments in children.** Evidence suggests that parents essentially customize their styles in caring for and disciplining each of their children depending on children's temperaments (Deater-Deckard, 2009). Those with mild temperaments elicit calm and patient reactions from parents, whereas siblings who are irritable push parents' buttons. Although most of the research on children's temperamental effects is conducted with parents, the same tendency may occur to a lesser extent with teachers, who also interact with children regularly. Thus, teachers and other professionals need to remain calm while interacting with oppositional children and make a point to teach these children how to cope with frustration, anger, and disappointment (Keogh, 2003).

Bioecology of Child Development
Evidence that different children who share a particular gene exhibit distinct characteristics depending on their family circumstances attests to the malleability of genetic expression.

Improving Your Observation Skills

Red card. The young man at right has been caught being disrespectful and belligerent during a soccer game. How might the young man's behavior reflect a genetically based temperament? Compare your response with the explanation at the end of the chapter.

Preparing for Your Licensure Examination
Your teaching test might ask you about the kinds of school personnel who can help you design effective learning plans for students with exceptional learning needs.

• **Encourage children to make growth-promoting choices.** Especially as they grow older, youngsters actively seek experiences compatible with their natural tendencies. Adults can present options for cultivating youngsters' talents and remediating any pronounced weaknesses. For instance, a socially outgoing boy with an excessive amount of energy and little self-control may be inclined to interrupt adults and peers. His teachers may need to remind him to hold his tongue and give others a chance to speak. They might also encourage the boy to join the drama club, a sports team, or other groups in which he can exercise leadership skills while increasing his self-control.

PRENATAL DEVELOPMENT

During **prenatal development**, the period of growth between conception and birth, a simple, single cell is transformed into a complex human being. During this remarkable developmental journey, the new being undergoes a series of changes, takes nourishment from the mother, and grows in an environment especially suited to its fragile capabilities.

Phases of Prenatal Growth

The developing baby-to-be must accomplish a wide range of tasks, including growing new cells, moving through the mother's body, settling into an interior wall of the mother's uterus, taking in nutrition and expelling wastes, forming and refining basic body structures, and activating rudimentary learning abilities. Prenatal development is divided into three phases: the periods of the *zygote, embryo*, and *fetus.*

Development of the Zygote

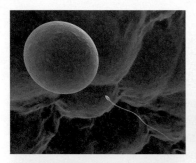
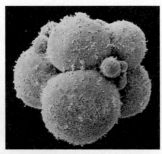
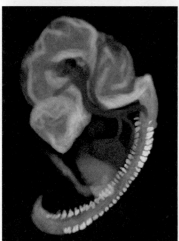
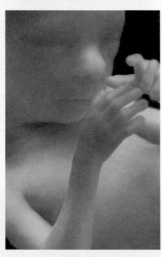

MIRACLES OF GROWTH. Human prenatal development begins at conception (top left) and then progresses through the periods of the zygote (top right), embryo (bottom left), and fetus (bottom right).

prenatal development
Growth that takes place between conception and birth.

mitosis
The process of cell duplication by which chromosomes are preserved and a human being or other biological organism can grow.

During the middle of a woman's menstrual cycle, an *ovum* (female gamete) emerges from one of her two *ovaries* (see Figure 4-6). Several protective cells surround the ovum. The ovum enters the adjacent *fallopian tube,* a narrow and curved pipe that connects the ovary to the uterus. The ovum is guided toward the uterus by pliant fringes in the fallopian tube. When a man ejaculates during sexual intercourse, he releases millions of sperm into the woman's vagina, but only about 200 will find their way into the uterus and move toward the fallopian tube (K. L. Moore & Persaud, 2008). As the ovum is gently ushered down the fallopian tube, sperm swim first slowly up the vagina and then more rapidly as they enter the uterus and proceed up the fallopian tube. When a conception takes place, a single sperm attaches to the ovum and enters it. The ovum cooperates by rearranging its exterior layers so that no other sperm can enter. The ovum and the sperm then combine their chromosomes, and the zygote, a new being, is formed.

The zygote creates new cells as it travels through the fallopian tube and toward the uterus. In a process called **mitosis**, the zygote duplicates its cells such that each of its new cells shares the original 46 chromosomes. During mitosis, the spiral staircase of DNA straightens itself up and splits down the middle, and each half re-creates the original structure. After two exact copies of each chromosome have been formed, one copy from each pair moves to opposite sides of the cell, the cell gradually splits, and two new cells are formed. This process of mitosis continues throughout the life span and permits both growth and replacement of worn out cells.

In the zygote, mitosis takes place in the following manner. The first cell divides into two cells; these two cells divide to make four cells; four divide into eight; and by the time the zygote has 16 cells, it is entering the uterus (see Figure 4-6). These cells align themselves as the exterior lining of a sphere (see the *blastocyst* in Figure 4-6). Now about a week old, the zygote attaches itself to the wall of the uterus. The zygote separates into two parts: One is a tiny being that will develop further into an embryo, and the other becomes the *placenta,* the spongy structure in the uterus that provides nourishment. Cells begin to specialize and merge with other similar cells to form distinct structures, such as the nervous system and brain. The implanted zygote releases hormones, telling the ovaries that a conception has occurred and that menstruation should be prevented. In 2 short weeks, the new being has initiated growth, taken a journey, and found a hospitable home.

Development of the Embryo

The period of the **embryo** extends from 2 through 8 weeks after conception. Tasks of the embryonic period are to instigate life-support systems and form basic body structures. The placenta becomes larger, stronger, and more elaborate as it goes about its job of supplying food, liquid, and oxygen; removing wastes; and secreting hormones that sustain the pregnancy. An *umbilical cord* forms and connects the embryo to the placenta.

The embryo itself undergoes rapid structural changes and increases in size. During prenatal development, growth tends to occur from top to bottom (head first, feet last) and from inside to outside (torso before limbs, arms and legs before hands and feet). Consistent with these trends, the head and heart are among the first structures to develop (see Figure 4-7). The growth of the neural tube that will give rise to the brain and spinal cord is well under way early in the embryonic period. Neurons—the cells that form connections in, and to and from, the brain—emerge and move to their proper places. Buds of limbs begin to develop, and by the eighth week, fingers and toes are recognizably distinct as separate digits. Also during this phase, internal organs appear and begin to develop.

Development of the Fetus

The period of the **fetus** lasts from week 9 until birth. During this period, the developing being grows rapidly, receiving finishing touches that will permit life outside the womb (see Figure 4-8). The many organs and structures that were initiated earlier are now expanded,

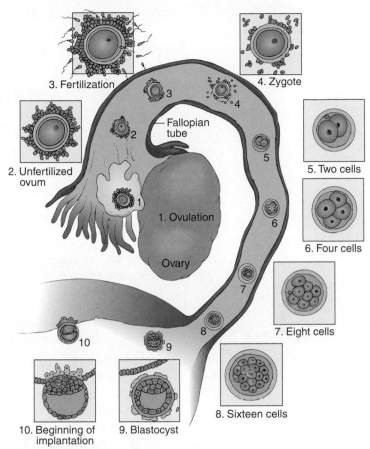

FIGURE 4-6 Development of the zygote.
Based on K. L. Moore, Persaud, & Shiota, 2000.

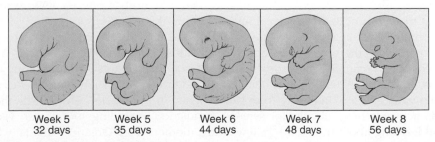

| Week 5 | Week 5 | Week 6 | Week 7 | Week 8 |
| 32 days | 35 days | 44 days | 48 days | 56 days |

FIGURE 4-7 Development of the embryo.
Based on K. L. Moore et al., 2000.

embryo
During prenatal weeks 2 through 8, the developing offspring that is in the process of forming major body structures and organs.

fetus
During prenatal week 9 until birth, the developing offspring that is growing in size and weight and in sensory abilities, brain structures, and organs needed for survival.

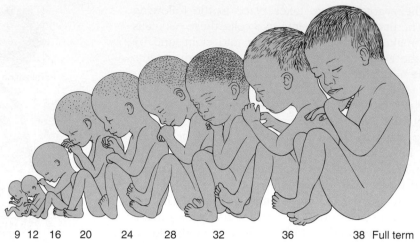

9 12 16   20   24   28   32   36   38 Full term

FIGURE 4-8 Development of the fetus during specific weeks.
Based on K. L. Moore & Persaud, 2008.

and they become coordinated with other systems in the body. The fetus's body is elaborated through a series of specific changes:

- *Third month*. The head is large in comparison to the rest of the body but now slows down in rate of growth. The eyes move to their proper places, and the fetus becomes increasingly human looking. The external genitalia grow. The fetus begins to show reflexes and muscular movement. The mother does not yet feel these movements.
- *Fourth month*. The fetus grows rapidly in length (height). Weight increases slowly. Hair grows on the head and eyebrows. Eye movements occur.
- *Fifth month*. The fetus continues to grow rapidly in length. Fine hair covers the body, and a greasy substance protects the fetus's delicate skin. The mother can usually feel the fetus's movement by now.
- *Sixth month*. The fetus has red, wrinkled skin and a body that is lean but gaining weight. Fingernails are present. The respiratory system and central nervous system are still developing and coordinating their operations.
- *Seventh month*. Eyes open and eyelashes are present. Toenails grow. The body begins to fill out. The brain has developed sufficiently to support breathing.
- *Eighth month*. Skin is pink and smooth. Fat grows under the skin. The testes (in males) descend. (K. L. Moore & Persaud, 2008; Sadler, 2010)

During the final months of prenatal development, the fetus is refining its basic body structures and also gaining weight, slowly at first and more steadily as birth approaches. On average, the fetus at 6 months of prenatal growth weighs approximately 1 pound, 13 ounces; at 7 months, 2 pounds, 14 ounces; and at 8 months, 4 pounds, 10 ounces (K. L. Moore & Persaud, 2008). Birth weights vary, of course, but on average, the newborn infant weighs 7 pounds, 8 ounces. These last few weeks of weight gain increase the chances of an infant's survival after birth. In fact, infants rarely survive when they are born before 5½ half months of prenatal development or at weights of less than 1 pound, 2 ounces. (We examine the health and treatment of early and small infants later in this chapter.)

The brain also expands and matures during the final weeks and months of prenatal growth. Structurally, the outer layers of the brain (those closest to the skull) bunch up into folds and creases, creating a staggering number of potential circuits for transmitting information. Functionally, the fetus's brain is being prepared to carry out such vital reflexes as sucking, swallowing, and looking away from bright lights. In the weeks before birth, the fetus's brain also activates brain circuits for sensing stimulation, including sounds and visual patterns, and learning about the world. In one study, mothers from Ontario, Canada, who were in the final weeks of pregnancy were randomly assigned to one of two treatments (Kisilevsky et al., 2009). Both groups of mothers lay on their backs with audio speakers placed about

10 centimeters above their abdomens. One group of mothers rested while listening to guitar music and while a prerecording of a passage they had previously recited from *Bambi* was played through headphones above their abdomen. The second group also rested and listened to guitar music as a different prospective mother's prerecording of the same *Bambi* passage was emitted over their abdomen. As the mothers rested, their fetus's heart rate was examined. Results indicated that the heart rates of fetuses exposed to their own mother's voice were higher than those of fetuses exposed to an unfamiliar woman's voice. Presumably, fetuses recognized their own mother's voice, having been previously exposed to their mother's conversations. Studies such as this one suggest that rudimentary abilities to learn simple patterns are present before birth.

In summary, the formation of a human life is the outcome of many changes. The body grows step by step, carefully managed by nature, constantly drawing from nurture. In spectacular feats of coordination, new cells extend body parts so that these structures become increasingly defined—for example, simple paddles turn into elongated arms, arms add hands, and hands add fingers. Both genetic expression and prenatal development show a wonderful balance between nature and nurture, universality and diversity, and qualitative and quantitative change, as you can see in the Basic Developmental Issues table "Biological Beginnings" on the following page.

Medical Care

Prospective parents invariably hope for healthy children. To enhance their chances of giving birth to strong, well-formed infants, prospective mothers can look after themselves and address any serious medical issues before getting pregnant. When they do become pregnant, women can shield their developing offspring from harmful substances and obtain ongoing medical care.

Preparing for Pregnancy

A woman can increase her chances of having a healthy infant by caring for herself *before* becoming pregnant. Physicians and nurses advised of a woman's wish for a child may suggest that she watch her diet, take approved vitamin supplements, exercise moderately, and avoid alcohol and drugs. They may also review her prescriptions and over-the-counter medicines, because some can be harmful to fetuses. For example, the antianxiety drug diazepam (Valium) increases the chances the offspring will develop a cleft lip, and the acne medication isotretinoin (Accutane) in some cases appears to cause serious malformations in offspring (M. R. Davidson, London, & Ladewig, 2008; Sadler, 2010). Obviously, these and other potentially dangerous substances are not recommended for women who are pregnant or likely to conceive. Medical personnel may also address particular health problems that can become complicated during a pregnancy, such as hypertension or diabetes. Finally, physicians and nurses may discuss any concerns that they or the woman have about age. Pregnant women under age 17 sometimes have poor nutrition and give birth to infants with low birth weight. Advanced age in mothers and fathers (35 or older for mothers, 40 or older for fathers) is associated with slightly elevated risks for genetic problems, and older mothers are at minor risk for complications during the pregnancy and for giving birth to a baby with physical malformations (M. R. Davidson et al., 2008).

Yet the responsibility for avoiding toxic substances must not rest entirely on mothers-to-be. Prospective fathers, too, should take precautions in the days, weeks, and months before conceiving a child. Evidence is growing that men's exposure to mercury, lead, alcohol, cigarettes, and other substances is associated with miscarriage (spontaneous loss of the offspring), low birth weight, and birth defects in their offspring (Sadler, 2010).

A man and woman concerned about conceiving a child with significant birth defects may consult a genetic counselor. Prospective parents are most likely to work with a genetic counselor when they have had several miscarriages; have given birth to a child with a genetic defect or chromosomal abnormality; have a particular concern that can be addressed with investigations into genetic risk; or are aware of a family history of a genetic disorder, intellectual disability, or birth defects (S. Dolan, Biermannn, & Damus, 2007; Meyerstein, 2001). The genetic counselor examines the family's medical records and information the couple provides about the health of siblings, parents, and other biological relatives. Diagnostic tests may be conducted, including

BASIC DEVELOPMENTAL ISSUES
Biological Beginnings

ISSUE	GENETIC FOUNDATIONS	PRENATAL DEVELOPMENT
Nature and Nurture	Nature forms gametes (the sperm and ovum) and fuses them to form a future child with a unique genetic make-up. Nurture is evident in environmental effects on the parents' chromosomes, as can occur when radiation and illness create errors in reproductive cells. During and after prenatal development, nature and nurture work in concert: Genes do their work in collaboration with the offspring's physiology, nutrition, and experience.	Nature and nurture are closely intertwined during the offspring's prenatal development. The effects of nature are evident in predictable, ordered changes to body structures and in the formation and operation of supporting physical structures, such as the placenta. The effects of nurture are seen with nutrition, protection from harmful substances, and the mother's stress management.
Universality and Diversity	The vast majority of children are born with 46 chromosomes. Most genes take the form of uniform instructions for necessary proteins to build human bodies and brains. Some genes vary systematically across children and permit individual differences in height, weight, physical appearance, motor skills, intellectual abilities, and temperament. Errors in chromosomes and genes are another source of diversity.	In healthy prenatal beings, there is considerable universality in the sequence of changes. The small being proceeds through phases of the zygote, embryo, and fetus, and ultimately is born after approximately 9 months. Diversity occurs because of variations in mothers' health and exposure to harmful substances, the genetic vulnerabilities of the fetus, and the efficiency with which physical structures in the womb sustain life.
Qualitative and Quantitative Change	Qualitative changes are made possible by the careful sequence with which particular genes are triggered. At appropriate times, selected genes spring into action and create qualitative changes in the child's body, such as the makeovers of puberty. When genes direct the body to mature and grow larger, they also permit quantitative changes, as occurs in steady increases in height and weight.	The future baby undergoes a series of predictable qualitative transformations. As a zygote it moves through the fallopian tubes, grows new cells, and burrows into the inside wall of the uterus; as an embryo it creates many new cells, which form the basic organs and structures of the body; and as a fetus it builds and refines these preliminary structures, activating physiological processes needed for survival. Quantitative changes are present in the rapid production of new cells, particularly in the brain and body prior to birth.

an analysis of the potential parents' chromosomes. Genetic counselors inform the couple of medical facts, inheritance patterns, estimated risks for having a child with a birth defect or disorder, and ways to deal with risks. Counselors may recommend that prenatal diagnostic tests be conducted during a pregnancy and make appropriate referrals to mental health professionals.

Avoiding Harmful Substances

During prenatal development, some babies-to-be are unfortunately exposed to potentially harmful substances, or **teratogens**. Examples of teratogens include many prescription and nonprescription drugs; alcohol; infectious agents such as rubella, syphilis, and human immunodeficiency virus (HIV); and dangerous environmental chemicals, including lead and polychlorinated biphenyls.

Prenatal development includes a series of *sensitive periods* for forming physical structures. Certain body parts are most vulnerable to teratogens when the formations are first emerging, growing speedily, and laying the foundation on which more refined extensions are built. Thus the timing of exposure to teratogens partly determines their impact. A newly formed *zygote* has not yet begun to form separate body parts and tends not to sustain structural defects when exposed to teratogens. Occasionally, exposure to teratogens can cause death of the zygote, but frequently a few cells will die or become damaged, and these cells will be replaced with healthy cells (K. L. Moore & Persaud, 2008). For the *embryo,* however, damage can be serious. The principal parts of the body, including the limbs and the internal organs, are formed during this phase, and exposure to drugs, alcohol, and other teratogens can cause major problems. Limbs are particularly sensitive to harm 24 to 36 days after conception (K. L. Moore & Persaud, 2008). Keep in mind that during this early phase of the pregnancy, women may not yet know they are pregnant. As a general rule, the *fetus* is less susceptible to serious structural damage, although there are some exceptions: Notably, the brain continues to grow until (and after) birth and, as a result, the brain can be damaged then.

teratogen

Potentially harmful substance that can cause damaging effects during prenatal development.

The genetic makeup of both mother and baby moderates the effects of teratogens. For example, phenytoin (Dilantin) is an anticonvulsant medication prescribed for some people who have epilepsy. Between 5 and 10 percent of children exposed to phenytoin as embryos develop a small brain, an intellectual disability, wide spaces between eyes, a short nose, and other distinctive facial features (K. L. Moore & Persaud, 2008). About a third of exposed embryos show minor congenital problems, and approximately half are unaffected. Presumably, genetic factors are partly responsible for these different outcomes.

The amount of teratogen exposure is also important: The greater the exposure, the more severe and widespread the effects. Clearly, women who are pregnant must exercise caution in the food and substances they ingest and the toxins they encounter in the environment. In fact, this need for caution extends to all women who are sexually active and capable of becoming pregnant, because women are not always aware that they are carrying rapidly growing offspring. Here are some examples of particular teratogens and their potential effects on offspring:

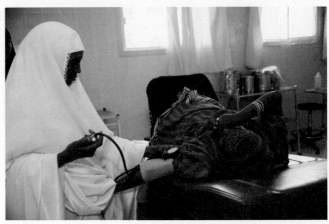

HOW'S MY BABY? To protect their children, pregnant women can eat healthfully, reduce their stress, avoid potentially harmful substances, and, like this woman in Somaliland, see a midwife, doctor, or nurse.

- *Alcohol.* Women who drink alcohol excessively during pregnancy can give birth to infants with *fetal alcohol syndrome*. Cells in the brain are disrupted, physical development is delayed, facial abnormalities occur, intellectual disabilities are common, and children become impulsive and exhibit other behavioral problems. In less severe cases, children may develop learning disabilities or minor physical problems.
- *Nicotine.* Women who smoke cigarettes are at risk for giving birth to small, lightweight babies and (less often) to lose their offspring through miscarriage.
- *Cocaine.* Women using cocaine during pregnancy are likely to have a miscarriage; give birth prematurely; and have babies with low birth weight, small head size, lethargy, and irritability.
- *Heroin.* Pregnant women who use heroin may miscarry or give birth prematurely. After birth, exposed infants may be irritable, suffer respiratory complications, and even die, and those who survive may have a small head size.
- *Organic mercury.* Pregnant women who ingest high levels of mercury from diets rich in fish are at risk for giving birth to children with abnormal brains, intellectual disabilities, and motor problems.
- *Rubella.* Pregnant women who become infected with the virus rubella (also known as German or three-day measles) early in their pregnancy may give birth to children with cataracts, heart problems, and deafness.
- *Herpes simplex.* Pregnant women with the herpes simplex virus are at risk for having a miscarriage or giving birth prematurely to infants with physical problems.
- *HIV infection and AIDS.* Unless treated medically, pregnant women with the HIV virus are at risk for passing on the virus to their children, and children who become infected may initially show delays in motor skills, language, and cognitive development, and ultimately develop more serious health impairments. (Buka, Cannon, Torrey, Yolken, and the Collaborative Study Group on the Perinatal Origins of Severe Psychiatric Disorders, 2008; M. R. Davidson et al., 2008; K. S. Montgomery et al., 2008; Slotkin, 2008; C. B. Smith, Battin, Francis, & Jacobson, 2007)

Maternal anxiety can also create problems for the fetus. Pregnant women who experience high levels of stress are apt to give birth to infants with low birth weight and short-tempered dispositions and, later in life, with difficulties in focusing attention and dealing with negative emotions (Bekkhus, Rutter, Barker, & Borge, 2011; Buss, Davis, Muftuler, Head, & Sandman, 2010; Huizink, Mulder, & Buitelaar, 2004). Of course, most women experience some level of stress during their pregnancy, and mild emotional strain is probably harmless and may even help stimulate growth of the fetus's brain (DiPietro, 2004).

Implementing Medical Procedures

Several medical procedures are available to check on the status of prenatal offspring. An *ultrasound examination* (also known as ultrasonography) has become a routine part of the obstetric care of pregnant women in many countries. Ultrasound devices emit high-frequency sound waves that bounce off tissues of varying densities. The apparatus is passed over the woman's abdomen or inserted in her vagina. Echoes from the waves are converted into two-dimensional images of the fetus and displayed on a television monitor. Ultrasound examinations provide good estimates of the age of the fetus, detect multiple fetuses, and reveal some major abnormalities (London, Ladewig, Ball, & Bindler, 2007; K. L. Moore & Persaud, 2008). Ultrasounds are also used as anatomical guides during the implementation of other prenatal tests. Finally, ultrasound examinations confirm the reality of the pregnancy for expectant parents, as one father reported:

> Yes, when (she) got pregnant I didn't really understand it. But after we had the ultrasound I did. . . . It was the most exciting thing I have done as far as the baby is concerned. It was more exciting than when I heard that we were going to have a baby. (Ekelin, Crang-Svalenius, & Dykes, 2004, p. 337)

Several other prenatal diagnostic techniques are implemented only with high-risk pregnancies. *Chorionic villus sampling* (CVS) is an invasive diagnostic procedure performed sometime between 10 and 12 weeks after conception (London et al., 2007). A needle is inserted into the woman's abdomen, or a tube is guided through her cervix (see Figure 4-9A), and tiny amounts of chorionic villi (blood vessels that grow on the membrane surrounding the developing embryo or fetus) are collected. Abnormalities detected by CVS include chromosomal abnormalities, such X-chromosome-linked disorders as Tay-Sachs disease, and some diseases of the blood, for example sickle cell disease. Test results are typically available within a few days. The procedure entails a small risk for damage to an arm or leg of the embryo or fetus, and miscarriage is possible but unlikely (Sadler, 2010).

Amniocentesis is an invasive diagnostic procedure usually performed sometime between 14 and 18 weeks after conception. A needle is inserted into the woman's abdomen to draw a small amount of fluid from the uterus (see Figure 4-9B). The fluid is analyzed for high concentrations of a fetal protein, which are present when fetuses have *neural tube defects* and some abdominal problems. Fetal cells floating in the amniotic fluid are also analyzed

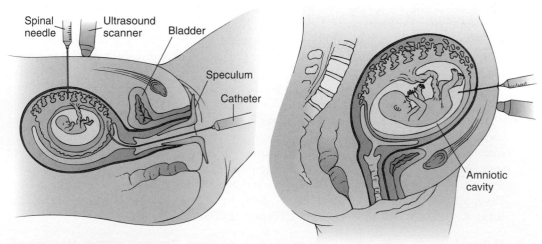

A. Chorionic villus sampling with a 7-week-old embryo

B. Amniocentesis with a 13-week-old fetus

FIGURE 4-9 Prenatal diagnostic methods. In both chorionic villus sampling (A) and amniocentesis (B), an ultrasound procedure guides the test.

Based on K. L. Moore et al., 2000.

for possible chromosomal abnormalities. Other problems detected by amniocentesis are biochemical defects, prenatal infections, gene defects, and blood diseases. Results from cell cultures usually take 2 to 4 weeks to analyze. Risks associated with amniocentesis are trauma to the fetus, infection, and miscarriage (fetal loss rates are 1 percent; Sadler, 2010).

Other tests are performed occasionally. The mother's blood can be tested for the presence of fetal cells. Normally, not many fetal cells cross the placenta into the mother's circulation, but some do, and the mother's blood can be tested for high rates of fetal protein, which might indicate a neural tube defect in the fetus. In consultation with the mother, a physician may also use a *fetoscope,* an instrument with a tiny camera and light, to examine the fetus for defective limbs or other deformities. Corrective surgery is performed in rare circumstances.

When couples learn that their offspring has a chromosomal abnormality or other serious defect, they may be shocked initially and subsequently ask for support from counselors, medical personnel, and family and friends (C. L. Anderson & Brown, 2009; Lalor, Begley, & Galavan, 2009). Depending on their values and circumstances, some couples choose to terminate the pregnancy, concerned that they will not be able to care adequately for a child with special needs. Other couples want practical tips and emotional support in preparing for the birth of a child with a disability, believing in the fetus's right to life and their ability to be caring parents for the child.

Supporting Parents, Protecting Babies

If you have the opportunity to work with prospective parents, you can educate them about prenatal development and their future child's need for protection. Here are some specific tactics to take:

• **Encourage women to evaluate their health before becoming pregnant.** Women who are planning a pregnancy or capable of becoming pregnant can consult their physician. In particular, women who take over-the-counter or prescription medications need to talk with their doctor about risks for a pregnancy and alternative ways of managing chronic conditions.

• **Remind sexually active women and men to take care of themselves.** Women may be several weeks along (or longer) in a pregnancy before they become aware of it. Consequently, women who might be pregnant should watch their diet, restrict their exposure to teratogens, including alcohol, and avoid x-rays. Men may need to be advised that they, too, can put their future children at risk by exposing themselves to harmful substances.

• **Urge pregnant women to seek medical care.** A number of pregnant women are reluctant to seek medical care. Yet prenatal care can be necessary in order to detect and treat problematic conditions in mothers and offspring. For example, pregnant women with HIV can be treated with antiretroviral therapy, helping to control the infection and in many cases preventing transmission of the virus to their offspring. When pregnant women visit nurses and other medical care providers, their risks will be assessed, questions answered, and conditions treated. Under the guidance of a doctor, pregnant women often follow an exercise program. Getting regular exercise can help pregnant women keep up their stamina, prepare for birth, and ease stress. Getting adequate rest is another important goal for pregnant women, even though doing so is sometimes difficult, especially when they have other children, jobs, and ongoing household responsibilities.

• **Use well-researched strategies when trying to reach women who are at risk for late or no prenatal care.** Outreach is critical but it must be done effectively. Public health personnel occasionally seek the advice of pregnant women in the local community for guidance about how best to convince *other* expectant mothers to get appropriate medical and nutritional care. Effective recruitment strategies take a variety of forms, including toll-free hotline numbers, radio spots, and posters in various public locations (P. A. Doyle et al., 2006).

• **Advise pregnant women about nutritional resources.** All expectant mothers need a healthful diet. Yet some women may not remember to eat well and others cannot afford to do so. You can encourage women to become more thoughtful about nutrition than they were previously, and you can advise them of community resources that will help them get the food they need. For example, the U.S. Special Supplemental Nutrition Program for Women, Infants, and Children (WIC) offers supplemental foods with nutrients that are vital for healthy prenatal development yet often lacking in the diets of low-income populations (e.g., protein, iron, calcium, and vitamins A and C) (Connor et al., 2010).

• **Urge pregnant women to stay clear of teratogens.** Smokers can be encouraged to reduce the number of cigarettes they smoke or, better yet, to quit smoking altogether. Twenty-year-old Veronica, first-time mother and smoker since the age of 13, was concerned that her smoking would harm her baby and decided to phase out cigarette smoking one cigarette at a time, until the fourth month of her pregnancy, when she quit altogether and commented, "I have done what I can, now the rest is up to God" (Nichter et al., 2007, p. 754). Expectant women who drink alcohol or take drugs need to be confronted with the dreadful and permanent damage these substances can cause in children.

Obviously, pregnant women who are physiologically dependent on alcohol or drugs need immediate professional help. For their own sake and that of their children, women who continue to abuse substances after their babies are born also need professional treatment. Many of these mothers additionally need guidance with parenting skills (J. V. Brown, Bakeman, Coles, Platzman, & Lynch, 2004; M. R. Davidson et al., 2008). Community counselors and family educators can advise families about helpful programs in their area.

• **Ask pregnant women to speak their minds.** Many pregnant women have experiences they want to share. For example, they may have concerns about possible birth defects or simply want to communicate excitement, for instance, when they first feel the fetus stir within them. Many women appreciate sympathetic listeners who let them talk about their changing and conflicting feelings.

• **Ask fathers to talk about their experiences.** Many fathers are mystified with the physical changes their partners undergo during pregnancy. Some fathers feel excluded during pregnancy. Although they had an obvious hand in creating the new being, they may believe they are not needed for further development (Genesoni & Tallandini, 2009). In reality, fathers can play an enormously important role in supporting expectant mothers. And many prospective fathers gain just as much as mothers from having a sensitive listener with whom to share their worries and hopes related to the baby.

• **Advise new parents about appropriate care when children have been exposed to teratogens.** Sadly, the brains and bodies of some children are impaired due to prenatal exposure to drugs, alcohol, infection, and other teratogens. Some of these effects are lasting, but even so, affected children certainly benefit from responsive, predictable, and developmentally appropriate care. For example, many children who have been exposed to cocaine and other serious teratogens develop good language, communication, and interpersonal skills when they receive high-quality care (J. V. Brown et al., 2004). Special educational services can likewise enhance the academic and social skills of teratogen-exposed children.

Unlike many other developmental accomplishments, for instance, learning to talk, walk, and ride a bicycle, many aspects of prenatal development cannot be observed directly. Nonetheless, the mother has firsthand experience with the pregnancy, and scientific evidence provides accurate benchmarks as to what is happening to the baby-to-be during the various phases of growth. The Developmental Trends table "Prenatal Development" provides a useful synopsis of key prenatal developments and discernible signs of growth.

DEVELOPMENTAL TRENDS
Prenatal Development

PHASE OF PRENATAL GROWTH	WHAT YOU MIGHT OBSERVE	DIVERSITY	IMPLICATIONS
Zygote (Conception to 2 Weeks After)	• The zygote begins to develop at conception with the fusing of the sperm and ovum. The offspring's first cell divides into two cells, two divide into four, four divide into eight, and so forth. The zygote is a ball of cells as it travels down the fallopian tube and into the uterus. • No signs of pregnancy are typically noticeable to the prospective mother.	• Couples vary in their chances of conceiving a child. • Some children are conceived with the assistance of reproductive technologies. • A large number of zygotes perish because errors in chromosomes cause them to be seriously malformed and unable to grow. • Hormonal factors in the woman can also cause loss of zygotes.	• Encourage prospective parents to plan for a pregnancy by first taking stock of their health, talking with a physician, and, if they have concerns about potential genetic problems in their children, seeing a genetic counselor. • Persuade prospective parents to follow a physician's recommendations regarding appropriate uses of prescription medications, over-the-counter drugs, and vitamins. • Persuade sexually active women to avoid alcohol and drugs.
Embryo (2 Through 8 Weeks After Conception)	• Body parts and organs are being formed as the embryo rapidly develops. At the end of the period, the little being shows a head structure and limbs that are recognizably human. • The prospective mother may notice that her menstrual period is late. She may experience early signs of pregnancy, including nausea, fatigue, abdominal swelling, and tender breasts.	• The embryo is especially susceptible to damage from harmful substances. The extent of harm done by teratogens will depend on the timing and duration of exposure, the amount of the dose, and the biological vulnerability of the embryo. • Miscarriage is fairly common during this period.	• Encourage a prospective mother to see a nurse or physician if she believes she might be pregnant. • Encourage pregnant women to shield themselves from potentially harmful substances. Educate prospective mothers and fathers about the impact of teratogens on the developing offspring.
Fetus (9 Weeks After Conception Until Birth)	• Organs and body parts continue to grow and mature. • The mother can feel the fetus moving, lightly at first and actively over time. • The mother's abdomen swells, and the mother gains weight.	• Many pregnant women feel strong and healthy during the final months of pregnancy, but some continue to experience nausea and fatigue. • Fetuses vary in many respects, including their movements, growth rates and birth weights, and readiness for survival at birth.	• Advise pregnant women to follow the advice of their nurse or physician regarding diet and exercise. • Listen to prospective mothers and fathers talk about their hopes, fears, and expectations related to the baby. • Continue to advocate for abstinence from alcohol and drugs; discourage cigarette smoking. • Encourage pregnant women to manage their stress levels. • Inform pregnant women about prepared childbirth classes in their area.

Source: K. L. Moore & Persaud, 2008.

BIRTH OF THE BABY

Childbirth is a complex bioecological occasion. The events that culminate in a birth are affected by the health of mother and baby; support the mother receives from family, friends, midwives, medical personnel, and other members of the community; the mother's preferences for coping with the physical strains of labor and delivery; and her cultural traditions and beliefs.

Bioecology of Child Development

Childbirth is affected by numerous biological processes and by the mother's choices and experiences in her social and cultural environment.

In many societies, childbirth is a natural event, unaccompanied by drugs or medical procedures. Emefa, a woman in Ghana, gave birth to her fourth child in the corner of her hut:

> She lay curled into a small ball on her left side, her pregnant and contracting uterus protruding from her thin frame. No sound came from her. No sound came from the midwife either. She was seated in the corner of the dark hot hut, waiting. Suddenly, Emefa gave a low whimper and hauled herself into a sitting and then squatting position. The midwife crept over to her and gently supported Emefa's back as she bore down. No words, no commands, no yelling. . . . Once it was over, Emefa lay down on the ground again to rest until she was required to continue the process of giving birth. . . . Another contraction gripped Emefa and she lumbered up into her squatting position again. . . . The baby's head appeared gradually, slowly making its progress into the world. . . . A soft whoosh and the baby's body was born into the steady and confident hands of the midwife. . . . The baby was breathing and at once handed to his mother. (Hillier, 2003, p. 3)

Numerous women in Western societies also strive for a natural childbirth, as you saw in Laurie and Tom's experience in our chapter-opening case study. Yet women in industrialized countries frequently use medical practices that ease their discomfort or protect their baby from complications. Women who choose to take medication and permit one or more procedures typically have good outcomes, and in some births medical interventions save the life of mother or baby. However, in a sizable number of births women are pressured into medical procedures that are probably unnecessary and in some cases potentially harmful to them or their babies (Janssen et al., 2009).

In Western and non-Western societies alike, a clash often arises between traditional customs and the procedures of modern medicine. As you can see in the Development in Culture feature "Having Babies in Nepal," numerous contemporary health providers try to overcome these tensions by allowing women to select from the best features of traditional methods of childbirth *and* from the advantages of medical techniques (Gabrysch et al., 2009).

Preparation for Birth

A human childbirth provokes a range of feelings in parents—excitement, fear, pain, fatigue, and joy, to name a few. The events of birth are managed best when families prepare ahead of time, take advantage of adequate care, and hold reasonable expectations about the baby's abilities.

Although some anxiety is common, parents are highly individual in their feelings about pregnancy and birth. One first-time mother may be eager to have her baby but anxious about changes to her life, new financial pressures, and her lack of experience with children, whereas another prospective woman has plenty of support from her family and takes the changes in stride. Such feelings, along with any concerns about controlling pain, may influence the actual birth experience (Hall et al., 2009; Soet, Brack, & Dilorio, 2003). Excessive levels of stress make for an unpleasant experience for parents and can prolong the early stages of labor, raise the mother's blood pressure, and decrease oxygen to the baby. Parents can reduce their anxiety by seeking out information, getting organized for the baby, and preparing other children in their family for the new arrival.

Health care providers and family educators can give useful information and reassurance to parents during the pregnancy. They may teach relaxation techniques; offer tips for posture, movement, and exercise; and persuade women to eliminate potentially risky behaviors. In Western societies, *prepared childbirth classes* are common. These programs typically include the following elements:

- Information about changes in, and nutritional needs of, the prospective baby
- Preparation for the baby's arrival, including arrangements for the baby at home and decisions about breast or bottle feeding
- Relaxation and breathing techniques that encourage the mother to stay focused, manage pain, reduce fear, and use muscles effectively during the various phases of the labor
- Support from a spouse, partner, friend, or family member who coaches the mother throughout labor and delivery, reminds her to use the breathing techniques she has learned, massages her, and otherwise encourages her

DEVELOPMENT IN CULTURE
Having Babies in Nepal

Nepal is a small developing country nestled between China and India. Three rivers and a rough mountainous terrain make it difficult for the Nepalese to grow crops and travel between villages. These harsh conditions have given rise to a hardy people, most of whom are Hindus or Buddhists who advocate for loyalty within the family, respect for elders, nonviolence, and a commitment to meditation (Rolls & Chamberlain, 2004).

Sex roles are clearly demarcated in Nepalese culture, especially in the sparsely populated regions. In rural areas, women collect water, prepare meals, wash clothes, and aspire to live by ethics of modesty, obedience, and self-sacrifice. Men make the major decisions for the family, carry out strenuous agricultural tasks, and trade with other men in the village. Marriages typically take place between young women in their teens and young men in their early twenties. Most newly married couples eagerly await their first child and proceed to have three or more additional offspring.

Nepalese women are expected to remain self-sufficient during pregnancy and childbirth. Prenatal development is presumed to be a natural process that progresses with divine support (Matsuyama & Moji, 2008). Medical care was not historically available in the rural areas, nor could women easily travel to hospitals or for that matter did they want to be examined by unfamiliar doctors, nurses, or midwives. In recent years, more and more clinics have been built but are not always used. When pregnant women determine they require help, they generally ask mothers-in-law for practical advice and traditional healers for assistance in banishing evil spirits (Justice, 1984; Regmi & Madison, 2009).

A BLESSING. Many Nepalese women have their first child during their teenage years, welcome a baby as a divine blessing, and bear the discomforts of pregnancy and childbirth without complaint.

Most Nepalese women are strong and robust. They work throughout their pregnancies, have smooth deliveries, and resume their household toils soon after their babies are born. More than 9 out of 10 deliveries occur at home or in a cowshed (Regmi & Madison, 2009). Nepalese women typically give birth without medication, using such postures as kneeling, squatting, or standing (Carla, 2003). They regularly take herbal remedies to ease recovery after the birth.

But not every Nepalese woman has an easy time with pregnancy or birth. Occasional serious problems, including poor nutrition and health complications, go untreated and as a result, the mortality rate of Nepalese pregnant mothers is distressingly high—539 deaths per 100,000 live births (Kulkarni, Christian, LeClerq, & Khatry, 2009; Matsuyama & Moji, 2008). Moreover, almost 1 in 20 infants dies during childbirth due to serious difficulties during the delivery or before their first birthday due to such problems as inadequate nutrition, impure water, prolonged exposure to the cold, and contraction of infectious diseases (Central Intelligence Agency, 2010; Justice, 1984).

In recent decades, international agencies and local authorities have tried to prevent and treat medical problems of Nepalese women. Medical personnel have had mixed success, in part because their interventions have failed to address barriers in local conditions or been incompatible with cultural practices. In one program young women trained as midwives came primarily from the urban areas and were shunned in the villages because of the widespread belief that young women should not travel on their own or work side by side men (Justice, 1984). Some women have avoided going to hospitals because of the reputation that medical staff had in discouraging local childbirth traditions, including beneficial delivery postures that allow mobility (Carla, 2003; Regmi & Madison, 2009). One 20-year-old mother, Anu, went to a modern hospital and felt like an observer at her own childbirth:

> The nurse took me to the delivery table. There were several young males and females in white coats surrounding the delivery table. Their job was to shout in a monotonous voice "bal gar . . . jor gar" [push down]. Then they said I needed a cut down into my private part [episiotomy]. I didn't like the idea, but they said that it had to be done otherwise the baby could get stuck. Finally, going through all these uncomfortable procedures I delivered this baby. Now I am asking myself, what have I done to deliver this baby? I simply watched the health workers delivering this baby. (Regmi & Madison, 2009, pp. 384–385)

Health initiatives have begun to accommodate the traditions and beliefs of Nepalese culture while offering mothers the benefits of modern medicine. A few programs are educating mothers-in-laws about maternal health, prenatal care, and danger signs during pregnancy and labor (Regmi & Madison, 2009). Many health care workers are now showing respect for cultural traditions, encouraging women to make their own choices, and selectively implementing intrusive medical procedures only with mothers who have defined risks (Barker, Bird, Pradhan, & Shakya, 2007; Safe Motherhood Network Federation, 2010).

- Education about the physiology and mechanics of delivery, types of positions during delivery, and pain medications and common medical interventions. (Dick-Read, 1944; Jaddoe, 2009; Lamaze, 1958)

The pregnant woman and her partner, if she has one, may decide ahead of time where the birth will take place and who will attend to it. Hospitals offer the latest technology, well-trained medical staff, arrangements for insurance coverage, and pain medication, but they have definite disadvantages. As occurred with Laurie and Tom in our introductory case study, some parents perceive hospitals as instituting unnecessary treatments and as creating an impersonal climate that separates rather than unites family members during a momentous occasion. Hospitals have responded to concerns about their lack of family orientation by creating birthing rooms that are attractive, comfortable, and large enough to accommodate several family members. Community birth centers are homelike, inexpensive, and welcoming of extended contact with the newborn; however, they are less appropriate for women with high-risk deliveries, those who need emergency care, and those whose insurance does not cover costs. Home settings offer families a familiar and comforting environment, allow family members to participate, are inexpensive, and give extended contact with the newborn. They have disadvantages similar to those of community birth centers and in many cases offer no pain medication, few emergency procedures, and minimal access to trained birth attendants (Symon, Winter, Inkster, & Donnan, 2009).

In North America, physicians most often deliver babies, but other common attendants include certified *midwives* who may or not be trained as nurses. Midwives have less medical training than physicians but are generally well educated and experienced. Midwives typically assume responsibility for a mother's prenatal care, delivery, and recovery after the birth. Increasingly mothers also turn to *doulas*, attendants at the birth who do not provide medical care but do offer emotional and physical support. Doulas help the mother develop a birth plan ahead of time and then stay by a mother's side throughout the childbirth, guiding her in effective breathing techniques, massaging her back, and coaching her through the process (Deitrick & Draves, 2008). Doulas supplement rather than replace the mother's partner if she has one, and some hospitals offer the services of a doula to laboring women without partners.

In addition to seeking conventional medical treatment, many women avail themselves of *complementary therapies* during pregnancy and childbirth (M. R. Davidson et al., 2008; Fontaine, 2011; D. Walls, 2009). Complementary therapies supplement standard medicine and offer some benefits in health and relaxation. In other cases, women use *alternative therapies*, healing practices that are tried *instead* of conventional treatments. As examples, as either complementary therapies or in lieu of conventional medical procedures, some women obtain *acupuncture*, a traditional Chinese treatment in which thin stainless steel needles stimulate precise locations on the body so as to relieve pain and promote wellness. Other women choose *biofeedback*, a method for controlling muscle tension, or *self-hypnosis*, a self-induced state of relaxation and receptivity to suggestions about reducing distress. Many women derive a sense of well-being from *prayer*, during which they address (silently or vocally) the divine being of their faith, or from *meditation*, a quiet transcendent state during which the mind is still, peaceful, and uncluttered. Other common complementary and alternative therapies include *massage therapy*, relaxing manipulation of the body's soft tissues to reduce tension and promote comfort; *hatha yoga*, an Eastern practice of gentle exercises and breathing techniques; and use of herbs and essential oils.

Complementary and alternative therapies offer the advantages of being relatively low in cost, emphasizing wellness, and being noninvasive. Unfortunately, childbirth risks cannot always be anticipated and do not always respond to complementary and alternative therapies. In rare situations surgery or other medical procedures are needed to save the life of the mother or infant.

The Birth Process

Amazingly, medical researchers are still not able to pinpoint the cascade of changes necessary to trigger the uterine contractions that begin a woman's labor (M. R. Davidson et al., 2008). Currently, medical researchers believe that a combination of factors precipitates labor, including hormonal changes in the mother's body and hormones released by the baby's brain.

Typically, the mother's uterus begins preparations for birth 38 to 40 weeks into the pregnancy. Here is the incredible sequence of events that constitutes the birth process:

- As the pregnancy advances, the mother experiences *Braxton Hicks contractions*. These irregular contractions exercise the mother's uterine muscles without causing the cervix to open.
- In most cases (95%), the baby settles in a head-downward position, which facilitates its passage through the birth canal. When babies are in breech position (situated to come out buttocks or legs first) or in a sideways position (a shoulder would likely come out first), the mother is monitored closely and often undergoes a *cesarean delivery*, a surgical procedure in which the baby is removed after an incision is made in the mother's abdomen and uterine wall.
- A few events may occur in the days immediately before labor begins. The mother may experience a descent of the baby into the pelvis, feel a rush of energy, lose 1 to 4 pounds as her hormonal balance changes, and notice vaginal secretions. Sleep is difficult at this time. Accordingly, health providers may help mothers use relaxation techniques and reassure them that sleep disturbances prior to labor do not usually interfere with its progression.
- In the *first stage of labor*, the mother experiences regular uterine contractions that widen the cervix opening (see Figure 4-10A). These contractions last until the cervix is dilated to about 10 centimeters (approximately 4 inches). Mothers feel pain, especially in their pelvis and back. This first stage typically takes about 12 to 16 hours for mothers who are having their first baby and 6 to 8 hours for mothers who have previously delivered one or more babies. Medical personnel keep track of the cervix opening and monitor the fetal heartbeat. They may offer pain medication and encourage the mother to walk around. At the beginning of the first stage of labor, contractions are spaced widely apart (e.g., every 15 to 30 minutes) and are mild to moderate in intensity. When the cervix dilates to 3 centimeters, an "active" phase begins and lasts until full dilation. Contractions become stronger and longer (they last 30 to 60 seconds) and occur every 2 to 3 minutes.
- In the *second stage of labor*, the cervix is fully dilated, the baby proceeds down the birth canal, and the child is born (see Figures 4-10B, C, and D). This stage may take about half an hour, but in first pregnancies it often lasts up to 2 hours. Contractions come often and hard. They appear every other minute and last for a minute at a time. Mothers must push hard to help move the baby down and out. Medical personnel continue to watch the fetal heartbeat. The doctor may use forceps or call for a cesarean delivery if uterine contractions slow down or the baby does not move quickly enough. Too fast is not good either, however, because the pressure might tear the mother's tissues or the baby's head. Thus, the doctor or midwife may place a hand on the part of the baby coming out and ease it out methodically. Medical personnel may also help rotate the baby's head so that it can get past the mother's pelvic bones. As the head comes out, the doctor or midwife checks to make sure the umbilical cord is not wrapped around the head, and if it is, the cord is moved. The nose and mouth are cleansed of fluids. The mother continues to push to eject the baby's shoulders and the rest of the body. The baby is gently wiped dry, and after the blood has drained from the umbilical cord into the baby's body, the cord is clamped and cut. The baby is born! The baby is placed on the mother, and the father or other coach may take a turn holding him or her. Oftentimes the baby is alert and looks around the room—a stunning and memorable event for the mother, father or other partner, and other friends and family. You can observe the final moments of a normal birth and the extensive testing of the newborn that takes places immediately after birth in many Western countries in a video on MyEducationLab.
- In the *third stage of labor*, the placenta and fetal membranes (collectively known as the *afterbirth*) are expelled by the uterus (see Figure 4-10E). Usually, this process happens

MyEducationLab

To observe the final moments of a normal birth and the extensive testing of the newborn that takes places immediately after birth, go to the Video Examples section in Topic 4 of MyEducationLab.

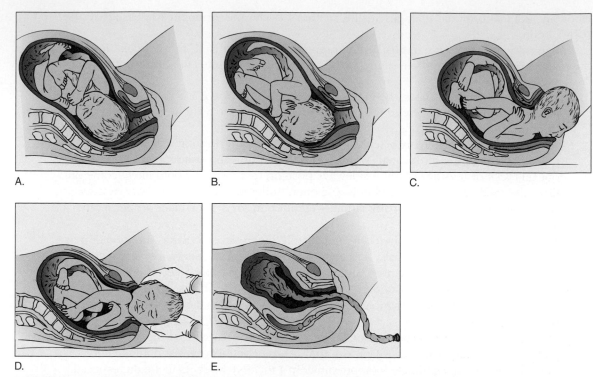

FIGURE 4-10 Stages of a typical birth. In the first stage of labor, the mother's cervix dilates (A). After numerous contractions the cervix opens completely, the baby's head moves down the vagina, and the second stage of labor begins (B). The second stage continues with the mother pushing with each contraction, the baby moving down the vagina, and the baby's head appearing (C). Gradually, the shoulders and the rest of the body emerge (D). The third stage of labor is the delivery of the placenta (E).
Based on Demarest & Charon, 1996.

without assistance, although medical personnel must watch to make sure it happens. The mother is checked to see if lacerations have occurred or if medical treatment is needed.

- In the *fourth stage of labor*, 1 to 4 hours after birth, the mother's body begins to readjust after its considerable exertion. Having lost some blood, the mother may experience a slight decrease in blood pressure, shake and feel chilled, and want to drink water and get something to eat. (M. R. Davidson et al., 2008; Demarest & Charon, 1996; Sherwen, Scoloveno, & Weingarten, 1999)

Medical Interventions

Medical personnel, midwives, and the mother's partner can do many things to comfort the mother as she goes through labor and delivery. Following are some examples of interventions that are typical in many Western societies:

- Physicians may *induce labor*—that is, start it artificially—with medications (e.g., Pitocin). Candidates for an induced labor include women past their due dates and those with diabetes or pregnancy-induced hypertension.
- Midwives, doulas, partners, and medical staff may help relieve the mother's pain by using methods that do not require medication. Some mothers are assisted by a warm whirlpool bath, visual images of the cervix opening, music, hypnosis, biofeedback, and massage.
- Physicians sometimes offer *analgesics,* medicines that reduce pain without loss of consciousness. Medications injected into the mother's spine (such as *epidural analgesia*) are an especially common method for labor relief. Generally, these medications are

not offered early in labor, because they may slow progress, but also not too late, because physicians want the medicine to be metabolized by mother and baby prior to birth. Some analgesic medications can increase the need for other medical interventions, such as use of forceps and cesarean deliveries, and they may reduce breathing in the newborn.

- Physicians may offer *anesthetics* to women in active labor if extreme pressure must be applied (such as occurs in the use of forceps) or when a cesarean delivery must be performed. Anesthetics cause loss of sensation and in some cases also lead to loss of consciousness.

- Women sometimes take *opioids* (also known as narcotics), medicines that reduce the sensation of pain by changing the way it is perceived by the brain. Opioids have several disadvantages, including limited effectiveness in reducing pain, occasional side effects such as nausea and drowsiness, and tendency to adversely affect the baby's breathing and breastfeeding.

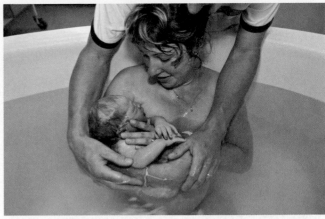

WATER BIRTH. This new mother delivered her baby in a warm bathtub at the hospital with the help of a midwife. For women who choose water births, the warm water provides a relaxing atmosphere.

- Almost 30 percent of babies born in the United States are delivered through cesarean surgery, a rate that many people suggest is higher than it should be (Centers for Disease Control and Prevention, 2005b). Cesarean deliveries are performed when the physician believes the safety of the mother, child, or both is at stake. Examples of conditions that might lead to a cesarean delivery are fetal distress, health problems of the mother, failure to progress in labor, infections in the birth canal, and the presence of multiple babies. You can watch a cesarean delivery in a video on MyEducationLab.

Regardless of the specific medical treatments expectant mothers receive, they and their families invariably appreciate consideration of their individual needs and preferences. Nurses, midwives, doulas, and other attendants can be compassionate caregivers whose sympathetic reassurance helps women to cope with the pain and loss of control that accompanies the birthing process. Depending on their cultural traditions, women may also appreciate the presence and support of their husbands, other partners, friends, or close family members during labor and delivery (S. Price, Noseworthy, & Thornton, 2007).

Many medical personnel do their best to accommodate women's cultural practices related to birth. For example, some Hispanic women prefer to stay at home during the early stages of labor, and when they do arrive at the hospital, they want their partners to remain at their side (Spector, 2004). Many Muslim women are distressed when unfamiliar male doctors and nurses see them uncovered; thus medical personnel might take measures to ensure that these women are covered and accompanied by husbands, mothers, or mothers-in-law during examinations (Rassin, Klug, Nathanzon, Kan, & Silner, 2009). Some Korean women remain silent during labor and delivery, and attendants must be alert to the fact that labor may be progressing without the women's vocalizations. Women from a few cultural groups (e.g., some Native Americans and the Hmong from Laos) may ask to take the placenta home for burial in the ground because of their religious beliefs (M. R. Davidson et al., 2008; Fadiman, 1997).

MyEducationLab

Go to the Video Examples section in Topic 4 of MyEducationLab to watch a cesarean delivery.

Babies at Risk

Some babies are born before they are able to cope with the demands of life outside the womb. Two categories of babies require special care:

- *Babies born early.* The **premature infant** is born before the end of 37 weeks after conception (Sherwen et al., 1999). Premature labor may be triggered by several factors, including infection, presence of two or more babies, abnormalities in the fetus, death of the fetus, abnormalities in the mother's uterus or cervix, and serious disease in the mother. Extremely early babies (born after only 32 or fewer weeks of prenatal growth) face serious risk factors, including higher than typical rates of death during infancy. Immediately after birth, premature infants are also at risk for health problems, including breathing

premature infant
Infant born early (before 37 weeks of prenatal growth) and sometimes with serious medical problems.

HUSH, LITTLE BABIES. In this hospital in Manila, mothers hold their infants on their chests for part of each day in a technique known as *kangaroo care.* Kangaroo care has definite therapeutic properties, including facilitating breastfeeding and helping small infants to relax and grow.

problems, anemia, brain hemorrhages, feeding problems, and temperature instability.

• *Babies born small for date.* Some infants are small and light given the amount of time they have had to develop in the mother's uterus. These babies are at risk for many problems, including neurological deficiencies, structural problems with body parts, breathing difficulties, vision problems, and other serious health problems (Sadler, 2010). Small babies may have chromosomal abnormalities or may have been exposed to infections or harmful substances or received inadequate nutrition during their prenatal development.

Developmental Care for Babies at Risk

Babies born especially early or small may not have the physical maturity to breathe independently, regulate their body's changes in temperature, or suck adequately to meet nutritional needs. Despite these challenges, babies can often survive with access to life-sustaining devices and medicines. Physicians and nurses strive to create a therapeutic atmosphere that is nurturing and developmentally appropriate. The following guidelines are recommended for those who care for a fragile infant:

• Reduce the infant's exposure to light and noise.
• Regulate the amount of handling of the infant by medical staff.
• Position the baby to increase circulation.
• Encourage parents to participate in the care of the infant.
• Inform parents about the infant's needs.
• Arrange diapering, bathing, and changing of clothes so that interruptions to sleep and rest are minimized.
• Encourage parents to cuddle with the infant and carry him or her often and for long periods.
• Swaddle the baby in a blanket or with arms bent and hands placed near the mouth to permit sucking on fingers or hands.
• Massage the baby.
• Educate parents about caring for the child as he or she grows older. (L.-L. Chen, Su, Su, Lin, & Kuo, 2008; T. Field, 2001; Sherwen et al., 1999)

When fragile babies become strong enough to leave the hospital and go home with their families, they may continue to need specialized treatments. Their families may also benefit from support because these babies often show a lot of distress and are not easily soothed. If parents of premature and health-impaired infants learn to fulfill infants' needs confidently and tenderly, however, these infants are likely to calm down and develop healthy habits for responding to distress (J. M. Young, Howell, & Hauser-Cram, 2005). Furthermore, fragile infants who repeatedly relax in the arms of their caregivers are apt to form close bonds with caregivers and gain needed mental energy for attending to the environment.

Thus, the developmental journeys of premature and sick newborn infants are typically *not* destined to be rocky ones (Bronfenbrenner, 2005). In fact, many premature and small infants go on to catch up with peers in their motor, intellectual, and communication skills, particularly when families, educators, and other professionals meet their special needs (Sheffield, Stromswold, & Molnar, 2005). Others have intellectual delays or persisting medical problems, such as visual problems or asthma, and these children benefit from appropriate medical care, advocacy from families, and educational services that help them progress academically and socially. As they grow older, children may also require continued services, such as speech therapy and other individualized educational interventions (Sheffield et al., 2005). Without sensitive care and, if needed, effective intervention, some premature and low-birth-weight infants continue to face later problems in coping with negative emotions and in learning at school (Nomura, Fifer, & Brooks-Gunn, 2005; Shenkin, Starr, & Deary, 2004).

DEVELOPMENT AND PRACTICE
Showing Sensitivity to the Needs of Newborn Infants

Carefully observe the sensory abilities of newborn infants.

- A pediatric nurse watches a newborn infant scanning her parents' faces. The nurse explains to the parents that infants have only limited visual acuity at birth, but they can see some shapes and patterns, are especially attracted to human faces, and develop better vision in their first few months. (Infancy)
- A doctor notices a 3-day-old infant turn his head after his mother begins speaking. The doctor comments softly to the baby in front of the mother, "Oh, you hear your mother talking, don't you, young man?" (Infancy)

Point out the physiological states of newborn infants.

- A family educator talks with parents about their newborn infants, commenting that infants commonly sleep for long periods but usually have brief periods each day when they are receptive to quiet interaction. (Infancy)
- A child care director watches the gaze of a newborn infant as her parents tour the child care center. "Hello little one," says the director. "My goodness you are taking it all in now, aren't you?" (Infancy)

Notice the kinds of stimuli that attract infants' attention.

- A mother watches her newborn infant while he is awake and alert. She notices that her son intently inspects her face and certain other stimuli, such as the edges of the bassinet. (Infancy)
- A 2-week-old infant stares at his father's face while sucking on the bottle. His father smiles back at him. (Infancy)

Encourage parents to articulate infants' preferences for being soothed.

- A pediatrician asks a new mother how she is getting along with her baby. When the mother reports that the baby cries a lot, the doctor asks her how the baby likes to be comforted. The doctor explains that most infants find it soothing to be held tenderly, but some infants also calm down while riding in a car or stroller. The doctor suggests that the mother keep informal records of the infant's fussy times and the kinds of care that eventually prove calming. (Infancy)
- A visiting nurse asks a new mother and her partner about the infant's frequent crying. The parents express their frustration and listen appreciatively when the nurse demonstrates several ways for calming the baby. (Infancy)

Model sensitive care for new parents.

- A family educator shows a new father how to hold the baby, change her diaper, and interact quietly and sensitively with her. (Infancy)
- A grandmother demonstrates to her daughter how to bathe her newborn son. The grandmother carefully tests the temperature of the water in the kitchen sink and assembles all of the bathing supplies before holding the baby in a few inches of warm, sudsy water and gently patting down the baby's skin with a clean cloth. (Infancy)

Offer appropriate care to fragile infants.

- A hospital offers lifesaving care to fragile infants and attends to their sensory abilities and psychological needs by reducing light, noise, and unnecessary medical procedures, and by massaging the infants a few times each day. (Infancy)
- In the neonatal intensive care unit of the hospital, mothers and fathers are allowed to hold their premature infants for an hour or two every day in a procedure known as Kangaroo Care. One of the parents lies down on a bed and holds the infant on his or her bare chest. The baby's head is placed to one side to allow the baby to hear the parent's heartbeat. A blanket is then placed over the baby, and the parent is encouraged to relax and allow the baby to do the same. (Infancy)

Enhancing Parents' Sensitivity to Newborn Infants

To give infants a healthy start on life, parents and other caregivers must recognize infants' abilities, interests, and styles of self-expression. Family educators and other professionals can support infants indirectly—yet powerfully—when they teach family members how to observe their infants closely and respond sympathetically to infants' individual needs. To get a sense of how you might enhance caregivers' awareness of infant needs, see the examples in the Development and Practice feature "Showing Sensitivity to the Needs of Newborn Infants." Also consider these recommendations:

    • **Reassure new mothers that they will be able to find the necessary energy and insight to take good care of their baby.** Many new mothers return home from the hospital feeling tired, sore, and overwhelmed by the demands of an infant, as reflected in these comments:

- "I guess I expected that our lives would change dramatically the moment we walked in the door with him . . . which they did!"
- "It's hard, and sometimes I don't want the responsibility."
- "I felt very much like I didn't know what to do!"
- "Some people are giving too much advice."
- "[The pain was] . . . more than expected." (George, 2005, pp. 253–254)

These observations reveal the need for a series of adjustments by new parents. Although mothers and fathers may want information about infants and their care, they are best able to act on this information when they have caught up on their rest and feel supported by friends, family, and health care professionals.

- **Share what you know about infants' sensory and perceptual abilities.** Infants learn a lot about the world from their sensory and perceptual abilities. **Sensation** refers to the infant's detection of a stimulus; for example, a newborn baby may sense a father's stroking movements on her hand. Infants (and adults, for that matter) sense many things that they don't necessarily focus on or think about. When infants do attend to and interpret a sensation, **perception** takes place, such as when the baby, now 6 months old, watches a moving image and perceives it to be his father.

At birth, many newborn infants look intently at the faces of parents and others, giving people the impression that infants are learning from the beginning of life. In fact, they are. What newborn infants actually *perceive* cannot be determined with certainty, but researchers have established that newborn infants are able to *sense* basic patterns and associations. The majority of infants can see well-defined contrasts and shapes, such as large black-and-white designs on checkerboards, but it takes time for the various parts of the eye to work efficiently and to connect with the brain structures necessary for making sense of visual stimuli.

During the first year of life, vision improves dramatically (D. L. Mayer & Dobson, 1982; Ricci et al., 2007; van Hof-van Duin & Mohn, 1986). Infants can see best from a distance of about 6 to 12 inches, develop a preference for looking at faces, and explore the visual properties of objects. The sense of hearing is actually more advanced at birth than is vision. Recall that late in prenatal development, fetuses begin to hear and recognize their mothers' voices. Typically developing infants are also born with the ability to experience touch, taste, and smell. Sensory and perceptual abilities continue to develop, and these abilities will, of course, make critical contributions to infants' rapidly expanding knowledge about the world.

- **Point out the physiological states of newborn infants.** Unless they have previously had a child or been around newborn infants, parents may be surprised at how their infants act, how long they sleep, and how they respond to stimuli. Family educators and medical personnel can educate parents by explaining the nature of infants' **states of arousal**, the physiological conditions of sleepiness and wakefulness that infants experience throughout the day. Infant practitioners can also point out infants' **reflexes**, their automatic motor responses to stimuli. One example of a reflex is an infant blinking his eyes when his father moves him close to a bright light. Take a look at the Observation Guidelines table "Indicators of Health in Newborn Infants" on page 143 for the kinds of physical states you might show to parents.

- **Encourage families to watch infants' responses to particular stimuli.** Infants give off clues about what they like and dislike, find interesting, and experience as pleasant or painful. However, it may take a while for caregivers to decipher infants' signals and the circumstances that elicit them. When infants are drowsy, asleep, or agitated, they do not show curiosity. When they are rested, comfortable, and awake, they may scan the visual environment, intently study the properties of a mobile over the crib, and smile at familiar vocalizations from a parent. By observing the textures, tastes, sounds, and visual properties that attract infants' sustained attention, parents and other caregivers can guess about concepts of interest to infants. For instance, perhaps they are learning that the blanket feels soft, the juice tastes sweet, the melody is pleasing, and the rubber duck is visually attractive.

- **Discuss the kinds of stimulation infants might find soothing.** Babies have distinct preferences for being comforted. Different babies may relax to varying sensations—listening to the rumble of the clothes dryer, nursing at Mother's breast, sleeping on Father's chest, or going for a ride in the car. Mothers and fathers who have not yet found the antidote to their infants' fussy periods may be grateful for suggestions about a range of soothing techniques.

- **Model sensitive interactions with infants.** Not all caregivers know how to interact in a gentle, reassuring manner with infants. Practitioners can show parents and other caregivers how to slow their pace, hold the baby gently but firmly, speak quietly, and watch for signs

sensation
Physiological detection of stimuli in the environment.

perception
Interpretation of stimuli that the body has sensed.

state of arousal
Physiological condition of sleepiness or wakefulness.

reflex
Automatic motor response to a particular kind of stimulus.

OBSERVATION GUIDELINES
Indicators of Health in Newborn Infants

CHARACTERISTIC	LOOK FOR	EXAMPLE	IMPLICATION
Adjustment After Birth	• *First breaths* are taken within a half minute after birth (the doctor may suction fluid from the mouth and throat). • *Attempts to nurse* at the breast or suck on the nipple of a bottle occur within a few hours after birth (the baby may lose a few ounces of weight during the first few days). • *First urination and bowel movements* occur within first 2 days. • *Head* may be elongated after birth but gradually regains round appearance; skin may be scratched and contain discolored spots that disappear within a few days.	Immediately after birth, Trinisha begins crying. Her head is misshapen and she has some blotchy spots on her skin. Her mother places Trinisha on her chest, and the baby quiets down, opens her eyes, and scans the room.	Before birth, encourage parents to arrange for appropriate medical care for their newborn babies. After birth, reassure parents about the appearance of newborn infants.
States of Arousal	• *Quiet sleep:* The infant lies still with closed eyelids and relaxed facial muscles. • *Active sleep:* Although the infant is sleeping, eyes may open and shut and move from side to side, facial expressions change and include grimaces, and breathing is irregular. • *Drowsiness:* The infant's eyelids may open and close without focus, and breathing is regular and rapid. • *Quiet alert:* The infant is awake, calm, happy, and engaged with the world. • *Active waking:* The infant wriggles and shows bursts of vigorous movements, breathes in an irregular tempo, has flushed skin, and may moan or grunt. • *Crying:* The infant cries and thrashes and has a flushed and distressed face.	In the first few days after birth, baby Kyle spends most of his time sleeping. Some of his sleep appears peaceful, and at times he appears to be dreaming. When Kyle is awake, he sometimes looks intently at people and objects close to him. At other times he appears agitated, and these episodes tend to escalate into loud and persistent crying.	Help parents notice infants' distinct states of arousal. Encourage them to develop a sensitive style of responding to infants' distress. Advise parents that when infants are in the quiet, alert state, this is a good time to interact calmly.
Reflexes	• *Rooting:* When touched near the corner of the mouth, the infant turns toward the stimulus, as if in search of breast or bottle. • *Sucking:* When a nipple or finger touches the infant's mouth, he or she begins to suck it. • *Swallowing:* Transferring liquids from mouth to stomach with muscles in the throat. • *Grasping:* The infant grasps onto a finger or other small object placed in his or her hand. • *Moro reflex:* When startled, the infant stretches arms outward and then brings them together in a hugging, embracing motion. • *Babinski reflex:* When the inner side of the infant's foot is rubbed from heel to toe, the infant's big toe moves upward and the other toes fan inward toward the bottom of the foot. • *Stepping:* When the baby is held upright under the arms with feet dangling and touching a hard surface, the legs take rhythmic steps. • *Tonic neck reflex:* If the infant is lying on his or her back and the head is moved toward one side, the arm on that side extends out and away from the body, and the other side is flexed close to the head with clenched fist (resembling a fencing position).	Little Josefina lies on her back on a blanket as her mother washes the dishes. When her mother accidentally drops and breaks a dish, Josefina appears alarmed, extends her arms, and seems to be grasping for something in midair.	Gently demonstrate infants' reflexes to family members. Family members, including the baby's siblings, may begin to use the grasping reflex as a way to interact with the baby. Explain that reflexes show that infants' brains and bodies are operating as they should.

Sources: Jadcherla, Gupta, Stoner, Fernandez, & Shaker, 2007; Shevell, 2009; C. W. Snow & McGaha, 2003; Wolff, 1966.

MyEducationLab

Go to the Video Examples section in Topic 4 of MyEducationLab to watch a nurse shows a new mother how to hold her baby while breastfeeding.

that the baby is ready to interact (e.g., the baby looks into caregivers' faces) or is distressed by the interaction (e.g., the baby looks away).

• **Show parents how to care for the baby.** First-time parents may appreciate some hands-on tips for administering to the physical needs of a new baby. Unless they have seen a baby being bathed, nursed, fed a bottle, diapered, or carried, new parents may not know how to perform these caretaking functions. You can watch a nurse show a new mother how to breastfeed her baby in a video on MyEducationLab.

• **Offer early and continued support to parents of fragile infants.** Infants who are at risk for one reason or another—for example, those who are premature or have serious disabilities—can require unusually high levels of attention from parents. Infants might cry often, be difficult to console, or need an intensive medical treatment. Some infants with health problems may be sluggish and seek out little interaction from their parents. In such cases family members may have practical questions about optimal care for their children, and they may also benefit from counseling and other services.

SUMMARY

Genetic Foundations of Child Development

All children have a set of genetic instructions that influence their characteristics at birth and emerging physical features as they grow. Most of the genes that children inherit are ones they share with other children, giving them a common human heritage. Other genes contribute to children's individuality by disposing them to look and act in certain unique ways. Genes exert their effects on children through complex and interactive processes in cells and body systems. Children's health, other physiological processes, and experiences in particular environments mediate the effects of genes. Teachers and other professionals can accept that all children have genetically based characteristics that make certain kinds of relationships, behaviors, and accomplishments relatively easy or difficult for them. Practitioners can also express their confidence that, whatever children's natural abilities, they have the potential to achieve high personal and academic standards.

Prenatal Development

At conception, the new offspring inherits a unique genetic makeup that guides the lifelong process of growing, changing, and interacting with the environment. Development begins at conception, when the *zygote,* a one-celled being, divides multiple times and becomes a ball of cells that burrows into the uterus. From weeks 2 through 8 after conception, the *embryo* grows rapidly, forming structures needed to sustain future growth and developing rudimentary organs and body parts. Between week 9 and birth, the *fetus* continues to grow quickly, now putting the finishing touches on body and brain and becoming sufficiently heavy and strong to live in the outside world. Professionals can support healthy prenatal growth by informing prospective parents (and all sexually active individuals) about the damaging effects of teratogens; the need to evaluate their health and medical regimens before a pregnancy; and the value of stress reduction, a healthful diet, appropriate exercise, and ongoing medical care during pregnancy.

Birth of the Baby

The birth of the baby is an exciting event for parents, who can reduce their stress by preparing for childbirth. Birth is a multistage process that is grounded in culture and often helped along by family members and doctors, nurses, midwives, and doulas. The health and medical needs of newborn infants depend on their birth weight, size, prior exposure to teratogens, and genetic vulnerabilities. Family educators and other professionals can help parents develop realistic expectations about their newborn infants and respond sensitively to their physical and psychological needs.

APPLYING CONCEPTS IN CHILD DEVELOPMENT

The exercises in this section will help you build your ability to apply your knowledge of child development in your work with children.

Improving Your Observation Skills

On page 116, you examined a photograph of two girls and were asked, *"Are these two sisters from Brazil monozygotic or dizygotic twins?"* The young women have similar facial expressions and seem to be the same height.

The sisters definitely *appear* to be monozygotic twins, but without a comparison of their chromosomes, it is not possible to know for sure. Monozygotic twins come from the same fertilized egg and have the same genes. Dizygotic twins come from two different fertilized ova, meaning that they are as similar genetically as ordinary siblings of the same two parents.

On page 123, you examined a photograph of an adolescent boy being charged with an infraction for being disrespectful and belligerent during a soccer game and were asked, *"How might the young man's behavior reflect a genetically based temperament?"* This young man may be genetically inclined to be irritable, impulsive, and aggressive. It is also possible that he has learned to be impolite and combative from environmental experiences. In any case, the young man can learn to solve his conflicts more constructively, and the referee may be assisting him by pointing out his inappropriate behaviors.

Practicing for Your Licensure Examination

Many teaching tests require students to use what they have learned about child development in responses to brief vignettes and multiple-choice questions. You can practice for your licensure examination by reading the following case study and answering a series of questions.

Adolescent Childbearing

Read the case and then answer the questions that follow it.

Three young women from Reykjavik, Iceland, talked with an interviewer about their feelings about being pregnant and becoming mothers. Each of the girls had previously considered having an abortion but ultimately decided to have and raise her child. Read these responses from the author who interviewed them and then answer the questions that follow.

Karen (age 15): Karen found it difficult to describe changes that might take place in her life after the child was born. When asked what kind of changes she could foresee she replied, "I don't know." After rephrasing the question a few times, we managed to discuss to some degree the possible positive and negative sides of motherhood, but her expressions were very concrete. She said she had some experiences in taking care of children but not newborns. She had not started to think about breastfeeding and revealed some misinformation. She explained that her mother would be responsible for the child in the beginning and that she herself would not dare to hold a newborn baby. Regarding the mothering role she said: "My mother will just be the mother of the child for the first months and then I will take over." When asked about care of the child she said: "I need of course to make it happy and of course to be good to it and to be there if it needs something." About her future with the child, she said: ". . . just that I have enough money for it. That it will not be on the streets. That is all." (S. S. Bender, 2008, p. 868)

Sophie (age 17) Sophie was aware that it would take her some time to get adjusted to the newborn and she described her role as a mother by saying: "I am, of course the mother of the baby, I will feed the baby, put it to sleep and will do the laundry and all that." She also said: "If my baby wakes up I also need to wake up, change the diapers and all that." Still she found the thought of having a newborn baby strange. She said: "Having a child is okay, but having a newborn, is strange." She felt great security in being able to go to her parents for support, and she knew they would be able to provide her with some freedom. She said her parents understood her need for being a teenager. She felt confident about her new roles since she had considerable babysitting experience. She said she was very fond of children and believed in her ability to take care of a baby. She described herself as having a rich imagination which she used when playing with children. She and her boyfriend had talked about their parenting roles and possible changes that would take place after the child was born. (S. S. Bender, 2008, p. 871)

Mary (age 20) Mary ". . . felt completely unprepared for the mothering role. 'I do not know anything about newborns. I think it has been ten years since I last changed a diaper. I have never been very fond of children.' She also expressed uncertainty about the role of being a mother: 'Now, after I became pregnant, I have been thinking about how I should go about it [take care of the child]. I sense that I am now having a baby. I have never thought about it this way before.' She described her role as a mother: 'I will always have one eye open during the night and day caring for the baby. I think of the difficulties adjusting to all the changes, all the new things taking place, both regarding myself and others.' Further on she said: 'One is just scared—if everything will go well, how this will turn out.' She was also concerned about her well being: 'Maybe it is not primarily the baby that I am [concerned about] . . . rather myself. I need to change myself and my life. Everything will change.'" (S. S. Bender, 2008, pp. 873–874)[a]

[a] Excerpts from "Three Cases of Adolescent Childbearing Decision-Making: The Importance of Ambivalence" by Soley S. Bender, from *ADOLESCENCE*, Volume 43(172) winter 2008. Copyright © by Soley S. Bender. Reprinted with permission of Libra Publishers, San Diego, CA.

Constructed-Response Question

1. What is the range of experiences that these young women are having as they anticipate becoming parents?

Multiple-Choice Questions

2. Given the recommendations in Chapter 4, what kinds of support can educators or other practitioners provide to these young women?

    a. Convince the young women that they are destined to be bad parents and should place their infants up for adoption.
    b. Encourage the young women to relax, avoid such potentially damaging substances as cigarettes and alcohol, obtain medical care, and prepare for their parenting role.
    c. Arrange for the young women to drop out of school so they can concentrate on their new parenting roles.
    d. Encourage the young women to allow their own mothers, the babies' grandmothers, to raise the children due to the grandmothers' superior parenting skills.

3. How might a midwife or prepared childbirth educator help these young women prepare for labor and delivery?

    a. Advise the mothers about the nutritional needs of their baby.
    b. Encourage mothers to decide whether they will breast-feed or bottle feed their baby.
    c. Talk with mothers about typical deliveries, types of positions, and possible pain medications and medical procedures.
    d. All of the above.

Once you have answered these questions, compare your responses with those presented in Appendix A.

Improving Your Ability to Interpret Children's Artifacts and Reflections

Consider chapter concepts as you analyze the following artifacts created by a child.

Horses by Nadia

Autism spectrum disorders are a group of related disabilities in communicating and acquiring basic social and cognitive skills (Centers for Disease Control and Prevention, 2007; National Institute of Mental Health, 2008a). The most severe of the autism spectrum conditions is commonly known as *autism*. Children with autism typically have difficulty learning to speak and comprehend language. They also generally withdraw from eye contact and other social interaction; do not understand social gestures or participate in pretend games; tend to repeat particular actions incessantly (e.g., repeatedly turning the pages of a book); resist changes in routine; and exhibit unusual reactions to sensory experiences (e.g., they may shudder at the sensation of being draped with silk yet not react with pain after running into a wall). Autism appears to be caused by both genetics and such environmental factors as exposure to teratogens (Arndt, Stodgell, & Rodier, 2005; Freitag, 2007).

Nadia, an English child of Ukrainian immigrants, was identified as being autistic at age 6 (Selfe, 1977). By age 3, Nadia had spoken only 10 words, and she uttered these few words rarely. Her language

did not progress much further in the following years, and she found it especially difficult to learn abstract and superordinate concepts (e.g., "furniture") (Selfe, 1995). Nadia was also clumsy, showed no concern for physical danger, and displayed regular temper tantrums. Yet like a small minority of other children with autism (Treffert & Wallace, 2002; Winner, 2000), Nadia was an exceptionally talented artist. After noticing her unusual artistic ability, Nadia's parents and a psychologist gave her paper and pens. Nadia drew several times a week, reproducing pictures she had studied days before in children's books, newspapers, or other printed material. Nadia's drawings were

Artwork by Nadia. Horse; age 3½ years (left). Horse and rider; age 5½ years (right). Originally published in Selfe, Lorna (1977). *Nadia: A Case of Extraordinary Drawing Ability in an Autistic Child*. London: Academic Press. Used with permission of Lorna Selfe.

realistic but also creative representations of images she had seen—she occasionally reversed the orientation, changed the size, or constructed a composite of several images. As you examine two of her drawings, shown on the previous page, answer these questions:

- Nadia was not able to describe her art in any depth using words. How might *nature* have played a role in Nadia's artistic ability and her language delay?
- Horses were Nadia's favorite topic. How might *nurture* have played a role in Nadia's interest in horses?

Once you have analyzed Nadia's artifacts, compare your ideas with those presented in Appendix B. For further practice in analyzing children's artifacts and reflections, go to the Activities and Applications section in Chapter 4 of MyEducationLab.

Key Concepts

gene (p. 112)
chromosome (p. 112)
DNA (p. 112)
gamete (p. 114)
meiosis (p. 114)
zygote (p. 116)
monozygotic twins (p. 116)

dizygotic twins (p. 116)
alleles (p. 117)
dominant gene (p. 117)
recessive gene (p. 117)
codominance (p. 117)
multifactorial trait (p. 117)
inclusion (p. 121)

canalization (p. 121)
niche construction (p. 122)
prenatal development (p. 124)
mitosis (p. 124)
embryo (p. 125)
fetus (p. 125)
teratogen (p. 128)

premature infant (p. 139)
sensation (p. 142)
perception (p. 142)
state of arousal (p. 142)
reflex (p. 142)

PEARSON myeducationlab

Now go to www.myeducationlab.com to:
- Take a Quiz to test your mastery of chapter objectives.
- Study chapter content with an individualized Study Plan.
- Deepen your understanding of particular concepts and principles with Review, Remediation, and Enrichment Exercises.
- Apply what you have learned in the chapter to your work with children in Building Teaching Skills and Dispositions exercises.
- Observe children and their unique contexts in Video Examples.

Chapter Five

Physical Development

CASE STUDY: Project Coach

Sam Intrator and Donald Siegel, professors in exercise and sports science, have devoted their careers to getting children actively involved in high-quality athletic programs (Intrator & Siegel, 2008). For Sam and Donald, helping children develop proficiency in sports is not an end in and of itself but rather a means to foster children's health, confidence, academic achievement, and communication skills.

Central to their work has been addressing characteristics in the community that make sports accessible and appealing to children. As one of their ventures, Sam and Donald reviewed children's participation in sports in Springfield, Massachusetts, an economically distressed city with high rates of teenage pregnancy, unfit youth, and low-achieving students. Children there had few prospects to immerse themselves in sports, primarily because adults were not available to supervise the leagues. Few parents were able to serve as coaches, and no one else seemed willing to volunteer. The situation looked bleak to Sam and Donald.

Or were they missing something? In a conversation with Jimmy, the parks and recreation director, Sam and Donald came up with a creative solution: Perhaps teenagers in the community might have an interest in working as coaches. The teenagers could benefit from the leadership training, and the children would finally have a viable sports league. Jimmy was enthusiastic about the idea, and *Project Coach* was launched.

In the training program, adolescents were recruited into an after-school program that taught them technical skills in sports, methods of coaching, and benefits from being a leader on the athletic field, at school, and in the community. Adolescent coaches acquired other advantages as well. They observed themselves improving in their ability to take initiative and developing a reputation as responsible citizens, rather than, as formerly, "problems to be managed" (Intrator & Siegel, 2008, p. 22).

With teen leaders now at the helm, elementary children had a chance to play soccer and other sports. They also had adolescent mentors from their own neighborhoods who expressed an interest in their welfare. Sam and Donald's notes reveal the rousing environment that the teen coaches created for their young athletes:

Fifteen-year-old Kenny walks into an energetic and bustling group of elementary school-age boys and girls, puts his whistle to his mouth, and gives one short, decisive tweet. "Okay, Nikey-Nikes, gather around for a meeting." Twelve boys and girls promptly scamper over and sit in a circle. Kenny and another teenager, both wearing a blue tennis shirt emblazoned with "Coach," join the group. "Coach Pedro and I are happy to see you today. Before we begin playing, I have a question for you. What does it mean to be a good sportsperson?" Coach Kenny and Coach Pedro listen intently as each of the players shares an idea. They ask follow-up questions like "How do you think it feels if your opponent celebrates too much after scoring a goal?" After each of the students contributes, Coach Pedro claps his hands, points to a 30-foot square demarcated by orange cones and says, "Everybody grab a soccer ball. There is the ocean. You are fishies—Coach Kenny and I are sharks. You know the game—let's go!" In an instant the students are tearing around the field chased by their teenage coaches. (Intrator & Siegel, 2008, p. 17).

GAME TIME. Organized sports can allow children to exercise, improve physical skills, and make productive use of leisure time.

Art by Eric, age 12.

- What kinds of physical needs did the children in Springfield have?
- How did the sports league affect the young athletes and their mentors?

OBJECTIVES

5.1: Outline the basic principles of children's physical development.

5.2: Identify the brain's basic structures and developmental processes.

5.3: Describe ways that teachers and other practitioners can support the brain development of youngsters of various ages.

5.4: Identify physical characteristics for each of the five developmental periods.

5.5: Summarize basic issues related to children's physical health and well-being.

5.6: Explain how professionals can assist all children, including those with special physical needs, to develop health-promoting habits.

As children develop, they undergo numerous physical changes. They learn to crawl, walk, run, and play sports. They grow taller and stronger. They become increasingly proficient at handling small objects. But these healthy developments depend on practice, nutrition, and protection from harm. As occurs in many communities, young people in Springfield were undergoing physical changes but also facing some risks to their health, notably teen pregnancy and inactivity.

Fortunately, concerned adults Sam and Donald believed in the power of youth. They realized that the children could become physically fit and that local adolescents were part of the solution. The sports leagues that were introduced allowed the elementary school children to rehearse athletic skills, forge friendships, and have fun, and the adolescents to gain memorable lessons in leadership. In this chapter we examine age-related changes in physical development and the strategies adults can use to foster children's health and well-being.

PRINCIPLES OF PHYSICAL DEVELOPMENT

A child's physical development is the outcome of countless orderly changes. Let's look at the remarkable principles of growth that characterize physical development.

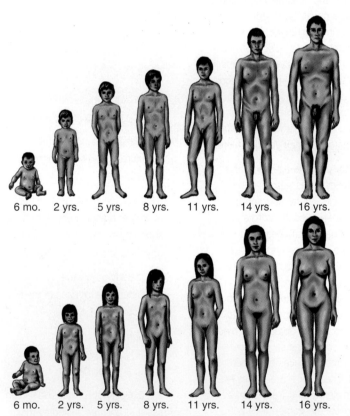

FIGURE 5-1 Physical development during childhood and adolescence. Children grow taller and heavier as they develop, and the characteristics and relative proportions of their body parts change as well.
Based on Diagram Group, 1983.

6 mo. 2 yrs. 5 yrs. 8 yrs. 11 yrs. 14 yrs. 16 yrs.

6 mo. 2 yrs. 5 yrs. 8 yrs. 11 yrs. 14 yrs. 16 yrs.

Different parts of the body mature at their own rates. Genes tell certain parts of the body to grow during distinct time periods. As a result, the relative body proportions change throughout childhood and adolescence (see Figure 5-1). Early in development heads are proportionally closer to adult size than are torsos, which are more advanced than arms and legs. In the upper limbs, the hand approaches adult size sooner than the forearm does; the forearm approaches adult size sooner than the upper arm does. Likewise in the lower limbs, the foot is more advanced than the calf, which is more advanced than the thigh.

Internally, separate systems grow at different rates as well (London, Ladewig, Ball, Bindler, & Cowen, 2011; J. M. Tanner, 1990). The lymphoid system (e.g., tonsils, adenoids, lymph nodes, and the lining of the small intestines) grows rapidly throughout childhood and then slows in adolescence. Lymphoid organs help children resist infection, which is particularly important during the early and middle childhood years when children are exposed to many contagious illnesses for the first time. Taking a different trajectory, reproductive organs expand slowly until adolescence, when a substantial burst of growth occurs.

The outcome of separate systems growing at distinct rates is that the body as a whole increases in size, albeit with its parts progressing somewhat unevenly. Typical growth curves for height and weight reveal rapid increases during the first 2 years, slow but steady growth during early and middle childhood, an explosive spurt during adolescence, and a leveling off to mature levels by early adulthood (Hamill et al., 1979; London et al., 2011). Patterns of growth are similar for boys and girls, although girls tend to have their adolescent growth spurts about a year and a half earlier, and boys, on average, end up a bit taller and heavier.

differentiation

A gradual transition from general possibility to specialized functioning over the course of development.

Functioning becomes increasingly differentiated. Every cell in the body (with the exception of sperm and ova) contains the same genetic instructions. As cells grow, they take on specific functions, some aiding with digestion, others transporting oxygen, still others transmitting information to various places in the body, and so on. Thus individual cells "listen" to only a subset of the many instructions they have available. This progressive shift from having the *potential* to become many things to actually carrying out a specialized function is known as **differentiation**.

Differentiation characterizes many aspects of development. During prenatal development, the arms first protrude as tiny, round shoots and then these buds become longer, sprout globular hands, and eventually differentiate into fingers. Motor skills, too, become increasingly differentiated: They first appear as rough, unsteady actions but gradually evolve into precise, controlled motions. You can see a clear developmental progression toward fine motor control by comparing the writing-implement grips of 16-month-old Corwin, 4-year-old Zoe, and 9-year-old Elena in three videos in MyEducationLab.

Functioning becomes increasingly integrated. As cells and body parts differentiate, they must also work together. Their increasingly coordinated efforts are known as **integration** (J. M. Tanner, 1990). The various parts of the eye coordinate their mechanical movements to permit vision; separate areas of the brain form connections that allow exchanges between thoughts and feelings; and fingers become longer and more adept at synchronizing movements for handling small objects (see Figure 5-2).

Each child follows a unique growth curve. Children's bodies appear to pursue predetermined heights—not as specific as 4′9″ or 6′2″, but definite ballpark targets for height, nonetheless. Growth curves are especially evident when things go temporarily awry in children's lives. Circumstances such as a serious illness or poor nutrition may briefly halt height increases. But when health and adequate nutrition are restored, children grow rapidly. Before you know it, they're back on track—back to where we might have expected them to be, given their original rate of growth. Sadly, exceptions to this self-correcting tendency occur when severe malnutrition is present very early in life or extends over a lengthy time period. Thus, children who are seriously undernourished during the prenatal phase are not able to follow their genetically based growth curve and instead become at risk for delayed maturation, brain damage, mental and behavioral deficiencies, and motor difficulties (Rees, Harding, & Inder, 2006; Roseboom, de Rooij, & Painter, 2006; M.-Q. Xu et al., 2009; Zeisel, 2009).

Physical development is characterized by both quantitative and qualitative changes. Quantitative changes are perhaps most obvious. Children continually eat, of course, and in most cases gain weight on an incremental basis. Motor skills, which may seem to the casual observer to appear overnight, typically result from numerous gradual advancements. A young girl may slowly improve in dexterity with shoelaces and eventually tie her shoes independently. Yet qualitative changes in motor skills occur as well (see Figure 5-3). Children's posture, use of limbs, and transfer of weight are transformed with motor experience (Gallahue & Ozmun, 1998; C. Hyde & Wilson, 2011).

Children's bodies function as dynamic, changing systems. The specific parts in the body change over time, as do the relationships among them, and children's own activity is an important part of the equation. To illustrate, infants apply considerable effort in coordinating the various muscles needed for reaching for objects with their arms and hands. Having moved their limbs spontaneously during the prenatal period and immediately after birth, infants gradually gain experience with movement and by 3½ to 4 months of age, they begin to reach for objects, first shakily and then more smoothly (Thelen & Smith, 2006). After some small improvements, though, infants often exhibit temporary *declines* in speed, directness, and smoothness in reaching, as if they must figure out how to address changes in muscle tone or deal with a new factor. With considerable practice and typically before 12 months of age, most infants can reach easily and quickly. You can see 7-month-old Madison adeptly reach for objects and transfer objects from one hand to the other in the "Emotional Development: Infancy" video in MyEducationLab.

MyEducationLab

Observe developmental differentiation in hand grips by comparing three children holding writing utensils: Corwin in "Literacy: Infancy," Zoe in "Neighborhood: Early Childhood," and Elena in "Neighborhood: Middle Childhood." (Find Video Examples in Topic 5 of MyEducationLab.)

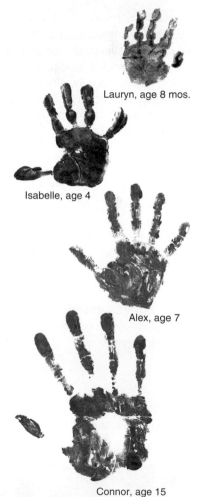

Lauryn, age 8 mos.

Isabelle, age 4

Alex, age 7

Connor, age 15

FIGURE 5-2 Growing apart, coming together. The separate fingers on a child's hand start out rather similar looking but become increasingly distinct (differentiated) and better able to coordinate their movements (integrated). These handprints are shown at 25% of actual size.

	Initial Motor Activity	Practiced Motor Activity	Mature Motor Activity
Walking	a.	b.	c.
Throwing	a.	b.	c.

FIGURE 5-3   Qualitative changes in walking and overhand throwing. In *walking,* children tend to progress from (a) having difficulty maintaining balance and using short steps with flat-footed contact, to (b) a smoother pattern, where arms are lower and heel-toe contact occurs, to (c) a relaxed gait, with reflexive arm swing. In *overhand throwing,* children progress from (a) stationary feet and action mainly from the elbow, to (b) ball held behind head, arm swung forward and high over shoulder, and a definite transfer forward with body weight, to (c) movement of foot on same side as throwing arm; definite rotation through hips, legs, spine, and shoulders; and a step with foot opposite to the throwing arm as weight is shifted.
Based on Gallahue & Ozmun, 1998.

Children gradually discover how to coordinate their different body parts and offset personal limitations. Infants who make vigorous, spontaneous movements in their first few months of life must learn to control their arms before they can successfully reach for objects. In contrast, infants who generate few and slow movements have a different set of problems to solve: They must learn to apply muscle tone while extending arms forward and holding them stiffly. Thus the act of reaching, like so many motor skills, shows dramatic individual differences in pathways to proficiency.

integration
An increasing coordination of body parts over the course of development.

Children's health is affected by their involvement in numerous environments. Applied to children's physical development, the bioecological model identifies the numerous people and settings that directly and indirectly influence children's health-related decisions and habits

Improving Your Observation Skills

Watch me grow. A boy is wearing the same t-shirt in photos taken at ages 1, 5, 9, 13, and 17. How does the boy's physical appearance change over the years? Compare your response with the explanation at the end of the chapter.

(Gardiner & Kosmitzki, 2008; Pfefferbaum, Pfefferbaum, & Norris, 2010). Children's families are especially important to their health. From their countless experiences at home, children learn to like particular foods and dislike others, follow an active or sedentary lifestyle, and take or avoid physical risks. Parents' jobs indirectly affect children's health through the resources generated for food, safe housing, and medical insurance (Y. R. Harris & Graham, 2007; Repetti & Wang, 2010). Outside the family, peers may congregate at fast-food restaurants or at the gym. At school, personnel may restrict or encourage children's movement and allow access to nutritious or non-nutritious meals on the lunch line. External societal forces, particularly the media and community, also affect children's physical development. Youngsters may head to the basketball court in the hope of emulating the lean bodies of famous athletes, and they may take illicit drugs after seeing neighbors do the same. In addition, community agencies may or may not effectively enforce laws regarding use of cigarettes and alcohol (Steinberg, 2007).

THE BRAIN AND ITS DEVELOPMENT

The brain is an extraordinary organ that senses information in the environment, guides movement, and regulates other systems in the body. The brain also permits advanced human abilities: It forms associations among environmental stimuli and previously learned ideas, fills everyday experience with emotional meaning, translates thoughts and feelings into words and behaviors, and determines actions needed to achieve desired outcomes.

Altogether, the brain has trillions of cells, the two primary kinds of which are *neurons* and *glia*. Historically scientists have emphasized the 100 billion **neurons**, cells that transmit information to other cells (Naegele & Lombroso, 2001; R. W. Williams & Herrup, 1988). Each neuron has numerous branchlike extensions called **dendrites** that react to chemicals released by nearby neurons, as well as a long, armlike **axon** that sends information on to other neurons (Figure 5-4). The dendrites and axons come close to one another at junctions called **synapses**. When any particular neuron is stimulated by a sufficient amount of chemicals from one or more of its neighbors, it either "fires," generating an electrical impulse that triggers the release of its own chemicals (culminating in the stimulation and subsequent firing of adjacent neurons), or it is inhibited from firing. Neurons fire or are inhibited from firing depending on the amount and types of chemicals that neighbors send their way.

Observe Madison reaching for objects in the "Emotional Development: Infancy" video. (Find Video Examples in Topic 5 of MyEducationLab.)

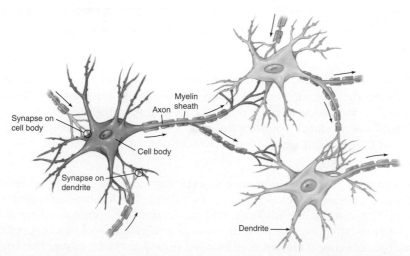

FIGURE 5-4   Neurons. The neuron on the left is receiving information from other cells and will subsequently fire and incite neurons at right to fire. Arrows show the direction of messages being sent.
Based on N. R. Carlson (2011).

neuron
Cell that transmits information to other cells; also called a *nerve cell*.

dendrite
Branchlike part of a neuron that receives information from other neurons.

axon
Armlike part of a neuron that sends information to other neurons.

synapse
Junction between two neurons.

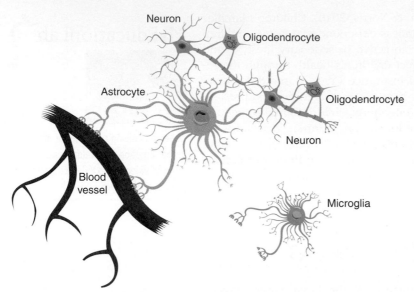

FIGURE 5-5 Glial cells take numerous forms, three of which are represented here. *Oligodendrocytes* insulate neurons and increase their efficiency in firing. *Microglia* rid the brain of infectious and damaged material. *Astrocytes* play numerous roles, including communicating with one another and nourishing and controlling neurons.

glial cell

Cell in the brain that provides structural or functional support for, and in some cases direction to, one or more neurons.

astrocyte

Glial cell that regulates blood flow in the brain, brings nutrients to and metabolizes chemicals for neurons, and communicates with other similar cells and with neurons.

hindbrain

Part of the brain controlling the basic physiological processes that sustain survival.

midbrain

Part of the brain that coordinates communication between the hindbrain and forebrain.

forebrain

Part of the brain responsible for complex thinking, emotions, and motivation.

cortex

Part of the forebrain that enables conscious thinking processes, including executive functions.

Most of the brain's neurons have thousands of synapses, so obviously a great deal of cross-communication occurs. Furthermore, groups of neurons grow together as "communities" that specialize in certain functions. Following the principle that there is strength in numbers, these communities, called *circuits,* are laid out in side-by-side wires that reach out to other groups of neurons. The outcome is that important processes of the brain (such as feeling emotions, paying attention, and learning new ideas) are supported by robust structures.

Intermingling with neurons are a trillion or more **glial cells**. Glial cells perform numerous functions (Figure 5-5). *Oligodendrocytes* coat the axons of neurons with insulating myelin, allowing electrical signals to propagate rapidly. *Microglia* rid the brain of damaged neurons, bacteria, and viruses. **Astrocytes** are glial cells that regulate blood flow to the brain, bring nutrients to neurons, metabolize chemicals released by neurons, and communicate with one another and with neurons. When stimulated, individual astrocytes release calcium, triggering other nearby astrocytes to activate. Several features of astrocytes hint at their significance. Scientists have begun to speculate that astrocytes may partly control the actions of neurons and help to consolidate information in the brain (Fields, 2009; Koob, 2009). Compared to other species, human beings have a higher ratio of astrocytes to neurons as well as larger and more complex astrocytes (Banaclocha, 2007; Koob, 2009; Oberheim et al., 2009). Furthermore, astrocytes are especially plentiful in areas of the brain responsible for higher thinking processes. Ultimately scientists may find that it is the close interplay between neurons and astrocytes, rather than the separate functioning of either, that is at the root of thinking.

Structures and Functions

On a more global scale, the brain is organized into three main parts: the hindbrain, the midbrain, and the forebrain (Figure 5-6). Each of these parts is organized further into specialized systems with identifiable functions:

- The **hindbrain** controls basic physiological processes that sustain survival, including breathing, blood pressure, sleep, arousal, balance, and movement (thank your hindbrain for your slow, methodical breathing as you sleep blissfully at night).
- The **midbrain** connects the hindbrain to the forebrain and acts as a kind of relay station between the two; for instance, it sends messages to the forebrain about priorities for attention ("Hello! Alarm clock ringing! Hello! Time to rise!").
- The **forebrain** produces complex thinking, emotional responses, and the forces of motivation ("Ugh! I can sleep another 10 minutes if I skip breakfast. No . . . I better get up.").

The *forebrain* is of special relevance to educators and other practitioners because it allows children to learn and develop distinct personalities. The forebrain contains the **cortex**, a wrinkled cap that rests on the midbrain and hindbrain. The cortex is where interpreting, reasoning, communicating, and purposeful, conscious thinking processes (e.g., planning and decision making, collectively known as **executive functions**) take place. The cortex is also the seat of many personality traits, such as being enthusiastic and sociable or quiet and introverted, and of habitual ways of responding to physical events and novel information. One 10-year-old girl's cortex would control the way she snuggles up to her father on the sofa in

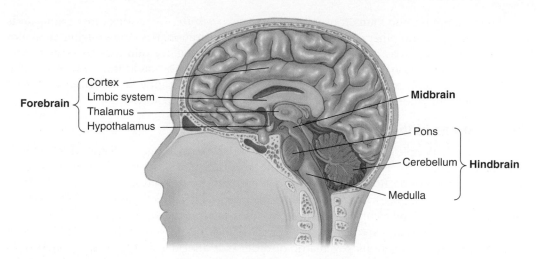

FIGURE 5-6   Structure of the human brain. The human brain is an enormously complex and intricate structure with three main parts: the hindbrain, midbrain, and forebrain.
Based on N. R. Carlson (2011).

the evening, her exuberant style in social groups, her understanding of how to read, and, of course, much more.

Physiologically, the cortex is extremely convoluted. Bundles of neurons repeatedly fold in on themselves. This physical complexity permits a huge capacity for storing and transmitting information throughout the brain. Consistent with the principle of differentiation, various parts of the cortex develop specific functions, which we now examine.

Areas of Specialization within the Cortex

The cortex consists of regions (called *lobes*) that specialize in particular functions, notably decision making and planning (front), understanding and production of language (sides), and visual processing (rear). In addition, the cortex is divided into two halves, or *hemispheres.* In right-handed individuals, the **left hemisphere** controls the right side of the body, and the **right hemisphere** manages the left side. In most people the left hemisphere dominates in *analysis,* breaking up information into its constituent parts and extracting order in a sequence of events, as occurs in talking, understanding speech, reading, writing, mathematical problem solving, and computer programming (N. R. Carlson, 2011; Goulven, Ferath, Guillaume, Seghier, & Price, 2009; Pinel & Dehaene, 2009). It is usually the right hemisphere that excels in *synthesis,* pulling together information (especially nonlinguistic information) into a coherent whole, as when we recognize faces; detect geometrical patterns; read body language; and appreciate musical melodies, humor, and emotions (N. R. Carlson, 2011; Gainotti, 2007). Left-handed individuals often have reversed patterns, with the right hemisphere dominant in analysis and the left hemisphere more involved in synthesis (Toga & Thompson, 2003).[1] Apparently, some of the many genes that guide brain development are expressed asymmetrically during prenatal development, directing different circuits to be formed in each side of the brain (Pinel & Dehaene, 2009).

Despite their separate specialties, the two hemispheres are in constant communication, trading information through a thick bundle of connecting neurons. Therefore, both hemispheres almost always work together. For example, the right hemisphere may process a complex emotion, such as the mixed feelings people experience at a high school graduation, while the left hemisphere searches for the right words to communicate these feelings.

executive functions
Purposeful and goal-directed intellectual processes (e.g., planning, decision making) made possible by higher brain structures.

left hemisphere
Left side of the cortex; largely responsible for sequential reasoning and analysis, especially in right-handed people.

right hemisphere
Right side of the cortex; largely responsible for simultaneous processing and synthesis, especially in right-handed people.

[1] Other individuals (particularly those who use both hands equally well) blend psychological functions within hemispheres (Sheehan & Smith, 1986).

Supplementing the numerous circuits existing *within* the cortex are connections *between* the cortex and other parts of the brain. As an illustration, basic "energizing" activities that reside partly in areas of the brain outside the cortex (e.g., certain aspects of attention, emotion, and motivation) regularly interact with more reflective "intellectual" processes that take place in the cortex. Hence, children who feel alert and happy would readily grasp a classroom lesson, whereas children who are sleepy or distracted would not.

Malformations in the Brain

In some cases, people's brains have unusual circuits or missing or distorted structures, malformations that can interfere with learning and behavior. Too many or too few cells may form, or the connections among cells may be laid out in unusual ways (C. A. Nelson, Thomas, & de Haan, 2006). These neurological irregularities affect children's ability to pay attention, learn efficiently, control impulses, and deal with negative emotions.

Some neurological disorders are not obvious at birth, or even in the first few years of life. **Schizophrenia**, a serious psychiatric disorder that affects 1 in 100 people, often does not surface until adolescence or adulthood (Anjum, Gait, Cullen, & White, 2010). Individuals with schizophrenia display such symptoms as thought disorders (e.g., irrational ideas and disorganized thinking), hallucinations (e.g., "hearing" nonexistent voices), delusions (e.g., worrying that "everyone is out to get me"), and social withdrawal (e.g., avoiding eye contact or conversation with others). These symptoms appear to result, at least in part, from structural abnormalities or overactive synapses in certain parts of the brain (de Castro-Manglano et al., 2011; Goghari, Sponheim, & MacDonald, 2010; Gogtay & Thompson, 2010).

What factors cause serious malformations in brain development? Errors in genetic instructions can trigger problems in brain chemistry and architecture. Other neurological abnormalities may be due to a mother's drug or alcohol use, illness, or stress during pregnancy. Prenatal exposure to rubella (German measles) can reduce the number of neurons formed and culminate in a small brain (C. A. Nelson et al., 2006). In the case of schizophrenia, a variety of factors, including genes, viral infections and malnutrition during prenatal development, childbirth complications, and stressful environments during childhood, may share responsibility for the condition (A. S. Brown et al., 2009; Schlotz & Phillips, 2009; Sinkus et al., 2009; E. Walker & Tessner, 2008).

Developmental Changes in the Brain

The magnificent intricacy of the human brain is made possible by a lengthy course of forming, refining, and connecting basic parts. Together, nature and nurture guide this sculpting process throughout prenatal development, infancy, childhood, adolescence, and well into the adult years.

Prenatal Development

During prenatal development, the brain's most basic parts are formed. The brain begins as a tiny tube approximately 25 days after conception, as illustrated in Figure 5-7. This seemingly simple tube grows longer in places and folds inward to form pockets (Tierney & Nelson, 2009). Three bulges appear early on and become the forebrain, midbrain, and hindbrain. Soon the brain takes on more complex features, with the forebrain cleaving down the middle and beginning to specialize into the left and right hemispheres (Stephan, Fink, & Marshall, 2007).

Before the brain can develop any further, it must become a factory for neurons. Beginning in the fifth week, neurons reproduce in the inner portion of the tube. This production peaks between the third and fourth prenatal months, when several hundred thousand new neurons are generated *each minute* (C. A. Nelson et al., 2006). The vast majority of neurons that will ever be used by a person are formed during the first 7 months of prenatal development (Rakic, 1995).[2]

schizophrenia
A psychiatric condition characterized by irrational ideas and disorganized thinking.

[2] Some new neurons are formed later in development, including during the adult years, in a structure of the brain that forms memories (C. A. Nelson et al., 2006). Astrocytes continue to duplicate throughout life.

Once formed, neurons move, or *migrate,* to specific brain locations where they will do their work. Some young neurons push old cells outward, creating brain structures underneath the cortex. Others actively seek out their destination, climbing up pole-like glial cells and ultimately giving rise to the cortex. When in place, neurons send out axons, which grow together as teams, reaching toward other groups of neurons (their targets) that attract them by secreting certain chemicals. As axons get close to neighboring neurons, they generate branches that become dendrites, which in turn differentiate into synapses with the target cells. The target cells do their part as well, forming small receptors with their dendrites. Only about half of neurons ultimately make contact with other cells. Those that do make contact survive; the others die. Nature's tendency to overproduce neurons and eliminate those that fail to connect ensures that the brain invests in workable connections (M. Diamond & Hopson, 1998; P. R. Huttenlocher, 1990).

In the last few months of prenatal growth, the brains of developing babies form the necessary circuits for breathing, sucking, swallowing, crying, forming simple associations, and learning about people and the physical world. These final touches prepare newborn infants to survive and learn.

The rapid changes that occur in the prenatal offspring's brain make this phase of life highly susceptible to environmental influence and therefore a *sensitive period.* Disruptions in neurons and glial cells can occur due to infection, genetic irregularities, poor nutrition, and exposure to toxins. Such problems can permanently affect the number of neurons that are formed, the circuits they build, and the chemical reactivity of neurons later in life. Therefore, practitioners must advise pregnant women to obtain adequate nutrition; protect themselves from toxins, drugs, alcohol, and excessive stress; and obtain prenatal care from a physician or other health care provider.

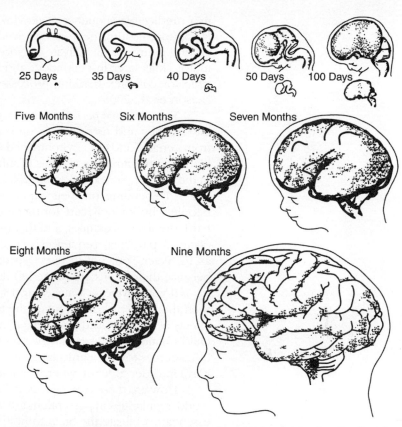

FIGURE 5-7 Prenatal growth of the human brain. During the first few months, the basic structures appear (in the top row of drawings, the relative size of the brains has been increased to show detail in the structures). During the middle months of prenatal development, basic structures are refined. During the final weeks prior to birth, the cortex folds in and out of itself, preparing the fetus for learning as a baby.
Figure from "The Development of the Brain" by Tom Prentiss, from SCIENTIFIC AMERICAN Edition 241, p. 106. Illustration copyright © 1979 by Nelson H. Prentiss. Reprinted by permission of Nelson H. Prentiss.

Infancy and Early Childhood

At birth and for a couple of days afterward, astrocytes and other glial cells proliferate and find their places near neurons. Also at birth, the brain forms countless new connections (synapses) among neurons, a phenomenon called **synaptogenesis**. In the first few years of life, so many new synapses appear that their number far exceeds adult levels (C. A. Nelson et al., 2006).

Then, following this fantastic proliferation of synapses, frequently used connections become stronger, and rarely used connections wither away in a process known as **synaptic pruning**. Particular regions of the brain take their turns growing and shedding synapses over a period of many years (P. R. Huttenlocher, 1990; C. A. Nelson et al., 2006). Psychologists speculate that by generating more synapses than will ever be needed, human beings can adapt to a wide variety of conditions and circumstances. Synaptic pruning, then, may be Mother Nature's way of making the brain more efficient in a particular environment.

Early brain development is also marked by **myelination**, a process in which glial cells grow around the axons of neurons to form a fatty coating (*myelin*) that insulates axons and enables neurons to conduct electrical charges quickly. Just as synaptic proliferation and pruning proceed through areas of the brain in a particular order, myelination also occurs

synaptogenesis
A process in brain development whereby many new synapses appear during the first few years of life.

synaptic pruning
A process in brain development whereby many previously formed synapses wither away, especially if they have not been used frequently.

myelination
The growth of a fatty sheath around neurons that allows them to transmit messages quickly.

in a predictable sequence (Yakovlev & Lecours, 1967). It actually begins during the prenatal period, coating neurons involved in basic survival skills. Myelination then takes place around neurons that activate sensory abilities during infancy, followed by those involved in motor skills later in childhood, and eventually (well into adolescence) with those responsible for complex thinking processes and judgment (M. Diamond & Hopson, 1998; C. A. Nelson et al., 2006).

The *sensitive period* for brain growth that begins during the prenatal period persists into infancy and now focuses on support for learning. An infant's brain is primed to learn from certain kinds of environmental stimuli. The American psychologist **Alison Gopnik** has identified the amazing abilities of infants to form generalizations from patterns they observe in the environment (A. Gopnik, 2009a, 2009b, 2009c; R. Wu, Gopnik, Richardson, & Kirkham, 2011). Depending on their experiences, infants may notice that their parents are special people who lovingly care for them; that their toys are typically colorful, shiny, and made of hard, durable substances; and that their native language is composed of various sounds that occur in particular sequences (e.g., "p" and "t" often occur together within English words, as in "Peter," but not in direct succession, as in "Pteer"). Infants can form generalizations because their brains are primed to detect patterns as they interact with people and objects.

If you have ever watched an 18-month-old child play with a new toy, you have probably seen the child pick it up, rotate the toy carefully while looking at its various sides, watch its effects as it is handled and shaken, and listen for any sound it makes. Gopnik argues that a child's brain specializes in *exploration*, whereas an adult's mind concentrates on *exploitation* of resources toward particular goals (A. Gopnik, 2009c). In other words, a young child's brain plays in order to learn, whereas an adult's brain works to achieve specific purposes.

How are these experiences etched into the young child's brain? As infants interact in their world, regularities in perceptions are transformed into foundational brain circuits. These circuits essentially obligate the brain to notice features of later stimuli that are consistent with earlier patterns. The brain's tendency to convert preliminary distinctions into circuits that support and constrain future learning has been described as making *neural commitments* (Kuhl, 2007; Kuhl, Conboy, Padden, Nelson, & Pruitt, 2005). When infants regularly hear certain sounds in their native language (e.g., the sound *ba* in English), they form neural commitments for these sounds, enabling the infants to recognize these sounds in full-blown words (e.g., *ba*ll). Such neural commitments almost certainly help young children learn their native language but later *limit* their ability to learn a second language with somewhat different sounds.

Research on early brain development offers several practical applications. During infancy and early childhood much of the motivation for learning emanates from the children themselves. Instead of learning best from flash cards, teacher-directed lessons, or television programs, young children acquire knowledge most effectively when immersed in a reasonably complex environment and allowed to play, explore, and communicate with others. In fact, because some neurological changes do not take place until middle childhood or later, young children are typically not able to benefit from educational experiences that require sustained attention and inhibition of distractions.

Middle Childhood

By the time a child enters kindergarten, his or her brain is well formed, with some areas achieving full maturation and other areas continuing to grow (Fusaro & Nelson, 2009). Sensory and perceptual functions have generally reached adult levels of maturity during this period. Areas that support other basic psychological processes, including memory and emotion, are also essentially complete although they continue to form connections with other parts of the brain. This process of connecting previously separate neurological centers makes it increasingly possible for children to reflect on their thoughts and persist with their goals (Fusaro & Nelson, 2009).

Synaptic pruning of weak connections becomes a major force of change during childhood. Yet even as unused synapses are being pruned back, new ones continue to be formed during learning, especially in the cortex (National Research Council, 1999; C. A. Nelson et al., 2006). The process of myelination also continues, protecting neurons and speeding up transmission of messages (Yakovlev & Lecours, 1967). This practice of solidifying useful neurological circuits allows children to become knowledgeable about whatever strikes their fancy—comic books, dance movements, cake decorating, or hunting strategies. Likewise, children learn much about the habits and motives of people in their lives, helping them to fit comfortably into their family and peer groups. Children also become increasingly proficient in their native tongue, flexibly and expertly using sophisticated words and grammatical structures.

One other outcome of neurological changes in childhood is that children become capable of handling a growing number of ideas in mind and carrying out multiple mental tasks simultaneously. You can see this capacity being tapped in the "Memory: Early Child-hood" video clip in MyEducationLab. In the clip 6-year-old Brent listens to 12 words and tries to recall them. He is able to recall 6 words. A year or so earlier he probably would have recalled fewer words, and in a few more years, he likely will recall more. Yet in part because their brain circuits are still under construction, children in the elementary grades have limited attention spans and restricted abilities to plan for the future. As a result, they cannot recall lengthy instructions and frequently forget belongings.

Teachers and other practitioners can accommodate the abilities and limitations of el-ementary school children's growing brains. Adults can foster children's interests in patterns by asking them to identify the characteristics of changing seasons, tidal movements, holidays, artistic designs, musical rhythms, and historical themes. Adults can also help children exer-cise fragile executive skills by posting a calendar, offering reminders, setting interim goals for complex tasks, and encouraging children to keep track of their progress on projects. In addition, adults can support children's tentative efforts to regulate their emotions by talking with them about their feelings and teaching them productive ways to convey anger, disap-pointment, and sadness. Finally, children of this age continue to learn new vocabulary and sophisticated grammatical structures and can benefit from exposure to literature, poetry, and second languages.

Adolescence

The cortex continues to change in important ways during adolescence (Casey, Giedd, & Thomas, 2000; Sowell et al., 2001). Synaptic pruning and myelination continue in parts of the brain used in sophisticated thought processes (Giorgio et al., 2010). As a result of these numerous long-term changes, adults' brains are more efficient than children's brains, both in terms of their connections (through synapses) and insulation (through myelination).

Given the significant developmental transformations that brains go through at this age, young people can now look beyond the surface of things. The capac-ity to consider multiple ideas simultaneously grows steadily over childhood and culminates in abstract thinking in adolescence. Yet as adolescents are developing these high-brow intellectual abilities, they also are gaining a taste for adventure (Banich, 2010; Steinberg, 2007; Strauch, 2003). Many previously compliant chil-dren suddenly violate basic rules, perhaps stealing, getting suspended at school, taking drugs, coloring their hair purple, or driving recklessly. How is it that ado-lescents can act intelligently one minute and rashly the next? The answer seems to lie in a temporary imbalance that occurs in the adolescent brain. At this time, circuits in the brain devoted to enjoying immediate rewards (e.g., laughing up-roariously with friends when a peer is ridiculed) mature before other circuits for avoiding adverse consequences (e.g., noticing that the peer is within earshot and telling the friends to cool it; Cauffman et al., 2010; Somerville, Jones, & Casey, 2010). Gradually, neurological systems constraining impulsive behavior catch up, making it increasingly easy for young people to control their impulses in the heat of the moment.

Of course, precisely how youth respond to impetuous feelings depends largely on the expectations of adults and conduct of peers. Some societies accept the inevitability of hot-headed exploration whereas others try to discourage, limit, or redirect it. The Amish, a peaceful, traditional Christian sect in rural areas of Pennsylvania and Indiana, tolerate a period of "Rumspringa," during which time Amish adolescents engage in such misbehavior as wearing nontraditional clothing,

MyEducationLab

Observe Brent as he tries to keep a few words in mind in the "Memory: Early Childhood" video. (Find Video Examples in Chapter 5 of MyEducationLab.)

AIRBORNE! Brain development during adolescence can incite risky activities. This young man enjoys the thrill of snowboarding—without a helmet.

driving automobiles instead of horse-drawn vehicles, drinking alcohol, and engaging in pre-marital sex (Stevick, 2007). At the end of this period, Amish youth are encouraged to resume traditional ways, become baptized, and marry. In comparison, many Japanese adults do not view adolescence as an age of unrest but rather as a crucial period for forming career goals (H. Montgomery, 2009; M. White, 1993). When typically obedient Japanese adolescents violate social norms, adults expect them to remain committed to their schoolwork. Other societies ask young people to profess their commitment to adult roles after an identified period for instruction, as you can learn about in the Development in Culture feature, "Initiation Ceremonies."

The complex neurological changes of adolescence have implications for practitioners. Adults can foster abstract thinking by providing opportunities to test hypotheses in science, analyze characters' motivations in literature, and identify conflicting perspectives of different factions in history. Adults can similarly encourage adolescents to polish skills in their individual areas of interest, perhaps computer programming or film production. Given the penchant for impetuous behavior at this age, adults must also try to shield young people from harm by restricting their access to hazardous activities. Adolescents are generally able to appraise the risks of dangerous behaviors (e.g., drinking and driving, having unprotected sex), but they can temporarily lose good judgment when overwhelmed by immediate social pressures (Cauffman et al., 2010; V. F. Reyna & Farley, 2006; Somerville et al., 2010; Steinberg, 2007). As a result, efforts to educate adolescents about the consequences of risk-taking behaviors tend to be only modestly effective unless paired with mechanisms that limit exposure to health-compromising activities. For instance, adults can educate adolescents about problems with underage drinking but also make it not only illegal but also expensive and inconvenient for them to obtain alcoholic beverages.

Applications of Research on Brain Development

We previously offered some recommendations for accommodating the characteristics of children's brains during specific developmental periods. Let's now look at some broader applications.

- **Be optimistic that children can learn essential skills throughout childhood and adolescence.** Some people exaggerate the need for stimulating the brains of infants and forget that *everyone* can learn throughout life. Certainly early stimulation *is* necessary for normal development of visual processing and depth perception. Some cats, monkeys, and people who have had reduced or abnormal visual stimulation in their first few months have developed lifelong difficulties with visual perception, apparently as a result of irreversible neurological change. On the other hand, varied experiences around the world provide sufficient stimulation for normal development in visual areas of the brain (Bruer, 1999; Greenough, Black, & Wallace, 1987).

Virtually no evidence suggests that structured stimulation must occur during early development for areas of the brain that support learning in reading, mathematics, and music (Bruer, 1999; Greenough et al., 1987). On the contrary, we know from a large number of studies that human beings learn new information and skills quite successfully across the life span (Kolb, Gibb, & Robinson, 2003; C. A. Nelson et al., 2006). Thus you can have an important impact *throughout* the childhood and adolescent years if you offer such "brain-friendly" experiences as properly designed instruction, exposure to rich cultural contexts (visits to museums, libraries, and the like), and warm social relationships.

- **Give children opportunities to exercise their emerging executive functions.** As you have learned, infants and toddlers do not acquire knowledge through teacher-directed academic lessons. Instead, they detect all kinds of patterns and regularities in the world by spontaneously exploring objects, listening to language, playing, and interacting with people (Thompson-Schill, Ramscar, & Chrysikou, 2009). Around age 3 or 4 and after, children become increasingly able to direct their behavior toward the goals that they and their teachers establish. Their executive skills remain fragile for some time, making it helpful for adults to adjust to children's limited attention by keeping explanations brief, teaching children overt steps for self-control (e.g., counting to 10 before responding when angry), and asking children to break up challenging assignments into manageable pieces (Calkins & Marcovitch, 2010).

DEVELOPMENT IN CULTURE
Initiation Ceremonies

To help young people remain committed to productive pathways despite temptations around them, some societies arrange for *initiation ceremonies*, rites of passage in which boys and girls are shepherded through an educational process and ultimately accepted as men and women. In Latin American cultures, a 15-year-old girl may take part in a *Quinceañera* celebration after publically affirming her religious faith. A 13-year-old Jewish boy may become a *Bar Mitzvah* and a 12-year-old girl a *Bat Mitzvah* after reading from the Torah during a religious ceremony. Many Christian youth take part in *Confirmation* ceremonies, during which time they profess their faith and become full members of their religious community.

In nonindustrialized societies, initiation ceremonies also prepare girls for womanhood and boys for manhood (H. Montgomery, 2009). In the Tswapong culture of Botswana, a girl who has had her first menstrual period is designated a "mothei" and secluded to a hut for 7 days. The mothei is ushered through several intense rituals, including observing village women dancing, being smeared with python dung and swatted on the back, eating special food, and listening to women recite codes of conduct (Werbner, 2009). An anthropologist who observed the initiation ceremony and interviewed village women described the significant conversion that the adolescent girl undergoes:

> Seen as a whole, the mothei is framed by a series of transformations: from weakness to potency, dependence to independence, darkness to shaded protection. (Werbner, 2009, p. 451)

Many boys in nonindustrialized societies also take part in initiation ceremonies, often as part of groups (Lancy, 2008; Schlegel & Barry, 1980). For instance, the Tapirapé, an indigenous tribe in the Amazon rain forest of Brazil, brought young adolescent boys into the "takana," a men's club that socialized the boys for manhood (Wagley, 1977). An anthropologist who studied the Tapirapé described a boy's induction into the takana:

> During his first night of residence there his mother brought water in a pot to the door of the takana for him to bathe and his father brought him a bow and arrow tipped with beeswax, with which he had to kill two birds for his father to eat. The next morning the men rubbed red annatto paste [a dye from a local fruit] into his hair. Until the red annatto paste wore off, the men called him each morning to bathe. Then, when the red dye had disappeared, his hair was cropped short and a portion of his scalp was shaven. (Wagley, 1977, p. 149)

Boys stayed in the takana for several months—some for up to a year—and learned about such masculine traditions as making bows and arrows. When the boys were considered mature and ready to find a spouse, they underwent another ceremony during which time they danced for a full day and night and were thereafter considered men.

The road to adulthood is not always an easy one, but guidance from adults in the form of initiation ceremonies and other supportive gestures can ease the transition.

COMING OF AGE. Initiation ceremonies prepare adolescent boys and girls for adult roles. These Aboriginal boys in Arnhem Land, Australia, are heading into the bush with elders to celebrate their manhood.

• **Consider the connections that exist among cognitive processes, emotional experiences, and bodily sensations.** To leave a favorable impression on children, adults need to consider the several interconnected domains in which children are developing. Although we adults occasionally prioritize children's cognitive abilities over their social-emotional and physical needs, the reality is that children's thoughts regularly trigger emotions, which in turn play out as sensations in the body (Immordino-Yang & Damasio, 2007). For example, a group of third graders may become distressed as they listen to a teacher's description about a recent famine, with their faces tensing, fists clenching, and bodies fidgeting. Noticing their reaction, the teacher might talk about her own feelings, reassure them about the productive responses officials are taking in response to the tragedy, and solicit the children's ideas about how they, too, could play a role in addressing the problem.

• **Accommodate the needs of children with neurological delays and disabilities.** Individualizing instruction is especially important for children who have neurological conditions that hinder their learning. For example, children who have difficulty distinguishing among various sounds of speech often benefit from intensive training in speech processing, presumably because of its beneficial effects on brain pathways (T. A. Keller & Just, 2009; Simos et al., 2007). Similarly, some children who have difficulty performing basic numerical operations have brain circuits that do not easily process mathematical information but do respond favorably to intervention (Posner & Rothbart, 2007).

Furthermore, some children with genetic problems and those who were exposed to alcohol, cocaine, and other drugs during their prenatal development have brain circuits that impair certain kinds of learning. As a result, these youngsters may need assistance in understanding abstract ideas (e.g., a teacher's request to be "responsible"), inhibiting inappropriate responses (e.g., hitting bothersome peers), and generalizing rules to multiple settings (e.g., "keep your hands to yourself" applies to the playground as well as to the classroom). Ultimately, adults must remember that, with proper guidance and instruction, most children with unusual brain circuits can lead productive and fulfilling lives. One 17-year-old girl with fetal alcohol syndrome expressed this idea eloquently:

> There are two things I want you to know: Do not call me a victim, and do not tell me what I cannot do. Help me to find a way to do it. (Lutke, 1997, p. 188)

• **Coach young children in expressing their emotions productively.** As they grow, children typically learn many skills related to *self-regulation,* the ability to direct and control personal actions and emotions. Yet not all children receive adequate support for self-regulation at home, and others are born with neurological circuits that predispose them to be tense or combative and thus find it difficult to express their needs in ways that adults find acceptable (Eisenberg, 2006). By the time children enter school, there are marked individual differences in children's self-regulatory abilities. Some children begin school able to deal productively with disappointment and frustration, whereas others cannot easily restrain themselves (Blair, 2002). Children who lack self-regulatory skills need the same loving, sensitive care as do other children, but they also need extra guidance in waiting patiently in line, keeping their hands to themselves, and expressing their emotions in healthy and culturally appropriate ways.

• **Help children who have been neglected or abused to form warm, trusting, and stable relationships.** Children develop expectations, tentatively written into their neurological circuits, regarding relationships (e.g., whether caregivers are affectionate or rejecting), emotions (e.g., whether anger dissipates or explodes into a turbulent outburst), and themselves (e.g., whether they are intrinsically worthy people or not; W. A. Cunningham & Zelazo, 2010; S. Hart, 2011; Siegel, 2001). When children learn negative lessons, it is up to caring adults to help them realize that other kinds of relationships, emotional expressions, and self-perceptions are possible. Early and repeated interventions are necessary when expectations have solidified over time.

PHYSICAL DEVELOPMENT DURING CHILDHOOD

As you are learning, systematic changes take place in physical size, bodily proportions, and neurological structures throughout childhood and adolescence. With these changes come new opportunities to practice motor skills, develop healthy habits, engage in physical activity, and relate to peers in unprecedented ways. We describe the physical characteristics of developmental periods in more detail in the next few pages.

Infancy (Birth–Age 2)

Infancy is an impressive period of rapid physical growth that builds on a foundation of remarkable reflexes. Before the umbilical cord is cut, the first reflex, *breathing*, begins, providing oxygen and removing carbon dioxide. Breathing and a few other reflexes beginning in infancy operate throughout life. Other reflexes of the infant, such as automatically grasping small objects placed in hands and responding to loud noises by flaring out arms and legs, last

Preparing for Your Licensure Examination
Your teaching test might ask you about the major milestones in physical development during childhood and adolescence.

only a few months. Abnormal reflexes at birth are associated with serious health problems (M. V. Johnston, 2008; Ohgi, Akiyama, & Fukuda, 2005; Touwen, 1974).

As infants grow older, they add motor skills to their physical repertoire. In the first 12 to 18 months, infants learn to hold up their heads, roll over, reach for objects, sit, crawl, and walk. In the second year, they walk with increasing coordination and manipulate small objects with their hands. In the "Cognitive Development: Infancy" video in MyEducationLab, you can observe 16-month-old Corwin walking confidently and competently. Corwin holds his arms high to maintain balance, but he is also agile enough to walk quickly and stay upright while reaching down into a bag.

Motor skills emerge in a particular order, following *cephalocaudal* and *proximodistal* trends (W. J. Robbins, Brody, Hogan, Jackson, & Green, 1928). The **cephalocaudal trend** refers to the vertical order of emerging skills, proceeding from the head downward. Infants first learn to control their heads, then shoulders and trunk, and later their legs. The **proximodistal trend** refers to the inside-to-outside pattern in which growth progresses outward from the spine. Infants first learn to control their arms, then their hands, and finally, their fingers. As you learned in the earlier discussion of infants' reaching behaviors, these general motor trends coexist with sizable stylistic variations in pathways to proficiency.

Because infants cannot use words to communicate physical needs, practitioners must seek information from families about their babies' sleeping, eating, drinking, diapering, and comforting preferences, needs, and habits. We offer ideas of what to look for in the Observation Guidelines table "Assessing Physical Development in Infancy."

MyEducationLab

Observe Corwin walk with good balance in the "Cognitive Development: Infancy" video. (Find Video Examples in Topic 5 of MyEducationLab.)

cephalocaudal trend
Vertical ordering of motor skills and physical development; order is head first to feet last.

proximodistal trend
Inside-outside ordering of motor skills and physical development; order is inside first and outside last.

OBSERVATION GUIDELINES
Assessing Physical Development in Infancy

CHARACTERISTIC	LOOK FOR	EXAMPLE	IMPLICATION
Eating Habits	• *Ability to communicate hunger* to adults • *Developing ability to suck, chew, and swallow* • *Ability to enjoy and digest food* without abdominal upset • *Cultural and individual differences* in how families feed infants	Wendy Sue is a listless eater who doesn't seem as interested in food as other infants in her child care program. The caregiver tells her supervisor she is worried, and the two decide to talk with the parents.	To understand an infant's health, talk with parents and families. Ask the parents what they believe is appropriate care of children.
Mobility	• *Coordination of looking and touching* • *Growing ability to move* toward objects • *Temperamental factors* that might affect exploration • *Physical challenges*, including hearing and visual impairments, that might affect exploration • *Temporary declines* in exploration, such as when first separating from parents	Due to neurological damage at birth, Daniel's left arm and leg are less strong than those on his right side. His new teacher notices that he is reluctant to move around in the center. During a home visit, the teacher finds that Daniel's movements are somewhat lopsided, but he crawls around energetically. The teacher realizes that Daniel needs to feel secure at the center before he can freely explore there.	Set up the environment so infants will find it safe, predictable, attractive, and interesting. Help individual children find challenges and opportunities that match their abilities.
Resting Patterns	• *Typical moods and responses* prior to napping • *Families' expectations* for sleeping arrangements • *Difficulty falling asleep* • *Evidence that families understand risk factors* for sudden infant death syndrome (SIDS)	Angie cries a lot when falling asleep, in part because she is used to sleeping on her stomach at home. Her teacher explains to her parents that he places babies on their backs in order to reduce the risk of SIDS. He rubs Angie's abdomen as she adjusts to her new sleeping position.	Talk to parents about risk factors for SIDS (see the upcoming section on "Rest and Sleep"). Explain why babies should be placed on their backs when they are falling asleep.
Health Issues	• *Possible symptoms of infections*, such as unusual behavior, irritability, fever, and respiratory difficulty • *Suspicious injuries and unusual behaviors* that may indicate abuse • *Possible symptoms of prenatal drug exposure*, including difficulty sleeping, extreme sensitivity, and irritability • *Physical disabilities* requiring accommodation	A teacher enjoys having 18-month-old Michael in her care. Michael has cerebral palsy, making it difficult for him to scoot around. His teacher encourages him to move toward objects, but she also occasionally brings faraway toys to him to examine. When he has a fever, she calls his mother or father, as she would for any child.	Remain alert to signs of illness and infection in children. Contact family members when infants have a fever or show other unusual physical symptoms.

MyEducationLab

Observe Acadia and Cody playing actively and spontaneously at the park in the "Physical Activity: Early Childhood" video. (Find Video Examples in Topic 5 of MyEducationLab.)

gross motor skills
Large movements of the body that permit locomotion through and within the environment.

fine motor skills
Small, precise movements of particular parts of the body, especially the hands.

Early Childhood (Ages 2–6)

Movement is a hallmark of early childhood, and dramatic changes occur in both gross motor skills and fine motor skills. **Gross motor skills** (e.g., running, hopping, tumbling, climbing, and swinging) permit large movement within the environment. **Fine motor skills** (e.g., drawing, writing, cutting with scissors, and manipulating small objects) involve more limited, controlled, and precise movements, primarily with the hands.

During the preschool years, children typically learn such culture-specific motor skills as riding a tricycle and throwing and catching a ball. Motor skills become smoother and better coordinated over time as a result of several factors—practice, development of longer arms and legs, and genetically guided increases in muscular control. Determination plays a role as well. When Teresa's son Alex was 4, he repeatedly asked his parents to throw him a softball as he stood poised with his bat. Not at all deterred by an abysmal batting average (about 0.05), Alex would frequently exclaim, "I almost got it!" His efforts paid off, as he gradually did learn to track the ball visually and coordinate his swing with the ball's path.

A lot of chatter, fantasy, and sheer joy accompany gross motor movements in early childhood. Often young children infuse pretend roles into their physical play. They become superheroes and villains, cowboys and cowgirls, and astronauts and aliens. You can observe creative and cooperative interactions between two 4-year-old children, Acadia and Cody, as they play on climbing equipment in the "Physical Activity: Early Childhood" video in MyEducationLab. These two children practice a variety of gross motor skills (running, climbing, throwing a ball), all in the name of play.

 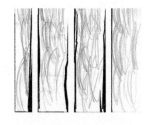

ARTIFACT 5-1 I can write and cut. Isabelle, age 3½, traced shapes and wrote her name in the artwork on the left. Learning to spell her name, Isabelle included two *E*s and two *L*s. In the artwork on the right, she practiced her cutting, attempting to follow the black lines, and correcting her work in the third rectangle from the left, showing her desire to meet a standard of straightness.

Young children also make major strides in fine motor skills. They begin to dress and undress themselves and eat with utensils. Some children develop an interest in building blocks, putting small pieces of puzzles together, or stringing beads. Other children spend considerable time drawing and cutting, forming creative shapes (e.g., by combining circles and lines to represent human beings), representing objects from the real world, and mimicking adults' cursive writing with wavy lines or connected loops (Braswell & Callanan, 2003; Kellogg, 1967).

Educators often notice large individual differences in young children's fine motor skills. Children born with certain disorders (e.g., Turner syndrome or autism) and those exposed to alcohol during prenatal development tend to show delays in fine motor skills (Connor, Sampson, Streissguth, Bookstein, & Barr, 2006; Provost, Lopez, & Heimerl, 2007; Starke, Wikland, & Möller, 2003). Girls sometimes find certain fine motor activities (e.g., cursive handwriting) easier than do boys, although many girls do have trouble with fine motor skills and plenty of boys find it easy and even pleasurable to write, draw, and cut (M. R. Cohen, 1997; Rohr, 2006). Fortunately, explicit instruction and practice can help children improve fine motor skills, even if some differences in dexterity may persist (Bruni, 1998; Case-Smith, 1996; Maraj & Bonertz, 2007).

Middle Childhood (Ages 6–10)

Over the course of middle childhood, youngsters typically show slow but steady gains in height and weight. Their bodies grow larger without undergoing alterations to the basic structures. As a result, proportions of separate body parts change less than in infancy or early childhood. With these slow, continuous gains come a few losses: Children lose their 20 primary ("baby") teeth one by one, replacing them with permanent teeth that at first appear oversized in the small mouths of 6-, 7-, and 8-year-olds. Girls mature somewhat more quickly than do boys, erupting permanent teeth sooner and progressing toward skeletal maturity earlier.

In middle childhood, children build on their emerging physical capabilities. Many gross motor skills, once awkward, are now executed smoothly. Whereas preschoolers run for the sheer joy of it, elementary school children put running to use in games and sports. Children at this point intensify their speed and coordination in running, kicking, catching, and dribbling. You can observe the pleasure that 9-year-old Kyle and 10-year-old Curtis experience as they practice basketball skills in the "Physical Activity: Middle Childhood" video in MyEducationLab.

Children within this age period also improve in fine motor skills. Their drawings, supported by physiological maturation and cognitive advances, are more detailed, and their handwriting becomes smaller, smoother, and more consistent. They also begin to tackle such fine motor activities as sewing, model building, and arts and crafts projects.

As children progress through middle childhood, they become increasingly sensitive about their physical appearance. Consider this fourth grader's self-critical viewpoint:

> I am the ugliest girl I know. My hair is not straight enough, and it doesn't even have the dignity to be curly. My teeth are crooked from sucking my thumb and from a wet-bathing-suit-and-a-slide accident. My clothes are hand-me-downs, my skin is a greenish color that other people call "tan" to be polite, and I don't say the right words, or say them in the right way. I'm smart enough to notice that I'm not smart enough; not so short, but not tall enough; and definitely, definitely too skinny. (Marissa Arillo, in Oldfather & West, 1999, p. 60)

For many children, self-consciousness increases as they get close to puberty. And it is not only the children themselves who notice their physical appearance. In fact, people generally respond more favorably to children they perceive to be physically attractive. In a variety of cultures, physical attractiveness is correlated with, and probably a causal factor in, self-esteem (Dohnt & Tiggemann, 2006; Eccles, 2010; Harter, 1999; Lau, Cheung, & Ransdell, 2008). Thus, although many children exaggerate their own physical flaws, the reality is that appearance *is* influential in social relationships, and it does affect how children feel about themselves.

Teachers and other practitioners can support the healthy physical development of children. In the Development and Practice feature "Accommodating the Physical Needs of Children," we give examples of strategies for meeting children's needs for physical care, creating a hazard-free environment, and integrating physical activity into the curriculum.

Early Adolescence (Ages 10–14)

The most obvious physical change in early adolescence is the onset of **puberty**. Ushered in by a cascade of hormones, puberty involves a series of biological changes that lead to reproductive maturity. It is marked not only by the maturation of sex-specific characteristics but also by a **growth spurt**, a rapid increase in height and weight. The release of hormones has other physiological repercussions as well, such as increases in bone density, facial oil production (often manifested as acne), and sweat gland activity (Styne, 2003).

Girls typically progress through puberty before boys do. Puberty begins in girls sometime between ages 8 and 13 (on average, at age 10). It starts with a growth spurt, "budding" of the breasts, and the emergence of pubic hair. Such changes are typically gradual; however, first menstruation, **menarche**, is an abrupt event that can be either exciting or frightening depending on a girl's preparation. The first menstrual period occurs rather late in puberty, usually between 9 and 15 years of age. Nature apparently delays menstruation, and with it the possibility of conception, until girls are physically strong and close to their adult height and therefore physiologically able to have a successful pregnancy.

For boys, puberty starts between 9 and 14 years (on average, at 11½ years), when the testes enlarge and the scrotum changes in texture and color. A year or so later, the penis grows larger and pubic hair appears; the growth spurt begins soon after. At about 13 to 14 years, boys have their first ejaculation experience, **spermarche**, often while sleeping. Boys seem to receive less information about this milestone than girls do about menstruation,

MyEducationLab

Observe Kyle and Curtis practicing basketball skills in the "Physical Activity: Middle Childhood" video. (Find Video Examples in Topic 5 of MyEducationLab.)

ARTIFACT 5-2 I like to move. When asked to choose five things he liked to do, 6-year-old Alex identified five athletic activities: kicking, running, swimming, skating, and boating.

puberty
Physiological changes that occur during adolescence and lead to reproductive maturation.

growth spurt
Rapid increase in height and weight during puberty.

DEVELOPMENT AND PRACTICE
Accommodating the Physical Needs of Children

Meet the physical needs of individual infants rather than expecting them collectively to conform to a universal schedule.

- A caregiver in an infant program keeps a schedule of times infants usually receive their bottles and naps. That way, she can plan her rotations among infants, giving each child as much attention as possible. (Infancy)
- A child care director recruits volunteers from a local senior group to drop in to the center in the early afternoon when the majority of infants want to be held before their afternoon nap. The director encourages each of the seniors to get to know a couple of infants and to hold them one at a time. (Infancy)

Integrate the physical needs of young children into the curriculum.

- An infant caregiver understands the importance of meeting physical needs in ways that deepen relationships with each child. She uses one-to-one activities, including diaper changing and bottle feeding, as occasions to interact. (Infancy)
- A preschool teacher involves children in the preparation of healthful midmorning snacks, having the children place crackers and apples slices on plates and then serve peers. (Early Childhood)

Make sure the environment is safe for exploration.

- After new carpet is installed in his classroom, a preschool teacher notices that a few children complain of headaches. He wonders if the recently applied carpet adhesive is to blame and asks the preschool's director to evaluate the situation. Meanwhile, he conducts most of the day's activities outdoors or in other rooms. (Early Childhood)
- The principal and a few teachers in a new elementary school design their new playground with climbing structures that are sturdy and securely anchored in the ground. (Middle Childhood)

Provide frequent opportunities for children to engage in physical activity.

- A preschool teacher schedules "Music and Marching" for midmorning, "Outdoor Time" before lunch, and a nature walk to collect leaves for an art project after nap time. (Early Childhood)
- Elementary school teachers organize a walking club in which students stroll around the school grounds three times a week with pedometers (small instruments that measure the number of steps taken; Satcher, 2010). (Middle Childhood)

Plan activities that help children develop their fine motor skills.

- A toddler teacher introduces spoons and bowls when children begin to show an interest in feeding themselves with utensils. (Infancy)
- An after-school caregiver invites children to make mosaics that depict different kinds of vehicles. The children glue a variety of small objects (e.g., beads, sequins, beans, colored rice) onto line drawings of cars, trains, boats, airplanes, and bicycles. (Middle Childhood)

Design physical activities so that students with widely differing skill levels can successfully participate.

- During an outdoor play session, a teacher makes balls of a variety of sizes available so that individual children with different levels of motor proficiency can each successfully throw and catch balls. (Early Childhood)
- During a unit on tennis, a physical education teacher has children practice the forehand stroke with tennis rackets. First, she asks them to practice bouncing and then hitting the ball against the wall of the gymnasium. If some students master these basic skills, she asks them to see how many times in succession they can hit the ball against the wall. When they reach five successive hits, she tells them to vary the height of the ball from waist high to shoulder high (Logsdon, Alleman, Straits, Belka, & Clark, 1997). (Middle Childhood)

Intersperse physical activity between or within academic lessons.

- When teaching about molecules and temperature, a fifth-grade teacher asks children to stand in a cluster in an open area of the classroom. To show children how molecules behave when something is cold, she asks them to move slowly while staying close together. To show them how molecules behave when something is hot, she asks them to spread farther apart and move more quickly. (Middle Childhood)
- A preschool teacher reads *Alphabet Under Construction* by D. Fleming (2002) and then takes the children for a walk to examine the architecture of local buildings (Bredekamp, 2011). (Early Childhood)

Give children time to rest.

- After a kindergarten class has been playing outside, their teacher offers a snack of apple slices, crackers, and milk. Once they have removed milk cartons and dirty napkins, the children gather around him on the floor while he reads a story. (Early Childhood)
- A third-grade teacher arranges for children to read books quietly after returning from lunch. (Middle Childhood)

Respect children's physical self-care.

- A teacher shows toddlers how to wash their hands after toileting and before eating. The teacher stands with the children, uses warm and soapy water, and helps them rub their hands together before rinsing. (Infancy)
- In an after-school program, a teacher allows the children to go to the restroom whenever they need to. He asks children to hang a clothespin with their name on an "out rope" when they leave the room and then return the pin to the "in rope" when they get back. (Middle Childhood)

IN GIRLS	IN BOYS
Initial elevation of breasts and beginning of growth spurt (typically between 8 and 13 years; on average, at 10 years)	Enlargement of the testes and changes in texture and color of scrotum (typically between 9 and 14 years; on average, at 11$\frac{1}{2}$ years)
Appearance of pubic hair (sometimes occurs before elevation of breasts)	Increase in penis size and appearance of pubic hair
Increase in size of uterus, vagina, labia, and clitoris	Beginning of growth spurt (on average, at 12$\frac{1}{2}$ years)
Further development of breasts	*Spermarche*, or first ejaculation
Peak of growth spurt	Peak of growth spurt, accompanied by more rapid penis growth
Menarche, or onset of menstrual cycle (typically between 9 and 15 years)	Appearance of facial hair
	Deepening voice, as size of larynx and length of vocal cords increase
Completion of height gain (about 2 years after menarche) and attainment of adult height	Completion of penis growth
	Completion of height gain and attainment of adult height
Completion of breast development and pubic hair growth	Completion of pubic hair growth

FIGURE 5-8 Maturational sequences of puberty.

and little is known about boys' feelings about it. Later developments include growth of facial hair, deepening of the voice, and eventually attainment of adult height. (The course of puberty for both boys and girls is depicted in Figure 5-8.)

In addition to differences in their reproductive organs, boys and girls become increasingly distinct in other ways. Boys end up on average being taller than girls. Boys have a longer period of steady prepubescent growth, and they grow a bit more during their growth spurt. With the onset of puberty, boys also gain considerably more muscle mass than girls, courtesy of the male hormone *testosterone*.

Accompanying the physical changes of puberty are alterations to adolescents' cognitive capacities, social relationships, and feelings about themselves (Brooks-Gunn & Paikoff, 1992; E. Reese, Yan, Fiona, & Hayne, 2010). Continuing development of the cortex allows more abstract thought, as we have seen, and hormonal fluctuations and additional changes in the brain affect emotions. Adolescents' rapidly changing physical characteristics can be a source of either excitement or dismay. Anne Frank looked positively on puberty, as this entry in her diary shows:

> I think what is happening to me is so wonderful, and not only what can be seen on my body, but all that is taking place inside. I never discuss myself or any of these things with anybody; that is why I have to talk to myself about them.
>
> Each time I have a period—and that has only been three times—I have the feeling that in spite of all the pain, unpleasantness, and nastiness, I have a sweet secret, and that is why, although it is nothing but a nuisance to me in a way, I always long for the time that I shall feel that secret within me again. (A. Frank, 1967, p. 146)

Others are not at all happy with their changing bodies. They may believe they are too thin, fat, flabby, or unattractive, or developing too quickly or too slowly.

Timing of puberty accounts for some of the variations in adjustment among adolescents. The age at which puberty begins is strongly affected by heredity and also is influenced by nutrition, exercise, and stress (R. Carter, Jaccard, Silverman, & Pina, 2009; Mustanski, Viken, Kaprio, Pulkkinen, & Rose, 2004). Young people who enter puberty early, girls especially,

menarche
First menstrual period in an adolescent female.

spermarche
First ejaculation in an adolescent male.

are often dissatisfied with their bodies and vulnerable to anxiety, eating disorders, and precocious sexual activity with older peers (Reardon, Leen-Feldner, & Hayward, 2009; Zehr, Culbert, Sisk, & Klump, 2007). Young people who enter puberty later than peers are apt to become self-conscious about their appearance and worried that something is wrong with them (Lindfors et al., 2007).

Puberty, whenever it happens, seems to loosen restraints on problematic behaviors. In many cultures the onset of puberty is associated with misconduct, including use of alcohol, drugs, and cigarettes and experimentation with such misbehaviors as lying, shoplifting, and burglary (R. Carter et al., 2009; Martino, Ellickson, Klein, McCaffrey, & Edelen, 2008). As we suggested earlier, adolescents' risk taking may be based partly in new brain circuits. Having a teenage brain, it seems, encourages young people to try new things, be daredevils, and affiliate with like-minded peers.

School personnel can help youngsters adjust to adolescence by giving advance warning about physiological changes, reassuring youngsters that considerable variations in timing are well within the "normal" range, encouraging them to work hard in school, and restricting their access to unhealthy experiences. In the Development and Practice feature "Accommodating the Physical Needs of Adolescents," we give additional examples of strategies for accommodating both the changes of puberty and the diversity that exists among young adolescents.

Late Adolescence (Ages 14–18)

On average at about age 15 for girls and age 17 for boys, the growth spurt ends, and in the later teenage years, most adolescents reach sexual maturity. With sexual maturation comes increasing interest in sexual activity, including hugging, kissing, and, for many teens, more intimate contact as well (DeLamater & MacCorquodale, 1979). Later in this chapter, we consider the health risks associated with unprotected sexual contact among peers.

DEVELOPMENT AND PRACTICE
Accommodating the Physical Needs of Adolescents

Show understanding of the self-conscious feelings that adolescents have about developing normally.

- A middle school basketball coach gives students plenty of time to shower and change clothing after practice in stalls that protect privacy with curtains. (Early Adolescence)
- A high school teacher advising the Yearbook Club asks student photographers to take shots of boys and girls from different ethnicities and of varying heights, weights, and appearances so as to represent the full diversity in the student population. (Late Adolescence)

Be sensitive to adolescents' feelings about early or late maturation.

- A middle school's health curriculum describes the typical sequence of biological changes that accompany puberty for boys and girls. It also stresses that the timing of these changes varies widely from one person to the next. (Early Adolescence)
- During an advising session, a high school teacher asks a late-developing freshman boy about his goals for the year. The adviser admits that his primary goal at the same age was to grow a few inches. (Early Adolescence)

Keep in mind that menstruation can begin at unexpected times and be accompanied by discomfort.

- An eighth-grade girl comes into class obviously upset, and her best friend approaches their teacher to explain that the two of them need to go to the nurse's office right away. The teacher realizes what has probably just happened and gives them permission to go. (Early Adolescence)
- A high school nurse allows girls to rest on a sofa in her office when they have menstrual cramps. (Late Adolescence)

Make sure adolescents understand what sexual harassment is, and do not tolerate it when it occurs.

- A middle school includes a sexual harassment policy in its student handbook. Homeroom teachers explain the policy at the beginning of the school year. (Early Adolescence)
- When a high school junior teases a classmate about her "big rack," his teacher takes him aside and privately explains that his comment not only constitutes sexual harassment (and so violates school policy) but also makes the girl feel unnecessarily embarrassed. The boy admits that he spoke without thinking and, after class, tells the girl he's sorry. (Late Adolescence)

TABLE 5-1   Percentages of U.S. Students Grades 9–12 Who Reported
Engaging in Risky Behaviors

RISKY BEHAVIOR	GIRLS	BOYS
Substance Use		
Alcohol (in last 30 days)	44.6	44.7
Cigarettes (in last 30 days)	18.7	21.3
Marijuana (in last 30 days)	17.0	22.4
Cocaine (in last 30 days)	2.5	4.0
Inhalants (in lifetime)	14.3	12.4
Heroin (in lifetime)	1.6	2.9
Methamphetamine (in lifetime)	4.1	4.6
Ecstasy (MDMA; in lifetime)	4.8	6.7
Hallucinogenic drugs (e.g., LSD, PCP angel dust; in lifetime)	6.1	9.5
Illegal steroids (in lifetime)	2.7	5.1
Sexual Behaviors		
Had sexual intercourse (in lifetime)	45.9	49.8
Sexually active (had intercourse in past 3 months)	35.6	34.3
No condom use during last intercourse (among sexually active adolescents)	45.1	31.5
Alcohol or drug use at last sexual intercourse (among sexually active adolescents)	17.7	27.5
Had four or more sexual partners (in lifetime)	11.8	17.9
Behaviors That Contribute to Unintentional Injuries		
Rarely or never wore seat belts in car	8.5	13.6
Bicycle riding without helmets (among those who rode bicycle in last 12 months)	82.2	87.4
Rode with a driver who had been drinking alcohol (in last 30 days)	28.8	29.5
Drove car after drinking alcohol (in last 30 days)	8.1	12.8
Weapon Use		
Carried a weapon (e.g., knife, club, gun; in last 30 days)	7.5	28.5
Carried a gun (in last 30 days)	1.2	9.0

Source: Centers for Disease Control and Prevention (CDC), 2008.

As you have learned, the brain continues to refine its pathways during adolescence, permitting more thoughtful control of emotions and more deliberate reflection about possible consequences of various behaviors. Nevertheless, some older adolescents continue to engage in behaviors that could undermine their long-term physical health—for instance, abusing alcohol and drugs and not wearing a seat belt while riding in an automobile (Briggs, Lambert, Goldzweig, Levine, & Warren, 2008; Wallander, Eggert, & Gilbert, 2004). Table 5-1 presents risky behaviors commonly seen in high school students in the U.S.

The Developmental Trends table "Physical Development at Different Age Levels" summarizes the key characteristics of each age-group and provides implications for teachers and other professionals. In the next section we examine the practices that contribute to good health and, conversely, the choices that undermine it.

PHYSICAL WELL-BEING

With age, children become more aware of "good health," but they don't always make decisions that are best for their physical well-being. In the following sections, we consider issues related to health, including eating habits, physical activity, rest and sleep, and health-compromising behaviors. We also identify strategies that adults can use to encourage young people to develop healthful lifestyles.

DEVELOPMENTAL TRENDS
Physical Development at Different Age Levels

AGE	WHAT YOU MIGHT OBSERVE	DIVERSITY	IMPLICATIONS
Infancy (Birth–2 Years) 	• Emergence of reflexes • Rapid growth and weight gain • Increasing ability to move around, first by squirming; then rolling, crawling, creeping, or scooting; finally by walking • Increasing ability to coordinate vision with small muscles of hands • Increasing self-help skills in feeding, dressing, washing, toileting, and grooming	• Children vary in timing and quality of gross motor skills (e.g., rolling over, crawling, and sitting up) depending on genetic and cultural factors. • Fine motor skills and eye–hand coordination may appear earlier or later depending on genetic makeup and encouragement from caregivers. • Self-help skills appear earlier when encouraged, but virtually all children learn them eventually, and sooner is not necessarily better.	• Celebrate each child's unique growth patterns, but watch for unusual patterns or differences that may require intervention. • Provide choices of appropriate indoor and outdoor activities for practicing motor skills. • Don't push infants to reach milestones. Allow them to experience each phase of physical development thoroughly.
Early Childhood (2–6 Years) 	• Loss of rounded, babyish appearance, with arms and legs lengthening and taking on more mature proportions • Boundless energy for practicing new gross motor skills, such as running, hopping, tumbling, climbing, and swinging • Acquisition of fine motor skills, such as functional pencil grip and use of scissors • Transition away from afternoon nap, which may initially be marked by periods of fussiness in the afternoon	• Children differ considerably in the ages at which they master various motor skills. • On average, boys are more physically active than girls, but girls are healthier overall; these differences continue throughout childhood and adolescence. • Some home environments (e.g., small apartments, as well as larger houses in which parents restrict movement) limit vigorous physical activity; others may present hazardous environmental conditions (e.g., lead paint, toxic fumes). • Children with an intellectual disability may have delayed motor skills.	• Provide frequent opportunities to play outside or (in inclement weather) in a gymnasium or other large indoor space. • Intersperse vigorous physical exercise with rest and quiet time. • Encourage development of fine motor skills through puzzles, blocks, doll houses, and arts and crafts. • Choose activities that accommodate diversity in gross and fine motor skills.
Middle Childhood (6–10 Years) 	• Steady gains in height and weight • Loss and replacement of primary teeth • Refinement and consolidation of gross motor skills and integration of these skills into structured play activities • Participation in organized sports • Increasing fluency in fine motor skills, such as handwriting and drawing	• Variations in weight and height are prominent at any single grade level. • Children begin to show specific athletic talents and interests. • Gender differences appear in children's preferences for various sports and physical activities. • Some neighborhoods do not have playgrounds or other safe play areas that foster gross motor skills. • Some children have delays in fine motor skills (e.g., their handwriting may appear sloppy and irregular) as a result of neurological conditions or lack of opportunity to practice these skills. • Some children spend much of their nonschool time in sedentary activities, such as watching television or playing video games.	• Integrate physical movement into academic activities. • Provide daily opportunities for children to engage in self-organized play activities. • Teach children the basics of various sports, and encourage them to participate in organized athletic programs. • Encourage practice of fine motor skills, but don't penalize children whose fine motor precision is delayed.
Early Adolescence (10–14 Years) 	• Periods of rapid growth • Beginnings of puberty • Self-consciousness about physical changes • Some risk-taking behavior	• Onset of puberty may vary over a span of several years; puberty occurs earlier for girls than for boys. • Leisure activities may or may not include regular exercise. • Young teens differ considerably in strength and physical endurance, as well as in their specific talents for sports. Noticeable gender differences occur, with boys being generally faster, stronger, and more confident than girls in physical abilities. • Peer groups may or may not encourage risky behavior.	• Be a role model by showing a commitment to physical fitness and good eating habits. • Provide privacy for changing clothes and showering during physical education classes. • Explain what sexual harassment is, and do not tolerate it in jokes, teasing, or physical contact. • Encourage after-school clubs and pursuits that help teenagers spend their time constructively. • Supervise adolescents and restrict their access to risky activities.

DEVELOPMENTAL TRENDS (continued)

AGE	WHAT YOU MIGHT OBSERVE	DIVERSITY	IMPLICATIONS
Late Adolescence (14–18 Years)	• In girls, completion of growth spurt and attainment of mature height • In boys, ongoing increases in stature • Ravenous appetites • Sexual arousal and in some cases sexual activity with peers • Some serious risky behaviors (e.g., drinking alcohol, taking illegal drugs, engaging in unprotected sexual contact, driving under the influence of drugs or alcohol), due in part to greater independence and acquisition of driver's licenses	• Gender differences in physical abilities increase; boys are more active in organized sports programs. • Some teens begin to limit risky behaviors and make better decisions. • Eating disorders may appear, especially in girls. • Adolescents are less likely than younger children to get regular medical care. • Adolescents differ in their exposure to risky substances (e.g., drug use is more prevalent in some neighborhoods than others).	• Make sure that adolescents know "the facts of life" about sexual intercourse and conception. • Encourage abstinence when adolescents are not sexually active. • When adolescents are sexually active and committed to remaining so, encourage them to use protective measures and to restrict the number of partners. • Encourage young people to form worthwhile goals for the future (e.g., going to college, developing athletic skills). • Reduce adolescents' exposure to potentially risky situations. • Develop and enforce policies related to sexual harassment.

Sources: Bredekamp, 2011; Bredekamp & Copple, 1997; Gallahue & Ozmun, 1998; V. F. Reyna & Farley, 2006; Steinberg, 2007; J. M. Tanner, 1990.

Eating Habits

Food affects all aspects of children's physical well-being. In many but unfortunately not all circumstances, the nutrition children consume is sufficient to ensure their health, growth, energy, and ability to learn and remember.

At birth, breastfeeding is the preferred source of nutrition because breast milk is rich in vitamins, provides antibodies against illness, and is easier to digest than infant formulas (London et al., 2011). Breast milk also gives the developing brain the nutrients it needs to form protective myelinating layers around neurons. Of course, some mothers cannot easily breastfeed, others do not want to, and still others (e.g., mothers who carry the human immunodeficiency virus or who are undergoing certain medical treatments) cannot do so safely, because it is possible to pass on infections and medications in breast milk. As an alternative, many families select one of the iron-fortified formulas that have been commercially prepared from the proteins of cow's milk or soybeans to match infants' digestive abilities and needs for calories, vitamins, and minerals. Other specialty formulas are available for infants with food allergies and intolerances. Professional caregivers generally try to support families' preferences but also suggest medically advisable strategies, for example introducing nutritious soft cereals and fruits at around 4 to 6 months of age and avoiding hard foods that infants cannot easily chew and swallow.

As children grow, they remain strongly influenced by meals prepared at home or purchased by families. For some children, mealtime is a chance to refuel, learn cultural customs, and talk about their day. For other children, meals can be unhealthy, especially when parents have few financial resources or are homeless, mentally ill, or simply tired and strapped for time. When children are underfed or given primarily non-nutritious foods, some outcomes are serious. Half of children in developing countries and more than 1 in 20 children under age 5 in the United States have anemia (iron deficiency), a condition that can cause developmental delays and behavioral disturbances (Killip, Bennett, & Chambers, 2007; S. P. Walker et al., 2007). Other outcomes are less grave but can have negative effects on children, as when children raised on fast food develop a preference for meals that are high in fat, sugar, and salt (Azzam, 2009/2010).

What, exactly, *should* children be eating? The U.S. Department of Agriculture (2010) recommends that children consume foods mainly from five food groups: grains (especially whole grains), vegetables, fruits, milk and dairy foods, and meat and other sources of protein

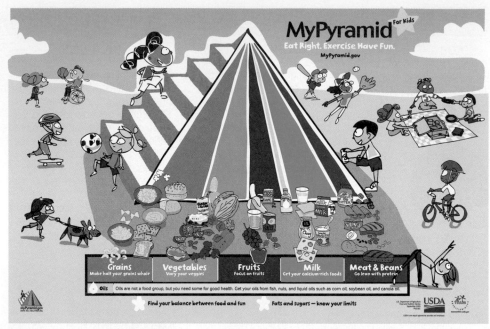

FIGURE 5-9 MyPyramid for Kids.
U.S. Department of Agriculture (2005b). MyPyramid print materials: Poster, simplified version. Retrieved March 31, 2010, at http://teamnutrition.usda.gov/Resources/mpk_poster.pdf

(see Figure 5-9). A 10-year-old boy or girl who typically consumes about 1,800 calories would eat 6 ounces of grains (half of which are whole grain), 2½ cups of vegetables, 1½ cups of fruits, 3 cups of milk, and 5 ounces of meats and beans (U.S. Department of Agriculture, 2005a). A few small snacks (e.g., cookies and potato chips) are considered acceptable as long as children are physically active and obtain needed nutrition from the five essential food groups.

Most children between ages 2 and 17 do *not* meet the full complement of dietary requirements established by the U.S. Department of Agriculture (Federal Interagency Forum on Child and Family Statistics, 2009). The diets of young American children (between 2 and 5 years of age) generally include adequate amounts of fruit, milk, and meat and beans but insufficient servings of vegetables and whole grains. As children grow older and make more decisions on their own, their nutrition deteriorates. Between the ages of 6 and 17, youngsters typically do not get enough fruit, vegetables, legumes, or whole grains. In general, youngsters also eat far too much "bad" stuff—the fatty, sugary, and salty foods. In addition, many children become less inclined to eat breakfast with age, resulting in difficulty concentrating at school (CDC, 2005a).

Overweight Youth

In part because of children's increasing consumption of processed foods, a staggering number of children have become overweight during the past few decades. Children are considered overweight when their body mass index, a measure of weight in relation to height, is at or above the 85th percentile for children of the same age and sex. About one in ten infants and toddlers, one in five young children ages 2 to 5, one in three children ages 6 to 11, and one in three adolescents ages 12 to 19 years are overweight (C. L. Ogden, Carroll, Curtin, Lamb, & Flegal, 2010). Boys and girls are represented about equally as often among overweight children.

Some children are extremely overweight. **Obesity**, the condition of being seriously overweight, is considered a global health epidemic by the World Health Organization (2000). Children are considered obese if their body mass index is at or above the 95th percentile for someone of their same age and gender (C. L. Ogden et al., 2010). Approximately one in ten children ages 2 to 5, one in five children ages 6 to 11, and one in five adolescents

obesity
Condition in which a person's body mass index, a measure of weight in relation to height, is at or above the 95th percentile for someone of the same age and gender.

ages 12 to 19 are obese. Childhood obesity is a concern because it is associated with serious health risks in childhood, including asthma, and may lead to even more deadly problems in adulthood, for example continued weight problems and diabetes, high blood pressure, and high cholesterol (CDC, 2009a; Jelalian, Wember, Bungeroth, & Birmaher, 2007). It also can have detrimental social consequences. Sadly, some peers torment obese youngsters, calling them names and excluding them from social activities.

For some obese children, their weight problems have a genetic basis, but environmental experiences, including family eating patterns and restricted exercise, contribute in most cases (H. Thomas, 2006). Acquiring an appetite for unhealthy foods, eating too much and too often, sitting for long periods in front of televisions and computers, and spending little time in physical activity are additional factors for many children. Fortunately, interventions in clinics, dietary counseling, calorie restriction, increases in physical activity, and use of behavioral techniques (e.g., setting specific goals, monitoring progress toward goals, and recognizing and rewarding progress) are often effective.

Increasingly, educators are realizing that schools are another important setting for addressing children's weight problems. Many educators are appropriately adjusting cafeteria menus and replacing the sweet, salty, and fatty snacks and carbonated and caffeinated drinks in school vending machines with more nutritious items (Fetro, Givens, & Carroll, 2009/2010; Geraci, 2009/2010; Lumeng, 2006). Teachers are also decreasing time spent in sedentary activities (e.g., sitting for hours at a time without getting up) and incorporating physical activity into lessons (Budd & Volpe, 2006; Lumeng, 2006). Some schools have asked students to set dietary goals and keep track of their fat intake, soft drink consumption, and physical activity (Haerens et al., 2006). Such record keeping, when coupled with motivational techniques, can have desirable effects on youngsters' weight and health.

Eating Disorders

Whereas some young people eat too much, others eat too little and develop eating disorders that seriously threaten their health. People with **anorexia nervosa** eat little, if anything. In contrast, people with **bulimia** eat voraciously, especially fattening foods, and then purge their bodies by taking laxatives or forcing themselves to vomit. Unfortunately, extreme weight control methods, such as not eating, taking diet pills, vomiting, and taking laxatives, are fairly widespread among adolescents. In one national study among U.S. high school students, about 15 percent of girls and 4 percent of the boys reported behaviors that indicated an eating disorder (Austin et al., 2008).

Individuals with eating disorders often have a distorted body image (believing they are "fat" even when they appear grossly thin to others), and they may exercise compulsively to lose additional weight. In addition to jeopardizing physical health, eating disorders tend to slow down the bodily changes associated with puberty (London et al., 2011). Moreover, the malnutrition that accompanies anorexia in particular can cause heart failure; tragically, anorexia is also associated with higher-than-usual thoughts related to, and attempts at, suicide.

Many experts believe that society's obsession with thinness is partly to blame for anorexia nervosa and bulimia (Ahern & Hetherington, 2006). It is fashionable for girls and women in particular to be slender; thin is "in." Psychological factors, some of which may be partly inherited, may also come into play. Individuals with eating disorders are sometimes lonely, depressed, and anxious, and some have experienced child abuse or have problems with substance abuse (Brietzke, Moreira, Toniolo, & Lafer, 2011; Dominé, Berchtold, Akré, Michaud, & Suris, 2009; U.S. Department of Health and Human Services, 2000). You can listen to a young woman describing her experience with anorexia nervosa in a video in MyEducationLab.

Anorexia nervosa and bulimia are not easily corrected simply by encouraging individuals to change their eating habits. Young people with these conditions frequently require intensive and long-term intervention from medical and psychological specialists. Educators should be alert to common symptoms such as increasing thinness, complaints of being "too fat," and a lack of energy. When they suspect an eating disorder, they can consult with a counselor, a school psychologist, or principal. Fortunately, many young people with eating disorders do respond favorably to treatment.

MyEducationLab

Go to the Video Examples section of Topic 5 to watch a video of a young woman describing her experience with Anorexia Nervosa.

anorexia nervosa
Eating disorder in which a person eats little or nothing for weeks or months and seriously jeopardizes health.

bulimia
Eating disorder in which a person, in an attempt to be thin, eats a large amount of food and then purposefully purges it from the body by vomiting or taking laxatives.

AND THEY'RE GOOD FOR YOU, TOO. Teachers and practitioners can help children to develop healthy diets by making nutritious food available at snack time and in the cafeteria.

I think I have ate to many sweets on Sunday. I had 1 to many things from the dairy groop. I had the right amount of meat, but not anof vegetables, I had only one vegetble. You wone't belve this, I had no fruits at all! I realy need to eat more fruits and vegetbles. If I ate two more things from bread groop I would have had anof.

ARTIFACT 5-3 Too many sweets. Charlotte (age 8) reflects on her eating habits over the weekend.

Promoting Good Eating Habits

We end this section with thoughts about what teachers and other practitioners can do to foster good nutrition and eating habits:

• **Provide between-meal snacks when young children are hungry.** Crackers, healthy cookies, and fruit slices can invigorate active preschool and elementary children. Nutritious snacks are particularly important for children who are growing rapidly and those who receive inadequate meals at home. In providing refreshments, educators must be aware of food allergies, family food preferences, and possible limitations in chewing and swallowing hard substances.

• **Offer healthful foods at school.** Teachers and other school personnel can advocate for healthful foods and drinks on the cafeteria line and in the vending machines at school (Azzam, 2009/2010; Budd & Volpe, 2006; Lumeng, 2006). When children are permitted to bring snacks, teachers can send home written recommendations for children and their families (e.g., carrot sticks, pretzels, and granola bars). As a fourth grader, Teresa's son Alex was advised that chocolate (a culinary passion for him) was *not* a good idea for a midmorning snack. He began to bring other snacks instead, such as granola bars (and, as you might suspect, he was happy to find granola bars sprinkled with chocolate chips).

• **Regularly review the basics of good nutrition, and ask children to set goals for improving their eating habits.** A reasonable first step is to introduce children to basic food groups and ask them to evaluate their own diets based on recommended servings for each group. Other important steps include asking youngsters to set specific goals (e.g., reducing consumption of salty snacks), encouraging them to chart their progress toward these goals, showing them that they can stick with new eating patterns, and taking cultural practices into account (Schinke, Moncher, & Singer, 1994; H. Thomas, 2006; D. K. Wilson, Nicholson, & Krishnarmoorthy, 1998).

• **Encourage children to experiment with unfamiliar nutritious foods.** Children who have grown accustomed to processed food may initially resist fresh food. Young children may not muster up the courage to try a new food until they have seen it multiple times, sometimes only after 10 to 15 presentations (Zero to Three, 2010). Some strategies that successfully encourage children to try new foods include offering new foods next to preferred foods; using such healthy dips as yogurt, hummus, ketchup, and low-fat salad dressings when presenting new vegetables and fruits; and enlisting the help of children in preparation of the meal (Zero to Three, 2010). Educators in the Baltimore City public schools have included a piece of fresh fruit in every lunch and implemented a program called "No thank you bites," in which children can try small portions of a new fruit, vegetable, or entrée item, asking for more if they like it or saying "No thank you" and moving on down the cafeteria line if they don't (Geraci, 2009/2010). Another strategy of Baltimore schools has been to open an organic farm that produces fresh food and allows students to work there.

• **Make referrals when you suspect children have eating disorders.** If you suspect a girl or boy has an eating disorder, you will want to contact the principal or another authority figure immediately. Youngsters with eating disorders urgently need medical intervention. Even with such care, they may have trouble concentrating at school and need services from school counselors or psychologists. Associated underlying problems with depression and anxiety are unlikely to be resolved overnight and will require your continued consideration.

• **Educate everyone about good and bad diets.** Children can learn about foods that are essential and about those that undermine a person's health. In one school, a supermarket was created in the building and used to instruct children about food and food labels (Fetro et al., 2009/2010). Teachers and other professionals can also take the glamour out of being excessively thin by educating children about body image and eating disorders (R. R. Evans,

Roy, Geiger, Werner, & Burnett, 2008). Teresa's son Connor first learned about anorexia nervosa when his third-grade teachers talked about eating disorders as part of a unit on the human body.

• **Follow up when you suspect serious nutritional problems.** Malnutrition can occur as a result of many factors. When low family income is the cause, practitioners can help families obtain free or reduced-cost lunches at school. When parental neglect or mental illness is possibly involved, teachers can report their suspicions to principals, counselors, or school nurses to find the best approach for protecting vulnerable children.

• **Convey respect for the feelings of children and adolescents.** Youngsters who struggle with obesity or eating disorders are certainly as distressed as their peers—and often even more so—when others comment on their appearance. Unfortunately, unflattering comments are frequently made, as recalled by these overweight adolescents: "'Kids make fun of me, they say, 'You fat ugly cow, you make a whale look small,' 'In the gym, they laugh and talk behind my back,' and 'It hurts me when they say, "Hey there, fat kid." I try to ignore them, but it does not stop'" (M. J. Smith & Perkins, 2008, p. 392). Adults must insist that classrooms, child care centers, and after-school programs be "no-tease zones" regarding weight and other physical conditions.

Physical Activity

Infants and toddlers are highly motivated to master new physical skills. As they wiggle, squirm, reach, and grasp, they exercise physical skills and also learn a lot about the world. For young children, physical activity is so enjoyable—and increasingly controllable—that they become even more active during the preschool years.

Children continue to need physical activity as they grow. Unfortunately, children are not always given sufficient outlets to move. One of the problems is that adults tend to want children to remain still and quiet, particularly in groups, whereas many children prefer more rambunctious activities. A common quality of physical activity in early and middle childhood is **rough-and-tumble play**, or good-natured mock "fighting" (A. P. Humphreys & Smith, 1987; L. J. Nelson, Hart, & Evans, 2008; Pellegrini, 2006). Children often derive considerable pleasure from it, find it a healthy release from intellectually demanding tasks, and defend it to adults as just "playing" or "messing around." Yet in schools and other institutions, boisterous play is rarely considered acceptable. Thus educators face the challenge of protecting children while allowing them to run, shout, and be exuberant. Many educators handle this dilemma sensibly by arranging for a safe playground and reasonable rules that reduce the chances of injury.

Another deterrent to physical activity is the perception that physical education and outdoor play take time away from academic lessons. In fact, a series of studies shows that reductions in physical education are *not* associated with increases in academic achievement (Ahamed et al., 2007; Trost & van der Mars, 2009/2010). Some evidence even indicates that physical activity and participation in physical education actually *increase* achievement (S. A. Carlson et al., 2008; Kristjánsson, Sigfúsdóttir, & Allegrante, 2010; Tremarche, Robinson, & Graham, 2007). Furthermore, research findings increasingly demonstrate that recess and other breaks that allow movement help children regain their energy and refocus their attention (Pellegrini & Bjorklund, 1997; Pellegrini & Bohn, 2005). With older children, organized walks or other energetic activity in the morning or at lunchtime can allow children to relax and concentrate on school learning (Jeffrey, 2009/2010). In some schools, children are given a chance to move around within the classroom between and sometimes during lessons.

As youngsters reach adolescence, exercise can help them maintain physical fitness and cope effectively with life's frustrations and stresses (J. D. Brown & Siegel, 1988). However, school tasks become increasingly sedentary in middle school and high school, and so adolescents are most likely to find opportunities for vigorous activity *outside* of school walls (Pate, Long, & Heath, 1994). Yet many do not get the exercise they need. In a recent national survey with U.S. high school students, only 26 percent of girls and 44 percent of boys participated in recommended levels of physical activity—vigorous exercise that increased their heart rate and made them sweat or breathe hard for an hour during 5 or more of the previous

rough-and-tumble play
Playful physical "fighting" common in early and middle childhood.

7 days (CDC, 2008). Children and adolescents in European countries similarly exhibit relatively low rates of physical activity (Knisel, Opitz, Wossmann, & Ketelhut, 2009).

Organized Sports and Individual Athletic Activities

In this chapter's opening case study, a group of adolescents became trained as coaches, giving them and their elementary school athletes a valuable outlet for exercise. Organized sports offer the means for maintaining and enhancing physical strength, endurance, and agility. Sports can also promote social development by fostering communication, cooperation, and leadership skills. Particularly when parents and coaches encourage children to try hard and work together as a team, children often derive a great deal of enjoyment from sports and come to see themselves as reasonably competent athletes (Ullrich-French & Smith, 2006).

Organized sports can have a downside when adults promote unhealthy competition, put excessive pressure on children to perform well, and encourage athletically talented children at the expense of their less gifted teammates. Well-meaning coaches can bolster children's athletic skills and team spirit but occasionally rob children of their intrinsic enjoyment of sports and cause them to overexercise and become injured (Holt, Tink, Mandigo, & Fox, 2008; R. E. Smith & Smoll, 1997). And as we authors have personally witnessed, some parents are extremely critical of their children's athletic performance on the sidelines of public games.

Some children do *not* like team sports but nevertheless want to exercise. A few are drawn to such individual athletic activities as running, skateboarding, snowboarding, and mountain biking. Although not part of teams, youngsters who engage in individual sports may spend time with peers while participating in these activities. Individual athletic activities have the advantages of requiring initiative and at least moderate levels of exercise. However, some individual sports (e.g., hang gliding, wakeboarding) incur risk for injury and are not always well supervised. You can watch a video in MyEducationLab about youngsters' participation in risky sports and the kinds of guidance that adults may offer about protective measures.

Encouraging Physical Activity

Physical activity is an essential part of every child's day. Here are some specific strategies educators can follow to promote physical activity:

• **Be "pro-ACTIVE."** Teachers can incorporate physical movement into many activities, particularly at the preschool and elementary school levels. Regular breaks that include physical activity can actually increase children's attention to more sedentary, cognitively demanding tasks (Pellegrini & Bjorklund, 1997; Pellegrini & Bohn, 2005; Trost & van der Mars, 2009/2010).

• **Provide appropriate equipment and guidance so children can safely engage in physical activity.** Open space, playground equipment, balls, and other athletic props encourage physical exercise. Equipment should be chosen carefully to allow children to experiment freely yet safely, ideally minimizing times when adults have to say no to certain activities (Bronson, 2000). Equipment and exercise facilities should also be properly designed to fit children's body sizes and abilities (Frost, Shin, & Jacobs, 1998).

• **Make exercise an enjoyable pastime.** By the time they reach high school, many young people have had unpleasant experiences with physical exercise and, as a result, associate exercise with regimentation, discomfort, failure, embarrassment, competitiveness, boredom, or injury (Rowland, 1990). Furthermore, many adolescents do not see physical exercise as a regular part of the daily lives of their parents or other family members. By talking with youngsters, adults can learn about intrinsic interests in particular skills (e.g., in karate), pleasure in physical self-expression (e.g., through dance), and the camaraderie they gain from group

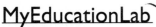

Go to the Video Examples section in Topic 5 of MyEducationLab to watch a video about youngsters' participation in risky sports (e.g., ski racing, rock climbing, and wakeboarding) and the kinds of guidance nurses may offer about protective measures youth can take.

ARTIFACT 5-4 My favorite time at school. Regular recess and breaks for physical movement not only promote children's physical well-being but also lead to improved attention and concentration in more cognitively oriented activities. Art by Grace, age 11.

activities (e.g., exercising together in an aerobics class; W. C. Taylor, Beech, & Cummings, 1998).

• **Plan physical activities with diversity in mind.** Not everyone can be a quarterback, and not everyone likes football. But nearly all children and adolescents can find enjoyment in physical activity of some form. Offering a range of activities, from dance to volleyball, and modifying them for children with special needs can maximize the number of students who participate. A child who is unusually short might look to such activities as soccer, cycling, or gymnastics that do not require exceptional height (Rudlin, 1993). Another child in a wheelchair might go up to bat in a softball game and then have a classmate run the bases for her.

Ensuring that boys and girls and members of different ethnic groups are all encouraged to participate in athletic activities is another important diversity concern. According to *Title IX* of the Educational Amendments of 1972, educators in the U.S. must give boys and girls the same opportunities to participate in athletic programs and, in fact, in all aspects of academic life. Thus, boys and girls must receive comparable quality in coaching, practice, and locker facilities.

• **Focus on self-improvement rather than on comparison with peers.** Focusing on one's own improvement is, for most children, far more motivating than attending to how well one's performance stacks up against that of peers. Dwelling too much on one's relative standing with others leads children to believe that physical ability is largely a matter of "natural talent," when in fact most physical skills depend on considerable practice (Ames, 1984; R. W. Proctor & Dutta, 1995). Thus adults can direct children to progress they are making as individuals (e.g., "Wow, Libby, you have become one fine kicker this week").

Another way to promote self-improvement is to teach skills in progression, from simple to complex (Gallahue & Ozmun, 1998). A preschool teacher could ask children to hop on one foot as they pretend to be the "hippity hop bunny." Once they have mastered that skill, the teacher might demonstrate more complex skills, such as galloping and skipping. Carefully sequenced lessons give children feelings of success and make physical activities enjoyable. A similar tactic is to ask children to chart their progress on particular athletic skills and exercises (CDC, 2002).

FEELING FINE. Adults can help young people see how enjoyable exercise can be.

Improving Your Observation Skills

Record of 15-year-old Connor's physical activity. Connor kept a kept a record of his performance on sit-ups, push-ups, and up-downs over a 5-day period. How did Connor's performance change as he adjusted to the new exercise routine? Compare your response with the explanation at the end of the chapter.

Form adapted from *Planning for Physical Activity* (a BAM! Body and Mind Teacher's Corner resource) by the CDC, Fall 2002. Retrieved January 19, 2003, from http://www.bam.gov/teachers/activities/planning.htm.

Your Name: Connor   Your Age: 15   Adult Supervising: MOM

Record of Physical Activity

Day 1-5: Exercise	Activity 1: Sit ups		Activity 2: push ups		Activity 3: up-downs	
	How many did you do?	How did it feel?	How many did you do?	How did it feel?	How many did you do?	How did it feel?
1	37	Good	26	Hard to Keep Back Straight.	21	Hard to Keep Balance
2	22	Stomach Sore from yesterday. Sore	30	Easy	25	Harder
3	26	Stomach is better ok	22	Sore	23	Sore
4	15	Hurt really Bad!	20	Sore	25	Hard
5	30	tried to beat #1 But to Sore to	31	Bent It	25	use a lot of Energy
Day 6: Reflect	What parts of your body did you use? Stomach Muscles!		What parts of your body did you use? Upper Body.		What parts of your body did you use? A Full body work out	
	What did you do to prevent injury? Stopped when It hurt.		What did you do to prevent injury? Tried to keep Balance		What did you do to prevent injury? Stopped when I needed to	

Even in competitive sports, the emphasis should be more on how well children have "played the game"—on whether they worked well together, treated members of the opposing team with respect, and were all-around good sports—than on whether they won or lost.

• **Make sure that children don't overdo it.** Becoming fanatically involved in exercise can create medical problems for children. The soft and spongy parts of bones in growing children are susceptible to injury from repeated use, and especially from excessive weight-bearing forces (R. H. Gross, 2004; Micheli, 1995). Weight-training machines are almost always designed for adult-sized bodies, exacerbating children's chances for injury. Overuse injuries are also seen in distance running, competitive swimming, and gymnastics (Gallahue & Ozmun, 1998). Furthermore, obsessive concern about being successful in athletics can lead youngsters to make health-compromising choices (taking steroids, gaining or losing weight too quickly, etc.). Medical experts recommend that children be discouraged from concentrating solely on one sport before adolescence, that they never be asked to "work through" stress fractures, and that they receive regular care from a physician who can monitor the possible health effects of intensive training (e.g., delays in sexual maturation; American Academy of Pediatrics [AAP] Committee on Sports Medicine and Fitness, 2000).

Rest and Sleep

Rest and sleep are essential to growth and health. Sleep actually helps young people grow, because growth hormones are released at higher rates as children snooze than when they're awake. In addition to promoting growth, sleep may help the brain maintain healthy functioning (N. R. Carlson, 2011).

Infancy

Newborn babies spend a long time sleeping—16 to 18 hours a day according to some estimates (Wolff, 1966). Gradually, infants develop wake/sleep cycles that correspond to adults' day/night cycles (St. James-Roberts & Plewis, 1996). They begin to sleep through the night when they are ready to, depending in part on their own biological rhythms. Teresa recalls that her sons as infants were oblivious to a pediatrician's guideline that they should be able to sleep through the night by 10 weeks of age and 10 pounds in weight. Infants' sleeping habits are also affected by cultural practices, suggesting that there is no single "best" way to put babies to sleep (Shweder et al., 1998).

Although there may be no best way, there is definitely one *wrong* way to put babies to sleep. Medical experts advise caregivers *not* to place babies on their stomachs for sleeping because this position puts babies at risk for **sudden infant death syndrome (SIDS)**, a death that occurs (usually during sleep) without an apparent medical cause. SIDS is a leading cause of death among infants from 1 month through 1 year in age (AAP Task Force on Infant Sleep Position and Sudden Infant Death Syndrome, 2000). During the period that SIDS is most common (between 2 and 4 months), infants' brains are developing circuits that control arousal, breathing, heart rate, and other basic physiological functions. Minor abnormalities in these areas in the brain may prove fatal if infants are under physical stress, for example, if they have a respiratory infection, are especially warm due to excessive clothing or blankets, or have an obstructed airway with their face nestled into the bed (Kinney, 2009; E. A. Mitchell, 2009; F. M. Sullivan & Barlow, 2001).

Infant caregivers need to be aware of current advice not only for reducing the risk of SIDS but also for preventing suffocation generally. Recommendations include placing babies on their backs (face up) to sleep, refraining from smoking nearby, keeping babies at a comfortable temperature, using a firm mattress, and avoiding soft surfaces and loose bedding (AAP Task Force on Infant Sleep Position and Sudden Infant Death Syndrome, 2000). You can watch a video on measures to reduce SIDS in a video in MyEducationLab.

Early Childhood through Adolescence

Time spent sleeping decreases steadily over the course of childhood and adolescence. Two-year-olds typically need 12 hours of sleep, 3- to 5-year-olds need 11 hours, 10- to 13-year-olds need 10 hours, and 14- to 18-year-olds need 8 1/2 hours (Roffwarg, Muzio, & Dement,

MyEducationLab

To learn more about measures to reduce the risk of sudden infant death syndrome (SIDS), watch a video on the topic in the Video Examples section in Topic 5 of MyEducationLab.

sudden infant death syndrome (SIDS)
Death of an infant in the first year of life, typically during sleep, that cannot be explained by a thorough medical examination; the risk of SIDS is highest between 2 and 4 months of age.

1966). These figures, of course, are averages. The number of hours of sleep children of a particular age need to feel rested varies somewhat.

Occasional sleep problems occur. Nightmares are common between ages 3 and 6, and children may ask adults to help them battle the demons of the night that seem so real. Pronounced sleep disturbances (e.g., waking repeatedly during the night) may be due to serious health problems, excessive stress, use of street drugs, or side effects from prescribed medications. Repeated nightmares are especially common among children who have been victims of abuse or other traumatic incidents (Durand, 1998; C. Humphreys, Lowe, & Williams, 2008). Also, children with certain disabilities (e.g., cerebral palsy, severe visual impairment, autism, attention-deficit hyperactivity disorder) often have difficulty sleeping (Cotton & Richdale, 2010; Durand, 1998).

Especially as they grow older, children and adolescents may get insufficient sleep because of poor sleep habits. Adolescents in particular are at risk for *sleep deprivation*, a state of being tired and irritable and having difficulty in reasoning, learning, and remembering. Although they require less sleep than they did in their earlier years, adolescents are still growing rapidly, and their bodies need considerable time for sleep and rest (Mitru, Millrood, & Mateika, 2002). However, out-of-school obligations—extracurricular activities, part-time jobs, social engagements, and homework assignments—may keep teenagers up until the wee hours of the morning.

When children and adolescents lose sleep, they are likely to become short tempered and impatient. Depending on their age, sleep-deprived youngsters may become aggressive and depressed, have trouble concentrating, perform at low levels academically, and engage in high-risk behaviors (Bergin & Bergin, 2009/2010; Dahl & Lewin, 2002; Durand, 1998; Sadeh, Gruber, & Raviv, 2002). Of course, some youngsters who are staying up late and finding it hard to sleep may experience a good deal of stress independent of their sleeping problems.

Accommodating Children's Needs for Rest and Sleep

Educators often have youngsters in their classrooms who do not sleep easily and soundly, including some who are truly sleep deprived. With this in mind, we offer the following suggestions:

• **When appropriate, provide time for sleep during the day.** Infants and toddlers *must* sleep during the day. It is a common custom, and most certainly good practice, to include an afternoon nap time in the schedule of preschoolers who attend child care or school in the afternoon. A few older children and adolescents—for instance, youngsters with brain injuries or other chronic health conditions—may need an hour or two of sleep as well, perhaps on a couch in the school nurse's or counselor's office (Lewandowski & Rieger, 2009; Ormrod & McGuire, 2007).

• **Include time for rest in the daily schedule.** Young children typically give up their afternoon nap sometime between ages 2 and 5, but for quite some time after that, they need to recharge their batteries with quiet and restful activities (e.g., listening to stories or music) in the afternoon. Children at any age level learn most effectively when they take an occasional, restful break from intense activity.

• **Communicate with families about the importance of sleep.** Teachers and other practitioners can speak tactfully with family members when they think chronic fatigue is causing children's difficulty in concentrating, maintaining reasonably good spirits, and resisting aggressive impulses. The topic of sleep can also be addressed in tips to parents in school newsletters.

• **Encourage youngsters to make steady progress on lengthy assignments.** At the high school level, adolescents may have several hours of homework each night. Add to this workload extracurricular events, social activities, family commitments, and part-time jobs, and you have adolescents who are seriously overstretched. When assigning major projects, teachers can encourage regular progress by giving interim deadlines for various *parts* of the assignment.

• **Schedule school events with reasonable ending times.** Athletic practices, plays and musical performances, clubs meetings, and other school events can be planned with definite

BASIC DEVELOPMENTAL ISSUES
Physical Development

ISSUE	PHYSICAL GROWTH	MOTOR SKILLS	HEALTH AND ACTIVITY
Nature and Nurture	Genetic instructions specify the particular changes that occur as bodies grow larger and provide individual targets for mature height and weight. Normal progressions depend on adequate nutrition, movement, stimulation, affection, and protection from toxic substances.	Nature sets firm boundaries as to the motor skills a child can execute at any age range. A 6-month-old cannot run and a 10-year-old cannot clear 15 feet in the standing high jump. However, organized sports programs and other opportunities for regular exercise allow children to expand and refine their motor skills.	Nature influences children's activity level and susceptibility to infection and illness. Nurture affects children's daily activities. Children learn many habits related to eating and exercising from their parents, peers, and others in their community.
Universality and Diversity	Children tend to show similar sequences in physical development (e.g., in the emergence of sexual characteristics associated with puberty) across a wide range of situations. However, the rate of development differs from one child to the next as a result of genetic diversity, personal choices, family stresses, and cultural variations.	Motor skills often develop in a similar sequence. Children can, on average, pick up crumbs at age 1, scribble with a crayon at age 2, and build a tower 10 blocks high at age 4 (Sheridan, 1975). Diversity is present in the specific ages at which children master motor skills, due to genetic differences and variations in environmental support.	All children and adolescents need good nutrition, plenty of rest, and a moderate amount of physical activity to be healthy. Huge disparities are present in the activity levels and eating habits of youngsters. In addition, children differ in their susceptibility to illness.
Qualitative and Quantitative Change	Many physical advancements are the result of a series of quantitative changes (e.g., gradual increases in strength and dexterity). Qualitative changes are revealed in new physical characteristics that emerge with puberty.	As a general rule, children must practice motor skills for a long time before they can execute them easily and gracefully, and a series of quantitative improvements allow more complex skills to emerge. Some motor skills, such as walking and throwing a ball, also change qualitatively.	During middle childhood, children gradually gain control over what they eat and how they spend their leisure time (a quantitative change). Reorganization in thinking about safety and danger occurs in adolescence. Young people may shift from a preoccupation with safety to a thrill-seeking mind-set (a qualitative change).

starting and ending times that allow students to wrap up commitments early enough that they can go home at sensible hours (Bergin & Bergin, 2009/2010). Occasionally, such events as school dances extend far into the night (and even into the morning), but late-night activities should be the exception rather than the rule.

• **Deliberate over the starting time for high school.** Some high schools are delaying the start of morning classes to allow students to sleep in an extra hour or so (Bergin & Bergin, 2009/2010; Wahlstrom, Davison, Choi, & Ross, 2001). These schedule revisions have been well received, especially by the adolescents themselves, who actually do seem to get more sleep rather than staying up even later at night (Wolfson & Carskadon, 2005). However, the implications of schedule changes for families and school personnel must also be considered during any discussions.

• **Recognize that sleep problems can be a sign of illness or emotional stress.** Words of acknowledgment and kindness ("You look tired today, Darragh. Did you sleep all right last night?") may give children permission to share their troubles and, as a result, take the first step toward resolving them.

As you have seen, advances that occur in physical development take many forms and depend on several distinct factors, including maturational processes, adequate nutrition, physical activity, and sleep. In the Basic Developmental Issues table "Physical Development," we summarize how physical development shows nature and nurture, universality and diversity, and qualitative and quantitative change. Because good health comes not only from acquiring health-promoting habits but also from avoiding negative substances, we now focus on the important topic of health-compromising behaviors.

Health-Compromising Behaviors

Especially as they grow older and gain increasing independence from adult supervision, children and adolescents face many choices about how to spend their leisure time. With freedom comes an element of danger: Young people sometimes make decisions that undermine their health. Here we look at three health-compromising behaviors: cigarette smoking, alcohol and drug use, and unsafe sexual activity.

Cigarette Smoking

An alarming percentage of young people smoke cigarettes (see Table 5-1). Unfortunately, teens often continue to use tobacco when they become adults.

Because the health risks are so well publicized, it is difficult for many adults to understand why adolescents choose to smoke. Undoubtedly, "image" is a factor. Teens may smoke cigarettes to look older, rebel, and affiliate with certain peer groups. Advertising plays a role as well. The majority of teen smokers choose from only a few cigarette brands, perhaps because of the youthful, fun-loving images that certain tobacco companies cultivate in the media. Regardless of the reasons adolescents begin smoking, those who make it a habit may develop health problems that they would otherwise avoid.

Alcohol and Drug Use

Alcohol and drugs are among the most serious threats to physical health that adolescents face today. Occasionally a single episode with a particular drug leads to permanent brain damage or even death. Losing judgment under the influence of alcohol and drugs, adolescents can become vulnerable in other ways, such as engaging in unprotected sexual activity. Those who are intravenous drug users may share needles, putting themselves at risk of contracting the human immunodeficiency virus (HIV) (described later in the chapter) and other diseases (J. L. Evans, Hahn, Lum, Stein, & Page, 2009). Figure 5-10 lists substances used by some adolescents.

Alcohol depresses the central nervous system, sometimes gives a sense of elation, and impairs coordination, perception, speech, and decision making; for instance, heavy drinkers may talk incoherently and walk with a staggering gait. Teens who drink excessively are more likely to have car accidents and commit rape.

Methylene dioxymethamphetamine (MDMA, or "ecstasy") gives users a sense of euphoria and exuberance, sensory enhancements and distortions, and feelings of being at peace with the world and emotionally close to others (it is sometimes called the "hug drug"). However, the sense of euphoria often leads users to ignore such bodily distress signals as muscle cramping and dehydration; more serious effects include convulsions, impaired heart function, and occasionally death. It is often available at dance clubs ("raves"), where music and flashing lights intensify its effects.

Inhalants are attractive to many adolescents because they cause an immediate "high" and are readily available in the form of such household substances as glue, paint thinner, aerosol paint cans, and nail polish remover. These very dangerous substances can cause loss of sensation, brain damage, and death.

Marijuana delays reaction time, modifies perception, and instills a mild feeling of euphoria, but it can also heighten fears and anxieties and impair thinking. Teens who smoke marijuana may have red eyes, dry mouths, mood changes, and loss of interest in former friends and hobbies, and they may exhibit impaired driving.

Methamphetamine ("speed") is a stimulant that gives users a sense of energy, alertness, confidence, and well-being.

Overdoses are possible, addiction frequently results, and changes to the brain and heart may occur. People who use speed regularly combat psychiatric problems, such as becoming violent and confused and believing that "everyone is out to get me."

Cocaine (including *crack*, a particularly potent form) overstimulates neurons in the brain and gives users a brief sense of energy and intense euphoria; it can also cause tremors, convulsions, vomiting, respiratory problems, over-heating, strokes, and heart failure. Cocaine users may be energetic, talkative, argumentative, and boastful; long-time users may appear anxious and depressed. Crack users are prone to violence and crime.

Prescription medications are used by a growing number of adolescents. Prescription painkillers, including OxyContin and Vicodin, are potentially addictive narcotics that reduce sensations of discomfort and increase feelings of pleasure. Anabolic steroids are another type of medication for which there is an illicit market among teenagers. Some adolescents use nonprescribed doses of anabolic steroids to increase muscle development, but they also inadvertently experience unwanted side effects (e.g., in boys, shrinking testicles and breast development; in girls, growth of facial hair and menstrual changes; in both, liver damage, high blood pressure).

Sources: G. R. Adams, Gullotta, & Markstrom-Adams, 1994; Atwater, 1996; DanceSafe, 2000a, 2000b; S. S. Feldman & Wood, 1994; L. D. Johnston, O'Malley, Bachman, & Schulenberg, 2007; Kulberg, 1986; National Institute on Drug Abuse, 2010a, 2010b, 2010c, 2010d, 2010e, 2010f, 2010g, 2010h; Neinstein, 2004; L. Smith, 1994; J. M. Taylor, 1994.

FIGURE 5-10 Effects and symptoms of adolescent substance abuse.

Given the hazards of alcohol and drugs, why do some adolescents frequently use them? As you learned earlier about brain development, adolescence is a time of trying new things. For some, it's a matter of mild curiosity: After hearing about alcohol and drugs, not only from their peers but also from adults and the media, teens may want to experience the effects firsthand. For others, trying alcohol and drugs is an impulsive event with little forethought.

Adult behaviors, too, influence substance abuse. Many adolescents who use drugs or alcohol have parents who fail to supervise their whereabouts and do little to promote adolescents' self-confidence, willingness to abide by society's rules, or ability to stay focused on long-term goals in the presence of immediate, conflicting interests (Botvin & Scheier, 1997; Jessor & Jessor, 1977; P. Wu, Liu, & Fan, 2010). Drug and alcohol use is more typical when people in the local community are relatively tolerant of such behavior (Poresky, Daniels, Mukerjee, & Gunnell, 1999).

Peer group norms and behaviors are yet another factor affecting adolescents' substance abuse (J. A. Epstein, Botvin, Diaz, Toth, & Schinke, 1995; P. Wu et al., 2010). To a great extent, use of alcohol and drugs is a social activity, and teenagers may partake to a certain extent as a means of "fitting in." In other cases, teens inclined to violate laws may actively seek out peer groups similarly disposed to get in trouble (A. M. Ryan, 2000).

Regardless of their initial reasons for trying alcohol and drugs, youngsters' continued use often creates serious problems for them. If these substances give adolescents pleasure, satisfy a desire for thrills, alleviate anxieties, or deaden feelings of pain and depression, they may begin to use the substances regularly (Conner, Hellemann, Ritchie, & Noble, 2010; Ozechowski & Waldron, 2010). Unfortunately, some users eventually develop an **addiction** to, or biological and psychological dependence on, drugs or alcohol. They grow physiologically accustomed to using the substance and need increasing quantities to produce a desired effect. If they try to stop, addicts experience intense cravings and severe physiological and psychological reactions (Hussong, Chassin, & Hicks, 1999; National Institute on Drug Abuse, 2009).

Unsafe Sexual Activity

Learning about sexuality is an important part of coming of age, and many adolescents become sexually active during the secondary school years.[3] On average, about 4 or 5 in every 10 high school students in the United States reports having had sexual intercourse (CDC, 2008; see Table 5-1). More than 1 in 10 high school students have had four or more sexual partners (CDC, 2008). From the perspective of physical health, early sexual activity is problematic because it can lead to sexually transmitted infections, pregnancy, or both.

Sexually transmitted infections. Sexually transmitted infections (STIs) vary in their severity. Syphilis, gonorrhea, and chlamydia can be treated with antibiotics, but affected teens do not always seek prompt medical help. Without treatment, serious problems can occur, including infertility and sterility, heart problems, and birth defects in future offspring. Genital herpes has no known cure, but medication can make its symptoms less severe.

Undoubtedly the most life-threatening STI is acquired immune deficiency syndrome (AIDS), a medical condition in which the immune system is weakened, permitting severe infections, pneumonias, and cancers to invade the body. AIDS is caused by HIV, which can be transmitted through the exchange of body fluids (e.g., blood and semen) during just a single contact. Sexual transmission is the primary means of HIV transmission during adolescence (AAP Committee on Pediatric AIDS and Committee on Adolescence, 2001; Letourneau, Ellis, Naar-King, Cunningham, & Fowler, 2009).

addiction
Physical and psychological dependence on a substance, such that increasing quantities must be taken to produce the desired effect and withdrawal produces adverse physiological and psychological effects.

[3] Sexual intimacy is examined in Chapter 15.

Pregnancy. Pregnancy rates in U.S. adolescents have decreased slightly during the past few decades in large part due to increased use of condoms and other contraception methods (Santelli, Orr, Lindberg, & Diaz, 2009). Nevertheless, numerous pregnancies do occur in teens, some of which end in miscarriage or abortion, and others of which go to full term. The current birthrate for American adolescent girls ages 15 to 19 is 4 births per 100 girls (Federal Interagency Forum on Child and Family Statistics, 2009). Many girls who become teenage mothers are from low-income families, have records of weak academic performance, believe they have few career options, achieve status within their community with the birth of the baby, and yearn for an emotional connection with their baby (Coley & Chase-Lansdale, 1998; Sieger & Renk, 2007).

Addressing Health-Compromising Behaviors

Schools and community organizations can do a great deal to reduce physical risk. We offer a few thoughts on appropriate support:

- **Provide healthy options for free time.** Children and adolescents are less likely to engage in health-compromising behaviors when they have better things to do with their time. In our chapter-opening case study, a new coaching program afforded youth a productive form of leisure. Community leaders can advocate for after-school programs and community athletic leagues. As an example, the *First Choice* program, which has been implemented at more than 80 sites in the United States, is targeted at students who are at risk of dropping out of school or getting in serious trouble with the law (Collingwood, 1997; PE 4 Life, n.d.). The program focuses on fitness and prevention of drug use and violence. Elements that contribute to its success include physical activity classes, a peer fitness leadership training program, parent support training, and coordination with mental health agencies and recreational facilities.

- **Prevent problems.** It is much easier to teach children and adolescents to resist cigarettes, alcohol, and drugs than it is to treat dependence on these substances. Effective prevention programs take advantage of the protective factors that children might have, perhaps strong support from families, by sending home newsletters about drug prevention programs, and they reduce or reverse risk factors, for example eliminating easily accessible drugs by implementing a "no tolerance" policy on school grounds (Bukstein & Deas, 2010; National Institute on Drug Abuse, 2003).

Effective prevention programs are also designed to address age-typical abilities and risk factors. At the elementary level, prevention programs minimize potential problems with aggression and academic failure by fostering self-control, emotional awareness, communication skills, social-problem solving, and academic achievement. In middle, junior high, and high school, successful programs address similar abilities as well as drug-resistance skills, antidrug attitudes, and commitments against drug and alcohol use. Exposure to the same antidrug messages across multiple settings, for example, at school, in the home, in faith-based organizations, and in the media, is also valuable.

- **Implement programs that have demonstrated success in particular settings.** The kinds of programs educators implement are determined largely by their particular professional duties and the needs of youngsters with whom they work. Coaches and other staff members in the Forest Hills School District in Cincinnati, Ohio, designed an effective drug prevention program that addressed local needs (see Figure 5-11). This comprehensive program enlisted participation by school coaches, principals, other school staff, team captains, parents, and the adolescents themselves (U.S. Drug Enforcement Administration, 2002). Coaches spoke openly about substance use. Peer pressure was used to discourage alcohol and drug use. When athletes did break the rules, they were given defined consequences, but in a way that communicated hope that they would try harder next time.

- **Encourage adolescents to protect themselves.** Approaches to preventing adolescent pregnancy and transmission of STIs are somewhat controversial. Many parents object to schools' distribution of condoms and advocacy of "safe sex." (And, of course, at the present

Bioecology of Child Development

Health-compromising behaviors and their prevention are affected by numerous bioecological factors.

<table>
<tr><td>

Student's Pledge

As a participant in the _____ High School Athletic Program, I agree to abide by all training rules regarding the use of alcohol, tobacco, and other drugs. Chemical dependency is a progressive but treatable disease, characterized by continued drinking or other drug use in spite of recurring problems resulting from that use. Therefore, I accept and pledge to abide by the training rules listed in the athletic handbook and others established by my coach.

To demonstrate my support, I pledge to:

1. Support my fellow students by setting an example and abstaining from the use of alcohol, tobacco, and other drugs.

2. Not enable my fellow students who use these substances. I will not cover up for them or lie for them if any rules are broken. I will hold my teammates responsible and accountable for their actions.

3. Seek information and assistance in dealing with my own or my fellow students' problems.

4. Be honest and open with my parents about my feelings, needs, and problems.

5. Be honest and open with my coach and other school personnel when the best interests of my fellow students are being jeopardized.

Student _____ Date _____

**PARENTS: We ask that you co-sign this pledge to show your support.

</td><td>

Sample Letter from Coach to Parent about a Drug or Alcohol Violation

Dear Parent:

Your daughter _____ has violated the _____ High School extra-curricular activities code of conduct. She voluntarily came forward on Thursday afternoon and admitted her violation of the code, specifically, drinking alcohol. The code is attached.

We respect her honesty and integrity and hope you do as well. Admitting a mistake such as this is very difficult for her. Not only does she have to deal with authorities such as us, she must face you, her parents, as well as her peers—which is probably the most difficult. We understand that no one is perfect and that people do make mistakes. Our code, and the resulting consequences of violating the code, is a nationally recognized model and is designed to encourage this type of self-reporting where the student can seek help and shelter from guilt without harsh initial penalties. She has admitted to making a mistake and is willing to work to alleviate the negative effects of the mistake.

As you can see in the enclosed code, we require that your daughter complete 10 hours of drug and alcohol in-service education and counseling. In addition, she must sit out 10 practice days of competition. She is still part of the team and must attend practices and competition; she is just not allowed to compete or participate in games for 10 days.

We hope you understand and support our effort to provide a healthy athletic program for the students. If you have any questions, please call either one of us at the high school.

Sincerely,

</td></tr>
</table>

FIGURE 5-11 Team Up drug prevention materials from high school athletic coaches.
From Team Up: A Drug Prevention Manual for High School Athletic Coaches, by the U.S. Drug Enforcement Administration, 2002, Washington, DC: U.S. Department of Justice Drug Enforcement Administration.

time condom use is no guarantee of protection against either infection or pregnancy.) Evidence suggests, however, that having condoms available in schools moderately increases condom use for those students who are already sexually active (and so may offer some protection against HIV infection) and does not necessarily increase rates of sexual activity (Alan Guttmacher Institute, 2001; D. Kirby & Laris, 2009). Programs that encourage sexual abstinence are a less-controversial alternative and can be effective in the short run, although such programs appear to be relatively ineffective over the long run (Dreweke & Wind, 2007; Kirby & Laris, 2009). Some programs encourage both abstinence and use of protection, and it appears that young people easily grasp the merits of these two strategies and are *not* confused by the dual message (D. Kirby & Laris, 2009).

• **Get help for young people who have become addicted to drugs or alcohol.** Teachers and other practitioners can share suspicions with parents and counselors that youngsters have become dependent on drugs or alcohol. Various kinds of treatment, including medication, counseling, and residential programs, frequently help young people manage painful withdrawal from drugs and alcohol and learn to resist these substances in the future (National Institute on Drug Abuse, 2009). Some adolescents go through treatment voluntarily, whereas others are required by families and court orders to participate in treatment. Relapses in drug and alcohol use are relatively common and signify the need for additional intervention.

The four areas we've discussed in this section—eating habits, physical activity, rest and sleep, and health-compromising behaviors—all have major effects on youngsters' physical development. In the Observation Guidelines table "Assessing Health Behaviors and Characteristics of Children and Adolescents," we identify attributes of good and poor health. (Obviously, practitioners should not make inferences about health or provide treatment for which they are not trained.) We turn now to children who have special physical needs and the practices that can help these children achieve their full potential.

OBSERVATION GUIDELINES
Assessing Health Behaviors and Characteristics of Children and Adolescents

CHARACTERISTIC	LOOK FOR	EXAMPLE	IMPLICATION
Eating Habits	• *Frequent consumption* of junk food (candy, chips, carbonated beverages, etc.) • *Unusual heaviness or thinness*, especially if these characteristics become more pronounced over time • *Lack of energy* • *Reluctance or inability to eat anything* at lunchtime	Melissa is a good student, an avid runner, and a member of the student council. She is quite thin but wears baggy clothes that hide her figure, and she eats only a couple of pieces of celery for lunch. Her school counselor suspects an eating disorder and contacts Melissa's parents to share her suspicion.	Observe what children eat and drink during the school day. Seek free or reduced-rate breakfasts and lunches for children from low-income families. Consult with parents and specialists when eating habits seem to be seriously compromising children's health.
Physical Activity	• *Improvements in speed, complexity, and agility* of gross motor skills (e.g., running, skipping, jumping) • *Restlessness, lethargy, or inattention* during lengthy seatwork (possibly reflecting a need to take a break or release pent-up energy) • *Overexertion* (increasing the risk of injury)	During a class field day, a fifth-grade teacher organizes a soccer game with her students. Before beginning the game, she asks them to run up and down the field, individually accelerating and decelerating while kicking the ball. She then has them practice kicking the ball in ways that allow them to evade another player. Only after such practice does she begin the game (Logsdon et al., 1997).	Incorporate regular physical activity into the daily schedule. Choose tasks and activities that are enjoyable and allow for variability in skill levels. Make sure youngsters have mastered necessary prerequisite skills before teaching more complex skills.
Rest and Sleep	• *Listlessness* and lack of energy • *Inability to concentrate* • *Irritability* and overreaction to frustration • *Sleeping in class*	A teacher in an all-day kindergarten notices that some of his students become cranky during the last half-hour or so of school, and so he typically reserves this time for storybook reading and other quiet activities.	Provide regular opportunities for rest. When a youngster seems unusually tired day after day, talk with him or her (and perhaps with parents) about how lack of sleep can affect attention and behavior. Jointly seek possible solutions to the problem.
Health-Compromising Behaviors	• *Smell of cigarettes* on clothing • *Physiological symptoms of drug use* (e.g., red eyes, dilated pupils, tremors, convulsions, respiratory problems) • *Distortions in speech* (e.g., slurred pronunciation, fast talking, incoherence) • *Poor coordination* • *Impaired decision making* • *Mood changes* (e.g., anxiety, depression) • *Dramatic changes in behavior* (e.g., unusual energy, loss of interest in friends) • *Signs of sensory distortions or hallucinations* • *Rapid weight gain* and a tendency to wear increasingly baggy clothes (in girls who may be pregnant)	A school counselor notices a dramatic change in James's personality. Whereas he used to be eager to engage in activities, he now begins to "zone out" during counseling sessions. He slumps in his chair, looking out the window. His limited speech is unintelligible. The counselor asks James if he is using drugs, but James denies it. The counselor advises his parents about her fears and talks about a drug treatment center in their community.	Educate children and adolescents about the dangers of substance abuse and unprotected sexual activity; teach behaviors that will help youngsters to resist temptations, tailoring instruction to their ages and cultural backgrounds. Enforce alcohol and drug policies on school grounds and in extracurricular activities. Encourage participation in enjoyable and productive leisure activities that allow young people to interact with health-conscious peers. Consult with a counselor, psychologist, or social worker when you suspect that a youngster is pregnant or abusing drugs or alcohol.

SPECIAL PHYSICAL NEEDS

Some children have long-term physical conditions that affect school performance, friendships, and leisure activities. Here we look at chronic medical conditions, serious injuries, and physical disabilities in children and adolescents. We then identify strategies for accommodating these conditions.

Chronic Medical Conditions

All children get sick now and then, but some have ongoing, long-term conditions as a result of genetic legacies (e.g., cystic fibrosis), environmentally contracted illnesses (e.g., AIDS), or

Preparing for Your Licensure Examination

Your teaching test might ask you about exceptionalities in physical development.

an interaction between the two (e.g., some forms of asthma and cancer). As many as 1 or 2 in 10 children have a chronic condition that causes them to experience noticeable limitations in strength, vitality, and alertness (Nabors, Little, Akin-Little, & Iobst, 2008).

Teachers obviously are not doctors, but they may have occasion to notice how well children are caring for themselves. For instance, most children with diabetes can monitor blood sugar levels and take appropriate follow-up action. Yet these children and others with chronic conditions sometimes forget to take prescribed medication and are not always completely reliable in assessing their own symptoms (Bearison, 1998; Koinis-Mitchell et al., 2009). Accordingly, educators may need to keep an eye on children's symptoms, seek family help when conditions deteriorate, and obtain medical assistance in cases of emergency.

Teachers can also help children with chronic illnesses develop social skills and relationships. Some children who are ill feel so "different" that they are hesitant to approach peers (A. Turnbull, Turnbull, & Wehmeyer, 2010). Furthermore, they may blame their physical condition (perhaps accurately, perhaps not) for any problems they have in social relationships (Kapp-Simon & Simon, 1991). As a result, sick children may become isolated and have few opportunities to develop interpersonal skills. Furthermore, absences from school are common among children with chronic illnesses because of flare-ups of conditions, doctor visits, and hospitalizations.

Unfortunately, some healthy children actively reject peers who have serious illnesses. To some extent, such reactions reflect ignorance. Many children, young ones especially, have naive notions about illness. Preschoolers sometimes believe that people catch colds from the sun or get cancer by being in the same room as someone else with cancer (Bibace & Walsh, 1981). As children get older, their conceptions of illness gradually become more accurate, they grow more attuned to internal body cues, and they can better understand the effects of germs and are able to differentiate among types of illness (T. K.-F. Au et al., 2008; Bearison, 1998).

In many cases teachers and other professionals can help address the unique needs of sick children. Practitioners can help especially unwell children make up unfinished work, find a sympathetic peer to talk with, and contact a school counselor when sad or withdrawn. Other needs of youngsters with chronic illnesses vary significantly by developmental level, as do the accommodations that best address their needs, as you can see in the Developmental Trends table "Chronic Health Conditions in Children and Adolescents." You can also watch two videos in MyEducationLab, one about cultural differences in treating illness and the other about children's concerns regarding hospitalization.

MyEducationLab

Go to the Video Examples section in Topic 5 of MyEducationLab to watch two videos, one about cultural differences in the treatment of illness and the second on children's concerns regarding hospitalization.

Serious Injuries and Health Hazards

Injuries represent a major threat to children and adolescents. Around the world, more children between the ages of 1 and 14 die from unintentional injury than from any other cause (Odendaal, van Niekerk, Jordaan, & Seedat, 2009). Young children are prone to such hazards as ingesting poisons, drowning in pools, falling from heights, and getting burned on the stove. As children get older, their increasing independence makes them susceptible to other kinds of injuries. In the United States, injuries from firearms and motor vehicle crashes are the primary causes of death during the adolescent years (National Center for Health Statistics, 2005).

Although some injuries heal quickly, others have long-term effects that must be accommodated. Each year approximately 1 to 3 in every thousand children, adolescents, and young adults sustain traumatic brain injuries from playground falls, bicycle mishaps, skiing and vehicle accidents, assaults, and other traumatic events (McKinlay et al., 2008). Depending on location and severity, brain injuries can have temporary or lasting effects on physical functioning (e.g., seizures, headaches, poor motor coordination, fatigue) and psychological processes (e.g., impairments in perception, memory, concentration, language, decision making, or anger management). Numerous young people experience less serious brain injuries, known as concussions, often from sports injuries, that cause a brief loss of consciousness or sense of being disoriented and a loss of memory for events immediately before or after the accident. These youngsters may have headaches, nausea, and trouble concentrating for several months after the injury. Depending on the symptoms, a teacher might minimize distractions in the classroom, allow extra time to complete assignments, or adjust expectations for performance, at least for the first few weeks or months (A. Turnbull et al., 2010).

DEVELOPMENTAL TRENDS
Chronic Health Conditions in Children and Adolescents

AGE	WHAT YOU MIGHT OBSERVE	DIVERSITY	IMPLICATIONS
Infancy **(Birth–2 Years)** 	• Irregular sleep and wake cycles • Trouble being soothed • Digestive problems • Breathing problems	• Some genetic conditions, such as cystic fibrosis, may be diagnosed during infancy. • Some infants initially show normal developmental advances, such as making eye contact, babbling, and smiling, and then slow down in their physical growth as an illness progresses.	• Provide emotional support to families struggling with the news that children have a chronic or serious illness. • Determine the kinds of physical care that infants find comforting and soothing.
Early Childhood **(2–6 Years)** 	• Eating problems • Regular medication schedule • Some toileting problems • Greater susceptibility to many mild illnesses, such as the common cold • Belief that "being bad" is the cause of getting sick	• Some children have special nutritional needs. • A number of children begin to take dietary supplements. • Children may fail to take prescribed medicines if their parents believe they are unnecessary or cannot afford to purchase them.	• Encourage children to adhere to diets advised by medical personnel. • Allow children to use the toilet whenever necessary. • Safeguard small children from environmental substances that exacerbate their symptoms (e.g., shield children with asthma from secondhand smoke).
Middle Childhood **(6–10 Years)** 	• Frequent teasing and inappropriately personal questions from other children • Periods of health interspersed with states of deterioration • Some efforts by the child to manage symptoms at school (e.g., a child with asthma may monitor his or her lung function with a peak flow meter) • Greater than average number of absences from school	• A particular illness affects a child's ability to manage his or her health in distinct ways. • Absences from school vary depending on the child's illness, frequency of flare-ups, and the family's anxiety about the illness. • Some children are hospitalized occasionally or regularly. • Many children show some adverse reactions to particular treatments (e.g., becoming nervous or jittery after taking asthma medicine).	• Ask families for ideas about how you can support their child's physical well-being. • Advise family members of significant changes in their child's symptoms and health-management routines. • Insist that other children show understanding of peers with chronic illnesses. • When children are absent due to hospitalizations, keep in touch through phone calls, e-mail, and notes from classmates. • Allow children (particularly those with diabetes) to eat nutritious snacks regularly throughout the school day.
Early Adolescence **(10–14 Years)** 	• Heightened concern about physical appearance • Some self-consciousness about being different due to illness • Growing knowledge of how to monitor health conditions • Transition from family care to self-care of chronic illnesses • Some feeling of being invincible to threats to health	• Some adolescents who were previously conscientious about their health now become inconsistent in adhering to good medical regimens. • Some adolescents with chronic health conditions may need accommodations at school. • Some adolescents may now show noticeable manifestations of their disease (e.g., adolescents with cystic fibrosis may develop enlarged and rounded fingertips). • Adolescents with diabetes may have an increase in symptoms when they are growing rapidly.	• Offer reassurance that all adolescents are valued members of the class and school. • Advise adolescents about the services of school counselors. • Facilitate contact with classmates and teachers when adolescents are hospitalized or recuperating at home. • Talk privately with adolescents about seeing the school nurse as needed (e.g., to take inhaled medications).

(continued)

DEVELOPMENTAL TRENDS (continued)

AGE	WHAT YOU MIGHT OBSERVE	DIVERSITY	IMPLICATIONS
Late Adolescence (14–18 Years)	• Growing knowledge of health condition and management • Some difficulties in physical education classes (e.g., breathing problems, fatigue, and weakness on hot days) • Some negative feelings when illness necessitates continued dependence on parents (e.g., being unable to obtain a driver's license because of a seizure disorder)	• Several adolescents who regularly miss school due to illness feel isolated and lonely when at school. • Some adolescents manage their health conditions effectively and make plans that realistically address their conditions. • Adolescents who engage in risky behaviors or follow chaotic lifestyles may fail to take prescribed medicines. • Some adolescents with serious health conditions are vulnerable to depression. • Some adolescents face declining health as well as the prospect of dying in early adulthood.	• At the beginning of the year, develop a plan for dealing with school absences and making up missed academic work. • Encourage adolescents to assume increasing responsibility for management and treatment of their condition. • Consult with a school counselor to learn appropriate ways to help an adolescent who is terminally ill.

Sources: Annett, 2004; Dahan & McAfee, 2009; Lemanek, 2004; Quittner, Modi, & Roux, 2004; Shapiro & Manz, 2004; R. A. Smith, Martin, & Wolters, 2004; Wallander et al., 2004; J. Williams, 2004; Young-Hyman, 2004.

Many childhood injuries are avoidable, of course, and schools can play a key role in educating children about preventive measures. Adults can teach children to use seat belts while riding in motor vehicles, wear helmets while biking and skating, and install smoke detectors at home (e.g., Klassen, MacKay, Moher, Walker, & Jones, 2000). Educators should also be aware of youngsters who are more vulnerable than others. For instance, children with Down syndrome are particularly susceptible to sprains and dislocations because of limited muscle tone and excessive mobility in their joints (P. L. Krebs, 1995).

Finally, practitioners can learn about hazardous substances that may be present in their community. For example, children can come into contact with lead in the dirt of play areas and in paint chips of older homes (Agency for Toxic Substances and Disease Registry, 1999; Nigg, Nikolas, Knottnerus, Cavanagh, & Friderici, 2010). Depending on the amount of lead they ingest, children can develop blood anemia, kidney damage, colic, muscle weakness, and brain damage. Young children are affected more seriously by exposure to toxic substances than are adults because children's brains and bodies are growing quickly (S. M. Kroger, Schettler, & Weiss, 2005). Some health problems may disappear if toxic substances are removed, but lasting reductions in intelligence may nevertheless persist. Obviously, teachers and other professionals will want to do all they can to protect children from harmful substances in schools and community settings.

Physical Disabilities

Children with physical disabilities, such as cerebral palsy, muscular dystrophy, and blindness, have the same essential physical needs as other children, namely, a good diet, regular exercise, and adequate rest and sleep. In addition, children with disabilities may need specially adapted equipment (e.g., a wheelchair, a speech synthesizer, or a computer printer that produces Braille) and an environmental layout that permits safe movement.

Because exercise is central to health, adults must find ways to adapt physical activities for children with special physical needs. Basically, such adaptation involves giving appropriate support that enables successful movement. A teacher can assist students who have visual impairments by guiding their bodies into correct positions and inserting bells or other noisemakers inside playground balls (Poel, 2007). For a student who likes baseball but lacks strength and endurance, a teacher might allow another student to run around the bases after a hit (Pangrazi & Beighle, 2010). With students who lack coordination, adults can teach catching with a soft and lightweight ball that supports attempts to track its movement visually. Finally, with students who lack balance, adults can make chairs available for temporary propping and teach them to focus on their feet and center of gravity (Pangrazi & Beighle, 2010).

Preparing for Your Licensure Examination

Your teaching test might ask you about accommodations that permit children with physical disabilities to participate in sports.

Promoting Physical Well-Being in All Children

Children with chronic illnesses, serious injuries, and physical disabilities often require individualized accommodations so they can achieve optimal health. Several general guidelines apply to *all* children but especially to those with special physical needs:

- **Seek guidance from parents and from specialized organizations.** Parents and guardians often have helpful suggestions about adjustments that will enable their children to participate in school and extracurricular activities. And professional organizations—most are easily found on the Internet—offer a wealth of ideas about adapting instruction and equipment for children with chronic physical conditions and disabilities. Two broadly focused organizations are the American Alliance for Health, Physical Education, Recreation and Dance and the National Consortium for Physical Education and Recreation for Individuals with Disabilities. Specific disabilities are the focus of other organizations, such as the American Athletic Association for the Deaf and the U.S. Association for Blind Athletes.

- **Encourage children to monitor their health conditions.** Children gradually learn to cope with the everyday demands of chronic health conditions, but they may need reminders to check on critical physiological states (e.g., to test blood glucose levels if they have diabetes), go to the nurse's office at appropriate times (e.g., to take medicines), and look after their recurring physical needs (e.g., to eat nutritious snacks and use the toilet regularly).

- **Encourage children and their families to take protective measures.** Caregivers and teachers can teach young children how to handle emergencies, for example, how and under what circumstances to make an emergency phone call, what to do when they are lost, and what to do if they find a gun (Pan-Skadden et al., 2009; M. C. Roberts, Brown, Boles, & Mashunkashey, 2004). In elementary school, teachers can explain (and enforce) safety rules for climbing and using slides. Schools can distribute safety brochures on topics such as seat belts, bicycle helmets, and fire and smoke safety.

- **Design environments to minimize injuries.** Careful attention to equipment can reduce children's injuries (M. C. Roberts et al., 2004). For example, an infant caregiver can purchase cribs with slats close together to prevent babies' heads from getting stuck between them. The caregiver can also examine toys for choking hazards, set the temperature of water heaters below what would cause scalding, and confirm that the refrigerator door will not lock from the inside (M. C. Roberts et al., 2004). A principal can ensure that a playground has no sharp edges; that the ground's surface has soft, cushioning materials; and that smoke detectors in the school building are installed properly and regularly checked for working batteries.

- **Know what to do in a health emergency.** Some children have conditions that occasionally result in life-threatening situations. A child with diabetes could go into insulin shock, a child with asthma might have trouble breathing, or a child with epilepsy may have a seizure. When teachers learn that a child has a chronic health condition, they should consult with parents and school medical personnel to find out ahead of time how to respond to such emergencies.

- **Educate children about physical disabilities.** Children are more likely to show kindness to a peer with a physical impairment if they understand the nature of the disability. Children should know, for example, that cancer cannot be spread through breathing the same air and that epileptic seizures, though frightening, are only temporary. Keep in mind, however, that a teacher should talk about a particular child's physical condition *only* if the child and his or her parents have given permission for the teacher to do so (Shapiro & Manz, 2004).

- **Keep lines of communication open with children who are hospitalized or homebound.** Sometimes children's physical conditions keep them out of school for lengthy periods of time. In such circumstances, children can often participate in classroom lessons, activities, and social events by telephone or computer hook-up. When they cannot, they may be especially appreciative of correspondence and photographs from classmates and other important people in their lives.

- **Teach social skills to children who find themselves excluded from friendship groups.** School absences and the stresses of a chronic condition (and occasional overprotection from parents) can put a strain on children's peer relationships. Teachers can keep an eye out for the inclusion of children with chronic illnesses, particularly when they reenter school after repeated or lengthy absences. Teachers can also coach children to try particular social skills, such as listening sympathetically, resolving conflicts, and gaining entry into an existing group of children (Kapp-Simon & Simon, 1991).

• **Address any problems in learning that accompany children's illnesses.** Depending on their conditions and the medicines they take, children with chronic illnesses may develop attention problems and have difficulty staying organized (Shapiro & Manz, 2004). Teachers can encourage children to stay focused and teach them how to organize their work, set interim goals for complex assignments, and so forth. Teachers can also arrange for hospitalized children to make up missed work when they begin to recuperate.

• **Use precautions when caring for children who are sick or injured.** Educators can teach children basic safety precautions, such as sneezing into one's elbow, staying away from a friend's bloody knee, and washing hands after using the toilet. Adults also need to take precautions themselves. The use of appropriate barrier precautions for blood (e.g., latex gloves) is advisable when helping children who have skinned their knees or who have open wounds. Experts also direct caregivers to wash their hands after changing diapers and wiping noses (AAP Committee on Pediatric AIDS and Committee on Infectious Diseases, 1999).

Thoughtful attention to children's physical needs can enhance children's health. Such short-term effects pay dividends for future health, because good habits in childhood pave the way to healthy living later in life.

SUMMARY

Principles of Physical Development

The body is a complex, dynamic system that grows and changes in a multilayered environmental setting. Over time, physiological functioning becomes increasingly differentiated (e.g., cells take on different roles depending on their location in the body) and integrated (e.g., different body parts work more closely together). Children's bodies seem to aim for general targets in physical growth, even if growth is temporarily deterred by illness or inadequate nutrition.

The Brain and Its Development

The human brain is an intricate organ that regulates basic physiological functions (e.g., heart rate), sensations of pleasure and pain, motor skills and coordination, emotional responses, and intellectual processes. The brain consists of millions of interconnected circuits of neurons and glial cells that make up the distinct parts of the brain. During prenatal development, neurons form and migrate to places where they will do their work. During infancy, the brain creates many connections among neurons; areas of the brain that support perceptual learning show particularly rapid growth. During early and middle childhood, the brain protects those connections that are used most often and lets the others die out; particular refinements solidify language skills and complex learning processes. During adolescence, the brain makes new interests and passions possible, sparks impetuous behavior, and grows in areas that play key roles in forethought and judgment.

Physical Development During Childhood

Predictable changes in physical functioning occur during childhood and adolescence. During infancy, survival mechanisms, such as reflexes, are implemented, feeding moves from milk to a combination of milk and soft solids, and motor skills permit exploration. Early childhood is marked by vigorous physical activity and the acquisition of new motor skills. Middle childhood is a time of consolidation, when children's growth rate slows down and they put motor skills to purposeful use. Puberty marks the onset of adolescence and extends over several years' time. Adult height and sexual maturation are attained in late adolescence.

Physical Well-Being

Health depends on several factors, including eating habits, physical activity, and rest and sleep. Some children and adolescents show patterns of behavior (e.g., eating disorders, overreliance on sedentary activities, overcommitments that result in insufficient sleep) that jeopardize their physical well-being. In adolescence, additional health-compromising behaviors may emerge as youths struggle with such temptations as cigarette smoking, alcohol, drugs, and unprotected sexual activity.

Special Physical Needs

Youngsters with chronic illness, serious injuries, and physical disabilities often benefit from modifications in instruction, equipment, and the physical environment. Ultimately, educators should strive to include these children in physical activity and help them with any disruptions to their education.

APPLYING CONCEPTS IN CHILD DEVELOPMENT

The exercises in this section will help you build your ability to apply your knowledge of child development in your work with children.

Improving Your Observation Skills

On page 152, you examined five photographs of a boy wearing the same t-shirt several times between his infancy and late adolescent years and were asked, *"How does the boy's physical appearance change over the years?"* The developmental patterns of different parts of the body are evident. The boy's head is well developed during his first couple of years, after which time the torso and limbs accelerate. The boy grows taller, his arms and legs get longer, his trunk also increases in length, his face changes from being round to angular, and his hair color darkens.

On page 177, you examined the record 15-year-old Connor kept after trying out new exercises and were asked, *"How did Connor's performance change as he adjusted to the new exercise routine?"* Connor found that his muscles needed time to recover after he used them in unfamiliar exercises. Connor complained that his stomach muscles hurt after his first attempts and only gradually recovered but also reported enjoying the challenge of trying to beat his own records. The activities seem to be appropriate because he stopped when the exercises began to hurt, and an adult supervised his efforts.

Practicing for Your Licensure Examination

Many teaching tests require students to use what they have learned about child development in responses to brief vignettes and multiple-choice questions. You can practice for your licensure examination by reading about the following young women's perspectives and answering a series of questions.

Lucy

Read the case and then answer the questions that follow it.

> In her early teenage years, Lucy had leukemia. After a long hospitalization, plus radiation and chemotherapy treatments that resulted in temporary hair loss, Lucy's disease finally went into remission. Eventually, Lucy was healthy enough to return to school, but her life at school was quite different from what it once had been. Her therapist, Mary Pipher (1994), explains:
>
> > It had been hard for her to return to school. Everyone was nice to Lucy, almost too nice, like she was a visitor from another planet, but she was left out of so many things. Her old friends had boyfriends and were involved in new activities. When she was in the hospital they would visit with flowers and magazines, but now that she was better, they didn't seem to know what to do with her.

Frank [her father] said, "Lucy's personality has changed. She's quieter. She used to clown around. Now she is more serious. In some ways she seems older; she's suffered more and seen other children suffer. In some ways she's younger; she's missed a lot."

Lucy had missed a great deal: ninth-grade graduation, the beginning of high school, parties, dating, sports, school activities and even puberty (the leukemia had delayed her periods and physical development). She had lots of catching up to do. She'd been so vulnerable that her parents were protective. They didn't want her to become tired, to eat junk food, to forget to take her medicines or to take any chances. Her immune system was weak and she could be in trouble with the slightest injury. Lucy, unlike most teens, didn't grimace at her parents' worries. She associated them with staying alive. (p. 84)[a]

Constructed-Response Question

1. How did Lucy's illness affect her physical, social, and cognitive development?

Multiple-Choice Questions

2. How did Lucy's illness affect the rate of her development?

   a. In some respects, Lucy's illness led her to develop more rapidly, whereas in other areas, she was delayed.
   b. Lucy's illness speeded up all aspects of her development.
   c. Lucy's illness put a halt to all aspects of her development.
   d. Lucy's illness had no effect on any aspect of her development.

3. Given the recommendations in Chapter 5, how might a teacher ease Lucy's adjustment as she returns to school?

   a. Ask Lucy's parents about her condition, the symptoms she may have, how she can be supported at school, and if the teacher has permission to tell the other children about Lucy's illness and recovery.
   b. Teach academic skills that Lucy might have missed during her treatment and hospitalization.
   c. Encourage Lucy to see the school nurse as necessary and carry out any warranted health protective measures such as applying sunscreen when medications cause extreme sensitivity to sunlight.
   d. All of the above.

Once you have answered these questions, compare your responses with those presented in Appendix A.

Improving Your Ability to Interpret Children's Artifacts and Reflections

Consider chapter concepts as you analyze the following responses from a young adolescent boy.

MyPyramid Worksheet by Alex

Twelve-year-old Alex is 4 feet, 11 inches tall and weighs 73 pounds. Alex is slender, athletically inclined, and reasonably attentive to his health. He is a rather picky eater, however, and has a decidedly sweet tooth. One Saturday morning, Alex agreed to record everything he ate and drank on that day (besides water) using a form prepared by the U.S. Department of Agriculture. The form is customized to a person's age, height, and weight (go to www.mypyramidtracker.gov). As you examine Alex's completed worksheet, consider these questions:

- What kinds of dietary goals are present on the worksheet? (Look under the fourth column.)
- Which of the dietary goals did Alex come closest to achieving?
- Which dietary goals did Alex fail to achieve?
- How did Alex fare in his physical activity?
- What insights did Alex have as he evaluated his diet and physical activity?

Once you have analyzed Alex's worksheet, compare your ideas with those presented in Appendix B. For further practice in analyzing children's artifacts and reflections, go to the Activities and Applications section in Chapter 5 of MyEducationLab.

MyPyramid Worksheet by Alex, Age 12.

From form published by U.S. Department of Agriculture (2008). *MyPyramid Plan.* Retrieved January 16, 2008, from *http://wwww.mypyramid.gov*

Key Concepts

differentiation (p. 150)
integration (p. 152)
neuron (p. 153)
dendrite (p. 153)
axon (p. 153)
synapse (p. 153)
glial cell (p. 154)
astrocyte (p. 154)
hindbrain (p. 154)

midbrain (p. 154)
forebrain (p. 154)
cortex (p. 154)
executive functions (p. 155)
left hemisphere (p. 155)
right hemisphere (p. 155)
schizophrenia (p. 156)
synaptogenesis (p. 157)
synaptic pruning (p. 157)

myelination (p. 157)
cephalocaudal trend (p. 163)
proximodistal trend (p. 163)
gross motor skills (p. 164)
fine motor skills (p. 164)
puberty (p. 165)
growth spurt (p. 165)
menarche (p. 167)
spermarche (p. 167)

obesity (p. 172)
anorexia nervosa (p. 173)
bulimia (p. 173)
rough-and-tumble play (p. 175)
sudden infant death syndrome
   (SIDS) (p. 178)
addiction (p. 182)

PEARSON
myeducationlab

Now go to www.myeducationlab.com to:
- Take a Quiz to test your mastery of chapter objectives.
- Study chapter content with an individualized Study Plan.
- Deepen your understanding of particular concepts and principles with Review, Remediation, and Enrichment Exercises.
- Apply what you have learned in the chapter to your work with children in Building Teaching Skills and Dispositions exercises.
- Observe children and their unique contexts in Video Examples.

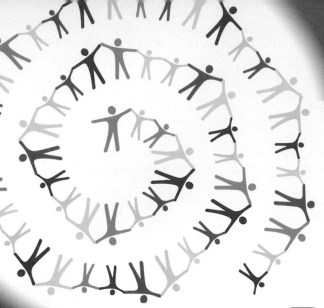

Chapter Six

Cognitive Development: Piaget and Vygotsky

CASE STUDY: Museum Visit

Four-year-old Billy is fascinated by dinosaurs. He and his mother have read many children's books about dinosaurs, so he already has some knowledge about these creatures and the geological time periods in which they lived. As Billy and his mother visit a dinosaur exhibit at a natural history museum, they have the following conversation:

Mother: This is a real dinosaur rib bone. Where are your ribs? Where are your ribs? No that's your wrist. Very close.

Billy: Oh, yeah, right here.

Mother: Yeah, that's right. Here. Protecting your heart . . . and your lungs. And this was one from a dinosaur from the Jurassic period, also found from our country. In a place called Utah.

Mother: And this one . . . [Mother picks up a piece of fossilized dinosaur feces, known as *coprolite*] Oh! You're not . . . guess what that is. Look at it and guess what that is.

Billy: Um, what?

Mother: Guess. What's it look like?

Billy: His gum? What? Mom!

Mother: It's dinosaur poop.

Billy: Ooooo! (laughs)

Mother: That's real dinosaur poop.

Billy: I touched it! (laughs)

Mother: It's so old that it doesn't smell anymore. It turned to rock. It's not mushy like poop. It's like a rock. And that's from the Cretaceous period but we don't know what dinosaur made it. And this was also found in our country in Colorado. I think that's pretty funny.

Billy: What's this?

Mother: So this one. . . . Oh, that's called . . . that's a stone that dinosaurs . . . remember in your animal book it says something about how sometimes chickens eat stones to help them digest—it helps them mush up their food in their tummy?

Billy: Yeah.

Mother: Well, dinosaurs ate stones to mush up their food in their tummy and this was one of the stones that they ate. They're so big, that to them this was a little stone. Right? And that also comes from Colorado. (dialogue is from Crowley & Jacobs, 2002, p. 346; "Billy" is a pseudonym.)[a]

- What knowledge does Billy already have that can help him understand what he sees in the dinosaur exhibit?
- What does Mother do to help her son make sense of the exhibit?

[a] Excerpt from LEARNING CONVERSATIONS IN MUSEUMS by Kevin Crowley. Copyright © 2002 by Kevin Crowley. Reprinted with permission via Copyright Clearance Center.

OBJECTIVES

6.1: Identify and explain the seven key principles in Piaget's theory of cognitive development.

6.2: Describe the abilities and limitations of children at each of Piaget's four stages of cognitive development.

6.3: Evaluate Piaget's stage theory in light of contemporary research in cognitive development, including neo-Piagetian perspectives.

6.4: Design learning experiences for children that are consistent with Piaget's principles and stages.

6.5: Identify the nine key principles in Vygotsky's theory of cognitive development, and note the ways in which this theory is similar to and unlike Piaget's theory.

6.6: Evaluate Vygotsky's theory and the contemporary perspectives that have built on his ideas.

6.7: Use principles from Vygotsky's theory and from Vygotsky's followers to support children's learning.

Thanks to the many books that 4-year-old Billy and his mother have previously read together, Billy appears to know a lot about dinosaurs and other animals. He is familiar with the words *Jurassic* and *Cretaceous,* and he knows that some animals have stones in their stomachs to aid digestion. Mother helps him connect what he is seeing to his prior knowledge—not only about geological periods and stomach stones but also about more commonplace concepts such as ribs and "poop." Yet Billy, like all children, is not simply a "sponge" who passively soaks up the information that his environment provides. Instead, his cognitive development is in large part the result of his *own active efforts* to make sense of his world.

As we begin our examination of cognitive development in this chapter, we consider the classic developmental theories of Jean Piaget and Lev Vygotsky, both of whom examined the active manner in which children learn. The perspective of children actively creating rather than passively absorbing knowledge is known as **constructivism**. Formulated in the first few decades of the 20th century, these two constructivist theories have provided much of the foundation for our current understanding of how children think. Between them, the two theories tell us a great deal about how children make sense of everyday events both on their own and in collaboration with adults and peers. As you will find out, the two theories also have much to say about how parents, teachers, and other adults can help children learn effectively.

PIAGET'S THEORY OF COGNITIVE DEVELOPMENT

constructivism

Theoretical perspective proposing that learners construct a body of knowledge and beliefs, rather than absorbing information exactly as it is received.

clinical method

Procedure in which an adult probes a child's reasoning about a task or problem, tailoring questions in light of what the child has previously said or done in the interview.

Jean Piaget (1896–1980) was formally trained as a biologist. But he had an interest in philosophy as well and was especially curious about the nature of knowledge and how it changes with development. In the 1920s he began to observe the everyday actions of infants and children and to draw inferences about the thinking and reasoning that seemed to underlie their behavior. In his laboratory in Geneva, Switzerland, Piaget pioneered the **clinical method**, a procedure in which an adult presents a task or problem and asks a child a series of questions about it, tailoring later questions to the child's previous responses. Drawing from these observations and interviews, Piaget developed a theory of cognitive development that has contributed a great deal to our understanding of how children and adolescents think and learn (e.g., Piaget, 1928, 1952b, 1959, 1985).

Key Ideas in Piaget's Theory

Central to Piaget's theory are the following seven principles:

EUREKA! Piaget explained that children develop cognitively as they explore their world.

Children are active and motivated learners. In the chapter-opening case study, Billy seems quite eager to make sense of the fossils he sees in the natural history museum. Piaget proposed that children are naturally curious about their world and actively seek out information that can help them interpret and understand it (e.g., Piaget, 1952b). They often experiment with the objects they encounter, manipulating them and observing the effects of their actions. For example, we authors think back to the days when our children were in high chairs, experimenting with their food (pushing, squishing, dropping, and throwing it) as readily as they would eat it.

Many contemporary theorists share Piaget's view that much of a human being's motivation for learning comes from within. It appears that growing children are naturally inclined to try to make sense of the people, objects, and events around them (e.g., K. Fischer, 2005; Hunnius & Bekkering, 2010; K. Nelson, 1996a).

You can see an example of such *intrinsic motivation* in the "Cognitive Development: Early Childhood" video in MyEducationLab, in which 2-year-old Maddie encounters an intriguing new object and actively manipulates it to discover its properties.

Children organize what they learn from their experiences. Children don't just amass the things they learn into a collection of isolated facts. Instead, they pull their experiences together into an integrated view of how the world operates. By observing that food, toys, and other objects always fall down (never up) when released, children begin to construct a basic understanding of gravity. As they interact with family pets, visit zoos, look at picture books, and observe creatures around them, they develop an increasingly complex understanding of animals. Piaget depicted learning as a very *constructive* process: Children create (rather than simply absorb) their knowledge about the world.

In Piaget's terminology, the things that children learn and can do are organized as **schemes**, groups of similar actions or thoughts that are used repeatedly in response to the environment. Initially, children's schemes are largely behavioral in nature, but over time they become increasingly mental and, eventually, abstract (Inhelder & Piaget, 1958; Piaget, 1952b, 1954). An infant may have a behavioral scheme for putting things in her mouth, an action that she uses in dealing with a variety of objects, including her thumb, toys, and blanket. A 7-year-old may have a mental but relatively concrete scheme for identifying snakes, one that includes their long, thin bodies, their lack of legs, and their slithery nature. As a 13-year-old, Jeanne's daughter Tina had her own opinion about what constitutes fashion, an abstract scheme that allowed her to classify various articles of clothing on display at the mall as being either "totally awesome" or "really stupid."

Piaget proposed that children use newly acquired schemes over and over in both familiar and novel situations. For example, in the "Cognitive Development: Infancy" video in MyEducationLab, you can observe 16-month-old Corwin repeatedly taking a toy out of a paper bag and then putting it back in. In the process of repeating their schemes, children refine them and begin to use them in combination. Eventually, they integrate schemes into larger systems of mental processes called **operations**. This integration allows children to think in increasingly sophisticated ways. For example, a child may integrate separate schemes for ordering blocks by size and placing one block on another into a new ability for building a stable pyramid tower.

Children adapt to their environment through the processes of assimilation and accommodation. According to Piaget, children's developing schemes allow them to adapt in ever more successful ways to their environment. Such adaptation occurs as a result of two complementary processes: assimilation and accommodation (e.g., Piaget, 1954). **Assimilation** entails responding (either physically or mentally) to an object or event in a way that is consistent with an existing scheme.[1] An infant may assimilate a ball into her putting-things-in-the-mouth scheme, and a 7-year-old may quickly identify a new slithery object in the backyard as a snake.

Yet children must typically adjust their existing schemes at least a little bit in order to respond to a new object or event. Thus one of two forms of **accommodation** is likely to occur. Children will either modify an existing scheme to account for the new object or event or else form an entirely new scheme to deal with it. For example, an infant may have to open her mouth wider than usual to accommodate a large plastic ball or teddy bear's paw. The 7-year-old may find a long, slithery thing with a snakelike body that cannot possibly *be* a snake because it has four legs. After making inquiries, he will develop a new scheme—*salamander*—for this creature.

Assimilation and accommodation work hand in hand as children develop understandings of the world. Children interpret each new event within the context of their existing knowledge (assimilation) but at the same time modify their knowledge as a result of the new event (accommodation). In the chapter-opening case study, Billy initially thinks that the piece of coprolite is a large wad of dinosaur gum—that is, he mistakenly assimilates the

[1]Note that Piaget's concept of *assimilation* is quite different from the process of *cultural assimilation* described in Chapter 3.

MyEducationLab

Observe Maddie experiment with a new object in the "Cognitive Development: Early Childhood" video. (Find Video Examples in Topic 6 of MyEducationLab.)

MyEducationLab

Observe Corwin repeatedly using his "putting-in" and "taking-out" schemes in the "Cognitive Development: Infancy" video. (Find Video Examples in Topic 6 of MyEducationLab.)

scheme
In Piaget's theory, an organized group of similar actions or thoughts that are used repeatedly in response to the environment.

operation
In Piaget's theory, an organized and integrated system of logical thought processes.

assimilation
In Piaget's theory, process of responding (either physically or mentally) to a new event in a way that is consistent with an existing scheme.

accommodation
Process of responding to a new event by either modifying an existing scheme or forming a new one.

object into his "chewing gum" scheme. But with his mother's help, he creates a new scheme, "fossilized dinosaur poop," that more accurately accounts for what he is seeing. Later Mother helps Billy assimilate a large stone into a "stones-that-help-digestion" scheme he has previously acquired. In the process, however, he must also modify this scheme so that it applies to dinosaurs as well as to chickens.

Interaction with the physical environment is critical for cognitive development. By exploring and manipulating the world around them—by conducting many little "experiments" with various objects and substances—children learn the nature of their physical world and continue to revise their existing schemes. The following anecdote from a preschool teacher illustrates this process:

> Tommy. . . had built a tower on a base of three regular blocks on end, with a round, flat piece of Masonite on top. Then on top of this were three more blocks and Masonite, supporting in turn a third story. . . . The tower was already taller than Tommy, and he had a piece of triangular Masonite in hand and was gently testing the tower's steadiness against his taps. Small taps and the tower would lean, settle, and become still. Again and again he varied the strength and place of the taps; watched, waited, tapped again, and finally—on purpose—did hit hard enough to topple the structure. Then the entire process of building the tower and testing it was repeated. (Hawkins, 1997, p. 200)[2]

Interaction with other people is equally critical. Piaget suggested that children learn a great deal from interacting with their fellow human beings. As you will discover shortly, preschoolers can have difficulty seeing the world from anyone's perspective but their own. By conversing, exchanging ideas, and arguing with others, they gradually come to realize that individuals often see things differently and that their own view of the world is not necessarily completely accurate. Likewise, older children and adolescents may begin to recognize logical inconsistencies in what they say and do when someone else points out these discrepancies.

The process of equilibration promotes increasingly complex forms of thought. Piaget proposed that children are sometimes in a state of **equilibrium**: They can comfortably address new situations using their existing schemes and operations. But equilibrium doesn't continue indefinitely. In their daily lives children regularly encounter circumstances for which their present knowledge and skills are inadequate. These circumstances create **disequilibrium**, a sort of mental "discomfort" that spurs children to try to deal with the situation at hand. By replacing or reorganizing certain schemes, children may be better able to address the situation, and so they can return to equilibrium. This process of moving from equilibrium to disequilibrium and back to equilibrium again is known as **equilibration** (e.g., Inhelder & Piaget, 1958). In many instances the end result is a better integrated, more inclusive, and more stable set of schemes and operations than children had previously. Thus, Piaget suggested, the equilibration process gradually leads to increasingly complex levels of thought and knowledge.

Piaget was a bit vague about how the processes of assimilation, accommodation, and equilibration actually work (e.g., diSessa, 2006; Klahr, 1982; Morra et al., 2008). Nevertheless, contemporary developmentalists accept that children's new ideas are based on their earlier ones and that inconsistencies can sometimes spur children to develop more sophisticated understandings and abilities. Developmentally speaking, then, more advanced knowledge, skills, and cognitive processes don't just appear out of thin air—they emerge out of children's quest for understanding, creative thinking processes, and discontent with their current knowledge.

Children think in qualitatively distinct ways at different age levels. Piaget proposed that as a result of brain maturation, environmental experiences, and children's natural desire to make sense of their world, cognitive abilities continue to undergo qualitative changes over the course of childhood and adolescence. He characterized youngsters' cognitive abilities as

Bioecology of Child Development

Piaget testified to the informative lessons a child receives during his or her dynamic interactions with the physical and social environments.

equilibrium
State of being able to address new events using existing schemes.

disequilibrium
State of being unable to address new events with existing schemes.

equilibration
Movement from equilibrium to disequilibrium and back to equilibrium; a process that promotes the development of increasingly complex forms of thought and knowledge.

[2]Excerpt from JOURNEYS WITH CHILDREN by Frances Hawkins. Copyright © 1997 by University Press of Colorado. Reprinted with permission of the publisher.

falling into four general stages of development (e.g., Piaget, 1971). The abilities at any one stage are constructed out of the accomplishments of any preceding stages. Thus, the four stages are *hierarchical*—each one depends on its predecessors—and so children progress through them in a predictable order. To a considerable degree, they are also assumed to be *universal,* characterizing the cognitive development of children throughout the world.

As you will discover later in the chapter, many psychologists question the notion that cognitive development is as stagelike as Piaget suggested. Nevertheless, Piaget's stages provide helpful insights into the nature of children's thinking at different age levels, and so we will look closely at them.

Piaget's Stages of Cognitive Development

Piaget's four stages are summarized in Table 6-1. The ages of onset for all but the sensorimotor stage are *averages:* Some children show characteristics associated with a particular stage a bit earlier, others a little later. Keep in mind, too, that many children are apt to be in *transition* from one stage to the next, displaying characteristics of two adjacent stages at the same time. Furthermore, children and adolescents don't always take advantage of their advanced

TABLE 6-1 Examples of Acquisitions Associated with Each of Piaget's Four Stages

STAGE	AGE OF ONSET[a]	GENERAL DESCRIPTION	EXAMPLES OF ACQUISITIONS
Sensorimotor	Begins at birth	Schemes are based largely on behaviors and perceptions. Especially in the early part of the stage, children cannot think about things that are not immediately in front of them, and so they focus on what they are doing and seeing at the moment.	• *Trial-and-error experimentation:* Exploration and manipulation of objects to determine their properties • *Goal-directed behavior:* Intentional behavior to bring about a desired result • *Object permanence:* Realization that objects continue to exist even when removed from view • *Symbolic thought:* Representation of physical objects and events as mental entities *(symbols)*
Preoperational	Appears at about age 2	Thanks in part to their rapidly developing symbolic thinking abilities, children can now think and talk about things beyond their immediate experience. However, they do not yet reason in logical, adult-like ways.	• *Language:* Rapid expansion of vocabulary and grammatical structures • *Extensive pretend play:* Enactment of true-to-life or fanciful scenarios with plots and assigned roles (e.g., mommy and daddy, hunter and prey, or hero and villain) • *Intuitive thought:* Some logical thinking based on "hunches" and "intuition" rather than on conscious awareness of logical principles (especially after age 4)
Concrete Operations	Appears at about age 6 or 7	Adult-like logic appears but is limited to reasoning about concrete, real-life situations.	• *Distinction between one's own and others' perspectives:* Recognition that one's own thoughts and feelings may be different from those of others and do not necessarily reflect reality • *Class inclusion:* Ability to classify objects as belonging to two or more categories simultaneously • *Conservation:* Realization that amount stays the same if nothing is added or taken away, regardless of alterations in shape or arrangement
Formal Operations	Appears at about age 11 or 12	Logical reasoning processes are applied to abstract ideas as well as concrete objects and situations. Many capabilities essential for advanced reasoning in science and mathematics appear.	• *Reasoning about abstract, hypothetical, and contrary-to-fact ideas:* Ability to draw logical deductions about situations that have no basis in physical reality • *Separation and control of variables:* Ability to test hypotheses by manipulating one variable while holding other variables constant • *Proportional reasoning:* Conceptual understanding of fractions, percentages, decimals, and ratios • *Idealism:* Ability to envision alternatives to current social and political practices (sometimes with little regard for what is realistically possible in a given time frame)

[a]The ages presented for the preoperational, concrete operations, and formal operations stages are *averages:* For some children, characteristics associated with each stage appear a bit earlier; for others, they appear a little later.

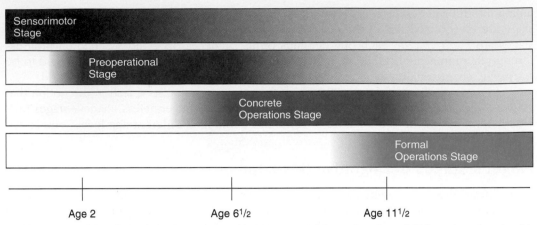

FIGURE 6-1 Emerging and continuing abilities. Children develop abilities associated with more advanced Piagetian stages slowly over time, and they don't entirely leave behind the characteristics associated with previous stages.

cognitive abilities, and so they may show considerable variability in level of thinking in their day-to-day activities (Chapman, 1988; Piaget, 1960b). Figure 6-1 depicts the transitional and flexible nature of children's progress through the stages.

Sensorimotor Stage (beginning at birth)

Piaget believed that in the first month of life, infants' behaviors are little more than biologically built-in responses to particular stimuli—that is, they are *reflexes* (e.g., sucking on a nipple)—that help keep them alive. In the second month infants begin to exhibit voluntary behaviors that they repeat over and over, reflecting the development of perception- and behavior-based *sensorimotor schemes*. Initially, such behaviors focus almost exclusively on infants' own bodies (e.g., putting one's fist in one's mouth), but eventually they involve nearby objects as well. For much of the first year, Piaget suggested, infants' behaviors are largely spontaneous and unplanned. Seven-month-old Madison is clearly intrigued by a variety of toys that happen to be nearby her in the "Emotional Development: Infancy" video in MyEducationLab.

Late in the first year, after repeatedly observing that certain actions regularly lead to certain consequences, infants gradually acquire knowledge of cause-and-effect relationships. At this point, they begin to engage in **goal-directed behavior:** They behave in ways that they know will bring about desired results. An infant who pulls a blanket to retrieve a small object lying on it shows goal-directed behavior. At about the same time, infants acquire **object permanence**, an understanding that physical objects continue to exist even when they are out of sight. In the "Cognitive Development: Infancy" video in MyEducationLab, 16-month-old Corwin shows object permanence when he looks for a toy elephant that his mother repeatedly hides. His searches under a pillow are directed toward a particular goal: finding the elephant.

Piaget believed that for much of the sensorimotor period, children's thinking is restricted to objects in their immediate environment—that is, to the here and now. But in the latter half of the second year, young children develop **symbolic thought**, the ability to represent and think about objects and events in terms of internal, mental entities, or *symbols* (Piaget, 1962). They may "experiment" with objects in their minds, first predicting what will happen if they do something to an object—say, if they give a toy car a hard push toward the edge of a tabletop—and then putting their plans into action. They may also recall and imitate behaviors they have seen other people exhibit—for instance, "talking" on a toy telephone or "driving" with a toy steering wheel.

The acquisitions of the sensorimotor stage are basic building blocks on which later cognitive development depends. The Observation Guidelines table "Assessing Cognitive Advancements in Infants and Toddlers" presents some of the behaviors you might look for as you work with these small learners.

MyEducationLab

Observe exploratory and goal-directed behaviors in the "Emotional Development: Infancy" and "Cognitive Development: Infancy" videos. (Find Video Examples in Topic 6 of MyEducationLab.)

Preparing for Your Licensure Examination

Your teaching test might ask you about the major cognitive advancements that children achieve during each of Piaget's four stages.

goal-directed behavior
Intentional behavior aimed at bringing about an anticipated outcome.

object permanence
Realization that objects continue to exist even when they are out of sight.

symbolic thought
Ability to mentally represent and think about external objects and events.

OBSERVATION GUIDELINES
Assessing Cognitive Advancements in Infants and Toddlers

CHARACTERISTIC	LOOK FOR	EXAMPLE	IMPLICATION
Repetition of Gratifying Actions	• *Repetition of actions involving the child's own body* • *Repetition of actions on other objects* • *Evidence that the child repeats an action* because he or she notices and enjoys it	Myra waves her arms, stops, and waves her arms again. She makes a sound and repeats it, as if she enjoys listening to her own voice.	Provide a variety of visual, auditory, and tactile stimuli; for instance, play "This little piggy" with an infant's toes, hang a mobile safely over the crib, and provide age-appropriate objects (e.g., rattles, plastic cups). Be patient and responsive when infants repeat seemingly "pointless" actions (e.g., dropping favorite objects).
Exploration of Objects	• *Apparent curiosity about the effects* that different behaviors have on objects • *Use of multiple behaviors* (feeling, poking, dropping, shaking, etc.) to explore an object's properties • *Use of several sensory modalities* (i.e., seeing, listening, feeling, tasting, and smelling)	Paco reaches for his caregiver's large, shiny earring. The caregiver removes the earring and holds its sharp end between her fingers while Paco manipulates the silver loop and multicolored glass beads that hang from it.	Provide objects that infants can explore using multiple senses, making sure the objects are free of dirt and toxic substances; lack sharp edges, loose cords, and bags that could cause strangulation or suffocation; and are large enough to prevent swallowing.
Experimentation	• *Creativity and flexibility* in the behaviors the child uses to discover how things work • *Specific problems that the child tackles* and the approaches he or she uses to solve them	Jillian drags a step stool to her dresser so that she can reach the toys on top of it. One by one, she drops the toys, watching how each one lands and listening to the sound it makes on impact.	Childproof the environment so that experiments and problem-solving activities are safe. Provide objects that require a sequence of actions (e.g., stacking cups, building blocks, pull toys). Closely supervise children's activities.
Imitation and Pretending	• *Imitation of actions modeled by another person* • *Imitation of actions when the model is no longer present* • *Use of one object to stand for another*	Darius holds a doll and sings to it in the same way his mother sings to him. He combs the doll's hair with a spoon and uses an empty plastic vitamin bottle to feed the doll.	Engage children in reciprocal, imitative games (e.g., peekaboo, hide-and-seek). Provide props that encourage pretend play (miniature shopping carts, plastic carpentry tools, dolls, etc.).

Preoperational Stage (beginning at about age 2)

The ability to represent objects and events mentally (i.e., symbolic thought) gives children in the preoperational stage a more extensive worldview than they had during the sensorimotor stage. They can now recall past events and envision future ones that might be similar to their previous experiences. In addition, they begin to tie their experiences together into an increasingly complex understanding of the world.

Language skills virtually explode during the early part of the preoperational stage. The words in children's rapidly increasing vocabularies provide labels for newly developed mental schemes and serve as symbols for thinking about objects and events even when not directly in sight. Furthermore, language provides the basis for a new form of social interaction, verbal communication. Children can express their thoughts and receive information from other people in a way that was not possible during the sensorimotor stage.

The emergence of symbolic thought is reflected not only in rapidly expanding language skills but also in the changing nature of children's play. Preschoolers often engage in fantasy and make-believe, using realistic objects or reasonable substitutes to act out the behaviors of people they see around them. Piaget proposed that such pretend play enables children to practice newly acquired symbolic schemes and familiarize themselves with the various roles they see others assume in society. This idea is illustrated in the following scenario, in which 5-year-olds Jeff and Scott construct and operate a "restaurant":

In a corner of Jeff's basement, the boys make a dining area from several child-sized tables and chairs. They construct a restaurant "kitchen" with a toy sink and stove and stock it with plastic dishes and "food" items. They create menus for their restaurant, sometimes asking

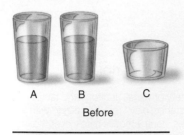

A   B   C

Before

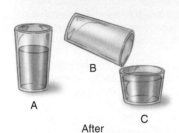

B

A

C

After

FIGURE 6-2 Conservation of liquid. Do Glasses A and C contain the same amount of water after the water in Glass B is poured into Glass C?

Jeff's mother how to spell certain words and sometimes using their knowledge of letter-sound relationships to guess how a particular word might be spelled.

Jeff and Scott invite their parents to come to the new restaurant for lunch. The boys pretend to write their customers' meal orders on paper tablets and then scurry to the kitchen to assemble the requested lunch items. Eventually, they return to serve the meals (hamburgers, French fries, and cookies—all of them plastic—plus glasses of imaginary milk), which the adults "eat" and "drink" with gusto. After the young waiters return with the final bills, the parents pay for their "meals" with nickels and leave a few pennies on the tables as tips.

With the emergence of symbolic thought, young children are no longer restricted to the here and now and so can think and act far more flexibly than they did previously. At the same time, preoperational thinking has some definite limitations, especially when compared to the concrete operational thinking that emerges later. Piaget described young children as exhibiting **egocentrism**, an inability to view situations from another person's perspective.[3] Preschoolers may play games together without ever checking to be sure that they are all playing according to the same rules. And they may say things without considering the perspective of the listener—for instance, leaving out critical details as they tell a story and giving a fragmented version that a listener cannot possibly understand. Here we see one reason why, in Piaget's view, social interaction is so important for development. Only by getting repeated feedback from other people can children learn that their thoughts and feelings are unique to them and not necessarily shared by others.

Preoperational thinking is also illogical (at least from an adult's point of view), especially during the preschool years. Following is an example of reasoning that characterizes preoperational thought:

> We show 4-year-old Lucy the three glasses at the top of Figure 6-2. Glasses A and B are identical in size and shape and contain an equal amount of water. We ask Lucy if the two glasses of water contain the same amount, and she replies confidently that they do. We then pour the water in Glass B into Glass C. We ask her if the two glasses of water (A and C) still have the same amount. "No," Lucy replies. She points to Glass A and says, "That glass has more because it's taller."

Piaget used this task to assess a logical thought process known as **conservation**, the recognition that an amount must stay the same if nothing is added or taken away, despite any changes in shape or arrangement. Lucy's response reveals that she is not yet capable of *conservation of liquid:* The differently shaped glasses lead her to believe that the actual amount of water has changed. Similarly, in a *conservation of number* task, a child engaging in preoperational thought might say that a row of five pennies spread far apart has more than a row of five pennies spaced close together, even though she has previously counted the pennies in both rows and found them to have the same number. Young children often confuse changes in appearance with changes in amount. Piaget suggested that such confusion is often seen in young children's reasoning because the preoperational stage depends more on perception than on logic.

Another ability that young children find challenging is **class inclusion**, the recognition that an object can belong both to a particular category and to one of its subcategories simultaneously. Preschool age children demonstrate lack of class inclusion in response to questions such as "Are there more brown beads or more wooden beads?" in a situation where there are 10 brown beads and 2 white beads and all beads are made of wood (Piaget, 1952a). They may insist that there are more brown beads whereas in reality there are more wooden beads.

Sometime around age 4 or 5, children show early signs of thinking more logically than they have previously. For example, they occasionally draw correct conclusions about conservation problems (e.g., the water glasses problem) and class inclusion problems (e.g., the

egocentrism
Inability of a child in Piaget's preoperational stage to view situations from another person's perspective.

conservation
Realization that if nothing is added or taken away, an amount stays the same regardless of any alterations in shape or arrangement.

class inclusion
Recognition that an object simultaneously belongs to a particular category and to one of its subcategories.

---

[3]Consistent with common practice, we use the term *egocentrism* to refer to the egocentric thinking that characterizes preoperational thought. Piaget actually talked about different forms of egocentrism at *each* of the four stages of development. For instance, he described egocentrism in the formal operations stage as involving an inability to distinguish one's own logical conclusions from the perspectives of others and from constraints of the real world. Adolescents' unrealistic idealism about social issues is one manifestation of this formal operational egocentrism.

wooden beads problem). But they base their reasoning on hunches and intuition rather than on any conscious awareness of underlying logical principles, and so they cannot yet explain *why* their conclusions are correct.

Concrete Operations Stage (beginning at about age 6 or 7)

In the early primary grades, children become capable of thinking about and integrating various qualities and perspectives of a situation. For example, children now know that other people may have perceptions and feelings different from their own. Accordingly, they realize that their own views may reflect personal opinion rather than reality, and so they may seek out external validation for their ideas ("What do you think?" "Did I get that problem right?").

See how children respond to various conservation tasks in the "Conservation" video. (Find Video Examples in Topic 6 of MyEducationLab.)

Children in the concrete operations stage show many forms of logical thought, and they can readily explain their reasoning. They can also easily classify objects into two categories simultaneously, making it easier for them to solve class inclusion problems. And they are capable of conservation: They readily understand that if nothing is added or taken away, an amount stays the same despite changes in shape or arrangement. For example, the second girl depicted in the "Conservation" video in MyEducationLab is quite confident that juice poured from a short, wide glass into a tall, thin glass hasn't changed in amount: "Just because this is skinny doesn't mean it's . . . this one is just wider, this one is skinnier, but they have the same amount of juice."

Children continue to develop their newly acquired logical thinking capabilities throughout the elementary school years. Over time they become capable of dealing with increasingly complex conservation tasks. Some forms of conservation, such as conservation of liquid and conservation of number, appear at age 6 or 7. Other forms don't appear until later. Consider the task involving *conservation of weight* depicted in Figure 6-3. Using a balance scale, an adult shows a child that two balls of clay have the same weight. One ball is removed from the scale and smashed into a pancake shape. The child is then asked if the pancake weighs the same as the unsmashed ball or if the two pieces of clay weigh different amounts. Children typically do not achieve conservation of weight—that is, they don't realize that the flattened pancake weighs the same as the round ball—until age 9 or 10 (Piaget, 1950).

Although children displaying concrete operational thought show many signs of logical thinking, their cognitive development is not yet complete. In particular, they have trouble reasoning about abstract or hypothetical ideas (hence the term *concrete* operations stage). In language, this weakness may be reflected in an inability to interpret the underlying, non-literal meanings of proverbs. In mathematics, it may be reflected in confusion about such concepts as *pi* (π), *infinity*, and *negative number*. And in social studies, it may limit children's comprehension of such abstract notions as *democracy, communism,* and *human rights*.

Formal Operations Stage (beginning at about age 11 or 12)

Sometime around puberty, Piaget found, children become capable of thinking and reasoning about things that have little or no basis in physical reality. They can think logically about abstract concepts, hypothetical ideas, and statements that contradict what they know to be

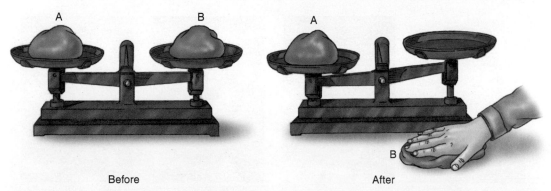

FIGURE 6-3   Conservation of weight. Balls A and B initially weigh the same. When Ball B is flattened into a pancake shape, how does its weight now compare with that of Ball A?

true in the real world. Also emerging are scientific reasoning abilities that enable children to identify cause-and-effect relationships in physical phenomena. As an example, consider the following task:

> An object suspended by a rope or string—a pendulum—swings indefinitely at a constant rate. Some pendulums swing back and forth very quickly, whereas others swing more slowly. Design an experiment that can help you determine what factor or factors affect a pendulum's oscillation rate.

To successfully tackle this problem, you must first *formulate hypotheses* about possible variables affecting a pendulum's swing. You might consider (a) the weight of the suspended object, (b) the length of the string that holds the object, (c) the force with which the object is pushed, and (d) the height from which the object is initially released. You must then *separate and control variables,* testing one factor at a time while holding all others constant. To test the hypothesis that weight makes a difference, you should try different weights while keeping constant the length of the string, the force with which you push each weight, and the height from which you release it. Similarly, if you hypothesize that the length of the string is critical, you should vary the length of the string while continuing to use the same weight and starting the pendulum in motion in the same manner. If you carefully separate and control variables, your observations should lead you to conclude that only *length* affects a pendulum's oscillation rate.

Once formal operational thinking appears, more advanced verbal and mathematical problem solving is also possible. Adolescents become able to see beyond literal interpretations of such proverbs as "A rolling stone gathers no moss" and "An ant may well destroy a dam" to identify their underlying meanings. Adolescents also become better able to understand such concepts as *negative number* and *infinity* because they can now comprehend how numbers can be below zero and how two parallel lines will never touch even if they go on forever. Furthermore, they can understand the nature of proportions (e.g., fractions, ratios, decimals) and correctly use proportions when working on mathematical problems. And they gain an appreciation for contrary-to-fact ideas, as you can learn more about in the "Thinking Logically About Contrary-to-Fact Premises" in MyEducationLab.

The emerging capacity to think about hypothetical and contrary-to-fact ideas allows adolescents to envision how the world might be different from, and possibly better than, the way it actually is. Thus they may be idealistic about and devoted to social, political, religious, and ethical issues—climate change, world hunger, animal rights, and so on.

Improving Your Observation Skills

Building blocks. How might Piaget have explained the age-related thinking of these children as they interact with building materials? Describe the possible thinking of the infant (left), young child (second from left), elementary-school student (third from left), and adolescent (far right). Compare your response with the explanation at the end of the chapter.

Sometimes they offer recommendations for change that seem logical but aren't practical in today's world. For example, they may argue that racism would disappear overnight if people would just begin to "love one another." Piaget suggested that adolescent idealism reflects an inability to separate one's own logical abstractions from the perspectives of others and from practical considerations. Only through experience do adolescents eventually begin to temper their optimism with some realism about what is possible in a given time frame and with limited resources.

Current Perspectives Related to Piaget's Theory

Piaget's theory has sparked a great deal of research about children's cognitive development. In general, this research supports Piaget's proposed *sequence* in which different abilities emerge. Children's early reasoning does depend more heavily on perception than on logic, and logical reasoning about concrete objects and events emerges before logical reasoning about abstract ideas (Flavell, Miller, & Miller, 2002; Ginsburg, Cannon, Eisenband, & Pappas, 2006; Morra, Gobbo, Marini, & Sheese, 2008). However, contemporary developmental researchers have found that many abilities appear considerably earlier or later than Piaget suggested and that often these abilities depend on particular experiences and cultural contexts.

Capabilities of Different Age-Groups

Using different research methods than those that were available to Piaget, present-day researchers have found that infants and preschoolers are apparently more competent than portrayed in Piaget's descriptions of sensorimotor and preoperational stages. When Piaget studied the development of object permanence, he focused largely on whether infants looked and reached for an object that was no longer in view. In contrast, contemporary researchers look at more subtle measures of object permanence, such as how long infants look at an object and how their heart rates change as they watch it. These researchers have found that infants spend more time looking toward an object that disappears in one spot and then immediately reappears in a very different spot—an event that apparently violates their basic understandings of how physical objects should behave. Such modern techniques reveal that infants show preliminary signs of object permanence as early as 2 to 6 months old and gradually solidify this understanding and connect it with their reaching behaviors (Baillargeon, 2004; Charles & Rivera, 2009; L. B. Cohen & Cashon, 2006).

Contemporary methods with preschoolers have taken a slightly different tact, with researchers making cognitive tasks and questions less artificial and easing demands on children's memories. When tasks are modified in such ways, preschoolers are often quite capable of conservation and class inclusion (M. Donaldson, 1978; R. Gelman & Baillargeon, 1983; Rule, 2007).

Piaget may have underestimated the capabilities of elementary school children as well. Many elementary students—and occasionally even 4-year-olds—show some ability to think abstractly and hypothetically about events that haven't been observed or have not yet occurred (S. R. Beck, Robinson, Carroll, & Apperly, 2006; S. Carey, 1985; Schulz, Goodman, Tenenbaum, & Jenkins, 2008). Also, even kindergarteners and first and second graders can understand simple ratios and proportions (e.g., fractions such as ½, ⅓, and ¼) if they can relate these concepts to everyday objects (Boyer, Levine, & Huttenlocher, 2008; Empson, 1999). And some elementary school children can separate and control variables in science, especially when given hints about the importance of controlling all variables except the one they are testing (Danner & Day, 1977; Metz, 1995; Strand-Cary & Klahr, 2008).

Yet Piaget probably *overestimated* what adolescents can do. Formal operational thinking processes emerge much more gradually than Piaget suggested, and adolescents don't use these skills as regularly as Piaget would have us believe (Kuhn, Pease, & Wirkala, 2009; Pascarella & Terenzini, 1991; Shayer & Ginsburg, 2009). A related issue is whether formal operational reasoning is really the final stage of cognitive development, as Piaget suggested. Some theorists have proposed that many adults progress to a fifth, postformal stage in which they can envision multiple approaches to the same problem and recognize that each approach may be valid from a particular perspective (Cartwright, Galupo, Tyree, & Jennings, 2009; Sinnott, 2009; P.-L. Wu & Chiou, 2008). Other theorists disagree, arguing that adult life simply poses different kinds of problems than the academically oriented ones that adolescents encounter at school (Schaie & Willis, 2000).

Effects of Prior Knowledge and Experience

Piaget acknowledged that as children gain new logical thinking skills, they may apply the skills in one content area but not necessarily in another (Chapman, 1988; Piaget, 1940). It is becoming increasingly apparent that for people of all ages, the ability to think logically in a particular situation depends on background experiences relevant to the situation. Children as young as age 4 or 5 begin to show class inclusion and conservation after having practice with such tasks, especially if they can actively manipulate the task materials and discuss their reasoning with someone who already exhibits these logical abilities (D. Field, 1987; Halford & Andrews, 2006; Siegler & Svetina, 2006). Children ages 10 to 12 years old can solve logical problems involving hypothetical ideas if they are taught relevant problem-solving strategies, and they become increasingly able to separate and control variables when they have numerous experiences that require them to do so (Kuhn & Dean, 2005; Kuhn et al., 2009; S. Lee, 1985; Schauble, 1990). Adolescents and adults as well often apply advanced reasoning to topics about which they have a great deal of knowledge and yet think concretely about topics with which they are unfamiliar (Klein, 2006; Kuhn, 2008; M. C. Linn, Clement, Pulos, & Sullivan, 1989). Thus it appears that what young people learn, with support, is how to think systematically about a few particular concepts rather than how to use all-purpose logical principles in all circumstances.

As an illustration of how prior knowledge affects formal operational thinking, consider the fishing pond shown in Figure 6-4. In a study by Pulos and Linn (1981), 13-year-olds were shown a similar picture and told, "These four children go fishing every week, and one child, Herb, always catches the most fish. The other children wonder why." If you look at the picture, it is obvious that Herb is different from the three other children in several ways, including the bait he uses, the length of his fishing rod, and his location by the pond. Children who had fished frequently more effectively separated and controlled variables for this situation than they did for the pendulum problem described earlier, whereas the reverse was true for children without fishing experience. In the "Cognitive Development" videos for middle childhood and late adolescence in MyEducationLab, 10-year-old Kent and 14-year-old Alicia both consider the problem as they look at the picture in Figure 6-4. Notice how Kent, who appears to have some experience with fishing, considers several possible variables and remains open minded about the causal one. In contrast, Alicia, who is older but admittedly unfamiliar with fishing strategies, considers only two variables and jumps to a conclusion about causation:

Kent: He has live . . . live worms, I think. Fish like live worms more, I guess 'cause they're live and they'd rather have that than the lures, plastic worms. . . . Because he might be more patient or that might be a good side of the place. Maybe since Bill has a boombox thing [referring to the radio], I don't think they would really like that because . . . and he doesn't really have anything that's extra. . . . But he's the standing one. I don't get that. But Bill, that could scare the fish away to Herb because he's closer. . . .

Alicia: Because of the spot he's standing in, probably. . . . I don't know anything about fishing. Oh, OK! He actually has live worms for bait. The other girl's using saltine crackers [she misreads *crickets*]. . . . She's using plastic worms, he's using lures, and she's using crackers and he's actually using live worms. So obviously the fish like the live worms the best.

MyEducationLab

Observe how experience with fishing affects Kent's and Alicia's ability to identify variables in the "Cognitive Development" videos. (Find Video Examples in Topic 6 of MyEducationLab.)

One general factor that promotes more advanced reasoning is formal education. Going to school and receiving instruction are associated with mastery of concrete operational and formal operational tasks (Artman & Cahan, 1993; Gauvain & Munroe, 2009; Rogoff, 2003). For instance, you may be happy to learn that taking college courses in a particular area (in

FIGURE 6-4 Gone fishing. What are some possible reasons why Herb is catching more fish than the others?
Based on Pulos & Linn, 1981.

child development, perhaps?) leads to improvements in reasoning skills related to that area (Lehman & Nisbett, 1990; T. M. McDevitt, Jobes, Sheehan, & Cochran, 2010).

Effects of Culture

Piaget acknowledged that children grow intellectually as they reflect on their exchanges with people and objects in their cultural environments. He further recognized that cultural variations in intellectual opportunities could lead to modest differences in children's skills (Piaget, 1972). Yet many contemporary theorists now conclude that Piaget did not fully understand how powerfully culture shapes children's minds or how strongly his own theory reflected the Western position that scientific reasoning is the pinnacle of human development (Maynard, 2008).

Considerable research indicates that Piaget was more on target about younger children developing similar abilities in a wide range of cultural situations than he was in his assumption about universal advancements in older children. Infants in all known cultures learn a lot from exploring their physical environment, and young children in the preschool years universally represent their ideas with language and intuitive logic. In comparison, concrete and formal operational abilities are more susceptible to particular cultural experiences. For example, Mexican children whose families make pottery for a living seem to acquire conservation skills earlier than Piaget found to be true for Swiss children (Price-Williams, Gordon, & Ramirez, 1969). Apparently, creating pottery requires children to make frequent judgments about needed quantities of clay and water—judgments that must be fairly accurate regardless of the specific form of the clay or water container. In other cultures, especially in some where children don't attend school, conservation may appear several years later than Piaget proposed, and some aspects of formal operational reasoning—at least as measured by Piaget and colleagues—do not appear when abstract reasoning has little relevance to people's daily lives (M. Cole, 1990; Fahrmeier, 1978; Maynard, 2008; J. G. Miller, 1997). For instance, adults in some Asian societies find little purpose in applying rules of logic to artificial, contrary-to-fact situations and so don't nurture such thinking in children (Norenzayan, Choi, & Peng, 2007).

Does Cognitive Development Occur in Stages?

In light of all the evidence, does it still make sense to talk about discrete stages of cognitive development? Even Piaget acknowledged that the characteristics of any particular stage don't necessarily hang together as a tight, inseparable set of abilities (Chapman, 1988; Piaget, 1940). Most contemporary developmental theorists now believe that children do *not* universally go through stages in all-encompassing logical structures. Today's theorists further suggest that Piaget's evidence about children's abilities may better describe how children *can* think, rather than how they typically *do* think (K. W. Fischer, Stein, & Heikkinen, 2009; Halford & Andrews, 2006; Klaczynski, 2001).

In addition to reformulating the essence of thinking, contemporary scholars are recasting the nature of developmental change. One group of theorists, *information processing theory* scholars, subscribe to the view that development can be described in terms of gradual *trends*—for instance, in gradual movements toward increasingly abstract thought—rather than discrete stages (e.g., Flavell, 1994; Kuhn & Franklin, 2006; Siegler & Alibali, 2005).[4] Another group, *developmental systems* scholars, believe that each child's thinking is unique and develops at an uneven pace, at any given moment improving rapidly, slowly or through a combination of progressions and temporary regressions (K. W. Fischer, 2008; Hohenberger & Peltzer-Karpf, 2009).

Despite their reservations about Piaget's global structures and stages, present-day developmental scholars remain sympathetic to Piaget's search for qualitative transformations in children's constructivist thinking. They believe that, by entirely rejecting Piaget's search for stages and constructivist ideas, we may be throwing the baby out with the bath water. Some of these psychologists have combined Piaget's ideas with precise research methods to construct **neo-Piagetian theories** of how children's learning and reasoning capabilities change over time.

Key Ideas in Neo-Piagetian Theories

Neo-Piagetian theorists share Piaget's belief that children's skills and understandings change in distinct, qualitative ways over time. Unlike Piaget, however, they suggest that children's abilities are strongly tied to personal experiences in particular contexts. Following are several principles that are central to neo-Piagetian approaches:

Cognitive development is constrained by the maturation of information processing mechanisms. Neo-Piagetian theorists have echoed Piaget's belief that cognitive development depends on brain maturation. A mechanism in the brain known as **working memory** is especially important for cognitive development (e.g., Case, 1985, 1991; Davidse, de Jong, Bus, Huijbregts, & Swaab, 2011; Morra et al., 2008). Working memory is that part of the human memory system in which people hold and actively think about new information. (For instance, you are using your working memory right now to make sense of what you're reading about cognitive development.) Children's working memory capacity increases with age, and so their ability to think about several things simultaneously increases as well. Neo-Piagetian theorists propose that young children's limited working memory capacity restricts their ability to acquire complex thinking, reasoning, and language skills (Barrouillet, Gavens, Vergauwe, Gaillard, & Camos, 2009; K. W. Fischer & Bidell, 1991; Morra & Camba, 2009).[5]

Children acquire new knowledge through both unintentional and intentional learning processes. Many contemporary psychologists agree that children learn some things with little or no conscious awareness or effort. Consider this question about household pets: "On average, which are larger, cats or dogs?" Even if you've never intentionally thought about this issue, you can easily answer "Dogs" because of the many characteristics (including size) you've learned to associate with both species. Children unconsciously learn the consistent patterns and associations that characterize many aspects of their world.

Yet, especially as children's brains mature in the first year or two of life, they increasingly think actively about their experiences, and they begin to devote considerable mental

neo-Piagetian theory
Theoretical perspective that combines elements of Piaget's theory with more contemporary research findings and suggests that development in specific content domains is often stagelike in nature.

working memory
Component of memory that enables people to actively think about and process a small amount of information.

---

[4]*Information processing theory*, described in Chapter 7, characterizes the general trends in cognitive processes that we are likely to see as children develop.
[5]You'll learn more about the development of working memory in Chapter 7.

attention to solving the little problems that come their way each day (Case & Okamoto, 1996; Pascual-Leone, 1970). As they do so, they draw on what they've learned (some of which they have absorbed unconsciously) about common patterns in their environment, and they may simultaneously strengthen their knowledge of those patterns. Thus both the unintentional and intentional learning processes work hand in hand as children tackle day-to-day tasks and, in the process, enhance their knowledge about the world (Case, 1985; Case & Okamoto, 1996; Weinert, 2009).

Children acquire cognitive structures that affect their thinking in particular content domains. Neo-Piagetian theorists reject Piaget's proposal that children develop general-purpose systems of mental processes (operations) that they can apply to a broad range of tasks and content domains. Instead, they suggest, children acquire more specific systems of concepts and thinking skills that influence reasoning in particular areas.

Canadian psychologist **Robbie Case** (1944–2000) and his colleagues have proposed that integrated networks of concepts and cognitive processes, called **central conceptual structures**, form the basis for much of children's thinking, reasoning, and learning in certain areas (Case, 1991; Case & Okamoto, 1996; S. Griffin, 2009). A central conceptual structure related to *number* underlies children's ability to reason about and manipulate mathematical quantities. This structure reflects an integrated understanding of how such mathematical concepts as numbers, counting, addition, and subtraction are interrelated.[6] A central conceptual structure related to *spatial relationships* underlies children's performance in such areas as drawing, construction and use of maps, replication of geometric patterns, and psychomotor activities (e.g., writing in cursive, hitting a ball with a racket). This structure enables children to align objects in space according to one or more reference points (e.g., the *x*- and *y*-axes used in graphing). A central conceptual structure related to *social thought* underlies children's reasoning about interpersonal relationships, their knowledge of common patterns in human interaction, and their comprehension of short stories and other works of fiction. This structure includes children's general beliefs about human beings' thoughts, desires, and behaviors. Case has found evidence indicating that the three conceptual structures develop in a wide variety of cultural and educational contexts (Case & Okamoto, 1996).

Development in specific content domains can sometimes be characterized as a series of stages. Although neo-Piagetian theorists reject Piaget's notion that a single series of stages characterizes cognitive development, they speculate that cognitive development in specific content domains often has a stagelike nature (e.g., Case & Okamoto, 1996; K. W. Fischer & Immordino-Yang, 2002; Morra et al., 2008). Children's entry into a particular stage is marked by the acquisition of new abilities, which children practice and gradually master over time. Eventually, they integrate these abilities into more complex structures that mark their transition into a subsequent stage.

Even in a particular subject area, however, cognitive development is not necessarily a simple sequence of stages through which children progress as if they were climbing rungs on a ladder. In some cases development might be better characterized as progression along "multiple strands" of skills that occasionally interconnect, consolidate, or separate in a weblike fashion (K. W. Fischer, 2008; K. W. Fischer & Daley, 2007; K. W. Fischer & Immordino-Yang, 2002). From this perspective, children may acquire more advanced levels of competence in a particular area through any one of several pathways. For instance, as they become increasingly proficient in reading, children may gradually develop word decoding skills, comprehension skills, and so on and draw on these assorted skills when reading a book. However, the rate at which each of the skills is mastered will vary from one child to the next.

central conceptual structure
Integrated network of concepts and cognitive processes that forms the basis for much of one's thinking, reasoning, and learning in a specific content domain.

[6]See Chapter 10 for more details about a possible central conceptual structure in number.

CENTRAL CONCEPTUAL STRUCTURES. According to Robbie Case's neo-Piagetian perspective, children develop central conceptual structures in number, spatial relationships, and social thought (and perhaps in other areas as well). These structures affect children's reasoning and performance on a variety of relevant tasks.

Preparing for Your Licensure Examination
Your teaching test might ask you about Piaget's major contributions to educational practice.

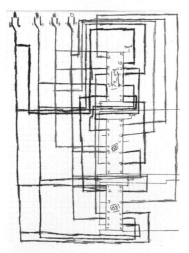

ARTIFACT 6-1 Habtom's circuit board. Fifteen-year-old Habtom designed a circuit board with the help of his engineering teacher, who advised him about the characteristics of electronic chips (see vertical boxes with internal numbers toward the middle-right of the artifact) and connections among the binary switches. Using formal reasoning, Habtom designed the circuit board, built it, and confirmed that it actually worked.

Applying the Ideas of Piaget and His Followers

Educators and practitioners who have taken Piaget's theory to heart respect the natural curiosity of children, give children many opportunities to make choices, and appeal to children's interests. Adults who are inspired by Piaget have tried these specific strategies:

• **Provide opportunities for children to experiment with physical objects.** Learners of all ages, but particularly children, can learn a great deal by exploring the physical world in a hands-on fashion (Ginsburg et al., 2006; Parton & Hancock, 2008; B. Y. White & Frederiksen, 1998). In infancy this might involve having regular access to objects with visual and auditory appeal, such as mobiles, rattles, stacking cups, and pull toys. At the preschool level, it might involve playing with water, sand, wooden blocks, and age-appropriate manipulative toys. During the elementary school years, hands-on exploration might entail throwing and catching balls, working with clay and watercolor paints, and constructing Popsicle-stick structures. Despite their increased capability for abstract thought, adolescents also benefit from opportunities to manipulate and experiment with concrete materials—perhaps equipment in a science laboratory, food and cooking utensils, or wood and woodworking tools. Such opportunities allow teens to discover laws of the natural world firsthand and to tie their newly emerging abstract ideas to the concrete physical world.

A potential downside, however, is that children and adolescents sometimes misinterpret what they observe, either learning the wrong thing or confirming their existing misconceptions about the world (M. H. Lee & Hanuscin, 2008; Myant & Williams, 2008; Schauble, 1990). Consider the case of Barry, an 11th grader whose physics class was studying the idea that an object's mass and weight do *not*, in and of themselves, affect the speed at which the object falls. Students were asked to design and build an egg container that would keep an egg from breaking when dropped from a third-floor window. They were told that on the day of the egg drop, they would record the time it took for the eggs to reach the ground. Convinced that heavier objects fall faster, Barry added several nails to his egg's container. Yet when he dropped it, classmates timed its fall at 1.49 seconds, a time very similar to that for other students' lighter containers. He and his teacher had the following discussion about the result:

Teacher: So what was your time?
Barry: 1.49. I think it should be faster.
Teacher: Why?
Barry: Because it weighed more than anybody else's and it dropped slower.
Teacher: Oh really? And what do you attribute that to?
Barry: That the people weren't timing real good. (Hynd, 1998, p. 34)

At the elementary and secondary levels, the misconceptions that can arise from spontaneous explorations can be addressed by adding structure to the activities. Carefully planned lessons that allow both exploration and guided interpretation can help children construct appropriate understandings (R. G. Fuller, Campbell, Dykstra, & Stevens, 2009; Hardy, Jonen, Möller, & Stern, 2006; D. T. Hickey, 1997). The Development and Practice feature "Facilitating Discovery Learning" illustrates several recommendations for enhancing the effectiveness of discovery learning activities.

• **Explore children's reasoning with problem-solving tasks and probing questions.** By presenting a variety of Piagetian tasks involving either concrete or formal operational thinking skills and probing students' reasoning with a series of follow-up questions—that is, by

DEVELOPMENT AND PRACTICE
Facilitating Discovery Learning

Make sure students have the necessary prior knowledge for discovering new ideas.

- A first-grade teacher asks students what they already know about air (e.g., people breathe it, wind is air that moves). After ascertaining that the students have some awareness that air has substance, she and her class conduct an experiment in which a glass containing a crumpled paper towel is turned upside-down and completely immersed in a bowl of water. The teacher eventually removes the glass from the water and asks students to explain why the paper towel didn't get wet. (You can see part of this lesson in the "Properties of Air" video in MyEducationLab.) (Middle Childhood)
- Before asking students to study an interactive website on earth science and build a simulated volcano, a high school science teacher introduces types of magma and defines important terms such as *cinder cone*, *lava dome*, *caldera*, and *flood basalt*. (Late Adolescence)

Show puzzling results to create disequilibrium.

- A middle school science teacher shows her class two glasses of water. In one glass an egg floats at the water's surface. In the other glass an egg rests on the bottom. The students give a simple and logical explanation for the difference: One egg has more air inside and so must be lighter. But then the teacher switches the eggs into opposite glasses. The egg that the students believe to be "heavier" now floats, and the "lighter" egg sinks to the bottom. The students are quite surprised and demand to know what is going on. (Ordinarily, water is less dense than an egg, so an egg placed in it will quickly sink. But in this demonstration, one glass contains salt water—a mixture denser than an egg and so capable of keeping it afloat.) (Early Adolescence)
- A high school social studies teacher asks students to decide whether adolescents in the past 60 years can be better characterized as conforming and obedient or rebellious and innovative. The teacher distributes two sets of readings that support each of the conclusions and asks students to study the evidence, determine why there might

be a discrepancy in viewpoints, and ultimately justify a position. (Late Adolescence)

Structure a discovery session so that students proceed logically toward discoveries you want them to make.

- Many students in an eighth-grade science class believe that some very small things (e.g., a tiny piece of Styrofoam, a single lentil bean) are so light that they have no weight. Their teacher asks them to weigh a pile of 25 lentil beans on a balance scale, and the students discover that all of the beans together weigh approximately 1 gram. In the ensuing class discussion, the students agree that if 25 beans have weight, a single bean must also have weight. The teacher then asks them to use math to estimate how much a single bean weighs. (Early Adolescence)
- Students in a high school chemistry class bring in samples of household water and beverages and then analyze the amount of carbon dioxide and other chemicals in the fluids. After it is determined that the fluids contain unhealthful levels of acid, the teacher asks the students to brainstorm ways that society can reduce acid rain. (Late Adolescence)

Help students relate their findings to concepts in the academic discipline they are studying.

- A teacher distributes slices of five kinds of apples—Granny Smith, Golden Yellow, Red Delicious, Fuji, and McIntosh—for purposes of taste testing. The teacher asks the children to indicate their first preference for apples, and together they aggregate the results into a graph. The class identifies the most and least favorite apples. Afterwards, the teacher shows the class other examples of graphs and explains how these diagrams are used in various fields of study. (Middle Childhood)
- After students in a social studies class have collected data on average incomes and voting patterns in different counties within their state, their teacher asks, "How can we interpret these data using what we've learned about the relative wealth of members of the two major political parties?" (Late Adolescence)

Sources: Blevins, 2010 (apple chart example); Bruner, 1966; Center for History and New Media, 2006 (teenage conformists and rebels example); de Jong & van Joolingen, 1998; Frederiksen, 1984; Hardy et al., 2006; D. T. Hickey, 1997; R. E. Mayer, 2004; Minstrell & Stimpson, 1996; Palmer, 1965 (egg example); C. L. Smith, 2007 (Styrofoam example); Smithsonian National Museum of Natural History, 2010 (volcano example); Water Educational Training Science Project, 2002 (acid rain example); B. Y. White & Frederiksen, 1998, 2005.

using Piaget's clinical method—adults can gain valuable insights into how children and adolescents think about their world. The Observation Guidelines table "Assessing Piagetian Reasoning Processes in Children and Adolescents" lists some of the characteristics you might look for.

In probing youngsters' reasoning, however, teachers and other practitioners need not stick to traditional Piagetian tasks. On the contrary, Piaget's clinical method is applicable to a wide variety of content domains and subject matter (e.g., diSessa, 2007; Ginsburg, 2009). In the "Research: Early Adolescence" video in MyEducationLab, you can hear an interviewer asking 12-year-old Claudia a series of questions to probe her reasoning during a categorization task (e.g., "How did you decide which shells to put where?" "What makes [those shells] different from the other ones?").

MyEducationLab

Observe the use of probing questions in the "Research: Early Adolescence" video. (Find Video Examples in Topic 6 of MyEducationLab.)

• **Keep Piaget's stages in mind when interpreting children's behavior and when planning activities, but don't take the stages too literally.** Although Piaget's four stages are not always accurate descriptions of children's and adolescents' thinking capabilities, they do provide a rough idea of the reasoning processes you are apt to see at various age levels (Crain, 2011; Feldman, 2004; Kuhn, 1997). For example, infant caregivers should remember that repetitive behaviors, even those that make a mess or cause inconvenience (dropping food, throwing toys), are an important means through which infants master basic motor skills and learn cause-and-effect relationships. Preschool teachers should not be surprised to hear young

OBSERVATION GUIDELINES
Assessing Piagetian Reasoning Processes in Children and Adolescents

CHARACTERISTIC	LOOK FOR	EXAMPLE	IMPLICATION
Concrete Thought	• *Heavy reliance on concrete manipulatives* to understand concepts • *Difficulty understanding abstract ideas*	Tobey solves arithmetic word problems more easily when he can draw pictures of them.	Use concrete objects and examples to illustrate abstract situations and problems.
Abstract Thought	• *Ability to understand strictly verbal explanations* of abstract concepts and principles • *Ability to reason about hypothetical or contrary-to-fact situations*	Elsa can imagine how two parallel lines might go on forever without ever coming together.	When working with adolescents, occasionally use verbal explanations (e.g., short lectures) to present information, but assess students' understanding frequently to make sure they understand.
Idealism	• *Idealistic notions* about how the world should be • *Difficulty taking other people's needs and perspectives into account* when offering ideas for change • *Inability to adjust ideals* in light of what can realistically be accomplished	Martin advocates a system of government in which all citizens contribute their earnings to a common "pool" and then withdraw money only as they need it.	Engage adolescents in discussions about challenging political and social issues.
Scientific Reasoning Skills	• *Identifying multiple hypotheses* for a particular phenomenon • *Separation and control of variables*	Serena proposes three possible explanations for a result she has obtained in her physics lab.	Have middle school and high school students design and conduct simple experiments. Include experiments about issues related to their backgrounds and interests.
Mathematical Reasoning Skills	• *Understanding and using abstract mathematical symbols* (e.g., π, the variable x in algebraic equations) • *Understanding and using proportions* in mathematical problem solving	Giorgio uses a 1:240 scale when drawing a floor plan of his school building.	Initially, introduce abstract mathematical concepts and tasks using simple examples (e.g., when introducing proportions, begin with fractions such as $\frac{1}{3}$ and $\frac{1}{4}$). Progress to more complex examples only when youngsters appear ready to handle them.

children arguing that the three pieces of a broken candy bar constitute more candy than a similar, unbroken bar (a belief that reflects lack of conservation). Elementary school teachers should recognize that their students may have trouble with proportions (e.g., fractions, decimals) and with such abstract concepts as *time* in astronomy and *negative number* and *pi* in mathematics (B. Adams, 2008; Kaufmann, 2008; Tourniaire & Pulos, 1985). Educators and other professionals should expect to hear passionate arguments from adolescents that reflect idealistic yet unrealistic notions about how society should operate.

Piaget's stages also provide guidance about strategies that are apt to be effective in teaching children of different age levels. For instance, given the abstract nature of historical time, elementary school teachers planning history lessons should probably limit talk about specific dates in favor of active investigations into people's motivations, conflicts, and accomplishments (Barton & Levstik, 1996; Levstik, 2008). Especially in the elementary grades (and to a lesser degree in middle and high school), instructors should find ways to make abstract ideas more concrete for their students. As one example, a third-grade teacher, realizing that the abstract concept of *place value* might be a difficult one for 8- and 9-year-olds, showed her students how to depict two-digit numbers with blocks, using ten-block rows for the number in the tens column and single blocks for the number in the ones column.

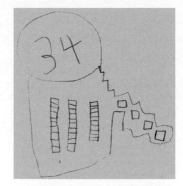

ARTIFACT 6-2   **Thirty-four.** Eight-year-old Noah uses rows of 10 squares and single squares to depict the number 34.

• **Present situations that children cannot easily explain using their existing understandings.** Events and information that conflict with youngsters' current understandings create disequilibrium that may motivate them to reevaluate and perhaps modify what they "know" to be true (e.g., M. G. Hennessey, 2003; Pugh, 2011; C. L. Smith, 2007; Vosniadou, 2009). For instance, if they believe that "light objects float and heavy objects sink" or that "wood floats and metal sinks," an instructor might present a common counterexample: a metal battleship (floating, of course) that weighs many tons.

• **Use familiar content when asking children to reason in sophisticated ways.** Earlier we presented evidence to indicate that children and adolescents display more advanced reasoning skills when they work with topics they know well. With such evidence in mind, teachers and other practitioners might ask young people to do the following:

- Conserve liquid within the context of a juice-sharing task.
- Separate and control variables within the context of a familiar activity (perhaps fishing, designing a paper airplane, or using various combinations of ingredients in baking cookies).
- Consider abstract ideas about subject matter that has already been studied in depth in a concrete fashion (e.g., introducing the concepts *inertia* and *momentum* to explain such everyday experiences as throwing a ball and driving quickly around a sharp curve).

• **Informally assess the individual strategies that children use when attempting to solve problems.** Observing the learning procedures and struggles of individual children is an important feature of constructivist teaching. The Neo-Piagetians have made an especially good case for determining and adjusting to the particular challenges that children face as they work on problems. Teachers might find that children have a preestablished idea about a task (e.g., mistakenly assuming that the arithmetic problem $4 + \_\_ = 7$ requires them to add the two numbers, thus writing "11" as the answer); have an inadequate memory capacity to complete the task (e.g., remembering only a few steps in a teacher's lengthy verbal instructions); misinterpret the requirements of a problem (e.g., not realizing that "=" in mathematics means "make the same"); and do not have the constituent skills (e.g., submitting the wrong answer on a long-division problem because of simple errors in subtraction) (Case, 1980; Morra et al., 2008). Once teachers determine children's abilities and difficulties, they can tailor their assistance accordingly, perhaps instructing children in missing skills or alleviating the memory load.

• **Plan group activities in which young people share their perspectives with one another.** As noted earlier, Piaget proposed that interaction with peers helps children realize that others often view the world very differently than they themselves do and that their own ideas are not always completely reasonable. Interactions with age-mates that involve differences of opinion—situations that create **sociocognitive conflict**—can cause disequilibrium that may spur children to reevaluate their current perspectives.

Many contemporary psychologists share Piaget's belief in the value of sociocognitive conflict. They have offered several reasons why interactions with peers may help promote cognitive growth:

- Peers speak at a level that children can understand.
- Whereas children may accept an adult's ideas without argument, they are more willing to disagree with the ideas of their peers.
- When children hear competing views held by peers—individuals who presumably have knowledge and abilities similar to their own—they may be motivated to reconcile the contradictions. (Damon, 1984; De Lisi & Golbeck, 1999; C. Howe, 2009; Murphy & Alexander, 2008; Rubin, Bowker, & Kennedy, 2009)

When sharing their views with one another, however, children can also acquire misinformation (Good, McCaslin, & Reys, 1992). It is essential, then, for teachers to monitor group discussions and correct any misconceptions or misinterpretations that youngsters may pass on to their peers.

Although children learn a great deal from their interactions with others, cognitive development is, in Piaget's theory, largely an individual enterprise: By assimilating and accommodating to new experiences, children develop increasingly advanced and integrated schemes over time. Thus Piaget's perspective depicts children as doing most of the mental "work" themselves. In contrast, Lev Vygotsky's theory places much of the responsibility for children's development on the adults in their society and culture. We turn to this theory now.

VYGOTSKY'S THEORY OF COGNITIVE DEVELOPMENT

Whereas Piaget had a background in biology, Russian psychologist **Lev Vygotsky** (1896–1934) had early training in law, history, philosophy, literature, and education. Vygotsky was deeply influenced by Karl Marx's proposal that historical changes in society have a significant impact on how people think and behave. And like Marx's colleague Friedrich Engels, Vygotsky saw much value in the use of *tools* for moving a society forward (M. Cole & Scribner, 1978; Gredler & Shields, 2008; Vygotsky, 1997e). A variety of tools influence thinking, many of which are tangible, including paper, the alphabet, writing utensils, books, and in today's industrialized societies, computers, calculators, cell phones, and an increasing array of other educational and recreational technologies. In Vygotsky's mind, however, *cognitive* entities—concepts, theories, problem-solving strategies, and so on—are also influential tools.

Vygotsky believed that the adults in any society foster children's learning in an intentional and somewhat systematic manner. In particular, adults engage children in meaningful and challenging activities, show them how to use various physical and cognitive tools to facilitate their performance, and help them make sense of their experiences. Because Vygotsky emphasized the importance of adult guidance in promoting cognitive advancements— and more generally because he emphasized the influence of social and cultural factors in children's cognitive development—his perspective is known as a *sociocultural theory*.

With the assistance of his students, Vygotsky conducted numerous studies of children's thinking from the 1920s until his early death from tuberculosis in 1934. In his major writings, he typically described his findings only in general terms, saving the details for technical reports that he shared with the small number of research psychologists working in Russia at the time (Kozulin, 1986). However, Vygotsky wrote persuasively about the qualities of research that should be included in order for scientific progress in cognitive development to take place. According to Vygotsky, research with children should have a coherent theoretical foundation instead of being based in a hodgepodge of ideas, it must focus on essential mental processes rather than on isolated responses, and it ideally examines developmental

sociocognitive conflict
Situation in which one encounters and has to wrestle with ideas and viewpoints different from one's own.

changes in mental processes and is not simply a record of thinking at one moment in time (Gredler & Shields, 2008; Vygotsky, 1987, 1997a, 1997d).

In their investigations, Vygotsky and his collaborators gave primary attention to how children improved in their use of cultural materials, especially when assisted by others. In Figure 6-5 you can see an example of the type of study Vygotsky conducted. Interested in how children might use external stimuli to augment their basic memory processes, Vygotsky told children he would show them a long list of words that would be impossible to remember without assistance. He encouraged children to form associations with pictures on cards that would be made available to them later. For young children, the pictures did not help and in some cases were actually distracting. In contrast, older children were able to use the pictures effectively as memory aids. An older child might associate the word "crab" with the picture of theater by connecting the two together in an image: "The crab is looking at the stones on the bottom, it is beautiful, for him it is a theater" (Vygotsky, 1997c, p. 181). Later, this child would easily remember the word "crab" when shown the picture of the theater.

In his book *Thought and Language*, Vygotsky explained that his approach to studying children's cognitive development was radically different from that of Piaget and other psychologists of his era. Rather than determine the kinds of tasks children could successfully perform *on their own* (as Piaget did), he often examined the kinds of tasks children could complete *only with adult assistance*. For example, he described two hypothetical children who could, without help, do things that a typical 8-year-old might be able to do. He would give each of the children progressively more difficult tasks and offer some help, perhaps asking a leading question or suggesting a reasonable first step. With such assistance, both children could almost invariably tackle more difficult tasks than they could handle on their own. However, the *range* of tasks that the two children could complete with assistance might be quite different, with one child "stretching" his or her abilities to succeed at typical 12-year-old-level tasks and the other succeeding only with typical 9-year-old-level tasks (Vygotsky, 1934/1986, p. 187).

Western psychologists were largely unfamiliar with Vygotsky's work until the last few decades of the 20th century, when his major writings were translated from Russian into

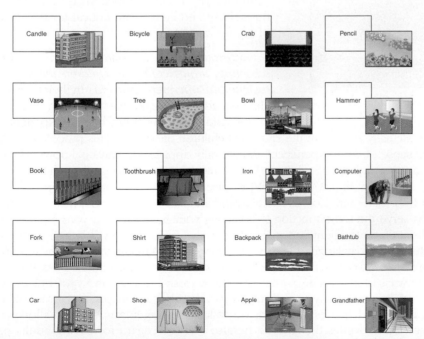

FIGURE 6-5 Learning to use memory aids. Vygotsky showed two sets of cards to children, asking the children to think of a possible connection between each word and the picture with which it was paired (e.g., they could remember "candle" by imagining trees next to a tall building lit up with candles). Afterwards, the word cards were removed and children were shown the picture cards and asked to recall as many of the words as possible using the word cards alone.
Based on Vygotsky, 1997c.

English (e.g., Vygotsky, 1934/1986, 1978, 1997b). Although Vygotsky's premature death meant he did not have the chance to develop his theory fully, his views remain evident in many contemporary theorists' discussions of learning and development today. In fact, while Piaget's influence has been on the wane in recent years (Bjorklund, 1997; Bredekamp, 2011), Vygotsky's influence has become increasingly prominent.

Key Ideas in Vygotsky's Theory

Vygotsky acknowledged that biological factors (e.g., brain maturation) play a role in development. Children bring certain characteristics and dispositions to the situations they encounter, and their responses to those situations vary accordingly. Furthermore, children's inherited traits affect their behavior, which in turn influences the particular experiences that they have (Vygotsky, 1997b). However, Vygotsky's primary focus was on the role of nurture, and especially on the ways in which a child's social and cultural environments foster cognitive growth. Following are central ideas in Vygotsky's theory:

Some cognitive processes are seen in a variety of species; others are unique to human beings. Vygotsky distinguished between two kinds of mental processes, which he called *functions.* Many species exhibit *lower mental functions:* certain basic ways of learning and responding to the environment, such as discovering what foods to eat and how best to get from one location to another. Human beings are unique in their additional use of *higher mental functions:* deliberate, focused cognitive processes that enhance learning, memory, and logical reasoning. In Vygotsky's view, the potential for acquiring lower mental functions is biologically built in, but society and culture are critical for the development of higher mental functions.

Through both informal interactions and formal schooling, adults convey to children the ways in which their culture interprets the world. In their interactions with children, adults share the *meanings* they attach to objects, events, and, more generally, human experience. As they do so, they actually *transform* the situations children encounter. This process of helping children make sense of their experiences in culturally appropriate ways is known as **mediation**. Meanings are conveyed through a variety of mechanisms—language, mathematical symbols, art, music, and so on. In the "Museum Visit" case at the beginning of the chapter, Mother helps 4-year-old Billy make sense of several dinosaur artifacts. She points out how dinosaur ribs and human ribs serve the same function ("Protecting your heart . . . and your lungs"). She relates some of the artifacts to scientific concepts that Billy already knows (*Jurassic, Cretaceous*). And she substitutes everyday language ("dinosaur poop") for an unfamiliar scientific term (*coprolite*).

Informal conversations are one common method by which adults pass along culturally appropriate ways of interpreting situations. But no less important in Vygotsky's eyes is formal education, where teachers systematically impart the ideas, concepts, and terminology used in various academic disciplines. Although Vygotsky, like Piaget, saw value in allowing children to make some discoveries themselves, he also showed regard for having adults pass along the discoveries of previous generations (Vygotsky, 1934/1986).

Increasingly, contemporary developmental psychologists are recognizing the many ways in which culture shapes children's cognitive development. Culture ensures that each new generation benefits from the wisdom that preceding generations have accumulated. A society guides children in certain directions by encouraging them to pay attention to particular stimuli (and not to others) and to engage in particular activities (and not in others).

Improving Your Observation Skills

What's this? How is this teacher mediating children's interpretations of their physical environment? Compare your response with the explanation at the end of the chapter.

Bioecology of Child Development

Vygotsky proposed that guidance from adults is essential to children's use of cultural symbols, strategies, and tools.

mediation
In Vygotsky's theory, a process through which adults help children make culturally appropriate sense of their experiences, perhaps by attaching labels to objects or explaining the nature of certain phenomena.

And it provides a lens through which children come to construct culturally appropriate interpretations of their experiences.

Every culture passes along physical and cognitive tools that make daily living more efficient. Not only do adults teach children specific ways of interpreting experience, but they also pass along specific tools that can help children tackle the various tasks and problems they are apt to face. Some tools, such as shovels, sewing machines, and computers, are physical objects. Others, such as writing systems, maps, and spreadsheets, are partly physical and partly symbolic. Still others, such as using rounding rules and mental arithmetic to estimate the cost of one's purchases at a store, may have little physical basis at all. In Vygotsky's view, acquiring tools that are partly or entirely symbolic or mental—**cognitive tools**—greatly enhances children's cognitive abilities.

Different cultures pass along different cognitive tools. Thus Vygotsky's theory leads us to expect greater diversity among children than Piaget's theory does. For instance, recall a point made earlier in the chapter: Children acquire conservation skills at a younger age if conservation of clay and water is important for their family's pottery business. Similarly, children are more likely to acquire map-reading skills if maps (perhaps of roads, subway systems, and shopping malls) are a prominent part of their community and family life (Liben & Myers, 2007). Children are more apt to have a keen sense of time if clocks and calendars regulate cultural activities (Graesch, 2009; K. Nelson, 1996a). In the opening case study, Billy can relate museum exhibits to certain time periods—cognitive tools from the field of geology—only because aspects of his culture (children's books, museums, etc.) have enabled him to acquire those organizational tools.

Thought and language become increasingly interdependent in the first few years of life. One very important cognitive tool is language. For us as adults, thought and language are closely interconnected. We often think by using the specific words that our language provides. For example, when we think about household pets, our thoughts contain such words as *dog* and *cat*. In addition, we usually express our thoughts when we converse with others. In other words, we "speak our minds."

But Vygotsky proposed that thought and language are separate functions for infants and young toddlers. In these early years, thinking occurs independently of language, and when language appears, it is first used primarily as a means of communication rather than as a mechanism of thought. Sometime around age 2, thought and language become intertwined: Children begin to express their thoughts when they speak, and they begin to think in words (see Figure 6-6).

When thought and language first merge, children often talk to themselves, a phenomenon known as **self-talk** (you may also see the term *private speech*). Vygotsky suggested that self-talk serves an important function in cognitive development. By talking to themselves, children learn to guide their own behaviors through complex maneuvers in much the same way that adults have previously guided them. Self-talk eventually evolves into **inner speech**, in which children "talk" to themselves mentally rather than aloud. They continue to direct themselves verbally through tasks and activities, but others can no longer see and hear them do it (Vygotsky, 1934/1986).

Recent research has supported Vygotsky's views regarding the progression and role of self-talk and inner speech. The frequency of children's audible self-talk decreases during the preschool and early elementary years, but this decrease is at first accompanied by an increase in whispered mumbling and silent lip movements, presumably reflecting a transition to inner speech (Bivens & Berk, 1990; Ostad & Askeland, 2008; Winsler & Naglieri, 2003). Furthermore, self-talk increases when children are performing more challenging tasks, at which they must exert considerable effort to be successful (Berk, 1994; Corkum, Humphries, Mullane, & Theriault, 2008; Schimmoeller, 1998; Vygotsky, 1934/1986). As you probably know from your own experience, even adults occasionally talk to themselves when they face new challenges.

Complex mental processes begin as social activities and gradually evolve into internal mental activities that children can use independently. Vygotsky proposed that complex thought processes, including the use of cognitive tools, have their roots in social interactions.

In infancy, thought is nonverbal in nature, and language is used primarily as a means of communication.

At about 2 years of age, thought becomes verbal in nature, and language becomes a means of expressing thoughts.

With time, children begin to use *self-talk* to guide their own thoughts and behaviors.

Self-talk gradually evolves into *inner speech*, whereby children guide themselves silently (mentally) rather than aloud.

FIGURE 6-6 Fusing of thought and language. Vygotsky proposed that thought and language initially emerge as separate functions but eventually become intertwined.

cognitive tool
Concept, symbol, strategy, or other culturally constructed mechanism that helps people think more effectively.

self-talk
Talking to oneself as a way of guiding oneself through a task.

inner speech
"Talking" to oneself mentally rather than aloud as a way of guiding oneself through a task.

As children discuss objects and events with adults and other knowledgeable individuals, they gradually incorporate into their own thinking the ways in which people around them talk about and interpret the world, and they begin to use the words, concepts, symbols, and strategies that are typical for their culture.

The process through which social activities evolve into internal mental activities is called **internalization**. The progression from self-talk to inner speech just described illustrates this process: Over time, children gradually internalize adults' directions so that they are eventually giving *themselves* directions.

Not all mental processes emerge as children interact with adults, however. Some develop as children interact with peers. For example, children frequently argue with one another about a variety of matters—how best to carry out an activity, what games to play, who did what to whom, and so on. According to Vygotsky, childhood arguments help children discover that there are often several ways to view the same situation. Eventually, he suggested, children internalize the "arguing" process, developing the ability to look at a situation from several different angles *on their own*.

Children acquire their culture's tools in their own idiosyncratic manner. Recall that Vygotsky was a constructivist. He believed that children do not necessarily internalize *exactly* what they see and hear in a social context. Rather, they often transform ideas, strategies, and other cognitive tools to make these tools uniquely their own. You may sometimes see the term **appropriation** used to refer to this process of internalizing but also selectively implementing some skills rather than others and adapting the ideas and strategies of one's culture for personal use.

Individual differences in 4- and 5-year-old children's responses to dramatic performances in a classroom reveal the process of appropriation. The teacher had encouraged children to act out such popular stories as *Little Red Riding Hood* and then encouraged children to dictate and act out their own stories. Most children enthusiastically made up stories and participated in other children's dramatic plays but a few stood on the periphery or tried to change the rules to suit their own needs. Their teacher described two children who initially avoided the drama project:

> Sonya was a shy girl, seldom spoke during large-group activities, and was reluctant to participate in any group activity in the classroom including morning meeting. She told her mother that she did not participate because she was shy. Her conversations with an adult involved a minimum number of words and she spoke mostly in a soft whisper. Sonya was the last to volunteer to be the storyteller and avoided taking part in plays. She had to be encouraged and cajoled into trying to write her first story which was very brief with the process requiring a lot of prompting and scaffolding by the teacher.… But the experience of writing and directing that first story was so positive for her that she immediately told the teacher she wanted to do another story. (Gupta, 2009, p. 1049–1050)

In comparison, another child, Alec, did not like to write but wanted to be selected for every play:

> Alec rarely used to leave the block area to work in the other centres. Blocks were his favourite activity and he very seldom worked on any art and writing work. Further, Alec was easily frustrated if he was not included in the acting out of the story. He would cry out loudly, fling himself on the floor and prevent the activity from proceeding. With time, however, there was a marked change in his behaviour. Although he continued to exhibit initial disappointment if not chosen to act in a story, he began to quickly reconcile to being part of the audience, showed more patience and enthusiastically began to offer feedback at the end of each play. (Gupta, 2009, p. 1050)

internalization
In Vygotsky's theory, the gradual evolution of external, social activities into internal, mental activities.

appropriation
Gradual adoption of (and perhaps also adaptation of) other people's ways of thinking and behaving for one's own purposes.

As Sonya and Alec reveal, children do not necessarily learn all cultural pastimes easily or enthusiastically. Instead, individual children approach educational activities using their own motivations, prior understandings, and creative learning processes.

Children can perform more challenging tasks when assisted by more advanced and competent individuals. Vygotsky distinguished between two kinds of abilities that children are apt to have at any particular point in their development. A child's *actual developmental level* is the upper limit of tasks that he or she can perform independently, without help from anyone else. A child's *level of potential development* is the upper limit of tasks that he or she can perform with the assistance of a more competent individual. To get a true sense of children's cognitive development, Vygotsky suggested, teachers should assess children's capabilities both when performing alone *and* when performing with assistance.

As we noted earlier, Vygotsky found that children typically accomplish more difficult things in collaboration with adults than they can do on their own. With the assistance of a parent or teacher, they may be able to read more complex prose than they are likely to read independently. They can play more difficult piano pieces when an adult helps them locate some of the notes on the keyboard or provides suggestions about which fingers to use. And notice how a student who cannot independently solve division problems with remainders begins to learn the correct procedure through an interaction with her teacher:

Teacher:	[writes $6\overline{)44}$ on the board] 44 divided by 6. What number times 6 is close to 44?
Child:	6.
Teacher:	What's 6 times 6? [writes 6]
Child:	36.
Teacher:	36. Can you get one that's any closer? [erasing the 6]
Child:	8.
Teacher:	What's 6 times 8?
Child:	64 . . . 48.
Teacher:	48. Too big. Can you think of something . . .
Child:	6 times 7 is 42. (A. L. Petitto, 1985, p. 251)

Challenging tasks promote maximum cognitive growth. The range of tasks that children cannot yet perform independently but *can* perform with the help and guidance of others is, in Vygotsky's terminology, the **zone of proximal development**, or **ZPD** (see Figure 6-7). A child's zone of proximal development includes learning and problem-solving abilities that are just beginning to emerge and develop. You can observe children working within their ZPD in the two "Zone of Proximal Development" videos in MyEducationLab.

Vygotsky proposed that children learn very little from performing tasks they can already do independently. Instead, they develop primarily by attempting tasks they can accomplish only in collaboration with a more competent individual—that is, when they attempt tasks within their zone of proximal development. In a nutshell, it is the challenges in life, not the easy successes, which promote cognitive development.

Whereas challenging tasks are educational, tasks that children cannot do even with considerable structure and assistance are of no benefit whatsoever. (For example, it is probably pointless to ask a typical kindergartner to solve for *x* in an algebraic equation.) A child's ZPD therefore sets a limit on what he or she is cognitively capable of learning.

Naturally, any child's ZPD will change over time. As some tasks are mastered, other, more complex ones appear on the horizon to take their place. Furthermore, as we discovered

MyEducationLab

Observe examples of children working within their zone of proximal development in the two "Zone of Proximal Development" videos. (Find Video Examples in Topic 6 of MyEducationLab.)

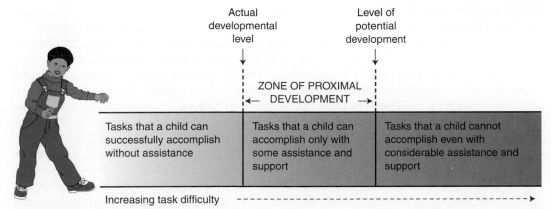

FIGURE 6-7   Entering the zone. Tasks within a child's zone of proximal development are optimal for promoting cognitive advancements.

zone of proximal development (ZPD)
Range of tasks that one cannot yet perform independently but can perform with the help and guidance of others.

IN THE ZONE. A San Bushman father operates within his son's zone of proximal development during a hunting trip. The father demonstrates how to use a bow and arrow and gives the boy a chance to try his hand at various steps of hunting.

earlier, children's ZPDs may vary considerably in "width." Whereas some children may, with assistance, be able to "reach" several years above their actual (independent) developmental level, others may be able to handle tasks that are only slightly more difficult than what they can currently do on their own.

Play allows children to stretch themselves cognitively. Recall the scenario of Jeff and Scott playing "restaurant" presented earlier in the chapter. The two boys take on several adult roles (restaurant manager, server, cook) and practice a variety of adult-like behaviors: assembling the necessary materials for a restaurant, creating menus, keeping track of customers' orders, and tallying final bills. In real life such a scenario would, of course, be impossible. Very few 5-year-old children have the cooking, reading, writing, mathematical, or organizational skills necessary to run a restaurant. Yet the element of make-believe brings these tasks within the boys' reach (e.g., Lillard, 1993). In Vygotsky's words:

> In play a child always behaves beyond his average age, above his daily behavior; in play it is as though he were a head taller than himself. (Vygotsky, 1978, p. 102)

Many contemporary psychologists share Vygotsky's and Piaget's belief that play provides an arena in which youngsters can practice skills they will need in later life. Not only does play promote social skills (e.g., cooperation and conflict resolution strategies), but it also helps children experiment with new combinations of objects, identify cause-and-effect relationships, learn more about other people's perspectives, and direct their behavior according to real-life plans (Chafel, 1991; Gredler & Shields, 2008; Lillard, 1998; Rubin, Fein, & Vandenberg, 1983; Vygotsky, 1966; Zervigon-Hakes, 1984).

To some degree, play probably serves dissimilar purposes for different age-groups. For infants, one primary goal of play activities seems to be to discover what objects are like and can do, as well as what people can do *to* and *with* the objects. Through such discoveries, infants learn many basic properties of the physical world (Gopnik, 2009b; Morris, 1977). Through more social games, including peekaboo, pat-a-cake, and playful exchanges of sounds, infants practice imitation and acquire rudimentary skills in cooperation and turn-taking (Bruner & Sherwood, 1976; Flavell et al., 2002; Powers & Trevarthen, 2009).

When play takes on an element of make-believe sometime around age 2, children begin to substitute one object for another and perform behaviors involving imaginary objects—for instance, "eating" imaginary food with an invented fork (M. Lewis & Carmody, 2008; O'Reilly, 1995; Pederson, Rook-Green, & Elder, 1981). As Vygotsky suggested, pretense probably helps children distinguish between objects and their symbolic representations and respond to internal representations (e.g., to the concept of *fork*) as much as to immediate appearance of external objects (Bodrova & Leong, 1996; W. L. Haight, 1999; Karpov, 2003). When, in the preschool years, children expand their pretend play into elaborate scenarios—sometimes called **sociodramatic play**—they can also practice such roles as "parent," "teacher," or "server," and they learn how to behave in ways that conform to cultural standards and expectations. Furthermore, children engaging in sociodramatic play are apt to gain a greater appreciation of what other people might be thinking and feeling (Göncü, 1993; Lillard, 1998; Sobel, 2009).

As children reach school age, role-playing activities gradually diminish, and other forms of play take their place. For instance, elementary school children often spend time with friends constructing things from cardboard boxes or Legos, playing cards and board games, and engaging in team sports. Many of these activities continue into adolescence. By adhering to rules of games and restrictions on their behavior, youngsters learn to plan

sociodramatic play
Play in which children take on specific roles and act out a scenario of imaginary events.

DEVELOPMENT IN CULTURE
Playing Around

As children enjoy carefree feelings during physical play, companionship during structured games, and shared fantasies during pretend play, they acquire knowledge about their culture (F. P. Hughes, 2010). To some degree, lessons in cultural practices change as children grow and make more of their own choices about what and with whom to play.

To begin with, adults guide the direction of play. Mothers, fathers, and other adults may invite infants to join games of peekaboo, pat-a-cake, and other good-humored exchanges that vary somewhat from one cultural group to another. One psychologist, Heidi Keller, found distinct patterns in the affectionate interactions of mothers and infants from urban German middle-class families and rural Camroonian Nso families (H. Keller, 2003). German mothers tended to spend a considerable amount of time interacting verbally with their infants—talking with them and encouraging their eye contact. German mothers also promoted play with toys and other objects. In comparison, Nso mothers attended to the physical needs of their infants by breastfeeding, soothing, and providing close body contact. The Nso mothers also gently jiggled and tugged at infants' limbs. As infants from both groups were enjoying their social interactions, they were simultaneously obtaining guidance in conducting themselves in their respective societies—developing verbal skills and exploring the properties of objects in the case of the German families and staying physically close to mothers and exercising new motor skills in the case of the Nso families.

After infancy, children integrate familiar cultural routines into play. In societies that encourage children to take on serious chores, children often pretend to be adult laborers (F. P. Hughes, 2010). In Botswana, men herd oxen, and boys regularly play the "cow game." Taking on complementary roles, some boys pretend to be oxen yoked with twine and others acts as drivers who control the oxen (Bock & Johnson, 2004). Girls in Botswana often observe women pounding grain and pretend to pummel grain themselves with reeds, sticks, dirt, and imaginary mortars (Bock & Johnson, 2004). In industrialized cultures that separate children from the daily work of adults, children are apt to bring fantasy figures that they have seen on television and in video games into their play (Farver & Shin, 1997; Haight, Wang, Fung, Williams, & Mintz, 1999; F. P. Hughes, 2010). Not every culture values or encourages pretend play, and in some groups children play creatively with objects and with one another without taking on defined fantasy roles (Farver & Shin, 1997; F. P. Hughes, 2010; Smilansky, 1968).

In middle childhood and after, youngsters often participate in structured games. Children in many societies play competitive games, wherein participants follow prescribed rules and vie to be winner (Bonta, 1997; F. P. Hughes, 2010). The nature of these competitive games varies among cultural groups. In hunting societies, children tend to play games of physical dexterity, including foot races and contests of tracking and spear-throwing, pursuits that allow for practice of valuable motor skills. In nomadic groups, children frequently play games whose outcomes are determined by chance, perhaps preparing them for experiences similar to those of their parents in adjusting to largely uncontrollable environmental conditions. In cultures that are technologically advanced, children play games that require some degree of strategy (e.g., chess, checkers, and computer games with defined objectives and tactics), possibly advancing their facility with complex systems. In societies that do not encourage competitive games, children may play cooperative games, tell one another stories, and copy adult roles (Bonta, 1997; F. P. Hughes, 2010).

Play provides children with a pleasurable forum for practicing roles, responsibilities, and skills. From the perspective of cultural learning, play is a productive medium through which children voluntarily socialize themselves into their community's traditions.

PLAYTIME. These boys enjoy a morning swim at a lake in Sri Lanka. Even as the boys enjoy a lighthearted moment, they are actively acquiring cultural knowledge about social interactions.

ahead, think before they act, cooperate and compromise, solve problems, and engage in self-restraint—skills critical for successful participation in the adult world (Christie & Johnsen, 1983; Hromek & Roffey, 2009; Sutton-Smith, 1979).

Play, then, is hardly a waste of time. Instead, it provides a valuable training ground for the adult world. Perhaps for this reason it is seen in children worldwide. In the Development in Culture feature "Playing Around," you can learn how playing alone and with others helps children gain proficiency in cultural practices.

Current Perspectives Related to Vygotsky's Theory

Vygotsky focused more on the processes through which children develop than on the abilities seen in children of particular ages. He did identify stages of development but portrayed them in only the most general terms (we refer you to Vygotsky, 1997b, pp. 214–216, if you would like to learn more about them). In addition, Vygotsky's descriptions of developmental processes were often imprecise and lacking in detail (Gauvain, 2001; Haenan, 1996; Wertsch, 1984). For these reasons, Vygotsky's theory has been more difficult for researchers to test and either verify or disprove than has Piaget's theory.

Despite such weaknesses, many contemporary theorists and practitioners have found Vygotsky's theory extremely insightful. Although they have taken Vygotsky's notions in many different directions, we can discuss much of their work within the context of several general ideas: social construction of meaning, scaffolding, participation in adult activities, and acquisition of teaching skills.

Social Construction of Meaning

Contemporary psychologists have elaborated on Vygotsky's proposal that adults help children attach meaning to the objects and events around them. They point out that an adult (e.g., a parent or teacher) often helps a child make better sense of the world through joint discussion of a phenomenon or event that the two of them have mutually experienced (Crowley & Jacobs, 2002; Feuerstein, 1990; Kozulin et al., 2010). Such an interaction, sometimes called a **mediated learning experience**, encourages the child to think about the phenomenon or event in particular ways: to attach labels to it, recognize principles that underlie it, draw certain conclusions from it, and so on. In such a conversation, the adult must consider the prior knowledge and perspectives of the child and tailor the discussion accordingly, as Billy's mother does in the chapter-opening case study (Newson & Newson, 1975).

In addition to co-constructing meanings with adults, children often talk among themselves to derive meaning from their experiences. School is one obvious place where children and adolescents can toss around ideas about a particular issue and perhaps reach consensus about how best to interpret and understand the topic in question. As an example of how members of a classroom might work together to construct meaning, let's look in on Ms. Lombard's fourth-grade class, which has been studying fractions. Ms. Lombard has never taught her students how to divide a number by a fraction. Nevertheless, she gives them the following problem, which can be solved by dividing 20 by ¾:

> Mom makes small apple tarts, using three-quarters of an apple for each small tart. She has 20 apples. How many small apple tarts can she make? (J. Hiebert et al., 1997, p. 118)[7]

Ms. Lombard asks the students to work in small groups to figure out how they might solve the problem. One group of four girls—Jeanette, Liz, Kerri, and Nina—has been working on the problem for some time and so far has arrived at such answers as 15, 38, and 23. We join the girls midway through their discussion, when they've already agreed that they can use three-fourths of each apple to make a total of 20 tarts:

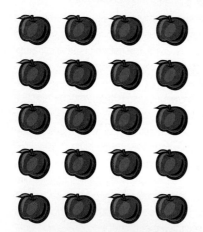

If you can make a single apple tart with ¾ of an apple, how many tarts can you make with 20 apples?

Jeanette:	In each apple there is a quarter left. In each apple there is a quarter left, so you've used, you've made twenty tarts already and you've got a quarter of twenty see—
Liz:	So you've got twenty quarters *left*.
Jeanette:	Yes, . . . and twenty quarters is equal to five apples, . . . so five apples divided by—
Liz:	Six, seven, eight.
Jeanette:	By three-quarters equals three.
Kerri:	But she can't make only three apple tarts!
Jeanette:	No, you've still got twenty.

[7] Excerpts from MAKING SENSE: TEACHING AND LEARNING MATHEMATICS WITH UNDERSTANDING by J. Hiebert et al. Copyright © 1997 by J. Hiebert. Published by Heinemann.

Liz:	But you've got twenty quarters, if you've got twenty quarters you might be right.
Jeanette:	I'll show you.
Liz:	No, I've drawn them all here.
Kerri:	How many quarters have you got? Twenty?
Liz:	Yes, one quarter makes five apples and out of five apples she can make five tarts which will make that twenty-five tarts and then she will have, wait, one, two, three, four, five quarters, she'll have one, two, three, four, five quarters. . . .
Nina:	I've got a better. . .
Kerri:	Yes?
Liz:	Twenty-six quarters and a remainder of one quarter left. (J. Hiebert et al., 1997, p. 121)[8]

The discussion and occasional disagreements continue, and the girls eventually arrive at the correct answer: Mom can make 26 tarts and then will have half an apple left over.

Scaffolding

Theorists have given considerable thought to the kinds of assistance that can help children successfully accomplish challenging tasks and activities. The term **scaffolding** is often used to describe the guidance or structure provided by more competent individuals to help children perform tasks in their ZPD. To understand this concept, think of the scaffolding used in the construction of a new building. The *scaffold* is an external structure that provides support for the workers (e.g., a place where they can stand) until the building itself is strong enough to support them, other people, furniture, and its own materials. As the building gains substance and stability, the scaffold becomes less necessary and is gradually removed.

In much the same way, an adult guiding a child through a new task may initially provide a scaffold to support the child's early efforts. In the following example, notice how a mother helps her 4-year-old daughter Sadie assemble a toy from Duplo blocks (larger versions of Legos) by following a set of instructions:

Mother:	Now you need another one like this on the other side. Mmmmmm . . . there you go, just like that.
Sadie:	Then I need this one to go like this? Hold on, hold on. Let it go. There. Get that out. Oops!
Mother:	I'll hold it while you turn it. *(Watches Sadie work on toy.)* Now you make the end.
Sadie:	This one?
Mother:	No, look at the picture. Right here *(points to plan)*. That piece.
Sadie:	Like this?
Mother:	Yeah. (Gauvain, 2001, p. 32)[8]

Scaffolding can take a variety of forms. Here are just a few of the many possibilities:

- Demonstrate the proper performance of the task in a way that children can easily imitate.
- Divide a complex task into several smaller, simpler tasks.
- Provide a structure or set of guidelines for how the task should be accomplished.
- Provide a calculator, computer software (word processing program, spreadsheet, etc.), or other technology that makes some aspects of the task easier.
- Ask questions that get children thinking in appropriate ways about the task.
- Keep children's attention focused on the relevant aspects of the task.
- Give frequent feedback about how children are progressing. (Bodrova & Leong, 2009; A. Collins, 2006; Gallimore & Tharp, 1990; Pentimonti & Justice, 2010; Rogoff, 1990; Torres-Guzmán, 2011; D. Wood, Bruner, & Ross, 1976)

scaffolding
Support mechanism, provided by a more competent individual, that helps a child successfully perform a task within his or her zone of proximal development.

[8] Excerpt from THE SOCIAL CONTEXT OF COGNITIVE DEVELOPMENT by Mary Gauvain. Copyright © 2001 by Mary Gauvain. Reprinted with permission of Guilford Publications, Inc.

MyEducationLab

In the "Scaffolding" video, observe examples of how adults scaffold young children's efforts at assembling puzzles. (Find Video Examples in Topic 6 of MyEducationLab.)

Depending on their particular knowledge and ability levels, different children at any single age or grade level may need different kinds of scaffolding to support their success (Lodewyk & Winne, 2005; Puntambekar & Hübscher, 2005; Rittle-Johnson & Koedinger, 2005). As children become more adept at performing a new task, their scaffolding is gradually phased out so that they eventually accomplish it entirely on their own.

Learning to offer just the right level of support to individual children takes considerable sensitivity and experience. In a Building Teaching Skills and Dispositions exercise in MyEducationLab, you can gain practice in applying the concepts *cognitive tool*, *zone of proximal development*, and *scaffolding* in elementary and high school lessons. You can also observe examples of adults scaffolding young children's efforts at assembling puzzles in the "Scaffolding" video in MyEducationLab.

Participation in Adult Activities

Virtually all cultures allow—and in fact usually require—children to be involved in adult activities to some degree. Children's early experiences are often at the fringe of an activity. As children acquire greater competence, they gradually take a more central role in the activity until, eventually, they are full-fledged participants (S. Gaskins, 1999; Lave & Wenger, 1991; Rogoff et al., 2007).

TO THE BEAT. Many communities in Rwanda have elevated traditional drum rhythms to a complex art form. Notice how the two boys at the end are closely observing the adults as the group performs for visitors.

In most cases children's early involvement in adult activities is scaffolded and supervised through what is sometimes known as **guided participation** (Rogoff, 2003). When our own children were preschoolers, we authors often had them help us bake cookies by asking them to measure, pour, and mix ingredients, but we stood close by and offered suggestions about how to get the measurements right, minimize spilling, and so on. Similarly, when taking our children to the office with us, we had them press the appropriate buttons in the elevator, check our mailboxes, open envelopes, or deliver documents to the department secretary, but we kept a close eye on what they were doing and provided guidance as necessary. In later years we gave them increasing responsibility and independence. By the time they were in high school, they were baking their own pastries, and they sometimes ran errands for us as we worked on our books and articles.

Parents are not the only ones who engage children in adult activities. Schools sometimes invite students to be members of faculty decision-making committees, and parent-teacher organizations ask students to help with school fund-raising efforts. Girl Scout troops introduce girls to salesmanship, accounting, and other adult business practices during annual cookie drives (Rogoff, 1995, 2003). Many local newspapers take on high school students as cub reporters, movie reviewers, and editorial writers, especially during the summer months.

In some instances adults work with children and adolescents in formal or informal **apprenticeships**, one-on-one relationships in which adults teach young people new skills, guide their initial efforts, and present increasingly difficult tasks as proficiency improves and the ZPD changes. Many cultures use apprenticeships as a way of gradually introducing children to particular skills and trades in the adult community—perhaps weaving, tailoring, or playing a musical instrument (D. J. Elliott, 1995; Lave & Wenger, 1991; Rogoff, 1990; Tehrani & Riede, 2008).

In apprenticeships, children learn not only the behaviors but also the language of a skill or trade (Lave & Wenger, 1991). When master weavers teach apprentices their art, they might use such terms as *warp, weft, shuttle,* and *harness* to focus attention on a particular aspect of the process. Similarly, when teachers guide students through scientific experiments, they use words like *hypothesis, evidence*, and *theory* to help the students evaluate their procedures and results (Perkins, 1992). Furthermore, an apprenticeship can

guided participation
Active engagement in adult activities, initially with considerable direction from an adult or other more advanced individual and subsequently with opportunities for increasing responsibility and independence.

apprenticeship
Mentorship in which a novice works intensively with an expert to learn how to accomplish complex tasks in a particular domain.

show children how adults typically think about a task or activity—a situation known as a **cognitive apprenticeship**. For instance, an adult and child might work together to accomplish a challenging task (perhaps sewing a patchwork quilt, solving a mathematical brainteaser, or collecting data samples in biology fieldwork). In the process of talking about various aspects of the task, the adult and child together analyze the situation and develop the best approach to take, and the adult models effective ways of thinking about and mentally processing the situation (Bodrow & Magalashvili, 2009; A. Collins, 2006; Shreyar, Zolkower, & Pérez, 2010).

From a Vygotskian perspective, gradual entry into adult activities increases the probability that children will engage in behaviors and thinking skills within their ZPD. It also helps children tie newly acquired skills and thinking abilities to the specific contexts in which they are apt to be useful later on (Carraher, Carraher, & Schliemann, 1985; A. Collins, 2006; P. Light & Butterworth, 1993).

Acquisition of Teaching Skills

When learning new techniques from more experienced members of their community, children observe the teaching process and subsequently have occasions to teach other children basic skills (Gauvain, 2001). For instance, children in the Gambia help peers or siblings learn new clapping games by giving verbal directions and also moving the other children's hands into the appropriate position (Koops, 2010).

With age and experience, children become increasingly adept at teaching others what they have learned. In a study in rural Mexico (Maynard, 2002), Mayan children were observed as they worked with younger siblings in such everyday activities as preparing food and washing clothes. The children's earliest form of "instruction" (perhaps around age 4 or 5) was simply to let a younger brother or sister join in and help. At age 6 or 7, children tended to be directive and controlling, giving commands and taking over if something wasn't done correctly. By the time they were 8, however, they were proficient teachers, using a combination of demonstrations, explanations, physical guidance, and feedback to scaffold their siblings' efforts.

For an example of how skillfully children can teach one another, consider the game of Monopoly. Four 8-year-old girls are playing the game while a researcher videotapes their interactions (Guberman, Rahm, & Menk, 1998). One girl, Carla, has limited math skills and little experience playing the game. On her first turn, she lands on Connecticut Avenue:

Nancy:	Do you want to buy it?
Carla:	Hmmmm . . . [There is a long pause and some unrelated discussion among the players.] How much is it again? Twelve hundred. . . .
Nancy:	A hundred and twenty dollars.
Carla:	A hundred and twenty [She starts to count her money] . . . a hundred [She is referring to a $10 bill]. . . .
Sarah:	You give her one of these and one of these. [She holds up first a $100 bill and then a $20 bill of her own money.] (Guberman et al., 1998, p. 436; format adapted)

Notice how Nancy and Sarah scaffold Carla's initial purchase. Nancy asks her to consider buying the property and tells her the purchase price. When it is clear that Carla is having trouble counting out $120 (she thinks that a $10 bill is worth $100), Sarah gives her sufficient guidance that she can identify the needed bills by color alone. Later in the game, as Carla becomes more competent, the other girls reduce their support. At one point Carla lands on Virginia Avenue, with a purchase price of $160:

Carla hesitates making the payment, looking through her money. Eventually, she takes a $100 bill from her money and appears unsure how to continue.

Nancy: Just a fifty and a ten.

Carla gives a $50 bill and a $10 bill to the banker. (Guberman et al., 1998, p. 437; format adapted)

cognitive apprenticeship Mentorship in which an expert and a novice work together on a challenging task and the expert suggests ways to think about the task.

When children help others, the "teachers" often benefit as much as the "students" (D. Fuchs, Fuchs, Mathes, & Simmons, 1997; Karcher, 2009; Webb & Palincsar, 1996). For instance, when youngsters study something with the expectation that they will be teaching it to someone else, they are more motivated to learn it, find it more interesting, and learn it more effectively (Benware & Deci, 1984; Choo, 2009; Semb, Ellis, & Araujo, 1993).

Applying the Ideas of Vygotsky and His Followers

Vygotsky's work and the recent theoretical advances it has inspired have numerous implications for teaching and working with children and adolescents. Educators taking a Vygotskian perspective strategically direct children to take on increasing levels of responsibility for cultural tasks.

• **Help children acquire the basic cognitive tools necessary for succeeding in academic disciplines.** Mastering concepts that undergird a cultural activity helps children to engage more successfully in the activity. Children can become better musicians when they can read music and understand what *keys, chords,* and *thirds* are. In the disciplines of science, mathematics, and social studies, our culture passes along other key concepts (e.g., *molecule, negative number, democracy*), symbols (e.g., H_2O, π, x^3), and visual representations (e.g., graphs, maps) that help growing children organize and interpret the physical and social worlds in which they live.

• **Use group learning activities to help children internalize cognitive strategies.** Contemporary researchers have found that, as Vygotsky suggested, children often do internalize—and so eventually use independently—the complex thinking processes they first use in social interaction (e.g., Andriessen, 2006; Murphy, 2007). We find an example in **reciprocal teaching**, an approach to reading instruction that has had great success in enhancing children's reading comprehension skills (Alfassi, Weiss, & Lifshitz, 2009; A. L. Brown & Palincsar, 1987; Palincsar & Brown, 1984; Pilonieta & Medina, 2009). This approach is designed to foster four effective reading strategies:

- *Summarizing*—Identifying the main ideas of a reading passage
- *Questioning*—Asking oneself questions to check comprehension of ideas
- *Clarifying*—Taking steps to better understand a confusing point
- *Predicting*—Anticipating what points an author is apt to make in later sentences or paragraphs

In this approach, a teacher and several students meet in a group to read a piece of text, occasionally stopping to discuss and process the text aloud. Initially, the teacher leads the discussion, asking questions about the text to promote summarizing, questioning, clarifying, and predicting. He or she gradually turns this "teaching" role over to a few students, who for a short time take charge of the discussion and ask one another the same kinds of questions that their teacher has modeled. Eventually, the students can read and discuss a text almost independently of the teacher, working together to make sense of it and checking one another for comprehension and possible misunderstandings.

As an illustration, consider the following reciprocal teaching session for a group of six first graders reading a passage about snowshoe rabbits. In this particular case the teacher reads the text in small segments (at higher grade levels, the children themselves take turns reading). After each segment, the teacher pauses while the children discuss and make sense of the segment. As you read the dialogue, look for examples of summarizing, questioning, clarifying, and predicting (there is at least one instance of each).

> The children were reading about the snowshoe rabbit, and it was the 16th day of dialogue. The teacher had just read a segment of text describing the season in which baby rabbits are born and the ways in which the mother rabbit cares for her babies. A student named Kam is the dialogue leader.

> Kam: When was the babies born?
> Teacher: That's a good question to ask. Call on someone to answer that question.
> Kam: Robby? Milly?

reciprocal teaching
Approach to teaching reading comprehension in which students take turns asking teacher-like questions of their classmates.

Milly: Summer.

Teacher: What would happen if the babies were born in the winter? Let's think.

Several children make a number of responses, including: "The baby would be very cold." "They would need food." "They don't have no fur when they are just born."

Kam: I have another question. How does she get the babies safe?

Kris: She hides them.

Kam: That's right but something else. . . .

Teacher: There is something very unusual about how she hides them that surprised me. I didn't know this.

Travis: They are all in a different place.

Teacher: Why do you think she does this?

Milly: Probably because I heard another story, and when they're babies they usually eat each other or fight with each other.

Teacher: That could be! And what about when that lynx comes?

Several children comment that that would be the end of all the babies.

Travis: If I was the mother, I would hide mine, I would keep them all together.

Kris: If the babies are hidden and the mom wants to go and look at them, how can she remember where they are?

Teacher: Good question. Because she does have to find them again. Why? What does she bring them?

Milly: She needs to bring food. She probably leaves a twig or something.

Teacher: Do you think she puts out a twig like we mark a trail?

Several children disagree and suggest that she uses her sense of smell. One child, recalling that the snowshoe rabbit is not all white in the winter, suggests that the mother might be able to tell her babies apart by their coloring.

Teacher: So we agree that the mother rabbit uses her senses to find her babies after she hides them. Kam, can you summarize for us now?

Kam: The babies are born in the summer. . . .

Teacher: The mother. . . .

Kam: The mother hides the babies in different places.

Teacher: And she visits them. . . .

Kam: To bring them food.

Travis: She keeps them safe.

Teacher: Any predictions?

Milly: What she teaches her babies . . . like how to hop.

Kris: They know how to hop already.

Teacher: Well, let's read and see.[9] (dialogue courtesy of A. S. Palincsar)

Notice how the teacher scaffolds the children's teaching strategies, in part by giving hints ("Kam, can you summarize for us now?") and in part by modeling effective questions ("What would happen if the babies were born in the winter?"). Notice, too, how the children support one another in their meaning-making efforts (Kris: "She hides them." Kam: "That's right but something else. . . .").

Reciprocal teaching has been used successfully with a wide variety of students, ranging from first graders to college students, to teach effective reading and listening comprehension skills. In many cases students become far more effective readers and apply their new reading strategies when studying a wide variety of subject areas (Alfassi et al., 2009; A. L. Brown & Palincsar, 1987; Palincsar & Brown, 1984, 1989; Rosenshine & Meister, 1994; Stricklin, 2011).

• **Present challenging tasks, and provide sufficient scaffolding to enable children to accomplish them successfully.** To promote cognitive development, teachers and other adults must present some assignments that a child can perform successfully only with assistance— that is, tasks within the child's ZPD. Children at any single age level are likely to have

ARTIFACT 6-3 I can count! In this simple worksheet a preschool teacher scaffolds 4-year-old Hannah's efforts to write numerals.

different zones of proximal development and so may need different tasks. In other words, instruction is most effective when it is individually tailored to children's unique strengths and limitations (Bodrova & Leong, 2009; Horowitz, Darling-Hammond, & Bransford, 2005).

Children need some degree of support in tackling challenges, of course. The Development and Practice feature "Scaffolding Children's Efforts at Challenging Tasks" presents several additional examples. One of the strategies listed in this feature—*teach children how to talk themselves through a complex new procedure*—makes use of Vygotsky's concept of *self-talk* to enable children to create their *own* scaffolding. Teaching children how to give themselves instructions and thereby guide themselves through a new task might proceed through five steps (Meichenbaum, 1977, 1985):

1. *Cognitive modeling.* An adult model performs the desired task while verbalizing instructions that guide performance.
2. *Overt, external guidance.* The child performs the task while listening to the adult verbalize the instructions.
3. *Overt self-guidance.* The child repeats the instructions aloud (*self-talk*) while performing the task.
4. *Faded, overt self-guidance.* The child whispers the instructions while performing the task.
5. *Covert self-instruction.* The child silently thinks about the instructions (*inner speech*) while performing the task.

In this sequence of steps, depicted in Figure 6-8, the adult initially serves as a model both for the behavior itself and for the process of self-guidance. Responsibility for performing the task is soon turned over to the child. Eventually, responsibility for guiding the performance is turned over as well.

TASK PERFORMANCE	TASK INSTRUCTIONS
Step 1 The adult performs the task, modeling it for the child.	The adult verbalizes instructions.
Step 2 The child performs the task.	The adult verbalizes instructions.
Step 3 The child performs the task.	The child repeats the instructions aloud.
Step 4 The child performs the task.	The child whispers the instructions.
Step 5 The child performs the task.	The child thinks silently about the instructions.

FIGURE 6-8 Self-talk. In a five-step process, a child shifts from adult help to independent self-regulation.

• **Assess children's abilities under a variety of work conditions.** To foster children's cognitive development, educators need to determine under what conditions the children are most likely to accomplish various tasks successfully. For instance, can children accomplish a task entirely on their own? If not, can they do it in collaboration with one or two peers? Can they do it if they have some adult guidance and support? By addressing such questions, teachers can get a better sense of the tasks that are in each child's ZPD (Bodrova & Leong, 2009; Calfee & Masuda, 1997; Haywood & Lidz, 2007; Horowitz et al., 2005).

• **Provide opportunities to engage in authentic activities.** As we've already seen, children's participation in adult activities plays a critical role in their cognitive development. However, children spend much of their day at school, which is far removed from the working world of adults. A reasonable alternative is **authentic activities**—classroom tasks and projects that closely resemble typical adult activities. Following are examples:

- Writing an editorial
- Participating in a debate
- Designing an electrical circuit
- Conducting an experiment
- Creating and distributing a class newsletter
- Organizing a volunteer campaign to address a community need
- Performing in a concert
- Planning a personal budget
- Conversing in a foreign language
- Creating a museum display
- Developing a home page for the Internet
- Filming and editing a video production

authentic activity
Instructional activity similar to one that a child might eventually encounter in the outside world.

By placing classroom activities in real-world contexts, teachers can enhance a variety of skills in students, including their mastery of classroom subject matter and ability to work effectively in groups (Bereiter & Scardamalia, 2006; A. Collins, Brown, & Newman, 1989; Kirshner, 2008). For instance, students may show greater improvement in writing skills when they practice writing stories, essays, and letters to real people, rather than completing short, artificial

DEVELOPMENT AND PRACTICE
Scaffolding Children's Efforts at Challenging Tasks

Ask questions that get children thinking in suitable ways about a task.

- A middle school teacher asks her students a series of questions as they prepare to deliver a persuasive speech to members of a community organization: *What are the main points you want to make? Who will make them? What kind of objections and counterarguments can you anticipate? How will you respond to them?* (Early Adolescence)

- As students in a high school science class begin to plan their experiments for an upcoming science fair, their teacher encourages them to separate and control variables with the following questions: *What do I think causes the phenomenon I am studying? What other possible variables might cause or influence it? How can I be sure that these variables are not influencing the results I obtain?* (Late Adolescence)

When learners are unfamiliar with a task, provide explicit guidance and give frequent feedback.

- A preschool teacher watches the attempts of children to write their names. With a girl who writes the letters of her name backward, the teacher puts a green dot under the first letter of her name and tells her to start with that letter. With a boy who forgets a few letters, the teacher writes the missing letters and highlights them with a color pen and encourages the boy to include these special letters next time. With another boy who has trouble writing a letter that is difficult to write (perhaps "S" or "W"), the teacher writes that letter for him and encourages him to add the other letters himself. (Early Childhood)

- When an outdoor educator takes 12-year-olds on their first camping trip, he has the children work in pairs to pitch their tents. Although he has previously shown the children how to put up a tent, this is the first time they've actually done it themselves, and so he provides written instructions that they can follow. In addition, he circulates from campsite to campsite to check on each group's progress and provide assistance as necessary. (Early Adolescence)

Provide a calculator, computer software, worksheet, or other material that makes some aspects of the task easier.

- Children in a third-grade class have mastered basic addition, subtraction, and multiplication facts. They are now applying their knowledge of arithmetic to determine how much money they would need to purchase a number of recreational items from a mail-order catalog. Because the list of items is fairly lengthy and includes varying quantities of each item, their teacher gives them calculators to do the necessary multiplication and addition. (Middle Childhood)

- A high school history teacher distributes a worksheet with a partially completed table of cultural accomplishments during ancient African and Middle Eastern history. A few cells contain summaries and serve as models for notes students can take as they read their textbook and fill in the missing cells. (Late Adolescence)

Teach children how to talk themselves through a complex procedure.

- A school psychologist teaches children with cognitive disabilities to classify shapes by asking themselves questions (e.g., Does the object have three or more sides? Is it round? How large is the shape?). The children begin to ask themselves these questions and learn to classify shapes more accurately. (Middle Childhood)

- A physical education teacher shows beginning tennis players how to use self-instructions to remember correct form when swinging the racket:
  1. Say *ball* to remind yourself to look at the ball.
  2. Say *bounce* to remind yourself to follow the ball with your eyes as it approaches you.
  3. Say *hit* to remind yourself to focus on contacting the ball with the racket.
  4. Say *ready* to get yourself into position for the next ball to come your way. (Early Adolescence)

Divide a complex assignment into several smaller, simpler tasks, and perhaps ask children to tackle it in small groups.

- A fourth-grade teacher has his students create a school newspaper that includes news articles, a schedule of upcoming events, a couple of political cartoons, and classified advertisements. Several students work together to create each feature, with different students assuming distinct roles (e.g., fact finder, writer, editor) and occasionally switching the parts they play. (Middle Childhood)

- A high school film analysis teacher helps students to dissect movies by breaking up their assignments into manageable parts. After the class watches *Citizen Kane*, the teacher gives pieces of poster paper to four groups of students and encourages members in each group to answer particular questions. One group pieces together flashbacks of the life of Charles Foster Kane, another reads the screenplay of the movie, a third group examines the movie's filmmaking innovations, and a fourth group looks into the original reception the movie received. (Late Adolescence)

Gradually withdraw guidance as children become more proficient.

- A preschool teacher has 2- and 3-year-olds take turns distributing the crackers, fruit, and napkins at snack time, and she asks all of them to bring their dishes and trash to the kitchen after they have finished eating. Initially, she must show the children how to carry the food so that it doesn't spill. She must also remind servers to make sure that every child gets a snack. As the year progresses, reminders are usually not necessary, although she must occasionally say, "I think two of you have forgotten to bring your cups to the kitchen. I'm missing the one with Big Bird on it and the one with Cookie Monster." (Early Childhood)

- In a group of high school volunteers concerned about economic poverty, an adult facilitates the young people's discussion and eventually encourages them to develop solutions that can be tried in their community. As the adolescents move closer to generating possible tactics, the adult grows silent and allows students to formulate an action plan. (Late Adolescence)

Sources: Bodrova & Leong, 2009 (kindergarten writing example); Gallimore & Tharp, 1990; Good et al., 1992; Kirshner, 2008 (persuasive speech example); Lajoie & Derry, 1993; Lou et al., 1996; Meichenbaum, 1985; Rogoff, 1990; Rosenshine & Meister, 1992; Stevens & Slavin, 1995; D. Wood et al., 1976; Ziegler, 1987 (tennis example).

writing exercises (E. H. Hiebert & Fisher, 1992). Likewise, they may gain a more complete understanding of how to use and interpret maps when they construct their own maps than when they engage in workbook exercises involving map interpretation (Gregg & Leinhardt, 1994a).

• **Give children the chance to play.** Many developmental theorists advocate for the inclusion of play in children's daily schedules, especially in the preschool and early elementary years (P. M. Cooper, 2009; Elkind, 2007; Hirsh-Pasek, Golinkoff, Berk, & Singer, 2009; Van Hoorn, Nourot, Scales, & Alward, 1999). Following are several suggestions for promoting the play of children in preschool and kindergarten:

- Partition the classroom into small areas (e.g., a corner for blocks, a "housekeeping" area, an art table) that give children numerous options.
- Provide realistic toys (e.g., dolls, dress-up clothes, plastic dishes) that suggest certain activities and functions, as well as more versatile objects (e.g., Legos, wooden blocks, cardboard boxes) that allow children to engage in fantasy and imagination.
- Encourage children to set goals in their play, for example, pretending to run a shop together, and help them solve conflicts before they escalate ("It sounds as if you both want to be the cashier. Your shop needs a cashier *and* a stocker. Could you trade off in these jobs?").
- Provide enough toys and equipment to minimize potential conflicts, but keep them limited enough in number that children must share and cooperate (Bodrova & Leong, 2009; Bredekamp, 2011; Frost, Shin, & Jacobs, 1998).

By observing children during play, teachers also can gain insights into the abilities and skills that individual children have acquired. Examples of things to look for are presented in the Observation Guidelines table "Observing the Cognitive Aspects of Young Children's Play."

OBSERVATION GUIDELINES
Observing the Cognitive Aspects of Young Children's Play

CHARACTERISTIC	LOOK FOR	EXAMPLE	IMPLICATION
Exploratory Play with Objects	• *Interest in exploring objects* in the environment • *Ability to manipulate objects* • *Use of multiple senses* in exploratory play	When Tyler sees a new toy guitar among the toys in the playroom, he picks it up, inspects it on all sides, and begins to turn the crank (although not enough to elicit any musical notes). After Tyler leaves it to play with something else, Sarah picks up the guitar, sniffs it, puts the crank in her mouth, and begins to suck and chew on it.	Provide a wide variety of toys and other objects for infants and toddlers to explore, making sure that all are safe, clean, and nontoxic. Recognize that children may use these things in creative ways (and not necessarily in the ways their manufacturers intended) and will move frequently from one object to another.
Group Play	• *Extent to which children play* with one another • *Extent to which children in a group cooperate* in their play activities	LaMarr and Matthew are playing with trucks in the sandbox, but each boy seems to be in his own little world.	Give children opportunities to play together, and provide toys that require a cooperative effort.
Use of Symbolic Thought and Imagination	• *Extent to which children use an object* to stand for another • *Extent to which children incorporate imaginary objects* into their play	Julia tells her friend she is going to the grocery store, then opens an imaginary car door, sits on a chair inside her "car," steers an imaginary steering wheel, and says, "Beep, beep" as she blows an imaginary horn.	When equipping a play area, include objects (e.g., wooden blocks, cardboard boxes) that children can use for a variety of purposes.
Role Taking	• *Extent to which children use language* (e.g., tone of voice, specific words and phrases) *and behaviors* (e.g., mannerisms, characteristic actions of a person with a specific job) that reflect a particular person or role • *Extent to which children coordinate and act out multiple roles* within the context of a complex play scenario	Mark and Alisa are playing doctor. Alisa brings her teddy bear to Mark's "office" and politely says, "Good morning, Doctor. My baby has a sore throat." Mark holds a Popsicle stick against the bear's mouth and instructs the "baby" to say "Aaahhh."	Provide toys and equipment associated with particular roles (e.g., toy medical kit, cooking utensils, play money).

COMPARING PIAGETIAN AND VYGOTSKIAN PERSPECTIVES

Together, Piaget's and Vygotsky's theories and the research they've inspired give us a more complete picture of cognitive development than either theory provides alone. The Developmental Trends table "Thinking and Reasoning Skills at Different Age Levels" draws on elements of both perspectives to describe characteristics of children and adolescents in different age ranges.

Common Themes

If we look beyond the very different vocabulary Piaget and Vygotsky used to describe the phenomena they observed, we notice four themes that their theories share: constructive processes, readiness, challenge, and the importance of social interaction.

Constructive Processes in Learning

Neither Piaget's nor Vygotsky's theory depicts cognitive development as a process of simply "absorbing" one's experiences. Rather, both frameworks portray the acquisition of new knowledge and skills as a very constructive process. In Piaget's view, children increasingly organize their thoughts as schemes and, later, as operations that apply to a wide variety of circumstances. In Vygotsky's view, children gradually internalize—in their own idiosyncratic ways—the interpretations and cognitive tools they first encounter and use in social contexts.

Thus, these two perspectives on constructivism are complementary. Piaget's theory focuses largely on how children construct knowledge *on their own;* his perspective is sometimes labeled **individual constructivism**. In contrast, the ideas of Vygotsky and his followers focus more on how children construct meanings in collaboration with adults and peers; thus they are sometimes collectively called **social constructivism**. Without doubt, children acquire increasingly sophisticated thinking processes through *both* their own individual efforts and joint meaning-making efforts with others.

Readiness

Both Piaget and Vygotsky suggested that at any point in time a child is cognitively ready for some experiences but not for others. Both theorists acknowledged that brain maturation places some limits on what children can do at various points in development. In addition, however, Piaget proposed that children accommodate to new objects and events only when they can also assimilate the information into existing schemes, and they can think logically about new problems only if they have constructed the relevant logical operations. Vygotsky, meanwhile, portrayed children's readiness for tasks as comprising an ever-changing zone of proximal development. As children master some skills and abilities, other, slightly more advanced ones emerge in immature forms that are ready for adult nurturance and support.

For Piaget and Vygotsky, all children are ready to learn *something*. For Piaget, children are continually ready to learn based on their boundless curiosity about the world. For Vygotsky, children are ready to learn concepts and skills that are used by people in their culture, and especially those abilities that children can accomplish with a smidgen of help.

Challenge

We see the importance of challenge most clearly in Vygotsky's concept of the zone of proximal development: Children benefit most from tasks that they can perform only with the assistance of more competent individuals. Yet challenge, albeit of a somewhat different sort, also lies at the heart of Piaget's theory: Children develop more sophisticated knowledge and thought processes only when they encounter phenomena they cannot adequately understand using their existing schemes—in other words, phenomena that create disequilibrium.

ARTIFACT 6-4   Under the sea. The idea that children construct rather than absorb knowledge has stood the test of time. This drawing reflects 6-year-old Laura's self-constructed conception of underwater ocean life. The air bubbles rising up from the fish and sea horse reveal her belief that sea creatures exhale in a manner similar to people.

individual constructivism
Theoretical perspective that focuses on how people independently construct meaning from their experiences.

social constructivism
Theoretical perspective that focuses on people's collective efforts to impose meaning on the world.

DEVELOPMENTAL TRENDS
Thinking and Reasoning Skills at Different Age Levels

AGE	WHAT YOU MIGHT OBSERVE	DIVERSITY	IMPLICATIONS
Infancy (Birth–2 Years) 	• Exploratory actions in the environment becoming increasingly complex, flexible, and intentional over time • Growing awareness of simple cause-and-effect relationships • Emergence of ability to represent the world mentally (e.g., as revealed in daily conversations and make-believe play)	• Temperamental differences (e.g., the extent to which infants are adventuresome vs. more timid and anxious) influence exploratory behavior. • Infants and toddlers who are emotionally attached to their caregivers are more willing to venture out and explore their environment. • In some cultures adults encourage infants to focus more on people than on the physical environment. When people rather than objects are the priority, children may be less inclined to touch and explore their physical surroundings.	• Set up a safe, age-appropriate environment for exploration. • Provide objects that stimulate different senses—for instance, things that babies can look at, listen to, feel, and smell. • Suggest age-appropriate toys and activities that parents can provide at home.
Early Childhood (2–6 Years) 	• Rapidly developing language skills • Reasoning that is, by adult standards, often illogical • Limited perspective-taking ability • Frequent self-talk • Sociodramatic play • Limited understanding of how adults typically interpret events	• Shyness may limit children's willingness to talk with others and engage in cooperative sociodramatic play. • Adult-like logic is more common when children have accurate information about the world (e.g., about cause-and-effect relationships). • Children learn to interpret events in culture-specific ways.	• Provide numerous opportunities for children to interact with one another during play and other cooperative activities. • Introduce children to a variety of real-world situations through picture books and field trips. • Talk with children about their experiences and possible interpretations.
Middle Childhood (6–10 Years) 	• Conservation, class inclusion, and other forms of adult-like logic • Limited ability to reason about abstract or hypothetical ideas • Emergence of group games and team sports that involve coordinating multiple perspectives • Ability to participate to some degree in many adult activities	• Development of logical thinking skills is affected by the importance of those skills in a child's culture. • Formal operational reasoning may occasionally appear for simple tasks and in familiar contexts, especially in 9- and 10-year-olds. • Regular involvement in adult activities is more common in some cultures than in others.	• Use concrete manipulatives and experiences to illustrate concepts and ideas. • Supplement verbal explanations with concrete examples, pictures, and hands-on activities. • Allow time for organized play activities. • Introduce children to various adult professions, and provide opportunities to practice authentic adult tasks.
Early Adolescence (10–14 Years) 	• Increasing ability to reason about abstract ideas • Emerging scientific reasoning abilities (e.g., formulating and testing hypotheses, separating and controlling variables) • Increasing ability to reason about mathematical proportions • Some idealism about political and social issues, but often without taking real-world constraints into consideration • Increasing ability to engage in adult tasks	• Adolescents can think more abstractly when they have considerable knowledge about a topic. • Adolescents are more likely to separate and control variables for situations with which they are familiar. • Development of formal operational reasoning skills is affected by the importance of those skills in one's culture. • Adolescents' idealistic notions may reflect their religious, cultural, or socioeconomic backgrounds.	• Present abstract concepts central to various academic disciplines, but tie them to concrete examples. • Have students engage in scientific investigations, focusing on familiar objects and phenomena. • Assign math problems that require use of simple fractions, ratios, or decimals. • While demonstrating how to do a new task, also talk about how to effectively *think* about the task.
Late Adolescence (14–18 Years) 	• Abstract thought and scientific reasoning skills becoming more prevalent, especially for topics about which adolescents have considerable knowledge • Idealistic notions tempered by more realistic considerations • Ability to perform many tasks in an adult-like manner	• Abstract thinking tends to be more common in some content areas (e.g., mathematics, science) than in others (e.g., history, geography). • Formal operational reasoning skills are less likely to appear in cultures that don't require those skills. • Teenagers' proficiency in particular adult tasks varies considerably from individual to individual and from task to task.	• Study particular academic disciplines in depth; introduce complex and abstract explanations and theories. • Encourage discussions about social, political, and ethical issues; elicit multiple perspectives regarding these issues. • Involve adolescents in activities that are similar or identical to the things they will eventually do as adults. • Explain how experts in a field think about the tasks they perform.

Importance of Social Interaction

In Piaget's eyes, the people in a child's life can present information and arguments that create disequilibrium and, as a result, can foster greater perspective taking or more logical thinking processes. For instance, when young children disagree with one another, they begin to realize that different people may have discrepant yet equally valid viewpoints, and they gradually shed the egocentrism that characterizes preoperational thought.

In Vygotsky's view, social interactions provide the very foundation for thought processes. Children internalize the processes they use when they converse with others until ultimately, they can use these processes independently. Furthermore, tasks within the ZPD can, by definition, be accomplished only when others assist in children's efforts.

Theoretical and Educational Differences

Despite sharing several ideas about children's learning, Piaget and Vygotsky held opposing views on other significant matters. First we highlight their key theoretical differences and then consider distinctions in educational implications.

Theoretical Differences

Following are four questions that capture key distinctions between Piaget's and Vygotsky's theories of cognitive development.

To what extent is language essential for cognitive development? According to Piaget, language provides verbal labels for many of the concepts and other schemes that children have already developed. It is also the primary means through which children interact with others and begin to incorporate multiple perspectives into their thinking. Yet in Piaget's view, much of cognitive development occurs independently of language.

For Vygotsky, however, language is absolutely critical for cognitive development. Children's thought processes are internalized versions of social interactions that are largely verbal in nature. Through two language-based phenomena—self-talk and inner speech—children begin to guide their own behaviors in ways that others have previously guided them. Furthermore, in their conversations with adults, children learn the meanings that their culture imposes on particular events and gradually interpret the world in these culture-specific ways.

The truth of the matter probably lies somewhere between Piaget's and Vygotsky's perspectives. Piaget clearly underestimated the importance of language: Children acquire more complex understandings of phenomena not only through their own interactions with the world but also (as Vygotsky suggested) by learning how others interpret these occurrences. On the other hand, Vygotsky may have overstated the case for language. Some concepts clearly emerge *before* children have verbal labels to attach to them (Gopnik, 2009b; Halford & Andrews, 2006; L. M. Oakes & Rakison, 2003). Furthermore, verbal exchanges may be less important for cognitive development in some cultures than in others. For instance, adults in some rural communities in Guatemala and India place heavy emphasis on gestures and demonstrations, rather than on verbal instructions, to teach and guide children (Rogoff, Mistry, Göncü, & Mosier, 1993).

What kinds of experiences promote development? Piaget maintained that children's independent, self-motivated explorations of the physical world form the basis for many developing schemes, and children often create these schemes with little guidance from others. In contrast, Vygotsky argued for activities that are facilitated and interpreted by more competent individuals. The distinction, then, is one of primarily self-exploration versus guided exploration and instruction. Children almost certainly need both kinds of experiences: opportunities to manipulate and experiment with physical phenomena on their own and opportunities to draw on the wisdom of prior generations (Brainerd, 2003; Karpov & Haywood, 1998).

What kinds of social interactions are most valuable? Both theorists saw value in interacting with people of all ages. However, Piaget emphasized the benefits of interactions with peers (who could create conflict and disequilibrium), whereas Vygotsky placed greater importance on interactions with adults and other more advanced individuals (who could support children in challenging tasks and help them make appropriate interpretations).

Some contemporary theorists have proposed that interactions with peers and adults play different roles in children's cognitive development (Damon, 1984; Hartup, 2009; Rogoff, 1991; Webb & Palincsar, 1996). When children's development requires that they abandon old perspectives in favor of new, more complex ones (e.g., regarding their understanding of the purposes of friendship in a person's life), the sociocognitive conflict that often occurs among age-mates (and the multiple perspectives that emerge from it) may be optimal for bringing about such change. But when children's development instead requires that they learn new skills (e.g., on how to operate a microscope), the thoughtful, patient guidance of a competent adult may be more beneficial.

How influential is culture? Although Piaget eventually acknowledged that different cultural groups might foster different ways of thinking, he gave only modest attention to culture as a factor in cognitive development (Chapman, 1988). In Vygotsky's view, culture is of paramount importance in determining the specific thinking skills that children acquire. Vygotsky was probably more on target here. Earlier in the chapter we presented evidence to indicate that children's reasoning skills do not necessarily appear at the same ages in different countries. In fact, some reasoning skills (especially those involving formal operational thought) may never appear at all unless a child's culture specifically cultivates them.

TABLE 6-2 Interpretations of Children's Needs by Teachers Taking Piagetian and Vygotskian Perspectives

GENERAL SITUATION WITH CHILDREN'S LEARNING	TEACHER TAKING A PIAGETIAN PERSPECTIVE	TEACHER TAKING A VYGOTSKIAN PERSPECTIVE
A second-grade class takes a field trip to the hands-on exhibits at an aquarium. As the children walk around the exhibits, the teacher recalls her plans for interacting with the children.	At the aquarium, Miss Sánchez takes children to the hands-on tide pool, advises them of rules regarding touching marine life, encourages them to learn about the animals, and then listens intently to their conversations. She asks the parent chaperones to enforce rules that ensure the safety of children and animals but to otherwise allow children to explore freely. Miss Sánchez endorses Piaget's notion that children learn a great deal in response to their own curiosity.	At the aquarium, Mr. Avraham reminds the children of the words they learned back at school: *camouflage*, *hide*, *enemy*, and *disguise*. He distributes pencils and sheets of papers and encourages the parent chaperones to help the children draw pictures of any animals that seem to be hiding or are well camouflaged near sand, rocks, coral, and seaweed. Mr. Avraham accepts Vygotsky's ideas that children learn a lot from using cultural tools, being exposed to cultural concepts, and receiving educational support from adults who are knowledgeable about a topic.
Five-year-old Berlinda sits at a table completing a puzzle that has imprints of pieces in the tray. She frowns as she stares at the shapes of the pieces and the outlines in the tray. After a few unsuccessful attempts at inserting pieces, she grows frustrated and tosses the puzzle pieces onto the floor. Yet she seems interested in the puzzle later in the day.	Berlinda's teacher, Mr. Moses, concludes that the girl is motivated to complete puzzles. Over the next few days, he continues to make puzzles available in the classroom and observes Berlinda. He notices that she keeps choosing puzzles during free time and gradually improves in her ability to complete puzzles. Mr. Moses applies Piaget's ideas that adults need to be sympathetic observers of children's initiatives and make available the kinds of experiences to which children are naturally drawn.	Ms. de la Cruz sits next to Berlinda and demonstrates the strategy of first locating and inserting pieces that have straight edges and then filling in other pieces. She then stands back and encourages Berlinda to try a few pieces by herself. When Berlinda struggles, Ms. de la Cruz gently directs the girl's attention to a particular shape in the inlaid outline, and together they search for its match. Ms. de la Cruz applies Vygotsky's ideas that adults should provide carefully attuned levels of help on worthwhile tasks.
A group of 3- and 4-year-old children sit side-by-side in the sandbox, moving their vehicles this way and that and building tunnels and towers. Elliott says, "I'm going to the rocky quarry." Roz says, "My castle is getting bigger."	Mrs. Dean smiles at the children, interpreting their language as being benignly self-centered, a charming quality of early childhood that will disappear as they move into concrete operations. Mrs. Dean agrees with Piaget's conclusion that children's speech is often egocentric during their preschool years.	Mr. Sidorov interprets the speech of children as externalized thought that helps guide their activities. He shares Vygotsky's view that children generally emit less audible speech with development while continuing to talk to themselves when completing especially difficult tasks.

Teachers and other practitioners must keep in mind, however, that there isn't necessarily a single "best" or "right" way for a culture to promote cognitive development (Rogoff, 2003). Despite their diverse instructional practices, virtually all of the world's cultures have developed effective strategies for helping growing children acquire the knowledge and skills they will need to be successful participants in adult society.

Educational Differences

Given these disparities between Piaget's and Vygotsky's core ideas, we can anticipate that there would be some different educational implications as well. Piaget believed that educators should honor the direction of children's curiosity and allow children to explore their physical worlds freely. Vygotsky believed that educators needed to guide children in using cultural tools. In Table 6-2 (on the previous page), you can see how teachers firmly committed to either a Piagetian or Vygotskian perspective might respond in particular situations.

In the Basic Developmental Issues table "Contrasting Piaget and Vygotsky," we compare the two perspectives in terms of our three general themes: nature and nurture, universality and diversity, and qualitative and quantitative change. Obviously, neither theorist was completely "right" or completely "wrong." Both offered groundbreaking insights into the nature of children's learning and thinking, and as you will discover in the next chapter, both have influenced more recent theories of cognitive development.

BASIC DEVELOPMENTAL ISSUES
Contrasting Piaget and Vygotsky

ISSUE	PIAGET	VYGOTSKY
Nature and Nurture	Piaget believed that biological maturation probably constrains the rate at which children acquire new thinking capabilities. However, his focus was on how interactions with both the physical environment (e.g., manipulation of concrete objects) and the social environment (e.g., discussions with peers) promote cognitive development.	Vygotsky acknowledged that children's inherited traits and talents affect the ways in which they deal with the environment and hence affect the experiences they have. But his theory primarily addresses the environmental conditions (e.g., engagement in challenging activities, guidance from more competent individuals, exposure to cultural interpretations) that influence cognitive growth.
Universality and Diversity	In Piaget's view, children make similar advancements in their logical reasoning capabilities despite the particular environment in which they grow up. Children differ in the ages at which they acquire new abilities, however.	From Vygotsky's perspective, the specific cognitive abilities that children acquire depend on the cultural contexts in which the children are raised and the specific activities in which they are encouraged to engage.
Qualitative and Quantitative Change	Piaget proposed that children's logical reasoning skills progress through four qualitatively distinct stages. Any particular reasoning capability continues to improve in a gradual (quantitative) fashion throughout the stage in which it first appears.	Vygotsky acknowledged that children undergo qualitative changes in their thinking but did not elaborate on the nature of these changes. Much of his theory points to gradual and presumably quantitative improvements in skills. A child may initially find a particular task impossible, later be able to execute it with adult assistance, and eventually perform it independently.

SUMMARY

Piaget's Theory of Cognitive Development

Piaget portrayed children as active and motivated learners who, through numerous interactions with their physical and social environments, construct an increasingly complex understanding of the world around them. He proposed that children's thinking progresses through four stages: (a) the sensorimotor stage, when cognitive functioning is based primarily on behaviors and perceptions; (b) the preoperational stage, when symbolic thought and language become prevalent, but reasoning is "illogical" by adult standards; (c) the concrete operations stage, when logical reasoning capabilities emerge but are limited to concrete objects and events; and (d) the formal operations stage, when thinking about abstract, hypothetical, and contrary-to-fact ideas becomes possible.

Developmental researchers have found that Piaget probably underestimated the capabilities of infants, preschoolers, and elementary school children and overestimated the capabilities of adolescents. Furthermore, children's reasoning on particular tasks depends heavily on their prior knowledge, experience, and formal schooling relative to those tasks. Contemporary developmentalists doubt that cognitive development can really be characterized as a series of general stages that pervade children's thinking across diverse content domains. A few theorists, known as neo-Piagetians, propose that children acquire more specific systems of concepts and thinking skills relevant to particular domains and that these systems may sometimes change in a stagelike manner. Many others instead suggest that children exhibit more gradual trends in a variety of abilities. However, virtually all contemporary theorists acknowledge the value of Piaget's research methods, his portrayal of cognitive development as a constructive process, and the appearance of qualitative changes in cognitive development.

Vygotsky's Theory of Cognitive Development

Vygotsky suggested that human beings are different from other species in their acquisition of complex mental processes, which are largely the legacy of a social group's cultural heritage. In his view, adults promote children's cognitive development by sharing the meanings that their culture assigns to objects and events, introducing children to the many physical and cognitive tools that previous generations have created, and assisting children with challenging tasks. Social activities are often precursors to, and form the basis for, complex mental processes: Children initially use new skills in the course of interacting with adults or peers and slowly internalize these skills for their own, independent use. Children first experiment with adult tasks and ways of thinking within the context of their early play activities and later are inducted into mature tasks with guidance from more experienced social partners.

Contemporary theorists have extended Vygotsky's theory in several directions. Some suggest that adults can help children benefit from their experiences through joint construction of meanings, guided participation, and cognitive apprenticeships. Others recommend that adults engage children and adolescents in authentic, adult-like tasks, initially providing enough scaffolding such that youngsters can accomplish those tasks successfully, and gradually withdrawing support as proficiency increases.

Comparing Piagetian and Vygotskian Perspectives

Constructive processes, readiness, challenge, and social interaction are central to the theories of both Piaget and Vygotsky. However, the two perspectives differ on the role of language in cognitive development, the relative value of free exploration versus more guided activities, the relative importance of interactions with peers versus adults, and the influence of culture. The two theories also offer somewhat different educational applications.

APPLYING CONCEPTS IN CHILD DEVELOPMENT

The exercises in this section will help you build your ability to apply your knowledge of child development in your work with children.

Improving Your Observation Skills

On page 204, you examined photographs of four children from infancy through adolescence and were asked, "How might Piaget have explained the age-related thinking of these children as they interact with building materials?" These four children appear to be responding to building materials quite differently—exploring the sensory properties of blocks during infancy (sensorimotor stage), imaginatively creating new structures during early childhood (preoperational stage), classifying and aligning shapes during middle childhood (concrete operations stage), and inventing a new building during adolescence (formal operations stage). Each of the children is actively learning and exploring, but the mental schemes that they use depend on their developmental level of thinking.

In a photo on page 216, you observed a teacher showing children in her class a circle and were asked, "How is this teacher mediating children's interpretations of their physical environment?" Providing labels for objects, such as the word circle for round things, is one way in which the teacher is mediating children's interpretations of their environment. The children will now probably notice the ubiquity of shapes around them, including shapes on the bulletin board beside their seating area. In addition, the teacher is teaching the children some basic words and may regularly draw their attention to the alphabet on the bulletin board. Children are learning essential elements of literacy that will become an increasingly important tool in their education as they grow and encounter books, lists, signs, and other written materials.

Practicing for Your Licensure Examination

Many teaching tests require students to use what they have learned about child development in responses to brief vignettes and multiple-choice questions. You can practice for your licensure examination by reading about the learning of adolescents in a science class in the following case study and answering a series of questions.

Adolescent Scientists

Read the case and then answer the questions that follow it.

Scott Sowell has just introduced the concept of *pendulum* in his seventh-grade science class. When he asks his students to identify variables that might influence the frequency with which a pendulum swings, they suggest three possibilities: the amount of weight at the bottom, the length of the pendulum, and the "angle" from which the weight is initially dropped. You can watch this lesson in the "Designing Experiments" video in MyEducationLab.

Mr. Sowell divides his students into small groups and gives each group a pendulum composed of a long string with a paper clip attached to the bottom (Figure A). He also provides extra paper clips that the students can use to increase the weight at the bottom. He gives his students the following assignment: *Design your own experiment. Think of a way to test how each one of these variables affects the frequency of swing. Then carry out your experiment.*

Jon, Marina, Paige, and Wensley are coming to grips with their task as Mr. Sowell approaches their table.

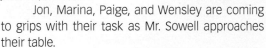

Figure A

Marina: We'll time the frequency as the seconds and the . . . um . . . what? [She looks questioningly at Mr. Sowell.]

Mr. S.: The frequency is the number of swings within a certain time limit.

The group agrees to count the number of swings during a 15-second period. After Jon determines the current length of the string, Wensley positions the pendulum 25 degrees from vertical. When Jon says "Go" and starts a stopwatch, Wensley releases the pendulum. Marina counts the number of swings until, 15 seconds later, Jon says "Stop." Jon records the data from the first experiment: length = 49 cm, weight = 1 paper clip, angle = 25°, frequency = 22.

The group shortens the string and adds a second paper clip onto the bottom of the first clip. The students repeat their experiment and record their data: length = 36 cm, weight = 2 paper clips, angle = 45°, frequency = 25.

Wensley: What does the weight do to it?

Marina: We found out that the shorter it is and the heavier it is, the faster it goes.

Mr. Sowell joins the group and reviews its results from the first two tests.

Mr. S.: What did you change between Test 1 and Test 2?

Marina: Number of paper clips.

Mr. S.: OK, so you changed the weight. What else did you change?

Wensley: The length.

Marina: And the angle.

Mr. S.: OK, so you changed all three between the two tests. So what caused the higher frequency?

Wensley: The length.

Marina: No, I think it was the weight.

Jon: I think the weight.

Paige: The length.

Mr. S.: Why can't you look at your data and decide? [The students look at him blankly.] Take a look at the two tests. The first one had one paper clip, and the second had two. The first test had one length, and the second test had a shorter length. Why can't you come to a conclusion by looking at the two frequencies?

Marina: All of the variables changed.

Mr. Sowell nods in agreement and then moves on to another group. The four students decide to change only the weight for the next test, so they add a third paper clip to the bottom of the second. Their pendulum now looks like Figure B. They continue to perform experiments but are careful to change only one variable at a time, or so they think. In reality, each time the group adds another paper clip, the pendulum grows longer. Mr. Sowell visits the students once again.

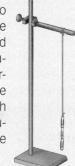

Figure B

Mr. S.: One thing you're testing is length, right? And another thing is weight. Look at your system. Look at how you might be making a slight mistake with weight and length. [He takes two paper clips off and then puts one back on, hanging it, as the students have done, at the bottom of the first paper clip.]

Marina: It's heavier *and* longer.

Mr. S.: Can you think of a way to redesign your experiments so that you're changing only weight? How can you do things differently so that your pendulum doesn't get longer when you add paper clips?

Jon: Hang the second paper clip from the bottom of the string instead of from the first paper clip.

When Mr. Sowell leaves, the students add another paper clip to the pendulum, making sure that the overall length of the pendulum stays the same. They perform another test and find that the pendulum's frequency is identical to what they obtained in the preceding test. Ignoring what she has just seen, Marina concludes, "So if it's heavier, the frequency is higher."

Constructed-Response Question

1. In what ways does Mr. Sowell scaffold the students' efforts during the lab activity?

Multiple-Choice Questions

2. Which one of Piaget's stages is the students' reasoning most consistent with?

    a. The sensorimotor stage
    b. The preoperational stage
    c. The concrete operations stage
    d. The formal operations stage

3. Given the current perspectives on Piaget's theory, how might a teacher help students to separate and control variables?

    a. Teachers should simply wait a few years until the students mature.
    b. Teachers can lecture students on the merits of scientific reasoning.
    c. Teachers can give students practice in pouring liquids to and from smaller and larger containers and asking students if the amount remains the same despite being poured into different containers.
    d. Teachers can give students practice in separating and controlling variables, for example, by growing sunflowers under varying conditions or charting their progress in a particular athletic skill using various training regimens.

Once you have answered these questions, compare your responses with those presented in Appendix A.

Improving Your Ability to Interpret Children's Artifacts and Reflections

Consider chapter concepts as you analyze the following artwork from an adolescent boy.

Fish in a Boat

Combining his pen-and-ink drawing skills and computer technology, 14-year-old Brady created this cartoon of a fish rowing a boat

START BAILING, HOWARD, WE'RE TAKING ON AIR FAST!

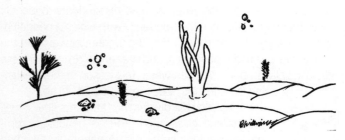

upside-down at the water's surface. As you look at the cartoon, consider these questions:

- Brady used at least three physical tools in creating his cartoon: pen, paper, and a computer. Identify at least three *cognitive tools* that Brady also took advantage of in creating the cartoon.
- Identify a logical reasoning ability that creating this cartoon required. Also identify the Piagetian stage associated with this ability.

Once you have answered these questions, compare your ideas with those presented in Appendix B. For further practice in analyzing children's artifacts and reflections, go to the Activities and Applications section in Chapter 6 of MyEducationLab.

Key Concepts

constructivism (p. 196)
clinical method (p. 196)
scheme (p. 197)
operation (p. 197)
assimilation (p. 197)
accommodation (p. 197)
equilibrium (p. 198)
disequilibrium (p. 198)
equilibration (p. 198)
goal-directed behavior (p. 200)

object permanence (p. 200)
symbolic thought (p. 200)
egocentrism (p. 202)
conservation (p. 202)
class inclusion (p. 202)
neo-Piagetian theory (p. 208)
working memory (p. 208)
central conceptual structure (p. 209)
sociocognitive conflict (p. 214)
mediation (p. 216)

cognitive tool (p. 217)
self-talk (p. 217)
inner speech (p. 217)
internalization (p. 218)
appropriation (p. 218)
zone of proximal development
   (ZPD) (p. 219)
sociodramatic play (p. 220)
mediated learning experience
   (p. 222)

scaffolding (p. 223)
guided participation (p. 224)
apprenticeship (p. 224)
cognitive apprenticeship (p. 225)
reciprocal teaching (p. 226)
authentic activity (p. 228)
individual constructivism (p. 231)
social constructivism (p. 231)

PEARSON
myeducationlab

Now go to www.myeducationlab.com to:
- Take a Quiz to test your mastery of chapter objectives.
- Study chapter content with an individualized Study Plan.
- Deepen your understanding of particular concepts and principles with Review, Remediation, and Enrichment Exercises.
- Apply what you have learned in the chapter to your work with children in Building Teaching Skills and Dispositions exercises.
- Observe children and their unique contexts in Video Examples.

Chapter Seven

Cognitive Development: Cognitive Processes

CASE STUDY: How the United States Became a Country

Our colleague Dinah Jackson worked for many years in the Colorado public schools. At one point she asked students in grades 2 through 8 to write essays addressing the following question: *The land we live on has been here for a very long time, but the United States has been a country for only a little more than 200 years. How did the United States become a country?* Here are some of their responses:

Second grader:

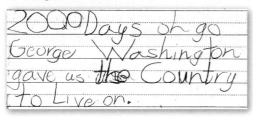

> 2000 Days oh go George Washington gave us the Country to Live on.

Third grader:

> The pilgrims came over in 17 hundred, when they came over they bilt houses. The Idians tihout they were mean. Then they came fraends and tot them stuff. Then winter came and alot died. Then some had babies. So thats how we got here.

Sixth grader:

> The U.S.A. became a contry by some of the British wanting to be under a different rule than of the kings. So, they sailed to the "new world" and became a new country. The only problem was that the kings from Britin still ruled the "new world". Then they had the revolutionary war. They bet Britin, and became an independent country.

Eighth grader:

> We became a country through different processes. Technology around the world finally caught up with the British. There were boats to travel with, navigating tools, and the hearts of men had a desire to expand. Many men had gone on expeditions across the sea. A very famous journey was that of Christopher Columbus. He discovered this land that we live. More and more people poured in, expecting instant wealth, freedom, and a right to share their opinions. Some immigrants were satisfied, others were displeased. Problems in other countries forced people to move on to this New World, such as potato famins and no freedom of religions. Stories that drifted through people grew abolt this country. Stories of golden roads and free land coaxed other families who were living in the slums. Unfortunately, there were slums in America. The people helped this country grow in industry, cultures, religions, and government. Inventions and books were now better than the Europeans. Dime-novels were invented, and the young people could read about heroes of this time. May the curiosity and eagerness of the children continue.

- What do the four compositions reveal about developmental changes in children's knowledge of written language?
- What do they reveal about developmental changes in children's knowledge of American history?

OBJECTIVES

7.1: Describe the operations of basic cognitive processes.

7.2: Trace the development of metacognition and cognitive strategies.

7.3: Explain how teachers can facilitate children's basic information processes and metacognitive strategies.

7.4: Combine the principles of information processing theories with key ideas from sociocultural theories to explain developmental trends in intersubjectivity, memory, and collaborative strategy use.

7.5: Provide evidence to support the idea that children construct integrated belief systems about various content domains.

7.6: Describe how teachers can facilitate children's construction of new knowledge.

7.7: Identify possible challenges in information processing children may face and offer recommendations for assisting children with these needs.

Certainly children know *more* as they get older, both about writing mechanics (spelling, punctuation, and capitalization) and about American history. But if you look closely at what the children have written, changes in the *quality* of children's writing and knowledge of history are evident as well. Whereas the third grader describes the nation's history as a list of seemingly unrelated facts, the sixth and eighth graders have pulled what they have learned into an integrated whole that hangs together. In addition, the younger children's descriptions reflect very simplistic and concrete understandings (e.g., the country was a gift from George Washington, the Pilgrims came over and built houses). In contrast, the eighth grader uses abstract concepts (e.g., technological progress, freedom of religion, and optimistic expectations for wealth) to explain immigration to the United States.

In this chapter our focus is on contemporary research on children's thinking. As you will discover, today's developmental scientists build on the foundational work of Piaget and Vygotsky.[1] Like these prominent figures, contemporary theorists assume that children actively make sense of their worlds. In contrast to the work of Piaget and Vygotsky, however, modern-day theorists use more precise research methods, search for continuous changes in the breadth of children's knowledge and the efficiency of their mental processes, and view children's thinking as being derived from experiences with specific content rather than as reflecting broadly applicable stages and general social influences.

BASIC COGNITIVE PROCESSES

Do children become better able to pay attention as they grow older? Do they learn and remember things more effectively as they move through the elementary and secondary grades? In what ways does their knowledge change with age? Such questions reflect the approach of **information processing theories**, a family of theoretical perspectives that address how human beings mentally acquire, interpret, and remember information and how such cognitive processes change over the course of development.[2]

Information processing theories emerged in the late 1950s and early 1960s and continued to evolve in the decades that followed. Many early information processing theorists tried to draw parallels between how people think and how computers operate. As a result, computer terms are sometimes used to describe human thought processes. For example, information processing theories portray people as *storing* (i.e., putting) symbolic information in memory and *retrieving* it from memory (i.e., finding it) when they need it at a later time.

Increasingly, however, informational processing researchers have found that people often think in distinctly non–computer-like ways. Unlike most computer programs, human beings actively pursue self-chosen goals and create understandings in somewhat idiosyncratic and unpredictable ways. Many information processing theories now have a *constructivist* flavor similar to that of Piaget's and Vygotsky's theories. As an example, consider the second grader's explanation in the opening case study:

2000 Days oh go George Washington gave us the Country to Live on.

Almost certainly, no one has ever told her that the United States was a gift from George Washington. Instead, she uses something she has learned—that Washington was a key figure in the country's early history—to construct what is, to her, a logical explanation of her country's origin. Furthermore, not knowing how to spell *ago*, she uses two words she does know (*oh* and *go*) to construct a reasonable (albeit incorrect) spelling. Following in the footsteps of Piaget and Vygotsky, information processing theorists would acknowledge the second grader's creative amalgamation of prior understandings. As you will learn, information processing theorists would also extend the work of these pioneering giants by carefully examining several additional aspects of the second grader's thinking—the manner in which

information processing theories
Theoretical perspectives that focus on the specific ways in which people mentally acquire, interpret, and remember information and how such cognitive processes change over the course of development.

[1]The theories of Jean Piaget and Lev Vygotsky are examined in detail in Chapter 6.
[2]No single information processing theorist has achieved comparable recognition to that of Piaget or Vygotsky. Instead, numerous information processing scholars have pitched in to identify the characteristics of children's cognitive processes.

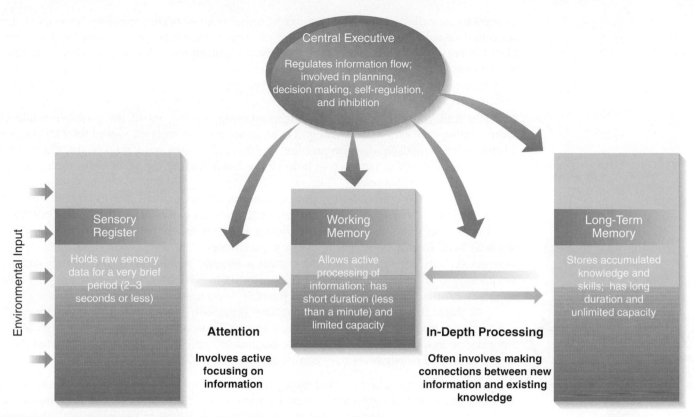

FIGURE 7-1 A model of the human information processing system.
Adapted from the theoretical frameworks of R. C. Atkinson and Shiffrin (1968), Baddeley (1981), and Neisser (1976).

her thoughts were shaped by memory limitations, the evolving strategies she uses to solve problems, and the distinctive understandings she has in particular areas, in this case in history and writing.

Key Ideas in Information Processing Theories

Figure 7-1 presents a model of what the human information processing system might look like. Although information processing theorists don't always agree about the specific mechanisms involved in learning and remembering information, many of them agree on several points.

Input from the environment provides the raw material for learning and memory. Human beings receive input from the environment through the senses (e.g., by seeing, hearing, or touching) and translate that raw input into more meaningful information. The first part of this process, detecting stimuli in the environment, is *sensation*. The second part, interpreting those stimuli, is *perception*.

Even the simplest interpretation (perception) of an environmental event takes time. Thus many theorists believe that human memory includes a mechanism that allows people to remember raw sensory data for a very short time (perhaps 2 to 3 seconds for auditory information and less than a second for visual information). This mechanism goes by a variety of names, but we'll refer to it as the **sensory register**.

In addition to a sensory register, human memory includes two other storage mechanisms: working memory and long-term memory. **Working memory** is that part of the human memory system in which people actively hold and think about new information.[3] Working memory is where children try to solve a problem or make sense of what they are reading. It can keep information for only a very short time (probably less than a minute), so it

[3]Working memory is introduced in Chapter 6.

Preparing for Your Licensure Examination
Your teaching test might ask you to identify key features of children's basic cognitive processes.

sensory register
Component of memory that holds incoming information in an unanalyzed form for a very brief time (2 to 3 seconds or less).

working memory
Component of memory that enables people to actively think about and process a small amount of information.

is sometimes called *short-term memory*.[4] Furthermore, working memory appears to have a limited capacity—only a small amount of "space" in which people can hold and think about events or ideas. As an illustration, try computing the following division problem in your head:

$$59\overline{)49,383}$$

Did you find yourself having trouble remembering some parts of the problem while you were dealing with other parts? Did you ever arrive at the correct answer of 837? Most people cannot solve a multistep division problem like this unless they write it on paper. There simply isn't "room" in working memory to hold all the numbers in your head while simultaneously trying to solve the problem.

Long-term memory is the component that allows human beings to save the many things they've learned from their experiences. For instance, it might include such knowledge as where cookies can be found in the kitchen and how much 2 and 2 equal, as well as such skills as how to ride a bicycle and use a microscope. Things in long-term memory don't necessarily last forever, but they do last for a lengthy period, especially if they are used frequently. In addition, long-term memory appears to have an unlimited capacity, "holding" as much information as a person could possibly need to save.

To think about information people have previously stored in long-term memory, they must retrieve and reflect on it in working memory. Thus, although people's capacity to keep information in long-term memory may be boundless, their ability to *think about* what they've stored is limited to whatever they can hold in working memory at any one time.

Attention is essential to the learning process. Many information processing theorists suggest that attention is the primary process through which information moves from the sensory register into working memory. Thus attention plays a key role in the interpretation, storage, and later recall of information. In the "Memory: Middle Childhood" video in MyEducationLab, you can see what happens when a child isn't focusing on the task. Ten-year-old David remembers only 3 of the 12 words that the interviewer reads to him. He realizes that his lapse in attention was the reason he did not recall more words: "My brain was turned off right now."

A variety of cognitive processes are involved in moving information from working memory to long-term memory. Whereas attention is instrumental in moving information from the sensory register to working memory, more complex processes are needed if people are to remember information for longer than a minute or so. Occasionally simply repeating information over and over (*rehearsing* it) is sufficient for its long-term storage. More often, however, effective storage requires making connections between new information and the ideas that already exist in long-term memory. For instance, people might use their existing knowledge either to *organize* or expand (i.e., *elaborate*) on newly acquired information. We'll look at the development of such processes later in this chapter.

People control how they process much of the information they encounter. Some sort of cognitive "supervisor" is almost certainly necessary to ensure that a person's learning and memory processes work effectively. This component, sometimes called the **central executive**, oversees the flow of information throughout the memory system and is critical for planning, decision making, self-regulation, and inhibition of unproductive thoughts and behaviors.[5]

Cognitive development involves gradual changes in various components of the information processing system. Many information processing theorists reject Piaget's notion of discrete developmental stages. Instead, they believe that children's cognitive abilities develop primarily through ongoing, gradual *trends*. Hence children are portrayed as gradually developing increasingly efficient mental processes and strategies. Qualitative transformations that do emerge in information processing analyses tend to be a series of short-lived states that are

MyEducationLab

Observe David's realization that attention affects memory in the "Memory: Middle Childhood" video. (Find Video Examples in Topic 7 of MyEducationLab.)

long-term memory
Component of memory that holds knowledge and skills for a relatively long period of time.

central executive
Component of the human information processing system that oversees the flow of information throughout the system.

---

[4]In everyday language, people often use the term "short-term memory" to refer to memory that lasts for a few days or weeks. Notice how, in contrast, information processing theorists characterize short-term memory as lasting *less than a minute*.

[5]The central executive oversees the executive functions you learned about in Chapter 5.

not universal across individuals. In the following sections, we look at developmental trends in various aspects of the human information processing system.

Sensation and Perception

Most sensory and perceptual development occurs in infancy and early childhood. Researchers have reached the following conclusions about infants' sensory and perceptual abilities.

Some sensory and perceptual capabilities are present at birth, and others emerge within the first few weeks or months of life. Even newborns can sense and discriminate among different sights, sounds, tastes, and smells (El-Dib, Massaro, Glass, & Aly, 2011; Gervain, Macagno, Cogoi, Peña, & Mehler, 2008; Ricci et al., 2008; Sann & Streri, 2008; Winberg, 2005).[6] And their ability to perceive—that is, to *interpret*—this sensory information appears quite early. For instance, newborns have some ability to determine the direction from which a sound originates (Morrongiello, Fenwick, Hillier, & Chance, 1994). Within the first week they seem to understand that objects maintain the same shape and size even when the objects are rotated or moved farther away and, hence, *look* different (Slater, 2000; Slater, Mattock, & Brown, 1990).

Many sensory and perceptual capabilities continue to improve during the first few years of life. At birth visual acuity is less than 20/600, but by 8 months of age it is around 20/80 (Courage & Adams, 1990). Young infants can nevertheless do a great deal with their limited eyesight. When they are only a few days old, they can recognize the contours of their mother's face and detect and imitate facial expressions depicting happiness, sadness, and surprise (de Heering et al., 2008; T. Field, Woodson, Greenberg, & Cohen, 1982; Werker, Maurer, & Yoshida, 2010). However, visual perception is probably not fully developed until the preschool years or after, when the visual cortex—that part of the brain that handles complex visual information—becomes similar to that of an adult (T. L. Hickey & Peduzzi, 1987; Vedamurthy, Suttle, Alexander, & Asper, 2008).

Infants show consistent preferences for certain types of stimuli, especially social ones. As early as the first week of life, infants are drawn to new and interesting stimuli, particularly social ones (Haith, 1990). Within 3 days of birth, they recognize their mother's voice and will suck vigorously on a synthetic nipple if doing so turns on a recording of their mother speaking (DeCasper & Fifer, 1980). Similarly, infants only 1 to 4 days old exhibit more coherent brain patterns when listening to human speech than when listening to music (Kotilahti et al., 2010). In the first month, infants prefer to look at spatial configurations that look like faces, that is, those that are bordered and have large visible elements resembling eyes at the top (Werker et al., 2010). This early inclination to focus on social stimuli is, of course, advantageous for dependent infants, who must focus in on people around them in order to acquire essential social skills, language, and cultural traditions.

Perceptual development is the result of both biological maturation and experience. We find an example of the integration of nature and nurture in research on depth perception. To determine when infants acquire depth perception, researchers sometimes use a *visual cliff,* a large glass table with a patterned cloth immediately beneath the glass on one side and the same pattern on the floor on the other side (see Figure 7-2). In a classic study (E. J. Gibson & Walk, 1960), infants ages 6 to 14 months were placed on a narrow platform between the "shallow" and "deep" sides of a visual cliff. Their mothers stood at one end of the table and actively coaxed them to crawl across the glass. Although most infants willingly crawled off the platform to the "shallow" side, very few ventured onto the "deep" side, suggesting that infants can perceive depth.

FIGURE 7-2 Visual cliff. By refusing to crawl to the "deep" side of this glass-covered table, infants demonstrate a fear of heights.

[6]The amazing abilities of infants in distinguishing among basic sensory stimuli are introduced in Chapter 4.

Certainly neurological maturation is involved in depth perception. Visual acuity must be suitably developed to enable infants to perceive edges, inclines, and the relative distances between objects. Some species that can walk almost immediately after birth (e.g., chicks, lambs, baby goats) show avoidance of the deep side of a visual cliff within the first days of life (E. J. Gibson & Walk, 1960), suggesting that neurological foundations for a fear of heights are fairly common in the animal kingdom. But learning also appears to be involved. Infants who have had experience with self-locomotion, either through crawling or using a walker (a framed seat with wheels attached to the base),[7] show greater fear of drop-offs than infants without such experience (Bertenthal, Campos, & Kermoian, 1994; Witherington, Campos, Anderson, Lejeune, & Seah, 2005).

From an evolutionary perspective, it makes sense that both heredity and environment should play a role in perceptual development. Because perception of one's surroundings and emotional connections with caregivers are essential for survival, the human species has undoubtedly evolved biologically built-in perceptual abilities (Rakison, 2005). At the same time, the specific environments to which individual children must adapt vary from place to place, so the human brain has also evolved to be responsive to local circumstances (J. J. Gibson, 1979; Greenough & Black, 1992; M. H. Johnson, 2009). Thus, infants look intently at all faces from birth but rather quickly learn to recognize the faces of their own beloved caregivers and later distinguish among faces of different people outside the family (Werker et al., 2010).

Attention

The development of attention is also due, in part, to brain maturation (M. L. Dixon, Zelazo, & De Rosa, 2010; Ruff & Rothbart, 1996). The brain appears to have at least three attention networks that develop and interconnect as children grow (Cowan & Alloway, 2009; Posner, 2004; van de Weijer-Bergsma, Wijnroks, & Jongmans, 2008; Waszak, Li, & Hommel, 2010). An *orienting system* develops in the first year of life and allows children to direct their mental energies to interesting objects and events. The orienting system is at work when children show a preference for looking at one toy or another, visually track a moving ball as it rolls across the floor, and look away in boredom when they have finished inspecting a picture on the wall. An *arousal system* permits children to maintain a state of focused alertness when thinking about something. The arousal system becomes obvious as children show increasingly lengthy periods of sustained attention while exploring toys, conversing with others, and participating in lessons at school. Finally, the *executive control system*, which takes many years to mature, lets children plan ahead, keep their goals in mind, and disregard potentially distracting or irrelevant stimuli. The maturation of these three attentional systems contributes to the following developmental trends.

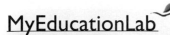

Observe how Corwin's attention is drawn to a novel object in the "Cognitive Development: Infancy" video. (Find Video Examples in Topic 7 of MyEducationLab.)

Children's attention is affected by stimulus characteristics and, later, also by familiarity. In the "Cognitive Development: Infancy" video in MyEducationLab, 16-month-old Corwin is captivated by an unusual, multicolored toy he finds in a paper bag. Like all human beings, infants quickly turn their attention to new, unusual, and perhaps intense stimuli—for instance, orienting to a flash of light, loud noise, or sudden movement (Bahrick, Gogate, & Ruiz, 2002; K. A. Snyder, 2007; van de Weijer-Bergsma et al., 2008). Once they have gained some knowledge about their everyday world, familiarity comes into play as well. In particular, they are most likely to be drawn to objects and events that are moderately different, but not too different, from those they have previously experienced (McCall, Kennedy, & Applebaum, 1977; Shinskey & Munakata, 2010; van de Weijer-Bergsma et al., 2008).[8]

With age, distractibility decreases and sustained attention increases. Children as young as 6 months are capable of focused attention for brief periods when they are captivated by an object or event (Richards & Turner, 2001; van de Weijer-Bergsma et al., 2008). Yet by and large, young children's attention moves quickly from one thing to another

---

[7]Traditional walkers are now considered unsafe by some medical experts.

[8]This tendency to prefer novelty in moderation is consistent with Piaget's belief that children can accommodate to (and so benefit from) new stimuli only to the extent that they can also assimilate those stimuli into their existing schemes.

(Dempster & Corkill, 1999; Ruff & Lawson, 1990; M. E. Schmidt, Pempek, Kirkorian, Lund, & Anderson, 2008). You can see age-typical shifts in attention in the "Cognitive Development: Early Childhood" video in MyEducationLab. As children move through the elementary school years, they become better able to focus and sustain their attention on a particular task despite the presence of distracting stimuli (Cowan, Morey, AuBuchon, Zwilling, & Gilchrist, 2010; M. L. Dixon et al., 2010; Ruff & Lawson, 1990).

As you might expect, developmental progressions in attention show some variability. How long young children can sustain their attention is partly a function of their temperament. Some toddlers become quite engrossed in an activity when the task is self-chosen, intriguing, and free from interference by others. Others are more prone to move quickly from one activity to the next. As you will learn later in this chapter, some children continue to be sufficiently distractible during the school years that they require special assistance in staying focused on academic lessons.

Attention becomes increasingly purposeful. By the time children are 3 or 4 months old, they show some ability to anticipate where a moving object will soon appear and focus their attention accordingly (Haith, Hazan, & Goodman, 1988; Reznick, 2009). In the preschool years they intentionally use attention to help them learn and remember something, and their ability to concentrate continues to improve during the elementary and middle school years (Hagen & Stanovich, 1977; Luna, 2009; P. Miller & Seier, 1994). Indeed, children's learning increasingly becomes a function of what they think they need to remember.

As an illustration of the purposeful nature of attention, imagine that you have the six cards shown in Figure 7-3 in front of you on a table. You are told to remember only the *colors* of the cards. Now the cards are flipped over, and you are asked where the green card is, where the purple card is, and so on. You are then asked to name the object that appeared on each card. Chances are, you will remember the colors far more accurately than the objects because you deliberately focused on the color of cards.

In one study (Maccoby & Hagen, 1965), children in grades 1 through 7 were asked to perform a series of tasks similar to the one just described. The older children remembered the background colors more accurately than the younger children did. Yet the older children were no better than younger ones at remembering the objects pictured on the cards. In fact, the oldest group in the study remembered the *fewest* objects. These results suggest that older children are better at paying attention to and learning the things they need to know, but they are not necessarily better at learning information irrelevant to their goals.

Working Memory and the Central Executive

Working memory and the central executive are closely connected and jointly responsible for what children pay attention to, how they think about the information, and how well they remember it. Three developmental trends in working memory and the central executive enable children to handle increasingly complex cognitive tasks with age:

Processing speed increases. As youngsters move through childhood, they execute many cognitive processes more quickly and efficiently than they did in earlier years (Fry & Hale, 1996; Kail & Ferrer, 2007; Luna, 2009; Shin, 2011). Some of this increased speed and efficiency is undoubtedly due to the genetically driven *myelination* of neurons in the brain.[9] Yet experience and practice are involved as well. By frequently practicing certain mental and physical tasks, children and adolescents develop **automatization** for these tasks. That is, they eventually become capable of performing the tasks rapidly and with little or no conscious effort. Once thoughts and actions become automatized, they take up very little "space"

[9]Chapter 5 describes myelination, the maturational process in which a fatty sheath grows around neurons and allows messages to be transmitted rapidly.

MyEducationLab

Observe Maddie's age-typical shifts in attention in the "Cognitive Development: Early Childhood" video. (Find Video Examples in Topic 7 of MyEducationLab.)

FIGURE 7-3 Incidental memory. Imagine that you are told to remember the *colors* of each of these cards. After the cards are flipped over, do you think you would remember where each color appeared? Would you also remember what *object* appeared on each card, even though you were not asked to remember the objects? *Modeled after stimuli used by Maccoby & Hagen, 1965.*

Preparing for Your Licensure Examination

Your teaching test may ask you to recognize developmental changes in attention.

automatization
Process of becoming able to respond quickly and efficiently while mentally processing or physically performing certain tasks.

BUILDING ON THE BASICS. Practice with basic skills frees up mental energy for other challenging mental processes. This Indian girl is proficient in writing at the chalkboard and is able to focus on other aspects of a lesson arranged for her by her teacher.

in working memory, enabling children to devote more working memory capacity to other, more challenging tasks and problems.

As an example of the benefits of automatization, consider how children's reading ability improves over time. When children first begin to read, they devote considerable mental effort to identifying the words on the page—for instance, figuring out what the letters *f-r-i-e-n-d* spell—and may recall little about the *meaning* of what they've read. But with increasing exposure to a variety of reading materials, word identification gradually becomes an automatized process, such that children immediately recognize most of the words they see. At this point, they can focus their efforts on understanding and remembering what they're reading.

The capacity of working memory increases with age. One common way of measuring the capacity of working memory is to ask people to remember a sequence of unrelated items, perhaps a series of digits or unrelated objects or words. Toddlers can remember more items than infants can, older children can remember more items than younger children can, and adolescents can remember even more. Much of this increase in working memory capacity is probably due to the fact that cognitive processes become faster and more efficient with age and so take up less "room." Basic maturational processes in the brain, including myelination, synaptic pruning, and increased connections among neurons, seem to contribute to the speed of processing and hence to working memory capacity (Luna, 2009).[10]

The central executive increasingly takes charge of cognitive processes. Thanks in large part to continuing maturation of the brain, youngsters gain ever-increasing control of their cognitive processes (Kuhn, 2006; Luna, 2009; Zelazo, Müller, Frye, & Marcovitch, 2003). With such control comes a variety of new and improved abilities. Youngsters become better able to plan and direct their actions toward goals and standards. They also better inhibit inappropriate thoughts and behaviors. And they can reflect on and think *about* their thinking, as we'll see in our discussion of *metacognition* later in the chapter. Keep in mind, however, that the central executive is still a "work in progress" even in adolescence and does not fully mature until adulthood.

Long-Term Memory

Some knowledge in long-term memory is virtually universal among children. Most children around the globe soon learn that people typically have two legs but cats and dogs have four. Other understandings depend on children's unique experiences and on the cultural contexts in which they grow. In the four children's compositions in the opening case study, we consistently see a European American perspective on the early days of the United States: The focus is on immigration and early European colonization. Were we to ask Native American children how the United States came into being, we might get very different interpretations, perhaps ones based on invasion or confiscation of property.

Regardless of their particular background, all children place a mounting number of ideas in long-term memory. The following trends in long-term memory enhance children's ability to understand and respond to their world.

The capacity to remember information in long-term memory appears very early and improves with age. Before birth, children have some ability to learn from and remember their experiences. Infants develop some initial taste preferences based on flavors they were

CONCENTRATION. With maturation and experience, young people gain increasing control over their attention and cognitive processes. This young man focuses intently while reading in a noisy classroom.

[10]Chapter 5 introduces synaptic pruning as the universal process in brain development whereby many previously formed synapses wither away, especially if they have not been used frequently.

previously exposed to in the amniotic fluid (as a result of their mother's diet; Mennella, Jagnow, & Beauchamp, 2001). Similarly, experience in hearing their mother's speech, muffled in the womb, helps infants recognize their mother's voice after birth (Kisilevsky et al., 2009). In infancy, the capacity for long-term memory manifests itself in additional ways. When a ribbon connected to a mobile is tied to a 2-month-old baby's foot, the baby easily learns that kicking makes the mobile move and remembers the connection over a period of several days—even longer if he or she is given an occasional reminder (Rovee-Collier, 1999). At age 6 months, infants can also recall and imitate actions they saw 24 hours earlier, and their memory for such actions increases in duration in the months that follow. By the time children reach their second birthday, they are able to retain a complex sequence of actions for a year or more (Bauer, DeBoer, & Lukowski, 2007). Such advancements in long-term memory ability are probably due, in large part, to brain maturation (Bauer, 2009; Fujioka, Mourad, & Trainor, 2011; Hayne, 2007).

Children increasingly have conscious awareness of events. Early memories are by and large acquired through an *implicit memory* process—infants are not knowingly aware that they are learning information and cannot articulate their memories through language (Lloyd & Newcombe, 2009). Implicit memories are evident in infants' selective responses to parents over unfamiliar adults; preferences for some foods above others; and displays of recognition of a favorite book, blanket, or toy. Yet as they grow, children cannot necessarily recall these memories in any detail. In fact, children typically have little if any *conscious* recall of things that happened during their first 2 years—a phenomenon known as **infantile amnesia**. For much of the preschool period as well, recall of past events continues to be rather sketchy. A variety of explanations for infantile amnesia have been offered, including the immaturity of brain structures and the absence of cues later in life that would be necessary for triggering recollections from infancy (Lloyd & Newcombe, 2009; H. L. Williams & Conway, 2009). The condition of infantile amnesia is overcome when the child develops symbolic thinking and an emerging sense of self that catalogs personal memories.

Of course, the fact that children cannot recall their earliest experiences does not mean that these memories do not serve a vital function in life. On the contrary, first experiences form the foundation for long-term knowledge (Hayne & Simcock, 2009). Thus the early years of life yield understandings that children subsequently reflect on consciously. Particularly when people engage children in conversations about shared experiences, children's awareness of past events improves dramatically (M. L. Howe, Courage, & Rooksby, 2009; C. A. Nelson & Fivush, 2004; K. Nelson, 1996b). It appears that talking about events enables children to store the events in a verbal (language-based) form, making the events easier to recall at a later time.

The amount of knowledge stored in long-term memory increases many times over. This trend is an obvious one, and the four essays in the opening case study illustrate it clearly. Yet the obviousness of the trend does not diminish its importance in cognitive development. In particular, long-term memory provides the **knowledge base** from which children draw as they encounter, interpret, and respond to new events. As their knowledge base grows, children can interpret new events more effectively.

On average, older children and adults learn new information and skills more easily than do younger children. A key reason is that they have more knowledge that they can use to make sense of new information and experiences (Kail, 1990; P. A. Ornstein & Haden, 2009). When the tables are turned—when young children know more about a particular topic than adults or older children do—the younger children are often the more effective learners (Chi, 1978; Schneider, Korkel, & Weinert, 1989). In one classic study, elementary and middle school children who were expert chess players could better remember where chess pieces were located on a chess board than could college-educated adults who were relative novices at chess (Chi, 1978).

Dear Diary,
  Guess what!! We have all most made it to the west cost. I can't whate to lye down on CA. Sand in a Calafona Beach. Hot and sunny. Out like Floida.
  The first place we went today was Bandelier National Monument. It is a Monument with lots of Hopi tribe houses. It is a place where a Hopie tribe has bilt a village that has been abandoned and is now a museum/monument.
  Well, we where going on this tour through thes ancient adobe houses. Suddenly, the house we are standing in begins to skweek. We rush outside to find that a 7-8 year old child is swinging on the old wooden "poles" that help support the floor above, like monkey bars. The kid reaches for the next pole and it crables into dust.
  It finally tured out to be all right. The mom was having a spazz about, we need to call 911, and, Does he need CPR? The tour guide was trying to calm her down and then came over to u He thanked us and bussled up out,
      More to morrow
        Amaryth

ARTIFACT 7-1 Dear diary. Ten-year-old Amaryth describes a day when her family visited a national monument that was once a Hopi village. Travel opportunities such as this will undoubtedly enhance Amaryth's ability to learn about Native American civilizations in her social studies classes.

infantile amnesia
General inability to recall events that have occurred in the early years of life.

knowledge base
One's knowledge about specific topics and the world in general.

Improving Your Observation Skills

Loveland. Three children drew maps of their hometown, Loveland, Colorado. How do the maps drawn by a first grader (top), fifth grader (middle), and seventh grader (bottom) reflect different levels of knowledge about their local community? Compare your response with the explanation at the end of the chapter.

Maps courtesy of Dinah Jackson.

Children's knowledge about the world becomes increasingly integrated. Children begin categorizing their experiences as early as 3 or 4 months of age (more about this point a bit later). Even so, much of what young children know about the world consists of separate, isolated categories and facts. In contrast, older children's knowledge includes many associations and interrelationships among ideas (Bjorklund, 1987; M. C. Wimmer & Howe, 2009). This developmental change is undoubtedly one reason why older children can think more logically and draw inferences more readily: They have a more cohesive understanding of the world around them.

As an example, let's return to the essays in the opening case study. Notice how the third grader presents a chronological list of events without any attempt at tying them together:

> The Idiuns thout they were mean. Then they came friends, and tot them stuff. Then winter came, and alot died. Then some had babies.

In contrast, the eighth grader frequently identifies or implies cause-and-effect relationships among events:

> More and more people poured in, expecting instant wealth, freedom, and a right to share their opinions. Some immigrants were satisfied, others were displeased. Problems in other countries forced people to move on to this New World, such as potato famins and no freedom of religions. Stories that drifted through people grew about this country. Stories of golden roads and free land coaxed other families who were living in the slums.

Children and adults alike sometimes organize their knowledge into schemas and scripts. **Schemas** (similar, but not identical, to Piaget's *schemes*) are tightly integrated sets of ideas about specific objects or situations. You might have a schema for what a typical horse looks like (e.g., it's a certain height, and it has a mane and an elongated head) and a schema for what a typical office contains (it probably has a desk, computer, bookshelves, and file cabinets). **Scripts** encompass knowledge about the predictable sequence of events related to particular activities. You probably have a script related to how weddings typically proceed, and even many 3-year-olds can tell you what typically happens when you go to McDonald's for a meal (K. Nelson, 1997). Schemas and scripts help children make sense of their experiences and predict what is likely to happen on future occasions.

Schemas and scripts increase in number and complexity as children grow older (Flavell et al., 2002; Hudson & Mayhew, 2009). Like Piaget's sensorimotor schemes, children's earliest schemas and scripts tend to be behavioral and perceptual in nature. For instance, toddlers can act out typical scenarios (scripts) with toys long before they have the verbal skills to describe what they are doing (Bauer & Dow, 1994). As children get older, their mental structures presumably become less tied to physical actions and perceptual qualities.

Thinking and Reasoning

From an information processing perspective, many developmental changes occur in mental activities. Here we look at three general developmental trends in thinking and reasoning. A bit later we'll examine changes in specific strategies that children use to learn and problem solve.

Thought increasingly makes use of symbols. In Piaget's theory of cognitive development, the content of infants' and toddlers' schemes is predominantly sensorimotor—that is, based on perceptions and behaviors.[11] Near the end of the sensorimotor stage (at about 18 months, Piaget suggested), children begin to think in terms of **symbols**, mental entities (e.g., words) that do not strictly reflect the perceptual and behavioral qualities of the objects or events they represent (e.g., a "ball" is called by different names in different languages). Such symbolic thought enables children to infer characteristics they haven't directly observed. When a 3-year-old who is familiar with common household pets hears her father use the word "cat," she might easily visualize a small animal that has pointy ears and whiskers, walks on four legs, and purrs.

Piaget was probably correct in believing that sensorimotor representations of objects and events precede symbolic representations. However, the shift from one to the other is much more gradual than Piaget thought. Long before children reach school age, they begin to use such symbols as words, numbers, pictures, and miniature models to represent and think about real-life objects and events (DeLoache, 2011; DeLoache & Ganea, 2009; J. Huttenlocher, Newcombe, & Vasilyeva, 1999; K. Nelson, 1996a). Yet when children begin elementary school, they may initially have only limited success in dealing with the wide variety of symbols they encounter. Elementary school teachers often use blocks and other concrete objects to represent numbers or mathematical operations, but not all kindergartners and first graders make the connection between these objects and their related concepts (DeLoache, Miller, & Rosengren, 1997; E. Mundy & Gilmore, 2009; Uttal, Liu, & DeLoache, 2006). Maps, too, are largely symbolic in nature, and children in the early grades often interpret them literally, perhaps thinking that a road that is red on a map is actually painted red (Liben & Myers, 2007). As children grow older, their use of symbols to think, remember, and solve problems grows in frequency and sophistication. Eventually, their symbolic abilities allow them to transcend everyday realities, think about what could or should happen in the future, and develop abstract understandings about their physical and social worlds (Bandura, 2006; Kuhn, 2009; Tattersall, 2006).

Logical thinking abilities improve with age. The initial manifestations of logical thinking appear in infancy and are related to perceptions of physical events. Long before their first birthdays children can perceive a cause-and-effect relationship in a sequence of events. When 6-month-olds see one object hit another and watch the second object move immediately after the impact, they seem to understand that the first object has essentially "launched" the second one (L. B. Cohen & Cashon, 2006; Luo, Kaufman, & Baillargeon, 2009).

By preschool age, children can draw logical inferences from language-based information—for instance, they draw appropriate conclusions about events depicted in children's stories (M. Donaldson, 1978; R. Gelman & Baillargeon, 1983; Van Kleeck, 2008). However, preschoolers and elementary school children do not always draw *correct* inferences, and they have difficulty distinguishing between what *must* be true versus what *might* be true given the evidence before them (Galotti, Komatsu, & Voelz, 1997; Pillow, 2002).

[11]Piaget's description of sensorimotor thinking is introduced in Chapter 6.

QUINCEAÑERA. This fifteen-year-old girl from Mexico is celebrating her Quinceañera. In Mexico, Quinceañera festivities typically begin with a Catholic Mass and also include a party at the girl's home or at a local banquet hall where everyone enjoys a meal, takes part in a series of toasts, and dances to a musical band. The well-developed script for what typically happens during a Quinceañera contributes to the family's anticipation before the event and enjoyment on the day.

Preparing for Your Licensure Examination

Your teaching test may ask you to recognize how children represent their knowledge through organized networks of ideas.

schema
Tightly integrated set of ideas about a specific object or situation.

script
Schema that involves a predictable sequence of events related to a common activity.

symbol
Mental entity that represents an external object or event, typically without reflecting its perceptual and behavioral qualities.

The ability to reason logically improves in childhood and adolescence. Yet even in these years, reasoning ability varies widely from one young person to another, and it is often influenced by personal motives and biases (Goswami, 2011; Klaczynski, 2001; Kuhn, 2009; Kuhn & Franklin, 2006).

Gestures sometimes foreshadow the emergence of more sophisticated thinking and reasoning. As children make the transition to more advanced forms of reasoning—perhaps about traditional Piagetian tasks or mathematical problems—they often show such reasoning in their gestures before they show it in their speech (Goldin-Meadow, 2006; Pine, Lufkin, Kirk, & Messer, 2007). The following scenario illustrates this trend:

> [A] 6-year-old child [is] attempting to justify her belief that the amount of water changed when it was poured from a tall, skinny glass into a short, wide dish. The child says, "It's different because this one's tall and that one's short," thus making it clear that she has focused on the heights of the two containers. However, in the very same utterance, the child indicates with her hand shaped like a C first the diameter of the glass and then, with a wider C, the larger diameter of the dish. The child speaks about the heights but has also noticed—not necessarily consciously—that the containers differ in width as well. (Goldin-Meadow, 1997, p. 13)

Gestures, like the 6-year-old's C-shaped hand gestures, appear to provide a way for children to "experiment" (cognitively) with new ideas. Gestures may also alleviate the strain on working memory as children first begin to wrestle with more complex ways of thinking (Goldin-Meadow, 2006; Goldin-Meadow, Nusbaum, Kelly, & Wagner, 2001).

Facilitating Basic Cognitive Processes

Our discussion of information processing theories thus far leads to several implications for working with children and adolescents.

See examples of safe environments for infants and young children in the "Environments" videos in the Video Examples section in Topic 7 of MyEducationLab.

• **Provide a variety of sensory experiences for infants and young children.** In the first few years of life, children learn many things about the physical world through direct contact—by looking, listening, feeling, tasting, and smelling. Experiences that ensure optimal perceptual development are *not* those that involve intense, nonstop visual and auditory stimulation, however. Instead, needed stimuli are ones that children with normal sensory abilities encounter in any reasonably nurturing environment—everyday contact with faces, voices, toys, and the like. Thus, adults can offer an enriched environment but not overdo it. Infants, toddlers, and preschoolers should have a wide variety of objects to manipulate and play with, and their environment should be set up for safe movement and exploration. You can see examples of safe environments for infants and young children in the "Environments" videos in MyEducationLab. In addition, the Development and Practice feature "Providing Appropriate Stimulation for Infants and Young Children" offers several suggestions for structuring materials and caregiving settings for small children.

• **Watch for and address significant problems in perception.** By the time they enter preschool, most but not all children will have been previously screened by a pediatrician or nurse for limitations in seeing and hearing or unusual sensitivities to stimuli of various kinds—tastes, smells, sights, or tactile sensations (Turnbull, Turnbull, & Wehmeyer, 2010). Yet not every child with a perceptual impairment will have been identified. With their daily observations of children, teachers and other practitioners may notice that a child has a perceptual problem that they can address. A teacher might relocate a child who complains about the muted noises of a vent fan to a different part of the classroom. A school psychologist might refer a child with limited language to an audiologist. Because the young brain is being wired in part through its exposure to perceptual stimulation, it is important to arrange for children with sensory problems to receive treatment from knowledgeable professionals.

• **Help children pay attention to things that are important for them to learn and remember.** As we've seen, attention is a critical factor in learning. Yet many children, young ones especially, are easily distracted from planned activities by extraneous sights and sounds. Even highly motivated high school students can't keep their minds on a single task indefinitely. Several strategies for helping children and adolescents focus their attention

DEVELOPMENT AND PRACTICE
Providing Appropriate Stimulation for Infants and Young Children

Give children some choice in their sensory experiences.

- A home caregiver offers a variety of simple toys for infants to explore and play with. She often places several items within reach, and she respects infants' occasional rejection and apparent dislike of certain items. (Infancy)
- A preschool teacher makes available a variety of sensory materials that children can observe and manipulate. The teacher includes an array of jars that contain various scents (e.g., herbs, vanilla, and orange slices), sound boxes with small objects (e.g., rice, beans, and coarse salt), and a water table with funnels, containers, and other pouring toys. (Early Childhood)

Allow children periods of quiet and calm.

- A teacher in an infant center realizes that his room is often busy and noisy. Knowing that too much stimulation can be unsettling, he monitors the sights, sounds, textures, and smells that are present at any one time. He tries to tone down the environment a bit when introducing a new child to the center. (Infancy)
- A preschool teacher includes a brief rest period after snack time to allow children to recharge their batteries. Children who need a nap can lie down on mats, while non-nappers can complete puzzles or participate in other quiet activities. (Early Childhood)

Read cues.

- A father helps a caregiver understand the signals his daughter typically gives. "She often turns away when she's had enough of something," he explains. "But at other times, she just acts sleepy. If she's truly tired, she quickly goes to sleep." (Infancy)
- A kindergarten teacher observes the different ways that children respond to varied levels of stimulation. Maggie gets anxious during story time as other children sit quietly, Alicia is aggressive during transitions between activities, and Hollister remains focused even when peers are loud and raucous. (Early Childhood)

Avoid the "better baby" trap.

- A child care provider attends a workshop on brain development, where several presenters make a strong pitch for certain new

products that are supposedly essential for intellectual growth. Fortunately, she knows enough about cognitive development to realize that children benefit from a wide variety of toys and that an intensive "sensory stimulation" approach is *not* in children's best interest. (Infancy)
- A toddler teacher designs his curriculum carefully, exposing children to a wide range of developmentally appropriate objects, including blocks, sensory materials, dolls, trucks, durable books, and coloring materials. When parents ask about his plans to "multiply the intelligence" of children, he explains that he does not use flash cards or structured academic lessons with toddlers. Instead, he cultivates their intelligence through a carefully selected curriculum that fosters children's natural curiosity and nurtures their budding sense of self, language development, and knowledge of the world. (Infancy)

Recognize that temperamental and cultural differences help determine the optimal amount of stimulation for each child.

- A teacher in a child care center has noticed that some of the toddlers in her group seem to respond to sensory overload by getting excited and animated, whereas others fuss, go to sleep, or in some other way indicate that they have had enough. Although she herself prefers a quiet, peaceful room, one of her coworkers enjoys lively salsa music and often plays it while the children are awake. The two teachers often compare notes about how different children respond to quiet versus more active environments. (Infancy)
- A kindergarten teacher observes that children from different backgrounds respond very differently to discussions during story time. Some children are animated and make spontaneous comments, whereas others remain still and quiet. The teacher realizes that the children have been acquiring customs at home for acting in a group and responding to authority figures. The teacher makes a point to ask silent children about their perceptions of stories as the large group disperses. (Early Childhood)

productively are presented in the Development and Practice feature "Getting and Keeping Children's Attention."

- **Relate new information to children's existing knowledge.** People of all ages learn new information more effectively when they can relate it to what they already know. Yet children don't always make meaningful connections on their own. For instance, they may not realize that subtraction is simply the reverse of addition or that Shakespeare's *Romeo and Juliet* is in some ways similar to modern-day ethnic clashes around the world. By pointing out such connections, adults can foster a more integrated knowledge base (Ormrod, 2008; Vosniadou, 2009; J. J. White & Rumsey, 1994).

- **Remember that children can think about only a small amount of information at any one time.** Although working memory capacity increases during childhood, young people

DEVELOPMENT AND PRACTICE
Getting and Keeping Children's Attention

Capture children's interest with bright colors, intriguing sounds, and objects that invite manipulation and exploration.

- An elementary music teacher provides several instruments (e.g., a xylophone, toy guitar, and set of drums) for children to explore. The teacher also allows the children to take turns composing simple songs on the classroom piano. (Middle Childhood)
- An elementary teacher takes his class on a trip to a local pond to create small biospheres. Children fill their jars with water, mud, and algae. During the next few weeks, the children observe changes in the color of water, growth of plants, and presence of hatched snails. (Middle Childhood)

Minimize loud noises and potential distractions when working with children who are easily diverted from task completion.

- A school psychologist is administering a battery of tests to a 7-year-old boy who is suspected of having a significant learning disability. Before the testing session, the psychologist puts away the Russian nesting dolls that decorate her office shelves. She also removes all of the testing materials from sight, putting items in front of the boy only when it is time to use them. (Middle Childhood)
- When administering a test at the end of a term, a high school mathematics teacher closes the classroom door, answers students' questions individually in a hushed voice, and reminds students to remain quiet while waiting for others to finish. (Late Adolescence)

Present stimulating activities in which children *want* to pay attention.

- In a unit on nutrition, a high school biology teacher has students determine the nutritional value of various menu items at a popular local fast-food restaurant. (Late Adolescence)
- In a photo editing class, high school students are especially engaged when asked to help with the yearbook. Students design double-page spreads, crop photos, and apply special effects on the images. (Late Adolescence)

Get children physically involved in tasks and lessons.

- A middle school history teacher plans a special event late in the school year when all of his students will "go back in time" to the American Civil War. In preparation for the occasion, the students spend several weeks learning about the Battle of Gettysburg, researching typical dress and meals of the era, gathering appropriate clothing and equipment, and preparing snacks and lunches. On the day of the "battle," students assume various roles: Union and Confederate soldiers, government officials, merchants, housewives, doctors and nurses, etc. (Early Adolescence)
- In a high school earth systems class, students go outside to examine the relationships among different ecological systems: a hydrosphere (e.g., pond), a biosphere (e.g., tree), and a geosphere (e.g., floodplain). The teacher gives the students a worksheet and asks them to describe and draw the different systems and speculate about their interdependences. (Late Adolescence)

Incorporate a variety of activities into the daily schedule.

- After explaining how to calculate the areas of squares and rectangles, a fourth-grade teacher has her students practice calculating areas in word problems. She then breaks the class into small cooperative groups. Each group is given a tape measure and calculator and asked to determine the area of the classroom floor, excluding those parts of the floor covered by built-in cabinets. To complete the task, the students must divide the room into several smaller rectangles, compute the area of each rectangle separately, and add the figures together. (Middle Childhood)
- In a high school drama class, a teacher introduces students to various forms of comedy. Students watch and critique a brief recording of a stand-up comedian and then read a couple of pages from a comedic play. Students end the lesson by forming teams and performing brief improvisational skits about awkward high school moments. (Late Adolescence)

Provide frequent breaks from sedentary activities.

- To provide practice with the alphabet, a kindergarten teacher occasionally has students make letters with their bodies: one child standing with arms extended up and out to make a *Y,* two children bending over and joining hands to form an *M,* and so on. (Early Childhood)
- After a class discussion about a book they are reading together, a middle school literacy teacher allows students to move quietly around the room as they plan the key ideas that they will elaborate on in their written reports. (Early Adolescence)

Preparing for Your Licensure Examination

Your teaching test may ask you how to address children's basic cognitive processes during instruction.

can mentally manipulate only a very limited amount of material in their heads at once. Thus teachers and other adults who instruct children should pace any presentation of new information slowly enough that the children have time to "process" it all. Educators might also write complex directions or problems on a chalkboard or ask children to write them on paper.

• **When determining what children know or are ready to learn, consider not only what they say but also what they do and create.** Earlier we described a 6-year-old who said that a tall, thin glass had more water than a short, wide dish because of the height difference between the two containers. At the same time, she showed through her gestures that the tall container had a smaller diameter than the short one. Such discrepancies in what children say and do suggest a possible readiness for developing new ideas and logical reasoning skills—for instance, a readiness for acquiring conservation of liquid (Goldin-Meadow, 1997, 2006). In some instances adults might assess children's current knowledge by asking them to draw rather than describe what they have learned.

   • **Give children ongoing practice in basic information and skills.** Some information and skills are so fundamental that children must learn to retrieve and use them quickly and effortlessly. To write well, children should be able to form letters and words without having to stop and think about how to make an uppercase *G* or spell the word *friend*. And to solve mathematical word problems, they should have such number facts as "2 + 4 = 6" and "5 × 9 = 45" on the tips of their tongues.

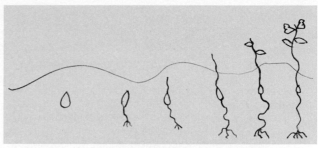

ARTIFACT 7-2   Noah's sprout. Eight-year-old Noah draws a seed becoming a plant. His picture reveals understandings that roots typically go down before a stalk grows up and that leaves gradually increase in size and number.

   Ultimately, children can automatize basic information and skills only by using and practicing them repeatedly (J. C. Anderson, 1983; Berninger et al., 2010; W. Schneider & Shiffrin, 1977). This is definitely *not* to say that teachers should fill each day with endless drill-and-practice exercises involving isolated facts and procedures. Automatization can occur just as readily when the basics are embedded in a variety of stimulating, challenging (and perhaps authentic) activities.

   The Developmental Trends table "Basic Information Processing Characteristics at Different Age Levels" summarizes the capabilities of children and adolescents in various age-groups. We now focus on two manifestations of the *central executive:* metacognition and cognitive strategies.

METACOGNITION AND COGNITIVE STRATEGIES

In the process of learning and remembering information, children gain insights into their own cognitive processes. These reflections on thoughts and memories help children to understand how their minds work and give them insights into how they can take active control of their mental processes. Such knowledge and control of one's own mental processes are collectively known as **metacognition**. The specific mental processes that children intentionally use to regulate their own thinking are known as **cognitive strategies**. In this section we look at development in five important aspects of metacognition: learning strategies, problem-solving strategies, metacognitive awareness, self-regulated learning, and epistemic beliefs.

Learning Strategies

As you are finding out, children are able to remember some but not all of the information they encounter on a daily basis. As they progress through school, it becomes necessary for children to identify key points and store essential ideas in ways that facilitate later recall.

   Toddlers as young as 18 months occasionally show conscious attempts to remember things (Bjorklund, Dukes, & Brown, 2009; DeLoache, Cassidy, & Brown, 1985). When asked to remember where a doll has been hidden in their home, they may stare or point at the location where they saw it being placed until they are able to go get it. Yet overall, young children rarely make a point of trying to learn and remember something. In fact, 4- and 5-year-olds can remember a set of objects more successfully by playing with the objects than by intentionally trying to remember them (L. S. Newman, 1990).

   As they progress through the elementary and secondary grades, children and adolescents develop an increasing number of *learning strategies*—techniques that they intentionally use to learn something—that help them remember information more effectively. Three that appear during the school years are rehearsal, organization, and elaboration.

Preparing for Your Licensure Examination
Your teaching test may ask you to distinguish metacognition from basic cognitive processes.

metacognition
Knowledge and beliefs about one's own cognitive processes, as well as efforts to regulate those cognitive processes to maximize learning and memory.

cognitive strategy
Specific mental process that people intentionally use to acquire or manipulate information.

DEVELOPMENTAL TRENDS
Basic Information Processing Characteristics at Different Age Levels

AGE	WHAT YOU MIGHT OBSERVE	DIVERSITY	IMPLICATIONS
Infancy (Birth–2 Years) 	• Some ability to learn and remember evident from birth • Adult-like hearing acuity within hours after birth • Considerable improvement in visual acuity during the first year • Preference for moderately complex stimuli • Attention easily drawn to intense or novel stimuli • By 3 or 4 months of age, some ability to integrate information (e.g., acquisition of general concepts such as *dog* and *chair*)	• Variations in attention spans are partly due to differences in temperament, but persistent inability to focus on any one object may signal a cognitive disability. • Exploration tendencies vary considerably: Some children constantly seek new experiences, whereas others are more comfortable with familiar objects.	• Change some toys and materials regularly to capture infants' interests and provide new experiences. • Provide objects that can be easily categorized (e.g., colored blocks, plastic farm animals). • Allow for differences in interest, attention span, and exploratory behavior; offer choices of toys and activities.
Early Childhood (2–6 Years) 	• Short attention span • Distractibility • Conscious recall of past events • Some understanding and use of symbols • Limited knowledge base with which to interpret new experiences	• Pronounced disabilities in information processing (e.g., attention-deficit hyperactivity disorder, dyslexia) begin to reveal themselves in children's behaviors or academic performance. • Children's prior knowledge differs markedly depending on their cultural and socioeconomic backgrounds.	• Change activities often. • Keep unnecessary distractions to a minimum. • Provide a variety of experiences (field trips to the library, fire department, etc.) that enrich children's knowledge base. • Consult experts when delays in acquisition of basic academic skills suggest a possible learning disability.
Middle Childhood (6–10 Years) 	• Increasing ability to focus on important stimuli and ignore irrelevant stimuli • Increasingly symbolic thought and knowledge • Gradual automatization of many basic skills • Increasing exposure to environments beyond the home and family, leading to an expanding knowledge base • Knowledge of academic subject matter consisting largely of discrete, unintegrated facts, especially in science and social studies	• Many children with learning disabilities or attention-deficit hyperactivity disorder have short attention spans and are easily distracted. • Some children with learning disabilities have a smaller working memory capacity than their peers. • Mild cognitive disabilities may not become evident until the middle or upper elementary grades.	• Intersperse sedentary activities with physically active ones to help children maintain attention. • Provide many opportunities to rehearse basic knowledge and skills (e.g., number facts, word recognition), often through authentic, motivating, and challenging tasks. • Begin to explore hierarchies, cause and effect, and other interrelationships among ideas in various disciplines.
Early Adolescence (10–14 Years) 	• Ability to attend to a single task for an hour or more • Largely automatized skills in reading, writing, and mathematics (e.g., word identification, common word spellings, basic math facts) • Growing (although not necessarily well integrated) knowledge base related to various topics and academic disciplines	• Many adolescents with information processing difficulties have trouble paying attention for a typical class period. • Many adolescents with sensory or physical disabilities (e.g., those who are visually impaired or in a wheelchair) have less-than-average knowledge about some topics, due to fewer opportunities to explore the world around them.	• Provide variety in learning activities as a way of keeping young adolescents' attention. • Frequently point out how concepts and ideas are related to one another, both within and across content domains. • Provide extra guidance and support for those with diagnosed or suspected information processing difficulties.
Late Adolescence (14–18 Years) 	• Ability to attend to a single task for lengthy periods • Extensive and moderately integrated knowledge in some content domains • Ability to engage in fairly sophisticated symbolic reasoning	• High school students have choices in course selection, leading to differences in the their knowledge base in various content areas. • Students' attention can vary considerably from one class to another, depending on their intrinsic interest in the subject matter at hand.	• Occasionally give assignments that require adolescents to focus on a particular task for a long period. • Consistently encourage adolescents to think about the "hows" and "whys" of what they are learning. • Assess learning in ways that require adolescents to depict relationships among ideas.

Rehearsal

What do you do if you need to remember a telephone number for a few minutes? Do you repeat it to yourself over and over as a way of keeping it in your working memory until you can dial it? Such repetition of information as a way of remembering it is known as **rehearsal**.

Rehearsal is rare in preschoolers but increases in frequency and effectiveness throughout the elementary school years. By age 7 or 8, many children spontaneously rehearse individual pieces of information as a way of remembering the information. By age 9 or 10, they become more strategic, combining several items into a single list as they rehearse. If they hear the list "cat, dog, horse," they might say "cat" after the first item, "cat, dog" after the second, and "cat, dog, horse" after the third. Repeating items in this cumulative manner helps children remember items more successfully, at least for a minute or so (Bjorklund, Dukes, et al., 2009; Kunzinger, 1985; Lehmann & Hasselhorn, 2007). Yet rehearsal is a relatively *in*effective strategy for remembering information over the long run unless, in the process, children also try to make sense of the information by relating it to something they already know (Cermak & Craik, 1979).

Organization

Take a minute to study and remember the following 12 words, then cover them and try to recall as many as you can:

shirt	table	hat
carrot	bed	squash
pants	potato	stool
chair	shoe	bean

In what order did you remember the words? Did you recall them in their original order, or did you rearrange them somehow? If you are like most people, you grouped the words into three semantic categories—clothing, furniture, and vegetables—and recalled them category by category. In other words, you used **organization** to help you learn and remember the information.

As early as 3 or 4 months old, children begin to organize their experiences mentally into categories (Kovack-Lesh, Horst, & Oakes, 2008; Quinn, 2002). After seeing pictures of various dogs, they may gradually lose interest, but their interest is apt to pick up again when, for a change, they see a picture of a cat.[12] By 6 to 12 months, some of their categories seem to be based on perceptual similarity (e.g., *balls* are round, *blocks* are cubes), but they also show emerging knowledge of more general, abstract categories (e.g., *vehicles, furniture*) (Bornstein, Arterberry, & Mash, 2010; Horst, Oakes, & Madole, 2005; Mandler, 2007b). By age 2, children may physically pick up objects and sort them by theme or function, perhaps using classifications such as "things for the feet" or "kitchen things" (Bornstein & Arterberry, 2010; DeLoache & Todd, 1988; Mandler, Fivush, & Reznick, 1987).

As children move through the elementary, middle school, and secondary grades, they become increasingly effective in using organization as a learning strategy (Bjorklund, Dukes, et al., 2009; Lucariello, Kyratzis, & Nelson, 1992; Pressley & Hilden, 2006). Their organizational strategies become more sophisticated, reflecting a variety of hierarchical and often fairly abstract categories. Children also come to be more flexible in their organizational schemes. For example, consider the several alternatives that 17-year-old Paul identifies for organizing shells in the "Intelligence: Late Adolescence" video in MyEducationLab:

> Yeah, I could do them by color, smoothness. Some are rough, some got little jagged edges on them. Some are just smooth. And these big ones, they could do like patterns and stuff.

Elaboration

If we authors tell you that we've both spent many years living in Colorado, you will probably conclude that we either live or have lived in or near the Rocky Mountains. In this situation you're not only learning the information we told you, you're also learning some information

[12]Children who grow bored with repeated exposure to the same stimulus are showing *habituation*, a process that is introduced in Chapter 2.

MyEducationLab

Notice Paul's ability to consider multiple organizational structures for sorting shells in the "Intelligence: Late Adolescence" video. (Find Video Examples in Topic 7 of MyEducationLab.)

rehearsal
Attempt to learn and remember information by repeating it over and over.

organization
Process of identifying interrelationships among pieces of information as a way of learning them more effectively.

that you yourself supplied. This process of using your existing knowledge to embellish on new information is known as **elaboration**. Elaborating on new information typically facilitates learning and memory, sometimes quite dramatically.

Children begin to elaborate on their experiences in the preschool years (Fivush, Haden, & Adam, 1995). As a strategy that they *intentionally* use to help them learn, however, elaboration appears relatively late in development (usually around puberty) and gradually increases throughout the teenage years (Bjorklund, Dukes, et al., 2009; W. Schneider & Pressley, 1989). Even in high school, it is primarily students with high academic achievement who use their existing knowledge to help them expand on and remember new information. Low achievers are much less likely to use elaboration when they study, and many students of all ability levels resort to rehearsal for difficult, hard-to-understand material (J. E. Barnett, 2001; Pressley, 1982). The following interview with 15-year-old "Beth," who earns mostly As in her classes but must work hard to get them, illustrates how infrequently some high school students elaborate on classroom subject matter:

Adult: Once you have some information that you think you need to know, what types of things do you do so that you will remember it?

Beth: I take notes . . . [pause].

Adult: Is that all you do?

Beth: Usually. Sometimes I make flash cards.

Adult: What types of things do you usually put on flash cards?

Beth: I put words I need to know. Like spelling words. I put dates and what happened then.

Adult: How would you normally study flash cards or your notes?

Beth: My notes, I read them over a few times. Flash cards I look at once and try to remember what's on the other side and what follows it. (interview courtesy of Evie Greene)

Notice how Beth emphasizes taking notes and studying flash cards, approaches that typically require little or no elaboration. In fact, the repetitive use of flash cards is really just a form of rehearsal.

Why do some children tend to use advanced learning strategies whereas others do not? Instruction appears to be key. When teachers talk regularly about memory (e.g., "What are some good ways to remember that formula? Can you form a picture in your mind?") and encourage children to use various memory strategies, children tend to deploy memory strategies themselves and achieve at high levels academically (Moely, Santulli, & Obach, 1995; P. A. Ornstein, Grammer, & Coffman, 2010).

Problem-Solving Strategies

By the time children are a year old, they have some ability to think about and solve problems. Imagine that an infant sees an attractive toy beyond her reach. One end of a string is attached to the toy, and its other end is attached to a cloth closer at hand. But between the cloth and the infant is a foam rubber barrier. The infant puts two and two together, realizing that to accomplish her goal (getting the toy), she has to do several things in sequence. She removes the barrier, pulls the cloth toward her, grabs the string, and reels in the toy (Willatts, 1990). This ability to break a problem into two or more subgoals and work toward each one in turn continues to develop during the preschool and elementary school years (e.g., Klahr & Robinson, 1981; Welsh, 1991). Children gradually learn to inhibit the impulse to act on responses that come immediately to mind, and they slowly develop proficiencies in generating a range of possible solutions and shifting their attention flexibly as they execute the various steps of a complex plan (Agostino, Johnson, & Pascual-Leone, 2010; Baughman & Cooper, 2007).

As children get older, their problem-solving strategies become increasingly mental rather than behavioral. Often their mental problem solving involves applying certain *rules* to a problem, with more complex and effective rules evolving over time. As an example, consider the balancing task depicted in Figure 7-4. The top half of the figure shows a metal beam

elaboration
Process of using prior knowledge to embellish new information and thereby learn it more effectively.

balancing on a fulcrum at its midpoint. In the bottom half of the figure, we hold the beam steady while hanging 3- and 6-pound weights at particular locations (nine notches to the left of the fulcrum and four notches to the right, respectively). Will the beam continue to be balanced when we let go of it, or will one side fall?

Children acquire a series of increasingly complex rules to solve such a problem (G. Andrews, Halford, Murphy, & Knox, 2009; Siegler, 1976, 1978). Initially (perhaps at age 5), they consider only the amount of weight on each side of the beam. Comparing 6 pounds (at right) to 3 pounds (at left), they would predict that the right side of the beam will fall. Later (perhaps at age 9), they begin to consider distance as well as weight. They realize that weights located farther from the fulcrum have a greater effect, but their reasoning is not precise enough to ensure correct solutions. For the problem in Figure 7-4, they would merely guess at how greater distance compensates for greater weight. Eventually (perhaps in high school), they may develop a rule that reflects a multiplicative relationship between weight and distance:

> For the beam to balance, the product of weight and distance on one side must equal the product of weight and distance on the other side. In cases where the two products are unequal, the side with the larger product will fall.

Applying this rule to the problem in Figure 7-4, they would determine that the product on the left side ($3 \times 9 = 27$) is greater than the product on the right side ($6 \times 4 = 24$) and so would correctly predict that the left side will fall.

The equipment: Balance and weights

The problem

FIGURE 7-4 Balancing act. A beam without weights balances on a fulcrum located at its center. After weights are hung from the beam in the manner shown here, will the beam continue to balance? If not, which side of the beam will drop?

Strategy Development as "Overlapping Waves"

Children tend to acquire new learning and problem-solving strategies gradually over time. Initially, they are likely to use a strategy infrequently and ineffectively. With time and practice, they become more adept at applying it efficiently, flexibly, and successfully to tackle challenging tasks (P. A. Alexander, Graham, & Harris, 1998; Siegler & Alibali, 2005).

By the time children reach elementary school, they may have several strategies to choose from when dealing with a particular learning or problem-solving task, and the specific strategy they use may vary from one occasion to another. Some strategies are apt to be more advanced than others, yet because children initially have trouble using the more advanced ones effectively, they may resort to less efficient but more dependable "backup" strategies. For example, even after children have learned their basic math facts ($2 + 4 = 6$, $9 - 7 = 2$, etc.), they sometimes resort to counting on their fingers to solve simple addition and subtraction problems. Eventually, however, children acquire sufficient proficiency with their new strategies that they can comfortably leave their less efficient ones behind (P. A. Alexander et al., 1998; Kuhn & Pease, 2010; Siegler & Alibali, 2005).

From an information processing perspective, then, development of strategies does not occur in discrete, one-step-at-a-time stages. Instead, each strategy develops slowly and increases in frequency and effectiveness over a lengthy period, perhaps over several months or years. Later it may gradually fade from the scene as a better strategy emerges to take its place. American psychologist **Robert Siegler** and colleagues have observed that the rise and fall of various strategies is similar to the *overlapping waves* depicted in Figure 7-5 (Siegler, 1996; Siegler & Alibali, 2005). Children use several strategies, gradually favoring ones that produce successful performances, in areas as

FIGURE 7-5 Strategic development as overlapping waves. Children gradually replace simple strategies with more advanced and effective ones. Here we see how five different strategies for dealing with the same task might change in frequency over time.

From Children's Thinking *(4th ed., p. 98), by R. Siegler and M. W. Alibali, 2005, Upper Saddle River, NJ: Prentice Hall. Copyright 2005 by Prentice Hall. Adapted with permission of Prentice-Hall, Inc., Upper Saddle River, NJ.*

diverse as crawling, spelling, and counting (Chetland & Fluck, 2007; Heineman, Middelburg, & Hadders-Algra, 2010; Kwong & Varnhagen, 2005).

Metacognitive Awareness

In addition to acquiring new learning and problem-solving strategies, children acquire increasingly sophisticated knowledge about the nature of thinking. This **metacognitive awareness** includes a conscious appreciation of one's thought processes, an understanding of the limits of human memory, and knowledge of the relative effectiveness of various learning strategies.

Awareness of the Existence of Thought

By the time children are 3 years old, they are aware of thinking as an entity in its own right (Balcomb & Gerken, 2008; Flavell, Green, & Flavell, 1995). Their initial understanding of thought is quite simplistic, however. They are likely to say that a person is "thinking" only when he or she appears to be physically engaged in a challenging task and has a thoughtful or puzzled facial expression. They also view thinking and learning as relatively passive activities (e.g., the mind acquires and holds information but doesn't do much with it), rather than as the active, constructive processes they actually are (Flavell et al., 1995; Wellman, 1990).

Awareness of One's Own Thought Processes

Young children have only a limited ability to look inward at their own thoughts and knowledge (Flavell, Green, & Flavell, 2000). Although many preschoolers have the words *know, remember,* and *forget* in their vocabularies, they don't fully grasp the nature of these mental phenomena in themselves. Three-year-olds use the term *forget* simply to mean "not knowing" something, regardless of whether they knew the information at an earlier time (Lyon & Flavell, 1994). And when 4- and 5-year-old children are taught a new piece of information, they may say that they've known it for quite some time (M. Taylor, Esbensen, & Bennett, 1994). The following interview, which a kindergarten teacher aide conducted with a bright 5-year-old whom we'll call "Ethan," illustrates the relatively superficial awareness that young children have of thought processes:

Aide:	When you learn a new song, like "The Horne Street School Song," how do you remember the words?
Ethan:	I just remember. I didn't know how to sing it for a while until I listened to the words enough to remember them.
Aide:	When I ask you during group time to "put on your thinking caps," what do I mean?
Ethan:	It means think. You think hard until you know what you are trying to think about. . . . I don't really know how you think, you just do. . . .
Aide:	How do you remember to give Mommy and Papa papers that we send home?
Ethan:	My good memory.
Aide:	Why do you have a good memory?
Ethan:	It's just good. It started when I turned three. I still had it when I was four, and now when I am five. (interview courtesy of Betsy Hopkins)

During the elementary and secondary school years, young people become better able to reflect on their own thought processes and are increasingly aware of the nature of thinking (Jaswal & Dodson, 2009; Wellman & Hickling, 1994).

Understanding of Memory Limitations

Young children tend to be overly optimistic about how much they can remember. As they grow older and encounter a wide variety of learning tasks, they discover that some things are more difficult to learn than others (Bjorklund, Dukes, et al., 2009; Flavell et al., 2002; Grammer, Purtell, Coffman, & Ornstein, 2011; B. L. Schwartz & Perfect, 2002). They also

metacognitive awareness Extent to which one is able to reflect on the nature of one's own thinking processes.

begin to realize that their memories are not perfect and that they cannot possibly remember everything they see or hear. In one study (Flavell, Friedrichs, & Hoyt, 1970), preschoolers and elementary school children were shown pictures of 1 to 10 objects and asked to predict how many objects they could remember for a short time period. The average predictions of each of four age-groups and the average number of objects the children actually remembered were as follows:

Age-Group	Predicted Number	Actual Number
Preschool	7.2	3.5
Kindergarten	8.0	3.6
Grade 2	6.0	4.4
Grade 4	6.1	5.5

Notice that children in all four age-groups predicted that they would remember more objects than they actually did. But the older children were more realistic about the limitations of their memories.

Being naive is a mixed blessing for young children. Anticipating that they will be successful in remembering information, young children fail to apply extra procedures that might help with memory. Yet their overly optimistic assessment of their mental abilities has a distinct benefit for cognitive development. It may give them the necessary confidence to try new and difficult tasks—challenges that are likely to promote cognitive growth (Bjorklund, Dukes, et al., 2009).

Knowledge about Effective Learning and Memory Strategies

Imagine that it's winter and you live in a cold climate. Just before you go to bed, some friends ask you to go ice skating with them after class tomorrow. What might you do to be sure you will remember to take your ice skates to class with you? Older children typically generate more strategies than younger children for remembering to take a pair of skates to school. Yet even 5- and 6-year-olds can identify one or more effective strategies—perhaps writing a note to themselves, recording a reminder on a tape recorder, or leaving their skates next to their school bag (Kreutzer, Leonard, & Flavell, 1975).

Not only do children acquire more effective learning strategies (e.g., organization, elaboration) as they grow older, but they also become increasingly aware of what strategies are effective in different situations (Lovett & Flavell, 1990; Schneider & Lockl, 2002; Short, Schatschneider, & Friebert, 1993). Consider the simple idea that when you don't learn something the first time you try, you need to study it again. This is a strategy that 8-year-olds use, but 6-year-olds do not (Masur, McIntyre, & Flavell, 1973). Similarly, 10th graders are more aware than 8th graders of the advantages of using elaboration to learn new information (H. S. Waters, 1982). Even so, many children and adolescents seem relatively uninformed about which learning strategies work most effectively in different situations (Joseph, 2010; Kuhn, Garcia-Mila, Zohar, & Andersen, 1995; J. W. Thomas, 1993). The following interview with "Amy," a 16-year-old with a history of low school achievement, illustrates how metacognitively naive some adolescents are:

Adult: What is learning?

Amy: Something you do to get knowledge.

Adult: What is knowledge?

Amy: Any information that I don't know.

Adult: What about the things you already know?

Amy: That doesn't count.

Adult: Doesn't count?

Amy: As knowledge, because I already know it.

Adult: How do you know when you have learned something?

Amy: When I can repeat it, and it is the same as what the teacher said or what I read, and I can remember it forever or a really long time. (interview courtesy of Jennifer Glynn)

Notice how Amy thinks she has learned something when she can repeat what a teacher or textbook has told her. She says nothing about *understanding* classroom subject matter. And curiously, she thinks of knowledge as things she *doesn't* know.

Self-Regulated Learning

As children and adolescents gain awareness of their learning and memory processes, they become more capable of **self-regulated learning**—that is, they begin to control and direct their own learning. Self-regulated learning involves strategies such as these:

- Setting goals for a learning activity
- Planning an effective use of study time
- Keeping attention on the subject matter to be learned
- Motivating oneself to persist while studying
- Identifying and using appropriate learning strategies
- Monitoring progress toward learning goals
- Evaluating the effectiveness of learning strategies
- Adjusting goals or learning strategies depending on progress
- Evaluating the final knowledge gained from the learning activity. (Boekaerts, 2006, 2009; Meltzer & Krishnan, 2007; Muis, 2007; S. M. Reis, 2011; B. J. Zimmerman & Schunk, 2004)

The experiences of a group of middle school students who had been supported by their teacher in setting short-term academic goals illustrate the benefits of self-regulation (T. M. McDevitt et al., 2008). Students regularly analyzed their own test score results regarding how they fared in meeting state standards in literacy (e.g., being able to differentiate fact from opinion and discern the main idea in a passage; Colorado Department of Education, 2007). After analyzing their performance on tests, students set specific targets and designed steps to meet these aspirations during the coming weeks. When asked what they liked about setting their own goals, students reported such advantages as these:

- Satisfaction in making their own choices (e.g., "I like being able to do what I want and read what I want.")
- Academic benefits of personalized study (e.g., "I like that by setting these goals, I can accomplish them and improve my reading.")
- Enjoyment of the challenge (e.g., "It helps to motivate you to get your work done."). (T. M. McDevitt et al., 2008, p. 129)

Of course, carrying out the multifaceted process of self-regulation can be difficult. Students reported several challenges, including these:

- Uncertainty as to how to meet their goals (e.g., "I don't know which activities will help me most.")
- Vacillations over optimal levels of challenge (e.g., "The kinds of difficulties I have faced were trying not to pick really easy goals and to pick goals that would make me think.")
- Insufficient time or commitment (e.g., "If I don't keep practicing them, I won't ever learn them."). (T. McDevitt et al., 2008, p. 130)

SELF-REGULATED LEARNING. Children who engage in self-regulated learning set goals for themselves, choose effective learning strategies, and monitor their learning progress.

Rudimentary capacities for self-regulated learning are evident beginning in early childhood, when many children show flashes of self-control, perhaps by ignoring rather than hitting an annoying classmate or staying focused on a plan to build a tall tower even when it wobbles (Demetriou, 2000; Kopp, 1982). Some preschool teachers encourage children to keep their plans in mind in the face of distractions and temptations, for example, by asking children to plan a specific activity (perhaps playing with a friend in the housekeeping area or riding a tricycle outside), carry it out, and return with a report on their play (Bodrova & Leong, 2009; Hohmann &Weikart, 2002).

self-regulated learning
Directing and controlling one's own cognitive processes in order to learn successfully.

Of course, self-regulatory skills are a long time in the making. In many circumstances, elementary school children and adolescents have difficulty effectively regulating their own learning on academic tasks (Bronson, 2000; B. J. Zimmerman & Risemberg, 1997). This delay is due in part to the difficulty of remaining introspective and acting strategically when engaged in a multistep activity (Moschner, Anschuetz, Wernke, & Wagener, 2008). Fortunately, teachers can foster children's capacity for self-regulatory learning by giving children numerous opportunities to set goals and practice particular strategies (Perels, Merget-Kullmann, Wende, Schmitz, & Buchbinder, 2009; Tracy, Reid, & Graham, 2009; Yoon, 2009). Of particular importance is that at least some of the goals that children pursue are of personal interest so that they develop their own sense of curiosity (A. Kohn, 2008).

Epistemic Beliefs

As someone who learns new things every day, you undoubtedly have ideas about what "knowledge" and "learning" are. Such ideas are collectively known as **epistemic beliefs**. Included in people's epistemic beliefs are their views about the stability, certainty, structure, and source of knowledge, as well as about the purpose and speed of learning activities.

As children develop, many (though not all) of them change their beliefs about knowledge and learning. Typical changes are shown in Table 7-1. Most children in the elementary grades think that the absolute truth about any topic is "out there" somewhere, waiting to be discovered (Astington & Pelletier, 1996; Kuhn & Weinstock, 2002). Late in the elementary school years, children occasionally realize that two people can have the same information yet come to a very different interpretation about it (Chandler, Hallett, & Sokol, 2002). Nevertheless, it is generally not until they reach adolescence that they apply this insight regularly. During adolescence, many young people realize that knowledge is a subjective entity and that two or more perspectives on a topic may each have some merit (Schommer, 1994b; Schommer, Calvert, Gariglietti, & Bajaj, 1997; Tabak & Weinstock, 2008). Eventually some realize that certain interpretations have more merit than others—that each must be evaluated on the basis of research evidence and logical arguments (Kuhn & Weinstock, 2002).

Additional changes may occur in high school. Twelfth graders are more likely than ninth graders to believe that knowledge consists of complex interrelationships (rather than

Bioecology of Child Development

Children develop capacities for self-regulated learning through neurological maturation; practice in setting and pursuing goals; and guidance from parents, teachers, and cultural traditions.

epistemic belief
Belief regarding the nature of knowledge and knowledge acquisition.

TABLE 7-1 Developmental Changes in Epistemic Beliefs

WITH REGARD TO . . .	CHILDREN INITIALLY BELIEVE THAT . . .	AS THEY DEVELOP, THEY MAY EVENTUALLY BEGIN TO REALIZE THAT . . .
The stability and certainty of knowledge	Knowledge about a topic is a fixed, unchanging, absolute "truth" that should not be questioned.	Knowledge about a topic (even that of experts) is tentative and dynamic. It continues to evolve as ongoing research adds new insights and ideas. Multiple interpretations of an issue are possible, but each should be critically examined and evaluated on the basis of objective evidence and logical arguments.
The structure of knowledge	Knowledge is a collection of discrete, largely unrelated facts.	Knowledge is a set of complex and interrelated ideas.
The source of knowledge	Knowledge comes from outside the learner, perhaps from firsthand observation of the physical world or perhaps from a teacher or other authority figure.	Knowledge is derived and constructed by learners themselves.
The goal of a learning activity	Learning involves committing certain facts and procedures to memory.	Learning involves gaining deep understanding of complex concepts and their interrelationships.
The speed of learning	Knowledge is acquired quickly, and in an all-or-nothing fashion, or else not at all. As a result, people either know something or they don't.	Knowledge is acquired gradually over time. Thus people can have greater or lesser degrees of knowledge about a topic.

Sources: Astington & Pelletier, 1996; B. K. Hofer & Pintrich, 1997, 2002; B. K. Hofer & Sinatra, 2010; Kuhn & Franklin, 2006; Kuhn & Park, 2005; Kuhn & Weinstock, 2002; M. C. Linn, Songer, & Eylon, 1996; Muis, 2007; Perkins & Ritchhart, 2004; Schommer, 1994a, 1994b; Schommer et al., 1997.

discrete facts), that learning happens slowly (rather than quickly), and that learning can be enhanced by practice and better strategies (Schommer et al., 1997). Some high school students continue to have very superficial views of knowledge and learning, however. Recall how 16-year-old Amy defined *learning* simply as "something you do to get knowledge" and *knowledge* as "any information that I don't know."

Some epistemic beliefs are specific to particular content domains (Buehl & Alexander, 2006; J. A. Chen & Pajares, 2010; Muis, Bendixen, & Haerle, 2006). Adolescents may believe that knowledge in mathematics, the natural sciences, and history is pretty much a "sure thing," whereas knowledge in some social sciences (e.g., psychology) is more tentative (D. Estes, Chandler, Horvath, & Backus, 2003; Haenen, Schrijnemakers, & Stufkens, 2003; B. K. Hofer, 2000; Muis, 2007; Schommer, 1994b). Many adolescents think that learning in math and physics classes means memorizing procedures and formulas and finding single "right" answers to problems (Muis, 2004; Schoenfeld, 1988). In comparison, when they search the Internet for information, adolescents may realize from experience that some websites include invalid and untrustworthy information (Mason, Boldrin, & Ariasi, 2010).

Youngsters' epistemic beliefs influence the ways in which they study and learn at school (J. A. Chen & Pajares, 2010; B. K. Hofer & Pintrich, 2002; Schommer et al., 1997). When students believe that knowledge consists of discrete facts that are indisputably right or wrong, that one either has that knowledge or doesn't, and that learning happens quickly if at all, they may focus on rote memorization of the subject matter and easily give up if they find themselves struggling to understand it. In contrast, when students believe that knowledge is a complex body of information that is learned gradually with time and effort, they are apt to use a wide variety of learning strategies and persist until they've made sense of what they're studying (D. L. Butler & Winne, 1995; Kardash & Howell, 1996; Schommer, 1994b). Not surprisingly, then, students with more advanced epistemic beliefs achieve at higher levels in the classroom (J. A. Chen & Pajares, 2010; B. K. Hofer & Pintrich, 1997; Schommer, 1994a).

More advanced levels of achievement may, in turn, bring about more sophisticated views about knowledge and learning (Schommer, 1994b; Strike & Posner, 1992). The more that students get beyond the "basics" and explore a discipline in depth—whether it is science, mathematics, history, or some other academic domain—the more they discover that learning involves acquiring an integrated and cohesive set of ideas, that even experts don't know everything about a topic, and that truly complete and accurate "knowledge" of how the world operates may ultimately be an unattainable goal.

We speculate, however, that naive epistemic beliefs may have some benefits for young children. Children may initially be more motivated to learn about a topic if they think it involves absolute, unchanging facts that they can easily learn and remember (Ricco, Pierce, & Medinilla, 2010). And even though children ultimately construct many of their own understandings, it is often efficient for them to turn to parents, teachers, and the library as authoritative sources of desired information.

Cultural Roots of Metacognition

Children's metacognitive beliefs and strategies are, in part, the result of the particular social and cultural environments in which they grow up. From the perspective of mainstream Western culture, the acquisition of knowledge is largely for one's personal benefit: People learn in order to understand the world and acquire new skills and abilities. But for many people in China, learning also has moral and social dimensions: It enables an individual to become honorable and to contribute in significant ways to the betterment of society. From a traditional East Asian perspective, true learning is not a quick-and-easy process. Rather, it comes only with a great deal of diligence, concentration, and perseverance (Dahlin & Watkins, 2000; H. Grant & Dweck, 2001; J. Li & Fischer, 2004; Q. Wang & Pomerantz, 2009).

Cultural differences have also been observed in children's willingness to critically evaluate the knowledge and beliefs that adults pass along to them. Some cultures place high value on respecting one's elders or certain religious teachings. In doing so they may foster the epistemic belief that truth in certain domains is a matter of faith and best acquired from revered authority figures (Kuhn, Daniels, & Krishnan, 2003; Qian & Pan, 2002; Tabak &

Weinstock, 2008). In addition, a cultural emphasis on maintaining group harmony may discourage children from discussing and critiquing diverse perspectives on a controversial topic (Kağitçibaşi, 2007; Kuhn & Park, 2005).

Consistent with a belief that learning requires diligence and perseverance, many East Asian parents and teachers encourage frequent use of rehearsal and rote memorization as learning strategies (Dahlin & Watkins, 2000; D. Y. F. Ho, 1994; Purdie & Hattie, 1996). Rehearsal and memorization are also common in cultures that value committing oral histories or verbatim passages of sacred text to memory (MacDonald, Uesiliana, & Hayne, 2000; Rogoff et al., 2007; Q. Wang & Ross, 2007). In contrast, many schools in mainstream Western societies ask students to focus on making sense of classroom material rather than memorizing it word for word. Even so, Western schools typically do insist that students learn certain things (e.g., word spellings, multiplication tables) by heart (Q. Wang & Ross, 2007).

The Developmental Trends table "Cognitive Strategies and Metacognitive Understandings at Different Age Levels" summarizes developmental changes in children's cognitive strategies and metacognitive understandings, as well as some of the metacognitive diversity you are likely to see in any age-group.

Bioecology of Child Development

Children acquire views about learning from their personal experiences in cultural communities.

Promoting Metacognitive and Strategic Development

Most sophisticated cognitive processes involve metacognition; hence, metacognitive development is central to cognitive development. Children are more likely to acquire and use

DEVELOPMENTAL TRENDS
Cognitive Strategies and Metacognitive Understandings at Different Age Levels

AGE	WHAT YOU MIGHT OBSERVE	DIVERSITY	IMPLICATIONS
Infancy (Birth–2 Years) 	• Use of one object to obtain another (in the second year) • Emerging ability to plan a sequence of actions to accomplish a goal (appearing sometime around age 1) • General absence of intentional learning strategies; however, toddlers may look or point at a location to remember where a desired object is hidden • Little awareness and knowledge of thought processes (may have some awareness that other people have intentions[13])	• Emergence of early problem-solving strategies is somewhat dependent on opportunities to experiment with physical objects. • Willingness to engage in trial-and-error problem solving and other exploratory behavior is partly a function of temperamental differences and physical abilities.	• Model tool use and other simple problem-solving strategies. • Pose simple problems for infants and toddlers to solve (e.g., place desired objects slightly out of reach), but monitor children's reactions to make sure they are not unnecessarily frustrated in their efforts to solve problems.
Early Childhood (2–6 Years) 	• Some rehearsal beginning in the preschool years, but with little effect on learning and memory • Occasional use of organization with concrete objects • Some ability to learn simple strategies modeled by others • Awareness of thought in oneself and others, albeit in a simplistic form; limited ability to reflect on the specific nature of one's own thought processes • Belief that learning is a relatively passive activity • Overestimation of how much information one can typically remember	• Children's awareness of the mind and mental events depends partly on the extent to which adults talk with them about thinking processes. • Many young children with autism have little conscious awareness of the existence of thought, especially in other people.[14]	• Talk often about thinking processes (e.g., "I *wonder* if . . . ," "Do you *remember* when . . . ?"). • Model strategies for simple memory tasks (e.g., pinning permission slips on jackets to remind children to get their parents' signatures).

(continued)

[13]Children's understanding of other people's thoughts is explored in Chapter 12.
[14]The characteristics of children with autism are examined in Chapter 12.

DEVELOPMENTAL TRENDS (continued)

AGE	WHAT YOU MIGHT OBSERVE	DIVERSITY	IMPLICATIONS
Middle Childhood (6–10 Years) 	• Use of rehearsal as the predominant intentional learning strategy • Gradual increase in organization as an intentional, conscious learning strategy • Emerging ability to reflect on the nature of one's own thought processes • Frequent overestimation of one's own memory capabilities • Little if any self-regulated learning • Belief that true knowledge about a topic is "out there" somewhere and can often be gained from authority figures	• Some Chinese and Japanese children rely more heavily on rehearsal than do some of their peers in Western schools; this difference continues into adolescence. • Children with cognitive disabilities are less likely to organize material as they learn it. • A few high-achieving children are capable of sustained self-regulated learning, especially in the upper elementary grades.	• Encourage children to repeat and practice the things they need to learn. • To encourage organization as a learning strategy, ask children to study information that is easy to categorize. • Ask children to engage in simple, self-regulated learning tasks; give them suggestions about how to accomplish the tasks successfully.
Early Adolescence (10–14 Years) 	• Emergence of elaboration as an intentional learning strategy • Few and relatively ineffective study strategies (e.g., weak note-taking skills) • Increasing flexibility in the use of learning strategies • Emerging ability to regulate one's own learning • Belief that knowledge about a topic consists of a collection of discrete facts • Recognition that diverse perspectives may all have some merit, but without a critical evaluation of each perspective	• Adolescents differ considerably in their use of effective learning strategies. • Some adolescents, including many with cognitive disabilities, have few strategies for engaging effectively in self-regulated learning.	• Ask questions that encourage adolescents to elaborate on new information. • Teach and model effective strategies within the context of various subject areas. • Assign homework and other tasks that require independent learning, but provide sufficient structure to guide students' efforts. • Give adolescents frequent opportunities to set goals and assess their own learning.
Late Adolescence (14–18 Years) 	• Increase in elaboration • Growing awareness of which cognitive strategies are most effective in different situations • Increasing self-regulatory learning strategies (e.g., setting of goals and keeping track of progress) • Increasing realization that knowledge involves understanding of the interrelationships among ideas • Emerging ability and willingness to critically evaluate conflicting perspectives on an issue (in some students)	• High-achieving teenagers are most likely to use sophisticated learning strategies (e.g., elaboration); low-achieving ones typically resort to simpler, less effective strategies (e.g., rehearsal). • Many teenagers with cognitive disabilities have insufficient reading skills to learn successfully from typical high school textbooks; furthermore, their study skills tend to be relatively ineffective. • Willingness to reflect on and critically evaluate others' ideas is, in part, a function of adolescents' cultural and religious upbringings.	• Continue to teach and model effective learning strategies both in and out of school. • Assign more complex independent learning tasks, giving the necessary structure and guidance for those who are not yet self-regulating learners. • Present various subject areas as dynamic entities that continue to evolve with new discoveries and theories. • Teach specific criteria (e.g., presence of research evidence, logical consistency) by which to evaluate diverse perspectives.

effective strategies when they are aware of the various strategies they use and monitor how well each one helps them reach their goals (M. Carr, 2010; Kuhn, 2001b). Following are several suggestions for fostering the development of metacognition and cognitive strategies.

• **Engage children in discussions about the mind.** As you've seen, even preschoolers have some awareness of the mind and its activities. Adults enhance this awareness by regularly referring to mental activities in day-to-day conversations—for example, by asking children to put on their "thinking caps," describing someone's mind as "wandering," and encouraging children to explain the tactic they might take in learning to ride a bicycle (Perels et al., 2009; Wellman & Hickling, 1994).

As children become more introspective in the elementary and secondary school years, they become better able to reflect on and describe the kinds of things they do mentally as they study and learn. At earlier points in the chapter, we've presented interviews in which children describe their views about thinking, learning, and studying to adults. Such interviews can shed light on young people's study strategies that adults in turn can accommodate in instruction. These conversations may also have educational value for children. Their explanations in mathematics, for example, help children to identify inconsistencies and gaps in their understandings of mathematical concepts (Carr, 2010).

- **Model and teach effective cognitive strategies.** Adults can foster more effective problem-solving strategies by modeling them for children. Infants as young as 6 to 10 months can overcome obstacles to obtain an attractive toy if someone shows them how to do it (Z. Chen, Sanchez, & Campbell, 1997; Horne, Erjavec & Lovett, 2009; Want & Harris, 2001).

Learning strategies, too, can clearly be modeled and taught. Four- and five-year-olds can be taught to organize objects into categories as a way of helping them remember the objects (Carr & Schneider, 1991; Lange & Pierce, 1992). As children encounter increasingly challenging learning tasks at school and elsewhere, simple categorization alone is, of course, not enough. By the time they reach high school, students need to learn—and often must be explicitly taught—strategies such as elaboration, goal setting, note taking, and time management. Ideally, such instruction should be integrated into lessons about specific academic topics, rather than in a separate course or unit (Carr, 2010; K. R. Harris, Santangelo, & Graham, 2010; R. E. Mayer, 2010; Pressley, El-Dinary, Marks, Brown, & Stein, 1992). Once adolescents become proficient in advanced strategies, they are apt to find these strategies more rewarding than simple rehearsal. In the "Memory: Late Adolescence" video in MyEducationLab, 16-year-old Hilary describes her feelings about rehearsal this way:

> Just felt like I was trying to memorize for a test or something. . . . Sometimes it's kind of boring or repetitious, [just] going over it.

Small-group learning and problem-solving activities, especially when structured to encourage effective cognitive processes, can also promote more sophisticated strategies (e.g., Carr, 2010; A. King, 1999; Kuhn & Pease, 2010; Palincsar & Herrenkohl, 1999). One approach is to teach children how to ask one another thought-provoking questions about the material they are studying. The following exchange shows two fifth graders using such questions as they study material about tide pools and tidal zones:

MyEducationLab

Hear Hilary express her view of rehearsal in the "Memory: Late Adolescence" video. (Find Video Examples in Topic 7 of MyEducationLab.)

Janelle:	What do you think would happen if there weren't certain zones for certain animals in the tide pools?
Katie:	They would all be, like, mixed up—and all the predators would kill all the animals that shouldn't be there and then they just wouldn't survive. 'Cause the food chain wouldn't work—'cause the top of the chain would eat all the others and there would be no place for the bottom ones to hide and be protected. And nothing left for them to eat.
Janelle:	O.K. But what about the ones that had camouflage to hide them? (A. King, 1999, p. 95)

Notice how Janelle's questions don't ask Katie to repeat what she has already learned. Instead, Katie must use what she's learned to speculate and draw inferences; in other words, she must engage in elaboration. Questioning like Janelle's appears to promote both better recall of facts and increased integration of ideas, undoubtedly because it encourages more sophisticated learning strategies (Kahl & Woloshyn, 1994; A. King, 1999; E. Wood et al., 1999).

Why are collaborative learning and problem-solving activities so beneficial? For one thing, group members scaffold one another's efforts, providing assistance on difficult tasks and monitoring one another's progress toward a particular goal. Second, group members describe and explain their strategies, allowing others to observe and possibly model them. Third, in a Vygotskian fashion, group members may internalize their group-based strategies.

Preparing for Your Licensure Examination

Your teaching test may ask you how to foster children's metacognitive knowledge and strategies.

Thus, when they engage in mutual question asking, they may eventually ask *themselves,* and then answer, equally challenging questions as they read and study.

- **Expect and encourage increasingly independent learning over time.** On average, self-regulating learners achieve at higher levels in the classroom than do non–self-regulators (Blair & Razza, 2007; Duckworth & Seligman, 2005; Tracy et al., 2009). But self-regulated learning is a complex endeavor that involves many abilities (goal setting, attention control, flexible use of cognitive strategies, etc.) and takes many years to master. Throughout the elementary and secondary school years, teachers and other adults must encourage and scaffold learning in age-appropriate ways. For instance, they might provide examples of questions that encourage elaboration (e.g., "Explain why _____," "What is a new example of _____ ?"). They might provide a general organizational framework that children can follow while taking notes. They might provide guidance about how to develop a good summary (e.g., "Identify or invent a topic sentence," "Find supporting information for each main idea"). Such scaffolding is most likely to be helpful when children are studying subject matter they find difficult to comprehend yet *can* comprehend if they apply appropriate strategies—in other words, when the subject matter is within their zone of proximal development.[15] As children develop increasing proficiency with each self-regulating strategy, the scaffolds can gradually be removed (Meltzer & Krishnan, 2007; Pressley et al., 1992).

In the following mathematics lesson, a first-grade teacher offers what appears to be just the right amount of support in children's strategy use. The teacher instructs children in place value and uses rods to represent 10s, boxes 5s, and squares and tallies both 1s. Notice how she directs children to use a strategy but gives them leeway with their approach:

Teacher: And each box is worth how much?

Student 1: Five.

Teacher: Five, so each tally mark is worth one, each box is worth five. And she's doing a wonderful strategy of putting the amount underneath, counting by fives. Five, 10, 15, and now she's going to add the rest. Will she make another box?

Student 2: No.

Teacher: No, she does not have enough to make a box, but she has her amount. Beautiful! That's how your tally boxes should look for that number. Five, 10, 15, and then 16, 17. (*The teacher is showing the students each box/tally on the board as she calls out the numbers.*) Who will take a risk, and show us that number using place values?

The students raise their hands. The teacher looks around and calls on a student, and he comes up to the overhead.

Teacher: You have two choices. You can use the overhead rods if you'd like, or you can draw them if you'd like. What's a good strategy to do with the number 17 before he even starts with the place values? Is there a good strategy?

Student 3: Yes.

Teacher: Yes. What's a good strategy?

Student 3: You . . . do the 10's and then the 1's. (dialogue from P. A. Ornstein, Coffman, & Grammer, 2009, p. 116)[16]

From this and previous lessons, children are learning that they should identify and implement an effective learning strategy when solving mathematical problems.

---

[15]You can find a description of Vygotsky's notion of the zone of proximal development, the range of tasks that one can perform only with guidance, in Chapter 6.

[16]Table 6.3 from Chapter 6, "Learning to Remember" from HANDBOOK OF CHILD DEVELOPMENT AND EARLY EDUCATION by Oscar A. Babarin and Barbara Hanna Wasik. Copyright © 2009 by Oscar A. Babarin and Barbara Hanna Wasik. Reprinted with permission of Guilford Publications, Inc.

• **Provide opportunities for children to evaluate their own learning, and help them develop mechanisms for doing so effectively.** As noted earlier, self-regulating learners monitor their progress throughout a learning task and then evaluate their ultimate success in mastering what they've been studying. Experts make several recommendations for promoting self-monitoring and self-evaluation:

- Teach children to ask themselves, and then answer, questions about the topic.
- Have children set specific objectives for each session and then describe how they've met each one.
- Provide specific criteria that children can use to judge their performance.
- Encourage children to evaluate their performance realistically, and then reinforce them (e.g., with praise or extra-credit points) when their evaluations match an established standard.
- Have children compile portfolios that include samples of their work, along with a written reflection on the quality and significance of each sample. (Carr, 2010; McCaslin & Good, 1996; M. Morgan, 1985; Paris & Ayres, 1994; Perry, 1998; Rosenshine, Meister, & Chapman, 1996; Schraw, Potenza, & Nebelsick-Gullet, 1993; Silver & Kenney, 1995; Tracy et al., 2009; Winne, 1995b; G. A. Zuckerman, 1994).

You can observe eight-year-old Keenan's self-evaluation in the "Portfolio" video in MyEducationLab. By engaging in ongoing self-evaluation of her performance, Keenan is developing appropriate standards and applying those standards regularly to her accomplishments—true hallmarks of a self-regulating learner.

MyEducationLab

Observe 8-year-old Keenan's self-evaluation of her work in the "Portfolio" video. (Find Video Examples in Topic 7 of MyEducationLab.)

• **Promote more sophisticated epistemic beliefs.** If they are to achieve at high levels in the high school and college years, young people must become aware that knowledge is not merely a cut-and-dried set of facts and that effective learning is not simply a process of mindlessly repeating those facts over and over. One way to foster more advanced epistemic beliefs is to talk openly about the nature of knowledge and learning—for example, to describe learning as an active, ongoing process of making connections among ideas (Schommer, 1994b). Another effective approach is to provide experiences that lead children to discover for themselves that knowledge is dynamic rather than static, that multiple perspectives on an issue may all have some validity, and that successful learning sometimes occurs only through effort and persistence. For example, teachers might give their students complex problems that have no clear-cut right or wrong answers, have students read conflicting accounts and interpretations of historical events, or ask students to compare several different explanations of a particular scientific phenomenon (Britt, Rouet, Georgi, & Perfetti, 1994; Leinhardt, 1994; M. C. Linn et al., 1996; Schommer, 1994b; Tabak & Weinstock, 2008).

In addition, discussions about controversial topics (e.g., various interpretations of a classic work of literature) can help children gain an understanding that there is not always a simple "right" answer to a question or issue (Kuhn, Shaw, & Felton, 1997; C. L. Smith, Maclin, Houghton, & Hennessey, 2000). Furthermore, by struggling as a group with difficult subject matter, children may begin to appreciate that one's knowledge about a topic is likely to evolve and improve gradually over time. And when children have opportunities to formulate questions, discuss one another's explanations, and compare and evaluate potential solutions, they gain practice in all-important strategies (P. Bell & Linn, 2002; Kuhn & Pease, 2010; Muis et al., 2006).

ADDING A SOCIOCULTURAL ELEMENT TO INFORMATION PROCESSING THEORIES

Earlier in the chapter we noted that children show a preference for social stimuli (e.g., human faces, their mother's voice) very early in life. This preference is rooted in the information processing circuits in the brain. Within the first hours after birth, infants show preliminary signs of mimicking other people's facial expressions (e.g., by opening their mouths or

SENSITIVITY TO SOCIAL CUES. Children have distinctively social brains that prompt them to attend to human faces and voices, imitate others' actions, and enter into a state of mutual recognition with caregivers.

sticking out their tongues; Kugiumutzakis, 1999; Meltzoff & Moore, 1977). Evidence is emerging that some primate species, including human beings, have certain neurons, called *mirror neurons*, that fire either when they perform a particular action themselves *or* when they watch another person perform it (Arbib, 2005; Del Giudice, Manera, & Keysers, 2009; Iacoboni & Woods, 1999).

With the distinctly social nature of human beings in mind, some theorists have suggested that a combination of information processing and sociocultural perspectives (such as those of Vygotsky and his followers) provides a better explanation of how cognitive development occurs than either perspective can provide alone. Information processing theories may tell us a great deal about *what* changes over time, and sociocultural views may help us explain *how* those changes occur (Gauvain, 2001; Hobson, 2004; Mareschal et al., 2007). Here we look at three aspects of this blend of information processing theories and sociocultural theories: intersubjectivity, social construction of memory, and collaborative use of cognitive strategies.

Intersubjectivity

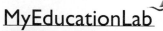

Observe joint attention in the "Literacy: Infancy" video. (Find Video Examples in Topic 7 of MyEducationLab.)

intersubjectivity
Awareness of shared perceptions and understandings that provide the foundation for social interaction.

joint attention
Phenomenon in which two people (e.g., a child and caregiver) simultaneously focus on the same object or event, monitor each other's attention, and coordinate their responses.

social referencing
Looking at someone else (e.g., a caregiver) for clues about how to respond to a particular object or event.

For two people to interact and communicate, they must have shared understandings on which to build. Each member of the pair should have some awareness of what the other person sees, knows, thinks, and feels. Such mutual understanding is known as **intersubjectivity**. The beginnings of intersubjectivity are seen at about 2 months of age, when infants and their caregivers focus on one another through eye contact, exchanges of smiles and the give-and-take of vocalizations (Adamson & McArthur, 1995; Kingstone, Smilek, Ristic, Friesen, & Eastwood, 2003; E. Nagy, 2008).

Sometime around 9 or 10 months of age, intersubjectivity becomes more complex and takes the form of **joint attention**. At this point, an infant and caregiver can simultaneously focus on a single object, with both members of the pair monitoring the *other's* attention to the object and coordinating their behaviors toward the target of their common interest (Adamson & McArthur, 1995; M. Carpenter, 2011; Gaffan, Martins, Healy, & Murray, 2010; Trevarthen & Hubley, 1978). You can see joint attention in action as 16-month-old Corwin and his mother read a book together in the "Literacy: Infancy" video in MyEducationLab.

Early in the second year, infants also begin to show **social referencing**, the act of looking at someone else for clues about how to respond to or feel about a particular object or event (Feinman, 1992; Klinnert, Emde, Butterfield, & Campos, 1986; G. Stenberg, 2009). Children are most likely to engage in social referencing when they encounter a new and uncertain situation. In one study (Klinnert, 1984), 1- and 1½-year-old infants were shown three new toys to which their mothers had been instructed to respond with a happy, fearful, or neutral expression. Upon seeing each new toy, most infants looked at their mother and chose actions consistent with her response. They typically moved toward the toy if Mom showed pleasure, but moved away from it if she showed fear.

As information processing theorists tell us, attention is critical to learning and cognitive development. As we bring the sociocultural perspective into the picture, we see that awareness of a *partner's* attention is critical as well (Gauvain, 2001; P. Mundy & Newell, 2007). For instance, when an adult uses a word that a toddler has never heard before, the toddler will often look immediately at the speaker's face and follow the speaker's line of vision to the object being inspected. In this way, children probably learn many object labels (D. A. Baldwin, 2000; Kwisthout, Vogt, Haselager, & Dijkstra, 2008). In general, a child can learn from a person with more experience only if both people are focusing on the same thing and *know* that they are sharing their focus.

Because intersubjectivity is so critical for children's ability to learn from more experienced members of their community, it appears to be a universal phenomenon across cultures

(Adamson & Bakeman, 1991; R. A. Thompson & Virmani, 2010). However, the manner in which intersubjectivity develops varies slightly in different cultures. In one investigation 5-month-old infants from Tokyo were encouraged by their mothers to look at objects in the environment when the infants were currently gazing at the mothers, and to look at the mothers when focusing on objects in the environment, suggesting that the mothers were actively guiding their children's exploration (Bornstein, Toda, Azuma, Tamis-LeMonda, & Ogino, 1990). In comparison, infants of the same age from New York City were encouraged by mothers to explore wherever the infants were currently inspecting, suggesting that these mothers were fostering independent initiative. In both settings, the infants were probably aware that they and their mothers shared an interest in immediate stimuli in the environment.

Social Construction of Memory

Another arena in which an adult and child can find common ground is their personal history together. Almost as soon as children are old enough to talk, their parents begin to engage them in conversations about past events (Fivush, 2009; Gauvain, 2001; Ratner, 1984). Initially, the parents do most of the work, reminiscing, asking questions, prompting recall, and so on, but by the time children are 3 years old, many are active participants in the conversations (Fivush, 2009). By the end of the preschool years, young children can typically give detailed and coherent narratives of important events, for example, what they did on their last birthday.

Discussions about past events have several benefits (Fivush, Haden, & Reese, 2006; Gauvain, 2001). First, as noted in the earlier discussion of infantile amnesia, children are more likely to remember the experiences they talk about. Second, because adults focus on certain aspects of events and not others, children learn what things are important to remember. Third, such conversations help children to develop an **autobiographical self**, a mental history of important events in their lives. Finally, because adults are apt to interpret events in particular ways (e.g., finding some things amusing, desirable, or distasteful), children acquire perspectives and values appropriate for their culture, as you can read more about in the Development in Culture feature "Memory."

Talking about events occasionally has a downside, however, especially for impressionable young children. Imagine that a man identified as "Sam Stone" briefly visits a preschool classroom. He comments on the story the teacher is reading to the children, strolls around the perimeter of the room, waves good-bye, and leaves. Later another adult asks, "When Sam Stone got that bear dirty, did he do it on purpose or was it an accident?" and "Was Sam Stone happy or sad that he got the bear dirty?" When asked such questions, children may recall that Sam soiled a teddy bear, even though he never touched a stuffed animal during his visit (Leichtman & Ceci, 1995, p. 571). Such susceptibility to leading questions is more common in 3- and 4-year-olds than in 5- and 6-year-olds.

When teachers and other professionals ask young children to describe events they have witnessed—say, a fight on the playground or a possible theft in the classroom—they should be careful to ask questions that do not communicate any foregone conclusions about what children may have experienced or witnessed (Pipe & Salmon, 2009). An adult might simply say, "Tell me what happened as best as you can remember it." Furthermore, adults should, whenever possible, seek additional evidence that might either corroborate or cast doubt on young children's recollections of serious matters.

Collaborative Use of Cognitive Strategies

Earlier in the chapter we mentioned that children acquire more sophisticated cognitive strategies when adults model and teach those strategies. A sociocultural perspective suggests that adults should go a step further, engaging children in activities that require collaborative use of the strategies. Through joint discussion and considerable adult guidance, children gradually internalize strategies and begin using them independently (Freund, 1990; Gauvain, 2001; Nader-Grosbois, Normandeau, Ricard-Cossette, & Quintal, 2008). The following example illustrates such internalization:

> Ben, age 4, shuffles into the family room with a jar of pennies that he has been saving. He announces to his mother that he wants to count them to see how much money he has. With

autobiographical self
Mental "history" of important events in one's life.

DEVELOPMENT IN CULTURE
Memory

Across a wide range of environmental circumstances, children develop some similar memory characteristics, including an increasingly efficient working memory capacity and an expanding array of schemas and scripts about people and events. Coexisting with these common trends are cultural variations in memory.

Obviously, daily experiences affect the *content* of children's memory. At the kitchen table, on city streets, and in the classroom, children form specific memories about how institutions in their culture operate and how they themselves are expected to behave. Distinct *methods* of remembering also are acquired during cultural exchanges. Repeated exposure to some information is sufficient to form memories when meaningful patterns are present in the material. Thus children easily learn and remember songs, stories, dances, woodcarvings, games, and configurations of objects in familiar environments (Gaunt, 2006; Kearins, 1981; Rogoff, 2003). In industrialized societies, children are generally taught to use memory strategies for learning and retrieving abstract information (Bjorklund, Dukes, et al., 2009).

Cultural experiences also influence children's autobiographical memory. As children reminisce with their parents and other adults, they learn customs related to telling life stories (Fivush, 2009). Children who are regularly asked to talk about personal experiences seem to retain especially early images of their lives. The Māori, an indigenous people of New Zealand, speak in great detail with children about such significant early experiences as the occasion of their birth (E. Reese, Hayne, & MacDonald, 2008). Of course, children cannot recall their own births because of memory limitations in infancy but these discussions seem to help Māori children remember important occasions at later ages. The earliest memories of Māori adults date back to 2½ years on average whereas other cultures exhibit later ages for first memories—typically at about 3½ to 4 years (E. Reese et al., 2008).

The kinds of questions adults ask during daily conversations guide children's memories as well. Many mothers from European American families prompt children with numerous questions and fill in the gaps when children show lapses in memory. In the following interaction, a European American mother asks her 3-year-old son to expand on his description of their shared experience at a craft fair:

Mother: Tell me about the craft fair. Mommy and Daddy went to the craft fair. What did we go there for, do you remember?
Child: Yeah. Christmas time.
Mother: It was Christmas time, we were getting some Christmas presents. Did you want to be there?
Child: No.
Mother: And what did you start to do?
Child: Hit.
Mother: And you started to hit and what else?
Child: Scratch.
Mother: Do you remember why you were so mad?
Child: Yell.
Mother: You were yelling very loud, I sure agree with that.
Child: And crying.
Mother: And crying too. Why were you so mad?
Child: Because I just want to do whatever I want to do.
Mother: You want to do whatever you want to do. I see.[a] (dialogue is from Q. Wang, 2006, p. 186)

DO YOU REMEMBER WHEN? As this girl talks with her mother about an event they experienced together, she develops memorable images of her childhood.

With each question and comment, the mother scaffolds an interpretation of the events—the boy hit, scratched, and yelled because he did not want to be with his parents at the fair. Parents from European American families tend to ask a lot of questions that evoke details from children, particularly about children's personal feelings and motivations (Fivush, 2009; M. L. Howe et al., 2009; Q. Wang, 2006).

Parents from several other cultures do not offer as many requests for additional information and sometimes dwell on alternative features of events. In the following conversation, a Chinese mother asks her 3-year-old son to focus on the moral dimensions of an event:

Mother: What did Teacher Lin tell you at school?
Child: "Qiu Shao-yun." He didn't move even when his body was on fire.
Mother: The teacher taught you to follow the rules, right?
Child: Um.
Mother: Then why did you cry last night?
Child: You and Grandma didn't let me watch TV.
Mother: Do you know why we didn't let you watch TV?
Child: You were worried that my eyes would get hurt. I wanted to watch "Chao-Tian-Men." I was mad. I insisted on watching it.
Mother: So you got spanked, right?
Child: Um.[a] (dialogue is from Q. Wang, 2006, p. 186)

This mother asks her son to articulate a moral lesson learned at school and infer its relevance to his home life. She invites him to speculate on why she enforced a restriction on television viewing and encourages him to notice the connection between his misbehavior and the punishment he received. Many parents from Chinese families regularly ask their children to focus on moral lessons and shared experiences with family members (Fivush, 2009; M. L. Howe et al., 2009; Q. Wang, 2006).

Through countless conversations with parents about their collective experiences, young children form distinct memories. These conversations convey all sorts of cultural principles, although variations exist within all societies, and generally those parents within a society who frequently ask young children to elaborate on past experiences foster an early ability to narrate life experiences (Fivush, 2009).

mother looking on, Ben dumps the coins on the coffee table and begins to count the pennies, one by one. All is going well until he counts some pennies a second time. Mother interrupts and suggests that he put the pennies in rows so that he doesn't count any twice. Ben agrees to do this, but he aligns his rows poorly. Mother shows him how to straighten them by making a few sample rows herself. She also tells him that it is important to put 10 coins in each row and no more. They finish building the rows together and then they count the pennies: there are 47. A few days later Ben tells his mother that his father gave him some more pennies so he needs to count them again. Mother looks on as Ben dumps the pennies on the coffee table and begins, on his own, to set up rows of 10.[17] (Gauvain, 2001, p. 140)

Strategies associated with self-regulated learning, too, may have their roots in social interaction. At first, other people (e.g., parents, teachers) might help children through a particular learning task by setting goals for the activity, keeping children's attention focused on the task, monitoring learning progress, and so on. Developmentally speaking, a reasonable bridge between other-regulated learning and self-regulated learning is **co-regulated learning**, in which an adult and one or more children share responsibility for directing the various aspects of the learning process (Kutnick & Berdondini, 2009; McCaslin & Good, 1996; Meltzer & Krishnan, 2007). An adult and a group of children might mutually agree on the specific goals of a learning endeavor, or the adult might describe the criteria that indicate successful learning and then have children evaluate their own performance in light of those standards. Initially, the adult provides considerable scaffolding for the children's learning efforts but gradually removes it as children become self-regulating.

Enhancing Information Processing Through Social Interaction

In this and the preceding chapter, we've identified numerous implications of the information processing and sociocultural perspectives. Following are additional implications that emerge when we consider both frameworks simultaneously:

• **Regularly engage infants in social exchanges.** In the early months, social interaction with infants may simply involve making eye contact, smiling and talking, extending a finger to be grabbed, and holding infants in a different way in response to a shift in their position. Later it is more likely to involve jointly looking at, manipulating, experimenting with, and talking about objects. Such activities, simple though they may be, foster the mutual awareness (intersubjectivity) so essential for later information sharing (Hobson, 2004; K. Nelson, 2005; R. A. Thompson & Virmani, 2010).

• **Talk with children about their experiences.** Children begin to talk about their experiences almost as soon as they begin to speak, and by age 2 they do it fairly often (van den Broek, Bauer, & Bourg, 1997). Adults should join in: Talking with children about joint experiences not only enhances children's memories of what they are seeing and doing but also helps children interpret their experiences in culturally appropriate ways (Fivush, 2009; Leichtman, Pillemer, Wang, Koreishi, & Han, 2000).

• **Involve children and adolescents in joint activities that require new strategies.** Information processing theorists point out that a good deal of cognitive development involves the acquisition of increasingly effective and efficient cognitive strategies. Vygotsky suggested that children often internalize the processes they first use in a social context and that they are most likely to benefit from challenging tasks when they have the support of more experienced individuals. Taken together, the two perspectives highlight the importance of having adults work closely with youngsters to scaffold the use and eventual mastery of advanced approaches to learning, memory, and problem solving (Hoskyn, 2010; McCaslin & Good, 1996; Meltzer & Krishnan, 2007).

co-regulated learning
Process through which an adult and child share responsibility for directing various aspects of the child's learning.

[17]Excerpt from THE SOCIAL CONTEXT OF COGNITIVE DEVELOPMENT by Mary Gauvain. Copyright © 2001 by Mary Gauvain. Reprinted with permission of Guilford Publications, Inc.

CHILDREN'S CONSTRUCTION OF THEORIES

Piaget, Vygotsky, and contemporary information processing and sociocultural theorists have all suggested that children *construct* their own understandings of their physical and social worlds. Some developmental psychologists suggest that children gradually combine these self-constructed understandings into integrated belief systems, or *theories,* about particular topics. This approach to cognitive development is known as **theory theory**. No, you're not seeing double here. Although the term *theory theory* may seem rather odd, to us it suggests that many psychologists, dry as their academic writings might sometimes be, do indeed have a sense of humor.

Children's theories about the world begin to emerge quite early in life. As an illustration, by 5 or 6 months of age, children appear to have some understanding that human beings and other animals are different from inanimate objects—for instance, that living and nonliving entities move in distinctly different ways (L. B. Cohen & Cashon, 2006; Mandler, 2007b). As children grow older, they increasingly understand that the *insides* of living creatures are as important as, and perhaps more important than, outside appearance (S. A. Gelman, 2003). Even though they have not yet learned about genetics, DNA, and the like, they realize that biological entities are defined primarily by their origins and internal properties (Keil, 1989). In contrast, children understand that nonliving, human-made objects are largely defined by their functions, not their internal makeup (Greif, Kemler Nelson, Keil, & Gutierrez, 2006; Keil, 1989). Told that bowling balls are reshaped into objects that hold liquid for drinking, children conclude that these objects are cups rather than bowling balls. More generally, within the first 3 to 5 years of life, children form theories about the physical world, the biological world, the social world, and the nature of thinking (Geary, 2005; Wellman, Cross, & Watson, 2001; Wellman & Gelman, 1998). By age 5, children realize that living things grow and reproduce whereas nonliving things do not (Erickson, Keil, & Lockhart, 2010). As they grow older, they expand on and refine their theories, integrating many of the facts, concepts, and beliefs they acquire and identifying numerous interrelationships among ideas (J. A. Dixon & Kelley, 2007; Keil, 1994; Wellman & Gelman, 1998). We now explore children's theories of the physical world as an example.[18]

Children's Theories of the Physical World

Young infants are amazingly knowledgeable about the physical world. By age 3 or 4 months, they show signs of surprise when one solid object passes directly through another one, when an object seems to be suspended in midair, or when an object appears to move immediately from one place to another without traveling across the intervening space to get there (Baillargeon, 1994; Newcombe, Sluzenski, & Huttenlocher, 2005; Spelke & Kinzler, 2007). Such findings suggest that young infants know that objects (a) are substantive entities with definite boundaries, (b) fall unless something holds them up, and (c) move in a continuous manner across space. These findings also suggest to some theorists that infants are endowed with some basic knowledge about the physical world at birth or at least are primed to construct workable understandings after only a few brief experiences (Baillargeon, 2008; Flavell et al., 2002; Spelke & Kinzler, 2007).

The idea that some knowledge and inclinations might be biologically preprogrammed is known as **nativism**.[19] Built-in knowledge about the world would have an evolutionary advantage, of course—it would give infants a head start in learning about their environment— and evidence for it has been observed in other species as well (S. A. Gelman & Kalish, 2006; Spelke, 2000). Nevertheless, the extent to which the human brain is hardwired with certain knowledge, or at least with built-in predispositions to acquire that knowledge very early and easily, is, at present, an unresolved issue (M. Cole & Hatano, 2007; K. Nelson, 2005; Rakison, 2005).

theory theory
Theoretical perspective proposing that children construct increasingly integrated and complex understandings of physical and mental phenomena.

nativism
Theoretical perspective proposing that some knowledge is biologically built-in and available at birth or soon thereafter.

---

[18]We explore children's theories about other people's thoughts, feelings, and actions—collectively known as *theory of mind*—in Chapter 12.

[19]As you will discover in Chapter 9, nativism also figures prominently in some theories of language development.

Whatever their origins may be, children's early conceptions of objects provide a foundation for constructing an integrated and increasingly elaborate theory of the physical world. Especially in the preschool and early elementary years, children's theories develop with little or no direct instruction from adults and so often include naive ideas about how the world operates. A belief that people play a significant role in influencing physical phenomena (e.g., forming mountains, making clouds move, causing hurricanes) is common in the preschool and early elementary years, and some cultures actually promote it (O. Lee, 1999; Piaget, 1929, 1960a). Young children may also believe that natural objects and phenomena have a particular purpose. For instance, they may believe that pointy rocks exist so that animals can scratch themselves when they have an itch (Kelemen, 1999, 2004; Piaget, 1929). Perceptions trigger other beliefs, for example, that the sun revolves around the earth—that at night, it "goes" to the other side of the world (Vosniadou, 2009).

Some misconceptions persist well into adolescence. For example, many high school and college students believe that an object continues to move only if a force continues to act on it and that an object dropped from a moving train or airplane will fall straight down (diSessa, 1996; diSessa, Gillespie, & Esterly, 2004; M. McCloskey, 1983). In reality, of course, an object continues to move at the same speed in a particular direction unless a force acts to *change* its speed or direction (reflecting the law of inertia), and an object dropped from a moving train or plane not only falls but also continues to move forward (reflecting the laws of gravity and inertia).

ARTIFACT 7-3   Lake formation. Children's early theories often include naive beliefs about the world. When 4-year-old Isabelle is asked "How were lakes made?" she offers an unlikely—but in her mind quite plausible—explanation: "You get a bucket and you fill it up with water. You get lots and lots of buckets." She illustrates her theory with the picture shown here.

Several factors probably contribute to inaccuracies in children's theories about the world (D. B. Clark, 2006; Glynn, Yeany, & Britton, 1991b; Vosniadou, 2009). As we have seen, misconceptions result from how things appear to be. From our perspective here on earth, the sun looks as if it moves around the earth, rather than vice versa. Several misconceptions are encouraged by common expressions in language (e.g., the sun "rises" and "sets"). Various cultural mechanisms—fairy tales, television shows, local folklore, occasionally even textbooks—may also play a role. For example, after cartoon "bad guys" run off the edge of a cliff, they usually remain suspended in air until they realize that there's nothing solid holding them up, and at that point they fall straight down.

Earlier in the chapter you learned that, in general, children's growing knowledge base about the world helps them make sense of and learn new information. But when children's "knowledge" is inaccurate, it often has a counterproductive effect, in that children's erroneous beliefs about a topic interfere with their understanding of new information related to the topic (P. K. Murphy & Mason, 2006; Vosniadou, 2003). Consider the fact that many children in the early elementary grades believe that the earth is flat rather than round. When adults tell them the earth is actually round, they may interpret that information within the context of what they already "know" and hence think of the earth as being *both* flat and round—in other words, shaped like a pancake (Vosniadou, 2009).

Facilitating Children's Theory Construction

Theory theory yields several practical implications for parents, teachers, and other adults who work with young people.

- **Encourage and answer children's why and how questions.** Young children ask many *why* and *how* questions: "Why is the sky blue?" "How does a cell phone call know how to connect with another phone?" Such questions often pop up within the context of shared activities with adults (Callanan & Oakes, 1992; Frazier, Gelman, & Wellman, 2009). Although some adults find them bothersome, children's queries typically reflect their genuine desire to make sense of their world and to refine their theories about what causes what and why things are the way they are (Chouinard, 2007; Engel & Randall, 2009; Kemler Nelson, Egan, & Holt, 2004).

- **When teaching a new topic, determine what children already know and believe about it.** Adults can more successfully address children's misconceptions when they know what those misconceptions are (P. K. Murphy & Alexander, 2008). When beginning a new curriculum unit, teachers should probably assess students' existing beliefs about the topic, perhaps simply by asking a few informal questions that probe what students know and misunderstand.

• When children have misconceptions about a topic, work actively to help them acquire more accurate understandings. Even as children encounter more accurate and adult-like perspectives about the world, their existing misunderstandings do not necessarily disappear. In fact, because early "knowledge" influences the interpretation of subsequent experiences, misconceptions are often quite resistant to change even in the face of blatantly contradictory information (Kuhn, 2001b; P. K. Murphy & Mason, 2006). Thus, teachers and other adults must make a concerted effort to help youngsters revise their early, inaccurate theories to incorporate more accurate and productive worldviews. In other words, they must help youngsters undergo **conceptual change**. Theorists and researchers have offered several strategies for promoting conceptual change:

- Ask children to articulate their current beliefs, either verbally or in pictures.
- Present phenomena that children cannot adequately explain within their existing perspectives—in other words, create *disequilibrium*.
- Engage children in discussions of the pros and cons of various explanations of observed phenomena.
- Explicitly point out what the differences between children's beliefs and "reality" are.
- Show how the scientifically accepted explanation of an event or phenomenon makes more sense than any alternative explanation children themselves can offer.
- Provide children with compelling evidence (e.g., video of the earth from outer space) that addresses particular misconceptions that children typically have (e.g., that the earth is flat).
- Arrange for children to gain hands-on experiences during experiments that address the underlying presuppositions children have about a topic.
- Have children study a topic for an extended period so that accurate explanations are thoroughly understood rather than learned in a superficial, rote manner.
- Share historical cases with children in which there has been a significant progression of thought about a scientific topic. (D. B. Clark, 2006; P. K. Murphy & Alexander, 2008; P. K. Murphy & Mason, 2006; C. L. Smith, 2007; Vosniadou, 2009)

COMPARING AND CRITIQUING CONTEMPORARY APPROACHES TO COGNITIVE DEVELOPMENT

The Basic Developmental Issues table "Contrasting Contemporary Theories of Cognitive Development" compares information processing theories and theory theory with respect to nature and nurture, universality and diversity, and qualitative and quantitative changes. Both theories have extended our understanding of cognitive development far beyond Piaget's and Vygotsky's early ideas. Information processing theories have made significant inroads into the question of how human beings mentally process and learn new information and how cognitive processes change over the course of childhood and adolescence. Theory theory helps us understand why children's naive beliefs (e.g., "The world is flat") may persist even in the face of contradictory evidence. Together such approaches lead us to conclude that cognitive development involves more gradual changes and that the evolution of children's reasoning capabilities is more domain specific than Piaget suggested.

In their present forms, however, both the information processing and theory theory perspectives have limitations. Theory theory offers rather vague descriptions of a limited number of self-constructed theories by children (K. Nelson, 1996a; Siegler & Alibali, 2005). The particular ideas that children have about any domain can be unstable, shifting from one setting to another; furthermore, individual differences in these ideas can be significant (M. E. Martinez, 2010). Therefore, work on children's self-constructed theories can be difficult to address in the classroom. Information processing theories are more precise, but their precision may not provide a completely accurate description of how human memory works.

conceptual change
Revision of one's knowledge and understanding of a topic in response to new information about the topic.

BASIC DEVELOPMENTAL ISSUES
Contrasting Contemporary Theories of Cognitive Development

ISSUE	INFORMATION PROCESSING THEORIES	THEORY THEORY
Nature and Nurture	Nature endows children with certain brain mechanisms that enable them to direct their attention to particular stimuli, to actively deliberate about an event or task at hand, and to retain acquired knowledge and skills for lengthy periods. Furthermore, information processing difficulties (e.g., learning disabilities, attention-deficit hyperactivity disorder) often have biological origins. Nevertheless, the focus is primarily on environmental factors, in particular, on how environmental input is interpreted, stored, integrated, and remembered and on how formal instruction can best facilitate learning and cognitive development.	Rudimentary understandings of the physical world—or at least predispositions to divide up and interpret the world in particular ways—seem to be in place within the first few weeks or months after birth and may possibly be biologically built-in. As children observe and interact with their physical and social environments, they construct increasingly elaborate and integrated understandings and beliefs about various physical, social, and mental phenomena.
Universality and Diversity	The components of the information processing system (e.g., working memory, long-term memory, the central executive) are universal. However, some children use their information processing capabilities more effectively than others. Children's prior knowledge and their mastery of various cognitive strategies influence the degree to which they can learn new information and skills effectively.	Any biologically built-in knowledge and predispositions are universal across cultures. However, informal experiences, formal schooling, and community practices and beliefs—things that are apt to differ from one culture to the next—lead children to embellish on their initial understandings in somewhat culture-specific ways.
Qualitative and Quantitative Change	Over the course of development, children and adolescents acquire a variety of new cognitive strategies that are qualitatively different from earlier ones. Each strategy evolves gradually over a lengthy period and becomes increasingly efficient and effective—a trend that reflects quantitative change.	As children gain more information about their world, they may add to their theories in a quantitative manner. Under certain conditions, new and compelling experiences spur children to overhaul their theories in a way that reflects qualitative change.

Human beings seem to learn and remember many things that they don't consciously pay attention to and think about in working memory (Frensch & Rünger, 2003). In addition, mounting research evidence indicates that working memory and long-term memory are closely interconnected and possibly overlapping entities, rather than the two distinctly separate components depicted in Figure 7-1 (Kirschner, Sweller, & Clark, 2006; Ormrod, 2008).

Perhaps the biggest challenge for today's developmental psychologists is to explain exactly how and why cognitive development occurs (Gauvain, 2001; Siegler & Alibali, 2005). Theorists have made some progress on this front, to be sure. Children appear to have an innate need to adapt to their environment, and they almost certainly acquire more complex strategies when adults nurture such strategies. But we do not yet have a detailed understanding of how various aspects of heredity and environment work in concert in the transformation of newborn infants into cognitively sophisticated adults. To arrive at such an understanding, psychologists must pull together the concepts and research findings of multiple theoretical perspectives—for instance, by integrating elements of information processing theories and sociocultural theories in the ways we did earlier.

Although we do not yet have a complete picture of cognitive development, existing theories and research findings tell us a great deal about what to look for in children's development and how to work effectively with various age-groups (see the Observation Guidelines table "Assessing Cognitive Processing and Metacognition"). What we have learned about cognitive development can also help us identify children who may be having difficulties in processing certain kinds of information, as we shall see now.

OBSERVATION GUIDELINES
Assessing Cognitive Processing and Metacognition

CHARACTERISTIC	LOOK FOR	EXAMPLE	IMPLICATION
Intersubjectivity	• Reciprocal interactions with caregivers • Attempts to coordinate one's own actions toward an object with the actions of another person • Social referencing (i.e., responding to an object or event based on how an adult responds to it)	A teacher at a child care center is obviously frightened when a large dog appears just outside the fenced-in play yard, and she yells at the dog to go away. Fifteen-month-old Owen observes her reaction and begins to cry.	Regularly engage infants in affectionate and playful interactions (smiles, coos, etc.). Remember that your own reactions toward objects and events will communicate messages about the value, appeal, and safety of those objects and events.
Attention	• Sustained attention to human beings and inanimate objects • Ability to stay on task for an age-appropriate period • On-task behavior when distracting stimuli are present	During story time, a second-grade teacher has been reading Roald Dahl's *Charlie and the Chocolate Factory*. Most of the children are attentive, but Ben fidgets and squirms, and soon he finds a new form of entertainment: making silly faces at nearby classmates.	Monitor children's ability to pay attention. If children have exceptional difficulty staying on task, minimize distractions, teach them strategies for focusing their attention more effectively, and give them opportunities to release pent-up energy regularly.
Automatization of Basic Skills	• Retrieval of simple facts in a rapid, effortless fashion • Ability to use simple problem-solving strategies quickly and efficiently	Elena easily solves the problem $\frac{4}{12} = \frac{X}{36}$ because she realizes almost immediately that $\frac{4}{12}$ is the same as $\frac{1}{3}$.	Give children numerous opportunities to use and practice essential facts and skills; do so within the context of interesting and motivating activities.
Learning Strategies	• Use of rehearsal in the elementary grades • Use of more integrative strategies (e.g., organization, elaboration) in the secondary grades • Flexible use of strategies for different learning tasks	Terri studies each new concept in her high school physics class by repeating the textbook definition aloud three or four times. Later she can barely remember the definitions she has studied, and she is unable to apply the concepts when trying to solve physics problems.	Show struggling learners that their difficulties may be due to ineffective strategies, and teach them strategies that can help them learn more successfully.
Self-Regulated Learning Capabilities	• Initiative in identifying and seeking out needed information • Intentional efforts to keep attention focused on an assigned task • Effective planning and time management	At wrestling practice one day, John tells his coach that he has just read several articles about the pros and cons of using steroids to increase muscle mass. "I'm confused about why most experts advise against them," he says. "Can you help me understand their logic?"	When youngsters fail to complete independent assignments in a timely or thorough manner, provide more structure for subsequent tasks. Gradually remove the structure as they become better able to regulate their own learning and performance.
Beliefs About Knowledge and Learning	• Optimism that knowledge improves when one focuses on understanding (rather than memorization) • Attempts to master interrelationships among ideas (e.g., cause and effect, similarities and differences) • Eagerness to compare and critique various perspectives and theories	Several middle school students are studying for a test on westward migration in North America during the 1800s. Some students focus on cause-and-effect relationships among events. Others make a list of facts from the textbook and study them in a piece-meal fashion.	Convey the message that mastering any single domain is an ongoing task that requires efforts to understand. Especially when working with adolescents, communicate that knowledge about a topic includes an understanding of how various concepts and ideas are interrelated. Suggest that competing perspectives each may have some merit but must be critically evaluated on the basis of evidence and logic.

EXCEPTIONALITIES IN INFORMATION PROCESSING

Every child learns and processes information in a unique manner. But the information processing capabilities of some children are sufficiently different from peers that they require the use of specially adapted instructional practices and materials.[20] Here we consider two kinds of exceptionalities in information processing: learning disabilities and attention-deficit hyperactivity disorder.

[20]In Chapters 8 and 9, respectively, we examine individual differences in intelligence and language. Children with these exceptionalities also respond well to customized interventions.

Learning Disabilities

A **learning disability** is a significant difficulty in one or more specific cognitive processes that cannot be attributed to a sensory impairment, a general intellectual disability, an emotional or behavioral disorder, or lack of instruction. The difficulty interferes with academic achievement to such a degree that special educational services are warranted (J. M. Fletcher, Lyon, Fuchs, & Barnes, 2007; National Joint Committee on Learning Disabilities, 1994).

Many learning disabilities appear to have an inherited biological basis. Some children with learning disabilities have minor abnormalities in certain brain structures, and others seem especially vulnerable to "interference" from brain signals irrelevant to the task at hand (Dempster & Corkill, 1999; Kovas, Haworth, Dale, & Plomin, 2007; Manis, 1996).

Children with learning disabilities are a diverse group, with a wide variety of talents, ability levels, and personalities. For instance, some children easily gain proficiency in mathematics but have exceptional difficulty with reading, whereas others show the reverse pattern.[21] Yet many children with learning disabilities do seem to have certain characteristics in common. They are apt to have trouble with executive functions—focusing their attention, self-regulating their learning, inhibiting inappropriate thoughts and behaviors, and so on (Andersson, 2010; Meltzer, 2007; Turnbull et al., 2010). With few effective learning and problem-solving strategies at their disposal, some children with learning disabilities take a rather "passive" approach to learning tasks—for instance, mindlessly staring at a textbook instead of actively thinking about what the words mean (Brownell, Mellard, & Deshler, 1993; Meltzer & Krishnan, 2007). Some of them appear to have less working memory capacity than their age-mates, making it difficult to engage in several cognitive processes simultaneously and to inhibit thoughts that are irrelevant to the task at hand (Geary, 2010; J. A. Stein & Krishnan, 2007; H. L. Swanson & Jerman, 2006). They may also suffer from low self-esteem and emotional problems, due at least partly to frustration about their repeated academic failures (Horowitz, Darling-Hammond, & Bransford, 2005; Leichtentritt & Shechtman, 2010).

As students reach the secondary school grades, the school curriculum becomes increasingly challenging, textbooks are written in more sophisticated language, and teachers expect greater independence and self-regulated learning. Unless they have considerable scaffolding to help them study and learn, students with learning disabilities become discouraged. Perhaps for this reason, adolescents with learning disabilities are often among those students most at risk for dropping out of school (Barga, 1996; Deshler, 2005).

Attention-Deficit Hyperactivity Disorder

Children with **attention-deficit hyperactivity disorder (ADHD)** have either or both of the following characteristics (American Psychiatric Association, 2000; Barkley, 1998):

- *Inattention.*—Children are easily distracted by either external stimuli or their own thoughts. They may daydream, have trouble listening to and following directions, or give up easily when working on difficult tasks.
- *Hyperactivity and impulsivity.*—Children have an excess amount of energy. They may be fidgety, move around at inappropriate times, talk excessively, or have difficulty working or playing quietly. They may also show such impulsive behaviors as blurting out answers, interrupting others, making careless mistakes, and acting without thinking about potential consequences of their behavior.

A deficit in executive functions, and more specifically in the inhibition of inappropriate thoughts and actions, may be at the heart of ADHD (Denckla, 2007; Holmes et al., 2010). Limitations in reward mechanisms in the brain, especially favoring immediate over delayed rewards, may share responsibility (Carmona et al., 2009). In most cases the condition is probably the result of specific brain abnormalities, but in a few situations it may reflect a delay in normal neurological maturation processes (Doehnert, Brandeis, Imhof, Drechsler, & Steinhausen, 2010; Gatzke-Kopp & Beauchaine, 2007; Sabbagh, Xu, Carlson, Moses, & Lee, 2006).

In addition to inattentiveness, hyperactivity, and impulsivity, children identified as having ADHD may have difficulties with cognitive processing, academic achievement, interpersonal

[21]See discussions about *dyslexia* and *dyscalculia* in Chapter 10.

learning disability
Significant deficit in one or more cognitive processes, to the point where special educational services are required.

attention-deficit hyperactivity disorder (ADHD)
Disability characterized by inattention, by hyperactivity and impulsive behavior, or by all of these characteristics.

Preparing for Your Licensure Examination
Your teaching test may ask you to identify the needs of children with learning disabilities and attention disorders.

skills, or classroom behavior (Barkley, 1998; Danckaerts et al., 2010; S. Goldstein & Rider, 2006). Many adolescents outgrow some aspects of hyperactivity but continue to show some delays in attention (Doehnert et al., 2010; E. L. Hart, Lahey, Loeber, Applegate, & Frick, 1995). Adolescents with ADHD have greater difficulty than their peers in successfully meeting the challenges of the teenage years—the physical changes of puberty, more complex classroom assignments, increasing demands for independent and responsible behavior, and so on. And they are more prone to use tobacco and alcohol, get in traffic accidents, and drop out of school (Barkley, 1998; S. Goldstein & Rider, 2006; Whalen, Jamner, Henker, Delfino, & Lozano, 2002).

Working with Children Who Have Information Processing Difficulties

Children with either a learning disability or ADHD are apt to be more different than they are similar. Hence teachers and other practitioners who work with them must consider the unique needs of each child. Yet several general suggestions are applicable to many children with information processing difficulties.

• **Examine children's work for clues about specific processing difficulties.** Writing samples, math homework, and other academic work can be a rich source of information about cognitive deficits that hinder children's ability to learn and master classroom subject matter. For example, a child who solves a subtraction problem this way:

$$\begin{array}{r} 85 \\ -29 \\ \hline 64 \end{array}$$

may be applying an inappropriate rule ("Always subtract the smaller number from the larger one") to subtraction. A child who reads the sentence *I drove the car* as *I drove the cat* may be having trouble using context clues in reading words and sentences.

• **Help children keep their attention on the task at hand.** Many children with information processing difficulties are easily distracted. Thus adults who work with them should minimize the presence of other stimuli likely to compete for their attention, perhaps by finding a quiet room for tasks requiring considerable concentration or by pulling down window shades when interesting events are unfolding outside. Many children also benefit from specific training in attention-focusing strategies, such as keeping one's eyes directed toward a speaker or moving to a new location if the current one presents too many distracting sights and sounds (Buchoff, 1990).

• **Provide children with opportunities to practice learning strategies.** Many children with learning disabilities and attention problems need to learn how to acquire, store, and recall information (Turnbull et al., 2010). Teachers can ask students to use such learning strategies as formulating a goal when undertaking a task, dividing complex activities (e.g., reading a long passage) into manageable units, and identifying key concepts to look for when starting a lesson.

• **Teach strategies for controlling hyperactivity and impulsivity.** All children, but especially those with information processing difficulties, need regular opportunities to release pent-up energy, perhaps in the form of recess, sports, or hands-on activities (Panksepp, 1998; Pellegrini & Bohn, 2005). In addition, after a period of high activity, adults might give children a "settling-in" time that allows them to calm down gradually (Pellegrini & Horvat, 1995). As an example, when children return from lunch, many elementary teachers begin the afternoon by reading a chapter from a relaxing storybook.

Teaching children to use self-talk can help them resist the tendency to respond too hastily to situations and problems. Notice

Improving Your Observation Skills

Halloween. A few days before Halloween, Nathan, age 7, created and illustrated the writing sample shown here. Writing in small print, his first-grade teacher clarified what he intended to say: "I drew this pumpkin" and "A bat." What patterns of errors do you notice in Nathan's word spellings? Compare your response with the explanation at the end of the chapter.

how one formerly impulsive child learned to talk himself while completing matching tasks in which he needed to find two identical pictures among several very similar ones:

> I have to remember to go slowly to get it right. Look carefully at this one, now look at these carefully. Is this one different? Yes, it has an extra leaf. Good, I can eliminate this one. Now, let's look at this one. I think it's this one, but let me first check the others. Good, I'm going slow and carefully. Okay, I think it's this one. (Meichenbaum & Goodman, 1971, p. 121)

• **Provide extra scaffolding in delayed areas and while studying, doing homework, and completing other learning tasks.** Obviously, children with significant delays in foundational academic areas, especially reading and mathematics, need customized instruction that addresses the difficulties they face. For example, a child who struggles with mathematics needs one-on-one tutoring in basic arithmetic calculations whereas another child who struggles in reading requires extra practice in recognizing common words. In addition, children with information processing difficulties often need considerable support completing tasks on their own. Such support might take a variety of forms: structured note-taking, handouts that list major ideas, memory tricks for remembering tidbits of information, teacher-supervised after-school homework programs, and the like (T. Bryan, Burstein, & Bryan, 2001; Cosden, Morrison, Albanese, & Macias, 2001; Meltzer, 2007).

[22] Chapters 12, 14, and 15 identify a variety of strategies for promoting effective interaction with others.

SUMMARY

Basic Cognitive Processes

Information processing theories focus on how children acquire, interpret, and remember information and on how these cognitive processes change over the course of development. Information processing theorists propose that cognitive capabilities improve gradually with age and experience. Infants have many sensory and perceptual capabilities at birth or soon thereafter. In general, however, children are less efficient learners than adults are. They have shorter attention spans, a smaller working memory capacity, and a smaller and less integrated knowledge base to which they can relate new information and events.

Metacognition and Cognitive Strategies

The term *metacognition* encompasses both the knowledge that people have about their own cognitive processes and their intentional use of certain cognitive processes to facilitate learning and memory. Children's metacognitive knowledge and cognitive strategies improve throughout the school years. Children become more proficient in such learning strategies as rehearsal, organization, and elaboration, and they acquire increasingly powerful and effective ways of solving problems. With age, they become more aware of the nature of thinking, learning, and knowledge, and they develop strategies for regulating their own learning.

Adding a Sociocultural Element to Information Processing Theories

Information processing theories can tell us a great deal about what abilities change over time, and sociocultural views can help us explain how those changes occur. Combining elements of both perspectives can give us a more complete picture of cognitive development than we might get from either one alone. Children learn what to pay attention to in part by watching what other people pay attention to. And adults can help children become more effective, self-regulating learners by giving them control of a learning activity in a gradual, step-by-step manner.

Children's Construction of Theories

Some theorists propose that children gradually construct integrated belief systems (theories) about the physical world, the biological world, the social world, and mental events. Such theories are not always accurate, however. Children's theories about the physical world may include erroneous beliefs about the solar system and laws of motion. To the extent that children's theories include misconceptions, they may interfere with children's ability to acquire more sophisticated understandings.

Comparing and Critiquing Contemporary Approaches to Cognitive Development

Contemporary theories (e.g., information processing theories, theory theory) have added considerably to Piaget's and Vygotsky's early notions of children's thinking and knowledge-building processes. Taken together, various theoretical perspectives give us a more complete picture of cognitive development than any single perspective can give us alone.

Exceptionalities in Information Processing

The information processing capabilities of some children (e.g., those with learning disabilities and those with attention-deficit hyperactivity disorder) are different enough that they require specially adapted instruction and materials. Although children with such disabilities have diverse abilities and needs, all of them benefit from explicit instruction in effective cognitive strategies and teacher scaffolding for completing learning tasks.

APPLYING CONCEPTS IN CHILD DEVELOPMENT

The exercises in this section will help you build your ability to apply your knowledge of child development in your work with children.

Improving Your Observation Skills

On page 250, you examined maps of Loveland, Colorado, and were asked, "*How do the maps drawn by a first grader (top), fifth grader (middle), and seventh grader (bottom) reflect different levels of knowledge about their local community?*" The first grader's map includes only a few features of her town that she knows well (her house and school, nearby mountains) and distorts spatial relationships among the features. The third grader's map shows many features of his immediate neighborhood and their proximity to one another. The seventh grader's map encompasses numerous town landmarks and their relative locations on major streets. It also makes greater use of symbols—for instance, single lines for roads, squares for buildings, and distinctive letter *M*s to indicate McDonald's restaurants. This collection of maps reflects age-related increases in detailed knowledge about the community and accuracy in representing connections among roads, buildings, and lakes (see Forbes, Ormrod, Bernardi, Taylor, & Jackson, 1999).

On page 280, you examined 7-year-old Nathan's writing sample and were asked, "*What patterns of errors do you notice in Nathan's word spellings?*" With the exception of the *L* in the first line, Nathan correctly captured some of the sounds in the words he was trying to spell. He acknowledged the *d* in *drew*, the *s* in *this*, and the *b* and *t* in *bat*. But he omitted several other consonants, as well as all of the vowel sounds except for the initial *I*. We might suspect that Nathan has difficulty hearing all the distinct sounds in spoken words and matching them with the letters he sees in written words. Such difficulties are common in young elementary school students who have significant reading disabilities.[23]

Practicing for Your Licensure Examination

Many teaching tests require students to use what they have learned about child development in responses to brief vignettes and multiple-choice questions. You can practice for your licensure examination by reading about library research by eighth graders and answering a series of questions.

The Library Project

Read the case and then answer the questions that follow it.

In the final year of her teacher education program, Jessica Jensen is a teacher intern in four eighth-grade social studies classes. She has recently assigned a month-long group project that involves considerable library research. Midway through the project, Jessica writes the following entry in her journal:

> Within each group, one student is studying culture of the region, one has religion, one has economy, and one government. The point is for the students to become "experts" on their topic in their region. There are a lot of requirements to this assignment. I'm collecting things as we go along because I think a project this long will be difficult for them to organize . . . ?
>
> So we spent all week in the library. I collected a minimum of two pages of notes yesterday, which will be a small part of their grade. The one thing that surprised me in our work in the library was their lack of skills. They had such difficulty researching, finding the information they needed, deciding what was important, and organizing and taking notes. As they worked, I walked around helping and was shocked. The librarian had already gotten out all of the appropriate resources. Even after they had the books in front of them, most did not know what to do. For instance, if they were assigned "economy," most looked in the index for that particular word. If they didn't find it, they gave up on the book. After realizing this, I had to start the next day with a brief lesson on researching and cross-referencing. I explained how they could look up *commerce, imports, exports,* and how these would all help them. I was also shocked at how poor their note-taking skills were. I saw a few kids copying paragraphs word for word. Almost none of them understood that notes don't need to be in full sentences. So, it was a long week at the library.
>
> Next week is devoted to group work and time to help them work on their rough drafts. With the difficulty they had researching, I can imagine the problems that will arise out of turning their notes into papers. (journal entry courtesy of Jessica Jensen)

Constructed-Response Question

1. Initially, the intern realizes that her students will need some structure to complete the project successfully. In what ways do she and the librarian structure the assignment for the students?

Multiple-Choice Questions

2. How does the students' prior knowledge (or lack thereof) influence the effectiveness of their strategies?

    a. Students' lack of knowledge about such terms as *economics* makes it difficult for them to use the index and to cross-reference terms.
    b. Students' limited knowledge about their topic makes it difficult for them to make sense of the material they read.
    c. Students' lack of exposure to the topics they are researching makes it difficult for them to paraphrase and summarize what they've read.
    d. All of the above.

3. Given the information on metacognition in this chapter, how might the intern teach students about strategy usage?

    a. The intern needs to realize that due to their age, the eighth-grade students are not yet capable of acquiring learning strategies.
    b. The intern can model and give the students practice in using such strategies as identifying the main point of a passage, paraphrasing the material they read, referring to an index in a book, and keeping notes organized.

[23]You can read about reading disabilities in Chapter 10.

c. None, because with additional reflection, the intern will come to the conclusion that students already know how to use learning strategies and simply need to be told to try harder.
d. The intern should teach students to memorize the assertions experts make and repeat these comments verbatim in their reports.

Once you have answered these questions, compare your responses with those presented in Appendix A.

Improving Your Ability to Interpret Children's Artifacts and Reflections

Consider chapter concepts as you analyze the following interview with 9-year-old Aletha, a fourth grader:

Interview with Aletha

Adult: What is paying attention?
Aletha: What they are talking about is interesting and it's fun. Before we learn about anything new, my teacher asks us questions [about the new topic] and nobody knows the answers. When we are done, she asks us questions and you know all the answers. It's cool! To learn new things you have to pay attention. If you don't, then you won't know what's going on. If you are talking with your friends or fiddling, you are not paying attention, so the teacher will call on you and you won't know the answer. If you are not listening, then you are not paying attention. When it's interesting, I'm

really paying attention. It's hard if you're not interested, but that's not how it works. You have to pay attention.
Adult: How do you pay attention if it's not interesting?
Aletha: I think of questions in my head and I have to pay attention to see if the teacher answers my questions before I want the answers. Then I have something to say when the teacher calls on me.
Adult: Can you do other things when you pay attention?
Aletha: Some things. You can't read a book because it's hard to do both. Sometimes in science we watch movies and we are allowed to keep notes because we have a test on the movie later. I write the stuff down so I can memorize it. That was easy [to take notes], but it's hard because I had to write while I was listening.
Adult: Is paying attention just listening?
Aletha: Not necessarily. You can listen and not have a clue. But if you don't listen, you obviously won't get it. (interview courtesy of a former student who wishes to remain anonymous)

- What beliefs does Aletha have about the nature of human learning and memory?
- What evidence do you see to indicate that Aletha is taking steps toward becoming a self-regulating learner?

Once you have answered these questions, compare your ideas with those presented in Appendix B. For further practice in analyzing children's artifacts and reflections, go to the Activities and Applications section in Chapter 7 of MyEducationLab.

Key Concepts

information processing theories (p. 242)
sensory register (p. 243)
working memory (p. 243)
long-term memory (p. 244)
central executive (p. 244)
automatization (p. 247)
infantile amnesia (p. 249)

knowledge base (p. 249)
schema (p. 251)
script (p. 251)
symbol (p. 251)
metacognition (p. 255)
cognitive strategy (p. 255)
rehearsal (p. 257)
organization (p. 257)

elaboration (p. 258)
metacognitive awareness (p. 260)
self-regulated learning (p. 262)
epistemic belief (p. 263)
intersubjectivity (p. 270)
joint attention (p. 270)
social referencing (p. 270)
autobiographical self (p. 271)

co-regulated learning (p. 273)
theory theory (p. 274)
nativism (p. 274)
conceptual change (p. 276)
learning disability (p. 279)
attention-deficit hyperactivity disorder (ADHD) (p. 279)

PEARSON
myeducationlab

Now go to www.myeducationlab.com to:
- Take a Quiz to test your mastery of chapter objectives.
- Study chapter content with an individualized Study Plan.
- Deepen your understanding of particular concepts and principles with Review, Remediation, and Enrichment Exercises.
- Apply what you have learned in the chapter to your work with children in Building Teaching Skills and Dispositions exercises.
- Observe children and their unique contexts in Video Examples.

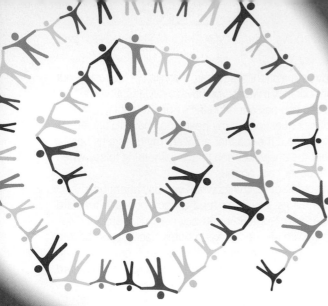

Chapter Eight

Intelligence

CASE STUDY: Gina

Seventeen-year-old Gina has always been an enthusiastic learner. As a toddler, she talked early and often. As a 4-year-old, she asked her mother to identify a few words in a reading primer her aunt had given her, used the words to deduce many letter-sound relationships, and then deciphered additional words on her own. By the time she reached kindergarten, she was reading first- and second-grade-level storybooks.

In elementary school Gina consistently achieved straight As on her report cards until finally, in sixth grade, she broke the pattern by getting a B in history. Since then, she has earned a few more Bs, but As continue to dominate her record. Her performance has been highest in her advanced math courses, where she easily grasps the abstract concepts that many of her classmates find difficult to understand.

Gina has other talents as well. She won her high school's creative writing contest 2 years in a row. She has landed challenging roles in her school's drama productions. And as president of her school's National Honor Society during her senior year, she has masterfully coordinated a peer-tutoring program to assist struggling students.

Gina's teachers describe her as a "bright" young woman. Her friends affectionately call her a "brainiac." Test results in her school file bear out their assessments: An intelligence test that she took in junior high school yielded a score of 140, and this year she performed at the 99th percentile on college aptitude tests.

This is not to say that Gina is strong in every arena. She shows little artistic ability in her paintings or clay sculptures. Her piano playing is mediocre despite 5 years of weekly lessons. In athletic events she has little stamina, strength, or flexibility. She is shy and unsure of herself at social events. And she hasn't earned an A in history since fifth grade, in large part because her idea of how best to learn history involves simply memorizing people, places, and dates.

- What evidence is there that Gina is intelligent?
- In which abilities does Gina exhibit her strongest talents?
- In which abilities is Gina apparently less advanced?

Every child is intelligent to a certain degree. Gina's performance reflects exceptional intelligence: She has earned high marks in many subjects throughout her school career. Yet intelligence is not a set-in-concrete characteristic that youngsters either do or don't have. Gina has definite talents as well as a few areas that are challenging for her. Among her assets are academic areas that rely on advanced verbal skills, organizational abilities, and mathematical reasoning. Similarly, she excels at dramatic self-expression. Gina does not show the same extraordinary potential in history, art, music, athletics, or social situations, yet she will certainly be able to advance in these competencies if she puts her mind to it and is assisted in her efforts. Like Gina, every child is poised to make the most of his or her unique abilities if given appropriate support at home and school and in the community.

DEFINING INTELLIGENCE

Theorists think of intelligence in a variety of ways, but most agree that it has several distinctive qualities:

- It is *adaptive,* such that it can be used flexibly to meet a person's goals in a variety of situations.
- It involves *learning ability.* People who are intelligent in particular domains learn new information and behaviors more quickly and easily than people who are less intelligent in those domains.

OBJECTIVES

8.1: Differentiate among the five theoretical perspectives on intelligence.

8.2: Describe four ways in which general intelligence can be tested, and contrast general intelligence tests with dynamic assessments and developmental assessments.

8.3: Describe and evaluate research findings regarding general developmental trends in IQ scores.

8.4: Review evidence of the separate and interactive influences of heredity and environment on intelligence.

8.5: Recognize and foster the kinds of intelligence that children exhibit during classroom lessons and everyday activities.

8.6: Describe ways to nurture the abilities of exceptional children at each end of the intelligence continuum.

- It involves the *use of prior knowledge* to analyze and understand new situations effectively.
- It involves the complex interaction and coordination of *many different mental processes*.
- It is *culture specific*. In separate societies, being intelligent might mean reasoning about complex and abstract ideas, getting along with others, acquiring strong moral values, respecting one's elders, or exhibiting coordinated motor skills (Crago, 1988; Greenfield, 1998; H. Keller, 2003; Laboratory of Comparative Human Cognition, 1982; J. Li, 2004; Neisser et al., 1996; Nisbett, 2009; Sternberg, 2007; Sternberg, Jarvin, & Grigorenko, 2011)

With these qualities in mind, we offer one possible (but intentionally broad) definition of **intelligence**: the ability to apply past knowledge and experiences flexibly and in a culturally appropriate manner to accomplish challenging new tasks.

THEORETICAL PERSPECTIVES ON INTELLIGENCE

Views on intelligence have evolved considerably over the past two centuries. Initial concerns were based on the practical needs to measure intelligence and customize instruction for individual children. In the early 1900s, school officials in France asked the psychologist **Alfred Binet** (1857–1911) to develop a way of identifying students who would have exceptional difficulty in regular classrooms without special educational services. To accomplish the task, Binet devised a test that measured general knowledge, vocabulary, perception, memory, and abstract thought. He found that students who performed poorly on his test tended to perform poorly in the classroom as well. Binet's test was the earliest version of what we now call an **intelligence test**.

PUTTING INTELLIGENCE TO WORK. Children learn to apply their intellectual skills in a variety of domains. These young Tibetan monks are investing intellectual resources in determining how to get along with peers, develop self-discipline, and gain spiritual insights from their religious community.

intelligence
Ability to apply past knowledge and experiences flexibly to accomplish challenging new tasks.

intelligence test
General measure of current cognitive functioning, used primarily to predict academic achievement over the short run.

Such down-to-earth concerns came to be supplemented with theoretical discussions on the underlying structure of intelligence. Scholars have debated whether intelligence is essentially one characteristic that a child has to a greater or lesser degree, or alternatively if it is a compilation of several distinct abilities, each of which represents a strength or weakness for the child. As you will find out, evidence is strong for both positions, and many theorists now conclude that children have more or less of a general ability that permits them to solve novel problems in a wide range of situations, as well as a collection of specific abilities (e.g., understanding spoken words or holding a lot of information in memory) that they employ in circumscribed situations.

Another theoretical issue that has garnered analysis has been the extent to which the capacity for intelligence is inherited or derived from experience. Originally, scholars were impressed with data indicating genetic origins of intelligence, yet increasingly experts have found even stronger evidence about the effects of child rearing, schooling, nutrition, and other environmental factors. Currently, experts in intelligence are resoundingly optimistic that a child's intelligence can be increased with appropriate conditions and, when necessary, intervention (Dweck, 2009; D. J. Matthews, 2009; Nisbett, 2009). These themes—determining practical implications, underlying structures, and origins of intelligence—are addressed to varying degrees in the following five theories of intelligence.

Spearman's *g*

In the early 1900s, British psychologist **Charles Spearman** (1863–1945) proposed that intelligence comprises both (a) a single, pervasive reasoning ability (a *general factor*) that is used on a wide variety of tasks and (b) a number of narrow abilities (*specific factors*) involved in executing particular tasks (Spearman, 1904, 1927). From Spearman's perspective, children's performance on any given task depends both on the general factor and on any specific factors that the task involves. Measures of various language skills (vocabulary, word recognition, reading comprehension, etc.) are all highly correlated, presumably because they all reflect both general intelligence and the same specific factor: verbal ability. A score on language skills will correlate to a lesser extent with a score on mathematical problem solving because the two measures tap into general intelligence but also employ somewhat different specific abilities.

Many contemporary psychologists have found sufficient evidence in the substantial positive correlations among diverse intellectual abilities to conclude that a general factor in intelligence exists (e.g., N. Brody, 2006; Kovas et al., 2007). This factor is often known simply as Spearman's *g*. Some contemporary theorists suspect that the ability to process information quickly may be at the heart of *g*, because substantial correlations have been found between measures of children's general intelligence and information processing speed (e.g., in rapidly pressing the M key every time the number 5 appears on the right side of a computer screen; Demetriou, Mouyi, & Spanoudis, 2008). Other recent evidence indicates that high levels of general intelligence are associated with having a large number of neurons and glial cells, especially in the front area of the brain (where circuits for planning and decision making reside), and with the brain's consumption of low levels of energy during simple cognitive processes (Gläscher et al., 2010; Luders, Narr, Thompson, & Toga, 2009; van den Heuvel, Stam, Kahn, & Hulshoff Pol, 2009). Apparently, children who are especially intelligent develop brains that allow for efficient comparison, integration, and control of ideas.

Not all psychologists agree that a *g* factor exists, however. Some suggest that the evidence for a single general factor can be either strong or weak depending on the specific abilities measured and on the particular statistical methods used to analyze the data (Neisser, 1998a; Sternberg, 2003a; Sternberg & Grigorenko, 2000). Others argue that the appearance of a general factor is an artifact of test items having been taken from skills valued in a limited number of societies, especially in mainstream cultures of Europe and North America (Gardner, 2006). A few psychologists point out that even if *g* exists, children may additionally possess specific abilities that would be more constructive to address (Mather, 2009; McGrew, 2005). Hence it could be quite helpful for a teacher to learn that a child has trouble identifying sounds and matching them with letters because these skills can be taught. In contrast, knowing the child's most recent general intelligence score provides virtually no information about specific interventions that would benefit the child.

Cattell-Horn-Carroll Theory of Cognitive Abilities

The Cattell-Horn-Carroll theory of cognitive abilities is a blend of views that was originally inspired by the work of **Raymond Cattell** (1905–1998), a British psychologist who worked in the United States. Extending the ideas of Spearman, Cattell (1963, 1987) found evidence for two distinctly different components of general intelligence. First, Cattell proposed, children differ in **fluid intelligence**, the ability to acquire knowledge quickly and adapt to new situations effectively. Second, they differ in **crystallized intelligence**, the knowledge and skills they have accumulated from their experiences, schooling, and culture. These two components may be more or less relevant to different kinds of tasks. Fluid intelligence relates more to novel tasks, especially those that require rapid decisions and are largely nonverbal in nature. Crystallized intelligence is more important for familiar tasks, especially those that are heavily dependent on language and prior knowledge.

According to Cattell, fluid intelligence is largely the result of inherited biological factors, whereas crystallized intelligence depends on both fluid intelligence and experience and so is influenced by both heredity and environment (Cattell, 1980, 1987). Fluid intelligence peaks in late adolescence and begins to decline gradually in adulthood. In contrast, crystallized intelligence continues to increase throughout childhood, adolescence, and most of adulthood (Cattell, 1963).

More recent work has led to refinements in Cattell's abilities. Psychologists John Horn and John Carroll obtained evidence indicating that Cattell's distinction between fluid and crystallized abilities needed further differentiation. Other scholars joined an initiative to distinguish these global capacities, and a new integrative framework emerged,

g
General factor in intelligence that influences performance in a wide variety of tasks and content domains.

fluid intelligence
Ability to acquire knowledge quickly and thereby adapt effectively to new situations.

crystallized intelligence
Knowledge and skills accumulated from one's prior experience, schooling, and culture.

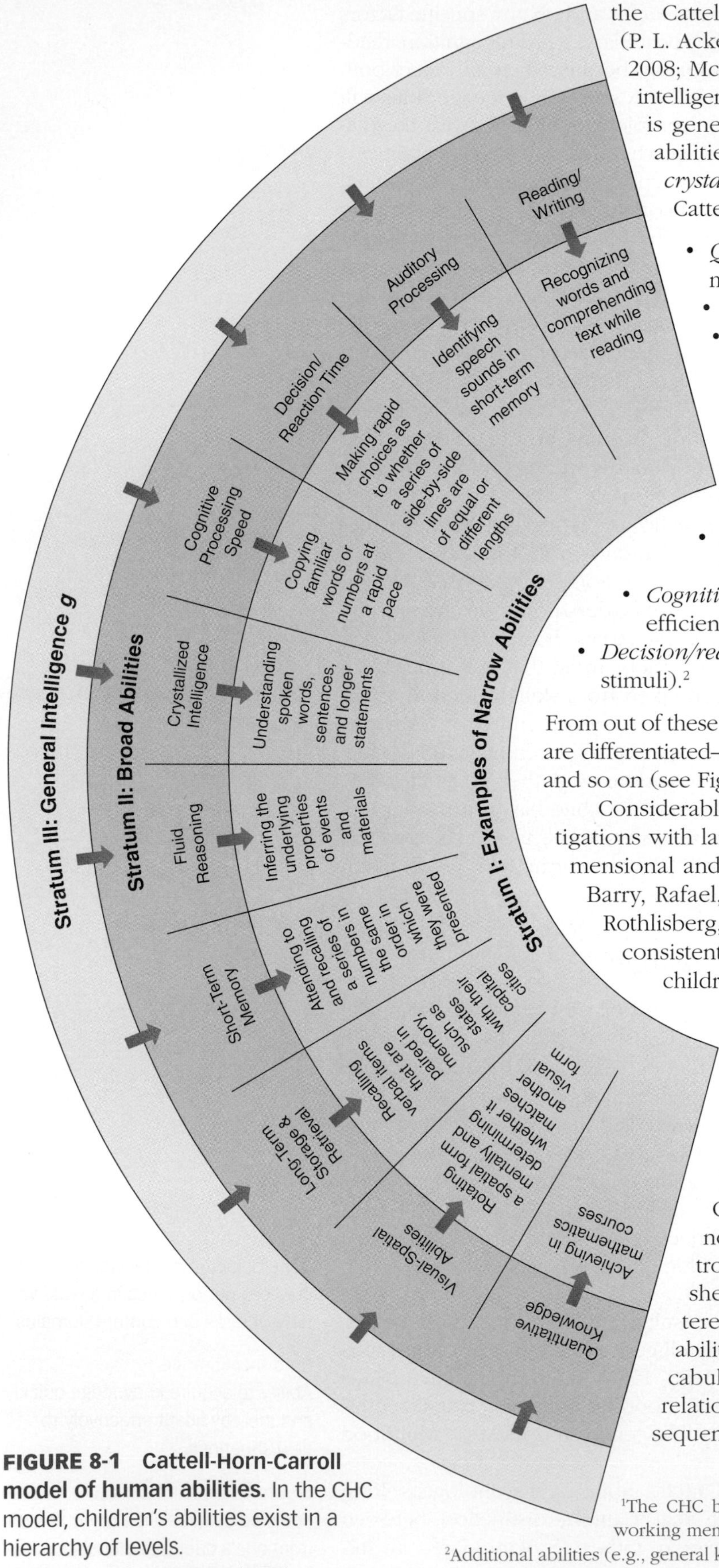

Stratum III: General Intelligence g

Stratum II: Broad Abilities

Stratum I: Examples of Narrow Abilities

Reading/Writing — Recognizing words and comprehending text while reading

Auditory Processing — Identifying speech sounds in short-term memory

Decision/Reaction Time — Making rapid choices as to whether a series of side-by-side lines are of equal or different lengths

Cognitive Processing Speed — Copying familiar words or numbers at a rapid pace

Crystallized Intelligence — Understanding spoken words, sentences, and longer statements

Fluid Reasoning — Inferring the underlying properties of events and materials

Short-Term Memory — Attending to and recalling a series of numbers in the same order in which they were presented

Long-Term Storage & Retrieval — Recalling verbal items that are paired in memory, such as states with capital cities

Visual-Spatial Abilities — Rotating a spatial form mentally and determining whether it matches another visual form

Quantitative Knowledge — Achieving in mathematics courses

FIGURE 8-1 Cattell-Horn-Carroll model of human abilities. In the CHC model, children's abilities exist in a hierarchy of levels.

Abilities based on McGrew (2005).

the Cattell-Horn-Carroll (CHC) theory of cognitive abilities (P. L. Ackerman & Lohman, 2006; Carroll, 1993, 2003; J. L. Horn, 2008; McGrew, 2005; Golay & Lecerf, 2011). In the CHC theory, intelligence has three layers, or *strata*. At the top layer (Stratum III) is general intelligence, or *g*. Emerging out of *g* are 10 broad abilities (in Stratum II), including *fluid intelligence* and *crystallized intelligence*, the two abilities originally identified by Cattell. The other eight broad abilities are:

- *Quantitative knowledge* (applying knowledge about mathematical operations)
- *Reading/writing* (performing complex literacy skills)
- *Long-term storage and retrieval* (putting information into memory and remembering it)
- *Short-term memory* (attending to and remembering a small number of items for a short time)[1]
- *Visual-spatial abilities* (generating visual images and identifying patterns in an incomplete visual display)
- *Auditory processing* (analyzing and synthesizing sound elements and auditory patterns)
- *Cognitive processing speed* (performing easy and familiar tasks efficiently)
- *Decision/reaction time* (making decisions quickly about simple stimuli).[2]

From out of these broad abilities, 70 to 100 very specific abilities (Stratum I) are differentiated—reading speed, mechanical knowledge, visual memory, and so on (see Figure 8-1).

Considerable evidence supports the CHC model. Numerous investigations with large samples and statistical models validate the multidimensional and hierarchical structure of intelligence (Floyd, McGrew, Barry, Rafael, & Rogers, 2009; Golay & Lecerf, 2011; K. E. Morgan, Rothlisberg, McIntosh, & Hunt, 2009). The model is also generally consistent with research on the brain, developmental changes in children's intelligence, and evidence of hereditary and environmental influences on intelligence (McGrew, 2005).

In addition, many school psychologists suggest that the CHC model can productively guide services for individual children who achieve at exceptionally advanced or delayed levels in particular academic areas (Bergeron & Floyd, 2006; Fiorello & Primerano, 2005; Floyd, Bergeron, & Alfonso, 2006; Volker, Lopata, & Cook-Cottone, 2006). For example, when one teacher noticed that a sixth-grade girl appeared to be having trouble with short-term memory and basic reading skills, she consulted with a school psychologist who administered a battery of tests and found that most of the girl's abilities were strong (i.e., she had good language skills, vocabulary, long-term memory, and knowledge of letter-sound relationships), but a few reflected difficulty remembering a sequence of spoken words (i.e., a problem with working

---

[1]The CHC broad ability of short-term memory reflects the limited capacity of working memory, described in Chapters 6 and 7.

[2]Additional abilities (e.g., general knowledge, kinesthetic abilities, general cognitive speed) are currently under investigation for possible inclusion as broad abilities in the middle stratum (McGrew, 2005).

memory for auditory information; Fiorello & Primerano, 2005). The psychologist recommended that the girl receive drills in spelling and letter-sound combinations so that these operations could be used without major demands on memory. Other recommendations included allowing her to use a tape recorder during class, obtain notes from a classmate, and review assigned books on tape.

A disadvantage of the CHC model is that it is still evolving and obviously very complex, making the full range of implications unclear. In addition, although it has been informed by numerous kinds of data, it is based primarily on existing intelligence tests. The CHC theory could be enhanced with additional data about human abilities, particularly children's performance in non-Western cultures and on nontraditional tasks.

Gardner's Multiple Intelligences

American psychologist **Howard Gardner** argues that traditional definitions of intelligence are too narrow (Gardner, 1995, 2003, 2009). He concedes that a general factor of intelligence may exist but questions its usefulness in explaining people's performance in particular situations. In his view, children and adults have at least eight distinctly different abilities, or *multiple intelligences* (MI), which are described and illustrated in Table 8-1.

TABLE 8-1 Gardner's Multiple Intelligences

TYPE OF INTELLIGENCE[a]	EXAMPLES OF RELEVANT BEHAVIORS
Linguistic Intelligence Ability to use language effectively	• Making persuasive arguments • Writing poetry • Identifying subtle nuances in word meanings
Logical-Mathematical Intelligence Ability to reason logically, especially in mathematics and science	• Solving mathematical problems quickly • Generating mathematical proofs • Formulating and testing hypotheses about observed phenomena[b]
Spatial Intelligence Ability to notice details in what one sees and to imagine and manipulate visual objects in one's mind	• Conjuring up mental images • Drawing a visual likeness of an object • Making fine discriminations among very similar objects
Musical Intelligence Ability to create, comprehend, and appreciate music	• Playing a musical instrument • Composing a musical work • Showing a keen awareness of the underlying structure of music
Bodily-Kinesthetic Intelligence Ability to use one's body skillfully	• Dancing • Playing basketball • Performing pantomime
Interpersonal Intelligence Ability to notice subtle aspects of other people's behaviors	• Correctly perceiving another's mood • Detecting another's underlying intentions and desires • Using knowledge of others to influence their thoughts and behaviors
Intrapersonal Intelligence Awareness of one's own feelings, motives, and desires	• Identifying subtle differences in one's experiences of such similar emotions as sadness and regret • Identifying the motives guiding one's own behavior • Using self-knowledge to relate more effectively with others
Naturalist Intelligence Ability to recognize patterns in nature and differences among natural objects and life-forms	• Identifying members of particular plant or animal species • Classifying natural forms (e.g., rocks, types of mountains) • Applying one's knowledge of nature in such activities as farming, landscaping, or animal training

[a]Gardner has also suggested the possibility of an existential intelligence dedicated to philosophical and spiritual issues, but he acknowledges that evidence for it is weaker than is the case for the eight intelligences described here.
[b]This example may remind you of Piaget's theory of cognitive development. Many of the stage-relevant characteristics that Piaget described fall within the realm of logical-mathematical intelligence.

Sources: Gardner, 1983, 1993, 1999, 2000, 2009; Gardner & Hatch, 1990.

Improving Your Observation Skills

Multiple intelligences. In their everyday lives, children exercise a variety of intellectual abilities. *How might each child be exercising one of Gardner's intelligences?* Look at the label under each photo and describe how the child appears to be employing the designated intelligence. Compare your response with the explanation at the end of the chapter.

1. Linguistic intelligence

2. Logical-mathematical intelligence

3. Spatial intelligence

4. Musical intelligence

5. Bodily-kinesthetic intelligence

6. Interpersonal intelligence

7. Intrapersonal intelligence

8. Naturalist intelligence

Three of the intelligences—linguistic, logical-mathematical, and spatial abilities—resemble the kinds of abilities that are tapped by conventional intelligence tests. According to Gardner, the remaining intelligences—musical, bodily-kinesthetic, interpersonal, intrapersonal, and naturalist abilities—are legitimate intellectual domains but have been neglected by test developers. Gardner also speculates that there may be a ninth, "existential" intelligence dedicated to philosophical and spiritual issues (e.g., Who are we? Why do we exist?). Because Gardner himself is on the fence about whether sufficient data distinguish an existential ability as a separate intelligence, it is not included in the table (Gardner, 1999, 2003, 2009). From Gardner's vantage point, it is not as important to agree on a specific number of intelligences as it is to accept that abilities exist in a plurality and span a breadth of intellectual domains.

Gardner presents some evidence to support the existence of multiple intelligences. He describes people who are quite skilled in one area (perhaps in composing music) and yet have seemingly average abilities in the other areas. He also points out that people who suffer brain damage sometimes lose abilities that are restricted primarily to a single intelligence. One person might show deficits primarily in language, whereas another might have difficulty with tasks that require spatial reasoning. Furthermore, Gardner argues that each of the intelligences has its own symbolic operations and has played an important role over the course of human evolution, allowing people to adapt successfully to their environments. Thus, whereas Spearman's theory and the Cattell-Horn-Carroll model are based heavily on traditional test scores, Gardner and his colleagues claim that other kinds of data (e.g., studies of people with exceptional talents, documentation of people with brain injuries) must be seriously considered to get a good picture of human beings' abilities (Gardner, 2008, 2009; Gardner & Moran, 2006).

Gardner and his colleagues have identified several implications of his theory. One important application is that children should have some choices in how they demonstrate their knowledge. Gardner also recommends that teachers help children acquire increasingly refined skills that match their unique profiles of abilities, for example, by implementing computer programs that personalize training. In addition, teachers can vary their instructional modalities, for example, by asking students to show their mastery of mathematics with written formulas (logical-mathematical abilities) on one occasion, self-reflections into their accomplishments (intrapersonal abilities) on another, and analyses of data collected from the local ecology (naturalistic abilities) on yet another occasion. Soliciting a range of intellectual abilities increases the chances that the special talents of every child will be exercised at one time or another and that children will develop well-rounded understandings of subject matter (Gardner, 2009).

DEVELOPMENT IN CULTURE
Multiple Intelligences in China

Three aspects of Howard Gardner's theory of MI have led to its appeal around the world (Armstrong, 2009; Gardner, 2009). First, integral to Gardner's theory is the idea that each of the eight or nine intelligences is represented in unique ways in virtually all cultures (Gardner, 1983). Thus people in varied circumstances can easily recognize the everyday uses that they make of language, mathematics, spatial images, movement, music, personal insights, interpersonal understandings, and knowledge of nature (Armstrong, 2009). Second, the theory's advocacy for the arts, creative expression, and physical education has been compelling to educators in many corners who believe that restriction to a narrow range of academic skills, which occurs in a number of classrooms, robs students of the joy of learning (Gardner, 2009). Finally, educators have appreciated Gardner's interest in reaching underserved students with inclusive methods.

Educators in China have been particularly enthusiastic about applying lessons from the theory of MI. In fact, hundreds of thousands of Chinese educators have received training in this theory (J.-Q Chen, 2009). Chinese educators increasingly recognize that traditional methods of instruction, which have emphasized memorization of basic facts, yield an inadequate skill set for a rapidly changing society. In welcome contrast, the active learning, respect for individual differences, and innovation endorsed by MI theory make it a desirable model for optimizing human potential (J.-Q. Chen, 2009; H. H.-P. Cheung, 2009).

MI theory has also been warmly embraced because of its compatibility with cultural ideals about learning. Dating back to the days of Confucius, Chinese culture has admired the plurality of human abilities (J.-Q. Chen, 2009; Shen, 2009). Today, an appreciation for individual differences has helped teachers respond sympathetically to learners who do not perform well on traditional academic tasks. One Chinese teacher said, "Unlike before, when I look at my students now, they are all good students. Everyone has shining points to appreciate" (H. H.-P. Cheung, 2009, p. 45). Another teacher made a similar observation, "I noticed some of my students who did not have high scores in school turned out to be more successful. MI theory shows me the reason. Those students' interpersonal intelligences might be higher. Each of them is unique" (H. H.-P. Cheung, 2009, p. 45).

In the process of absorbing basic tenets of MI theory, Chinese educators have adapted the framework to fit two unique features of their culture. First, intelligence in young children is considered inseparable from the abilities of their families (J.-Q. Chen, 2009). In other words, intelligence is a property of the family, not a quality of the individual child. Each family has its own profile of intellectual strengths, interests, and skills, and each member of the family complements and supports the intelligence of other members. To reach out to families, educators trained in MI theory hold classes in the evening and on weekends for parents. At school, children are encouraged to learn about their parents' values, interests, and child-rearing strategies so as to increase children's receptivity to family lessons and to increase children's insights into family relationships. Second, the cultural ideal of harmony is integrated into interpretations of MI theory. Chinese educators view children's intellectual strengths as being balanced with their weaknesses. To be effective, teachers must take into account the entire package of abilities and limitations in children. The notion of harmony also applies to offering a good balance of lesson formats so that everyone has a chance to succeed (J.-Q. Chen, 2009).

INTELLIGENCE IN THE FAMILY. In China, Gardner's theory of Multiple Intelligences has drawn attention to the growth of intellectual development within the family.

Chinese educators wrestle with certain challenges in translating the principles of MI theory to instruction (H. H.-P. Cheung, 2009). Large class sizes make it difficult to individualize innovative instructional methods. Pressures to prepare high school students for college entrance examinations undermine the ease with which educators can apply the theory with older adolescents. Finally, some Chinese educators have the misconception that the framework directs them to train every child to an extremely high level of accomplishment in each of the eight or nine intelligences, rather than allowing children freedom in the particular talents in which they excel.

Many educators around the world have wholeheartedly embraced the insight that students can accomplish a great deal when instructional methods are adapted to reflect a wide spectrum of abilities (Armstrong, 2009; L. Campbell, Campbell, & Dickinson, 1998; Rizzo, 2009). You can learn how educators in China have integrated Gardner's theory in the Development in Culture feature, "Multiple Intelligences in China."

In psychological circles, reviews of Gardner's theory are mixed. Some psychologists do not believe that Gardner's evidence is sufficiently compelling to support the notion of eight or nine distinctly different abilities (N. Brody, 2006; A. R. Jensen, 2007; Sternberg, 2003b). Others agree that people may have a variety of relatively independent abilities but argue for intelligences other than the ones Gardner has described (e.g., J. L. Horn & Noll, 1997; Sternberg et al., 2000). Still others reject the idea that abilities in specific domains, such as in music or bodily movement, are really "intelligence" per se (Bracken, McCallum, & Shaughnessy, 1999; Sattler, 2001).

Sternberg's Theory of Successful Intelligence

American psychologist **Robert Sternberg** has developed a series of interrelated theories on how people use their cognitive abilities to achieve personal goals. Sternberg sees intelligence as a multifaceted capacity that allows an individual to select and adapt effectively to his or her environments (see Figure 8-2). He suggests that people may be more or less intelligent in three sets of abilities (Sternberg, 1985, 2005, 2009). *Analytical intelligence* involves making sense of, analyzing, contrasting, and evaluating the kinds of information and problems often seen in academic settings and on intelligence tests. *Creative intelligence* involves imagination, invention, and synthesis of ideas within new situations. *Practical intelligence* involves applying knowledge and skills effectively to manage and respond to everyday problems and social situations. Children blend these three types of intelligence in everyday tasks and gradually learn to recognize their personal strengths in each, use them to their advantage, and correct or compensate for their weaknesses.

Successful Intelligence

- Is comprised of analytical, creative, and practical abilities
- Helps a person achieve personal goals
- Requires a balancing among particular abilities
- Draws from memory and engages specific cognitive processes
- Allows a person to adapt, shape, and select their environment

FIGURE 8-2 Sternberg's theory of successful intelligence. According to Sternberg, a child uses a multifaceted collection of abilities to achieve personal goals.

These three types of intelligence involve the interplay of three additional factors, all of which vary from one occasion to the next: (a) the environmental *context* in which the behavior occurs, (b) the way in which one's memory of prior *experiences* is brought to bear on a particular task, and (c) the *cognitive processes* required by the task (Sternberg, 1985, 1997, 2003b).

Role of Environmental Context

As noted earlier, intelligence involves adaptation. In Sternberg's view such adjustment might take one of three forms: (a) modifying a response to deal successfully with specific environmental conditions, (b) modifying the environment to better fit one's own strengths and needs, or (c) selecting an alternative environment more conducive to success. Thus a given action may be considered more or less intelligent depending on the demands of different settings. Learning to describe events in explicit detail may be considered intelligent behavior in some contexts (e.g., at school), whereas speaking in an informal manner with reference to shared experiences may be thought of as clever behavior in other settings (e.g., at home).

Role of Prior Experience

Intelligent behavior sometimes involves the ability to deal successfully with a brand-new situation. At other times, it involves the ability to respond to familiar situations rapidly and efficiently. In both cases, a child's prior experiences play a critical role. When children encounter a new task or problem, they must draw on past experiences and consider the kinds of reactions that have been effective in similar circumstances. When they deal with familiar tasks, basic skills are well practiced so that the necessary processes can be completed quickly and effortlessly.

Role of Cognitive Processes

In addition to examining how context and prior experience affect behavior, we must also consider how a child thinks about (mentally processes) a particular situation. Sternberg suggests that numerous cognitive processes are involved in intelligent behavior: interpreting a new situation in productive ways, sustaining concentration on a task, separating important

TABLE 8-2 Activities Related to Light Using Sternberg's Theory of Successful Intelligence

LESSON	ANALYTICAL ABILITIES	CREATIVE ABILITIES	PRACTICAL ABILITIES
Straight from the Sun	Interpret observational data.	Create new transparent and translucent objects by combining as many materials as possible.	Plan and construct a scoring sheet to enable judges to fairly judge translucent and transparent objects.
Exploring Mirrors	Make and verify predictions.	Design a mirror "Exploratorium."	Use mirrors to direct light around corners.
Can You Bend a Pencil Without Breaking It?	Compare and contrast observational data and draw conclusions.	Write the memoirs of a light beam, *One Week on Earth: A Light Beam's Story*.	Use knowledge of refraction to improve one's ability to catch a fish in an aquarium.
Where Did All the Colors Go?	Make and verify predictions about color filters.	Create a cartoon strip illustrating the key concepts learned in this unit.	Make sample toys for a book on light.

Sources: Table 52 from "Balancing Analytical, Creative, and Practical Activities in an Elementary/Middle School Science Unit on Light" from WISDOM, INTELLIGENCE, CREATIVITY, AND SUCCESS by Elena L. Grigorenko. Copyright © 2009 by Elena L. Grigorenko. Reprinted with permission via Copyright Clearance Center.

information from irrelevant details, identifying possible problem-solving strategies, finding relationships among seemingly different ideas, and making effective use of external feedback. Different cognitive processes are likely to be relevant to different situations, and so a child may behave more or less "intelligently" depending on specific demands.

Sternberg and his colleagues recommend that teachers diversify the particular abilities they target across the curriculum. Although it is not realistic to address the full spectrum of children's abilities in any single lesson, teachers can diversify their teaching repertoire over a period of time (Sternberg, Jarvin, & Grigorenko, 2009). In Table 8-2, you can see some illustrations of activities that solicit various abilities. In research by Sternberg and his colleagues, students who took part in a well-balanced curriculum with exercises in analytical, practical, and creative intelligence performed at higher levels than did students who received conventional instruction (Sternberg, Torff, & Grigorenko, 1998).

A modest amount of research supports Sternberg's theory. Some evidence indicates that analytical, creative, and practical skills exist and are somewhat independent of one another and of general intelligence (Sternberg, 2009). Other results indicate that Sternberg's abilities are associated with later academic success, sometimes more strongly than are conventional tests of ability. However, several scholars worry that certain aspects of Sternberg's theory (e.g., how various factors work together) are described in such general terms that they are difficult to test empirically (Sattler, 2001; Siegler & Alibali, 2005). A few intelligence specialists are not yet convinced that the practical abilities identified in Sternberg's theory are really different from general intelligence (N. Brody, 2006; Gottfredson, 2003). Despite these limitations, Sternberg's perspective helps us understand the specific cognitive processes that underlie a child's multifaceted abilities. Furthermore, it reminds us that a child's ability to behave intelligently varies considerably depending on the context and specific knowledge required by a task.

Distributed Intelligence

Implicit in our discussion so far has been the assumption that intelligent behavior is something that children and adolescents engage in with little if any help from external resources. But some psychologists point out that youngsters are far more likely to behave intelligently when they have the support of their physical, social, and cultural environments (A. Bennett et al., 2007; Pea, 1993; Perkins, 1995; Sternberg, Grigorenko, & Bridglall, 2007). For example, it's easier for many adolescents to solve for x in the equation

$$\frac{7}{25} = \frac{x}{375}$$

if they have pencil and paper with which to work out the problem. And they are more likely to write a convincing persuasive essay if they brainstorm their ideas with peers before beginning to compose their notes.

This idea that intelligent behavior depends on physical, social, and cultural support mechanisms is sometimes referred to as **distributed intelligence**. Learning specialists **Roy Pea** and **David Perkins** have observed that children and adolescents can "distribute" their thinking (and therefore think more intelligently) in at least three ways (Pea, 1993; Perkins, 1992, 1995). First, young people can use physical objects, especially technology (e.g., calculators, computers), to handle and manipulate large amounts of information. Second, they can work with others to explore ideas and solve problems. Third, they can represent and think about the situations they encounter using the various symbolic tools their culture provides—for instance, the words, diagrams, charts, mathematical equations, and so on that help them simplify or make better sense of complex topics and problems.

The framework of distributed intelligence has considerable appeal to many educators who recognize that *all* children—not just those who have the advantage of "smart" genes or those whose families foster their academic skills at home—deserve to have their abilities nurtured at school (Barab & Plucker, 2002; Hoerr, 2003). In fact, children often develop more advanced skills when working together, using new technologies, and tackling realistic problems (Gomez, Schieble, Curwood, & Hassett, 2010; Greeno, 2007). Theorists have only begun to explore the implications of a "distributed" view of intelligence, however. Much work remains to be done, both in identifying the specific ways in which the environment can support intelligent behavior and in determining how great an effect such support is likely to have.

The five perspectives just presented provide diverging views of human intelligence. Differences with respect to three themes—nature and nurture, universality and diversity, and qualitative and quantitative change—are presented in the Basic Developmental Issues table "Contrasting Theories of Intelligence."

MEASURING INTELLIGENCE

Although psychologists have not been able to agree on exactly what intelligence is, they have been trying to measure it for more than a century. Today intelligence tests are widely used to assess children's cognitive functioning and predict academic achievement, especially when a child may possibly have special educational needs.

Tests of Intelligence

Most intelligence tests in use today have been developed to do the same thing that Alfred Binet's first test was intended to do: identify children with special needs who might benefit from customized educational services. In many cases, a diagnostic battery of intelligence tests is administered to determine why certain children are showing developmental delays or academic difficulties. In other instances, intelligence tests are used to identify children with exceptionally high abilities who require more in-depth instruction or advanced classwork to nurture their cognitive growth.

Intelligence tests typically include a wide variety of questions and problems for children to tackle. By and large, the focus is not on what children have specifically been taught at school, but rather on what they have learned and deduced from their general, everyday experiences.

Examples of Intelligence Tests

To give you a feel for the nature of intelligence tests, we briefly describe four of them.[3]

distributed intelligence
Thinking facilitated by physical objects and technology, social support, and concepts and symbols of one's culture.

---

[3]You can find descriptions of several widely used standardized tests at www.ctb.com (for CTB and McGraw-Hill), www.riverpub.com (for Riverside Publishing), and www.pearsonassessments.com (for Pearson Assessments and PsychCorp tests).

BASIC DEVELOPMENTAL ISSUES
Contrasting Theories of Intelligence

ISSUE	SPEARMAN'S GENERAL FACTOR (g)	CATTELL-HORN-CARROLL THEORY OF COGNITIVE ABILITIES	GARDNER'S THEORY OF MULTIPLE INTELLIGENCES	STERNBERG'S THEORY OF SUCCESSFUL INTELLIGENCE	THEORY OF DISTRIBUTED INTELLIGENCE
Nature and Nurture	Spearman did not specifically address the issue of nature versus nurture. Researchers have subsequently found evidence that *g* is related to both heredity and environment.	Proponents of the Cattell-Horn-Carroll model claim that fluid intelligence is strongly determined by inherited factors. Crystallized intelligence is influenced by both heredity and environment, and practitioners can teach children to improve their specific abilities.	Gardner believes that heredity provides some basis for individual differences in the various intelligences. However, culture influences the form that each intelligence takes, and informal experiences and schooling influence the extent to which each intelligence flourishes.	Sternberg emphasizes the roles of environmental context (e.g., culture), prior experience in intelligent behavior, and the person's own goals and choices in particular environments. Thus his focus is on nurture.	Environmental support mechanisms (physical tools, social interaction, and the symbolic representations of one's culture) influence a person's ability to behave intelligently.
Universality and Diversity	Spearman assumed that the existence of *g* is universal across cultures. However, people vary both in their general intellectual ability and in more specific abilities.	Substantial evidence suggests that the multidimensional structure of abilities is universal. Individual children differ in levels of general intelligence, broad abilities, and specific abilities.	According to Gardner, the various intelligences are products of human evolution and are seen worldwide. However, any particular intelligence will manifest itself in its own way in different environments and cultures.	The three factors that influence intelligent behavior (context, experience, cognitive processes) are universal. Different cultures place distinct demands on analytical, creative, and practical abilities, so intelligence may take unique forms in each culture.	The physical, social, and symbolic support mechanisms at one's disposal vary widely from situation to situation and from one cultural group to another.
Qualitative and Quantitative Change	Spearman derived his theory from various tests of cognitive abilities. Implicit in such tests is the assumption that abilities change quantitatively over time.	Evidence indicates a quantitative increase in fluid analytical abilities in childhood and a gradual decline in adulthood (Cattell, 1963). Other evidence indicates that abilities change qualitatively. Intelligence is seen in 2-month-olds' responsiveness to the environment, in 8-month-olds' imitation of others' actions, and in 2-year-olds' labeling of objects (Tusing & Ford, 2004).	Growth in each intelligence has both quantitative and qualitative elements. In logical-mathematical intelligence, children gain skills in increments (quantitatively) but also acquire new (and qualitatively different) abilities.	The effects of relevant prior experiences, more automatized knowledge and skills, and more efficient cognitive processes involve quantitative change. The acquisition of new strategies over time involves qualitative change.	Some contexts enhance intelligence quantitatively (e.g., children might remember more from a book when they not only read it but also listen to an audiotape of it). Some instruction enhances intelligence qualitatively (e.g., children are more likely to elaborate on a book's content when they are taught how to ask one another thought-provoking questions about the material).

Wechsler Intelligence Scale for Children. One widely used intelligence test is the fourth edition of the *Wechsler Intelligence Scale for Children,* or *WISC-IV,* designed for children and adolescents ages 6 to 16 (O'Donnell, 2009; Wechsler, 2003). The WISC-IV consists of 15 subtests, with certain subtest scores being combined to obtain composite scores in Verbal Comprehension, Perceptual Reasoning, Working Memory, and Processing Speed. Many of

Following are descriptions of 6 of the 15 subtests on the WISC-IV, along with items similar to those included in the subtests.

Similarities

This subtest is designed to assess a child's verbal reasoning and concept formation.

- In what way are a lion and a tiger alike?
- In what way are an hour and a week alike?
- In what way are a circle and a triangle alike?

Comprehension

This subtest is designed to assess a child's understanding of general principles and social situations.

- What should you do if you see someone forget his book when he leaves a restaurant?
- What is the advantage of keeping money in a bank?
- Why is copper often used in electrical wires?

Information

This subtest is designed to assess a child's general knowledge about a broad range of topics.

- How many wings does a bird have?
- What is steam made of?
- What is pepper?

Letter-Number Sequencing

This subtest is designed to assess a child's working memory capacity. In each item, a letter-number sequence is presented, and the child is asked to repeat first the numbers (in numerical order) and then the letters (in alphabetical order).

- Q-3 [Response: 3-Q]
- M-3-P-6 [Response: 3-6-M-P]
- 5-J-4-A-1-S [Response: 1-4-5-A-J-S]

Arithmetic

This subtest is designed to assess a child's ability to solve orally presented arithmetic problems within a certain time limit, tapping into both working memory capacity and knowledge of arithmetic.

- Sam had three pieces of candy and Joe gave him four more. How many pieces of candy did Sam have altogether?
- Three women divided eighteen golf balls equally among themselves. How many golf balls did each person receive?
- If two buttons cost $.15, what will be the cost of a dozen buttons?

Block Design

This subtest is designed to assess a child's ability to analyze and reproduce geometric designs, thus tapping into visual-spatial ability. The child looks at a series of designs, such as the one below, and is asked to re-create them using blocks that are solid red on two sides, solid white on two sides, and diagonally red and white on the remaining two sides.

FIGURE 8-3 WISC-IV. Items similar to those found on the *Wechsler Intelligence Scale for Children*®—Fourth Edition.

the subtest scores are also combined to determine a total score, known as a Full Scale IQ. Illustrations of items like those on the WISC-IV are presented in Figure 8-3.

Stanford-Binet Intelligence Scales.   A second commonly used instrument is the fifth edition of the *Stanford-Binet Intelligence Scales* (Roid, 2003; Roid & Tippin, 2009). The Stanford-Binet can be used with children (as young as age 2), adolescents, and adults. The individual being assessed is asked to perform a wide variety of tasks, some involving verbal material and responses (e.g., defining vocabulary words, finding logical inconsistencies in a story, or interpreting proverbs) and others involving objects or pictures (e.g., remembering a sequence of objects, copying geometric figures, or identifying absurdities in pictures). The Stanford-Binet yields an overall IQ score, and its most recent edition also yields Verbal and Nonverbal IQs, plus more specific scores in Fluid Reasoning, Knowledge, Working Memory, Visual-Spatial Processing, and Quantitative Reasoning.

Universal Nonverbal Intelligence Test. The WISC-IV and Stanford-Binet depend heavily on language: Even when tasks involve reasoning about strictly nonverbal, visual material, the child is usually given verbal instructions about how to complete them. In contrast, some measures of intelligence involve no language whatsoever. An example is the *Universal Nonverbal Intelligence Test,* or *UNIT* (Bracken & McCallum, 1998, 2009; McCallum & Bracken, 2005). Designed for children and adolescents ages 5 to 17, the UNIT consists of six subtests involving memory or reasoning regarding visual stimuli. Its content (e.g., people, mice, cheese) was chosen from objects and symbols presumed to be universal across all industrialized cultures. Instructions are given entirely through gestures, pantomime, and modeling, and the child responds by either pointing or manipulating objects. For example, the child may trace a path through a maze or construct a three-dimensional design using colored cubes.

Nonverbal tests such as the UNIT are especially useful for children who have hearing impairments or language-related learning disabilities, as well as for children for whom English is a second language. Children who are deaf and children who have been raised speaking a language other than English perform better on the UNIT than on more traditional language-based intelligence tests (Krivitski, McIntosh, Rothlisberg, & Finch, 2004; Maller, 2000; McCallum, 1999).

The Cognitive Assessment System. The Cognitive Assessment System (CAS) is a multidimensional measure of cognitive processes (Naglieri & Conway, 2009). The CAS was founded on the premise that cognitive processes identified in neurological research are the basis for intelligence. It includes four scales: an *Attention* scale (examines selective attention to a particular stimulus, e.g., finding particular numbers on a page despite many distracters); a *Simultaneous* scale (tests the ability to integrate separate stimuli into a single representation, e.g., after looking at a geometric figure, finding it embedded in a more complex pattern); a *Planning scale* (checks the ability to formulate a plan for solving a novel problem, e.g., rapidly matching letters and numbers on separate pages); and a *Successive Subtest* scale (assesses the ability to process information in a specific order, e.g., repeating words in the same order as stated by the examiner).

Intelligence Scores

In the early 20th century, some psychologists began to calculate scores for intelligence tests by comparing a child's *mental age* (referring to the age-group of students whose performance is most similar to the child's performance) with his or her chronological age (W. Stern, 1912; Terman, 1916). The mathematical formula involved division, and so the resulting score was called an *intelligence quotient,* or **IQ score.**[4] Even though we still use the term *IQ,* intelligence test scores are no longer based on the old formula. Instead, they are determined by comparing a person's performance on the test with the performance of others in the same age-group. Scores near 100 indicate average performance: People with a score of 100 have performed better than half of their age-mates on the test and not as well as the other half. Scores well below 100 indicate below-average performance on the test, and scores well above 100 indicate above-average performance.

Figure 8-4 shows the percentage of people getting scores at different points along the scale (e.g., 12.9 percent get scores between 100 and 105). Notice how the curve is high in the middle and low

IQ score

Score on an intelligence test, determined by comparing one's performance with the performance of same-age peers.

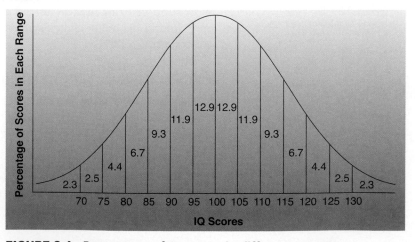

FIGURE 8-4 **Percentage of IQ scores in different ranges.**

[4]Alfred Binet himself objected to the use of intelligence quotients, believing that his tests were too imprecise to warrant such scores. Lewis Terman, an American psychologist, was largely responsible for popularizing the term *IQ* (Montagu, 1999).

at both ends. This shape tells us that many more people obtain scores close to 100 than scores very much higher or lower than 100. If we add up the percentages in different parts of Figure 8-4, we find that approximately two-thirds (68 percent) of individuals in any particular age-group score within 15 points of 100 (i.e., between 85 and 115). In contrast, only 2 percent score as low as 70, and only 2 percent score as high as 130.[5] Figure 8-4 does not include scores below 70 or above 130. Such scores are possible but relatively rare. You might recall that Gina, in the opening case study, once obtained a score of 140 on an intelligence test. A score of 140 is equivalent to a percentile rank of 99.4. In other words, only 6 people out of every 1,000 would earn a score as high as or higher than Gina's.

Keep in mind that use of an IQ score rests on the validity of the notion of general intelligence. As you have learned, not everyone believes that *g* is a meaningful concept, and practically speaking, knowing a child's relative standing on an aggregate of varied items is arguably less informative than finding out the particular intellectual domains in which a child excels and struggles (Mather, 2009; Stanovich, 1999). Consider the performance of elementary student Gary on the scales of the Cognitive Assessment System (Naglieri & Conway, 2009). Gary performed well below average but still in the normal range on the full-scale CAS (specifically, he scored better than 19 percent of children who took the CAS, meaning that approximately eight in ten children outperformed him; the CAS scales are defined on p. 297). What is more illuminating, however, is his uneven performance across the four scales and especially his score on the *Planning* scale. Gary performed better than 55 percent of peers on the *Attention* scale, 23 percent on the *Simultaneous* scale, 5 percent on the *Planning scale*, and 39 percent on the *Successive Subtest* scale. After receiving test score results, Gary's teacher focused on the challenges that Gary faced in planning and asked him to reflect on his strategies for completing mathematics worksheets:

> Gary reported that he developed and used several methods for completing the math pages. First, Gary informed his teacher that it was very difficult to concentrate because he was sitting next to someone who was disturbing him. He moved to a quieter part of the room so he could do his work and not be distracted by this person. Second, he noticed that he needed to review his basic math facts. Gary found that making flashcards and working with one of his friends at his teacher's suggestion was an enjoyable way to review this information. Third, Gary reported that in the past he rushed through his math problems without checking his work. His work was often written in a sloppy and messy manner. This caused errors, for example, when he subtracted columns that were not aligned properly. (Naglieri & Conway, 2009, p. 44)

Preparing for Your Licensure Examination

Your teaching test might ask you about the kinds of information provided by intelligence tests.

With support from his teacher related to planning and evaluating his performance, Gary improved in his mathematics achievement, more than doubling the number of problems he got correct.

Validity and Reliability of Intelligence Tests

If tests are to be used to make decisions about services for children, the test scores must be accurate. In general, the *validity* of an intelligence test is the extent to which it actually measures intelligence. The *reliability* of an intelligence test is the extent to which it yields consistent, dependable scores.[6]

Researchers take a variety of approaches to determine the validity of intelligence tests. For instance, they look for evidence that older children perform better on test items than do younger children—a result consistent with the assumption that children think more intelligently with age. As an example of age differences in performance on test questions, observe

[5]This symmetrical and predictable distribution of scores happens by design rather than by chance. If you have some knowledge of descriptive statistics, you probably recognize Figure 8-4 as a normal distribution. IQ scores are based on a normal distribution with a mean of 100 and, for most tests, a standard deviation of 15.
[6]In Chapter 2 we introduced the concepts of validity and reliability.

how three children define the word *freedom* in the "Intelligence" videos for middle childhood, early adolescence, and late adolescence in MyEducationLab:

Kate (age 8):   You want to be free. Or you want to play something . . . and you got caught and they have to keep you like in jail or something like in a game and you want to get free.

Ryan (age 13):   It means that you can, like, do stuff that you want.

Paul (age 17):   Basically something that everyone has these days or should have. It's the right to be able to make your own decisions and choose for yourself what you want to do or want to be.

Notice how, with age, the responses get increasingly abstract and complex. Kate limits her definition to a specific behavior, getting out of "jail" in a game. Ryan defines the term more broadly, implying that it has relevance to a wide variety of situations. Paul offers an abstract definition as well, but his is more precise than Ryan's.

Researchers also examine the validity of intelligence tests by determining how closely IQ scores correlate with school achievement and other indicators of intelligence. Many studies indicate that traditional measures of general intelligence, such as the WISC-IV, the Stanford-Binet, and the CAS, have considerable validity in this respect. On average, children and adolescents who earn higher scores on these tests have higher academic achievement and complete more years of education than their lower-scoring peers (Alloway & Alloway, 2010; N. Brody, 1997; S. D. Mayes, Calhoun, Bixler, & Zimmerman, 2009; Naglieri, De Lauder, Goldstein, & Schwebech, 2006). To a lesser extent, intelligence scores also predict later performance in the adult workplace (Baum & Bird, 2010; Sattler, 2001; Sternberg, 1996). We have less information about the UNIT, because it has only recently arrived on the scene, but emerging evidence indicates that it, too, has some validity as a measure of intelligence (M. M. Farrell & Phelps, 2000; McCallum & Bracken, 1997, 2005; E. L. Young & Assing, 2000).

It is also important that tests do not discriminate among different groups. A test has **cultural bias** when one or more of its items either offend or unfairly penalize people of a particular ethnic background, gender, or socioeconomic status, to the point that the validity of the test results is affected. Certain characteristics of intelligence tests may lead some children to attain scores that underestimate their intelligence. For instance, many contemporary intelligence tests focus on abstract thinking and other cognitive processes that are important in industrialized Western societies but less relevant to other cultures (Greenfield et al., 2006; Laundra & Sutton, 2008; Ogbu, 1994). Lack of familiarity with a test's question format may also hamper children's performance (Heath, 1989; Neisser et al., 1996). Facility with the English language is a factor as well: Children for whom English is a second language perform relatively poorly on test items that are primarily verbal in nature (E. C. Lopez, 1997). Publishers of intelligence tests routinely employ individuals from diverse backgrounds to ensure that test content is fair and appropriate for students of all races and ethnicities (R. L. Linn & Miller, 2005). Nevertheless, tests can be biased in ways that are not always anticipated by test developers.

To determine the reliability of intelligence tests, researchers look at various indications of consistency, especially the extent to which the same test yields similar scores on two different occasions, different subtests within a particular test yield similar results for a particular child, and two different examiners score a child's performance in the same way. Children's scores on the WISC-IV, Stanford-Binet, UNIT, and CAS are highly reliable in these respects (Anastasi & Urbina, 1997; Naglieri & Conway, 2009; Sattler, 2001; P. E. Williams, Weiss, & Rolfhus, 2003; E. L. Young & Assing, 2000).

Dynamic Assessment

The approaches described so far focus on what children can *currently* do with little or no assistance from anyone else. In contrast, **dynamic assessment** focuses on assessing children's ability to learn in new situations, usually with an adult's assistance (Feuerstein, 1979; Feuerstein, Feuerstein, & Gross, 1997; Haywood & Lidz, 2007; Lidz & Gindis, 2003; Navarro & Mora, 2011; Tzuriel, 2000). Typically, dynamic assessment involves (a) identifying one or more tasks that

MyEducationLab

Notice how children's word definitions become increasingly sophisticated with age in the "Intelligence" videos for middle childhood, early adolescence, and late adolescence in the Video Examples section in Topic 8 of MyEducationLab.

Preparing for Your Licensure Examination

Your teaching test might ask you about the degree to which intelligence tests are valid and reliable.

cultural bias
Extent to which an assessment instrument offends or unfairly penalizes some individuals because of their ethnicity, gender, or socioeconomic status.

dynamic assessment
Systematic examination of how a child's knowledge or reasoning may change as a result of learning a specific task or performing it with adult guidance.

children cannot initially do independently, (b) providing in-depth instruction and practice in behaviors and cognitive processes related to the task(s), and then (c) determining the extent to which each child has benefited from the instruction. Accordingly, dynamic assessment is sometimes called *assessment of learning potential.*

Dynamic assessment is consistent with several theoretical perspectives. As Sternberg has pointed out, intelligence involves adaptation to new situations (Sternberg, 2009). And as the concept of distributed intelligence reminds us, intelligent behavior is heavily context dependent. But Vygotsky's theory of cognitive development is probably most relevant here.[7] Vygotsky proposed that we get a more complete picture of children's cognitive development when we assess not only their *actual developmental level* (the upper limit of tasks they can successfully accomplish on their own), but also their *level of potential development* (the upper limit of tasks they can accomplish when they have the assistance of more competent individuals).

Dynamic assessment is a fairly new approach to assessing intelligence, so psychologists are only beginning to discover its strengths and weaknesses. On the plus side, it often yields more optimistic evaluations of children's abilities than traditional measures of intelligence (Jeltova et al., 2007; H. L. Swanson & Lussier, 2001; Tzuriel, 2000). Dynamic assessment can provide a wealth of qualitative information about children's experiences and approaches to learning and so may be helpful in guiding future instruction (Feuerstein, 1979; Hamers & Ruijssenaars, 1997; Moore-Brown, Huerta, Uranga-Hernandez, & Peña, 2006; Tzuriel, 2000). To illustrate, a boy named Justin was initially able to tell only a very simple story but after a brief period of instruction, he articulated complex ideas, expressed varied vocabulary, and used advanced grammar. In studying Justin's responses and records, his assessment team realized that his previous academic delays had probably been due to his frequent absences, tardiness, and weak educational foundation—not to limited intelligence. Accordingly, the team was optimistic that Justin could benefit from instruction that addressed his missing academic skills. In this manner, dynamic assessments can be especially effective in determining the academic concepts and learning strategies that children need to practice in order to progress academically (Lin, 2010; T.-H. Wang, 2010).

Yet disadvantages of dynamic assessment are also emerging. A dynamic assessment often involves considerable training before it can be used appropriately, and it typically requires a great deal of time to administer (Anastasi & Urbina, 1997; Tzuriel, 2000). Furthermore, questions have been raised about how best to determine the validity and reliability of dynamic assessment instruments, and those instruments that have been evaluated have fared poorly in comparison to more traditional measures of intelligence (Swanson & Lussier, 2001; Tzuriel, 2000). Accordingly, when educators and psychologists use dynamic assessment to assess children's capabilities, they should do so cautiously and always within the context of other data. Generally, practitioners will find dynamic assessment to be of greater value in determining what a child is capable of learning with assistance than in determining how much the child can apply independently (Haywood & Lidz, 2007).

Developmental Assessments with Infants and Young Children

If an adult is to assess a child's cognitive abilities accurately, the child must, of course, be a cooperative participant in the process—for instance, by staying alert, paying attention, and maintaining interest in the assessment tasks. Yet infants and young children are not always able to cooperate. Infants may be sleepy, fussy, or afraid of the stranger conducting the assessment. Young children regularly have short attention spans, lose interest in the test questions, or misinterpret instructions. Because of such factors, which can vary considerably from one occasion to the next, assessments for infants and young children are not always reliable (Anastasi & Urbina, 1997; L. Ford & Dahinten, 2005; C. E. Snow & Van Hemel, 2008).

Nevertheless, teachers, child care providers, and other professionals sometimes need to monitor the cognitive development of infants and young children, perhaps to identify

---

[7]You learned about Vygotsky's theory of cognitive development in Chapter 6.

significant developmental delays that require intervention or perhaps to determine readiness for various kinds of educational experiences. Here we briefly describe the nature of tests available for infants, toddlers, and preschoolers.

Assessments with Infants and Toddlers

Infants born in hospital settings are typically assessed as soon as they are born. At both 1 minute and 5 minutes after birth, a doctor or nurse evaluates their color, heart rate, reflexes, muscle tone, and breathing, giving each characteristic a rating between 0 and 2. A perfect score on this *Apgar Scale* is 10. You can observe an Apgar Scale being performed on a newborn child in the video "An Apgar Assessment" in MyEducationLab. A more in-depth assessment for young infants from birth until 2 months is the *Neonatal Behavioral Assessment Scale* (Brazelton, 2009; Brazelton & Nugent, 1995). Often used to identify significant neurological abnormalities, it assesses alertness and attention, the quality of visual and auditory processing, and a variety of reflexes and behaviors.

Perhaps the most widely used test for older infants and toddlers is the third edition of the *Bayley Scales of Infant Development* (Albers & Grieve, 2007; Bayley, 2006). Designed for children ages 1 month to 3½ years, it includes five scales. Three scales—for cognitive development (attention, memory, concept formation, etc.), language, and motor skills—are assessed through interactions with the child. Two additional scales—for social-emotional functioning and adaptive behavior—are assessed through parent questionnaires.

Developmental assessments appear to determine current abilities reasonably well. You can observe tasks similar to those on infant assessments of cognitive abilities in the "Intelligence: Infancy" video of MyEducationLab. Such assessments can be helpful in identifying significant cognitive disabilities if used in combination with other information (Bradley-Johnson, 2001; Sattler, 2001; C. E. Snow & Van Hemel, 2008). When combined with observations of a child, interviews with parents, and medical records, developmental assessments can help identify particular needs before they become serious problems. However, caregivers should keep in mind that measures of cognitive growth in the first few years of life are only modestly related to intelligence in later years (Fagan, Holland, & Wheeler, 2007; McCall, 1993; C. E. Snow & Van Hemel, 2008). "Bright" babies do not necessarily become the brightest fourth graders, and toddlers who appear slow to learn may eventually catch up to, or even surpass, their peers (more about this point in the discussion of IQ stability a bit later in the chapter).

Assessments with Preschoolers

As you've previously learned, the Stanford-Binet Intelligence Scales can be used for children as young as 2 years. Another commonly used test for young children is the third edition of the *Wechsler Preschool and Primary Scale of Intelligence,* or WPPSI-III (Wechsler, 2002). Suitable for children ages 2½ to 7, the WPPSI-III has 14 subtests, some similar to those on the WISC-IV, and others (e.g., naming a pictured object) more appropriate for young children. In addition to an overall IQ, it yields a Verbal IQ (based on subtests that depend heavily on a child's language skills), a Performance IQ (based on subtests that require only minimal use of language), a score for General Language, and (for children ages 4 and older) a measure of Processing Speed.

As measures of intelligence for young children, both the Stanford-Binet and WPPSI-III correlate with other measures of intelligence and provide reasonable estimates of children's current cognitive functioning. In other words, their scores have some validity and reliability (Lichtenberger & Kaufman, 2003; McCallum, 1991; Roid & Tippin, 2009; Sattler, 2001). Although young children's IQ scores correlate somewhat with their scores in later years, the correlations are modest at best—no doubt because many young children have high energy levels, short attention spans, and little interest in sitting still for more than a few minutes. Thus measures of IQ obtained in the preschool years should *not* be used to make predictions about children's academic performance over the long run.

Other tests for preschoolers, known as *school readiness tests*, are designed to determine whether children have acquired the cognitive skills that many kindergarten and first-grade teachers view as essential foundations for their curricula (e.g., abilities to pay attention; count and perform simple mathematical procedures; and identify letters, colors, and shapes).

MyEducationLab

Observe an Apgar Scale being performed on a newborn child in the video "An Apgar Assessment." (Find Video Examples in Topic 8 of MyEducationLab.)

MyEducationLab

Observe tasks similar to those on infant tests of cognitive abilities in the "Intelligence: Infancy" video. (Find Video Examples in Topic 8 of MyEducationLab.)

Although widely used in school districts, such tests have come under fire in recent years, for two reasons. First, the scores they yield correlate only moderately at best with children's academic performance even a year or so later (Duncan et al., 2007; La Paro & Pianta, 2000; Stipek, 2002). Second, by age 5, most children are probably ready for some sort of structured educational program. Rather than determining whether children can adapt to a particular educational curriculum and environment, it is probably more beneficial to determine how instruction can be adapted to fit each child's needs (Lidz, 1991; Stipek, 2002). In this manner, children who do not yet have basic numeracy and literacy skills can receive appropriate intervention that nurtures these competencies (P. L. Harrison, 2009).

DEVELOPMENTAL TRENDS IN IQ SCORES

In one sense, children definitely become more "intelligent" as they develop: They know more, think in more complex ways, and solve problems more effectively. However, IQ scores are based not on how much children develop over time, but rather on how well children perform in comparison with their age-mates. By definition, the average IQ score for any age-group is 100 and does not increase with age.

Nevertheless, IQ scores do change in two important ways over the course of development:

• *IQ scores become increasingly stable.* As noted previously, children's early performance on infant assessments are not terribly predictive of their later intelligence. We've already encountered one reason for the poor predictive powers of these instruments: Infants' moods and priorities may be at odds with the demands of testing. A second reason is that the various genes contributing to intelligence are activated at different times over the course of development.[8] A third reason is that the types of items on assessments for young children are considerably different than items on tests for older children and adolescents. The Developmental Trends table "Intelligence at Different Age Levels" identifies some commonly used indicators of intelligence at various age levels, along with important considerations to keep in mind at each level.

As children progress through the school years, their IQ scores tend to hover within an increasingly narrow range. Although children continue to develop cognitively, each child's

DEVELOPMENTAL TRENDS
Intelligence at Different Age Levels

AGE	WHAT YOU MIGHT OBSERVE	DIVERSITY	IMPLICATIONS
Infancy (Birth–2 Years)	• Success on test items that involve recognition of previously seen objects, visual preferences, and eye–hand coordination • Distractibility and short attention span • Differentiated responses to familiar adults and strangers • Variability in performance from one assessment to the next • Performance dependent on examiner's ability to establish a positive relationship with the infant	• Temperamental differences (e.g., a tendency to be shy or cautious) affect infants' willingness to interact with the examiner and test materials. • Compared to full-term infants, infants born prematurely are less physically developed and more easily fatigued and so tend to obtain somewhat lower test scores. With good medical care and families' responsive involvement, many premature infants gradually develop into healthy, intelligent individuals. • Exposure to drugs or alcohol before birth may adversely affect test performance.	• Create a secure and comfortable examiner–child relationship before beginning an assessment. • Use results only to identify significant developmental delays requiring immediate intervention; refrain from making long-term predictions about intellectual growth. • Communicate honestly with parents about their child's performance on an assessment, while also describing the assessment's strengths and weaknesses as a tool for learning about children's abilities.

[8]Chapter 4 explains that particular genes come into play depending on the child's state of maturation and other factors.

DEVELOPMENTAL TRENDS (continued)

AGE	WHAT YOU MIGHT OBSERVE	DIVERSITY	IMPLICATIONS
Early Childhood (2–6 Years) 	• Success on test items that involve naming objects, stacking blocks, drawing circles and squares, remembering short lists, and following simple directions • Short attention span, influencing test performance • Variability in test scores from one occasion to the next	• Significant developmental delays in the early years may indicate an intellectual disability. • On average, children from economically disadvantaged families perform at lower levels on measures of cognitive development than children from middle-income families; however, enriching preschool experiences can narrow and occasionally eliminate the gap.	• Use cognitive assessments primarily to identify significant delays in development; follow up by seeking intervention programs for children with such delays. • Provide preschool experiences that foster children's language skills, knowledge of numbers and counting, and visual-spatial thinking.
Middle Childhood (6–10 Years) 	• Success on test items that involve defining concrete words, remembering sentences and short sequences of digits, understanding concrete analogies, recognizing similarities among objects, and identifying absurdities in illogical statements • Some consistency in test scores from one occasion to the next • Noticeable differences among children in mastery of classroom subject matter	• For this age range, many intelligence tests become increasingly verbal in nature; thus proficiency with the English language can significantly affect test performance. • Children with learning disabilities may perform poorly on some parts of an intelligence test. • Children from some ethnic groups may perform poorly in situations where the examiner has not established rapport.	• On some lessons, individualize instruction to match children's abilities to learn in particular ways. • Do *not* assume that poor performance in some domains necessarily indicates limited ability to learn in other areas. • Take children's cultural and linguistic backgrounds into account when interpreting IQ scores.
Early Adolescence (10–14 Years) 	• Success on test items that involve defining commonly used abstract words, drawing logical inferences from verbal descriptions, and identifying similarities between opposite concepts • Considerable individual differences in the ability to understand abstract material	• Some adolescents (especially those from certain ethnic groups) may not perceive a high test performance as personally advantageous and so may not be motivated to perform at their best. • Some adolescents who are gifted may try to hide their talents; cultures that stress traditional gender roles may actively discourage girls from achieving at high levels in mathematics and science and boys from achieving at high levels in literacy.	• Expect considerable diversity in adolescents' ability to master abstract classroom material, and individualize instruction accordingly. • Make sure that school enrichment programs include students from all ethnic groups; do not rely exclusively on IQ scores to identify students as gifted.
Late Adolescence (14–18 Years) 	• Success on test items that involve defining infrequently encountered words, identifying differences between similar abstract words, interpreting proverbs, and breaking down complex geometric figures into their component parts • Relative stability in most adolescents' IQ scores • Increasing independence to seek out opportunities consistent with existing ability levels	• Concerns about appearing "too smart" may continue into the high school years. • Some adolescents of color may underperform because their awareness of negative group stereotypes creates debilitating anxiety during a test (see the discussion of *stereotype threat* on p. 311).	• Provide challenging activities for teenagers who are gifted. • Encourage bright adolescents from lower-income families to pursue a college education, and help them with the logistics of college applications (e.g., applying for financial aid).

Source: Bayley, 2005; Brooks-Gunn, 2003; Brooks-Gunn, Klebanov, & Duncan, 1996; Colombo, 1993; G. A. Davis & Rimm, 1998; S. I. Greenspan & Meisels, 1996; Luckasson et al., 2002; D. J. Matthews, 2009; L. C. Mayes & Bornstein, 1997; McLoyd, 1998b; Meisels, Wen, & Beachy-Quick, 2010; Ogbu, 1994; Steele, 1997; Terman & Merrill, 1972; A. Thomas & Chess, 1977; Thorndike, Hagen, & Sattler, 1986; Wechsler, 2002, 2003.

relative intelligence in comparison with peers changes less as time goes on (N. Brody, 1992; Neisser et al., 1996; Sattler, 2001). As an example, look once again at the chapter's opening case study. Gina obtained an IQ score of 140 (equivalent to the 99th percentile) in junior high school and performed at a similar level on college aptitude tests several years later.

Despite the increasing stability of IQ scores, we must remember that each individual score reflects a youngster's performance on a particular test at a particular time. Some degree of change (sometimes as much as 10 to 20 points' worth, and occasionally even more) can reasonably be expected over the years. The longer the time interval between two administrations of an intelligence test, the greater the change in IQ we are likely to see, especially when young children are involved (B. S. Bloom, 1964; L. G. Humphreys, 1992; McCall, 1993; Sattler, 2001). The magnitude and kind of changes in intelligence depend on children's access to nutrition, health status, and exposure to stimulating activities, as you will learn more about in a moment.

• *IQ scores become increasingly accurate predictors of future academic achievement.* As IQ scores become more stable with age, their usefulness in predicting classroom performance increases. Yet educators should remember two things about the relationship between IQ and academic achievement. First, intelligence by itself does not *cause* achievement. Intelligence certainly plays an important role in school performance, but many other factors—motivation, quality of instruction, family resources and support, peer group norms, and so on—are also involved. Second, the relationship between IQ scores and achievement is an imperfect one, with many exceptions. For a variety of reasons, some children with high IQ scores do not perform well in the classroom. And other children achieve at higher levels than would be predicted from their IQ scores alone.

BIOECOLOGY OF INTELLIGENCE

Bioecology of Child Development

As children develop their intellectual abilities, they are affected by an assortment of individual and environmental factors.

A variety of factors blend together in the development of children's intelligence. Children have unique genetic profiles and also contribute to their own developing intellectual abilities through their choices of activities. At the same time, children experience distinct opportunities, pressures, and sometimes threats related to intellectual development through their family relationships, access to nutrition, exposure to toxins, and participation in early childhood programs, schools, and other settings.

Evidence for Hereditary Influences

Earlier we mentioned that measures of information processing speed correlate with IQ scores. Speed of processing depends on neurological efficiency, which in turn is largely genetically controlled. From this standpoint, we have some support for a hereditary basis for intelligence. The fact that children with certain genetic defects (e.g., Down syndrome) have, on average, significantly lower IQ scores than their nondisabled peers provides further evidence of heredity's influence (Keogh & MacMillan, 1996; Rihtman et al., 2010). But perhaps the most convincing evidence comes from twin studies and adoption studies.

Twin Studies

Numerous studies have included monozygotic (identical) twins and dizygotic (fraternal) twins to get a sense of how strongly heredity affects IQ. Because monozygotic twins begin as a single fertilized egg, which then separates, their genetic makeups are virtually equivalent. In contrast, dizygotic twins are conceived as two separate fertilized eggs. Dizygotic twins share about 50 percent of their genes, with the other 50 percent being unique to each twin. Most twins of both types are raised together by the same parent(s) and in the same home, so they share similar environments. Thus comparisons between the correlations of IQs in monozygotic and dizygotic twins can inform us about the impact of heredity on intelligence.

In one study, children were studied over several years to determine how their IQ scores correlated with siblings' scores (E. G. Bishop et al., 2003). If you take a look at the two columns for twins in Table 8-3, you will notice that the correlations for monozygotic twins are consistently higher than the correlations for dizygotic twins, non-twin siblings, and adopted siblings.[9] This pattern has been observed in many other investigations and suggests that intelligence has a sizable genetic basis. In fact, even when twins are raised separately (perhaps because

---

[9]In our teaching experiences, we have found that some students erroneously interpret the higher correlations as indicating that identical twins have higher intelligence. This is not the case. The size of each correlation indicates the *strength of the relationship* between twins' IQs, not the level of twins' intelligence per se.

TABLE 8-3 Correlations Between IQs of Sibling Pairs Living Together

AGE OF CHILDREN[a]	MONOZYGOTIC TWINS	DIZYGOTIC TWINS	NON-TWIN BIOLOGICAL SIBLINGS	ADOPTED SIBLINGS
Age 1	.59	.40	.38	.07
Age 3	.77	.51	.37	.26
Age 7	.76	.40	.47	.04
Age 9	.80	.21	.40	.24

[a]Tests of ability were administered to the same children repeatedly over several years in a longitudinal study.
Sources: E. G. Bishop et al., 2003.

they have been adopted and raised by different parents), they typically have similar IQ scores (T. J. Bouchard & McGue, 1981; W. Johnson et al., 2007; Plomin & Petrill, 1997; Segal & Hur, 2008). Twin studies also provide data for environmental effects, as we will see in a moment.

Adoption Studies

Another way to identify the effects of heredity is to compare adopted children with both their biological and adoptive parents. Adopted children tend to be similar to their biological parents in genetic makeup. Their environment, of course, more closely matches that of their adoptive parents. Researchers have found that adopted children's IQ scores are more highly correlated with their biological parents' IQs than with their adoptive parents' IQs. In other words, in a group of people who place their infants up for adoption, those with the highest IQs tend to have offspring who, despite being raised by other people, also have the highest IQs. Furthermore, the IQ correlations between adopted children and their biological parents become stronger, and those between the children and their adoptive parents become weaker, as the children grow older, especially during late adolescence (T. J. Bouchard, 1997; McGue, Bouchard, Iacono, & Lykken, 1993; Plomin, Fulker, Corley, & DeFries, 1997; Plomin & Petrill, 1997). (If you find this last research result puzzling, we'll offer an explanation later in the chapter.)

Researchers also compare correlations among the IQs of adopted siblings with correlations among twins and nonadopted siblings (ordinary biological brothers and sisters). If you look again at Table 8-3, you can see that the IQ correlations for dizygotic twins and non-adopted siblings are generally higher than most of the correlations for adopted siblings. In other words, children who are genetically related resemble one another intellectually more than do children who are unrelated biologically. Although other factors are at work in such associations (which we will soon examine), twin and adoption studies point convincingly to a genetic component in intelligence (T. J. Bouchard, 1997; N. Brody, 1992; J. M. Horn & Loehlin, 2010; Hunt, 1997).

Evidence for Environmental Influences

Numerous sources of evidence indicate that the environment has a significant impact on intelligence. We find some of this evidence in twin and adoption studies. Investigations into the effects of nutrition, toxic substances, home environment, early intervention, and formal schooling provide additional support for the influence of environment. Also, a steady increase in performance on intelligence tests during the past several decades—known as the *Flynn effect,* to be discussed shortly—is probably at least partly attributable to environmental factors.

Twin Studies and Adoption Studies Revisited

Twin studies reveal evidence for environmental effects. Comparing across multiple separate investigations, researchers have found an average correlation of .85 for monozygotic twins reared together and an average correlation of .74 for monozygotic twins reared apart (Devlin, Daniels, & Roeder, 1997; Nisbett, 2009). In other words, twins raised in different homes have less similar IQs than twins raised in the same home. Adoption studies, too, indicate that intelligence is affected by environmental experiences (Capron & Duyme, 1989; Devlin, Fienberg, Resnick, & Roeder, 1995; Nisbett, 2009). In one study, children of low-income parents (with unknown IQs) were adopted by middle-class parents with IQs averaging 118 to 121 (Scarr & Weinberg, 1976). Other children remained with their low-income biological parents. IQ averages of adopted children were 105, whereas IQ averages of nonadopted children were 90. Although the adopted children's IQ scores were, on average, lower than those of their adoptive parents, they were about 15 points higher than the scores for the children who were raised by their biological parents. In another investigation, French children adopted by high-income parents had IQs that were 12 points higher than IQs of other French children adopted by low-income parents (Capron & Duyme, 1989).

Consider also that twin and adoption studies do not fully disentangle environmental effects (W. A. Collins, Maccoby, Steinberg, Hetherington, & Bornstein, 2000; Wahlsten & Gottlieb, 1997). An adopted child has shared a common environment for at least 9 months—the period of prenatal development—with his or her biological mother. Likewise, monozygotic twins who are separated at birth are often placed by adoption agencies in families that are similar in educational backgrounds and income levels. Furthermore, twin studies and adoption studies do not allow researchers to examine the ways in which heredity and environment interact in their effects on measured intelligence. In genetic studies, interactive effects are included on the "heredity" side of the scoreboard (W. A. Collins et al., 2000; Nisbett, 2009; Turkheimer, 2000).

Still other clues in the data suggest that environmental effects may be stronger than they appear at first blush. For one thing, twin studies are generally drawn from middle-income families because these individuals are most inclined to participate in longitudinal research (Nisbett, 2009). It is a well-documented trend for genetic effects to be stronger in high-income families than in low-income families (Turkheimer, Haley, Waldron, D'Onofrio, & Gottesman, 2003). In a group of children who grow up in an advantaged environment, most have access to the experiences they need to express potential intellectual abilities. In comparison, among other children who grow up in a low-income environment, many do not routinely have the opportunities they need to develop their abilities, and genetic effects are low. Because twin studies tend to overrepresent high-income families, the estimates of genetic contributions are larger than they would be with a more diverse sample.

Thus, in a range of comprehensive studies examining genetic contributions to intelligence, there is almost always some indication of strong effects from the environment. Let's look at some specific ways that the environment affects intelligence.

Early Nutrition

Severe malnutrition, either before birth or during the early years of life, can limit neurological development and have a long-term impact on cognitive development (Lynn, 2009; McDermott, Durkin, Schupf, & Stein, 2007; Ricciuti, 1993). Attention, memory, abstract reasoning, intelligence, and general school achievement are all likely to suffer from inadequate nutrition. Children sometimes recover from short periods of poor nourishment (due, perhaps, to war or illness), but the adverse effects of long-term deprivation are apt to be enduring (Sigman & Whaley, 1998).

Aware of these long-term effects, some investigators have provided medically approved food supplements and vitamins to infants and young children who would not otherwise have adequate nutrition. Such interventions improve the development of motor skills, and in some instances cognitive development is enhanced as well (D. Benton, 2001; Pollitt & Oh, 1994; Sigman & Whaley, 1998).

Toxic Substances

A variety of toxic substances, or *teratogens*, in children's prenatal environments—for instance, alcohol, drugs, radiation, lead-based paint dust—affect neurological development and IQ scores (e.g., Carpenter & Nevin, 2010; Dilworth-Bart & Moore, 2006; Michel, 1989; Streissguth, Barr, Sampson, & Bookstein, 1994). Children with fetal alcohol syndrome have mothers who consumed large amounts of alcohol during pregnancy; as a result these children show poor motor coordination, delayed language, and an intellectual disability.[10] Exposure to toxic substances can also threaten intelligence during infancy and early childhood because children's brains are growing rapidly and are especially vulnerable to harm.

Home Environment

One likely explanation for the beneficial effects of adoption is that adoptive parents, who typically have adequate financial resources and high levels of education, can provide a more stimulating home environment than the biological parents might have been able to offer. Correlational studies indicate that stimulating home environments (e.g., those in which parents interact frequently with their children, make numerous reading materials available, encourage the development of new skills, and use complex sentence structures in conversation) are associated with higher IQ scores in children (R. H. Bradley & Caldwell, 1984; Nisbett, 2009; Tong, Baghurst, Vimpani, & McMichael, 2007). Furthermore, when two biologically *un*related children of the same age are raised by the same parents (typically because one or both children are adopted), the children's IQs tend to be more similar than we would expect by chance alone, a relationship that can be attributed primarily to the influence of a common home environment (Segal, 2000).

We find additional evidence for the beneficial effects of stimulating home environments in Romania (C. A. Nelson, 2005; Smyke, Zeanah, Fox, & Nelson, 2009). As a result of previous government policies, most Romanian orphans were at one time raised in large institutions. After a change in government and the intervention of a team of developmental psychologists, some institutionalized infants (randomly selected) were placed with adults willing to serve as foster parents. (Sadly, the intervention team could not find foster families for all of the infants.) As researchers periodically assessed the children's physical and cognitive development, they found dramatic differences between the two groups. Despite adequate nutrition, children remaining in an institution throughout infancy and the preschool years had smaller head circumferences and less brain activity than did the foster children. When intelligence was assessed, the institutionalized children had an average IQ of 64, which is on par for a person with an intellectual disability, whereas the foster children, on average, had IQs in the normal range.

Early Intervention

When children live in impoverished or neglectful home environments, enriching preschool programs and other forms of early intervention can make an appreciable difference. Children who participated in the Head Start preschool program in the United States have shown short-term IQ gains and other cognitive benefits (Bronfenbrenner, 1999; NICHD Early Child Care Research Network, 2002; Zigler, 2003). The intellectual effects of such programs don't continue indefinitely, however. Unless they receive follow-up interventions during the elementary school years, children lose some of the cognitive advantages over time (Brooks-Gunn, 2003). Despite experiencing fading benefits, children who attended Head Start programs did exhibit other advantages later in life: They less often repeated grade levels, achieved at higher levels in school, more often attended college, enjoyed greater health, and exhibited less criminal behavior (Garces, Thomas, & Curry, 2002; Ludwig & Miller, 2007; Zigler & Styfco, 2010).

Other early interventions have also shown long-term improvements in areas not reflected in IQ scores. In the Perry Preschool Program, children from economically disadvantaged families attended preschool and had teachers visit their homes once a week to coach mothers in supporting children's development. Participants in the program showed short-term gains in IQ and later in school were infrequently placed in special education classes. At age 14 they scored higher on academic achievement tests, and at age 40 they had completed more schooling, had higher earnings, and were more likely to be in stable families than was the case with individuals who had not attended preschool or had visiting teachers at home (W. S. Barnett, 1992; Muennig, Schweinhart, Montie, & Neidell, 2009; Schweinhart & Weikart, 1993).

---

[10]You may recall reading about teratogens and fetal alcohol exposure in Chapter 4.

INTELLECTUAL ENRICHMENT.
Research indicates that stimu-
lating preschool experiences
often increase IQ in economi-
cally disadvantaged children,
at least over the short run, and
yield other benefits later in life.

Still other programs offering intensive services in early childhood have yielded long-term increases in intelligence. In the Abecedarian Program, children from disadvantaged backgrounds were assigned to one or more interventions (F. A. Campbell, Pungello, Miller-Johnson, Burchinal, & Ramey, 2001; F. A. Campbell & Ramey, 1995; C. T. Ramey et al., 2000; S. L. Ramey & Ramey, 1999). Children who received high-quality care beginning in infancy showed an IQ advantage in early childhood that persisted into the adult years. They also were less likely to be assigned to special education classes and to repeat a grade and were more likely to be accomplished readers, to graduate from high school, and to attend college than were individuals who had not received an intervention beginning in infancy.

In brief, early childhood interventions that begin in children's first years and offer intensive support during early childhood foster children's intelligence. Although intellectual gains fade slightly during the school years, some intellectual advantages persist, particularly when children attend high-quality elementary schools. Furthermore, other significant life benefits accrue, including higher achievements in secondary school and college and better life outcomes in adulthood (Nisbett, 2009).

Formal Schooling

The very act of attending school leads to small increases in IQ. In Western societies, children who begin their educational careers early and attend school regularly have higher IQ scores than children who do not. When children must start school later than is typical, their IQs are at least 5 points lower for every year of delay. In addition, children's IQ scores decline slightly (usually only temporarily) over the course of the summer months, when children are not attending school. Other things being equal, children who drop out of school have lower IQ scores than children who remain in school, losing an average of almost 2 IQ points for every year of high school not completed (Ceci, 2003; Ceci & Williams, 1997).

The intellectual benefits of schooling are seen in a wide variety of cultures. As Vygotsky pointed out, schooling provides a systematic means through which children can acquire cultural tools, such as alphabets, that were developed by previous generations. Participation in school also generally encourages the acquisition of advanced cognitive processes (e.g., elaboration, organization, metacognition) that enhance learning of a broad range of concepts[11] (M. Cole, 2006; Nettelbeck & Wilson, 2005).

The Flynn Effect

The past few decades have seen a slow, steady increase in people's average performance on IQ tests throughout the industrialized world (Flynn, 1987, 2007; D. F. Marks, 2011; Neisser, 1998b). This trend is commonly known as the **Flynn effect**[12]. A similar change has been observed in children's performance on traditional Piagetian tasks (Flieller, 1999).

Why might populations of children be becoming smarter? Conceivably some genetic factors may be having an impact here. Recent decreases in the numbers of children conceived by first cousins and other close relatives appear to have strengthened the overall intelligence of human beings[13] (Mingroni, 2007). Yet most theorists believe that the Flynn effect is largely the result of changes in children's environments worldwide. Better nutrition, protection from infectious diseases, smaller family sizes, higher quality home environments, better schooling, and more enriching and informative stimulation (access to television, reading materials, etc.) are all possible contributing factors (Daley, Whaley, Sigman, Espinosa, & Neumann, 2003; Eppig, Fincher, & Thornhill, 2010; Flynn, 2003; Neisser, 1998b).

Flynn effect
Gradual increase in intelligence test performance observed in many countries during the past several decades.

[11]Chapter 7 describes the processes and benefits of elaboration, organization, and metacognition.
[12]The Flynn Effect was named in recognition of the work of James R. Flynn in promoting recognition of this phenomenon.
[13]Genetic problems, including dispositions for intellectual disability, are more likely in children of closely related parents than in children of unrelated parents.

How Nature and Nurture Interact in Their Influence on Intelligence

Clearly both nature and nurture influence intelligence. What is less clear is *how much* influence each of these factors has. Most psychologists now believe that it may ultimately be impossible to separate the relative effects of heredity and environment. They suggest that the two factors combine to influence children's intellectual development in ways that can never be disentangled (e.g., W. A. Collins et al., 2000; Rogoff, 2003; Turkheimer et al., 2003). However, theorists are reasonably certain about how nature and nurture interact in intellectual development:

Heredity establishes a range rather than a precise figure. Heredity does not dictate that a child will have a particular IQ score. Instead, it appears to set a range of abilities that a child will eventually develop, with the actual level depending on his or her specific environmental experiences (Weinberg, 1989). Heredity may also affect how susceptible or resistant a child is to particular environmental influences (Rutter, 1997). In the opening case study, Gina learned how to read before she attended school and with only minimal help from her mother. Yet other, equally intelligent children may learn to read *only* when they have systematic reading instruction tailored to their individual needs.

Genetic expression is influenced by environmental conditions. Genes are not self-contained, independent "carriers" of particular characteristics but rather flexible instructions that respond directly to circumstances in the child's body and indirectly to features in the environment.[14] In an extremely impoverished setting—one with a lack of adequate nutrition and little if any stimulation—heredity may have little to say about the extent to which children develop intellectually. In an ideal environment—one in which nutrition, parenting practices, and educational opportunities are optimal and age-appropriate—heredity can have a significant influence on children's IQ scores (Ceci, 2003; Turkheimer et al., 2003).

Furthermore, intelligence is the result of many genes, each contributing a small amount to the efficiency of thinking processes (Sattler, 2001). These genes may "kick in" at different points in development, and their expression will be influenced by particular environmental conditions at those times. Thus we do not have a single heredity–environment interface, but rather a number of heredity–environment interactions, all contributing to intellectual growth (Simonton, 2001).

Especially as they get older, children choose their environments and experiences. Children may actively seek out environmental conditions that match their inherited abilities—a phenomenon known as **niche-picking** (Benbow & Lubinski, 2009; Halpern & LaMay, 2000; Scarr & McCartney, 1983). Children who, genetically speaking, have exceptional quantitative reasoning ability may enroll in advanced mathematics courses, voluntarily tackle mathematical brainteasers, and in other ways nurture their own inherited talents. Children with average quantitative ability are less likely to take on such challenges and so have fewer opportunities to develop their mathematical skills. Given the ubiquity of such choices, the relative effects of heredity and environment are difficult to tease apart.

Earlier we mentioned that the IQ correlations between adopted children and their biological parents become stronger over time. We now have a possible explanation for this finding. Children gain increasing independence as they get older. Especially as they reach adolescence, they spend less time in their home environments, and they make more of their own decisions about the kinds of opportunities to pursue—decisions undoubtedly based, in part, on their natural talents and tendencies (McGue et al., 1993; Petrill & Wilkerson, 2000). Similarly, correlations between the IQs of monozygotic twins increase in strength with age and presumably the growing ability to act on the genetic tendencies they share (you can see an age-related increase in IQ correlations for monozygotic twins in Table 8-3) (Hoekstra, Bartels, & Boomsma, 2007).

niche-picking
Tendency to actively seek out environments that match one's inherited abilities.

---

[14]Chapter 4 examines the physiological processes by which genes and environmental experiences interact over time in a child's body.

Demographic Factors

The experiences that children have as boys and girls, recipients of varying levels of financial security, and members of ethnic and racial groups also affect their intellectual development to some degree. As you will find out, differences among groups tend to be small and due primarily to discrepancies in society's allotment of resources to children with particular characteristics.

Gender

Apart from a greater frequency of intellectual disabilities in boys than girls, there are rarely any significant gender differences in IQ scores (Halpern et al., 2007; Neisser et al., 1996). This finding is at least partly a function of how intelligence tests are developed: As a general rule, test constructors eliminate any test items on which one gender performs better than the other.

Average differences in specific cognitive abilities are sometimes found but are usually small. Girls are often slightly better at such verbal tasks as reading and writing (Calvin, Fernandes, Smith, Visscher, & Deary, 2010; Halpern, 2006; Maccoby & Jacklin, 1974). Especially after puberty, boys perform somewhat better on tasks involving visual-spatial thinking (which require people to imagine two- or three-dimensional figures and mentally manipulate them), and adolescents with extremely high mathematical ability are more likely to be male than female (Benbow, Lubinski, Shea, & Eftekhari-Sanjani, 2000; Calvin et al., 2010; Hegarty & Kozhevnikov, 1999). In verbal, visual-spatial, and mathematical domains, however, there is typically a great deal of overlap between the two genders.

These minor gender differences in specific intellectual abilities may be partly due to hormonal differences or subtle anatomical differences in the brain (Hahn, Jansen, & Heil, 2010; Halpern, 2004; Halpern & LaMay, 2000). Environmental factors appear to play a role as well. In many cultures boys and girls have distinctly different experiences growing up. In many Western cultures boys are more likely to have toys that require physical manipulation in space (e.g., blocks, model airplanes, and footballs), and such items can foster the development of visual-spatial skills. In contrast, girls are more likely to have dolls, housekeeping items (e.g., dishes, plastic food), and board games—items that are apt to encourage verbal communication with peers (Halpern, 1992; Leaper & Friedman, 2007; D. D. Tobin et al., 2010).

In recent years, perhaps because of the push for more equitable educational opportunities, males and females have become increasingly similar in their abilities (Jacklin, 1989; Spelke, 2005). For all intents and purposes, educators should expect boys and girls to have similar potential in virtually all subject areas.[15]

Socioeconomic Status

Intelligence test scores are correlated with socioeconomic status (SES).[16] On average, children from lower-SES families earn somewhat lower IQ scores, and they also perform at lower levels in school, than children from middle-SES families (Brooks-Gunn, 2003; Linver et al., 2002). Children who grow up in persistently impoverished conditions are at greatest risk for poor performance, but children who endure only short-term poverty may also fall behind their peers (McLoyd, 1998b).

Several factors contribute to differences in IQ and school achievement among socioeconomic groups (Berliner, 2005; McLoyd, 1998b; L. S. Miller, 1995). Poor nutrition, lack of health care, and greater-than-average exposure to environmental toxins can impede neurological development among economically impoverished children. Parents who work long hours (especially single parents) may have little time to spend with their children and may be unable to afford high-quality child care (Marshall, 2004). Some parents with limited educational backgrounds have little knowledge about how to help children acquire academic skills

---

[15]Boys and girls don't always *believe* they have similar abilities, however, as you will discover in Chapter 12.
[16]Socioeconomic status is defined and described in Chapter 3.

(P. A. Edwards & Garcia, 1994; Portes, 1996). And a family without a dependable income must, in general, place higher priority on survival than on toys, books, and other materials that nurture children's cognitive growth. Once children from low-income families begin school, they may lack the knowledge (e.g., familiarity with letters and numbers) on which more advanced learning depends. Their lower school attendance rates, due to health problems, family crises, and frequent changes of residence, further decrease their opportunities for acquiring the academic skills so critical for school success.

In addition, some teachers—especially those who have grown up in middle-SES families—often have lower academic expectations for children from lower-income homes. As a result, teachers may give these children less time and attention, fewer opportunities to learn, and less challenging assignments (K. Alexander, Entwisle, & Thompson, 1987; McLoyd, 1998b; Rosenthal, 1994). Without intending it, these teachers thus increase any socioeconomic differences in cognitive ability that already exist.

As you read earlier, high-quality preschool programs can boost IQ scores (at least over the short run) and enhance school achievement, and the benefits seem to be greatest for children from low-SES families (e.g., Magnuson, Meyers, Ruhm, & Waldfogel, 2004). Programs that teach parents how to provide stimulating activities for, and interact effectively with, their growing children can also make a difference (F. A. Campbell & Ramey, 1994; Ceci, 2003). When teachers have high expectations for students from lower-income backgrounds, the students are more likely to perform at high levels (Midgley, Feldlaufer, & Eccles, 1989; M. Phillips, 1997).

Ethnicity and Race

Every ethnic, racial, and cultural group has child-rearing practices and traditions that nurture the intellectual development of young people. Yet not every group in a diverse society is given the same opportunities. The minor variations in intelligence that result are most certainly the outcome of such environmental experiences. On average, Asian Americans and European Americans slightly outperform African Americans and Hispanic Americans (Ang, Rodgers, & Wänström, 2010; N. Brody, 1992; Neisser et al., 1996; Nisbett, 2005).

The primary reason for the minor disadvantage in average IQ scores of African American and Hispanic American children is that these children are apt to grow up in families and neighborhoods with somewhat lower incomes than European American children (Brooks-Gunn et al., 1996; McLoyd, 1998b). As we've seen, socioeconomic status can affect the quality of nutrition, availability of stimulating toys and books, and value of educational experiences. Even when different ethnic and racial groups have similar economic resources, long-term discrimination (e.g., exclusion from better schools and jobs, lower expectations for classroom performance) can limit some children's opportunities for intellectual growth (Ogbu, 1994).

As they grow, some children of color are affected by perceptions of other people that they lack intelligence. With time, they may have little motivation to do well on intelligence and achievement tests. Some children give minimal answers (e.g., "I don't know") as a way of shortening a testing session that they find confusing or unsettling (Zigler & Finn-Stevenson, 1992). Other children may simply not see the point of answering questions that contradict their own cultural perspectives on what intelligence is (Sternberg et al., 2007). Still others may exhibit a phenomenon known as **stereotype threat**: They perform more poorly—unintentionally and perhaps as a result of excessive anxiety—if they believe that members of their group typically do not do well on particular kinds of tests (Guyll, Madon, Prieto, & Scherr, 2010; A. H. Jordan & Lovett, 2007; Steele, 1997).

An encouraging trend is that the IQ scores and other measures of cognitive ability of various ethnic and racial groups have, in recent years, become increasingly similar. Such a trend can be attributed to more equitable environmental conditions across society (Ceci, Rosenblum, & Kumpf, 1998; Dickens & Flynn, 2001; Nisbett, 2009). Nevertheless, it remains a serious concern that not every child has a reasonable chance to develop his or her emerging intellectual skills.

stereotype threat
Reduction in performance (often unintentional) as a result of a belief that one's group typically performs poorly.

CRITIQUE OF CURRENT PERSPECTIVES ON INTELLIGENCE

The study of intelligence is at a crossroads, having shifted from a belief that intelligence is a largely inherited, one-dimensional characteristic to the realization that intelligence is a multifaceted core of abilities, each of which is influenced by experience. In the context of this change in thinking, several concerns about contemporary work in intelligence remain:

Research continues to rely heavily on traditional intelligence tests. Existing intelligence tests have been designed primarily to identify individuals who require special interventions or educational services, and in this context they can be quite helpful. Yet researchers have used them in other ways as well—for instance, to make cross-group comparisons, draw conclusions about the relative effects of heredity and environment in intellectual development, and evaluate the effectiveness of preschool programs for low-income children—without due consideration of the appropriateness of IQ tests for such purposes. Traditional intelligence tests are most certainly too limited to help researchers completely answer broad theoretical questions about the origins and development of intelligence.

IQ scores are often interpreted out of context. Over the years, the use of intelligence tests has been quite controversial. In earlier decades (as recently as the 1970s), IQ scores were frequently used as the sole criterion for identifying children with an intellectual disability. In part as a result of this practice, children from racial and ethnic minority groups were disproportionately represented in special education classes, where their potential for academic achievement was tragically underestimated and ineffectively nurtured.

Most clinical and school psychologists, counselors, and other specialists now have sufficient training in assessment to understand that a single IQ score should never warrant a diagnosis of an intellectual disability. Decisions about special educational placement and services must always be based on multiple sources of information about a child. Yet many other people (including a few teachers) view IQ scores as permanent characteristics. We occasionally hear remarks such as "She has an IQ of such-and-such" spoken in much the same matter-of-fact manner as someone might say "She has brown eyes."

For most children, IQ scores are reasonably accurate reflections of their general learning potential. But for some children, IQ scores are poor summaries of what they can do at present or in the future. Teachers and other professionals must be extremely careful not to put too much stock in any single intelligence score, especially when working with children from diverse backgrounds. Furthermore, the use of global IQ scores obscures the differentiated profiles of intellectual strengths and abilities that most children have.

Assessment of intelligence focuses almost exclusively on skills valued in mainstream Western culture. The items found on traditional intelligence tests focus on cognitive skills (logical reasoning, abstract thought, etc.) that are valued primarily in middle-class North American, European, and Australian societies (Gardner, 2006; Sternberg et al., 2007). Such a bias enhances the tests' ability to predict students' school achievement because schools in these societies place heavy emphasis on the same set of skills. However, traditional intelligence tests do not do justice to the range of skills that every child applies in daily life.

Intelligence tests overlook dispositions and metacognitive strategies that are important contributors to intellectual functioning. Most descriptions and measures of intelligence focus on specific things that a child *can* do (abilities), with little consideration of what a child is *likely* to do (dispositions). Intelligence tests don't evaluate the extent to which children view a situation from multiple perspectives, examine data with a critical eye, regulate their own learning, and reflect on their thoughts and actions. Nor do they assess children's self-discipline. Yet such qualities are often just as important as intellectual abilities in determining success in academic and real-world tasks (Duckworth & Seligman, 2005; Kuhn, 2001a; Nisbett, 2009; Perkins, 1995).

Preparing for Your Licensure Examination

Your teaching test might ask you about appropriate cautions to follow when interpreting the results of intelligence tests.

Many theorists have placed higher priority on <u>measuring</u> current intelligence than on <u>developing</u> future intelligence. Implicit in the practice of intelligence testing is the assumption that intelligence is a relatively fixed, and perhaps largely inherited, ability. Fortunately, some psychologists and educators are now calling for a shift from the assessment of intelligence to its enhancement (Boykin, 1994; Nisbett, 2009; Sternberg et al., 2000). As theorists and researchers gain a better understanding of the nature of intelligence and the environmental factors that promote it, schools can, we hope, adopt a more proactive approach, one in which all children are given the opportunities and resources they need to maximize their learning.

IMPLICATIONS OF RESEARCH ON INTELLIGENCE

Given existing knowledge about the nature and development of intelligence, as well as our concerns about shortcomings in the field, we offer the following suggestions to teachers and other practitioners who work with infants, children, and adolescents:

- **Maintain a healthy skepticism about the accuracy of IQ scores.** Intelligence tests can, in many cases, provide a general idea of children's current cognitive functioning. Yet IQ scores are rarely dead-on measures of what children can do. As we have seen, the scores of young children can vary considerably from one testing to the next and are not always accurate predictors of children's future academic success. Furthermore, the scores of children are affected by their background experiences, motivation, and English proficiency. We cannot stress this point enough: IQ scores should *never* be used as the sole criterion in making diagnoses and decisions about children.

- **Support early intervention programs in your community.** Early intervention is especially important for infants and toddlers with developmental disabilities, as well as for small children living in low-income neighborhoods or unstable family settings. Interventions can take the form of regular checkups and nutritional support for pregnant women, stimulating infant care and preschool programs for young children, and suggestions and materials for helping inexperienced parents nurture their children's cognitive growth at home. Interventions are most effective when they begin early, integrate a variety of services into a single support network, and address children's physical, social, and emotional needs as well as their cognitive development (Loeb, Fuller, Kagan, & Carroll, 2004; Shonkoff & Phillips, 2000).

- **Cultivate youngsters' intellectual abilities throughout the school years.** Research evidence strongly supports the role that schools can play in fostering children's potential throughout their school years (A. Bennett et al., 2007; Nisbett, 2009; Sternberg et al., 2007). In particular, youngsters from economically disadvantaged families are positively affected when teachers foster their curiosity and explicitly teach advanced intellectual abilities. Teachers can help fill in any gaps in children's knowledge, make sure children are familiar with basic mathematical concepts and reading processes, and scaffold children's ability to apply what they learn to new contexts (A. Bennett et al., 2007).

- **Be open minded about the ways in which children might demonstrate intelligence.** As we've seen, some psychologists believe that human intelligence isn't a single entity—that it is, instead, a collection of relatively separate abilities that children may have to varying degrees depending on their individual characteristics, experiences, and cultural backgrounds (Gardner, 1995; Neisser et al., 1996; Perkins, 1995; Sternberg, 1985). The Observation Guidelines table "Seeing Intelligence in Children's Daily Behavior" presents a variety of behaviors that may reveal higher intelligence than children's IQ scores indicate.

- **Capitalize on children's individual strengths when teaching new topics and skills.** Gardner's and Sternberg's theories, in particular, encourage educators to use a variety of approaches to instruction that collectively build on the unique abilities that individual

OBSERVATION GUIDELINES
Seeing Intelligence in Children's Daily Behavior

CHARACTERISTIC	LOOK FOR	EXAMPLE	IMPLICATION
Oral Language Skills	• *Sophisticated vocabulary* • *Colorful speech* • *Creative storytelling* • *Clever jokes and puns*	Jerome entertains his friends with clever jokes, vivid images, and wild exaggerations about events and the characteristics of other people.	Look for unusual creativity or advanced language development in children's everyday speech.
Learning Ability	• *Ability to learn new information quickly* • *Exceptional knowledge* about a variety of topics • *Ability to find relationships* among diverse ideas • *Excellent memory*	Four-year-old Gina teaches herself to read using several reading primers she finds at home. Initially, her mother identifies a few words for her. From these words she deduces many letter-sound correspondences that enable her to decipher additional words.	Make note of situations in which children learn and comprehend new material more quickly than their peers. Look for creative analogies and interconnections in their ideas.
Problem-Solving Skills	• *Ability to solve challenging problems* • *Flexibility* in applying previously learned strategies to new kinds of problems • *Ability to improvise* with common-place objects and materials	A fourth-grade class plans to perform a skit during an upcoming open house. When the children puzzle over how to hang a sheet from the ceiling (to serve as a stage curtain), Jeff suggests that they turn their desks to face the side of the classroom rather than the front, allowing a sheet to be hung from a light fixture that runs the length of the room.	Present unusual tasks and problems for which children have no ready-made strategies.
Cognitive and Metacognitive Strategies	• *Use of sophisticated learning strategies* • *Desire to understand* rather than memorize • *Effective comprehension monitoring*	Shannon, a sixth grader, explains that she learned the countries on South America's west coast (Colombia, Ecuador, Peru, Chile) by creating the sentence "*C*olin *e*ats *p*eas and *c*hocolate."	Ask children to describe how they think about the things they are trying to learn and remember.
Curiosity and Inquisitiveness	• *Voracious appetite for knowledge* • *Tendency to ask a lot of questions* • *Intrinsic motivation* to master challenging subject matter	Alfredo reads every book and article he can find about outer space. He has a particular interest in black holes.	Find out what children like to do in their free time and then direct them to relevant resources.
Leadership and Social Skills	• *Ability to persuade* and motivate others • *Exceptional sensitivity* to other people's feelings and body language • *Ability to mediate disagreements* and help others reach reasonable compromises	As a high school student, Gina organizes and directs a schoolwide peer tutoring program.	Observe how children interact with their peers at play, in cooperative group work, and in extracurricular activities.

Source: B. Clark, 1997; A. W. Gottfried, Gottfried, Bathurst, & Guerin, 1994; Lupart, 1995; Maker, 1993; Maker & Schiever, 1989; Perkins, 1995; Sousa, 2009; Torrance, 1995; Turnbull et al., 2010; Winner, 1997.

children are likely to have. The following scenario illustrates how some children may learn more effectively when they can use their visual-spatial skills:

> In third grade, Jason loved to build with blocks, Legos, toothpicks, Popsicle sticks, anything that fit together. During a unit on ancient history, Jason built an object for every culture studied. He fashioned Babylonian ziggurats out of Legos, Egyptian pyramids with toothpicks and small marshmallows, the Great Wall of China from miniature clay bricks which he made, the Greek Parthenon from Styrofoam computer-packing, Roman bridges out of popsicle sticks and brads, and Mayan temples with molded plastic strips resurrected from an old science kit. While appearing apathetic during most classroom activities, Jason was highly animated during his building projects. History came alive for Jason when he could build the structures of each era and culture studied. (L. Campbell et al., 1998, p. 79)

• **Consider the specific cognitive abilities that classroom lessons require of children.** Teachers generally target specific intellectual skills when designing classroom lessons. Some children will have difficulty with one or more abilities that are required by a lesson, such as visual-spatial abilities when doing geometry, auditory processing when learning to read, or short-term (working) memory when listening to lengthy instructions. When children struggle with one or more skills, teachers may find it helpful to offer specific kinds of support until children have developed the necessary prerequisite mental processes. School psychologists and other specialists are regularly available to offer advice about guiding children with various intellectual strengths and limitations.

• **Promote more "intelligent" cognitive strategies.** Look again at this chapter's opening case study. Gina's relative weakness in history is due largely to her ineffective study strategies. In fact, teachers, parents, and other adults can promote more effective learning, studying, and problem solving—and in doing so can promote more intelligent behavior—by teaching children more sophisticated and effective cognitive and metacognitive strategies (Cornoldi, 2010; Perkins, 1995; Sternberg, 2002).[17]

Improving Your Observation Skills

Sunflower. Which of Gardner's multiple intelligences did 10-year-old Amaryth use in creating the drawings of a sunflower and insect? You may want to refer back to Table 8-1 (p. 289) as you do this exercise. Compare your response with the explanation at the end of the chapter.

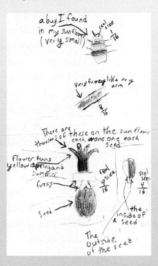

• **Give children the support they need to think more intelligently.** The notion of distributed intelligence tells us that intelligent behavior should be relatively commonplace when children have the right physical tools, social groups, and symbolic systems with which to work. Rather than asking the question "How intelligent are these children?" educators might instead ask themselves "How can I help these children think as intelligently as possible? What tools and social networks can I give them? What useful concepts and procedures can I teach them?"

For the most part, educators can easily accommodate such variability within the context of normal instructional practices. In some cases, however, young learners have ability levels so different from those of age-mates that they require special educational services to reach their full potential. We turn now to exceptionalities in intelligence.

EXCEPTIONALITIES IN INTELLIGENCE

No matter how we define or measure intelligence, we find that some children and adolescents show exceptional talent and others show significant cognitive delays relative to their peers. The two ends of the intelligence continuum are commonly known as *giftedness* and *intellectual disability*.[18]

Children Who Have Gifts and Talents

Gina, first introduced in the opening case study, is an example of someone who is gifted (you may also see the term *gifted and talented*). **Giftedness** is unusually high ability or aptitude in one or more areas (e.g., mathematics, science, creative writing, art, or music) to the point where special educational services are necessary to help a youngster meet his or her full potential (e.g., C. M. Ackerman & Fifield, 2005; Gromko, 2004; U.S. Department

giftedness
Unusually high ability in one or more areas, to the point where children require special educational services to help them meet their full potential.

[17]Cognitive and metacognitive strategies are examined in Chapter 7.
[18]In the United States, different states may establish somewhat different criteria for these two categories, especially with regard to determining eligibility for special educational services.

of Education, 1993). Some school districts identify students as gifted primarily on the basis of general IQ scores, often using 125 or 130 as a minimum cutoff point. But many experts argue that IQ scores should not be the only criterion for selection into special services, and that such factors as creativity, motivation, and children's everyday accomplishments should also be considered. These less formal indicators may be especially useful for identifying talented children from diverse backgrounds who, perhaps because of a language barrier, lack of confidence, or weak academic preparation, are not as likely to score at exceptionally high levels on intelligence tests (Council for Exceptional Children, 1995; S. Graham, 2009; Sousa, 2009; Sternberg & Zhang, 1995).

Individual children who are gifted are very different from one another in their particular strengths and talents, but as a group they tend to share certain characteristics. Compared to children not identified as gifted, these youngsters process information more quickly and remember it more easily, have more advanced reasoning and metacognitive skills, and use more effective learning and problem-solving strategies (K. R. Carter & Ormrod, 1982; Steiner & Carr, 2003; Winner, 1997, 2000). Often they have an abundant curiosity and an exceptional drive to learn, seek out new challenges, make their own discoveries, express themselves creatively, and master tasks with little instruction from others (D. A. Greenspan, Solomon, & Gardner, 2004; Smutny, Fremd, & Artabasy, 2009; Winner, 2000). They tend to set extremely high standards for their performance, sometimes to the point of unrealistic perfectionism (W. D. Parker, 1997; Tsui & Mazzocco, 2007). Most have high self-esteem, good social skills, and above-average emotional adjustment, although a few extremely gifted children have social or emotional difficulties, such as being overly sensitive to criticism (Edmunds & Edmunds, 2005; A. W. Gottfried et al., 1994; Sousa, 2009).

Giftedness may be partly an inherited characteristic, but environment clearly plays a significant role as well (B. Clark, 1997; A. W. Gottfried, Gottfried, & Guerin, 2009; Shavinina & Ferrari, 2004). Children who are gifted are more likely to be firstborn or only-born children and thus generally have more attention from their parents than other children do. Children who are gifted also tend to have many opportunities to practice and enhance their abilities from an early age, long before they have been identified as being gifted. And they are more likely to seek out enriching opportunities—an example of the *niche-picking* phenomenon described earlier.

As is true for Gina in the opening case study, a child's giftedness is often evident throughout childhood and adolescence. Some gifted children use unusually advanced language beginning in infancy, and others show signs of giftedness in early childhood, exhibiting intense curiosity and persistent interests (Colombo, Shaddy, Blaga, Anderson, & Kannass, 2009; C. Harrison, 2004). Yet others are "late bloomers"; their talents become evident relatively late in the game, perhaps as environmental conditions bring such talents to fruition.

Fostering the Development of Children with Gifts and Talents

Gifted students tend to be among our schools' greatest underachievers. When required to progress at the same rate as their nongifted peers, they achieve at levels far short of their capabilities (K. R. Carter, 1991; J. J. Gallagher, 1991; Rogers, 2002). Drawing on Vygotsky's theory of cognitive development, we could say that children who are gifted are unlikely to be working within their zone of proximal development if they are limited to the same tasks assigned to their peers, diminishing their opportunities to develop more advanced cognitive skills (Lubinski & Bleske-Rechek, 2008).

Children who are gifted often appreciate encouragement to take on demanding work in certain areas. In the "Intrinsic Motivation: Middle Childhood" video in MyEducationLab, 9-year-old Elena reveals her desire for challenge in her description of PEAK, a program at her school for students who are gifted:

Adult:	What do you like best about school?
Elena:	I like PEAK. . . . It's for smart kids who have, like, good ideas for stuff you could do. And so they make it more challenging for you in school. So instead of third-grade math, you get fourth-grade math.

MyEducationLab

Dear Mr. P—— [the school principal]:

I have found in recent months that it is time for me to make the next step in my life. This step is graduation. I would like to graduate a year early in May, this year, with the class of 2002.

This is a step I have chosen as the best for me for several reasons. The first reason is that I would like to spend a semester studying abroad in Austria. I have chosen Austria because it is a country where German is spoken and this is the language I have been learning for four years....

I have also decided to graduate because several people have suggested that this is my best option, as they believe that I am at a maturity level that indicates I should move on. These people, among others, are primarily my parents, my advisor, and the school counselor. They suggest that I am ready to graduate, but perhaps not ready for college, which is why I've chosen to do a foreign exchange and give myself time to further mature and prepare for college.

Besides these reasons, I personally believe that I would have extreme difficulty attending school next year and succeeding.

I have been told that this same thing is seen every year, when seniors become tired of attending, as they lack the motivation to succeed. I am afraid that this would happen to me, but on a higher level, as I already feel that I am losing motivation. Attending school next year could mean dire consequences for my transcript, my G.P.A., and my life.

When speaking with [the school counselor], we decided that I need to finish an internship and one job shadow, and I will have the credits necessary to graduate by the end of the school year. I plan to set up several internships over a period of five days in five different fields of engineering, so I can get an idea of what each field is like....

I hope you understand my reasons for leaving and I am sure that you will support me in my decision to graduate early. It will be difficult to change in such a gigantic way, but it will be very beneficial for me in the end.

Sincerely,

Geoff A——

ARTIFACT 8-1 **I hope you understand my reasons.** Here are excerpts from a letter in which Geoff, an 11th grader, requests permission to graduate early. School officials found his rationale convincing and granted his request.

Many students with special gifts and talents become bored or frustrated when their school experiences don't provide assignments that allow them to develop their unique abilities (Feldhusen, 1989; Feldhusen, Van Winkle, & Ehle, 1996; Winner, 2000). They may lose interest in school tasks and put in only the minimum effort they need to get by in the classroom, as Geoff, a gifted 11th grader, reveals in the letter shown in Artifact 8-1.

Yet some young people try to hide their exceptional talents. They may fear that peers will ridicule them for their high academic abilities and enthusiasm for academic topics, especially at the secondary school level (Covington, 1992; DeLisle, 1984; Stormont, Stebbins, & Holliday, 2001). Girls in particular are likely to hide their talents, especially if they have been raised in cultures that do not value high achievement in females (Covington, 1992; G. A. Davis & Rimm, 1998; Nichols & Ganschow, 1992).

Keep in mind that a child can be gifted and also have a disability. Some children with exceptional gifts and talents have learning disabilities, ADHD, autism, emotional disorders, or physical or sensory challenges (e.g., Hettinger & Knapp, 2001; S. Moran & Gardner, 2006). In such situations teachers and other practitioners must, when planning instruction, address the disabilities as well as the areas of giftedness. A few gifted children—for example, those with a limited English background or those who have specific learning disabilities—may need some training in basic skills (Brown-Mizuno, 1990; C. R. Harris, 1991; Udall, 1989).

Several strategies for helping children and adolescents with exceptional abilities maximize their potential are presented and illustrated in the Development and Practice feature "Addressing the Unique Needs of Children and Adolescents with Gifts and Talents."

GIFTED AND CHALLENGED. Some children who are gifted also have disabilities—possibly learning disabilities, emotional disorders, or physical challenges. This girl's teacher must take both her exceptional intelligence and her physical disability into account when planning instruction.

Children with Intellectual Disabilities

Children with an **intellectual disability** show developmental delays in most aspects of their academic and social functioning.[19] Two characteristics must both

intellectual disability
Disability marked by significantly below-average general intelligence and deficits in adaptive behavior.

---

[19] Although readers may be more familiar with the term *mental retardation* for the condition of low general intelligence, many advocates for children with special needs prefer the term *intellectual disability* because it has less of a social stigma (American Association on Intellectual and Developmental Disabilities, 2008).

DEVELOPMENT AND PRACTICE
Addressing the Unique Needs of Children and Adolescents with Gifts and Talents

Continually watch for unusual gifts and talents in children and adolescents.

- A preschool teacher hears from a 3-year-old boy's mother that he is already riding a two-wheel bicycle proficiently. The teacher marvels at the accomplishment and tells his mother about athletic programs in the local community. (Early Childhood)
- A third-grade teacher notices that one of her students has an exceptional skill with spatial and mechanical tasks. The boy repairs the class's broken digital clock, navigates with a homemade map as he rides the bus, completes intricate mazes, and draws plans for robots. Although the boy achieves at only average grades in school, the teacher is impressed with his talents and mentions them to a school psychologist, who can help determine whether he may qualify for special services. In the meantime the teacher provides opportunities for him to use his exceptional spatial and mechanical skills in a few classroom activities. (Middle Childhood)

Individualize instruction in accordance with students' specific talents.

- With help from the kindergarten teacher, a school librarian selects numerous nonfiction picture books about a variety of topics (e.g., books focused on animal life, historical figures, astronomy, and airplanes). Children select one book of interest, examine its pages, and then draw a few pictures of their own on the topic. With assistance from the teacher, they create their own booklets on topics of personal interest (Early Childhood)
- Two mathematically gifted junior high school students study calculus with a retired mathematician who volunteers her time three mornings a week. A classmate with exceptional reading skills is assigned classic works of literature appropriate to his reading level. (Early Adolescence)

Form study groups of gifted students who have similar abilities and interests.

- A music teacher provides semiweekly instruction and practice sessions for a quintet of musically talented 10- and 11-year-olds. As the group members gains skills, they begin meeting daily and occasionally ask their teacher for guidance in advanced techniques. (Early Adolescence)
- A high school dramatic arts teacher arranges for students to write a brief play in their study groups. Several active members of the school's theater club spend the entire weekend scripting the play and subsequently perform it enthusiastically for the class. (Late Adolescence)

Teach complex cognitive skills within the context of specific school topics rather than independently of the standard school curriculum.

- An elementary teacher has an advanced science group conduct a series of experiments. To promote critical thinking, she gives the students several questions about hypotheses, procedures, and rival explanations they should ask themselves as they conduct the experiments. (Middle Childhood)
- In an earth science class, a middle school teacher gives students a variety of projects related to weather. For students who have little background on the topic, the teacher provides basic information and

asks students to prepare a public service announcement about an upcoming weather system (Sousa, 2009). For students who want more of a challenge, the teacher asks students to prepare and administer a survey about people's awareness of weather patterns. (Early Adolescence)

Provide opportunities for independent study.

- A second-grade teacher finds educational software through which a mathematically gifted 8-year-old can study decimals, exponents, square roots, and other advanced concepts. (Middle Childhood)
- A high school student who is exceptionally talented in the arts is encouraged by her advisor to offer recommendations about the kind of studios, stages and theatrical supplies, musical instruments, and other resources that the school needs to offer basic support for budding artists. (Late Adolescence)

Encourage students to set high goals for themselves, but without expecting perfection.

- A middle school literacy teacher encourages students to set increasingly high goals for themselves in reading and writing. She makes available test score results and information on state standards in literacy so that students can select their own short-term goals for bridging the gap between their current levels of proficiency and the higher standards. (Early Adolescence)
- A high school counselor encourages a student from a low-income, single-parent family to consider going to a prestigious college. He also helps the student find sources of financial assistance for higher education. (Late Adolescence)

Challenge children to express themselves creatively.

- An elementary teacher encourages children to challenge themselves to express their knowledge creatively. The teacher asks children to compose poems, write speeches, detect patterns in mathematics, and design multimedia presentations. (Middle Childhood)
- In a high school lesson on romanticism, a teacher asks students to imagine that Ralph Waldo Emerson is coming to their school. For the assignment, the students write an essay on conditions in their community and speculate on how Emerson might respond to the environment. (Late Adolescence)

Seek outside resources to help students develop their exceptional talents.

- A high school student with an aptitude for learning foreign languages takes a Russian course at a local university. Through her new contacts in the class, she finds correspondence buddies in Russia and talks with them on *Skype.* (Late Adolescence)
- A high school requires students to complete a series of requirements across their four years of study—community service as freshmen, job shadowing as sophomores, an extended internship as juniors, and a major project during their senior year. In planning each activity, students are encouraged to obtain advice from experts in their community (Late Adolescence)

Sources: Ambrose, Allen, & Huntley, 1994; Feldhusen, 1989; Fiedler, Lange, & Winebrenner, 1993; Kulik & Kulik, 1997; Lupart, 1995; Milner & Ford, 2007; Moon, Feldhusen, & Dillon, 1994; W. D. Parker, 1997; Piirto, 1999; Smutny et al., 2009; Sousa, 2009; Spicker, 1992; Stanley, 1980; Sternberg et al., 2009; Turnbull et al., 2010; Winner, 2000.

be present in order for a child to be diagnosed with an intellectual disability (American Association on Intellectual and Developmental Disabilities, 2008):

- *Significantly below-average general intelligence.* Children with an intellectual disability perform poorly on traditional intelligence tests, with IQ scores being no higher than 65 or 70 (reflecting performance in the bottom 2 percent of the age-group). In addition, they learn slowly and perform quite poorly on school tasks in comparison with age-mates, and they show consistently poor achievement across virtually all academic areas.
- *Deficits in adaptive behavior.* Low intelligence test scores and poor academic performance are insufficient evidence to classify children as having an intellectual disability. An additional criterion is a deficit in **adaptive behavior**, which includes *practical intelligence* (management of the ordinary activities of daily living) and *social intelligence* (appropriate conduct in social situations). In these areas children and adolescents with an intellectual disability often exhibit behaviors typical of individuals much younger than themselves.

Children with an intellectual disability show impairments in many aspects of information processing. Some have weak attention and working memory skills (Schuchardt, Gebhardt, & Mäehler, 2010; Trezise, Gray, & Sheppard, 2008). Others have trouble generalizing what they learn to new situations and may exhibit a sense of helplessness about their ability to learn new things (Dempster & Corkill, 1999; Seligman, 1975; Turnbull et al., 2010). Furthermore, the play activities of children with an intellectual disability are the kinds that would ordinarily be observed in much younger children (F. P. Hughes, 1998; Malone, Stoneham, & Langone, 1995; Matson & Fodstad, 2010). For instance, some children with an intellectual disability intrude into peers' activities, ask inappropriately personal questions, and fail to take turns during conversations.

Intellectual disabilities are often caused by abnormal genetic conditions (e.g., Down syndrome). Sometimes an intellectual disability runs in families, such that many family members' abilities fall at the lower end of the normal distribution of intelligence (Kail, 1998). Yet heredity is not always to blame. Some instances of intellectual disabilities are due to noninherited biological causes, such as severe malnutrition or substance abuse during the mother's pregnancy (e.g., recall our earlier discussion of fetal alcohol syndrome), oxygen deprivation associated with a difficult birth, or environmental toxins (Keogh & MacMillan, 1996; Streissguth et al., 1994; Wodrich, Tarbox, Balles, & Gorin, 2010). Conditions in the home, including parental neglect and an extremely impoverished and unstimulating home life, may also be at fault (Batshaw & Shapiro, 1997; Feuerstein, 1979; M. M. Wagner, 1995).

Fostering the Development of Children with Intellectual Disabilities

The great majority of children and adolescents with intellectual disabilities attend school, and many of them are capable of mastering a wide range of academic and vocational skills. The Development and Practice feature "Maximizing the Development of Children and Adolescents with Intellectual Disabilities" illustrates several effective strategies.

Teachers and other adults must remember that children with intellectual disabilities have many strengths and that they are more likely to master new knowledge and skills when instruction builds on what they know and do well. When classroom adults trust in the potential of children with intellectual disabilities and accommodate the occasionally distinctive ways in which they learn, these children are most likely to thrive.

Preparing for Your Licensure Examination
Your teaching test might ask you about the characteristics of children with intellectual disabilities.

Preparing for Your Licensure Examination
Your teaching test might ask you about instructional strategies for fostering the academic and life skills of children and adolescents with intellectual disabilities.

adaptive behavior
Behavior related to daily living skills and appropriate conduct in social situations.

DEVELOPMENT AND PRACTICE
Maximizing the Development of Children and Adolescents with Intellectual Disabilities

Encourage young children to use the strengths they have, and offer support for acquiring new knowledge and skills.

- An 18-month-old who has intellectual and physical disabilities has recently begun attending an infant care center. His caregiver thinks creatively about how to help him interact with his physical environment. She glues Popsicle sticks to the pages of cardboard books so that he can easily grab them and turn the pages. To help him feel secure in his infant chair, she puts skid-proof material on the seat of the chair and cushions at the sides to keep him upright. (Infancy)
- A preschool teacher encourages a 4-year-old child, Sierra, to verbalize her desires. When Sierra points at a cabinet, her teacher suspects that Sierra wants her favorite ball, which is typically stored there. The teacher prompts Sierra, "Do you want to play with the ball, Sierra?" Sierra smiles and nods affirmatively. The teacher asks her, "Can you say 'ball,' Sierra?" Sierra says, "Bah." The teacher replies, "Good job, Sierra, you asked for your ball. Let me get it for you now." (Early Childhood)

Introduce new material at a slower pace, and provide many opportunities for practice.

- A fourth-grade teacher gives a student only two new addition facts a week, primarily because any more than two seem to overwhelm him. Every day, the teacher has the student practice writing the new facts and review the addition facts learned in previous weeks. (Middle Childhood)
- A paraprofessional stands by as 13-year-old Yarah completes a mathematics worksheet with single-digit multiplication problems. Yarah completes the problems and occasionally asks for help. Yarah will work on a similar worksheet tomorrow and a few days next week to solidify her memory of multiplication facts. (Early Adolescence)

Explain tasks concretely and in very specific language.

- An elementary art teacher gives a student explicit training in the steps she needs to take at the end of each painting session: (1) Rinse the paintbrush at the sink, (2) put the brush and watercolor paints on the shelf in the back room, and (3) put the painting on the counter by the window to dry. Initially, the teacher needs to remind the student of every step in the process. However, with time and practice, the student eventually carries out the process independently. (Middle Childhood)

- In preparation for an internship, a teacher tells students about general requirements of jobs—being on time, following directions, using a quiet voice, and so forth. The teacher asks students to anticipate some potential problems and consider how they might respond—for example, how they will get to work if their parents are unable to drive them. (Late Adolescence)

Give explicit guidance about how to study.

- An elementary teacher tells a student, "When you study a new spelling word, it helps if you repeat the letters out loud while you practice writing the word. Let's try it with *house,* the word you are learning this morning. Watch how I repeat the letters—H . . . O . . . U . . . S . . . E—as I write the word. Now you try doing what I just did." (Middle Childhood)
- A high school teacher advises a student how to take a standardized test. The teacher tells the student that it's important to write your name at the top of the first page, to fill in the bubbles, to check when done to see that all the items have been answered, and to do one's best without worrying about the result. (Late Adolescence)

Give feedback about specific behaviors rather than about general areas of performance.

- A fourth-grade teacher notices that a student in his class is showing a lot of progress in library skills. He tells the student, "I saw how interested you have been in your progress at the library. You returned your two books from last week and checked out three books this week. I can't wait to hear about your new books." (Middle Childhood)
- A vocational educator tells a high school student, "You did a good job in wood shop this week. You followed the instructions correctly, and you put away the equipment when you were finished with it." (Late Adolescence)

Encourage independence.

- An elementary teacher shows a boy how to find a seat during lunchtime. The teacher encourages the boy to find a familiar face from class, ask politely if he can join the others, and listen to the conversation before making a relevant comment. (Middle Childhood)
- A life skills instructor shows a high school student how to use her calculator to figure out how much she needs to pay for lunch every day. The instructor also gives the student considerable practice in identifying the correct bills and coins to use when paying various amounts. (Late Adolescence)

Sources: K. L. Fletcher & Bray, 1996; Patton, Blackbourn, & Fad, 1996; Perkins, 1995; Turnbull et al., 2010.

SUMMARY

Defining Intelligence

Intelligence involves effective learning processes and adaptive behaviors. Intelligent behavior is embedded in a particular setting. In separate societies, intelligence means slightly different things.

Theoretical Perspectives on Intelligence

Some theorists believe that intelligence is a single entity (a general factor, or *g*) that influences children's learning and performance across a wide variety of tasks. This belief is reflected in the widespread use of IQ scores as general estimates of academic ability. Other theorists (e.g., Gardner, Sternberg) propose that intelligence consists of a number of somewhat independent abilities and therefore cannot be accurately reflected in a single IQ score. There is also increasing evidence that children are more likely to behave "intelligently" when they have physical, social, and symbolic support systems to help them in their efforts.

Measuring Intelligence

Most intelligence tests have been developed primarily to identify individuals who have special needs (e.g., those who are gifted or have an intellectual disability). Contemporary intelligence tests include a variety of tasks designed to assess what people have learned from their everyday experiences. Performance on these tests is usually summarized by one or more IQ scores, which are determined by comparing an individual's performance with the performance of others of the same age. In some instances dynamic assessments may be more useful for evaluating children's capabilities in specific areas or for predicting their ability to benefit from certain kinds of instruction. Developmental assessments for infants and young children are often helpful in identifying those who have significant delays. However, results of tests given to small children should not be used to make long-term predictions about cognitive development.

Developmental Trends in IQ Scores

Performance on intelligence tests predicts school achievement to some degree, with IQ scores becoming increasingly stable and having greater predictive power as children grow older. Nevertheless, some children's IQ scores change considerably over time, especially during the early years.

Bioecology of Intelligence

Studies with twins and adopted children indicate that intelligence may be partly an inherited characteristic. But environmental conditions, including nutrition, exposure to toxic substances, home environment, preschool programs, and formal schooling, can also have a significant impact on IQ scores. Heredity and environment interact in their influence, to the point where it may be virtually impossible to separate the relative effects of these two factors on children's intellectual development.

Critique of Current Perspectives on Intelligence

Research on intelligence has relied heavily on traditional intelligence tests, which emphasize skills valued in mainstream Western culture and overlook dispositions and metacognitive strategies as important contributors to intellectual performance. Some theorists are now calling for a shift in focus from the assessment of intelligence to its development.

Implications of Research on Intelligence

Used within the context of other information, intelligence tests can provide a general idea of children's current cognitive functioning. Yet educators and other practitioners should remain optimistic about every child's potential for intellectual growth. Adults can anticipate that different children will be intelligent in different ways and should capitalize on children's unique strengths and abilities to promote learning and achievement. Adults should also give children the social support and the physical and symbolic tools that can enhance intelligent thinking and performance.

Exceptionalities in Intelligence

Children and adolescents identified as having gifts and talents show exceptional achievement or promise in one or more domains. Giftedness may be manifested differently in different cultures, but in general, gifted individuals demonstrate rapid learning, advanced reasoning, and sophisticated cognitive strategies. In contrast, children with an intellectual disability exhibit low general intellectual functioning and deficits in adaptive behavior. In individual children, either kind of exceptionality may have genetic roots, environmental causes, or both. Children with unusually high or low intelligence maximize their cognitive development when instruction is geared to their specific strengths and weaknesses.

APPLYING CONCEPTS IN CHILD DEVELOPMENT

The exercises in this section will help you build your ability to apply your knowledge of child development in working with children.

Improving Your Observation Skills

On page 290, you examined a series of photographs of children in various activities and were asked, "*How might each child be exercising one of Gardner's intelligences?*" In Photo 1, a young boy is exercising linguistic intelligence by producing and comprehending verbal information as he converses with his father. In Photo 2, a boy is exercising logical-mathematical intelligence as he learns about prices and profits at his family's produce stall. In Photo 3, a girl is exercising spatial intelligence as she examines a three-dimensional model of the solar system. In Photo 4, a teenager uses musical intelligence while playing the guitar.

In Photo 5, a young Columbian girl exercises bodily-kinesthetic intelligence while performing dance steps. In Photo 6, two girls are using interpersonal intelligence as they coordinate their turns and anticipate one another's next moves during a board game. In Photo 7, a girl applies intrapersonal intelligence as she contemplates her recent experiences and their meaning to her. In Photo 8, a boy uses naturalist intelligence as he learns about small critters and plants.

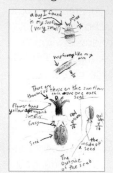

On page 315, you examined two drawings and were asked, *"Which of Gardner's multiple intelligences did 10-year-old Amaryth use in creating the drawings of a sunflower and insect?"* Amaryth certainly needed to rely on her naturalist intelligence to detect patterns in the sunflower's seeds. She also made good use of her spatial intelligence to measure the insect and various parts of the sunflower and then to magnify the objects as she sketched them (notice her references to "real size"). And to some degree she drew on her linguistic intelligence as she tried to capture in words the nonverbal essence of what she was seeing. For example, notice how she used an analogy to describe the sunflower's stem ("very fuzzy like my arm").

Practicing for Your Licensure Examination

Many teaching tests require students to use what they have learned about child development in responses to brief vignettes and multiple-choice questions. You can practice for your licensure examination by reading about an adolescent boy and answering a series of questions.

Fresh Vegetables

Read the case and then answer the questions that follow it.

Twelve-year-old Steven had no known genetic or other organic problems but had been officially labeled as having an intellectual disability (mental retardation) based on his low scores on a series of intelligence tests. His prior schooling had been limited to just part of one year in a first-grade classroom in inner-city Chicago. His mother had kept him home after a bullet grazed his leg while he was walking to school one morning. Fearing for her son's safety, she would not let him outside the apartment after that, not even to play, and certainly not to walk the six blocks to the local elementary school.

When a truant officer finally appeared at the door one evening 5 years later, Steven and his mother quickly packed their bags and moved to a small town in northern Colorado. They found residence with Steven's aunt, who persuaded Steven to go back to school. After considering Steven's intelligence and achievement test scores, the school psychologist recommended that he attend a summer school class for students with special needs.

Steven's summer school teacher soon began to suspect that Steven's main problem might simply be a lack of the background experiences necessary for academic success. One incident in particular stands out in her mind. The class had been studying nutrition, and so she had asked her students to bring in some fresh vegetables to make a large salad for their morning snack. Steven brought in a can of green beans. When a classmate objected that the beans weren't fresh, Steven replied, "The hell they ain't! Me and Momma got them off the shelf this morning!"

If Steven didn't know what *fresh* meant, the teacher reasoned, then he might also be lacking many of the other facts and skills on which any academic curriculum is inevitably based. She and the teachers who followed her worked hard to help Steven make up for all those years in Chicago during which he had experienced and learned so little. By the time Steven reached high school, he was enrolling in regular classes and maintaining a 3.5 grade point average.

"Fresh Vegetables" from CASE STUDIES: APPLYING EDUCATIONAL PSYCHOLOGY, 2nd Edition, by Jeanne Ellis Ormrod and Dinah McGuire. Copyright © 2007 by Jeanne Ellis Ormrod and Dinah McGuire. Reprinted by permission of Pearson Education, Inc., Upper Saddle River, NJ. Adapted by permission of the publisher.

Constructed-Response Question

1. Did Steven really seem to have an intellectual disability? Why or why not?

Multiple-Choice Questions

2. What factors have contributed to Steven's current abilities and intellectual weaknesses?

   a. Steven's skills and limitations are due solely to genetic factors.

   b. Steven's skills and limitations are exclusively from environmental experiences.

   c. Steven's skills and limitations derive from a combination of genetic and environmental factors.

   d. Steven's skills and limitations change from moment to moment and thus cannot be analyzed for their origins.

3. Given information on intelligence in this chapter, what can we expect about Steven's academic performance?

   a. Steven's limited knowledge and skills make it highly unlikely that he could initially succeed in a general education classroom without intensive instruction addressing the areas in which he lags behind age-mates.

   b. Given evidence of Steven's low intelligence, we can expect that he will never succeed in any arena of school.

   c. The skills that Steven has exhibited thus far are irrelevant to the demands of later academic tasks, therefore no prediction about his future performance or needs can be made.

   d. Because the underlying character of verbal skills and other intellectual abilities changes with development, it is difficult to determine what Steven's needs will be in the future.

Once you have answered these questions, compare your responses with those presented in Appendix A.

Improving Your Ability to Interpret Children's Artifacts and Reflections

Consider chapter concepts as you analyze the following accomplishments of a child with high intelligence.

Jermaine's Life

Jermaine has strong verbal skills and an active imagination (Hébert & Beardsley, 2001). An African American first-grade boy growing up in a rural community in Alabama, Jermaine has become inspired by the storytelling of his grandfather, and he receives ample encouragement from a few teachers at school who have noticed his remarkable talents. Yet Jermaine also faces some distinct hardships. His family is economically poor, and his single mother is frequently away from home. Jermaine and his older sister are expected to care for their brother and an elderly aunt. Neighbors ostracize Jermaine and his sister as "odd" or "crazy" because their brother and aunt have disabilities and also because the family fails to worship at the local church, as is the custom in their community (Hébert & Beardsley, 2001, p. 92). Not every teacher likes Jermaine either. One teacher who observed him on the school bus commented, "that boy is just too hard to handle," and the assistant principal has referred to him as "that bad little boy I have to keep an eye on" (Hébert & Beardsley, 2001, p. 93).

So far, Jermaine is managing to draw on his strengths and overcome his obstacles. Blending his natural talents with his personal life experiences, Jermaine has developed a keen sense of curiosity and a love of words. He likes to daydream at school and conjure up new worlds late at night as he gazes at the stars. Jermaine has decided to write about his life and fantasies in a book he calls "Jermaine's Life." Following is an excerpt he wrote in first grade:

> I was leaving Jermaine's world. I needed to go see my sister. It was soon to be her wedding. I wanted to stop her from marrying a jerk. I was riding my dragon through the hills. My dragon and I bumped into a gate. I wanted to show off my powers, so I burned the gate down with my powerful triton. We walked to where the gate had been. Suddenly, thousands of dragons arrived. They were breathing fire and smoke. I looked around. I knew we had to get out of there. I saddled up my dragon, grabbed my triton, and tried to escape. One of the dragons fired at my bottom. One fried my hair until I was bald. Another tried to claw me. I spoke out in my kingly voice, "What is this NONSENSE?" A dragon said, "Who ARE you talking to?" "Who ARE YOU talking to? I am the most powerful king you will ever meet." "OH HO! Fried King for supper tonight!" All the dragons were happy to hear that. "Fried! No, not fried," I said. "I would taste better boiled. And if you are going to boil me, you'll need some water." The dragons turned and began to walk toward a pond several miles away. Dragons do not like to have water too close. It might put out their fire. It took them many hours to get to the pond. They walked so slowly because they were afraid. I turned south and went back to my world. I decided to never return. My dragon agreed with me. He was glad that none of the other dragons had noticed that he was toothless. (Hébert & Beardsley, 2001, p. 93)[a]

- Jermaine earns high scores in verbal abilities on standardized tests, distinguishes himself in literature arts, and is identified as gifted. How does the excerpt from Jermaine's book offer additional evidence of his talent in verbal abilities?
- What kinds of educational services might help Jermaine reach his full potential?

Once you have answered these questions, compare your ideas with those presented in Appendix B. For further practice in analyzing children's artifacts and reflections, go to the Activities and Applications section in Chapter 8 of MyEducationLab.

[a]Hébert, T. P., & Beardsley, T. M. (2001). Jermaine: A critical case study of a gifted black child living in rural poverty. *Gifted Child Quarterly, 45,* 85–103.

Key Concepts

intelligence (p. 286)
intelligence test (p. 286)
g (p. 287)
fluid intelligence (p. 287)

crystallized intelligence (p. 287)
distributed intelligence (p. 294)
IQ score (p. 297)
cultural bias (p. 299)

dynamic assessment (p. 299)
Flynn effect (p. 308)
niche-picking (p. 309)
stereotype threat (p. 311)

giftedness (p. 315)
intellectual disability (p. 317)
adaptive behavior (p. 319)

PEARSON
myeducationlab

Now go to www.myeducationlab.com to:
- Take a Quiz to test your mastery of chapter objectives.
- Study chapter content with an individualized Study Plan.
- Deepen your understanding of particular concepts and principles with Review, Remediation, and Enrichment Exercises.
- Apply what you have learned in the chapter to your work with children in Building Teaching Skills and Dispositions exercises.
- Observe children and their unique contexts in Video Examples.

Chapter Nine

Language Development

CASE STUDY: Mario

As a young boy growing up in rural Vermont, Mario had the good fortune to learn two languages. At home, his parents spoke Spanish almost exclusively, in part because they wanted to pass their cultural heritage along to their son. Most of Mario's early exposure to English was in the English-speaking child care centers and pre-schools he attended off and on from the time he was 2 years old.

When Mario was 5, his dominant language was Spanish, but he was proficient in English as well. After his first 2 months in kindergarten, his teacher wrote the following in a report to Mario's parents:

[Mario is] extremely sociable. He gets along fine with all the children, and enjoys school. He is quite vocal. He does not seem at all conscious of his speech. His slight accent has had no effect on his relations with the others. Whenever I ask the class a question, he is always one of the ones with his hand up.

His greatest problem seems to be in the give and take of conversation. Since he always has some-thing to say, he often finds it difficult to wait his turn when others are talking. When he talks, there are moments when you can see his little mind thinking through language—for he sometimes has to stop to recall a certain word in English which he might not have at his finger tips. (Fantini, 1985, p. 28)

The "slight accent" in Mario's English led a speech therapist to recommend speech therapy, which Mario's parents declined. In fact, all traces of an accent disappeared from Mario's speech by age 8, and his third-grade teacher was quite surprised to learn that he spoke a language other than English at home.

Standardized tests administered over the years attested to Mario's proficiency in English. Before he began kindergarten, his score on a standardized English vocabulary test was at the 29th percentile, reflecting performance that, though a little on the low side, was well within an average range. Later, when he took the California Achievement Test in the fourth, sixth, and eighth grades, he obtained scores at the 80th percentile or higher (and mostly above the 90th percentile) on the reading, writing, and spelling subtests. When Mario spent a semester of fifth grade at a Spanish-speaking school in Bolivia, he earned high marks in Spanish as well, with grades of 5 on a 7-point scale in reading, writing, and language usage.

As Mario grew older, his vocabulary and written language skills developed more rapidly in English than in Spanish, in large part because most of his school instruction was in English. His father described the situation this way:

[B]y about fifth grade (age ten), he had entered into realms of experience for which he had no counterpart in Spanish. A clear example was an attempt to prepare for a fifth grade test on the topic of "The Industrial Revolution in England and France." It soon became clear that it was an impossibility to try to constrain the child to review materials read and discussed at school—in English—through Spanish. With this incident, [use of English at home] became a fairly well established procedure when discussing other school topics, including science, mathematics, and the like. (Fantini, 1985, p. 73)[a]

- What aspects of language did Mario learn?
- How did the distinctly different environments in Mario's everyday life affect his language development?

[a]Excerpts from "Case Study: Mario" from LANGUAGE ACQUISITION OF A BILINGUAL CHILD: A SOCIOLOGICAL PERSPECTIVE by A. E. Fantini. Copyright © 1985 by Alvino E. Fantini Reprinted by permission of the author.

OBJECTIVES

9.1: Differentiate among and critique the five theoretical frameworks of language development.

9.2: Trace the development of language from infancy through adolescence in six key domains.

9.3: Describe ways to foster children's fundamental language skills, including semantics, syntax, listening, speaking skills, pragmatics, and metalinguistic awareness.

9.4: Summarize and apply research on the development of a second language.

9.5: Discuss diversity and exceptionalities in children's acquisition of language.

Acquiring the language of one's culture is an extremely complex and challenging undertaking. To understand and use a language effectively, children must master four basic components of the language. First, they must master **phonology**: They must know how words sound and be able to produce the sequence of sounds that make up any given word. Second, they must master **semantics**, the meanings of a large number of words. Third, they must have a good command of **syntax**, rules for how words can legitimately be combined to form understandable phrases and sentences. Finally, children must master the **pragmatics** of language, the use of social conventions and speaking strategies that enable effective communication with others.

Mastering these four components of language is a remarkable achievement for any child. For children like Mario who acquire more than one language, the task is even more challenging. Given the multifaceted nature of human language, it is not surprising that Mario needed some extra time to acquire basic skills in both English and Spanish. At age 5, he had minor difficulties with English phonology (the kindergarten teacher mentioned a "slight accent"), semantics (his score on a vocabulary test was a tad on the low side), and pragmatics (especially turn taking). Over the long run, however, Mario's bilingual upbringing clearly did *not* hinder his language development. The accent in his English disappeared by age 8, and test scores in the fourth and fifth grades were well above average. All in all, Mario most certainly benefited from learning two languages.

In this chapter we often revisit Mario as we explore the multifaceted nature of human language and its development over childhood. We begin our discussion by looking at several theoretical perspectives on how children acquire their first language—that is, their **native language**.

THEORETICAL PERSPECTIVES OF LANGUAGE DEVELOPMENT

By age 3 or 4, most children have acquired sufficient proficiency in language that they are able to carry on productive conversations with the people around them. How they accomplish this monumental task in such a short time is one of the great mysteries of child development.

Theorists have offered numerous explanations for how children learn their native language. Here we describe an early framework based on modeling and reinforcement plus four more contemporary perspectives: nativism, cognitive process theories, sociocultural theories, and functionalism.

Modeling and Reinforcement

Some early theorists suggested that language development is largely the result of modeling—that children simply imitate the speech of others. Observation and imitation of others are certainly involved in language development to some degree (e.g., Arbib, 2005; Dabrowska, Rowland, & Theakston, 2009). Infants occasionally imitate the specific sounds and general sound patterns that parents and other caregivers make (Balog, 2010; M. H. Goldstein & Schwade, 2008; Theodore, Demuth, & Shattuck-Hufnagel, 2011; Tronick, Cohn, & Shea, 1986). And older children sometimes pick up other people's words and expressions. When Mario began attending an English-speaking preschool, he came home using such expressions as "Shut up!" and "Don't do dat!" which he had apparently acquired by listening to his classmates (Fantini, 1985, p. 97).[1]

The behaviorist B. F. Skinner (1957) suggested that *reinforcement* also plays a role, in that parents and other adults in a child's environment praise or in some other way reward increasingly mature language use. In Skinner's view, when infants make a variety of speech sounds in a seemingly random fashion, adults respond favorably to—and so encourage children to repeat—only those sounds used in the local language. As children grow older, Skinner proposed, adults begin

phonology
The sound system of a language; how words sound and are produced.

semantics
The meanings of words and word combinations.

syntax
Rules consistently used to put words together into sentences.

pragmatics
Conventions and strategies used in effective and socially acceptable verbal interactions.

native language
The first language a child learns.

[1]Excerpt from "Case Study: Mario" from LANGUAGE ACQUISITION OF A BILINGUAL CHILD: A SOCIOLOGICAL PERSPECTIVE by A. E. Fantini. Copyright © 1985 by Alvino E. Fantini Reprinted by permission of the author.

to reinforce the use of actual words, then the use of multiword combinations, and eventually only word combinations that are, from an adult's perspective, grammatically correct.

As complete explanations of how children acquire language, however, these early theories have not held up under the scrutiny of research. The speech of young children includes many phrases (e.g., "Allgone milk") that people around them neither say nor reinforce (N. Chomsky, 1959; V. Cook & Newson, 1996; D. Lightfoot, 1999). Moreover, parents usually reinforce their children's statements based on what is factually accurate rather than what is grammatically correct (R. Brown & Hanlon, 1970; Byrnes & Wasik, 2009). Even in the elementary and secondary school years, the great majority of grammatical errors in children's speech go uncorrected (Bohannon, MacWhinney, & Snow, 1990). And children may continue to produce grammatically incorrect sentences despite feedback that the sentences need revision, as the following dialogue illustrates:

Child:	Nobody don't like me.
Mother:	No, say "nobody likes me."
Child:	Nobody don't like me.

[Eight repetitions of this dialogue]

Mother:	No, now listen carefully; say "nobody likes me."
Child:	Oh! Nobody don't likes me. (McNeill, 1966, p. 68)

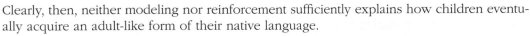

DADDY, TELL ME A STORY. Although parents and other adults certainly model and reinforce children's early efforts at speech, other factors are essential for language learning, including children's inherited abilities, their ongoing efforts to detect regularities in others' speech, and their initiative during conversation.

Clearly, then, neither modeling nor reinforcement sufficiently explains how children eventually acquire an adult-like form of their native language.

Nativism

In an approach known as **nativism**, theorists have turned to biology to explain language development.[2] One early pioneer, **Noam Chomsky** (1965, 1976, 2006), proposed that growing children have a biologically built-in mechanism—a **language acquisition device**—that enables them to learn many complex aspects of language in a very short time. This mechanism provides certain "prewired" knowledge and skills that make the task of learning language much simpler than it would be if children had to start from scratch.

Many psychologists share Chomsky's belief that human beings, though certainly not born knowing any particular language, nevertheless inherit some predispositions that assist them in acquiring linguistic knowledge and skills. Beginning at a very early age, infants can detect subtle differences among very similar speech sounds. They can divide a steady stream of sound into small segments (e.g., syllables) and identify common patterns in what they hear. They seem to have a few built-in concepts (e.g., colors such as red, pink, and yellow) that predispose them to categorize their experiences in certain ways. They may also have a *Universal Grammar,* a set of parameters that predispose them to form certain kinds of grammatical structures but not others (Boeckx, Fodor, Gleitman, & Rizzi, 2009; N. Chomsky, 2006; M. Gopnik, 1997).

Several lines of research converge on the conclusion that language has roots in biology. First, children from diverse cultural and linguistic backgrounds tend to reach milestones in language development at similar ages. Virtually all children, even those who are born deaf and have never heard a human voice, begin to produce speechlike syllables at about 6 or 7 months of age (Kuhl & Meltzoff, 1997; Lieven & Stoll, 2010; Locke, 1993). In general, children who have had regular exposure to a particular language—either spoken or manually signed—make similar progress in producing meaningful words and stringing them together into interpretable sequences (Crago, Allen, & Hough-Eyamie, 1997; L. A. Petitto, 1997; Snedeker, Geren, & Shafto, 2007).

nativism
Theoretical perspective proposing that some knowledge is biologically built-in and available at birth or soon thereafter.

language acquisition device
Biologically built-in mechanism hypothesized to facilitate language learning.

---

[2]You have also seen the influence of nativism in the discussion of *theory theory* in Chapter 7.

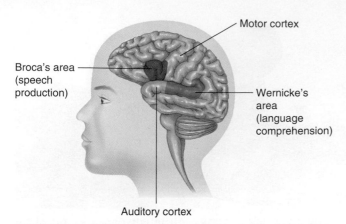

Motor cortex

Broca's area
(speech
production)

Wernicke's
area
(language
comprehension)

Auditory cortex

FIGURE 9-1 Primary language centers in the left hemisphere of the brain. Wernicke's area processes sounds and comprehends speech. Broca's area permits production of speech.

A second body of evidence comes from brain research. For most people, including children who are deaf and use a visual-manual sign system, the left hemisphere of the brain dominates in language production and comprehension (A. J. Newman, Supalla, Hauser, Newport, & Bavelier, 2010). Two specific regions of the left cortex specialize in language functions (see Figure 9-1). *Broca's area*, located near the forehead, plays a key role in producing speech. *Wernicke's area*, behind the left ear, is heavily involved in understanding speech. The right hemisphere offers complementary support, sifting through multiple possible meanings of statements, perceiving humor and sarcasm, and keeping track of events in a story (Neville & Bavelier, 2001; A. J. Newman et al., 2010; R. Ornstein, 1997). In addition, the right hemisphere dominates in language activities for a sizable number of left-handers, as well as for some children who incur serious injuries in their left hemispheres before age 1 (Beharelle et al., 2010; R. Ornstein, 1997; Stiles & Thal, 1993).

Additional evidence for the nativist view comes from the finding that there are *sensitive periods* in certain aspects of language development. Children who have little or no exposure to *any* language in the early years often have trouble acquiring advanced grammatical structures later on, even with intensive language instruction (Arshavsky, 2009; Curtiss, 1977; Newport, 1990). And acquiring phonological and syntactic skills in a second language is usually easier if the process begins in childhood or early adolescence instead of late adolescence or adulthood. Youngsters typically learn how to pronounce a second language flawlessly only if they study it before midadolescence or, even better, in the preschool or early elementary years, as Mario did (Bialystok, 1994a; Flege, Munro, & MacKay, 1995; Gluszek & Dovidio, 2010). They may also have an easier time mastering complex aspects of a second language's syntax when they are immersed in the language within the first 5 to 10 years of life (Arshavsky, 2009; Bialystok, 1994b; J. S. Johnson & Newport, 1989). From a nativist perspective, the predictable timing of such sensitive periods suggests the influence of genetically driven maturational processes.

Despite such findings, researchers have yet to obtain clear evidence that human beings do, in fact, inherit a specific neurological mechanism—Chomsky's hypothesized *language acquisition device*—that is dedicated solely to learning language. Even if research eventually confirms the existence of such a mechanism, questions would remain about the cognitive and motivational processes that enable children to acquire the language of their cultural group (Pinker, 1987). The theoretical perspectives that follow better address these factors.

Cognitive Process Theories

In contrast to Chomsky's position, certain other theories assert that children are born not with a specific capacity for learning language but rather with perceptual abilities and general thinking skills that allow them to infer the underlying patterns of their native language. Cognitive process theories represent a fairly diverse collection of frameworks that have in common their identification of the specific intellectual operations used by children to make sense of language (MacWhinney, 2010; Rumelhart & McClelland, 1987).[3] These perspectives show how children use strategies, often unconsciously, that allow them to discover how their native language works, for example, by paying attention to the ends of words and searching for ways that grammatical rules must make sense (Slobin, 1985). These perspectives also reveal that children identify and refine rules of varying levels of abstraction, sometimes using knowledge of one element of language (e.g., word meaning) to make sense of other features (e.g., grammatical category; Gleitman, Cassidy, Nappa, Papafragou, & Trueswell, 2005; Pinker, 1987).

From a cognitive process perspective, one essential ingredient to many aspects of language learning is attention (M. Harris, 1992; Koenig & Woodward, 2010; Pruden, Hirsh-Pasek, Golinkoff, & Hennon, 2006). Infants pay attention to human speech from a very early age.

[3]Cognitive process theories are introduced in Chapters 1 and 7.

Within a few days after birth, they show a preference for human voices over other sounds, distinguish between familiar and unfamiliar voices, and in some instances expend considerable effort to hear a familiar voice (DeCasper & Fifer, 1980; DeCasper & Prescott, 2009; J. L. Locke, 1993).

Yet cognitive processes must be sufficiently flexible that they allow children around the world to acquire language despite the varied ways in which adults support their language learning. Many U.S. and European parents engage their infants in dyadic exchanges, using short, simple, high-pitched language and pointing to the people or objects under discussion, ostensibly to secure their children's attention and ease the challenges inherent in comprehending new words (M. Harris, 1992; Lieven & Stoll, 2010; Sterponi, 2010). In societies that use such **infant-directed speech**, children are inducted into conversations and make increasingly appropriate verbal contributions. You can hear examples of infant-directed speech in the infancy video clips related to "Cognitive Development," "Intelligence," and "Literacy" in MyEducationLab.

Children are resourceful detectives and find many other ways to discern the underlying rules of language when not exposed to infant-directed speech. Among the Kaluli in Papua New Guinea, mothers carry their infants around all day and hold infants facing outward, not speaking to them directly but rather giving them an opportunity to listen in on conversations with older children and with other adults (Schieffelin, 1985, 1990). After children speak their first words, adults tell children what they should say in particular situations. Children in the Kaluli become skilled eavesdroppers as infants, learn to identify the rhythms of speech long before they utter their first words, and become accomplished communicators in early childhood.

In listening to their native language, children carefully analyze clues in ongoing speech. Some analyses take a lot of time, allowing for predictable sequences in language acquisition. In most languages researchers have examined to date, children learn nouns before verbs, probably because children find it easier to map a word to an object than to discern a distinct process from a continuous stream of action (Gentner, 2006; Golinkoff & Hirsh-Pasek, 2008; Lieven & Stoll, 2010). Children gradually notice that people regularly use certain words (i.e., verbs) to describe salient events. Moreover, they learn verbs for actions they can see (e.g., running) before actions they cannot see (e.g., thinking; Golinkoff & Hirsh-Pasek, 2008).

Reasoning is another critical player in language development (M. Atkinson, 1992; Cromer, 1993; Frazier et al., 2009). Young children seem to form hypotheses about the meanings of words based on the context in which the words are used. In one study (Au & Glusman, 1990), researchers showed preschoolers an unfamiliar animal and consistently called it a *mido*. Later they presented a collection of odd-looking animals (including some midos) and asked the children to find a *theri* in the set (see Figure 9-2). Although the children had no information to guide their selection, they always chose an animal other than a mido. Apparently, they deduced that because the midos already had a name, a theri had to be a different kind of animal.

Sociocultural Theories

Whereas cognitive process theorists consider the intellectual operations involved in acquiring and using language, sociocultural theorists look more at how social interactions foster language development. From this perspective children are *socialized* to use language (Ochs, 2002; Ochs & Schieffelin, 1995; Sterponi, 2010). Such **language socialization** involves both explicit instruction about language (e.g., parents may insist that children say "please" and "thank you") and more indirect means of communicating appropriate linguistic behaviors (e.g., parents may model turn taking and other cultural conventions of social interaction). Furthermore, social interactions provide a means through which children *internalize* language. Consistent with Vygotsky's theory of cognitive development, children use words first in their interactions with others, and then,

MyEducationLab

Hear examples of infant-directed speech in the infancy clips of the "Cognitive Development," "Intelligence," and "Literacy" videos. (Find Video Examples in Topic 9 of MyEducationLab.)

Preparing for Your Licensure Examination
Your teaching test might ask you about cultural influences on language learning.

This is a *mido*.

Which one of these is a *theri*?

FIGURE 9-2   Which one of these is a theri? Children are more likely to attach new words to objects for which they don't already have labels. In this situation, a child is likely to choose either the purple crocodile-like creature or the yellow dinosaur-like creature as being a *theri*.
After Au & Glusman, 1990.

infant-directed speech
Short, simple, high-pitched speech often used when talking to young children.

through the process of internalization, gradually incorporate these words into their everyday thought processes (Hobson, 2004; K. Nelson, 1996a; McCafferty, 2008).

From a sociocultural perspective, a process critical for language acquisition is *intersubjectivity*, the mutual understanding that two or more people are thinking about the same thing at the same time.[4] If children are to learn new words in their interactions with others, they must share with their conversation partners an awareness of their mutual focus (D. A. Baldwin, 2000; Mundy & Newell, 2007; Tomasello, 1999). As an illustration, imagine that a father and his 3-year-old daughter are shopping at the local supermarket. "Oh good," the father exclaims, "a carambola. I love carambolas!" If the daughter has never heard the word *carambola* before, she will likely look at her father's face and then follow his gaze to the object in question (in this case, a yellow-green, star-shaped fruit). But she is apt to do this only if she realizes that her father is probably looking at the object he is talking about.

This state of mutual attention is achieved in a variety of ways. As you have learned, parents do not universally simplify their speech and use a high-pitched, singsongy style with young children. To return to the Kaluli people mentioned earlier, mothers hold their children up to face another person and, when they notice their children being provoked (e.g., when the other person takes the child's food), tell them what to say (Schieffelin, 1985). The child is generally able to grasp the mother's focus in such a personally relevant circumstance.

As early as the second year, and quite possibly before that, children use what they know or can surmise about other people's thoughts to assist them in learning word meanings (Golinkoff & Hirsh-Pasek, 2006; Mundy & Newell, 2007; Tomasello, 1999). In one study, 18-month-olds were looking at one new toy while an adult looked at another (D. A. Baldwin, 1993). When the adult exclaimed, "A modi!" the children typically turned their attention to see what the adult was looking at. A short time later, when the children were asked to get the modi, they were most likely to choose the toy the adult had been looking at, even though they themselves had been looking at something different when they first heard the word.

Functionalism

Another important question involves motivation: Why do children *want* to learn the language of their society? Some psychologists argue that over the course of evolution, human beings developed language skills in large part because language serves several useful functions—hence the term **functionalism**. Language helps children acquire knowledge, establish productive interpersonal relationships, control their own behavior, and influence the behavior of others (L. Bloom & Tinker, 2001; Karniol, 2010; O'Connell & Kowal, 2008). When Mario attended preschool as a 3-year-old, he quickly learned such expressions as "No do dat no more!" and "Get auto here!" (Fantini, 1985, pp. 97–98).[5] We can reasonably guess that such language enabled Mario to influence his classmates' behaviors in ways that more gentle speech might not have.

Functionalists point out that language development is closely intertwined with—and, in fact, is critical for—development in other domains (L. Bloom & Tinker, 2001; Langacker, 1986). Language enhances cognitive development in several ways: by providing symbols with which children can mentally represent and remember events, by allowing children to exchange information with others, and by enabling children to internalize processes they first use in their social interactions. Language is essential for social and moral development as well. Through conversations and conflicts with adults and peers, children learn socially acceptable ways of behaving toward others and, in most cases, eventually establish a set of principles that guide their moral decision making.[6]

Language is so important for the human species that children seem to have the ability not only to learn it but also to *create* it. We find an example in a study of children attending a school for the deaf in Nicaragua (Senghas & Coppola, 2001). Before coming to the school, the children had little or no exposure to sign language, and teachers at the school focused primarily on teaching them how to lip-read and speak Spanish. Although many of the children made little progress in Spanish, they became increasingly adept at communicating with

language socialization
Direct and indirect means through which other people teach children the language and verbal behaviors deemed to be appropriate in their culture.

functionalism
Theoretical perspective of language development that emphasizes the purposes language serves for human beings.

---

[4]Intersubjectivity is examined in Chapter 7.
[5]Excerpt from "Case Study: Mario" from LANGUAGE ACQUISITION OF A BILINGUAL CHILD: A SOCIOLOGICAL PERSPECTIVE by A. E. Fantini. Copyright © 1985 by Alvino E. Fantini. Reprinted by permission of the author.
[6]Moral development is the focus of Chapter 14.

one another through a variety of hand gestures, and they consistently passed this sign language along to newcomers. Over a period of 20 years, the children's language became more systematic and complex, with a variety of syntactic rules taking shape.

Critiquing Theories of Language Development

The Basic Developmental Issues table "Contrasting Contemporary Theories of Language Development" summarizes how nativism, cognitive process theories, sociocultural theories,

BASIC DEVELOPMENTAL ISSUES
Contrasting Contemporary Theories of Language Development

ISSUE	NATIVISM	COGNITIVE PROCESS THEORIES	SOCIOCULTURAL THEORIES	FUNCTIONALISM
Nature and Nurture	By and large, children develop language only when they are exposed to it; thus, environmental input is essential. But children also rely on one or more biological mechanisms that provide predetermined "knowledge" about the nature of language and skills that help them decipher linguistic input.	Most cognitive process theorists assume that language learning involves a complex interplay among inherited inclinations, abilities to detect regularities in language input, and experiences that facilitate effective language learning (e.g., attention-getting actions by parents, frequent practice in using words).	Sociocultural theorists don't necessarily discount the role of heredity, but they prioritize the social contexts that promote development and the cultural legacy (e.g., culture-specific interpretations of words and phrases) that a society passes along from one generation to the next.	As their needs and desires become increasingly ambitious and complex, children propel their own language development through their efforts to communicate more effectively. Their needs and desires are probably the result of both heredity and environment.
Universality and Diversity	Although human languages differ in many respects, most have certain things in common (e.g., they include both nouns and verbs). Furthermore, children speaking different languages reach milestones in language development at similar ages. Diversity exists primarily in the specific phonological, semantic, syntactic, and pragmatic features of various languages.	Cognitive mechanisms that affect language acquisition (e.g., attention, analysis of speech sounds) are universally relevant across cultures. Children's unique language experiences, which vary among and within cultures, lead to differences in the language(s) that children speak, the pathways they take to language proficiency, and the precise meanings they assign to specific words.	Some mechanisms that promote language development (e.g., intersubjectivity) may be universal across cultures. At the same time, different societies support common mechanisms in their own distinctive ways and cultivate many culture-specific linguistic practices.	The drive to understand and be understood by others is universal. Different cultural groups may be more responsive to, and so nurture, certain ways of communicating more than others.
Qualitative and Quantitative Change	Children often acquire specific syntactic structures in a predictable sequence, with noticeable, stage-like changes in linguistic constructions occurring after each new acquisition (e.g., see the discussion of question formation in the upcoming section "Syntactic Development").	Many changes in language development—for instance, children's ever-enlarging vocabularies, ongoing refinement of word meanings, increasingly correct pronunciation, and expanding working memory capacities (enabling production of longer and more complex sentences)—come about in a trendlike, quantitative fashion.	The nature of adult–child relationships that nurture language development may change both quantitatively and qualitatively over time. Qualitative change occurs in the development of intersubjectivity. Initially intersubjectivity involves only an interaction between an adult and a child but later involves a mutual focus on, as well as shared understandings of, an object. Trendlike increases occur in the absorption of language conventions from the community.	With development, children's expressions of needs and desires change in both quality and intensity. Whereas a 2-year-old might simply be interested in getting "more cookie" sometime within the next few minutes, a 15-year-old might ask, "When I'm old enough to drive, can I have my own car if I earn the money for it?" Thus both qualitative changes (e.g., use of new grammatical structures, such as dependent clauses) and quantitative changes (e.g., increasing sentence length) occur.

Bioecology of Child Development

In the bioecological framework, children contribute to their own language development through their active analysis of semantic, syntactic, phonological, and pragmatic features of their native language. Parents, other adults, and children of various ages provide language input and occasions for practicing speech. As they grow, children interact with people in different communities that are regulated by distinct conventions of use.

Preparing for Your Licensure Examination

Your teaching test might ask to recognize key developmental milestones in learning language.

MyEducationLab

Hear 16-month-old Corwin's early words in the "Literacy: Infancy" video. (Find Video Examples in Topic 9 of MyEducationLab.)

and functionalism differ with respect to the broad themes of nature and nurture, universality and diversity, and qualitative and quantitative change. Another important difference among various theoretical perspectives is one of focus: Nativism focuses largely on syntactic development, cognitive process and sociocultural theories look more closely at semantic development (with sociocultural theories also considering pragmatic skills), and functionalism considers how motivation fits into the overall picture. Therefore, theorists often shift from one perspective to another or combine elements of two or more perspectives into a more comprehensive framework.

TRENDS IN LANGUAGE DEVELOPMENT

Children's first form of communication is crying. Soon thereafter, they also communicate by smiling and cooing and, a bit later, by pointing and gesturing (e.g., Goldin-Meadow, 2006; Tomasello, Carpenter, & Liszkowski, 2007). On average, they begin using a few recognizable words sometime around their first birthday and put words together, two at a time, before their second birthday. During the preschool years, their vocabulary grows considerably, and their sentences become longer. By the time they enroll in elementary school, at age 5 or 6, they use language that seems adult-like in many respects. Yet throughout the elementary and secondary school years, children and adolescents learn thousands of new words, and they become capable of comprehending and producing increasingly complex sentences. They also continue to develop skills for conversing appropriately with others and acquire a better understanding of the nature of language. In the following sections, we explore numerous aspects of language development over the course of infancy, childhood, and adolescence.

Semantic Development

Infants begin categorizing objects as early as 3 or 4 months of age, understand the meanings of some words as early as 8 months of age, and typically say their first word at about 12 months (Byrnes & Wasik, 2009; Fenson et al., 1994; M. Harris, 1992). By the time children are 16 to 18 months old, many have 50 words in their expressive vocabularies (Byrnes & Wasik, 2009; O'Grady, 1997). There is considerable variability from child to child, however. For example, Mario did not say his first word until he was 16 months old, and by his second birthday he was using only 21 words (Fantini, 1985). You can hear 16-month-old Corwin's first words in the "Literacy: Infancy" videos in MyEducationLab.

At some point during the end of the second year or beginning of the third year, a virtual explosion in speaking vocabulary occurs, with children using 30 to 50 new words a month and, later, as many as 20 new words each day (M. Harris, 1992; O'Grady, 1997). In the preschool years, children also begin to organize their knowledge of various words into general categories (e.g., *juice*, *cereal*, and *morning* are all related to *breakfast*), hierarchies (e.g., *dogs* and *cats* are both *animals*), and other interword relationships (S. A. Gelman & Kalish, 2006; M. Harris, 1992).

At 6 years of age, children's semantic knowledge typically includes 8,000 to 14,000 words, of which they use about 2,600 in their own speech (Byrnes & Wasik, 2009; Carey, 1978). By the sixth grade, they understand on average, 50,000 words in what they hear and read although cannot necessarily produce these words appropriately in context. By high school, it includes approximately 80,000 words (G. A. Miller & Gildea, 1987; Nippold, 1988; Owens, 2008). Thus by age 3 or so, children learn several thousand new words each year and so, on average, must learn numerous new words *every day* (Byrnes & Wasik, 2009; W. E. Nagy, Herman, & Anderson, 1985).

The dramatic increase in the number of words that children can use and understand is the most obvious aspect of semantic development. Yet several other principles also characterize semantic development, as we see now.

Young children divide the continuous stream of speech they hear into its individual word "pieces." Doing so is not as easy as you might think: Even in the simplified infant-directed speech described earlier, one word flows quickly into the next, without pause (Jusczyk, 1997). Despite such nonstop verbal action, infants begin to identify the specific words in speech by 7 or 8 months of age (Aslin, Saffran, & Newport, 1998; Bortfeld, Morgan, Golinkoff, & Rathbun, 2005). Exactly how they do it remains a mystery, but they probably rely on the characteristic rhythm, stress patterns, and consistencies in sound sequences they hear in their native language (K. G. Estes, Evans, Alibali, & Saffran, 2007; Gervain & Mehler, 2010; Jusczyk, 2002). They probably notice that some sound combinations regularly co-occur in sequence in a particular language, whereas other combinations are not permissible Byrnes & Wasik, 2009; Jusczyk, 1997). Consider the English statement, "Call Peter for dinner" ("C" (*Cuh*), "a" (*ahh*), and "l" (*ahl*) flow easily together, but "l" (*luh*) and "p" (*puh*) do not, signaling to the listener that "call" is one word but "call" and "Peter" are probably separate words. Similarly, "r"(*err*) and "f" (*fuh*) do not unfold fluently, providing a cue that "Peter" and "for" are also separate words. As children learn which sounds can and cannot be bundled together, listen to the stress on syllables, and notice other clues, they divide an ongoing stream of sounds into distinguishable words.

Children use many ingenious strategies for learning the meanings of words. Once children have identified the specific words in speech, they must zero in on their meanings. In some cases adults provide instruction, perhaps by labeling objects or by asking questions ("Where is the _____?") while looking at picture books with children (M. F. Collins, 2010; Dunham, Dunham, & Curwin, 1993; Manolitsis, Georgiou, & Parrila, 2011; Sénéchal, Thomas, & Monker, 1995). More often, however, caregivers, teachers, and other individuals don't explicitly identify what they are referring to when they use new words. As a result, youngsters must infer the meaning of many words from clues intrinsic to speech as well as from the contexts in which the words are used.

Infants and young toddlers sometimes need numerous repetitions of a particular word before they understand and use it (A. M. Peters, 1983; Pruden et al., 2006; Woodward, Markman, & Fitzsimmons, 1994). But by the time children are age 2 or 3, they can often infer a word's general meaning after only one exposure—a process known as **fast mapping** (Carey & Bartlett, 1978; Mayor & Plunkett, 2010; Pinker, 1982). Young children seem to use a number of general "rules" to fast-map word meanings. Here are some examples:

- If I see several objects and know labels for all of them except one, the new word is probably the name of the unlabeled object. (Recall the research study involving the words *mido* and *theri* described earlier.)
- If someone uses a word while pointing to a particular object, the word probably refers to the *whole* object rather than to just a part of it.
- Generally speaking, when a word is used to refer to a particular object or action, it refers to *similar* objects or actions as well.
- If a word is preceded by an article (e.g., "This is a *ball*"), it refers to a category of objects. If it has no article in front of it (e.g., "This is *Tobey*"), it is the name of a *particular* object (i.e., it is a proper noun). (Au & Glusman, 1990; Choi & McDonough, 2007; S. A. Gelman & Raman, 2003; S. A. Gelman & Taylor, 1984; Golinkoff, Hirsh-Pasek, Bailey, & Wenger, 1992; M. Hansen & Markman, 2009; Jaswal & Markman, 2001; Markman, 1989; Spiegel & Halberda, 2011)

Improving Your Observation Skills

Monkey. A mother points at an animal at the zoo and says to her toddler son, "It's a monkey." What cues in the language and context might the boy use to interpret his mother's utterance? Compare your response with the explanation at the end of the chapter.

fast mapping
Inferring a word's general meaning after a single exposure.

As children get older, they continue to refine their understandings of words through repeated encounters with words in different contexts and sometimes through explicit instruction and feedback (Byrnes & Wasik, 2009; Carey & Bartlett, 1978). As an example, consider how three children in the same family once defined the word *plant:*

Andrew (age 7):	Something that people plant in a garden or somewhere.
Amaryth (age 10):	A growing thing that's sometimes beautiful.
Anthony (age 13):	A life-form that uses sunlight and carbon dioxide to live.

Notice how Andrew's definition is quite concrete and limited (apparently) to contexts in which his parents and other people might have used the word. Amaryth's definition is more general, in that it includes a characteristic of all plants: growth. Only Anthony's definition includes characteristics that a biologist might identify. Presumably Anthony had acquired this understanding of the word *plant* in one of his science classes at school.

Comprehension usually, but by no means always, precedes production. Psychologists studying language development frequently make a distinction between receptive and expressive language skills. **Receptive language** is the ability to understand what one hears and reads. In other words, it involves language *comprehension*. In contrast, **expressive language** is the ability to communicate effectively either orally or on paper. In other words, it involves language *production*.

It would be quite reasonable to assume that receptive language skills must precede expressive language skills—that children must understand what words and sentences mean before using them in speech and writing. You can see that 16-month-old Corwin shows greater facility in understanding words than in producing them in the "Intelligence: Infancy" video in MyEducationLab. Yet many theorists don't believe the relationship between receptive and expressive language is always clear-cut (Owens, 2008). Children sometimes use words and expressions whose meanings they don't completely understand. Teresa recalls a 3-year-old preschooler who talked about the "accoutrements" in her toy purse, presumably after hearing others use the word in a similar context. Although the girl used the word appropriately in that situation, she did not understand all of its connotations. That is, her production exceeded her comprehension. Ultimately, receptive and expressive language skills probably develop hand in hand, with language comprehension facilitating language production, and language production also enhancing language comprehension.

Children initially focus on lexical words; grammatical words come a bit later. All languages have two main categories of words (Shi & Werker, 2001). **Lexical words** have some connection, either concrete or abstract, to objects or events in people's physical, social, and psychological worlds. They include nouns (e.g., *horse, freedom*), verbs (e.g., *swim, think*), adjectives (e.g., *handsome, ambiguous*), and adverbs (e.g., *quickly, intentionally*). **Grammatical words** (also known as *function words*) have little meaning by themselves but affect the meanings of other words or the interrelationships among words or phrases. They include articles (e.g., *a, the*), auxiliary verbs (e.g., the *have* in *I have swum*), prepositions (e.g., *before, after*), and conjunctions (e.g., *however, unless*). By the time children are 6 months old, they can distinguish between lexical words and grammatical words and show a distinct preference for lexical words (Bornstein & Cote, 2004; Shi & Werker, 2001).

Over time, children continue to refine their understandings of lexical words. Children initially have a general idea of what certain words mean but define them imprecisely and may use them incorrectly. One common error is **underextension**, in which children attach overly restricted meanings to words, leaving out some situations to which the words apply. For example, Jeanne once asked her son Jeff, then 6, to tell her what an *animal* is. He gave this definition:

It has a head, tail, feet, paws, eyes, nose, ears, lots of hair.

Like Jeff, young elementary school children often restrict their meaning of *animal* primarily to nonhuman mammals, such as dogs and horses, and insist that fish, birds, insects, and people are *not* animals (Carey, 1985; Saltz, 1971). Another frequent error is **overextension**: Words

MyEducationLab

Notice how Corwin has greater facility in understanding words (receptive language) than in pronouncing them (expressive language) in the "Intelligence: Infancy" video. (Find Video Examples in Topic 9 of MyEducationLab.)

receptive language
Ability to understand the language one hears or reads.

expressive language
Ability to communicate effectively through speaking and writing.

lexical word
Word that in some way represents an aspect of one's physical, social, or psychological world.

grammatical word
Nonlexical word that affects the meanings of other words or the interrelationships among words in a sentence.

underextension
Overly restricted meaning for a word that excludes some situations to which the word applies.

are given meanings that are too broad and so are applied to inappropriate situations. For example, a child might say "I'm *barefoot* all over!" or "I'll get up so early that it will still be *late*" (Chukovsky, 1968, p. 3; italics added).

In addition to underextending and overextending word meanings, children sometimes confuse the meanings of similar words. The following conversation illustrates 5-year-old Christine's confusion between *ask* and *tell:*

Adult:	Ask Eric his last name. [Eric Handel is a classmate of Christine's.]
Christine:	Handel.
Adult:	Ask Eric this doll's name.
Christine:	I don't know.
Adult:	Ask Eric what time it is.
Christine:	I don't know how to tell time.
Adult:	Tell Eric what class is in the library.
Christine:	Kindergarten.
Adult:	Ask Eric who his teacher is.
Christine:	Miss Turner. (dialogue from C. S. Chomsky, 1969, p. 55; format adapted)

In a similar manner, young children often confuse comparative words, sometimes interpreting *less* as "more" or thinking that *shorter* means "longer" (Owens, 2008; Palermo, 1974).

Children have difficulty with grammatical words throughout the elementary and middle school years. Children's mastery of a particular grammatical word typically evolves slowly over a period of several years. For instance, although 3-year-olds can distinguish between the articles *a* and *the*, children as old as 9 are occasionally confused about when to use each one (Owens, 2008; Reich, 1986). Children in the upper elementary and middle school grades have trouble with many conjunctions, such as *but, although, yet, however,* and *unless* (E. W. Katz & Brent, 1968; Nippold, 1988; Owens, 2008). As an illustration, consider the following two pairs of sentences:

Jimmie went to school, but he felt sick.
Jimmie went to school, but he felt fine.

The meal was good, although the pie was bad.
The meal was good, although the pie was good.

Even 12-year-olds have trouble identifying the correct sentence in pairs like these, reflecting only a vague understanding of the connectives *but* and *although* (E. W. Katz & Brent, 1968). (The first sentence is correct in both cases.)

Understanding of abstract words emerges later than understanding of concrete words. Children's increasing ability to think abstractly is reflected in their semantic development (e.g., Anglin, 1977; Haskill & Corts, 2010; Quinn, 2007).[7] Young children in particular are apt to define words (even fairly abstract ones) in terms of the obvious, concrete aspects of their world. For example, when Jeanne's son Jeff was 4, he defined *summer* as the time of year when school is out and it's hot outside. By the time he was 12, he knew that scientists define summer in terms of the earth's tilt relative to the sun—a much more abstract notion.

Fostering Semantic Development

Researchers have identified several strategies that teachers, parents, and other caregivers can use to help children learn word meanings:

• **Talk regularly to, with, and around infants, toddlers, and preschool children.** Even when young children do not yet talk themselves, they learn a great deal from hearing their native language. Initially, they learn its basic characteristics, such as its typical rhythms and stress patterns and the specific sounds (phonemes) that it does and does not include. Later,

[7]Children's ability to think abstractly is examined in Chapter 6.

overextension
Overly broad meaning for a word, such that it is used in situations to which it does not apply.

as they begin to mentally "divide" others' speech into individual words, they also begin to draw inferences about what some of those words mean. Although the simple sentences and attention-grabbing tones some parents use may initially attract infants into conversation, over the long run it's the richness of language—a wide variety of words, complex syntactic structures, and so on—that facilitates children's vocabulary development (B. Hart & Risley, 1995; Hoff & Naigles, 2002; Pan, Rowe, Singer, & Snow, 2005). Thus, early childhood educators can label objects that might be unfamiliar to children, elaborate on children's simple utterances, occasionally let children take the lead in conversation, and so on (C. Bouchard et al., 2010).

• **Give definitions.** By the time children are school age, they often learn words more easily when they are told specifically what the words mean—in other words, when they are given definitions (Tennyson & Cocchiarella, 1986). Definitions are especially helpful when the essential characteristics of a concept are abstract or otherwise not obvious. Children can usually learn what a *circle* is and what *red* means even without definitions, because roundness and redness are characteristics that are easily noticed. But the important characteristics of such conceptually based ideas as *polygon* and *fragile* are more subtle, and for words like these, definitions can be very helpful.

• **Provide examples and nonexamples.** Children often acquire a more accurate understanding of a word when they are shown several examples (Barringer & Gholson, 1979; Tennyson & Cocchiarella, 1986). Ideally, such examples should be as different from one another as possible so that they illustrate a word's entire range. If adults limit their examples of *animal* to dogs, cats, cows, and horses, children will understandably draw the conclusion that all animals have four legs and fur (a case of underextension). If, instead, adults also present goldfish, robins, beetles, earthworms, and people as examples of *animal*, children are apt to realize that animals can differ considerably in physical appearance.

In addition to having examples, children benefit from having nonexamples of a word, especially those that are "near misses" (Winston, 1973). For instance, to learn what a *salamander* is, a child might be shown several salamanders and such similar animals as a snake and a lizard and told that the latter two critters are "not salamanders." By presenting nonexamples, including the near misses, adults minimize the extent to which children are likely to overextend their use of words.

TOAD, NOT FROG. Children acquire more accurate understandings of a word when they are advised of examples and nonexamples of the category.

• **Give feedback when children use words incorrectly.** Misconceptions about word meanings reveal themselves in children's speech and writing. Astute teachers and caregivers listen closely not only to what children say but also to how they say it, and they also look at how children use words in their writing. A preschooler might mistakenly refer to a rhinoceros as a "hippo," an elementary school student might deny that a square is a rectangle, and a high school student might use the term *atom* when she is really talking about molecules. In such situations adults should gently correct the misconceptions, perhaps by saying something along these lines: "A lot of people get hippos and rhinoceroses confused, because both of them are large and gray. This animal has a large horn on its nose, so it's a rhinoceros. Let's find a picture of a hippo and see how the two animals are different."

• **Encourage children to read as much as possible.** Avid readers learn many more new words and so have larger vocabularies than do children who read infrequently (Fukkink & de Glopper, 1998; Stanovich, 2000; Swanborn & de Glopper, 1999). Similarly, when an adult reads storybooks to young children, the children are more likely to develop their vocabularies if the adult occasionally stops to talk about potentially unfamiliar words (Brabham & Lynch-Brown, 2002).

What dose worrisome meen?
what is and dose prevaricate mean?
Sobreuctl?

ARTIFACT 9-1 **Worrisome.** Regular reading introduces children to new vocabulary. On this page of her fifth-grade journal, 10-year-old Amaryth has jotted down unfamiliar words from a book she is reading.

Syntactic Development

Which one of the following sentences is grammatically correct?

- Growing children need nutritious food and lots of exercise.
- Experience students find to be many junior high school an unsettling.

You undoubtedly realized that the first sentence is grammatically correct and the second is not. But *how* were you able to tell the difference? Can you describe the specific grammatical rules you used to make your decisions?

Rules of syntax—the rules we use to combine words into meaningful sentences—are incredibly complex (e.g., N. Chomsky, 2006). Yet much of our knowledge about syntax is unconscious. Although we can produce acceptable sentences and readily understand the sentences of others, we cannot always put our finger on exactly what it is we know about language that allows us to do these things.

Despite the complex and elusive nature of syntactic rules, children seem to pick up on them rather quickly. By the time children reach school age, they have mastered many of the basics of sentence construction (Haskill & Corts, 2010; McNeill, 1970; Reich, 1986). Even so, they are apt to show gaps in their syntactic knowledge throughout the elementary school years and, to a lesser extent, in the secondary school years as well. Following are noteworthy aspects of syntactic development over the course of childhood and adolescence.

Early syntactic knowledge builds on awareness of patterns in speech. In one study, 7-month-olds heard a series of "sentences" each comprised of three nonsense syllables (e.g., *ga*, *na*, *ti*, *li*). Infants in Group 1 consistently heard them in a predictable "ABA" pattern (e.g., "Ga ti ga," "Li na li"), whereas infants in Group 2 consistently heard them in an "ABB" pattern (e.g., "Ga ti ti," "Li na na"; Marcus, Vijayan, Bandi Rao, & Vishton, 1999). After losing interest in these sentences (reflecting *habituation*), they heard another series of "sentences" with new nonsense syllables.[8] Some of these sentences followed the ABA pattern (e.g., "Wo fe wo"), whereas others followed the ABB pattern (e.g., "Wo fe fe"). The infants paid greater attention when listening to the pattern that was new to them, showing that the pattern they had heard before was "the same old thing," even though new sounds were involved.

Some syntax appears in children's earliest word combinations. Initially, children use only single words to express their thoughts. At 18 months, Teresa's son Connor would simply say "mo" if he wanted more of whatever he was eating or playing with at the time. And like many toddlers, he would stretch out his arms and plead "Up!" when he wanted to be carried or cuddled. Developmentalists sometimes use the word **holophrase** to refer to such one-word "sentences" (Byrnes & Wasik, 2009). As toddlers begin to combine words into two-word "sentences" in the latter half of their second year, simple syntactic rules guide their constructions. Their two-word combinations frequently reflect description ("Pillow dirty"), location ("Baby table"), or possession ("Adam hat") (R. Brown, 1973, p. 141). Children's early multiple-word sentences, known as **telegraphic speech**, include lexical words (rather than grammatical words) almost exclusively. By using such words, children maximize the meaning their short sentences convey—they get "the most bang for the buck"—just as many adolescents and adults do when they send text messages. As children's sentences increase in length, they also increase in syntactic complexity—for instance, by including a subject, verb, and object (e.g., "I ride horsie") or describing both an action and a location ("Put truck window," "Adam put it box") (R. Brown, 1973, p. 205). Sometime before age 3 children begin to include grammatical words—*the*, *and*, *because*, and so on—in their sentences (O'Grady, 1997; Owens, 2008).

Young children rely heavily on word order when interpreting sentences. By the time they are 1½, children have some understanding that, at least in English, word order affects meaning (Gertner, Fisher, & Eisengart, 2006; Hirsh-Pasek & Golinkoff, 1996). For instance, they know that "Big Bird is washing Cookie Monster" means something different from

---

[8]Habituation is defined in Chapter 2.

holophrase
A single word used to express a complete thought; commonly observed in children's earliest speech.

telegraphic speech
Short, grammatically incomplete sentences that include lexical (rather than grammatical) words almost exclusively; common in toddlers.

"Cookie Monster is washing Big Bird." Yet young children are sometimes misled by the order in which words appear (O'Grady, 1997). Many preschoolers seem to apply a general rule that a pronoun refers to the noun that immediately precedes it. Consider the sentence "John said that Peter washed him." Many 4-year-olds think that *him* refers to *Peter* and so conclude that Peter washed himself. Similarly, kindergartners are apt to have trouble with the sentence "Because she was tired, Mommy was sleeping" because no noun appears before *she*.

Children also use information about the prevalence of particular kinds of word combinations. Some theorists suggest that acquiring syntax involves discovering the probabilities with which various word combinations appear in sentences (MacWhinney & Chang, 1995; Saffran, 2003; Sirois, Buckingham, & Shultz, 2000). Children may notice that *the* is usually followed by names of things or by "describing" words (e.g., they might hear "the dog," "the picnic," or "the pretty hat"). In contrast, *the* is rarely followed by words that identify specific actions (e.g., they never hear "the do" or "the went").

Children attend to word meaning when making inferences about syntactic rules. Children occasionally engage in **semantic bootstrapping**, the process of using word meanings as a basis for forming syntactic categories (Bates & MacWhinney, 1987; S. A. Gelman & Kalish, 2006; Pinker, 1984, 1987). They may notice that labels for people and concrete objects always serve particular functions in sentences, that action words serve other functions, that spatial-relationship and direction words serve still others, and so on. Through this process they gradually acquire an intuitive understanding of nouns, verbs, prepositions, and other parts of speech—an understanding that allows them to use various kinds of words appropriately in sentences.

Children's questions increasingly incorporate multiple syntactic rules. In some languages it's very easy to ask questions. In Chinese, for instance, a person can change a statement into a question simply by adding *ma* to the end of the sentence. In English, asking questions is more complicated and requires switching the order of the subject and verb (from "You are hungry" to "Are you hungry?"). When past tense is involved, asking a question requires putting the auxiliary verb but *not* the main verb first ("Have you eaten yet?"). And when something other than a yes or no answer is called for, a question word (e.g., *who, what, where, how*) must also appear at the beginning ("What did you eat?").

English-speaking children seem to master these question-asking rules one step at a time. Initially, their questions may be nothing more than telegraphic sentences with a rise in pitch at the end (e.g., "Kitty go home?") (R. Brown, 1973, p. 141). At about age 2½, they attach question words to the beginning, and sometime in their third year, they add an auxiliary verb such as *is* or *does*. However, preschoolers often neglect one or more of the rules for asking questions. For instance, they may ask "What you want?" (forgetting to add the auxiliary verb) or "What you will do?" (forgetting to put the auxiliary verb before the subject) (de Villiers, 1995, pp. 516, 518). But by the time they are 5, most English-speaking children have mastered the correct syntax for questions (de Villiers, 1995).

Children tend to learn general rules for word endings before they learn the many exceptions. Knowledge of syntax includes awareness of when to use word endings (suffixes) such as *-s, -er,* and *-ed.* When children first learn the rules for using suffixes (e.g., *-s* indicates plural, *-er* indicates a comparison, and *-ed* indicates past tense), they often apply these rules indiscriminately, without regard for exceptions. Thus a child might say "I have two *foots*," "Chocolate is *gooder* than vanilla," or "I *goed* to Grandma's house." This phenomenon, known as **overregularization**, is especially common during the preschool and early elementary years. It gradually diminishes as children master the irregular forms of various words: The plural of *foot* is *feet*, the comparative form of *good* is *better*, the past tense of *go* is *went*, and so on (Cazden, 1968; Marcus, 1996; Siegler, 1994).

Yet most high school students (and many adults as well) haven't completely mastered the irregularities of the English language (Marcus, 1996). For instance, throughout his high school years, Jeanne's son Jeff consistently said "I have *broughten.* . ." despite Jeanne's frequent reminders that he should say "I have *brought.* . ."

semantic bootstrapping
Using knowledge of word meanings to derive knowledge about syntactic categories and structures.

overregularization
Use of a syntactic rule in situations where an exception to the rule applies.

The ability to comprehend passive sentences evolves gradually during the preschool and elementary school years. In a passive sentence, the subject of the sentence is the recipient, rather than the agent, of the action that the verb conveys. Passive sentences frequently confuse young children, who may incorrectly attribute the action to the subject. Consider these two sentences:

> The boy is pushed by the girl.
> The cup is washed by the girl.

Preschoolers are more likely to be confused by the first sentence—that is, to think that the boy is the one doing the pushing—than by the second sentence (Karmiloff-Smith, 1979). The first sentence has two possible "actors," but the second sentence has only one: Both boys and girls can push someone else, but cups can't wash girls. Complete mastery of passive sentences doesn't appear until the late elementary school years (O'Grady, 1997; Sudhalter & Braine, 1985).

Children can be confused by sentences with multiple clauses. At about age 4 children begin to produce simple subordinate clauses, such as those that follow and modify nouns (e.g., "This is the toy *that I want*") (Owens, 2008, p. 295). Yet throughout the elementary school years children struggle to understand certain kinds of multiple-clause sentences. Sentences with one clause embedded in the middle of another clause seem to be especially difficult, particularly if the noun tying the clauses together has a different function in each clause. Consider the sentence "The dog *that was chased by the boy* is angry" (Owens, 2008, p. 346). The dog is the subject of the main clause ("The dog . . . is angry") but is the recipient of the action in the embedded clause (". . . [dog] was chased by the boy"). Seventh graders easily understand such sentences, but younger children overrely on word order to interpret them and so may conclude that the boy, rather than the dog, is angry (Owens, 2008).

Knowledge of syntactic rules continues to develop in the later elementary and secondary levels. Beginning in the upper elementary and middle school grades, children may be taught to identify the various parts of a sentence (e.g., subject, direct object, prepositional phrase, subordinate clause) about which they acquired intuitive knowledge years earlier. They also study various verb tenses (e.g., present, past, present progressive) even though they have been using these tenses in their everyday speech for quite some time. In middle school and high school, adolescents learn more subtle aspects of syntax, such as subject–verb and noun–pronoun agreement, correct uses of *that* versus *which* to introduce subordinate clauses, functions of punctuation marks such as colons and semicolons, and so on. They rarely develop such knowledge on their own, however. Instead, most of their syntactic development probably occurs as the result of formal instruction, especially through courses in language arts, English composition, and foreign languages (e.g., Pence & Justice, 2008).

Fostering Syntactic Development

Especially as they are learning the more complex and subtle aspects of syntax, children and adolescents often benefit from ongoing instruction and practice in various syntactic structures. Following are several examples of how caregivers and teachers can promote youngsters' syntactic development.

• **Expand on young children's telegraphic speech.** When young children speak in telegraphic sentences, caregivers can engage in **expansion** by repeating the sentences in a more mature form. When a toddler says, "Doggy eat," mother might respond by saying, "Yes, the doggy is eating his dinner." Expansion gives children gentle feedback about the incompleteness of their own utterances and possibly encourages them to use more complex syntactic forms (C. Bouchard et al., 2010; N. Scherer & Olswang, 1984; Strapp & Federico, 2000).

• **Teach irregular forms of verbs and comparative adjectives.** Children do not always hear the irregular forms of verbs and adjectives in everyday speech (Owens, 2008). Their young playmates may talk about what's *badder* or *worser,* and many adults confuse the past tenses of the verbs *lay* and *lie* (which are *laid* and *lay*, respectively). Some formal instruction

expansion
Repetition of a child's short utterances in more complete and grammatically correct forms.

NONRESTRICTIVE CLAUSE? Especially in adolescence and adulthood, many advances in language development probably occur as a result of formal instruction.

in irregular forms may therefore be the only way that children discover which terms are correct and which are not.

• **Describe various sentence structures, and give children considerable practice in their use.** Having children examine and practice common syntactic structures (active and passive voice, independent and dependent clauses, etc.) has at least two benefits. First, children should be better able to vary their sentence structure as they write—a strategy associated with more sophisticated writing (Beers & Nagy, 2009; Spivey, 1997). Second, learning the labels for such structures (e.g., *passive voice*) in English should help them acquire analogous structures in other languages they study at a later time.

• **Provide ample opportunities for children to express their ideas in relatively formal contexts, and give feedback about appropriate syntax.** In typical everyday conversation, adults and children alike often use incomplete sentences and are lax in their adherence to grammatical rules (Cook & Newson, 1996; D. Lightfoot, 1999). But what's common in casual speech is often frowned on in writing and public speaking. In formal and public situations (e.g., a letter to the editor of a local newspaper or a presentation to a large group), correct grammar is, in many people's minds, an indication that the writer or speaker is educated and someone to take seriously (Purcell-Gates, 1995; H. L. Smith, 1998).

Development of Listening Skills

As you might guess, children's ability to understand what they hear is closely related to their semantic and syntactic development. The development of listening skills is characterized by several additional trends as well.

In the first year, infants learn to focus primarily on sounds important in their native language. The basic elements of spoken language—all the consonants and vowels a language includes—are collectively known as **phonemes**. Phonemes are the smallest units of speech that indicate differences in meaning in a particular language. For instance, the word *bite* has three phonemes: a "buh" sound, an "eye" sound, and a "tuh" sound. If we change any one of these sounds—for instance, if we change *b* to *f (fight)*, long *i* to long *a (bait)*, or *t* to *k (bike)*—we get a new word with a different meaning.

As you have already learned, the ability to identify and distinguish sounds is a crucial part of language development. Beginning on day one, infants can discriminate among a wide variety of phonemes, including many that they don't hear in the speech around them (Aldridge, Stillman, & Bower, 2001; Jusczyk, 1995; Werker & Lalonde, 1988). They prefer human speech over nonspeech sounds and regular speech over recordings of the same speech that has been distorted by playing it backward (Gervain & Mehler, 2010). Newborn babies even prefer to listen to their native language over other languages, suggesting that they have learned something about language patterns from exposure to their mother's speech during prenatal development (Mehler et al., 1988; Moon, Cooper, & Fifer, 1993). Several months after birth, infants show a noticeable preference for sounds and words they hear frequently. Five-month-olds pay more attention to their own names than to other, similar-sounding words (Mandel, Jusczyk, & Pisoni, 1995). When infants reach 8 or 9 months, they also prefer listening to the rhythms of their native language (Jusczyk & Aslin, 1995; Saffran, Aslin, & Newport, 1996).

This early tuning-in to a particular language gradually alters what infants "hear" and "don't hear" in speech. By the time children are a year old, they primarily hear the differences that are important in their own languages (Gervain & Mehler, 2010; Jusczyk, 1997; Werker & Tees, 1999). One-year-old infants in English-speaking countries continue to hear the difference between the "L" and "R" sounds, a distinction critical for making such discriminations as *lap* versus *rap* and *lice* versus *rice*. In contrast, Japanese children gradually lose the ability to

phonemes
Smallest units of a spoken language that signify differences in meaning.

tell this difference, presumably because the Japanese language treats the two sounds as a single phoneme. Similarly, babies in English-speaking societies lose the ability to distinguish among various "S" sounds that comprise two or more different phonemes in certain other languages.

As you can see, the first year of life is an important one for learning which differences among speech sounds are essential for understanding one's native language. Yet children continue to fine-tune their discriminative powers throughout early and middle childhood. For instance, they may have some difficulty distinguishing between words that differ by only one phoneme until they are 5 years old (Gerken, 1994; Rayner, Foorman, Perfetti, Pesetsky, & Seidenberg, 2001). Furthermore, they may continue to hear some sound differences not important in their own language until they are 8 to 10 years old (Siegler & Alibali, 2005).

Young children rely more heavily on context than older children, but young-sters of all ages take context into account. Children do not necessarily need to focus on every sound, or even every word, when they listen to what other people say. Eighteen-month-olds often know from the context which word a speaker is going to say after hearing only the first two phonemes (Fernald, Swingley, & Pinto, 2001). Furthermore, using various contextual clues, children often realize that what a speaker says is different from what the speaker actually means (M. Donaldson, 1978; Flavell et al., 2002; Paul, 1990). Hence, kindergartners may correctly conclude that a teacher who asks "Whose jacket do I see lying on the floor?" is actually requesting the jacket's owner to pick it up and put it where it belongs.

Sometimes young children are *too* dependent on context for determining the meaning of language, to the point where they don't listen carefully enough to understand a spoken message accurately. They may instead "hear" what they think the speaker means based on their beliefs about the speaker's intentions. As an example, look at the cows and horses in Figure 9-3. *Are there more cows or more black horses?* There are four cows but only three black horses, so obviously there are more cows. Yet if you ask 6-year-olds this question, they are apt to tell you that there are more black horses. In probing the children's reasoning, it becomes clear that most of them interpret the question as a request to compare only the *black* cows with the black horses. For example, one child defended his incorrect answer by saying, "There's more black horses 'cos there's only two black cows" (M. Donaldson, 1978, p. 44).[9]

Older children and adolescents consider the context in a somewhat different way, in that they compare a message to the reality of the situation. Such a comparison enables them to detect sarcasm—to realize that the speaker actually means the exact opposite of what he or she is saying (Capelli, Nakagawa, & Madden, 1990; Glenwright & Pexman, 2010). They understand that someone who says "Oh, that's just *great!*" in the face of dire circumstances doesn't think the situation is "great" at all.

Cognitive factors influence oral comprehension. Not only does children's ability to understand what they hear depend on their knowledge of word meanings and syntax, but it also depends on their general knowledge about the world. Children can better understand a friend's story about a trip to a fast-food restaurant if they have a script for what such visits typically entail. Children's schemas, scripts, and other knowledge about the world enable them to draw inferences from the things they hear, thus filling gaps in the information actually presented.[10]

In addition, children's ability to understand and remember what they hear is limited to what they can reasonably hold in working memory at a single time (Anthony, Lonigan, & Dyer, 1996; Florit, Roch, Altoè, & Levorato, 2009). When information exceeds their working

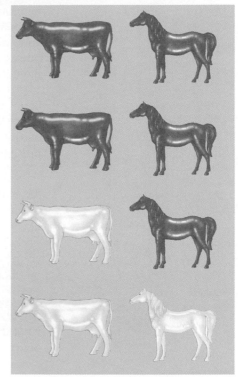

FIGURE 9-3 **Are there more cows or more black horses?** Many young children interpret the question as a request to compare the numbers of *black* cows and black horses.

---

[9]This task might remind you of Piaget's *class inclusion* problems. Piaget interpreted children's responses from the perspective of logical reasoning processes, but here we see a different factor at work: Children's inferences about a speaker's intentions overshadow their attention to the question's literal meaning.

[10]To refresh your memory about *schemas* and *scripts*, reread the section "Long-Term Memory" in Chapter 7.

memory capacity, it will, as a common expression puts it, "go in one ear and out the other."[11] Because young children tend to have less working memory capacity than older children and adults, they will be especially limited in their ability to understand and remember what others tell them. Preschoolers, for instance, often have trouble remembering and following directions with multiple steps (L. French & Brown, 1977).

Children's general cognitive abilities play a role as well. Interpreting messages in non-literal ways requires abstract thinking and an ability to draw analogies across diverse situations (Winner, 1988). Given what we know about the development of abstract thought, it is hardly surprising that children have difficulty understanding metaphors and proverbs in the preschool and early elementary years.

Young children have an overly simplistic view of what "good listening" is. Children in the early elementary grades believe they are good listeners if they simply sit quietly without interrupting the person speaking. Older children (e.g., 10- and 11-year-olds) are more likely to recognize that good listening also requires an understanding of what is being said (T. M. McDevitt, Spivey, Sheehan, Lennon, & Story, 1990.). And in adolescence, many youngsters begin to realize that being a *socially effective* listener also involves listening to others in an open-minded, nonjudgmental, and empathic manner (Imhof, 2001).

Preschool and elementary school children do not always listen actively or critically or follow up when confused. Children regularly ignore ambiguities and blatant inconsistencies in what they hear and read. Children's **comprehension monitoring**—the process of evaluating one's comprehension of oral and written material—develops slowly over childhood and well into the adolescent and adult years (Markman, 1979; Skarakis-Doyle & Dempsey, 2008).

Children may also fail to ask for assistance when they do feel confused. In a series of studies (T. M. McDevitt, 1990; T. M. McDevitt et al., 1990), children in grades 1, 3, and 5 were given the following dilemma:

> This is a story about a girl named Mary. Mary is at school listening to her teacher, Ms. Brown. Ms. Brown explains how to use a new computer that she just got for their classroom. She tells the children in the classroom how to use the computer. Mary doesn't understand the teacher's directions. She's confused. What should Mary do? (T. M. McDevitt, 1990, p. 570)

Some children responded that Mary should ask the teacher for further explanation. But others said that Mary should either listen more carefully or seek clarification of the procedure from other children. Many children, younger ones especially, believe it is inappropriate to ask a teacher for help, perhaps because they lack confidence or have previously been discouraged from asking questions at school or home (Marchand & Skinner, 2007; T. M. McDevitt, 1990; Puustinen, Lyyra, Metsäpelto, & Pulkkinen, 2008).

Older children and adolescents become increasingly able to find multiple meanings in messages. As children move into the middle and secondary grades, they become aware that some messages are ambiguous and have two or more possible meanings (Bearison & Levey, 1977; Nippold, 1988; Owens, 2008). They also become better able to understand and explain **figurative speech**, language that communicates meaning beyond a literal interpretation of its words. For instance, they understand that idioms should not be taken at face value—that a person who "hits the roof" doesn't really hit the roof and that someone who is "tied up" isn't necessarily bound with rope. In addition, they become increasingly adept at interpreting similes and metaphors (e.g., "Her hands are like ice," "That man is the Rock of Gibraltar"). And in the late elementary years, they begin to draw generalizations from such proverbs as "Look before you leap" and "Don't put the cart before the horse." In MyEducationLab, you can observe how children's ability to understand proverbs improves with age. Whereas 10-year-old Kent seems baffled by the old adage "A rolling stone gathers no moss," 14-year-old Alicia offers a reasonable explanation: "Maybe when you go through things too fast, you don't collect anything from it." Adolescents' ability to interpret proverbs in a generalized, abstract fashion continues to develop throughout the secondary school years (Owens, 2008).

MyEducationLab

Observe the developmental progression in understanding figurative speech as you listen to Kent and Alicia interpret proverbs in the "Cognitive Development" videos for middle childhood and late adolescence. (Find Video Examples in Topic 9 of MyEducationLab).

comprehension monitoring
The process of evaluating one's comprehension of oral messages or written material.

figurative speech
Speech that communicates meaning beyond a literal interpretation of its words.

---

[11]You can remind yourself of the characteristics of working memory by returning to Chapter 7.

Promoting Listening Comprehension

Parents, teachers, caregivers, and others who work with children must take into account their limited listening comprehension skills. Following are three suggestions for adults who work with young people.

• **Take children's semantic and syntactic development into account when speaking to them, and check frequently to be sure they understand.** Although children profit from exposure to a rich corpus of language, adults must be careful to use vocabulary and syntactic structures that do not significantly exceed children's grasp in situations when children need to understand the gist of the message. Furthermore, rather than assuming that their messages have been understood, adults should in some way assess children's understandings, perhaps by asking questions, having children restate ideas in their own words, or arranging for them to demonstrate what they've learned through actions or pictures (Jalongo, 2008).

• **Adjust the length of verbal presentations to the attention span of the age-group.** As cognitive process theorists tells us, people of all ages can understand a message only when they are paying attention, and they can handle only a limited amount of information at a time. Given such limitations, children and adolescents alike often benefit from brief and repeated messages (e.g., Wasik, Karweit, Burns, & Brodsky, 1998).

• **Encourage critical listening.** Sometime around ages 3 to 6, children begin to realize that what people say is not necessarily what is true (e.g., Koenig, Clément, & Harris, 2004; K. Lee, Cameron, Doucette, & Talwar, 2002). Yet throughout the elementary and secondary school years, children and adolescents sometimes have difficulty separating fact from fiction in the messages they hear. Children who are taught not to believe everything they hear are more likely to evaluate messages for errors, falsehoods, and ambiguities. For example, when children are reminded that television commercials are designed to persuade them to buy something, they are less likely to be influenced by the commercials (Calvert, 2008; Halpern, 1998; D. F. Roberts, Christenson, Gibson, Mooser, & Goldberg, 1980).

In the context of the conversations and instructions that take place in the classroom and other group settings, adults can find many ways to enhance children's capacity for effective listening. You can see examples of adults fostering these abilities in the Development and Practice feature "Promoting Listening Skills in Children."

Development of Speaking Skills

As children become more adept at understanding what other people say, they also become more skilled at expressing their own thoughts, feelings, and wishes. Children's increasing proficiency in oral language is the result of many things: better muscular control of the lips, tongue, and other parts of the vocal apparatus; more semantic and syntactic knowledge; growing awareness of what listeners are apt to know and believe; and so on. But to a considerable degree, the development of speaking skills also comes from children's desire to communicate effectively. Following are several trends that characterize the development of speech and other means of communication in infancy, childhood, and adolescence.

In the first year of life, children become increasingly proficient in making speech sounds. Between 1 and 2 months of age, infants typically begin **cooing**, making vowel sounds in an almost "singing" manner (e.g., "aaaaaaa," "ooooooo"). Sometime around 6 months, they begin **babbling**, combining consonant and vowel sounds into syllables that they repeat over and over (e.g., "mamamamama," "doodoodoo") without apparent meaning. With time, babbling becomes increasingly speechlike in nature, as infants combine different syllables into language-like utterances. Also with time, infants gradually drop the sounds they don't hear in the speech around them (Locke, 1993). In essence, infants first babble in a universal "language" that includes a wide variety of phonemes but later babble only in their native tongue.

Infants and young children sometimes use gestures to communicate. During their first year of life, infants try to communicate through their actions. An infant might put his fingers in his mouth to indicate that he wants something to eat. A toddler might wrinkle her nose and sniff as a way of "talking" about flowers. To some degree, the use of such gestures seems

cooing
Making and repeating vowel sounds (e.g., "oooooo"); common in early infancy.

babbling
Repeating certain consonant-vowel syllables over and over (e.g., "mama-mama"); common in the latter half of the first year.

DEVELOPMENT AND PRACTICE
Promoting Listening Skills in Children

Present only small amounts of information at one time.

- A preschool teacher helps the 3- and 4-year-olds in her class make "counting books" to take home. She has previously prepared nine sheets of paper (each with a different number from 1 to 9) for each child. She has also assembled a variety of objects that the children can paste on the pages to depict the numbers (two buttons for the "2" page, five pieces of macaroni for the "5" page, etc.). As she engages the children in the project, she describes only one or two steps of the process at a time. (Early Childhood)

- As a kindergarten teacher reads aloud a story to children, she stops at the end of each page, allowing children time to absorb the segment and make comments or ask questions. After allowing children a brief time to contribute to the discussion, the teacher resumes with the story. (Early Childhood)

Expect children to listen attentively only for short periods.

- An infant caregiver notices that the babies in her care like to watch her face as she talks to them during diaper changes and bottle feedings. After a few minutes of listening and watching her facial expressions, however, the infants are apt to look away. (Infancy)

- A kindergarten teacher has learned that most of his students can listen quietly to books on tape for no more than 10 or 15 minutes at a stretch, and he plans his daily schedule accordingly. (Early Childhood)

Discuss the components of good listening.

- At the beginning of the school year, a kindergarten teacher explains how children are to act during storytime. After soliciting input from

the children, the teacher posts several guidelines: (1) Pay attention to the story. (2) Stay seated. (3) Keep your hands to yourself. (4) Take your turn in discussions. (Early Childhood)

- A second-grade teacher explains to her students that "good listening" involves more than just sitting quietly, that it also involves paying attention and trying to understand what the speaker is saying. Later, after a police officer has visited her class to discuss bicycle safety, she asks the children to repeat some of the safety precautions the officer mentioned. (Middle Childhood)

Discuss courses of action that children should take when they don't understand a speaker.

- A preschool teacher tells children it is time for free choice. The children move around the room, selecting one activity or another, but a new boy walks aimlessly. The teacher talks with him privately, explaining what free choice means and encouraging him to ask her questions when he's confused by her instructions. (Early Childhood)

- At the beginning of the year, a middle-school teacher explains to students that he will try to be clear in his explanations but there will be times when he forgets to mention information necessary to understand a lesson or assignment. Students have several solutions they can try when unclear about something—they can figure it out themselves, ask for help from another student, or ask him to clarify. He tells the students that each of these strategies is appropriate in certain circumstances and he would rather they try to get help somehow instead of remaining confused. (Early Adolescence)

MyEducationLab

Observe one girl's effective use of gestures in the "Conversation with a Five-Year-Old" video. (Find Video Examples in Topic 9 of MyEducationLab.)

to pave the way for later language development (Goodwyn & Acredolo, 1998; McGregor, Rohlfing, Bean, & Marschner, 2009; Volterra, Caselli, Capirci, & Pizzuto, 2005).[12] Youngsters don't entirely abandon gestures as they gain proficiency in spoken language, however. You can observe a young girl's effective use of gestures while speaking in the "Conversation with a Five-Year-Old" video in MyEducationLab.

Pronunciation continues to improve in the early elementary years. As you've discovered, children say their first word sometime around their first birthday, and by age 2 or so most children talk a great deal. Yet children typically do not master all the phonemes of the English language until they are about 8 years old (Hulit & Howard, 2006; Owens, 2008). During the preschool years, they are likely to have difficulty pronouncing *r* and *th* (they might say "wabbit" instead of "rabbit" and "dat" instead of "that"). Most children have acquired these sounds by the time they are 6, but at this age they may still have trouble with such consonant blends as *spl* and *thr* (Byrnes & Wasik, 2009; Owens, 2008; Pence & Justice, 2008). Recall the kindergarten teacher's reference to Mario's "slight accent." Mario mastered Spanish pronunciation by age 3. A few months later, he could produce many of the additional phonemes required for English. Nevertheless, Spanish sounds occasionally crept into Mario's English for several years thereafter (Fantini, 1985).

---

[12]Gestures also play a role in young children's reasoning (see Chapter 7).

As children grow older, their conversations with others increase in length, coherence, and depth. Early conversations tend to be short. Most young children are quite willing and able to introduce new topics into a conversation, but they have difficulty maintaining a sustained interchange about a single topic (Brinton & Fujiki, 1984; Byrnes & Wasik, 2009; K. Nelson, 1996a). As they grow older, they can carry on lengthier discussions about a single issue or event. And in adolescence, the content of their conversations gradually becomes more abstract (Owens, 2008).

Children become increasingly able to adapt their speech to the characteristics of their listeners. As early as age 3, preschoolers use simpler language with toddlers than they do with adults and peers (Shatz & Gelman, 1973). Yet preschoolers and elementary school children don't always take their listeners' visual perspectives and prior knowledge into account and so may provide insufficient information for listeners to understand what they are saying (Glucksberg & Krauss, 1967). For instance, a child might ask "What's this?" without regard for whether the listener can see the object in question. To some extent, such speech may reflect *egocentrism*.[13] However, it may also be the result of young children's lack of proficiency in precisely describing the objects and events they are currently experiencing or have previously witnessed (T. M. McDevitt & Ford, 1987).

As children grow older, they become increasingly able to take other people's knowledge and perspectives into account and so are better able to make their meanings clear (D. Matthews, Lieven, & Tomasello, 2007; Sonnenschein, 1988). They also become better able to read the subtle nonverbal signals (e.g., puzzled brows, lengthy silences) that indicate others' confusion about their messages. Children who spend a lot of time interacting with different kinds of listeners may become especially proficient in adapting to listeners' characteristics. For instance, children of the Ituri Forest of the Democratic Republic of Congo regularly interact with children who are younger or older themselves, giving them numerous occasions to adjust their speech to listeners with varied perspectives (Rogoff, Morelli, & Chavajay, 2010).

Over time, children become more skillful at narratives. Beginning in the preschool years, children can tell a story, or **narrative**—an account of a sequence of events, either real or fictional, that are logically interconnected (McKeough, 1995; Sutton-Smith, 1986). Young children's narratives are usually quite short, as illustrated by one 5-year-old's account of what she did at her preschool earlier in the day:

> My class and me went outside to play. And we played in the sprinkler and we played on the toys and we made soap.

By age 5 or 6, many children can create a narrative that reflects a reasonable sequence of events and includes simple cause-and-effect relationships between characters' mental states and behaviors (Kemper, 1984; McKeough, 1995; Nicolopoulou & Richner, 2007). Narratives become increasingly complex during the elementary years. Definite plot lines begin to emerge, and descriptions of people's thoughts, motives, and emotions become increasingly sophisticated (Bauer, 2006; Kemper, 1984; Owens, 2008). You can observe the development of narratives in three videos in MyEducationLab: "Conversation with a Five-Year-Old," "A Seven-Year-Old's Nonfictional Narrative," and "A Thirteen-Year-Old's Fictional Narrative."

Improving Your Observation Skills

Look and listen, bro. The young boy at left is communicating with his baby brother at right. What evidence is there that the boy is adjusting his speech according to his perceptions of his younger brother's needs? Compare your response with the explanation at the end of the chapter.

MyEducationLab

Observe the development of narratives in three videos in the Video Examples section in Topic 9 of MyEducationLab: "Conversation with a Five-Year-Old," "A Seven-Year-Old's Nonfictional Narrative," and "A Thirteen-Year-Old's Fictional Narrative."

narrative
Verbal account of a temporal sequence of logically interconnected events; a story.

---

[13]Piaget's concept of egocentrism is examined in Chapter 6.

Preparing for Your Licensure Examination

Your teaching test might ask you about how community membership affects a child's language development.

In learning to relay events and experiences, children acquire a cultural perspective on what other people want to hear. In her classic research, linguistic anthropologist **Shirley Brice Heath** (1983) identified two distinct styles of narrating events in working class communities in the Piedmont Carolinas of the United States. In the predominantly European American community of Roadville, children relayed factual accounts of their personal experiences, whereas in the mostly African American community of Trackton, children learned to tell entertaining and sometimes far-fetched fictional stories. Children's narratives in other cultures also communicate such cultural qualities as moral standards, gender roles, and political orientations (Sterponi, 2010).

Creative and figurative expressions emerge during the elementary years and continue into adolescence. Many children enjoy "playing" with language in some way (Nippold, 1988; Owens, 2008). Good friends might converse in "pig Latin" in which any initial consonants are moved to the ends of words, and a long-*a* sound is added to each word. (As an illustration, the sentence *This sentence is written in pig Latin* would be "Is-thay entence-say is-ay itten-wray in-ay ig-pay atin-lay.") Children also take delight in jokes and riddles that play on the multiple meanings of words or similar-sounding phrases ("How much do pirates pay for their earrings?" "A buccaneer"). Creative wordplay is especially common in many African American communities (e.g., Smitherman, 2007). It sometimes takes the form of **playing the dozens**, playful teasing of one another through exaggerated insults—for example, "Your mama's so fat she's got to sleep in the Grand Canyon" (Goodwin, 2006, p. 232; J. Lee, 2009).

Adolescents sometimes use their own teen lingo in conversing with peers. Many adolescents express themselves in ways that are unique to their age-group, or perhaps to a small group of friends. For example, over the years, teenagers have used a variety of adjectives—*cool, boss, radical, wicked awesome,* and so on—to describe something they really like. At age 16, Jeanne's son Alex insisted on addressing everyone (including his mother) as "Dude." Such expressions help adolescents communicate affection and establish themselves as belonging to particular groups (Androutsopoulos & Georgakopoulou, 2010; J. R. Harris, 1995).

Promoting Speaking Skills

To help children and adolescents develop their speaking skills, teachers and other adults should, of course, give them many opportunities to speak. The following strategies can be beneficial:

• **Regularly invite infants to join you in "conversation."** In the "Cognitive Development," "Intelligence," and "Literacy" videos for infancy in MyEducationLab, you can observe several "conversations" that 16-month-old Corwin has with his mother. Although Corwin says few words distinctly enough to be understood, he knows how to take turns in the dialogue and understands enough of what his mother says to respond appropriately to her questions.

As you have learned, not every infant participates in a cultural pattern of dyadic conversations with adults. Some infants gain more experience by eavesdropping on adults' conversations and conversing with other children than by taking part in dyadic interactions with parents. Given this diversity in language socialization, it seems prudent for caregivers to invite infants to interact verbally without forcing these exchanges. Gentle attempts to encourage verbal interaction are generally well received by infants when adults respect infants' right to opt out of the conversation. For example, young infants as early as 3 or 4 months of age are able to take turns in verbal interactions with adults, and many enjoy mimicking the intonations (e.g., changes in pitch and stress) that a caregiver uses (Masataka, 1992). When a caregiver mimics *their* vocalizations, infants' speechlike sounds increase in frequency (K. Bloom, Russell, & Wassenberg, 1987). Another effective strategy is to teach infants gestures they can use to communicate their wishes. For instance, caregivers might teach babies signs for *more* and *please* (see Figure 9-4). Infants as young as 6 months old can successfully learn a few hand signs to communicate with caregivers (Acredolo & Goodwyn, 1990; Góngora & Farkas, 2009).

MyEducationLab

Observe Corwin's turn-taking ability in the "Cognitive Development," "Intelligence," and "Literacy" videos for infancy in the Video Examples section in Topic 9 of MyEducationLab.

playing the dozens
Friendly, playful exchange of insults, common in some African American communities; also called *joaning* or *sounding.*

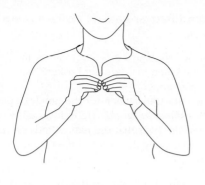

"More"

Place your fingertips together in front of your chest, as if adding something to the top of a pile.

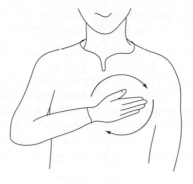

"Please"

Hold your hand close to your heart with palm facing toward your chest, and move it clockwise (from an observer's viewpoint) to indicate pleasure.

FIGURE 9-4   More, please. Children as young as 6 months can be taught to communicate through simple gestures. Examples of useful gestures are the signs for *more* and *please* in American Sign Language.

• **Let children know when their messages are difficult to understand.** People of all ages occasionally have trouble communicating their thoughts clearly to others. Young children may have particular difficulty because of their limited ability to consider the knowledge and perspectives of their listeners. Asking questions or expressing confusion when children describe events and ideas ambiguously should gradually help them express their thoughts more precisely and take into account what their listeners do and do not know (e.g., D. Matthews et al., 2007).

• **Ask children to recall real events and speculate about fictional ones.** Adults often pose questions that encourage children to respond in narrative form. For instance, a teacher might ask, "What did you do this weekend?" or say "Make up a story about what might happen if someone brought a cow to show-and-tell." Giving children opportunities to narrate events, either actual incidents or fictional creations, provides a context in which they can practice speaking for sustained periods and build on the rich traditions of their cultures (Hale-Benson, 1986; Hemphill & Snow, 1996; McCarty & Watahomigie, 1998).

Storytelling ability can be enhanced by training and practice (McKeough, 1995; J. R. Price, Roberts, & Jackson, 2006). Consider how 6-year-old Leanne's ability to tell a story improved over a 2-month period as a result of specific instruction in how to conceptualize and tell stories:

> **Before instruction:**
> A girl—and a boy—and a kind old horse. They got mad at each other. That the end. (McKeough, 1995, p. 170)

> **After instruction:**
> Once upon a time there was a girl. She was playing with her toys and—um—she asked her mom if she could go outside—to play in the snow. But her mom said no. And then she was very sad. And—and she had to play. So she she [sic] asked her mom if she could go outside and she said yes. She jumped in the snow and she was having fun and she had an idea and she jumped in the snow and she feeled happy. (McKeough, 1995, p. 170)

• **Encourage creativity in oral language.** Linguistic creativity can be expressed in many ways, including through stories, poems, songs, rap, jokes, and puns. Such forms of language not only encourage creative language use but also help children identify parallels between seemingly dissimilar objects or events. Recognizing commonalities enables children to construct similes, metaphors, and other analogies. Hyperbole can be encouraged as well, as long as children realize that they are intentionally stretching the truth.

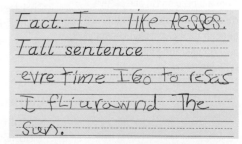

ARTIFACT 9-2   Tall tale. Morris (age 6) shows that he knows the difference between a fact ("I like recess") and a "tall sentence" ("Every time I go to recess I fly around the sun").

The playful use of language can help children discover general characteristics of language, as an incident in Mario's childhood illustrates:

> Seven-year-old Mario tells his parents a joke that he has heard at school earlier in the day. He relates the joke in English: "What did the bird say when his cage got broken?" His parents have no idea what the bird said, so he tells them, "Cheap, cheap!"
>
> Mario's parents find the joke amusing, so he later translates it for the family's Spanish-speaking nanny: *"¿Qué dijo el pájaro cuando se le rompió la jaula?"* He follows up with the bird's answer: *"Barato, barato."* Mario is surprised to discover that the nanny finds no humor in the joke. He knows that he has somehow failed to convey the point of the joke but cannot figure out where he went wrong. (Fantini, 1985, p. 72)[14]

The joke, of course, gets lost in translation. The Spanish word *barato* means "cheap" but has no resemblance to the sound that a bird makes. Only several years later did Mario understand that humor that depends on wordplay does not always translate from one language to another (Fantini, 1985). His eventual understanding of this principle was an aspect of his growing *metalinguistic awareness*, a topic we examine shortly.

Development of Pragmatics

MyEducationLab

Observe many pragmatic skills (e.g., maintaining eye contact, making polite requests) in the "Conversation with a Five-Year-Old" video. (Find Video Examples in Topic 9 of MyEducationLab.)

The pragmatic aspects of language include verbal and nonverbal strategies for communicating effectively with others. Strategies for initiating conversations, changing the subject, telling stories, and arguing persuasively are all forms of pragmatic knowledge. Also falling within the domain of pragmatics are **sociolinguistic behaviors**—behaviors that are considered polite and socially acceptable in verbal interactions in one's particular culture.

Most children begin to acquire pragmatic skills (e.g., prefacing a request with "please" and responding politely to other people's questions) long before they reach school age. Preschoolers also learn that certain ways in which they might speak to their peers ("Shut up!" "Get auto here!") are unacceptable when talking to adults (J. B. Bryant, 2001). Children continue to refine their knowledge of pragmatics throughout the preschool years and elementary grades (Byrnes & Wasik, 2009; Garvey & Berninger, 1981; Warren-Leubecker & Bohannon, 1989). You can observe a young girl trying to be polite in the "Conversation with a Five-Year-Old" video in MyEducationLab. Our own observations indicate that this developmental process continues into the middle and high school years as well.

By and large, conversational etiquette and other sociolinguistic conventions are the result of language socialization in children's local cultural groups (Ochs, 2002; Rogoff, 2003). Sometimes adults explicitly teach sociolinguistic behaviors. Mario once explained to his parents how his kindergarten teacher encouraged students to take turns when speaking in class (we present an English translation of Mario's Spanish):

> [A]t school, I have to raise my hand . . . and then wait a long, long time. And then the teacher says: "Now you can speak, Mario," and she makes the other children shut up, and she says, "Mario's speaking now." (Fantini, 1985, p. 83)[15]

Bioecology of Child Development

From a bioecological perspective, children learn rules for communication through their participation in families, peer groups, and other community settings.

Children also learn many conventions through imitating the behaviors of others—perhaps mimicking the way their parents answer the telephone, greet people on the street, and converse with friends and relatives. In addition, the feedback youngsters receive from others (sometimes blatant, sometimes more subtle) may encourage them to behave in certain ways and not others.

Culture and Sociolinguistic Behaviors

Sociolinguistic rules are generally learned sufficiently well that they essentially go underground in a person's mind—they become unconscious standards for guiding speech and

sociolinguistic behaviors
Social conventions (often culture specific) that govern appropriate verbal interaction.

[14]Excerpt from "Case Study: Mario" from LANGUAGE ACQUISITION OF A BILINGUAL CHILD: A SOCIOLOGICAL PERSPECTIVE by A. E. Fantini. Copyright © 1985 by Alvino E. Fantini. Reprinted by permission of the author.
[15]See footnote 14.

OBSERVATION GUIDELINES
Identifying Cultural Differences in Sociolinguistic Conventions

CHARACTERISTIC	LOOK FOR	EXAMPLE	IMPLICATION
Talkativeness	• *Frequent talking*, even about trivial matters, *or* • *Silence* unless something important needs to be said	When Muhammed unexpectedly stops talking to his peers and turns to read his book, the other children think his action is rude.	Don't interpret a child's sudden or lengthy silence as necessarily reflecting apathy or intentional rudeness.
Style of Interacting with Adults	• *Willingness to initiate conversations* with adults, *or* • *Speaking to adults only when spoken to*	Elena is exceptionally quiet in class and answers questions only when her teacher directs them specifically at her. At lunch and on the playground, however, she readily talks and laughs with her friends.	Keep in mind that some children won't tell you when they're confused. If you think they may not understand, take them aside and ask specific questions to assess what they have learned. Provide additional instruction to address any gaps in understanding.
Eye Contact	• *Looking others in the eye* when speaking or listening to them, *or* • *Looking down* or away in the presence of adults	Herman always looks at his feet when an adult speaks to him.	Don't assume that children aren't paying attention just because they don't look you in the eye.
Personal Space	• *Standing quite close* to a conversation partner, perhaps touching that person frequently, *or* • *Keeping distance* between oneself and others when talking with them	Michelle is noticeably uncomfortable when other people touch her.	Give children some personal space during one-on-one interactions. To facilitate cross-cultural interactions, teach children that what constitutes personal space differs from culture to culture.
Responses to Questions	• *Answering questions readily*, *or* • *Failing to answer very easy questions*	Leah never responds to "What is this?" questions, even when she knows the answers.	Be aware that some children are not accustomed to answering the types of questions that many Western adults ask during instruction. Respect children's privacy when they are reluctant to answer personal questions.
Wait Time	• *Waiting several seconds* before answering questions, *or* • *Not waiting at all*, and perhaps even interrupting others	Mario often interrupts his classmates during class discussions.	When addressing a question to an entire group, give children several seconds to think before calling on one child for an answer. When some children interrupt regularly, communicate a procedure (e.g., hand raising and waiting to be called on) to ensure that everyone has a chance to be heard.

evaluating other people's adherence to them. Children's violations of these standards may evoke emotional responses from adults, as when a teacher reacts with irritation when a child makes a request that is impolite (e.g., saying "Give me a pencil" rather than "May I please have a pencil, Ms. Martinez?"). Following are some cultural differences that may lead to misunderstandings in classrooms and other group settings. The implications for spotting these characteristics are summarized in the Observation Guidelines table "Identifying Cultural Differences in Sociolinguistic Conventions."

Talking versus Being Silent. Relatively speaking, mainstream Western culture is a chatty one. People often say things to one another even when they have very little to communicate, making small talk as a way of maintaining interpersonal relationships and filling awkward silences (Irujo, 1988; Trawick-Smith, 2010). In some African American communities in particular, people speak frequently and often with a great deal of energy and enthusiasm (Gay, 2006; Lein, 1975). In certain other cultures, however, silence is golden. Many Brazilians and Peruvians greet their guests silently, some Arabs stop talking to indicate a desire for privacy, and several

Preparing for Your Licensure Examination
Your teaching test might ask you about how cultures determine conventions for speaking and listening.

I'M LISTENING. In some cultures, looking an adult in the eye is a sign of respect. In other cultures, it is interpreted as *dis*respect.

Native American communities value silence in a few circumstances (Basso, 1972; Menyuk & Menyuk, 1988; Trawick-Smith, 2010).

Interacting with Adults. In many European American families, children feel they can speak freely when they have comments or questions. Yet in many communities, children learn very early that they should engage in conversation with adults only when their participation has been directly solicited. In such cultures, speaking directly and assertively to adults is seen as rude, perhaps even rebellious (Banks & Banks, 1995; Delgado-Gaitan, 1994; Paradise & Rogoff, 2009). In some parts of Mexico and in the Yup'ik culture of Alaska, children are expected to learn primarily by close, quiet observation of adults. Accordingly, these children rarely ask questions or otherwise interrupt what adults are doing (García, 1994; Gutiérrez & Rogoff, 2003).

Making Eye Contact. Among many people from European American backgrounds, looking someone in the eye is a way of indicating that they are trying to communicate or are listening intently. But for many people from African American, Hispanic, and Native American backgrounds, a child who looks an adult in the eye is showing disrespect. Children in such cultures may be taught to look down in the presence of adults (Torres-Guzmán, 1998; Trawick-Smith, 2010). The following anecdote shows how accommodation to this culturally learned behavior can make a difference:

> A teacher [described a Native American] student who would never say a word, nor even answer when she greeted him. Then one day when he came in she looked in the other direction and said, "Hello, Jimmy." He answered enthusiastically, "Why hello Miss Jacobs." She found that he would always talk if she looked at a book or at the wall, but when she looked at him, he appeared frightened. (Gilliland, 1988, p. 26)

Maintaining Personal Space. In some groups, such as in some African American and Turkish communities, people stand close together when they talk and may touch one another frequently (Hale-Benson, 1986; A. Ozdemir, 2008). In contrast, European Americans and Japanese Americans tend to keep a fair distance from one another—they maintain more **personal space**—especially if they don't know one another very well (Irujo, 1988; Trawick-Smith, 2010). Adults can try to be sensitive to the personal space that children from various cultural backgrounds need in order to feel comfortable in interactions with others.

MyEducationLab

Observe an IRE cycle in the "Literacy: Infancy" video. (Find Video Examples in Topic 9 of MyEducationLab.)

personal space
A child's personally and culturally preferred distance from other people during social interaction.

IRE cycle
Adult–child interaction pattern marked by adult *initiation*, child *response*, and adult *evaluation*; in Western cultures, such a pattern is often seen in instructional settings.

Responding to Questions. A common interaction pattern in many Western classrooms is the **IRE cycle**: A teacher *initiates* an interaction by asking a question, a student *responds* to the question, and the teacher *evaluates* the response (Mehan, 1979). Similar interactions are frequently found in parent–child interactions in middle-income European American homes. These parents might ask their toddlers such questions as "Where's your nose?" and "What does a cow say?" and praise them for correct answers. You can observe an IRE cycle in the "Literacy: Infancy" video in MyEducationLab. But children from some other backgrounds are unfamiliar with such question-and-answer sessions when they first come to school. Such is the case for some children raised in lower-income homes, as well as for children raised in several Mexican American, Native American, and Hawaiian communities (Losey, 1995; Rogoff, 2003).

Furthermore, different cultural groups teach children to answer different kinds of questions. European American parents frequently ask their children questions that they themselves know the answers to. Parents from certain other cultures rarely ask such questions (Crago, Annahatak, & Ningiuruvik, 1993; Heath, 1989; Rogoff & Morelli, 1989). Parents in some African American communities in the southeastern United States are more likely to ask questions involving comparisons and analogies. Rather than asking "What's that?" they may instead ask "What's that *like?*" (Heath, 1980). Also, children in these communities are specifically taught *not* to answer questions that strangers ask about personal and home life (e.g., "What's your name?" "Where do you live?").

Waiting and Interrupting. Teachers frequently ask their students questions and then wait for an answer. But exactly how long do they wait? The typical **wait time** for many teachers is a second or even less, at which point they either answer a question themselves or call on another student (M. B. Rowe, 1974, 1987). Yet people from some cultures leave lengthy pauses before responding as a way of indicating respect, as this statement by a Northern Cheyenne illustrates:

> Even if I had a quick answer to your question, I would never answer immediately. That would be saying that your question was not worth thinking about. (Gilliland, 1988, p. 27)

For some cultural groups, then, children are more likely to participate in class and answer questions when given several seconds to respond (C. A. Grant & Gomez, 2001; Mohatt & Erickson, 1981; Tharp, 1989).

Conversely, children from certain other backgrounds may interrupt adults or peers who haven't finished speaking—an action that some of their teachers might interpret as rudeness. In some African American, Puerto Rican, and Jewish families, however, family discourse often consists of several people talking at once. In fact, people who wait for their turn might find themselves excluded from the discussion altogether (Condon & Yousef, 1975; Farber, Mindel, & Lazerwitz, 1988; Trawick-Smith, 2010).

Taking Sociolinguistic Differences into Account

When the sociolinguistic behaviors expected at home differ significantly from those expected at school and in other group settings, a sense of confusion, or **culture shock**, can result. Such culture shock can interfere with children's adjustment to the group setting and, ultimately, with their behavior and achievement as well (Banks & Banks, 1995; Phalet, Andriessen, & Lens, 2004; Phelan, Yu, & Davidson, 1994). Adults further compound the problem when, interpreting children's behaviors as being unacceptable or "odd," they jump too quickly to the conclusion that these youngsters are unable or unwilling to make productive contributions to the group (Bowman, 1989; Hilliard & Vaughn-Scott, 1982).

Clearly, teachers and other practitioners must educate themselves about the diverse sociolinguistic patterns they are likely to encounter in day-to-day interactions with children. Furthermore, they must keep children's varying conversational styles in mind as they design group lessons and activities. Thus, teachers might vary the questions they ask in class to include those that different students are accustomed to answering at home. And they should allow sufficient wait time for all students to think about and respond to questions. Finally, they should observe the distinct styles of communicating that individual children use. Ms. Miller exhibits this sensitivity when she realizes during a conversation that one of her children, Ding Fang, is not refusing to cooperate but instead seems to be following the Chinese custom of remaining silent during a threatening social situation:

Ms. Miller:	What's going on over here? It seems like you two are having an argument.
Ding Fang:	(Looks down, says nothing)
Maura:	(In an angry tone) She took my car. (Now shouting at her peer) I was playing with that, you know!
Ding Fang:	(Says nothing, does not establish eye contact)
Ms. Miller:	Is that right, Ding Fang? Did you take Maura's car?
Ding Fang:	(Remains silent)
Ms. Miller:	Ding Fang? Can you tell me what happened?
Ding Fang:	(Still silent)
Ms. Miller:	Well, you don't seem to want to talk about it right now.
Ding Fang:	(Remains silent; looks as if she might cry)
Ms. Miller:	(Recognizes that Ding Fang is upset) You know, maybe this isn't such a good time to talk about it. Why don't we just go look at a book for a while. Would you like to do that? (Trawick-Smith, 2010, pp. 280–281)[16]

Development of Metalinguistic Awareness

Children's **metalinguistic awareness** is their conscious understanding of the nature and functions of language. Language skills and metalinguistic awareness develop hand in hand, as you can see in the Developmental Trends table "Language Skills at Different Age Levels."

[16]Excerpt from EARLY CHILDHOOD DEVELOPMENT: A MULTICULTURAL PERSPECTIVE, 5th Edition by Jeffrey Trawick-Smith. Copyright © 2010 by Jeffrey Trawick-Smith. Reprinted by permission of Pearson Education, Inc., Upper Saddle River, NJ.

wait time
The length of time a teacher pauses, after either asking a question or hearing a student's comment, before saying something.

culture shock
Sense of confusion that occurs when one encounters an environment with expectations for behavior very different from those in one's home environment.

metalinguistic awareness
Extent to which one consciously understands and thinks about the nature and functions of language.

DEVELOPMENTAL TRENDS
Language Skills at Different Age Levels

AGE	WHAT YOU MIGHT OBSERVE	DIVERSITY	IMPLICATIONS
Infancy (Birth–2 Years) 	• Interest in listening to the human voice and in exchanging vocalizations with adults • Repetition of vowel sounds (cooing) at age 1–2 months and consonant-vowel syllables (babbling) at about 6 months • Understanding of some common words at about 8 months • Use of single words at about 12 months • Use of two-word combinations at about 18 months • Rapid increase in vocabulary in the second year	• In the latter half of the first year, babbling increasingly reflects phonemes of the native language. • Temperament may influence the development of expressive language; more cautious children may wait a bit before beginning to speak. • Chronic ear infections can interfere with early language development. • Infants with severe hearing impairments orally babble, but the quality of their babbling changes little over time. They may also "babble" manually if their caregivers regularly use sign language to communicate with them. • Adults' cultural patterns of communicating with infants (e.g., verbal interaction or nonverbal contact) affect infants' language learning.	• Engage young infants in "conversations," using simplified and animated speech (i.e., infant-directed speech) and responding when they vocalize. • Label and describe the objects and events children observe. • Ask simple questions (e.g., "Is your diaper wet?" "What does a cow say?"). • Repeat and expand on children's early "sentences" (e.g., follow "Kitty eat" with "Yes, the kitty is eating his dinner"). • Teach simple hand signs that preverbal infants can use to communicate.
Early Childhood (2–6 Years) 	• Rapid advances in vocabulary and syntax • Incomplete understandings of many simple words (e.g., underextension, overextension, confusion between simple comparatives such as *more* vs. *less*) • Overregularization (e.g., *foots*, *gooder*, *goed*) • Overdependence on word order and context (instead of syntax) when interpreting messages • Superficial understanding of what "good listening" is • Difficulty pronouncing some phonemes and blends (e.g., *r*, *th*, *spl*) • Increasing ability to construct narratives	• Children raised in bilingual environments may show slight delays in language development, but any delays are short lived and rarely a cause for concern. • Major language impairments (e.g., abnormal syntactic constructions) reveal themselves in the preschool years. • The richness of parents' language affects children's vocabulary growth.	• Read age-appropriate storybooks as a way of enhancing vocabulary. • Give tactful corrective feedback when children's use of words indicates inaccurate understandings. • Work on simple listening skills (e.g., sitting quietly, paying attention, asking questions when confused). • Ask follow-up questions to make sure that children accurately understand important messages. • Ask children to construct narratives about recent events (e.g., "Tell me about your camping trip last weekend").
Middle Childhood (6–10 Years) 	• Increasing understanding of temporal words (e.g., *before*, *after*) and comparatives (e.g., *bigger*, *as big as*) • Incomplete knowledge of irregular word forms • Literal interpretation of messages (especially before age 9) • Pronunciation mastered by age 8 • Consideration of a listener's knowledge and perspective when speaking • Sustained conversations about concrete topics • Construction of narratives with plots and cause-and-effect relationships • Linguistic creativity and wordplay (e.g., rhymes, word games)	• Some minor language impairments (e.g., persistent articulation problems) become evident and can be addressed by specialists. • Children from certain groups (e.g., some children who are African American) often show advanced ability to use figurative language (e.g., metaphor, hyperbole). • Bilingual children are apt to show advanced metalinguistic awareness. • Reading habits may affect children's metalinguistic awareness and other aspects of language development.	• Use group discussions as a way to explore academic subject matter. • Have children develop short stories that they present orally or in writing. • Teach irregular word forms (e.g., the superlative form of *bad* is *worst*, the past tense of *bring* is *brought*). • Encourage jokes and rhymes that capitalize on double meanings and homonyms (sound-alike words). • When articulation problems are evident in the upper elementary grades, consult with a speech-language pathologist.

DEVELOPMENTAL TRENDS (continued)

AGE	WHAT YOU MIGHT OBSERVE	DIVERSITY	IMPLICATIONS
Early Adolescence (10–14 Years) 	• Increasing awareness of the terminology used in various academic disciplines • Ability to understand complex, multiple-clause sentences • Emerging ability to look beyond literal interpretations; comprehension of simple proverbs • Emerging ability to carry on lengthy conversations about abstract topics • Significant growth in metalinguistic awareness	• Frequent readers tend to have larger vocabularies. • Girls are more likely than boys to converse about intimate and confidential matters. • Certain adolescents (e.g., some African American teens) may bandy insults back and forth in a creative and playful manner. • Adolescents may prefer to use their native *dialects* even if they have mastered *Standard English* (see discussion in upcoming "Bioecology of Language Development" section).	• Begin to use the terminology preferred by experts in various academic disciplines (e.g., *simile* in language arts, *theory* in science). • Use classroom debates to explore controversial issues. • Present proverbs and ask adolescents to consider possible underlying meanings. • Explore the nature of words and language as entities in and of themselves.
Late Adolescence (14–18 Years) 	• Acquisition of many terms related to specific academic disciplines • Subtle refinements in grammar, mostly as a result of formal instruction • Mastery of a wide variety of connectives (e.g., *although*, *however*, *nevertheless*) • General ability to understand figurative language (e.g., metaphors, proverbs, hyperbole)	• Boys are apt to communicate their thoughts in a direct and straightforward manner; girls are more likely to be indirect and tactful. • A preference for one's native dialect over Standard English continues into the high school years. • The kinds of slang adolescents use vary depending on their particular peer groups.	• Consistently use the terminology associated with various academic disciplines. • Distinguish between similar abstract words (e.g., *weather* vs. *climate*, *velocity* vs. *acceleration*). • Explore complex syntactic structures (e.g., multiple embedded clauses). • Consider the underlying meanings and messages in poetry and fiction. • When teenagers have a native dialect other than Standard English, encourage them to use it in informal conversations and creative writing; encourage Standard English for more formal situations.

Sources: C. Baker, 1993; Bruer, 1999; Bruner, 1983; Byrnes & Wasik, 2009; N. Chomsky, 1972; Eilers & Oller, 1994; Elias & Broerse, 1996; Fantini, 1985; Fenson et al., 1994; Fifer & Moon, 1995; Goodwyn, Acredolo, & Brown, 2000; Hale-Benson, 1986; Imhof, 2001; J. L. Locke, 1993; T. M. McDevitt, 1990; K. Nelson, 1973; Nicolopoulou & Richner, 2007; O'Grady, 1997; Ortony, Turner, & Larson-Shapiro, 1985; Owens, 2008; Pence & Justice, 2008, L. A. Petitto, 1997; H. L. Smith, 1998; R. H. Thompson, Cotnoir-Bichelman, McKerchar, Tate, & Dancho, 2007.

In the late preschool or early elementary school years, children become consciously aware that words are the basic units of language, that spoken words are comprised of phonemes, and that different phonemes tend to be associated with different letters or letter combinations (Lonigan, Burgess, Anthony, & Barker, 1998; T. A. Roberts, 2005; Tunmer, Pratt, & Herriman, 1984). As they move into the upper elementary and middle school grades, they also begin to recognize and label the component parts of speech, at least partly as a result of formal instruction about nouns, verbs, and so on (e.g., Sipe, 2006; Vavra, 1987). During this age level, young people begin to understand some nonliteral references and also identify and repair errors in speech (Haskill & Corts, 2010). More sophisticated aspects of metalinguistic awareness, such as recognizing and interpreting phrases and sentences with multiple meanings, continue to develop throughout adolescence (Nippold & Taylor, 1995; Owens, 2008).

Theoretical accounts of metalinguistic development focus almost exclusively on the effects of experience. One factor that probably promotes metalinguistic awareness is "playing" with language through rhymes, chants, jokes, puns, and so on. For example, rhymes help children discover the relationships between sounds and letters. Jokes and puns help children discover that words and phrases can have more than one meaning (L. Bradley & Bryant, 1991; Cazden, 1976; Yuill, 2009).

Children's early experiences with books also promote metalinguistic awareness (Ravid & Geiger, 2009; Yaden & Templeton, 1986). The very process of reading to children helps them realize that printed language is related to spoken language. In addition, some children's books playfully address the nature of language. An example is *Amelia Bedelia*

Goes Camping (Parish & Sweat, 2003), one in a series of books featuring a rather obtuse maid who takes everything her employers say quite literally. For instance, when they tell Amelia it's time to "hit the road," she hits the road with a stick—a response that our own children found quite amusing.

Formal language instruction further fosters metalinguistic awareness. By exploring parts of speech, various sentence structures, and the like, children and adolescents gain a better grasp of the underlying structure of language. By reading and analyzing poetry and classic literature, they discover a variety of mechanisms (similes, metaphors, symbolism, etc.) that a writer might use to convey multiple layers of meanings.

Finally, research consistently indicates that knowledge of two or more languages (bilingualism) promotes metalinguistic awareness (X. Chen et al., 2004; Moran & Hakuta, 1995; Reyes & Azuara, 2008). By the time Mario was 5, he showed considerable awareness of the nature of language:

> Mario was well aware that things were called in one of several possible ways, that the same story could be retold in another language (he was capable of doing this himself), and he knew that thoughts were convertible or translatable through other forms of expression. . . . He knew that a [language] could be varied so as to make it sound funny or to render its messages less transparent, such as in Pig Spanish. . . .
>
> [As Mario grew older,] he became increasingly analytical about the medium which so many take for granted as their sole form of expression. He demonstrated interest, for example, in the multiple meaning of some words ("'right' means three things"); and in peculiar usages ("Why do you call the car 'she'?"); as well as intuitions about the origins of words ("'soufflé' sounds French"). (Fantini, 1985, pp. 53–54)[17]

Promoting Metalinguistic Development

Factors that promote metalinguistic awareness—language play, reading experiences, formal instruction, and bilingualism—have several implications for teaching and working with children.

• **Explore multiple meanings through ambiguities, jokes, riddles, and the like.** Having fun with language can be educational as well as entertaining. Teachers, parents, and other practitioners might ask children to identify the double meanings of such sentences as *He is drawing a gun* and *This restaurant even serves crabs* (Wiig, Gilbert, & Christian, 1978). Jokes and riddles provide another vehicle for exploring multiple meanings (Shultz, 1974; Shultz & Horibe, 1974; Yuill, 2009):

> Call me a cab.
> Okay, you're a cab.
>
> Tell me how long cows should be milked.
> They should be milked the same as short ones, of course.

• **Read literature that plays on the nature of language.** One of our favorites is *The Phantom Tollbooth* (Juster, 1961), which has considerable fun with word meanings and common expressions. In one scene the main character (Milo) asks for a square meal and is served (you guessed it) a plate "heaped high with steaming squares of all sizes and colors." Among the all-time classics in English wordplay are Lewis Carroll's *Alice's Adventures in Wonderland* and *Through the Looking Glass*. These books are packed with whimsical uses of double word meanings, homonyms, and idioms, as the following excerpt from *Through the Looking Glass* illustrates:

> "But what could [a tree] do, if any danger came?" Alice asked.
> "It could bark," said the Rose.
> "It says, 'Boughwough!'" cried a Daisy. "That's why its branches are called boughs."

• **Encourage children to learn a second language.** Promoting metalinguistic awareness is just one of several benefits of learning a second language. In the next section we look more closely at second-language learning and bilingualism.

---

[17]See footnote 14 on p. 348.

DEVELOPMENT OF A SECOND LANGUAGE

The presence of several language communities in a single society provides children with the chance to become proficient in two or more languages. Here we address three issues related to the development of a second language: the timing of second-language learning, the nature of bilingualism, and approaches to teaching a second language.

The Timing of Second-Language Learning

The human brain is quite capable of learning *two* or more languages from the beginning of life (e.g., Kuhl, 2004). When, like Mario, human beings are regularly exposed to two languages within the first few years of life, the same language-specific areas of the brain (usually concentrated in the left hemisphere) appear to handle both languages (K. H. Kim, Relkin, Lee, & Hirsch, 1997; L. Petitto, 2009). When people learn a second language quite a bit later, perhaps later in childhood or early adulthood, they must enlist a larger number of distinct neural structures from both hemispheres (K. H. Kim et al., 1997; L. Petitto, 2009).

Exposure to a second language in the first few years of life may be especially important for acquiring flawless pronunciation and the complex syntactic structures of that second language. Early exposure to a second language is especially advantageous if the second language is very different from the first. Thus, a native English speaker benefits more from an early start in Japanese or Arabic than from an early start in, say, Spanish or German (Bialystok, 1994a; Strozer, 1994).

The challenges of learning and keeping two languages straight actually strengthen certain brain functions, especially flexibility in the brain's executive functions[18] (e.g., shifting easily from one intellectual task to another in accordance with task demands; Bialystok & Viswanathan, 2009). Nevertheless, some of the advantages young children have because of neurological flexibility are counterbalanced by the greater cognitive maturity, world knowledge, and metalinguistic sophistication on which adolescents and adults can build (Bialystok, 1994b; Collier, 1989; Long, 1995). Therefore, people of all ages can acquire proficiency in a second language and face somewhat distinct challenges in the process.

Acquiring a second language during childhood, at whatever particular age, benefits children in other ways as well (Bialystok & Viswanathan, 2009; T. H. Cunningham & Graham, 2000; Diaz, 1983; A. Doyle, 1982; A. M. Padilla, 2006; Reich, 1986). Learning a second language leads, on average, to higher achievement in reading, vocabulary, and grammar. Furthermore, it sensitizes youngsters to the international and multicultural nature of the world in which they live. Children who learn a second language during the elementary school years express more positive attitudes toward people who speak that language, and they are more likely to enroll in foreign language classes in high school. And in classrooms in which children speak only one of two different languages (perhaps some speaking only English and others speaking only Spanish), instruction in the second language promotes communication with peers.

Bilingualism

Bilingualism is the ability to speak two languages fluently. Bilingual individuals can easily switch from one language to the other, and they readily distinguish the contexts in which they should use each one. At least half of the world's children are bilingual or multilingual (speaking three or more languages fluently), typically because they've been exposed to more than one language from an early age (Hoff, 2001). Children raised in bilingual environments from birth or soon thereafter sometimes show initial delays in language development, but by elementary school they have generally caught up to their monolingual peers and easily keep the two languages separate (C. Baker, 1993; Bialystok, 2001; Fennell, Byers-Heinlein, & Werker, 2007). And when they are truly fluent in both languages, children are apt to perform better on intelligence tests and on tasks requiring creativity (Bialystok & Senman, 2004; Diaz & Klingler, 1991; García, 1994; Mora, 2009).

Being bilingual often yields personal advantages as well. Perhaps most importantly, it allows children to maintain interpersonal relationships with important people in their

bilingualism
Knowing and speaking two languages fluently.

[18]Executive functions are introduced in Chapter 5.

lives. For instance, some children are bilingual in English and American Sign Language as a way of communicating effectively with one parent who can hear and another who is deaf (L. A. Petitto, 1997). In many Native American groups, the ancestral language is important for conducting local business and communicating oral history and cultural traditions, yet adults in those groups also believe that mastery of spoken and written English is essential for children's long-term success (McCarty & Watahomigie, 1998). Although most Puerto Rican children have more valuable professional opportunities if they know English, they often speak Spanish at home and with peers, thereby showing respect to their elders and maintaining their cultural identity (Nieto, 1995; Torres-Guzmán, 1998). A statement by Marisol, a high school student, illustrates the latter point:

> I'm proud of [being Puerto Rican]. I guess I speak Spanish whenever I can. . . . I used to have a lot of problems with one of my teachers 'cause she didn't want us to talk Spanish in class and I thought that was like an insult to us, you know? (Nieto, 1995, p. 127)

Teaching a Second Language

In the United States, several million children are members of families who speak a language other than English at home (D. Meyer, Madden, & McGrath, 2005; National Association of Bilingual Education, 1993). A sizable minority of these children has had little exposure to English before beginning school. Currently, more than 5% of the public school population in the United States has limited proficiency in English (Federal Interagency Forum on Child and Family Statistics, 2010). School-age children who are fluent in their native language but not in English are often referred to as **English language learners (ELLs)**. Many English language learners enjoy definite advantages in life, including having warm support from an involved and extended family, but they sometimes face distinct challenges, as you can discover in MyEducationLab (García, Jensen, & Scribner, 2009).

Just as very young children typically learn their native language through daily exposure, so, too, can they learn two languages simultaneously if (like Mario) they have frequent, ongoing exposure to both languages. But when children begin to learn a second language at an older age, perhaps in the elementary grades or even later, they often learn it more quickly if their language-learning experiences are fairly structured (Strozer, 1994). The particular model of instruction that a school selects depends on political pressures (how willing the community is to support second-language learning) and policy mandates (what the local authorities require). Cultural practices are also influential, as you can read more about in the Development in Culture feature, "Learning Second Languages in Cameroon."

Several approaches to second-language instruction have been used in schools, including bilingual education, submersion, structured English immersion programs, immersion, and foreign language instruction. The first three of these programs are typically used with English language learners, and the latter two programs are usually offered to help native English speakers learn a second language.[19]

In **bilingual education**, English language learners receive intensive instruction in English while studying other academic subject areas in their native language. The sequence might be as follows:

1. Students join native English speakers for classes in subject areas that do not depend too heavily on language skills (e.g., art, music, physical education). They study other subject areas in their native language and also begin classes in *English as a Second Language* (ESL).
2. Once students have acquired some English proficiency, instruction in English begins for one or two additional subject areas (perhaps for math and science).
3. When it is clear that students can learn successfully in English in the subject areas identified in step 2, they join their English-speaking classmates in regular classes in these subjects.
4. Eventually students are sufficiently proficient in English to join the mainstream in all subject areas, and they may no longer require their ESL classes (Krashen, 1996; A. M. Padilla, 2006; Valdés, Bunch, Snow, & Lee, 2005).

[19]Similar models of second-language instruction are used in many other countries.

English language learner (ELL)
School-age child who is not fully fluent in English because his or her family speaks a language other than English at home.

bilingual education
Approach to second-language instruction in which students are instructed in academic subject areas in their native language while simultaneously being taught to speak, read, and write in a second language.

Educational anthropologist Leslie Moore spent several years in northern Cameroon, first as a Peace Corps volunteer and later as a researcher. During observations in Maroua, Cameroon, Moore observed children whose first language was Fulfulde and who were learning French at the local public school and Arabic during religious lessons with Islamic authorities (L. C. Moore, 2006, 2010).

Moore noticed both similarities and differences in the ways that children were taught French and Arabic. In both cases, *guided repetition* was a primary way by which children learned the languages. Teachers would model a phrase and ask children to repeat it in unison. Children eagerly complied and gradually grew proficient in their pronunciation of French and Arabic sounds, words, and phrases.

Yet the underlying purposes of learning French and Arabic were different and led to subtle distinctions in how instruction was implemented. The purpose of learning French was to become educated within a modern society. Children were taught French as a second language and were also taught their basic subjects in French. Children needed to acquire sufficiently high levels of proficiency that they could understand a teacher's instructions and comprehend basic vocabulary in academic lessons in mathematics, civics, hygiene, and national culture. The purpose of learning Arabic was more specific—it prepared children to recite the *Qur'an*, the Islamic book of sacred scriptures. Children did not learn to speak Arabic conversationally but rather gained the particular abilities they needed to read along in the Qur'an. Being able to recite the Qur'an prepared children to develop Muslim identities and become reverent in matters of faith.

Guided repetition in French is evident in observations Moore made of a young girl:

Six-year-old Halima sat at her desk, which she shared with another girl and two boys, and listened attentively to her first grade teacher, Mr. Garza. In a loud, clear voice, he began the language lesson, "Bonjour, Papa. Répétez?" Halima and most of her 150 classmates repeated loudly after him the first line of dialogue that he had introduced the day before: "Bonjour, Papa." Mr. Garza said again, "Bonjour, Papa," and the class repeated after him, "Bonjour, Papa." Then Mr. Garza modeled the second line of the dialogue, "Bonjour, mon fils." There was a second of silence. Mr. Garza prompted

REPEAT AFTER ME. In a number of Cameroon schools, imitation and rehearsal are primary means for learning second languages.

the class to speak, and several students (but not Halima) produced a repetition of the second line, "Bonjour, mon fils." The teacher approved the repetition and then elicited more of the same: "Très bien. Encore? Bonjour, Papa." The class practiced the two lines of dialogue under Mr. Garza's direction for another 30 minutes, chorally, by row, by desk, and in pairs. On this day, Halima was not one of the children called on to perform the dialogue with a classmate at the front of the classroom. After the language lesson came a mathematics lesson, followed by recess, followed by a writing lesson. All the lessons were conducted entirely in French, while at recess children chatted and shouted in local languages, including Fulfulde, which was Halima's native language and the regional lingua franca. At noon, it was time to go home.[a] (L. C. Moore, 2010, p. 207)

The focus of this lesson was on learning phrases from everyday conversation. Later in the day, Moore followed Halima to her Qur'an lessons. During Halima's afternoon lesson, she received guided repetition in order to recite verses with correct pronunciation and a sense of piety:

Halima walked the kilometer home with her big sister and two boy cousins. She had lunch and a short rest before heading to her Qur'anic school just down the street, around 1:30. Her teacher, Mal Buuba, was not at home when she arrived, but his teenage son was there to supervise the students. Halima took her *alluha* (a wooden tablet on which Qur'anic verses are written for a child to study) from where she had left it the evening before, leaning against the wall of the entryway of Mal Buuba's family compound. She sat down on the gravel-covered ground with her back against the mud wall, crossed her legs, lay her alluha on her lap, and resumed her study of the 108th chapter of the Qur'an. For almost two hours, she practiced her recitation of the *basmalah* (the brief invocation that precedes all but one chapter of the Qur'an) and the three short verses. She repeated the Arabic text over and over in a very loud voice, sometimes bent over her alluha, sometimes sitting up straight. Five other girls from the neighborhood sat along the same wall as Halima, and against the facing wall sat her two boy cousins (who were also in her first grade class) and four other neighborhood boys. Each child recited a different text in a loud voice. Whenever the volume began to fade, Mal Buuba's son commanded them in Fulfulde to recite "with force." At the sound of the call to the afternoon prayer, Halima and the other children stopped reciting, put away their alluhas, and went home. After dinner, Halima returned for the evening session, practicing her recitation for another hour and a half before the call to the night prayer signaled that it was time to go home and go to bed.[a] (L. C. Moore, 2010, p. 208)

Moore identified advantages and disadvantages of guided repetition in the two contexts. Rote memorization is a familiar method for teaching a second language in Cameroon. The method appeared to work especially well in teaching children to recite the Qur'an because young children were to recite scripture as a matter of faith and not ask questions about its meaning. Guided repetition worked reasonably well in the public school, yet had definite limitations in fostering advanced mastery of French. Many children did not develop the French expertise they needed to understand challenging material in the upper school grades, and a high proportion of children repeated grades and dropped out of elementary school.

[a]Excerpts from "Learning in Schools" by Leslie C. Moore, from THE ANTHROPOLOGY OF LEARNING IN CHILDHOOD, Edited by D. F. Lancy, J. Block, and S. Gaskins. Reprinted with permission of Rowman & Littlefield Publishers, Inc.

In reality, these four steps are often carried out fairly quickly, completed within 2 to 3 years. Rushing children's language learning is a concern because simple knowledge of basic conversational English is not enough for success in an English-only curriculum (A. M. Padilla, 2006). After all, students must have sufficient mastery of English vocabulary and grammar that they can readily understand and learn from English-based textbooks and lectures, and such mastery takes considerable time to achieve—often 5 to 7 years (Cummins, 1981, 2000). Moreover, concerns have been raised that children in transitional programs do not develop high levels of literacy in either their native language or in English (Estrada, Gómez, & Ruiz-Escalante, 2009). In one variant of this model, *transitional bilingual education*, children are taught by a bilingual teacher who teaches regular subjects in the children's first language and English as a separate subject. English is gradually introduced for other subjects.

In another type of bilingual program, *developmental bilingual education*, both the native language and English are maintained. Developmental bilingual teachers instruct the children in both languages for an indefinite period. In a related model, *dual language instruction*, a mixed group of children who are native English speakers and others who are English language learners (and usually speak Spanish) receive instruction in both languages together throughout their time in school (Estrada et al., 2009). Dual language programs have resulted in high levels of academic achievement, motivation, and student enthusiasm (Estrada et al., 2009).

Many schools have limited funds, relatively few children who speak the same native language, and an insufficient number of bilingual teachers to justify bilingual education programs. As a result, some schools simply place English language learners in a regular classroom with other native English speakers. In the **submersion approach**, children are essentially left to their own devices in acquiring English. In **structured English immersion** programs, children receive intensive instruction in English over or year or so. Teachers offer instruction in the English language as well as specially adapted instruction in English in academic subjects (K. Clark, 2009). The main emphasis is on teaching English, with educators hoping children will gain proficiency in English rapidly so that they can enter the regular classroom and catch up on academic subjects with peers.

Two other programs are commonly used with native *English* speakers learning a second language at school. In **immersion** programs, children receive instruction in language arts in their first language and instruction in a second language in other subjects. Immersion programs begin as early as kindergarten and as late as sixth grade or after. For native English speakers, immersion in the second language for part or all of the school day helps students acquire basic proficiency in the language fairly quickly, and any adverse effects on achievement in other academic areas appear to be short lived (Collier, 1992; T. H. Cunningham & Graham, 2000; Genesee, 1985; A. M. Padilla, 2006).

In traditional **foreign language instruction**, children are taught a second language as a subject occasionally as early as elementary school and regularly in middle school and high school. Children receive instruction in the foreign language for approximately 20 to 50 minutes daily or a couple of times weekly. Instruction that is based on drills and grammatical lessons seems less effective than lessons that emphasize cultural awareness, oral communication, and community involvement (Otto, 2010).

Which models are most effective, and why? For non-native English speakers, children need to learn English so that they can master academic subjects and ultimately communicate with other English-speaking citizens, yet they also need to continue to communicate with family members, friends, and others in their neighborhoods. If English language learners are taught exclusively in English, they may very well lose proficiency in their native language before developing adequate proficiency in English—a phenomenon known as **subtractive bilingualism**—and their cognitive development will suffer in the process. In this regard, bilingual programs may be superior to submersion and structured English immersion models. Because bilingual education is designed to foster growth in *both* English and a child's native language, it is apt to promote cognitive as well as linguistic growth (Estrada et al., 2009; McBrien, 2005b; Pérez, 1998; Tse, 2001; Winsler, Díaz, Espinosa, & Rodriguez, 1999). Furthermore, bilingual programs, and especially dual language instruction programs, tend not to isolate English language learners from their peers, which is a growing a concern with English immersion models (Rios-Aguilar, González-Canche, & Moll, 2010).

submersion
Approach to second-language instruction in which English language learners are placed in the regular classroom and expected to acquire the new language simply through exposure.

structured English immersion
Approach to second-language instruction for English language learners in which the children receive intensive lessons in English for a year or so and are then placed in the regular classroom.

immersion
Approach to second-language instruction in which native English speakers hear and speak the second language almost exclusively in the classroom.

foreign language instruction
Approach to second-language instruction in which native English speakers receive lessons in a new language for less than an hour once or twice a week or occasionally more often.

subtractive bilingualism
Phenomenon in which immersion in a new-language environment leads to deficits in one's native language.

DEVELOPMENT AND PRACTICE
Working with English Language Learners

Teach literacy skills in a student's native language.

- When working with students whose families have recently emigrated from Mexico, a first-grade teacher teaches basic letter-sound relationships and word decoding skills in Spanish (e.g., showing how the printed word *dos* can be broken up into the sounds "duh," "oh," and "sss"). (Middle Childhood)
- In a first-grade classroom, most of the children speak English but several speak primarily Spanish or Vietnamese. The teacher makes read-along books available in English, Spanish, and Vietnamese and posts the days of the week on the calendar and messages in the board in the three languages. (Middle Childhood)

If you don't speak a student's native language yourself, recruit and train parents, community volunteers, or other students to assist in providing instruction in that language.

- A boy in a kindergarten class has grown up speaking Hmong, a language spoken in some Asian immigrant communities in the United States. His teacher recruits a fourth grader who can read an English picture book to the boy and translate it into Hmong. At one point the teacher points to a lily pad on a page of the book and asks the fourth grader to describe a lily pad in Hmong, because the younger child has never seen these plants in his own environment. (You can see this example in action in the "Reading a Picture Book to a Hmong Student" in MyEducationLab.) (Early Childhood)
- A second-grade teacher invites the mother of a Salvadoran child to come to school and share something from her culture. The mother shares tamales with the class and talks about the different wrappers that people use to form the tamales, including corn husks, banana leaves, and paper. The children ask a lot of questions about Salvadoran culture and other societies that make tamales. (Middle Childhood)

When using English to communicate, speak more slowly than you might otherwise, and clearly enunciate each word.

- A third-grade teacher is careful that he always says "going to" rather than "gonna" and "want to" rather than "wanna." (Middle Childhood)
- A high school speech teacher provides a rubric for presentations. In addition to including criteria for organization, persuasive appeal, and an animated delivery, the teacher includes standards that benefit English language learners, especially requirements that key terms are defined in a handout and words pronounced clearly. (Late Adolescence)

Use visual aids to supplement verbal explanations.

- Before introducing a lesson on the desert habitat, a fifth-grade teacher draws a picture of a desert on a poster, labels a few common plants and animals that live there, prepares a list of key biological adaptations in harsh environments (e.g., conserving water, keeping predators away), and writes down a few vocabulary words (e.g., *desert*, *conserve*, *predator*). (Middle Childhood)
- A high school history teacher uses photographs she's downloaded from the Internet to illustrate a short lecture on ancient Egypt. (Late Adolescence)

During small-group learning activities, encourage same-language students to communicate with one another in their native language.

- When a middle school science teacher breaks students into cooperative groups to study the effects of weight, length, and amount of push on a pendulum's oscillation rate, she puts three native Chinese speakers into a single group. She suggests that they can talk in either English or Chinese as they do their experiments. (Early Adolescence)
- A high school chemistry teacher asks a couple of Vietnamese students to brainstorm a few ways that chemistry plays a role in contemporary Vietnamese society. The students then share their ideas with other groups, who have been asked to define ways that other cultures are affected by chemistry. (Late Adolescence)

Have students work in pairs to make sense of textbook material.

- As two middle school students study a section of their geography textbook, one reads aloud while the other listens and takes notes. They frequently stop to talk about what's been read, and then they switch roles. (Early Adolescence)
- A high school literature teacher guides a small group of English language learners by asking them a series of questions about a story. Students answer questions about information that is explicitly described in the story, other information that is implied, and their own perspectives about dilemmas raised in the story. (Late Adolescence)

Have students, read, write, and report about their native countries.

- A second-grade teacher asks children to write a report about people who have made a difference in the region or country in which they or their parents grew up. The teacher encourages the children to talk with their parents as well as find books about their culture from the library. (Middle Childhood).
- A middle school social studies teacher has students conduct research on a country from which they or their ancestors have immigrated. The students create posters to display what they've learned, and they proudly talk about their posters at an "International Day" that students from other classes attend. (Early Adolescence)

Sources: Agirdag, 2009; Comeau, Cormier, Grandmaison, & Lacroix, 1999; Espinosa, 2007; García, 1995; Herrell & Jordan, 2004; Igoa, 1995; Krashen, 1996; McClelland, 2001; McClelland, Fiez, & McCandliss, 2002; A. M. Padilla, 2006; Peregoy & Boyle, 2008; Ramirez & Soto-Hinman, 2009; Rothenberg & Fisher, 2007; Slavin & Cheung, 2005; Valdés et al., 2005.

For native English learners, immersion and foreign language instruction that permits conversation and fosters ties to the culture of the new language community seem beneficial. Native English speakers who live in an English-speaking country and are immersed in a different language at school still have many opportunities—at home, with their friends, and in the local community—to continue using and developing their English.

Second-language instruction is a controversial topic that will continue to inspire new instructional models and related research. Nevertheless, teachers can effectively support children in their own classrooms, as you can see in the Development and Practice feature "Working with English Language Learners."

Bioecology of Child Development

Children bring their individual qualities to the task of learning language; are affected by such characteristics as gender, family socioeconomic status, and ethnicity; and use forms of speech that allow them to achieve personal goals in their language communities.

BIOECOLOGY OF LANGUAGE DEVELOPMENT

The bioecological framework provides a useful way to highlight the numerous factors that affect the individuality of language development. Children contribute to their own development, actively searching for regularities in language and taking initiative to achieve their goals. The manner in which children go about tackling language acquisition depends partly on their personal qualities. Shy or reserved children may begin to speak somewhat later than more outgoing ones (Coplan & Evans, 2009; K. Nelson, 1973). In learning to express themselves through language, children also draw on resources they have as a boy or girl, member of a family, and participant in an ethnic community. These various influences interact, making each child's language development unique.

Gender

As infants and toddlers, girls are, on average, more verbally active than boys. Girls begin to speak about a month earlier, form longer sentences sooner, and have a larger vocabulary (C. Bouchard, Trudeau, Sutton, Boudreault, & Deneault, 2009; Halpern & LaMay, 2000; Reznick & Goldfield, 1992). Once they reach the school years, girls outperform boys on tests of verbal ability. This gender difference in verbal ability is quite small, however, with considerable overlap between the two groups.[20]

Qualitative gender differences exist as well, for children and adults alike. On average, boys, who see themselves as information providers, speak more directly and bluntly. Conversely, girls, who seek to establish and deepen relationships through their conversations, are more likely to be indirect, tactful, and polite (C. M. Mehta & Strough, 2009; Owens, 2008; Tannen, 1990). Furthermore, at least in European American middle-class families, girls tend to talk more about emotions and relationships than do boys (Fivush, 1994; Fivush & Buckner, 2003).

Socioeconomic Status

As mentioned in the earlier discussion of nativism, children from diverse backgrounds tend to reach language milestones at similar ages. However, children from higher-income homes tend to have larger vocabularies (Black, Peppé, & Gibbon, 2008; B. Hart & Risley, 1995; Hoff, 2003; Wasik & Bond, 2001). This difference appears to be at least partly due to the quantity and quality of language that parents use with their children. Although mothers from all income levels in Western societies tend to interact frequently with their children, on average mothers from higher-SES families talk with their babies more, ask more questions, elaborate more on topics, and, in general, expose their children to a greater variety of words (B. Hart & Risley, 1995, 1999; Hoff, 2003). Nevertheless, children from low-income families are a highly variable group and show tremendous resilience in their language development and academic achievement, particularly when enrolled in high-quality schools (Obradović et al., 2009).

Ethnicity

As you've already learned, sociolinguistic conventions, use of figurative language, and narrative styles often differ from one group to another. In addition, children from some ethnic and

Preparing for Your Licensure Examination

Your teaching test might ask you how gender, socioeconomic status, and ethnicity influence children's language development.

---

[20]Gender differences in verbal ability are discussed in Chapter 8.

cultural groups may use a form of English different from the **Standard English** (sometimes known as Mainstream American English) that is typically valued in schools, the media, government, and other formal settings. Specifically, some children of color and those from non-dominant cultural groups may speak in a **dialect**, a form of English (or, more generally, a form of any language) that includes some unique pronunciations and syntactic structures. Dialects tend to be associated either with particular geographical regions or with particular ethnic and cultural groups.

Perhaps the most widely studied ethnic dialect is **African American English** (also known as *Black English Vernacular* or *Ebonics*). This dialect, which is actually a group of similar dialects, is used in many African American communities throughout the United States and is characterized by certain unique pronunciations, idioms, and grammatical constructions.[21] For example:

- The *th* sound at the beginning of a word is often pronounced as *d* (e.g., *that* is pronounced "dat").
- The *ng* sound at the end of a word is typically pronounced as *n* (e.g., *bringing* is pronounced "bringin").
- The *-ed* ending on past-tense verbs is often dropped (e.g., "We walk to the park last night").
- The present- and past-tense forms of the verb *to be* are consistently *is* and *was*, even if the subject of the sentence is the pronoun *I* or a plural noun or pronoun (e.g., "I is runnin'," "They was runnin'").
- The verb *is* is often dropped in simple descriptive sentences (e.g., "He a handsome man").
- The word *be* is used to indicate a constant or frequently occurring characteristic (e.g., "He be talking" describes someone who talks much of the time). (Hulit & Howard, 2006, pp. 345–346)

At one time many researchers jumped to the conclusion that an African American dialect represented a less complex form of speech than Standard English. They urged educators to teach students to speak "properly" as quickly as possible. But psychologists now realize that African American dialects and most other dialects are, in fact, very complex languages with their own predictable idioms and grammatical rules and that these dialects promote communication and complex thought as readily as Standard English (Fairchild & Edwards-Evans, 1990; Hulit & Howard, 2006; B. Z. Pearson, Velleman, Bryant, & Charko, 2009).

Many children and adolescents view their native language and dialect as an integral part of their cultural identity (Agirdag, 2009; Ogbu, 2003; A. W. Tatum, 2008). Children generally develop a sense of loyalty to those who share their mother tongue, and this link certainly exists for those speaking a dialect, especially when they find that others in their vicinity are apt to misunderstand them. Obviously, when a local dialect is the language most preferred by residents of a community, it is often the most effective means through which youngsters can communicate in daily interactions. Unfortunately, many children are growing up being discouraged from using familiar dialects at school and have consequently been made to feel that they (and their people) are not welcome there. Unless children are respected by teachers and classmates for who they are—and how they speak—they may naturally withdraw from the school setting.

At the same time, children who have proficiency in Standard English have an easier time learning to read and may gain access to a wider variety of jobs and other opportunities in society (Charity, Scarborough, & Griffin, 2004; Hudley, 2009; T. A. Roberts, 2005). For this reason, most experts recommend that all youngsters acquire proficiency in Standard English (e.g., Craft, 1984; DeBose, 2007; Ogbu, 1999).

ARTIFACT 9-3 Yesterday. A local dialect is evident in this writing sample from a fifth grader who lives in the Northern Mariana Islands of the Pacific Ocean. The student blends present and past tenses in a description of an event. *Writing sample courtesy of the Commonwealth of the Northern Mariana Islands Public School System.*

Standard English
Form of English generally considered acceptable in school (as reflected in textbooks, grammar instruction, etc.) and in other formal institutions by teachers and others.

dialect
Form of a language characteristic of a particular geographic region or ethnic group.

African American English
Dialect of some African American communities that includes pronunciations, idioms, and grammatical constructions different from those of Standard English.

---

[21]Obviously, not all African Americans speak an African American dialect, and individuals who do use the dialect may restrict its use to certain settings. Furthermore, particular words and pronunciations in African American English vary considerably across different regions of the United States (Eberhardt, 2009). Moreover, some people who do not identify as African American use language that has characteristics of African American English (Hudley, 2009).

Ultimately, children and adolescents function most effectively when they can use both their local dialect and Standard English in appropriate settings. Although teachers may wish to encourage Standard English in most written work and in formal oral presentations, they should be receptive to other dialects in creative writing and informal classroom discussions (DeBose, 2007; Ogbu, 1999, 2003; D. Paris, 2009). They certainly can encourage children who speak a dialect to read authors from a similar background who may write in their dialect (A. W. Tatum, 2008). In addition, they should not be surprised when children use certain dialects selectively, perhaps sharing a secret with one classmate in a dialect and using Standard English with another classmate when communicating about an assignment (Dowdy, 2002).

EXCEPTIONALITIES IN LANGUAGE DEVELOPMENT

Language delays are often seen in children with general intellectual disabilities or severe forms of autism.[22] Here we describe language difficulties for two additional groups of children: those with specific language impairments and those with sensory impairments.

Specific Language Impairments

Some children develop normally in all respects except for language. Children with **specific language impairments** have delays or abnormalities in spoken language or in language comprehension that significantly interfere with their performance at school. Such impairments may involve problems in one or more of the following:

- Receptive language (e.g., inability to distinguish among different phonemes, difficulty understanding or remembering directions)
- Articulation (e.g., mispronunciations or omissions of certain speech sounds)
- Fluency (e.g., stuttering, an atypical rhythm in speech)
- Syntax (e.g., abnormal syntactic patterns, incorrect word order)
- Semantics (e.g., infrequent use of grammatical words, such as prepositions and conjunctions; frequent use of words with imprecise meanings, such as *thing* or *that*; difficulty interpreting words that have two or more meanings)
- Pragmatics (e.g., talking for long periods without letting others speak). (American Speech-Language-Hearing Association, 1993; Hulit & Howard, 2006; Joanisse, 2007)

Specific language impairments are also suspected when children don't demonstrate age-appropriate language. However, speech patterns that reflect a regional or ethnic dialect and those that are due to a bilingual background do *not* fall within the realm of specific language impairments. (Recall the speech therapist who inappropriately recommended that Mario have speech therapy.)

In comparison with their nondisabled peers, children with specific language impairments have greater difficulty mentally processing particular aspects of spoken language—perhaps the quality, pitch, duration, or intensity of specific sounds in speech (Corriveau, Pasquini, & Goswami, 2007; P. R. Hill, Hogben, & Bishop, 2005; Thatcher, 2010). Some of these children have problems with reading and writing (Catts, Adlof, Hogan, & Weismer, 2005; J. R. Johnston, 1997; Leonard, 2009). Personal and social problems may also emerge. Some youngsters feel so self-conscious about their language disability that they are reluctant to speak to peers (Patton et al., 1996). And if they sound "odd" or are difficult to understand, they may suffer the ridicule of thoughtless classmates (Durkin & Conti-Ramsden, 2007; LaBlance, Steckol, & Smith, 1994; Rice, Hadley, & Alexander, 1993).

In some cases specific language impairments are inherited (D. Bishop, 2010; F. M. Spinath, Price, Dale, & Plomin, 2004). In other instances they are associated with specific brain abnormalities that occur for unknown reasons (Basu, Krishnan, & Weber-Fox, 2010; Locke, 1993). Often

specific language impairment Disability characterized by abnormalities in producing or understanding spoken language, to the point where special educational services are required.

[22]We discuss autism spectrum disorders in Chapter 12.

the exact cause of the impairment is unknown (T. F. Campbell et al., 2003; Hulit & Howard, 2006; P. P. Wang & Baron, 1997).

Although trained specialists typically work with children who have impaired language skills, parents, teachers, and other adults can also facilitate the language development of these youngsters. Several recommendations are presented in the Development and Practice feature "Working with Children Who Have Specific Language Impairments."

DEVELOPMENT AND PRACTICE
Working with Children Who Have Specific Language Impairments

Be on the lookout for children who exhibit significant delays or other language problems unusual for their age-group.

- An expert caregiver is familiar with milestones in language development and watches for red flags indicating a significant delay (e.g., absence of babbling, pointing, and gestures by the end of the first year; no words by about 16 months; and no two-word phrases by the second year). Without overreacting, the caregiver talks with parents of children who show major delays in language development and suggests that a pediatrician or speech-language pathologist may be able to offer appropriate assessment. (Infancy)
- A preschool teacher consults with a speech-language pathologist about a 4-year-old girl who communicates only by pointing and gesturing. "She's certainly not shy," the teacher explains. "She often tries to get other children's attention by poking them, and she loves to sit on my lap during story time." (Early Childhood)

Encourage children to speak.

- A fourth-grade teacher has a couple of children in class who repeat themselves a lot, hesitate while speaking, change the topic during the middle of a sentence, and say "um . . ." a lot. The teacher offers several guidelines to the entire class that may help children generally and children with oral disfluencies in particular. He arranges for children to practice reading in pairs, encourages children to practice their stories individually before reading them in front of the class, and tells all children that they can take their time when responding to questions. (Middle Childhood)
- An 11-year-old has trouble pronouncing the *s* sound (e.g., he says "thpethial" for *special*) and is meeting regularly with a speech therapist to address the problem. Nevertheless, his fifth-grade teacher encourages him to speak in class, especially in small-group settings. When he does so, she models acceptance of his disability, and if a classmate makes fun of his speech, she discreetly takes the classmate aside and explains that all children have strengths and weaknesses and that everyone in her class deserves respect. (Early Adolescence)

Listen patiently.

- Before children read their stories out loud for the class, an elementary teacher discusses expectations on how to listen. She tells the children

that everyone is expected to listen quietly and respectfully and to make comments, give compliments, and offer tactful suggestions that will help their classmates become better writers. (Middle Childhood)
- A high school student often stutters when she speaks and sometimes struggles for several seconds midway through a sentence to pronounce a particular word. Her teachers know that she is able to complete her thoughts if they give her time. (Late Adolescence)

Ask for clarification when a message is unclear.

- A preschool teacher sits down with a child who has a language delay and helps him to formulate his thoughts during dramatic play. The teacher comments on his actions and expands on his simple phrases. When she is not clear on his meaning, she asks for clarification, providing him with options if she can guess what he might be trying to say. When he says "wrenchit," she asks, "Are you pretending that you are fixing the clock with a special wrench?" (Early Childhood)
- An 8-year-old boy often says "this" or "that thing there" when referring to objects in the classroom. Suspecting that he may have an undiagnosed language disability, his third-grade teacher talks with his parents and then refers him to a school psychologist for evaluation and encourages him to call objects by their names. (Middle Childhood)

Provide guidance about how to talk effectively with others.

- During storybook sharing, third-grade children form small groups of two or three students and talk about the books they had read. Before the groups meet, their teacher gives brief instruction to a girl with a language delay. The teacher suggests that the way to be a good listener is to offer a compliment to the person who gives a report or to make a comment on a feature of the book that seems interesting. (Middle Childhood)
- A middle school student often dominates conversations in small-group discussions, rambling on at such length that her classmates have trouble getting a word in edgewise. Her teacher meets with her during lunch one day to remind her of the importance of letting everyone participate. Together they identify a strategy that will help her restrict her comments: Whenever she starts to speak, she will look at the second hand on her watch and yield the floor after a maximum of 30 seconds. (Early Adolescence)

Sources: L. Bloom & Lahey, 1978; Otto, 2010; Patton et al., 1996; Turnbull et al., 2007.

Happy Mother's Day!

ARTIFACT 9-4 For Mom. Children with hearing loss can interact more effectively with classmates who know sign language. Here, Marianne, a hearing child, has created a Mother's Day card using the sign for "I love you."

Sensory Impairments and Language Development

Children with severe visual impairments (e.g., blindness) typically have normal syntactic development but are apt to have more limited vocabularies than their sighted age-mates (M. Harris, 1992). Because they cannot always see the objects and events around them, they simply don't have as many opportunities to make connections between words and their meanings (Hobson, 2004; M. B. Rowe, 1978).

Children with hearing impairments (e.g., deafness) are at risk for delays in both syntactic and semantic development, especially if an impairment was present at birth or emerged early in life (M. Harris, 1992). Furthermore, children who have been completely deaf from birth or soon thereafter typically need special training to develop proficiency in speaking. Yet these children are apt to show normal language development in *sign language* if family members and others use it as the primary means of communicating with them (Mann, Marshall, Mason, & Morgan, 2010; Newport, 1990; L. A. Petitto, 1997). Deaf infants who are regularly exposed to sign language often begin to "babble" with their hands at 7 to 10 months, are apt to sign their first word at around 18 to 22 months, and use multiword phrases soon thereafter. Like hearing children, children who use sign language appear to construct rules that guide their language use, and they gradually expand on and refine these rules over time (Goldin-Meadow & Mylander, 1993; L. A. Petitto, 1997).

A case study of BoMee (Wilcox, 1994) illustrates just how much is possible when parents provide a linguistically rich environment through sign language. BoMee was born in Korea 8 weeks prematurely. Although she could hear at birth, early illnesses or medications apparently caused profound hearing loss early in life. At age 2½, BoMee was adopted by American parents, who regularly communicated with her in sign language. Within a few weeks after BoMee's arrival, they also began to sign their self-talk as a way of "thinking aloud." For instance, BoMee's mother might have signed "What goes next in this recipe?" or "Where are my shoes?" Within a week, BoMee began signing her own self-talk, such as "Where my shoes are?" Soon self-talk was a regular feature in BoMee's problem-solving activities. On one occasion, BoMee was trying to put a dress on her doll, but the dress was too small. She signed to herself:

> Hmmm, wrong me. This dress fit here? Think not. Hmmm. For other doll here. (Translation: *Hmmm, I'm wrong. Does this dress go on this doll? I don't think so. Hmmm. It goes on this other doll.*) (Wilcox, 1994, p. 119)

BoMee showed other normal linguistic behaviors as well. She adapted her language when she signed to her baby brother. And just as hearing children typically read aloud in the early stages of reading, BoMee signed "out loud" when she began to read.

Like Mario, BoMee may have had an advantage in the development of metalinguistic awareness. She was exposed to both English-based signs and American Sign Language (which have somewhat different vocabularies and syntactic structures) and quickly became bilingual in her knowledge of the two language systems. She also understood very early that some people talk and others use sign language. Furthermore, shortly after her third birthday, she appropriately signed "This Little Piggy" in two different ways—in English-based signs and in American Sign Language—to people who understood only one of the two languages. Clearly, then, children with hearing loss can have very normal cognitive and linguistic development when their language environment is appropriate for them.

Children who have sensory impairments typically work with specialists to develop strategies for communicating effectively with others. Teachers, parents, and other adults can also help these children in many ways. Examples are presented in the Development and Practice feature "Working with Children Who Have Hearing Impairments."

DEVELOPMENT AND PRACTICE
Working with Children Who Have Hearing Impairments

Intervene as early as possible to address correctable hearing impairments.

- Among the children in a preschool class is a 3-year-old boy who is deaf. His mother expresses interest in a cochlear implant but cannot afford one. The boy's teacher and an audiologist locate a charitable organization that will pay for the cost of surgery. With the implant, the boy begins to hear the language around him, and both his receptive and expressive language rapidly develop. (Early Childhood)

- A third-grade teacher wonders whether a boy in her class might have a hearing difficulty. She notices that he responds to her only when she is in face-to-face interaction with him. During large-group instruction, he does not follow directions without hearing them several times and seems to misunderstand a lot of what she and classmates say. The teacher talks with the boy's parents, and together they decide to have him referred to a speech-language pathologist for testing. (Middle Childhood)

Communicate messages through multiple modalities.

- During a large-group meeting of the class, a fifth-grade teacher places a girl with a hearing impairment nearby so that she has a good view of the teacher and can see the pictures more clearly. (Middle Childhood)

- A 15-year-old who is deaf has a student-specific aide who accompanies her to all of her classes and manually translates the content of teachers' lectures and explanations. Even so, her teachers make sure that they communicate as much as possible through sight as well as sound. They write important points on the chalkboard and illustrate key ideas with pictures and other graphics. (Late Adolescence)

Learn elements of American Sign Language and finger spelling, and teach them to children's peers.

- A teacher in a combined first- and second-grade class has several students who are deaf, and so she both speaks and signs to her class as she presents new information and describes assignments. All of her students know enough American Sign Language to converse easily with one another. (The teacher and students are depicted in the two "Language Classroom" videos in Topic 9 of MyEducationLab.) (Middle Childhood)

- An elementary school with a large population of children who have hearing impairments offers a weekly workshop in American Sign Language. Several parents and other family members of these children who sign attend, as do a few parents of hearing children who volunteer in the classroom and want to be able to communicate with all of the children. (Middle Childhood)

Sources: Bruer, 1999; Newport, 1990; Otto, 2010; Svirsky, Robbins, Kirk, Pisoni, & Miyamoto, 2000.

SUMMARY

Theoretical Perspectives of Language Development

Although modeling, reinforcement, and feedback almost certainly play some role in language development, early theories based on such processes could not adequately account for the fact that most children acquire a complex language system in a very short period, and with only limited guidance from adults. Several more recent theoretical perspectives have emerged, each focusing on somewhat different aspects of language development. *Nativists* propose that young children have certain inherited knowledge and skills that facilitate language acquisition. *Cognitive process theorists* apply general principles of cognition (e.g., the importance of attention, the detection of patterns in language input) to explain how some aspects of language may develop. *Sociocultural theorists* emphasize the role that social interactions play in language learning. *Functionalists* propose that children develop language primarily because it enhances their effectiveness in social groups and increases their ability to satisfy their own needs. Many theorists draw from elements of two or more of these perspectives when explaining how language develops.

Trends in Language Development

Children and adolescents develop their linguistic knowledge and skills throughout infancy, childhood, and adolescence. School-age children add several thousand new words to their vocabulary each year. Over time, children rely less on word order and more on syntax to interpret other people's messages, and they can comprehend and produce sentences with increasingly complex syntactic structures. Their conversations with others increase in length, they become better able to adapt the content of their speech to the characteristics of their listeners, and they become more aware of the unspoken social conventions that govern verbal interactions in their culture. They also acquire a growing understanding of the nature of language as an entity in and of itself.

Development of a Second Language

Individuals easily learn two languages during infancy and early childhood but retain the ability to learn a second language later in childhood, during adolescence, or as adults. Research consistently indicates that knowing two or more languages enhances achievement in reading and other language arts, promotes greater metalinguistic awareness, and fosters multicultural sensitivity. Several instructional models exist for teaching English to English language learners. Research is still ongoing, but serious concerns are being raised about the effectiveness of instruction in English for English language learners, the need for instructional models to ensure that English language learners make adequate progress in academic subjects, and the importance of supporting children's proficiency in their native language so that they can continue to communicate with family and community members.

Different models of instruction exist for teaching native English speakers a second language, and these are effective to the degree that instruction embeds the new language in cultural issues.

Bioecology of Language Development

Children develop language as individuals with personal characteristics and experiences. Subtle qualitative differences have been observed in the conversational styles of males and females. Children from higher-SES backgrounds tend to have larger vocabularies, probably because they are likely to be exposed to a wider variety of words. Different ethnic groups may show differences in sociolinguistic behaviors, storytelling traditions, use of figurative language, and dialects. Numerous personal and environmental influences interact in highly individual ways in language development.

Exceptionalities in Language Development

Some children have disabilities that affect their language development. Specific language impairments include abnormalities in receptive or expressive language that significantly interfere with children's performance and accomplishments in and out of school. Children with hearing impairments and, to a lesser extent, those with visual impairments may have more limited language proficiency because of reduced exposure to language or reduced awareness of the meaningful contexts in which it is used.

APPLYING CONCEPTS IN CHILD DEVELOPMENT

The exercises in this section will help you build your ability to apply your knowledge of child development in working with children.

Improving Your Observation Skills

On page 333, you examined a photograph of a mother showing her son a monkey and were asked, *"What cues in the language and context might the boy use to interpret his mother's utterance?"* The boy would probably realize that he and his mother are attending to the same creature, a monkey. The boy would also probably be familiar with sound combinations in English generally and the phrase "It's a . . ." in particular, providing a clue that his mother is telling him the name of something. Finally, the boy is probably assuming that his mother is providing a label for the entire organism rather than its color or some other specific feature of it.

On page 345, you examined a photograph of a boy interacting with his baby brother and were asked, *"What evidence is there that the boy is adjusting his speech according to his perceptions of his younger brother's needs?"* The preschool-aged boy is doing several things that suggest he is adapting his speech according to his perceptions of his baby brother's language abilities. The boy successfully attracts the baby's attention with his loving posture and eye contact. We cannot know what he says, but if you look closely, you can see that the boy is using a sign with his hands that the baby seems to be inspecting. If you examine the art on p. 364, you may notice the same sign: "I love you," in American Sign Language.

Practicing for Your Licensure Examination

Many teaching tests require students to use what they have learned about child development in responses to brief vignettes and multiple-choice questions. You can practice for your licensure examination by reading about language learning at a boarding school and answering a series of questions.

Boarding School

Read the case and then answer the questions that follow it.

Some parts of Alaska are so sparsely settled that building local high schools makes little economic sense. So in certain Native American communities, older students are sent to boarding school for their high school education. A high priority for boarding school teachers is to help students master Standard English. With this information in mind, consider the following incident:

Many of the students at the school spoke English with a native dialect and seemed unable to utter certain essential sounds in the English language. A new group of speech teachers was sent in to correct the problem. The teachers worked consistently with the students in an attempt to improve speech patterns and intonation, but found that their efforts were in vain.

One night, the boys in the dormitory were seeming to have too much fun, and peals of laughter were rolling out from under the door. An investigating counselor approached cautiously and listened quietly outside the door to see if he could discover the source of the laughter. From behind the door he heard a voice, speaking in perfect English, giving instructions to the rest of the crowd. The others were finding the situation very amusing. When the counselor entered the room he found that one of the students was speaking. "Joseph," he said, "You've been cured! Your English is perfect." "No," said Joseph returning to his familiar dialect, "I was just doing an imitation of you." "But if you can speak in Standard English, why don't you do it all of the time?" the counselor queried. "I can," responded Joseph, "but it sounds funny, and I feel dumb doing it." (Garrison, 1989, p. 121)

Constructed-Response Question

1. Why might Joseph prefer his native dialect to Standard English?

Multiple-Choice Questions

2. The counselor told Joseph that he had "been cured." What beliefs about Joseph's native dialect does this statement reflect?

   a. The belief that Joseph's dialect was inferior to Standard English
   b. The belief that the dialect was a problem that needed to be corrected
   c. The belief that the counselor could benefit from learning the Native American dialect
   d. Both a and b

3. Considering the information in this chapter, how might teachers deal effectively with the language proficiencies of children in Joseph's school?

   a. Teachers should continue to insist that children use only Standard English at school.

b. Teachers should revert to teaching all subjects in the local dialect.

c. Teachers might encourage Standard English in most written work and in formal oral presentations but welcome the local dialect in creative writing and informal class discussions.

d. Teachers might allow children to use the local dialect in formal communication and Standard English in letters home to families.

Once you have answered these questions, compare your responses with those presented in Appendix A.

Improving Your Ability to Interpret Children's Artifacts and Reflections

Consider chapter concepts as you analyze the following accomplishments of a child's understanding of a figure of speech.

Figure of Speech

In response to an assignment in his third-grade class, 8-year-old Jeff drew his interpretation of the common expression *Your eyes are bigger than your stomach*. As you look at Jeff's drawing, consider these questions:

- What aspects of language has Jeff mastered?
- What aspect of language has he apparently *not* yet mastered?
- Is Jeff's performance on this assignment usual or unusual for his age?

Once you have answered these questions, compare your ideas with those presented in Appendix B. For further practice in analyzing children's artifacts and reflections, go to the Activities and Applications section in Chapter 9 of MyEducationLab.

Key Concepts

phonology (p. 326)	expressive language (p. 334)	figurative speech (p. 342)	English language learner (ELL) (p. 356)
semantics (p. 326)	lexical word (p. 334)	cooing (p. 343)	bilingual education (p. 356)
syntax (p. 326)	grammatical word (p. 334)	babbling (p. 343)	submersion (p. 358)
pragmatics (p. 326)	underextension (p. 334)	narrative (p. 345)	structured English immersion (p. 358)
native language (p. 326)	overextension (p. 335)	playing the dozens (p. 346)	immersion (p. 358)
nativism (p. 327)	holophrase (p. 337)	sociolinguistic behaviors (p. 348)	foreign language instruction (p. 358)
language acquisition device (p. 327)	telegraphic speech (p. 337)	personal space (p. 350)	subtractive bilingualism (p. 358)
infant-directed speech (p. 329)	semantic bootstrapping (p. 338)	IRE cycle (p. 350)	Standard English (p. 361)
language socialization (p. 329)	overregularization (p. 338)	wait time (p. 351)	dialect (p. 361)
functionalism (p. 330)	expansion (p. 339)	culture shock (p. 351)	African American English (p. 361)
fast mapping (p. 333)	phonemes (p. 340)	metalinguistic awareness (p. 351)	specific language impairment (p. 362)
receptive language (p. 334)	comprehension monitoring (p. 342)	bilingualism (p. 355)	

PEARSON
myeducationlab

Now go to www.myeducationlab.com to:
- Take a Quiz to test your mastery of chapter objectives.
- Study chapter content with an individualized Study Plan.
- Deepen your understanding of particular concepts and principles with Review, Remediation, and Enrichment Exercises.
- Apply what you have learned in the chapter to your work with children in Building Teaching Skills and Dispositions exercises.
- Observe children and their unique contexts in Video Examples.

Chapter Ten

Development in the Academic Domains

CASE STUDY: Osvaldo's Story

Suzanne Peregoy, a specialist in language and literacy development, spent several days in a kindergarten class-room with English language learners whose native tongue was Spanish. She observed the children's daily experiences in writing, listening to stories, and playing in dramatic play centers (Peregoy & Boyle, 2008). During one English language arts lesson, Suzanne asked the children if they might like to write a story in English that she would bring home to her husband. She handed out pieces of paper with blank spaces at the top for drawings and lines at the bottom for written text.

The children took pen to paper. Lisa wrote, "I love my mom" and illustrated her story with a picture of her-self, her mother, and several hearts (Peregoy & Boyle, 2008, p. 153). Rosa drew her family of seven and filled in a few lines with evenly spaced block letters. Osvaldo was last to finish. He first wrote a series of letters, which were unintelligible to Suzanne, and then drew a boy with a soccer ball. Suzanne asked him numerous times what he was writing. He replied that he didn't know and eventually, after her persistent questioning, responded, "I won't know what my story is about until I finish my picture!" (Peregoy & Boyle, 2008, p. 153).

When Suzanne returned to the classroom at a later time, Osvaldo asked her, "How'd your daddy like the story?" (Peregoy & Boyle, 2008, p. 153). Osvaldo had meant her husband, of course, and was genuinely interested in how his story had been received.

- What did Osvaldo understand about writing?
- Which tasks of writing would Osvaldo need to master in the years ahead?

Osvaldo understands a great deal about writing. He realizes that stories communicate an author's intentions. He understands that readers have their own responses to text. He appreciates that print and art are linked and views his artwork as having the commanding voice in his own story.

In the years ahead, Osvaldo will learn even more about how to write. He may continue to illustrate his stories but will find that he can communicate many of his thoughts through words alone. He will learn to use conventional spelling, follow the rules of grammar and punctuation, and represent a topic cohesively. With guidance from his teachers, the foundations Osvaldo has already achieved will help him to tackle these and other challenges in learning to write.

As children enter preschool and kindergarten, they bring relevant background knowl-edge about many academic subjects—reading, writing, arithmetic, geography, music, and so on. Schools build on these initial mental frameworks and extend them with instruction. In this chapter, we look at how competences in a variety of academic disciplines develop over the course of childhood and are fostered with age-appropriate instruction.

READING DEVELOPMENT

Children's literacy skills—their abilities in reading and writing—obviously build on their knowledge of spoken language. The thousands of words and innumerable grammatical structures that children master in speech are basic elements of written language as well.[1]

---

[1] Language development is described in depth in Chapter 9.

However, written language differs from spoken language in important ways. To learn to read and write, children must understand the relationships between how words sound and how they look and are written on paper. Children must also master the nuances of a written symbol system that have no counterparts in spoken language, such as punctuation marks and appropriate uses of upper- and lowercase letters (D. Coker, 2007; S. G. Paris & Cunningham, 1996; Stephenson, 2010). In the upcoming sections, we look at children's acquisition of basic knowledge about written language and then examine the development of several critical aspects of reading.

Emergent Literacy

Through early exposure to reading and writing, young children learn many things about written language. For instance, they learn the following:

- Print conveys meaningful information.
- Different kinds of printed matter (storybooks, newspapers, grocery lists, greeting cards, etc.) serve different purposes.
- Spoken language is transcribed according to certain rules (e.g., specific alphabet letters are associated with specific sounds, words are always spelled the same way).
- Written language includes some predictable elements and conventions (e.g., fairy tales often begin with "Once upon a time," and in English, writing proceeds from left to right and from the top of the page to the bottom). (Cabell, Justice, Konold, & McGinty, 2010; Lonigan, Farver, Phillips, & Clancy-Menchetti, 2011; S. G. Paris & Cunningham, 1996; Pérez, 1998; Serpell, Baker, & Sonnenschein, 2005; Treiman, Cohen, Mulqueeny, Kessler, & Schechtman, 2007; Weiss & Hagen, 1988)

Such basic knowledge about written language, which lays a foundation for reading and writing development, is known as **emergent literacy**.

Parents and other adults encourage emergent literacy in numerous ways. They provide easy access to reading and writing materials. They model reading and writing behavior. They take children on frequent trips to the library. They talk about the things they've read and written. They demonstrate that reading and writing are useful and enjoyable activities. But perhaps most importantly, they read to children regularly (L. Baker, Scher, & Mackler, 1997; Huebner & Payne, 2010; Serpell et al., 2005). Reading to children is especially valuable when adults ask children questions, invite their responses, and connect story concepts to events in children's lives (Huebner & Payne, 2010; Panofsky, 1994; Whitehurst et al., 1994).[2]

Young children whose parents read to them frequently learn to read more easily once they reach elementary school than do young children without this exposure (Myrberg & Rosén, 2009; Sénéchal & LeFevre, 2002; Whitehurst et al., 1994). Associating literacy activities with pleasure is especially important. Children who enjoy their early reading experiences often become enthusiastic readers in their later years (L. Baker et al., 1997; Vandermaas-Peeler, Nelson, Bumpass, & Sassine, 2009).

By observing young children interact with books and writing implements, teachers and other caregivers can determine what children have learned about the nature of written language. The Observation Guidelines table "Assessing Emergent Literacy in Young Children" offers several ideas about what to look for. You can also observe age-appropriate books for infants and a young child's emergent literacy in the "Emotional Development: Infancy" and "Literacy: Early Childhood" videos respectively in MyEducationLab.

Letter Recognition and Phonological Awareness

Knowing letters and the sounds that each one represents is an obvious prerequisite for learning to read (M. Harris & Giannouli, 1999; Piasta & Wagner, 2010; Scarborough, 2001). But in addition, children are more successful readers when they have **phonological**

MyEducationLab

Observe appropriate books for infants in the "Emotional Development: Infancy" video. (Find Video Examples in Topic 10 of MyEducationLab.)

MyEducationLab

Observe Carrie's emergent literacy in the "Literacy: Early Childhood" video. (Find Video Examples in Topic 10 of MyEducationLab.)

emergent literacy
Knowledge and skills that lay a foundation for reading and writing; typically develops in the preschool years from early experiences with written language.

---

[2] By talking about what they have read together, adults engage children in the *social construction of memory* we discuss in Chapter 7.

OBSERVATION GUIDELINES
Assessing Emergent Literacy in Young Children

CHARACTERISTICS	LOOK FOR	EXAMPLE	IMPLICATION
Attitudes Toward Books	• *Frequent manipulation and perusal of books* • *Interest and attentiveness* when adults read storybooks • *Eagerness to talk about stories* that are read	Martina often mentions the Berenstain Bears books that her father reads to her at home.	Devote a regular time to storybook reading, choose books with colorful pictures and imaginative story lines, and occasionally stop to discuss events in a story. Make regular trips to the library.
Behaviors with Books	• *Correct handling of books* (e.g., holding them right-side up, turning pages in the appropriate direction) • *Pretend reading* • *Use of pictures* to construct a logical sequence of events when pretending to read • *Asking "What does this say?"* when coming across repeated phrases in the text	Rusty doesn't seem to know what to do with the books in his preschool classroom. He opens them haphazardly and apparently sees nothing wrong with ripping out pages.	If children have had only limited experience with books, occasionally read one-on-one with them. Let them hold the books and turn the pages. Gently show young children how to take care of books so that pages don't tear.
Letter and Word Recognition	• *Recognition of product names* when they appear in logos and other familiar contexts • *Correct identification* of some alphabet letters • *Recognition of own name* in print	Katherine sees a take-out bag from a local fast-food restaurant and correctly deduces that it says "Burger King."	Prominently label any coat hooks, storage boxes, and other items that belong to individual children. Write children's names in large letters on paper and encourage them to trace or copy the letters. When children are ready, ask them to put their first name (or first initial) on their artwork.
Writing Behaviors	• *Production of letter-like shapes* • *Writing in a left-to-right sequence* (in English and certain other languages) • *Ability to write some letters* correctly or almost correctly • *Ability to write own name*	Hank can write his name, but he frequently reverses the *N* and sometimes leaves it out altogether.	Give children numerous opportunities to experiment with writing implements (paper, crayons, markers, pencils, etc.) in both structured tasks and unstructured situations. Guide letter and word formation when children show an interest in being helped with letter formation
Knowledge About the Nature and Purposes of Written Language	• *Awareness that specific words are always spelled in the same way* • *Correct identification of reference materials*, perhaps telephone books, calendars, and computer manuals • *Pseudowriting* for particular purposes	When Shakira and Lucie pretend to shop, they write several lines of squiggles on a piece of paper. They say that this is a list of items they need to get at the store.	Encourage play activities that involve pretend writing (e.g., writing and delivering "letters" to friends or classmates). Let children see you engaging in a wide variety of reading and writing activities.

Source: Cabell et al., 2010; Dickinson, Wolf, & Stotsky, 1993; Hawkins, 1997; McLane & McNamee, 1990; S. G. Paris, Morrison, & Miller, 2006; D. W. Rowe & Harste, 1986; Serpell et al., 2005; Share & Gur, 1999; Sulzby, 1985; Treiman et al., 2007.

awareness—when they can hear the distinct sounds that make up words (Boscardin, Muthén, Francis, & Baker, 2008; Corriveau, Goswami, & Thomson, 2010; Stanovich, 2000). Phonological awareness includes abilities such as these:

- Hearing the specific syllables within words (e.g., hearing "can" and "dee" as separate parts of *candy*)
- Dividing words into discrete word sounds, or *phonemes* (e.g., hearing the sounds "guh," "ay," and "tuh" in *gate*)[3]
- Blending separate phonemes into meaningful words (e.g., recognizing that, when put together, the sounds "wuh," "eye," and "duh" make *wide*)
- Identifying words that rhyme (e.g., realizing that *cat* and *hat* end with the same sounds).

phonological awareness
Ability to hear the distinct sounds of which spoken words are comprised.

[3] This aspect of phonological awareness is sometimes called *phonemic* awareness.

Phonological awareness develops gradually during the preschool and early elementary years (Byrnes & Wasik, 2009; Goswami, 2007; Lonigan et al., 1998). Most children can detect syllables within words by age 4, well before they begin school and start learning to read. Soon after, perhaps around age 5, they begin to realize that many syllables can be divided into two parts: an *onset* (one or more consonants that precede the vowel sound) and a *rime* (the vowel sound and any consonants that follow it). By the time they are 6 or 7, many children can identify the individual phonemes in spoken words. This last ability seems to emerge hand in hand with learning to read (Anthony & Francis, 2005; Goswami, 1999; M. Harris & Giannouli, 1999).

Researchers have consistently found letter recognition and phonological awareness to be important factors in children's early reading ability (e.g., Anthony & Francis, 2005; Byrnes & Wasik, 2009; J. R. Kirby, Parrila, & Pfeiffer, 2003). Children acquire these important skills after repeated experiences in identifying patterns in speech. Parents and teachers also cultivate phonological awareness by reading to children and challenging them in various word games (Muter, 1998). The Development and Practice feature "Promoting Phonological Awareness and Letter Recognition in Young Children" presents several useful strategies.

Word Recognition

Many preschool children can correctly identify certain words that appear in familiar contexts. For example, numerous young children correctly identify the word *stop* when it appears on a red, octagonal sign beside the road. They might also "read" the word *Cheerios* on a cereal box. And they know that a word at a fast-food restaurant is *McDonald's* when the *M* takes the form of the well-known golden arches (Ehri, 1994; Homer, 2005; Juel, 1991).

DEVELOPMENT AND PRACTICE
Promoting Phonological Awareness and Letter Recognition in Children

Read alphabet books that use colorful pictures, amusing poems, or entertaining stories to teach letters and their sounds.

- A teacher reads *The Ocean Alphabet Book* (Pallotta & Mazzola, 1986) to an 18-month-old boy. It is the boy's favorite book, and he points at the pictures as his teacher reads the words. (Infancy)
- A preschool teacher shares *Alphabet Adventure* (Wood & Wood, 2001) with her group of 4-year-olds. The children eagerly follow along as the main character, "Little i," looks for her lost dot, and they delight in finding various letters on each page. (Early Childhood)

Have children think of words that rhyme.

- A grandmother reads Dr. Seuss's (1968) *The Foot Book* to her 3-year-old granddaughter, stopping at the end of familiar phrases to allow the little girl to chime in with the anticipated rhyming word. (Early Childhood)
- A kindergarten teacher challenges his students to think of at least five words that rhyme with *break*. (Early Childhood)

Ask children to identify words that begin (or end) with a particular sound or group of sounds.

- A preschool teacher asks children to join her in finding words that end with an "oo" sound. She says, "'Zoo' and the number 'two' end with an 'oo' sound. Can you think of other words that end with an 'oo' sound?" Children volunteer, "Achoo!" "Do," and "True." (Early Childhood)

- A first-grade teacher says, "Listen to the 'str' sound at the beginning of *string*. What are some other words that begin with 'str'?" (Middle Childhood)

Say several words and ask children which one begins (or ends) in a different sound.

- After reading Robert McCloskey's (1948) book *Blueberries for Sal*, a preschool teacher asks his children, "Do you hear the difference between *kuplink*, *kuplank*, and *kuplunk*?" (Early Childhood)
- A second-grade teacher asks, "Listen carefully to these four words: *end*, *dent*, *bend*, and *mend*. Which one ends in a different sound than the others? Listen to them again before you decide: *end*, *dent*, *bend*, and *mend*." (Middle Childhood)

Have children practice forming alphabet letters on paper and through other mediums.

- A preschool teacher gives children pieces of paper with large letters she has prepared with glue and colored sand. Children trace the letters with their fingers. (Early Childhood)
- A kindergarten teacher has children make letters with their bodies. One child stands with his arms outstretched like a *Y*, and two others bend over and clasp hands to form an *M*. (Early Childhood)

Sometime around age 5, children begin to look more closely at words. Initially, they are apt to focus on one or two visually distinctive features, perhaps seeing the "tail" hanging down at the end of *dog* or the two "ears" sticking up in the middle of *rabbit*. Soon after, they begin to use some of a word's letters for phonetic clues about what the word must be. For instance, they might read *box* by looking at the *b* and *x* but ignoring the *o* (Ehri, 1991, 1994).

Once children have mastered letter-sound relationships, they initially rely heavily on these relationships as they read (Byrnes & Wasik, 2009; Ehri, 1991, 1994; Farrington-Flint & Wood, 2007). Doing so allows them to identify such simple words as *cat*, *bed*, and *Jane*. However, they have difficulty when they encounter words that violate general pronunciation rules. For instance, using the rule that *ea* is pronounced "ee" (as in *meat* and *treat*), they might read *head* as "heed" or *sweater* as "sweeter."

By the middle elementary grades, most children have a reasonable **sight vocabulary**: They can recognize a sizable number of words immediately and with little effort. That is, a good deal of word recognition has become *automatized*.[4] When they encounter words that aren't in their sight vocabulary, they draw on letter-sound relationships, familiar prefixes and root words, common spelling patterns, and the meaning of other words in the passage (Ehri & Robbins, 1992; Kuo & Anderson, 2006; Solity & Vousden, 2009).

Reading Comprehension

In its most basic form, reading comprehension involves understanding the words and sentences on the page. But for advanced readers, it also means going *beyond* the page to identify main ideas, make inferences and predictions, and detect an author's assumptions and biases (Perfetti, 1985). Thus reading comprehension is a very *constructive* process: Readers combine what they see on the printed page with their existing knowledge to derive meaning from text. Several general trends characterize the development of reading comprehension:

Children's growing knowledge base facilitates better reading comprehension. As children grow older, they become better able to understand what they read, in part because they know more regarding the topics about which they are reading (Rayner et al., 2001). In fact, reading comprehension ability at *any* age is influenced by topic knowledge (Cromley & Azevedo, 2007; I. W. Gaskins et al., 2007; Lipson, 1983; Snyder & Caccamise, 2010). For example, when second graders read about spiders, those who already know a lot about spiders remember more and draw inferences more easily than peers who know less about the topic (P. D. Pearson, Hansen, & Gordon, 1979).

Children become familiar with common structures in fictional and nonfictional texts. Most 5- and 6-year-olds can distinguish between books that tell stories and those that provide information (S. L. Field, Labbo, & Ash, 1999). As children get older, they also learn how various kinds of texts are typically organized, and such knowledge helps them make better sense of what they read. They gradually acquire a **story schema** that represents the typical components of fictional narratives (main characters, plot, problem resolution, etc.) and use this schema to impose a coherent structure on a short story or novel (Graesser, Golding, & Long, 1991; N. L. Stein, 1982; Van Kleeck, 2008). With age, they also begin to use common structures in nonfiction to enhance their comprehension. When reading a textbook, they may rely on headings and subheadings to help identify key ideas and organize what they are studying.

Children become increasingly able to draw inferences from what they read. The ability to draw inferences is a key factor in children's reading comprehension. Especially as children

LEARNING TO READ. Young readers become increasingly proficient at sounding out new words. With time and practice, they develop a sizable sight vocabulary and recognize many words quickly and easily.

sight vocabulary
Words that a child can immediately recognize while reading.

story schema
Knowledge of the typical elements and sequence of a narrative.

[4] In Chapter 7, *automatization* is defined as the process of becoming able to respond quickly and efficiently while mentally processing or physically performing certain tasks. When skills are automatized, working memory is freed up for other challenging tasks.

HE CANNOT BE SERIOUS. By the time they reach high school, many adolescents no longer take everything they read at face value. Instead, they begin to read text with a critical eye.

Bioecology of Child Development

In the bioecological framework, children contribute to their own reading through their personal abilities and interests. Children's experiences at home and school and with peers influence their enthusiasm for reading and their choices of reading materials.

reach the upper elementary grades, they become more adept at drawing inferences and, hence, more effectively learn new information from what they read (Bowyer-Crane & Snowling, 2010; S. G. Paris & Upton, 1976). At this point, however, they tend to take the things they read at face value, make little attempt to evaluate the quality of ideas, and fail to notice blatant contradictions (Chall, 1996; Markman, 1979; Walczyk, Marsiglia, Johns, & Bryan, 2004). As youngsters reach adolescence and move into the secondary grades, they read written material with a more critical eye (Chall, 1996).

Metacognition in Reading

Metacognition, a person's understandings of his or her own cognitive processes and efforts to control these processes in order to learn more effectively, is an important part of reading.[5] One of the first aspects of metacognition to emerge is the awareness that reading involves more than identifying the words on a page—that it involves making *sense* of text. This awareness probably depends, in part, on how adults portray the process of reading to young children. For instance, when a researcher asked a first grader named Marissa if something she had just read made sense to her, she responded, "What I read never makes sense. The teacher just gives us books so we can practice reading words—they don't have to make sense" (I. W. Gaskins et al., 2007, pp. 196–197).

Successful readers obviously *do* realize that reading is largely a process of sense-making (I. W. Gaskins et al., 2007). As children gain more experience with reading, and especially with reading textbooks and other informational text, they also develop strategies for comprehending written material and improve in their ability to identify main ideas (van den Broek, Lynch, Naslund, Ievers-Landis, & Verduin, 2003). Compared to children in the upper elementary and middle school grades, high school students are more likely to monitor their comprehension as they read and also to backtrack (i.e., reread) when they don't understand something the first time (Garner, 1987; I. W. Gaskins et al., 2007; Hacker, 1995). Not all adolescents use effective metacognitive reading strategies, however, and those who engage in little metacognition often have considerable difficulty understanding and remembering what they read (Alvermann & Moore, 1991; Cromley & Azevedo, 2007; Hacker, 1995).

With ample support, children and adolescents regularly learn to use effective metacognitive strategies and improve their reading comprehension as a result. The Development and Practice feature "Promoting Effective Reading Comprehension Strategies" presents several suggestions.

As young people move through the school years, they generally read with greater fluency and flexibility and comprehend increasingly complex and challenging material. The Developmental Trends table "Reading at Different Age Levels" traces the development of reading over the course of childhood and adolescence.

Bioecology of Reading Development

As you have learned, children's experiences at home affect their reading development. The kind of reader a child becomes also depends on support at school (e.g., the presence of interesting and age-appropriate books), from peers (e.g., whether friends talk about books they've read), and within the broader society (e.g., the role that literacy plays in an ethnic community) (A. B. Jordan, 2005). Connections among settings can be equally important. A young person may have learned to read at home but become an unenthusiastic reader at school if culturally relevant books are not available.

Children's own characteristics strongly influence their reading. Many (but not all) children who are later identified as intellectually gifted begin to read earlier than their peers, and some read frequently and voraciously (L. Olson, Evans, & Keckler, 2006; Piirto, 1999).

[5] Metacognition is described in Chapter 7.

DEVELOPMENT AND PRACTICE
Promoting Effective Reading Comprehension Strategies

Teach reading comprehension skills in all subject areas.

- A middle school mathematics teacher instructs students to read word problems carefully and ask themselves a series of questions: Can I tell what this question is really asking? What other options are there to interpret the problem? What options do I have for solving the problem? How will I know if I have a good solution? (Early Adolescence)

- When a life skills instructor tells his students to read a section of their first aid manual, he suggests several strategies they might use to help them remember what they read. As students begin each section, they should look at the heading and ask a question they think the section will address. At the end of the section, they should stop and consider whether their question was answered. (Late Adolescence)

Model effective reading strategies.

- A girl in a seventh-grade history class reads aloud a passage describing how, during Columbus's first voyage across the Atlantic, many members of the crew wanted to turn around and return to Spain. Her teacher says, "Let's think of some reasons why the crew might have wanted to go home." One student responds, "Some of them might have been homesick." Another suggests, "Maybe they thought they'd never find their way back if they went too far." (Early Adolescence)

- A high school literacy teacher advises students that it may be difficult for them to keep track of all the characters in the novel they will be reading. She says, "When I was reading it, I had to jot down a few notes on who everyone was so I could follow the plot." (Late Adolescence)

Encourage children to relate what they are reading to things they already know.

- Children in a third-grade classroom are reading books on a particular topic in science (e.g., on dinosaurs, insects, or outer space). Before they begin reading a book, their teacher asks them to write answers to three questions: (a) What do you already know about your topic? (b) What do you hope to learn? and (c) Do you think what you learn in your books will change what you already know? (Middle Childhood)

- While reading individually selected autobiographies, students answer questions on a worksheet about basic aspects of the writers' lives (e.g., who was in their family, where they grew up, what kind of education they had). Students also write about how the writers' upbringing was similar to, and different from, their own. (Early Adolescence)

Ask children to identify key elements in stories.

- A fourth-grade teacher instructs his students to ask themselves a series of questions as they read stories: (a) Who is the main character? (b) Where and when did the story take place? (c) What did the main characters do? (d) How did the story end? and (e) How did the main character feel? (Middle Childhood)

- A high school literature teacher asks students to reflect on how the various genres they have examined during the year—short stories, poetry, dramatic texts, and novels— used different strategies to convey mood and emotion. (Late Adolescence)

Suggest that children create mental images that capture what they are reading.

- A second-grade teacher asks children to come up with creative ways to represent challenges faced by characters in a story. Children draw characters with distressed facial expressions and also use various images, including a person falling off a cliff, a prison cell, and a fist-fight, to show the turmoil in characters' lives. (Middle Childhood)

- When a high school English class reads Nathaniel Hawthorne's *The Scarlet Letter*, the teacher suggests that students try to envision what the two main characters, Arthur Dimmesdale and Hester Prynne, might look like. She then asks several students to describe their mental images. (You can see this example in action in the "Scarlet Letter" video in MyEducationLab.) (Late Adolescence)

Scaffold children's early efforts to use complex strategies.

- A middle school science teacher asks her students to write summaries of short textbook passages. She gives them four rules to use as they develop their summaries: (a) Identify the most important ideas, (b) delete trivial details, (c) eliminate redundant information, and (d) identify relationships among the main ideas. (Early Adolescence)

- In a high school chemistry course, students use a computer program to structure their observations and notes. The program asks students to respond to questions such as these: What calculations are necessary? What data must be gathered? What steps are needed to gather the data? (Late Adolescence)

Source: Deeters, 2008; Gambrell & Bales, 1986; I. W. Gaskins et al., 2007; Pressley et al., 1994; Rinehart, Stahl, & Erickson, 1986; Sejnost & Thiese, 2010; Short & Ryan, 1984; H. Thompson & Carr, 1995.

Children with intellectual disabilities are apt to learn to read more slowly than their age-mates, and they acquire fewer effective reading strategies. In some instances they may develop excellent word identification skills yet understand little or nothing of what they read (Cossu, 1999).

Children with visual or hearing impairments face particular challenges when learning to read. Youngsters who are visually impaired cannot see the printed page when caregivers read to them and so may develop strong listening skills but limited knowledge about the

DEVELOPMENTAL TRENDS
Reading at Different Age Levels

AGE	WHAT YOU MIGHT OBSERVE	DIVERSITY	IMPLICATIONS
Infancy (Birth–2 Years) 	• Manual exploration of cloth and cardboard books • Increasing enjoyment of storybooks • More attention to pictures than to story lines • Attention to and enjoyment of rhythm and rhymes in spoken language	• Individual infants vary in their exposure to stories depending on the reading habits of their families. • Some toddlers who are read to regularly participate actively in storybook reading (e.g., by pointing to and labeling objects in pictures), whereas others listen quietly while an adult reads.	• Read books with catchy rhythms and rhymes to capture and maintain attention. • During story time, label and talk about the pictures in books. Recognize that toddlers may not be able to sit still for an entire story.
Early Childhood (2–6 Years) 	• Attention focused largely on pictures rather than print during adult storybook reading (especially before age 6) • Incorporation of books and familiar story lines into play activities • Some knowledge of conventions of written language (e.g., left-to-right direction) by age 4 • Increasing knowledge of letters and letter-sound correspondences • Identification of a few words in well-known contexts (e.g., words on commercial products) • Use of a word's distinctive features (e.g., a single letter or overall shape) in attempts to identify it	• Children who have had little exposure to books before starting school may have less knowledge about the nature of reading. Some cultures emphasize oral language more than written language. • When parents speak a language other than English, they may provide early literacy experiences in their native tongue; such experiences provide a good foundation for reading and writing in English. • Some children begin school knowing the alphabet and may have a small sight vocabulary as well. Others may need to start from scratch in learning letters and their sounds.	• Read to young children using colorful books with high-interest content. • Teach letters of the alphabet through engaging, hands-on activities. • Teach letter-sound relationships through storybooks, games, rhymes, and enjoyable writing activities. • Encourage children to read words that can easily be identified from their contexts. • Encourage parents to read regularly to children and to make frequent visits to the local library.
Middle Childhood (6–10 Years) 	• Ability to hear individual phonemes within words • Increasing proficiency in identifying unfamiliar words • Growing sight-word vocabulary, leading to greater reading fluency • Beginning of silent reading (at age 7 or 8) • Emerging ability to draw inferences • Tendency to take things in print at face value, without critically evaluating the content or looking below the surface for underlying themes	• Children with deficits in phonological awareness have a more difficult time learning to read. • Children with hearing impairments may be slower to master letter-sound relationships. • On average, girls develop reading skills earlier than boys. • Children vary widely in their use of effective comprehension strategies. • Children with strong vocabularies may learn to read more easily than children with limited vocabularies.	• Explore "families" of words (e.g., "fight," "sight," and "light") that are spelled similarly. • Assign well-written trade books (e.g., children's paperback novels) as soon as children are able to read and understand them. • Engage children in discussions about books. Focus on interpretation, inference drawing, and speculation. • For students who struggle with reading, explicitly teach phonological awareness and word identification skills, especially within the context of meaningful reading activities.
Early Adolescence (10–14 Years) 	• Automatized recognition of most common words • Ability to learn new information through reading • Emerging ability to go beyond the literal meaning of text • Developing metacognitive processes that aid comprehension (e.g., comprehension monitoring, backtracking)	• Adolescents with deficits in phonological awareness continue to lag behind their peers in reading development. • Individuals who were poor readers in elementary school often continue to be weak readers in adolescence. • Some individuals (e.g., a number of students with intellectual disabilities) may have excellent word identification skills yet not fully understand what they read. • Individuals with sensory challenges may have less general world knowledge on which to build as they construct meaning from what they read.	• Assign age-appropriate reading materials in various academic areas; provide scaffolding (e.g., questions to answer) to guide youngsters' thinking and learning as they read. • Begin to explore classic works of poetry and fiction. • Seek the advice and assistance of specialists to help promote the reading skills of youngsters who lag far behind their peers.

DEVELOPMENTAL TRENDS (continued)

AGE	WHAT YOU MIGHT OBSERVE	DIVERSITY	IMPLICATIONS
Late Adolescence (14–18 Years)	• Automatized recognition of many abstract and discipline-specific words • Ability to consider multiple viewpoints about a single topic • Ability to critically evaluate what is read • More sophisticated metacognitive reading strategies	• Poor readers draw few if any inferences from what they read and exert limited metacognitive control over their reading. • As classroom learning becomes more dependent on reading textbooks and other written materials, adolescents with reading disabilities may become increasingly frustrated in their attempts to achieve academic success. • Girls are more likely than boys to enroll in advanced literature classes. • Some adolescents are interested in reading assignments from school, whereas other adolescents prefer to make their own choices.	• Expect that many teenagers can learn effectively from textbooks and other reading materials, but continue to scaffold reading assignments, especially for poor readers. • Encourage adolescents to draw inferences and make predictions from what they read. • Ask students to critically analyze classic works of poetry and fiction. • Modify reading materials and paper-pencil assessments for individuals with delayed reading development.

Source: Byrnes & Wasik, 2009; K. Cain & Oakhill, 1998; Chall, 1996; Dryden & Jefferson, 1994; Ehri, 1994; M. A. Evans & Saint-Aubin, 2005; Felton, 1998; M. Harris & Hatano, 1999; Hedges & Nowell, 1995; Hulme & Joshi, 1998; P. Johnston & Afflerbach, 1985; Y. Kim, Petscher, Schatschneider, & Foorman, 2010; Kyle & Harris, 2010; Mancilla-Martinez, Kieffer, Biancarosa, Christodoulou, & Snow, 2011; McBride-Chang & Treiman, 2003; McLane & McNamee, 1990; W. E. Nagy, Berninger, Abbott, Vaughan, & Vermeulen, 2003; S. G. Paris et al., 2006; Owens, 2008; Raikes et al., 2006; L. Reese, Garnier, Gallimore, & Goldenberg, 2000; T. A. Roberts, 2005; Serpell et al., 2005; Share & Gur, 1999; Trawick-Smith, 2003; Treiman et al., 2007; Trelease, 1982; Wigfield, Eccles, & Pintrich, 1996; Yaden & Templeton, 1986.

conventions of written language (the left-to-right progression of words, the use of punctuation, etc.; Edmonds & Pring, 2006; Tompkins & McGee, 1986). Children with hearing impairments who have learned a manual language (e.g., American Sign Language) cannot take advantage of letter-sound relationships and may have limited knowledge of the idioms and other regularities of day-to-day speech (J. F. Andrews & Mason, 1986; Chall, 1996).

Some children with learning disabilities have considerable difficulty learning to read. In its extreme form, this difficulty is known as **dyslexia**, a disability that can manifests itself in several distinct ways and often has biological roots (Galaburda & Rosen, 2001; R. L. Peterson & Pennington, 2010; Shaywitz, Mody, & Shaywitz, 2006). Contrary to popular belief, dyslexia is typically *not* a problem of visual perception, such as reading words or letters backwards. Instead, many children with dyslexia have deficits in phonological awareness (Goswami, 2007; H. L. Swanson, Mink, & Bocian, 1999; J. M. Thomson & Goswami, 2010).[6] Others have deficits in the ability to identify visual stimuli quickly, which translates into difficulty automatizing connections between printed words and their meanings (Menghini et al., 2010; Wimmer, Mayringer, & Landerl, 2000; Wolf & Bowers, 1999). Some children with reading disabilities may also have general information processing difficulties, such as a smaller working memory capacity or a tendency to process information at a slower-than-average rate (Beneventi, Tønnessen, Ersland, & Hugdahl, 2010; Henry & Winfield, 2010).

We find further diversity in children's reading development as a function of their gender, socioeconomic status, and ethnicity.

Gender Differences

On average, girls read better than boys (Weaver-Hightower, 2003). And in the high school grades, girls are more likely than boys to enroll in advanced literature classes (Wigfield et al., 1996). Boys tend to have less interest in reading than girls do, in part because boys find fewer books at school that pique their curiosity and in part because many of

[6] The writing sample in the "Halloween" Improving Your Observation Skills exercise in Chapter 7 (p. 280) shows unusual difficulty with letter-sound relationships. Its author, 7-year-old Nathan, was diagnosed as having a reading disability.

dyslexia
Inability to master basic reading skills in a developmentally typical time frame despite normal reading instruction.

them prefer more physically active pastimes (Freedman, 2003; Marinak & Gambrell, 2010; D. Taylor & Lorimer, 2002–2003). A tenth grader named Devin expressed the latter reason this way: "Why should I want to read about doing things when I can actually *do* them?" (Newkirk, 2002, p. 54). Many boys prefer nonfiction to fiction and, when they do read novels, like to read books focused on action and adventure, science fiction, fantasy, comedy, and horror (Hébert & Pagnani, 2010). Some boys are interested in reading materials on the Internet, for example, the content of websites and gaming manuals.

Socioeconomic Differences

On average, children from low-income families come to school with fewer literacy skills than children from middle- and upper-income families (Serpell et al., 2005). This socioeconomic disparity in reading ability not only persists, but in fact *increases*, over the course of the elementary and secondary school years (Jimerson et al., 1999; Portes, 1996).

Even when low-income parents regularly read to their children and in other ways foster literacy development, children do not always develop the advanced reading skills that are typical of their peers from more advantaged backgrounds (Jimerson, Egeland, & Teo, 1999; G. Li, 2010; McLane & McNamee, 1990). Part of the problem seems to be that teachers are not attuned with the literacy practices that are used by parents in low-income families. In one study of three low-income families, parents read and wrote frequently (G. Li, 2010). They helped children with homework, read for pleasure, corresponded with relatives, and communicated with teachers. Despite being actively involved in their children's schooling, parents found themselves at odds with teachers. Teachers misunderstood the cultural backgrounds of families, for example referring a Sudanese child to an Arabic teacher even though the child did not speak Arabic. Another teacher advised Vietnamese parents to read *with* children when the parents could not speak English well and preferred to supervise children's reading rather than actually reading to them.

Ethnic and Cultural Differences

Most people in Western society believe that literacy is essential for children's eventual success in the adult world (Gallimore & Goldenberg, 2001; Pérez, 1998; Spera, 2005). Yet the particular literacy practices parents use with children vary somewhat by culture. Furthermore, the interpretations that children make of what they read depend in large part on their upbringing in a specific cultural setting. As an example, Rosenna Bakari, a colleague of ours who specializes in African-centered education, describes an incident involving her 7-year-old daughter Nailah:

> [An event] that always stands out in my mind is a reading comprehension question that Nailah had in a workbook. The question asked why two brothers drew a line down the middle of a messy room to clean it. The answer was pretty obvious: The boys were dividing the room in half so that they could each clean their part. However, Nailah could not get to that answer no matter how I scaffolded her. When I told her the answer, she replied, "Why would they divide the room up? They should just both clean it together." I immediately realized that in her African-centered world, division rarely takes place. Most things in our house are communal. Each child is responsible for the other. So for her to get to that answer would have taken something beyond reasonable reading comprehension. She would have had to understand that there are people in the world who operate under different views about sharing and responsibility. That's a more difficult task for a seven-year-old. (R. Bakari, personal communication, 2002)

Young people from all backgrounds respond more favorably to literature that reflects their own culture's customs (Gollnick & Chinn, 2002). In working with African American high school boys, one educator found that the young men were inspired to read books by African American men who wrote about their personal struggles (A. W. Tatum, 2008). One boy, Quincy, previously a nonreader, described his response to Anthony Davis and Jeffrey Jackson's (1998) book, *"Yo, Little Brother . . .": Basic Rules of Survival for Young African American Males*:

> I don't know what made me read it, but I was, like, totally involved in what he's saying. To tell you the truth, I read this book in one day. I ain't started it until that Monday, and I sat down 'cause I wasn't going to read it at first, but I sat down, and said, let me read this book. So as

I flip over the pages and I start out reading, I'm like, I like this book for a reason, so I'm going to try to read, and then I seen this say "Street Smarts" right at the top. I know I know a lot about the street, so I just read to see what they was talking about. Then some of the things they was saying was true. . . . As I was going along I wanted to stop, but I couldn't. I was like, I started it, and I ain't going to sleep 'til about six in the morning. That's how into it I was, and I didn't know I could get into a book like that. To tell you the truth, I forgot I was reading. . . . This is a good book, it helped you out a lot. (A. W. Tatum, 2008, pp. 170–171)

Promoting Reading Development

Traditionally, reading is taught primarily during the elementary grades. Many teachers and other adults assume that middle school and high school students read well enough to learn successfully from textbooks and other printed materials. But as you have learned, this assumption is not always warranted. Even at the high school level, many adolescents have not yet mastered all of the skills involved in reading effectively. Furthermore, children who have trouble reading in elementary school often continue to be poor readers in the secondary grades (Adlof, Catts, & Lee, 2010; Felton, 1998; Shaywitz, 2004) and so may be in particular need of ongoing instruction in reading skills. Consider the following general strategies:

• **Help parents of young children acquire effective storybook reading skills.** In the "Literacy: Infancy" video in MyEducationLab, Corwin's mother enthusiastically engages her son in a discussion about the book they are looking at:

Mother:	Do you wanna see the cow? Would you like to read with Mama? You ready for the cow? Where is he? [turns the page] Huh! The cow says . . .
Corwin:	Mooo!
Mother:	What's that? [points to something in the book]
Corwin:	Boon.
Mother:	Balloon! We can count! One . . .
Corwin:	Two.
Mother:	Two! [reading book] This is my nose. Where's your nose?
Corwin:	[touches his nose]
Mother:	Nose! Where's your toes?
Corwin:	[grabs his toes]
Mother:	There's your toes!

MyEducationLab

Observe strategies Corwin's mother uses during picture book reading in the "Literacy: Infancy" video. (Find Video Examples in Topic 10 of MyEducationLab.)

Notice how Mother models enthusiasm for the book and uses its content to review object labels (*balloon, nose, toes*) and general world knowledge (numbers, what a cow says) with Corwin. When parents use such strategies as they read to their children, their children acquire larger vocabularies, better knowledge of written language, and appreciation for literature (P. A. Edwards & Garcia, 1994; E. Reese, Sparks, & Leyva, 2010; Whitehurst et al., 1994). Yet some parents have little awareness of how to read to young children, perhaps because they themselves were rarely read to when they were young. Such parents may benefit from explicit instruction in strategies for reading to children—labeling and describing pictures, asking questions that encourage inferences and predictions, and inviting children to make comments.

• **Use engaging activities to teach basic reading skills.** Explicit instruction in basic reading skills—relating letters to sounds, identifying simple words, finding main ideas, and so on—facilitates reading development, especially for poor readers (Ehri, Dreyer, Flugman, & Gross, 2007; Elbro & Petersen, 2004; Karemaker, Pitchford, & O'Malley, 2010). To become truly effective readers, children must automatize the most basic aspects of reading, including letter-sound relationships and recognition of common words (K. J. Brown, 2009; Stainthorp, Stuart, Powell, Quinlan, & Garwood, 2010; Stanovich, 2000). Automaticity of reading skills develops primarily through practice. One approach, of course, is to provide drill-and-practice activities—workbook exercises, flash cards, and so on—that help children automatize specific reading skills. Unfortunately, such activities are not always effective and can seem boring to children (C. C. Block, Parris, Reed, Whiteley, & Cleveland, 2009; E. H. Hiebert & Raphael, 1996; J. C. Turner, 1995). Instruction in basic skills does not *have* to be dull, however. With a

Meggie   10/10 ★

1. rode   6. pole
2. note   7. mole
3. nose   8. woke
4. bone   9. code
5. rose   10. stove

ARTIFACT 10-1 Long o, silent e. In this assignment, 7-year-old Meggie, a first grader, practices words with a long o sound and silent e. Instruction in specific letter-sound relationships and common spelling patterns helps children with both reading and spelling. However, too much focus on such drill and practice may lead children to conclude that reading and writing are joyless activities.

MyEducationLab

Observe Alicia's preference for self-chosen literature in the "Literacy: Late Adolescence" video. (Find Video Examples in Topic 10 of MyEducationLab.)

little thought, teachers, parents, and other adults can develop enjoyable, meaningful activities to teach almost any basic reading skill. For instance, to promote phonological awareness in young children, adults might conduct a game of "Twenty Questions" (e.g., "I'm thinking of something in the room that begins with the letter *B*") or ask children to bring something from home that begins with the letter *T*. To foster greater automaticity in word recognition, teachers might encourage children to create "sound boards" (e.g., identifying and listing words that end in "ack," perhaps *black*, *slack*, and *track*; Bear, Invernizzi, Templeton, & Johnston, 2008). Of course, many children are able to improve basic reading skills in the course of reading, so teachers should also arrange for children to read books of interest to them (C. C. Block et al., 2009; Solity & Vousden, 2009).

While espousing an approach known as *whole-language* instruction, some educators have suggested that virtually all basic literacy skills—knowledge of letter-sound relationships, root words, common spelling patterns, and so on—be taught within the context of children's books and other authentic written materials (e.g., Goodman, 1989, 2008; Weaver, 1990). Studies with kindergartners and first graders have found that whole-language approaches are often quite effective in promoting emergent literacy—familiarity with the nature and purposes of books, pretend reading, and so on (Purcell-Gates, McIntyre, & Freppon, 1995; Sacks & Mergendoller, 1997; Stahl & Miller, 1989). On the downside, however, letter-sound relationships and phonological awareness are often shortchanged in strictly whole-language instruction (Juel, 1998; Kauffman & Sasso, 2006; T. A. Roberts & Meiring, 2006). Thus, many theorists urge that teachers strike a balance between whole-language activities and basic-skills exercises, and in fact this is what many teachers do (Biemiller, 1994; Ryder, Tunmer, & Greaney, 2008; Savage, Abrami, Hipps, & Deault, 2009).

• **Keep in mind that some literacy skills transfer from one language to another.** Even in an English-speaking country, reading instruction doesn't necessarily need to begin in English. English language learners often learn to read more quickly and successfully when they are initially taught to read in their native language (Slavin & Cheung, 2005). As they gain proficiency in English and begin to tackle English reading materials, they readily apply some of the knowledge they've acquired in one language—phonological awareness, vocabulary, and so on—to the other language (Huennekens & Xu, 2010; C. P. Proctor, August, Carlo, & Snow, 2006).

• **Identify and address reading problems early.** If children initially struggle with reading, they are apt to read as little as possible and thereby limit their opportunities for practice, improvement, and automatization of basic skills. As a result, the gap between them and their peers widens over time (Stanovich, 2000). To minimize the damage, children should make up any reading deficits early in the game, ideally with explicit training in basic skills in first grade or even earlier. Numerous children with early reading difficulties benefit from intensive training in letter recognition, phonological awareness, word identification, and comprehension strategies (e.g., Bursuck & Blanks, 2010; Dion, Brodeur, Gosselin, Campeau, & Fuchs, 2010; Schneider, Roth, & Ennemoser, 2000). Of course, children with learning delays also need to gain experience with books that they find personally appealing.

• **Use high-interest works of fiction and nonfiction.** Children and adolescents read more energetically and persistently, use more sophisticated metacognitive strategies, and remember more content when they are interested in what they are reading (R. C. Anderson, Shirey, Wilson, & Fielding, 1987; E. Fox, 2009; Guthrie et al., 1998). In the "Literacy: Late Adolescence" video in MyEducationLab, 14-year-old Alicia describes the importance of being able to choose what she reads:

> I really don't like it when the reading is required. I can't read books if they're required. I just avoid reading them because they don't seem very interesting. And even after you read them, even though they might be interesting, they're not as interesting as if you picked them up by yourself.

As much as possible, then, teachers, parents, and other adults should make available reading materials that are likely to be relevant to young people's own lives and concerns, and they should give youngsters some choices about what to read.

We Wear the Mask
by Paul Laurence Dunbar

We wear the mask that grins and lies,
It hides our cheeks and shades our eyes,—
This debt we pay to human guile;
With torn and bleeding hearts we smile,
And mouth with myriad subtleties.

Why should the world be overwise,
In counting all our tears and sighs?
Nay, let them only see us, while
We wear the mask.

We smile, but, O great Christ, our cries
To thee from tortured souls arise.
We sing, but oh the clay is vile
Beneath our feet, and long the mile;
But let the world dream otherwise,
We wear the mask!

ARTIFACT 10-2 **The mask.** Sixteen-year-old Jeff illustrated the poem "We Wear the Mask" by Paul Laurence Dunbar for his American Literature class. Jeff's brightly colored painting is the cheerful face ("mask") that its African American owner presents in public. The black face is the flip side of the mask, as viewed by the person wearing it. Depicted in the holes of the mask are a lynching (left eye); a whipping (right eye); an African American woman and a white baby (nostrils), reflecting white owners' rape of slaves; and a slave ship with someone being thrown overboard (mouth).

• **Conduct group discussions about novels.** Children often construct meaning more effectively when they discuss what they read with peers. Adults can form "book clubs" in which children lead small groups of peers in discussions about specific books (Fish, Rabidoux, Ober, & Graff, 2009; McMahon, 1992; Rief & Heimburge, 2007). Similarly, adults can hold "grand conversations" about a particular work of literature, asking youngsters to share their responses to questions with no single right answers—perhaps questions related to interpretations or critiques of various aspects of a text (Eeds & Wells, 1989; E. H. Hiebert & Raphael, 1996). By tossing around possible interpretations of what they are reading, children often model effective reading and listening comprehension strategies for one another (R. C. Anderson et al., 2001).

• **Have children use a variety of media to capture their interpretations of what they read.** Children might perform skits to illustrate stories, write personal letters that one character in a story might send to another character, or create works of art that illustrate the setting or characters of a novel or the underlying meaning of a poem.

• **Encourage reading outside of school.** Reading beyond school walls—for instance, reading after school and during the summer months—probably accounts for a significant portion of young people's growth in reading (D. P. Hayes & Grether, 1983; Sheldon, Arbreton, Hopkins, & Grossman, 2010; Stanovich, 2000). Providing books that children can take home to read (perhaps accompanied by audiotapes) encourages outside reading and can significantly enhance reading comprehension skills (Koskinen et al., 2000). Visits to the local library can also encourage outside reading.

WRITING DEVELOPMENT

Children must coordinate numerous abilities as they learn to write. Let's examine the age-related trends that occur as children gain increasing experience in writing.

MyEducationLab

Observe 16-month-old Corwin's early attempt at scribbling in the "Literacy: Infancy" video. (Find Video Examples in Topic 10 of MyEducationLab.)

Early Childhood

Children write long before they reach school age, especially if they see people around them writing. By 18 months of age—sometimes even earlier—many toddlers can hold a pencil or crayon and scribble enthusiastically (McLane & McNamee, 1990; Winner, 2006). Children's early efforts with writing implements are largely exploratory, reflecting experimentation with different kinds of marks on paper and other surfaces. You can observe 16-month-old Corwin's attempts at scribbling in the "Literacy: Infancy" video in MyEducationLab.

With the increasing motor coordination they acquire during the preschool years, children better control their hand movements and produce recognizable shapes. By age 4, their writing is clearly different from drawing (Graham & Weintraub, 1996; Sulzby, 1986). It may consist of wavy lines or connected loops that loosely resemble adults' cursive writing. Children's early writing—or more accurately, *pseudowriting*—often reveals considerable knowledge about written language, including the need to pay attention to the orientation of letters and preserve small spaces in between individual print letters.

Improving Your Observation Skills

John's writing. Four-and-a-half-year-old John prepared these writing samples, all on the same day. In the artifact at left, John wrote a letter to his mother. When later asked about what he wrote, he recognized words on the first, third, and fourth lines. He stated that he had included the number "4" in the second line but was not sure what the line said. In the middle artifact, he prepared a shopping list. In the artifact at right, John created a page for a book on dinosaurs, a topic of considerable fascination for him. Which aspects of written language does John exhibit in the writing samples? Compare your response with the explanation at the end of the chapter.

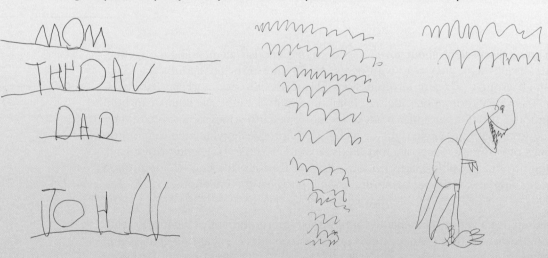

By age 5, children frequently incorporate letters and letter-like forms in their pseudowriting (Byrnes & Wasik, 2009; Graham & Weintraub, 1996). Some preschoolers don't yet realize that writing must take a particular form to have meaning, however, and even those who do may be unable to distinguish between true writing and meaningless marks on a page. For instance, children may scribble something and ask an adult, "What did I write?" (McLane & McNamee, 1990).

Middle Childhood and Adolescence

True writing is, of course, much more than simply putting letter-like forms on paper. To become proficient writers, growing children must not only master handwriting and spelling but also learn conventions of capitalization and punctuation. They must discover how to communicate thoughts clearly and regulate the entire writing effort using metacognitive skills. Unless basic processes are automatized, virtually any writing task exceeds the limits of a typical child's working memory capacity (e.g., Bourke & Adams, 2010; S. Graham, 2006b; Hoskyn & Tzoneva, 2008).

Progress in writing occurs on several fronts as youngsters gain experience in elementary, middle school, and high school. Children show improvements in handwriting, spelling, syntax and grammar, and composition skills.

Handwriting

During the elementary school years, children's handwriting gradually becomes smaller, smoother, and more regular (Graham & Weintraub, 1996). Little if any improvement in handwriting occurs after elementary school, although youngsters generally learn to simplify their letters and write more quickly and efficiently (Olive, Favart, Beauvais, & Beauvais, 2009). Some legibility may be lost during adolescence due to this increased speed. Rapid, automatized handwriting and keyboarding are important factors in effective writing (Berninger, 2004; Graham, Harris, & Fink, 2000; Olive et al., 2009).

Spelling

As you might guess, phonological awareness is as important in spelling as it is in reading (A. Holm, Farrier, & Dodd, 2007; Y. Kim, 2010; Lennox & Siegel, 1998). Children learn the correct spellings of a few words (such as their names) almost as soon as they learn how to write letters of the alphabet. But in their early writing they tend to engage in considerable guesswork about how words are spelled, creating **invented spellings** that correctly capture certain sounds but may only vaguely resemble actual words (Bear et al., 2008; Treiman, 1998). Consider the invented spellings in this kindergartner's creation entitled "My Garden" (note that "HWS" is *house*):

THIS IS A HWS

THE SUN

WL SHIN

ND MI

GRDN

WL GRO (Hemphill & Snow, 1996, p. 192)

As children develop greater phonological awareness, their spellings increasingly represent most or all of the phonemes they hear (Bear et al., 2008; Hemphill & Snow, 1996). Sometime around first or second grade, they also begin to incorporate common letter patterns (e.g., *-ight*, *-ound*, and *-ing* in English) into their spelling (P. Bryant, Nunes, & Aidinis, 1999; Critten, Pine, & Steffler, 2007; Nation & Hulme, 1998). All along, of course, they are learning more and more *correct* spellings, and eventually they automatize many of these spellings, retrieving them quickly and easily as they write (Bear et al., 2008; Rittle-Johnson & Siegler, 1999).

Syntax and Grammar

As children grow older, they use longer sentences and more varied sentence structures in their writing. By the time they are 12 or 13 years old, the syntactic structures they use in written work are considerably more complex than those they use in speech. With age, too, comes an increasing ability to use punctuation and capitalization rules without reminders from adults (Gillam & Johnston, 1992; Nippold, Ward-Lonergan, & Fanning, 2005; Ravid & Zilberbuch, 2003).

Composition Skills

When preschool children engage in early writing activities at home, they often do so with a particular purpose in mind, such as labeling a possession or writing a letter to a grandparent. Only when children enter kindergarten or first grade do most of them begin to write for

invented spelling
A child's early, self-constructed word spelling, which may reflect only some of the word's phonemes.

writing's sake. Children's earliest compositions are usually narratives, such as recollections of personal experiences or short, fictional stories (Hemphill & Snow, 1996). Expository writing (e.g., research reports, persuasive essays) arrives on the scene considerably later (Owens, 2008), possibly because teachers typically don't ask for such writing until the upper elementary grades.

The quality of compositions changes in many ways throughout the elementary and secondary school years, as reflected in the following trends:

Children develop topics in greater depth as they grow older. When children of various ages are asked to write about a particular topic, older ones tend to include more ideas than younger ones do (Byrnes & Wasik, 2009; Donovan, 1999; Scardamalia & Bereiter, 1986). Such growth continues throughout the school years. For instance, when writing persuasive essays, high school students include more arguments than elementary and middle school students do, and 12th graders include more arguments than 9th graders (Knudson, 1992; McCann, 1989).

Children increasingly take their audience into account when they write. Just as children become ever more able to adapt their speech to the characteristics of their listeners, they become more attentive to their readers' needs.[7] With age and experience, children become better able to envision the audience to whom they are writing and tailor their text accordingly (Byrnes & Wasik, 2009; Graham, 2006; Perfetti & McCutchen, 1987).

We became a country by way of common sense. The inhabitants on American soil thought it rather silly and ridiculus to be loyal to, follow rules and pay taxes to a ruler who has never seen where they live. King George III had never set foot (as far as I know) on American soil, but he got taxes and other things from those who lived here. When America decied to unit and dishonnor past laws and rules, England got angry. There was a war. When we won, drew up rules, and accepted states America was born.

In a more poetic sense, we became a country because of who lived here and what they did. They actions of heros, heroines, leaders, followers and everyday people made America famous, an ideal place to live. The different cultures and lifestyles made America unique and unlike any other place in the world. If you think about it, it's like visiting the worlds at Epcot in Florida. You can go from country to country without leaving home.

ARTIFACT 10-3 Common sense. In her account of how the United States became a country, an eighth grader tries to help the reader understand what she is saying—an approach known as *knowledge transforming.* (We've kept her spelling errors intact.)

knowledge telling
Writing down ideas in whatever order they come to mind, with little regard for communicating the ideas effectively.

knowledge transforming
Writing about ideas in such a way as to intentionally help the reader understand them.

Especially in adolescence, a knowledge-telling approach gradually evolves into a knowledge-transforming approach. Young writers often compose a narrative or essay simply by writing down ideas in the order in which the ideas come to mind. Such an approach is known as **knowledge telling** (Bereiter & Scardamalia, 1987; Graham, Harris, & Olinghouse, 2007; Olive et al., 2009). But with age, experience, automatization of basic writing skills, and an increasing ability to take the characteristics of potential readers into account, some adolescents (and a few younger children as well) begin to think of writing as a process of helping potential readers *understand* what they're saying, an approach known as **knowledge transforming**.

With age comes a growing ability to write a cohesive composition. In the elementary grades, children use few if any devices to tie their compositions together. For instance, they may write a story by beginning with "Once upon a time," listing a sequence of events that lead only loosely to one another, and then ending with "They lived happily ever after" (McLane & McNamee, 1990). Their nonfiction, too, may be little more than a list of facts or events. Older children, and especially adolescents, are more capable of analyzing and synthesizing their thoughts as they write, and so they compose more cohesive, integrated texts (Byrnes & Wasik, 2009; McCutchen, 1987; Owens, 2008).

Metacognition in Writing

Good writers think about a topic ahead of time and carefully plan how they are going to write about it. They also critically evaluate their work, looking not only for grammatical and spelling errors but also for omissions, ambiguities, logical flaws, and contradictions (Graham, 2006; Tracy et al., 2009). Such editing skills emerge slowly and are incomplete even by the end of adolescence, in large part because youngsters' metacognitive capabilities are still

[7] We describe children's consideration of listeners' perspectives in Chapter 9.

developing. Young people of various ages have considerable difficulty identifying problems in their own writing, particularly those related to clarity and cohesiveness (Beal, 1996; Berninger, Fuller, & Whitaker, 1996; Fitzgerald, 1987). Because they have trouble reading their own writing as another person might read it, students are apt to think they are expressing themselves more clearly than they really are. As a result, they often don't revise their work unless an adult specifically urges them to do so. When they *do* rewrite, they tend to make only small, superficial changes (Beal, 1996; C. A. Cameron, Hunt, & Linton, 1996; Francis & McCutchen, 1994). Yet with instruction in how to plan and revise stories and reports, students are generally able to reflect on their writing and improve subsequent drafts (Tracy et al., 2009).

With appropriate support from adults, children gradually learn to express themselves effectively. The Developmental Trends table "Writing at Different Age Levels" identifies changes in writing seen during infancy and the preschool, elementary school, and secondary school years.

DEVELOPMENTAL TRENDS
Writing at Different Age Levels

AGE	WHAT YOU MIGHT OBSERVE	DIVERSITY	IMPLICATIONS
Infancy (Birth–2 Years) 	• Development of eye–hand coordination, including the *pincer grasp*, through which infants use thumb and forefinger to pick up and hold objects • Appearance of scribbling at 18 to 24 months • Interest in mimicking "writing"; experimentation with writing implements	• Individual differences appear in the development of fine motor skills. • Infants can imitate only what they see, so those who never see anyone writing are unlikely to mimic writing or understand that some objects are used for writing.	• Allow toddlers to manipulate small objects that do not present choking hazards. • Have a variety of tools available for supervised scribbling and coloring (e.g., fat crayons or washable, non-toxic markers). • Tape writing paper to the table or floor to permit easier writing.
Early Childhood (2–6 Years)	• Increasing muscular control in writing and drawing • Pseudowriting (e.g., wavy lines, connected loops) in preschool play activities • Ability to write own name (perhaps at age 4) • Ability to write most letters of the alphabet (at age 4 or later) • Invented spellings (at ages 5 to 6)	• Some cultures place greater emphasis on writing than others. • Some children have little exposure to written materials at home and so have less knowledge of letters. • Children with visual impairments have less awareness of print conventions (left-to-right progression, use of punctuation, etc.).	• Make writing implements (pencils, markers, paper) easily accessible. • Give children opportunities to write their names and a few other meaningful words. • Have children act out stories they have orally composed.
Middle Childhood (6–10 Years) 	• Gradual increase in smoothness of handwriting; gradual decrease in handwriting size • Increasing use of letter-sound relationships and common letter patterns when spelling words • Predominance of narratives in writing • Difficulty identifying problems (especially problems of clarity) in own writing	• Better readers tend to be better writers, presumably because general language ability provides a foundation for both competencies. • Children with deficits in phonological awareness have a more difficult time learning to spell. • Girls show higher achievement in writing and spelling beginning in the elementary years. • Children with dyslexia often have poor handwriting skills.	• Engage children in authentic writing activities (e.g., writing letters to relatives, creating a newsletter). • Provide regular practice in spelling, grammar, and punctuation (often within authentic activities). • Explore various ways in which particular phonemes and phoneme combinations are spelled in the English language. • Introduce expository forms of writing (e.g., descriptions, lab reports). • Build opportunities for editing into the schedule; provide criteria with which children can self-evaluate and revise their writing.

(continued)

DEVELOPMENTAL TRENDS (continued)

AGE	WHAT YOU MIGHT OBSERVE	DIVERSITY	IMPLICATIONS
Early Adolescence (10–14 Years) 	• Automatized spelling of most common words • Increasing use of expository forms of writing • Use of longer and more complex syntactic structures • Tendency not to edit and revise very much unless strongly encouraged to do so	• Some students (e.g., those with learning disabilities) may have exceptional difficulty with spelling and sentence structure. • A few adolescents write in their spare time (e.g., keeping diaries, writing notes to friends), whereas others write only when required to do so at school.	• Provide continuing instruction in spelling, punctuation, and grammar. • Introduce persuasive and argumentative forms of writing. • Suggest a specific audience for whom to write. • Give feedback on first drafts, including guidance on how to improve clarity and cohesiveness. • Encourage adolescents to use local dialects in creative writing projects.
Late Adolescence (14–18 Years) 	• Ability to write about a particular topic in depth • More organized and cohesive essays • Increasing tendency to knowledge-transform rather than knowledge-tell • More revisions than at younger ages, but with a focus on superficial rather than substantive problems	• Individuals with learning disabilities may focus largely on mechanics (spelling, use of correct grammar, etc.) while writing, perhaps because such skills are not yet automatized. • Individuals from some cultural backgrounds (e.g., a few from some East Asian countries) may be reluctant to put their thoughts on paper unless they are certain that their thinking is correct.	• Assign and scaffold lengthy writing projects. • Teach specific strategies for organizing and synthesizing ideas. • Show examples of effective writing (e.g., writing that illustrates knowledge transforming). • For teens who have language-based learning disabilities, downplay the importance of correct spelling and grammar when evaluating written work; teach strategies for overcoming or compensating for weaknesses.

Source: Beal, 1996; Berninger et al., 1996; Byrnes, 1996; Cameron et al., 1996; Dickinson et al., 1993; Dien, 1998; J. M. Fletcher et al., 2007; Gentry, 1982; Glaser & Brunstein, 2007; Graham, 2006; Graham et al., 2007; Graham & Perin, 2007; Graham & Weintraub, 1996; Halpern, 2006; J. Hansen & Kissel, 2009; M. Harris & Hatano, 1999; Hedges & Nowell, 1995; Hemphill & Snow, 1996; Kellogg, 1967; MacArthur & Graham, 1987; McLane & McNamee, 1990; Owens, 2008; Rittle-Johnson & Siegler, 1999; Robin, Berthier, & Clifton, 1996; Rochat & Bullinger, 1994; Rochat & Goubet, 1995; Shanahan & Tierney, 1990; Smitherman, 1994; Spivey, 1997; Trawick-Smith, 2003; Yaden & Templeton, 1986.

Bioecology of Child Development

Children learn to express themselves as writers in several settings.

Bioecology of Writing Development

As is true for reading development, a child's writing development is influenced by individual characteristics and by experiences at home, with peers, at school, in the community, and by compatible—and sometimes conflicting—expectations across various settings. Thus a boy may compose stories at home but not at school if he feels that his writing is valued by his parents but likely to be judged harshly by his teacher. Some boys, for example, prefer to write about such topics as hunting, comics, video games, and war, but find that teachers want them to address interpersonal relationships or other topics (R. Fletcher, 2006).

The numerous intellectual demands of writing affect children differently depending on their personal characteristics. Some children who are gifted exhibit extraordinary writing talent. In contrast, most children with intellectual disabilities or with specific learning disabilities have problems in handwriting, spelling, and expressing themselves coherently on paper (J. M. Fletcher et al., 2007). Children with writing disabilities typically focus their writing efforts more on addressing mechanical issues (spelling, grammar, etc.) than on communicating clearly (Graham, Schwartz, & MacArthur, 1993). The quality of their writing improves considerably when demands on the mechanical aspects of writing are minimized (e.g., when they can dictate their stories and other compositions) and when they are given specific steps to follow as they write (Hallenbeck, 1996; MacArthur & Graham, 1987; R. J. Sawyer, Graham, & Harris, 1992).

The bioecological framework also reminds us that writing is learned in social settings. Children observe their parents and other family members writing for particular purposes and later imitate these actions, perhaps keeping a journal at night or regularly posting witty reflections on a Facebook account. At school, children are affected by formal writing assignments, instruction from teachers, and interactions with peers. In one study with fourth- and fifth-grade students, researchers focused on Juan, an English language learner who had previously failed to complete his written assignments. When an activity called for children to pair up for a writing assignment, Juan teamed up with his friend Ned and made much more progress. In the following excerpt, the boys speculate about why turtles are disappearing, and Juan is motivated to take notes for the assignment:

Ned: Another way he could get drown is a crab could get him.

Juan: He puts his head in his shell?

Ned: If he sticks his head in his shell, he can't get it out. Then it gets trapped. Then the crab will stick his claws inside it, and sometimes they eat turtles. They stick their claws inside and eat turtles. Sea turtles. He sticks his claws inside and gets the turtle's head and starts eating it. (Juan is writing.)

Juan: Or . . . putting . . . his . . . head . . . in . . . his . . . shell . . . can drown him, too?

Ned: What?

Juan: Putting his head in his shell can drown him too?

(Juan is writing. He continues his questioning to fill in the matrix where there are question marks.)

Juan: What about the leatherback? (Bicais & Correia, 2008, p. 370)

Juan improved in his confidence as a writer with help from his friend. Let's now consider additional ways that children's writing skills can be enhanced.

Promoting Writing Development

Promoting writing development must be a long-term effort (S. Graham, 2006). Psychologists and experienced educators have offered several suggestions for facilitating youngsters' writing development:

• **Provide tools for drawing and writing as soon as children are old enough to use them.** Quite early in life, children can begin to explore—and so discover what they can do with—drawing, writing, and painting tools. As fine motor skills, cognitive abilities, and knowledge of written symbols continue to improve during the preschool years, children become increasingly able to produce recognizable shapes and letters. You can observe a preschool drawing and writing center in the "Environments: Early Childhood" video in MyEducationLab.

• **Present authentic writing tasks.** Youngsters write more frequently, and in a more organized and communicative (e.g., knowledge-transforming) manner, when they can write for a "real" audience (not just for their teacher) and when they're interested in their topic (S. L. Benton, 1997; S. Graham, 2006; McCourt, 2005). When one high school English teacher noticed that several very capable students weren't completing assigned writing tasks, he began asking students to write about their personal experiences and share their work with others on the Internet. The students suddenly began writing regularly, presumably because they could write for a real audience and could now choose what they wrote about (Garner, 1998). Similarly, in the Development and Culture feature "Summer Camp in Bosnia," a group of girls were motivated to write stories for younger children at camp.

• **Scaffold children's writing efforts.** Such scaffolding can take a variety of forms, including the following:

- Ask children with limited writing skills to dictate rather than write their stories.
- Ask children to set specific goals for their writing, and help them organize their thoughts before beginning to write.
- Help children brainstorm ideas for communicating effectively (e.g., by using examples, analogies, and similes).
- Provide an explicit structure for children to follow as they write (e.g., for a persuasive essay, ask students to include a main argument, supporting arguments, and rebuttals to possible counterarguments).
- Suggest that children initially focus on communicating clearly and postpone attention to writing mechanics (e.g., spelling, punctuation) until later drafts.

Observe a preschool drawing and writing center in the "Environments: Early Childhood" video. Also, observe students' preference for self-chosen writing topics in the "Literacy" videos for middle childhood, early adolescence, and late adolescence. (Find Video Examples in Topic 10 of MyEducationLab.)

ARTIFACT 10-4   Finger painting. Once infants are old enough to sit up on their own, they can begin to explore the properties of paper and paint, as 5-month-old Lauryn did in this early painting. Such activities should be closely supervised, of course, and only nontoxic substances used.

DEVELOPMENT IN CULTURE
Summer Camp in Bosnia

Jacqueline Darvin, a college professor in literacy education, attended a conference one spring and became impressed with the work of the Global Children's Organization (GCO) (Darvin, 2009). GCO is a group of educators, professionals, and other volunteers who offer summer camps for children growing up with unrest, violence, and intolerance in their society. Jacqueline learned that GCO had implemented programs for children in Los Angeles and Northern Ireland and was planning a program in the former Yugoslavia. She joined the group and traveled to a summer camp in Bosnia.

Children at the Bosnian camp had grown up in communities afflicted with ethnic conflicts, high rates of unemployment, and political corruption. Children's families had strong allegiances as Bosniaks, Bosnian Serbs, or Bosnian Croats, ethnic groups that had previously fought one another in a brutal war. Some of the children who attended camp had lost their parents in the war, and others had witnessed violence firsthand, sometimes in their schools.

At the camp, children were warmly welcomed through community-building exercises. Children also participated in numerous relaxing sports and leisure activities, including artwork, horseback riding, and hiking. Jacqueline's contribution to the activities was a literacy project. She invited the oldest girls at the camp (between 10 and 13 years old) to compose and illustrate books that they would share with the younger children. Girls individually selected one of three themes to write about: peace and freedom, preservation of nature, or funny stories about horses. Children wrote their books in their native Serbo-Croatian language, and English-speaking native speakers translated the books for Jacqueline.

A few girls wrote about horses, but the majority focused on peace and friendship or the beauty of the natural world. Among girls who wrote about peace and friendship, an interest in developing new relationships with people from dissimilar backgrounds was evident. Melita wrote about her desire to make friends with other children from different backgrounds:

NEW FRIENDS. These Bosnian children race on inflatable beach mattresses with new friends at their summer camp. Such experiences provide fruitful content for personal writing.

When I was small, I always thought about meeting many friends and wanted to be surrounded by many people. Always, I was thinking and dreaming about this. I was in the dark, but one day, my eyes were opened. The people I met were different religions, from different countries, had different feelings, but the one thing we had in common was friendship and love. . . . It didn't matter that we had different colour skin, that we prayed to God in a different way and talked to Him about our eminent departure (from camp) and the pain we would feel. But sure enough, it was time to leave. We were all sad. But in a way, we were happy because we knew that we would see each other again and forever carry each other in our hearts.[a] (Darvin, 2009, p. 55)

Similarly, Ana wrote about how gratifying it was to make friends who had diverse faiths:

My biggest dream in life was to have many friends. This dream came true in camp. Our camp is full of peace and friendship. We play together and we stick together through the rough times. We're friendly to each other, we like each other, and we share our feelings. . . . In our camp, nobody makes fun of each other or cares about the fact that we are different religions. . . . Sometimes we get on each other's nerves, but in the end, it works out. . . . When we're riding the horses, I feel like we're all the same and we're all excited to be here.[a] (Darvin, 2009, p. 55)

Jacqueline had selected preservation of nature in Bosnia as a second option because of people's growing concern there about pollution, water shortages, and illegal stripping of forests. Many children were aware of these concerns and appreciative of their time in a scenic rural setting. Children who selected this theme wrote about the natural beauty around them. Zerina described the marvelous sights she saw:

My country BiH (Bosnia and Herzegovina) is blessed with many natural wonders. Among these natural wonders are: rivers, mountains, hills, springs, prairies, the sea, etc. It's the only country where beauty grows.[a] (Darvin, 2009, p. 54)

Another student, Anela, communicated a sense of awe in a poem:

One night,
A little star was shining in the sky.
In the morning,
The birds woke up from their nests.
The flowers bloomed from their green buds
To please the missing stars.[a] (Darvin, 2009, p. 54)

As they prepared their books, the girls exchanged ideas and helped one another with illustrations. Local camp counselors assisted with spelling and grammar when asked. As final touches, the girls wrote brief autobiographies, added photographs of themselves on the back covers, and laminated the books. Having completed the stories, the girls hosted a story hour for the 6- to 8-year-old children at camp. The authors were pleased with their accomplishments, and the younger children were impressed with the books.

- Provide specific questions that children should ask themselves as they review their writing (e.g., "Are the ideas logically organized?").
- Ask children to collaborate on writing projects, or to read and respond to one another's work.
- Encourage use of word processing programs. (Benton, 1997; Boyle & Charles, 2011; Glaser & Brunstein, 2007; Graham & Perin, 2007; J. Hansen & Kissel, 2009; K. R. Harris & Graham, 1992; McLane & McNamee, 1990; Sitko, 1998; Sperling, 1996; Tracy et al., 2009)

• Include writing assignments in all areas of the curriculum. Writing shouldn't be a skill that only elementary teachers and secondary English teachers teach. In fact, writing takes different forms in different disciplines. Writing fiction is very different from writing a science lab report, which in turn is very different from preparing an analysis of historical documents. Particularly at the secondary level, teachers need to teach writing skills specific to their own academic disciplines (De La Paz, 2005; Newell, Koukis, & Boster, 2007; Sejnost & Thiese, 2010).

MATHEMATICS DEVELOPMENT

Mathematics is a cluster of domains—arithmetic, algebra, geometry, statistics, and so on—that use somewhat different methods for representing and solving quantitative problems. Our focus here will be on the development of knowledge and skills that are central to all of these domains, notably number sense, counting, basic concepts and procedures, and metacognition.

Number Sense and Counting

By 5 or 6 months of age, infants have some awareness of quantity. Although they certainly aren't counting at this age, they do seem to notice the difference between two small collections of varying amounts (e.g., a set of two objects and a set of three objects), and they distinguish between two large collections with significantly different amounts (e.g., a set of 16 dots and a set of 32 dots) (Wynn, 1995; F. Xu & Spelke, 2000; Zamarian, Ischebeck, & Delazer, 2009). As they approach their first birthday, they also show some understanding of *more* versus *less*. For example, 9- to 11-month-olds notice the difference between sequences of pictures that reflect increases versus decreases in quantity (Brannon, 2002; McCrink & Wynn, 2009).

Except for small groupings (e.g., sets of two or three objects), infants' awareness of quantity is imprecise. The ability to count is necessary to distinguish between larger, roughly comparable quantities—say, between collections of seven versus eight objects (Geary, 2006; Lipton & Spelke, 2005; Siegler & Robinson, 1982). Many children in Western cultures begin counting before their third birthday, and many 3- and 4-year-olds can correctly count to 10 (Ginsburg et al., 2006; Griffin, 2009). Five-year-olds can often count far beyond 10 (perhaps to 50), although they may get confused about the order of such numbers as 70, 80, and 90 (Fuson & Hall, 1983). As children work with two- and three-digit written numbers in the elementary grades, they increasingly master the correct sequence of numbers well into the hundreds and beyond (Case & Okamoto, 1996).

Counting itself takes a developmental course. When children first begin to count, they don't necessarily do so in a way that accurately determines amount (Geary, 2006; Wynn, 1990). They may say two successive numbers (e.g., ". . . three, four . . .") while pointing to a single object and so count it twice. Or, instead, they may point to two successive objects while saying only one number. But by the time they are age 4 or 5, most children have mastered several basic principles of counting, including the following:

- *One-one principle.* Each object in the set being counted must be assigned one and only one number word. In other words, you say "one" while pointing to one object, "two" while pointing to another object, and so on until every object has been counted exactly once.

ARTIFACT 10-5 Similes of sadness. Teachers can help children by providing structures that scaffold initial writing efforts. After her class brainstorms the kinds of similes a writer might use, 11-year-old Charlotte practices using similes in a description of sadness.

- *Cardinal principle.* The last number word counted indicates the number of objects in the set. In other words, if you count up to five when counting objects, then there are five objects in the set.
- *Order-irrelevance principle.* A set of objects has the same number regardless of the order in which individual objects are counted. (Bryant & Nuñes, 2011; Gallistel & Gelman, 1992; Griffin, 2009; Stock, Desoete, & Roeyers, 2009)

Initially children apply these principles primarily to small number sets (e.g., of 10 objects or fewer), but within a few years they can apply the principles to larger sets as well. As they do so, their ability to recognize that quantity stays the same regardless of changes in arrangement also improves (Geary, 2006).[8]

Mathematical Concepts and Principles

In addition to building on a basic understanding of numbers, mathematical reasoning requires an understanding of many other concepts and principles. An especially critical one in the early elementary grades is the *part-whole principle*, the idea that any single number can be broken into two or more smaller numbers (e.g., 7 can be broken into 1, 2, and 4) and that any two or more numbers can be combined to form a larger number. This principle is probably central to children's understanding of addition and subtraction (Baroody, Tiilikainen, & Tai, 2006; Sophian & Vong, 1995).

Another important concept in mathematical reasoning is the idea of *proportion*, as reflected in fractions, ratios, and decimals. Proportional reasoning emerges very gradually over the course of childhood and adolescence.[9] As early as 6 months of age, infants show some intuitive awareness of different proportions—for instance, distinguishing visual displays reflecting 2-to-1 and 4-to-1 ratios, and noticing a difference between containers that are ¼ and ¾ full of liquid (Jeong, Levine, & Huttenlocher, 2007; Krasa & Shunkwiler, 2009; McCrink & Wynn, 2007). By about age 3 children can distinguish smaller and larger proportions in fractions of circles. By the early elementary grades children can understand simple, specific fractions (e.g., ½, ⅓) if they can relate these fractions to everyday objects (Empson, 1999; Van Dooren, De Bock, Hessels, Janssens, & Verschaffel, 2005). Yet they are apt to continue to struggle with more complex fractions and other proportions until well into adolescence (Geary, 2006; Modestou & Gagatsis, 2010; Van Dooren et al., 2005). It seems that they regularly misapply their knowledge of whole numbers (Ni & Zhou, 2005). For example, because 4 is greater than 3, they are apt to conclude that ¼ is greater than ⅓. And because 256 is greater than 7, they are apt to think that 0.256 must be greater than 0.7.

Middle school and high school math classes increasingly focus on abstract concepts, such as *pi* (π), *irrational number*, and *variable*. Mathematical principles, such as *the product of two negative numbers is a positive number* and *the angles of a triangle always have a total of 180°*, also become increasingly abstract. Because such concepts tend to be far removed from the concrete realities with which children and adolescents are familiar, formal instruction about them is usually necessary (Byrnes, 1996; Geary, 1994; R. S. Nickerson, 2010).

Basic Arithmetic Operations

Two of the most basic mathematical operations are, of course, addition and subtraction. Infants seem to have a preliminary understanding of these processes well before their first birthday (McCrink & Wynn, 2009; Wynn, 1992). Imagine that two Mickey Mouse dolls are placed on a table in front of you. An experimenter lowers a screen to block your view of the dolls, and then you watch the experimenter take one of the dolls from behind the screen and put it away. You assume that only one doll remains on the table, but as the screen is

---

[8] Realizing that the quantity of objects has not changed with rearrangement of their placement reflects the *conservation of number* of which we spoke in Chapter 6.

[9] As you might recall from Chapter 6, Piaget suggested that children become capable of proportional reasoning when they enter the formal operations stage, sometime around age 11 or 12. More recent research indicates that children exhibit glimmerings of proportional reasoning before Piaget expected but continue to solidify these abilities over an extended period of time.

raised, you still see *two* dolls there. Even 5-month-olds seem to be surprised by this outcome, indicating an awareness that something isn't as it should be.

By age 2½ or 3 years of age, children clearly understand that adding objects to a set increases quantity and that subtracting objects from a set decreases quantity (J. Huttenlocher, Jordan, & Levine, 1994). By age 3 or 4, many begin to apply their knowledge of counting to simple addition and subtraction problems, typically using procedures they develop on their own (Bermejo, 1996; Krasa & Shunkwiler, 2009; Siegler & Jenkins, 1989). One early strategy is to use fingers to represent the objects in question. Consider the problem *If I have 2 apples and you give me 3 more apples, how many apples do I have altogether?* A child might put up two fingers and then three more fingers and count all the fingers to reach the solution, "5 apples." Somewhat later, children may begin to use a *min* strategy, in which they start with the larger of the two numbers (for the apple problem, they would start with 3) and then add on, one by one, the smaller number (e.g., counting "three apples . . . then four, five . . . five apples altogether") (Siegler & Jenkins, 1989). They might do something similar for subtraction, starting with the original number of objects and then counting down the number of objects removed: "Five . . . then four, three . . . three apples left." Still later, of course, children learn and retrieve many basic addition and subtraction facts (e.g., $2 + 3 = 5, 5 - 3 = 2$) that allow them to bypass the more cumbersome counting strategies.

By the early elementary years, children use a variety of strategies for solving simple addition and subtraction problems, including physically counting objects, counting on fingers, and retrieving addition and subtraction facts from memory. As they get older, they increasingly rely on memory and depend less on fingers and other objects (Ashcraft, 1982; Griffin, 2009; Siegler & Jenkins, 1989).[10]

In North America, formal instruction in multiplication usually begins in second or third grade. Once again, children typically learn and use a mixture of strategies (J. B. Cooney & Ladd, 1992; Geary, 2006). When working with small numbers, they may simply use addition (e.g., solving "$3 \times 3 = ?$" by adding $3 + 3$ and then adding another 3 to the sum). Sometimes they count by twos, fives, or some other number (e.g., solving "$5 \times 4 = ?$" by counting "five, ten, fifteen, twenty"). At other times they apply certain rules, such as *anything times zero is zero* or *anything times 1 is itself*. Gradually, retrieval of basic multiplication facts replaces such strategies (Cooney, Swanson, & Ladd, 1988; De Brauwer & Fias, 2009). Children often encounter simple division problems in the preschool years (e.g., when they must share food or toys with others), and even some 3-year-olds may use counting to divide quantities somewhat equitably (K. Miller, 1989). With formal instruction, children become more efficient. As they tackle division problems, children often rely on their knowledge of other arithmetic facts, especially multiplication facts (e.g., if $5 \times 4 = 20$, then $20 \div 5 = 4$) (Geary, 1994).

When children encounter arithmetic problems involving two-digit or larger numbers, and especially when the problems involve "carrying" or "borrowing" across columns, they must also master the concept of *place value*. This idea that digits reflect different quantities depending on the column (whether they are in the ones column, tens column, and so on) is a fairly abstract one that many children have trouble with in

ONE . . . TWO . . . THREE . . . FOUR . . . FIVE! Long before receiving formal instruction in addition at school, young children often develop addition and multiplication strategies on their own by building on their finger-counting skills.

Improving Your Observation Skills

Arithmetic errors. For each of these problems, a child has correctly retrieved basic math facts but arrived at an incorrect solution. Which inappropriate strategy has each child used? Compare your response with the explanation at the end of the chapter.

```
  26        603
 +47       -305
 ----      ----
 613        208
```

[10] The changing frequency of various addition strategies over time reflects the *overlapping waves* idea presented in Chapter 7 (see Figure 7-5 on p. 259).

the elementary grades (Fuson & Kwon, 1992; Geary, 2006; J.-A. Jordan, Mulhern, & Wylie, 2009). And when children don't understand place value, they are apt to make errors when they tackle problems that require carrying or borrowing.

Developmental Patterns in Mathematical Skills and Understandings

Neo-Piagetian theorist Robbie Case and his colleagues have suggested that during the preschool and elementary school years, children gradually develop a *central conceptual structure* that integrates much of what they know about numbers, counting, addition, subtraction, and place value (Case & Okamoto, 1996; Case, Okamoto, Henderson, & McKeough, 1993; Griffin, 2009; Griffin, Case, & Siegler, 1994).[11] In Case's view, 4-year-olds understand the difference between "a little" and "a lot" and recognize that adding objects leads to more of them and subtracting objects leads to fewer of them. Furthermore, many 4-year-olds can accurately count a small set of objects and conclude that the last number they count equals the total number of objects in the set (the cardinal principle). Thus 4-year-olds can visually compare a group of 5 objects with a group of 6 objects and tell you that the latter group contains more objects, and they may also count accurately to either 5 or 6. Yet they cannot answer a question such as "Which is more, 5 or 6?" because the question involves knowledge of counting and a more-versus-less comparison.

By the time children are 6 years old, they can easily answer simple "Which is more?" questions. Case proposed that at the age of 6, children have integrated their understanding of *more* and *less* with counting. Children's knowledge and reasoning about numbers now include several key elements:

- Children understand and can say the verbal numbers "one," "two," "three," and so on.
- They recognize the written numerals 1, 2, 3, and so on.
- They have a systematic process for counting objects: They say each successive number as they touch each successive object in a group. Eventually, children count by mentally "tagging" (rather than physically touching) each object.
- They also use their fingers for representing small quantities (e.g., 3 fingers equals 3 objects). Their use of fingers for both counting objects and representing quantities may be a key means through which they integrate the two processes into a single conceptual structure.
- They equate movement toward higher numbers with such concepts as "a lot," "more," and "bigger." Similarly, they equate movement toward lower numbers with such concepts as "a little," "less," and "smaller."
- They understand that movement from one number to the next is equivalent to either adding one unit to the set or subtracting one unit from it, depending on the direction of movement.

In essence, the more comprehensive conceptual structure at age 6 forms a mental "number line" that children can use to facilitate their understanding and execution of such processes as addition, subtraction, and comparisons of quantities.

At age 8, Case proposed, children have sufficiently mastered this central conceptual structure such that they can begin using two number lines simultaneously to solve mathematical problems. They can now answer such questions as "Which number is bigger, 32 or 28?" and "Which number is closer to 25, 21 or 18?" Such questions require them to compare digits in both the ones column and tens column, with each comparison taking place along a separate number line. In addition, 8-year-olds presumably have a better understanding of operations that require transformations across columns, such as "carrying 1" to the tens column during addition or "borrowing 1" from the tens column during subtraction. Finally, at about age 10, children become capable of generalizing the relationships of two number lines to the entire number system. They now understand how the various columns (ones, tens, hundreds, etc.) relate to one another and can expertly move back and forth among the

---

[11] See Chapter 6 for a more general discussion of *central conceptual structures* in neo-Piagetian theory.

columns. They can also treat the answers to mathematical problems as mental entities in and of themselves and so can answer such questions as "Which number is bigger, the difference between 6 and 9 or the difference between 8 and 3?"

Case tracked the development of children's central conceptual structure for number only until age 10. He acknowledged, however, that children's understanding of numbers continues to develop well into adolescence. He pointed out that teenagers often have trouble with questions such as "What is a half of a third?" and suggested that their difficulty results from an incomplete conceptual understanding of division and the results (e.g., fractions) that it yields.

Other researchers have obtained data on later advancements in mathematics. By the time children reach middle school, most are relatively proficient in solving simple arithmetic problems with whole numbers (Byrnes, 1996). As they move through the middle school and high school grades, much of the math curriculum involves procedures for working with proportions, negative numbers, roots, exponents (e.g., $\sqrt{18}$, 4^3), and unknown variables (e.g., x, y). Children are able to tackle more complex problems to the extent that they have largely automatized basic procedures, permitting them to retrieve and use relevant mathematical facts in advanced problems (Geary, 1994, 2010).

Advanced proficiency in mathematics also requires young people to *make sense of* these procedures, rather than simply applying them in a rote, meaningless fashion. In other words, understanding of advanced mathematical procedures is closely tied to comprehension of mathematical concepts and principles, in much the same way that understanding of addition and subtraction is closely connected to mastery of numbers and counting (Geary, 1994; Hecht, Close, & Santisi, 2003; N. C. Jordan, Glutting, & Ramineni, 2010). In the "Intrinsic Motivation: Early Adolescence" video in MyEducationLab, 12-year-old Claudia reveals such sense making: "You can explain it all." When children *cannot* make sense of mathematical procedures—perhaps because they haven't yet mastered the abstract concepts on which the procedures are based or perhaps because no one has shown them why certain manipulations are mathematically logical—they are apt to use the procedures incorrectly and have trouble applying them to real-world problems.

Metacognition is another element of sophisticated work in mathematics. Not only should youngsters understand what they're doing when they tackle mathematical problems, but they should also plan, monitor, and assess their problem-solving efforts. Such metacognitive oversight might involve setting goals for a problem-solving task, monitoring the effectiveness of various problem-solving strategies, and evaluating a final solution to determine whether it's a logical one (Cardelle-Elawar, 1992; Desoete, 2009; L. S. Fuchs et al., 2003). Only a child who reflects on his or her problem-solving efforts will recognize that a sum of 613 is *not* a reasonable answer to the problem 26 + 47. When children and adolescents are asked to engage in metacognitive processes, they can begin to focus on how they know what they are doing and what their mathematical work really means (Carr, 2010).

Bioecology of Mathematics Development

Virtually all children have a general awareness that objects and substances can vary in quantity and amount (Geary, 2006). But youngsters differ considerably in the ways they go about learning mathematics, the specific uses for which they see mathematics being used in their society, and the kind of instruction they receive in this subject.

Some children grasp challenging mathematics principles in a seemingly effortless fashion and enjoy solving challenging problems. Other children have learning disabilities that impede their ability to understand number concepts, automatize math facts, and solve simple arithmetic problems quickly—disabilities that in an extreme form are known as **dyscalculia** (N. C. Jordan, Hanich, & Kaplan, 2003; Mussolin, Mejias, & Noël, 2010; A. J. Wilson & Dehaene, 2007). Dyscalculia may be present in children who struggle to learn basic arithmetic and continue to use finger counting of small numbers well into middle childhood. This condition is probably neurologically based for at least some children with serious delays in mathematics.

Gender differences in mathematics exist but are smaller than many people believe. Some researchers find a slight advantage for one gender or the other depending

MyEducationLab

Hear 12-year-old Claudia explain why she likes math in the "Intrinsic Motivation: Early Adolescence" video. (Find Video Examples in Topic 10 of MyEducationLab.)

dyscalculia
Inability to master basic numerical concepts and operations in a developmentally typical time frame despite normal instruction.

1. When the figure on the left is folded along the dotted lines, it becomes a three-dimensional object. Which one or more of the four figures on the right represent(s) how this object might appear from different perspectives?

2. When the object on the left is rotated in three-dimensional space, it can look like one or more of the objects on the right. Which one(s)?

Model   a   b   c   d

Model   a   b   c

Answer Key: (1) Depending on the direction from which it is viewed, the object might look like either *a* or *d.* (2) The object can be rotated to look like either *a* or *c.*

FIGURE 10-1 **Examples of tasks requiring visual-spatial ability.** *Tasks modeled, respectively, after G. K. Bennett, Seashore, & Wesman, 1982; and Shepard & Metzler, 1971.*

on the age-group, cultural setting, and task in question (Else-Quest, Hyde, & Linn, 2010; A. M. Gallagher & Kaufman, 2005). However, boys show greater *variability* in math. More boys than girls have very high mathematical ability, especially in high school, and more boys than girls have significant disabilities in this field (Else-Quest et al., 2010; Halpern et al., 2007; Hedges & Nowell, 1995; Penner, 2003). The prevalence of adolescent males at the upper end of the math-ability continuum may be partly due to biology, and in particular to sex-related hormones (e.g., estrogen, testosterone) that differentially affect brain development before and after puberty (Halpern, 1992; Hegarty & Kozhevnikov, 1999; Lippa, 2002). One area in which these hormones may come into play is in the development of **visual-spatial ability**, the ability to imagine and mentally manipulate two- and three-dimensional figures (see Figure 10-1). On average, boys and men perform better than girls and women on measures of visual-spatial ability, which appears to give them an advantage in certain kinds of mathematical tasks (Halpern et al., 2007; Reynolds, Keith, Ridley, & Patel, 2008).

Yet environmental factors also play a role in gender differences in mathematics. In many Western societies, mathematics has historically been viewed as a "male" domain more suitable for boys than for girls. Some parents and (unfortunately) some teachers pick up on this stereotype and expect boys to do better than girls in mathematics and also offer boys more encouragement (Bleeker & Jacobs, 2004; Halpern et al., 2007; Tiedemann, 2000). Perhaps partly as a result of such differential expectations and encouragement, boys tend to express greater confidence about their mathematical ability than girls do, even when actual achievement levels for the two genders have been similar (G. Nagy et al., 2010; Steinmayr & Spinath, 2009; Vermeer, Boekaerts, & Seegers, 2000).

Cultural practices and resources determine many experiences with mathematics. For instance, unschooled 10- to 12-year-old candy sellers in Brazil are able to solve arithmetic and ratio problems with large numerical values, presumably due to their many experiences calculating change and determining profits and losses in the marketplace (Saxe, 1988). Children also are affected by the kinds of formal education that cultures offer in mathematics. For example, Asian teachers are apt to provide thorough explanations of mathematical concepts, focus classroom discussions on making sense of problem-solving procedures, and assign a lot of math homework (Schleppenbach, Perry, Miller, Sims, & Fang, 2007; J. Wang & Lin, 2005). Curiously, even the terminology for numbers in a native language can direct children to attend to particular features of numerical systems. Many theorists speculate that the structure of number words in Asian languages (Chinese, Japanese, Korean) may facilitate Asian children's mathematical development (Fuson & Kwon, 1992; K. F. Miller, Smith, Zhu, & Zhang,1995; Miura, Okamoto, Vlahovic-Stetic, Kim, & Han, 1999). In these languages the base-10 number system is clearly reflected in number words. The word for 11 is literally

visual-spatial ability
Ability to imagine and mentally manipulate two- and three-dimensional figures.

"ten-one," the word for 12 is "ten-two," and the word for 21 is "two-ten-one." Furthermore, words for fractions reflect what a fraction *is*. For example, the word for ¼ is literally "of four parts, one." In contrast, English has many number words (e.g., *eleven, twelve, thirteen, twenty, thirty, one-half, one-fourth*) that "hide" the base-10 structure somewhat and don't reveal much information about the nature of proportions.

With appropriate education, children from various backgrounds evolve from intuitive observers of simple mathematical patterns into disciplined thinkers who adeptly handle abstract mathematical symbols. The Developmental Trends table "Mathematics at Different Age Levels" characterizes some of the mathematical knowledge and abilities commonly seen in infants, children, and adolescents.

DEVELOPMENTAL TRENDS
Mathematics at Different Age Levels

AGE	WHAT YOU MIGHT OBSERVE	DIVERSITY	IMPLICATIONS
Infancy (Birth–2 Years) 	• Some awareness that adding or subtracting something affects quantity (appearing at around 5 months) • Rudimentary ability to discriminate among different proportions (by 6 months) • Discrimination between sequences that show increases versus decreases in amount	• Some toddlers have familiarity with small-number words (e.g., *two, three*), usually because their parents often use the words in parent–child interactions. • Children with visual impairments may have fewer opportunities to make more-versus-less comparisons.	• Use small-number words (e.g., *two, three*) when talking with infants and toddlers if doing so makes sense within the context of everyday activities. • Provide age-appropriate toys that encourage children to focus on size or quantity (e.g., nesting cups, stacking blocks).
Early Childhood (2–6 Years)	• Clear understandings that adding objects results in an increase and removing objects results in a decrease (by age 2½ or 3) • Appearance of counting (at around age 3) • Increasing ability to count correctly (perhaps to 50 by age 5) • Emergence of self-constructed strategies for addition and subtraction (e.g., counting objects or using fingers) • Some familiarity with division in everyday sharing tasks	• On average, Chinese children learn to count at a younger age than children whose native language is English. The more "transparent" nature of Chinese number words is thought to be at least partly responsible for this difference. • At age 5, Chinese- and Japanese-speaking children typically have a better grasp of place value than English-speaking children (apparently because Chinese and Japanese number words make place value quite obvious). • On average, children from middle-income families begin counting at an earlier age than children from low-income families.	• Occasionally ask mathematical questions (e.g., "How many are there?" "Where's the triangle?") • In storybook reading sessions, occasionally read books that engage children in counting activities (e.g., *The Icky Bug Counting Book*, Pallotta & Masiello, 1992). • Use concrete manipulatives to help children learn counting and simple addition and subtraction.
Middle Childhood (6–10 Years) 	• Increasing ability to count correctly into the hundreds and beyond • Acquisition of more efficient addition and subtraction strategies, including retrieval of number facts • Increasing mastery of multiplication and division strategies • Growing understanding of place value and its relevance to carrying and borrowing • Some understanding of simple fractions • Increasing ability to solve word problems	• Children vary considerably in the strategies they use at any given age level. Some 8-year-olds have most basic math facts automatized, whereas others continue to rely heavily on fingers. • Children who speak certain Asian languages (e.g., Mandarin Chinese) generally master multidigit addition and subtraction at an earlier age than English-speaking children. • Some children begin to dislike math, typically because they have consistently been frustrated in their efforts to understand and master it.	• Help children understand the logic underlying basic mathematical procedures (e.g., show the relevance of the concept of *place value* to carrying and borrowing). • Provide frequent practice in basic arithmetic as a way of promoting automaticity. • Introduce number lines as a way of helping children understand how numbers relate to one another. • Have low-achieving fourth and fifth graders tutor first and second graders in basic arithmetic skills.

(continued)

DEVELOPMENTAL TRENDS (continued)

AGE	WHAT YOU MIGHT OBSERVE	DIVERSITY	IMPLICATIONS
Early Adolescence (10–14 Years) 	• Increasing ability to understand abstract concepts (e.g., π, *variable*) • Increasing ability to understand and work with proportions • Naive epistemic beliefs about mathematics (e.g., that it involves memorizing procedures without necessarily understanding them)	• Young adolescents who have not yet automatized basic arithmetic facts are apt to struggle when they encounter challenging mathematical concepts and procedures. • Some adolescents tend to misapply their knowledge about whole numbers to problems involving fractions and decimals. • Young adolescents vary widely in their ability to understand and apply abstract mathematical concepts.	• Conduct small-group activities in which students must devise and explain multiple approaches to solving a single problem. • Teach metacognitive strategies for solving problems (e.g., identify the goal to be achieved, break a complex problem into smaller steps, consider whether an obtained solution is reasonable).
Late Adolescence (14–18 Years) 	• Increasing facility in working with abstract concepts and principles (e.g., *unknowns* such as *x* and *y*) • Difficulty translating word problems into algebraic expressions • Tendency for many teens to memorize and mindlessly apply mathematical procedures, rather than to reflect on and understand the procedures	• Individual differences in mathematical abilities increase in the high school years, due both to course "tracking" according to students' achievement and to the prevalence of elective mathematics courses in high school. • On average, girls have less confidence about their ability to do mathematics even when they achieve at the same level as boys.	• Ask teenagers to apply their math skills to real-life contexts and problems. • Allow teens to use calculators when performing complex mathematical operations (this strategy allows them to devote most of their working memory capacity to the overall problem-solving effort). • Minimize competition for grades and other rewards for mathematical achievement (this strategy is especially important for girls).

Source: Brannon, 2002; Byrne & Shavelson, 1986; Byrnes, 1996; Cardelle-Elawar, 1992; M. Carr & Biddlecomb, 1998; Case & Okamoto, 1996; Chipman, 2005; Cooney & Ladd, 1992; Cooney et al., 1988; Davenport et al., 1998; De Corte et al., 1996; De Corte, Op't Eynde, & Verschaffel, 2002; Eccles, Freedman-Doan, Frome, Jacobs, & Yoon, 2000; Empson, 1999; Fuson & Hall, 1983; Fuson & Kwon, 1992; Gallistel & Gelman, 1992; Geary, 2006; Ginsburg et al., 2006; Greeno, Collins, & Resnick, 1996; Griffin, 2009; Griffin, Case, & Capodilupo, 1995; C. S. Ho & Fuson, 1998; J. Huttenlocher et al., 1994; Inglis & Biemiller, 1997; Klibanoff, Levine, Huttenlocher, Vasilyeva, & Hedges, 2006; Krasa & Shunkwiler, 2009; McCrink & Wynn, 2004, 2007; K. Miller, 1989; K. F. Miller et al., 1995; Schoenfeld, 1988, 1992; Siegler & Jenkins, 1989; Van Dooren et al., 2005; Wynn, 1990; F. Xu & Spelke, 2000; Zamarian et al., 2009.

Promoting Development in Mathematics

Mathematics probably causes more confusion and aggravation for young people than any other academic subject. The hierarchical nature of the discipline is partly to blame. To the extent that youngsters don't completely master mathematics concepts and procedures at one grade level, they lack necessary prerequisites in later grades. Frustration can mount when children develop the belief that mathematics requires quick responses to questions posed by teachers that have nothing to do with the real world (De Corte, Op't Eynde, Depaepe, & Verschaffel, 2010). Developmental factors also figure prominently. When children have difficulty with abstract ideas, proportional thinking, and other developmental acquisitions on which mathematics depends, they are apt to struggle with mathematical reasoning. We offer the following suggestions for teachers to help children and adolescents make steady progress in mathematics:

• **Teach numbers and counting in preschool and the primary grades.** A basic understanding of numbers and counting forms the foundation for virtually every aspect of mathematics. When young children haven't acquired these basics at home, teachers can often make up the difference. Activities and games involving counting, comparing quantities, adding, and subtracting are apt to be beneficial (Bird, 2009; Ginsburg, Lee, & Boyd, 2008; Ramani & Siegler, 2008). Regular practice in counting objects and comparing quantities (e.g., determining which of three groups of apples has the *most* apples) leads to improved performance not only in these tasks but in other quantitative tasks as well (Case & Okamoto, 1996; L. Fuchs et al., 2010).

• **At all age levels, use manipulatives and visual displays to tie mathematical concepts and procedures to concrete reality.** Concrete manipulatives (beans, blocks, Cuisenaire rods, toothpicks bundled in groups of 10 and 100, etc.) can often help children grasp the nature of addition, subtraction, place value, and fractions (Fujimura, 2001; Fuson & Briars, 1990; Greeno et al., 1996). Visual aids such as number lines and pictures of pizzas depicting various fractions can be helpful in the early elementary grades, and graphs and diagrams of geometric figures are useful for secondary students (Greeno et al., 1996; C. Lee & Chen, 2010; J. L. Schwartz, Yarushalmy, & Wilson, 1993).

• **Encourage visual-spatial thinking.** Although boys may have a biological advantage in visual-spatial thinking, structured experiences that *encourage* such thinking can help to reduce the gender gap (Ginsburg et al., 2008; Nuttall, Casey, & Pezaris, 2005; Sprafkin, Serbin, Denier, and Connor, 1983). In the preschool and early elementary grades, such experiences might involve blocks, Legos, puzzles, simple graphs, and basic measurement tools. As children move into the middle elementary grades and beyond, visual-spatial tasks might also include complex graphs and three-dimensional geometry (Ginsburg et al., 2006; Nuttall et al., 2005; Sandamas, Foreman, & Coulson, 2009).

• **As youngsters work on new and challenging mathematical problems, provide the physical and cognitive scaffolding they need to find successful solutions.** Complex mathematical tasks and problems often put a strain on working memory and in other ways stretch children to their cognitive limits (H. L. Swanson, Jerman, & Zheng, 2008). Fortunately, Western cultures have devised a variety of tools for easing the burden. For children in the early elementary grades, such tools may simply be pencil and paper for keeping track of quantities, calculations, and other information. Once children have mastered basic mathematical facts and understand the logic behind arithmetic operations, they might use calculators or computers while working with large numbers or cumbersome data sets (Horowitz et al., 2005). Yet cognitive scaffolds are valuable as well. A teacher might encourage students to brainstorm possible approaches to problems, model the use of new problem-solving strategies, and teach students various metacognitive strategies for checking their progress (Calin-Jageman & Ratner, 2005; Carr, 2010; Staples, 2007). When teaching algebra, a teacher might ask a student a conceptually focused question about how the x intercepts of a graph are related to the factors of an equation instead of simply asking the student to solve the equation (Rakes, Valentine, McGatha, & Ronau, 2010).

• **Encourage children to invent, use, and defend their own strategies.** As we've seen, young children often invent strategies (e.g., the *min* strategy) for adding and subtracting objects well before they have formal instruction in addition and subtraction. Rather than ignore strategies children have developed on their own, teachers should encourage those that seem to be effective. As children acquire more efficient strategies over time, they will gradually abandon their earlier ones (Geary, 1994; Siegler, 1989). Also beneficial is specifically asking children to reflect on and explain in writing why they solved a problem as they did (Carr & Biddlecomb, 1998; Johanning, D'Agostino, Steele, & Shumow, 1999; Rittle-Johnson, 2006).

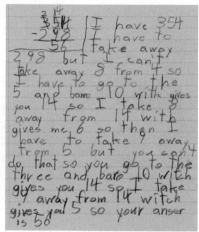

ARTIFACT 10-6 354 – 298. Children can often benefit by explaining their solutions. In this assignment, Noah explains what he did when he solved a subtraction problem.

SCIENCE DEVELOPMENT

As scientists observe physical and biological phenomena in nature, they use certain strategies (formulating and testing hypotheses, separating and controlling variables, etc.) to conduct systematic investigations, and they form theories to explain their findings. Development in science, then, involves both theory building and acquisition of scientific reasoning skills. It also involves advancements in beliefs about science.

Children's Theories About the Biological and Physical Worlds

In studying children's growing understandings of scientific phenomena, many developmental theorists take a *theory theory* approach, suggesting that children construct (rather than absorb) their knowledge and beliefs about physical and biological phenomena. Some theorists are *nativists*, arguing that infants' brains are neurologically "preprogrammed" with some basic knowledge about their world, or at least with some preliminary dispositions to interpret events in certain ways.[12] Even young infants (i.e., those between 2 and 5 months old) seem to know that an object maintains its existence and shape as it moves, that two objects cannot occupy the same space at the same time, and that one object can influence another object only when the two come into contact (Baillargeon, 1994, 2004; Kaufman & Needham, 2010; Spelke, 1994).

One important step in children's early theory building is making a distinction between biological and nonbiological entities. By the time infants are 6 months old, most have some awareness that people and other animals move in ways that nonliving things do not. By age 3 or 4, children know that humans and other animals, but not nonliving objects, can move *themselves* and that living and nonliving entities change in different ways—living things grow, and nonliving things may increase in size but do not development naturally due to a physiological process (Jipson & Callanan, 2003; Massey & Gelman, 1988). At about age 4, children also realize that two living creatures in the same category, even if they look quite different, are apt to share many characteristics—for instance, that a blackbird has more in common with a flamingo (because both are birds) than it does with a bat (S. A. Gelman & Markman, 1986). By the middle elementary school years, children understand that both plants and animals are defined largely by their genetic heritage and internal makeup—for instance, that round, reddish fruits that come from pear trees must be pears rather than apples.[13]

Infants' early understandings of nonliving physical objects (e.g., the realization that two objects cannot occupy the same space at the same time) are consistent with classical principles of physics. As children get older and gain more experience with the physical world, they construct increasingly elaborate, but usually fairly concrete, theories about physical entities. Many school-age children view all physical phenomena either as actual substances (i.e., touchable "things" that have specific, although possibly changeable, locations) or as properties of those substances (Reiner, Slotta, Chi, & Resnick, 2000). This **substance schema** can be quite useful in explaining many everyday events (e.g., holding a ball, touching a hot stove). Yet children and adolescents tend to apply it inappropriately to such phenomena as light, heat, fire, and force, which in and of themselves have little or no substance (Megalakaki, 2008; Reiner et al., 2000). Children are likely to think of *force* as something that a pitched ball "contains," rather than as the initial impetus for the ball's motion. And they are apt to think of *heat* as something that can "flow" from one object to another.

Another idea that children acquire quite early but eventually overapply is the concept of *gravity*. At 3 or 4 months of age, children have some understanding that objects fall down (never up) when there is nothing to support them (Baillargeon, 1994). This "downward" view of gravity works quite well on a small scale. But imagine the situation depicted in Figure 10-2. A rock is dropped at the equator, at the entrances to two tunnels that go through the earth. Tunnel A comes out at the equator on the opposite side of the earth. Tunnel B comes out at the South Pole. Into which tunnel will the rock fall? Many middle school students say that the rock will fall into Tunnel B, apparently thinking that gravity always pulls something "down." They respond in this way even if they have explicitly learned that gravity pulls objects toward the center of the earth (Pulos, 1997).

To some degree, children's not-quite-right theories undoubtedly reflect a limited ability to think about abstract ideas. Even though these theories don't always jibe with scientific explanations, they almost certainly reflect children's genuine desire to make sense of their experiences.

Scientific Reasoning Skills

Even in the first year of life children seem predisposed to identify cause-and-effect relationships in the world around them.[14] But children's ability to think as scientists appears much later, and then only gradually. **Scientific reasoning** encompasses a number of cognitive

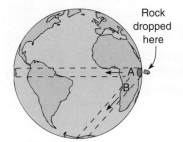

Rock dropped here

FIGURE 10-2 Which way? If a rock is dropped into a hole near the equator, into which of the two tunnels will it fall?

substance schema
General view of all physical phenomena as being either touchable substances or properties of those substances.

scientific reasoning
Cognitive processes central to conducting scientific research and interpreting findings appropriately.

[12] See Chapter 7 if you need a brief refresher about *theory theory* and *nativism*.

[13] Children's understandings about the properties of objects and living things are also explored in Chapter 7.

[14] Chapter 7 describes children's emerging inferences about cause-and-effect relationships.

processes, including planning an investigation, analyzing evidence, and drawing appropriate conclusions (Kuhn & Franklin, 2006). Taken together, such processes are often called the *scientific method*. Common to all of them is a conscious intention to acquire and evaluate new knowledge.

Conducting a scientific investigation requires two abilities, formulating hypotheses and then separating and controlling variables while testing those hypotheses. Such abilities emerge gradually over the course of middle childhood and adolescence. Formulating hypotheses depends on at least two things that change with age: (a) the ability to think about abstract and potentially contrary-to-fact ideas, and (b) a knowledge base that can help a person generate a *variety* of ideas. The ability to separate and control variables seems to depend partly on children's working memory capacity, which increases somewhat with age (M. Bullock & Ziegler, 1999). Elementary school children can often distinguish between experiments that do and do not control variables appropriately, yet they are apt to have trouble controlling variables in their *own* experiments—a task that requires them to keep track of several things simultaneously (M. Bullock & Ziegler, 1999; Kuhn et al., 2009; Metz, 2004).

Although adolescents are better able than elementary school children to separate and control variables, even adolescents occasionally have difficulty doing so (Barchfeld, Sodian, Thoermer, & Bullock, 2005; Kuhn, Amsel, & O'Loughlin, 1988; Kuhn et al., 2009). Furthermore, in their hypothesis testing, adolescents tend to focus on and test hypotheses they think are correct and to ignore hypotheses that, in their minds, are *in*correct (Byrnes, 1996). Such *try-to-prove-what-I-already-believe* thinking reflects a *confirmation bias*. A confirmation bias appears not only when adolescents test hypotheses but also when they analyze and interpret their data (Klaczynski, 2000; Kuhn et al., 1988; Kyza, 2009).[15] In general, they tend to overlook results that conflict with their favorite hypotheses. And they often try to explain away unexpected results that they *cannot* ignore. For example, when students in a high school science laboratory observe results that contradict what they expected to happen, they might complain that "Our equipment isn't working right" or "I can never do science anyway" (Minstrell & Stimpson, 1996, p. 192). Even high school graduates and many adults are apt to think in such "unscientific" ways (Byrnes, 1996; Kuhn & Franklin, 2006; McAuliff, Kovera, & Nunez, 2009).

INVESTIGATORS AT WORK. Children and adolescents often collect data enthusiastically but struggle to evaluate the quality of their evidence.

Metacognition in Science

Ultimately, children must discover that science is, like other disciplines, a dynamic body of ideas that will continue to evolve as new data come in. They must also be able to reflect on and critically evaluate their own beliefs and theories. And, of course, they must be willing to change their views in the face of disconfirming evidence. Such understandings, abilities, and dispositions emerge only gradually over childhood and adolescence (Elder, 2002; Kuhn & Pearsall, 2000; C. Zimmerman, 2007). Giuliana, an eighth grader, reveals beliefs and attitudes about science that are fairly sophisticated for her age-group:

> I think nothing is true. You can say about the Egyptians, for example, that once such and such was believed, but now there's another truth, we aren't sure of anything. We weren't there at the time of the Egyptians, and so we can only hypothesize about it. Historians rely on documents, studies, findings, but I really don't know how true it is what they say. We can say it's true now, but tomorrow another scientist may say "I've found another document that proves something else" and then we'll have two different things and we'll no longer know which is true and which is false. When the atom was discovered, it was considered the smallest particle, but now the quark's been discovered. What we believed before, now we don't believe anymore because the quark is smaller. Perhaps in fifty years' time an even smaller particle will turn up and then we'll be told that what we believed in before was false. It's really something to do with progress. (Mason, 2003, p. 223)

---

[15] *Confirmation bias* is examined in Chapter 7.

MyEducationLab

Observe Colin's epistemological beliefs about science in the "Memory: Early Adolescence" video. (Find Video Examples in Topic 10 of MyEducationLab.)

Youngsters' epistemic beliefs about the nature of science will undoubtedly affect the approaches they take (mentally) when they study science.[16] In the "Memory: Early Adolescence" video in MyEducationLab, 12-year-old Colin seems to view science largely as a collection of facts he needs to memorize. When asked what things are really hard to remember, he says this:

I think long things like science and stuff where you have to remember a lot of stuff and stuff that really isn't . . . you really wouldn't want to remember it that much.

Students who believe that "knowing" science means understanding the connections between concepts and related evidence are going to study and learn more effectively than students who think that learning science means remembering isolated facts (M. C. Linn et al., 1996; Yang & Tsai, 2010). And students who recognize that scientific theories will inevitably change over time are more likely to evaluate theories (including their own) with a critical eye (Bereiter, 1994; Kuhn, 1993, 2001a; M. C. Linn et al., 1996).

As you are learning, scientific development reflects transformations in reasoning skills, ideas about everyday phenomena, and reflections about the nature of science. The Developmental Trends table "Science at Different Age Levels" presents examples of scientific knowledge and reasoning you are apt to see in infancy, childhood, and adolescence.

Bioecology of Science Development

The bioecological framework suggests that children contribute to their own science development through personal initiative and environmental experiences. Influential personal characteristics include children's interests, abilities, and disabilities. Youngsters with sensory impairments may have fairly limited opportunities to observe certain scientific phenomena firsthand. For example, a child who is blind may be unaware that wood changes in size and color when it burns (M. B. Rowe, 1978). In comparison, youngsters with strong visual-spatial skills have a relatively easy time imagining and understanding interrelationships among objects in space (L. Friedman, 1994; Halpern, 2006). For example, children who can easily picture objects in their minds can better grasp the idea that the moon revolves around the earth while the earth simultaneously revolves around the sun.

As is true with mathematics, science has traditionally been regarded as a "male" domain (Halpern et al., 2007; Ullman, 2010a). Perhaps for this reason, boys tend to like science more than girls do, and they are more likely than girls to aspire to careers in science (Bandura, Barbaranelli, Caprara, & Pastorelli, 2001). On average, girls get higher grades in science than boys do, but boys tend to come out slightly ahead on national science achievement tests, especially in the physical sciences (Halpern et al., 2007; Leaper & Friedman, 2007). Yet with encouragement and exposure to women in scientific and technological fields and classes that build on their interests, girls are well able to achieve in these subjects (Ullman, 2010a).

Cultural environments shape many children's beliefs about the biological and physical worlds. Japanese children are more likely than European American children to think of plants (e.g., a tree, a blade of grass) and certain nonliving objects as having some sort of "mind" that thinks (M. Cole & Hatano, 2007; Hatano & Inagaki, 1996). And cultural differences in schooling may influence youngsters' epistemic beliefs about the nature of science. Schools in China tend to encourage respect for authority figures and to downplay differences of opinion among experts. Possibly as a result, high school students in China are more likely than U.S. students to believe that science is simple rather than complex—that it involves discrete facts rather than interrelationships and unresolved issues (Qian & Pan, 2002).

Religion also comes into play when youngsters develop their theories about the world. In the elementary grades, some children are apt to think that supernatural forces (e.g., God, the devil, witchcraft) are largely responsible for illness or natural disasters (O. Lee, 1999; Legare & Gelman, 2007). And young people's acceptance or nonacceptance of Darwin's

---

[16] Children's epistemic beliefs pertain to their ideas about the nature of knowledge, in particular, its stability, certainty, structure, and source, as well as their views of the goals and speed of learning activities. Epistemic beliefs are introduced in Chapter 7.

DEVELOPMENTAL TRENDS
Science at Different Age Levels

AGE	WHAT YOU MIGHT OBSERVE	DIVERSITY	IMPLICATIONS
Infancy (Birth–2 Years) 	• Knowledge of a few basic principles of physics (e.g., two objects cannot occupy the same space at the same time) • Emerging awareness that humans and animals are fundamentally different from nonliving things • Increasing ability to infer cause-and-effect relationships	• Infants differ in the number and diversity of opportunities to explore interesting objects and surroundings. • Infants with sensory impairments (e.g., blindness, hearing loss) are more limited in the scientific phenomena they can observe.	• Put infants and toddlers in contexts in which they can safely explore and experiment with physical objects. • Let toddlers interact with small, gentle animals (e.g., rabbits, cocker spaniels) under your close supervision.
Early Childhood (2–6 Years) 	• Increasing differentiation between living and nonliving things (e.g., they change differently, with living things growing due to intrinsic physiological processes and nonliving things changing due to other factors) • Increasing understanding that members of a biological category (e.g., *birds*) share many characteristics despite differences in appearance • Naive beliefs about the solar system (e.g., the earth is flat)	• Children in some cultures (e.g., Japanese children) are more likely to think of plants and nonliving objects as having "minds." • Children who grow up in inner-city environments may have little exposure to life cycles (e.g., calves being born, trees losing leaves in the fall and growing blossoms in the spring).	• Read simple nonfiction picture books that depict wild and domesticated animals. • Take children to zoos, farms, arboretums, and other sites where they can see a variety of animals and plants. • Talk with children about natural phenomena, pointing out the physical properties of objects (e.g., some objects float and others sink). • Engage children in simple hands-on investigations of natural phenomena.
Middle Childhood (6–10 Years) 	• Intuitive understanding that biological entities are defined by their genetic heritage and internal makeup • Tendency to think of all physical phenomena as having a physical and potentially touchable substance • Some ability to discriminate between valid and invalid tests of hypotheses	• Children differ considerably in their early exposure to scientific concepts (e.g., through family visits to natural history museums and access to age-appropriate science books). • Some children are apt to view supernatural forces (e.g., God, the devil, witchcraft) as being largely responsible for natural disasters or illness.	• Have children conduct simple experiments with familiar materials, for example, have them raise sunflowers with varying amounts of light and water. • Obtain computer programs that let students "explore" human anatomy or "dissect" small animals in a virtual "laboratory."
Early Adolescence (10–14 Years) 	• Some ability to think abstractly about scientific phenomena and to separate and control variables • Formulation and testing of hypotheses influenced by existing beliefs (confirmation bias) • Some tendency to misapply scientific concepts (e.g., thinking that gravity pulls objects toward the South Pole)	• Especially in adolescence, boys tend to have more positive attitudes toward science than do girls. Girls are more likely than boys to underestimate their science abilities. • Influences of religion on beliefs about natural phenomena (e.g., evolution) become especially noticeable in early adolescence.	• Have adolescents explore individual interests in science fair projects, scaffolding their efforts at forming hypotheses and controlling irrelevant variables. • Provide scientific explanations that are sufficiently concrete that young adolescents can understand and apply them.
Late Adolescence (14–18 Years) 	• Increasing ability to understand abstract scientific concepts • Increasing ability to separate and control variables • Continuing confirmation bias in experimentation and interpretation of results • Increasing awareness that science is a dynamic and changing (rather than static) discipline	• On average, boys achieve at higher levels in science than girls, especially in the physical sciences; the gender gap in science achievement has decreased in recent years. • Boys are more likely than girls to aspire to careers in science. • Cultures that place high value on honoring authority figures tend to promote the belief that scientific findings should not be questioned.	• Gradually introduce abstract explanations for phenomena, such as the idea that heat results from molecules colliding at a certain rate. • To increase girls' interest and involvement in science, occasionally form same-gender groups in science labs and activities. • Arrange internships for students with men and women who are scientists and exemplify diverse ethnic and cultural backgrounds.

Source: Baillargeon, 1994; Bandura et al., 2001; Barchfeld et al., 2005; M. Bullock & Ziegler, 1999; L. B. Cohen & Cashon, 2006; E. M. Evans, 2001; Flavell, Miller, & Miller, 2002; S. A. Gelman & Markman, 1986; Kyza, 2009; Halpern et al., 2007; Hatano & Inagaki, 1996; Jipson & Callanan, 2003; Keil, 1989; Klaczynski, 2000; Kuhn et al., 2009; Kuhn & Franklin, 2006; Leaper & Friedman, 2007; O. Lee, 1999; Lee-Pearce, Plowman, & Touchstone, 1998; Legare & Gelman, 2007; M. C. Linn & Muilenburg, 1996; Massey & Gelman, 1988; Metz, 2004; Nakazawa et al., 2001; Patrick, Mantzicopoulos, & Samarapungavan, 2008; Pomerantz, Altermatt, & Saxon, 2002; Pulos, 1997; Qian & Pan, 2002; Reiner et al., 2000; M. B. Rowe, 1978; Schauble, 1990; Spelke, 1994; Tamburrini, 1982; Ullman, 2010a; Vosniadou, 1991; B. Y. White & Frederiksen, 1998; Wigfield et al., 1996.

theory of evolution is closely connected to what their religion or philosophy has taught them about how human beings and other living creatures came into existence (E. M. Evans, 2001; Haider-Markel & Joslyn, 2008; Southerland & Sinatra, 2003).

The bioecological framework reminds us that scientific views learned by the child in one context affect his or her interpretation of related views espoused in another setting (Simpson & Parsons, 2008). In one school in northern California, teachers invited children and parents who came from a predominantly Mien (Laotian) background to plant a garden and build a garden house at the school (Hammond, 2001). Families had extensive technological expertise from previous experiences in hunting, farming, preserving food, building houses, producing fabrics, forging metals, and creating elaborate jewelry. The Mien parents and children applied many of their indigenous abilities in planting the garden and building the house, creating a basis for discussion about scientific matters, and motivating everyone to attend family science nights.

Promoting Development in Science

In the first few years of life, children's science "education" is usually limited to informal experiences. At this point, perhaps the best strategy is simply to provide objects and experiences—blocks, water tables, sand piles, field trips to farms and zoos, and so on—that help children acquire general knowledge on which more formal science instruction can later build.

Once children reach kindergarten or first grade, the curriculum typically includes some science topics. As we've seen, children's scientific reasoning capabilities and their ability to separate and control variables are fairly limited. Thus, elementary school teachers tend to focus most science instruction on descriptions of natural phenomena rather than on explanations of why those phenomena occur (Byrnes, 1996). Yet even at the elementary level, it is counterproductive to portray science as primarily a collection of facts. By having students engage in simple investigations almost from the very beginning of the science curriculum, children gain experiences in evaluating data and unraveling the mysteries of our world (Khalid, 2010; Kuhn, 2007).

At the middle school level, students' increasing ability to think about abstract ideas makes it possible to address some of the causal mechanics that underlie natural phenomena. Even so, middle school teachers may not want to introduce ideas completely removed from students' everyday, concrete experiences (Hammerman, 2008; M. C. Linn et al., 1996; Reiner et al., 2000). When students reach high school, they are more likely to have acquired the scientific knowledge and reasoning skills they need to think abstractly about natural phenomena (M. C. Linn et al., 1996). Nevertheless, teachers should continue to engage students in frequent hands-on science activities, not only through systematic experiments but also through informal, exploratory activities that relate scientific concepts to everyday experiences. Secondary students in general, but especially high school girls, are likely to achieve at higher levels when they have regular hands-on experiences with the phenomena they are studying (Burkam, Lee, & Smerdon, 1997).

Several additional instructional strategies can be helpful for a wide variety of age groups:

• **Engage students regularly in authentic scientific investigations.** Many school laboratory activities are little more than cookbook recipes: Students are given specific materials and instructions to follow step by step. Such activities can certainly help make scientific phenomena more concrete for students. However, they are unlikely to encourage youngsters to engage in thinking processes (formulating and testing hypotheses, separating and controlling variables, and so on) that characterize true scientific reasoning (Keil & Silberstein, 1996; M. J. Padilla, 1991; J. Singer, Marx, Krajcik, & Chambers, 2000). So in addition, teachers should give students many opportunities to conduct investigations in which the procedures and outcomes are not necessarily predetermined. For instance, teachers might ask students

ARTIFACT 10-7   Just follow the instructions. In this pencil drawing, 9-year-old Corey depicts his perception of scientific "research" as something in which an adult tells him the steps to follow.

to address such questions as "Does one fast-food restaurant provide more meat in a hamburger than others?" or "Is the local drinking water really safe to drink?" (M. J. Padilla, 1991; J. Singer et al., 2000).

Youngsters typically need some scaffolding for such activities, however. For instance, a teacher might do the following:

- Present situations in which only two or three variables need to be controlled.
- Ask students to identify several possible hypotheses about cause-and-effect relationships before beginning to experiment.
- Provide regular guidance, hints, and feedback regarding the need to control variables and evaluate observations objectively.
- Ask questions that encourage students to make predictions and critically analyze their observations (e.g., "What do you think will happen?" "What is your evidence?" "Do you see things that are inconsistent with what you predicted?"). (Byrnes, 1996; Carey, Evans, Honda, Jay, & Unger, 1989; Kuhn et al., 1988; Kuhn & Dean, 2005; Legaspi & Straits, 2011; Minstrell & Stimpson, 1996; Thatch, 2008)

- **Provide age-appropriate explanations for physical and biological phenomena.** Although youngsters can discover a great deal through their own experimentation, they also need to learn the concepts, principles, and theories that scientists use to make sense of the world (Vygotsky, 1934/1986). Ideally, they should pull the things they learn into integrated, meaningful bodies of knowledge. Often teachers can make interrelationships concrete for students by presenting diagrams, flowcharts, or two- or three-dimensional models (Glynn, Yeany, & Britton, 1991a; Schwarz & White, 2005; Vosniadou, 2009).

- **Actively work to promote conceptual change.** Existing misconceptions probably interfere with children's development in science more than in any other academic discipline. Thanks to confirmation bias, youngsters are apt to seek out information that confirms, rather than contradicts, what they currently believe.[17] Perhaps one of the most effective approaches for facilitating conceptual change is to give students opportunities to discuss competing perspectives within a classroom environment that communicates the message "It's okay to make errors and change our minds" (Minstrell & Stimpson, 1996; C. L. Smith, 2007; Vosniadou, 2009).

Yet a single discussion or exercise is generally not sufficient to enact meaningful conceptual change. Take the example of accepting the notion that the earth is a solid sphere, not a flat surface. From children's everyday experiences, they live on a level plane, so when first exposed to the notion that the earth is a round ball, they try to protect their prior belief by supplementing it with subtle revisions that the earth is a hollow sphere with a flat surface inside or that the earth is a sphere with a flattened surface on its top (Vosniadou, 2009). It typically takes a series of discussions and exposures to spherical models before children accept the scientific view that the earth is really a solid ball floating in space.

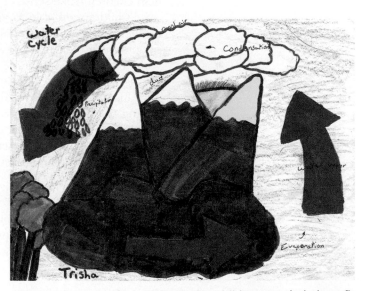

ARTIFACT 10-8   The water cycle. Children regularly benefit from requests that they identify cause-and-effect relationships. In this drawing, 9-year-old Trisha shows her understanding that various phenomena in nature are interrelated.

DEVELOPMENT IN OTHER ACADEMIC DOMAINS

In their studies of children's development in academic subject areas, researchers have focused largely on reading, writing, mathematics, and science. Yet they have also learned a few things about children's development in social studies, art, and music. We now look briefly at trends in each of these domains.

[17] Chapter 7 suggests several general strategies for promoting conceptual change.

Social Studies

The field of *social studies* examines a wide range of topics from history, political science, geography, anthropology, and government, whose collective mastery prepares a young person to become an informed and responsible citizen (National Council for the Social Studies, 2010). In preschool and elementary school, social studies lessons are generally taught in an interdisciplinary manner around such issues as how the lives of people in the past are similar to, and different from, our own lives today. As youngsters move into middle and high school levels, they frequently take courses that are focused on a specific aspect of a single discipline (e.g., U.S. History or Human Geography).

Children's experiences at home and in the community affect their interpretations of concepts in social studies. Children are generally able to extrapolate from their own lives to those of other people and in so doing appreciate their need for shelter, food and water, and love and respect. Yet children frequently misunderstand *why* other people choose to live in certain ways.

Children are more likely to understand decisions other people make about their livelihoods when teachers discuss available natural resources and local climates (Brophy, Alleman, & Knighton, 2009). For example, although many children are interested in the kinds of houses that Native American tribal groups have historically built, they may not realize *why* tribes chose to design particular kinds of dwellings—that tribes moving with migrating buffalo needed portable structures (and therefore created tipis), that other tribes in eastern states could count on an abundance of wood (and thus could build longhouses), and that groups in the southwest had a plentiful supply of mud and clay (and hence built pueblos) (Brophy et al., 2009). By pointing out the kinds of resources that a society did and did not have access to, teachers can help children make sense of types of dwellings, modes of transportation, and the like.

Children are able to view people from other eras and cultures sympathetically when teachers explain how seemingly exotic customs are actually sensible strategies that helped people meet their basic needs. One teacher, Barbara Knighton, had had extensive contact with first- and second-grade children and was able to anticipate children's reactions to *rites of passage*, ceremonies that signal transitions from one stage of life to another. Barbara initially introduced these rites by talking about markers of maturity that were familiar to children—staying home alone, babysitting, going on dates, getting a driver's license, and undergoing certain religious rituals, for example, participating in a Catholic First Communion or Jewish Bar Mitzvah. Next, she described a Kenyan ceremony for boys and scaffolded children's responses to this unfamiliar custom:

Barbara:	Here is one I hadn't heard about until I read about it just the other day. Kenya is right here [shows on globe], so it's on the same continent but just a little ways from Ghana, where we read about before. In Kenya, they have a special ceremony called safana. I'll write this for you here [writes word]. This is really going to surprise you. This is really different from mine [her own rites of passage described earlier]. You're going to be surprised at what they do. Are you ready? . . . They take the boys who are the right age to have their rites of passage—to start becoming considered adults—and they take them and cut off their hair. That was a lot different from mine, right?
Students:	Yeah.
Barbara:	Then they take mud and make it into a kind of hat or a cap—almost like a ball cap. Now, remember what we said the other day about discrimination—things that seem different or strange to you. What you might say is, "Wow, that's kind of a surprise. That's really different. I hadn't expected to hear that." But you're not going to do this: "Eeuooo!" or "Gross!" or "Yuck!" That's discrimination. So what you will say in your head is, "Wow, that would be really strange."
Student:	Horrible.
Barbara:	Not horrible—you don't know—but they're pretty excited. They're probably looking forward to it because it means they're going to be

	looked on as an adult. Don't you look forward to when you're an adult and you get to be the boss of yourself?
Students:	Yeah.
Barbara:	Well, that's what they think. I'm sure they think the same thing. Every kid I've ever known thought that same way. So they take the mud and they make a cap out of it, and because it's so hot there, the cap will eventually dry. After it's dry, they take it off very carefully and they save it and they paint it. That's part of their ceremony. Sound different?
Students:	Yeah.
Barbara:	Different from any of these [points to terms and illustrations associated with more familiar rites of passage]?
Students:	Yeah.
Barbara:	But the point is still the same. He's starting to become . . .
Students:	A grown-up. (dialogue from Brophy et al., 2009, pp. 120–121)[18].

Barbara depicted the Kenyan ceremony as similar to Western customs and fostered children's respect for the Kenyan boys. Like Barbara, teachers can communicate that people invariably pursue reasonable goals in the context of their current knowledge, customs, and opportunities. Thus, children can learn that people sometimes go to war to gain control over land, take voyages to satisfy their curiosity and obtain resources, and immigrate to other lands to escape oppression or gain more favorable economic conditions (Brophy et al., 2009).

As you might expect, children's understandings of social studies begin as personal concerns and only gradually evolve into symbolic and abstract understandings. Let's look at developmental progressions in social studies in two specific domains, history and geography.

History

Children's first awareness of history typically involves their *own* history. Sometime between ages 2 and 4, children begin to construct an *autobiographical self:* They can recall past events in their own lives and realize that they exist *in time*, with a past and a future as well as a present.[19] As their improving language skills allow an increasing exchange of ideas with family members and playmates, they gradually expand their sense of history to include other people whom they know well.

Children's knowledge of history on a broader scale emerges largely as a result of formal instruction. In the elementary grades, children's awareness of history tends to be concrete and simplistic. They may conceptualize the birth of the United States as resulting from a single, specific event (e.g., the Boston Tea Party) or as involving nothing more than constructing new buildings and towns (Ormrod, Jackson, Kirby, Davis, & Benson, 1999). Another source of difficulty for elementary school children is a limited ability to understand historical time. They might refer to events that happened "a long, long time ago" or "in the old days" but tell you that such events happened in 2005. And they tend to lump historical events into two general categories: those that happened very recently and those that happened many years ago.

At around age 10, children acquire some ability to put historical events in sequence and to attach them to particular time periods (Barton & Levstik, 1996). Accordingly, systematic history instruction usually begins in fourth or fifth grade. Yet when children first study the broader scope of history, they have little direct knowledge on which to build. They haven't lived in most of the time periods they study, nor have they seen most of the locations they learn about. What they *can* build on, as you are learning, is their knowledge of human beings. Children can better understand historical events when they discover that historical figures had

2000 Days oh go George Washington gave us the Country To Live on.

ARTIFACT 10-9 **George Washington gave us the country.** As shown in this response to the question *How did the United States become a country?,* a second grader has only a limited ability to understand historical time.

[18] Excerpt from "Discussion of Rite of Passage" from INSIDE THE SOCIAL STUDIES CLASSROOM by Jere Brophy. Copyright © 2009 by Jere Brophy. Reprinted with permission via Copyright Clearance Center.
[19] Chapter 7 introduces the concept of autobiographical self.

I'm Pocahontas. I am an Indian girl. My father's name was Cheif Powhatan. My brothers name was Nantequas. Some white man had come to My fatherland in three tall ships. The white man had fire sticks that thundered and killed. My people found Jhon Smith on our land. When the indians where going to Jhon Smith for traspassing I Pocahontas layd over Jhon Smith and yelled, please Father let him live! My Father did. A few days later My Father adopted Jhon Smith and called him Nantaquwe. I wished Jhon Smith could stay forever but he had to go back to his village. Jhon Smith village was starving so I asked father to give them food. He did. Jhon Smith made Cheif Powtan a Crown and placed it on is head. I never saw Jhon Smith agian I thoght he had died. After a couple of years I found Jhon Rolfe. We fell in love and got marryed we had One child. After I found out Jhon Smith was still alive. We became good friends agian.

ARTIFACT 10-10 Pocahontas. In this history assignment, 10-year-old Kaitlyn takes on the perspective of Pocahontas to describe events in the early 1600s.

particular goals, motives, and personalities—in other words, that people in history were, in many respects, just ordinary folks (Brophy et al., 2009; Brophy & VanSledright, 1997; Yeager et al., 1997). Following are several additional strategies that can help children and adolescents gain a "human" understanding of history:

- Assign works of fiction that realistically depict people living in particular times and places.
- Role-play family discussions that focus on making decisions during critical times in history (e.g., deciding whether to send a teenage son off to war).
- Have "journalists" (two or three students) interview people (other students) who "participated" in various ways in a historical event.
- Assign readings from original documents, including diaries, letters, newspaper articles, and so on. (Afflerbach, VanSledright, & Dromsky, 2003; Brophy & Alleman, 1996; Brophy et al., 2009; Brophy & VanSledright, 1997; Nokes, Dole, & Hacker, 2007; M. B. W. Wolfe & Goldman, 2005)

Geography

The discipline of geography is concerned not only with where various natural features and cultural groups are located but also with why and how they got there. Geographers study how rivers and mountain ranges end up where they do, why people are more likely to settle in some locations than in others, and how people in various locations make a living.

Many children and adolescents have a simple view of geography as a discipline. Typically, they conceive of geography as being little more than the names and locations of various countries, capital cities, rivers, mountain ranges, and so on—perhaps, in part, because teachers often present geography this way (Bochenhauer, 1990; VanSledright & Limón, 2006). Even in the high school years, students rarely reflect on why various locations have the physical features they do or on how the economic and cultural practices of various social groups might be partly the result of their physical environment.

An essential cognitive tool in geography is, of course, the *map*. Central to geographical thinking is an understanding that maps depict the arrangement and characteristics of particular locations. By age 3 or 4, children have some ability to recognize relationships between simple graphics and the physical locations that the graphics represent (J. Huttenlocher et al., 1999; Peralta & Maita, 2007). During the next several years, children can increasingly use maps to identify locations in their immediate, familiar surroundings (Blades & Spencer, 1987; C. Davies & Uttal, 2007). However, their ability to use maps to navigate through *un*familiar territory remains fairly limited until adolescence at the earliest (C. Davies & Uttal, 2007; Liben, Kastens, & Stevenson, 2002).

When children in the early elementary grades look at larger-scale maps—perhaps those depicting a state or country—they tend to take what they see somewhat literally (Gardner, Torff, & Hatch, 1996; Liben 2009). They may think that lines separating states and countries are actually painted on the earth or that an airport denoted by a picture of an airplane has only one plane. Young children also have trouble maintaining a sense of scale and proportion when interpreting maps. They might deny that a road could actually be a road because "it's not fat enough for two cars to go on" or insist that a mountain depicted on a three-dimensional relief map can't possibly be a mountain because "it's not high enough" (Liben & Downs, 1989b; Liben & Myers, 2007, p. 202). As children get older, and especially as they reach adolescence, they become more proficient in dealing with the symbolic and proportional nature of maps (Forbes et al., 1999; Liben & Myers, 2007).

In social studies units, and in particular in geography lessons, children are regularly exposed to maps. Eventually youngsters learn that different maps are drawn to different scales, reflecting various proportions between graphic representation and reality (Liben & Downs, 1989b). One effective strategy is to ask children to create their *own* maps, perhaps of their neighborhood or town (Enyedy, 2005; Forbes et al., 1999; Gregg & Leinhardt, 1994a). Teachers and other adults might also ask youngsters to look for patterns in what they see in maps and to speculate about why those patterns exist (Gregg & Leinhardt, 1994b; Liben & Downs, 1989a).

Art

As budding artists, children exercise a variety of skills. They imagine new worlds; express their thoughts and emotions; interpret the meaning of pictures, sculptures, and performances; practice fine motor skills; reason spatially; explore perspective and dimensions; and analyze such compositional elements as shape, proportion, light, and color (Smutny & von Fremd, 2009).

The particular artistic skills children use depend on their age and experience. As early as age 2, some children begin to represent their experiences on paper—for instance, by making a series of dots to mimic how an animal hops (J. Matthews, 2010; Winner, 2006). They also begin to experiment with geometric figures, especially lines and circles. At age 3, their repertoire of shapes expands to include squares, rectangles, triangles, crosses, and Xs, and they soon begin combining such shapes to create pictures (Beaty, 1998; Golomb, 2004; Kellogg, 1967). Many of their early drawings are of people, which might initially consist of

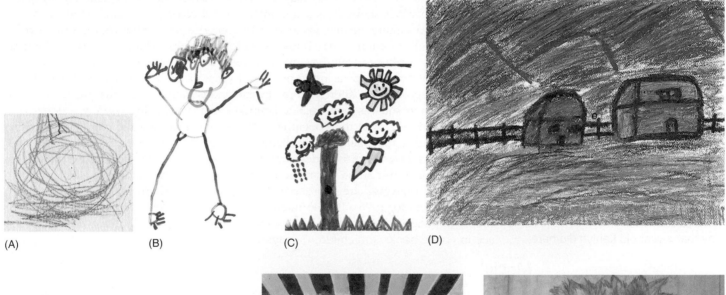

(A)   (B)   (C)   (D)

ARTIFACT 10-11 Artistic development. Developmental progressions in children's art are clearly seen in these pieces by (A) Tina at age 2½, (B) Corey at age 5, (C) Corey at age 6, (D) Trisha at age 11, (E) Elizabeth at age 14, and (F) Joey at age 17.

(E)   (F)

a circle (depicting either a head or a head plus body) with a few facial features (e.g., eyes, mouth) within it and four lines (two arms, two legs) extending from it. With age, preschoolers increasingly add features—perhaps hair, hands, fingers, and feet—to their human figures.

Sometime around age 4, children begin to combine drawings of several objects to create pictures of groups or nature scenes. Initially, they may scatter things haphazardly around the page, but eventually place objects on the page in an orientation that is somewhat consistent with everyday reality. In the elementary grades, children become capable of producing a wide variety of shapes and contours, and their drawings and paintings become more detailed, realistic, and appropriately proportional (N. R. Smith et al., 1998; Winner, 2006). By the upper elementary grades, children represent depth in their drawings (Braine, Schauble, Kugelmass, & Winter, 1993).

Some youngsters draw and paint very little once they reach adolescence, especially if art is not a regular part of the school curriculum, and so their artistic skills may progress very little beyond this point (S. Moran & Gardner, 2006; Winner, 2006). Young adolescents frequently hold themselves to a very high expectation for representing images in a realistic manner and become disappointed when they cannot achieve a desired standard (Luehrman & Unrath, 2006). Those who continue to create art refine their abilities to show texture, depth, perspective, and spatial relationships (N. R. Smith et al., 1998; Willats, 1995). They may also try to convey mood and emotion by selectively using various shapes, hues, and intensities of color (N. R. Smith et al., 1998).

When a culture neither values nor encourages art, children's art skills evolve slowly if at all (Gordon, 2004; Trawick-Smith, 2003). But when drawing implements are readily available to children—as they are in many cultures—certain universals in artistic development appear in the preschool years (Case & Okamoto, 1996; Golomb, 2004; Kellogg, 1967). Children from diverse industrialized cultures are also apt to draw houses as squares with smaller, internal squares depicting windows, doors, and perhaps chimneys. And they begin to compose more complex pictures in the same sequence and at approximately the same ages regardless of their cultural background.

Other aspects of artistic development are more culture specific. If children receive extensive instruction in artistic techniques, as many children do in Japan and China, their drawings are more elaborate, detailed, and true-to-life (Alland, 1983; Case & Okamoto, 1996). By the middle elementary grades, some children begin to mimic popular images in their local cultural environment, such as the drawings they see in comic books and children's magazines (B. Wilson, 1997; Winner, 2006).

ARTIFACT 10-12 My house. Young children in a variety of industrialized cultures draw houses in much the same way that 4-year-old Kaitlyn did here.

Music

Human beings of all ages clearly enjoy music. Six-month-olds pay more attention to their mother when she is singing (rather than talking) to them (Nakata & Trehub, 2004). Mother's lively songs help capture infants' attention and keep infants on an even keel, perking them up a bit if they seem low on energy but soothing them if they are overly aroused (Longhi, 2009; Shenfield, Trehub, & Nakata, 2003). Five- to 24-month-old infants are more likely to sway, rock, and make other rhythmic movements to music than to speech (Zentner & Eerola, 2010).

Just as young infants can hear subtle differences in spoken language that adults don't hear, so, too, do they pick up on subtle changes in music that adults don't notice.[20] When a melody changes slightly (say, by a note or two within the same key), 8-month-olds are more likely than adults to notice the difference (Trainor & Trehub, 1992). But as youngsters grow older, and especially as they progress through the preschool and early elementary school years, they increasingly perceive patterns (melodies, keys, complex rhythms, etc.) rather than individual notes (Gromko & Poorman, 1998; Winner, 2006).

Children also gain considerable proficiency in singing during the early and middle childhood years (Persellin & Bateman, 2009; Winner, 2006). At around age 2, they begin to repeat some of the song lyrics they hear. They soon add a rhythmic structure and up-and-down "melody" of sorts. By the time they are 5 or 6, most can sing a recognizable tune and keep it

---

[20] The shift in infancy from initially discriminating all sounds in the world's many languages to becoming a specialist in the sounds present in one's own native language is described in Chapter 9.

largely within the same key and meter. For most youngsters, further development in singing comes primarily from explicit voice training (Winner, 2006). Formal instruction is usually necessary for children to gain proficiency in playing a musical instrument as well (D. J. Elliott, 1995).

Another important aspect of musical development is **music literacy**, the ability to read and understand musical notation. As early as age 4, children can, when asked, invent ways to represent musical sounds with objects—for instance, using large, heavy objects to represent loud notes and smaller objects to represent softer notes (Gromko, 1996). At about the same age, they can also invent strategies for representing music on paper. For instance, they may make small circles or mountain "peaks" for high notes and make larger circles or "valleys" for lower pitches (Gromko, 1994, 1996, 1998). Standard musical notation is, of course, a cultural creation, and so children must be instructed in its interpretation. Youngsters' ability to read music can enhance their ability to hear and remember the subtle nuances of a musical piece (Gromko & Poorman, 1998).

Virtually all cultures have some form of music, and the types of music with which children grow up certainly affect their musical sensitivities and preferences (J. Davidson, Faulkner, & McPherson, 2009; Hannon & Trehub, 2005; Werker & Tees, 1999; Winner, 2006). But within any single culture, children have varying abilities to hear and appreciate music. About 4 percent of children in any age-group have **amusia** (or tone deafness), an inability to detect the small changes in pitch that are common in melodies. Such youngsters show little or no improvement in their perception of musical tones despite instruction and practice, suggesting that the ability to hear music *as* music may have a biological basis (Gardner et al., 1996; K. L. Hyde & Peretz, 2004). In contrast, some children not only hear, but can also *remember*, subtle differences in pitch. Although most people can remember the relative pitches of notes in a melody, individuals with *absolute pitch* can also recall the *exact* pitch of a note they have repeatedly heard in, say, a popular song or soundtrack (Shellenberg & Trehub, 2003). Absolute pitch is more common in infants and preschoolers than in older children or adults, so possibly children lose this ability if everyday demands in their culture don't require it (Saffran & Griepentrog, 2001; Winner, 2006). It is also more common in children who begin music lessons before age 7 (Takeuchi & Hulse, 1993).

The ability to *produce* music seems to draw from both nature and nurture as well (D. J. Elliott, 1995; Treffert & Wallace, 2002). Some children with autism have exceptional instrumental talent. After watching a movie on television one evening, 14-year-old Leslie Lemke sat down at the family piano and played Tchaikovsky's Piano Concerto No. 1, which had been a sound track for portions of the movie. He had never heard the concerto before that night, yet his rendition was flawless. Lemke is now a world-renowned pianist, even though he has autism and an intellectual disability, is blind, and has never had a piano lesson (Treffert & Wallace, 2002).

Some policy makers view art and music as luxuries that can easily be dropped from a school curriculum when budgets are tight. In reality, however, formal instruction in these domains appears to have distinct benefits for growing children. For instance, creating paintings or collages that capture certain events or moods can help children add descriptive words and other details to their short stories and poetry (Olshansky, 1995; Olshansky, O'Connor, & O'Byrne, 2006). Drawing illustrations of scientific phenomena or historical events can enhance children's understanding and memory of these situations (Edens & Potter, 2001; J. H. Davis, 2008). Entertaining others in a selective singing group enhances the self-esteem, resilience, and academic achievement of children who are otherwise at risk for school failure (Jenlink, 1994). And instruction in both art and music can promote the development of certain cognitive processes and dispositions—including pattern recognition, sustained attention, executive control processes, and a willingness to take risks and "think outside the box"—that are potentially applicable to other academic domains as well (J. H. Davis, 2008; Schellenberg, 2006; Smutny & von Fremd, 2009).

Children undergo similar progressions in the academic domains, shifting from initially approaching academic material personally, concretely, and spontaneously, to later applying increasingly sophisticated symbolic systems and learning strategies. The Basic Developmental Issues table "Developmental Progressions in the Academic Domains" summarizes how three general themes—nature and nurture, universality and diversity, and qualitative and quantitative change—play out in the subject areas you've learned about in this chapter.

music literacy
Ability to read and understand musical notation.

amusia
Inability to detect the small changes in pitch that are common in melodies; an extreme form of tone deafness.

BASIC DEVELOPMENTAL ISSUES
Developmental Progressions in the Academic Domains

ISSUE	READING AND WRITING	MATH AND SCIENCE	SOCIAL STUDIES	ART AND MUSIC
Nature and Nurture	Although children appear to have a biological predisposition to learn spoken language, facility with *written* language is largely the result of exposure to printed materials. Nature can interfere with normal literacy development, however: Some children with biologically based disabilities have unusual difficulty learning to read and write.	Within the first few months of life, infants notice differences in quantity and appear to understand certain basic principles of physics (e.g., that no two objects can occupy the same space at the same time). Some theorists speculate that such early acquisitions reflect neurologically "preprogrammed" knowledge. By and large, however, children's knowledge of numbers and scientific phenomena develops through informal experiences and formal instruction.	The bodies of knowledge and cognitive tools that children acquire in social studies are the result of nurture, as provided by both formal instruction in school and informal experiences within the family (trips to historical sites, contact with other societies, use of maps on subway systems, etc.). However, maturational processes may partly determine the age at which children become able to think about historical time and understand the symbolic nature of maps.	Hereditary and maturational factors play some role in artistic and musical development. In the preschool years, children's ability to draw depends largely on maturation of fine motor skills. Furthermore, most children seem to have an inborn appreciation for music from birth. And some children show exceptional talent in art or music even without formal instruction. For the most part, however, development in art and music is the result of training and practice.
Universality and Diversity	Phonological awareness facilitates reading development even when written language is *not* based on how words are pronounced. However, children learn to read and write more easily when words have highly regular and predictable spelling patterns. Children's literacy development also depends on the extent to which their families and cultural groups model and encourage reading and writing.	Although children worldwide have some awareness of quantity, their precision in measuring and comparing quantities depends on the number concepts and operations that their culture provides. Many Asian children seem to be especially adept in mathematics, in part because Asian languages make the structure of the base-10 number system quite obvious. Children's basic scientific knowledge (e.g., knowing that animals are fundamentally different from human-made objects) is similar worldwide, but understandings of many natural phenomena (e.g., the origins of species) differ depending on cultural and religious upbringings.	Because children's knowledge of social studies is largely the product of the environment and culture in which they have been raised, universal acquisitions have not been identified. In industrialized societies, history is formally taught in school, and maps are widely used to aid navigation. In other cultures, however, children's knowledge of history comes from hearing stories from their elders, and people navigate largely by locating distinctive landmarks in the physical terrain.	Virtually all cultures have some form of art and music. Artistic styles and musical patterns differ considerably from culture to culture, however, and children's development in these areas varies accordingly. Although preschoolers' drawings tend to be quite similar across cultures (e.g., early drawings of people may consist of circles with rudimentary facial features and four lines extending outward to represent limbs), by middle childhood their artwork begins to mimic the styles and images they see in their environment.
Qualitative and Quantitative Change	Reading and writing skills show many qualitative changes over time. Children shift their primary focus from word identification to comprehension (in reading), eventually switch from knowledge telling to knowledge transforming (in writing), and increasingly incorporate metacognitive processes in their literate activities (in both reading and writing). Literacy development is quantitative in the sense that children become able to recognize and spell more and more words each year, and basic reading and writing skills become increasingly automatized.	As children get older, they acquire more knowledge about mathematical and scientific concepts and principles—a progression that reflects quantitative change. In addition, they acquire more complex and sophisticated—and qualitatively different—ways of thinking about math and science. Elementary school children begin to rely on retrieval rather than counting objects on fingers as they solve addition and subtraction problems, and adolescents gain new reasoning skills (e.g., separating and controlling variables) in their scientific experimentation.	A good deal of development in social studies is quantitative, in that children acquire more information about historical events and geographical locations. Qualitative changes are seen in how children *think* about history and geography. With appropriate instruction children begin to realize that knowledge of history is comprised not only of what *did* happen but also of varying perspectives of what *might have* happened. And as children gain proportional reasoning, they become better able to understand the various scales with which maps are constructed.	Many qualitative changes are seen in art and music development. With growth and experience, children's drawings begin to address composition (e.g., creating an organized scene rather than a random collection of objects), perspective, and texture. And in the preschool years, their songs begin to reflect a consistent rhythm and key. Quantitative change is seen in such things as children's increasing knowledge of musical notation and increasing automaticity in playing a musical instrument.

USING CONTENT AREA STANDARDS TO GUIDE INSTRUCTION

Formal instruction in academic domains must, of course, take into account the knowledge and abilities that children and adolescents are likely to have at various ages. Within the past two or three decades, numerous discipline-specific professional groups have compiled comprehensive lists of topics and skills they believe to be appropriate for different grade levels. Such lists, known as content area **standards**, are often used to guide instruction and assessment from kindergarten or first grade through high school. Table 10-1 lists websites at which you can find standards for a variety of academic domains.

In many countries, an additional source of guidance comes from standards created by state departments of education and other regional or local authorities. In the United States, the *No Child Left Behind Act* of 2001 requires that each of the 50 states have standards for reading, mathematics, and science. Sometimes known simply as *NCLB*, this legislation mandates that school districts annually administer achievement tests in grades 3 through 8 to determine whether students are making "adequate yearly progress" in meeting state-determined standards. Schools that do not show progress are subject to corrective actions

standards
In education, general statements regarding the knowledge and skills that students should gain and the characteristics that accomplishments should reflect.

TABLE 10-1 Websites with Standards for Various Academic Disciplines

ACADEMIC DOMAIN	ORGANIZATION	INTERNET ADDRESS	ONCE YOU GET THERE . . .[a]
English and language arts	National Council of Teachers of English	www.ncte.org	Select Resources from the home page and then select Standards
Foreign language	American Council on the Teaching of Foreign Languages	www.actfl.org	Select *Standards for Foreign Language Learning: Executive Summary* from the *Publications* menu.
Geography	National Council for Geographic Education	www.ncge.org	Select *National Standards* from the *Resources* menu.
Health, physical education, and dance	National Association for Sport and Physical Education	www.aahperd.org/naspe	Select *National Standards* from the *Standards and Position Statements* menu.
History	National Center for History in the Schools	www.sscnet.ucla.edu/nchs	Select Standards from the main menu.
Mathematics	National Council of Teachers of Mathematics	www.nctm.org	Select *Standards and Focal Points*, then select *Principles and Standards for School Mathematics* menu, then click on *Math Standards and Expectations*.
Music	National Association for Music Education	www.menc.org	Click on *Resources* and then on *National Standards*.
Reading	International Reading Association	www.reading.org	Select Resources by Topic and then Common Core and then click on Standards Link
Science	National Academy of Sciences	www.nap.edu (site for National Academies Press, which publishes reports for several scientific organizations)	Click on *Education* (under *Browse Topics*) and then on *Testing, Assessments, and Standards* (under *Browse Subtopics*), and finally select *National Science Education Standards*.
Social Studies	National Council for the Social Studies	www.socialstudies.org	Click on *Resources* and then select *Curriculum Standards*.
Visual arts	National Art Education Association	www.naea-reston.org	Click on *Research and Knowledge* and then on Store and *The National Visual Arts Standards*.

[a]These steps worked for us in October 2011. Given the dynamic nature of many websites, you may find that you have to do something different when you get to the site in question.

**Preparing for Your
Licensure Examination**

Your teaching test might ask you
about using national standards in
instructional planning.

(e.g., administrative restructuring, dismissal of faculty members), and students have the option of attending another public school at the school district's expense. Well intentioned as this legislation was, most research on its effects has not been fully favorable. Because their livelihoods depend on their students' test scores, teachers spend more time on literacy, math, and science—and especially on basic topics and skills they think will be on the statewide tests—and less time on social studies, foreign language, the arts, and other disciplines (McCarty, 2009; Pianta, Belsky, Houts, & Morrison, 2007; R. M. Thomas, 2005; Valli & Buese, 2007). And students who consistently perform poorly on the tests (many of whom come from low-income families) are likely to drop out of school rather than persist in academic endeavors that they perceive to be a lost cause (Hursh, 2007; McCarty, 2009; R. Ryan, 2005; R. M. Thomas, 2005).

Existing standards are certainly useful in helping teachers focus instruction on important educational goals in various academic domains. When teachers establish clear instructional goals toward clearly defined standards, all children, and especially those who struggle academically, are likely to make good progress (Hamre & Pianta, 2005). We worry, however, that many existing standards are based on topics and skills that are *typically taught* at various grade levels, rather than on developmental research regarding what youngsters can reasonably accomplish at different ages (e.g., VanSledright & Limón, 2006). We worry, too, that some lists of standards are so lengthy that teachers are able to provide only fragmented, superficial "coverage" of topics and are less inclined to design lessons that foster elaboration, comprehension monitoring, and other effective cognitive and metacognitive processes in the academic areas (e.g., M. E. Schmidt, 2008; M. S. Schwartz, Sadler, Sonnert, & Tai, 2009; Valli & Buese, 2007).

Furthermore, if teachers rely exclusively on standards for particular academic domains, they are apt to neglect other, equally important domains, such as the development of general learning strategies, social skills, and emotional well-being. This is *not* to say that teachers must choose between strong academic standards and students' social-emotional growth. Effective teachers pursue both sets of objectives by integrating academic standards with nonacademic agendas.

SUMMARY

Reading Development

When toddlers and preschoolers have multiple and varied experiences with reading materials, they learn a great deal about the nature of written language. They understand that spoken language is represented in consistent ways and that different kinds of printed materials serve different purposes. Such knowledge, known as *emergent literacy*, provides an important foundation for the reading and writing skills that children acquire once they begin school.

Skilled reading involves knowing letter-sound correspondences, recognizing letters and words quickly and automatically, constructing meaning from the words on the page, and regulating the reading process. Phonological awareness (hearing the distinct sounds within spoken words), word identification skills, and the automatic recognition of many common words typically emerge by the early and middle elementary school years. Reading comprehension and metacognitive strategies develop throughout childhood and adolescence.

Some children with sensory impairments or learning disabilities have more difficulty learning to read than their nondisabled peers. Researchers have also found gender, socioeconomic, and cultural differences in reading development. Strategies for fostering reading development include teaching parents strategies for effective storybook reading, promoting children's phonological awareness, providing many opportunities to read authentic literature, making culturally relevant reading materials available, and engaging children in discussions about what they read.

Writing Development

To become skillful writers, children not only must master handwriting and spelling but must also discover how to communicate their thoughts clearly; learn conventions of capitalization, punctuation, and syntax; and regulate the entire writing effort. Handwriting is usually mastered in the elementary grades, but other aspects of writing continue to develop throughout the school years. In the middle school and high school years, many youngsters gradually abandon a *knowledge-telling* approach to writing (in which they write ideas in whatever order the ideas come to mind) in favor of a *knowledge-transforming* approach (in which they conscientiously try to communicate their ideas to the reader). Self-evaluation and editing skills also improve somewhat during adolescence.

To a considerable degree, children's writing development depends on their general intellectual development, but some children have difficulty writing despite normal cognitive development in other areas. Gender and cultural differences in writing development have also been observed. Teachers and other adults can promote writing development by introducing preschoolers to simple writing activities (e.g., making alphabet letters, using pseudowriting in pretend play), assigning authentic writing tasks in the elementary and secondary grades, scaffolding youngsters' writing efforts, and requiring writing in all areas of the school curriculum.

Mathematics Development

Children have some awareness of quantity in the first year of life, but they learn to count only if their culture provides the cognitive tools (e.g., number words) that make counting possible. Often they create strategies for performing simple mathematical operations (e.g., adding and subtracting small numbers) on their own, but formal instruction is usually necessary for acquisition of complex concepts and procedures. For optimal mathematical development, children should truly understand (rather than simply memorize) mathematical procedures and learn that there is often more than one correct way to solve a problem.

Some children have learning disabilities that impede their ability to automatize arithmetic facts and solve simple math problems, and others have little exposure to numbers and counting before they begin school. Gender and cultural differences in mathematics have been observed as well. Concrete manipulatives and visual aids often facilitate children's mathematical development, especially in the preschool and elementary years. Also, once children have mastered and automatized basic facts and skills, tools that reduce the load on working memory (e.g., paper and pencil, calculators) can enhance their mathematical problem-solving abilities.

Science Development

Although children are possibly "prewired" with some basic knowledge of physics, by and large they acquire scientific knowledge through their informal experiences and formal instruction. As early as the preschool years, they begin to form theories (sometimes accurate, sometimes not) about categories of living creatures and cause-and-effect relationships in their physical world. The ability to reason as scientists do (e.g., formulating and testing hypotheses, drawing conclusions from collected data) improves in adolescence, but even many high school students have difficulty analyzing data objectively.

Children's individual abilities (e.g., visual-spatial skills) and disabilities (e.g., blindness) affect their development in science, as do gender stereotypes and cultural beliefs. Authentic scientific investigations, age-appropriate explanations, and intentional efforts to bring about conceptual change can all enhance youngsters' scientific understandings and reasoning skills.

Development in Other Academic Domains

Social studies, history, geography, art, and music have received less attention in developmental research, but researchers are finding some trends in these and other subject areas. Children in the early elementary grades are apt to have difficulty understanding the nature of historical time, and they may not appreciate that some historical "knowledge" is a matter of perspective rather than fact. Geographical reasoning requires understanding the symbolic and proportional nature of maps, which emerges gradually over the elementary and middle school years. Educators can help children to understand the traditions and motivations of other people by communicating the circumstances of their lives and resources available to them.

Art and music are found in virtually all cultures, but the specific forms that they take differ considerably from one society to another. Some universals are seen, to be sure. Infants around the world seem to enjoy music, and children's early drawings of people are similar regardless of where they grow up—but advanced art and music abilities are largely dependent on instruction and practice.

Using Content Area Standards to Guide Instruction

Groups of subject-matter experts in various academic disciplines have developed content area standards describing topics believed to be appropriate for study at various grade levels. State departments of education and many local school districts have also created standards to guide instruction, especially in reading, writing, math, and science. Such standards provide useful guidance when teachers plan lessons for their own classrooms. Teachers must remember, however, that standards, voluminous as they are, tend to be focused almost exclusively on academic achievement and neglect accomplishments in other areas (e.g., work habits, social skills, emotional well-being) that are equally important for students' long-term development.

APPLYING CONCEPTS IN CHILD DEVELOPMENT

The exercises in this section will help you build your ability to apply your knowledge of child development in working with children.

Improving Your Observation Skills

On page 382, you examined three writing samples of a four-and-a-half-year-old boy and were asked, "*Which aspects of written language does John exhibit in the writing samples*?" John realizes that people write for particular purposes, for example, to communicate important things in letters, lists, and books. He is able to print a few familiar words (Mom, Dad, and John; see the artifact at left). The number "4" is evident as the third symbol in the string in the second line. He also realizes that letters are sometimes interconnected in another form of writing, cursive (noticeable in the artifacts at middle and right). He appreciates that writing and drawing are distinct but complementary forms of communication (presumably the cursive he includes at the top of the artifact at right is intended to provide descriptive information about the tyrannosaurus rex he draws at bottom). It may not be obvious from the print samples here, but John wrote from left to right and top to bottom, revealing his additional awareness of this convention in writing English.

$$26 \atop +47 \atop \overline{6|3}$$
$$603 \atop -305 \atop \overline{2\;08}$$

On page 391, you examined two mathematical solutions and were asked "*Which inappropriate strategy has each child used?*" The child who solved the addition problem on the left simply put the sums of 6 + 7 (13) and 2 + 4 (6) side by side at the bottom. The child who solved the subtraction problem on the right apparently knew that borrowing was necessary to perform the subtraction in the ones column. Finding only a zero in the tens column, she instead borrowed "10" from the hundreds column. Thus, she subtracted 13 – 5 in the ones column and 5 – 3 in the hundreds column. Such mistakes are less common when children not only know *how* to carry and borrow but also know *why* carrying and borrowing make sense.

Practicing for Your Licensure Examination

Many teaching tests require students to use what they have learned about child development in responses to brief vignettes and multiple-choice questions. You can practice for your licensure examination by reading about an inspiring mathematics teacher and answering a series of questions.

Beating the Odds

Read the following case and then answer the questions that follow it.

James A. Garfield Senior High School is located in a low-income neighborhood in East Los Angeles, California. In the 1980s, many of the students' parents were recent immigrants from Mexico, had limited formal education, and spoke little or no English. Garfield had a high dropout rate, in part because apathetic teachers and frequent campus violence (often between rival gangs) gave students little reason to stay in school.

Despite such circumstances, math teacher Jaime Escalante, himself an immigrant from Bolivia, was convinced that many Garfield students had the ability to achieve at high levels. To prove his point, he urged students in his calculus class to take the Advanced Placement (AP) calculus test, an instrument developed by the Educational Testing Service (ETS) to assess the extent to which students had achieved at a level equivalent to that in an introductory college calculus course. Possible scores on the test range from 1 to 5, with 3 being a "pass" and most colleges offering college credit for scores of 3, 4, and 5.

During the 1981–1982 school year, Mr. Escalante had 18 students (10 boys and 8 girls, all with Mexican heritage) in his calculus class. He required all class members (and their parents as well) to sign contracts in which they promised to attend class, pay attention, try hard, and do all assigned homework. Throughout the school year, teacher and students worked intensively, not only during class time, but also before school, after school, and on Saturdays. During study sessions, Mr. Escalante continually drilled students in basic calculus procedures, presented a wide variety of challenging problems to solve, and encouraged students to help one another. In the last few weeks before the AP test, most of the students devoted themselves almost exclusively to calculus, withdrawing from girlfriends, boyfriends, hobbies, and after-school jobs to prepare for the exam. (One student even took his textbook into the bathroom with him.) The class became a close-knit group, with teacher and classmates offering support and encouragement as needed. Mr. Escalante often reminded his students of what their dedication might bring them: "You want to make your parents proud. You want to make your school proud. Think how good it will feel if you go to college and know you did the calculus AP. It isn't everybody who can do that" (Mathews, 1988, p. 14).

On May 19, the 18 students took the test under the supervision of the school counselor. Although they struggled with a few items, for the most part they were well prepared for the test and found it easier than they had expected. In fact, they performed at such high levels (and in some cases their answers were so similar) that ETS accused 12 of them of cheating. These students were vindicated when, on August 31 (this time under the watchful eye of ETS employees), they retook the test and all earned a score of 3 or higher.

At least 15 of the 18 students went on to college, many earned bachelor's degrees, and several attended graduate school. Mr. Escalante's 1981–1982 calculus class eventually produced teachers, accountants, medical technicians, and an aerospace engineer.[a]

Constructed-Response Question

1. In what ways did *nurture* clearly play a role in the students' mathematical achievement? How might *nature* also have been involved?

Multiple-Choice Questions

2. Would Mr. Escalante have been able to achieve similar results in calculus achievement with preschool or elementary school children if he tried the same instructional strategies as he used with high school students?

   a. No, because preschool and elementary children generally dislike mathematics.

   b. Yes, because younger children have the same ability to learn challenging mathematical concepts as do adolescents.

   c. No, because younger children would rarely have the abstract reasoning abilities that are necessary for learning calculus.

   d. Yes, because younger children would easily translate abstract mathematics concepts into ideas that have a tangible basis in reality.

3. There were slightly more boys (10) than girls (8) in Mr. Escalante's advanced mathematics class. What does the evidence suggest about gender differences in mathematics?

   a. Girls consistently outperform boys in mathematical problem solving, algebra, and calculus but show a slight weakness in arithmetic computation.

   b. Boys are invariably more skilled in mathematics but less confident in their abilities than are girls.

[a] Case based on Mathews, 1988; Menéndez, 1988.

c. There are absolutely no gender differences in mathematics achievement, confidence, or experiences.

d. On average, boys and girls tend to perform at roughly the same levels of mathematics, although boys show more variability in achievement, tend to have more advanced visual-spatial ability, are often more confident in their mathematical abilities, and frequently receive more encouragement to excel in mathematics.

Once you have answered these questions, compare your responses with those presented in Appendix A.

Improving Your Ability to Interpret Children's Artifacts and Reflections

Draw on what you've learned about the development of reading and writing as you analyze the writing sample in this exercise.

The Pet Who Came to Dinner

Seven-year-old Justin wrote the story shown here. As you read it, consider these questions:

- What can you conclude about Justin's phonological awareness?
- What can you conclude about his knowledge of alphabet letters?
- What can you conclude about his knowledge of capitalization, punctuation, and grammar?
- What can you conclude about his ability to create a narrative?

Once you have answered these questions, compare your ideas with those presented in Appendix B. For further practice in analyzing children's artifacts and reflections, go to the Activities and Applications section in Chapter 10 of MyEducationLab.

Key Concepts

emergent literacy (p. 370)	dyslexia (p. 377)	dyscalculia (p. 393)	music literacy (p. 409)
phonological awareness (p. 371)	invented spelling (p. 383)	visual-spatial ability (p. 394)	amusia (p. 409)
sight vocabulary (p. 373)	knowledge telling (p. 384)	substance schema (p. 398)	standards (p. 411)
story schema (p. 373)	knowledge transforming (p. 384)	scientific reasoning (p. 398)	

PEARSON
myeducationlab

Now go to www.myeducationlab.com to:
- Take a Quiz to test your mastery of chapter objectives.
- Study chapter content with an individualized Study Plan.
- Deepen your understanding of particular concepts and principles with Review, Remediation, and Enrichment Exercises.
- Apply what you have learned in the chapter to your work with children in Building Teaching Skills and Dispositions exercises.
- Observe children and their unique contexts in Video Examples.

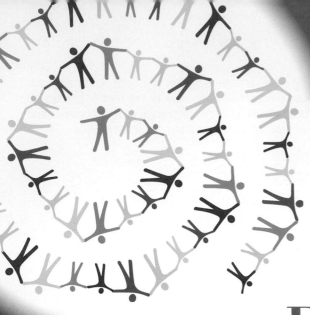

Chapter Eleven

Emotional Development

CASE STUDY: Merv

Merv had experienced a difficult childhood growing up in an economically poor family in Hawaii. Her father had been an alcoholic, and her mother had been regularly anxious, depressed, and preoccupied with her own troubles. Neither parent took adequate care of Merv or her six brothers and sisters. Merv's parents regularly fought and occasionally struck Merv and the other children. Food, shoes, clothing, and basic school supplies were scarce. And sadly, other parents in their neighborhood considered Merv and her brothers and sisters to be unworthy playmates for their own children (Werner & Smith, 2001).

Remarkably, Merv beat the odds. By the time she reached her forties, Merv was a productive, well-adjusted woman who worked as a parent educator and had been married since age 16 to "a pretty neat guy . . . a schoolteacher" (Werner & Smith, 2001, pp. 100–101). Merv and her husband raised their seven children in a manner that was gentle and loving. Merv also remained close to her own brothers and sisters. She led a happy, fulfilled life.

Merv credited four childhood experiences with making her a strong, secure person. First of all, Merv had learned to work hard, as she described in this memory:

> As children, we took care of the yard, the house, the clothes, each other, and the cars. We did everything. My father cooked when there was something to cook, and my mother simply coped. . . . When things got rough, I learned to dig in my heels and say, "How am I going to make this happen?" versus "This is too hard, I quit." (Werner & Smith, 2001, pp. 95–96)[a]

Second, Merv had "caring and supportive people" to guide and nurture her (Werner & Smith, 2001, p. 96). Merv thrived on the care she received from her grandmother Kahaunaele. During Merv's visits to Kahaunaele's house, Kahaunaele showered Merv with love, bathed the girl, and combed the tangles out of her long hair. Love from her grandmother was supplemented with kindness from several teachers and school staff. Merv's principal once said to her, "You are Hawaiian and you can be anything you choose to be" (p. 98). Merv was forever grateful for these words of encouragement.

Third, Merv received a good education. When she was 12 years old, she accepted an invitation to attend a prestigious school on another Hawaiian island. At the Kamehameha School, Merv was well cared for, and she progressed academically. At age 16, Merv became pregnant, married the father of her baby, and was expelled from school for becoming an unwed mother. Merv was soon allowed to return when a school counselor went "out on a major limb" for her, having realized that she was "not a bad student. She just made a mistake" (p. 100).

Finally, Merv learned to trust that there is goodness in the world. Merv saw hope as a vital quality for all young people, and noted that inspiration can be found in a variety of places:

> Somewhere, someplace down the line, somebody had taught me, "There is somebody greater than us who loves you." And that is my hope and my belief. Whatever that translates for you—a belief in God, a belief in a religion, a goal, a dream, something that we can hang on to. As adults, we need to give our young people hope and something to hang on to. As young people, we need to find our own. (Werner & Smith, 2001, p. 101)

- What basic need did Merv have that was ultimately fulfilled by people outside her immediate family?
- What does Merv's childhood experiences suggest about how teachers and other practitioners can contribute to children's emotional development?

[a]Excerpts from JOURNEYS FROM CHILDHOOD TO MIDLIFE: RISK, RESILIENCE, AND RECOVERY by Emmy E. Werner and Ruth S. Smith. Copyright © 2001 by Cornell University. Used by permission of the publisher, Cornell University Press.

OBJECTIVES

11.1: Identify the central challenges in each of Erikson's eight stages of psychosocial development, and describe strengths and criticisms of the theory.

11.2: Summarize the developmental course and implications of children's attachments to caregivers, and differentiate among the four common attachment styles.

11.3: Identify the primary tactics teachers and other practitioners can use to foster secure attachments in children.

11.4: Summarize general trends in the development of emotional expression and understanding from infancy through adolescence.

11.5: Describe at least three dimensions each in temperament and personality, and discuss how the development of these two characteristics may be related.

11.6: Describe ways to foster emotional development in typical children and adolescents as well as in those with emotional or behavioral problems.

**Preparing for Your
Licensure Examination**

Your teaching test might ask you
about the basic principles and
implications of Erikson's theory.

**BELOVED. Developing an expectation
that loving caregivers can be counted on
to meet one's needs is the child's first
social-emotional task.**

psychosocial stages
In Erikson's theory, eight periods
of life that involve age-related
challenges.

Every child needs to be loved. Merv's own parents neglected her, but fortunately several other people cherished her and fulfilled her need for affection. Her grandmother adored her, her brothers and sisters formed lasting bonds with her, and several teachers and school staff offered effective education. In this chapter you will find that warm, sensitive care is the mainstay of children's first relationships. When caregivers are kind and responsive, children begin to trust them and gain confidence in their own abilities. You will also learn that good relationships help children express their emotions productively and foster the necessary conditions for blossoming into healthy, one-of-a-kind personalities. Finally, you will see that educators can contribute immensely to the emotional development of youngsters, as they did with Merv.

ERIKSON'S THEORY OF PSYCHOSOCIAL DEVELOPMENT

In the past few chapters, you learned that many changes take place in children's cognitive abilities—in their memory capacity, reasoning skills, language competencies, academic concepts, and so forth. Equally momentous transformations occur in the social-emotional domain. To give you an overview of these significant social-emotional changes, we begin with Erikson's theory of psychosocial development.

Lessons Learned from Life's Challenges

Erik Erikson (1902–1994) was a *psychodynamic theorist* who believed that people grow from life's challenges.[1] In his own youth, Erikson had struggled with who he was as a person. He often felt different than others, having been born to a single Danish mother in Germany during an era when two-parent families were the norm, and having peers who questioned his Jewish heritage because he had blond hair and blue eyes and did not resemble the Jewish people they knew (Crain, 2011). Erikson had little interest in school and failed to earn a college degree, yet he eventually became a well-known scholar of human development.

In his theory, Erikson suggested that people experience eight "crises," in the form of **psychosocial stages**, as they progress from birth to old age (Erikson, 1963, 1972). Each of the eight crises is a turning point, the resolution of which directs a person's future concerns. He called these eight levels *psychosocial* stages because the various challenges refer to qualitatively different concerns about oneself *(psycho-)* and relationships with other people *(-social)*. Erikson observed that when individuals constructively address these eight challenges, they gain lasting personal assets, but when their efforts fall short, they are apt to dwell on their social-emotional problems. As they move from stage to stage, people build on their accumulated assets and deficits, occasionally revisiting unresolved crises during later personal experiences.

As they reflect on their life experiences, people navigate through each of the challenges. Let's look at the potential outcomes of the eight stages.

Trust versus Mistrust (Infancy)

According to Erikson, infants' primary task is to learn whether or not they can trust other people. When caregivers can be depended on to feed a hungry stomach, change an uncomfortable diaper, and provide affection at regular intervals, an infant learns *trust*—that others are dependable. When caregivers ignore an infant's needs, are inconsistent in their attention, or are abusive, the infant learns *mistrust*—that the world is an unpredictable and dangerous place.

Autonomy versus Shame and Doubt (Toddler Years)

As toddlers gain better control of their bodies, they become capable of satisfying their own needs. Toddlers learn to feed, wash, dress themselves, and use the toilet. When parents and other caregivers encourage self-sufficient behavior, toddlers develop *autonomy,* a sense

[1] Erik Erikson's theory is introduced in Chapter 1.

of being able to handle many problems on their own. But when caregivers demand too much too soon, refuse to let children perform tasks of which they are capable, or ridicule early attempts at self-sufficiency, children may instead develop *shame and doubt* about their inability to conduct themselves appropriately.

Initiative versus Guilt (Preschool Years)

If all goes well, children spend their infancy and toddler years learning that the world is a good place, people love them, and they can make things happen. With a growing drive toward independence, preschoolers begin to have their own ideas about activities they want to pursue. For example, they may undertake simple art projects, make houses and roadways in the sandbox, or share fantasies about being superheroes with other children. When adults encourage such efforts, children develop *initiative,* an energetic motivation to undertake activities independently. When adults discourage such activities, children may instead develop *guilt* about acting improperly.

Industry versus Inferiority (Elementary School Years)

When they reach elementary school, children are expected to master many new skills, and they soon learn that they can gain recognition from adults through their academic assignments, athletic accomplishments, artistic performances, participation in community activities, and so on. When children complete projects and are praised for their accomplishments, they demonstrate *industry,* a pattern of working hard, gaining mastery in tool use, and persisting at lengthy tasks. But when children are ridiculed or punished for their efforts or when they find that they cannot meet adults' expectations, they may develop feelings of *inferiority* about their own abilities.

THE WORK OF CHILDHOOD. Children derive a sense of accomplishment when they succeed at concrete tasks.

Identity versus Role Confusion (Adolescence)

As they make the transition from childhood to adulthood, adolescents wrestle with questions about who they are and how they fit into the adult world. Values learned during childhood are now reassessed in light of a new sexual drive and the desire to be true to oneself. Initially, youth experience *role confusion*—mixed feelings about the specific ways in which they fit into society—and may experiment with a variety of actions and attitudes (e.g., affiliating with various peer groups, trying several distinct sports and hobbies, and learning about the views of different political groups). In Erikson's view, most adolescents eventually achieve a sense of *identity* regarding who they are and where their lives are headed.

Intimacy versus Isolation (Young Adulthood)

Once people have established their identities, they are ready to make commitments to one or more other individuals. They become capable of *intimacy*—that is, they form close, reciprocal bonds with others (e.g., through marriage, other intimate relationships, or close friendships) and willingly make the sacrifices and compromises that such relationships require. When people cannot form intimate relationships (perhaps because of their reluctance or inability to forgo satisfaction of their own needs), a sense of *isolation* may result.

Generativity versus Stagnation (Middle Age)

During middle age, the primary developmental tasks are contributing to society and guiding future generations. When an individual makes a contribution, perhaps by raising a family or by working toward the betterment of society, a sense of *generativity,* or productivity, results. In contrast, an individual who is self-centered and unable or unwilling to help others develops a feeling of *stagnation*—dissatisfaction with lack of production.

Integrity versus Despair (Retirement Years)

According to Erikson, the final developmental task is a retrospective one. As individuals look back on their past experiences, they develop feelings of contentment and *integrity* if they believe they have led a happy, productive life. Alternatively, they may develop a sense of *despair* if they look back on a life of disappointments and unachieved goals.

For Erikson, successful progress through each stage is not an absolute accomplishment but rather a matter of degree. In other words, people advance at each stage when they develop *more* of the positive tendency and *less* of the negative tendency. Erikson believed that having modest deficits, balanced with adequate assets, helps people respond sensibly to the opportunities and threats they face in daily life. A young boy who has learned to trust his parents is hopeful when meeting a new teacher, yet having also known a few short-tempered grown-ups, he will be cautious until he gets to know the teacher better. Because his optimism is tempered with restraint, the boy is ready to form healthy relationships. In contrast, with too much of a deficit (e.g., when uneasiness outweighs peace of mind), a tipping point is reached and a person becomes unhappy, isolated, and socially impaired.

Contemporary Perspectives on Erikson's Theory

Three strengths of Erikson's theory make it a compelling framework of human development. First, Erikson argued convincingly that important changes occur *throughout* the life span. Thanks in part to Erikson's theory, developmental scholars now accept that catalysts for growth (e.g., a change in routine, an opportunity for a different kind of relationship, and new desires) surface at every age. Second, Erikson focused on truly significant social-emotional developments, including forming trusting relationships with other people and establishing one's identity. Finally, Erikson's stages reflect the idea that development is a dynamic synthesis of nature, nurture, and a person's own motivation to make sense of life (Côté, 2005; Dunkel & Sefcek, 2009; Lerner, 2002). Erikson's integrative model fits nicely with the contemporary view that developmental changes are complex blends of several interacting factors.

These contributions notwithstanding, Erikson's theory has some serious limitations. For one thing, Erikson's observations of the human condition were largely anecdotal and his conclusions rather vague (Crain, 2011). The systematic research findings that have accumulated since Erikson formulated his theory indicate that his stages are probably not completely accurate descriptions of what happens at each age period. For instance, Erikson believed that most people achieve a sense of identity by the end of adolescence. But in reality youth typically do not achieve a clear identity by late adolescence and instead continue to solidify their personal commitments during the young adult years (Bartoszuk & Pittman, 2010; Kroger, 2004). Also problematic is the fact that Erikson based his stages primarily on observations of men from a limited number of backgrounds. Women and individuals from non-Western cultures may face a different series of tasks than the ones Erikson identified in American and European men. Finally, Erikson probably underestimated just how differently various cultural groups think about particular assets. Many cultures intentionally discourage self-assertiveness *(autonomy)* in young children, sometimes as a way of protecting them from the very real dangers of their environments and at other times with the goal of deepening ties to family members (Kağitçibaşi, 2007; Morelli & Rothbaum, 2007; Rasmussen, 2009). You can see a summary of the research on each of Erikson's stages in Table 11-1.

Despite the holes in Erikson's theory, his framework does offer a valuable perspective on human life. As we mentioned earlier, Erikson's framework has several strong points, and it offers the additional advantage of inspiring optimism about young people's potential for growth. Most educators agree with Erikson that youngsters can usually find the inner strength they need to transform life's challenges into such worthwhile assets as a healthy self-confidence, a commitment to productive social values, and a solid work ethic. Although Erikson failed to provide detailed information about how to cultivate social-emotional skills in youngsters, other developmental scholars have taken up this cause. The developmental focus of Erikson's first stage, a trusting relationship with caregivers, has been thoroughly examined by researchers, and we look at this topic shortly. Other key tasks that Erikson examined—reflecting on one's personal characteristics, having the motivation to complete challenging tasks, living up to moral obligations, and forming close relationships with people outside the family—build on this initial sense of security and are the focus of later chapters in the book.[2]

[2]Children's sense of identity is examined in Chapter 12, motivation in Chapter 13, morality in Chapter 14, and peer relationships in Chapter 15.

TABLE 11-1   Developmental Research Related to Erikson's Stages

STAGE	AGE	RESEARCH
Trust vs. Mistrust	Birth to 1 year	Developmental investigations support Erikson's assertion that learning to trust others is a fundamental need for infants (Ainsworth, Blehar, Waters, & Wall, 1978; Bowlby, 1988). However, although Erikson indicated that infancy was a critical time for having a first trusting relationship, recent research indicates that children often get second chances. When children receive unresponsive care during early infancy, their first attachments are likely to be insecure, but if their later care is warm and sensitive, they can often develop trusting relationships.
Autonomy vs. Shame and Doubt	1 to 3 years	Evidence supports Erikson's conclusion that toddlers have a strong will to practice emerging skills without restriction. Toddlers are motivated to handle objects, walk on their own, and explore a home's forbidden areas. Yet not every culture agrees with Erikson that autonomy is a virtue: Some groups see young children's drive for independence as an immature impulse that must be tempered (Kağitçibaşi, 2007; Morelli & Rothbaum, 2007; Rasmussen, 2009).
Initiative vs. Guilt	3 to 5 years	Erikson aptly portrayed preschool-aged children as radiating a sense of purpose. Research confirms that young children show initiative in imaginative play and enthusiastic conversations. With his attention on shame, doubt, and guilt in young children, Erikson also paved the way for contemporary research on these emotions. Developmental studies indicate that young children tend to feel distressed when they break a rule or fail to live up to a standard (Kagan, 1984; Kochanska, 1993; R. A. Thompson & Newton, 2010).
Industry vs. Inferiority	6 to 10 years	Erikson saw middle childhood as a period for completing demanding tasks proficiently. Cross-cultural research indicates that adults routinely assign chores to children in this age range, reflecting a widespread recognition that school-aged children can act responsibly. Research also indicates that children compare their own abilities to those of peers and lose confidence if they see themselves coming up short relative to others in domains that they value (Harter, 2006; W. Wu, West, & Hughes, 2010).
Identity vs. Role Confusion	10 to 20 years	Erikson's focus on identity has spawned a lot of research. Studies generally confirm Erikson's assertion that young people actively engage in soul searching related to who they are, what they believe in, and where they are going (Marcia, 1980, 1988). This preoccupation with identity issues extends for a longer period than Erikson proposed, however (Bartoszuk & Pittman, 2010).
Intimacy vs. Isolation	Young adulthood	Evidence confirms that taking part in intimate relationships is a typical concern of the young adult years. However, some critics suggest that being closely connected with others is a human quality that transcends any single time period (Gilligan, 1982). Furthermore, the early adult years are more complex than Erikson suggested. Young adults are concerned not only with finding a mate but also with getting a good job and in many cases caring for their own small children.
Generativity vs. Stagnation	Middle age	During middle age, most adults organize their lives such that they contribute to the betterment of society, as Erikson proposed. One common critique of Erikson's theory is that he believed that men were primarily concerned with their careers and women with parenting their children. Yet in Western cultures today, both career and family are serious concerns for men and women alike (B. E. Peterson & Stewart, 1996).
Integrity vs. Despair	Retirement years	Looking back on one's life is an important task for many older adults, and Erikson was on the mark in this regard (R. N. Butler, 1963; B. K. Haight, 1992; Torges, Stewart, & Duncan, 2009). However, older adults tackle many other developmental tasks, including finding ways to cope with losses and make the best of their later years (Baltes, 1997). In other words, many older adults live in the present as well as the past.

ATTACHMENT

Human beings of all ages seem to have a fundamental need to feel socially connected to, and loved and respected by, other people. In other words, they have a **need for relatedness** (Moller, Deci, & Elliot, 2010; Park, Crocker, & Vohs, 2006; Pavey, Greitemeyer, & Sparks, 2011). Across the life span, this need is fulfilled with social bonds of various types, including friendships, romantic ties, marital partnerships, and family relationships.

The child's first bond, called an **attachment**, is an enduring emotional tie that unites the child to a caregiver and has far-reaching effects on the child's development (Ainsworth, 1973). In the past few decades, the dominant theoretical perspective on infant–caregiver

need for relatedness
Fundamental need to feel socially connected to, and loved and respected by, other people.

attachment
An enduring emotional tie uniting one person to another.

relationships has been **ethological attachment theory**, a perspective originally suggested by British psychiatrist **John Bowlby** (1907–1990) and later fleshed out by Canadian American psychologist **Mary Ainsworth** (1913–1999) (Ainsworth, 1963, 1973; Ainsworth et al., 1978; Bowlby, 1951, 1958).

Ethological attachment theory suggests that the human capacity for close relationships evolved over millions of years of human history. Attachment theorists speculate that severe environmental conditions in our ancestors' past made it necessary for small children to stay close to parents. Obviously, parents also had to be inclined to nurture and protect their children. These mutually close ties helped children to survive their infancy and develop into productive members of their society. The capacity for attachment was presumably passed down from generation to generation.

In today's world, attachments can be seen in infants' crying, clinging, and crawling toward parents and other caregivers when distressed. Under less stressful conditions, infants show affection with snuggles, smiles, and cooing. However, what develops in infants is not simply a collection of discrete behaviors, such as crying and smiling, but also an underlying system of relating to parents. This system has two important elements. First, infants learn to use their parents as a *safe haven*. Infants depend on parents for protection from harm and for comfort when feelings of hunger, fatigue, or fear escalate to unmanageable levels. Second, infants use parents as a *secure base*. Infants relax in the presence of their parents and feel sufficiently safe that they can venture here and there, crawling away but glancing back now and then for reassuring looks from Mom and Dad.

Developmental Course of Children's Attachments

In the process of forming attachments, infants learn a lot about themselves and other people. A baby slowly develops expectations about shared routines ("When Grandma says, 'Peekaboo,' I hide my eyes and we both laugh"), beliefs about other people's trustworthiness ("Mommy takes care of me"), emotional connections ("I love my Daddy"), and sense of self ("I am lovable"). To end up with this coherent system of expectations, infants must mature, develop cognitively, and gain social experience. Bowlby believed that there are four phases in attachment development:

Preattachment. From birth until about 6 to 12 weeks, infants use social signals (e.g., smiling, crying, and seeking eye contact) to elicit care from others. Infants initially treat adults in an equal opportunity fashion, allowing anyone with the right touch to comfort them (Schaffer, 1996). Nevertheless, rudimentary foundations for individualized attachments are being formed at this time. Infants begin to recognize familiar people through their faces, voices, smells, and characteristic behaviors.

Attachment-in-the-Making. From 6 to 12 weeks through 6 to 8 months after birth, infants learn that they cannot count on just anyone for affection and attention, but instead must turn to the few special people who regularly care for them. By the third month, infants smile selectively at people they know best (Camras, Malatesta, & Izard, 1991; Mendes, Seidl-de-Moura, & Siqueira, 2009). During this period, infants continue to depend on adults to carry most of the burden in initiating and maintaining a social exchange (Saarni, Campos, Camras, & Witherington, 2006). Caregivers notice when a baby is alert and calm, use this occasion to extend a greeting, and wait for the baby to make a simple response that functions as the baby's turn in the interaction. With experience, infants learn the rhythms of interaction and eagerly anticipate playful exchanges with caregivers, such as counting toes during a diaper change.

Clear-Cut Attachment. Between 6 to 8 months until a year and a half after birth, infants show full-fledged attachments to one person or a small number of people, including, perhaps, a mother, father, grandparent, employed caregiver, or some combination of these or other individuals. Attachments can be seen when infants reach out to be picked up by familiar caregivers; protest when separated from them; and wriggle, coo, and show unmistakable looks of recognition when adored caregivers walk into the room. When distressed, infants who have received sensitive care from parents regularly calm down with reassurance from parents (Hutman & Dapretto, 2009).

ethological attachment theory Theoretical perspective that emphasizes the benefits to children derived from close bonds with caregivers, particularly protection from harm and a secure base from which to explore the environment.

During this period, infants also begin to show intense fears. Just as infants are learning to crawl and motivated to explore, nature activates a useful fear of the unknown. Rather than crawling off into the hinterlands, infants generally stick within eyesight of familiar caregivers. When puzzling phenomena appear out of nowhere, such as a barking dog (woof!) or a jack-in-the-box's loud, unexpected effect (pop!), infants demand reassurance (now!).

Adults unknown to the baby now trigger fearful reactions. In the latter half of the first year of life and well into the second year, an unfamiliar adult often incites fear—**stranger anxiety** (Hahn-Holbrook, Holbrook, & Bering, 2010; Mangelsdorf, Shapiro, & Marzolf, 1995). This fear often intensifies into a red-faced, tearful, arm-flapping demand for the safe haven of a familiar caregiver. You can observe an infant's fear of an unfamiliar adult in the "Stranger Anxiety" video of MyEducationLab.

Reciprocal Relationship.   From about one and a half to two years, infants use their emerging cognitive and language abilities to make inferences about their parents' goals and plans. Toddlers regularly accept direction from parents but increasingly assert their own desires. Children also begin to take turns in a conversation, as you can see in 16-month-old Corwin's interchanges with his mother in the "Literacy: Infancy" video in MyEducationLab. Corwin's vocalizations are simple, but they serve nicely as contributions to the exchange.

Early Childhood

Children begin to reflect on their attachments during the early childhood years. Typically, young children appreciate the loving care they receive from parents and other beloved caregivers and actively reciprocate with affectionate gestures of their own.

As they did in their infant days, young children rely on familiar caregivers to be a safe haven, particularly when they are sick, scared, or distressed and when parents have previously cared for them with sensitivity (S. F. Waters et al., 2010). Urgent protests over separations are fewer now, and stranger anxiety also has become less intense, possibly because children are now convinced that their parents *will* return to get them at the end of the day, and in the meantime, warm, reliable teachers and relatives are nearby (Main & Cassidy, 1988; Schaffer, 1996). Increasingly, children also find that peers can play a supportive role in their daily lives. Particularly when they have enjoyed affectionate relationships with parents, young children play happily with peers in parents' absence (Howes, 1999; C. Hughes & Dunn, 2007).

Improving Your Observation Skills

I love Mommy. Three-year-old Ivy and four-year-old Alex prepared these notes (at the left and right, respectively) for their mothers. What are these two children trying to communicate? Compare your response with the explanation at the end of the chapter.

MyEducationLab

Observe an infant's fear of an unfamiliar adult in the "Stranger Anxiety" video. Also, observe Corwin taking turns in a conversation with his mother in the "Literacy: Infancy" video. (Find Video Examples in Topic 11 of MyEducationLab.)

stranger anxiety
Fear of unfamiliar adults in the latter half of the first year and into the second year of life.

MUTUAL SUPPORT. Even as youngsters begin to spend more time with friends and adults outside the family, they continue to cherish close attachments with parents.

Middle Childhood and Adolescence

Routine separations (such as going to school each day or to summer camp for a week) now induce little of the anxiety associated with late-infancy separations, although a few elementary school children continue to be anxious before and during separations. When relationships with parents are seriously disrupted, perhaps because of divorce or death, youngsters may become angry, aggressive, or physically ill, and they may withdraw from their customary activities (Pribilsky, 2001).

Although remaining crucial for youngsters, relationships with parents change during this period. Many adolescents now prefer to receive their affection behind the scenes, and they also become increasingly close to friends and romantic partners (Elmore & Huebner, 2010; K. A. Kerns, Brumariu, & Abraham, 2008; Mayseless, 2005; A. B. Nickerson & Nagle, 2005; Seibert & Kerns, 2009). At this age peers offer reassurance to one another when times are tough, providing a new kind of safe haven, one that permits equal participation. Adolescents do not usually renounce their ties to parents, but they do strengthen connections with peers and prepare (consciously or not) for their inevitable departure from the family nest.

The developmental course of attachments we have outlined is one that assumes a trusting relationship with parents and parental figures. As we see next, most caregivers earn the trust of children, but in unfortunate exceptions a few caregivers do not.

Individual Differences in Children's Attachments

If you look around at young children you know, you may notice variations in how they respond when afraid, hurt, or upset. Some children seek and find comfort in the reassuring arms of caregivers; some are clingy and fretful; and others want to be left alone.

To study such differences in the laboratory, Mary Ainsworth created a mildly stressful situation for 1-year-old infants. First, a mother and her infant were brought to a playroom and left alone. A stranger (a research assistant) soon entered the room and attempted to play with the baby. After 3 minutes, the mother left the room, leaving the baby alone with the stranger. Subsequently, the mother returned and the stranger departed, leaving mother and baby together. Next, mother departed, and baby was alone; the stranger returned at this point. Finally, the mother returned and the stranger departed (Ainsworth et al., 1978). This sequence, commonly known as the *Strange Situation,* has become a classic research tool for assessing attachment in young children.

In the Strange Situation, attention is focused primarily on the child's behavior. Observers rate the child's attempts to seek contact with a caregiver, the physical proximity of the to caregiver, the child's resistance to or avoidance of the caregiver, and the child's level of distress. From such ratings, the child is given one of several classifications:

- Infants who exhibit **secure attachment** use caregivers as a secure base. When caregivers are present, infants actively explore new toys and surroundings. When caregivers return after leaving the room, infants smile at or talk to them, move over to greet them, or in other ways seek proximity to them. In the "Strange Situation" video in MyEducationLab, you can see a securely attached infant's distress at his father's departure and relief at his father's return. About 60 percent of infants are classified as securely attached (R. A. Thompson, 2006).

- Infants who exhibit **insecure-avoidant attachment** seem oblivious to a caregiver's presence. They fail to greet the caregiver upon his or her return and may even look away. Instead, they go about their business independently, and they are somewhat superficial in their interactions with toys. About 15 percent of children participating in Strange Situation studies are classified as insecure-avoidant (R. A. Thompson, 2006).

- Infants who exhibit **insecure-resistant attachment** seem preoccupied with their caregivers, but they are not easily comforted during reunions. When caregivers return, these infants remain distressed and angry; they may rush to parents and other caregivers yet quickly struggle to be released. Insecure-resistant infants comprise about 10 percent of participants in Strange Situation studies (R. A. Thompson, 2006).

MyEducationLab

Observe an infant's distress at his father's departure, followed by the infant's relaxation during his father's return, in the "Strange Situation" video. (Find Video Examples in Topic 11 of MyEducationLab.)

secure attachment
Attachment classification in which children use attachment figures as a source of comfort in times of distress and as a secure base from which to explore.

insecure-avoidant attachment
Attachment classification in which children appear somewhat indifferent to attachment figures.

insecure-resistant attachment
Attachment classification in which children are preoccupied with their attachment figures but gain little comfort from them when distressed.

- More serious problems in attachment, which were not part of Ainsworth's original classification, have been subsequently identified. A **disorganized and disoriented attachment** style has been documented, in which infants lack a coherent way of responding to stressful events (Main & Solomon, 1986, 1990; Zilberstein & Messer, 2010). Infants classified in this manner may appear calm one minute yet, without provocation, become angry the next minute. They may interrupt their own actions midstream, for example, by crawling toward caregivers and then suddenly freezing with apprehension. In addition, a very few children show *no* attachment behaviors or exhibit other extremely serious problems, such as displaying fear of familiar caregivers rather than being comforted by them. Such serious problems frequently call for intervention by trained professionals. Approximately 15 percent of children show a disorganized and disoriented attachment, no attachment, or another serious attachment problem (R. A. Thompson, 2006).

The Observation Guidelines table "Assessing Young Children's Attachment Security" summarizes how children with particular kinds of attachments might act. In observing children, teachers and caregivers should guard against taking any single response from a child too seriously; they should instead look for patterns of behavior over time.

The Bioecology of Attachment Security

From a bioecological perspective, children develop attachments in social settings. The types of attachments that evolve are affected by the quality of the caregiver–child relationship, the child's own behavior, and the cultural setting.

Quality of Caregiver–Child Relationship

The relationship between a caregiver and a child is the primary basis of attachment security. When caregivers are sensitive and responsive to young children, protect them, and provide for their needs, children are inclined to develop secure attachments (Nievar & Becker, 2008; Svanberg, Mennet, & Spieker, 2010; R. A. Thompson, 2006). Caregivers who are sensitive and responsive show these qualities:

- *They consistently respond to infants' needs.* Caregivers establish routines for feeding, diapering, and holding infants. They do not run in response to every whimper, but they are faithfully available when infants are distressed and express genuine needs (Cassidy & Berlin, 1994; R. A. Thompson, Easterbrooks, & Padilla-Walker, 2003). Caregivers who fail to show this quality may be neglectful or available only occasionally; others are callous to infants' feelings.
- *They regularly express affection.* Caregivers dote on babies by caressing them, holding them gently, looking into their eyes, talking to them, and expressing tenderness and warmth. Caregivers who fail to show this quality may be withdrawn or even hostile and rejecting.
- *They permit babies to influence the pace and direction of their mutual interactions.* Caregivers let infants take the lead on occasion. They carefully note where infants are looking, notice their body posture, and recognize when infants want to interact (Bigelow et al., 2010; Isabella & Belsky, 1991; Nievar & Becker, 2008; D. N. Stern, 1977). They also act in synchrony with infants, letting them take a turn in an interaction by smiling, moving their hands, or babbling. Caregivers who fail to show this quality may be intrusive, perhaps to the point that babies look away from them, cry, or try to go to sleep. Other caregivers may fail to notice or respond to infants' bids for affection—for example, they may ignore infants' attempts to make eye contact.

Children's Activities and Characteristics

Children actively participate in their relationships with caregivers by making their needs known, relaxing when comforted, and reciprocating with affection. Through their unique ways of handling stress and relating to others, infants influence the manner in which caregivers respond to them. Whereas some fuss a lot when scared, others protest less adamantly.

Bioecology of Child Development
Children develop secure attachments by being cared for by responsive family members who follow cultural patterns in expressing affection. Children themselves play a role in their attachments by reciprocating affection to family members.

disorganized and disoriented attachment
Attachment classification in which children lack a single coherent way of responding to attachment figures.

OBSERVATION GUIDELINES
Assessing Young Children's Attachment Security

CHARACTERISTIC	LOOK FOR	EXAMPLE	IMPLICATION
Secure Attachment	• *Active, intentional exploration* of the environment in the presence of the caregiver • *Protest at being separated from a caregiver*; ability to be soothed when the caregiver returns • *Initial wariness of strangers*, with subsequent acceptance if reassured by the caregiver	Luis cries when his father drops him off at the child care center in the morning. After a few minutes, he settles down and crawls to a familiar and affectionate caregiver who is beginning to become an attachment figure for him.	It is natural for young children to resist separation from family members. Help them establish a routine of saying good-bye in the morning, and give them extra attention during this transition. Reassure parents and other family members by describing the activities their children typically turn to as they relax.
Insecure-Avoidant Attachment	• *Superficial exploration* of the environment • *Indifference to a caregiver's departure*; failure to seek comfort upon the caregiver's return • *Apparent discomfort around strangers*, but without an active resistance to their social overtures	Jennifer walks around her new child care center with a frown on her face. She parts easily with her mother and willingly explores her new environment, albeit without much enthusiasm. Jennifer glances up when her mother comes at the end of the day but doesn't seem overjoyed about her mother's return.	Independence from parents is often a sign of children's familiarity with child care or preschool settings. For children who seem at ease with separation, support them throughout the day. When children appear indifferent to family members, form your own affectionate relationships with the children, knowing that such ties could become children's first secure bonds.
Insecure-Resistant Attachment	• *Exceptional clinginess and anxiety with caregiver* • *Agitation and distress* at the caregiver's departure; continued crying or fussing after the caregiver returns • *Apparent fear of strangers*; tendency to stay close to caregiver in new situation	Irene tightly clutches her mother as the two enter the preschool building, and she stays close by as her mother signs her in for the morning. She is extremely upset when her mother leaves and remains distressed for a long time after her mother's return later in the day.	If children appear anxious when they enter a new child care or preschool setting, give them extra time to part from their parents. Sometimes a "comfort" object from home (a teddy bear or blanket) can help. Be patient as you interact with these children, knowing that they may eventually form a secure attachment to you.
Disorganized and Disoriented Attachment or Other Serious Attachment Problem	• *Unpredictable emotional responses* • *Cautious approaches to familiar caregiver* • *By end of first year, failure to contact caregiver* when distressed • *Reckless exploration* without use of caregiver as a secure base • *Reversed roles*, with excessive concern about caregiver • *No signs of attachment to family members* or other familiar caregivers, or fear of them • *Indiscriminately friendly behavior* with no preferential actions toward family members • *Signs of overwhelming grief* after the death of a primary caregiver	Myles seems lost at school. He arrives hungry, walks aimlessly for some time, and eventually sits and plays with blocks. He is aggressive with his peers, and his teacher sees bruises on his arms.	Provide special attention to and closely monitor children who seem disorganized and disoriented in their attachment. Be on the lookout for signs of abuse, and be ready to seek advice from authorities. Remember that these children are *not* doomed to serious lifelong problems, but you must work hard to establish positive, trusting relationships with them. Professional intervention may be necessary.

Sources: Ainsworth et al., 1978; Gervai, 2009; M. T. Greenberg, 1999; Main & Solomon, 1986, 1990; Svanberg et al., 2010; R. A. Thompson, 2006; Zeanah, 2000.

Infants who are exceptionally fearful and irritable can be somewhat difficult to care for, whereas those who are good natured and sociable invite positive interactions. Similarly, some fussy babies do not as readily notice that their parents are trying to comfort them and may find it difficult to relax in parents' arms (R. A. Thompson, 2006). Despite these possible influences of infants' dispositions, most parents are able to adjust to a wide range of emotional styles in children.

For most children with disabilities, their special circumstances play only a minor role in the security of their bonds to parents and other caregivers. Babies who are premature, show developmental delays, and are unusually fussy tend to develop secure attachments as long as their individual needs are met with patience and compassion (van IJzendoorn, Goldberg, Kroonenberg, & Frenkel, 1992). Likewise, babies with chromosomal or genetic disorders or other disabilities are apt to form secure attachments with parents who provide responsive and attentive care (F. A. Carlson, Sampson, & Sroufe, 2003; D. Howe, 2006).

Although most parents are able to respond to bids for reassurance from children who are unresponsive or demanding, risks accumulate in parents' lives and can result in their impatience, insensitivity, and withdrawal (Gervai, 2009). When parents experience marital conflict, are chronically ill, become emotionally depressed, or are economically poor, they may find it difficult to comfort infants who are exceptionally irritable. Conversely, children whose parents have social support and are invested in their parenting role are generally well able to offer good care to fussy infants (M. S. Wong et al., 2009).

Cultural Setting

Parents follow certain cultural practices in caring for infants themselves or sharing the responsibility with others, and infants in turn grow accustomed to these customs. For example, many Japanese infants become quite upset when their mothers leave the room and take a while to calm down when their mothers return (Miyake, Chen, & Campos, 1985; Takahashi, 1990). This reaction probably occurs because infants in this society rarely separate from mothers and when they do, it is in the care of close relatives (especially grandparents) rather than strangers (Saarni et al., 2006). In contrast, in Germany, many babies do not fret much when their mothers leave the room, nor do they move frantically toward mothers when they return (Grossmann, Grossmann, Huber, & Wartner, 1981; LeVine & Norman, 2008). German mothers regularly leave infants to do brief errands, and the infants seem to get used to being on their own for brief periods of time.

Cultures also prescribe appropriate methods for responding to infants' distress (Morelli & Rothbaum, 2007). Gusii mothers of Kenya continually hold, comfort, and watch their infants, and their infants rarely cry (LeVine, 2004). Gusii mothers are alarmed when they watch videos of Western mothers allowing infants to cry, even for a few moments. In comparison, some Western mothers believe that they are cultivating self-reliance in infants when they allow infants to comfort themselves. Consider the experience of a German aunt who is caring for Karl, almost 2 years of age, while his parents are away on a 2-week vacation:

> "Oh, he's a good boy, but a bit fussy," his aunt says. . . . The aunt tells of how early he wakes up in the morning, at six o'clock, "but I'm not to take him out of bed, Sigrid (Karl's mother) said, he's to stay there until nine or he'll just get used to it and she won't have it; she's done that from when he was a baby." So Karl is kept in bed, he stays quiet, she doesn't know what he does, hears him move about in his bed, babbling to himself. (LeVine & Norman, 2008, p. 134)

In addition, particular cultures have distinct patterns in showing warmth and involvement with infants (P. M. Cole & Tan, 2007; R. A. Thompson & Virmani, 2010). Many parents (especially those living in North America and Western Europe) frequently and tenderly respond to their infants' cooing and babbling. Consider an affectionate interaction between a U.S. father and his 3-month-old daughter Toto after a family event. In the following exchange, the father interacts good-naturedly with Toto, regularly waiting for, and then commenting on, her vocalizations:

Father:	5:30 p.m. Post-mortem on a party.
Toto:	Eh.
Father:	What was your reaction? What was your reaction? Did you like the food?
Toto:	Ah! Ahaa ah.
Father:	Yeah, that milk huh? It wasn't so bad, huh? And the guests—did you like the guests?
Toto:	Eh.
Father:	No, not so interesting.
Toto:	Eh! Ah ah.
Father:	What about the host and hostess?

Toto:	Aha aaaaah!
Father:	Yeah! Uncle Jim and Auntie Ann!
Toto:	Aaah!
Father:	Yeah, they're very nice.
Toto:	Ha! Ha! Ha! Oh.
Father:	Yeah; and did you enjoy yourself?
Toto:	Aha! Aaah! Aaah!
Father:	Yeah you had a good time. Well that's nice.
Toto:	Ah haa!
Father:	Well that's really nice.
Toto:	Heheh! Ahh! Hehh!
Father:	Did you think so as well? Yeah, I think so. Hmm? Yes?
Toto:	Hah! Aaaah! Ah!
Father:	You didn't cry at all and you were very polite!
	(dialogue from Reissland, 2006, p. 44)

From this exchange and other similar interactions, Toto is learning that her father can be trusted to be warm, reliable, and respectful of her efforts at communication. Many parents from different societies show their sensitivity through gentle touch and anticipation of infants' physical needs rather than through mutual vocalizations. Like Toto, infants in these other cultures learn that their parents can be trusted to love and care for them.

Variations in core beliefs appear to be at the root of cultural differences in attachment. In *individualistic societies,* parents encourage children to become independent, competitive, and assertive about their personal desires (Kağitçibaşi, 2007; Markus & Hamedani, 2007; Oyserman & Lee, 2007; Triandis, 2007).[3] Individualistic parents are apt to show their sensitivity treating vocalizations and emotional expressions as valid gestures (as Toto's father did) and respecting infants' independent explorations of their surroundings (Morelli & Rothbaum, 2007). Thus, separations from parents are usually only mildly stressful, and infants develop the habit of exploring the properties of nearby objects on their own.

In *collectivistic societies,* parents encourage children to be obedient and dependent, cooperative, respectful, and invested in the family's harmony. Many parents from collectivistic societies, such as those in many Hispanic and Asian cultures, show their sensitivity by maintaining physical closeness with infants, anticipating infants' experiences (e.g., being hungry or having a dirty diaper), and tending to these needs even before infants cry or protest (Morelli & Rothbaum, 2007). Parents from collectivistic societies foster close, dependent relationships. Many infants from collectivistic societies find separations stressful, prefer to remain in close contact with caregivers, and gradually learn to moderate their own demands in accordance with the needs of the family as a whole.

Multiple Attachments

Early investigators focused on *mothers* as primary attachment figures, probably because women physically bear children and often do most of the feeding, bathing, and diapering (Ainsworth et al., 1978; Bowlby, 1969/1982). Increasingly, research has examined the significant roles that fathers, other caregivers, and siblings play as attachment figures.

When two parents are present in the home, infants frequently show an initial preference for one parent and soon thereafter treat the second parent as an attachment figure. Both parents are likely to instill secure attachments when they respond sensitively to children's needs and are present in children's lives for an extended time (H. Freeman, Newland, & Coyl, 2010; Howes, 1999; R. A. Thompson et al., 2003). Nevertheless,

Improving Your Observation Skills

Mother and child. Parents in different societies use distinct ways of expressing sensitivity to children. What is this Native American mother doing to express her warmth to her toddler son? Compare your response with the explanation at the end of the chapter.

[3]Individualistic and collectivistic societies are introduced in Chapter 3.

mothers and fathers sometimes go about expressing their warmth in slightly different ways. Mothers tend to be more hands-on in caring for infants, enthusiastic while interacting with them, and thoughtful about what their infants might be experiencing, whereas fathers tend to engage infants in fun, physical play and are attuned to infants' need to explore the environment (H. Freeman et al., 2010; Iusitini, Gao, Sundborn, & Paterson, 2011; M. E. Lamb & Lewis, 2004; Malmberg et al., 2007). You can observe a father's playful style with his 7-month-old daughter in the "Emotional Development: Infancy" video in MyEducationLab.

Contemporary researchers have also examined the nurturing bonds that children form with other people besides parents. Children in numerous societies grow strongly attached to siblings, grandparents, and employed caregivers (M. Lewis, 2005; Seibert & Kerns, 2009). Networks of nurturing adults and siblings have important benefits for children, who can obtain different kinds of support over time (C. B. Fisher et al., 1998; Howes, 1999). For instance, a 1-year-old crawls to Grandma when a stranger enters the family home; at 6, the same child now seeks advice from his older sister as he faces bullies on the playground; and at 14, the youngster has heart-to-heart talks with an uncle about career options.

Children also form attachments to employed caregivers. Secure attachments with these individuals, as is the case with parents, depend on responsive care, sustained relationships, and mutual emotional investment (Ahnert, Pinquart, & Lamb, 2006; Howes, 1999). Yet children more easily achieve such close relationships with adults in some educational settings than others. During the preschool and elementary years, children often develop close bonds with teachers, thriving on teachers' affectionate care and gaining a sense of security in their presence (H. A. Davis, 2003; Pianta & Steinberg, 1992; Seibert & Kerns, 2009).

In the middle school years, close relationships with teachers occur but are now less common because young adolescents spend only a small portion of time with any single teacher, are in classes with large groups of students, and may feel anonymous in the classroom. When young adolescents do have supportive relationships with their teachers, they tend to enjoy school, feel competent, and achieve at high levels academically (H. A. Davis, 2003; Roeser, Eccles, & Sameroff, 2000; Roeser, Midgley, & Urdan, 1996). Unfortunately, the obstacles to close relationships with teachers intensify during high school. Adolescents often find relationships with teachers to be adversarial—it's "us" against "them"—possibly because many high school teachers view adolescents as rebellious, independent, and resistant to close relationships with them (H. A. Davis, 2003). Yet good relationships with teachers are possible and clearly beneficial for youth. High school students who have supportive relationships with teachers and other mentors are more likely to be well adjusted and to complete high school than are students without such relationships (Battin-Pearson et al., 2000; Cotterell, 1992; Georgiou, Demetriou, & Stavrinides, 2008).

Attachment Security and Later Development

A secure attachment during infancy predicts positive long-term outcomes in youngsters. In Western cultures, children who have been securely attached as infants tend to become relatively independent, empathic, socially competent preschoolers, especially in comparison with children who have been insecurely attached (Sroufe, 1983; Sroufe, Egeland, Carlson, & Collins, 2005; Vaughn, Egeland, Sroufe, & Waters, 1979). In middle childhood and adolescence, they tend to be self-confident, adjust easily to school environments, establish productive relationships with teachers and peers, do well at classroom tasks, and eventually graduate from high school (Aikins, Howes, & Hamilton, 2009; Lucas-Thompson & Clarke-Stewart, 2007; E. O'Connor & McCartney, 2006; Urban, Carlson, Egeland, & Sroufe, 1991). Security of attachment is also related to later parenting, with parents themselves who had been securely attached as infants looking after their own children in a responsive and sensitive way (Berlin, Cassidy, & Appleyard, 2008).

Of course, the kinds of long-term associations that occur with attachment are embedded in the customs of the child's community. In non-Western cultures, securely attached children develop adaptive characteristics that are valued in their particular society. As you learned earlier in this chapter, caregivers in Japan encourage

MyEducationLab

Observe 7-month-old Madison and her father interact playfully and affectionately in the "Emotional Development: Infancy" video. (Find Video Examples in Topic 11 of MyEducationLab.)

MULTIPLE ATTACHMENTS. Many children form close bonds with more than one family member. Children in this Hmong family cherish ties with one another and their parents and grandparents.

infants to rely on immediate family members. For Japanese children, close and affectionate relationships with caregivers foster dependence on caregivers' benevolence and a desire to act harmoniously with others (Morelli & Rothbaum, 2007).

How is it that early attachments affect children's later adjustment? Attachment theorists believe that a secure bond sets the stage for later relationships and helps children form positive, self-fulfilling expectations about other people. As children gain experience with primary caregivers, they begin to form a mental representation of what relationships with other people are like (Bowlby, 1969/1982, 1973; Ryan, Stiller, & Lynch, 1994). Especially when they are young, children's understanding of "typical" relationships is largely unconscious but nevertheless influential in directing how they relate to other individuals, including teachers (M. A. Hofer, 2006; S. C. Johnson et al., 2010; Maier, Bernier, Pekrun, Zimmermann, & Grossmann, 2004). Secure children expect other people to be trustworthy, and they give second chances to those who initially let them down—expectations and actions that sustain healthy interpersonal ties. In contrast, children with insecure attachments may form expectations of other people as untrustworthy and withdraw from relationships after being disappointed.

Early attachments also affect children through their influences on early emotional development. Caregivers who are affectionate and relaxed help children learn to calm down when overcome with fear, anger, and discomfort. Children whose caregivers are insensitive fail to offer these lessons, and as a result, children regularly respond to stressful events with maladaptive strategies, perhaps intensifying their negative feelings, pretending that nothing is wrong, or losing control under pressure (Borelli et al., 2010). These emotional responses to stress tend to become habitual, in part because of their physiological basis.

Although attachment theorists initially suggested that an infant's early attachments to primary caregivers (especially the mother) set the tone for *all* future relationships (e.g., Bowlby, 1973), more recent research has shown otherwise. As Merv's experience in the opening case study reveals, the kinds of bonds children form with their parents do not firmly dictate the bonds that they develop with other caregivers. Thus, children who have had an insecure attachment or other serious problem in relationships with parents may later develop secure attachments to caregivers outside the family (R. A. Thompson, 2006; Zilberstein & Messer, 2010).

Quality of parenting can also shift over time, leading to changes in children's attachments. In one investigation children whose parents were initially harsh and insensitive but later exhibited higher quality parenting were likely to develop increasingly productive social skills (NICHD Early Child Care Research Network, 2006b). The reverse trend also occurs, although perhaps less often. Children who initially form secure attachments but later live through one or more traumatic events (perhaps parents undergo a stormy divorce, a family member dies or suffers a debilitating illness, or children are physically or sexually abused by a family member) may have difficulty forming good relationships later as adolescents or adults (M. Lewis, Feiring, & Rosenthal, 2000; Mikulincer & Shaver, 2007; E. Waters, Merrick, Treboux, Crowell, & Albersheim, 2000).

Furthermore, as youngsters grow older, their attachments to peers (perhaps to best friends and, eventually, to romantic partners) may be significantly different from those they have previously formed with parents (M. W. Baldwin, Keelan, Fehr, Enns, & Koh-Rangarajoo, 1996; La Guardia, Ryan, Couchman, & Deci, 2000). Apparently, growing children and adolescents supplement their initial mental representation of what interpersonal relationships are like with new understandings of how relationships can unfold (M. W. Baldwin et al., 1996). Eventually, these various mental representations become integrated as a part of the child's personality (R. A. Thompson, 2006). In other words, children may initially develop trust in a parent and later become trusting people themselves.

Implications of Attachment Research

As we have seen, infants' attachments provide the foundation for later relationships. This foundation can be rebuilt if it's shaky, and it must occasionally be bolstered if, despite a solid beginning, it later weakens in the face of adverse circumstances. Drawing from

DEVELOPMENT AND PRACTICE
Offering Warm and Sensitive Care to Infants and Toddlers

Meet infants' needs in a timely fashion.

- An infant program has one caregiver for every three infants so that no child has to be left unattended for very long. When it is impossible to tend immediately to the needs of individual children, a caregiver reassures them that their needs are important and that she will be there as soon as possible. (Infancy)
- A mother is talking on her cell phone when her baby begins to cry. The mother tells her friend that she will call her back after she gives her baby a bottle and rocks the baby to sleep. (Infancy)

Respond positively to newly developed abilities.

- Caregivers in one center celebrate milestones as they notice them, including new teeth, advances in crawling, first steps, and first words. They share their admiration with family members but are sensitive to the desire of parents and other family members to be among the first to witness the accomplishment: "Raj is getting ready to walk, isn't he!" (Infancy)
- A father notices that his 6-month-old son has begun to flip over from his back to his front. The father gets on the floor beside his son and imitates his roll over. Together they laugh as they both roll back and forth. (Infancy)

Be polite but matter-of-fact when referring to infants' bodies.

- The director of an infant program trains staff members to use neutral terms for body functions. She asks a new teacher not to use the term "stinky baby," but instead to make a simple statement that an infant's diaper needs to be changed. (Infancy)
- A grandfather notices that his grandson has diarrhea and is developing diaper rash. As he changes the baby's diaper, he tells him, "Your bottom is getting very sore. I'm going to put some ointment on you after I wipe your bottom." (Infancy)

Set limits and redirect unacceptable behavior in a firm, but gentle way.

- The director of an infant-toddler program reminds teachers that their role is one of a *nurturer* who helps children learn self-control rather than an *authority figure* who doles out punishments. He suggests, "Tell children what they *can* do instead of telling them what they *cannot* do. You might say, 'Walk inside, please. Run outside.'" (Infancy)
- A quick-moving toddler has managed to unplug a humidifier and spill water from the tank. Her caregiver removes her from the scene and inserts safety plugs into the socket. She tells the little girl, "I made a mistake by placing the humidifier where you could reach it. Let me put it somewhere else so you don't get hurt." (Infancy)

Structure group infant care so that infants can maintain stable relationships with caregivers.

- An infant-toddler program is arranged into separate rooms so that each caregiver has a small number of infants with whom to form close relationships. Toddler teachers make a point to visit the infant room occasionally, so that they get to know children who will soon be moving to their room. (Infancy)
- In a child care center, caregivers arrange children into groups that stay together; as the infants outgrow the "Infant Room," for example, they "graduate" together to the "Toddler Room," and their caregiver goes with them. (Infancy)

---

attachment literature, we offer these recommendations for adults who work with children and adolescents:

• **Care for young children in a warm and sensitive manner.** Although family members are usually the recipients of children's first attachments, young children often form close bonds with employed caregivers, especially those who are familiar, responsive, and trustworthy. The Development and Practice feature "Offering Warm and Sensitive Care to Infants and Toddlers" illustrates such high-quality care.

• **Give children time to adjust to you.** It takes time for young children to form bonds with new caregivers, although the particular difficulties they face may depend partly on the quality of their relationships with parents. Infants who are securely attached to parents usually need several weeks to adjust to an unfamiliar caregiver's unique personality and style of interacting. In the meantime, the new caregivers need to offer lots of comfort during separations from parents. Infants who have not yet experienced sensitive care may feel anxious or withdrawn for weeks or even months before they decide that a new adult can be trusted. While children are adjusting, practitioners can be affectionate, meet children's needs, empathize with their feelings, and celebrate their accomplishments. In fact, children without prior secure attachments often benefit immensely when other caregivers act consistently and lovingly (Howes & Ritchie, 1998; NICHD Early Child Care Research Network, 1997; Zilberstein & Messer, 2010).

• **Promote emotional bonds in children of all ages.** The need for close attachments does not end with infancy. Children stand to gain immensely by having high-quality relationships with their teachers during the elementary, middle, and high school years. Generally, teachers and caregivers of infants, young children, and elementary school children find it easier to become acquainted with individual children than do practitioners working with adolescents. However, teachers of middle and high school students can also express their concern for individual students and get to know those adolescents they advise or see often (H. A. Davis, 2003). Adults can further promote ties among youngsters, giving them chances to become involved in clubs and sports teams, work together in projects, and so forth.

• **Model affectionate caregiving for family members.** Parents who had insecure relationships themselves may lack confidence in their parenting and obtain little pleasure from interacting with their children (Mikulincer & Shaver, 2007). One of the most effective tactics family educators can take with insensitive parents is to *show* them (in person or through videotapes) how infants devour affectionate gestures, especially during such routine games as playing peekaboo and sharing simple nursery rhymes (Bakermans-Kranenburg, van IJzendoorn, & Juffer, 2003; Svanberg et al., 2010). Caregivers and educators can demonstrate how to hold a baby tenderly and return the baby's smiles, vocalizations, and eye contact. They also can point out the signals infants give that indicate they are not ready to play (e.g., averting a gaze) or have had enough (e.g., pouting).

• **Encourage parents to watch their children's self-initiated actions.** Practitioners can encourage parents to watch their children carefully to determine interests and preferences. Babies learn a great deal by performing such simple activities as looking at their fingers, sucking on their toes, and listening to voices. When parents appreciate the significance of infants' spontaneous learning, they are more inclined to affirm and extend it ("Look at that mirror, Abigail! Is it shiny? Do you see yourself?").

• **Encourage parents to think about how infants and children understand events.** Parents do not always understand what makes their babies "tick" ("Why does Mike keep jumping out of his crib? Every time he does this, he gets hurt. What is he *thinking?*"). Professionals can share ideas about infants' motives, feelings, and understandings to help parents appreciate how babies might view the world ("Mike is one determined little guy, isn't he? He really wants to explore his environment!"). When parents reflect on how infants feel and construe events, attachments tend to be more secure (Koren-Karie, Oppenheim, Dolev, Sher, & Etzion-Carasso, 2002).

• **Advise parents about the special needs of children with disabilities.** Some parents feel so overwhelmed by the challenge of caring for a child with a disability that they find it difficult to identify their child's unique perspectives. Yet teachers and caregivers can help parents recognize their child's distinctive ways of communicating and expressing emotions. You might ask parents of a blind baby if the baby enjoys exploring their faces with her hands. Similarly, you could point out to parents of a child with Down syndrome that children with this condition sometimes express their discomfort in subtle, rather than insistent ways, and that these children often appreciate it when caregivers occasionally slow down during interactions and give them a chance to control the flow of the exchange (D. Howe, 2006).

• **When parents divorce, help children remain attached to both parents.** Many divorced parents share custody of children, making it likely that children will maintain attachments to both parents. Teachers can help by sending home duplicate copies of newsletters and correspondence to both parents' homes. Family educators and counselors can also talk with parents about ways in which children of different ages handle rotations between two households (J. B. Kelly & Lamb, 2000).

• **Acknowledge and encourage multiple attachments.** In the child care center and at school, children may talk about a variety of people in their lives (e.g., brothers and sisters, aunts and uncles, grandparents, and neighbors). Teachers and other practitioners can encourage children to invite some of these individuals to school events and orientation meetings. Educators can further help children by establishing a productive social climate in the classroom that fosters youngsters' relationships with one another.[4]

• **Offer a range of services when children are placed with new families.** When children are removed from families because of maltreatment or neglect, children often form healthy bonds with new caregivers (Chisholm, Carter, Ames, & Morison, 1995; Marcovitch et al., 1997; Zilberstein & Messer, 2010). However, professionals who work with children and their new families should not leave this adjustment to chance. Instead, they can prepare new families to recognize and meet children's individual needs. For example, a foster family might be advised to expect temper tantrums from an 8-year-old child who has recently joined the family. With coaching, family members can communicate their expectations for controlled behavior, follow through with agreed-on consequences when rules are violated, and persist in showing love even though the child does not yet reciprocate the affection.

COMMON CAUSE. Regularly scheduled educational, service, and recreational activities can help adolescents form bonds with peers.

• **Encourage sympathetic dispositions in children.** Some children who have had few affectionate relationships develop poor social skills and so may, in many people's eyes, be difficult children to like. These children may appear self-centered and unconcerned about others' distress; for example, they may hit a peer who has gotten hurt rather than offer sympathy (Volling, 2001). To help a child who seems uncaring, you can model appropriate reactions when someone is hurt, talk about the hurt person's feelings, and encourage the child to offer help and show sympathy.

• **Be especially sensitive with children who show insecurity or other attachment problems.** Children who have not yet developed secure attachments to parents may benefit from your extra efforts to keep social routines affectionate and consistent, especially during arrivals and departures. In addition, without prior history of a warm, mutually loving relationship, children may need repeated experiences with the pleasant give-and-take of social interaction (C. S. Cain, 2006; Mercer, 2006). Depending on the age of the child, you might sit quietly with the child in a relaxing activity, such as building blocks together or tossing a ball back and forth.

• **Address the needs of both parents and infants when parents struggle with unmet emotional needs.** When parents themselves are emotionally depressed, they may be unresponsive toward their infants, or even hostile and intrusive (Burrous, Crockenberg, & Leerkes, 2009; Teti, Gelfand, Messinger, & Isabella, 1995). Infants with depressed parents may themselves become chronically sad and withdrawn. Professional intervention that helps parents resolve their emotional needs may be a necessary step before they are able to use an involved, affectionate parenting style (Benoit & Parker, 1994; Main, Kaplan, & Cassidy, 1985). During the period in which a parent receives mental health treatment, the other parent or another family member may be able to pick up the slack and provide children with loving attention.

• **Seek professional guidance when attachment problems are serious.** Some attachment problems are so profoundly disruptive that families require the services of a counselor, psychologist, or social worker (C. S. Cain, 2006; Mercer, 2006; Zilberstein & Messer, 2010). Thus it is important for practitioners to be alert for signs of deeply troubled infant–family relationships. You should definitely seek professional guidance when you suspect a serious problem—for instance, when a distressed child never seeks comfort from a familiar caregiver, shows fear of a family member, or displays some other highly unusual style of responding to parents (see indicators of serious attachment problems in the Observations Guidelines table "Assessing Young Children's Attachment Security" on p. 426.

In their relationships with attachment figures, children learn to express their pleasure, distress, and other feelings. Expressing emotions is an important development in its own right and our focus now.

[4]We examine classroom climate and a sense of community in Chapter 15.

EMOTION

Emotions (sometimes referred to as *affective states*) are the feelings, both physiological and psychological, that people have in response to events that are personally relevant to their needs and goals (Campos, Frankel, & Camras, 2004). Emotions energize thinking and acting in ways that are often adaptive in present circumstances (Dennis, Cole, Wiggins, Cohen, & Zalewski, 2009; Goleman, 1995; Saarni et al., 2006). *Sadness* may lead a child to find comfort from others and reassess whether a goal is possible; *anger* may spur a child to try a new tactic or abandon an unrealistic goal; and *happiness* may prompt a child to share positive feelings with others and repeat a pleasurable experience in the future (Saarni et al., 2006). These and other emotions are described in the Observation Guidelines table "Assessing the Emotions of Children and Adolescents."

Developmental Changes in Emotions

How youngsters express, understand, and cope with emotions changes with age and experience. Emotional development is characterized by these specific trends:

Infants begin life with a few basic emotions and gradually add new feelings. Contentment, interest, and *distress* are felt within the first 6 months of life (Braungart-Rieker, Hill-Soderlund, & Karrass, 2010; Emde, Gaensbauer, & Harmon, 1976; Stenberg & Campos, 1990). Hungry babies most certainly feel pleasure when they begin to feed. A small smile may occur when infants are relaxed, happy, or enchanted with animated people. Infants show interest by watching objects carefully, inspecting their own body parts, mouthing fingers and toes, and tilting their heads to listen closely to the fine points of speech and music. Newborns exposed to a loud and sudden noise express distress, usually by crying; they do the same when hungry and tired.

As they mature, infants add to their basic emotions. Simple distress can become true *anger* when infants' desires are obstructed: Daddy does not come immediately to pick baby

emotion
Affective response to an event that is personally relevant to one's needs and goals.

OBSERVATION GUIDELINES
Assessing the Emotions of Children and Adolescents

CHARACTERISTIC	LOOK FOR	EXAMPLE	IMPLICATION
Happiness	• *Smiles* • *Laughter* • *Spontaneity*	Paul, age 17, chatters with his friends during his school's end-of-the-year athletic field day. He is happy about having schoolwork over and looks forward to his summer job and paychecks.	Happiness helps people enjoy life and seek similar pleasurable experiences. Help children and adolescents find appropriate outlets to express joy, and celebrate with them. Encourage them to talk about things they are happy about.
Anger	• *Frowns and angry expressions* • *Possible retaliation* toward the source of anger	Aranya, age 14, is furious that she wasn't admitted into an elective course, whereas her two closest friends were. Aranya is angry with the principal, who she thinks dislikes her.	Anger helps people deal with obstacles to their goals, often spurring them to try new tactics. Help youngsters express their anger appropriately and determine how they can redirect their energy toward reasonable solutions.
Fear	• *Frightened expression* • *Withdrawal* from circumstances • *Physiological responses*, such as sweating	Tony, age 2½, sits on his mat, eyes wide, body tense. He stares at a new poster of a clown in his preschool classroom. He is downright scared, runs to his teacher, and buries his head in her lap.	Fear occurs when people feel threatened and believe that their physical safety and psychological well-being are potentially at stake. Fear motivates people to flee, escape from harm, seek reassurance, and perhaps fight back. Help children articulate their fears. Offer reassurance.

(continued)

OBSERVATION GUIDELINES (continued)

CHARACTERISTIC	LOOK FOR	EXAMPLE	IMPLICATION
Sadness	• *Sad expression* • *Crying* • *Pouting* • *Being quiet* • *Possible withdrawal* from a situation	Greta, age 15, sits quietly on a bench near her locker. With her head hung low, she rereads the letter from a cheerleading organization. She has not been admitted to a prestigious cheerleading summer camp.	People are sad when they realize they cannot attain a desired goal or when they experience a loss, such as a friend moving to a distant city. Sadness causes some people to reassess their goals. Reassure children, ask them how they are doing, let them regroup, and encourage them to join familiar activities.
Disgust	• *Wrinkled nose* • *Remarks such as "Phew!"* • *Withdrawal* from the source of displeasure	Norton, age 8, looks skeptically at the meal he has just received in the school cafeteria. He wrinkles his nose and averts his gaze from the "tuna melt" on his plate.	Disgust occurs when people encounter food, smells, and sights they find repulsive. It is nature's way of getting people to be wary of something that is potentially troublesome or threatening to their health. Respect children's feelings of disgust, but also encourage them to reflect on why they might respond to particular substances in this way.
Anxiety	• *Frequent worrying* • *Excessive fidgeting*, hand wringing, or nail biting • *Avoidance* of source of anxiety	Tanesha, age 16, has to give an oral presentation to her class. She has spent a lot of time preparing but is worried that, when she is standing all by herself in front of the group, she might get so nervous that she forgets everything she wants to say.	As long as it is not excessive, anxiety can spur people to take steps to avoid problems and achieve valued goals. Teach youngsters strategies that keep anxiety at a manageable level, as well as tactics that help them achieve their goals.
Shame	• *Signs of embarrassment* • *Attempts to withdraw* from a situation • *Looking down and away* from other people	Luke, age 9, is stunned. He's just had an accident, urinating on the floor. He had felt a bit antsy beforehand but wasn't aware that he needed to use the toilet. Now 20 pairs of eyes are glued on him.	When children feel ashamed, they are aware of other people's standards for behavior and know they are not meeting those standards. Shame motivates children to try harder. Shame works best when it comes from within; in most cultures it would be considered inappropriate for adults to ridicule students. Help children redirect their behavior so they can meet their own standards.
Guilt	• *Sad expression* • *Self-conscious demeanor* • *Possible concern* for a person who has been harmed	A.J., age 12, regrets bad-mouthing his friend Pete to other classmates. A.J. sinks down low in his chair, feeling remorse for what he said behind Pete's back and for Pete's sadness.	Guilt occurs when people do something that violates their own standards. It leads people to right the wrong. More generally, it causes people to behave in socially appropriate ways that protect others from harm. Suggest to children that they can behave differently next time.
Pride	• *Happy expression* • *Desire to show off* work and accomplishments to other people	Jacinda, age 5, is beaming. For the last 20 minutes, she's painstakingly pasted sequins, stars, and feathers onto a mask. Her final product is a colorful, delicately adorned creation. She is happy with her work, as is evident from her ear-to-ear grin.	People are proud when they earn others' respect and meet their own goals. Pride fosters continued commitment to achieving high standards. Pride motivates people to share their accomplishments with others. Encourage children to identify things that make them proud. Share in their joy when they accomplish something meaningful for them.

Source: Adaptive functions of emotions based on material in Saarni et al., 2006.

up, and Mommy does not indulge baby's desire to press buttons on the DVD player. Infants show their anger by crying, thrashing, and looking directly, with accusation, at caregivers. Infants tend to show *fear* during the second half of the first year, as with the stranger anxiety we examined earlier. Animals and objects that move in unexpected ways also often scare infants.

Infants respond to other people's emotions. A basic ability to detect emotions in others is present even in infancy (Haviland & Lelwica, 1987; Hutman & Dapretto, 2009). This ability is illustrated by the **emotional contagion** of babies: When one starts crying, others soon join in (Eisenberg, 1992; Hatfield, Cacioppo, & Rapson, 1994; Hutman & Dapretto, 2009). Within the first few months of life, infants react to the emotional expressions of caregivers in meaningful ways. By 4 months, infants sometimes look away when other people show sad expressions, intently study the faces of people who look angry, and initially attend to others' fearful expressions and then look away (Montague & Walker-Andrews, 2001). When caregivers violate infants' expectations for a particular emotional expression (perhaps by showing no smiles after a period of social play), infants also react. Between 3 and 9 months, they may respond to a parent's deadpan face by crying, looking away, and using self-soothing behaviors such as sucking their thumbs (Conradt & Ablow, 2010; G. A. Moore, Cohn, & Campbell, 2001; Tronick, Als, Adamson, Wise, & Brazelton, 1978).

Children learn to guide their actions on the basis of other people's facial expressions, mannerisms, and tone of voice. In the first 2 years of life, children begin to monitor the emotions of others, particularly parents and trusted caregivers. Infants show *social referencing* early in their second year: They watch their parents' faces and body language and listen to emotional tones in their voices, especially in a novel or puzzling situation (Boccia & Campos, 1989; G. Kim, Walden, & Knieps, 2010).[5] For instance, a 14-month-old girl may glance at Mommy's face when a new babysitter enters the house. By determining whether Mommy is smiling or frowning, the little girl gets a sense of how to respond to the babysitter.

Children expand their repertoire of basic emotions to include self-conscious emotions. Simple emotions such as fear, anger, and pleasure in infancy are joined by **self-conscious emotions** in early childhood. These are affective states that reflect awareness of social standards (M. Lewis, 1993, 1995; R. A. Thompson & Newton, 2010). Self-conscious emotions include guilt, embarrassment, and pride. Teresa recalls early displays of guilt in both of her sons. As toddlers and preschoolers, the boys would often respond angrily when misbehavior resulted in their being sent to their room or having a privilege taken away. Occasionally they'd swat at her or stomp out of the room. However, they'd often return a while later, looking at her face for signs of sadness and affectionately rubbing her arm as they apologized.

Children increasingly reflect on emotions. As early as age 2 or 3, children talk about emotions that they and others experience ("Daniel got mad and pushed me"), and they realize that emotions are connected to people's desires ("Kurt loves to go down the slide and was really mad when he didn't get a turn") (Bretherton, Fritz, Zahn-Waxler, & Ridgeway, 1986; P. M. Cole, Armstrong, & Pemberton, 2010). By middle childhood, they realize that their interpretations of a situation determine how they feel about it and that other people may have different views and, as a result, different feelings ("Arlene feels bad because she thinks I don't like her") (P. L. Harris, 1989). Children also learn to connect words for emotions (*happy, sad, angry,* etc.) with particular facial expressions and with conditions under which these emotions are elicited.

By middle childhood, children appreciate that emotional expressions do not always reflect people's true feelings (Saarni et al., 2006; Selman, 1980). A 9-year-old may observe his teacher's cheerful demeanor yet know she just lost her brother to cancer and is probably sad inside. During the end of middle childhood and the beginning of adolescence, children also understand that they and other people can have ambivalent and conflicting feelings (S. K. Donaldson & Westerman, 1986; N. Stein, Trabasso, & Liwag, 2000). A 12-year-old girl

emotional contagion
Tendency for infants to cry spontaneously when they hear other infants crying.

self-conscious emotion
Affective state that reflects awareness of a community's social standards (e.g., pride, guilt, shame).

[5]Social referencing is introduced in Chapter 7.

may love her father but be angry with him for moving out of the house; she may like going to see him during custodial visits but not like the feelings of turmoil the visits evoke in her.

Children and adolescents gradually learn to regulate their emotions. One important aspect of *self-regulation* is **emotional regulation**, the management of affective states (Campos et al., 2004; Koole, 2009).[6] Children gradually acquire a constellation of strategies that help them cope with their feelings and deal with stressful situations (E. M. Brenner & Salovey, 1997; P. M. Cole et al., 2010).

As newborns, infants need help when they feel hungry, scared, or hurt. Most can count on caregivers to help them find relief. As parents and other family members tend to infants' needs, offer a soothing touch, and reassure them verbally, infants calm down and learn that distress can be relieved with certain tactics (P. M. Cole et al., 2010). Infants also learn to soothe themselves to some extent: They may suck on a thumb, avert their gaze from a stranger, or crawl away from a scary toy (Macklem, 2008; Mangelsdorf et al., 1995; R. A. Thompson et al., 2003).

Guidance from parents continues to help young children expand on their coping strategies (P. M. Cole et al., 2010; Saarni et al., 2006). Here a mother suggests a few actions a small child might take when upset:

Child:	[crying] Mommy!
Mother:	Are you okay?
Mother:	You want a tissue?
Mother:	Can I kiss it and make it better?
Mother:	You want to get your baby and make it better?
Mother:	Hug your baby.
Mother:	Wanna hug your baby? (P. M. Cole et al., 2010, pp. 67–68)

Emotional regulation skills expand dramatically during early childhood courtesy of sensitive care from adults and emerging verbal skills. Children identify their feelings using particular terms (e.g., being "disappointed") and talk themselves through challenging situations (e.g., reminding themselves to use their words rather than hit a peer when embroiled in a heated conflict; P. M. Cole et al., 2010). Parents serve an important role by modeling particular emotional responses, for example, expressing frustration verbally: "I'm angry that you promised to make dinner but didn't do it." Children may subsequently use a similar strategy with peers: "I'm angry that you said you'd give me a turn with the truck but never did." By the end of the early childhood period, many children have typically learned to talk comfortably about emotions, consider the perspective of others when expressing disappointment (e.g., when receiving an unwanted gift from a well-meaning relative), express their emotions in play, remain composed when faced with strong emotions, and anticipate the kind of situations that are likely to be enjoyable or upsetting (Macklem, 2008).

During the middle childhood and adolescent years, emotional regulation continues to evolve. Many young people realize that when they are upset they can substitute one activity for another (e.g., watching baseball on television after an injury rather than trying to play the game themselves), ask for support from peers or adults, or change the way they think about a troubling situation (e.g., by trying to forget about it, go to sleep, or reappraise the situation by focusing on its positive features) (E. L. Davis, Levine, Lench, & Quas, 2010). Elementary and secondary school students also tend to keep feelings to themselves that suggest they are vulnerable, for example, they may hide their disappointment about a low test score.

Throughout their school years, youngsters have many opportunities to regulate their emotions in the classroom. Children and adolescents regularly face circumstances in which they did not achieve as well as they would have liked or, in social settings, feel ostracized or ridiculed by peers (Macklem, 2008). Youngsters who express their emotions in a socially acceptable way are those most likely to be popular with peers (E. L. Davis et al., 2010; Fabes et al., 1999; Macklem, 2008).

[6]Chapter 3 introduces self-regulation as children's ability to control various aspects of their behavior.

ARTIFACT 11-1 I try not to hit and shout. Seven-year-old Miguel commented on his efforts to express anger appropriately.

emotional regulation
Strategies to manage affective states.

MyEducationLab

Listen to Brendan express empathic concern for injured birds in the "Neighborhood: Early Adolescence" video. (Find Video Examples in Topic 11 of MyEducationLab.)

Concern for others' feelings is an important emotional response that develops with age, especially when encouraged by adults. **Empathy** is the capacity to experience the same or similar feelings as another person, who perhaps may be in pain or distress (Eisenberg, Eggum, & Edwards, 2010; Hoffman, 1991). Children exhibit basic forms of empathy as infants, shedding tears in the presence of other crying infants. As children grow and gain insights into how other people's circumstances affect their emotional experiences, they show increasingly advanced forms of empathy. You can listen to Brendan express empathic concern for injured birds in the "Neighborhood: Early Adolescence" video in MyEducationLab. Young people are especially inclined to be empathic when their parents have previously been warm and responsive to them (Zhou et al., 2002).[7]

The upper elementary and secondary years bring new anxieties and pressures. As youngsters grow more independent, they may find their needs and desires conflicting with those of parents and other authority figures (Arnett, 1999; Moksnes, Moljord, Espnes, & Byrne, 2010; Shanahan, McHale, Osgood, & Crouter, 2007). Concerns about fitting in at school, making mistakes in front of others, completing difficult homework, achieving good grades, and having an ideal body type intensify during adolescence (Bokhorst, Westenberg, Oosterlaan, & Heyne, 2008; Knauss, Paxton, & Alsaker, 2007; Moksnes et al., 2010; Phelan et al., 1994).

Bioecology of Emotions

Children's personal characteristics and experiences in social groups affect their expression and control of emotions. In particular, children's gender, culture, and socioeconomic status affect their emotional pathways.

Gender

On average, male and female babies are similar in emotional states; any gender differences are subtle and situation dependent (J. E. O. Blakemore, Berenbaum, & Liben, 2009; Eisenberg, Martin, & Fabes, 1996). After the age of 2, however, consistent gender differences emerge. Boys show more anger than girls beginning in the preschool years, and girls more often report feeling sad, fearful, and guilty from the elementary grades onward (Blakemore et al., 2009; Eisenberg et al., 1996). Girls also respond more negatively to failures, to such an extent that their subsequent performance may suffer (Dweck, 2000). And some girls are inclined to dwell on their problems rather than taking action or distracting themselves. Such a ruminating style is a risk factor for becoming depressed (J. S. Hyde, Mezulis, & Abramson, 2008; Nolen-Hoeksema, Morrow, & Fredrickson, 1993). Meanwhile, as early as elementary school, boys are apt to put on a self-confident front when they feel vulnerable (Blakemore et al., 2009; Ruble, Martin, & Berenbaum, 2006). This style, too, has its disadvantages, especially when boys feel pressured to live up to unrealistic standards of personal strength.

Biology contributes to gender differences in emotions; for instance, rising hormonal levels at puberty are associated with increases in moodiness and depression in girls, and with aggressiveness and rebelliousness in boys (Buchanan, Eccles, & Becker, 1992; Davila, 2008). Yet socialization also determines gender differences in emotional responding. Parents are more likely to talk about fear and sadness with daughters and anger with sons (Kennedy Root & Denham, 2010; Malatesta & Haviland, 1982). At school, many teachers prefer the compliant, agreeable nature that girls are more likely to exhibit, and they discipline boys who have trouble sitting still and keeping their thoughts and feelings to themselves (R. E. Bennett, Gottesman, Rock, & Cerullo, 1993; Pianta, 2006; Pollack, 1998).

Obviously, both boys and girls have emotional needs. Being careful not to stereotype the sexes, concerned educators can look for occasions when children use styles of emotional regulation that make matters worse for them. For example, adults can watch for times when

ARTIFACT 11-2   Under pressure.
During his high school year, 17-year-old Jeff felt "locked in" by the combined pressures of a demanding course load, impending due dates for college applications, and his role as confidant for several troubled friends. Late one night, he put his schoolwork aside to create this picture. Because he had trouble drawing human figures, he combined two favorite things—a soft drink can and black-and-white cowhide—to represent himself. A cage and gigantic boulder hold him in, and so he cannot join his peers (represented by other soft drink cans) frolic freely in the distance

empathy
Capacity to experience the same feelings as another person, especially when the feeling is pain or distress.

[7]In Chapter 14, we examine the connection between children's empathic responses and their helping behaviors.

girls are ruminating over problems and help these girls work through their feelings, actively tackle the problems, and get on with life. Similarly, when boys seem to be trying hard to brush off a significant personal loss, adults can acknowledge that the event is, in fact, likely to be upsetting but can be tackled with active coping skills.

Culture

The language children speak defines aspects of emotion that are important in their culture. In English, words for emotions, for example, being anxious, happy, or excited, focus on internal, private states (Kagan, 2010). Some other languages emphasize the bodily sensations of emotions, such as being dizzy, having a headache, or feeling one's heart race away. A language also encodes nuances of emotion that are relevant in the culture. A child speaking English may hear about someone being "ashamed," whereas a child speaking Chinese encounters five distinct terms for shame, words that communicate different causes and effects of personal transgressions (H. Frank, Harvey, & Verdun, 2000).

Culture also directs children in how to express particular emotions in specific circumstances. In general, children in individualistic cultures are encouraged to express the full gamut of their emotions, including happiness, pride, frustration, and anger (Morelli & Rothbaum, 2007).[8] In individualistic cultures, it is considered healthy and appropriate to reveal one's innermost feelings. In contrast, collectivistic cultures disapprove of emotions that disrupt a group's harmony. Displays of frustration, anger, and pride are discouraged because they reflect self-absorption and may upset others.

Yet families within any single culture can differ markedly in how they socialize children's emotional expression. In a study with families in England, researchers listened to conversations among 3-year-old children, their mothers, and their older siblings; some children *never* mentioned emotions during an hour-long conversation at home, whereas one child mentioned emotions more than 27 times (J. Dunn, Brown, & Beardsall, 1991). On average, mothers were more likely to talk about feelings than were the children. When they occur, family "lessons" about feelings may help children to understand how emotions operate.

Socioeconomic Status

Children living in families that face ongoing economic hardships are at heightened risk for emotional and behavioral problems. Children whose families have low incomes are more prone to anxiety, depression, and behavior problems (e.g., physical aggression) than are children from advantaged backgrounds (Kagan, 2010; Tolani & Brooks-Gunn, 2006). Environmental factors are almost certainly the primary reason for this difference. Children living in impoverished circumstances have more than their share of reasons to feel sad, fearful, and angry. They may not know where their next meal is coming from, and they are more likely to encounter violence and drug addiction in their neighborhoods. Their parents may have limited resources to address children's needs (McLoyd, Aikens, & Burton, 2006). Furthermore, many children from low-income backgrounds, particularly those with histories of learning problems, have few positive interactions with teachers at school (R. M. Clark, 1983).

Obviously not every child who grows up in a low-income environment is emotionally burdened. Many children who face financial hardships receive stable, loving care from their immediate and extended families and in the process acquire good coping skills. For example, many children whose parents emigrated from Mexico to the United States with limited financial resources show fewer emotional and behavioral problems than do American-born children (Espinosa, 2008).

Nor are children from middle- and high-income backgrounds immune to stress. Some middle-income parents project their own aspirations onto their children, expecting children to follow unrealistic developmental timetables, such as cooperatively sharing toys with peers at 18 months or reading at 3 years. When children fail to meet these timetables, parents may become overly critical and controlling (Hyson, Hirsh-Pasek, Rescorla, Cone, & Martell-Boinske,

Bioecology of Child Development

Children's emotional development is influenced by their gender and experiences in social settings.

---

[8]Collectivistic and individualistic cultures are introduced in Chapter 3 and also examined earlier in this chapter in the context of attachment research.

1991). As a result, children may worry about parents' expectations, particularly when they think they are not measuring up (Hilt, Cha, & Nolen-Hoeksema, 2008; M. Levine, 2006).

Promoting Children's Emotional Development

Educators can promote children's emotional development if they consider emotions as *competencies*—that is, as valuable skills that can improve over time. We offer these suggestions for promoting children's abilities in emotional expression:

• **Help crying infants find comfort.** Caregivers can do several things to help infants in distress. First, they can strive to give timely reassurance—not always immediately, because they may have other demands, but not so late that crying escalates into turbulent agitation. Second, caregivers can allow and encourage actions that infants use to reduce stress. Searching for a favorite blanket, putting a finger in the mouth, tugging at an ear with a gentle hand—these are all positive signs that infants are learning to soothe themselves. Third, caregivers can consciously invite a baby to join them in a calm state—by showing baby a smiling face, holding baby close to the chest, and breathing in a shared rhythm (Gonzalez-Mena, 2002). Fourth, caregivers can investigate why an infant might be crying and try to meet the unfilled need or remove the painful stimulus. Finally, caregivers should try to stay calm and not take it personally—infants sometimes cry despite the most sensitive care.

• **Create an atmosphere of warmth, acceptance, and trust.** Children and adolescents alike learn most effectively when they experience positive emotions, for instance, when they feel secure, happy, or excited about an activity (Bauminger & Kimhi-Kind, 2008; Linnenbrink & Pintrich, 2004). And they are more likely to confide in an adult about troublesome issues if they know that the adult will continue to respect them no matter what they reveal about themselves in heart-to-heart conversations.

• **Consider using a research-based curriculum for fostering emotional development.** To have a significant impact on children's emotional expression, adults can implement a systematic program for educating children about their feelings. One illustration of a comprehensive emotional education program is the *Promoting Alternative Thinking Strategies (PATHS)* curriculum (Domitrovich, Cortes, & Greenberg, 2007). Second- and third-grade children are taught that all feelings are okay, some feelings are comfortable and others uncomfortable, feelings can help children learn what to do in certain situations, and some ways of dealing with emotions are better than others. Children keep a record of their feelings and use a poster showing a traffic signal as a guide to regulating their responses to feelings. Teachers encourage children to refer to the steps on a poster: to stop and calm down (red), slow down and consider their options (yellow), and try a plan (green). This program has been shown to increase emotional understanding and decrease problem behaviors in children with diverse ability levels. Well-designed social-emotional programs show significant effects in a variety of domains, including in reducing rates of substance abuse, antisocial behaviors, and misbehaviors at school and improving school attendance and achievement (Durlak, Weissberg, Dymnicki, Taylor, & Schellinger, 2011).

• **Offer age-appropriate outlets for emotional expression.** When they are young, children can find safe outlets for emotional expression in play. Through fantasy play with peers, children often work out their fears and anger (Kohlberg & Fein, 1987; Mathieson & Banerjee, 2010). For older children, writing about feelings, perhaps in essays or journals shared only with a teacher or counselor, can provide a confidential outlet.

• **Discuss emotions experienced by characters in literature and history.** Stories provide an occasion to talk about emotional states (Mar & Oatley, 2008). We have found in our own experience that children in the elementary grades are able to make appropriate inferences about characters' emotional states. For instance, in *Frog and Toad Are Friends* (Lobel, 1979), a book suitable for 4- to 8-year-olds, Frog waits impatiently

What Hits Me

Feeling excitment bubble inside know something great is waiting to happen to you. Feeling scared or nervous, want to dive under the covers and go back to sleep even though it is 8:30 and it is almost time to go to school. Feeling sad because your parents got divorced and you dad just moved out of the house. Feeling scared and excited at same time because you have discovered something that's mysterious and you are determind to figur it out.

ARTIFACT 11-3 **What hits me.** In this essay, 10-year-old Shea describes her experiences with various emotions.

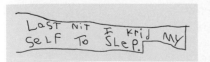

Last nit I krid my self to sleep.

ARTIFACT 11-4 **Last night.** In this journal entry, 8-year-old Noah reveals his sadness about his parents' recent divorce.

to play with his hibernating friend, Toad, and plays a trick on him to get him up early. The story provides a forum for discussions about feelings that may arise between friends, such as anger at being teased or misled (Solomon, Watson, Battistich, Schaps, & Delucchi, 1992). Meanwhile, older children and adolescents might read firsthand accounts of historical events and talk about how people in various contexts have responded emotionally to hostilities and inequities.

• **Ask children to guess what emotions people may feel in particular scenarios.** Children can practice analyzing situations and considering how those involved might feel. In Figure 11-1, you can see one situation that an elementary school counselor asks children to pretend they face. Adults can guide children to see that anger, fear, guilt, and other feelings are reasonable reactions to particular circumstances. In addition, they can ask children to think about how they might act when they have such uncomfortable feelings.

• **Take cultural differences into account.** Some cultures encourage open communication about feelings, whereas others actively discourage emotional expressiveness. Adults working with children from diverse cultures must be mindful of such differences when interpreting children's emotional expressions (or lack thereof). A girl who is pokerfaced when disappointed may actually be sad but controlling her emotional expressions, as she has learned at home.

• **Help children keep anxiety at a manageable level.** **Anxiety** is an emotional state characterized by worry and apprehension, often about future events with unknown outcomes. Children who are anxious may experience such physiological symptoms as muscle tension and headaches and have trouble concentrating. Educators can do a variety of things to help keep anxiety at a manageable level. When teachers assign oral reports, they can encourage students to create index cards or other memory "crutches." Before giving an important test (such as the standardized tests that many school districts require), they can administer a practice test that gives students a general idea of what to expect. In general, they should communicate realistic expectations for classroom performance and provide the support students need to *meet* those expectations.

• **Pay attention to your own emotions.** Practitioners who work with children and families often find themselves frustrated by the people they serve (Button, 2007; B. Davis, 2001). Teachers may become angry with rude children, harried parents, unrealistic external mandates, and inadequate resources for schools. Frustration and anger are natural emotions, but they must be handled with care. Exploding at the nearest bystander or retreating into personal despair are *not* good ideas; counting to 10 and finding another professional to talk with *can* be helpful in preserving one's mental health.

• **Model appropriate ways of dealing with negative emotions.** Youngsters often struggle with how to deal with anger, fear, and sadness; they can benefit from seeing adults express these emotions appropriately (Delaney, 2006). Teresa remembers how her fifth-grade teacher expressed anger: Rather than raising her voice, she lowered it to a whisper. The teacher's approach worked well: Students sensed her disappointment, responded with concern and guilt, and tried to make amends. Educators can enhance the benefits of modeling controlled, honest emotional reactions by offering an explanation: "I'm really angry now. Let's talk this out when we've all calmed down."

The Basic Developmental Issues table "Attachment and Emotional Development" shows how attachments and emotions draw from nature and nurture, show universality and diversity, and exhibit qualitative and quantitative change. As you have learned, nature furnishes children with inclinations to form attachments and express emotions, and nurture translates these abstract capacities into real-life relationships and abilities. In the next section, we reveal how individual differences in emotional responding, first manifested during infancy as distinct temperaments, are slowly integrated into well-defined personalities.

Marissa and Wendy Sue have been good friends for a long time. Marissa told Lucy about Wendy Sue's family. Wendy Sue had asked her not to tell anyone.

FIGURE 11-1 Respecting others' privacy. Counselors can ask children to pretend they are characters in particular situations, such as this one, and help them talk about how they might feel and respond. *Idea courtesy of Sally Tossey, Columbus, Ohio.*

WHAT IF YOU TRIED THIS? Adults can help relieve children's anxiety by talking through problems in a warm, supportive manner.

anxiety
Emotional state characterized by worry and apprehension.

BASIC DEVELOPMENTAL ISSUES
Attachment and Emotional Development

ISSUE	ATTACHMENT	EMOTIONAL DEVELOPMENT
Nature and Nurture	Children are biologically predisposed to form close bonds with their parents and other primary caregivers, but they are more likely to form secure attachments to adults when they are treated in a sensitive and responsible fashion. Parents, in turn, are by nature predisposed to care for their offspring, but they learn specific ways of interacting with children from other family members and from the community and culture in which they live.	The full range of emotions is made possible by human genetic instructions; the brain is wired to experience anger, pleasure, fear, and so on. Genetic factors also affect individual differences in temperament (e.g., activity level and ways of responding to new stimuli). Nurture affects how emotions are expressed. Children learn to control expression of negative emotions by observing other people and practicing various ways of dealing with feelings.
Universality and Diversity	The predisposition to form close social-emotional bonds is universal. Sensitive care is the common route to healthy attachments. However, not all children receive this responsive attention or form secure attachments. Being clingy and demanding may help infants who live in an environment with scarce resources. Similarly, being able to negotiate multiple relationships may enhance adjustment when numerous caregivers are present during the early years.	All children experience such basic emotions as happiness, sadness, anger, and fear. The tendency for emotional states to energize particular kinds of responses (e.g., fleeing in response to fear) is also universal. But substantial diversity is present in how children regulate their emotions (e.g., when trying to conceal their true feelings). Some children are more likely than others to respond to situations in a positive, upbeat fashion.
Qualitative and Quantitative Change	The development of attachments largely reflects quantitative change: Children gradually become more active as social partners, initiating conversations and other exchanges, taking turns to keep interactions going, and so on. Qualitative change occurs when young children, who have previously leapt into the arms of strangers, suddenly display stranger anxiety.	Children gradually gain the knowledge and skills needed to assess others' emotions. By watching facial expressions, listening to tones of voice, and drawing inferences from behaviors, children learn how others express and control emotions. The emergence of self-conscious emotions (pride, guilt, etc.) represents a qualitative change that reflects a new awareness of social standards.

TEMPERAMENT AND PERSONALITY

Visit any group of children—perhaps at a local child care center, a school, or an after-school program—and you are bound to notice dramatic differences in individual children's energy, mood, spontaneity, and attention to academic tasks. Such variations reflect differences in children's *temperaments* and *personalities*.

Temperament refers to a child's typical ways of responding to events and novel stimulation and of regulating impulses (Kagan & Fox, 2006; Rothbart, Sheese, & Conradt, 2009).[9] Individual differences in temperament are present even in infancy. Some infants are fussy and demanding; others are cheerful and easily pacified. Temperament has a genetic basis, as we shall see, but it also is very much affected by children's relationships and experiences.

As children grow older, they develop distinctive ways of behaving, thinking, and feeling. That is, they develop unique **personalities**. Temperament surely affects personality: A child who is timid relates to people and events differently than one who is socially confident. But personality includes more than temperament. Personality is affected by children's intellectual interests and the many habits they learn while growing up—for example, their traditions for fulfilling family obligations, strategies for dealing with stressful situations, styles of managing belongings, and preferences for spending leisure time.

Both temperament and personality help us understand how individual children respond to emotions, form relationships, and act within schools and other group settings. Temperament may be especially helpful to consider when children are infants and toddlers; personality may

personality
Characteristic way a person behaves, thinks, and feels.

[9]Temperament is introduced in Chapter 1.

be more relevant as youngsters move into their later childhood and adolescent years. Let's look more closely at both concepts and then consider their implications for educators.

Elements of Temperament and Personality

Temperament and personality are each made up of constellations of relatively independent dimensions. Individual children may have a lot, a little, or an in-between amount of each attribute.

Temperament

Much of the initial work on temperament was done using parents' reports and researchers' observations of infants' typical behaviors. Parents and researchers judged the extent to which the infants exhibited such qualities as activity level and adaptability to change. In considering the dramatic individual differences that emerged out of this research, psychologists and educators realized that infants' temperaments partly determine the particular kinds of care that are most effective for them as individuals (A. Thomas & Chess, 1977). Infants who exhibit a high activity level (squirming a lot, wiggling while having a diaper change) may benefit from many opportunities for safe exploration around the environment. In comparison, for children with low activity levels, adults might need to slow down their pace, enjoy quiet interaction with them, and invite more active play. Thus, children's well-being depends to some extent on the *goodness of fit* between their temperament and the particular environment in which they are raised (Chess & Thomas, 1992). Having a good fit does not mean that the adult shares the same temperament as a child but rather that the adult warmly accepts and accommodates the child's rhythms and dispositions.

More recent research has focused on the neurological basis of temperament. American psychologist **Mary Rothbart** and her colleagues suggest that particular temperaments emerge as children's brains develop distinctive capacities for responding to impulses and regulating attention, emotions, and activity (Rothbart, 2007; Rothbart & Bates, 2006; Rothbart et al., 2009). At birth, children react rather automatically to changes in stimuli by crying, thrashing their limbs, and looking away. But as they grow, children develop new ways to deal with sensations and environmental demands. For example, fear prompts children to be wary of potentially dangerous things, whereas a sense of initiative incites children to explore the world. Restraint emerges gradually, as children learn to direct their attention and actions flexibly, according to social rules and requirements and the likely consequences of possible decisions. These distinctive ways of responding to stimuli (i.e., reacting automatically, withdrawing out of fear, exploring with enthusiasm, and directing activity intentionally) are housed in different parts of the brain. As these various systems develop, they may be weak or strong, collectively creating individual differences in children's temperaments.

According to Rothbart and her colleagues, children may be low or high, or somewhere in between, on three dimensions of temperament:

- Children who score high on *extraversion/surgency* show high levels of optimistic anticipation, impulsivity, activity, and sensation seeking, and they smile and laugh often.
- Children who score high on *negative affectivity* tend to be shy and are often fearful, frustrated, sad, uncomfortable, and not easily soothed.[10]
- Children who show high levels of *effortful control* are proficient in strategically focusing and shifting their attention. They effectively plan for the future, suppress inappropriate responses, and take pleasure in complex and novel stimuli.

These three temperamental dimensions are fairly stable, partly due to genetic factors. Identical twins reared in different homes often have similar temperaments (N. D. Henderson, 1982; Malykh, Gindina, & Nadyseva, 2009; Tellegren, Lykken, Bouchard, & Wilcox, 1988). Children's genetic makeup apparently affects their temperaments through its effects on brain structure and chemistry (Kagan, Snidman, Vahn, & Towsley, 2007; Rothbart et al., 2009). That

---

[10] Some recent research indicates that negative affectivity may actually be two separate dimensions, one related to fear and distress, and the other based in frustration, irritability, and anger (Rothbart & Bates, 2006).

is, genes affect the density of synaptic connections in various parts of the brain and the concentrations of chemicals that make neurons fire or remain inactive.

Stability in temperament is further made possible by persistent characteristics in children's environments. The typical ways in which parents express or withhold affection and respond to children's displays of emotions influence the manner in which children deal with conflict, stressful circumstances, and novel events. Thus, children who live in a family that offers relatively little support tend to become irritable and aggressive as they grow (Fanti & Henrich, 2010). Conversely, children whose family members are affectionate are likely to become agreeable and well adjusted.

Yet environments also lead to modifications in children's temperament. Parents and other people socialize children to express their emotions in ways that are valued in their culture. In Western cultures, children are expected to be reasonably outgoing with peers. Parents sometimes encourage children who are shy to interact with peers in child care settings and schools, and as a result, children become more socially confident (Arcus, 2001; N. A. Fox, Henderson, Rubin, Calkins, & Schmidt, 2001). In China, acting in a socially restrained manner is valued, as you can learn more about in the Development in Culture feature "Temperament in China."

Personality

Over time, a child integrates biologically based emotional tendencies with his or her experiences, relationships, and intellectual interests. The result is a distinctive and somewhat stable personality. A child who is passionate about finding order in the material world may, as a 4-year-old, have an insatiable curiosity for dinosaurs; as an 8-year-old, be fascinated with space and aeronautics; as a 12-year-old, learn all he can about bridges and buildings; as a 16-year-old, become an expert in computers; and as a young man, prepare for a career in civil engineering.

Despite their relative stability, children's personalities can change slightly (and sometimes significantly) in response to the demands of particular situations. Thus a 12-year-old girl may be highly sociable (e.g., talking frequently, smiling at others, and befriending many peers) but find it difficult to make new friends when her family moves across the country and encounters unfamiliar customs and values. The demands of particular settings within a community can likewise affect which aspects of complex personalities children reveal. Hence, a given child may be spontaneous and cheerful on the playground but distracted and agitated in the classroom.

Recognizing that personality changes somewhat over time and across situations, psychologists have nevertheless found five relatively stable dimensions of personality:

- *Extraversion*—extent to which one is socially outgoing
- *Agreeableness*—extent to which one is warm and sympathetic
- *Conscientiousness*—extent to which one is persistent and organized
- *Neuroticism*—extent to which one is anxious and fearful
- *Openness*—extent to which one is curious and imaginative

These five dimensions were originally identified with adults, but they also characterize children to some degree (John, Caspi, Robins, Moffitt, & Stouthamer-Loeber, 1994; McCrae, Costa, & Busch, 1986; Woods & Hampson, 2010). As with constancy in temperament, the stability of personality dimensions is due partly to genetics and partly to consistency in children's environments.

Helping Children Be Themselves

Teachers can plan lessons and activities that address the varied temperaments and personalities of youngsters in their care. Here are some specific suggestions:

• **Identify the kinds of temperaments that you naturally prefer, as well as those that push your buttons.** Many teachers prefer to work with children who are curious, happy, obedient, hard working, cooperative, intelligent, cautious, and efficient (Keogh, 2003; Valiente, Lemery-Chalfant, Swanson, & Reiser, 2008; Wentzel, 2000). Teachers tend to find it less rewarding to work with children who are easily distracted, angry or irritable, disruptive, and exceptionally assertive. When teachers come to realize that they automatically (and often

DEVELOPMENT IN CULTURE
Temperament in China

China has a population of over 1.3 billion people, 265 million of whom are children ranging in age from infancy through 14 years (X. Chen & Wang, 2010). Fifty-six separate ethnic groups exist in China, and the country is rapidly shifting from reliance on a centrally planned financial system to a market economy with strong international ties.

Obviously, children throughout China are exposed to many distinct customs. Yet common cultural beliefs and practices pervade family and community life in China. Confucianism offers especially prominent guidelines (X. Chen & Wang, 2010). Confucius (551–479 B.C.) was a highly influential philosopher who lived during a time of significant social upheaval, when China was making the transition from slavery to a feudal society, and he espoused practices for restoring a harmonious social order. Moral standards in Confucianism include benevolence, righteousness, propriety, and wisdom. According to the Confucian code, children are expected to pledge obedience and respect to their parents, and parents in turn must guide and discipline their children. Children are similarly expected to respect their teachers and other authority figures and to be considerate of peers as well.

Taoism is another prevalent belief system in China. Taoism advocates internal harmony by being soft and tender (X. Chen & Wang, 2010). People are advised to be flexible, adjust to life circumstances, and refrain from struggles over material wealth. In the ideologies of both Confucianism and Taoism,

SERENITY. This young boy walks quietly with his grandmother In Shaxi Village in Yunnan Province, China.

children are directed to be calm, honorable, and attentive to the needs of the group.

Confucian and Taoist ideals both prescribe that children should remain relatively quiet, compliant, and emotionally restrained in the family, classroom, and peer settings so as to offer mutual support to others in the group. As you might anticipate, children require a lot of guidance from adults before they reliably overcome their own impulses and defer to the needs of others. This socialization begins early. Chinese parents regularly encourage young children to tone down emotional expressions to muted, socially acceptable levels. In one experimental study, Chinese infants produced less facial movement, fewer smiles, and less crying than did European American infants (Camras et al., 1998).

Chinese parents also encourage children to temper their independent exploratory behaviors. In an observational study, two-year-old Chinese children were more likely than Canadian children of the same age to stay close to mothers in the presence of a stranger and unfamiliar toys (X. Chen et al., 1998). In addition, Chinese children are expected to abide by basic rules even when parents are not present to oversee their conduct. In another experimental study, Chinese toddlers more willingly put away toys without their mother's intervention than did Canadian toddlers (X. Chen, Rubin, et al., 2003).

As they grow older, Chinese children prefer controlled behavior in peers. Shy Chinese preschool children are more likely to be accepted by peers than are shy Canadian children by their peers (X. Chen, DeSouza, Chen, & Wang, 2006). However, it appears that shyness is manifested in several distinct ways in China (Y. Xu, Farver, Chang, Zhang, & Yu, 2007). Children who exhibit *regulated shyness* show social restraint that is consistent with Chinese customs. They do not draw attention to themselves, are modest and unassuming, and are considerate of peers. In comparison, children who exhibit *anxious shyness* are overwhelmed with negative emotions such that they find it difficult to behave appropriately in social settings. These children find it too stressful to enter peer groups and instead stay on the periphery. Regulated-shy children have an advantage over anxious-shy children in China, probably because children with the former characteristics are able to insinuate themselves into groups whereas the latter are not (Y. Xu et al., 2007).

Curiously, biological factors seem to play a small role in Chinese children being emotionally controlled. Genetic factors appear partly responsible for Chinese infants displaying fewer smiles and more vigorously withdrawing from stressful circumstances than is the case with Caucasian infants (Kagan, 2010). Thus, it seems that Chinese society enhances a modest biologically based temperament for emotional restraint with cultural values for serenity.

---

unconsciously) respond in certain ways to particular temperaments, they can take the first steps toward holding their biases in check.

- **Adjust to young children's stylistic ways of responding to the world.** Warmly accepting children's personal ways of regulating their attention is an important service that adults can provide to children (Rudasill, Gallagher, & White, 2010). To meet the needs of active infants, caregivers might permit them to explore and move often. In contrast, infants who show a lower activity level may sit contentedly and let the world come to them (A. Thomas & Chess,

1977; Zero to Three, 2002). With infants who show a lower activity level, caregivers might sit quietly with them, talk softly about pictures in a book, and acknowledge their interests in toys. With older children, teachers can observe children's focus of attention, affectionately remind distractible children to stay engaged in lessons, and offer other opportunities for free choice.

• **Consider children's temperaments when forming groups.** Teachers can help children who are shy or impulsive by pairing them with peers who might compensate for their limitations. A first-grade teacher might plan a Halloween activity of making "dirt" cake, knowing she can count on one boy to be methodical in measuring cocoa and other ingredients. She could pair him with another boy who will attack the project enthusiastically but without restraint; together, they might make a good combination. However, because there is never any guarantee that temperamentally dissimilar children will work effectively together, you need to monitor the evolving dynamics of such groups once you form them.

• **Allow children to apply their natural strengths, but also encourage them to try out new strategies for learning.** Permitting children to choose from among a few specified options is an important way to respect children's individuality. For instance, when children are asked to report on a book they have read, they might choose from an array of formats, such as a written analysis, poster, or oral presentation. Yet children are naturally inclined to remain in their comfort zone and can benefit from occasional practice of their less developed talents. A child who has trouble concentrating may be taught to use attention-focusing strategies, and a child who chooses books impulsively might be asked to prepare a checklist of desirable topics to refer to when selecting a new book at the library.

• **Communicate your expectations about acceptable behaviors.** When adults make expectations explicit and consistently enforce compliance, children with many kinds of temperaments and personalities thrive (Denno, Carr, & Bell, 2010; Keogh, 2003). Those who are apprehensive about doing the right thing can be assured that they are indeed acting in an acceptable manner. Others who are inclined to act impulsively can be reminded of rules, consequences for misbehavior, and strategies they can use to keep track of their behaviors.

• **Set up routines that youngsters can follow.** Most children prefer a schedule that is somewhat predictable (H. A. Davis, 2003). Children adjust to activities more easily when they know what to expect, for example, when they know that after they arrive at school in the morning, they are to place their backpacks and jackets in preassigned places, go straight to their desks, and begin writing a new entry in their class journals. Of course, some variation is inevitable and desirable, but familiar routines help everyone relax. Children also need to be advised of the procedures of a classroom, such as how to line up or disperse for lunch, and the circumstances under which they can sharpen their pencils, use the restroom, and ask for assistance.

• **Help children cope with changes in routines.** Children with certain temperaments and personalities (for instance, those who are timid or irritable) may find alterations to routines to be difficult (Keogh, 2003). To help these children, educators can tell youngsters ahead of time about anticipated modifications in school personnel, schedules, or rules. Elementary school children can be introduced to a substitute teacher the week before their regular teacher departs for an extended family leave. Middle school adolescents can be shown the blueprints for a new auditorium before the existing structure is leveled, and high school students should receive a copy of a new code of conduct for their school before it is instituted. When changes *cannot* be anticipated ahead of time, children appreciate hearing as soon as possible about these alterations, especially those changes that may affect them personally.

• **Physically arrange the classroom to minimize disruptions and noise.** Defined pathways between desks and protected spaces in high-traffic areas can minimize tussles among children who are easily frustrated or lacking in social skills (K. Carter & Doyle, 2006; Emmer, Evertson, & Worsham, 2000). In addition, highly sensitive children may be overwhelmed by the chaos of the classroom and appreciate spending some time in a quieter setting. Children who are sensitive to sensory stimuli might occasionally be allowed to complete assignments in the school library.

• **Make appropriate adjustments for children who show unusually high or low levels on one or more personality dimensions.** Children with exceptional levels on particular personality dimensions stand out from other children. These children need to be accepted for who they are but also need accommodations that guide their learning, peer relationships, emotional expression, and motivation to follow rules. Let's consider how educators might adjust to some unusually high or low levels of the personality dimensions we introduced earlier:

- *Extraversion.* Extraverted children are active, assertive, emotionally expressive, talkative, enthusiastic, and socially outgoing. These children often appreciate opportunities to work on projects with peers. Teachers might occasionally offer a public forum (such as a dramatic performance) for self-expression. Teachers can intersperse opportunities for physical movement around quiet activities to give these children needed exercise. Yet some exuberant children have trouble attending to learning activities and need gentle reminders from teachers to stay focused (Rimm-Kaufman et al., 2002). In contrast, children who are shy may benefit from private conversations with teachers and friendly invitations from peers and adults to join in a game.

- *Agreeableness.* Agreeable children are warm, responsive, generous, kind, sympathetic, and trusting. They may be pleased when adults and other children notice and comment on their cooperative spirit. Children who are less prone to be agreeable and socially sensitive may benefit if teachers encourage them to compliment peers, share toys, offer comfort to others in distress, and voice opinions without insulting people. Extremely irritable children are at risk for developing behavior problems but usually can learn to adjust more effectively when assisted by school counselors, psychologists, or doctors (Aman et al., 2009; Ehrler, Evans, & McGhee, 1999).

- *Conscientiousness.* Conscientious children are attentive, persistent in activities, organized, and responsible. Teachers can admire the persistence and organization shown by these children and point out how their style pays off in well-designed work products. Children who follow lower standards can be taught to set appropriate goals, resist counterproductive urges, and monitor their own progress toward goals (Muris, Meesters, & Rompelberg, 2006).

- *Neuroticism.* Neurotic children are anxious, fearful, lacking in confidence, and self-pitying. These children need support in dealing with negative feelings (Kwok, Hughes, & Luo, 2007). They also need encouragement to try challenging tasks they might otherwise avoid. Children who are relaxed and confident thrive when given continuous support from adults. No one is self-assured all the time, however, and adults can express extra support when normally confident children face momentous losses, personal failures, or traumatic events.

- *Openness.* Children who are open are curious, eager to explore their world, and imaginative. They can be encouraged to exercise their budding skills in many contexts. However, curious children are not always motivated to achieve in school and may need encouragement from teachers to tackle conventional academic assignments (Abe, 2005). Those who are less driven to explore art, literature, history, and the scientific world may need to be shown the intrigue and beauty of these and other fields.

• **Recognize the complexity of children's personalities.** The various dimensions of temperament and personality combine in a myriad of creative ways that can both delight and tax adults. A teacher may have one child who is socially outgoing but a bit anxious and not terribly agreeable; another child who is self-confident and conscientious, but somewhat conforming and slow to exercise her imagination; another who worries constantly and craves approval from adults but is quietly curious and thoughtful; and many more other children, each with an individual profile. As you can see, every child has special needs when it comes to temperament and personality.

The Developmental Trends table "Emotional and Personal Development at Different Age Levels" encapsulates what you have learned about children's attachment, emotional qualities, and temperaments and personalities. By now it should be abundantly clear that children are well served when adults appreciate their individual qualities, a theme we explore further in the final section.

DEVELOPMENTAL TRENDS
Emotional and Personal Development at Different Age Levels

AGE	WHAT YOU MIGHT OBSERVE	DIVERSITY	IMPLICATIONS
Infancy (Birth–2 Years) 	• Attachment behaviors (seeking contact with caregiver when afraid, hurt, or hungry; being sufficiently relaxed in the presence of caregiver to explore the environment) • Distress at separation from caregiver • Increasing repertoire of ways to communicate feelings; crying and smiling gradually supplemented with laughter, hand gestures, and words • Beginning ability to soothe self by sucking thumb, hugging favorite blankets, pulling on ear, and so on	• Some children have multiple attachments and move easily from one caregiver to another, whereas other children may have a single close attachment and strongly protest separation from this person. • Some cultures encourage small children to express all their feelings, including anger and sadness. Other cultures place group harmony above self-expression and discourage infants and toddlers from expressing certain feelings; instead, they teach restraint.	• Model productive emotional expressions, and remain calm when infants and toddlers cry and shout. • Be responsive and sensitive to the needs of infants—they are learning to trust you as you help them satisfy their needs. • Seek professional guidance when you encounter infants who appear to have serious attachment problems. • Take infants' separation distress seriously, and provide them with lots of reassurance. • Tell parents and other family members what you do to comfort their babies after they leave and how long it takes for the children to settle down.
Early Childhood (2–6 Years) 	• Desire to be close to parents when afraid, hurt, or uncertain • Wide variety of emotions (e.g., happiness, sadness, fear, anger, disgust) • Familiarity with and use of labels for basic emotions • Emergence of self-conscious emotions (e.g., pride, embarrassment, guilt)	• Children vary in the number of close attachments they form, the extent to which they find reassurance in these attachment figures, and their responses to strangers. Some cling tightly to caregivers; others venture confidently to explore new environments and strangers. • Children vary in how they express their emotions. Some are very controlled, especially in masking anger and sadness. Others are more expressive.	• Realize that young children may initially be cautious or fearful in a new classroom or other group; they will become more confident as they begin to form attachments to their teachers. • Be patient in establishing relationships with young children; some may form attachments quickly, but others may take several weeks or months before trusting adults outside the home. • Teach appropriate ways of handling negative emotions. Encourage children to "use their words" rather than push or hit when angry.
Middle Childhood (6–10 Years) 	• Continued close relationships with family members • Increasing number of bonds with people outside the family, including peers, teachers, and other adults • Increasing ability to regulate emotions	• Children are emotionally affected by major family disruptions (e.g., divorce of parents, death or illness of a family member). Changes in family membership may temporarily undermine children's security. • Some children have strong role models for emotional regulation (e.g., a parent may express negative feelings in productive ways).	• Incorporate discussions of emotional states into the curriculum; for example, address the feelings of characters in literature and history. • Model appropriate ways of expressing feelings. • Respect cultural differences in regulating emotions.
Early Adolescence (10–14 Years) 	• Frequent fluctuations in mood, partly as a result of hormonal changes and everyday stressful experiences • Careful regulation of emotions (e.g., hiding joy about a good grade in order to appear "cool" to peers)	• Individual adolescents differ in the extent to which they conform to typical gender roles in expressing emotions. • Some adolescents tend to internalize their stresses (e.g., experiencing depression or anxiety); others respond with overt behaviors (e.g., being violent, breaking the law).	• Be a supportive listener when young people want to share their anxieties. • Keep in mind that some moodiness is normal in the middle school grades. However, talk with parents or the school counselor about the emotional well-being of youngsters who seem especially troubled.

DEVELOPMENTAL TRENDS (continued)

AGE	WHAT YOU MIGHT OBSERVE	DIVERSITY	IMPLICATIONS
Late Adolescence (14–18 Years)	• Seeking emotional intimacy with same-sex and opposite-sex peers • Continued attachments to parents, but with strong preferences for parental affection to be demonstrated in private rather than in public • Increasing ability to be comforted by peers when distressed	• For some adolescents, relationships with parents are full of conflict and offer little emotional support. • Some adolescents use drugs and alcohol to cope with negative emotions. • Some adolescents (girls especially) ruminate over small setbacks and disappointments. • Some adolescents (boys especially) hide their true feelings and project the impression that difficult experiences do not bother them.	• When adolescents are in minor conflicts with their parents, help them understand that most parents truly want the best for their children and behave accordingly (albeit sometimes punitively or coercively). • Refer youngsters to a school counselor when relationships with parents are extremely negative or the youngsters show signs of depression. • Ask adolescents to reflect on the emotional experiences of fictional characters and historical figures.

SUPPORTING CHILDREN AND ADOLESCENTS WHO FACE EMOTIONAL CHALLENGES

Some children and adolescents have more than their share of negative experiences, to the point where their ability to tackle everyday problems is disrupted. These youngsters may have trouble handling intense emotions, expressing emotions in culturally acceptable ways, or responding appropriately to other people's anger. Other children find it difficult to follow everyday rules in families, schools, and society, and to act with consideration for others' feelings and welfare. Yet as you saw in Merv's resilience in the opening case study and in Erik Erikson's optimism about the potential of people to recover from life's hardships, many youngsters overcome significant problems, especially when they receive steady support at home, in school, and in the community. Let's look at some of the serious emotional and behavioral problems children face as well as effective strategies for supporting their resilience.

Common Emotional and Behavioral Disorders

Emotional and behavioral problems in youngsters are more common than many adults realize. Approximately 25 percent of young people in the United States are affected by a mental health difficulty sometime during childhood (Braaten, 2011; Tolani & Brooks-Gunn, 2006).

Depression

People with **depression** feel exceptionally sad, discouraged, and hopeless; they may also feel restless, sluggish, helpless, worthless, or unusually guilty. Children and adolescents with depression may be unresponsive to caregivers, withdraw from social interactions with peers, report such physical complaints as headaches and stomach pain, and appear consistently sad and irritable (Braaten, 2011; Oltmanns & Emery, 2007). Depressed youngsters may have trouble concentrating, lose interest in their usual activities, have little appetite, and have difficulty sleeping (American Psychiatric Association, 1994). A variation of depression, *bipolar disorder,* occurs when individuals experience periods of extreme elation and hyperactivity as well as periods of deep depression.

The specific symptoms of depression vary somewhat from culture to culture. The American Psychiatric Association (APA) provides several examples of how depression might manifest itself in different cultures:

> Complaints of "nerves" and headaches (in Latino and Mediterranean cultures), of weakness, tiredness, or "imbalance" (in Chinese and Asian cultures), of problems of the "heart" (in Middle Eastern cultures), or of being "heartbroken" (among Hopi). (APA, 1994, p. 324)

Preparing for Your Licensure Examination

Your teaching test might ask you about how you can help children with emotional and behavioral disorders.

depression
Emotional condition characterized by significant sadness, discouragement, hopelessness, and, in children, irritability.

Many instances of depression and bipolar disorder probably have biological, and possibly genetic, roots (Cicchetti, Rogosch, & Toth, 1997; Griswold & Pessar, 2000; Hankin et al. 2009). These conditions tend to run in families, are often foreshadowed by temperamental moodiness, and may reflect chemical imbalances in the brain. Environmental factors also play a role in depression; for instance, the death of a loved one, mental illness or marital conflict in parents, child maltreatment, poverty, and inadequate schools may bring about or worsen depressive symptoms (Cicchetti et al., 1997; Hankin et al., 2009; Oltmanns & Emery, 2007). When individuals succumb to extreme stress with a depressive episode, the event may alter their neurological chemistry, making it more likely that they will suffer another depressive episode in the future (Akiskal & McKinney, 1973; Luby, 2010; Siever & Davis, 1985).

Depression rates in children vary by age and gender. Before adolescence, depression and bipolar disorder are rare. Their prevalence increases dramatically during adolescence. By the age of 19, approximately one in three girls and one in five boys has been seriously depressed one or more times (Oltmanns & Emery, 2007). Higher rates of depression may occur in girls beginning during adolescence because of hormone changes and the tendency of girls to ruminate on their problems (Hilt & Nolen-Hoeksema, 2009; Nevid, Rathus, & Greene, 2006).

Youth with serious depression or bipolar disorder are at risk for considering or committing suicide (M. G. Sawyer et al., 2010). Depressed individuals who contemplate suicide often believe that they face problems they cannot solve or have extreme emotional pain they wish to end. Suicide rates are low among 10- to 14-year-olds but increase eightfold among 15- to 24-year-olds (Nevid et al., 2006).

The overwhelming despair and high frequency of suicide that accompany depression make it a condition that educators must take seriously. Through their daily contact with youngsters, teachers have numerous opportunities to observe children's moods and so may become concerned about possible depression in children. (Friends and family, though they may have closer ties to youngsters, may not comprehend or accept how serious the problem is.) Educators will want to offer emotional reassurance to young people who appear troubled, but they should consult with principals and counselors if they suspect severe depression or another serious emotional disturbance.

Anxiety Disorder

In its milder forms, anxiety is a common and very "normal" emotion. But some people, including some children and adolescents, worry excessively and find it difficult to control their worrisome thoughts and feelings; in other words, they have an **anxiety disorder** (APA, 2000). Children with a *generalized anxiety disorder* tend to worry excessively about a wide variety of things, including their academic achievement and potential catastrophic events such as wars or hurricanes. Other individuals have more specific anxiety disorders, perhaps worrying excessively about gaining weight, having a serious illness, being away from family and home, feeling embarrassed in public, or being scared to go to school (Ollendick, Costa, & Benoit, 2010; Oltmanns & Emery, 2007).

Anxiety disorders tend to run in families (Last, Hersen, Kazdin, Francis, & Grubb, 1987; Ogliari et al., 2010). Family environment also seems to play a role in the onset of anxiety disorders. Some evidence suggests that a number of anxious children have had insecure attachments to their parents and have been exposed to aloof and critical parenting (Luijk et al., 2010; P. S. Moore, Whaley, & Sigman, 2004; Oltmanns & Emery, 2007).

Conduct Disorder

When children and adolescents display a chronic pattern of misbehavior and show little shame or guilt about their wrongdoings, they are sometimes identified as having a **conduct disorder**. Youngsters who display a conduct disorder ignore the rights of others in ways that are unusual for their age. Common symptoms include aggression toward people and animals (e.g., initiating physical fights, forcing someone into sexual activity, torturing animals), destruction of property (e.g., setting fires, painting graffiti), theft and deceitfulness (e.g., breaking into cars, lying about shoplifting so as not to be caught), and serious violations of

anxiety disorder
Chronic emotional condition characterized by excessive, debilitating worry.

conduct disorder
Chronic emotional condition characterized by lack of concern for the rights of others.

rules (e.g., ignoring reasonable curfews, being truant from school) (APA, 2000; Gelhorn et al., 2009). Approximately 2 to 6 percent of school-age youths could be classified as having a conduct disorder, with rates being three or four times higher for boys than for girls (Kazdin, 1997).

It is important to note that one or two antisocial acts do not necessarily indicate a serious conduct problem. Conduct disorders are more than a matter of "kids being kids" or "sowing wild oats." Instead, they represent deep-seated and persistent disregard for the rights and feelings of others. Youth with conduct disorders tend to see the world through conflict-colored glasses, for example, by always assuming that others have hostile intentions toward them (Dodge et al., 2003).

Conduct disorder is manifested somewhat differently depending on youngsters' gender and age. Among young people with conduct disorder, boys are more likely to steal and be aggressive; girls are apt to engage in sexual misbehavior. Conduct disorder is especially serious (and likely to foreshadow adjustment problems in the adult years) when it is manifested before adolescence begins (J. G. Barrett, 2005; Drugli, Fossum, Larsson, & Morch, 2010; Frick, Barry, & Kamphaus, 2010). Youngsters who exhibit conduct disorders beginning in childhood are likely to have many problems in adulthood, including antisocial and criminal behavior, frequent changes in employment, high divorce rates, little participation in families and community groups, and early death. In contrast, conduct disorders that don't emerge until adolescence are often the result of affiliation with peers who engage in delinquent behavior; as these late-onset offenders mature and find new social contacts, they tend to stop engaging in destructive acts.

As is true for the emotional disorders we've previously considered, biology may be *partly* to blame for conduct disorders. Children and adolescents with conduct disorders may have difficulty inhibiting aggressive impulses, perhaps as a result of brain damage or other neurological conditions (Fishbein et al., 2006; Nevels, Dehon, Alexander, & Gontkovsky, 2010). Families may be influential as well: Conduct disorders are more common when children's parents provide little affection and are highly critical and harsh in their physical punishment (Blackson et al., 1999; R. Chen & Simons-Morton, 2009; G. R. Patterson, DeBaryshe, & Ramsey, 1989). Neighborhoods can also be a factor in conduct disorders, as when children witness violence in their communities and later become physically aggressive themselves (Ridenour, Clark, & Cottler, 2009; Shahinfar, Kupersmidt, & Matza, 2001).

Supporting Youngsters with Emotional and Behavioral Problems

Despite their serious problems, young people with mental health conditions are generally able to adjust effectively when participating in counseling and other mental health treatments. Sensitive attention from teachers and other school staff can also be helpful. Educators can consider these strategies:

• **Show an interest in the well-being of all children and adolescents.** Many youngsters with emotional disorders have few positive ties with individuals outside of school, and so their relationships with caring teachers, school counselors, and other professionals are all the more important. Having a supportive relationship with a teacher protects a child from everyday stresses and gives the child extra assistance when necessary (Valiente et al., 2008). The many "little things" educators do each day, including greeting youngsters warmly, expressing concern when they seem worried, and lending a ready ear when they want to share their ideas or frustrations can make a world of difference for children (S. C. Diamond, 1991).

• **Teach social skills.** Many children and adolescents with emotional problems have difficulty maintaining friendships (Asher & Coie, 1990; Kingery, Erdley, Marshall, Whitaker, & Reuter, 2010). You can support these youngsters by encouraging them to practice particular social skills, such as saying something friendly to a peer and resolving conflicts by talking openly about the problem (Gillham, Reivich, Jaycox, & Seligman, 1995; Turnbull, Turnbull, & Wehmeyer, 2010).[11] Supervised volunteer activities, for example, joining community clean-up projects or tutoring younger children at school, provide an especially productive outlet for students with emotional and behavioral problems to practice social skills (Turnbull et al., 2010).

---

[11]We offer additional recommendations for fostering children's social skills in Chapters 12, 14, and 15.

• **Provide extra structure for youngsters who have high levels of anxiety.** One especially effective strategy is to communicate expectations for performance in clear and concrete terms. Highly anxious youngsters perform better in well-structured environments, such as classrooms with explicit expectations for academic achievement and social behavior (Stipek, 1993; Tobias, 1977). When they know what to expect and how they will be evaluated, these young people are more inclined to relax, enjoy themselves, and learn.

• **Set reasonable limits for behavior.** All children need to learn that aggression, destruction of property, and stealing are unacceptable. Establishing rules for appropriate behavior and imposing consequences (e.g., loss of privileges) for infractions provide the structure and guidance many children need to keep undesirable behaviors in check (Turnbull et al., 2010).

• **Give children and adolescents a sense that they have some control.** Some young people, especially those who consistently defy authority figures, often behave even less appropriately when people try to control them. With such youngsters, it is important that practitioners not get into power struggles, situations where only one person "wins" and the other inevitably loses (S. C. Diamond, 1991). Instead, adults might create situations in which children conform to expectations yet also know they have some control over what happens to them.

• **Advise parents about their children's needs.** Parents whose children have emotional and behavioral problems may appreciate advice on meeting children's emotional needs. Depending on the particular challenges that children face, parents may need guidance in establishing clear rules, recognizing children's good behaviors, and helping children to understand and regulate their emotions (Garland, Augustyn, & Stein, 2007; Turnbull et al., 2010).

• **Be alert for signs that a child or adolescent may be contemplating suicide.** Seriously depressed youngsters may fail to reach out for help when they believe that no one cares about them, think that they should be able to solve their problems on their own, or worry about their reputation if they were to disclose their mental anguish (Freedenthal & Stiffman, 2007). Fortunately, seriously depressed youngsters often give off signs (consciously or not) that they may be thinking about taking their own lives. Warning signs include the following (M. M. Jensen, 2005; L. L. Kerns & Lieberman, 1993; A. R. Roberts, 2008; B. M. Wagner, 2009):

- Signs of depression and helplessness
- Sudden withdrawal from social relationships (possibly after being rejected by peers or breaking up with a boyfriend or girlfriend)
- Disregard for personal appearance
- Serious health problems (e.g., a debilitating injury from an accident or a chronic condition resulting from an eating disorder)
- A dramatic personality change
- A sudden elevation in mood
- A preoccupation with death and morbid themes
- Serious problems at school, home, or in the community (e.g., expulsion from school, death of a friend, pregnancy, or arrest for illegal behavior)
- Overt or veiled threats (e.g., "I won't be around much longer")
- Actions that indicate "putting one's affairs in order" (e.g., giving away prized possessions)
- Substance abuse
- Preference for certain kinds of music (e.g., heavy metal rock music with morbid themes)
- Efforts to obtain suicidal means (e.g., medications, ropes, or guns)
- In some cases, impulsive personality

Adults must watch for these and other possible warning signs and take these behaviors seriously, particularly if they see more than one of the signs on the list. Educators should show genuine concern for potentially suicidal youngsters and seek trained help from a school psychologist or counselor *immediately* (McCoy, 1994; Spirito, Valeri, Boergers, & Donaldson, 2003).

SUMMARY

Erikson's Theory of Psychosocial Development

Erikson proposed that psychosocial characteristics emerge over the course of eight stages, with the first beginning in infancy and the last occurring in old age. Erikson blazed many trails for later developmental scholars, yet the volumes of research inspired by his work have revealed that his theory does not accurately describe all aspects of social-emotional development.

Attachment

Ideally, children's first attachments are close and enduring bonds between themselves and their caregivers. Sensitive and responsive attention is the necessary ingredient for secure attachments, but children also contribute by returning affection. Secure attachments in the early years lead to positive social-emotional outcomes later on. However, attachments manifest themselves somewhat differently in different cultures, and the nature of people's attachments can change over time.

Emotion

Emotions have adaptive functions for young people, helping them decide how to act. Children and adolescents become increasingly able to regulate their emotions in ways that are both socially acceptable and personally satisfying. Individual differences in emotional functioning are the result of both biology (e.g., gender-specific hormones) and environment (e.g., socialization by parents, peers, and culture). Dealing with youngsters' emotions is an important aspect of teaching and working with children and adolescents.

Temperament and Personality

Children are born with dispositions to respond to the world and express their emotions in certain ways. These constitutional inclinations, called temperaments, are also affected by experience and social relationships. As children grow, they integrate their temperamental dimensions with their intellectual interests, habits, and other experiences into distinctive personalities. Teachers and other practitioners can help children enormously when they make accommodations for children's unique temperaments and personalities.

Supporting Children and Adolescents Who Face Emotional Problems

Some youngsters face serious emotional and behavioral problems that require thoughtful accommodation from adults. Youngsters with depression, an anxiety disorder, or a conduct disorder often benefit from professional intervention. In addition, teachers and other adults can offer reassurance, communicate expectations for appropriate behavior, and address children's personal concerns, such as getting along with peers and needing to exert some control over everyday decisions.

APPLYING CONCEPTS IN CHILD DEVELOPMENT

The exercises in this section will help you build your ability to apply your knowledge of child development in working with children.

Improving Your Observation Skills

On page 423, you examined pictures from two young children and were asked, "*What are these two children trying to communicate?*" Children often create "love notes" for their parents. These two notes communicate the children's simple, heartfelt affection for their moms. Ivy and Alex have chosen the same graphic device, a stacks of hearts, to represent the depth of their feelings for their mothers. Hearts are a common symbol of love in Western cultures. Young children often choose other devices as well, such as drawing themselves holding hands with a loved one.

On page 428, you examined a photograph of a mother holding an infant and were asked, "*What is this Native American mother doing to express her warmth to her toddler son?*" This mother is gently holding her son as she goes about her work. She is keeping the young boy physically close to her and offering comforting touch. Her gentle touch by itself would be calming and soothing for the child. In addition, with this contact, the mother is able to anticipate the child's needs and intervene before discomfort escalates. For example, when the boy is hungry, the mother would be able to feed him before distress grew uncontrollably.

Practicing for Your Licensure Examination

Many teaching tests require students to use what they have learned about child development in responses to brief vignettes and multiple-choice questions. You can practice for your licensure examination by reading about an 8-year-old boy's emotional outbursts at school and answering a series of questions.

The Girly Shirt

Read the case and then answer the questions at the end.

Eight-year-old Tim caused quite a disruption in class this morning. His teacher, Amy Fox, isn't quite sure why things got out of hand, and so she is meeting with Tim while the rest of the class is at lunch to learn what happened.

Ms. Fox: Things got out of control in class this morning, didn't they, Tim?

Tim: I guess they did.

Ms. Fox: Tell me what happened.

Tim: John and Steven were teasing me about my shirt. They really made me mad.

Ms. Fox: They were teasing you about your shirt? What did they say?

Tim: That it's too pink. That it's a "girly" color.

Ms. Fox: Really? I don't think it's too "girly" at all. In fact, I rather like that color on you. But anyway, you say the boys teased you about it. What did you do then?

Tim: I yelled at them. Then when you gave me that dirty look, they kept on laughing, and so I kept on yelling.

Ms. Fox: I see. John and Steven were certainly wrong to tease you about your clothes. I'll speak to them later. But right now I'm concerned about how you reacted to the situation. You were so loud that the class couldn't possibly continue with the lesson.

Tim: I know. I'm sorry.

Ms. Fox: I appreciate your apology, Tim. And I'd like to make sure that the next time someone hurts your feelings—maybe intentionally, maybe not—you don't blow up the way you did today. Let's come up with a plan for how you might keep your temper under better control.

Constructed-Response Question

1. What kind of plan might be effective in helping Tim control his anger?

Multiple-Choice Questions

2. What aspect of emotional development is Tim struggling with in this incident?

   a. Emotional regulation, because he is having trouble controlling his temper.

   b. Emotional contagion, because he is absorbing the feelings of the other boys.

   c. Empathy, because he shares the disdain that the other boys have about his shirt.

   d. Insecure attachment, because he is not able to use his peers as a safe haven.

3. Let's assume that Tim has been somewhat irritable since starting school. What factors might account for this temperament?

   a. Tim's temperament is the simple outgrowth of his unique genetic profile.

   b. Tim's temperament is the result of harsh and punitive parenting.

   c. Tim's temperament is the complex result of his genetic disposition, his family relationships, and his own choices and experiences.

   d. Although it appears that Tim's irritability has been stable, temperament changes dramatically from month to month and year to year, therefore it is not possible to identify any factors that account for his temperament.

Once you have answered these questions, compare your responses with those presented in Appendix A.

Improving Your Ability to Interpret Children's Artifacts and Reflections

Draw on what you've learned about emotional development as you analyze an adolescent's poem in this exercise.

Paint Me Like I Am

Many young people express their innermost thoughts and feelings through poetry. WritersCorps, an organization that cultivates the literacy skills of youth from disadvantaged urban neighborhoods, has published the poems of numerous young people. Delia Garcia, an adolescent from San Francisco, California, wrote a poem, *Paint Me Like I Am*, which was published by WritersCorps (2003). As you read Delia's poem, consider these questions:

- What kinds of emotions does Delia express in her poem?
- How might poetry help Delia cope with her complex feelings?

Paint Me Like I Am
Why don't you paint me
Like I am?
Paint me happy,
Laughing, running down a path of happiness
Paint me with a smile on my face.
Paint me with long wavy black hair
And my rosy cheeks.
Paint me with sunflowers, red and white roses.
Paint me with bears, rabbits and baby deer
In my arms, dancing around me.
Paint me somewhere wonderful
Somewhere where there's sunshine and
A light blue sky
With butterflies floating
Around that lovely sky.
Paint me without my sadness.
Paint me without my sorrow,
Paint me without my tears.
Paint me so my pain won't show.
Can you see the face telling you to paint me happy,
Paint me with my life, but most of all
Paint me free.
Delia Garcia[a]

(WritersCorps, 2003, p. 5)

Once you have analyzed the poem, compare your ideas with those presented in Appendix B. For further practice in analyzing children's artifacts and reflections, go to the Activities and Applications section in Chapter 11 of MyEducationLab.

[a]"Paint Me Like I Am" by Delia Garria from PAINT ME LIKE I AM: TEEN POEMS FROM WRITERSCORPS. Copyright © 2003 by WritersCorps. Reprinted with permission from WritersCorps.

Key Concepts

psychosocial stages (p. 418)
need for relatedness (p. 421)
attachment (p. 421)
ethological attachment theory
    (p. 422)
stranger anxiety (p. 423)

secure attachment (p. 424)
insecure-avoidant attachment
    (p. 424)
insecure-resistant attachment (p. 424)
disorganized and disoriented
    attachment (p. 425)

emotion (p. 434)
emotional contagion (p. 436)
self-conscious emotion (p. 436)
emotional regulation (p. 437)
empathy (p. 438)
anxiety (p. 441)

personality (p. 442)
depression (p. 449)
anxiety disorder (p. 450)
conduct disorder (p. 450)

PEARSON
myeducationlab

Now go to www.myeducationlab.com to:
- Take a Quiz to test your mastery of chapter objectives.
- Study chapter content with an individualized Study Plan.
- Deepen your understanding of particular concepts and principles with Review, Remediation, and Enrichment Exercises.
- Apply what you have learned in the chapter to your work with children in Building Teaching Skills and Dispositions exercises.
- Observe children and their unique contexts in Video Examples.

Chapter Twelve

Development of Self and Social Understandings

CASE STUDY: Theodore

At age 16, Theodore had an assignment to write about who he was as a person. Following is his response:

Hello. I'm Theodore. I am 16 years old and come from America. I'm a very happy person and have an optimistic view on life. Although life can be very challenging and confusing at times, I always think to myself it will be all right later on. I think everybody is equal and everybody should be treated the same, even though this is close to impossible.

I love to hang out with my friends and family. I think family is one of the most important things in life. I love my family and feel very lucky, and I am very appreciative for all they have done for me. Not everybody can have such a loving family though, and that makes me very sad. Occasionally I get great urges to go out and try to help people all around the world who are in need of support. But also at times I feel very helpless, and I feel like I can't do much to help, which makes me upset. Living in a small city in America is very great, but I know there is more out there in the world, and I wish I could experience living in a developing country. I have been able to travel to several countries and have friends around the world that I keep in contact with on Facebook.

I am just a sort-of average kid who is medium in height and underweight. I have longish brown hair and big feet. I like girls and some like me back. I love to play video games and watch movies. I also like to play any kind of sports with my friends especially Ultimate Frisbee.

I have no idea what I will be when I grow up. I am interested in SO many things, and it seems I will never be able to narrow it down. I am interested in computers/engineering, being a medical doctor of sorts, being an airplane pilot, and more. My biggest dream in life is to travel around the world as much as I can and learn about people, culture, food, history, language, religions, everything else I can learn about, everywhere in the world.

Throughout my life I have changed a lot physically and mentally. I look at the world very differently than I did even a few months ago, and I will probably think differently a couple months down the road. I grow more and more patient and less egocentric every day. I think I am going in the right direction except for a few things. Although I am smart and get good grades, I could work a lot harder in school and on other academic things. I could do extra homework. I find it hard to muster the gumption to work harder and do more academic things such as enter a spelling bee or science contest or something.

Well that's who I am today. Ask me again in a couple of years and see what I say!

- What does Theodore say about his personal characteristics?
- What challenges does Theodore face?

From the beginning of life, children experience themselves as unique human beings. As they mature, they increasingly reflect on their physical, social, and cognitive characteristics, and they appreciate how being situated in a particular family and social setting affects them. They realize that they share some qualities with other people but ultimately are one-of-a-kind individuals.

Early self-perceptions are concrete, focusing on appearance and tangible habits, but as is the case for Theodore, young people become introspective about their inner thoughts and unique personal experiences. Theodore is especially thoughtful about the blessings he has received from his family and community. He also sees himself as a person in transition.

In addition to thinking about themselves, children become quite proficient in identifying other people's perspectives. Theodore mentions that he is becoming less and less egocentric. He most certainly uses his perspective-taking skills in his relationships with family and friends and also in consideration of the needs of people in other societies.

As we shall see, children face certain challenges in developing a sense of self and thinking about other people. They absorb many of the messages that other people communicate about their worth, and some individuals unfortunately conclude that they are incapable, unattractive, and unwanted. A small number of children have difficulty understanding the perspectives of other people, and without intervention their relationships may suffer. Several challenges are age-related, as Theodore reveals in his age-typical concerns with overcoming his egocentrism, finding a career pathway, and figuring out how he can contribute to the world.

In this chapter, we examine children's developing sense of self and understandings of other people. We find that, like Theodore, children learn a great deal about themselves and other people from their personal experiences and the guidance of thoughtful adults.

SENSE OF SELF

Children's knowledge, beliefs, judgments, and feelings about themselves are collectively known as their **sense of self**. Particular elements of self-perceptions go by a variety of names, including self-concept, self-esteem, and self-worth. In general, one's *self-concept* addresses the question "Who am I?" Self-concept includes knowledge and beliefs about one's own characteristics, strengths, and weaknesses ("I get high grades in school," "My nose is a bit crooked"). The terms *self-esteem* and *self-worth* are synonymous and address the question "How good am I as a person?" They include judgments and feelings about one's own value and worth (e.g., "I am proud of my academic record," "I hate my crooked nose!").

Children's self-concept and self-worth are closely related (Byrne, 2002; Harter, 2006; Richman, Hope, & Mihalas, 2010). Children who focus largely on their negative features tend to believe they are unworthy people. Those who hold favorable impressions of their own characteristics tend to have high self-esteem. In this chapter, we examine self-concept and self-esteem together, often calling them self-perceptions but occasionally using the more specific terms when distinctions in the research merit their separation.

Purpose of the Self

Children's sense of self serves several important functions. It helps children understand things that happen to them ("Other kids keep asking me to join their teams, so I must be good at sports"). It motivates them to engage in behaviors to which others might respond approvingly ("If I'm nice to Russell, maybe he'll ask me to play with him"). It influences their reactions to events ("I'm upset that I'm not reading as well as my classmates"). And once they begin to look seriously at a particular *future self*, it helps them make choices appropriate for their goals ("If I want to become a veterinarian, then I need to take a biology class").

Perhaps most importantly, a sense of self helps a person find a comfortable niche in a complex world, one in which the individual feels capable, cared for, and respected. Many psychologists believe that human beings have a basic need to think of themselves as

sense of self
Knowledge, beliefs, judgments, and feelings about oneself as a person.

self-handicapping
Action that undermines one's own success as a way of protecting self-worth during difficult tasks.

competent, likable, and worthy individuals—that is, to achieve a positive sense of self-worth (Covington, 1992; J. S. Lawrence & Crocker, 2009; Meadows, 2010). To maintain a strong self-worth, people use a variety of tactics, including affiliating with other individuals who treat them kindly and putting themselves in situations where they can be successful.

Most children do seem to focus more on what they do well than on what they do poorly, and so they are predisposed to think rather highly of themselves (Diesendruck & Lindenbaum, 2009; Jacobs, Lanza, Osgood, Eccles, & Wigfield, 2002; Salley, Vannatta, Gerhardt, & Noll, 2010). Often they downplay areas that give them trouble (e.g., "Math is dumb"). They may also explain their shortcomings in ways that enable them to maintain a positive sense of self. In the "Memory: Middle Childhood" video in MyEducationLab, you can see 10-year-old David give a healthy, upbeat spin on why he doesn't recall as many words as he expects to. He predicts that he might recall 12 out of 12 words but actually recalls only 3. Here is David's positive interpretation:

David: Okay, shirt, carrot, bed. I'm sorry, I can't remember the rest of it. It's just, I don't know. My brain was turned off right now. I use it a lot during school hours so then I just like to relax. . . .

Interviewer: What did you do to remember the ones that you remembered?

David: Even though I said 12, I was just trying to challenge myself a little.

The need to protect one's self-worth is so strong that it sometimes leads children to create obstacles that give them an excuse for failing. In other words, youngsters occasionally do things that actually *undermine* their chances of success—a phenomenon known as **self-handicapping**. Self-handicapping takes a variety of forms, including the following:

- *Reducing effort.* Putting forth an obviously insufficient amount of effort to succeed
- *Setting unattainably high goals.* Working toward goals that even the most capable individuals couldn't achieve
- *Taking on too much.* Assuming so many responsibilities that no one could possibly accomplish them all
- *Procrastinating.* Putting off a task until success is virtually impossible
- *Cheating.* Presenting others' work as one's own
- *Using alcohol or drugs.* Taking substances that will inevitably reduce performance (Covington, 1992; D. Y. Ford, 1996; Shih, 2009; Urdan, Ryan, Anderman, & Gheen, 2002; Waschbusch, Craig, Pelham, & King, 2007)

ARTIFACT 12-1 Future selves. In these spontaneously created drawings, 10-year-old Alex envisions a variety of possible roles he might take on, some realistic and others fanciful.

It might seem paradoxical that youngsters who want to be successful would actually try to undermine their own accomplishments. But if they believe they are unlikely to succeed no matter what they do—and especially if failure will reflect poorly on their intelligence and ability—they increase their chances of *justifying* the failure. Self-handicapping is seen as early as elementary school and becomes increasingly common in the high school and college years (L. H. Chen, Wu, Kee, Lin, & Shui, 2009; Määttä, Nurmi, & Stattin, 2007; Urdan, 2004; Waschbusch et al., 2007).

Factors Influencing Self-Perceptions

To a considerable degree, children base their self-perceptions on their own past behaviors and performances (Damon, 1991; Ferla, Valcke, & Cai, 2009; Marsh, Trautwein, Lüdtke, Köller, & Baumert, 2005; Meadows, 2010). Thus children are more likely to believe they will succeed in school and later in college if they have been successful in their previous classes. Conversely, those children who struggle recurrently see their abilities as limited and their

MyEducationLab

Listen to David put a positive spin on why he didn't remember as many words as he had predicted in the "Memory: Middle Childhood" video. (Find Video Examples in Topic 12 of MyEducationLab.)

academic futures as bleak. A second grader named Tom, who had dyslexia, once described how he felt when struggling with reading in first grade:

> I falt like a losr. Like nobad likde me. I was afrad then kais wod tec me. Becacz I wased larning wale . . . I dan not whet to raed. I whoe whte to troe a book it my mom.
>
> *(I felt like a loser. Like nobody liked me. I was afraid that kids would tease me. Because I wasn't learning well . . . I did not want to read. I would want to throw a book at my mom.)*
> (N. F. Knapp, 2002, p. 74)

Adults also influence children's sense of self, and in several ways. First, adults communicate messages about children's strengths, limitations, and overall worth through words and deeds. Such lessons begin in infancy and extend throughout childhood and adolescence. When caregivers regularly nurture infants and show affection, infants learn not only that their caregivers can be loving but also that they themselves are worthy of being loved (Bretherton, 1991). As children grow, parents enhance children's sense of self by treating children warmly and communicating expectations for mature behavior. Parents who accept children as they are—applauding children's abilities and taking *in*abilities in stride—are likely to have children with high self-esteem. Parents who punish children for things they cannot do, without also praising them for things done well, are apt to have children with low self-esteem (Harter, 1999; Mulvaney & Mebert, 2010). Adults outside the family are influential as well. Teachers foster a positive sense of self when they have high yet realistic expectations for children's performance and offer the support children need to succeed at challenging goals (Dweck, 2000; M. J. Harris & Rosenthal, 1985; Leflot, Onghena, & Colpin, 2010).

Meanwhile, peers communicate information about children's social and athletic competence, perhaps by seeking out a child's companionship or ridiculing the child in front of others (Dweck, 2000; Harter, 2006; Salley et al., 2010). Peers contribute to children's sense of self in a second way as well: They provide information about what children "should" be able to do. How children evaluate themselves often depends on how their own performance compares to that of peers (Guay, Boivin, & Hodges, 1999; Marsh & Hau, 2003; Salley et al., 2010). Children who see themselves achieving at higher levels than age-mates usually develop a more positive sense of self than those who, like Tom (the boy with dyslexia), consistently find themselves falling short.

Membership in one or more groups can also influence children's sense of self, especially in adolescence (R. K. Baker & White, 2010; Lave & Wenger, 1991; M. B. Spencer, 2006). If you think back to your own school years, you might recall taking pride in a regional championship earned by one of your school's athletic teams or feeling good about a community service project completed by your club. Some young people affiliate with others on Facebook and other social networking sites on the Internet and in the process gain a sense of being part of a circle of friends (R. K. Baker & White, 2010). Being a member of an ethnic group similarly affects a youngster's sense of self, as we discover later in this chapter in our analysis of ethnic identity.

So far our discussion has focused primarily on the effects of children's experiences—that is, the effects of environment—on their self-perceptions. Biology has an impact as well. Studies with twins and other siblings indicate a fairly substantial genetic basis for self-esteem (Caprara et al., 2009; Raevuori et al., 2007). Genes probably affect self-esteem indirectly through their effects on partially inherited characteristics (e.g., temperaments, physical skills, cognitive abilities, and physical and cognitive disabilities) that contribute to children's successes and failures in social, athletic, and academic pursuits. Physical appearance also makes a difference: Adults and peers alike respond more favorably to children who are physically attractive (Harter, Whitesell, & Junkin, 1998; S. H. W. Mares, de Leeuw, Scholte, & Engels, 2010).

Developmental Trends in the Self

Children's physical, cognitive, and social abilities change with age, and their perceptions of themselves shift accordingly. Researchers have observed the following developmental trends in sense of self:

Children construct increasingly multifaceted understandings of who they are. Young children define themselves in terms of a few specific, concrete, easily observable characteristics and behaviors. Children in the preschool and early elementary grades can distinguish between a few general aspects of themselves, for example, how competent they are in daily activities and how much family and friends seem to like them (Davis-Kean & Sandler, 2001; Harter, 2006; E. Reese, Yan, Jack, & Hayne, 2010). As they grow older, they make finer and finer discriminations. By the upper elementary grades, they realize that they may be more or less advanced in their academic work, athletic activities, classroom behavior, likability among peers, and physical attractiveness. By adolescence, they also have self-perceptions about their competence at adult-like tasks and romantic appeal. Adolescents begin to describe their characteristics and behaviors as reflecting such intangible qualities as being "technologically savvy" or "moody" (D. Hart, 1988; Harter, 2006; Meadows, 2010).

Improving Your Observation Skills

Comparing self-descriptions. When her children were younger, Jeanne once asked them to describe themselves. Read their self-descriptions, and then answer the following question: What kinds of developmental trends do you notice in these responses? Compare your response with the explanation at the end of the chapter.

Jeff (age 6): I like animals. I like making things. I do good in school. I'm happy. Blue eyes. Yellow hair. Light skin.

Alex (age 9): I have brown hair, brown eyes. I like wearing short-sleeved shirts. My hair is curly. I was adopted. I was born in Denver. I like all sorts of critters. The major sport I like is baseball. I do fairly well in school. I have a lizard, and I'm going to get a second one.

Tina (age 12): I'm cool. I'm awesome. I'm way cool. I'm twelve. I'm boy crazy. I go to Brentwood Middle School. I'm popular with my fans. I play viola. My best friend is Lindsay. I have a gerbil named Taj. I'm adopted. I'm beautiful.

Children become increasingly committed to certain standards for themselves. In general, youngsters have high self-esteem when they evaluate themselves as being strong in domains that are most important to them. For some, academic achievement may be the overriding factor, whereas for others popularity with peers may be more influential. Some children invest in athletic accomplishments, and others may value their contributions to the family or community. And for many youngsters around the world, physical attractiveness contributes heavily to overall self-esteem (D. Hart, 1988; Harter, 2006; S. H. W. Mares et al., 2010).

Most youngsters gradually internalize criteria that others use to evaluate their behavior and characteristics. Just as Vygotsky proposed that children internalize many of the cognitive strategies they first use in social interactions, so, too, do psychologists specializing in the self suggest that children gradually internalize other people's ideas about desirable characteristics and behaviors (Burton & Mitchell, 2003; Harter, 2006; R. A. Thompson & Virmani, 2010).[1] As youngsters acquire such criteria, their self-esteem is increasingly based on *self*-judgments rather than others' judgments. A boy whose parents regularly praise him for his high grades is likely to begin judging *himself* by the grades he earns. You can see such internalization in an interview with 15-year-old Greg in the "Intrinsic Motivation: Late Adolescence" video in MyEducationLab:

MyEducationLab

Observe how Greg has internalized his parents' standards for academic performance in the "Intrinsic Motivation: Late Adolescence" video. (Find Video Examples in Topic 12 of MyEducationLab.)

Interviewer:	What are the things that make you want to do well in school?
Greg:	My parents. [*Both laugh.*]
Interviewer:	Okay.
Greg:	My parents mostly. . . . And myself . . . sometimes.
Interviewer:	Okay. How do your parents influence you wanting to do well in school?
Greg:	I don't know. They did well so they want me to. . . .
Interviewer:	You said that sometimes you also want to do well for you. Can you tell me more about that?
Greg:	'Cause, I mean, you feel better if you get all As than Cs or Fs.

[1] Vygotsky's theory is described in depth in Chapter 6.

Yet the standards that youngsters internalize are not always realistic or productive. A girl whose friends place a premium on fashion-magazine standards for thinness may think she is "fat" even when she is dangerously underweight—a misperception commonly seen in youngsters who have eating disorders (Attie, Brooks-Gunn, & Petersen, 1990; McVey et al., 2010; K. A. Peterson, Paulson, & Williams, 2007).

Despite experiencing a general trend toward becoming progressively more certain of their own personal standards, some youngsters remain heavily dependent on others' opinions well into adolescence. They may be so preoccupied with approval from peers and adults that they base their own sense of self-worth largely on what others think—or at least on what *they think* others think—of them (Dweck, 2000; Harter, Stocker, & Robinson, 1996; McArdle, 2009). Teenagers who have such **contingent self-worth** are often on an emotional roller coaster, feeling elated one day and devastated the next, depending on how classmates, parents, and teachers have recently treated them.

As children grow older, their feelings of self-worth increasingly depend on peers' behaviors and opinions. In the early years, parents and other family members are key players in shaping children's sense of self. As children spend more time away from home, however, they become more aware of and concerned about what nonfamily members—and especially peers—think of them (Harter, 2006; Richman et al., 2010). Whereas parents often express approval for good behavior and high academic achievement, peers tend to prefer physical attractiveness, athleticism, and being a fun-loving playmate. Peers by no means replace the influence of parents, however. Well into the adolescent years, youngsters' self-perceptions continue to be strongly affected by interactions with parents (S. M. Cooper & Smalls, 2010; Harter, 2006).

Children increasingly behave in ways that mirror their self-perceptions. Those who see themselves as "good students" are more apt to pay attention in class, use effective learning strategies, and tackle challenging tasks, whereas those who believe they are "poor students" are apt to misbehave in class, study infrequently, and avoid difficult subject matter. Children who see themselves as friendly and likable are apt to seek the company of classmates and perhaps run for student council, whereas those who believe they are disliked may keep to themselves or behave aggressively toward peers. As you might guess, children who routinely *under*estimate their ability avoid the many challenges necessary for cognitive, social, and physical growth (Assor & Connell, 1992; D. Phillips & Zimmerman, 1990). Children who consistently view themselves and their abilities in a negative light are at risk for developing depression and other mental health problems (Nuijens, Teglasi, & Hancock, 2009).

Children's sense of worth becomes more stable over time. Beginning in middle childhood and continuing into adolescence and beyond, self-esteem becomes fairly stable, such that those with positive self-perceptions tend to continue to see themselves in favorable terms (J. Kim & Cicchetti, 2009; R. W. Robins & Trzesniewski, 2005). Conversely, children who think poorly of themselves in elementary school also tend to have low self-esteem in high school and adulthood. Several factors contribute to the increasing stability of self-perceptions:

- Children usually behave in ways consistent with what they believe about themselves, and their behaviors are apt to produce reactions from others that confirm their self-concepts.
- Children tend to seek out information that confirms what they already believe. Those with positive self-perceptions are more likely to seek out feedback about their strengths, whereas some with negative self-perceptions may actually look for information about their weaknesses (S. Epstein & Morling, 1995; LaGrange et al., 2008; Swann, 1997).
- Children seldom put themselves in situations where they believe they won't succeed, thus minimizing the chances of discovering that they *can* succeed in a domain about which they've been pessimistic. If a middle school student believes he is a poor athlete and so refuses to go out for the baseball team, he may never learn that, in fact, he has the potential to become a good player.
- Many factors affecting self-esteem—inherited abilities and disabilities, parents' behaviors, physical attractiveness, and so on—remain relatively stable throughout childhood (O'Malley & Bachman, 1983; Raevuori et al., 2007).

contingent self-worth
Overall sense of self that is highly dependent on others' opinions.

This is *not* to say that once children acquire an unfavorable sense of self, they will always think poorly of themselves. Quite the contrary can be true, especially when circumstances change significantly (Marsh & Craven, 1997; Rönnau-Böse & Fröhlich-Gildhoff, 2009).

Transformations in the Self During the Developmental Periods

The developmental trends just listed reflect gradual changes in sense of self over time. We now look at unique aspects of self-perceptions at five age levels: infancy, early childhood, middle childhood, early adolescence, and late adolescence.

Infancy (Birth–Age 2)

The first elements of children's sense of self emerge during infancy. Through repeated physical experiences, babies discover that they have bodies that bring them discomfort (through hunger, fatigue, and injury) and pleasure (through feeding, sucking thumbs, and snuggling in the arms of caregivers) (R. A. Thompson, 2006). Children also form impressions of themselves as being lovable (or not) from their relationships with parents and caregivers. Infants who form secure attachments with caregivers are apt to develop positive self-perceptions, whereas infants who form insecure attachments do not.[2]

In the first year, infants also develop a sense of self-awareness as they elicit predictable responses. As they drop a ball, kick a mobile, and engage a parent with a cry or smile, infants realize that their behavior elicits particular effects (R. A. Thompson & Virmani, 2010). Infants' ability to imitate other people's facial expressions further nourishes their early sense of self; likewise, they notice and appreciate when adults imitate their behavior (Lenzi et al., 2009; Meltzoff, 1990, 2007). As they improvise in their mimicking (e.g., opening and closing their mouths more quickly than their older brother does), it dawns on them that they and other people are separate entities. Late in the first year, activities involving joint attention come into play as well. When Mommy and baby examine a toy together, baby shifts her gaze between toy and Mommy's face. Baby begins to learn that she has a sense of "we-ness" with her mother but also is separate from Mommy (Emde & Buchsbaum, 1990).

In the second year, infants begin to recognize themselves in the mirror. In a clever study of self-recognition, babies 9 to 24 months were placed in front of a mirror (M. Lewis & Brooks-Gunn, 1979; R. A. Thompson & Virmani, 2010). Their mothers then wiped their faces, leaving a red mark on their noses. Older infants, especially those 15 months or older, touched their noses when they saw their reflections, as if they understood that the reflected images belonged to them.

Early Childhood (Ages 2–6)

In early childhood, language acquisition and other cognitive developments permit other advancements in the self. Once children begin to talk, their self-awareness becomes much more obvious. Children begin to refer to themselves by the pronouns *I* and *me,* and at ages 2 and 3 commonly exclaim "Mine!" during tussles with siblings and peers (L. Levine, 1983; M. Lewis & Brooks-Gunn, 1979; R. A. Thompson & Virmani, 2010). Learning about what is *mine* is a natural part of development and is probably a precursor to sharing. Young children also increasingly assert their competence and independence (e.g., by refusing assistance with putting on their jackets) and articulate their self-awareness by labeling emotions (e.g., "Happy me").[3]

Another acquisition that depends on cognitive development is the *autobiographical self,* the child's memory of important events in his or her life.[4] Children's early recollections are usually sparse, fragmented snippets that don't hang together in any meaningful way. On average, children remember few if any events that occurred before age 3½, and their recall of events before age 2 is virtually nonexistent. Memories for events become increasingly

Preparing for Your Licensure Examination

Your teaching test might ask you about some basic ways in which children's self-perceptions change during development.

---

[2] In Chapter 11, you can find more information about how children develop perceptions about themselves and others while forming close bonds with parents.

[3] Children's ability to label emotions is examined in Chapter 11.

[4] The autobiographical self is defined in Chapter 7.

464 CHAPTER 12 • DEVELOPMENT OF SELF AND SOCIAL UNDERSTANDINGS

detailed and integrated during the preschool years as children talk about their experiences with other people (Fivush & Nelson, 2004; M. L. Howe, 2003; R. A. Thompson & Virmani, 2010).

Initially, children see themselves largely in terms of obvious physical characteristics and simple psychological traits (Damon & Hart, 1988; Harter, 2006). As they learn from caregivers what things are "good" and "bad," they begin to apply these standards in evaluating themselves (Dweck, 2000; Kagan, 1981; R. S. L. Mills, Arbeau, Lall, & De Jaeger, 2010). Often they feel sad or angry when they don't measure up. Hence, a 5-year-old boy may become quite frustrated when he discovers he can't build a tower as tall as his friend's construction.

By and large, however, most young children have upbeat self-concepts and high self-esteem. Often they believe that they are more capable than they really are (Diesendruck & Lindenbaum, 2009; Harter, 2006; Lockhart, Chang, & Story, 2002). Such optimism is perhaps due to their tendency to base self-assessments on their continuing improvements in "big boy" and "big girl" activities. Their overconfidence is probably beneficial for their development in that it motivates them to persist at challenging tasks (Bjorklund & Green, 1992; Pintrich & Schunk, 2002).

Song of Myself

I am Shea
Above me are the bright colored leaves on the trees
Below me are seeds waiting to become flowers next spring
Before me are years to come full of new things to be learned
Behind me are memories I've forgotten
All around me are my friends lending me a helping hand
I see children having fun
I smell the sweet scent of flowers
I hear the birds talking to each other
I feel the fur of a helpless baby bunny
I move like wind as I run through the grass
I am old like the planets who have been here from the beginning
I am young like a seed waiting to sprout
I am the black of a panda's patches
I am the gold of the sun
I am the green of a cat's eye
I am the many colors of the sunset
I am a parrot, kangaroo, tiger, turtle
I am kind, responsible, pretty, smart
I think, plan, help, research
I give ideas to people that need them
I fear lightning
I believe that we all are equal
I remember my dreams
I dream of bad things as well as the good
I do not understand why some people pollute the Earth
I am Shea, a child of honesty
May I walk in peace

ARTIFACT 12-2 Song of Myself. During middle childhood, children see themselves as having specific characteristics in numerous distinct domains. Shea wrote this poem about herself using "stems" provided by her teacher (e.g., "Above me . . . ," "I feel . . . ," "I am . . . ," and "I dream . . .").

Middle Childhood (Ages 6–10)

During middle childhood, children tend to see themselves in more complex physical and psychological terms. Elementary school children are usually aware that they do some things well and other things poorly (Bouffard, Marcoux, Vezeau, & Bordeleau, 2003; Marsh & Craven, 1997; Wigfield, 1994). As they progress through the elementary school grades, they have many opportunities to compare themselves with others and become more cognitively able to *make* such comparisons. Most youngsters now receive some critical feedback from teachers and also observe some of their peers outshining them at least some of the time, and so their self-assessments typically decline from the overconfidence of the preschool years to levels that are more accurate (Harter, 2006; Marsh & Hau, 2003; Robins & Trzesniewski, 2005). Becoming more realistic about their talents and limitations probably helps children choose age-appropriate activities and work toward achievable goals (Baumeister, Campbell, Krueger, & Vohs, 2003; Harter, 2006). Generally, however—perhaps because they have so many domains to consider as they look for strengths—most children maintain reasonably positive self-esteem during the elementary school years (Bouffard et al., 2003; Kasanen, Räty, & Eklund, 2009; Wigfield & Eccles, 1994).

Early Adolescence (Ages 10–14)

A drop in self-esteem often occurs at about the time that youngsters move from elementary school to middle school or junior high school; this drop tends to be more pronounced for girls (Marsh, 1990b; A. K. Parker, 2009; Robins & Trzesniewski, 2005). The physiological changes of puberty may be one factor in the decline. Self-evaluations depend increasingly on perceptions of appearance and popularity, and boys and girls alike tend to think of themselves as being somewhat less attractive once they reach adolescence (Cornell et al., 1990; D. Hart, 1988; Harter et al., 1998). Changes in the school environment, such as disrupted friendships, more superficial teacher–student relationships, and more rigorous academic standards, probably also have a negative impact (Eccles & Midgley, 1989; Harter, 2006).[5]

Also with early adolescence come two new phenomena that have implications for self-perceptions. First, youngsters become more cognitively able to reflect on how others see

[5] We look more closely at youngsters' transitions to new school environments in Chapter 15.

them (Harter, 1999). They may initially go to extremes in this respect, to the point where they think that in any social situation, everyone else's attention is focused squarely on them (Alberts, Elkind, & Ginsberg, 2007; Meadows, 2010; P. D. Schwartz, Maynard, & Uzelac, 2008). This self-centered aspect of the young adolescent's sense of self is sometimes called the **imaginary audience**. Because they believe they are the center of attention, teenagers (girls especially) are often preoccupied with their physical appearance and can be quite self-critical. Many adolescents change the way they speak and act according to whom they are interacting with at the moment, increasing the chances they will gain others' approval. Yet young adolescents are generally not fully aware that they are acting somewhat inconsistently with different people.

A second noteworthy phenomenon in early adolescence is the **personal fable**. Young teenagers often believe they are completely unlike anyone else (Aalsma, Lapsley, & Flannery, 2006; Elkind, 1981a; P. L. Hill & Lapsley, 2011). They are apt to think their own feelings are unique—that the people around them have never had such experiences. Hence they may insist that no one else, least of all parents and teachers, can possibly know how they feel. They may also believe that they have special powers and are invulnerable to harm.

Adults should keep in mind that modest levels of the personal fable and the imaginary audience appear to serve important functions for adolescents. The personal fable—in particular, the sense of invulnerability—may encourage young people to venture out into the world and try new things (Bjorklund & Green, 1992; Lapsley, 1993). The imaginary audience keeps youngsters "connected" to their larger social context. Because they continually attend to how others might judge their actions, they are more apt to behave in ways that their society will view favorably (Lapsley, 1993; R. M. Ryan & Kuczkowski, 1994). However, excessive concern about the self is associated with some risks. Having a strong personal fable is associated with depression in adolescents, possibly because it reflects a tendency to ruminate about one's own shortcomings (Aalsma et al., 2006). At some point, both the imaginary audience and personal fable apparently outlive their purposes for most teens, because these tendencies slowly diminish in late adolescence and early adulthood (Lapsley, 1993; P. D. Schwartz et al., 2008).

Late Adolescence (Ages 14–18)

As their worlds expand, teenagers have a greater variety of social experiences with people from diverse backgrounds. With their increasing ability to reflect on their own behaviors, they become consciously aware that they themselves take on different personalities when interacting with parents, teachers, friends, and romantic partners. Thus their sense of self may include multiple qualities that they perceive to be somewhat contradictory (D. Hart, 1988; Harter, 2006; Wigfield et al., 1996). The contradictions can be a source of confusion, as a ninth grader revealed:

> I really don't understand how I can switch so fast from being cheerful with my friends, then coming home and feeling anxious, and then getting frustrated and sarcastic with my parents. Which one is the *real* me? (Harter, 1999, p. 67)

As high school students wrestle with the question *Who is the real me?*, they gradually broaden their sense of self to accommodate the range of personas that they see themselves projecting (Harter, 2006). For instance, they may resolve self-perceptions of being both "cheerful" and "depressed" by concluding that they are "moody" or explain inconsistent behaviors by deciding they are "flexible" or "open minded."

In the process of reconciling their "multiple selves," older adolescents make progress toward establishing a sense of **identity**, a self-constructed definition of who they are, what they find important, what they believe, and what they should do in life. You might recall from Erik Erikson's theory that a search for identity is a pivotal challenge for adolescents.[6] Contemporary research indicates that before youngsters achieve a true sense of their adult identity, most need considerable time to explore career options, political views, religious

---

[6] Erikson's stage of identity vs. role confusion is described in Chapter 11.

imaginary audience
Belief that one is the center of attention in any social situation.

personal fable
Belief held by many adolescents that they are unique beings invulnerable to normal risks and dangers.

identity
Self-constructed definition of who one is, what things one finds important, what one believes, and what goals one wants to accomplish in life.

convictions, and so on. Canadian psychologist **James Marcia** (1980, 1991) identified four distinct patterns of behavior that may characterize an adolescent's search for identity:

- *Identity diffusion.* The adolescent has made no commitment to a particular career path or ideological belief system. Possibly there has been some haphazard experimentation with particular roles or beliefs, but the adolescent has not yet embarked on a serious exploration of issues related to self-definition.
- *Foreclosure.* The adolescent has made a commitment to an occupation and a particular set of beliefs. The choices have been made without much deliberation or exploration of other possibilities; rather, they have been based largely on what others (especially parents) have prescribed.
- *Moratorium.* The adolescent has no strong commitment to a particular career or set of beliefs but is actively exploring and considering a variety of professions and ideologies.
- *Identity achievement.* The adolescent has previously gone through a period of moratorium and emerged with a clear choice regarding occupation and commitment to political and religious beliefs.

Foreclosure—identity choice without prior exploration—rules out potentially more productive alternatives, and identity diffusion leaves young people without a clear sense of direction. Being in moratorium can be an uncomfortable experience for some adolescents (consider the angst that Theodore expressed with not yet having decided on a career path in the introductory case study), but it is often an important step in achieving a healthy identity (Kunnen, 2009; Luyckx, Goossens, & Soenens, 2006; Marcia, 1988; Mullis, Graf, & Mullis, 2009).

For most older high school students, the search for identity is hardly complete. Even so, their self-esteem has largely recuperated from the unsettling experiences of the middle

It was during high school that I discovered who I was. Freshman and sophomore year I was a hermit crab, slowly trying to change to a new shell. I was eager to make the process yet I was yearning for something to hold on to help ease the way. For me my path of stepping stones was the — High School music department.

When I walked into chorus my freshman year, I was petrified. I felt like I was involved in a cult of some sort. Everyone either seemed extremely friendly or in love with the music department. I have to admit that at first I thought that the music department was pretty lame. Everyday I would walk in and see everyone hugging their friends or people crying on each other's shoulders, what was this? Everyone seemed so dependent on each other. I had my thoughts of quitting; I didn't know a lot of people and wasn't excited at the thought of making friends with them either, but I stuck it out, singing has always been my passion and I wasn't about to never perform again. This is who I was, I wasn't about to let some crazy group of people intimidate me.

By the middle of my sophomore year I was a full time band geek; besides the fact that I wasn't even in the band. I finally let my walls cave in and let the music department be my second home. I loved it. I could come in during the middle of a bad school day and always find a friend, always have someone their for me. The seniors in the rest of the school always seemed so big, so intimidating, but when I walked through the doors of the music department everyone was equal; there were no judgments and everyone felt welcome.

The music department changed me. I am no longer shy or timid but I am me to the fullest extent of the word. I now have the ability to walk into a group of people and make friends instantly. The music department helped me realize that performing is my passion, it's what I love; it's who I am. I am now ready to go audition, to go out and show the world what I am made of. Throughout high school nothing else has made such a lasting impression on me, I am not going to sit back one day as a mother and tell my children about my freshman PE class; my only eventful memories are contained within the walls of the music department. . . .

The music department has given me the strength to move on. When I am nervous I know I can always think back to my — years, and the confidence that slowly grew with the help of loving arms. I may be unsure about the future but I am excited. I will always remember the friends I made, the confidence I earned, and the love I shared within the four years; or better yet the four solid walls of the — High School music department

ARTIFACT 12-3 Hermit crab. As an assignment for one of her 11th-grade classes, 17-year-old "Kiley" (a pseudonym) wrote the essay shown here. (We have blanked out the name of Kiley's school but have left spelling and grammar errors intact.) Notice how Kiley describes her transformation from being a loner to identifying as a fellow musician.

school and early high school years (Harter, 2006). Several developmental advancements contribute to this rebound in sense of self. Most older adolescents have acquired the social skills they need to get along well with others. They have accepted many of the apparent inconsistencies in their self-perceptions and have considerable autonomy in choosing activities at which they are likely to be successful. And they increasingly judge themselves based on their *own* (rather than other people's) standards.

Even as older adolescents move rapidly toward independence, their attachments to family members, especially parents, continue to play a significant role in their sense of self. Adolescents who have strong emotional bonds with parents tend to have higher self-esteem (Harter, 2006; Josselson, 1988; Ryan & Lynch, 1989). This emotional support gives adolescents needed license to explore various aspects of their developing identities (Mullis et al., 2009). However, some parenting styles (e.g., uninvolved or rejecting parenting) can cause adolescents to feel alienated from their parents and become susceptible to the opinions of others; that is, these adolescents are more likely to have the *contingent self-worth* described earlier (Forthun, Montgomery, & Bell, 2006; Josselson, 1988; McArdle, 2009).

Self in a Bioecological Context

As you have learned, children reflect on their personal characteristics, affiliations with particular groups, and experiences in familiar settings as they construct self-perceptions. American psychologist **Margaret Beale Spencer** has created a bioecological model that examines these key influences in children from a wide variety of backgrounds (see Figure 12-1).[7]

Bioecology of Child Development
Children develop a sense of self while reflecting on their experiences in complex social environments.

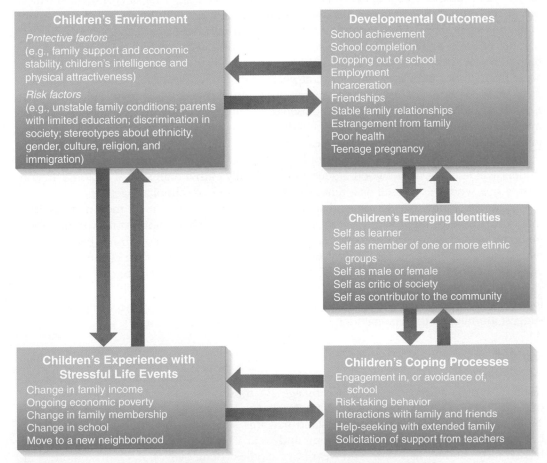

FIGURE 12-1   Emerging identities in the contexts of protection and risk.
Adapted from M. B. Spencer, 2006.

[7] Margaret Beale Spencer's work is introduced in Chapter 3.

According to Spencer, children encounter both *risk factors* (e.g., growing up in poverty and dealing with discrimination) and *protective factors* (e.g., being intelligent and having involved parents and dedicated teachers). A few of these risks and protections are based in part on experiences in ethnic groups. For example, many African American children regularly confront prejudice and discrimination. Yet these children also obviously enjoy numerous advantages, in many cases strong extended family support, an active spiritual life, and good coping skills (Barrow, Armstrong, Vargo, & Boothroyd, 2007; M. B. Spencer, 2006; S. A. Wilson, 2010). In comparison, many European American children benefit from access to good schools and ample family income yet grapple with challenges in acquiring effective coping skills, which in adverse situations may account for their comparatively high suicide rates (National Institute of Mental Health, 2008b; M. B. Spencer, 2006). These are extreme examples, of course, but they do suggest that children in different ethnic groups experience somewhat different pressures.

Of course, children do not passively react to circumstances in their environment. Instead, they actively interpret the implications of events and relationships for themselves. For example, many children welcome the addition of a new father figure into their family, especially when they perceive him as an affectionate provider who is concerned about their welfare. However, a few children feel threatened by the presence of a new stepfather, especially when they perceive him as displacing themselves with their mother or competing with their birth father for their loyalty. Thus individual children facing the same objective circumstances can show distinctly different responses.

To address the environmental pressures they experience, children develop an array of *coping skills*, behavioral strategies for overcoming the stresses of everyday life. Children regularly develop adaptive coping skills that allow them to make the best of a difficult situation, but at other times they adopt maladaptive strategies that actually hinder their adjustment. One adolescent girl may respond to decreased attention from her parents (perhaps due to a parent's new job or a family crisis) by spending more time with grandparents and asking for help from her school adviser. A second girl may respond to the same circumstance by staying away from home, associating with deviant peers, and getting into trouble.

In the process of using their emerging coping skills, children reflect on their own *identity*. Children may come to see themselves as effective or ineffective learners; as vital members of their families or as rejected children; and as productive members of society or as individuals who resort to illegal activities. These and other identities culminate in important developmental outcomes. An adolescent boy who sees himself as an academically talented student will likely try to get good grades and eventually earn a high school diploma. In contrast, a boy who sees himself as a renegade may drop out of school altogether.

The developmental outcomes that youngsters attain, in turn, affect their new environments. An adolescent girl who is on track to earn her high school diploma now thinks about going to college or working in her aunt's hair salon next year. Her cousin has been charged with various criminal acts, including vandalism, burglary, and assault on a classmate, and the cousin now spends most of her time with peers who commit delinquent acts.

Identity, then, is the outcome of many experiences and also serves as a catalyst for future growth. Let's look more closely at three characteristics that Spencer and colleagues suggest are integral to personal identity: gender, ethnicity, and culture.

Gender

From an early age, children show an interest in gender. By the end of the first year, infants can distinguish male and female faces, and by age 2½, most children know that they are a "boy" or a "girl" (J. E. O. Blakemore et al., 2009; Kohlberg, 1966; C. L. Martin, Ruble, & Szkrybalo, 2002). By age 4 or 5, children understand that this state is permanent—that boys do not become girls if they grow their hair long and wear ribbons, and that girls do not become boys if they cut their hair short and wear boys' clothes (Bem, 1989; J. E. O. Blakemore et al., 2009; Ruble et al., 2007). As children become increasingly aware of the typical characteristics and behaviors of boys, girls, men, and women, they begin to pull their knowledge together into self-constructed understandings, or **gender schemas**, of "what males are like" and "what females are like." These gender schemas become part of their self-concept and guide their behavior and characteristics—how they should dress, what toys they should play with, what interests and academic subject areas they should pursue, and so on (Bem, 1981; J. E. O. Blakemore et al., 2009; Ruble et al., 2006).

With the onset of puberty, being "male" or "female" takes on new meaning. Many youngsters show a surge in gender-specific interests beginning in adolescence (J. E. O. Blakemore et al., 2009; Galambos, Almeida, & Petersen, 1990; Ruble et al., 2006). Girls may show a newfound interest in their appearance, and boys may develop a heightened fascination with sports. To affirm their masculinity or femininity, many adolescents shy away from behaviors more closely associated with the opposite sex. In the "Emotional Development: Late Adolescence" video in MyEducationLab, 15-year-old Greg responds to the question "What are some things that kids do when they're sad?" by saying, "Cry . . . if you're a guy, you don't show it." Girls in general show less interest and confidence in subject areas that have been historically preferred by boys—for instance, in mathematics, science, and sports (Barkatsas, Kasimatis, & Gialamas, 2009; E. M. Evans, Schweingruber, & Stevenson, 2002; Leaper & Friedman, 2007).

Not only do behaviors and interests diverge by gender, but boys' and girls' sense of self-worth differs somewhat as well. From early adolescence and after, boys have slightly higher self-esteem overall (J. E. O. Blakemore et al., 2009; Wilgenbusch & Merrell, 1999). However, differences in self-evaluations vary by domain. Boys tend to rate themselves higher in mathematics, physical appearance, athletics, and emotional well-being. Girls have more favorable self-assessments in verbal skills, close friendships, and same-sex peer relationships.

The consistency of psychological differences between the sexes raises questions about how these divisions originate. Biology clearly has some influence on how boys and girls behave. The brain is permanently marked "male" or "female" by subtle differences in anatomy during prenatal development (J. E. O Blakemore et al., 2009; Knickmeyer & Baron-Cohen, 2006; Ruble et al., 2006). At puberty, gender differences are amplified as hormones accelerate the progression of gender-related characteristics. In a few cases these hormones increase the likelihood of problem behaviors and emotional responses. In boys, for example, these rising hormones are associated with increased aggression—a stereotypically male characteristic.[8]

The environment, too, plays a role by encouraging children to think about males and females in particular ways. Family and peers often model gender-typical behavior, reinforce children for "staying within bounds," and punish them (e.g., by ridicule or exclusion) when they violate accepted gender roles (Cassano & Zeman, 2010; Pipher, 1994; Ruble et al., 2006). A boy who cries after breaking his arm may be called a "sissy," and a girl who excels in mathematics might be teased for being a "math geek." Other people also influence children's gender schemas through the typical roles they play in society (backhoe operators are almost always men), the preferences and priorities they express ("Wait! I have to put on my makeup!"), and the behaviors they model and encourage ("Why don't you gals go shopping and let us guys watch the football game?") (C. K. Friedman, Leaper, & Bigler, 2007; Ruble et al., 2006; Tennenbaum & Leaper, 2002).

Yet much of the pressure to act "appropriately" according to one's gender comes from within rather than from others (Bem, 1981; C. L. Martin, 2000; Zosuls et al., 2009). This tendency for children and adolescents to conform to their own ideas about appropriate behaviors is known as **self-socialization**. For example, when teachers actively encourage children to engage in non–gender-stereotypical activities (boys playing with dolls, girls playing with toy cars, etc.), the children may comply for a short time but soon revert to their earlier, more gender-typical ways (Lippa, 2002).

As they gain social experience and develop cognitively, children gradually learn to apply more open-minded criteria for gender-appropriate behaviors (Ruble et al., 2006; Trautner, 1992). In other words, they soften previously rigid boundaries regarding the appearance and

[8] Aggression is examined in Chapter 14.

MyEducationLab

Listen to Greg express his belief that boys often hide their emotions in the "Emotional Development: Late Adolescence" video. (Find Video Examples in Topic 12 of MyEducationLab.)

Preparing for Your Licensure Examination
Your teaching test might ask you about gender differences in psychological characteristics.

gender schema
Self-constructed body of beliefs about the traits and behaviors of males or females.

self-socialization
Tendency to integrate personal observations and others' input into self-constructed standards for behavior and to choose actions consistent with those standards.

behaviors of boys and girls. Yet as we saw earlier, many adolescents temporarily embrace gender stereotypes once again, perhaps until they are comfortable with themselves as young men or women. Adolescents often begin looking at men and women in new ways, searching for masculine or feminine role models, sometimes in magazines and other media, as these teenage girls reveal in their discussions:

Sophie:	I think that *More!* is for older girls really. Like the younger ones [comics and mags] where you've got, you've got ponies and stuff.
Naomi:	And pictures of kittens.
Sophie:	Yeah, there's *Girltalk* and *Chatterbox* and you go up and you get *Shout* and then you get *Sugar* and *Bliss* and then it's like *Just Seventeen, Nineteen,* and it's *More!* And then *Women's Own* and stuff like that, so you get the range. (Nayak & Kehily, 2008, p. 135)

Some adolescents become preoccupied with images of slender, toned, and (for males) muscular bodies in the media. For girls and young women, extensive exposure to fitness and fashion magazines is associated with dissatisfaction with their body and a strong desire to be thin (Dohnt & Tiggemann, 2006; K. Harrison & Hefner, 2008; Tiggemann, 2003). Such self-perceptions increase the probability of developing an eating disorder, and they also are linked to depression in girls (Harter, 2006).[9]

FEMININE MYSTIQUE. Especially in adolescence, much of the pressure to act "appropriately" for one's gender comes from within rather than from other people.

Ethnicity

Children's self-perceptions are also influenced by their participation in one or more ethnic groups. By the time children reach kindergarten or first grade, they may be aware that they belong to a different "group" than many of their age-mates. A variety of characteristics may make them stand out in a crowd, including their skin color, facial features, and language. Already at this age, many children accurately classify themselves as being African, Mexican, Laotian, and so on and can describe some of the traditions of their group (R. D. Parke & Clarke-Stewart, 2011; Sheets, 1999). Parents and other family members may also give them labels (*Black, Chinese,* and so on) that communicate that they are special in some important way. By early adolescence, youngsters actively consider how their life is affected by being a member of a particular ethnic group. By late adolescence, a large number of youngsters achieve a strong *ethnic identity,* an awareness and pride in their ethnic heritage and willingness to adopt many of their ethnic group's behaviors (Kiang & Fuligni, 2010; Phinney, 1989; Sheets & Hollins, 1999).[10]

In forming an ethnic identity, children attend closely to the tactics used by family members to foster loyalty to their group; they also listen to their family's explanations of the group's status in society. For example, many African American parents speak with pride about their heritage, inform children about the valiant struggles of their ancestors, and teach children how to cope with racial prejudice (D. Hughes, 2003; Pahl & Way, 2006). Many Puerto Rican and Dominican families transmit cultural pride by posting flags, speaking Spanish, and celebrating the holidays of their native lands (French, Seidman, Allen, & Aber, 2006; Pahl & Way, 2006).

Children from ethnic minority backgrounds typically consider their cultural background to be a more central feature of their self-concept than do children from majority backgrounds (Aboud, 1988; Kiang & Fuligni, 2010; K. L. Turner & Brown, 2007). European American children tend to see their ethnicity as the norm and are usually not strongly motivated to learn more about it. In contrast, children from other ethnicities realize that they are different from peers and are interested in learning about these origins. In the process of exploring their ancestry, ethnic minority children sometimes develop more positive self-perceptions than do children from majority groups, possibly because they benefit from gestures from

[9] Eating disorders are examined in Chapter 5.
[10] We introduce the concept of ethnic identity in Chapter 3.

familiar adults to portray their ethnic heritage in a positive light (H. Cooper & Dorr, 1995; M. B. Spencer & Markstrom-Adams, 1990; Stevenson et al., 1990; van Laar, 2000).

Yet not all the messages that ethnic minority children receive are positive ones. Unfortunately, children from ethnic minority and immigrant backgrounds are often victims of prejudicial remarks. Sozan, an adolescent girl whose family members were Kurdish refugees to the United States, regularly heard other students criticize her thick eyebrows and the scarf she wore out of respect for her religion, suggesting that she had a "unibrow" (i.e., one long eyebrow extending across her forehead) and was bald (McBrien, 2005a, p. 66). These were deeply hurtful comments, but Sozan, like many other ethnic minority youngsters, held onto her faith and customs.

Some young people respond to discrimination by taking proactive steps to learn more about the strengths of their ethnic group and determine what they can do to combat negative race relations and inequities in the community. Yet repeatedly being the victim of prejudice during childhood can exceed the coping skills of children. In fact, exposure to discrimination and prejudice create a risk for low academic achievement and such mental health problems as depression (Kiang & Fuligni, 2010; Rivas-Drake, Hughes, & Way, 2009).

Children who have more than one ancestry, perhaps because of growing up in an immigrant or *multiethnic* family, often undergo a lengthy period during which they explore their various heritages. Occasionally, peers and adults outside the family communicate their belief that one or more aspects of a particular ethnic heritage are somehow undesirable, causing confusion or distress in children who affiliate with two or more distinct ethnic groups

ETHNIC IDENTITY. Many children incorporate a strong sense of ethnic identity into their sense of self.

ARTIFACT 12-4   Blending heritages. Sozan sees herself as a young Muslim woman who is committed to her cultural heritage and also wants to take advantage of the customs and opportunities in the United States.

"Sozan Self-Portrait from Dissertation" from DISCRIMINATION AND ACADEMIC MOTIVATION IN ADOLESCENT REFUGEE GIRLS by J. L. McBrien (Unpublished doctoral dissertation, Emory University, Atlanta, GA) DISSERTATION ABSTRACTS INTERNATIONAL SECTION A: HUMANITIES AND SOCIAL SCIENCES, 66 95-4). Copyright © 2005 by J. Lynn McBrien. Reprinted with permission.

(C. R. Cooper, Jackson, Azmitia, Lopez, & Dunbar, 1995; B. D. Tatum, 1997). For an extended period of time, youngsters who are the beneficiaries of multiple heritages may fluctuate back and forth between allegiances to one ethnic identity or another depending on the circumstances (A. M. Lopez, 2003; B. D. Tatum, 1997; Yip & Fuligni, 2002). Consider Alice, who migrated from China to the United States at age 8. Although she gained fluency in English fairly quickly, for several years she had trouble reconciling the Chinese and American aspects of herself:

> [A]t home my parents expect me to be not a traditional Chinese daughter . . . but they expect things because I was born in China and I am Chinese. And at school, that's a totally different story because you're expected to behave as an American. You know, you speak English in your school; all your friends speak English. You try to be as much of an American as you can. So I feel I'm caught somewhere in between. . . . I feel I can no longer be fully Chinese or fully American anymore. (Igoa, 1995, p. 85)

After an extended period of time in exploring numerous options for self-expression, many teens with multiethnic backgrounds ultimately emerge with a strong, often multifaceted, ethnic identity.

For the most part students with a positive ethnic identity (including those with a strong multiethnic identity) perform well academically (Chavous et al., 2003; Costigan, Hua, & Su, 2010; Rowley, Cooper, & Clinton, 2006). Having a clear ethnic identity is also linked to high self-esteem, a willingness to help other people, and decreased use of violence (Costigan et al., 2010; Phinney, Cantu, & Kurtz, 1997; Umaña-Taylor & Alfaro, 2006). Furthermore, pride in one's ethnic heritage can serve as an emotional "buffer" against the insults and discrimination that children and adolescents from minority groups sometimes encounter (Romero & Roberts, 2003). Other findings indicate that young people with a strong ethnic identity are less likely to use drugs and partake in other risky behaviors (Brook, Chenshu, Finch, & Brook, 2010; Umaña-Taylor & Alfaro, 2006).

Culture

Cultures tell children what they should think about, how they should relate to other people, and what it means to be a good person.[11] These core lessons are integrated into children's sense of self (Morelli & Rothbaum, 2007; R. A. Thompson & Virmani, 2010).

Particular cultures differ in the extent to which they encourage children to attend to personal needs (those of the individual self) or other people's needs (those of the collective group). Some societies (e.g., some groups in North America) place a lot of emphasis on the self. In *individualistic societies*, parents, teachers, and other adults encourage children to focus on their own wishes, motivations, and emotions (Markus & Hamedani, 2007).[12] Children are encouraged to become personally confident in their initiatives and gain a clear sense of self-worth. In comparison, children in *collectivistic societies* place more emphasis on the group. Adults in these cultures encourage children to take pride in the accomplishments of their families and communities. Thus, for children in collectivistic societies, sense of self tends to include a strong connection to family and community (Banks & Banks, 1995; A. O. Harrison, Wilson, Pine, Chan, & Buriel, 1990; Markus & Kitayama, 1991). Children in these societies place special importance on being members of esteemed, honorable groups. Furthermore, children in collectivistic societies (e.g., in Southeast Asia) are more willing to acknowledge their weaknesses than is true for other groups. For these children, admitting personal limitations is a sign of humility (a desirable quality) rather than an indication of poor self-esteem (Brophy, 2004).

Thus, as a result of being socialized in a particular culture, children learn to think of themselves as having personal qualities or as being in relationships with other people. A 6-year-old European American girl describes herself primarily in personal terms:

> I am a wonderful and very smart person. A funny and hilarious person. A kind and caring person. A good-grade person who is going to go to Cornell [University]. A helpful and cooperative girl. (Q. Wang, 2006, p. 182)

---

[11] The characteristics and influences of culture are introduced in Chapter 3.
[12] Other aspects of individualistic and collectivist societies are examined in Chapters 3 and 11.

In comparison, a Chinese boy of the same age mentions some of his own personal qualities but also emphasizes his ties to family:

> I'm a human being. I'm a child. I like to play cards. I'm my mom and dad's child, my grandma and grandpa's grandson. I'm a hard-working good child. (Q. Wang, 2006, p. 182)

Of course, children from both individualistic and collectivistic societies are likely to embrace both personal qualities and interpersonal connections. In our opening case study, Theodore described himself as having certain individual qualities (e.g., being American, smart, not as academically motivated as he might be) and as being closely connected with family and friends.

Children use their individual- and relationship-focused views of themselves to help remember events in their lives. European American children are likely to mention their own preferences, opinions, and accomplishments when recalling events, whereas Chinese children are likely to mention incidents with other people, such as going to family parties (Q. Wang, 2006). Thus the content of autobiographical selves also varies somewhat by culture.

The earlier anecdote about Sozan reveals that for many children, the process of incorporating cultural beliefs into a sense of self is enriched by, and occasionally complicated by, exposure to two or more cultures. Around the world, many children of immigrant families are exposed to their family's native customs as well as to the new community's way of life (Hernandez, 2010). Children thus encounter one culture at home and another in the community. Yet even the culture of home can be a mosaic of different customs. Children from immigrant families may see their parents integrating different cultural traditions in everyday life, as with "a business representative educated in a French school system but working for a Chinese company; Algerian women participating in an international football competition but afterward praying in a mosque; English-speaking employees living in India but giving technical training courses via the Internet to adolescents in the United States; and a scientist with university training in Zimbabwe desperately looking for a job as an immigrant in Great Britain" (Hermans & Dimaggio, 2007, p. 35).[13] Children take an approach that is similarly adaptive and resourceful, drawing here and there from the various traditions they encounter. You can read about a situation in which children actively acquire the customs of a new society in the Development and Culture feature "At Home in Ireland."

In the Observations Guidelines table "Observing Indicators of Children's Self-Perceptions," you can see some of the ways that children reveal their thoughts about who they are. The manner in which children manifest these self-perceptions changes dramatically across infancy, childhood, and adolescence, as you can see in The Developmental Trends table "Sense of Self at Different Age Levels."

Enhancing Children's Sense of Self

Adults have many opportunities to nurture productive self-perceptions in children. You may be able to try one or more of the following strategies:

• **Communicate a genuine interest in children's well-being.** As children observe how adults treat them and hear what adults say about them, they wonder, "What do these things mean about me?" Youngsters often interpret harsh words and thoughtless actions as indications that adults do not like them, possibly because they are not worthy of love. We urge all adults, but especially teachers, parents, and other caregivers, to think carefully about what they say and do to children. Messages of affection and high regard come in a variety of forms, including the following:

- Giving children a smile and warm greeting at the beginning of the day
- Complimenting children on a special talent, new skill, or exceptional effort
- Asking children to talk about important events in their lives
- Being a good listener when children appear angry or upset

---

[13] Chapter 3 illustrates situations in which children selectively adopt customs from the family's native culture as well as from the new society.

DEVELOPMENT IN CULTURE
At Home in Ireland

In the 19th and 20th centuries, millions of Irish citizens, including Teresa's four grandparents, emigrated from Ireland to other countries in search of employment. A strong educational system helped change the economic environment and in the 1990s Ireland boasted low unemployment, modest corporate tax rates, and a well-educated workforce. Not only did many Irish emigrants return home, but the "Celtic Tiger," as Ireland came to be called, took in a record-breaking number of immigrants, with a large proportion coming from eastern Europe, especially Poland.

A previously homogenous country comprised primarily of fair-skinned individuals of the Roman Catholic faith, Ireland welcomed the newcomers with interest, sympathy, and occasional trepidation. Recently, a couple of researchers conducted interviews with native Irish, immigrants, and asylum seekers living in refugee hostels in Cork, a large city in the southwest of the country (O'Sullivan-Lago & de Abreu, 2010).

Many of those interviewed expressed uncertainty about rapid cultural changes in Ireland. One native Irishman, Dermot, lamented the break from a traditional past, worrying that longstanding Irish customs would be replaced by practices from other European countries. Alejandro, an immigrant from Galicia, an autonomous community in northern Spain, was torn between his allegiance to Galicia and his increasingly strong recognition that he felt at home in his adopted city of Cork. Alike, an asylum seeker, was apprehensive about her personal future, specifically worrying about whether she would be able to make Ireland her permanent home.

Schools were commonly seen as a place of integration for children from different backgrounds. Irishman Dermot observed that children from different backgrounds were easily integrated in the classroom. Asylum seekers were eager to see their children attend school and acquire Irish accents and customs. Jumoke was enthusiastic that her daughter, who could already speak Arabic and English, would acquire an Irish accent so that she could easily blend in to Irish society.

IRRESISTIBLE FUN. These Irish children are members of a neighborhood hockey club and participants in St. Patrick's Day festivities. The children's enjoyable antics would likely be appealing to immigrant children.

Some of the immigrants and asylum seekers believed that in order for their children to fit in, their family would need to give up some of their own traditions. This was a bigger concern for the parents than for the children. Children in immigrant families eagerly practiced new customs, such as Irish sports, as they interacted with other children. Their parents were slower and more hesitant in acquiring the new customs. Thus, children essentially led the way in the family's adjustment, with parents marveling at the speed with which their children acquired an Irish accent, made friends, and became proficient in local sports. Despite a dramatic downturn in the Irish economy since the late 2000s, many immigrants and refugees have remained in Ireland, in large part due to their children having made good adjustments there.

OBSERVATION GUIDELINES
Observing Indicators of Children's Self-Perceptions

CHARACTERISTIC	LOOK FOR	EXAMPLE	IMPLICATION
Self-Concept	• *Increased time spent looking in mirror* and inspecting one's image (in infancy) • *Verbal references to self* (e.g., "I," "mine") (in infancy and early childhood) • *Self-assessments of areas of proficiency and weakness* (e.g., "I'm good at math but bad at reading") (in middle childhood and adolescence)	Fifteen-month old Sierra stands at the full-length mirror in her child care center. She looks up and down at her reflection, smiles, and, after noticing a scrape on her knee in the mirror, bends down to touch her knee and says "Ouch."	Express a genuine interest in the well-being of all youngsters. Encourage young children's emerging insights into their sense of self (e.g., "Look who's in the mirror!" and "I see you copying me! Can you make your hands do this?"). As children grow, compliment them on special accomplishments, extra effort on tasks, and unusual talents.

OBSERVATION GUIDELINES (CONTINUED)

CHARACTERISTIC	LOOK FOR	EXAMPLE	IMPLICATION
Self-Worth	• *Comments on the self's inherent goodness or capability* (e.g., "I'm a good boy") • *Attempts to protect the self from threatening information* (e.g., anger at hearing critical comments after a flawed high jump attempt, or self-handicapping gestures by not studying for a challenging test) • *Changes in mood* depending on most recent treatment by peers (reflecting *contingent self-worth*)	After obtaining his graded mathematics test, 13-year-old Emmett notices the low score written on the top, crumples up the paper, and throws it in the trash. The next time he has a mathematics test, he does not study at all, even though he knows he's confused about the math concepts his class has been studying.	Encourage children to take disappointments in stride, suggesting that although they may not have done as well on particular tasks as they would have liked, with renewed effort, a change in tactics, and perhaps a little assistance, they have the ability to make sizable progress. Provide a range of activities and content domains so that everyone has a chance to excel in one or more domains.
Autobiographical Self	• *Conversations with parents about past family events* in which the child participated • *Recollections about personally significant events* or family celebrations	Five-year-old Jeremiah draws a picture of himself with his parents, two sisters, and the family dog in front of a farm. He explains that he and his family used to live in rural Idaho and then moved to the Oregon coast when his parents changed jobs.	Create assignments that allow children to reflect on their family origins and early experiences (e.g., have kindergarten children bring in photographs of themselves as preschoolers and talk about what they remember from that time). Ask older children to create self-portraits and write essays about memories of their early school years.
Gender Schema	• *Insistence that boys must act one way and girls another* (especially in early childhood) • *Selection of toys that are stereotypical for one's gender*, for example toy cars, blocks, and action figures by boys and dolls and board games by girls • *Heightened interest in same-sex role models* in magazines and other media during adolescence	In her spare time, 13-year-old Janice likes to browse through her mother's fashion magazines, picking up tips on how to apply cosmetics. Her older brother Reggie reads his father's automotive mechanics magazines.	Recognize that during various points in their development, many youngsters go overboard in trying to be exceptionally feminine or masculine. Accept that young people may go through phases of rigidly endorsing traditional gender roles, but also point out that both men and women have many opportunities in life and that few individuals can live up to standards of physical attractiveness touted by the media.
Identity	• *Early in the process of identity formation, varied levels of concern about the future*, perhaps including: —Questions about jobs and lifestyles —Noncritical acceptance of career goals that parents have suggested —Expression of a desire to define personal lifelong goals for oneself • *During late adolescence, more serious attempts to form an identity*: —Active search for information about career options, political viewpoints, religious convictions, etc. —Occasional well-developed justifications for political and religious beliefs and future occupations	Mr. Decker asks the ninth graders in his advisee group to write a brief essay about the kinds of jobs they find personally appealing. Some of the students write about jobs their parents currently have, yet others write little, having apparently not given the issue much thought. A few of the students ask Mr. Decker if they can learn more about different jobs as part of their homeroom class.	Give children opportunities to examine and try out a variety of adult roles. With young children, rotate various props through a housekeeping area (e.g., dress-up clothes and equipment that might be found in a police station, gas station, or doctor's office) to foster children's imagination of themselves in different roles. With older children, ask parents to come to school to talk about their jobs. With adolescents, arrange internships in local businesses, community agencies, and other institutions.
Ethnic Identity	• *Comments about being a member of a particular ethnic group* • *Growing preference for customs of one's own ethnic group* (e.g., meal practices, holiday celebrations, tastes in music and art) • *Frustration* with discrimination toward one's ethnic group	Fourteen-year-old Diego is proud of his Latino heritage. He follows many of his parents' Mexican traditions, loves Mexican food, and regularly watches Spanish-speaking programs on television. Diego is angered by derogatory names for Hispanics used by a few students at his high school.	Foster ethnic pride by welcoming ethnic traditions at school. Encourage youngsters to write about ethnic customs in assignments, and infuse multicultural material into instruction. Also establish cooperative groups that cross ethnic lines and ensure that children from different ethnic groups take on equally responsible positions within groups. Adamantly discourage the use of ethnic slurs.

DEVELOPMENTAL TRENDS
Sense of Self at Different Age Levels

AGE	WHAT YOU MIGHT OBSERVE	DIVERSITY	IMPLICATIONS
Infancy (Birth–2 Years) 	• Increasing awareness that one is separate from caregivers (in the first year) • Emerging self-awareness of having an impact on other people and the environment (especially at the end of the first year) • Increasing recognition of self in mirror (in the second year) • Appearance of first-person pronouns, such as *I, me, mine* (late in the second year)	• The quality of child–caregiver relationships influences infants' beliefs that they are worthy of love. • The regularity with which adults comment on infants' images in a mirror and refer to infants' facial features (e.g., "We'd better wipe your runny nose") may affect infants' self-recognition.	• Communicate affection by cuddling and talking to infants and by attending to their physical needs in a timely and consistent manner. • Talk with infants and toddlers about their bodily features and possessions ("Where's your nose?" "Here's your teddy bear!").
Early Childhood (2–6 Years) 	• Frequent use of *I, me,* and *mine,* especially at ages 2 and 3 • Emergence of an autobiographical self (beginning at age 3 or 4) • Concrete self-descriptions (e.g., "I'm a boy," "I'm pretty") • Overconfidence about what tasks can be accomplished	• Children whom others treat affectionately tend to develop a positive sense of self. Those who are rejected, ridiculed, or ignored have a harder time seeing themselves in positive terms. • Some children gain an emerging awareness that they belong to a particular racial or ethnic group (by about age 5).	• Acknowledge children's possessions, but encourage sharing. • Engage children in joint retellings of recent events. • Don't disparage children's lofty ambitions ("I'm going to be president!"), but focus their efforts on accomplishable short-term goals.
Middle Childhood (6–10 Years) 	• Increasing distinction among various aspects of oneself (e.g., among academic performance, athletic ability, and personal likability) • Increasing tendency to base sense of self on how one's own performance compares with that of peers • Increasing internalization of others' standards for performance (continues into adolescence) • Generally good self-esteem in most children	• Different children place greater or lesser importance on various domains (e.g., on academic performance vs. athletic prowess) in deriving their overall sense of self-worth. • In middle childhood, girls begin to evaluate their physical appearance less favorably than boys do.	• Praise children for their talents and accomplishments in numerous areas (e.g., in physical activities, social relationships, and specific academic subjects). • Help children find arenas in which they can be especially successful. • If necessary, teach hygiene and personal grooming habits that enhance children's physical attractiveness.
Early Adolescence (10–14 Years) 	• Increasing tendency to define oneself in terms of abstract rather than concrete characteristics • Possible drop in self-esteem after the transition to middle school or junior high • Heightened sensitivity to what others think of oneself *(imaginary audience),* leading to a preoccupation with physical appearance • Belief in oneself as overly unique *(personal fable),* occasionally leading to a sense of invulnerability	• Drops in self-esteem, when sizable and not followed by a gradual rebound, can signal a problem. • On average, youngsters increasingly base their self-perceived strengths on gender stereotypes (e.g., boys see themselves as good in mathematics and science, girls see themselves as good in reading) even when actual achievement levels are similar. • Members of ethnic groups vary in the extent to which their ethnic status plays a role in their core identity.	• When students are making the transition to middle school or junior high, be especially supportive and optimistic about their potential for success. • Be patient when adolescents show exceptional self-consciousness; give them strategies for presenting themselves well to others (e.g., how they might introduce themselves to unfamiliar peers).
Late Adolescence (14–18 Years) 	• Decrease in the self-consciousness that was evident in early adolescence • Reconciliation of many apparent contradictions in oneself • Concern with identity issues: Who am I? What do I believe? What course should my life take?	• Adolescents whose sense of self-worth continues to depend heavily on others' behaviors and opinions (those who have *contingent self-worth*) are more susceptible to mood swings and peer pressure. • Some adolescents willingly accept the professional goals and ideologies that their parents offer. Others engage in more soul-searching as they piece together their identity.	• Provide opportunities for adolescents to explore diverse belief systems and try on a variety of occupational "hats." • Be on the lookout for teens whose self-worth seems especially dependent on peers' opinions; help them discover areas of talent that can contribute to a more stable sense of self-worth.

- Being well prepared for lessons and other activities with children
- Including children in decision making and in evaluations of their performance
- Acknowledging that children can occasionally have an "off" day and not holding it against them (L. H. Anderman, Patrick, Hruda, & Linnenbrink, 2002; Certo, Cauley, & Chafin, 2002; Cushman & Cowan, 2010; H. A. Davis, 2003; H. A. Davis, Schutz, & Chambless, 2001)

• Promote success on academic, social, and physical tasks. Experiences with success are powerful catalysts for the development of a positive sense of self (Cushman & Cowan, 2010; Damon, 1991; Marsh & Craven, 1997). Thus teachers should gear assignments to youngsters' capabilities—for instance, by making sure that they have already mastered any necessary prerequisite knowledge and skills. However, success at very easy activities is unlikely to have much of an impact. Mastering the significant challenges in life—earning the hard-won successes that come only with effort and persistence—brings more enduring and resilient self-perceptions (Dweck, 2000; Eisenberger, 1992; Winne, 1995a). Thus teachers and other practitioners are most likely to bolster youngsters' sense of self when they assign challenging tasks and provide the structure and support youngsters need to accomplish the tasks successfully. They should also help young people keep the little "failures" along the way in perspective: Mistakes are an inevitable part of learning something new.

• Focus children's attention on their own improvement rather than on how their peers perform. Youngsters are likely to be optimistic about their chances of future success if they see they are making regular progress—if they continually make gains through effort and practice. They are *un*likely to be optimistic if they focus their attention on how their age-mates are surpassing them (Deci & Ryan, 1992; Krampen, 1987; Stipek, 1996).

• Be honest about children's shortcomings, but also provide the guidance and support they need to overcome them. Youngsters are likely to be successful over the long run if they come to grips with their areas of weakness. If adults give only positive feedback—and especially if they provide inflated evaluations of children's performance—some children may be unaware of areas that need improvement (Dweck, 2000; T. D. Little, Oettingen, Stetsenko, & Baltes, 1995; Paris & Cunningham, 1996). And when adults praise children for successes on very easy tasks, children may conclude that they are not capable of handling anything more difficult (Pintrich & Schunk, 2002).

Realistically, then, adults must give children negative as well as positive feedback. When feedback must include information about children's shortcomings, the best approach is to give it within the context of high (yet achievable) expectations for future performance (Deci & Ryan, 1985; Pintrich & Schunk, 2002). Following are examples of how a teacher might put a positive spin on negative feedback:

- "You're generally a very kind person, but you hurt Jenny's feelings by making fun of her new outfit. Perhaps you can think of a good way to make her feel better."
- "In the first draft of your research paper, many of your paragraphs don't lead logically to the ones that follow. A few headings and transitional sentences would make a world of difference. Let's find a time to discuss how you might use these techniques to improve the flow of your paper."

When children have long-standing difficulties in certain domains, discovering that their failures are due to a previously undiagnosed disability, such as dyslexia or ADHD, sometimes helps repair damage to self-esteem. Such a discovery helps children make sense of *why* they can't perform certain tasks as well as their peers. It can also spur children and their teachers to identify effective coping strategies. In the following reflection, one young adolescent boy reveals how, in coming to terms with his dyslexia, he's acquired a healthy sense of self despite his disability:

> Dyslexia is your brain's wired differently and there's brick walls for some things and you just have to work either around it or break it. I'm dyslexic at reading that means I need a little bit more help. If you have dyslexia the thing you have to find is how to get over the hump, the wall. Basically you either go around it and just don't read and get along in life without it or you break down the wall. (Zambo, 2003, p. 10)

GOOD CITIZEN. An adolescent boy sees himself in a productive role as he works with younger children at summer camp.

Obviously, it can be detrimental if children are given labels for their conditions without simultaneously learning about strategies that will help them overcome or minimize their difficulties.

• **Provide opportunities to explore a wide variety of activities and domains.** Not all children and adolescents can achieve at superior levels in the classroom, nor can they all be superstars on the playing field. Youngsters are more likely to have a positive sense of self if they find an activity—perhaps singing, student government, or competitive jump-roping—in which they can shine (Harter, 1999). By exploring many different fields and career options and beginning to zero in on a few possible career paths, young people take an important step toward forming a sense of their adult identity.

• **Consider the unique needs of girls and boys.** Many youngsters place little value on characteristics and abilities that they think are more "appropriate" for members of the opposite sex. In addition, they may place high value on qualities they think they need to be "feminine" or "manly." Some teenage girls may strive for impossible standards of physical beauty. And some teenage boys may worry that they are maturing too slowly and lack the height and build of their classmates.

With these points in mind, teachers and other adults should probably use somewhat different tactics in nurturing the self-esteem of girls and boys. They might help girls identify realistic standards by which to judge their physical appearance. And given girls' tendency to react more negatively to failures, adults might encourage them to pat themselves on the back for their many successes, even those (and perhaps *especially* those) in traditionally male domains such as science and mathematics. But boys, too, have special needs. Many boys are often brought up to believe they should be "tough" and hide any feelings of self-doubt or inadequacy. Adults may want to take special pains to acknowledge a boy's "softer" sides—for instance, his compassion and skill in interacting with small children.

• **Communicate respect for diverse ethnic and cultural backgrounds.** Although most educators today are aware of the need to respect the diversity in children's backgrounds, they do not always know how best to show such regard. An important first step, of course, is *understanding* various ethnic and cultural groups—their traditions, values, priorities, and so on. In addition to showing appreciation for children's native languages and dialects, educators can communicate respect for diverse groups through strategies such as these:

- Treat all children as full-fledged members of the classroom and community, rather than as exotic "curiosities" who live in a strange and separate world.
- Call children by their given names unless they specifically request otherwise.
- Consistently look at historical and current events from diverse cultural perspectives—for instance, by considering American, European, African, and Arabic perspectives of recent events in the Middle East.
- Visit the communities in which children live, and invite their families to school to share their talents, origins, and traditions.
- Create situations in which youngsters from diverse backgrounds must collaborate to achieve success—for example, through cooperative group activities or community service projects. (Banks & Banks, 1995; Branch, 1999; Fantino & Colak, 2001; García, Arias, Murri, & Serna, 2010; Howard, 2007; Ladson-Billings, 1994; Oskamp, 2000; Villegas & Lucas, 2007; S. C. Wong, 1993)

In their efforts to be sensitive to children's cultural backgrounds, some well-meaning practitioners make the mistake of thinking of children

I had lots of friends back home, and I remember all of them, we used to play soccer together. I have also friends here now, well ... mostly classmates.

School is OK but there is one thing that bothers me. My name is Mohammed, no other. Here, my teacher calls me Mo, because there are five other kids with the same name. My friends sometimes call me M J, which is not too bad, but I wish they will call me by my real name. I like what my grandma called me: "Mamet." I like how she used to say it. One thing makes me really mad. I have a pen pal called Rudy. He lives in Toronto. Once I showed his letter to my teacher and she said: "That is nice name." Now, all my friends call me Rudy. I hate it, because that's not me, that's not my name. My name is "MO-HA-MMED." Do you understand me?

ARTIFACT 12-5 **My name is Mohammed.** For many children, their given name is an important part of their identity, as this reflection by a refugee child in Canada illustrates.
Excerpt from "Refugee Children in Canada: Searching for Identity," by A. M. Fantino and A. Colak, 2001, Child Welfare, 80, pp. 591–592, a publication of the Child Welfare League of America.

as belonging exclusively to a particular ethnic or cultural group. Yet in this age of increasing multiracial ethnicities and multicultural interminglings, many youngsters cannot be pigeonholed. Teachers must keep in mind that some of their students have a blended ethnic, racial, cultural, or religious heritage, and many students from minority-group backgrounds want to be integral parts of both their local cultural groups and mainstream Western society (C. R. Cooper et al., 1995; A. M. Lopez, 2003; Stroink & Lalonde, 2009). It also is worth bearing in mind that children of any ethnic heritage, however simple or complex, may or may not exhibit typical characteristics of people whose ancestry they share.

• **Give youngsters second chances to develop healthy self-perceptions.** Adolescents who struggle academically or have friendships with antisocial peers tend to see themselves as disconnected from school. These self-perceptions are not easily changed, but concerted efforts from a teacher can have a desirable effect. In one instance a group of adolescents with learning disabilities were moved from one school (Piney Ridge), where they were failing, to another school in which teachers got to know them individually and encouraged their success (Youngblood & Spencer, 2002). With time the adolescents came to see themselves as capable academically and socially, as one boy explains:

Interviewer:	What makes you. . . . Why do you think there's a difference between the student helping each other in this program and not helping each other at Piney?
Rashae:	Because they're. . . . Well half of them over there criminal. They're like they just got out of jail or whatever. I mean, they just. . . . I think Piney Ridge like a school for bad kids.
Interviewer:	So why do you think they're more likely to help you over here?
Rashae:	Because everybody over here nice. They don't think about just they self. Think about other people in the class. . . . Well we help one another in the class work or out of class. (dialogue from Youngblood & Spencer, 2002, p. 103)

• **Put self-esteem in its proper perspective.** The popular educational literature often overrates self-esteem as a target for intervention, sometimes to the point where it becomes the *only* target (Dweck, 2000). Certainly we want children and adolescents to feel good about themselves, but increasing evidence suggests that efforts to enhance self-esteem as *the* ultimate goal for children are ineffective for several reasons (Baumeister et al., 2003; Meadows, 2010). First, children appreciate optimistic evaluations from adults but are more likely to be convinced of their own capabilities when they see themselves surmounting challenges and fulfilling high standards of conduct. Thus, rather than telling children that they are smart and good, it makes more sense to create conditions where children achieve success.[14] Second, self-esteem seems to be closely linked to personal happiness and resilience yet, counter to society's expectations, it does *not* protect young people from numerous risks in life. Youngsters with high self-esteem do not avoid drugs, for example, any more than youngsters with low self-esteem do (Baumeister et al., 2003; Meadows, 2010). Hence, other developmental outcomes must receive equal billing from adults. Third, some children with an inflated sense of self are aggressive and callous to the feelings of others (Baumeister et al., 2003). Rather than simply being told about their own inherent goodness, these children need support in focusing on the needs of other people. Finally, not every culture aspires to high self-esteem in its children, at least as self-esteem is typically conceptualized in Western cultures. Instead, some cultures socialize children to focus more on being humble and respectful of friends, family members, and adults in authority.

SOCIAL COGNITION

As you have learned, children regularly think about who they are and what they are becoming. As they gain a sense of their own thoughts, feelings, and other characteristics, children also begin to realize that other people have qualities and perspectives that differ from their

---

[14] You will learn several strategies for helping children to succeed on academic tasks in Chapter 13.

own. Most children and adolescents devote a lot of mental energy to **social cognition**, their speculations about what other people are thinking and feeling.

As you might expect, social cognition has many facets. We begin our discussion with an analysis of children's understanding of what other people think and their ability to apply these skills during social interactions. We next examine biases in children's thinking that can lead to prejudice. We finally consider bioecological variations that exist in children's social-cognitive abilities and outline the many things adults can do to foster children's social cognition.

Understanding What Others Think

Just as children construct theories about their physical and biological worlds, so, too, do they construct theories about their psychological world. More specifically, they develop a **theory of mind** that eventually encompasses complex understandings of people's mental and emotional states—thoughts, beliefs, feelings, motives, intentions, and so on.

Children put these general understandings to work in particular social interactions, stepping into others' shoes and looking at the world from others' perspectives. Such **social perspective taking** helps children make sense of actions that might otherwise be puzzling. As children exercise their theory of mind by inferring others' people frames of mind in particular settings, they are better able to interact effectively with important people in their lives (Flavell, 2000; R. D. Parke & Clarke-Stewart, 2011; Selman, 2003).

Infancy (Birth–Age 2)

Infants quickly discover that, unlike inanimate objects, people are active, expressive, and responsive (Mandler, 2007a; Poulin-Dubois, Frenkiel-Fishman, Nayer, & Johnson, 2006). In the latter part of their first year, they also begin to realize that people have an "inner life" that objects do not. By about 9 or 10 months, infants show *intersubjectivity*, an awareness that they share a focus of attention with a caregiver.[15] At about the same time or shortly thereafter, they acquire some awareness of **intentionality**. That is, they know that other people behave in order to accomplish certain goals, and they begin to draw inferences about people's intentions from such actions as reaching for, pointing at, and gazing at objects (D. A. Baldwin, 2000; Kuhlmeier, Wynn, & Bloom, 2003; C. Moore & Barresi, 2010).

In the second year, infants become increasingly mindful of other people's mental states. Infants as young as 12 months engage in *social referencing*, the tendency to watch an adult react to an unfamiliar person, object, or event in a particular way and then show the same kind of response.[16] By 18 months, children clearly know that their own actions influence other people's emotions and behaviors. Infants are likely to offer an adult a food item to which the adult has previously reacted favorably, even though they themselves dislike that kind of food (Repacholi & Gopnik, 1997).[17] Early gestures to comfort others also suggest an attempt to consider others' perspectives (P. L. Harris, 2006). In some cases, toddlers may even behave in ways that they know will annoy or upset someone else (J. Dunn & Munn, 1985; Flavell et al., 2002). As a toddler, Jeanne's daughter Tina occasionally ran into the street and then looked tauntingly back at Mom as if to say, "Look at what I'm doing! I know this upsets you! Catch me if you can!"

Early Childhood (Ages 2–6)

In the preschool years, children become increasingly aware of people's mental states. Beginning at age 2 (sometimes even earlier), they spontaneously use words that refer to desires and emotions (e.g., *want, feel, sad*), and by age 3, "cognitive" words such as *think, know*, and *remember* appear in their speech (Astington & Pelletier, 1996; Bartsch & Wellman, 1995; Skelley & Crnic, 2010). By the time children are 3, they also realize that the mind is

social cognition
Process of thinking about how other people are likely to think, act, and react and choosing one's own interpersonal behaviors accordingly.

theory of mind
Awareness that people have an inner, psychological life (thoughts, beliefs, feelings, etc.).

social perspective taking
Imagining what someone else might be thinking or feeling.

intentionality
Engagement in an action congruent with one's purpose or goal.

---

[15] Intersubjectivity is introduced in Chapter 7.

[16] Social referencing is described in Chapter 7.

[17] In Chapter 6 we saw evidence that preschoolers are not as egocentric as Piaget said they were. Here we see evidence that even toddlers can occasionally take another person's perspective.

distinct from the physical world—that thoughts, memories, and dreams are not physical entities (J. A. Baird & Astington, 2005; Wellman & Estes, 1986; Woolley, 1995).

In the third and fourth year, children develop an appreciation that other people have desires that differ from their own (P. L. Harris, 2006). Preschoolers are often eager to learn why people do the things they do, as this conversation between 2½-year-old Adam and his mother illustrates:

Adam:	Why she write dat name?
Mother:	Because she wanted to.
Adam:	Why she wanted to?
Mother:	Because she thought you'd like it.
Adam:	I don't want to like it. (Wellman, Phillips, & Rodriguez, 2000, p. 908)

Inherent in Adam's question *Why she write dat name?* is an advancement in theory of mind: Preschoolers become increasingly aware of relationships between other people's desires and behaviors.

After gaining an appreciation that they and other people have desires, young children gradually gain an understanding of everyone's knowledge (P. L. Harris, 2006). Initially, preschoolers have trouble looking inward and describing their own thoughts. Furthermore, they may mistakenly assume that what *they* know is what other people know as well. Consider the following situation:

> Max puts a piece of chocolate in the kitchen cupboard and then goes out to play. While he is gone, his mother discovers the chocolate and moves it to a drawer. When Max returns later, where will he look for his chocolate? (based on Wimmer & Perner, 1983)

Max will look in the cupboard, of course, because that's where he thinks the chocolate is. However, 3-year-olds are quite certain he will look in the drawer, where the chocolate is actually located. Not until age 4 or 5 do children appreciate a *false belief:* They realize that circumstances may reasonably lead people to believe something different from what they themselves know to be true (Spritz, Fergusson, & Bankoff, 2010; Wimmer & Perner, 1983).

Gradually, then, children develop an understanding of how people's perceptions, emotions, and desires influence their actions, and they become increasingly adept at inferring people's intentions and other mental states from behaviors and other events (Astington & Pelletier, 1996; Fireman & Kose, 2010; Wellman et al., 2000). Look at the two scenarios in Figure 12-2. *Which boy would like to swing?* Obviously the boy in the lower picture is the one who has an *intention* of using the swing. Most 5-year-olds correctly answer the question we've just asked you, but few 3-year-olds do (Astington, 1991).

Middle Childhood (Ages 6–10)

As children reach the elementary grades, they become capable of more sophisticated inferences about people's mental states. They realize that people's actions do not always reflect their true thoughts and feelings (Flavell et al., 2002; Gnepp, 1989; Spritz et al., 2010). A person may intentionally lie about a situation to mislead someone else, and another person who appears happy may actually be sad.

Middle childhood heralds more complex understandings of the nature of thinking as well. In particular, children understand that people *interpret* an event, rather than simply "record" it, a phenomenon that allows for differences in perspectives among people (Chandler & Boyes, 1982; P. L. Harris, 2006). Finally, children now begin to recognize that people's thoughts and feelings are often closely intertwined. Thus different thoughts about a situation lead to different feelings about it (Flavell, Flavell, & Green, 2001; P. L. Harris, 1989). A 9-year-old might say, "Arlene feels bad because she thinks I don't like her. I *do* like her, though."

FIGURE 12-2   Which boy would like to swing? Children who can correctly answer this question can distinguish between intention and behavior.

"Which Boy Wants to Swing" by J W. Asington, from "Intention in the Child Theory of Mind" from CHILDREN'S THEORIES OF MIND: MENTAL STATES AND SOCIAL UNDERSTANDING by D. Frye. Illustration copyright © 2009 by J. W. Asington. Reprinted with permission via Copyright Clearance Center.

We were playing freeze-tag one day at recess. Leslie got tagged and asked me to step on her shadow before anyone else. I stepped on Becca's shadow before I stepped on Leslie's and she got mad. I told Leslie to stop being so selfish and bratty. She took it extremely personally and stormed off, told a teacher, and called her mom.

I later appologized and we became friends again. I invited her to my birthday and she came but I could tell she felt uncomfortable. So, I decided to do makeovers. I was playing around with lipsticks and accidentally messed up on Leslie's makeover, but laughed because I knew it could be fixed. She ran to see the "damage" in the mirror, started to cry, and called her mom and left.

From then on, I've never really understood her and we've never been close. We see each other and say "hi" in the halls, but that's it.

ARTIFACT 12-6 I've never really understood her. Young adolescents exert a lot of effort in deciphering the perspectives of other people but are especially effective in identifying the viewpoints of individuals they know well. In this reflective essay, 13-year-old Georgia expresses dismay over an acquaintance's interpretation of events.

Early Adolescence (Ages 10–14)

Theory of mind and perspective taking continue to develop during the adolescent years (Smetana & Villalobos, 2009). As children move into early adolescence, they begin to appreciate that people can have mixed feelings about events and other individuals (S. K. Donaldson & Westerman, 1986; Flavell & Miller, 1998; Harter & Whitesell, 1989). And they realize that people may simultaneously have multiple, and possibly conflicting, intentions (Chandler, 1987). They also become increasingly thoughtful about the divergent perspectives that people may have about a single event. In general, young adolescents seem to find it easier to think about the perspectives of people they know and like, presumably because these individuals have shared their views in the past (T. G. O'Connor & Hirsch, 1999; Smetana & Villalobos, 2009).

Courtesy of their expanding reasoning abilities, working memory capacity, and social awareness, young adolescents also begin to engage in **recursive thinking** (Abrams, Rutland, Cameron, & Ferrell, 2007; Müeller & Overton, 2010; Perner & Wimmer, 1985). That is, they now think about what other people might be thinking about them and eventually can reflect on their own and other people's thoughts through multiple iterations (e.g., "You think that I think that you think . . ."). This is not to say that adolescents always use this capacity. In fact, thinking only about one's own perspective, without regard for the perspectives of others, is a common phenomenon in the early adolescent years (recall our earlier discussion of the *imaginary audience*).

Late Adolescence (Ages 14–18)

Older adolescents can draw on a rich knowledge base derived from numerous social experiences, and so they become ever more skillful at identifying people's psychological characteristics, intentions, and needs (Eisenberg, Carlo, Murphy, & Van Court, 1995; Paget, Kritt, & Bergemann, 1984). In addition, they are more attuned to the complex dynamics—not only thoughts, feelings, and present circumstances, but also past experiences—that influence behavior (Flanagan & Tucker, 1999; Selman, 1980; Tynes, 2007). Furthermore, they realize that human beings are not always aware of why they act as they do (Selman, 2003). What we see emerging in the high school years, then, is a budding psychologist: an individual who can be quite astute in deciphering and explaining the motives and actions of others.

Social Perspective Taking in Action

Taking the perspective of another person is not simply an intellectual exercise. Drawing inferences about other people's thoughts, desires, and intentions allows children to better meet such personal goals as comforting a friend in distress, outsmarting an opponent in a game, and pleasing a demanding teacher. American psychologist **Robert Selman's** theory of social perspective taking portrays some of the developmental trends that occur in children's thinking during social exchanges.

Selman asked children to think about the various perspectives that different people had about a situation. Consider the following situation:

> Holly is an 8-year-old girl who likes to climb trees. She is the best tree climber in the neighborhood. One day while climbing down from a tall tree she falls off the bottom branch but does not hurt herself. Her father sees her fall. He is upset and asks her to promise not to climb the trees any more. Holly promises.
>
> Later that day, Holly and her friends meet Sean. Sean's kitten is caught up in a tree and cannot get down. Something has to be done right away or the kitten may fall. Holly is the only one who climbs trees well enough to reach the kitten and get it down, but she remembers her promise to her father. (Selman & Byrne, 1974, p. 805)

Children are asked if Holly understands Sean's feelings about the kitten, if Sean realizes why it will be difficult for Holly to decide whether or not to climb up the tree, and what

recursive thinking
Thinking about what other people may be thinking about oneself, possibly through multiple iterations.

Holly believes her father will think if he learns she eventually does climb the tree. To answer these questions, you must look at the situation from the perspectives of three different people: Sean, Holly, and Holly's father. By presenting situations like this one and asking children to view them from various perspectives, Robert Selman (1980; Selman & Schultz, 1990) found that with age, children show an increasing ability to take the perspective of others. He described a series of five levels that characterize the development of perspective taking:

- *Level 0: Egocentric perspective taking.* Children are aware of physical differences among people but have little awareness of psychological differences. They are incapable of looking at a situation from anyone's perspective but their own (hence the reference to Level 0). As an example, 3-year-old Andrea assumes that her preschool friends know how scared she is about climbing on the jungle gym. Hence she expresses indignation when Rose and Sue Ann ask her to climb with them.
- *Level 1: Subjective perspective taking.* Children realize that people have different thoughts and feelings as well as different physical features. However, they view someone else's perspective in a relatively simplistic, one-dimensional fashion (e.g., a person is simply happy, sad, or angry) and tend to equate behavior with feelings (e.g., a happy person will smile, and a sad person will pout or cry). For instance, 8-year-old Li-Wen realizes that her friend Tony is sad about his grandfather's recent death but does not understand that he also feels relief that his grandfather's suffering is over.
- *Level 2: Second-person, reciprocal perspective taking.* Children realize that people occasionally have mixed feelings about an event—for instance, that Holly might feel both compassion for the kitten and uneasiness about breaking her promise to her father. At this level, children also understand that people may feel differently than their behaviors indicate and that people may sometimes do things they didn't really want or intend to do. In this manner, 11-year-old Peter understands that his friend Mark has misgivings about his decision to experiment with inhalants. Peter perceives reservation in Mark's voice and body language as he brags about his escapades.
- *Level 3: Third-person, mutual perspective taking.* Children can take an outsider's perspective of interpersonal relationships: They can look at their own interactions with another person as a third individual might. They appreciate the need to satisfy both their own and another's needs simultaneously and therefore readily grasp the advantages of cooperation, compromise, and trust. To illustrate, two high school freshmen, Jasmine and Alethea, discover that they've each arranged a homecoming party for the same night. They learn that they've each sent invitations to mutual friends. Since they were both looking forward to hosting a party, they discuss options for rescheduling one of the parties and co-hosting the event.
- *Level 4: Societal, symbolic perspective taking.* Children realize that people are affected by the many factors in their environments and, furthermore, that people are not always aware of why they act as they do. In their psychology course, high school seniors Kent and Joaquin are preparing a joint oral report on strategies of social persuasion. They find magazine advertisements that are geared toward adolescents and discuss possible images and feelings that advertisers are trying to invoke.

Selman aptly captures general trends in children's perspective taking but his original work seems to have underestimated young children's capabilities. Convincing evidence by other theorists reveals perspective-taking abilities in young children. Even young preschoolers realize that another person can see an object only if he or she is looking in the object's direction and has a clear, unobstructed view. Older preschoolers also grasp that the same object may look different to people viewing it from different angles—for example, that a book that is right-side-up to one person will be upside-down to someone sitting across the table (Flavell, 2000). Furthermore, in their daily communication, children appear to be truly other-oriented a lot of the time; that is, they listen to what other people say, respond appropriately, and take into account how their listeners might be thinking and feeling (Garvey & Hogan, 1973; Rozendaal & Baker, 2010).

Selman's original theory is limited in another way. It seems to imply that progress through levels is almost inevitable. In more recent work, Selman has argued that children's social awareness is not guaranteed by basic maturational processes and instead is highly dependent on personal experience (Selman, 2003). For example, Selman and his colleagues have found that children integrate their social experiences into understandings of teasing and persuading others to take a certain position (Dray, Selman, & Schultz, 2009; S. L. Katz, Selman, & Mason, 2008).

All things considered, Selman's work suggests that adults can be confident that they can gradually nudge young people toward more advanced ways of thinking about the people around them—perhaps "one level up" in levels of perspective taking. Preschool teachers might point out how classmates' feelings may differ from children's own feelings (Level 1). Adults who work with children in the elementary grades can discuss situations in which people may have mixed feelings or want to hide their feelings—situations such as going to a new school, trying a difficult but enjoyable sport for the first time, or celebrating a holiday without a favorite family member present (Level 2). Adults who work with adolescents might, either informally (e.g., in free-flowing conversations) or formally (e.g., in a high school psychology class), explore the many ways in which people are affected by their past experiences and present understandings (Level 4).

The progressions in social cognition we've examined suggest that it's a long road from infants' initial flickers of social awareness to adolescents' far-reaching insights into how minds coordinate a broad array of mental states. In the Developmental Trends table "Social Cognition at Different Age Levels," you can see some of the primary social-cognitive accomplishments and common manifestations of diversity at each age level.

Social-Cognitive Bias and Prejudice

By now you understand just how much mental "work" is involved in thinking about social situations. Yet, people often take mental "shortcuts" to ease the load on working memory and make their dealings with others more efficient (L. A. Brenner, Koehler, Liberman, & Tversky, 1996; Tversky & Kahneman, 1990). Many of these shortcuts reflect **social-cognitive biases**, predispositions to interpret or respond to social situations in particular ways. For example, in various situations a child might assume that a single action reflects a person's typical behavior (Boseovski & Lee, 2006; Dweck, 2000; Karafantis & Levy, 2004). Eight-year-old Dwight may observe a new boy arguing with his friend on the playground and jump to the conclusion that the new boy is a bully.

Some social-cognitive biases are a minor nuisance; they lead to small distortions in thinking but don't cause grave harm. Others, however, have serious consequences. Children occasionally jump to hasty conclusions about others based on group membership (e.g., gender, ethnicity, sexual orientation, religious affiliation). In other words, they respond on the basis of a **stereotype**, a rigid, simplistic, and erroneous characterization of a particular group. Often a stereotype encompasses a host of negative attributes (e.g., "stingy," "lazy," "promiscuous") and leads children to exhibit negative attitudes, feelings, and behaviors—that is, **prejudice**—toward the group in question.

The roots of stereotypes and prejudice lie in the natural tendency of human beings to categorize their experiences. In their first few years, children learn that people belong to different groups, such as boys and girls, and "Blacks" and "Whites," and many preschoolers can identify members of various ethnic groups (Aboud, 1988). As children form these social categories, they tend to favor their own group and expect less desirable characteristics from members of other groups, especially if the different groups are in some form of conflict with one another (Aboud, 2005; Bigler & Liben, 2007; R. D. Parke & Clarke-Stewart, 2011; J. H. Pfeifer, Brown, & Juvonen, 2007).

On average, stereotypes and prejudice decrease as children move through the elementary grades (D. E. Carter, Detine-Carter, & Benson, 1995; F. H. Davidson, 1976; J. H. Pfeifer et al., 2007). This decline is probably due to children's increasing awareness of the limits of social categories. Many children gradually begin to realize that individuals who share membership in a category (e.g., "girls") are similar in some ways but very different in others. Yet other factors may work to maintain or strengthen stereotypes, and so some children show an increase in prejudice as they reach early adolescence (Aboud, 2005; Black-Gutman & Hickson, 1996;

social-cognitive bias
Mental shortcut used when thinking about other people or social events.

stereotype
Rigid, simplistic, and erroneous characterization of a particular group.

prejudice
Display of negative attitudes, feelings, and behaviors toward particular individuals because of their membership in a specific group.

DEVELOPMENTAL TRENDS
Social Cognition at Different Age Levels

AGE	WHAT YOU MIGHT OBSERVE	DIVERSITY	IMPLICATIONS
Infancy (Birth–2 Years) 	• Awareness of one's ability to share a focus of attention with caregiver *(intersubjectivity)* • Observation of other people's emotional reactions, followed by the child making a similar response *(social referencing)* • Emerging realization that other people have desires, goals, and intentions different from one's own	• Infants who receive inadequate care at home may be delayed in acquiring intersubjectivity and social referencing. • Infants who are autistic may avoid eye contact with caregivers and not understand the connection between where they are pointing and what they are thinking about.	• Get to know infants as individuals and the kinds of social interactions that each of them enjoys. • Use words such as *like, want,* and *think* regularly in descriptions of yourself and children. • Patiently explain why you must prohibit infants from pursuing tempting yet dangerous activities (protecting them from harm but also cultivating their awareness that your perspective differs from theirs).
Early Childhood (2–6 Years) 	• Increasing use of "feeling" and "thinking" words (e.g., *want, sad, know*) • Growing realization that the mind does not always represent events accurately (e.g., that a person may have a false belief) • Growing ability to take others' perspectives	• Children whose parents talk frequently about thoughts and feelings tend to have a more advanced theory of mind. • Children with certain cognitive impairments (e.g., autism spectrum disorders) and those with reduced exposure to language as a result of hearing impairments tend to have a more limited theory of mind than their peers.	• Talk about various people's thoughts, feelings, perspectives, and needs. • Establish fun routines (e.g., tossing a ball, turning the pages of a book together) with children who find it difficult to synchronize their behavior with others. • Recognize that selfish and territorial behaviors are common in early childhood, but encourage sharing.
Middle Childhood (6–10 Years) 	• Recognition that people's actions do not always reflect their true thoughts and feelings • Growing realization that other people interpret (rather than simply remember) their experiences • Decrease in rigid stereotypes of particular groups of people (for most children)	• Children with certain disabilities (e.g., ADHD, autism, general intellectual disability) are more apt to have difficulty making accurate inferences about people's motives and intentions. • Children whose families or communities consistently promote unflattering images of particular groups may continue to have strong prejudices.	• Assist children in their attempts to discern the viewpoints of characters in stories and of public figures during historical events. • When addressing the experiences of a particular ethnic group (perhaps their literary accomplishments or struggles during historical events), make a point to expose children to individuals within the group who hold distinctly different perspectives.
Early Adolescence (10–14 Years) 	• Recognition that people may have multiple and possibly conflicting feelings and motives • Emerging ability to think recursively about one's own and others' thoughts	• Some adolescents become so concerned about how other people see them that they succumb to peer pressure and take extreme measures to please other people. • Intellectual disabilities may hinder adolescents' abilities to consider multiple points of view.	• Conduct discussions that require adolescents to look at controversial issues from multiple perspectives. • Do not tolerate ethnic jokes or other remarks that show prejudice toward a particular group.
Late Adolescence (14–18 Years) 	• Recognition that people are products of their environment and that past events and present circumstances influence personality and behavior • Use of a peer group as a forum for self-exploration and self-understanding • Increasing awareness that members of any single category of people (e.g., women, people with disabilities) can be very different from one another	• Most high school students use their social perspective-taking abilities constructively, but a few students use their knowledge of other people's psychological vulnerabilities to inflict harm on them. • Adolescents who are familiar with people from diverse cultures may find it relatively easy to infer the perspectives of individuals from different backgrounds.	• Talk about other people's complex (and sometimes conflicting) motives, perhaps while discussing contemporary issues, historical events, or works of fiction. • Assign autobiographies and other readings that depict individuals who have actively worked for the greater good of society, asking students to write about the motivations, beliefs, and ideas of these individuals.

J. H. Pfeifer et al., 2007). Parents may encourage prejudice through both words and actions—for instance, by telling ethnic jokes, restricting playmates to same-race peers, or enrolling their children in schools with as little racial and ethnic diversity as possible (Ashmore & DelBoca, 1976; McGlothlin & Killen, 2005; Rodríguez-García & Wagner, 2009). Popular images in television and other media—where males are often depicted as strong and aggressive, females appear to be weak and passive, and members of certain ethnic groups are consistently cast as unimportant characters or "bad guys"—may also have an impact (B. S. Greenberg & Mastro, 2008; Huston et al., 1992; Maher, Herbst, Childs, & Finn, 2008).[18]

By adolescence and probably before, children who are victims of prejudice are well aware that others' treatment of them is unfair (Dessel, 2010; Phinney & Tarver, 1988; R. D. Taylor, Casten, Flickinger, Roberts, & Fulmore, 1994). Over time they acquire a variety of strategies—seeking the support and companionship of other group members, forming a positive ethnic identity, and so on—for coping with prejudice and discrimination (Carranza, 2007; Swim & Stangor, 1998). Even so, young people who are victims of prejudice are more likely than their peers to succumb to such distressing circumstances by becoming ill or depressed and performing at relatively low levels in school (Allison, 1998; Dessel, 2010; B. D. Tatum, 1997).

Bioecology of Social Cognition

The bioecological framework suggests that the personal characteristics of children and their experiences in complex environments contribute to their emerging social understandings. Let's look at two qualities affecting social cognition: having certain exceptionalities and growing up in a particular social setting.

Exceptionalities Affecting Social Cognition

Some children with disabilities are disadvantaged in their understanding of other people, in large part because their brains do not allow them to easily recognize faces, think about other people's perspectives, and detect emotions. Children with Fragile X syndrome, who have intellectual disabilities and are socially anxious, tend to perform at relatively low levels on theory of mind tasks (Cornish et al., 2005; P. Lewis et al., 2006).[19] When children have significant hearing impairments beginning at birth or soon thereafter, they miss out on many discussions about "thinking," "feeling," "wanting," and the like, and so their theory of mind may develop slowly (Dahlgren, Sandberg, & Larsson, 2010; C. C. Peterson, 2002). Some children with ADHD find it difficult to take the perspective of other people, possibly in part because they may have few friends—and therefore limited social experiences—as a result of their disruptive behaviors (Stormont, 2001; Uekermann et al., 2010).

One group of children with disabilities has an especially significant deficit in social cognition. Children with **autism spectrum disorders** have one of several conditions characterized by a serious impairment in social communication and restricted, repetitive behaviors (e.g., repeatedly flipping through the pages of a book or running water over one's hands). Children with these disorders vary considerably in the severity of their symptoms, hence the reference to being somewhere on the *spectrum* (American Psychiatric Association, 1994; Koegel, 1995; Lord & Bishop, 2010; Ozonoff, 2010; D. L. Williams, 2008). Children with *autistic disorder* (also known simply as *autism*) show abnormal behaviors by age 3, notably deficits in reciprocal social interactions, communication, and language; limitations in imitation or imaginative play; preoccupations with parts of objects; unusual sensory aversions or interests; restricted concerns; and, frequently, an intellectual disability. Children with *Asperger's syndrome* are similar to their peers with autism in that they have problems with social abilities and exhibit restricted, repetitive behaviors, but unlike children with autism they have normal intelligence and language. Children with *Rett syndrome* have a significant intellectual disability, an unsteady gait, repetitive hand movements (e.g., wringing hands), and problems with social interactions.

Common to autism spectrum disorders are marked deficits in social cognition (e.g., self-awareness, theory of mind, and perspective taking) and in social skills (e.g., gaining entry

Bioecology of Child Development

Children's own characteristics and their experiences in social groups affect how they understand other people's perspectives.

autism spectrum disorders

Disorders marked by impaired social cognition, social skills, and social interaction, as well as by repetitive behaviors; extreme forms are often associated with significant cognitive and linguistic delays and highly unusual behaviors.

[18] Children's experiences with media and technology are described in Chapter 15.
[19] Fragile X syndrome is described in Chapter 4.

into a peer group, interacting appropriately with others) (Baron-Cohen, Tager-Flusberg, & Cohen, 1993; Hobson, Chidambi, Lee, & Meyer, 2006; Ozonoff, 2010; Pellicano, 2010). Although children with autism spectrum disorders tend to form close emotional attachments to their caregivers, they often prefer to be alone and have difficulty making friends (Hobson, 2004; Oppenheim, Koren-Karie, Dolev, & Yirmiya, 2008). Children with these conditions may also have an undersensitivity or oversensitivity to sensory stimulation (R. C. Sullivan, 1994; D. Williams, 1996). Temple Grandin, a brilliant woman who has gained international prominence as a designer of livestock facilities, recalls what it was like to be a child with autism:

> From as far back as I can remember, I always hated to be hugged. I wanted to experience the good feeling of being hugged, but it was just too overwhelming. It was like a great, all-engulfing tidal wave of stimulation, and I reacted like a wild animal . . . .
>
> When I was little, loud noises were also a problem, often feeling like a dentist's drill hitting a nerve. They actually caused pain. I was scared to death of balloons popping, because the sound was like an explosion in my ear. Minor noises that most people can tune out drove me to distraction. (Grandin, 1995, pp. 63, 67)

Preparing for Your Licensure Examination
Your teaching test might ask you about the characteristics of children with autism and Asperger 's syndrome.

One reason for the characteristics of autism may be deficiencies in mirror neurons. **Mirror neurons** are specialized brain cells that are activated when a person performs a certain act, perhaps reaching for a cup or clapping his or her hands, or when the person observes someone else carry out that same behavior.[20] Mirror neurons seem to play a role in imitation and also allow an individual to draw reasonable inferences about what another person is doing. A few theorists have found irregularities in mirror neurons in children with autism (Rizzolatti & Fabbri-Destro, 2010). Other scholars have found irregularities in other parts of the brain. Some children with autism have larger than usual brains by the first year of life (suggesting excessive growth of neurons and failure of normal synaptic pruning mechanisms[21]) and abnormal structures in the cerebellum (which modulates controlled movements), brainstem (which controls automatic functions necessary for survival, including breathing, digestion, and circulation of blood), and the front part of the cortex (which controls planning, inhibiting of automatic responses, and coordinating of complex, multistep actions) (Fan, Decety, Yang, Liu, & Cheng, 2010; Minshew & Williams, 2007; Ozonoff, 2010).

Of course, children with an autism spectrum disorder also have numerous strengths. Many children with this condition are able to resist distractions and regularly become highly familiar with visual details in the objects and visual displays they study (Gernsbacher, Stevenson, Khandakar, & Goldsmith, 2008; Rondan & Deruelle, 2007). Occasionally, students with autism exhibit *savant syndrome*, in that they possess an extraordinary ability (e.g., exceptional artistic, mathematical, or musical talent) that is quite remarkable in contrast to other aspects of their mental functioning (Jones et al., 2009; Treffert & Wallace, 2002; Winner, 2000). One example of such a talent is the astonishing artistic ability that young Nadia revealed in her drawings of horses (see p. 146 in Chapter 4). Quite possibly, having weak connections among remote areas of the brain may allow for certain strengths, enabling individuals with autism to concentrate in specific domains that do not require much cross-talk within the brain (Casanova, 2008).

Many children with one of the autism spectrum disorders are in a general education classroom for all or part of the school day. Teachers can help these children feel secure by keeping the classroom layout and schedule fairly consistent. Capitalizing on children's strong visual-spatial skills, teachers can use objects, pictures, and photographs to convey ideas about academic topics (Hogdon, 1995; C. C. Peterson, 2002; Quill, 1995). When working with young children, teachers can strive to establish one-on-one relationships with them, initially getting to know them by sitting beside them, expressing an interest in their activities with objects, and encouraging (but not demanding) give-and-take in interactions (Schreibman, 2008; Wieder, Greenspan, & Kalmanson, 2008). Teachers can also teach vocabulary for such internal mental processes as "thinking," "wishing," and "planning."

As children with autism spectrum disorders grow older, they continue to need guidance in interpreting what other people are doing and how to interact with peers. Teachers can advise youngsters about what to expect during upcoming social events, such as sitting

mirror neuron
Specialized cell in the brain that either fires when the person performs a particular act or observes another individual performing the same act.

---

[20] Mirror neurons are examined in Chapter 7.
[21] The brain's process of *pruning* back on an overabundance of *synapses* is explained in Chapter 4.

with peers during a school play or holding hands with another child during a field trip. Teachers can discourage actions that other youngsters find disturbing, such as repetitive behaviors, so as to increase their social acceptance by peers (Turnbull et al., 2010). They can also teach appropriate ways to secure peers' attention and participate in pretend play with friends (K. Chung et al., 2007; Schreibman, 2008). Finally, some teachers set up buddy arrangements, in which a child without a serious disability is trained to interact with the child with autism and adjust to his or her needs, for example, by maintaining mutual attention with him or her and by commenting on ongoing activities (Kohler, Greteman, Raschke, & Highnam, 2007; Turnbull et al., 2010).

Social Setting

Children learn about other people in particular social settings. Discussions with adults about what people think, feel, want, and so on enhance children's awareness of thoughts and emotions (J. M. Jenkins, Turrell, Kogushi, Lollis, & Ross, 2003; Meadows, 2010; Meins et al., 2003). Parents who openly consider differing points of view during family discussions help children realize that multiple perspectives legitimately exist (Astington & Pelletier, 1996; Taumoepeau & Ruffman, 2008). In the early years, sociodramatic play activities, in which children take on a variety of roles ("mommy," "doctor," etc.), can help children imagine what people might think and feel in different contexts (Ashiabi, 2007; P. L. Harris, 1989; Lillard, 1998). Discussions and conflicts with siblings provide an especially motivating context in which to use perspective-taking skills (Randell & Peterson, 2009).

Children exposed to a wide variety of cultural customs acquire a basic theory of mind, often at similar ages (Callaghan et al., 2005; P. L. Harris, 2006; Liu, Wellman, Tardif, & Sabbagh, 2008). Children around the world first learn about other people's desires and then develop other specific abilities in social cognition depending on priorities in their culture. After grasping that other people are motivated to fulfill their desires, Chinese children next develop an appreciation that people can be either knowledgeable or ignorant, whereas children in the United States and Australia next come to realize that different people may have varying beliefs (Wellman, Fang, Liu, Zhu, & Zhu, 2006).

Cultures also influence *how much* children think about other people's thoughts and feelings (Lillard, 1999). Some cultures frequently explain people's behaviors in terms of mental events, whereas others are more likely to focus on external circumstances. In the United States, children who live in urban areas regularly refer to people's psychological states when explaining good and bad behaviors (e.g., "He helped me catch bugs, because he and I like to catch bugs"). In contrast, children in rural areas are more likely to attribute people's behaviors to situational factors (e.g., "She helped me pick up my books, because if she didn't I would have missed the bus"). The latter approach is also common in many Southeast Asian cultures (Lillard, 1999; J. G. Miller, 1987).

As you have learned in this chapter, a sense of self and basic social understandings about other people derive from both nature *and* nurture. In the Basic Developmental Issues table "Comparing Sense of Self and Social Cognition," you can see other ways that the two characteristics reflect developmental dimensions.

Fostering the Development of Social Cognition

The research findings just reviewed have several implications for teachers and other adults who work with children and adolescents:

• **Talk about psychological phenomena and other people's perspectives in age-appropriate ways.** Adults can talk with children about thoughts and feelings, and together they might speculate about what other people (e.g., peers, figures in historical and current events, or fictional characters) might be thinking and feeling. Adults should, of course, try to gear such discussions to children's cognitive capabilities. Preschoolers understand such straightforward feelings as *sad, disappointed*, and *angry* (Saarni et al., 2006). Adolescents have sufficient cognitive and social reasoning capabilities to consider abstract and complex psychological qualities (e.g., being *passive aggressive* or having an inner *moral compass*).

BASIC DEVELOPMENTAL ISSUES
Comparing Sense of Self and Social Cognition

ISSUE	SENSE OF SELF	SOCIAL COGNITION
Nature and Nurture	Human beings appear to have an inborn need to think of themselves as competent, likable, and worthy individuals. A positive sense of self is fostered in environments wherein adults communicate messages about children's strengths and arrange for children to be successful, and in circumstances in which children interact with one another cooperatively.	The ability to consider other people's perspectives (their intentions, desires, thoughts, and so on) depends on having a normally maturing human brain. The capacities of theory of mind and social perspective taking are nurtured by social experiences with other people and, in particular, with exposure to different viewpoints.
Universality and Diversity	General developmental trends in self-perceptions are fairly universal. Most children first develop fairly simple views of the self and then increasingly see the self in complex terms. A second prevalent trend is for children to integrate their many discrete self-perceptions into general abstractions of their qualities as persons. Diversity emerges due to unique experiences in families and peer groups. Diversity is also reflected in the self-perceptions of boys and girls and children from different cultures and distinct ethnic groups.	Theory of mind appears to be a nearly universal capacity. A few children (e.g., some with autism or serious intellectual disabilities) exhibit substantial delays in acquiring understandings of other people's desires, intentions, and thoughts and feelings. Diversity is present in the age at which children acquire specific elements of theory of mind. Children who have many opportunities to hear about other people's ideas, desires, and feelings tend to develop a theory of mind early. Culture influences the order in which children attain particular aspects of theory of mind and how often they think about other people's perspectives.
Qualitative and Quantitative Change	Infants' basic awareness of themselves (e.g., arising from their experiences with bodily sensations and shared focus of attention with caregivers) is transformed qualitatively when children begin to speak and exchange verbal information about thoughts and feelings with others. Qualitative changes also occur when adolescents fold their seemingly separate selves into unified abstract models that encompass complex psychological characteristics. Quantitative changes occur when children gradually increase their knowledge about things that they are good at and activities for which they lack proficiency.	A series of qualitative changes (e.g., the acquisition of *intersubjectivity* and *social referencing*) appears to set the stage for an emerging awareness that other people have their own (and potentially different) perspectives. Quantitative changes are evident in the increasingly sophisticated understandings that children have about other people's thoughts, intentions, desires, and feelings.

• **Encourage children to look at situations from other people's perspectives.** Classrooms and other group situations provide many opportunities for children to look at the world as others do, and over time such opportunities enhance children's theory of mind and perspective-taking capabilities. The Development and Practice feature "Encouraging Social Perspective Taking" illustrates additional effective strategies.

• **Help children tune in to the nonverbal cues that can help them "read people's minds."** Some children (girls especially) readily pick up on the body language that reveals companions' thoughts and feelings (Bosacki, 2000; Deaux, 1984). Other children are less perceptive. The latter group can benefit from explicit instruction in signals they might look for—the furrowed brow that indicates confusion, the agitation that indicates frustration or impatience, the "silent treatment" that suggests anger, and so on (e.g., Beaumont & Sofronoff, 2008; Minskoff, 1980).

• **Intervene with children who face substantial delays in comprehending psychological concepts.** Children who are significantly delayed in their theory of mind may benefit from systematic exposure to psychological words (e.g., *wanting, thinking*, and *believing*). Paula, a 9-year-old girl with fetal alcohol syndrome, was delayed in her cognitive and language development, had trouble interacting with other children, and rarely used terms for her own or others' mental states (Timler, Olswang, & Coggins, 2005). An intervention was designed to foster

Improving Your Observation Skills

Let's go *there*. A group of children are looking at a globe of the earth with their teacher. What aspects of the interaction may help individual children understand that their peers have unique perspectives? Compare your response with the explanation at the end of the chapter.

DEVELOPMENT AND PRACTICE
Encouraging Social Perspective Taking

Ask children to share their interpretations with one another.

- A first-grade teacher finds several children arguing over why Serena tripped and fell during a game of tag. The teacher comforts Serena and then asks the children about what happened. Some believe she stumbled over her loose shoelaces, others argue that one of the other girls got in her way, and one boy thinks Serena wasn't looking where she was going. The teacher suggests that each of them may be partly right. He also urges them to be more careful when they play running games, because it is easy to accidentally bump into one another. (Middle Childhood)

- After a field trip to a local museum, a high school art teacher asks her students to share their interpretations of how the artists used color in their paintings. The students learn that some of them thought the color combinations were aesthetically vibrant and appealing, whereas others thought the color palettes and combinations were garish. (Late Adolescence)

Encourage children to speculate about characters' thoughts, emotions, and motives in works of literature.

- As a teacher in a child care center reads a story to a group of young children, she occasionally stops to ask questions about what the different characters might be thinking and feeling. While reading *The Berenstain Bears' Trouble with Pets* (Berenstain & Berenstain, 1990), she asks, "Why does the Bear family let Little Bird fly away?" and "How do you think Mama and Papa Bear feel when Lady makes a mess in the living room?" (Early Childhood)

- In *The Corn Grows Ripe by* Dorothy Rhoads (1956), Tigre, a 12-year-old Mayan boy living in the Yucatán, must take on new responsibilities when his father is injured. Mr. Torres assigns the book to his middle school students and facilitates a discussion about Tigre's new responsibilities. The students express a variety of opinions about how they would feel about taking on these new tasks. (Early Adolescence)

Ask children to consider the perspectives of people they don't know very well.

- A preschool teacher makes a batch of cookies for senior citizens who regularly come to their class to read to children. The children prepare a basket for each of their senior friends, place a few cookies in it, and insert thank-you notes. She says to the children, "Imagine how surprised our senior friends are going to be! I bet they're going to be really happy when they see the baskets." (Early Childhood)

- During a discussion of a recent earthquake in South America, an eighth-grade social studies teacher asks students to imagine how people must feel when they lose their home and possessions and don't know whether their loved ones are dead or alive. (Early Adolescence)

CAN YOU HELP ME? Productive interactions with peers help children discover that everyone has valuable qualities.

Preparing for Your Licensure Examination

Your teaching test might ask you about fostering productive social relationships among children from diverse backgrounds.

Paula's awareness of how people in various settings experience events. Paula and two other children met with a speech-language specialist over several weeks and considered how characters in hypothetical scenarios might have thought about the events. After a few weeks, Paula regularly used mental state terms in her speech:

> "I *know* Marco didn't let me play soccer unless I gave him one dollar bill."
>
> "The teacher *thought* I was making this story up and I'm trying to get him in trouble because he told her a lie."
>
> "I *know* because I saw the toilet paper in the boy's hand."
>
> "She *knows* that we got the wrong pizza because we were arguing about where we wanted to go and we went to Dominoes."
>
> (Timler et al., 2005, p. 81)

- **Actively work to break down stereotypes and prejudice.** One effective strategy is to encourage children to see people as *individuals*—as human beings with their own unique strengths and weaknesses—rather than as members of particular groups (García, 1994; C. D. Lee & Slaughter-Defoe, 1995; Spencer & Markstrom-Adams, 1990). Also effective is to increase interpersonal contacts among people from diverse groups (and ideally to create a sense that "we are all in this together"), perhaps through cooperative group activities, multi-school community service projects, or pen pal relationships with children in distant locations (Dessel, 2010; Koeppel & Mulrooney, 1992; Rutland, Killen, & Abrams, 2010). Cross-racial friendships are fostered when children are shown one another's talents, hear about one's another's individual characteristics, and find that they can depend on one another during collaborative projects.

In addition, adults should challenge any stereotypes and prejudicial attitudes they encounter in children's speech or actions. If a teenager talks about "lazy migrant workers," a teacher might respond by saying, "I occasionally hear students express that view. I wonder where that stereotype came from. Migrant workers are often up before dawn and pick produce until dusk. Many take other demanding jobs when the growing season is over." Notice how the teacher confronts the "lazy migrant worker" stereotype tactfully and matter-of-factly and does not assume that the teen's remark has malicious intent. Playing on their interest to appear tolerant and open minded may be more effective than chastising them for attitudes they have not carefully thought through (Dovidio & Gaertner, 1999). Some educators have found it effective to train children to intervene as bystanders when they hear prejudicial remarks themselves (Aboud & Fenwick, 1999; Dessel, 2010).

SUMMARY

Sense of Self

Children's *sense of self* includes their beliefs about who they are as people (self-concept) and their judgments about their value and worth (self-esteem, self-worth). Most children tend to interpret events in ways that allow them to maintain a positive self-image. Realistic self-perceptions, or perhaps self-perceptions that are just slightly inflated, are optimal, in that they encourage children to set their sights on potentially achievable challenges.

To a considerable degree, children's sense of self is based on their own prior successes and failures. Yet other people also play a role, either by treating children in ways that communicate high or low regard, or (in the case of peers) by demonstrating the kinds of things children "should" be able to do at a certain age. Membership in various groups (e.g., athletic teams, ethnic groups) also has an impact, as do gender, culture, physical appearance, disabilities, and inherited characteristics.

With age, children construct increasingly complex and multifaceted understandings of who they are as people. In the early years, their self-perceptions are fairly simplistic, concrete, and categorical (e.g., "I have brown eyes," "I'm a boy"). But as they acquire the capacity for abstract thought, their self-descriptions increasingly include general, abstract qualities (e.g., "thoughtful," dependable").

In adolescence they also begin to wrestle with who they ultimately want to become as human beings.

Social Cognition

As children grow older, they become more attuned to and interested in the mental lives of those around them. In the process of developing a *theory of mind,* they gradually learn that people have thoughts, feelings, and motives different from their own and that these internal states can be complex and at times contradictory. Children also become increasingly skilled in taking the perspectives of others. Unfortunately, youngsters' growing beliefs about other people may also include rigid stereotypes about certain groups, leading them to act toward members of those groups in prejudicial ways.

Classrooms and other group settings are important contexts in which children and adolescents develop increasing awareness of other people's needs and perspectives. Teachers and other adults can foster greater awareness and knowledge in numerous ways—for instance, by talking frequently about people's thoughts and feelings, exposing youngsters to multiple and equally legitimate perspectives about complex topics and events, and confronting inaccurate and counterproductive stereotypes.

APPLYING CONCEPTS IN CHILD DEVELOPMENT

The exercises in this section will help you build your ability to apply your knowledge of child development in working with children.

Improving Your Observation Skills

| Jeff (age 6): | I like animals. I like making things. I do good in school. I'm happy. Blue eyes. Yellow hair. Light skin. |

On page 461, you examined self-descriptions from three children and were asked, *"What kinds of developmental trends do you notice in these responses?"* Jeff and Alex talked mostly about how they looked, how they behaved, and what they liked. In contrast, Tina described several abstract qualities—cool, awesome, boy crazy, popular, beautiful—that she had apparently derived from her many experiences over time. Notice, too, how both boys mentioned their

performance in school. Tina focused more on social and physical qualities than on academic achievement (or, we might add, modesty). As you've learned, social acceptance and physical appearance are often high priorities in the minds of young adolescents.

On page 489, you examined a photograph of a group of children examining a globe of the earth and were asked, *"What aspects of the interaction may help individual children understand that their peers have unique perspectives?"* The children are each looking at a different region on the globe, so as they share their observations, they are likely to talk about these different areas. From such remarks, children may notice that peers see the globe from a different vantage point than their own. Individual children are apt to prefer different places to visit as well. Such a conversation likely communicates to children that others have a different perspective than they do.

Practicing for Your Licensure Examination

Many teaching tests require students to use what they have learned about child development in responses to brief vignettes and multiple-choice questions. You can practice for your licensure examination by reading about a boy's search for identity and answering a series of questions.

Joachín's Dilemma

Read the case and then answer the questions that follow it.

Pedro Noguera reflects on the challenges that his son, Joachín, faced as an African American boy developing his identity:

> Joachín did extremely well throughout most of his early schooling. He was an excellent athlete (participating in soccer, basketball, and wrestling), played piano and percussion, and did very well in his classes. My wife and I never heard any complaints about him. In fact, we heard nothing but praise about his behavior from teachers, who referred to him as "courteous," "respectful," and "a leader among his peers." Then suddenly, in the tenth grade, Joachín's grades took a nosedive. He failed math and science, and for the first time he started getting into trouble at school. At home he was often angry and irritable for no apparent reason.
>
> My wife and I were left asking ourselves, "What's going on with our son? What's behind this sudden change in behavior?" Despite my disappointment and growing frustration, I tried not to allow Joachín's behavior to drive us apart. I started spending more time with him and started listening more intently to what he had to tell me about school and his friends. As I did, several things became clear to me. One was that all of the friends he had grown up with in our neighborhood in South Berkeley, California (one of the poorest areas of the city), were dropping out of school. These were mostly Black, working-class kids who didn't have a lot of support at home or at school and were experiencing academic failure. Even though Joachín came from a middle-class home with two supportive parents, most of his reference group—that is, the students he was closest to and identified with—did not.
>
> The other thing that was changing for Joachín was his sense of how he had to present himself when he was out on the streets and in school. As he grew older, Joachín felt the need to project the image of a tough and angry young Black man. He believed that in order to be respected he had to carry himself in a manner that was intimidating and even menacing. To behave differently—too nice, gentle, kind, or sincere—meant that he would be vulnerable and preyed upon. I learned that for Joachín, part of his new persona also involved placing less value on academics and greater emphasis on being cool and hanging out with the right people.
>
> By eleventh grade Joachín gradually started working out of these behaviors, and by twelfth grade he seemed to snap out of his angry state. He became closer to his family, his grades improved, he rejoined the soccer team, he resumed playing the piano, and he even started producing music. As I reflected on the two years of anger and self-destructiveness that he went through, I came to the conclusion that Joachín was trying desperately to figure out what it meant to be a young Black man. I realized that, like many Black male adolescents,

> Joachín was trapped by stereotypes, and they were pulling him down. During this difficult period it was very hard for me to help him through this process of identity formation. While he was in the midst of it the only thing I could do was talk to him, listen to him, and try to let him know what it was like for me when I went through adolescence.[a]
> (Noguera, 2003, pp. 19–20)

Constructed-Response Question

1. What challenges did Joachín face in establishing his identity?

Multiple-Choice Questions

2. How might the developmental theorist James Marcia describe Joachín's identity formation?

   a. Joachín remained in a state of *diffusion*, in which he failed to embark on serious exploration of his identity.

   b. Joachín was in *foreclosure*, a state of committing to particular ideals and ways of life established for him by his parents.

   c. Joachín spent several years in *identity achievement*, embracing clear choices with regard to occupation, political beliefs, and religious views, before returning to a state of *foreclosure*, a state of committing to particular ideals and ways of life established for him by his parents.

   d. Joachín went through a period of *moratorium*, in which he actively searched for a core sense of beliefs and commitments as to whom he was and what he stood for.

3. How would you describe Joachín's development from the perspective of Margaret Beale Spencer's model of identity development?

   a. Joachín enjoyed certain *protective factors*, including having involved and supportive parents and being an intelligent young man, but also faced the *risk factor* of having peers who were disengaged from school.

   b. As he reflected on his experiences with peers and family and his place in society, Joachín developed *coping skills*.

   c. In the process of developing coping skills, Joachín gained a sense of his own *identity*.

   d. All of the above.

Once you have answered these questions, compare your responses with those presented in Appendix A.

Improving Your Ability to Interpret Children's Artifacts and Reflections

Draw on what you've learned about emotional development as you analyze an adolescent's poem in this exercise.

---

[a] "Case Study: Joaquin's Dilemma" from JOAQUIN'S DILEMMA: UNDERSTANDING THE LINK BETWEEN RACIAL IDENTITY AND SCHOOL-RELATED BEHAVIORS by Pedro Noguera, from ADOLESCENTS AT SCHOOL: PERSPECTIVES ON YOUTH, IDENTITY, AND EDUCATION, 1st edition, edited by Michael Sadowski (Cambridge, MA: Harvard Education Press, 2003), pp.19-30. Copyright © by the President and Fellows of Harvard College. All rights reserved. For more information, please visit www.harvardeducationpress.org

Two Histories

Rachel Stephanie Bolden-Kramer is an adolescent from San Francisco, California. In her poem, *Two Histories*, Rachel tells what it's like to have a dual ethnic heritage (WritersCorps, 2003). As you read Rachel's poem, consider these questions:

- How have other people responded to Rachel's ethnicity?
- How does Rachel show her commitment to a multiethnic identity?

Two Histories

Daddy wanted to name me Wilhemina after his mother.
You know you're supposed to name your baby after
someone who's gone.
Not alive.
But then my mother protested.
I should carry her mother's name, Anne.
"Rachel" kept me from the arguments and sour family disputes.
But did it compromise or anger both sides?
And that's what I'm stuck with,
Every day
Every move
I'm a compromise
Light skin
But thick bone structure
Half 'n half Jewish girl who fights for BSU[a]

Latke and greens
The horah and the butterfly
Act White
Won't date Black men
Think she's better
Has good hair
Looks more Latina than half-breed
But that boy always called me mixed in such an ugly way
Some say, "Nigga get off the swing"
Others say, "You're really not like those other Black people"
And I get told it's better to pretend I'm White
But I got two histories in me
Both enslaved
And both warriors.
Rachel Stephanie Bolden-Kramer[b]

(WritersCorps, 2003, pp. 39–40)

Once you have analyzed the poem, compare your ideas with those presented in Appendix B. For further practice in analyzing children's artifacts and reflections, go to the Activities and Applications section in Chapter 12 of MyEducationLab.

[a] BSU refers to the Black Student Union.
[b] "Two Histories" by Rachel Stephanie Bolden-Kramer from PAINT ME LIKE I AM: TEEN POEMS FROM WRITERSCORPS. Copyright © 2003 by WritersCorps. Reprinted with permission from WritersCorps.

Key Concepts

sense of self (p. 458)	identity (p. 465)	social perspective taking (p. 480)	prejudice (p. 484)
self-handicapping (p. 458)	gender schema (p. 469)	intentionality (p. 480)	autism spectrum disorders (p. 486)
contingent self-worth (p. 462)	self-socialization (p. 469)	recursive thinking (p. 482)	mirror neuron (p. 487)
imaginary audience (p. 465)	social cognition (p. 480)	social-cognitive bias (p. 484)	
personal fable (p. 465)	theory of mind (p. 480)	stereotype (p. 484)	

PEARSON
myeducationlab

Now go to www.myeducationlab.com to:
- Take a Quiz to test your mastery of chapter objectives.
- Study chapter content with an individualized Study Plan.
- Deepen your understanding of particular concepts and principles with Review, Remediation, and Enrichment Exercises.
- Apply what you have learned in the chapter to your work with children in Building Teaching Skills and Dispositions exercises.
- Observe children and their unique contexts in Video Examples.

Chapter Thirteen

Development of Motivation and Self-Regulation

CASE STUDY: Making Kites

Janet Keany teaches a mathematics class for fifth and sixth graders who have a history of poor performance in mathematics.[a] She has recently shown her class how concepts in geometry relate to aerodynamics, emphasizing that the size and shape of an object affect the ease with which it can fly. As a follow-up to the lesson, she asks her students to experiment with a variety of sizes and shapes of kites and then to design a kite using what they have learned.

The kite project lasts several days. A researcher observes the class throughout the project and interviews the children afterward. She finds that different children take very different approaches to the task and have widely varying perspectives about it. A girl named Sara approaches the task as a scientist might: She is keenly interested in creating an aerodynamic kite design and realizes that doing so will take time and patience. She redesigns her kite three times to make it as aerodynamic as possible. After the project, she summarizes her results:

> . . . I wasn't completely successful, because I had a few problems. But I realized that most scientists, when they try experiments, well, they're not always right. . . . [I]f I can correct myself on [errors] then I don't really mind them that much. I mean, everybody learns from their mistakes. I know I do. . . . I think mistakes are actually good, to tell you the truth. . . .
>
> When I had my test flights, the shape flew really, really well, and I was going to stick with that shape. . . . I had no doubts because I knew that I could really do it; I knew I could put this together really well, 'cause I had a lot of confidence in myself. . . . (Meyer, Turner, & Spencer, 1997, pp. 511–512)

Unlike Sara, Amy sticks with a single kite design throughout the project even though she has trouble getting her kite to fly. Later, Amy tells the researcher:

> I knew from the start what shape I wanted. Once I had the materials it was very easy to make the kite. . . . [T]here wasn't enough wind for the kites to fly. (pp. 510, 513)

The researcher asks Amy how important the project was to her and whether she ever takes risks at school. She responds:

> I feel lazy because I don't like to make challenges for myself, to make goals. I just like to do it as I go along, not make goals or challenges. . . . I like to do well for [the teacher] and my parents, and myself, I guess. . . . [I]f it doesn't affect my grade, whether I do this or not, if I totally fail and do everything wrong, if it doesn't affect my grade, then I'll [take risks]. (pp. 510, 512)

Had her kite flown, how might Amy have explained it? Amy tells the researcher that it would probably have been "beginner's luck" (Meyer, Turner, & Spencer, 1994, 1997).

- What differences do you notice in how the two girls approach the kite-making activity?
- How might you characterize Sara's motivation for engaging in the activity? For whom does Amy say she wants to do well on the task?
- How does Sara explain her success? How does Amy explain her failure?

[a]Although the case is real, "Janet Keany" is a pseudonym.

OBJECTIVES

13.1: Differentiate between extrinsic and intrinsic motivation, and identify the factors influencing the development of each.

13.2: Describe the kinds of goals toward which children and adolescents are apt to strive.

13.3: Explain how children's attributions influence their behavior and how various attributions develop.

13.4: Describe bioecological influences on motivation, and apply concepts about motivation to the classroom and other settings.

13.5: Identify developmental trends in, and practical applications of, self-regulation.

Sara is willing to experiment and make mistakes so that she can construct the best kite possible, whereas Amy prefers an easier, though less successful, course of action. Sara seems to find satisfaction in her accomplishments, whereas Amy seems to be more interested in pleasing her teacher and parents. Sara attributes her successful kite to her own effort and ability, whereas Amy concludes that her failure was due to poor weather conditions and suspects that any success on the task would have been a matter of luck. All of these differences illustrate aspects of motivation, an important aspect of children's development that affects their academic achievement, behavior, and well-being.

Preparing for Your Licensure Examination

Your teaching test might ask you to distinguish between extrinsic and intrinsic motivation.

LOOK AT THIS! Learning is usually more effective when children are intrinsically rather than extrinsically motivated.

motivation
State that energizes, directs, and sustains behavior.

extrinsic motivation
Motivation provoked by the external consequences that certain behaviors bring.

intrinsic motivation
Motivation resulting from personal characteristics or from factors inherent in the task being performed.

EXTRINSIC AND INTRINSIC MOTIVATION

Motivation energizes, directs, and sustains behavior: It gets people moving, points them in a particular direction, and keeps them going. We usually see motivation reflected in a certain amount of *personal investment* in particular activities, as exemplified by the time and effort that Sara put into creating her kite.

Virtually all children and adolescents are motivated in one way or another. One person may express a keen interest in academic subject matter, seek out challenging course work, join in classroom discussions, complete assignments diligently, and earn high grades. Another may be more concerned about social affairs, interacting with peers frequently, participating in numerous extracurricular activities, and chatting incessantly with friends on a cell phone. Still another may be focused on athletics, excelling in physical education classes, watching sports most weekends, and working out daily in hopes of making the varsity soccer team. And yet another, perhaps because of an undetected learning disability, poor social skills, or a seemingly uncoordinated body, may be interested primarily in *avoiding* academics, social situations, or athletic activities.

Sometimes youngsters have **extrinsic motivation**: They are motivated to either attain or avoid certain consequences in the outside world. They may complete a classroom assignment in order to get adult approval (as Amy did in the opening case), or they may lie about a misdeed in order to avoid being punished ("I didn't do it, *he* did!"). At other times youngsters have **intrinsic motivation**: They are motivated by factors within themselves or inherent in a task they are performing. They might read a book simply for the pleasure it brings, experiment with various kite shapes to find out which one flies best (as Sara did), or return a wallet to its owner as a way of being true to an internal moral code.

Both extrinsic and intrinsic motivation can spur children to acquire new knowledge and skills and engage in productive behaviors. But intrinsic motivation has numerous advantages over extrinsic motivation. Intrinsically motivated children are eager to learn classroom material, willingly tackle assigned tasks, use effective learning strategies, and are likely to achieve at high levels in school. In contrast, extrinsically motivated children may have to be enticed or prodded, are apt to study classroom topics only superficially, and are often interested in performing only easy tasks and meeting minimal classroom requirements (A. E. Gottfried, Fleming, & Gottfried, 2001; Habgood & Ainsworth, 2011; Reeve, 2006; R. M. Ryan & Deci, 2009).

Factors Affecting Extrinsic Motivation

Human beings of all ages usually behave in ways that bring desired results. In an early theory of learning known as *operant conditioning*, the American behaviorist **B. F. Skinner** (1904–1990) proposed that children learn and engage primarily in behaviors that lead to pleasant consequences, which he called **reinforcers** (e.g., Skinner, 1953, 1968).[1] From Skinner's perspective, human behaviors are those that are currently being reinforced or have often been reinforced in the past. For instance, Miguel might practice the piano regularly if his parents continually praise him for his efforts. Brigita might throw frequent temper tantrums if she's learned that these fits are the only way she can get special toys or privileges. Peter might misbehave in class if doing so gains him the attention of his teacher and classmates. The last of these examples illustrates an important point: Reinforcers are not always what we would typically think of as "rewards." The attention Peter gets for his misbehavior may seem unpleasant to others: Peter's teacher may scold him for acting out, or his classmates might shake their heads in disgust. But if Peter's misbehaviors increase as a result, then the attention is indeed a reinforcer.

[1]Skinner's theory is introduced in Chapter 1.

In early infancy, children are largely concerned with **primary reinforcers**, which satisfy basic, built-in needs or desires. Some primary reinforcers, such as food and drinks, are essential for physiological well-being. Others, such as physical affection, cuddling, and smiles, are more social in nature. Human beings have probably evolved to appreciate these social reinforcers as a way of enhancing their connectedness to others and so, indirectly, enhancing their chances of survival (Harlow & Zimmerman, 1959; Vollmer & Hackenberg, 2001).

Over time, children begin to associate certain other consequences with primary reinforcers. A child might discover that praise from Mother often comes with a candy treat or that a good grade frequently leads to a hug from Father. Through such associations, consequences such as praise, money, good grades, and attention (sometimes even attention in the form of a scolding) become reinforcing in their own right. That is, they become **secondary reinforcers**. Because secondary reinforcers are consequences that children *learn* to appreciate, the effectiveness of any one of them will differ considerably from one child to the next.

In addition to customizing reinforcers according to a child's individual preferences, teachers are also apt to consider the particular behaviors the child needs to learn. Special educator Ann Turnbull and her colleagues illustrate this need with Jane, an adolescent girl with autism who needs assistance in learning adaptive behaviors for everyday life.[2] Jane appreciates praise from her teacher, and thus praise can be used as a reinforcer (Turnbull et al., 2010). In the process of learning to sort silverware, Jane is first shown a *discriminative stimulus*, a reminder that a particular response is necessary. Next, she emits the desired *response* of placing the utensils in their proper places and finally receives *reinforcement*, verbal praise. Here's how Jane might learn to sort silverware:

> You lay a spoon, a fork, and a knife in front of her and provide a discriminative stimulus by saying, "Jane, show me the spoon." Most likely, Jane will point to or touch one of the utensils, or, if she is not certain, not respond at all. If she points to the spoon, you immediately praise her, saying, "Great job, Jane! That's right, that's the spoon." Your praise constitutes the reinforcing stimulus. If she points to a different utensil or to none of them, she does not get your reinforcer (verbal praise); instead, you prompt her again to identify the spoon. Eventually, if you reinforce ("Great job!"), her correct response (pointing to the spoon) to your discriminative stimulus ("Show me the spoon"), while ignoring or not reinforcing Jane's other responses, she will respond more consistently to the stimulus with the appropriate response. (Turnbull et al., 2010, p. 322)

The developmental abilities of the child also determine how reinforcement can be effectively implemented. As children grow older, they become better able to **delay gratification**: They can forgo small, immediate reinforcers for the more substantial consequences their long-term efforts may bring down the road (Green, Fry, & Myerson, 1994; C. Moore, 2010; Vaughn, Kopp, & Krakow, 1984). A 3-year-old is apt to choose a small toy she can have *now* over a larger and more attractive toy she cannot have until tomorrow. In contrast, an 8-year-old is usually willing to wait a day or two for a more appealing item. Many adolescents can delay gratification for weeks at a time. As a 16-year-old, Jeanne's son Jeff worked long hours stocking shelves at the local grocery store (hardly a rewarding activity!) to earn enough money to pay half the cost of a $400-a-night limousine for his high school prom.

Once in a while children are neither intrinsically motivated to acquire important skills nor responsive to simple reinforcement. In rare cases when children persist with a particular misbehavior despite adults' best efforts to teach them an appropriate action, punishment is sometimes an option. Psychologists define **punishment** as a consequence that *decreases* the frequency of the response it follows.[3] Whereas children are likely to behave in ways that lead to reinforcement, they are *un*likely to behave in ways that lead to punishment. Punishment of undesirable responses (e.g., engaging in off-task behaviors during a lesson), especially when combined with reinforcement of more productive ones (e.g., sitting attentively during the lesson), can bring about improvements in children's behavior (Landrum & Kauffman,

Preparing for Your Licensure Examination
Your teaching test might ask you how reinforcement can be implemented in the classroom.

reinforcer
Consequence of a response that leads to an increase in the frequency of that response.

primary reinforcer
Stimulus or event that satisfies a built-in biological need.

secondary reinforcer
Stimulus or event that becomes reinforcing over time through its association with one or more other reinforcers.

delay gratification
Forgoing small immediate rewards for larger ones at a future time.

punishment
Consequence of a response that leads to a decrease in the frequency of that response.

[2]Autism and the autism spectrum disorders are examined in Chapter 12.
[3]Be aware that the term *negative reinforcement* is *not* a synonym for punishment. Negative reinforcement increases rather than decreases the behavior it follows by removing an unpleasant stimulus and thereby causing a sense of relief in the person.

2006; Ringdahl, Kopelman, & Falcomata, 2009; Walters & Grusec, 1977). When teachers work with children who have serious behavioral problems, they may award points (reinforcement) for appropriate behaviors and take away points (punishment) for misbehaviors. After a certain time interval (perhaps at the end of the day or week), children can exchange the points they've accumulated for small toys or privileges. Taking away previously earned points for unacceptable behavior (a strategy called *response cost*) can be effective in bringing about behavior change (Landrum & Kauffman, 2006; K. D. O'Leary & O'Leary, 1972). Many other forms of punishment are *not* effective, however, especially those that provide models of aggression, inflict physical or psychological harm, or involve suspension or expulsion from school (Brendgen, Wanner, Vitaro, Bukowski, & Tremblay, 2007; Luiselli, 2009). Generally, punishment is a tool of last resort and must be implemented with utmost care.

As social learning theorists have pointed out, children's motivation is affected not only by the consequences they experience themselves but also by the consequences they see *other people* experience (e.g., Bandura, 1965, 1977). In other words, observed consequences may affect children vicariously. In **vicarious reinforcement**, a child who observes a peer being reinforced for doing something is likely to behave similarly. In **vicarious punishment**, a child who sees a peer being punished for a particular behavior is *un*likely to behave in that way. By watching the consequences that their peers experience, children might learn that being elected to a student government office brings popularity, that acting out in class gets the teacher's attention, or that exhibiting unsportsmanlike conduct on the playing field results in being benched during the next game.

Factors Affecting Intrinsic Motivation

As the following principles reveal, some of the factors underlying intrinsic motivation are at work quite early in life, whereas others emerge over time as children learn more about themselves and their relationship with the environment.

Children seem to have a natural predisposition to explore their environment. Following in **Jean Piaget's** (1896–1980) footsteps, many developmental theorists believe that children are naturally curious about their world and actively seek out information to help them make sense of it (e.g., Flum & Kaplan, 2006; A. Lieberman, 1993; R. M. Ryan & Deci, 2009).[4] Even as infants, children are constantly experimenting to discover the properties of objects and the outcomes of various actions. Later, as children gain proficiency in their native language, their seemingly incessant questions (e.g., "How do they make statues?" "Why does it rain sometimes?") are an additional means through which they try to satisfy their curiosity about the world (Callanan & Oakes, 1992, p. 218; Kemler Nelson et al., 2004). You can observe young children's intrinsic motivation to explore their physical world in the infancy and early childhood videos on "Cognitive Development" and the infancy video on "Emotional Development" in MyEducationLab.

Children strive for consistency in their understandings of the world. Jean Piaget suggested that another key factor driving a child's learning and development is *disequilibrium*, an inconsistency between new information and what the child already believes to be true. According to Piaget, disequilibrium causes mental discomfort and spurs the child to integrate, reorganize, or in some cases replace existing schemes to accommodate to the new information. Like Piaget, many contemporary developmental theorists believe that beginning early in life, human beings have an innate need for coherence among the things they learn (e.g., Bronson, 2000; Egan, Santos, & Bloom, 2007; Keil, 2010).

Children tend to choose activities at which they think they can be successful. Some psychologists propose that an important source of intrinsic motivation is an innate need to feel *competent*—to believe that one can deal effectively with one's environment (Jacobs et al., 2002; R. M. Ryan & Deci, 2009). A need for competence pushes children to acquire effective ways of dealing with various environmental circumstances. It may be one important reason

MyEducationLab

Observe infants' and toddlers' intrinsic motivation to explore their physical world in the infancy and early childhood "Cognitive Development" videos and in the infancy "Emotional Development" video. (Find Video Examples in Topic 13 of MyEducationLab.)

vicarious reinforcement
Phenomenon in which a child increases a certain response after seeing someone else reinforced for that response.

vicarious punishment
Phenomenon in which a child decreases a certain response after seeing someone else punished for that response.

[4]Piaget's theory of cognitive development is examined in depth in Chapter 6.

why we human beings have, over the course of time, been able to adapt successfully to many different habitats (R. White, 1959).

To maintain and enhance their sense of competence, children are apt to choose and persist at activities for which they have high **self-efficacy**—that is, activities at which they believe they can be successful (Bandura, 1997; Ozdemir, 2010; Schunk & Pajares, 2009). In the opening case study, Sara reveals a high sense of self-efficacy about building a kite: "I had no doubts because I knew that I could really do it; I knew I could put this together really well" (Meyer et al., 1997, p. 512). Once youngsters have high self-efficacy for a task or activity, they eagerly seek out challenges that can further enhance their ability. In the "Intrinsic Motivation" videos for middle childhood and late adolescence in MyEducationLab, 9-year-old Elena and 15-year-old Greg both express their desire for challenge at school:

Interviewer:	What do you like best about school?
Elena:	I like PEAK [a program for students identified as gifted]. It's this thing where you go to this program. It's for smart kids who have, like, good ideas for stuff you could do. And so they make it more challenging for you in school. So instead of third-grade math, you get fourth-grade math.
Interviewer:	What do teachers do that encourage you to do well at school?
Greg:	[S]ome of them kind of make it a competition, like class rank and stuff. . . . And that makes you want to. . . . And the challenge. If it's a really hard class, then I . . . will usually try harder in harder classes.

When children have *low* self-efficacy for a particular activity or content domain, they may try to avoid it as much as possible. The following statements by students with reading disabilities reveal two common avoidance strategies, making excuses and blatantly refusing to perform assigned tasks:

When it comes time for reading I do everything under the sun I can to get out of it because it's my worst nightmare to read. I'll say I have to go to the bathroom or that I'm sick and I have to go to the nurse right now. My teacher doesn't know that I'll be walking around campus. She thinks I am going to the bathroom or whatever my lame excuse is. All I really want to do is get out of having to read. (Zambo & Brem, 2004, p. 5)

They (teachers) used to hand us all our homework on Mondays. One day my teacher handed me a stack about an inch thick and as I was walking out of class there was a big trash can right there and I'd, in front of everybody including the teacher, just drop it in the trash can and walk out. I did this because I couldn't read what she gave me. It was kind of a point that I wanted to get the teacher to realize. That while I'm doing it, inside it kind of like hurt because I really wanted to do it but I couldn't and just so it didn't look like I was goin' soft or anything like that I'd walk over to the trash and throw it in. (Zambo & Brem, 2004, p. 6)

Children also prefer activities for which they have some autonomy. As early as 6 months of age, many infants become frustrated and angry when a parent stops them from moving their arms freely or when a device they've learned to operate successfully unexpectedly stops playing music (Braungart-Rieker et al., 2010; M. W. Sullivan & Lewis, 2003). By 14 months, infants actively resist parents' requests that would prevent them from reaching their immediate goals (Dix, Stewart, Gershoff, & Day, 2007). In general, children are more intrinsically motivated when they have a **sense of self-determination**, a belief that they have some choice regarding the things they do and the direction their lives take (R. M. Ryan & Deci, 2009; Tsai, Kunter, Lüdtke, Trautwein, & Ryan, 2008). A child who thinks "I *want* to do this" or "I'd *like* to learn more about that" has a high sense of self-determination. In contrast, a child who thinks "I *must* do this" or "*My teacher wants* me to learn that" is thinking that someone or something else is directing the course of events. You can observe Alicia articulate her need for self-determination in the "Literacy: Late Adolescence" video in MyEducationLab.

MyEducationLab

Notice the importance of self-efficacy and challenge in the "Intrinsic Motivation" videos for middle childhood and late adolescence in the Video Examples section in Topic 13 of MyEducationLab.

MyEducationLab

Observe Alicia's need for self-determination in the "Literacy: Late Adolescence" video. (Find Video Examples in Topic 13 of MyEducationLab.)

Preparing for Your Licensure Examination

Your teaching test might ask you about educational strategies for supporting children's self-determination.

self-efficacy
Belief that one is capable of executing certain behaviors or reaching certain goals.

sense of self-determination
Belief that one has some choice and control regarding the future course of one's life.

Improving Your Observation Skills

Type of interest. Do these children seem to be exhibiting *personal interest* or *situational interest* in their chemistry lesson? Compare your response with the explanation at the end of the chapter.

Developmental Trends in Intrinsic Motivation

As you are learning, a child's intrinsic motivation is a vital capacity that evolves with age and experience. Let's consider several of the major changes.

As children grow older, their interests become increasingly stable. When we say that children have an *interest* in a particular topic or activity, we mean that they find the topic or activity intriguing and rewarding in and of itself. Interest, then, is one form of intrinsic motivation. Psychologists distinguish between two general types of interest (Hidi, Renninger, & Krapp, 2004; Schiefele, 2009). **Situational interest** is evoked by something in the environment—something that is perhaps new, unusual, or surprising. In contrast, **personal interest** comes from within the child and is largely unrelated to immediate circumstances.

In infancy and early childhood, interests are mostly situational and short lived: Young children are readily attracted to novel, attention-getting stimuli and events for, say, a few seconds or minutes (e.g., Courage, Reynolds, & Richards, 2006; Pérez-Edgar et al., 2010). Sometimes these stimuli and events plant the seeds from which longer-term personal interests begin to grow (Hidi & Renninger, 2006). By the middle to upper elementary grades—sometimes even earlier— many children acquire personal interests, perhaps in animal life or mechanical movements, which persist over a period of time and may ultimately become important parts of children's identities (J. M. Alexander, Johnson, Leibham, & Kelley, 2008; Hidi et al., 2004; K. E. Johnson, Alexander, Spencer, Leibham, & Neitzel, 2004). Joey displayed an exceptional interest in art beginning at age 3. Throughout his childhood and adolescence, he had a strong interest in drawing the human form and, later, in fashion design.[5]

Children and adolescents increasingly pursue activities that they perceive to be valuable. A task or activity has **value** when children believe there are direct or indirect benefits in performing it (Dweck & Elliott, 1983; Wigfield & Eccles, 2000; Wigfield, Tonks, & Klauda, 2009). Some activities are valued because they are associated with certain personal qualities. A boy who wants to be smart and thinks that smart people do well in school will place a premium on academic success. Other activities have high value because they are seen as means to desired goals. Much as she disliked mathematics, Jeanne's daughter Tina struggled through math classes throughout high school because many colleges require 4 years of math. Still other activities are valued simply because they bring enjoyment (Durik, Vida, & Eccles, 2006; Eccles & Wigfield, 1985; Eccles [Parsons], 1983). An adolescent may value watching movies or reading novels for the sheer pleasure of the activities.

In the elementary grades, children primarily choose activities that they perceive to be interesting and enjoyable. As they reach adolescence and proceed through the secondary grades, however, they increasingly choose activities that, in their minds at least, will be

Age 8

Age 11

Age 17

ARTIFACT 13-1 **Joey's portraits.** In these drawings, Joey shows his long-term personal interest in drawing the human form.

situational interest
Interest evoked temporarily by something in the environment.

personal interest
Long-term, relatively stable interest in a particular topic or activity.

value
Belief that a particular activity has direct or indirect benefits.

[5]Joey's self-portrait at age 17 appears as an artifact on page 407 of Chapter 10.

instrumental in helping them achieve their goals (Eccles, Wigfield, & Schiefele, 1998; Okagaki, 2006; Wigfield, Tonks, & Eccles, 2004).

In contrast, children tend *not* to value activities that seem to require more effort than they're worth. A teenager who would ideally like to get straight As in school may begin to downplay the importance of As if she finds that they require forgoing much of her social life (e.g., Otis, Grouzet, & Pelletier, 2005). Children may also *de*value activities that they associate with frequent frustration and failure ("I don't see why I need to do these stupid geometry proofs!") and that may lessen their sense of competence (Wigfield & Eccles, 2000).

Over time, children internalize the motivation to engage in certain activities. As children grow older, most begin to adopt some of the values and priorities of the people around them. Such **internalized motivation** typically develops gradually, perhaps in the sequence depicted in Figure 13-1 (R. M. Ryan & Deci, 2009). Initially, children may engage in some activities primarily because of the external consequences that result. Hence, students may do schoolwork to earn praise or avoid being punished for poor grades. With time other people's approval becomes increasingly important for children's sense of self. Eventually children internalize the "pressure" to perform certain activities and see these activities as important in their own right. Such internalization of values is most likely to occur if adults who espouse those values (parents, teachers, etc.) do the following:

- Engage in valued activities themselves.
- Provide a warm, supportive, and somewhat structured environment for children.
- Offer enough autonomy in decision making that children have a sense of self-determination about their actions. (Jacobs, Davis-Kean, Bleeker, Eccles, & Malanchuk, 2005; R. M. Ryan, Connell, & Grolnick, 1992; R. M. Ryan & Deci, 2000)

1. **External regulation.** Children may initially be motivated to behave (or not to behave) in certain ways based primarily on the external consequences that follow behaviors; that is, children are extrinsically motivated.

2. **Introjection.** Children begin to behave in ways that gain the approval of others, partly as a way of protecting and enhancing their sense of self. They feel guilty when they violate certain standards for behavior but do not fully understand the rationale behind these standards.

3. **Identification.** Children begin to regard certain behaviors as being personally important or valuable to themselves.

4. **Integration.** Children integrate certain behaviors into their overall system of motives and values. In essence, these behaviors become a central part of their sense of self.

FIGURE 13-1 Emergence of internalized motivation. *Based on R. M. Ryan & Deci, 2009.*

Some of our readers may think that internalized motivation is essentially the same as intrinsic motivation. Certainly internalized motivation is a *form* of intrinsic motivation, in that it comes from inside the child rather than from outside factors in the immediate, here-and-now environment. But in one important way it is quite different from other forms of intrinsic motivation. Intrinsic motivation that arises spontaneously within the child (e.g., curiosity about an intriguing object) can increase or decrease somewhat unpredictably. In contrast, because internalized motivation is a product of ongoing social and cultural factors and eventually becomes an integral part of children's sense of self—their beliefs about who they are as human beings—it remains fairly stable and dependable over time (Otis et al., 2005; Reeve, Deci, & Ryan, 2004; R. M. Ryan & Deci, 2009).

Intrinsic motivation for learning school subject matter declines during the school years. Young children are often eager and excited to learn new things at school. But sometime between grades 3 and 9, children become less intrinsically motivated to learn classroom topics (Corpus, McClintic-Gilbert, & Hagenga, 2009; Spinath & Steinmayr, 2008). Their intrinsic motivation may be especially low if their transition from elementary school to a secondary-school format provokes considerable anxiety (Eccles & Roeser, 2009; Lepper, Corpus, & Iyengar, 2005; Wigfield, Byrnes, & Eccles, 2006).[6]

The decline in intrinsic motivation for academic subject matter is probably due to several factors. As children move through the grade levels, evidence mounts that they are not necessarily as competent as some of their peers, and they may shy away from activities for which they have low self-efficacy (Harter, 1992, 1996; Wigfield et al., 2006). Frequent reminders of the importance of good grades for promotion, graduation, and college admission may undermine their intrinsic motivation and sense of self-determination (Deci & Ryan, 1992; Eccles & Roeser, 2009; A. E. Gottfried, Marcoulides, Gottfried, & Oliver, 2009). In addition, as youngsters grow older, they become more able to set and strive for long-term goals and

internalized motivation
Adoption of behaviors that others value, whether or not one's immediate environment reinforces those behaviors.

[6]Chapter 15 discusses this school transition in more detail.

OBSERVATION GUIDELINES
Recognizing Intrinsic Motivation in Children's Behaviors

CHARACTERISTIC	LOOK FOR	EXAMPLE	IMPLICATION
Inquisitiveness	• *Eagerness to explore and learn* • *Fascination* with objects, other people, or both • *Frequent and thoughtful questions* • *Lack of concern about external rewards* for learning	Jamie often takes great interest in the new toys he finds in his preschool classroom. He is especially drawn to objects that come apart and can be reassembled in various ways.	Pique children's curiosity with puzzling situations, unusual phenomena, and opportunities to explore the physical world. Make sure their environment is safe for exploration.
High Self-Efficacy	• *Obvious pleasure during learning* • *Eagerness to tackle challenging topics* and activities • *Willingness to take risks* and make mistakes	Luana delights in trying to solve the brainteasers that her math teacher occasionally assigns for extra credit.	Give children the academic and social support they need to succeed at challenging tasks. Use evaluation procedures that encourage risk taking and allow for mistakes.
Autonomy	• *Pursuit of self-chosen activities* • *Willingness to engage in minimally structured tasks*	Mark, Reggie, and Cynthia form a rock band and practice together every chance they get. They actively seek out "gigs" both at school and in the community.	Provide opportunities for children to pursue self-chosen activities. Give them only as much structure as they need to be successful and achieve instructional goals.
Effective Learning Strategies	• *Focus on making sense of subject matter*, rather than on rote memorization of facts • *Persistence* in trying to solve difficult problems and understand complex ideas	As homework, Lenesia reads an assigned chapter in her geography textbook. Despite reading the section on mountain formation several times, she is confused about how folded mountains form. The following day she asks her teacher to explain the process in a way she can better understand.	In both instruction and assessment activities, emphasize genuine understanding and integration of the subject matter, rather than rote memorization of isolated facts.
Long-Term Interests	• *Consistent selection of a particular topic* when choices are given • *Frequent initiation of activities* in a particular domain	Whenever his after-school group goes to the local library, Connor looks for books about military battleships and aircraft.	Relate instructional subject matter to children's interests and needs. Give them occasional choices regarding the topics they study and write about.
Priorities	• *Consistent pursuit of certain activities* and disregard of other alternatives • *Apparent adoption of other people's values* (e.g., a strong work ethic, the importance of maintaining a well-organized work space) as one's own (this characteristic reflects *internalized* motivation)	Audrey is clearly frustrated when unexpected events at home prevent her from doing a homework assignment as thoroughly as she'd like. "Even though I got an A," she says later, "I didn't do as well as I *could* have if I'd had more time."	Encourage activities that will be in youngsters' best interest over the long run. Do so in a warm, supportive environment in which youngsters have input into decision making.

begin to evaluate school subjects in terms of their relevance or *non*relevance to such goals, rather than in terms of intrinsic appeal (Otis et al., 2005). And they may grow increasingly bored and impatient with highly structured, repetitive activities (Battistich, Solomon, Kim, Watson, & Schaps, 1995; Eccles & Roeser, 2009; Larson, 2000). The following interview with a high school student named Alfredo illustrates this last point:

Adult: Do you think your classes are interesting?

Alfredo: Some of them are. But some of them are boring. You go to the same class every day and you just do the same type of work every day. Like biology, I like [the teacher of this] class. She's about the only one I like. And last year I had the same problem. The only class I liked last year was science. . . . We used to do different things every day . . . but like classes like Reading, you go inside, read a story with the same person every day. That's boring.

Adult: That's boring? So will you just not show up?

Alfredo: No, I'll go but I won't do nothing sometimes. (dialogue from Way, 1998, p. 198)

BASIC DEVELOPMENTAL ISSUES
Contrasting Extrinsic and Intrinsic Motivation

ISSUE	EXTRINSIC MOTIVATION	INTRINSIC MOTIVATION
Nature and Nurture	Primary reinforcers satisfy inborn and presumably inherited needs (e.g., hunger, thirst). Secondary reinforcers acquire their reinforcing effects through regular association with primary reinforcers in a child's environment.	Children appear to have a natural curiosity about their world. Their need to feel competent and resolve apparent inconsistencies may also be inborn. Other factors that contribute to intrinsic motivation, such as confidence in one's own abilities, depend largely on experiences in the environment.
Universality and Diversity	By and large, primary reinforcers are universal around the world. Secondary reinforcers (e.g., praise) are *learned* reinforcers; thus, their effectiveness differs from child to child.	Innate sources of motivation, such as curiosity and the need to feel competent, are universal, as is the goal-directed nature of human behavior. Yet children have diverse interests, values, and goals, and they attribute their successes and failures to different factors.
Qualitative and Quantitative Change	Children increasingly learn to delay gratification, a trend that reflects quantitative change. Occasionally children respond differently to certain reinforcers than they have previously—a shift that reflects a qualitative change. A child who responds favorably to a teacher's praise in the elementary grades may later, as an adolescent, *avoid* teachers' compliments out of fear of being ridiculed as "teacher's pet."	Children shift from exclusively pursuing their own interests to internalizing some of the priorities and values of people around them, reflecting qualitative change. But for many youngsters, intrinsic motivation for learning academic subject matter declines over the school years, reflecting quantitative change.

Despite the average downward trend in intrinsic motivation, some youngsters remain genuinely interested in academic subject matter throughout the school years, especially if they have internalized the importance of school learning or if they study in schools that offer appropriate levels of challenge and relate academic concepts to students' lives (Eccles & Roeser, 2009; Otis et al., 2005; Walls & Little, 2005). Virtually all children and adolescents have intrinsic motivation for *some* activities—perhaps for skateboarding, dance, or playing electronic games. The Observation Guidelines table "Recognizing Intrinsic Motivation in Children's Behaviors" lists characteristics and behaviors to look for.

Intrinsic and extrinsic motivation develop hand in hand and occasionally interact such that one of the two driving forces takes precedence in a particular domain. In other words, a child may act according to his or her genuine interests or alternatively focus on gaining tangible rewards for good behavior. The Basic Developmental Issues table "Contrasting Extrinsic and Intrinsic Motivation" explains how these two types of motivation relate to recurrent themes in children's growth.

DEVELOPMENT OF GOALS

Many psychologists believe that human beings are purposeful by nature: People set goals for themselves and choose behaviors they think will help them achieve those goals (Boekaerts, 2009; Dweck & Elliott, 1983; Maehr & Zusho, 2009). Some goals ("I want to finish reading my dinosaur book") are transitory. Others ("I want to be a paleontologist") are relatively enduring.

Short-term goals emerge in infancy. As infants develop their motor skills (reaching, grabbing, crawling, etc.), they become increasingly capable of getting things they want.

When one end of a string is attached to a 2-month-old baby's foot and the other end is attached to a mobile, at some point the baby realizes that foot motion makes the mobile move (Rovee-Collier, 1999; Rovee-Collier & Cuevas, 2009). The infant begins to shake his or her foot more vigorously, apparently as a way to accomplish a particular goal: to gain an interesting visual display.

As children grow older, they adopt longer-term and more broadly based goals. Being happy and healthy, doing well in school, getting along with peers, bringing honor to the family, and having a romantic partner are just a few of the many possibilities (M. E. Ford, 1996; M. E. Ford & Smith, 2009; Schutz, 1994). Of course, individual children differ in their foremost goals. Those who attain high levels of academic achievement typically make class-room learning a high priority. Those who achieve at lower levels are often more concerned with maintaining social relationships (Wentzel & Wigfield, 1998; Wigfield et al., 1996).

Achievement Goals

Let's return once again to the opening case study. Sara is primarily concerned with construct-ing a kite that flies well, and she redesigns it three times to make it more aerodynamic. She doesn't mind the occasional stumbling blocks she encounters: "I mean everybody learns from their mistakes. I know I do" (D. K. Meyer et al., 1997, p. 511). In contrast, Amy sticks with her initial kite design, one that is easy to make but never gets off the ground. She says that she is primarily concerned with pleasing her teacher and parents, acknowledges that she rarely takes risks at school if a good grade is at stake, and then adds, "I feel lazy because I don't like to make challenges for myself, to make goals. I just like to . . . do it as I go along, not make goals or challenges" (p. 510).

Both girls want to do well in school; that is, they both have *achievement goals*. How-ever, their reasons for wanting to do well are quite different. Sara has a **mastery goal**: She wants to acquire new knowledge and skills related to kites and their construction, and to do so she must inevitably make a few mistakes. Amy has a **performance goal**: She wants to present herself as competent in the eyes of others and so tries to avoid mistakes if at all possible (e.g., Dweck & Elliott, 1983; Dweck & Master, 2009; Nicholls, 1984).[7]

Researchers have found it helpful to distinguish between two kinds of performance goals. In a **performance-approach goal**, the focus is on achieving positive outcomes, such as good grades, adult approval, or the respect of classmates. In a **performance-avoidance goal**, the focus is more on *avoiding undesirable* outcomes, such as exhibiting poor perfor-mance in public or being the subject of peer ridicule. Performance goals sometimes have an element of social comparison, in that children are concerned with how their accomplish-ments compare to those of their peers (A. J. Elliot & McGregor, 2000; Harackiewicz, Barron, Pintrich, Elliot, & Thrash, 2002; Maehr & Zusho, 2009).

In most instances, mastery goals are the optimal situation. To the extent that children and adolescents have mastery goals, they engage in the very activities that will help them learn: They pay attention at school, study in effective ways, and learn from their mistakes. Furthermore, they have a healthy perspective about learning, effort, and failure: They realize that learning is a process of trying hard and persevering even after temporary setbacks (E. M. Anderman & Maehr, 1994; Dweck & Elliott, 1983; Maehr & Zusho, 2009).

In contrast, children with performance goals—especially those with performance-*avoidance* goals—may be so concerned about how others evaluate them that they stay away from challenging tasks that would help them master new skills (Dweck, 1986; Maehr & Zusho, 2009; Urdan, 1997). Performance-*approach* goals are a mixed bag: They sometimes have very positive effects, spurring children on to achieve at high levels, especially in com-bination with mastery goals (Hidi & Harackiewicz, 2000; Linnenbrink, 2005; Maehr & Zusho, 2009). Yet by themselves, performance-approach goals may be less beneficial than mastery goals: To accomplish them, children may exert only the minimal effort required and use relatively superficial learning strategies such as rote memorization. Performance-approach

mastery goal
Desire to acquire additional knowledge or master new skills (also known as a *learning goal*).

performance goal
Desire to demonstrate high ability and make a good impression.

performance-approach goal
Desire to look good and receive favorable judgments from others.

performance-avoidance goal
Desire not to look bad or receive unfavorable judgments from others.

[7]You may sometimes see the term *learning goal* or *task involvement* instead of *mastery goal* and the term *ego involvement* instead of *performance goal* (e.g., Dweck & Elliott, 1983; Locke & Latham, 2006; Nicholls, 1984).

goals appear to be most detrimental when children are fairly young (e.g., in the elementary grades) and have low self-efficacy for classroom tasks (Hidi & Harackiewicz, 2000; Kaplan & Midgley, 1997; Midgley, Kaplan, & Middleton, 2001).

Mastery goals, performance-approach goals, and performance-avoidance goals are not necessarily mutually exclusive. On many occasions children may simultaneously have two kinds, or even all three (Covington & Müeller, 2001; Hidi & Harackiewicz, 2000; Meece & Holt, 1993). However, the relative prevalence of different achievement goals changes with age. Most young children seem to be primarily concerned with mastery goals. But by the time they reach second grade, they begin to show signs of having performance goals as well, and such goals become increasingly prevalent as they move into middle school and high school (Eccles & Midgley, 1989; Elliot & McGregor, 2000; Nicholls, Cobb, Yackel, Wood, & Wheatley, 1990). The greater emphasis on performance goals at older ages is probably due partly to youngsters' growing awareness of how their performance compares with that of peers and partly to an increasing focus on grades and other evaluations at the upper grade levels (Duchesne & Ratelle, 2010; Eccles et al., 1998; Nicholls et al., 1990).

Social Goals

Human beings have a basic *need for relatedness*—that is, they want to feel socially connected with, and to secure the love and respect of, other people.[8] For infants and toddlers, this need is reflected in early efforts to engage other people through crying, smiling, eye contact, and imitation, and more generally in the close attachments they form with caregivers. For many school-age children and adolescents, it may be reflected in the high priority they put on interacting with friends, sometimes at the expense of finishing chores, schoolwork, or other assigned tasks (W. Doyle, 1986; Schiefele, 2009; Wigfield, Eccles, Mac Iver, Reuman, & Midgley, 1991). In an interview in the "Intrinsic Motivation: Late Adolescence" video in MyEducationLab, 15-year-old Greg reveals the importance of social relationships in his life at school:

Interviewer:	What do you like best about school?
Greg:	Lunch.
Interviewer:	Lunch?
Greg:	All the social aspects. . . . Just friends and cliques. . . .

Like Greg, many high school students find the nonacademic aspects of school to be the most enjoyable and rewarding parts of the day (Certo et al., 2002; Otis et al., 2005).

Consistent with their need for relatedness, children and adolescents are apt to have a variety of **social goals**, perhaps including the following:

- Forming and maintaining friendly or intimate relationships with other people
- Gaining other people's approval
- Becoming part of a cohesive, mutually supportive group
- Achieving status and prestige within a peer group
- Meeting social obligations and keeping interpersonal commitments
- Assisting and supporting others, and ensuring their welfare. (Berndt & Keefe, 1996; Dowson & McInerney, 2001; M. E. Ford & Smith, 2009; Hicks, 1997; Schiefele, 2009)

Young people's social goals affect their behavior and performance in the classroom and in other group settings. If they are seeking friendly relationships with peers or are concerned about others' welfare, they may eagerly engage in such activities as cooperative

[8]The need for relatedness is introduced in Chapter 11.

Improving Your Observation Skills

I won! This girl is being recognized for an exceptionally high score on an assignment. What kinds of goals might the award foster in her? Compare your response with the explanation at the end of the chapter.

Observe how social connections are a priority for Greg in the "Intrinsic Motivation: Late Adolescence" video. (Find Video Examples in Topic 13 of MyEducationLab.)

social goal
Goal related to establishing or maintaining relationships with other people.

learning and peer tutoring (Allodi, 2010; Dowson & McInerney, 2001). If they want to gain adults' attention and approval, they are apt to strive for good grades and in other ways shoot for performance goals (Hinkley, McInerney, & Marsh, 2001). A desire for peer approval can lead to a focus on performance goals as well, although elementary and middle school students are more likely to feel pressure from peers to perform well academically than are high school students, who are less inclined to value positive academic accomplishments (L. H. Anderman & Anderman, 1999; Wentzel, 2009).

Future Aspirations

Children begin to think about a few serious long-term goals for themselves (Harter, 1999; Oyserman & Markus, 1993; Usinger & Smith, 2010). They may want to go to college or pursue a career in a certain field. The earliest goals may be quite transitory, however. Young children regularly change their minds, perhaps wanting to be a firefighter one week and professional basketball player the next.

Thus, career development takes a developmental course. In learning about jobs, children initially absorb information about typical jobs held by men and women in their society (R. B. Miller & Brickman, 2004). A little later, perhaps in middle childhood and early adolescence, children begin to speculate about careers that seem feasible for them (Bandura, 1986). These initial interests are by no means firm commitments but rather general judgments of potentially desirable jobs based on their self-perceptions of what they are capable of in specific domains (e.g., how skilled they feel they would be working in a health career). Young people also consider obstacles to working in these fields (possibly financial impediments, reactions from peers). By middle to late adolescence, many (though by no means all) young people settle on a narrower range of careers they want to pursue (Marcia, 1980). Such preliminary preferences set the stage for more definite steps in career exploration, such as selecting high school classes necessary for college admission or vocational training.

For some young people, career exploration is difficult. A number of young people do not have much insight into their own talents, such as when an adolescent holds onto a dream about becoming a professional basketball player long after it becomes obvious to his parents and the high school coach that the boy's short stature, slight build, and uncoordinated motor skills make it unlikely he will reach this goal. Other youngsters are hampered because they have gained little exposure to the world of work, perhaps never having had a part-time job or been exposed to adults in challenging professions (S. L. Turner & Conkel, 2010).

Consequently, many young people need support in defining career goals. Being exposed to men and women in the community with a wide range of occupations is an important step for youngsters, especially when they lack these contacts themselves. Adolescents may also find it helpful to participate in career-exploration activities, for example, by completing surveys about their interests and values, reading about the academic requirements and specialized training necessary for possible jobs of interest, and setting some preliminary goals (S. L. Turner & Conkel, 2010). Many high schools require students to complete internships and other practical assignments in which students spend time in a job setting and observe the daily activities of employees (E. Levine, 2010). Such experiences can enhance students' knowledge about careers and intensify their commitment to particular jobs. It is especially important for educators to provide foundational experiences of young people from low-income backgrounds, perhaps introducing them to a person who holds a desirable job and helping them complete a college application. Internships are particularly valuable for students from low-income backgrounds, who do not typically have access to role models or practical experiences in professional settings.

Coordinating Multiple Goals

Most children and adolescents have numerous and varied goals that they must juggle. Sometimes they find activities that allow them to achieve several goals simultaneously. They might satisfy both achievement goals and social goals by forming a study group to prepare for an exam. But at other times they may believe they have to abandon one goal to satisfy another

(Boekaerts, 2009; Boekaerts, de Koning, & Vedder, 2006; Phelan et al., 1994). Youngsters who want to do well in school may choose not to perform at their best so that they can maintain relationships with peers who don't value academic achievement.

Students with mastery goals may find that the multiple demands of school lead them to focus on performance goals (e.g., getting good grades) rather than studying the subject matter as thoroughly as they'd like. Brian, a junior high school student, expresses his ambivalence about striving for performance goals over mastery goals:

> I sit here and I say, "Hey, I did this assignment in five minutes and I still got an A+ on it." I still have a feeling that I could do better, and it was kind of cheap that I didn't do my best and I still got this A. . . . I think probably it might lower my standards eventually, which I'm not looking forward to at all. . . . I'll always know, though, that I have it in me. It's just that I won't express it that much. (S. Thomas & Oldfather, 1997, p. 119)

Teachers' instructional strategies and grading practices influence the extent to which students successfully juggle mastery goals with social and performance goals (Midgley, 2002). Students are more likely to strive for mastery goals when assignments entice them to learn new skills (thus encouraging a focus on mastery), when they have occasional group projects (thus helping them also meet their social goals), and when evaluation criteria allow for risk taking and mistakes (thus helping them meet their performance goals). Students are unlikely to strive for mastery goals when assignments ask little of them (consider Brian's concern about low standards), when their teachers insist that they compete with one another for resources or high test scores, and when any single failure has a significant impact on final grades.

DEVELOPMENT OF ATTRIBUTIONS

In the opening case study, Amy has not gotten her kite to fly. Even though she has put little effort into designing and constructing the kite, she chalks up her failure to insufficient wind and speculates that a successful kite would have been a matter of luck. In contrast, Sara, who has created a more aerodynamic kite, takes ownership of both her success ("I knew that I could really do it") and her little failures along the way ("I mean, everybody learns from their mistakes" [Meyer et al., 1997, p. 511]).

The various explanations people have for their successes and failures—or in some cases for the successes and failures of others—are **attributions**. Children form a variety of attributions about the causes of events in their lives. They develop beliefs about why they do well or poorly on classroom assignments, why they are popular or have trouble making friends, why they are skilled athletes or total klutzes, and so on. They may attribute their successes and failures to such factors as aptitude or ability (how smart or proficient they are), effort (how hard they're trying), other people (how well an instructor teaches or how much other children like them), task difficulty (how easy or hard something is), luck, mood, illness, fatigue, or physical appearance. Such attributions differ from one another in three general ways (Graham & Williams, 2009; Weiner, 1986, 2000, 2004):

- *Internal versus external.* Children may attribute the causes of events to factors within themselves (*internal* things) or to factors outside themselves (*external* things). In the opening case study, Sara's attributions are clearly internal, whereas Amy's are mostly external.
- *Stable versus unstable.* Children may believe either that events are due to *stable* factors, which probably won't change much in the near future, or to *unstable* factors, which can vary from one occasion to the next. Sara attributes her success to her own, relatively stable ability ("I knew that I could really do it"). In contrast, Amy's explanations of "not enough wind" and "beginner's luck" are based on unstable factors that change unpredictably.
- *Controllable versus uncontrollable.* Children may attribute events to *controllable* factors, which they can influence and change, or to *uncontrollable* factors, which they cannot influence. Sara clearly sees herself in control of her success ("I knew I could put this together really well, 'cause I had a lot of confidence in myself"), whereas Amy of course has no control over bad weather conditions or a lucky break.

attribution
Belief about the cause of one's own or another person's success or failure.

Preparing for Your Licensure Examination

Your teaching test might ask you about the role that attributions play in children's achievement.

Children's attributions are self-constructed *interpretations* that don't always reflect reality. In general, children tend to attribute their successes to internal causes (e.g., high ability, hard work) and their failures to external causes (e.g., bad luck, other people's behaviors) (Marsh, 1990a; Whitley & Frieze, 1985). By patting themselves on the back for the things they do well and putting the blame elsewhere for poor performance, they can maintain a sense of competence (Clifford, 1990; S. G. Paris & Byrnes, 1989). Yet youngsters are most likely to be successful over the long run when they attribute successes and failures alike to *internal and controllable factors*—that is, to things they are doing or might do differently.

Researchers have observed several developmental trends in children's attributions:

Children increasingly distinguish among various attributions. Up until age 5 or 6, children don't clearly discriminate among the possible causes of their successes and failures— effort, ability, luck, task difficulty, and so on (Folmer et al., 2008; Graham & Williams, 2009; Nicholls, 1990). Especially troublesome for young children is the distinction between effort and ability, which they gradually get a better handle on over time:

- At about age 6, children begin to recognize that effort and ability are separate qualities. At this point they believe that people who try hardest are those who have the greatest ability and that effort is the primary determiner of successful outcomes.
- At about age 9, they begin to understand that effort and ability can compensate for each other: People with less ability may have to exert greater effort to achieve the same outcomes as their more able peers.
- By about age 13, children clearly differentiate between effort and ability. They realize that people differ both in their inherent ability to perform a task and in the amount of effort they exert. They also realize that a lack of ability sometimes precludes success no matter how much effort a person puts forth—that some people simply don't have what it takes to accomplish certain tasks.

Many children increasingly attribute their successes and failures to stable, uncontrollable characteristics rather than to effort. Children have varying ideas of what *ability* is. Some have an **incremental view** of ability, thinking that they will almost certainly become proficient in an activity if they try hard and persevere. Others have an **entity view** of ability, believing that their capacity to perform various tasks is an inherited trait or is in some other way beyond their control (Dweck, 2000; Dweck & Master, 2009).

In the elementary grades, children tend to attribute their successes to effort and hard work, and so they are usually relatively optimistic about their chances for success and may work harder when they fail. By adolescence, however, they are apt to attribute success and failure more to a fairly stable ability that is beyond their control. To some degree, then, children move from an incremental view of ability in the elementary years to an entity view in adolescence (Dweck, 2000; Nicholls, 1990). Probably for this reason, adolescents are more discouraged by temporary setbacks than elementary school children are (Eccles & Wigfield, 1985; Pressley, Borkowski, & Schneider, 1987). And if they believe that their own low ability makes mastery of a topic or skill impossible, they may increasingly focus on performance goals (Kaplan, Middleton, Urdan, & Midgley, 2002).

Yet there are individual differences here: Some young people continue to hold an incremental view throughout high school. Others gradually discover the impact of hard work and effective learning strategies as they move through the high school grades. Adolescents who have an incremental view of ability are more likely to have mastery goals, seek out challenges to enhance their competence in various domains, persist in the face of difficulty, and achieve at high levels (Blackwell, Trzesniewski, & Dweck, 2007; Dweck, Mangels, & Good, 2004; Dweck & Master, 2009).

As they get older, children and adolescents become more aware of the reactions that different attributions elicit. Adults are often sympathetic and forgiving when children fail because of something beyond their control (illness, lack of ability, etc.) but frequently get angry when children fail because they didn't try very hard. By the time children reach the upper elementary grades, most are aware of this fact and are apt to express attributions that elicit favorable reactions (Graham & Williams, 2009; Juvonen, 2000). A child who knows very

incremental view (of ability)
Belief that ability can and does improve with effort and practice.

entity view (of ability)
Belief that ability is a "thing" that is relatively permanent and unchangeable.

well that she did poorly on a school assignment because she didn't put forth her best effort may distort the truth, telling her teacher that she doesn't "understand this stuff" or "wasn't feeling well."

Children also learn to adjust their attributions for peers. Generally speaking, fourth graders believe that their peers value diligence and hard work. Thus, they are likely to say that they did well on an assignment because they worked hard. In contrast, many eighth graders believe that their peers will disapprove of those who exert much effort on academic tasks. Thus, older students often convey the impression that they aren't working very hard—for instance, that they didn't study very much for an important exam (Graham & Williams, 2009; Howie, 2002; Juvonen, 2000).

Children gradually develop predictable patterns of attributions for future performance. When young people have frequent success in new endeavors, they gain confidence that they can master a variety of tasks. They attribute their accomplishments to their own ability and effort and have an *I can do it* attitude known as a **mastery orientation**. Yet other youngsters, especially those who encounter a consistent string of failures, become increasingly pessimistic about their chances for future success. They develop an *I can't do it* attitude known as **learned helplessness**.

Even when children with a mastery orientation and those with learned helplessness initially have equal ability, those with a mastery orientation behave in ways that lead to higher achievement over the long run. In particular, they set ambitious goals, seek out new challenges, and persist in the face of obstacles. Children with learned helplessness behave quite differently. Because they underestimate their ability, they set goals they can easily accomplish, avoid challenges that might actually enhance their learning, and respond to failure in counterproductive ways (e.g., giving up quickly) that almost guarantee future failure (Altermatt & Broady, 2009; Dweck, 2000; Seligman, 1991).

Occasionally preschoolers develop learned helplessness about a particular activity if they consistently fail at it, and they may conclude that they are basically "bad" children (Altermatt & Broady, 2009; Burhans & Dweck, 1995; Dweck, 2000). By age 5 or 6, a few children begin to show a general inclination toward learned helplessness that persists over time. Such children express little confidence about tackling challenging tasks and quickly abandon activities at which they initially struggle (D. I. Ziegert, Kistner, Castro, & Robertson, 2001). By and large, however, children rarely exhibit extreme forms of learned helplessness before age 8, perhaps because they still believe that success is due largely to their own efforts (Eccles et al., 1998; Lockhart et al., 2002; S. G. Paris & Cunningham, 1996). Feelings of helplessness are more common in adolescence. Some adolescents believe they have no control over things that happen to them and are at a loss for strategies that might get them on the road to success (Ciarrochi & Heaven, 2008; S. G. Paris & Cunningham, 1996; C. Peterson, Maier, & Seligman, 1993).

Origins of Attributions

To some extent, children's attributions are the result of their previous success and failure experiences (Covington, 1987; S. Graham & Williams, 2009; Y. Hong, Chiu, & Dweck, 1995). Those who usually succeed when they give a task their best shot are likely to believe that success is due to internal factors such as effort or high ability. Those who frequently fail despite considerable effort are likely to believe that success is due to something beyond their control—perhaps to a lack of genetic potential or to such external factors as bad luck or an adult's arbitrary and capricious judgments.

But children also pick up on other people's beliefs about why they have done well or poorly (Cimpian, Arce, Markman, & Dweck, 2007; S. Graham & Williams, 2009; Hareli & Weiner, 2002). Sometimes others' attributions are quite explicit, as the following statements illustrate:

- "That's wonderful. Your hard work has really paid off, hasn't it?" *(effort)*
- "You did it! You're so smart!" *(fairly stable ability)*
- "Hmmm, maybe this just isn't something you're good at." *(ability once again)*
- "Maybe you're just having a bad day." *(luck)*

mastery orientation
General belief that one is capable of accomplishing challenging tasks, accompanied by an intent to master such tasks.

learned helplessness
General belief that one is incapable of accomplishing tasks and has little or no control of the environment.

A combination of observing chronic failure in oneself and hearing unflattering attributions from others can be devastating, as a journal entry by a high school student with an undiagnosed learning disability reveals:

> When I told one teacher in jr. high that I thought I had dyslexia, he told me that I was just lazy. Yeah, right! Me, lazy? I would end up with the same routine before every vocabulary test or important assignment. I would spend a week trying to memorize words that, no matter what I did, I couldn't spell right. On test days, I would turn in the test, and get an F. All I could do was hope that I'd do better on the next one.
>
> It only got worse in high school, where there were more spelling and essay tests, with more complicated words that seemed too impossible to memorize. Finally, I just started to think, "Why should I even try? I am just going to end up with an 'F' anyway." It seems that an "F" was going to symbolize what I would end up in the future. (The Freedom Writers, 1999, p. 147)

In some instances adults communicate attributions indirectly rather than explicitly. When adults criticize and express anger about children's poor performance, they imply that children have the ability to master the task and simply aren't trying hard enough. When they instead express pity, they imply that low ability is the reason for the failure (Pintrich & Schunk, 2002; Weiner, 1984). Adults communicate low ability, too, when they praise easy successes, provide unneeded assistance on easy tasks, or encourage children to abandon challenging ones (Hokoda & Fincham, 1995; Schunk & Pajares, 2004; Stipek, 1996).

BIOECOLOGY OF MOTIVATION

Bioecology of Child Development

Children's individual characteristics and their experiences in complex social environments affect their motivational states, goals, and attributions.

Children's personal characteristics and experiences in the environment affect their motivation. For example, children's maturational states and general developmental abilities affect the tangible rewards and activities that they find reinforcing. Temperament partly determines inclinations either to act on their curiosity or, in contrast, to stay on the sidelines of social activities (Keogh, 2003). Children with attention-deficit hyperactivity disorder (many of whom have poor impulse control) tend to have difficulty delaying gratification (Chelonis et al., 2011; J. R. Cohen & Lieberman, 2010; Hoerger & Mace, 2006). A number of children with significant physical disabilities have little sense of self-determination because they must depend heavily on other people to help them meet their needs and achieve their goals (Egilson & Traustadottir, 2009; Sands & Wehmeyer, 1996). Children with cognitive disabilities (e.g., intellectual disabilities or undiagnosed learning disabilities) may show signs of learned helplessness about classroom tasks if their past efforts have repeatedly met with failure (Hersh, Stone, & Ford, 1996; Vieillevoye & Nader-Grosbois, 2008; Zambo & Brem, 2004).

Children also have unique motivations associated with being boys or girls and as members of particular cultural and ethnic groups. Let's examine these effects in detail.

Gender

Girls and boys develop somewhat distinct interests, educational goals, and beliefs about their own abilities beginning as early as age 4. On average, young boys are more likely to develop interests that involve acquiring considerable knowledge about a specific topic (e.g., about frogs, dinosaurs, or a particular sport). In contrast, young girls show more interest in creative activities such as drawing and painting (J. M. Alexander et al., 2008; K. E. Johnson et al., 2004). In the elementary grades, boys and girls tend to find greater or lesser value in various academic domains depending, in part, on whether they view these domains as being appropriate for their gender. Many children (but certainly not all of them) perceive some subjects (e.g., writing, instrumental music) to be for girls and others (e.g., math, science) to be for boys (Eccles et al., 1998; C. L. Martin & Ruble, 2010; Pajares & Valiante, 1999).

On average, girls are more concerned about doing well in school: They are more engaged in classroom activities, work more diligently on school assignments, and are more likely to graduate from high school (J. E. O. Blakemore et al., 2009; Duckworth & Seligman, 2006; Halpern, 2006). Furthermore, girls are currently more interested in getting a college education than boys are, and in North American and European countries more women than men earn college degrees (J. E. O. Blakemore et al., 2009; Halpern et al., 2007; National Science Foundation, 2007). Nevertheless, men are more likely to pursue graduate degrees, especially in mathematics, engineering, and the physical sciences (J. E. O. Blakemore et al., 2009).

Despite girls' eagerness to achieve academically, they tend to have less confidence about their abilities. When researchers compare girls and boys who have equal achievement levels, they find that girls typically have higher self-efficacy in gender-stereotypical "girl" domains (e.g., reading, writing, the arts) and boys have higher self-efficacy in gender-stereotypical "boy" domains (e.g., science and mathematics; Andrade, Wang, Du, & Akawi, 2009; Wigfield et al., 2006). In general, however, girls tend to underestimate their competence, whereas boys tend to overestimate theirs (D. A. Cole, Martin, Peeke, Seroczynski, & Fier, 1999; Eccles et al., 1998; Pajares, 2005). In addition, girls (especially high-achieving girls) are more easily discouraged by failure than are boys (Dweck, 2000). We can explain this difference, at least in part, by looking at gender differences in attributions. Some researchers have observed a tendency for boys to attribute their successes to a fairly stable ability and their failures to lack of effort, thus displaying the attitude that *I know I can do this if I work at it*. Girls tend to show the reverse pattern: They attribute their successes to effort and their failures to lack of ability, believing that *I don't know whether I can keep on doing it, because I'm not very good at this type of thing*. When encountering failure, then, boys are apt to have an incremental view of ability and girls are apt to have an entity view. Gender differences in attributions, which can appear even when youngsters' previous achievement levels have been equal, are most often observed in stereotypically male domains such as mathematics and sports (Chedzoy & Burden, 2009; Dweck, 2000; Vermeer et al., 2000).

Historically, boys have had more ambitious career aspirations than girls (Deaux, 1984; Lueptow, 1984). In recent years, many girls—especially those in Western countries—have also begun to set their sights on challenging professions (Bandura et al., 2001; Lapan, Tucker, Kim, & Kosciulek, 2003). But even as traditional boundaries delineating "appropriate" professions for men and for women have begun to dissolve, many adolescents continue to limit themselves to gender-stereotypical careers (Lippa, 2002; Weisgram, Bigler, & Liben, 2010). Gender patterns in career choices appear to be partly due to differences in self-efficacy for various academic domains (Bandura et al., 2001; Jacobs et al., 2002). Also, girls are more likely than boys to be attracted to people-helping professions (e.g., teaching, counseling) and to be concerned about balancing a career with family life (Leaper & Friedman, 2007; Mahaffy & Ward, 2002; Weisgram et al., 2010).

Culture and Ethnicity

Children everywhere are naturally curious about their physical world and about the society in which they live. Similarly, all children want to exercise their autonomy and make at least some of their own choices. Yet each culture fosters such motivational qualities in ways that fit with prevailing cultural practices. For example, the amount and forms that children's autonomy and self-determination take differ considerably from group to group (Bao & Lam, 2008; d'Ailly, 2003; J. Kim, Schallert, & Kim, 2010; Soenens & Vansteenkiste, 2010). Adults in some Native American communities express confidence in young children by giving them a lot of freedom to make choices (Deyhle & LeCompte, 1999). In comparison, some African American parents believe that young children should be closely supervised out of concern for their safety (Hale-Benson, 1986; McLoyd, 1998b). And in some Asian cultures, young people prefer that trusted adults make important choices for them (Iyengar & Lepper, 1999; Vansteenkiste, Zhou, Lens, & Soenens, 2005).

Children from many ethnic and cultural groups place high value on getting a good education (Gallimore & Goldenberg, 2001; Okagaki, 2001; Suizzo, Robinson, & Pahlke, 2008). But to some degree, different cultural groups encourage their own distinct values related to school learning. Many people in China, Japan, and Russia emphasize learning for learning's sake: With knowledge comes personal growth, better understanding of the world, and greater potential to contribute to society. Important for these cultures, too, are

Preparing for Your Licensure Examination

Your teaching test might ask about how children learn to be motivated in a cultural context.

hard work and persistence in academic studies (Hess & Azuma, 1991; Hufton, Elliott, & Illushin, 2002; J. Li, 2006). Students from European American backgrounds are less likely to be diligent when classroom topics have little intrinsic appeal, but they often find value in academic subject matter that piques their curiosity and in assignments that require creativity, independent thinking, or critical analysis (Hess & Azuma, 1991; Kuhn & Park, 2005).

Attributions for academic tasks and activities are also socialized during cultural experiences, for example, while encountering explanations from adults about why children might not have succeeded at a task. Students from Asian cultures are generally more likely to attribute classroom success and failure to unstable factors (e.g., effort, temporary situational conditions) than are students brought up in Western cultures (J. Li & Fischer, 2004; Muramoto, Yamaguchi, & Kim, 2009; Weiner, 2004). Unfortunately, another finding is that children of color are socialized to be somewhat pessimistic about their academic abilities (e.g., Graham, 1989; Murdock, 2009; Weiner, 2004). After encountering racial prejudice in day-to-day activities and adults with low expectations who fail to give them second chances, these students may begin to believe that they have little chance of academic success.

Finally, children's cultural experiences inform them of the kinds of goals that are realistic for them to pursue. A girl in one community may envision herself as an astronaut, computer programmer, or civil engineer, whereas a second girl in another community may look forward to becoming a weaver or midwife. In the Development and Culture feature "Achievement Orientation in Tanzania," you can read about viable areas of achievement perceived by a group of Tanzanian children.

As you have learned, motivation changes in somewhat predictable ways with age but also responds systematically to individual experiences. The Developmental Trends table "Motivation at Different Age Levels" identifies motivational characteristics and the types of diversity you are likely to see in children of different age groups.

DEVELOPMENT IN CULTURE
Achievement Orientation in Tanzania

How can an adult determine what a child wants to accomplish in life? Simply asking children to describe their goals is an option but as a research method, it has disadvantages. Many children feel uncomfortable sharing their private dreams and fears with a stranger. Others cannot easily respond to abstract questions about events that have not yet taken place.

Priya Nalkur, an expert in human development, was aware of methodological difficulties in assessing children's ideas about achievement yet was committed to examining these ideas in children from the Kilimanjaro region of Tanzania, Africa (Nalkur, 2009). She needed a strategy that would put children at ease, give them something concrete to respond to, and allow them to use a familiar means of expression. She decided to interact individually with children, show them pictures of people engaged in a task, and ask them to make up stories about what was going on in the pictures.

In her research, Nalkur invited children to examine three cards drawn of human figures with east African features and clothing. Picture 1 had a boy sitting at his desk and staring at a violin; Picture 2 showed a young woman carrying books and looking off into a field; and Picture 3 had a man hanging onto a suspended rope with his hand. Nalkur selected these pictures because they typically elicit motivational themes: young people are apt to project their own desires into their interpretations of the drawings

Nalkur encouraged children to develop stories that explained what the person in the card was doing before, during, and after the scene in the picture. She believed that the method would provide a comfortable context for the children, who could focus on meaningful stimuli and create stories, a tradition that is celebrated in their culture. To further create a relaxing atmosphere, Nalkur enlisted the help of a small group of cooperating children who led warm-up games before the child participants looked at pictures and told their stories.

Nalkur drew from three groups of research participants. "Street children" lived primarily on the streets, in some cases having lost their parents to acquired immunodeficiency syndrome (AIDS) and in other situations having left home out of their own initiative due to parents' abandonment or abuse. "Former street children" were those who had previously lived on the streets but had been in a shelter for at least 1 year at the time of the interview. "Schoolchildren" lived with families and attended school. Nalkur decided to include only boys in her sample because street children in Tanzania consist mainly of boys. One hundred and eighty-three boys from ages 11 to 18 participated, with roughly a third in each of her groups.

Nalkur found that children's stories regularly included the theme of *maisha magumu*, a feeling of having a "difficult life"[a] (Nalkur, 2009, p. 1013). Children were affected by the widespread frustration they heard about from adults that the local economy was weak and offered inadequate access to employment, health care, or education. Yet children also routinely exuded resilience. They demonstrated a faith in their own self-reliance and communicated a belief that they could overcome a host of difficult challenges in life.

As you might expect, the particular achievement orientations that children expressed varied somewhat by group. Street children expressed hope in

LIVING IN THE PRESENT, PREPARING FOR THE FUTURE. This Masai boy proudly wears the traditional clothing of his tribe. As with all children, he is developing an outlook on the future that is infused with cultural values and practices.

the future and in people's obligation for making life better for children. One street child revealed such optimism in his interpretation:

The young man is wishing to finish his education, get a good job to help him take care of his family and to build a beautiful house and live a good life. He wishes he could educate his children to become as learned as he is, and when he gets rich he can help other street kids. They will be grateful and he can become the president as he is helping the public. (13 years, Picture 1)[a] (Nalkur, 2009, p. 1019)

Although their aspirations were for a bright future, the street children did not seem to know how to achieve their goals. They often described troubled characters who were unaware of how to make progress in life:

The young man is a street child and he is used to sleeping in trees so that criminals won't do bad things to him, he is wondering when that kind of life will end and when he will get a good place to sleep, good food, and live happily just like everyone else. (16 years, Picture 3)[a] (p. 1020)

The former street children told stories about taking charge of their lives. Friends and adults outside the family played an important role for former street children that was not fulfilled by parents:

One day in my life, I asked myself about my friends. What way shall I use to be close to my friends? Some of them seem to like guitar and I also had a friend, Hussen, who is good guitar player. I asked him to teach me. He agreed and I learned in a short time. I had found a way of being close to my friends. I also taught them and until now they are good players. (16 years, Picture 1)[a] (p. 1021)

The schoolchildren told stories that linked hard work in school to academic achievement. They talked about jobs, performance in school, and effort in studying. Here is one typical response:

One day Simon was thinking as follows: When I grow up, I want to work as a doctor but without education, we cannot be doctors. I hope that I will study diligently. (13 years, Picture 1)[a] (p. 1022)

The schoolchildren were aware of temptations around them but also articulated strategies for taking control of their lives:

There was once a young man who was a thief. Together with his friends, he made others join their behavior. He lived a very difficult life, and eventually decided to join adult education to avoid getting a bad name in the community. He became very keen in studying to have a better future. He in turn motivated his friends who were thieves to not continue with that lifestyle. He told them to continue with education so as not to have a bad reputation. Eventually, they too got educated and worked to improve the community as a whole. (12 years, Picture 3)[a] (p. 1023)

In her interpretations of the responses, Nalkur suggested that children's achievement orientations arose from their experiences. Street children expressed hope for protection from harm, yet did not seem to know how to achieve their goals. Former street children's emphasis on friendship may have derived from their recognition that it was primarily other children who could be counted on for affection. Finally, the schoolchildren saw a clear connection between being well educated and having a good life.

MOTIVATING CHILDREN AND ADOLESCENTS

A common misconception about motivation is that it is something children and adolescents "carry around" inside of them—for instance, that some students are consistently motivated to learn at school and others are not. It's certainly true that some sources of motivation *do* come from within. However, it's equally true that youngsters' immediate environments can have dramatic effects on their motivation to learn and achieve. Such environment-dependent motivation is known as **situated motivation** (Guthrie, 2008; D. T. Hickey & Granade, 2004; S. G. Paris & Turner, 1994). Yet simple pep talks ("I know you can do it if you try!") are not

situated motivation
Phenomenon in which aspects of the immediate environment enhance motivation to learn particular things or behave in particular ways.

DEVELOPMENTAL TRENDS
Motivation at Different Age Levels

AGE	WHAT YOU MIGHT OBSERVE	DIVERSITY	IMPLICATIONS
Infancy (Birth–2 Years) 	• Curiosity about objects and people • Enthusiasm for exploring the environment • Some goal-directed behavior as early as 3 months • Little or no need for praise, especially in the first year; greater appreciation of praise after age 1	• Temperament and culture influence children's willingness to explore and experiment with their physical environment. • Attachment security influences children's willingness to explore. • Children with significant disabilities may show less interest in physical exploration than their nondisabled peers.	• Create a predictable, affectionate environment in which children feel comfortable exploring and trying new things. • Provide new and unusual objects that pique children's curiosity. • Identify and provide objects and events that can capture the interest of children with disabilities.
Early Childhood (2–6 Years) 	• Preference for small, immediate rewards over larger, delayed ones • Overconfidence about one's ability to perform new tasks • Rapidly changing, situation-dependent interests; emergence of stable interests in some children • Focus on obtaining the approval of adults more than that of peers • Focus on mastery (rather than performance) goals • Little understanding of the probable causes of successes and failures	• Differences in desire for social interaction are evident as early as age 3 or 4. • Children who begin school without basic knowledge of colors, shapes, letters, or numbers may see obvious differences between their own abilities and those of peers—differences that may set the stage for poor self-efficacy down the road if the missing knowledge is not soon addressed. • Learned helplessness in a particular domain occasionally appears as early as age 4 or 5, especially after a history of failure.	• Provide a wide variety of potentially interesting toys, storybooks, props for dramatic play, and other equipment. • Praise (or in some other way reinforce) desired behaviors as soon as they occur. • Provide the guidance and support children need in order to experience success more often than failure.
Middle Childhood (6–10 Years) 	• Increasing ability to delay gratification • Increasing awareness of how one's own performance compares with that of peers; more realistic assessment of abilities • Increasing prevalence of performance goals • Increasing distinction between effort and ability as possible causes of success and failure; tendency to attribute successes to hard work	• As a result of low self-efficacy, children with a history of learning problems have less intrinsic motivation to learn academic subject matter. • Some very bright, talented girls may be reluctant to do their best because of concerns about appearing unfeminine or surpassing peers. • Children of color and children with disabilities are somewhat more likely to develop learned helplessness about their ability to achieve academic success.	• Communicate the message that with appropriate effort, strategies, and support, virtually *all* children can master basic knowledge and skills in academic subject matter. • Focus children's attention on the progress they are making, rather than on how their performance compares to that of peers. • Stress the importance of learning for the intrinsic pleasure it brings; downplay the importance of grades and other external evaluations.
Early Adolescence (10–14 Years) 	• Increasing interest in social activities; increasing concern about gaining approval of peers • Declining sense of competence, often accompanying the transition to middle school or junior high • Decline in intrinsic motivation to learn school subject matter; increasing focus on performance goals • Increasing belief that skill is the result of stable factors (e.g., inherited ability) rather than effort and practice • Increasing motivation to learn and achieve in stereotypically gender-appropriate domains	• Girls have a stronger desire to interact frequently with peers. • Some adolescents believe that demonstrating high achievement can interfere with popularity. • Adolescents from a few ethnic groups (e.g., some from several Asian cultures) continue to place high value on adult approval. • Some individuals develop a general sense of learned helplessness about achieving academic success.	• Evaluate adolescents on the basis of how well they are achieving instructional objectives, not on how well their performance compares with that of their classmates. • Assign cooperative group projects that allow adolescents to interact with one another, display their unique talents, and contribute to the success of the group. • When youngsters exhibit a pattern of failure, provide the support they need to become successful in their endeavors.

DEVELOPMENTAL TRENDS (continued)

AGE	WHAT YOU MIGHT OBSERVE	DIVERSITY	IMPLICATIONS
Late Adolescence (14–18 Years)	• Ability to postpone immediate pleasures in order to gain long-term rewards • Increasing stability of interests and priorities • Increasing focus on the utilitarian value of activities • Tendency to attribute successes and failures more to ability than to effort • Some tentative decisions about career paths	• Girls work harder on school assignments and are more likely to graduate from high school than are boys. • Adolescents from some Asian cultures often attribute their successes and failures to effort rather than ability. • Many teens have career aspirations that are stereotypically gender appropriate.	• Point out the relevance of various academic domains (e.g., mathematics) for adolescents' long-term goals. • Design assignments in which adolescents apply academic content to real-world adult tasks and problems. • Allow teens to pursue personal interests within the context of particular academic domains.

Sources: Bandura et al., 2001; L. A. Bell, 1989; Burhans & Dweck, 1995; H. Cooper & Dorr, 1995; Corpus, McClintic-Gilbert, & Hayenga, 2006; Deshler & Schumaker, 1988; Dweck & Master, 2009; Eccles & Midgley, 1989; Eccles & Roeser, 2009; Fewell & Sandall, 1983; S. Graham, 1989; L. Green et al., 1994; Halpern, 1992, 2006; Harter, 1992, 1996; Jacobs et al., 2002; Jacobsen, Lowery, & DuCette, 1986; K. E. Johnson et al., 2004; Juvonen, 2000; Leaper & Friedman, 2007; Lieberman, 1993; Lillard, 1997; T. W. Linder, 1993; Lockhart et al., 2002; Nicholls, 1990; Otis et al., 2005; S. G. Paris & Cunningham, 1996; Peak, 1993; C. Peterson, 1990; Portes, 1996; Rotenberg & Mayer, 1990; Rovee-Collier, 1999; R. M. Ryan & Deci, 2009; Schultz & Switzky, 1990; Schunk & Pajares, 2009; Seligman, 1991; Vaughn et al., 1984; Wigfield et al., 1991, 2006; Ziegert et al., 2001.

terribly helpful in motivating youngsters, especially over the long run (Brophy, 2004). Far more effective is providing scaffolding for challenging tasks, thereby enticing children to tackle those tasks largely for the pleasure and sense of competence they bring (Eccles, 2007; Hidi & Renninger, 2006; Lodewyk & Winne, 2005). The following strategies are also widely recommended:

• **Focus on promoting intrinsic (rather than extrinsic) motivation.** Externally imposed consequences—praise, money, good grades, and so on—often bring about desired changes in children's behavior. Such reinforcers have disadvantages, however. Although they provide a source of extrinsic motivation, they can undermine children's *intrinsic* motivation if children perceive them to be controlling, manipulative, or in some other way limiting their autonomy and sense of self-determination (R. M. Ryan & Deci, 2009; Vansteenkiste, Lens, & Deci, 2006). Furthermore, externally imposed reinforcers may communicate the message that assigned tasks are unpleasant chores (why else would a reinforcer be necessary?), rather than activities to be carried out and enjoyed for their own sake (B. A. Hennessey, 1995; Stipek, 1993).

Ideally, then, teachers, parents, and other adults should focus children's attention *not* on the external consequences of their efforts but on the internal pleasures (enjoyment, satisfaction, pride, etc.) that accompany certain tasks and activities. Adults can also increase children's intrinsic motivation for learning important topics and skills using strategies such as these:

• Communicating enthusiasm for a topic
• Piquing children's curiosity with new and intriguing objects and phenomena
• Incorporating fantasy, adventure, or suspense into activities
• Creating disequilibrium by presenting puzzling phenomena
• Getting children physically involved with a topic (e.g., through role playing or hands-on experimentation)
• Relating important skills and subject matter to children's interests and goals
• Offering choices when several alternatives will be equally effective in helping children acquire desired skills
• Accentuating children's choice in studying material (e.g., "You've selected some interesting books to read.")
• Identifying areas in which each child can be especially successful. (Brophy, 2004; Martens, de Brabander, Rozendaal, Boekaerts, & van der Leeden, 2010; Patall, Cooper, & Wynn, 2008; R. M. Ryan & Deci, 2009; Schraw, Flowerday, & Lehman, 2001)

• **Enhance children's self-efficacy for mastering important knowledge and skills.** One critical way to enhance children's self-efficacy in a particular domain is, of course, to help them achieve success in the domain—for instance, by tailoring instruction to their existing ability levels, scaffolding their efforts, and so on (Lodewyk & Winne, 2005; Schunk & Pajares, 2009; Valentine, Cooper, Bettencourt, & DuBois, 2002). Another effective approach is to show them *other people's* successes. When children see peers of similar age and ability successfully accomplish a task, they are more likely to believe that they, too, can accomplish it (Schunk & Hanson, 1985).

• **Maintain children's sense of self-determination when describing rules and giving instructions.** Every group needs a few rules and procedures to ensure that children act appropriately and activities run smoothly. Furthermore, teachers and other adults must often impose restrictions about how children carry out assigned tasks. The trick is to present rules, procedures, guidelines, and structure without communicating an intention to *control* children's behavior. Instead, adults should present these things as *information*—for instance, as conditions that can help children accomplish important goals and objectives (Hagger, Chatzisarantis, Barkoukis, Wang, & Baranowski, 2005; Perry, Turner, & Meyer, 2006; R. M. Ryan & Deci, 2009). Following are examples:

• "We can make sure everyone has an equal chance to speak if we listen without interrupting and if we raise our hands when we want to contribute to the discussion."

• "I'm giving you a particular format to follow when you do your math homework. If you use this format, it will be easier for me to figure out which concepts you understand and which ones you need more help with."

• "Let's remember that other children will be using the same paints and brushes later today, so we need to make sure everything we use now is still in tip-top shape when we're done. It's important, then, that we clean the brushes thoroughly when we're done painting."

• **Encourage children to shoot for specific goals.** Children often respond more favorably to goals they set for themselves than to goals set by others (Boekaerts, 2009; Lens, 2001; Wentzel, 1999). Yet many children and some adolescents have trouble conceptualizing a "future" that is abstract (e.g., getting a good education) and perhaps many years down the road (e.g., going to medical school) (Bandura, 1997; Husman & Freeman, 1999; Usinger & Smith, 2010). They may initially respond more favorably to short-term, concrete goals—perhaps learning a certain number of math facts in a given week, getting the next belt in karate, or earning a merit badge in a scout troop (E. S. Alexander, 2006; Brophy, 2004; R. B. Miller & Brickman, 2004; Schunk & Rice, 1989). By setting and working for a series of short-term goals, youngsters get regular feedback about the progress they are making, acquire a greater sense of self-efficacy that they can master new skills, and achieve at demonstrably higher levels (Kluger & DeNisi, 1998; Page-Voth & Graham, 1999; Schunk, 1996).

As children reach adolescence, their increasing capacity for abstract thought allows them to envision long-term goals (e.g., winning a spot on a varsity sports team or having a career in journalism). Yet perhaps as a result of low self-efficacy or limited financial resources, some of them set their sights quite low. Teachers and other adults should not only encourage these young people to think ambitiously but also convince them that high goals are achievable. When encouraging girls to consider stereotypically masculine career paths, adults might provide examples of women who have led successful and happy lives in those careers. When encouraging teens from low-income families to think about going to college, adults might assist with filling out scholarship applications and scheduling appointments with college financial aid officers.

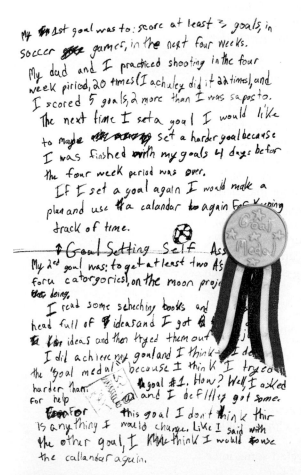

ARTIFACT 13-2 Amaryth's goals. Ten-year-old Amaryth describes how she worked toward goals on the soccer field and in the classroom. Her teacher had encouraged her to articulate her goals and recognized Amaryth's accomplishments when she met her goals.

- **Encourage mastery goals as well as (ideally even more than) performance goals.** To some degree, performance goals are inevitable in today's schools and in society at large. Children and adolescents will invariably look to their peers' performance when evaluating their own accomplishments, and many aspects of the adult world (gaining admission to college, seeking employment, working in private industry, etc.) are inherently competitive in nature. Yet adults do youngsters a disservice when they focus too much attention on "looking good" and surpassing peers. When adults instead explain how certain knowledge and skills will be useful down the road, highlight ongoing progress, and acknowledge that effective learning requires exerting effort and making mistakes, they are emphasizing mastery goals that will enhance achievement over the long run (Bong, 2001; Brophy, 2004; Maehr & Zusho, 2009).

- **Downplay the seriousness of failures.** Children and adolescents are more apt to accept responsibility for their failures—and therefore to learn from them—if adults don't make a big deal of mistakes and instead give students numerous opportunities to improve assignments and overall class grades (Ames, 1992; Dweck & Master, 2009; Katkovsky, Crandall, & Good, 1967; Perry & Winne, 2004). In some instances adults may also find it appropriate to focus children's attention on the *processes* they use to tackle assigned tasks and solve problems rather than on the final outcome of their efforts. A teacher may occasionally give an assignment with instructions like these:

> It doesn't matter at all how many you get right. In fact, these problems are kind of hard. I'm just interested in learning more about what [you] think about while [you're] working on problems like these. I want you to focus on the problem and just say out loud whatever you're thinking while you're working—whatever comes into your head. (Stipek & Kowalski, 1989, p. 387)

- **Help youngsters meet their social goals.** One of the reasons older children and adolescents focus so much on performance goals is that making a good impression helps them gain the respect and companionship of peers. They encounter most of their peers at school and in other large-group situations and naturally make social goals a high priority in these settings (B. B. Brown, Eicher, & Petrie, 1986; Ladd, Herald-Brown, & Kochel, 2009; Wentzel & Wigfield, 1998). The Development and Practice feature "Helping Children Meet Their Social Goals" suggests several ways in which educators can address youngsters' social needs within the context of academic instruction and other learning activities.

- **Give encouraging messages about the causes of successes and failures.** When commenting on children's successes, probably the best approach is to mention such controllable factors as effort and learning strategies (Dweck & Master, 2009; Schunk, 1990; Weiner, 1984). In this way, adults provide assurance that children are certainly capable of succeeding with hard work and perseverance. A teacher might say:

  - "You've done very well. I can see that you've been trying very hard to get better."
  - "Your project shows good strategies and a lot of hard work."

When identifying possible causes for failures, however, adults can also focus primarily on effort and better strategies and should usually give such feedback in private (Brophy, 2004; Cimpian et al., 2007; Dweck, 2000). Following are examples:

  - "The more you practice, the better you will get."
  - "Perhaps you need to study a little bit each night rather than waiting until the night before. And let's talk about how you might also study *differently* than you did last time."

When children's failures are consistently attributed to controllable factors such as lack of effort or ineffective strategies and when increased effort or new strategies do, in fact, produce success, children often work harder, persist longer in the face of failure, and seek help when they need it (Dweck & Elliott, 1983; Dweck & Master, 2009; Eccles & Wigfield, 1985).

The most effective feedback—no matter whether it commends successes or identifies weaknesses—also maintains children's sense of self-determination. More specifically, it provides information about children's performance but doesn't convey a desire to control their behavior (Brophy, 2004; Deci, 1992; R. M. Ryan & Deci, 2009). In complimenting a student

DEVELOPMENT AND PRACTICE
Helping Children Meet Their Social Goals

Continually communicate the message that you like and respect the young people with whom you are working.

- A second-grade teacher tells a student that she saw his karate exhibition at the local mall over the weekend. "You were great!" she says. "How many years have you been studying karate?" (Middle Childhood)

- A high school teacher reads about a group of students at school who produce informal movies in their free time and post them on *YouTube*. "I watched some of your movies," he says to one of the students. "Very clever. I'll be watching for any new videos that you post." (Late Adolescence)

Plan learning tasks that involve social interaction.

- A sixth-grade social studies teacher incorporates classroom debates, small-group discussions, and cooperative learning tasks into each month's lesson plans. (Early Adolescence)

- A high school chemistry teacher forms cooperative groups for conducting experiments. Every student is assigned a role essential to the overall functioning of the group—manager of equipment, recorder of notes, checker of observations, or spokesperson to the class. Students rotate through each of the roles during the span of the trimester. (Late Adolescence)

Get youngsters involved in large projects in which they must work toward the common good.

- The eighth graders at one middle school are sharply divided into "popular" and "unpopular" groups, and some students are routinely excluded from social interaction. The school music teacher suggests that a production of the musical *You're a Good Man, Charlie Brown* become a project for the entire class. All 92 eighth graders are either in the cast or working on costumes, scenery, or lighting. The ambitiousness of the project and the fact that the class's efforts will eventually be on public display instill a cohesive class spirit among the students, with formerly popular and unpopular students working respectfully with one another. (Early Adolescence)

- An environmental studies club organizes a Green Day for the school. Students in the club post flyers and *Facebook* requests for everyone to bring in objects that can be recycled, repurposed, or safely disposed. Students, teachers, and staff bring in used batteries, printer cartridges, eyeglasses, and cell phones. (Late Adolescence)

Teach strategies that enable youngsters to present themselves well to others.

- A preschool teacher welcomes a new boy, Fernando, to the classroom and introduces him to the other children. After noticing that the boy seems to be shy, the teacher observes him carefully and spots his exceptional skill in building intricate block structures. She encourages a few other children who also like to build with blocks to admire his work and see if he needs help, "Look at the amazing space station Fernando is making. I bet he could use help from some other engineers." (Early Childhood)

- As fourth graders prepare for upcoming oral reports on their small-group science projects, their teacher offers suggestions for capturing their audience's interest. "You might present a puzzling question your classmates would really like to know the answer to," she says. "Or you might show them something that will surprise them. Hands-on activities are good, too. Perhaps you can think of a short, simple experiment they might conduct to arrive at the same conclusion *you* did." (Middle Childhood)

Give praise in private when a student may be sensitive about peers' reactions.

- A middle school girl, Laura, has worked hard as student body president of the school. Her adviser, Mr. Gomez, has observed the results of her efforts in inspiring all of the officers to work together collaboratively for the betterment of the school community. Realizing that Laura would want to give credit to others in her group, Mr. Gomez takes her aside to compliment her on her effective leadership skills. (Early Adolescence)

- A high school English teacher reads a particularly creative story written by a young man who, she knows, is quite concerned about maintaining his "cool" image. On the second page of his story (which the student's classmates are unlikely to see), she writes, "This is great work, Tony! I think it's good enough to enter into the state writing contest. Can we meet before or after school some day this week to talk about the contest?" (Late Adolescence)

Respect individual differences.

- A preschool teacher notices that some of his students have a greater need for social contact than others. Some children really seem to enjoy cooperative play activities, while others are more interested in experimenting with physical objects. Although he interacts with all of the children regularly, he is careful not to interrupt when children are happily engrossed in play. (Early Childhood)

- An elementary student whose parents recently divorced is getting accustomed to new pickup routines after school. His father picks him up on Mondays through Wednesdays and his mother picks him up Thursdays and Fridays. The boy places great importance on his social life and wants to continue to see friends occasionally after school. When he is going home with a friend for a couple of hours, his teacher watches to make sure he takes his overnight bag if it's a day when he is shifting between his mother's and father's homes. (Middle Childhood)

Sources: M. E. Ford & Smith, 2007; Hamre & Pianta, 2005; Harter, 1999; Juvonen, 2000, 2006; Ladd et al., 2009; Ormrod, 2008; Stevens & Slavin, 1995; M. Thompson & Grace, 2001 (school play example); Wentzel & Wigfield, 1998; Wigfield et al., 1996.

who has written a good persuasive essay, a teacher might say, "Your arguments are well organized and quite convincing" (emphasis on what the student has done well), rather than saying, "Good job in following my guidelines" (emphasis on following the teacher's instructions). And in admonishing students for off-task behavior during a cooperative learning activity, a teacher might ask, "Are you three going to have time to work on your project tonight if you don't finish it during class?" (emphasis on students' own time management concerns), rather than saying, "How many times do I have to remind this group to *get to work*?" (emphasis on keeping the students under control).

- **Teach children to give themselves encouraging attribution messages as well.** Numerous research studies have shown that children can be taught more productive attributions for their successes and failures, with higher achievement and more persistence in the face of failure often being the result (e.g., Berkeley, Mastropieri, & Scruggs, 2008; Dweck, 1975; Robertson, 2000). In these *attribution retraining* studies, children are asked to engage in a particular task (e.g., reading challenging text, solving arithmetic problems, constructing geometric puzzles), with occasional failures interspersed among more frequent successes. Within this context, one viable approach for changing attributions is for an adult to interpret each success in terms of high effort or good strategies and each failure in terms of insufficient effort or ineffective strategies. But even more effective is teaching children to explicitly attribute their *own* successes and failures to amount of effort or specific strategies (Berkeley et al., 2008; Dweck & Master, 2009; Fowler & Peterson, 1981).

- **Use extrinsic reinforcers when necessary.** Despite adults' best efforts, children sometimes have little interest in acquiring knowledge or skills critical for their later success in life. To encourage learning or desired behaviors in such situations, adults may have to provide extrinsic reinforcers—not only praise but perhaps also free time, grades, special privileges, or points toward a small prize. How can adults use such reinforcers without undermining children's intrinsic motivation? One effective strategy is to reinforce children not simply for doing something but for doing it *well*. Another is to communicate that an extrinsic reinforcer is merely a concrete acknowledgment of significant progress or achievement—an accomplishment about which children should feel very proud (Brophy, 2004; J. Cameron, 2001). Especially when working with youngsters from cultures that place high priority on family or community ties, adults might point out the positive impact that children's actions have on other people (Abi-Nader, 1993; Dien, 1998; Suina & Smolkin, 1994). A teacher might say, "Think how proud your family will be!" or "Everyone in school will appreciate the beautiful wall murals you all have painted in the hallway."

STRATEGIC REWARDS. When used selectively over a short time period, extrinsic reinforcement can help children acquire foundational skills.

A more controversial use of extrinsic reinforcers is to pay students for earning advanced test scores or high grades or attending tutoring sessions (J. Henderson, 2009; Wright, 2009). Cash incentives have been tried in school districts in schools serving predominantly low-income students in several large U.S. cities, including New York City, Chicago, and Washington, D.C. Proponents of cash incentives have argued that low-income students need financial support so that they can afford to study after school rather than working long hours in part-time jobs. Others suggest that students from low-income families do not receive the same financial advantages of students from wealthier backgrounds and appreciate the opportunity to be awarded with financial incentives. So far the evidence on the impact has been mixed, with some studies indicating higher performance among those receiving incentives and others not finding this advantage (J. Henderson, 2009). Many educators are concerned about such initiatives, however, warning that if funding for these programs dries up, students will probably decrease their efforts.

- **Be especially attentive to the needs of students who are seriously behind classmates in academic skills.** Some students with weak academic skills have special educational needs, such as learning disabilities. Others have limited proficiency in English or cultural backgrounds that are not fully accepted at school. Still others may encounter serious personal problems (e.g., a pregnancy, an arrest) or come from home environments in which academic success is not encouraged (Behnke, Gonzalez, & Cox, 2010; Hirschfield, 2009; Steinberg, Blinde, & Chan,

1984). Regardless of the reasons for delayed progress, students who fail to acquire minimum academic skills are at risk for dropping out of school (Boling & Evans, 2008).

Low-achieving children and adolescents come from all socioeconomic levels, but youngsters from low-income, single-parent families are especially likely to leave school before high school graduation (Rumberger, 1995; Suh, Suh, & Houston, 2007). Boys are more likely to drop out than girls, and African Americans, Hispanic Americans, and Native Americans have higher dropout rates than other groups (L. S. Miller, 1995; Oguntoyinbo, 2009; Roderick & Camburn, 1999). Students who are struggling academically often have a long history of low achievement, ineffective learning strategies, poor relationships with teachers, and little emotional connectedness with their school (Belfiore & Hornyak, 1998; Christenson & Thurlow, 2004; V. E. Lee & Burkam, 2003; Suh et al., 2007).

Of course, low-achieving students almost always have the ability to succeed if given appropriate support from concerned adults. In a study with Canadian adolescents who were at risk for dropping out of high school but instead went on to earn their high school diploma, a group of researchers found that these young people established relationships with concerned adults outside the family (in many cases teachers), responded to challenges by reminding themselves of their own strong abilities, and made strategic choices for keeping themselves on track (e.g., distancing themselves from peers who took drugs) (Lessard, Fortin, Marcotte, Potvin, & Royer, 2009). One of the students, Aubrey, reported her experience:

> My father left when he learned that my mother was pregnant with me. I never knew him. My mother raised me on her own until she met my brother and sister's father, who lived with us until my sister was three years old. Then, it took a few years until my mother met another man. She never lived with him, though. We moved often, but we always stayed in the same town. I changed schools three times while in primary school. Being shy, it took me some time to make new friends each time.
>
> All went well in primary school. Teachers were really nice to me. They would come see me when they thought I did not understand. I loved English but had a really hard time with math. In class, I always paid attention. I never let others get me sidetracked. I did what was asked of me. In high school, math was still hard, but French was worse. I just couldn't handle it. I was failing. I saw the final exams coming and I kept telling myself that I had to succeed. I might have gone to ask for help, but I really did not get along with my French teacher. He was a dictator. I kept telling myself that I can do it. I did it, I passed my final exam and I got my high school diploma.[9] (Lessard et al., 2009, pp. 22–23)

The motivational strategies we've listed in the preceding pages are critical for most students who are low achieving. The Development and Practice feature "Encouraging Low-Achieving Students" offers additional suggestions.

SELF-REGULATION

As you've learned, children have a greater sense of self-determination and are more intrinsically motivated when they can make choices about what they do. But making *wise* choices and directing oneself along productive paths require *self-regulation*, the ability to direct and control personal actions and emotions.[10] Self-regulation is a multifaceted capability that includes several specific capabilities:

- *Impulse control.* Resisting sudden urges to engage in forbidden or counterproductive behaviors
- *Delaying gratification.* Forgoing small, immediate rewards in anticipation of larger rewards at a later time

[9]Excerpt from "Why Did They Not Drop Out? Narratives from Resilient Students" by A. Lessard, L. Fortin, D. Marcotte, P. Potvin, & É Royer from THE PREVENTION RESEARCHER, Volume 16, Issue 3, pp. 22–23. Copyright © 2009 Integrated Research Services, Inc., Eugene, OR. Reprinted with permission.
[10]Self-regulation is introduced in Chapter 3 and followed up throughout the book, namely as a quality in the child influenced by parenting in Chapter 3, as a characteristic that varies among children due to neurological characteristics and types of family support in Chapter 5, as the outcome of guidance from adults in Chapter 6, in the context of self-regulated learning in Chapter 7, and with reference to emotional regulation in Chapter 11.

Make the curriculum relevant to students' lives.

- In a unit on the physics of sound, a junior high school science teacher shows students how basic principles of sound reveal themselves in rock music. On one occasion the teacher brings in a guitar and explains why holding down a string at different points along its neck creates different frequencies and therefore higher and lower notes. (Early Adolescence)

- A middle school social studies teacher invites students to select an autobiography from an assortment of books by authors from a variety of cultural backgrounds. Students regularly choose books written by individuals who share their own cultural experiences. (Early Adolescence)

Use students' strengths to promote high self-efficacy in certain domains.

- An elementary school serving predominantly low-income families forms a singing group (the "Jazz Cats") for which students must try out. The group performs at a variety of community events, and the students enjoy considerable recognition for their talent. Group members exhibit confidence in their musical abilities, improvement in other school subjects, and greater teamwork and leadership skills. (Middle Childhood)

- A middle school science teacher encourages her students to enter a local science fair. Several students decide to participate, and they design innovative projects such as ones on chemical analyses of water from local estuaries and migration patterns of bees during periods of restricted access to pollen. After participating in the fair, students feel more capable in science. (Early Adolescence)

Provide extra support for academic success.

- At the beginning of class each day, a middle school teacher distributes a general outline that students can use to guide their note taking. She also writes two or three questions on the board that students should be able to answer at the end of the lesson. (Early Adolescence)

- A high school algebra teacher arranges with his principal to hire a tutor for students who are struggling in mathematics. The tutor works over the lunch hour and after school to offer help with homework. A local electronics company sponsors snacks for the students to munch on during the drop-in tutoring sessions. (Late Adolescence)

Communicate optimism about students' chances for long-term professional success.

- A kindergarten teacher equips the dramatic play area in her classroom with supplies and clothing from a wide array of professions—an airplane pilot's cap, a doctor's stethoscope, a beautician's hairbrush and rollers, a cash register with play money, and so forth. "What will you pretend to be today?" she asks the children. After they make their selections, she comments, "Isn't it wonderful to think about jobs you could have when you grow up?" (Early Childhood)

- A mathematics teacher in a low-income, inner-city high school recruits students to participate in an intensive math program. The teacher and students work evenings, Saturdays, and vacations, and all of them later pass the Advanced Placement calculus exam.[11] (Late Adolescence)

Show students that they are personally responsible for their successes.

- A high school teacher says to a student, "Your essay about recent hate crimes is very powerful. You've given the topic considerable thought, and you've clearly mastered several of the techniques of persuasive writing that we've talked about this semester. I'd like you to think seriously about submitting your essay to the local paper for its editorial page. Can we spend some time during lunch tomorrow fine-tuning the grammar and spelling?" (Late Adolescence)

- "Every single student in my advisee group is capable of going to college or a selective vocational program," a high school adviser tells his students at the beginning of the year. "But getting into college and choosing a major will be easier for you if you start planning now." During the year, students take a career inventory of interests; arrange for a 3-day internship with a professional in a job of personal interest; and search through catalogs from local colleges, universities, and vocational programs. (Late Adolescence)

Get students involved in extracurricular activities.

- A middle school encourages all its students to get involved in at least one of its many extracurricular activities and clubs. Students can choose from various athletic teams as well as an astronomy club, band, color guard, a hip-hop dance group, honor societies, science club, student council, school yearbook group, Peers for Peace group, school newspaper club, gay–straight alliance, and an ultimate Frisbee team. Each of the groups actively recruits members at the beginning of the year and conducts an additional membership drive halfway through the year. (Early Adolescence)

- A high school adviser encourages a student with a strong throwing arm to go out for the school baseball team and introduces the student to the baseball coach. The coach, in turn, expresses his enthusiasm for having the student join the team and asks several current team members to help welcome him. (Late Adolescence)

Involve students in school policy and management decisions.

- A teacher in a third-grade classroom encourages children to organize their own Valentine's Day party. With a little guidance from their teacher, children form several small groups, each of which is tasked with a particular job—bringing in decorations, asking parents to send in a drink or snack, creating bags for each child to store goodies, and typing up a list of children's names for those preparing Valentine's Day cards. (Middle Childhood)

- Students and teachers at one high school hold regular "town meetings" to discuss issues of fairness and justice and establish rules for appropriate behavior. Meetings are democratic, with students and teachers alike having one vote apiece, and the will of the majority being binding. (Late Adolescence)

Sources: Alderman, 1990; L. W. Anderson & Pellicer, 1998; Behnke et al., 2010; Christenson & Thurlow, 2004; Cosden et al., 2001; Fredricks, Blumenfeld, & Paris, 2004; S. Goldstein & Brooks, 2006; Hamre & Pianta, 2005; A. Higgins, 1995 (town meetings example); Jenlink, 1994 (Jazz Cats example); M. S. Knapp, Turnbull, & Shields, 1990; Lee-Pearce et al., 1998; Milner, 2006; Towne, 2009.

[11]See the case study on "Beating the Odds" at the end of Chapter 10.

- *Self-socialization.* Striving to act in accordance with society's standards for behavior
- *Emotional regulation.* Managing the expression of affective states so that it is socially appropriate
- *Goal setting.* Identifying and striving for self-chosen goals
- *Self-motivation.* Creating conditions that make a task more engaging or rewarding
- *Self-regulated learning.* Directing and monitoring one's attention and learning strategies in ways that promote effective cognitive processing

A child has countless opportunities to use self-regulation skills throughout the school day. An elementary student uses self-regulatory skills when keeping his focus on a teacher's explanations amid distractions from classmates. Self-regulatory skills are also at play when a high school student sets goals for completing a challenging project on time and then follows through by periodically checking on progress toward meeting the goal. Another girl applies a different form of self-regulatory skills as she holds her tongue after a boy calls her humiliating names.

The prevalent demands for self-regulatory skills raise the question of how they evolve. Let's examine their development.

Developmental Trends in Self-Regulation

Infants initially depend on adults for help in regulating their attention and physiological states. Parents direct infants' focus of thought by pointing to objects; face infants toward particular events; and use verbal labels for noteworthy people, processes, and things. Parents manage infants' moods by tending to their physical needs, holding them tenderly, and offering reassurance (Hrabok & Kerns, 2010). Yet from the beginning infants do their part as well, trying to moderate their own states and behaviors, for example, by choosing to follow a parent's gaze or avoid it or by soothing themselves by sucking on fingers or snuggling up with a favorite blanket.

As children grow, they develop an intensified motivation to direct their own behavior, albeit without a solid understanding of how to keep themselves safe and in good social standing. Some parents in Western cultures complain about the "terrible twos," a period between the second and third birthdays when children are mobile enough to get into almost anything and inclined to be fussy when they don't get their way. The immature state of the young brain makes it difficult for children to inhibit certain behaviors, especially those that would result in immediate rewards. Young children further lack sufficient working memory to think through what they want to do, how they might do it, and perhaps why they *shouldn't* do it.

Several developmental changes allow children to become increasingly able to guide their behavior in culturally approved ways. Researchers have identified four important development trends in self-regulation:

Children become better able to direct their behavior in light of future consequences. The young child is incited to act by an immediate reward: A single cookie received right now is infinitely preferable to two cookies obtained in an hour. Toward the end of early childhood, children become able to imagine themselves taking a couple of different actions and can now compare the short-term and long-term merits and disadvantages of these various scenarios (C. Moore, 2010). Children can conceive of themselves in the present as well as in the future and are able to consider both when choosing a response. They also begin to inhibit tempting acts, perhaps grabbing a toy out of the hands of another child in the sandbox, now showing consideration for the rights of others and wishing to avoid a teacher's punishment.

Children increasingly talk their way, and eventually think their way, through situations and tasks. The *self-talk* and *inner speech* that **Lev Vygotsky** (1896–1934) described seem to be key mechanisms through which children become able to regulate their behavior.[12] As children acquire language skills, they begin to talk themselves through new challenges ("To tie my shoe, I need to put one lace over and then under the other; then I need to make a loop . . ."). Children gradually internalize their self-talk, first whispering to themselves and

---

[12]Vygotsky's theory of cognitive development is introduced in Chapter 6.

eventually just *mentally* telling themselves what they should do. Such external and internal self-talk help children self-regulate not only simple physical tasks such as tying shoes but also more complex skills, for instance, resolving interpersonal conflicts and keeping their attention productively focused during a classroom test (Berk, 1994; Biemiller, Shany, Inglis, & Meichenbaum, 1998; Landry & Smith, 2010).

External rules gradually become internalized. Developing a **conscience**—an internalized sense of right and wrong—is an important part of the process by which children learn to act in socially appropriate ways. Having a close relationship with parents sets the stage for children accepting the legitimacy of parents' guidance and ultimately accepting parents' rules as their own (Hoffman, 1979; Kochanska, Koenig, Barry, Kim, & Yoon, 2010).

This process of internalization takes some time. Children comply with simple requests and restrictions by the time they are 12 to 18 months old (Kaler & Kopp, 1990; Kopp, 1982; Lindsey & Caldera, 2005). As they become increasingly verbal, they begin to use self-talk to prevent themselves from engaging in prohibited behaviors even when caregivers are absent—for instance, saying "no" or "can't" to themselves as they begin to reach for an electric outlet (Kochanska, 1993). By age 3 or 4, many children are acquiring flexible strategies for regulating their own behavior in accordance with adult rules and prohibitions. If they are asked to wait for a short time (e.g., 15 minutes), they might invent games or sing to themselves to pass the time more quickly (Mischel & Ebbesen, 1970). If a playmate has an enticing toy, they may turn away and engage in an alternative activity as a way of lessening the temptation to grab the toy (Kopp, 1982).

As children grow, they live up to progressively complex principles in their behavior—table etiquette, proper ways to address unfamiliar adults, tactics for saying "no" to drugs, and so forth. Children and adolescents increasingly take ownership of society's rules and regulations through the process of internalization portrayed earlier in Figure 13-1 (Kochanska, Coy, & Murray, 2001; R. M. Ryan & Deci, 2009). The first sign of internalization (the *introjection* phase) is evident when children feel some internal pressure (e.g., guilt) to comply with rules and regulations. Later (at the *identification* phase), children start to perceive rules and other desired behaviors to be important or valuable to them personally. This phase is evident in an interview with 9-year-old Elena in the "Neighborhood: Middle Childhood" video in MyEducationLab:

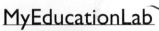

Observe Elena's understanding of the usefulness of laws in the "Neighborhood: Middle Childhood" video. (Find Video Examples in Topic 13 of MyEducationLab.)

Interviewer:	Neighborhoods and cities have lots of different laws. Why do you think people make these laws?
Elena:	For example, they closed this road because a lot of children were playing around here and some people just came zipping right through fast and fast and not going to the speed limit.
Interviewer:	What would it be like if we didn't have laws?
Elena:	If we didn't have these laws, by the time I step out of the door probably I would have a broken leg.

Finally (at the *integration* phase), rules and regulations become an integral part of children's sense of self. At this point, a teenage girl might define herself as being "law abiding" or "concerned about others' welfare" and so strive to behave in ways consistent with her self-definition.

Self-evaluation becomes more frequent. Infants do not seem to evaluate their own behavior, nor do they show much concern about how others evaluate it. In contrast, 2-year-olds often seek adults' approval for their actions (Stipek, Recchia, & McClintic, 1992). Sometime around age 3, children show the first signs of *self*-evaluation. For instance, they look happy when they're successful and sad when they fail (Heckenhausen, 1984, 1987).

As children move through the preschool, elementary, and middle school years, they show a marked increase in self-judgment (Bronson, 2000; van Kraayenoord & Paris, 1997; B. J. Zimmerman & Cleary, 2009). Previously their parents praised certain behaviors and criticized others, teachers evaluated their academic performance as having certain strengths and limitations, and their peers let them know in no uncertain terms about the effectiveness of their social skills. Children reflect on all of these comments, internalize many of these criteria, and direct their own behavior accordingly.

conscience
An internalized sense of right and wrong for guiding and evaluating one's behavior.

Bioecology of Child Development

Self-regulation is made possible by brain circuits for guiding behavior toward long-term goals and is fostered by encouragement from others.

Bioecology of Self-Regulation

The many facets of self-regulation draw on both nature and nurture. Nature provides the foundation for *executive functions*, those neurologically based abilities that allow for planning, restraint, and judgment. These abilities are specifically enabled by neurological connections within the front part of the cortex and develop throughout childhood, adolescence, and even into the early adulthood years (C. A. Nelson et al., 2006; Spear, 2007).[13]

Although virtually all children develop a basic biological infrastructure for executive functions, how robust these brain circuits are varies among children. Subtle features in the brain contribute to marked individual differences in children's ability to resist impulses and delay gratification (Birkas et al., 2006; Hrabok & Kerns, 2010; Lakatos, Birkas, Nemoda, & Gervai, 2007). Partly as a result of biological factors, children with impulsive temperaments as toddlers or preschoolers tend to have trouble inhibiting inappropriate behaviors when they move into elementary, middle, and high school (Eigsti et al., 2006; M. Pfeifer, Goldsmith, Davidson, & Rickman, 2002). And some children with some biology-based disabilities—for instance, those with brain injuries, learning disabilities, or mental illness—often have deficits in self-regulation (Hawley, 2005; Meltzer, 2007; Siegel, 1999).

Environmental factors—especially socialization practices—also play a strong role in the development of self-regulation abilities. Children and adolescents are more likely to become self-regulating when they have age-appropriate opportunities for independence. Infants are initially heavily externally regulated, as you have learned, even though they do make many of their own choices in attention and self-comfort. During the preschool years, parents socialize children to follow rules of basic safety and then more complex standards for proper social and cultural behaviors (Gralinski & Kopp, 1993; Hrabok & Kerns, 2010).

Youngsters can best benefit from opportunities to act independently if they are taught the skills they need to productively direct their own behaviors and overcome obstacles (Belfiore & Hornyak, 1998). When parents, other caregivers, and teachers have warm and supportive relationships with children, set reasonable boundaries for behavior, and take everyone's needs into consideration, they create optimal conditions for children making appropriate choices and working toward productive goals (Bronson, 2000; Reeve, Bolt, & Cai, 1999; B. J. Zimmerman, 2004). Parents also provide valuable verbal rules for proper behavior (e.g., "Eat your vegetables," "Honor your father and mother") that children may recall later when faced with a relevant situation (Hrabok & Kerns, 2010; Landry & Smith, 2010). Typically, adults gradually release the apron strings, shifting from lots of guidance to only occasional suggestions and reminders (Mithaug & Mithaug, 2003; Stright, Neitzel, Sears, & Hoke-Sinex, 2001; B. J. Zimmerman, 2004).

Adults promote self-regulation in another way as well: by modeling self-regulating behaviors (Bronson, 2000; B. J. Zimmerman & Cleary, 2009). In a classic study (Bandura & Mischel, 1965), fourth and fifth graders watched adult models make a series of choices between small, immediate rewards and more valuable, delayed ones (e.g., plastic chess pieces available that day versus wooden ones that they could have in 2 weeks). Some children observed a model choosing the immediate rewards (e.g., saying, "Chess figures are chess figures. I can get much use out of the plastic ones right away," p. 701). Others observed a model choosing the delayed rewards (e.g., saying, "The wooden chess figures are of much better quality, more attractive, and will last longer. I'll wait two weeks for the better ones," p. 701). Immediately after they had observed the models, and also on a second occasion several weeks later, the children themselves were asked to choose between small, immediate rewards and larger, delayed ones (e.g., a small plastic ball now or a much larger one in 2 weeks). The children were more likely to delay gratification if they had seen the model do likewise.

As you might expect, the particular opportunities children have for self-regulation are embedded in cultural traditions. By way of example, some Asian cultural groups place a high priority on self-discipline and other aspects of self-regulation (P. M. Cole & Tamang, 2001; Morelli & Rothbaum, 2007; Zahn-Waxler, Friedman, Cole, Mizuta, & Hiruma, 1996).

---

[13]Executive functions are described in Chapters 5 and 7.

Even as toddlers, children are strongly encouraged to control their feelings, minimizing the "terrible twos" phenomenon mentioned earlier (D. Y. F. Ho, 1994). Preschoolers are expected to work diligently and persistently on assigned tasks. Children in other societies learn different lessons in self-regulation, perhaps that they should interact cooperatively with peers, play imaginatively with toys, or complete routine chores for the benefit of the family and community.

Promoting Self-Regulation

Children and adolescents are more likely to engage in self-regulating behaviors when they are intrinsically motivated to accomplish certain goals or have internalized the need to live up to particular standards (Bronson, 2000; F. E. Cooney, 2008; Otis et al., 2005). As you have learned, teachers and other adults can foster intrinsic motivation by creating conditions in which youngsters have high self-efficacy and can maintain their sense of self-determination. To promote the internalization of culturally valued activities and behaviors (academic achievement, reasonable self-restraint, etc.), they should provide a warm, supportive environment in which youngsters are given reasonable guidance about how to behave. With these points in mind, we offer the following recommendations for promoting self-regulation:

- **Create an orderly and somewhat predictable environment.** Children are in a better position to make wise choices and direct their activities appropriately when they have some structure to guide them, know what to expect in the hours and days ahead, and can reasonably anticipate that certain behaviors will yield certain outcomes (Bronson, 2000; Holler & Greene, 2010; Meltzer, Pollica, & Barzillai, 2007). Communicating general guidelines for behavior, establishing regular routines for completing tasks and assignments, and identifying the locations of items that children may need during the day (glue, hole punches, dictionaries, etc.) are strategies can help children work productively with only minimal adult supervision.

- **Provide children with age-appropriate opportunities to make their own choices.** Although young children inevitably require adult supervision to keep them safe, they clearly benefit from having some choice (Holler & Greene, 2010; Perry, VandeKamp, Mercer, & Nordby, 2002). Young children might be invited to choose from among the puzzle area, dramatic play center, sensory table, or block zone during a free play period. At the same time, caregivers and teachers must anticipate and minimize problems that are likely to arise when children make their own decisions. Preschool and kindergarten teachers might create a few rules for taking turns and sharing materials, designate certain areas of the classroom for messy activities (e.g., painting, working with clay), and put potentially dangerous objects out of reach (Bronson, 2000).

Elementary school children also need frequent opportunities to make their own decisions. Independent assignments, computer-based instructional programs, group projects, homework, and the like often benefit students from middle childhood especially when the activities are structured so that youngsters know how to proceed and understand the expectations for their performance (H. Cooper, Robinson, & Patall, 2006; Corno & Mandinach, 2004; Landry & Smith, 2010). When children make poor choices, adults should offer constructive feedback that will nurture, rather than dampen, their enthusiasm for independence on future occasions.

- **Adjust to adolescents' self-regulatory abilities and vulnerabilities.** Adolescents have more advanced self-regulatory skills than do younger children but also face distinct challenges in resisting certain temptations. Particular areas in the brain mature unevenly during adolescence, causing some vexing problems with self-regulation (A. A. Baird, 2010; Ernst & Hardin, 2010; Van Leijenhorst & Crone, 2010). During this period, neurological circuits supporting emotions, sensitivity to rewards, and social interests outpace circuits enabling judgment and restraint. As a result, adolescents occasionally find it difficult to stay focused on academic tasks when peers entice them with alternative high-spirited, and occasionally, risky activities. Keep in mind, however, that adolescents are not destined to act impulsively and they certainly can benefit from appropriate intervention. Many secondary teachers provide outlets for adolescents' social needs by arranging for them to work together constructively in cooperative groups and in other social settings (Keramati, 2010; Slavin, Lake, & Groff, 2009).

Other teachers find ways for young people to develop passionate interests, perhaps for community service or cutting-edge technology, within the curriculum.

Adults can also address difficulties many adolescents have in staying organized and mobilized on challenging projects. Some middle and high school students lose track of their class materials and assignments, not because they do not care but because they have poor organizational skills. For such students, support with homework can be helpful (Bembenutty, 2009; Eilam, 2001; S. D. Miller, Heafner, Massey, & Strahan, 2003). In one approach (Belfiore & Hornyak, 1998), students report to a particular classroom at the end of the regular school day, where they find their homework assignments on a shelf. They learn to use a checklist such as that depicted in Figure 13-2, checking off steps they have completed. They also learn to administer **self-reinforcement**, giving themselves a reward (e.g., allowing themselves to play a board game or spend time on a computer) whenever they have completed all the steps. In addition, they learn problem-solving strategies for difficulties they might encounter (e.g., asking a teacher for assistance when they can't find needed materials). Initially, a teacher monitors whether their checklists accurately reflect what they've accomplished, but eventually such monitoring is no longer necessary. Over time, as students acquire a sense of accomplishment about completing their homework each day, the self-imposed extrinsic reinforcers become less critical. In the regular classroom as well, teachers can use similar resources to scaffold youngsters' ability to keep track of their books, supplies, and resources and make sure that they are making appropriate progress on ambitious projects. For example, young people can use checklists on the various steps in completing a lengthy report, perhaps initially brainstorming ideas, identifying key concepts, writing topic sentences, adding evidence, filling in the gaps, and editing (Meltzer, 2010).

• **Tailor levels of support to the individual characteristics of children with disabilities.** Independence is a major concern for children with disabilities, especially because adults monitor their behavior fairly closely (Minshawi, Ashby, & Swiezy, 2009; Sands & Wehmeyer, 1996). Adults can help by taking a long-term perspective on the self-regulation of children

STUDENT: _____		DATE: _____	
SUBJECT AREA: _____		GRADE: _____	
TEACHER: _____			

STEPS TO FOLLOW	YES	NO	NOTES
1. Did I turn in yesterday's homework?			
2. Did I write all homework assignments in my notebook?			
3. Is all homework in homework folder?			
4. Are all my materials to complete homework with me?			
5. BEGIN HOMEWORK?			
6. Are all homework papers completed?			
7. Did someone check homework to make sure it was completed?			
8. After checking, did I put all homework back in folder?			
9. Did I give this paper to teacher?			

FIGURE 13-2 Daily checklist for homework completion. *"The Daily Checklist for Homework Completion" from "Operant Theory and Application to Self-Monitoring in Adolescents" by P. J. Belfiore and R. S. Hornyak, from* SELF-REGULATED LEARNING: FROM TEACHING TO SELF-REFLECTIVE PRACTICE *by Dale H. Schunk and Barry J. Zimmerman. Copyright © 1998 by Dale H. Schunk and Barry J. Zimmerman. Reprinted with permission of Guilford Publications, Inc.*

self-reinforcement
Self-imposed pleasurable consequence for a desired behavior.

with disabilities, creating opportunities for independent activity that protect the children from harm yet encourage exercise of personal skills. A teacher might ask a student with a significant intellectual disability to take the daily attendance sheet to the office but remind her that as soon as she has done so, she should return immediately to class (Patton et al., 1996). Or a teacher might give a student who is blind a chance to explore the classroom before other students have arrived, locating various objects in the classroom (wastebasket, pencil sharpener, etc.) and identifying distinctive sounds (e.g., the buzz of a wall clock) that will help the student get his bearings (J. W. Wood, 1998).

- **Provide guidance when, but only when, children really need it.** Being self-regulating doesn't necessarily always mean doing something independently. It also involves knowing when assistance is needed and seeking it out (Bong, 2009; Karabenick & Sharma, 1994). Adult assistance often provides the scaffolding that children need to succeed at new and challenging tasks. Accordingly, adults should welcome any reasonable requests for help and not convey the message that children are "dumb" or bothersome for asking (R. S. Newman & Schwager, 1992). Sometimes, however, children ask for help when they really just want attention or companionship. If a 4-year-old asks for help on a puzzle, an astute preschool teacher might, after watching the child work at the puzzle, say, "I don't think you need help with this. But I can keep you company for a few minutes if you'd like" (Bronson, 2000).

- **Use suggestions and rationales rather than direct commands as much as possible.** Children are more likely to internalize and follow guidelines for behavior when adults make suggestions about how to accomplish goals successfully, elicit children's perspectives, and provide a rationale for why some behaviors are unacceptable (Baraldi & Iervese, 2010; Bronson, 2000; Hoffman, 1975). Consistent with what we have learned about cognitive development, younger children respond more favorably to suggestions that are concrete rather than abstract. To avoid incidents of bumping and pushing in the cafeteria, teachers at one school asked students to imagine they had "magic bubbles" around them. The students could keep their bubbles from "popping" if they kept a safe distance between themselves and others. This simple strategy resulted in fewer behavior problems at lunchtime (Sullivan-DeCarlo, DeFalco, & Roberts, 1998).

- **Teach specific self-regulation skills.** Children and adolescents become more self-regulating when they learn specific strategies for directing their own behavior. Such strategies include **self-monitoring**, **self-instructions**, **self-motivation**, and **self-evaluation**:

  - *Self-monitoring.* Children aren't always aware of how frequently they do something wrong or how infrequently they do something right. To help them focus on these things, adults can ask them to observe and record their own behavior. Such self-focused observation and record keeping often bring about significant improvements in children's academic and social behaviors (Flannery-Schroeder & Lamb, 2009; J. R. Sullivan & Conoley, 2004; Webber, Scheuermann, McCall, & Coleman, 1993). Initially some children may need assistance in monitoring their behavior accurately, for example, whether they have stayed on task during a lesson (DuPaul & Hoff, 1998).
  - *Self-instructions.* Sometimes children simply need a reminder about how to respond in particular situations. By teaching them specific ways of talking themselves through these situations, adults give them a means through which they remind *themselves* about appropriate actions, thereby helping them to control their own behavior. Such a strategy is often effective in helping young children and especially those with poor impulse control (Flannery-Schroeder & Lamb, 2009; Hains & Hains, 1988; Jutta, Jutta, & Karbach, 2008; Meichenbaum, 1985). Educators can try such simple methods as giving a child a line drawing of an ear as a reminder to listen quietly during a storybook reading (A. Diamond, Barnett, Thomas, & Munro, 2007; Tarullo, Obradovic, & Gunnar, 2009).
  - *Self-motivation.* Children may also need strategies to keep themselves motivated during dull but important tasks. For example, they might consciously identify several reasons why completing an activity will help them over the long run. They might embellish a task in some way to make it more interesting. Or they might learn how to divide a lengthy task into a number of small pieces and then reinforce themselves after completing each one (Wolters, 2003; B. J. Zimmerman & Cleary, 2009).

self-monitoring
Process of observing and recording one's own behavior.

self-instructions
Specific directions that one gives oneself while performing a complex behavior; a form of *self-talk*.

self-motivation
Intentionally using certain strategies to keep oneself on task during a dull but important activity.

self-evaluation
Judging one's own performance in accordance with predetermined criteria.

DEVELOPMENT AND PRACTICE
Teaching Self-Regulation Skills

Have children observe and record their own activities.

- When a third-grade student has trouble staying on task during class activities, her teacher asks her to stop and reflect on her behavior every 10 minutes (with the aid of an egg timer) and determine whether she has been on task during each interval. The student uses the checklist shown below to record her observations. Within a couple of weeks, the student's on-task behavior has noticeably improved. (Middle Childhood)

Self-Observation Record for _____ Karen _____

Every ten minutes, put a mark to show how well you have been staying on task.

+ means you were almost always on task
1/2 means you were on task about half the time
− means you were hardly ever on task

9:00-9:10	9:10-9:20	9:20-9:30	9:30-9:40	9:40-9:50	9:50-10:00
+	+	−	+	1/2	−
10:00-10:10	10:10-10:20	10:20-10:30	10:30-10:40	10:40-10:50	10:50-11:00
1/2	−	recess	+	1/2	
11:00-11:10	11:10-11:20	11:20-11:30	11:30-11:40	11:40-11:50	11:50-12:00

- A high school adviser notices that one of his advisees is getting low grades and after a discussion with him finds that the young man often forgets to do his homework and at other times forgets to check his backpack and turn in finished homework. The teacher develops a weekly calendar for the boy and checks with him to see that he has written his due dates on the calendar and crossed off homework assignments as he gives them to his teachers. (Late Adolescence)

Teach children instructions they can give themselves as reminders of what they need to do.

- A school counselor helps a fifth grader control his impulsive behavior on multiple-choice tests by having him mentally say to himself as he reads each question: "Read the entire question. Then look at each answer carefully and decide whether it is correct or incorrect. Then choose the answer that seems *most* correct." (Middle Childhood)
- A high school history teacher advises his students of what they can do to begin their homework. She tells them, "Remind yourself to follow the **POM** strategy: **P**repare your learning space, **O**rganize your materials by taking out your history book and a pen and paper for taking notes, and **M**inimize your distractions by turning the television off, silencing your cell phone, and getting to work." (Late Adolescence)

Help children identify ways to embellish tedious tasks to make them more rewarding.

- A third-grade teacher suggests that students practice writing the week's new spelling words at home every night. "That might not sound like much fun," she says, "but it's an important thing to do. Who can think of a way to make spelling practice more fun?" One student suggests making letters out of bits of straw and twig and gluing the words on a page. Another suggests trying to think of sentences that spell the words with first letters—for example, *"Eighty-nine overweight unicorns get hiccups"* spells enough. (Middle Childhood)
- A high school chemistry explains the order of elements in the periodic table and encourages students to attend to the similarity of atomic number (across) and chemical characteristics (down). He demonstrates how sodium and lithium in the first group both react vigorously when dropped in water to help students visualize a basic common property of these two elements. When students study the table, they remember the interesting properties of elements that they have observed. (Late Adolescence)

Teach children to reinforce themselves for appropriate behavior.

- A middle school teacher suggests that her students are more likely to develop regular study habits if they make a favorite activity—for example, shooting baskets or watching television—contingent on completing their homework first. (Early Adolescence)
- A high school geography class has been fascinated with recent lessons on cultural exchanges among people who have migrated from one country to another. After moving to a unit on properties of maps, the teacher finds that students have lost their enthusiasm for his class. The teacher acknowledges to the class that they may find certain topics within geography more interesting than others. To help them stay engaged with the subject, he encourages them to identify a reward (perhaps a pizza party, free period, or choice for an upcoming topic) that they can earn when they have successfully completed the project on mapping. (Late Adolescence)

Encourage children to evaluate their own performance.

- A middle school mathematics teacher has students grade their own mathematics homework. After totaling up their points, students enter their scores in their electronic assignment log. Students also enter a few narrative comments on how they are doing and whether or not they need help with any concepts. Those who decide they need help see the teacher during the last 10 minutes of class. (Early Adolescence)
- Early in baseball season, the coach of a high school boys' baseball team videotapes each boy as he practices batting, pitching, and fielding ground balls. The coach then models good form for each of these activities and lists several things the boys should look for as they watch themselves on tape. (Late Adolescence)

- *Self-evaluation.* To become truly self-regulating, children must acquire appropriate criteria by which to judge their accomplishments. For instance, teachers might ask students to reflect on their improvement ("What can we do that we didn't do before?") or complete self-assessment instruments that show them what to look for in their own performance (S. G. Paris & Ayres, 1994; Perry et al., 2002; B. J. Zimmerman & Cleary, 2009). At the secondary school level (and perhaps even sooner), young people might even play a role in identifying the criteria by which their performance might reasonably be evaluated.

The Development and Practice feature "Teaching Self-Regulation Skills" includes several illustrations of the strategies just described (see page 528). Adults must, of course, monitor children's ability to take charge of their own learning and offer guidance when children lose sight of their goals or implement ineffective methods of learning.

SUMMARY

Extrinsic and Intrinsic Motivation

Motivation energizes, directs, and sustains behavior. It can be either extrinsic (evoked largely by the external consequences that certain behaviors bring) or intrinsic (emanating from characteristics within a person or inherent in a task being performed). On average, children who are intrinsically motivated use more effective learning strategies and achieve at higher levels than those who are extrinsically motivated.

One key source of extrinsic motivation is the extent to which either primary reinforcers (things that satisfy built-in biological needs) or secondary reinforcers (things that have become reinforcing through frequent association with other reinforcing consequences) follow various behaviors. With age, children become increasingly able to forgo small, immediate rewards in favor of larger, delayed ones. An additional source of extrinsic motivation is punishment: Children tend to avoid behaviors that have previously led to unpleasant consequences either for themselves or for others.

Development of Goals

Children direct their behavior toward personal objectives from the beginning of life and increasingly pursue long-term goals that are encompassing in focus. When they enter school, most children want to do well in school but significant individual differences exist in how they go about achieving their goals. Some children want to acquire new knowledge and skills (i.e., they have *mastery goals*) whereas others want to look good or avoid looking bad in front of classmates and teachers (i.e., they have *performance goals*). Children's social goals are also important to children and can often be accommodated by thoughtful teachers.

Development of Attributions

Among the important factors influencing children's motivation are the attributions children make regarding their successes and failures in particular activities. Children are most optimistic when they attribute both successes and failures to internal factors that they can control (e.g., amount of effort and use of good strategies). Ultimately, some children acquire a general *I can do it* attitude (a *mastery orientation*), whereas others acquire an *I can't do it even if I try* attitude (*learned helplessness*).

Bioecology of Motivation

Children's motivational goals and beliefs are affected by their personal characteristics and presence in particular environments. Children's temperaments and any disabilities they might have can affect how they display their curiosity as well as their ability to delay gratification, self-determination, and learned helplessness. Boys and girls exhibit some differences in motivation, particularly in their interests, academic aspirations, and confidence in their abilities. Cultural values partly determine how children express their autonomy, persist with tasks, make attributions, and form aspirations for the future.

Motivating Children and Adolescents

To some degree, children's intrinsic motivation to tackle particular tasks depends on factors that develop gradually over time (e.g., self-efficacy, sense of self-determination, a mastery orientation) and are affected by environmental experiences. Piquing youngsters' curiosity and interest, helping them be successful in their efforts to master new skills, enhancing their sense of autonomy, and encouraging them to strive for specific goals are just a few of the many things adults can do to enhance youngsters' motivation to engage in productive activities.

Self-Regulation

With age and experience, most children and adolescents become increasingly able to control and direct their own behavior. They more effectively restrain their impulses and emotional reactions, gradually internalize adults' rules and restrictions, and begin to evaluate their own actions using appropriate criteria. Yet even at the high school level, some youngsters don't regulate their own behaviors very effectively. Adults promote self-regulation by establishing definite guidelines for behavior while also attending to children's needs, listening to children's perspectives, and providing a reasonable rationale for restrictions. Adults can also model self-regulating behaviors, give children age-appropriate opportunities for independence, and teach such specific skills as self-reinforcement, self-monitoring, self-instructions, self-motivation, and self-evaluation.

APPLYING CONCEPTS IN CHILD DEVELOPMENT

The exercises in this section will help you build your ability to apply your knowledge of child development in your work with children.

Improving Your Observation Skills

On page 500, you examined a photograph of a group of children observing their teacher conduct a chemistry demonstration and were asked, "*Do these children seem to be exhibiting personal interest or situational interest in their chemistry lesson?*" These children seem surprised at the chemical reaction occurring in the test tube. The teacher has captured their immediate attention, appearing to elicit their situational interest with a visually compelling chemical reaction. It is possible, but less likely, that these and other students in the class have a long-standing personal interest in chemistry that transcends their current engagement in the lesson. Long-term personal interests in any particular academic subject are not common: A limited number, but far from the majority, of students develop deep personal interests in science, mathematics, social studies, or other academic domains.

On page 505, you examined a photograph of a girl celebrating an award for an exceptionally high test score and were asked, "*What kinds of goals might the award foster in her?*" The ribbon probably draws the girl's attention to the extrinsic feature of being publicly honored for accomplishments rather than the intrinsic pleasure of developing high levels of expertise in a particular domain. Her teacher may be encouraging students to develop *performance goals*, specifically *performance-approach goals*.

Practicing for Your Licensure Examination

Many teaching tests require students to use what they have learned about child development in responses to brief vignettes and multiple-choice questions. You can practice for your licensure examination by reading about the motivation of an adolescent girl and answering a series of questions.

Derrika

Read the case and then answer the questions that follow it.

In a study conducted in the Chicago public schools, Roderick and Camburn (1999) investigated the academic progress of students who had recently made the transition from relatively small elementary or middle schools to much larger high schools. Many students in their research sample experienced considerable difficulty making the transition from eighth to ninth grade, as the case of Derrika illustrates:

> Derrika liked to be challenged and felt her eighth-grade teachers cared and made her work. Derrika entered high school with plans to go to college and felt that her strong sense of self would get her through: "Nobody stops me from doing good because I really wanna

go to college. . . . Nobody in my family's been to college . . . so I want to be the first person to go to college and finish."

> Derrika began having problems in eighth grade. Despite average achievement scores and previously high grades, she ended eighth grade with a C average and failed science. In high school, her performance deteriorated further. At the end of the first semester, Derrika received Fs in all her major subjects, had 20 absences, almost 33 class cuts for the last two periods of the day, and had been suspended for a food fight. Derrika is vague in explaining her performance, except for biology, in which she admits, "I don't never get up on time." She feels that her elementary school teachers were better because, "If you don't want to learn, they are going to make you learn," while her current teachers think, "If you fail, you just fail. It ain't our fault. You're the one that's dumb." (Roderick & Camburn, 1999, p. 304)

Constructed-Response Question

1. What strategies might a teacher, counselor, or other practitioner use to help Derrika get back on the road to academic success?

Multiple-Choice Questions

2. What evidence is there that Derrika faced difficulties in self-regulation?

   a. Derrika did not formulate any goals for the future.
   b. Even though Derrika would like to attend college, she frequently cut class and often didn't get up in time for biology class, suggesting that she was having trouble resisting temptations.
   c. Derrika had achieved academically at a low level since first grade, suggesting an inability to complete difficult schoolwork.
   d. Derrika disliked being challenged academically.

3. To what factors did Derrika's teachers apparently attribute any academic failures she had?

   a. Derrika's elementary teachers' attributed students' performance to hard work and effective strategies, whereas the secondary teachers attributed students' performance to lack of intelligence.
   b. All of Derrika's teachers attributed students' performance to genetic factors.
   c. Derrika's elementary teachers attributed students' performance to lack of intelligence, whereas the secondary teachers attributed students' performance to hard work and effective strategies.
   d. Derrika's teachers were not able to make attributions for Derrika's failures because her profile of accomplishments was inconsistent.

Once you have answered these questions, compare your responses with those presented in Appendix A.

Improving Your Ability to Interpret Children's Artifacts and Reflections

Consider what you've learned about self-regulation as you analyze the following essay written by an 11-year-old girl.

Tears of Pearls

When students in a sixth-grade class don't turn in homework assignments, a teacher intern insists that they write a 200-word essay explaining the missing homework and describing how they plan to be more diligent next time. In an essay shown on this page, 11-year-old Andrea explains why she didn't turn in her analysis of the lyrics to the song "Tears of Pearls," by the Australian singing duo Savage Garden. As you read the essay, consider these questions:

- What possible benefits might such an essay have?
- What evidence do you see that Andrea has developed some degree of self-regulation in her study habits?

Once you have analyzed Andrea's essay, compare your ideas with those presented in Appendix B. For further practice in analyzing children's artifacts and reflections, go to the Activities and Applications section in Chapter 13 of MyEducationLab.

---

200 word essay

I am very sorry this happened. I feel guilty that I forgot to pass the assignment Tears of Pearls in. Every time in social studies I will make sure I passed in <u>all</u> my assignments so that this will not happen again. I understand how hard it is for you to keep track of two classes work and I think it is a good idea you are doing this. I wish I wasn't so forgetful. Hopefully this will not happen to me again. Every night I will check my social studies folder to make sure the homework is complete. Now all I have to do is get it to school and put it in the pass in box. It was complete but I just forgot to pass it in. Every night I do my homework and my mom checks it and it goes in my back pack but sometimes I just forget to give it to you. I'm sorry. I really am. It is sometimes hard for us kids sometimes too. It is sometimes hard for us kids to be prepared but I guess that's just something we'll have to learn before middle school! Oh and sometimes we're packed with homework and the next day its hard to get it back together and into your and Mrs. Copeland's hands as soon as possible (A.S.A.P.). Like I said it's hard for you too and I can understand, but sometimes things (other) things are hard for us too. For the third time im really am sorry.

sincerly,
Andrea

Key Concepts

motivation (p. 496)
extrinsic motivation (p. 496)
intrinsic motivation (p. 496)
reinforcer (p. 497)
primary reinforcer (p. 497)
secondary reinforcer (p. 497)
delay of gratification (p. 497)
punishment (p. 497)
vicarious reinforcement (p. 498)

vicarious punishment (p. 498)
self-efficacy (p. 499)
sense of self-determination (p. 499)
situational interest (p. 500)
personal interest (p. 500)
value (p. 500)
internalized motivation (p. 501)
mastery goal (p. 504)
performance goal (p. 504)

performance-approach goal (p. 504)
performance-avoidance goal (p. 504)
social goal (p. 505)
attribution (p. 507)
incremental view (of ability) (p. 508)
entity view (of ability) (p. 508)
mastery orientation (p. 509)
learned helplessness (p. 509)

situated motivation (p. 513)
conscience (p. 523)
self-reinforcement (p. 526)
self-monitoring (p. 527)
self-instructions (p. 527)
self-motivation (p. 527)
self-evaluation (p. 527)

PEARSON
myeducationlab

Now go to www.myeducationlab.com to:
- Take a Quiz to test your mastery of chapter objectives.
- Study chapter content with an individualized Study Plan.
- Deepen your understanding of particular concepts and principles with Review, Remediation, and Enrichment Exercises.
- Apply what you have learned in the chapter to your work with children in Building Teaching Skills and Dispositions exercises.
- Observe children and their unique contexts in Video Examples.

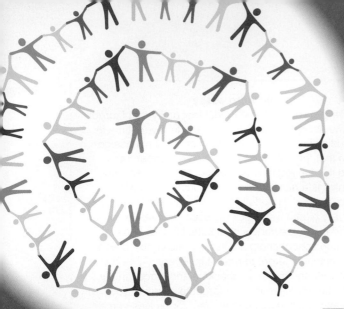

Chapter Fourteen

Moral
Development

CASE STUDY: Changing the World, One City at a Time

Alice Terry had worked as a middle school teacher with gifted and talented students in a rural area of Georgia. Over the years, Alice gave her students a chance to work on significant projects addressing pressing needs in their community, including restoring buildings, preparing a waste management plan for their county, and designing a walking tour past historic buildings and monuments (Terry, 2000, 2001, 2003, 2008; Terry & Panter, 2010). After students completed the projects, they talked with Alice about what they had learned.

Students reported that they acquired numerous benefits from participating in the projects, often gaining a sense of purpose in their work. Now in high school, several adolescents who had renovated a theater as middle school students described their accomplishments:

"Makes you feel like you have a—" Trina interrupted.

"A place in life," Kevin continued. "We, like, have our—we have, like, a place. No, not a place, but we have a a—a mark."

Anna blurted out, "We left our mark, yeah!"

"Our mark. When we were eighth graders," Kevin added, "we really made a difference."

"We'll go back," Ann responded, "and probably find some of our signatures somewhere."

"Our footprints are in there," Kevin mused. "Our breath will still be there."[a] (Terry, 2000, p. 126)

Along with gaining a sense of purpose, the adolescents acquired valuable social insights into relationships with peers. Students realized that they had to consider how their moods affected others:

"You can't be in a grouchy mood and do stuff like this," Anna began, "'cause folks are just gonna get mad at you—you can't do that . . . . You got to have a good attitude about it."

Kevin interjected, "Everybody has to have a good attitude."

Anna added, "Or nothing will get done." (Terry, 2000, p. 124)

A related social lesson was that cooperation was imperative to the group's progress. When asked to advise other adolescents who would be working on community service projects, the students emphasized teamwork:

"Learn to . . . work together," Kevin advised.

Anna added, "Work hard."

"Get along. To just, um, use their time wisely so they can get the most out of the project," Trina remarked. (Terry, 2000, p. 126)

In addition, students learned about themselves. Kat, now a young woman, had been impatient with her teammates and recalled lessons in self-control and tolerance:

I used to just blow up at people. . . . I guess we were working in such close quarters that, you know, if somebody that you didn't like was there, they were going to breathe on you at some point. You were going to have to put up with it. (Terry, 2001, pp. 126–127)

- What did Alice Terry understand about the moral needs of young people?
- What skills did the adolescents learn as they participated in community service projects?

[a] Excerpts from "An Early Glimpse: Service Learning from an Adolescent Perspective" by A. W. Terry, from JOURNAL OF SECONDARY GIFTED EDUCATION, Vol. 11, Issue 3, pp. 124, 126–128, 303–304. Copyright © 2000 by Prufrock Press, Inc. Reprinted with permission of Prufrock Press, Inc. http://www.prufrock.com

OBJECTIVES

14.1: Describe developmental trends in children's moral reasoning and factors influencing these progressions in children.

14.2: Identify key influences on the development of prosocial and aggressive behaviors.

14.3: Explain what teachers and other practitioners can do to promote children's moral development.

14.4: Apply information about prosocial and aggressive behaviors to classroom practice and safe school environments.

Although most children and adolescents readily acquire moral values, now and again they need guidance in treating others humanely. In the introductory case study, Alice Terry understood that adolescents could benefit from an opportunity to work together and serve their community. As a result of their experiences, these young people learned that their community needed them, that they had to compromise and act considerately in order to achieve common goals, and that they could derive considerable satisfaction from their collective accomplishments.

In this chapter, we examine children's moral development. We look specifically at children's reasoning about right and wrong and their tendencies to help and occasionally to hurt others. Just as you have discovered to be true about other aspects of development, you will learn that teachers and other adults play a vital role in children's ability to act decently and honorably.

MORAL REASONING

Moral development involves acquiring standards about right and wrong and acting in accordance with these standards. Three influential theories, those from Piaget, Kohlberg, and social domain scholars, explain regularities in children's moral reasoning.

Piaget's Theory of Moral Development

After conducting observations of children's social games (e.g., playing with marbles) and interviews with children about people's wrongdoings, the pioneering developmental theorist **Jean Piaget** (1896–1980) proposed that, over time, children construct increasingly mature understandings of "good" and "bad" behavior (Piaget, 1960b).[1] In the early elementary years, children believe that behaviors that are "bad" or "naughty" are those that cause serious damage or harm. Thus, a young child might say that a person who accidentally broke 15 dishes was more badly behaved than a person who intentionally broke just one dish. By the upper elementary grades, children consider people's motives when evaluating behaviors. At this age, they would see the person who intentionally broke one dish as the guiltier party.

Piaget noticed other changes in the ideas that children formed about moral issues. For preschoolers, "good" behavior consists of obeying adults and other authority figures. Around age 5, children begin to judge what is good and appropriate based on established *rules* for behavior. At this point, they see regulations as firm dictates to be obeyed without question. (Piaget called this rule-based morality *moral realism.*) Sometime around age 8 or 9, children begin to recognize that rules are created primarily to help people get along and can be changed if everyone agrees to the change.

WRONGDOING. Piaget believed that children construct their own ideas about morality. This three-year-old boy probably realizes he should not be in the kitchen cabinet and may be punished if caught.

Many developmental scholars find value in Piaget's notion that children construct their own ideas about moral behavior—often as a result of having discussions with adults and peers—rather than simply adopting the moral guidelines of those around them (Hoffman, 2000; Kohlberg, 1984; Smetana, 2006). Furthermore, theorists agree that development of children's moral understandings depends on advancing cognitive capabilities, such as social perspective taking and abstract thought (Eisenberg, 1995; Kohlberg, 1969). Nevertheless, researchers have found that Piaget was not always accurate about when various aspects of moral reasoning emerge; for instance, many preschoolers recognize that certain behaviors (e.g., pushing others or damaging their property) are wrong even if an adult tries to assure them that such behaviors are acceptable (Nucci, 2009; Tisak, 1993; Turiel, 1983). And as you will learn in the next section, another prominent theorist, Lawrence Kohlberg, found

moral development
Advancements in reasoning and behaving in accordance with culturally prescribed or self-constructed standards of right and wrong.

[1]Piaget's theory of cognitive development is described in Chapter 6.

significant developmental changes in moral thinking in adolescence and adulthood, periods that were not examined by Piaget.

Kohlberg's Theory of Moral Development

When the groundbreaking cognitive-developmental psychologist **Lawrence Kohlberg** (1927–1987) first began to examine other early theorists' descriptions of children's moral development, he was disappointed with much of what he read (Kohlberg, 1963, 1964).[2] At the time, several outspoken theorists (e.g., Sigmund Freud, B. F. Skinner) argued that people behave morally only in response to pressure from others. Kohlberg rejected this idea, siding instead with Piaget's view that individuals develop their own ideas about proper courses of action. Yet whereas Piaget studied moral development as one of several distinct topics he examined, Kohlberg made moral thinking his life's work and was therefore able to provide an especially detailed account of youngsters' moral thinking.

Kohlberg was the first researcher to look in depth at the age-related ways in which people analyze hypothetical conflicts. Consider the following situation:

> In Europe, a woman was near death from a rare form of cancer. There was one drug that the doctors thought might save her, a form of radium that a druggist in the same town had recently discovered. The druggist was charging $2,000, ten times what the drug cost him to make. The sick woman's husband, Heinz, went to everyone he knew to borrow the money, but he could only get together about half of what the drug cost. He told the druggist that his wife was dying and asked him to sell it cheaper or let him pay later. But the druggist said no. So Heinz got desperate and broke into the man's store to steal the drug for his wife. (Kohlberg, 1984, p. 186)

Should Heinz have stolen the drug? What would you have done if you were Heinz? Which is worse, stealing something that belongs to someone else or letting another person die a preventable death, and why?

The story of Heinz and his dying wife is an example of a **moral dilemma**, a situation in which two or more people's rights or needs are at odds and for which there is no clear-cut right or wrong solution. Following are three boys' responses to Heinz's dilemma. We have given the boys fictitious names so that we can talk about them afterwards.

> *Andrew (a fifth grader):* Maybe his wife is an important person and runs a store, and the man buys stuff from her and can't get it any other place. The police would blame the owner that he didn't save the wife. He didn't save an important person, and that's just like killing with a gun or a knife. You can get the electric chair for that. (Kohlberg, 1981, pp. 265–266)

> *Bradley (a high school student):* If he cares enough for her to steal for her, he should steal it. If not he should let her die. It's up to him. (Kohlberg, 1981, p. 132)

> *Charlie (a high school student):* In that particular situation Heinz was right to do it. In the eyes of the law he would not be doing the right thing, but in the eyes of the moral law he would. If he had exhausted every other alternative I think it would be worth it to save a life. (Kohlberg, 1984, pp. 446–447)

Each boy offers a different reason to justify why Heinz should steal the lifesaving drug. Andrew suggests that the druggist (whom he calls the owner) needs to be punished for not saving a life. Bradley takes a self-serving view, proposing that the decision to either steal or not steal the drug depends on how much Heinz loves his wife. Only Charlie considers the value of human life in justifying why Heinz should break the law.

After obtaining hundreds of responses to moral dilemmas, Kohlberg proposed that the development of moral reasoning is characterized by a sequence of six stages grouped into three general *levels* of morality: preconventional, conventional, and postconventional (Colby, Kohlberg, Gibbs, & Lieberman, 1983; Kohlberg, 1963, 1976, 1984) (see Table 14-1). **Preconventional morality** is the earliest and least mature form of moral reasoning, in that a child has not yet adopted or internalized society's conventions regarding what is right or

[2]Kohlberg's theory is introduced in Chapter 1.

Preparing for Your Licensure Examination
Your teaching test might ask you to describe how moral development is a constructive process that depends on experience and reflection.

moral dilemma
Situation in which there is no clear-cut answer regarding the morally right thing to do.

preconventional morality
In Kohlberg's theory, a lack of internalized standards about right and wrong; making decisions based on what is best for oneself, without regard for others' needs and feelings.

TABLE 14-1 Kohlberg's Three Levels and Six Stages of Moral Reasoning

LEVEL	AGE RANGE	STAGE	NATURE OF MORAL REASONING
Level I: Preconventional Morality	Seen in preschool children, most elementary school students, some junior high school students, and a few high school students	Stage 1: Punishment-avoidance and obedience	People make decisions based on what is best for themselves, without regard for others' needs or feelings. They obey rules only if established by more powerful individuals; they may disobey if they aren't likely to get caught. "Wrong" behaviors are those that will be punished.
		Stage 2: Exchange of favors	People recognize that others also have needs. They may try to satisfy others' needs if their own needs are also met ("You scratch my back, I'll scratch yours"). They continue to define right and wrong primarily in terms of consequences to themselves.
Level II: Conventional Morality	Seen in a few older elementary school students, some junior high school students, and many high school students (Stage 4 typically does not appear until the high school years)	Stage 3: Good boy/good girl	People make decisions based on what actions will please others, especially authority figures and other individuals with high status (e.g., teachers, popular peers). They are concerned about maintaining relationships through sharing, trust, and loyalty, and they take other people's perspectives and intentions into account when making decisions.
		Stage 4: Law and order	People look to society as a whole for guidelines about right or wrong. They know rules are necessary for keeping society running smoothly and believe it is their "duty" to obey them. However, they perceive rules to be inflexible; they don't necessarily recognize that as society's needs change, rules should change as well.
Level III: Postconventional Morality	Rarely seen before college (Stage 6 is extremely rare even in adults)	Stage 5: Social contract	People recognize that rules represent agreements among many individuals about appropriate behavior. Rules are seen as potentially useful mechanisms that can maintain the general social order and protect individual rights, rather than as absolute dictates that must be obeyed simply because they are "the law." People also recognize the flexibility of rules; rules that no longer serve society's best interests can and should be changed.
		Stage 6: Universal ethical principles	Stage 6 is a hypothetical, "ideal" stage that few people ever reach. People in this stage adhere to a few abstract, universal principles (e.g., equality of all people, respect for human dignity, commitment to justice) that transcend specific norms and rules. They answer to a strong inner conscience and willingly disobey laws that violate their own ethical principles.

Sources: Colby & Kohlberg, 1984; Colby et al., 1983; Kohlberg, 1976, 1984, 1986.

conventional morality
In Kohlberg's theory, acceptance of society's conventions regarding right and wrong; behaving to please others or to live up to society's expectations for appropriate behavior.

wrong—hence the label *preconventional*. Andrew's response to the Heinz dilemma is a good example of preconventional, Stage 1 thinking, in that he focuses on the consequences (death in the electric chair) of not providing the medicine. Kohlberg also classified Bradley's response as preconventional, in this case as a Stage 2 response. Bradley is beginning to recognize the importance of saving someone else's life, but the decision to do so ultimately depends on whether or not Heinz loves his wife. In other words, his decision depends on *his* feelings alone.

Conventional morality is characterized by an acceptance of society's conventions regarding right and wrong. At this level, an individual obeys rules even when there are no consequences for obedience or disobedience. Adherence to rules is somewhat rigid, however, and its appropriateness or fairness is seldom questioned. In contrast, people who exhibit **postconventional morality** view rules as useful but changeable mechanisms created to maintain the general social order and protect human rights, rather than as absolute dictates that must be obeyed without question. Postconventional individuals live by their own abstract principles about right and wrong—principles that typically include such basic human rights as life, liberty, and justice. They may disobey rules inconsistent with their principles, as we see in Charlie's Stage 5 response to the Heinz dilemma: "In the eyes of the law he would not be doing the right thing, but in the eyes of the moral law he would."

Younger children will reason primarily from within a preconventional framework but in the high school classroom, each of the three levels of reasoning may be evident at one time or another. You can listen to three young people give reasons for not spending money found in a lost wallet in the "Moral Development: Preconventional," "Moral Development: Conventional," and "Moral Development: Postconventional" videos in MyEducationLab.

A great deal of research on moral development has followed on the heels of Kohlberg's work. Some of it supports Kohlberg's sequence of moral reasoning: Generally speaking, children and adolescents make advancements in the order that Kohlberg proposed (Colby & Kohlberg, 1984; Nucci, 2009; Stewart & Pascual-Leone, 1992). Furthermore, Kohlberg's basic idea that moral development is a constructive process has stood the test of time—theorists remain intrigued with children's drive to create their own mental models of moral life (Nucci, 2006; Thornberg, 2010; Turiel, 2008a). Nevertheless, psychologists have identified several weaknesses in Kohlberg's theory. One set of problems is related to how Kohlberg defined morality. For one thing, Kohlberg included both *moral issues* (e.g., causing harm) and *social conventions* (e.g., having rules to help society run smoothly) into his views of morality, but as you will soon see, children view these two domains differently. In addition, he largely overlooked one very important aspect of morality: that of helping and showing compassion for others (Gilligan, 1982, 1987). Furthermore, although Kohlberg acknowledged that moral thinking is intertwined with emotions, he emphasized cognitive factors. In contrast, contemporary researchers have shown just how strongly emotions (e.g., empathy and guilt) are related to moral thought and action (Arsenio & Lemerise, 2010; R. A. Thompson & Newton, 2010; Turiel & Killen, 2010).

Another limitation of Kohlberg's theory is his proposal that environmental factors have only a modest impact on moral development. Kohlberg assumed that children's moral thinking is guided by their own introspection, largely without adult assistance. Yet recent research indicates that children are very much influenced by parents and other adults as well as by their many cultural experiences (J. Dunn, 2006; Grusec, 2006; Volling, Mahoney, & Rauer, 2009). Finally, Kohlberg disregarded situational factors that youngsters take into account when deciding what's morally right and wrong in specific contexts (Rest, Narváez, Bebeau, & Thoma, 1999; van IJzendoorn, Bakermans-Kranenburg, Pannebakker, & Out, 2010). For example, children are more apt to think of lying as immoral if it causes someone else harm than if it has no adverse effect—that is, if it is just a "white lie" (Turiel, Smetana, & Killen, 1991).

Social Domain Theory of Moral Development

American psychologist **Elliott Turiel** and his colleagues have followed the leads of Jean Piaget and Lawrence Kohlberg in examining children's beliefs about the appropriateness and inappropriateness of people's actions (Killen & Smetana, 2010; Nucci, 2009; Turiel, 2008b; Turiel & Killen, 2010). The unique contribution that Turiel and his collaborators have made is in demonstrating that young children easily distinguish issues about morality from concerns about society's conventions—an ability that was largely overlooked by Kohlberg. By comparing children's responses to carefully defined moral and social-conventional violations, Turiel and his colleagues have been able to demonstrate capabilities in reasoning that were not evident in Kohlberg's data.

MyEducationLab

Listen to three young people give reasons for not spending money found in a lost wallet in the "Preconventional Reasoning," "Conventional Reasoning," and "Postconventional Reasoning" videos. (Find Video Examples in Topic 14 of MyEducationLab.)

CLASSROOM RULES. Kohlberg suggested that children initially act appropriately in order to avoid punishment and only later abide by rules out of a sense of duty. These French students voluntarily work quietly, suggesting that they have internalized the need to follow rules.

Preparing for Your Licensure Examination
Your teaching test might ask you about the basic tenets and educational implications of Kohlberg's theory of moral development.

postconventional morality
In Kohlberg's theory, behaving in accordance with self-developed abstract principles regarding right and wrong.

Children identify important issues in three social domains. Young children understand that **moral transgressions** (e.g., hitting others, stealing their belongings, and calling them nasty names) are wrong because they cause damage or harm, violate human rights, or run counter to basic principles of equality, freedom, or justice (J. G. Miller, 2007; Nucci, 2009; Turiel, 2002, 2006a). Preschool and kindergarten children also realize that **conventional transgressions** (e.g., talking back to adults or burping at meals) violate widely held understandings about how one should act and are also wrong but not as serious as moral transgressions. Conventional transgressions are usually specific to a particular culture. Although burping is frowned on in mainstream Western culture, people in some cultures burp as a compliment to the cook. Moreover, young children see some choices, such as selecting a friend, as a **personal matter**; therefore, determining what is a right or wrong choice is up to the individual. The ability to distinguish moral violations, conventional transgressions, and personal choices appears to be universal, as you can learn more about in the Development in Culture feature on "Moral Development in Colombia."

Research in support of the social domain theory indicates that children construct understandings of rules in the various domains as they reflect on everyday experiences. When they or another person hurts someone else, the person who has been hurt tends to express anger, pain, or sadness, and adults may point out the negative outcomes of inappropriate acts for victims (Dunn, 2006; Parke & Clarke-Stewart, 2011). Conversely, children notice that when someone violates a social convention, everyone's responses tend to be less strident and focus instead on the rules that have been broken.

GET YOUR OWN DOLL. These young girls both want to take sole possession of a toy. As their conflict progresses, they may observe one another's reactions and regret their personal acts.

As children reflect on their social experiences, they develop an ever-growing appreciation for a person's responsibilities in the various domains. During early childhood, children describe violations in the moral domain in concrete terms, as causing physical harm to others, whereas older children express concern about abstract notions of inequality (Smetana, 2006). Similarly, children's awareness of social conventions is rudimentary in early childhood but increases throughout the elementary and secondary school years (Helwig & Jasiobedzka, 2001; Mullins & Tisak, 2006; Turiel, 2006b). A young child may suggest that it is wrong to call a teacher by his or her first name because of the school's custom of using the title "Mr.," "Miss," "Mrs.," or "Ms.," whereas an older child may be able to explain further that failing to use the proper title is disrespectful to the authority figure (Turiel, 1983). Concerns about the personal domain expand to include reflections on psychological issues, for example, matters affecting one's own safety, comfort, and health (Tisak & Turiel, 1984; Thornberg, 2010).

In the process of learning about specific domains, children gradually notice that particular actions can have repercussions across several domains. For example, adolescents may realize that a teacher's decision to place boys and girls into separate groups can be evaluated from several different perspectives (Killen, Margie, & Sinno, 2006). Morally, it might be considered unfair because one gender or the other could be denied an equal opportunity for learning. In its conventional dimensions, the decision might be considered acceptable because separating boys and girls is a common practice that can culminate in effectively functioning groups. In the personal domain, the decision might be considered an imposition that violates students' right to select their own groups.

Children also develop an increasingly thorough understanding of cultural practices in the various domains. Previously, you learned that children universally distinguish moral, conventional, and personal violations, but it is also the case that children learn culture-*specific* ways of classifying certain rules and violations. Social conventions in some areas of India include women wearing a sari (traditional apparel draped around the body) and a bindi (a forehead decoration), whereas some Mennonite and Amish women in the United States and Canada wear long dresses and bonnets (Parke & Clarke-Stewart, 2011). Such variations in dress are not simply fashion statements; they help to uphold the social order in traditional cultures. Moral rules also vary somewhat across culture. In Hindu society, fish is considered a "hot" food that would stimulate sexual desire and should not be consumed by widows who are seeking salvation for their deceased husbands (Shweder, Mahapatra, & Miller, 1987).

moral transgression
In social domain theory, action that causes damage or harm or in some other way infringes on the needs and rights of others.

conventional transgression
In social domain theory, action that violates society's general guidelines (often unspoken) for socially acceptable behavior.

personal matter
In social domain theory, action that is considered a choice that an individual can make without consulting others.

DEVELOPMENT IN CULTURE
Moral Development in Colombia

Children around the world develop several common ideas about social responsibility as well as some divergent views. Evidence of universality is present in children's ability to distinguish moral, social, and personal actions (Turiel, 2006b; Wainryb, 2006). By the preschool years, children realize that moral violations (e.g., hitting and pushing, or taking another's belongings) are hurtful acts that are rarely justified. Young children consider violations of social conventions (e.g., failing to say "please" or "thank you," or ignoring table etiquette) to be disrespectful but not as reprehensible as moral violations. With reference to the personal domain (e.g., selecting a friend or choosing a hairstyle), children typically say that individuals themselves should make their own decisions.

Research by Alicia Ardila-Rey and her colleagues in Colombia, South America, validates these understandings in children. As with children in many other cultures, Colombian children differentiate separate domains of social action. In one study, interviewers read stories to 3- to 7-year-old Colombian children from middle-class families (Ardila-Rey & Killen, 2001). Stories portrayed hypothetical children who were at odds with teachers over moral issues (e.g., hitting another child), social-conventional conflicts (e.g., drinking milk standing up rather than following the classroom's custom of doing so while sitting down), and personal disagreements (e.g., choosing to sit next to another classmate during a story other than the one chosen for the child by the teacher). Interviewers asked children about the proper course of action for teachers to take when the hypothetical children failed to live up to the teachers' expectations.

LEARNING RIGHT FROM WRONG. These Colombian children have daily experiences that help them to acquire important moral and social understandings.

Children stated that teachers should offer explanations when the hypothetical children violated moral rules. They believed that children in the stories had misbehaved because they were young and uninformed, not because they were being malevolent or intentionally disobedient. Therefore, the imaginary children were thought to need guidance, not punishment. In comparison, the interviewed children believed teachers should negotiate with fictional children who violated social-conventional rules or insisted on pursuing personal actions disapproved of by teachers. From the children's perspective, teachers should advise students about social-conventional and personal domains and then allow students to make their own decisions. In the following responses, children defended the rights of peers to exercise their independence in personal matters:

> "Children have their own rights, they have the right to choose what to play with" *("Los niños tienen sus propios derechos; ellos tienen derecho de jugar a lo que quieran jugar")*. "It is the child's play, not the teacher's play. The child can do whatever she wants to do" *("Es el juego de la niña, no es el juego de la profesora. La niña puede jugar a lo que ella quiera")*. "They can't force you to sit with a friend who is not your friend" *("A uno no lo pueden obligar a sentarse con un amigo que no es su amigo")*. (Ardila-Rey & Killen, 2001, p. 253)

Other research with Colombian children shows diversity in views about social conduct. In one investigation of children's evaluations of moral transgressions, 6- to 12-year-old Colombian children were recruited from two towns: Chía, a small and peaceful rural community with an educated population, and Soacha, a densely populated and economically impoverished community with high rates of crime and violence (Ardila-Rey, Killen, & Brenick, 2009). The vast majority of children from both groups evaluated the moral transgressions of hitting and refusing to share toys as being wrong. But children in the two groups differed in views about the acceptability of hitting or not sharing when another person had been aggressive ("Would it be okay to do it if they had teased or hurt her first? Why?" "Would it be okay to hit her back? Why?" Ardila-Rey et al., 2009, p. 189). Compared to children in Chía, who had grown up in a relatively peaceful setting, children from Soacha, who had been exposed to a lot of violence, more often responded that hurting and not sharing would be acceptable if the other person had acted aggressively or selfishly.

These and other studies indicate that Colombian children from very different backgrounds believe that children should be given considerable latitude in making their own social decisions, but should try to abide by moral rules that protect the welfare of other people. Subtle variations exist, however, in children's beliefs about the circumstances in which common moral rules are legitimately ignored. Children who have been exposed to excessive levels of violence are more inclined than peers who have grown up in peaceful communities to excuse a person's aggressive and selfish acts when that individual's own rights have been violated.

Widows in Western cultures would not be expected to refrain from eating fish but instead often wear black or follow other customs of respect for their deceased husband.

In summary, social domain theory offers a viable framework for understanding children's moral reasoning. This perspective has inspired an impressive volume of studies that collectively portrays children as perceptive evaluators of social action. As a limitation, this perspective has not yet inspired much research about the links among moral thinking, emotions, and behavior, but some scholars in the field have begun to make strides in analyzing these important connections (Arsenio & Lemerise, 2010; Smetana & Killen, 2008; Turiel & Killen, 2010).

Developmental Trends in Morality

Many contemporary developmental psychologists believe that moral development involves general *trends* rather than hard-and-fast stages. Contemporary psychologists have identified the following developmental changes in children's moral reasoning and behavior:

Children begin using internal standards to evaluate behavior at a very early age. Children apply their own standards for right and wrong even before age 2 (Kochanska, Casey, & Fukumoto, 1995; R. A. Thompson & Newton, 2010). Infants and toddlers may wince, cover their eyes or ears, or cry when they witness an aggressive interaction. Many toddlers distinguish between what's "good" and "bad," for example looking at a broken object and saying "uh-oh!" (Kagan, 1984; S. Lamb & Feeny, 1995). You can see 16-month-old Corwin's concern when his block tower falls down in the "Intelligence: Infancy" video in MyEducationLab. Sometime around age 3 or 4, children understand that causing physical harm to another person is wrong regardless of what authority figures might tell them and regardless of what consequences certain behaviors may or may not bring to themselves (Helwig, Zelazo, & Wilson, 2001; Smetana, 1981; Turiel, 2006b).

Children's capacity to respond emotionally to others' distress increases over the school years. Certain emotions tend to accompany and evoke moral actions, and these emotions emerge gradually as children grow older. Children begin to show signs of **guilt**—a feeling of discomfort when they know that they have inflicted damage or caused someone else suffering—as early as 22 months (Kochanska, Gross, Lin, & Nichols, 2002).[3] Children's capacity for guilt increases over the childhood years and seems to be an essential part of having a conscience. Feeling guilty deters future wrongdoing; children especially prone to guilt tend to refrain from serious misbehaviors (Kochanska et al., 2002; Tangney & Dearing, 2002). Excessive levels of guilt can be detrimental, however, leading children to become self-berating and depressed (Luby et al., 2009; Zahn-Waxler & Kochanska, 1990).

Children also develop a capacity for **shame**, the feeling of being embarrassed or humiliated when they realize that they are failing to meet others' standards for moral behavior. Precursors to shame emerge during early childhood and then evolve into conscious emotions in middle childhood. Toddlers sometimes avoid adults or appear anxious when they have done something wrong, but children generally are in the middle elementary grades before they reliably exhibit shame (Barrett, 2005; Damon, 1988; Hoffman, 1991). Feeling shame does not seem to inhibit wrongdoing as effectively as does guilt. In fact, some children who are ashamed tend to act out disruptively and aggressively (MacDermott, Gullone, Allen, King, & Tonge, 2010).

Guilt and shame emerge when children believe they have done something wrong. In contrast, *empathy,* the capacity to experience the same feelings as another person, and **sympathy**, a genuine feeling of sorrow and concern about another person's problems or distress, motivate moral behavior even in the absence of wrongdoing.[4] These emotions emerge in early childhood and continue to develop throughout middle childhood and adolescence (S. Lamb & Feeny, 1995; R. A. Thompson & Newton, 2010; Zahn-Waxler, Radke-Yarrow, Wagner, & Chapman, 1992). In the primary grades, children show empathy mostly for people they know, such as friends and classmates. But by the upper elementary and secondary

[3]The developmental course of guilt is examined in Chapter 11.
[4]Empathy is introduced in Chapter 11.

MyEducationLab

See evidence that Corwin has emerging internal standards in the "Intelligence: Infancy" video. (Find Video Examples in Topic 14 of MyEducationLab.)

I'M SORRY. Guilt, empathy, and sympathy are vital parts of children's moral development.

guilt
Feeling of discomfort when one inflicts damage or causes someone else pain or distress.

shame
Feeling of embarrassment or humiliation after failing to meet certain standards for moral behavior.

sympathy
Feeling of sorrow and concern about another's problems or distress.

school grades, youngsters also feel empathy for people they *don't* know—perhaps for the economically poor, the homeless, or those in catastrophic circumstances (Eisenberg, 1982; Hoffman, 1991; Markstrom, Huey, Stiles, & Krause, 2010). In the opening case study, the adolescents felt empathic for unfamiliar people in their community, wishing to preserve historical landmarks and natural resources for everyone's benefit. Also during adolescence, young people become better able to disregard their own personal distress in order to attend helpfully to another's misfortune (Eisenberg, Spinrad, & Sadovsky, 2006).

Children's understanding of fairness evolves throughout early and middle childhood. The ability to share with others depends on children's sense of **distributive justice**, their beliefs about what constitutes everyone's fair share of a valued commodity (food, toys, playground equipment, etc.). Children's notions of distributive justice change over time (Damon, 1977; Gummerum, Keller, Takezawa, & Mata, 2008; Kienbaum & Wilkening, 2009). In the preschool years, beliefs about what's fair are based on children's own needs and desires; for instance, it would be perfectly "fair" to give oneself a large handful of candy and give others smaller amounts. In the early elementary grades, children base their judgments about fairness on strict equality: A desired commodity is divided into equal portions. Sometime around age 8, children begin to take merit and special needs into account. They may think that people who contribute more to a group's efforts should reap a greater portion of the group's rewards and that people who are exceptionally poor might be given more resources than others.

As children get older, they increasingly make moral decisions that reflect a combination of several distinct factors. Children's moral behaviors are correlated with their moral reasoning (Brugman, 2010; Eisenberg, Zhou, & Koller, 2001; Turiel, 2008b). Those who, from Kohlberg's perspective, reason at higher stages are less likely to cheat, insult others, or engage in delinquent activities; more likely to help people in need; and more likely to disobey orders that would cause someone harm (Kohlberg, 1975; Kohlberg & Candee, 1984).

Yet as children decide how to act in particular circumstances, other factors besides moral reasoning come into play. Children's perspective-taking ability and emotions (in particular, their guilt, empathy, and sympathy) influence their decisions to behave morally or otherwise (Batson, 1991; Damon, 1988; Eisenberg et al., 2001; Malti, Gasser, & Gutzwiller-Helfenfinger, 2010). Children's personal goals typically affect their moral behavior as well. Although children may want to do the right thing, they may also be concerned about whether others will approve of their actions and about what positive or negative consequences might result. Children are more apt to behave in accordance with their moral standards if the benefits are high ("Will other people like me better?") and the personal costs are low ("How much will I be inconvenienced?") (Batson & Thompson, 2001; Narváez & Rest, 1995; Nunner-Winkler, 2007). In the opening case study, the group solidarity and shared pride students experienced certainly compensated for their hard work and discomfort in resolving interpersonal differences.

As you have learned, an extensive constellation of moral understandings and skills takes time to emerge in children. The Developmental Trends table "Moral Reasoning and Behavior at Different Age Levels" describes advancements you are likely to see in infancy, childhood, and adolescence.

Bioecology of Moral Development

According to the bioecological framework, children contribute to their own moral development through a number of actions—for example, by complying with adults' rules; occasionally misbehaving; reflecting on bystanders' reactions to their good manners and misdeeds; and classifying violations of social practices as moral, conventional, or personal matters. Children's existing cognitive abilities and self-perceptions affect these actions. An equally important part of moral development is experience in the environment—including their interactions with parents and peers, experiences as boys or girls, exposure to moral issues and religious teachings, and participation in cultural traditions. In the following sections we look at how children's cognitive development, sense of self, gender, and environmental experiences influence children's moral reasoning and behavior.

Bioecology of Moral Development
Children's personal characteristics and environmental experiences influence their moral development.

distributive justice
Beliefs about what constitutes people's fair share of a valued commodity.

DEVELOPMENTAL TRENDS
Moral Reasoning and Behavior at Different Age Levels

AGE	WHAT YOU MIGHT OBSERVE	DIVERSITY	IMPLICATIONS
Infancy **(Birth–2 Years)** 	• Acquisition of basic standards for behavior (e.g., saying "uh-oh!" after knocking over and breaking an object) • Reactions of distress when witnessing aggressive behavior	• In the second year, children begin to label objects and events in ways that reflect culture-specific standards (e.g., *good, bad, dirty, boo boo*). • Toddlers who are fearful and inhibited may experience considerable distress when parents respond harshly to their wrongdoings.	• Consistently discourage behaviors that cause harm or distress to others (e.g., hitting or biting peers). • Acknowledge undesirable events (e.g., spilled milk or a broken object), but don't overreact or communicate that children are somehow inadequate for having caused them.
Early Childhood **(2–6 Years)** 	• Some awareness that behaviors causing physical or psychological harm are morally wrong • Guilt for some misbehaviors (e.g., damaging a valuable object) • Greater concern for one's own needs than for those of others; complaining "It's not fair" when one's own needs aren't met • Realization that some violations of social practices reflect moral transgressions, whereas others are conventional transgressions or personal decisions	• Some cultures emphasize early training in moral values; for example, in many Hispanic communities, a child who is *bien educado* (literally, "well educated") knows right from wrong and tries to behave accordingly. • Children who show greater evidence of guilt about transgressions are more likely to adhere to rules for behavior. • At ages 2 and 3, girls are more likely to show guilt than boys; boys catch up at about age 4.	• Make standards for behavior very clear. • When children misbehave, give reasons why such behaviors are unacceptable, focusing on the harm and distress they have caused others (see the discussion on parents' use of *induction* in the description of bioecological factors in moral development).
Middle Childhood **(6–10 Years)** 	• Sense of distributive justice increasingly taking into account people's differing contributions, needs, and special circumstances (e.g., people with disabilities might get a larger share) • Increasing empathy for unknown individuals who are suffering or needy • Feelings of shame as well as guilt for moral wrongdoings	• Some cultures place greater emphasis on ensuring people's individual rights and needs, whereas others place greater value on the welfare of the community as a whole. • Children whose parents explain *why* certain behaviors are unacceptable show more advanced moral development.	• Talk about how rules enable classrooms and other group situations to run more smoothly. • Present simple moral dilemmas similar to circumstances children might encounter themselves (e.g., "What should a girl do when she has forgotten her lunch money and finds a dollar bill on the floor under a classmate's desk?").
Early Adolescence **(10–14 Years)** 	• Some tendency to think of rules and conventions as standards that should be followed for their own sake • Tendency to believe that distressed individuals (e.g., the homeless) are entirely responsible for their own fate	• Sometime around puberty, some youngsters begin to incorporate moral traits into their overall sense of self. • Youngsters' religious beliefs (e.g., their beliefs in an afterlife) influence their judgments about what behaviors are morally right and wrong.	• Involve adolescents in group projects that will benefit their school or community. • Encourage adolescents to think about how society's laws and practices affect people in need (e.g., individuals who are economically disadvantaged). • When imposing discipline for moral transgressions, point out harm caused to others (doing so is especially important when youngsters have deficits in empathy and moral reasoning).
Late Adolescence **(14–18 Years)** 	• Understanding that rules and conventions help society run more smoothly • Increasing concern about doing one's duty and abiding by the rules of society as a whole rather than simply pleasing certain authority figures • Genuine empathy for people in distress • Belief that society has an obligation to help those in need	• For some older adolescents, high moral values are a central part of their overall identity; these individuals often show a strong commitment to helping those less fortunate than themselves. • Adolescents who have less advanced moral reasoning—especially those who focus on their own needs almost exclusively (i.e., preconventional reasoners)—are more likely to engage in antisocial activities.	• Explore moral issues in social studies, science, and literature. • Give teenagers a political voice in decision making about rules at school and elsewhere.

Sources: Chandler & Moran, 1990; Damon, 1988; Eisenberg, 1982; Eisenberg & Fabes, 1998; Farver & Branstetter, 1994; Flanagan & Faison, 2001; D. Hart & Fegley, 1995; Helwig & Jasiobedzka, 2001; Helwig et al., 2001; Hoffman, 1975, 1991; Kochanska et al., 1995, 2002; Kohlberg, 1984; D. L. Krebs & Van Hesteren, 1994; Kurtines, Berman, Ittel, & Williamson, 1995; S. Lamb & Feeny, 1995; Laupa & Turiel, 1995; Nucci, 2009; Nucci & Weber, 1995; Rushton, 1980; Schonert-Reichl, 1993; Smetana & Braeges, 1990; R. A. Thompson & Newton, 2010; Triandis, 1995; Turiel, 1983, 2006a; Yates & Youniss, 1996; Yau & Smetana, 2003; Youniss & Yates, 1999; Zahn-Waxler et al., 1992.

Cognitive Development

Let's return once again to Charlie's response to the Heinz dilemma: "In the eyes of the law he would not be doing the right thing, but in the eyes of the moral law he would." Advanced moral reasoning—thoughtful consideration of moral law and such ideals as equality, justice, and basic human rights—requires reflection about intangible ideas (Kohlberg, 1976; Turiel, 2002). Thus, moral development depends to some extent on cognitive development. Children who are intellectually gifted are, on average, more likely than their peers to think about moral issues and to work hard to address injustices in the local community or the world at large (Silverman, 1994). In comparison, those with an intellectual disability tend to reason at lower levels regarding moral issues than do peers (Langdon, Clare, & Murphy, 2010).

Yet cognitive development does not *guarantee* moral development. It is quite possible to think abstractly about academic subject matter and yet reason in a self-centered, "preconventional" manner (Kohlberg, 1976). In other words, cognitive development is a necessary but insufficient condition for moral development.

Sense of Self

Children are more likely to engage in moral behavior when they think they are actually capable of helping other people—in other words, when they have high self-efficacy about their ability to make a difference (Narváez & Rest, 1995). Furthermore, in adolescence some youngsters begin to integrate a commitment to moral values into their personal goals and overall sense of *identity* (Arnold, 2000; Olthof, 2010). They think of themselves as moral, caring individuals and place a high priority on acting in accordance with this self-perception. Their acts of altruism and compassion are not limited to their friends and acquaintances but also extend to the community at large, as was the case with the young people in the opening case study.

Parenting

The nature of the parent–child relationship and the type of discipline a parent uses affect the child's moral development. Having a warm relationship with the parent motivates the child to learn and follow the parent's moral rules (R. A. Thompson & Newton, 2010). But no child adheres to a stringent moral code all of the time, and the way that a parent responds to this misbehavior influences the child's subsequent moral development. Certainly it is important to impose consequences for harmful actions and other immoral behaviors. However, punishment by itself often focuses children's attention on their own distress (Hoffman, 1975; Nucci, 2001). Children are more likely to make gains in moral development when they think about the harm that certain behaviors have caused for *others*. Giving children reasons why certain behaviors are unacceptable, with a focus on other people's perspectives, is known as **induction** (Hoffman, 1975). Consider these examples:

- "Having your hair pulled the way you just pulled Mai's can be really painful."
- "You probably hurt John's feelings when you call him names like that."
- "This science project you've just ridiculed may not be as fancy as yours, but I know that Michael spent many hours working on it and is quite proud of what he's done."

Consistent use of induction in disciplining children, especially when accompanied by *mild* punishment for misbehavior—for instance, insisting that children make amends for their wrongdoings—appears to promote compliance with rules and to foster the development of empathy, compassion, and altruism (Hoffman, 1975; R. A. Thompson & Newton, 2010; Volling et al., 2009). In contrast, power-assertive techniques, in which parents impose their will through spanking, making threats, expressing anger, and issuing commands (e.g., "Do this because I say so!"), are relatively *in*effective in promoting moral development (Damon, 1988; Kochanska et al., 2002; Zhou et al., 2002).

Parents also help their children to understand their moral responsibilities by talking with them about events earlier in the day or on previous days when children acted in consideration of, or with disregard for, the needs of another person. These conversations are not strictly disciplinary but rather occasions for making sense of a morally charged event. When

induction
Act of explaining why a certain behavior is unacceptable, usually with a focus on the pain or distress that someone has caused another.

Improving Your Observation Skills

Moral tutorial. This father is explaining to his daughter that it was wrong to tease her younger brother, who has become very upset. How might the father's style of parenting affect the little girl's moral development? Compare your response with the explanation at the end of the chapter.

parents draw attention to how other people were helped or hurt by something the child did, the child tends to develop a strong conscience (Laible, 2004; Laible & Thompson, 2000; R. A. Thompson & Newton, 2010).

Interactions with Peers

Children learn many moral lessons in their interactions with age-mates. When infants and toddlers interact with other children at home or in child care settings, they may notice others' reactions when they grab a toy or push the other children away. Beginning in the preschool years and continuing through middle childhood and adolescence, issues related to sharing, cooperation, and negotiation emerge during group activities (Damon, 1981, 1988; Galliger, Tisak, & Tisak, 2009; Turiel, 2006b). Conflicts frequently arise as a result of physical harm, disregard for another's feelings, mistreatment of possessions, and exclusion from social groups (Feigenberg, King, Barr, & Selman, 2008; Galliger et al., 2009; Killen & Nucci, 1995). To learn to resolve interpersonal conflicts successfully, children must engage in social perspective taking, show consideration for others' feelings and possessions, and satisfy both their own needs and those of others (Killen & Nucci, 1995; E. Singer & Doornenbal, 2006). (We elaborate on socially helpful and hurtful behaviors later in this chapter.)

Gender

On average, girls are somewhat more likely than boys to feel guilt, shame, empathy, and sympathy—emotions associated with moral behavior (Alessandri & Lewis, 1993; Mestre, Samper, Frías, & Tur, 2009; Zahn-Waxler & Robinson, 1995). Girls' greater tendency to feel guilt and shame may be related to their general tendency to attribute failures to internal qualities. In other words, girls are more likely than boys to take personal responsibility for their misdeeds (Alessandri & Lewis, 1993).

Although girls and boys may feel somewhat differently about moral situations, do they also *reason* differently? In presenting a variety of moral dilemmas to young adults of both genders, Kohlberg found that females reasoned, on average, at Stage 3, whereas males were more likely to reason at Stage 4 (Kohlberg & Kramer, 1969). But psychologist **Carol Gilligan** has argued that Kohlberg's stages do not adequately describe female moral development (Gilligan, 1982, 1987; Gilligan & Attanucci, 1988). In particular, Gilligan has suggested that Kohlberg's stages reflect a **justice orientation**—an emphasis on fairness and equal rights—that characterizes males' moral reasoning. In contrast, she has proposed, girls are socialized to take a **care orientation** toward moral issues—that is, to focus on interpersonal relationships and take responsibility for others' well-being. The following dilemma can elicit either a justice orientation or a care orientation:

> **The Porcupine Dilemma**
> A group of industrious, prudent moles have spent the summer digging a burrow where they will spend the winter. A lazy, improvident porcupine who has not prepared a winter shelter approaches the moles and pleads to share their burrow. The moles take pity on the porcupine and agree to let him in. Unfortunately, the moles did not anticipate the problem the porcupine's sharp quills would pose in close quarters. Once the porcupine has moved in, the moles are constantly being stabbed. The question is, what should the moles do? (Meyers, 1987, p. 141, adapted from Gilligan, 1985)

justice orientation
Focus on individual rights in moral decision making.

care orientation
Focus on nurturance and concern for others in moral decision making.

People with a justice orientation are apt to look at this situation in terms of someone's rights being violated. They might point out that the burrow belongs to the moles, and so the moles can legitimately throw the porcupine out. If the porcupine refuses to leave, the moles might rightfully harm him, perhaps even kill him. In contrast, people with a care orientation are likely to show compassion when dealing with the porcupine. They might suggest that the moles cover the porcupine with a blanket so his quills won't annoy anyone (Meyers, 1987).

Gilligan has raised a good point: There is more to moral thinking than a focus on justice. By including compassion for other human beings as well as respect for others' rights, she has broadened our conception of what morality encompasses (L. J. Walker, 1995). However, most research studies do not find major gender differences in moral reasoning (Leman & Björnberg, 2010; Nunner-Winkler, 1984; L. J. Walker, 1991, 2006). Minor differences (usually favoring females) sometimes emerge in early adolescence but disappear by late adolescence (Basinger, Gibbs, & Fuller, 1995). Furthermore, males and females typically incorporate both justice and care into their moral reasoning, applying different orientations (sometimes one, sometimes the other, sometimes both) to different moral problems (Rothbart, Hanley, & Albert, 1986; Smetana, Killen, & Turiel, 1991; L. J. Walker, 2006). Such findings are sufficiently compelling that Gilligan herself has acknowledged that both justice and care orientations are frequently seen in males and females alike (L. M. Brown, Tappan, & Gilligan, 1995; Gilligan & Attanucci, 1988).

Participation in Discussions About Moral, Conventional, and Personal Issues

Kohlberg proposed that children develop morally when they are challenged by moral dilemmas they cannot adequately deal with at their current stage of moral reasoning—in other words, when they encounter situations that create disequilibrium. Discussions of controversial topics and moral issues appear to promote the development of moral reasoning, especially when children are exposed to reasoning that's slightly more advanced than their own (DeVries & Zan, 1996; Power, Higgins, & Kohlberg, 1989; Schlaefli, Rest, & Thoma, 1985). Children may have opportunities to discuss various dilemmas at school, for example, whether it is right or wrong to steal food from a store to feed a hungry person (a moral issue), to wear casual clothing to a formal event (a conventional issue), or to wear a shirt with a rock band logo (a personal issue) (Nucci, 2009).

Religious Doctrine or Philosophical Stance

Having a religious faith or other clear philosophical position about the meaning of life plays an integral role in the moral development of many children. Even though religious beliefs do not typically enhance moral reasoning as Kohlberg defined it, perhaps most of the time, these beliefs *do* contribute to moral development by providing a compelling rationale for acting humanely (L. J. Walker & Reimer, 2006). Of course, many parents raise their children without a religious faith and have demonstrated that such an orientation is not a necessary condition for ethical development (McGowan, 2007). And in a few unfortunate cases, children are taught to use their faith as a justification for mistreating others, as has occurred in some white supremacy groups and certain terrorist organizations (P. E. King & Benson, 2006).

Culture

Each cultural group has a somewhat unique set of standards for which behaviors are "right" and which behaviors are "wrong." In mainstream Western culture, lying to avoid punishment for inappropriate behavior is considered wrong, but it is a legitimate way of saving face in certain other cultures (Triandis, 1995). Some cultures emphasize the importance of being considerate of other people (e.g., "Please be quiet so that your sister can study"), whereas others emphasize the importance of tolerating inconsiderate behavior (e.g., "Please try not to let your brother's radio bother you when you study") (M. L. Fuller, 2001; H. L. Grossman, 1994). Some societies teach children to emphasize individual rights and justice, others promote a sense of duty to family and society, and still others stress adherence to a sacred order (Haidt, 2008; J. G. Miller, 2007; Turiel, 2006a). Whereas many people in mainstream Western societies believe that males and females should have equal rights and opportunities, many Hindu people in India believe that a woman's obedience to her husband is integral to the social and moral order (Nucci, 2001; Shweder et al., 1987; Turiel, 2006a).

Despite these variations, different cultures also encourage several common values. Most cultures place value on both individual rights and concern for others (Turiel, 2006a; Turiel, Killen, & Helwig, 1987). And as you learned previously, children around the world learn to distinguish moral, conventional, and personal issues. Furthermore, children universally attend to the demands of situations, focusing on justice in some circumstances, compassion in other interactions, and a balance between the two in still others (J. G. Miller, 2007; Turiel, 1998; Turiel et al., 1987).

Children approach lessons about universal and culture-specific moral principles in an active and increasingly self-possessed manner. Rather than passively accepting adults' moral rules, children reflect on the emotional qualities of events, transform some of adults' ideas to fit their current understandings, and creatively address their personal responsibilities within the constraints of their abilities (Fung & Smith, 2010). In observations of Chubby Maata, an Inuit toddler in Arctic Canada, J. L. Biggs (1998) found that family members continually challenged her with dilemmas about her place in the family and community. One day a frequent visitor to Chubby Maata's house asked the little girl who she and her puppy would like to live with, scooping up the puppy and bringing it home, posing the fundamental question for her as to who matters most in her life. Repeated challenges such as this one helped Chubby Maata understand the complexities of her responsibilities in a close-knit community. For this growing girl, certain lessons, such as relinquishing the babyhood pleasure of relying on her mother for affectionate care, were more difficult than other lessons, such as not being too hard on herself when caught in wrongdoing.

Promoting Moral Development

Several strategies have been shown to promote advanced moral reasoning and behavior. Research findings point to the following recommendations for teachers, parents, and other adults who interact regularly with children and adolescents:

- **Clarify which behaviors are acceptable and which are not, and help children understand the reasons for regulations and prohibitions.** Adults must make it crystal clear that some behaviors (e.g., shoving, making racist remarks, bringing weapons to school) are not acceptable under any circumstances. Schools generally have written codes of conduct that specify prohibited behaviors, and classroom teachers can inform students of these rules at the beginning of the year. Adults also need to explain that some behaviors are appropriate in certain situations yet inappropriate in others. For example, copying a classmate's work may be permissible when a student is in the process of learning but is unacceptable (constituting fraud) during tests and other assessments of what a student has learned (Thorkildsen, 1995).

Adults should accompany any disciplinary actions or discussions of rules with explanations about *why* certain behaviors cannot be tolerated, with a particular emphasis on potential or actual harm (recall our earlier discussion of *induction*). A preschool teacher might say, "If we throw the blocks, someone may get hurt." (Bronson, 2000, p. 206; Riley, San Juan, Klinkner, & Ramminger, 2008). An elementary school teacher might remind students, "We walk when we are in line so nobody gets bumped or tripped" (Bronson, 2000, p. 205). Adults might also ask children to describe how they feel when they're the victims of certain misbehaviors and to speculate about how they would feel in a situation where someone else has been victimized (Doescher & Sugawara, 1989; Hoffman, 1991). In addition, adults can encourage children to make amends for misdeeds (Nucci, 2001). A middle school teacher might say, "I'm sure you didn't mean to hurt Jamal's feelings, but he's pretty upset about what you said. Why don't you think about what you might do or say to make him feel better?"

- **Engage children in discussions about moral issues.** Moral dilemmas often arise in conjunction with inappropriate behaviors (e.g., aggression, theft) that occur at school and in other group settings. One effective approach is to form a *just community*, in which students and their teachers hold regular "town meetings" to discuss recent interpersonal conflicts and moral violations and to establish rules that can help students be more productive and socially responsible (e.g., A. Higgins, 1995; Power et al., 1989).

Moral issues arise in classroom subject matter as well. An English class studying works of Shakespeare might debate whether Hamlet was justified in killing Claudius to avenge the murder of his father (Nucci, 2009). A social studies class might wrestle with the inhumane treatment that millions of people suffered during the Holocaust of World War II. A science class might discuss the ethical issues involved in using laboratory rats to study the effects of cancer-producing agents.

Classroom discussions can also help young people learn how to distinguish among moral, conventional, and personal matters, perhaps within the context of analyzing historical events. In American history a teacher might ask students to reflect on why George Washington refused to accept a letter from King George II of England. In Washington's mind, the letter violated an important social convention because it was addressed to "Mr. George Washington" rather than "President George Washington," thereby failing to recognize his status as leader of a legitimate nation (Nucci, 2001, 2006). Likewise, moral disputes, violations, and dilemmas have been plentiful throughout history and offer numerous occasions for analysis. For instance, students might discuss the moral dimensions of John Brown's 19th-century violent campaigns against slavery in the United States (Nucci, 2001, 2006).

Teachers and other adults can do several things to ensure that discussions about moral, conventional, and personal issues promote children's moral development (Nucci, 2001; Reimer Paolitto, & Hersh, 1983). First, they should create a trusting and nonthreatening atmosphere in which children feel free to express their ideas without censure or embarrassment. Second, they can help children identify all aspects of a dilemma, including the needs and perspectives of the various individuals involved. Third, they can encourage children to explore the underlying bases for their thinking—that is, to examine the extent to which particular moral, conventional, and personal principles are relevant to their concerns.

In discussions about misdeeds, adults must also help youngsters understand the diverse perspectives that can arise during a conversation. Adults might encourage children to look at social dilemmas from several different angles, perhaps considering the extent to which moral concerns, conventions, and personal choice are all involved (Nucci & Weber, 1991). Although classmates who deface their school building with graffiti might believe they are engaging in creative self-expression (personal choice), they are also breaking a rule (convention), disregarding other students' rights to study and learn in a clean and attractive setting (the moral dimension of justice), and thumbing their noses at the needs of those around them (the moral dimension of care).

- **Challenge children's moral reasoning with slightly more advanced reasoning.** Kohlberg's stages (see Table 14-1 on page 536) provide a useful framework for identifying moral arguments likely to create disequilibrium for youngsters. In particular, Kohlberg suggested that teachers offer reasoning that is one stage above a child's reasoning. Imagine that a teenage boy who is concerned primarily about gaining peer approval (Stage 3) often lets a popular cheerleader copy his homework. His teacher might present law-and-order logic (Stage 4), suggesting that homework assignments are designed to help students learn more effectively and so all students should complete them without classmates' assistance. If adults present arguments at a level that is too much higher than that of children's current reasoning, however, children will have trouble understanding the logic and so will probably not reconsider their thinking (Boom, Brugman, & van der Heijden, 2001; Narváez, 1998).

- **Encourage children to invite excluded classmates to participate in activities.** In almost every school, some children are excluded from social groups. Such rejection can occur as a result of prejudice and discrimination, with children occasionally perceiving peers with disabilities, those from low-income backgrounds, and individuals from different ethnic groups as undesirable playmates or as incompetent students (Killen & Smetana, 2010). Complicating matters, many children view the issue of selecting particular peers to eat lunch with or sit next to on the bus as their personal choice. Thus, they may feel justified when excluding certain peers. Yet teachers can appeal to children's sense of fairness and morality by pointing out that they collectively want to have a classroom where *all* children feel that they belong. Teachers might also explain that rejected classmates are likely to feel hurt when they are excluded. In

I tried to get the feeling of deep Sadness and Sorrow into my Picture. I whant the viewer to feel the emotion of what it was like for a Jew. I Didnt add any color becaus for a Jew ther life was gray dull and very Painfull, that is what I want the viewer to feel.

My Picture is Titled

A Jewish life.

ARTIFACT 14-1   The Holocaust. Children's moral beliefs influence their interpretations of school subject matter. Here Cody tries to imagine and capture the feelings of Jewish people during World War II in a seventh-grade unit on the Holocaust.

Preparing for Your Licensure Examination
Your teaching test might ask how you would facilitate discussions with children about important social issues.

addition, teachers can arrange for some assignments that require children to work together and encourage children to notice everyone's contributions to success on these projects.

• **Get children and adolescents actively involved in community service.** As you've learned, youngsters are more likely to adhere to strong moral principles when they have high self-efficacy for helping others and when they have integrated a commitment to moral ideals into their general sense of identity. Such self-perceptions don't appear out of the blue, of course, as the teacher in our opening case study, Alice Terry, understood. Children are more likely to have high confidence in helping others when they have the guidance, support, and feedback they need to carry out relevant behaviors successfully. Through ongoing **service learning**—food and clothing drives, visits to homes for the elderly, community cleanup efforts, and so on—children and adolescents can learn that they have the skills to help those less fortunate than themselves and in other ways make the world a better place in which to live. In the process, they also begin to think of themselves as concerned, compassionate, and moral citizens (Nucci, 2001; Youniss & Yates, 1999). To gain full advantage from such experiences, students need to have some choice in the projects they take on and to reflect on what they have accomplished by writing about their experiences or discussing them as a group (T. Gross, 2010; D. Hart, Atkins, & Donnelly, 2006; Nucci, 2006).

• **Foster a climate of religious tolerance.** In the United States, the First Amendment to the Constitution requires that matters of church and state be kept separate. Many other nations offer similar protections. Public school teachers can certainly discuss religions within the context of social studies or other appropriate academic topics. But teachers in U.S. public schools cannot incorporate religious ideas or practices into classroom activities or community events in any way that shows preference for one religion over another, or even express a preference for religion over atheism. Just as professionals foster respect for diverse cultural backgrounds, so, too, should they advance acceptance of diverse religious beliefs. Many school districts and other institutions for youngsters have specific policies that prohibit any name-calling that denigrates others' religious beliefs, practices, and affiliations.

Teaching respect for diverse religious perspectives does not necessarily mean communicating the message that all customs are equally acceptable. Teachers should certainly not embrace practices that blatantly violate some people's basic human rights. It *does* mean, however, that teachers and their students should work hard to understand other groups' behaviors within the context of their religious beliefs and assumptions.

PROSOCIAL BEHAVIOR AND AGGRESSION

Children's helping and hurting behaviors have an impact on other people's physical or psychological well-being and therefore have significant moral implications. **Prosocial behavior** is an action intended to promote the well-being of another person, perhaps by sharing, teaching, or comforting. **Aggression** is an action intentionally taken to hurt another person either physically (e.g., hitting, shoving, or fighting) or psychologically (e.g., embarrassing, insulting, or ostracizing). Let's consider the typical developmental course of these behaviors and then examine their origins and educational implications.

Development of Prosocial Behavior

Even young infants are attuned to others' distress, in that they may start to cry when they hear other babies crying (Eisenberg, 1992; Hatfield, Cacioppo, & Rapson, 1994; Hutman & Dapretto, 2009).[5] True prosocial behaviors—actions intended to help someone else—appear early in the second year (Farver & Branstetter, 1994; Kärtner, Keller, & Chaudhary, 2010; Zahn-Waxler et al., 1992). Toddlers may spontaneously give adults or peers assistance with everyday tasks, and they are apt to offer their favorite blanket or teddy bear to someone who seems to be unhappy or in pain. As a general rule, children behave more prosocially—for

service learning
Activity that promotes learning and skill development through volunteerism or community service.

prosocial behavior
Action intended to benefit another person (for example, sharing with or helping another person).

aggression
Action intentionally taken to hurt another either physically or psychologically.

[5]Infant's tendency to respond to others' emotions is summarized in Chapter 11.

instance, they become increasingly generous—as they grow older (Eisenberg, 1982; Eisenberg et al., 2010; Rushton, 1980).

Children engage in prosocial behaviors for a variety of reasons. Some motivations for prosocial behavior are self-serving. A 3-year-old boy may bring a toy to a distressed peer, hoping the other child will stop his annoying crying. A 7-year-old girl may help a classmate with schoolwork in order to gain her teacher's approval. Yet children also engage in prosocial behavior because they are genuinely concerned about the welfare of others. In the process of putting themselves in someone else's shoes, children experience some of the other person's feelings—that is, they have *empathy*. Many children who behave prosocially also feel *sympathy*, concern for another that does not necessarily involve sharing the same feeling as that person Batson, 1991; Eisenberg et al., 2010).

MY LITTLE BROTHER. Giving comfort and engaging in other prosocial behaviors contribute to healthy relationships.

Empathy and sympathy are probably the primary motivations of prosocial behavior, but the relationships among empathy, sympathy, and prosocial behavior are complex. As you have learned, a child can engage in prosocial behavior for self-serving motives that have nothing to do with an understanding of the other person's feelings and are not motivated by concern for his or her well-being. In addition, children can be empathic toward another's distress yet become so consumed by personal distress that they are unable to act helpfully (Eisenberg et al., 2010). Furthermore, children who are sympathetic toward the plight of others may provide needed assistance, but only if they are sufficiently confident about *how* to lend a hand.

As they grow older, children do increasingly help others at least in part as a result of feelings of empathy and sympathy. American psychologist **Nancy Eisenberg** and her colleagues have identified five different levels, or *orientations* to prosocial behavior, through which youngsters are apt to proceed over the course of childhood and adolescence. These orientations are described and illustrated in the Observation Guidelines table "Assessing Children's Prosocial Development." Children do not march through the orientations in a lock-step manner, however. Their behavior is apt to reflect two or more orientations in any particular time period, but with age they increasingly exhibit more advanced orientations (Eisenberg et al., 1995; Eisenberg, Miller, Shell, McNalley, & Shea, 1991).

In particular circumstances that might elicit prosocial behavior, children are more likely to actually help another individual if they themselves have been the cause of the person's pain or distress (Eisenberg, 1995). Thus, feeling guilty is also closely related to prosocial behavior (Eisenberg et al., 2010). Children are likewise more likely to behave prosocially if others' misfortunes are the result of an accident, disability, or other uncontrollable circumstance, rather than the result of something the distressed people might be construed as having brought upon themselves (Eisenberg & Fabes, 1998; Graham, 1997).

Finally, prosocial behaviors are more common when benefits outweigh the costs—for instance, when children think the beneficiary might eventually do them a favor in return (Eisenberg, Fabes, Schaller, Carlo, & Miller, 1991; L. Peterson, 1980). For some youngsters, however, the benefits of prosocial actions are strictly internal: A feeling of personal satisfaction about helping someone else more than makes up for any loss of time or convenience (see the "empathic" and "internalized values" orientations in the Observation Guidelines table on page 550). Unfortunately, some children believe that *aggression* yields more benefits than prosocial actions, as we shall see now.

Development of Aggression

Aggression takes a variety of forms. **Physical aggression** is an action that can potentially cause bodily injury. Examples are hitting, pushing, fighting, and using weapons. **Relational aggression** is an action that can adversely affect friendships and other interpersonal relationships. Examples are name-calling, spreading unflattering rumors, and ostracizing a peer from a desirable social group.

The capacity for aggression emerges early. By the latter half of the first year, infants may show anger toward caregivers who prevent them from reaching desired objects or otherwise restrain their movement (Hay et al., 2010; C. R. Stenberg & Campos, 1990). As they

physical aggression
Action that can potentially cause bodily injury (for example, hitting or scratching another person).

relational aggression
Action that can adversely affect interpersonal relationships (for example, calling another person names or socially excluding the person).

OBSERVATION GUIDELINES
Assessing Children's Prosocial Development

CHARACTERISTIC	LOOK FOR	EXAMPLE	IMPLICATION
Hedonistic Orientation *(common in preschool and the early elementary grades)*	• Tendency to help others only when one can simultaneously address one's own needs as well • Prosocial behaviors directed primarily toward familiar adults and peers	Several preschoolers are at a table drawing pictures. Peter is using the only black crayon at the table. Alaina asks him for the crayon so she can color her dog black, telling him, "I just need it for a second." Ignoring her, Peter continues to use the black crayon for several more minutes and then gives it to Alaina.	Point out that other people also have legitimate needs, and emphasize the importance of fairness and helping others. For example, ask children to be "reading buddies" for younger children, explaining that doing so will help them become better readers themselves.
Superficial Needs-of-Others Orientation *(common in the elementary grades)*	• Some willingness to help others even at personal sacrifice to oneself • Only superficial understanding of others' perspectives	During an annual holiday toy drive, many of the children in a third-grade class contribute some of their toys. They seem happy to do so, commenting that "Poor kids need toys too" and "This doll will be fun for somebody else to play with."	Commend youngsters for altruistic behaviors, and ask them to speculate on how their actions are apt to make others feel (e.g., "Can you imagine how these children must feel when they get your toys? Most of them escaped the flood with only the clothes on their backs. What must it be like to lose everything you own—your clothes, your books, your favorite toys—*everything*?!").
Stereotyped, Approval-Focused Orientation *(seen in some elementary and secondary students)*	• Tendency to behave prosocially as a means to gain others' approval • Simplistic, stereotypical views of what "good" and "bad" people do	When walking to school one day, Cari sees Stanley inadvertently stumble and drop his backpack in a puddle. She stops, asks him if he's okay, and helps him wipe off his backpack. As she describes the incident to her teacher later that morning, she says, "Maybe he'll be my friend now. Anyway, it's nice to help other people."	Provide numerous opportunities for youngsters to engage in prosocial activities. Choose activities that are apt to be enjoyable and in other ways rewarding in and of themselves.
Empathic Orientation *(common in the secondary grades)*	• Genuine empathy for other people's distress, even when one does not know the people personally • Willingness to help without regard for consequences for oneself	Members of a high school service club coordinate a schoolwide garage sale, with all proceeds going to a fund to help pay medical expenses of a classmate with a rare form of cancer. They spend several weekends collecting people's contributions to the sale, using their own money for the supplies they need to make the fund-raiser a success.	Alert youngsters to circumstances, both locally and internationally, in which people's basic needs are not being met or in which human rights are being violated. Ask youngsters to brainstorm ways in which they might in some small way make a difference for people living in dire circumstances.
Internalized Values Orientation *(seen in a small minority of high school students)*	• Generalized concern for equality, dignity, human rights, and the welfare of society as a whole • Commitment to helping others integrated into one's overall sense of self	Franklin spends much of his free time working with Habitat for Humanity, an organization of volunteers who build houses for low-income families. "This is as important as my schoolwork," he says. "It's the responsibility of all of us to help one another whenever we can."	Create opportunities—public service projects, fund-raisers, and so on—in which youngsters with an internalized-values orientation can share their enthusiasm for prosocial activities with their peers.

Sources: First two columns based on Eisenberg, 1982; Eisenberg et al., 1995; Eisenberg, Lennon, & Pasternack, 1986.

approach their first birthday, infants may swat at age-mates who take their toys (Caplan, Vespo, Pedersen, & Hay, 1991; Dodge, Coie, & Lynam, 2006). By 18 months of age, children regularly hit, kick, push, and bite others (Flanders et al., 2010; Tremblay et al., 2004). Conflicts over possessions are fairly common during the preschool years (S. Jenkins, Bax, & Hart, 1980). For most children, physical aggression declines after early childhood, partly because children learn to control their impulses, partly because they acquire better strategies for resolving conflicts, and partly because they become increasingly skillful at relational aggression (Dodge et al., 2006; Flanders et al., 2010; Mischel, 1974). You can observe a young boy begin to use physical aggression only to be reminded by his teacher to use his words instead in the "Preschool Aggression" video in MyEducationLab.

The developmental decline in physical aggression is not universal, however. Children who fail to show the expected pattern of diminished fighting generally exhibit one of two profiles, although extremely aggressive children may blend both. Children who exhibit **reactive aggression** act aggressively primarily in response to frustration, anger, or provocation (Crick & Dodge, 1996; Hubbard, Morrow, Romano, & McAuliffe, 2010; Poulin & Boivin, 1999). When an age-mate teases a child for losing a game, the child may impulsively hit the teaser. In comparison, children who engage primarily in **proactive aggression** deliberately initiate aggressive behaviors—physical aggression, relational aggression, or both—as a means of obtaining desired goals. A child may callously push another child out of the way at a vending machine when he hears that there is only one remaining can of soda in the dispenser. Of the two groups, children who exhibit proactive aggression are more likely to have difficulty maintaining friendships with others (Poulin & Boivin, 1999). They may also direct considerable aggression toward particular peers, and those who do so are often known as **bullies**. The hapless victims of bullies tend to be children who are immature, anxious, friendless, and lacking in self-confidence—some also have disabilities—and so are relatively defenseless (Bierman, 2004; L. Little, 2001; Marsh, Parada, Yeung, & Healey, 2001; Pellegrini, Bartini, & Brooks, 1999).

Aggressive children tend to have problems handling emotions and understanding social relationships. These children tend to be less empathic than their age-mates, and, as you have learned, reactively aggressive children in particular find it difficult to cope when angry (Eisenberg et al., 2010). Aggressive children are also apt to have one or more of the following problems in social cognition:[6]

- *Misinterpretation of social cues.* Children who are either physically or relationally aggressive toward peers tend to interpret others' behaviors as reflecting hostile intentions, especially when such behaviors have ambiguous meanings. This **hostile attributional bias** is especially prevalent in children who are prone to *reactive* aggression (Crick & Dodge, 1996; Dodge et al., 2003; Hubbard et al., 2010). Thus, if a clumsy peer bumps gently into a reactively aggressive child, the child is prone to assume that the act was intentionally aggressive and to retaliate with a push.
- *Prevalence of self-serving goals.* For most young people, establishing and maintaining interpersonal relationships are high priorities. For aggressive children, however, self-serving goals—perhaps maintaining an inflated self-image, seeking revenge, or gaining power and prestige—often take precedence (G. Bender, 2001; Crick & Dodge, 1996; Sijtsema, Veenstra, Lindenberg, & Salmivalli, 2009).
- *Ineffective social problem-solving strategies.* Aggressive children often have little knowledge of how to persuade, negotiate, or compromise, and so they resort to hitting, shoving, barging into play activities, and using other ineffective strategies (Honig, 2009; Lochman & Dodge, 1994).
- *Beliefs about the appropriateness and effectiveness of aggression.* Many aggressive children believe that violence and other forms of aggression are acceptable ways of resolving conflicts and retaliating for others' misdeeds. They may believe they need to teach someone a "lesson." Those who display high rates of *proactive* aggression are also apt to believe that aggressive action will yield positive results—for instance, that it will enhance their social status (Hubbard et al., 2010).

[6]Social cognitive abilities are examined in detail in Chapter 12.

MyEducationLab

Observe a young boy start to engage in reactive aggression before being asked by a teacher to use his words in the "Preschool Aggression" video. (Find Video Examples in Topic 14 of MyEducationLab.)

Improving Your Observation Skills

HE'S *MY* BABY! These two girls argue over who can play with the doll at preschool. How do the girls exhibit typical aggressive behavior for children of their age? Compare your response with the explanation at the end of the chapter.

reactive aggression
Aggressive response to frustration or provocation.

proactive aggression
Deliberate aggression against another as a means of obtaining a desired goal.

bully
Child or adolescent who frequently threatens, harasses, or causes physical or psychological injury to particular peers.

ARTIFACT 14-2   Batman. In his drawing of a superhero, 6-year-old Myron shows his understanding that aggression is a way of gaining power and dominance over others.

Bioecology of Prosocial Development and Aggression

Children's prosocial development and aggression are affected by nature, nurture, and the children's own experiences.

As you have learned, helping and hurting behaviors change steadily over the childhood years. In the Developmental Trends table "Prosocial and Aggressive Behavior at Different Age Levels," we present characteristics that teachers and other practitioners are likely to see in infants, children, and adolescents, as well as common forms of diversity in the different age-groups.

Bioecology of Prosocial Behavior and Aggression

Children's helping and hurting behaviors draw from an amalgamation of heredity, activity, and environmental experiences. In this section we look at biological foundations of these behaviors, the experiences children have in social environments, their experiences as boys or girls, and the impact of such individual characteristics as temperament on their prosocial and aggressive behaviors. As we explain, the outcomes of numerous separate and interacting factors contribute to individual profiles of helping and hurting behaviors.

Hereditary and Other Biological Influences

From an evolutionary perspective, both prosocial and aggressive tendencies have enabled human beings to survive and are part of humans' genetic endowment (Dodge, Coie, & Lynam, 2006; Hoffman, 1981; McCullough, Kurzban, & Tabak, 2011). Prosocial behavior provides the basis for close relationships, promotes group cohesion, and helps people pull together in harsh conditions. Some kinds of aggression, though antisocial in nature, also increase chances of survival. Squabbling and warfare cause people to spread apart (thereby improving people's chances of finding food and other essential resources) and, in times of battle, to compete such that only the strongest members survive and give birth to future, stronger generations.

An evolutionary perspective of such behaviors is, of course, speculative at best. Twin studies provide more convincing evidence that both prosocial and aggressive behaviors have biological origins. Monozygotic (identical) twins tend to be more similar than dizygotic (fraternal) twins with respect to altruistic behavior, empathy for others, and aggression (Eisenberg, Fabes, & Spinrad, 2006; Huesmann, Dubow, & Boxer, 2011; Rushton, Fulkner, Neal, Nias, & Eysenck, 1986; Son & Wilson, 2010).

Precisely how heredity affects children's tendencies to be especially helpful or hurtful is unknown, but genes probably determine aspects of the brain's physiology that affect the way that children experience emotions and interpret social cues. Specific areas of the brain become active when people listen to sad stories or witness another person's distress, indicating that these regions are devoted to empathic responses (S. Light et al., 2009; Ruby & Decety, 2001). Possibly, slight variations in both the structure of the brain and the amount of certain chemical substances within it are affected by genes and contribute to individual differences in prosocial behavior.

A similar picture emerges with the biological bases of aggression. Chemical substances in the brain affect children's aggressive tendencies, perhaps by influencing children's ability to inhibit aggressive impulses (Dodge et al., 2006; Mehta & Beer, 2010). Aggressive behavior also appears to be triggered partly by the male hormone testosterone. On average, males are more aggressive than females, and after puberty, males with high testosterone levels tend to be more aggressive than males with lower levels (Archer, 1991; Carney & Mason, 2010; Susman et al., 1987). Finally, children with irregularities to certain areas of the brain, especially damage to an area in the front of the cortex that is involved in planning and behavior control, display heightened aggression (Pennington & Bennetto, 1993; Raine & Scerbo, 1991; Sterzer & Stadler, 2009).

Environmental Influences

Close relationships provide children with emotional foundations for helping and hurting behaviors. Children whose parents are compassionate with them tend to become empathic, cooperative, and helpful to others (R. A. Thompson & Newton, 2010). Conversely, those whose parents are harsh or neglectful tend to become aggressive. Presumably, affectionate parents guide children in coping effectively with anger and disappointment, whereas hostile

hostile attributional bias
Tendency to interpret others' behaviors as reflecting hostile or aggressive intentions.

DEVELOPMENTAL TRENDS
Prosocial and Aggressive Behavior at Different Age Levels

AGE	WHAT YOU MIGHT OBSERVE	DIVERSITY	IMPLICATIONS
Infancy **(Birth–2 Years)** 	• Appearance of simple prosocial behaviors (e.g., offering a teddy bear to a crying child) in the second year • Anger at caregivers who prevent reaching toward desired goals • Conflicts with peers about toys and other objects • Occasional biting, hitting, or scratching of peers	• Infants may be more inclined to show prosocial behaviors when caregivers model these behaviors. • Some children have "difficult" temperaments; they may be especially contrary in the second year, biting others or exhibiting frequent temper tantrums.	• Allow infants to interact with one another under your guidance and protection. • Verbalize expressions of empathy and sympathy toward a child within earshot of other children. • Warmly acknowledge infants' prosocial behaviors. • Set up the environment to reduce frustration and aggression by providing duplicates of favorite toys and creating separate areas for quiet play and active movement. • Explain to aggressive toddlers that hitting another child is hurtful and leads to consequences (e.g., by being placed in a brief time-out).
Early Childhood **(2–6 Years)** 	• Some signs of empathy for people in distress • Increasing sharing and coordination of play activities • Attempts to comfort people in distress, especially those whom children know well; comforting strategies not always effective • Some aggressive struggles with peers about possessions; increasing ability to inhibit aggressive impulses	• Children who are impulsive may use more physical aggression than children who are more patient and self-regulating. • Children are more apt to behave prosocially if they are consistently reinforced for such behavior. • On average, boys are more physically aggressive than girls.	• Recognize that selfish and territorial behaviors are common in early childhood. • Model sympathetic responses; explain what you are doing and why you are doing it. • Encourage children to give one another comfort when they can. • Praise any gentle, controlled, and constructive responses to frustration or provocation. • Comfort the victims of aggression, and administer appropriate consequences for the perpetrators. Explain why aggressive behavior cannot be tolerated.
Middle Childhood **(6–10 Years)** 	• Growing repertoire of conflict-resolution skills • Increasing empathy for unknown individuals who are suffering or needy • Increasing desire to help others as an objective in and of itself • Decrease in overt physical aggression, but with an increase in relational aggression and more covert antisocial behaviors (e.g., lying, stealing)	• Children whose parents value prosocial behavior are more likely to appreciate helping gestures and to have genuine concern for others. • Some children consistently misinterpret peers' thoughts and motives (e.g., by interpreting accidents as deliberate attempts to cause harm). • Some children become increasingly aggressive in the elementary grades. • Some children are bullies who regularly victimize vulnerable peers (e.g., those without friends or those with disabilities).	• Assist children in their attempts to resolve interpersonal conflicts by asking them to consider one another's perspectives and develop solutions that address everyone's needs. • Draw attention to a comforted child's relief when another child helps ("Look how much better Sally feels now that you've apologized for hurting her feelings"). • Do not tolerate physical aggression or bullying. Make sure children understand rules for behavior, and follow through with appropriate consequences when children are aggressive. • Be on the lookout for children who seem to be frequent victims of others' aggression; help them form productive, supportive relationships with peers.

(continued)

DEVELOPMENTAL TRENDS (continued)

AGE	WHAT YOU MIGHT OBSERVE	DIVERSITY	IMPLICATIONS
Early Adolescence (10–14 Years)	• Decline in physical aggression • Frequent teasing and taunting of peers; emergence of sexual harassment • Teasing and bullying using social network sites and cell phones	• Beginning at puberty, an increased testosterone level in boys can intensify their aggressive tendencies. • Some adolescents with social-emotional problems (e.g., those with conduct disorders) show deficits in empathy for others. • Bullying behavior in some youngsters may temporarily increase after the transition to middle school or junior high.	• Communicate that giving, sharing, and caring for others should be high priorities. • Keep a watchful eye on students' between-class and after-school activities; make it clear that aggression is *not* acceptable on school grounds. • Talk with adolescents about their peer relationships and the pressures they feel to conform.
Late Adolescence (14–18 Years)	• For many, less motivation to engage in aggressive behavior, often as a result of forming more intimate and rewarding relationships with others • Some acts of relational aggression in the form of teasing, excluding others, or engaging in cyberbullying • Ability to offer constructive help to others as individuals and as members of volunteer groups	• Some high school students are exceptionally committed to making the world a better place. • On average, youngsters who live in violent neighborhoods are more apt to become aggressive than peers in safer neighborhoods. • Violence-prone adolescents often believe that hitting another person is reasonable retribution for unjust actions. • Substance abuse and sexual activity increase the probability of aggression.	• Encourage community service work so as to engender a commitment to helping others. Ask adolescents to reflect on their experiences through group discussions or written essays. • Enforce prohibitions against bringing weapons to school and other settings. • Provide intensive treatment to young people who exhibit especially aggressive tendencies.

parents cultivate aggression, particularly reactive aggression, because children grow accustomed to letting their frustrations escalate and lashing out at others (Fite et al., 2010).

Another way that families are influential is by serving as prosocial and aggressive models. Children who observe sympathetic and generous models tend to be more helpful than those without exposure to such models (R. Elliott & Vasta, 1970; M. Mares, Palmer, & Sullivan, 2008; Yarrow, Scott, & Waxler, 1973). A child notices and later emulates a parent's charitable acts in the community. In the same manner, children who observe aggressive models show a greater-than-average number of antagonistic acts (C. A. Anderson et al., 2003; Brendgen et al., 2008; Huesmann et al., 2011).

Parents' styles of interacting with their children and disciplining them also influence children's prosocial and aggressive tendencies. Children are more likely to imitate their parents' prosocial behaviors when parents exhibit an authoritative parenting style—that is, when parents are warm and loving, hold high standards for behavior, and explain why certain behaviors are unacceptable (Baumrind, Larzelere, & Owens, 2010; Eisenberg, 1995; Hoffman, 1988).[7] Children also tend to be more prosocial when their parents have work obligations outside the home and give them numerous responsibilities (e.g., taking care of younger siblings) to keep the household going (Carlo, Koller, Raffaelli, & de Guzman, 2007; Whiting & Whiting, 1975). By way of contrast, other family environments are virtual breeding grounds for aggression. Authoritar*ian* (rather than authoritat*ive*) parenting, especially when accompanied by frequent physical punishment or abuse, appears to foster aggression, but so occasionally does very permissive parenting, presumably because children are left to their own devices in dealing with negative urges (Chan, 2010; P. L. Harris, 2006; Straus, 2000).

Another mechanism for fostering prosocial and aggressive behavior is reinforcement. Over the short run, children engage in more prosocial behavior if they are rewarded (e.g., with candy or praise) for such behavior (J. H. Bryan, Redfield, & Mader, 1971; Eisenberg,

[7]Authoritative, authoritarian, and permissive parenting are examined in Chapter 3.

Fabes, Carlo, & Karbon, 1992; Ramaswamy & Bergin, 2009). However, tangible rewards such as candy appear counterproductive over the long run, perhaps because children begin to perform prosocial actions primarily to benefit themselves ("I gave her my candy because I knew Dad would give me an even bigger treat for sharing") rather than to gain personal satisfaction from helping others (Eisenberg & Fabes, 1998; Szynal-Brown & Morgan, 1983). Aggressive behavior is often reinforced by its outcomes: It may enable children to gain desired objects or get revenge (Crick & Dodge, 1996; Dodge et al., 2006; Lochman, Wayland, & White, 1993).

Thus far, we have emphasized family effects in our discussion of environmental factors, but children are also influenced by people at school and in other institutions of society. For instance, children are more likely to engage in prosocial behaviors, as well as to integrate qualities such as compassion into their overall sense of self, if teachers and other adults encourage empathic concern for one another and for others in the community (Conduct Problems Prevention Research Group, 2010; Sanders, 2010; Youniss & Yates, 1999). Violent aggression at schools is rare, but milder forms—racial and sexual harassment, vandalization, and so on—are fairly common (DeVoe et al., 2003; Garbarino, Bradshaw, & Vorrasi, 2002; Gregory et al., 2010). Unfortunately, domestic disputes and criminal assaults are common in many neighborhoods, providing vivid models for dealing with anger (Su, Mrug, & Windle, 2010). Community violence is strongly associated with proactive aggression, presumably because some children eventually imitate the vicious role models they have seen in their neighborhoods (Fite et al., 2010). Increasingly, many youngsters are exposed to *cyberbullying*, the posting of intentional and repeated harmful messages on cell phones, the Internet, and other electronic social networking systems (Bauman, 2011).

RESPONSIBILITY. Family chores, including caring for younger siblings, help this Indian girl gain a sense of responsibility.

Culture offers another important constellation of influences. A child's culture determines typical targets of, and circumstances for, compassion, prosocial behavior, and aggression. In the United States, parents often foster their young children's cooperation by engaging them in a playful manner, entering into their imaginative play, and facilitating their self-expression (Sirota, 2010). In the following episode, a mother helps her daughter to overcome her anger and cooperate during their errands:

> Kelly Morris, who is 42 years of age and a mother of three, prepares to embark with her two-year-old daughter, Tessa, on an errand-filled Saturday morning excursion. Kelly trundles Tessa in one arm, then pauses to retrieve Tessa's doll, Zoe, to accompany them on their outing. Kelly nestles Tessa snugly into her car seat. However, Tessa squirms restlessly and loudly exclaims, *"NO."* In response, Kelly adopts a playful tone. She presents the doll to Tessa with a dramatic flourish and animatedly announces to Tessa, "I've got something for you. I've got somebody *special*. Look who's *here.*" Noticeably calmer—and smiling now—Tessa immediately takes note. *"Zoe,"* Tessa proudly exclaims, as she laughs cheerfully and affectionately kisses the doll. (Sirota, 2010, p. 397)

Parents in other cultures use different methods for showing empathy and eliciting their children's cooperation. For instance, the Murik mothers in Papua New Guinea frequently express compassion for children during mealtime rituals (Barlow, 2010).

A culture also justifies particular kinds of aggression, prohibits others, and clarifies the meaning of hitting, ridiculing, and ostracizing in personal affairs. In a study comparing peer relationships in American and Japanese fourth graders, both groups of children exhibited relational aggression (e.g., excluding other children from their play groups), but Japanese children who were prone to use a lot of relational aggression tended to feel depressed, whereas comparable American children did not, presumably because of the stronger emphasis on intimacy, exclusivity, and harmony in Japanese relationships (Kawabata, Crick, & Hamaguchi, 2010). It is possible that Japanese children who ostracize other children are rejected by their peers and become distressed about their social standing. American children may receive fewer negative responses from peers when they engage in relational aggression.

Gender

Beginning in the preschool years, boys are more physically aggressive than girls (Dodge et al., 2006; Eagly, 1987; Ostrov & Godleski, 2010). This greater inclination toward physical aggression is probably the result of both biological factors (recall the link between testosterone and aggression) and socialization (parents are more likely to allow aggression in sons than in daughters) (J. E. O. Blakemore et al., 2009; Condry & Ross, 1985; Eisenberg et al., 1996). However, girls are at least as aggressive as boys (and sometimes more so) in relational aggression—for example, by tattling, gossiping, and snubbing their peers (Crick, Grotpeter, & Bigbee, 2002; Dodge et al., 2006; Ostrov & Godleski, 2010).

Boys also tend to be more assertive than girls. In mixed-sex work groups, boys sometimes dominate activities and take charge of needed equipment, and they are more likely to get their way when group members disagree (Jovanovic & King, 1998). Such assertiveness may be nurtured in same-sex activity groups over the years, because boys' friendships typically involve more conflict and competition than girls' friendships do (Eisenberg et al., 1996; Leaper & Smith, 2004). In contrast, girls make frequent small concessions to keep the peace, perhaps because they value group harmony more than boys do (Benenson et al., 2002; P. M. Miller, Danaher, & Forbes, 1986; Rudolph, Caldwell, & Conley, 2005).

Individual Profiles

Children's characteristics combine with their environmental experiences to affect their emerging approaches in helping and hurting others. Although a few environmental factors affect the child's helping and hurting behaviors in simple and straightforward ways, perhaps more often than not exposure to particular experiences interacts with the child's personal characteristics (Conduct Problems Prevention Research Group, 2010). Earlier you saw that authoritative parenting, a style in which mothers and fathers firmly but gently socialize children to act maturely, is associated with prosocial behavior in children. Yet now consider that children who are especially prone to be fearful are most likely to develop a strong conscience when exposed to this kind of parenting (Kochanska & Aksan, 2006). It appears that constitutionally anxious children easily find the direction they need in gentle induction. Other children who are relatively fearless are less responsive to authoritative discipline and instead develop a strong conscience when they have a close and secure bond with their parents. Aggression, too, shows interactive effects, with children who have inherited a somewhat irritable and impulsive temperament being especially vulnerable to acquiring excessively aggressive ways when reared in a harsh environment (Huesmann et al., 2011).

The many separate and interactive effects on children's social behaviors mount over time, crystallizing into unique and somewhat stable patterns of helping and hurting behaviors (Knafo, Zahn-Waxler, Van Hulle, Robinson, & Rhee, 2008; Tremblay, 2010). Thus, the child's choices in expressing compassion or injuring others become ingrained as habits. A given child may regularly comfort peers in distress or alternatively tease and harass classmates.

The stability of prosocial and aggressive habits becomes a concern when children are seriously delayed in the development of empathy or are unusually aggressive. Persistent impairments in empathy and aggressive behavior are associated with long-term problems in adjustment, peer relationships, and school failure (Eisenberg et al., 2010; S. Kim, Kim, & Kamphaus, 2010; Spilt, Koomen, Thijs, Stoel, & van der Leij, 2010). Children who are especially aggressive when they are young (e.g., regularly hitting others, bullying) sometimes become violent in their later years (e.g., participating in gang fights, physical assaults; C. A. Anderson et al., 2003; Di Giunta et al., 2010; Ladd & Burgess, 1999). And the victims of aggression—whether physical or relational—are apt to develop low self-esteem and suffer from depression (Crick, Casas, & Nelson, 2002). You can listen to a girl talk about what it is like to be the target of a bully's aggression in the "Bullying" video in MyEducationLab.

Generally, it is easier to intervene with aggressive children when they are young, but older children and adolescents also typically retain the capacity to acquire productive emotional and social capacities (Maldonado-Molina, Reingle, Tobler, Jennings, & Komro, 2010). In fact, some chronically aggressive individuals do not put a lid on their aggressive behaviors until their early adult years.

MyEducationLab

Listen to a girl talk about what it is like to be the target of a bully's aggression in the "Bullying" video. (Find Video Examples in Topic 14 of MyEducationLab.)

BASIC DEVELOPMENTAL ISSUES
Comparing Prosocial Behavior and Aggression

ISSUE	PROSOCIAL BEHAVIOR	AGGRESSION
Nature and Nurture	The capacity for prosocial behavior appears to be a natural, inborn human characteristic, but individual children have unique genetic endowments (e.g., temperaments) that predispose them to varying degrees of altruism. Affectionate caregiving, role modeling, and explicit requests for children to consider the needs of others in unfortunate circumstances are effective ways to nurture prosocial behavior in children.	The capacity for aggression has a biological basis and is to some degree inherited. Temperamental dispositions, hormone levels, and neurological structures in the brain influence aggressiveness in individual children. Yet the social environment influences how children express their aggressive impulses. Families, social institutions (e.g., schools), and communities may foster aggression through modeling, reinforcement, and harsh punishment.
Universality and Diversity	The capacity for prosocial behavior is universal in the human species. Furthermore, people in most cultures become increasingly prosocial as they mature. Significant diversity exists in the extent to which various cultural groups encourage prosocial activities (e.g., sharing, nurturing), as well as in children's exposure to adults who model prosocial behavior and articulate a commitment to caring for people in need.	Aggressive behavior is universal in human beings. Some general developmental sequences in aggressive expression, such as a gradual shift from physical aggression to verbal aggression, may also be universal. Substantial diversity is present in the ways that children and adolescents express aggression, in the amount of aggression young people encounter in their daily environments, and in the extent to which cultural groups condone aggression as a way of resolving conflict.
Qualitative and Quantitative Change	Qualitative changes may occur in children's understanding of why helping others is important and valuable. Young children often give help primarily to gain rewards or approval, whereas older children and adolescents are more likely to have a genuine concern for people in need. Quantitative increases occur in children's knowledge of effective prosocial strategies and in their ability to carry out such strategies.	A gradual shift from physical aggression in early childhood to more verbal and relational forms of aggression in later years reflects qualitative change. The decline in physical aggression over childhood and adolescence reflects a quantitative change.

Sources: Dodge et al., 2006; Eisenberg et al., 2010; Eisenberg & Fabes, 1998.

Both prosocial behavior and aggression can be seen at one time or another in youngsters of various ages and backgrounds. You can read about other similarities between these two types of behavior in the Basic Developmental Issues table "Comparing Prosocial Behavior and Aggression."

Encouraging Children to Act Prosocially and Curb Aggressive Impulses

Teachers and other practitioners who work with young people in social settings have many opportunities to foster prosocial skills and discourage aggressive behaviors. You can see illustrations of educators fostering productive social capacities in the Development and Practice feature "Promoting Prosocial Skills and Discouraging Aggression." In addition, consider the following strategies that researchers and experienced educators have found to be effective:

• **Treat children with compassion.** The root of empathy is love, of course, and children are especially inclined to express their concern about others' welfare when they themselves have been treated compassionately. Adults can set the stage for productive social behaviors in children by patiently addressing their concerns as an infant caregiver might do by responding sensitively to infants' distress while diapering or feeding (Gonzalez-Mena, 2010). As children grow older, adults can show their compassion by asking them about their activities, encouraging their progress, and forgiving rather than shaming them when they make mistakes (Sanders, 2010).

• **Expose children to models of prosocial behavior.** When educators model compassion and consideration for others, children are likely to emulate such qualities. Ideally, children

DEVELOPMENT AND PRACTICE
Promoting Prosocial Skills and Discouraging Aggression

Talk about other people's feelings and needs in a sympathetic manner.

- A kindergarten teacher notices that Farai is standing next to Ivan in the block area. The teacher says to Ivan, "It looks like Farai would like to help you build your tower. What do you think?" (Early Childhood)
- When reading a story about a homeless child, Lia, a second-grade teacher pauses and asks children to reflect on the girl's needs: "Lia is trying to figure out how her new classroom operates—its customs at the beginning and ending of the school day, rules for using classroom materials, procedures for using the bathroom, and so on. How do you think she feels when she doesn't understand these rules while everyone else does?" (Middle Childhood)

Communicate your concern for others who are hurt, and enlist children's support in caring for these individuals.

- A preschool teacher sympathizes with a child who has skinned his knee. She brings out the first-aid kit and asks another child to find a bandage as she applies the antiseptic. (Early Childhood)
- A high school English teacher walks over to Abril and another student, Maddie, who has recently broken her leg. "Good morning, young ladies. Today we're going to be doing a few activities that will involve moving around the room. Abril, would you mind helping Maddie carry her belongings when we shift seats?" (Late Adolescence)

Acknowledge children's good deeds.

- When a third-grade teacher notices a child helping a classmate who doesn't understand an assignment, she comments, "Thank you for helping Amanda, Jack. You're always ready to lend a hand!" (Middle Childhood)
- In an advising session with Jerald, a middle school teacher asks him about his goals for the year. The teacher is delighted to hear about Jerald's volunteer work as a swim instructor for children with physical disabilities. The teacher encourages him, "Jerald, that's good work. Can you write a story for the school newspaper? You can talk about how rewarding the experience is and let students know that there are chances for them to volunteer as well." (Early Adolescence)

Ask children to brainstorm approaches to solving social and moral dilemmas.

- A middle school teacher presents this situation to his class: "Imagine that one of your classmates comes up to you and asks if she can copy your homework. You don't want to let her copy it. After all, she won't learn what her teacher wanted her to learn by copying someone else's work. But you also don't want to make her angry or upset.

How might you refuse her request while also keeping her friendship?" (Early Adolescence)
- A boy in a middle school literature class is doing a class project on a book he recently read. He downloads a pirated copy of the movie that was based on the book. His teacher comments that showing a scene from the movie could inspire a lot of interesting discussion but worries about violating the rights of people who made the movie. His teacher asks him to think about how he might achieve his goal of showing a portion of the movie while not violating anyone's rights or doing anything illegal. The boy says he will look into finding a non-pirated source of the clip. (Early Adolescence)

Give concrete feedback about appropriate and inappropriate social behaviors.

- A fifth-grade teacher takes Marshall aside after he exercises good self-restraint during a difficult social interaction. Previously impulsive and aggressive, Marshall counted to 10 and walked away after Tanner called him a "douchebag." The teacher recognized the self-control Marshall showed: "Way to go, Marshall. What Tanner did was wrong, and you handled the situation well by controlling your temper." (Middle Childhood)
- During a cooperative learning activity, a high school teacher notices that the members of one cooperative group are getting increasingly angry. After briefly listening to their discussion, the teacher reminds them, "As we agreed yesterday, it's okay to criticize ideas, but it's *not* okay to criticize people." (Late Adolescence)

Encourage children and adolescents to think carefully before acting in difficult social situations.

- A soccer coach finds that several of her 9-year-old players react impulsively to any provocation. They might hit or yell at another player who unintentionally bumps into them on the playing field. The coach teaches the athletes four steps to follow in such situations: (a) Think about what just happened, (b) list three different ways to respond, (c) predict what might happen with each response, and (d) choose the best response. (Middle Childhood)
- With a rise in bullying in their school, teachers talk with children about what bullying is and how everyone can handle situations of being a victim of or bystander to harassment. One teacher tells her class, "Of course, no one needs to put up with bullying. If someone is picking on you, you can tell that person to stop it, but it's also important to step in when you see *someone else* being bullied. Say something. Tell the bully it's not right." (Middle Childhood)

should come into contact with other prosocial models as well. Teachers might invite public servants or members of charitable organizations to talk with students about the many intangible rewards of community service work (Honig, 2009). Teachers can also provide literature with prosocial models (Nucci, 2009). One example is Harper Lee's *To Kill a Mockingbird*, set in the highly segregated and racially charged Alabama of the 1930s, in which a lawyer defends an African American man falsely accused of raping a white woman and exemplifies a willingness to fight for social justice.

- **Give concrete guidelines for behavior.** Children should consistently hear the message that they must handle their conflicts non-violently. One way to communicate this message is to establish firm rules that prohibit physical aggression and possession of weapons. Behaviors that cause psychological harm—malicious gossip, prejudicial remarks, sexual harassment, intimidation, ostracism, and so on—must also be off-limits. And adults must consistently enforce these rules in the classroom, on the playground, in extracurricular activities, and elsewhere (Juvonen, Nishina, & Graham, 2000; Learning First Alliance, 2001).

- **Label appropriate behaviors as they occur.** Teachers can heighten children's awareness of effective social skills by identifying and validating behaviors that reflect those skills (Sanders, 2010; Vorrath, 1985; Wittmer & Honig, 1994). A teacher might say, "Thank you for *sharing* your art materials so helpfully" or "I think that you two were able to write a more imaginative short story by *cooperating* on the project." Researchers have found, too, that describing children as having desirable characteristics (generosity, empathy, etc.) has beneficial effects (Grusec & Redler, 1980; R. S. L. Mills & Grusec, 1989). Eight-year-olds who are told "You're the kind of person who likes to help others whenever you can" are more likely to share their belongings with others later on.

- **Integrate occasions for caring for others into the curriculum.** A preschool teacher might set up a dramatic play area for an animal shelter, doctor's office, baby's room, grocery store, or other theme that might elicit compassionate behavior. A teacher might also offer subtle suggestions for the theme: "My Grandma is preparing food baskets to take to people in need. I think I'll help her by buying some canned goods at your grocery store" (Sanders, 2010, p. 51). A school might sponsor an annual used clothing drive for individuals in the community who are homeless or abused, and a teacher might take a field trip with his class to visit senior citizens at a local retirement home and take them artwork (Sanders, 2010).

- **Plan cooperative activities.** When youngsters participate in cooperative activities rather than in competitive ones, aggressive behaviors tend to be infrequent (Bay-Hinitz, Peterson, & Quilitch, 1994; C. Howe, 2010). In cooperative learning activities, youngsters can practice help-giving, help-seeking, and conflict-resolution skills (Tolmie et al., 2010; Webb & Farivar, 1994). Furthermore, cooperative tasks that require a number of different skills can foster an appreciation for the various strengths that children with diverse backgrounds are likely to contribute (E. G. Cohen, 1994; Lotan, 2006). Cooperative activities are usually most successful when children have a structure to follow (e.g., when each group member is given a specific role to perform) and are given some guidelines about appropriate group behavior (E. G. Cohen, 1994; C. Howe, 2010; Webb & Palincsar, 1996). Certainly children should be told that disagreement is permissible but hitting, shoving, and calling one another derogatory names are not.

> **Preparing for Your Licensure Examination**
> Your teaching test might ask you about fostering prosocial behavior and discouraging aggressive behavior as part of a positive learning environment.

- **Document the circumstances of an aggressive child's behavior.** If a child regularly exhibits hurting behaviors, an adult should observe and record the forms that the aggression takes (e.g., Is the child biting, pushing, or name calling?) and the kinds of situations in which it occurs (e.g., Has the child planned the aggressive act in order to gain resources or prestige, or alternatively does the child seem to be reacting out of frustration? Does he or she choose the same victim or a different child each time? Is there a particular time of day or setting in which the child is prone to act out?). This information can then be used to formulate a plan to discourage acts of aggression and teach the child missing skills. For example, a teacher might make extra efforts to calm a child down who gets unsettled during transitions between lessons. Another teacher might coach a boy in the skill of compromise because he typically grabs toys rather than taking turns or sharing.

- **Nurture delayed abilities when children are particularly aggressive.** Children who display reactive aggression need practice in coping effectively with anger and identifying individuals' motivations and perspectives in various social situations (Hubbard et al., 2010). Children who exhibit proactive aggression need practice in productive social skills, including negotiation. Because proactively aggressive children also tend to be somewhat callous and unemotional in their interactions with others, adults also need to encourage them to act with consideration to the feelings of others.

• **Develop a peer mediation program.** Children and adolescents alike often benefit from **peer mediation** training that teaches them how to intervene effectively in their peers' interpersonal disputes (Daunic & Smith, 2010; Deutsch, 1993). In such training, youngsters learn how to help their peers resolve conflicts by asking opposing sides to express their differing points of view and then work together to devise a reasonable resolution. In one study (D. W. Johnson, Johnson, Dudley, Ward, & Magnuson, 1995), students in grades 2 through 5 were trained to help peers resolve interpersonal conflicts by asking the opposing sides to do the following:

1. Define the conflict (the problem).
2. Explain their own perspectives and needs.
3. Explain the *other* side's perspectives and needs.
4. Identify at least three possible solutions to the conflict.
5. Reach an agreement that addresses the needs of both parties.

Students took turns serving as mediator for their classmates, such that everyone had experience resolving the conflicts of others. As a result, the students more frequently resolved their *own* interpersonal conflicts in ways that addressed the needs of both parties, and they were less likely to ask for adult intervention, than were students who had not had mediation training.

Peer mediation is most effective when youngsters of diverse ethnic backgrounds, socioeconomic groups, and achievement levels all serve as mediators. Furthermore, it is typically most useful for relatively small, short-term interpersonal problems (hurt feelings, conflicts over use of limited academic resources, etc.). Even the most proficient of peer mediators may be ill prepared to handle conflicts that reflect deep-seated and emotionally charged behaviors, such as conflicts that involve sexual harassment or homophobia (Casella, 2001; K. M. Williams, 2001).

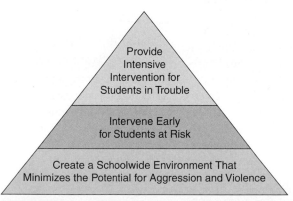

FIGURE 14-1   A three-level approach to preventing aggression and violence in schools. *Based on a figure in Safeguarding Our Children: An Action Guide (p. 3) by K. Dwyer and D. Osher, 2000, Washington, DC: U.S. Departments of Education and Justice, American Institutes for Research.*

peer mediation
Approach to conflict resolution in which one child or adolescent (the mediator) asks peers in conflict to express their differing viewpoints and then work together to identify an appropriate compromise.

Creating a Safe School Environment

Students can learn and achieve at optimal levels at school only if they know they are physically and psychologically safe. To be truly effective in combating aggression and violence at school, teachers and administrators must attack it on the three levels that are depicted graphically in Figure 14-1 (Dwyer & Osher, 2000; Hyman et al., 2006; H. M. Walker et al., 1996).

Level I: Creating a Nonviolent School Environment

One-shot "antiviolence" campaigns have little lasting effect on school aggression and violence (Burstyn & Stevens, 2001). Instead, creating a peaceful, nonviolent school environment must be a long-term effort that includes the following strategies:

• Make a joint, schoolwide commitment to supporting *all* students' academic and social success.
• Provide a challenging and engaging curriculum.
• Form caring, trusting faculty–student relationships.
• Insist on genuine and equal respect—among students as well as faculty—for people of diverse backgrounds, races, and ethnicities.
• Establish schoolwide policies and practices that foster appropriate behavior (e.g., give clear guidelines for behavior, consistently apply consequences for infractions, deliver instruction in effective social interaction and problem-solving skills).
• Involve students in decision making about school policies and procedures.
• Provide mechanisms through which students can communicate their concerns openly and without fear of reprisal.

- Emphasize prosocial behaviors (e.g., sharing, helping, cooperation).
- Establish close working relationships with community agencies and families.
- Openly discuss safety issues.
  (Burstyn & Stevens, 2001; Dwyer & Osher, 2000; Dwyer, Osher, & Warger, 1998; Gregory et al., 2010; Learning First Alliance, 2001; Meehan, Hughes, & Cavell, 2003; Morrison, Furlong, D'Incau, & Morrison, 2004; Pellegrini, 2002)

Many of these strategies have surfaced at one place or another in this book.[8] The final strategy on the list—an open discussion of safety issues—encompasses a variety of more specific techniques. For example, school faculty members should:

- Explain what bullying is (i.e., that it involves harassing and intimidating peers who cannot easily defend themselves) and why it is unacceptable.
- Solicit students' input on potentially unsafe areas (e.g., an infrequently used restroom or back stairwell) that require more faculty supervision.
- Convey willingness to hear students' complaints about troublesome classmates (such complaints can provide important clues about which students are most in need of assistance and intervention).

Communication with students should be a two-way street so that students' misconceptions about bullying can be cleared up and adults in turn can learn about students' experiences with aggression at school. In one study, a student alerted adults to areas they should be watching more carefully, " . . . some of the bullying happens near the portables [portable classrooms] because they're out of sight and there's not really any teachers usually on the grass for duty, they're usually on the pavement" (C. E. Cunningham, Cunningham, Ratcliffe, & Vaillancourt, 2010, p. 325). Another student revealed that students did not interpret anti-bullying policies as pertaining to relational aggression as was intended by adults, "I think we need to like really put it out there that like gossiping and all that stuff is like bullying. Like it's a form of bullying. Like I just learned that this year, that gossiping and I'm like really trying to stop. But you know, girls, it's really hard" (C. E. Cunningham et al., 2010, p. 328).

Level II: Intervening Early for Students at Risk

Students are at risk for negative adjustment in school, as well as in life more generally, when they use aggression often, exhibit poor coping skills, or are rejected by peers.[9] Effective interventions for students at risk cannot be a one-size-fits-all approach but must instead be tailored to individual students' strengths and needs. For some students it might take the form of social skills training. In other cases it might mean getting students actively involved in school clubs or extracurricular activities. In still others it may require well-planned, systematic efforts to encourage and reinforce productive behaviors. But regardless of their nature, interventions are more effective when they occur *early* in the game—before students go too far down the path of antisocial behavior—and when they are developed by a multidisciplinary team of teachers and other professionals who bring various areas of expertise to the planning table (Dryfoos, 1997; Dwyer & Osher, 2000).

Level III: Providing Intensive Intervention for Students in Trouble

When left unchecked, aggressive tendencies sometimes escalate into serious violence. For a variety of reasons, minor interventions will not always be sufficient when students are predisposed to be exceptionally violent. For instance, some students have serious mental illnesses (e.g., schizophrenia, bipolar disorder) that interfere with their ability to cope appropriately with everyday frustrations.[10] Typically, schools must work closely and collaboratively with other community groups—perhaps mental health clinics, police and probation officers, and social services—to help students at high risk for aggression and violence (Dwyer & Osher, 2000; M. T. Greenberg et al., 2003; Hyman et al., 2006).

Preparing for Your Licensure Examination

Your teaching test might ask you about enlisting the support of guidance counselors, school psychologists, other school personnel, and professionals in the community when working with potentially violent youth.

---

[8]We build on these tactics further in Chapter 15.

[9]We examine the nature of peer rejection in Chapter 15.

[10]Serious emotional problems and behavioral disorders are examined in Chapter 11.

Dear Diary,

Today there was a tragedy at school. Two people are now no longer with us. All because one person decided to bring a gun to school. This isn't fair to the parents, friends, and relatives of those people who died. My best friend is now gone. How could this happen? Why?

ARTIFACT 14-3 Tragedy at school. Occasionally physical aggression at school has tragic consequences, as shown in one child's diary entry.

Through their daily interactions with students, teachers may notice certain characteristics that suggest a need for professional intervention. Teachers can consult with their principals and other professionals if they notice several of these early warning signs of violence:

- *Social withdrawal.* Over time, a student interacts less and less frequently with teachers and with all or most peers. A student may directly or indirectly express the belief that he or she is friendless, disliked, or unfairly picked on.
- *Rapid decline in academic performance.* A student shows a dramatic change in academic performance and seems unconcerned about doing well. Cognitive and physical factors (e.g., learning disabilities, ineffective study strategies, brain injury) have been ruled out as causes of the decline.
- *Poor coping skills.* A student has little ability to deal effectively with frustration, takes the smallest affront personally, and has trouble bouncing back after minor disappointments. He or she frequently responds with uncontrolled anger to even the slightest injustice and may misdirect anger at innocent bystanders.
- *Sense of superiority, self-centeredness, and lack of empathy.* A student depicts himself or herself as smarter or in some other way better than peers, is preoccupied with his or her own needs, and has little regard for the needs of others.
- *Lengthy grudges.* A student is unforgiving of others' transgressions, even after considerable time has elapsed.
- *Violent themes in drawings and written work.* Violence predominates in a student's artwork, stories, and journal entries, and certain individuals (e.g., a parent or particular classmate) are regularly targeted in these fantasies. (Keep in mind that *occasional* violence in writing and art is not unusual, especially for boys.)
- *Intolerance of individual and group differences.* A student shows intense disdain for and prejudice toward people of a certain race, ethnicity, gender, sexual orientation, religion, or disability.
- *History of violence, aggression, and other discipline problems.* A student has a long record of seriously inappropriate behavior extending over several years.
- *Association with violent peers.* A student associates regularly with a gang or other antisocial peer group.
- *Inappropriate role models.* A student may speak with admiration about Satan, Hitler, Osama bin Laden, or another malevolent figure.
- *Frequent alcohol or drug use.* A student who abuses alcohol or drugs may have reduced self-control; in some cases substance abuse signals significant mental illness.
- *Access to firearms.* A student has easy access to guns and ammunition and may regularly practice using them.
- *Threats of violence.* A student has openly expressed the intent to harm someone else. ***This warning sign alone requires immediate action***. (Dwyer et al., 1998; Lebrun, 2009; Ormrod, 2011; O'Toole, 2000; U.S. Secret Service National Threat Assessment Center, 2000)

By themselves, most of the signs are unlikely to signal a violent attack, but several of them in combination necessitate consultation with school administrators and specially trained professionals. As we've stated, a child's stated intention to harm someone should always be considered seriously.

Although teachers must be vigilant about signs that a student may be planning to cause harm to others, it is essential that they keep several points in mind. First, despite media reports about school shootings, extreme violence is *very rare* in schools (DeVoe et al., 2003; Garbarino et al., 2002). Unreasonable paranoia about potential school violence will prevent teachers from working effectively with students. Second, the great majority of students who exhibit one or a few of the warning signs we've just examined will *not* become violent. Third, many teachers do not have sufficient information or professional training to make reliable judgments about certain aspects of children's personality (e.g., whether children hold grudges) and the nature of their home life (e.g., whether children have access to firearms) (Warnick, Johnson, & Rocha, 2010). And most importantly, a teacher must *never* use the warning signs as a reason to unfairly accuse, isolate, or punish a student (Dwyer et al., 1998). These signs provide a means of getting youngsters help if they need it, not of excluding them from the education that all children and adolescents deserve.

Gang-Related Problems

A frequent source of aggression at some schools is gang-related hostilities. Although gangs are more prevalent in low-income, inner-city schools, they are often found in suburban and rural schools as well (Howell & Lynch, 2000; Sharkey, Shekhtmeyster, Chavez-Lopez, Norris, & Sass, 2010).

The three-level approach to combating school aggression and violence just described goes a long way toward suppressing violent gang activities. Level I activities that ensure children have good relationships at school and access to an engaging curriculum discourage children from joining gangs in the first place (Sharkey et al., 2010). The Level II strategy of encouraging students to take part in appealing extracurricular activities may also preempt gang initiation (Sharkey et al., 2010). As suggested in our discussion of Level III, students who are already exhibiting violent behavior need intensive intervention to acquire productive coping skills and the necessary motivation to avoid overtures from gang leaders.

It is also important to limit the influence of gangs already present within the school setting. Educators can take measures to communicate that schools are neutral territories that do not favor one gang or another and, in fact, prohibit signs of gang affiliation. Recommended strategies include the following:

- Develop, communicate, and enforce clear-cut policies regarding potential threats to school safety.
- Identify the specific nature and scope of gang activity in the student population.
- Forbid clothing, jewelry, and behaviors that signify membership in a particular gang (e.g., bandanas, shoelaces in gang colors, certain hand signs).[11]
- Actively mediate between-gang and within-gang disputes. (Kodluboy, 2004; Sharkey et al., 2010)

In the last of these strategies—mediation— either adults or peers might serve as mediators, provided that they are familiar with the cultures and issues of the gang(s) involved (Kodluboy, 2004).

[11]A potential problem with this strategy is that it may violate students' civil liberties. For guidance on how to walk the line between ensuring students' safety and giving them reasonable freedom of expression, see Kodluboy (2004) and Rozalski and Yell (2004).

SUMMARY

Moral Reasoning

An ability to distinguish between right and wrong emerges early in life and continues to develop over time. Infants are clearly uncomfortable when they witness others being hurt. Most preschoolers have some awareness that actions that cause significant physical or psychological harm are wrong even if an authority figure tells them otherwise. Children of this age are able to distinguish transgressions that violate moral rules from conventional social practices and from other decisions that can be considered a matter of personal choice.

As children get older, they progress in their understanding of fairness and develop an increasing capacity to feel guilt, shame, and empathy about moral wrongdoings. As they advance in cognitive skills, and especially as they become capable of abstract thought, young people reason about moral issues and dilemmas in more sophisticated ways, and they are more likely to behave in accordance with general moral principles. Even at the high school level, however, youngsters do not always take the moral high road, because personal needs and self-interests often enter into their moral decisions.

To some degree, different cultures foster different moral values, but virtually all societies recognize the importance of fairness, justice, and concern for others. Adults can promote young people's moral development by explaining why certain behaviors are unacceptable (in that they cause harm to another or jeopardize another's rights and needs), engaging youngsters in discussions about moral issues and dilemmas, exposing them to diverse and slightly more advanced moral perspectives, and getting them actively involved in service to others.

Prosocial Behavior and Aggression

Most children become increasingly prosocial and less aggressive over the years, with such changes being partly the result of their growing capacity for perspective taking, empathy, and sympathy. However, some children and adolescents display troublesome levels of physical or relational aggression, perhaps partly as a result of temperamental characteristics, aggressive role models at home or in the community, or counterproductive social cognitive processes. These youngsters often need planned interventions to get them on the road to more productive relationships with others.

APPLYING CONCEPTS IN CHILD DEVELOPMENT

The exercises in this section will help you build your ability to apply your knowledge of child development in fostering the moral development of children.

Improving Your Observation Skills

On page 544, you examined a photograph of a father explaining why his little girl's misbehavior was wrong and were asked, "*How might the father's style of parenting affect the little girl's moral development?*" The father and daughter appear to have an affectionate relationship, which would inspire the little girl to accept her father's advice. By explaining to his daughter why her misbehavior was wrong, especially insofar as her brother has become upset, the father is using the parenting tactic of *induction*. Induction is an effective strategy for fostering children's moral development and in this situation may result in the girl becoming more considerate of her little brother in the future.

On page 551, you examined a photograph of two young girls arguing over who can play with the doll and were asked, "*How do the girls exhibit typical aggressive behavior for children of their age?*" Conflicts over toys are common during the preschool years. The two girls are arguing but their disagreement does not escalate into physical fighting. Physical aggression declines during early childhood as children learn to handle disagreements with words.

Practicing for Your Licensure Examination

Many teaching tests require students to use what they have learned about child development in responses to brief vignettes and multiple-choice questions. You can practice for your licensure examination by reading about gang mediation at one school and answering a series of questions.

Gang Mediation

Read the case and then answer the questions that follow it.

At Washington Middle School, many students belonged to one of several gangs that seemed to "rule the school." Fights among rival gangs were common, and nongang members were frequent victims of harassment. School officials tried a variety of strategies to keep the gang-related behavior in check—mandating dress codes, conducting regular weapon searches, counseling or suspending chronic trouble makers, and so on—but without success.

In desperation, two school counselors suggested that the school implement a peer mediation program. The program began by focusing on the three largest gangs, which were responsible for most of the trouble on school grounds. Interpersonal problems involving two or more gangs would be brought to a mediation team, comprised of five school faculty members and three representatives from each of the three gangs. The team would abide by the following rules:

1. Really try to solve the problem.
2. No name-calling or put-downs.
3. No interrupting.
4. Be as honest as possible.
5. No weapons or acts of intimidation.
6. All sessions to be confidential until an agreement is reached or mediation is called off. (Sanchez & Anderson, 1990, p. 54)

All team members would have to agree to and sign off on any decisions that the team reached. However, participation in the process was voluntary, and students could withdraw at any time.

To lay the groundwork for productive discussions, faculty members of the mediation team met separately with each of the three gangs to establish feelings of rapport and trust and to explain how the mediation process would work. After considerable discussion and venting of hostile intergroup feelings, many gang members agreed to try the new approach. Meanwhile, the buzz throughout the student body was that "something unusual and special was happening" at Washington.

Mediation sessions were held in a conference room, with team members sitting around a large table so that they could maintain eye contact with one another. In the first session, common grievances were aired. Students agreed that they didn't like being put down or intimidated, that they worried about their physical safety, and that they all wanted one another's respect. Curiously, each gang also complained that the school administration showed preferential treatment for the *other* gangs. Through all of this, the students got one message loud and clear: They could speak freely and honestly at the meeting, without fear of reprisal from faculty members or other students.

In several additional meetings during the next 2 weeks, the team reached agreement that a number of behaviors would be unacceptable at school: There would be no put-downs, name-calling, hateful stares, threats, shoving, or gang graffiti. After the final meeting, each gang was separately called into the conference room. Its representatives on the mediation team explained the agreement, and other members of the gang were asked to sign it. Despite some skepticism, most members of all three gangs signed the agreement.

A month later, it was clear that the process had been successful, at least in improving the school's social climate over the short term. Members of rival gangs nodded pleasantly to one another or gave one another a "high five" sign as they passed in the hall. Gang members no longer felt compelled to hang out in groups for safety's sake. Members of two of the gangs were seen playing soccer together one afternoon. And there had been no gang-related fights all month. (case described in Sanchez & Anderson, 1990)[a]

Constructed-Response Question

1. Why do you think the mediation approach was successful when other approaches had failed? Drawing on what you've learned about moral development, identify at least three possible reasons.

Multiple-Choice Questions

2. Considering the recommendations in this chapter on creating a safe school environment, which of the following strategies might reasonably supplement the mediation program used in this school?

   a. Look carefully at the curriculum to make sure it is engaging for students.
   b. Advise students individually about extracurricular activities that might be of personal interest to them.
   c. Provide individual counseling for students who have previously exhibited violent behavior.
   d. All of the above.

3. Given what you learned about aggression, which of the following explanations most accurately accounts for the reasons that children in the gangs might have become aggressive?

   a. As is the case with all children, these gang members can be persuaded to do anything depending on what others want them to do.
   b. The children were probably affected by a combination of factors, perhaps including exposure to parents and peers who handle their conflicts aggressively, the presence of individual temperaments that put them at risk

for responding impulsively, and the children's own interpersonal habits and interpretations of social events.
   c. The children most certainly had inferior genes, which can be considered fully responsible for the children's wrongdoings.
   d. None of the above.

Once you have answered these questions, compare your responses with those presented in Appendix A.

Improving Your Ability to Interpret Children's Artifacts and Reflections

Consider what you've learned about moral development as you analyze the following artwork. written by an 11-year-old girl.

Remembering 9/11

On September 11, 2001, several thousand innocent Americans lost their lives in a series of terrorist attacks. During the following months, scenes from the tragedy were shown repeatedly on television and in magazines. After seeing these images, many children expressed deep-seated concerns. Children wondered if they themselves were safe, asked a lot of questions, and wanted to help those who lost loved ones. In schools, teachers reassured children, answered their questions, kept up familiar routines, and arranged for the children to send artwork and cards to survivors and rescue workers.

Several months after the terrorists' attacks, elementary art teacher Jeanette Smith Anthos noticed that children in her school continued to be preoccupied with the events of September 11th (Anthos, 2004). She observed that children in her classes regularly drew pictures of explosions and destruction. She realized that the children needed an outlet to express their fears, sadness, and outrage about the injustices and horrors of the tragedy.

To structure her art lesson, Jeanette showed the children Pablo Picasso's *Guernica,* a painting of the 1937 bombings of a small Basque village,[12] and encouraged the children to talk about their present concerns about September 11th. She also showed her students how Picasso had conveyed the emotions of people affected by the bombing. She then asked the children to create their own drawings in memory of September 11th, communicating emotions and using symbols. Each child sat down with a regular pencil, a set of colored pencils, a black fine-tip marker, and a 12″ × 18″ piece of white drawing paper.

The children drew poignant pictures. Third-grader Antonio Villanueva created the picture shown here. If you have seen Picasso's *Guernica*, you might notice that Antonio has closely emulated Picasso's way of depicting human faces. As you examine Antonio's drawing, consider these questions:

- Does Antonio seem to interpret the events of September 11th as primarily a moral or conventional transgression?
- What emotions does Antonio convey in his drawing?
- What symbols does Antonio include in his art?

---

[a] List of Rules from "Gang Mediation: A Process That Works" by F. Sanchez and M. L. Anderson, from PRINCIPAL, Vol. 69, Issue 5, pp. 54. Copyright © 1990 by National Association of Elementary School Principals. Reprinted with permission. All rights reserved.

[12] Picasso's *Guernica* can be found on many Internet sites. To locate one of them, type the keywords "Guernica" and "Picasso" into a search engine such as Google or Yahoo!

"Remembering 9/11 Artifact" by Antonio Villanueva, from "The Healing Power of Art," from SCHOOL ARTS, September 2004, Edited by Jeanette Smith Anthos, Vol. 103(10), p. 47. Copyright © 2004 by Jeanette Smith Anthos. Reprinted with permission.

Once you have analyzed Antonio's art, compare your ideas with those presented in Appendix B. For further practice in analyzing children's artifacts and reflections, go to the Activities and Applications section in Chapter 14 of MyEducationLab.

Key Concepts

moral development (p. 534)
moral dilemma (p. 535)
preconventional morality (p. 535)
conventional morality (p. 536)
postconventional morality (p. 537)
moral transgression (p. 538)
conventional transgression (p. 538)

personal matter (p. 538)
guilt (p. 540)
shame (p. 540)
sympathy (p. 540)
distributive justice (p. 541)
induction (p. 543)
justice orientation (p. 544)

care orientation (p. 544)
service learning (p. 548)
prosocial behavior (p. 548)
aggression (p. 548)
physical aggression (p. 549)
relational aggression (p. 549)
reactive aggression (p. 551)

proactive aggression (p. 551)
bully (p. 551)
hostile attributional bias (p. 552)
peer mediation (p. 560)

PEARSON
myeducationlab

Now go to www.myeducationlab.com to:
- Take a Quiz to test your mastery of chapter objectives.
- Study chapter content with an individualized Study Plan.
- Deepen your understanding of particular concepts and principles with Review, Remediation, and Enrichment Exercises.
- Apply what you have learned in the chapter to your work with children in Building Teaching Skills and Dispositions exercises.
- Observe children and their unique contexts in Video Examples.

Chapter Fifteen

Peers, Schools, and Society

CASE STUDY: Life at School

Margaret Zoller Booth and Heather Chase Sheehan are interested in young adolescents' experiences at school and decide to ask 11- and 12-year-old students in Cleveland, Ohio and Manchester, England to describe their perceptions. In Cleveland, participating students attend one of two schools serving students from kindergarten through eighth grade or one of two middle schools. In Manchester, contributing adolescents are in one of three secondary schools. Margaret and Heather also conduct their own observations of the schools.

The ambiance of Schools 1 through 7 varies with the quality of the facilities, nature of the disciplinary policies, and age range of students served. Margaret and Heather find Schools 1 and 2, the two American middle schools, to be especially stark environments. As students enter the property they see chain-linked fences, pavement surfaces, and not a single patch of green grass. The insides of these schools are also dismal:

> Both buildings convey the feeling and appearance of a prison when a visitor arrives, first needing to be buzzed in through the front locked doors, then being given an approving look by a security guard, and finally signing in at the front-office desk. The buildings inside are dark as a result of the dark brick walls, low ceilings, and limited windows. The windows that are available on the outside walls of the buildings are so dark with soot or purposeful shading that very little, if any, natural light shines through.
>
> In addition to the gloomy atmosphere, the modus operandi of the day for both of these middle schools is control. The control of student behavior is apparent from the ever-present security guards on each floor, beeping walkie-talkies on all teachers and staff, automatically locking classroom doors, and lines of students outside the principal's office waiting for disciplinary action. On any given day, an alarm can sound and a "lock-out" ensues. Any student left standing in the hall, locked out of a classroom, immediately reports for punishment[a] (Booth & Sheehan, 2008, p. 730)

In comparison, the American elementary schools seem bright, warm, and inviting. One of these schools is a large brick building with attractive chandeliers and large windows. A few additional features of the school make the environment comfortable for students' learning:

> The lightly painted walls help reveal what is left of the beauty in the brick and old wood floors and doors. Touch-up paint is needed here and there, and ceiling tiles need replacing, however, there is an air of nurturing comfort to this building not found in School building 1 or 2. . . . No guards line the hallways and no constant walkie-talkies, or lines of students fighting exist outside the principal's office. Only an occasional student is sent to the office with an issue to be resolved (i.e., lateness, feeling ill, forgot article)[a] (Booth & Sheehan, 2008, p. 731).

Students of course have their own ideas about the schools. They occasionally comment on the facilities, for example suggesting that repairs are needed. Even more often, students talk about their relationships with people there. Friendships are important to students but other peers are also influential, particularly when they are aggressive. One boy in Cleveland laments, "I wish they would stop all the profanity, bullying, and fights in school"[a] (p. 734). Similarly, a girl in Manchester is saddened by aggression from peers: "People start bullying me—like calling me names in the classroom"[a] (p. 734).

When asked about any changes that they would like to see at their school, many adolescents comment on routines they like or dislike. Frequent suggestions are offered about cafeteria food, dress codes, and school uniforms. And the adolescents have plenty to say about school management, which they perceive as needing a thorough overall:

> Students complained, "Detentions don't work" and "Today's discipline does not work." Others said, "Nobody cares about suspensions" and there should be "No lockouts—it's just embarrassing." Rules having to do with lateness were also seen as "unfair" as students suggested, "Let the students go late to class" and "Let the kids use the bathroom sometimes"[a] (p. 735).

- What varying experiences do different students have at school?
- What characteristics of schools seem to support students?

[a]Excerpts from "Perceptions of People and Place: Young Adolescents' Interpretation of Their Schools in the United States and the United Kingdom," by Margaret Zoller Booth and Heather Chase Sheehan, from JOURNAL OF ADOLESCENT RESEARCH, 2008, 23(6), 722–744. Copyright © 2008 by Margaret Zoller Booth and Heather Chase Sheehan. Reprinted with permission of SAGE Publications.

OBJECTIVES

15.1: Characterize the development of friendships and other peer relationships during childhood and adolescence.

15.2: Explain what teachers and other practitioners can do to facilitate productive social skills and peer relationships in children.

15.3: Discuss three characteristics of school environments that positively affect children and adolescents.

15.4: Describe how a society's services, the media, and interactive technologies influence children's learning and behavior.

As children grow, they spend an increasing amount of time in social settings outside the family—with classmates and teachers at school, friends in the neighborhood, and adults in the community. In the opening case study, some students learn in cheerful buildings and enjoy good relationships with classmates and teachers while a few less fortunate students spend time in gloomy schools with peers who torment them and teachers who oppress their inner spirits. Whatever their experiences, students are deeply affected by the atmosphere at school. Generally, schools support students to the extent that they successfully engage their interests, teach them academic skills, build their confidence, supply sociable peers, and establish a sense of community. In this chapter you will find that schools can be positive catalysts for children's growth and that other elements of society, including peers, the media, interactive technologies, and after-school programs, also have the potential to promote healthy development.

PEERS

Peers, people of approximately the same age and position within a social group, make distinct and important contributions to children's development. In the next few pages, we examine various aspects of peer relationships, including their functions for children, their basis in emerging social skills, and the characteristics of different types of peer relationships. We also examine strategies adults can use to foster children's peer relationships.

Functions of Peer Relationships

Companionship with peers is one of children's top priorities. From a developmental standpoint, peer relationships serve multiple functions.

ARTIFACT 15-1 I had Katherine over yesterday. Seven-year-old Madison reveals her strong emotional bond with her friend, Katherine. Peers are desired companions beginning in early childhood.

Peers offer emotional support. The presence of familiar peers helps children relax in new environments and cope with mild aggression (Asher & Parker, 1989; Hartup, 2009; Wentzel, 1999). Although some youngsters adjust quite successfully to troubling situations on their own, as a general rule children and adolescents who have peers to turn to have higher self-esteem, fewer emotional problems (such as depression), and higher school achievement (Buhrmester, 1992; Erath, Flanagan, Bierman, & Tu, 2010; D. Schwartz, Gorman, Duong, & Nakamoto, 2008).

Peers serve as partners for practicing social skills. When children interact with their peers, they enter social exchanges on a more or less equal footing: No single individual has absolute power. By satisfying their own needs while also maintaining productive relationships with others, children acquire such fundamental skills as social perspective taking, self-regulation, and effective conflict resolution skills (Bierman, 2004; Selman, 2003; Sutton-Smith, 1979).[1]

Peers socialize one another. Children and adolescents socialize one another in several ways (Hartup, 2009; Rubin, Bukowski, & Parker, 2006; A. M. Ryan, 2000). Peers define options for leisure time, perhaps jumping rope in a vacant lot, getting together in a study group, or smoking cigarettes on the street corner. They offer new ideas, presenting arguments for becoming a vegetarian or playing a new computer game. They serve as role models, showing what is possible and what is admirable. Peers reinforce one another for acting in ways deemed appropriate for their age, gender, ethnic group, and cultural background. And they sanction one another, perhaps through ridicule, gossip, or ostracism, for stepping beyond acceptable bounds.

[1]Social perspective taking and self-regulation are examined in Chapters 12 and Chapter 13, respectively.

Peers contribute to a sense of identity. Association with peers helps children decide who they are and what they want to become (Clemens, Shipp, & Pisarik, 2008; Forthun et al., 2006; Hartup, 2009). Especially as they enter adolescence, young people are attracted to particular groups that allow them to explore certain parts of themselves. For instance, when Jeanne's son Alex was in middle school, he and his friends were avid skateboarders and spent long hours at a local skateboard ramp practicing and refining their technique. Alex proudly labeled himself a "skater" and wore the extra-large T-shirts and wide-legged pants that conveyed this identity.

"I KNOW WHAT YOU MEAN." Adolescents find it reassuring to talk with peers about everyday experiences.

Peers help one another make sense of their lives. During daily conversations, children share ideas that help one another interpret confusing and troubling events. Children may talk about similar experiences in getting along with a classmate, dealing with a difficult teacher, or being punished by parents. Such informally instructive conversations occur throughout childhood but take on special significance during adolescence, when teenagers are changing rapidly and appreciate reassurance from peers facing similar challenges (Richard & Schneider, 2005; Seltzer, 1982; H. S. Sullivan, 1953).

Peers achieve common ways of looking at the world. As an outcome of their interactions over time, children come to share views on the world. A long-standing group of children works out a general set of rules (often unspoken), expectations, and interpretations—a **peer culture**—that influences how group members behave (P. Davidson & Youniss, 1995; Ehrlich & Blum-Kulka, 2010; Killeya-Jones, Costanzo, Malone, Quinlan, & Miller-Johnson, 2007). You can read more about this aspect of children's lives in the Development and Culture feature "Peer Culture in the United States and Italy."

Social Skills

Not all peer relationships are alike, of course, and children are most likely to develop productive relationships when they have learned a range of **social skills**, strategies that facilitate effective interaction with others. Children who are adept with social skills are generally perceptive of other people's needs, able to establish and maintain high-quality relationships, and inclined to curb their own aggression. In other words, they are *socially competent* (Vaughn et al., 2009). Compared to children who are deficient in social skills, children who are socially competent achieve at higher levels academically, have higher self-esteem, are happier at school, exhibit fewer problem behaviors, and have better school attendance records (Bornstein, Hahn, & Haynes, 2010; Guay et al., 1999; Wentzel, 1999).

Developmental Trends in Social Skills

Socially competent children acquire a series of social skills as they interact with peers during each of the developmental periods.

Infancy (birth–2 years). Infants acquire some basic social skills during interactions with parents. Infants gradually are able to coordinate their focus of attention with adults by sharing eye contact, smiles, and utterances. In the latter half of the first year, infants who spend time with other small children may babble and smile at one another or look where the others point (Eckerman, 1979; Mueller & Silverman, 1989; S. T. Williams, Ontai, & Mastergeorge, 2010). As toddlers, they may imitate one another, offer one another toys, and assist others in simple tasks and play activities (P. L. Harris, 2006; Howes & Matheson, 1992; Meadows, 2010).

Early Childhood (2–6 years). With the capacity for coordinating attention with others well established, young children can interact more effectively with age-mates, especially within the context of play activities. One early researcher identified six different kinds of behaviors that preschool teachers might observe among 2- to 5-year-olds (Parten, 1932). These categories, most of which reflect a continuum of increasing social interaction, are described in the Observation Guidelines table "Observing the Social Aspects of Young Children's Play." Several of the categories are also illustrated in a MyEducationLab video, "Types of Play."

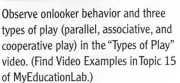

Observe onlooker behavior and three types of play (parallel, associative, and cooperative play) in the "Types of Play" video. (Find Video Examples in Topic 15 of MyEducationLab.)

peer culture
General set of rules, expectations, and interpretations that influence how members of a particular peer group behave.

social skills
Strategies used to interact effectively with others.

DEVELOPMENT IN CULTURE
Peer Culture in the United States and Italy

William Corsaro is a sociologist, a scientist who studies people's interactions in groups. Corsaro's specific interest is in how children relate to one another at school. In a series of *ethnographies* in the United States and Italy, he spent several months and in some cases over a year becoming familiar with preschool children's routines, the subtleties in their exchanges, and the logic of their customs.[a] He gained children's confidence by sitting down beside them, quietly watching and listening, and letting them react to him. Occasionally, he joined in their play, always following their leads.

Children in both societies gradually accepted Corsaro. In the U.S. preschools, the children came to think of Corsaro as "Big Bill," whom they readily welcomed into their playgroups (Corsaro, 2003, p. 7).[b] The children eventually insisted that he sit with them during birthday parties and that their parents include him in plans for cookies, cupcakes, and Valentine cards. In the Italian preschools, children initially treated Corsaro as "an incompetent adult" because of his lack of fluency with the Italian language (Corsaro, 2003, p. 15).[b] These children teased Corsaro when he made mistakes in speaking Italian but also regularly taught him new phrases. Corsaro recalled an early triumph in winning the children over:

> I was sitting on the floor with two boys (Felice and Roberto) and we were racing some toy cars around in circles. Felice was talking about an Italian race car driver as we played, but because he was talking so fast I could understand only part of what he was saying. At one point, however, he raced his car into a wall and it flipped over. Then I clearly heard him say "*Luis è morto*," and I knew this meant, "He's dead." I guessed that Felix must be recounting a tragic accident in some past Grand Prix event. At that moment I remembered and used a phrase that I had learned in my first Italian course: "*Che peccato!*" ("What a pity!"). Looking up in amazement Felice said, "Bill! Bill! *Ha ragione! Bravo Bill!*" ("Bill! Bill! He's right! Way to go, Bill!"). "*Bravo, Bill!*" Roberto chimed in. (Corsaro, 2003, pp. 17–18)[b]

As a result of his extended time with children in both countries, Corsaro gained an insider's perspective on children's *peer cultures* (Corsaro, 2003; Corsaro & Eder, 1990). During their time together, children in the two cultures developed their own informal routines. For example, in one American preschool, children became excited when they heard the characteristic noises of trash collectors attaching the dumpster to a lift. The truck was visible from the top of the jungle gym, and whichever child noticed it coming shouted to the others that the "garbage man" had arrived (Corsaro, 2003, p. 49).[b] Others quickly climbed the bars to get a good look. Corsaro described the first time he viewed the routine:

> The kids were very excited and were imitating the noise of the truck lift: "Whirr!" "Whirr!" "Whirr!" I was surprised to see there were now four more kids on the bars: ten in all, with one more, Barbara, climbing up. I looked around the yard and noted that all but two of the children who were outside were now on the bars. As the dumpster reached its apex and the trash tumbled into the truck, the kids seemed to reach their own peak of excitement. They waved and "whirred" in near

perfect unison. At exactly this point, the garbage man outside the truck looked up and waved back to his admirers. The lift then lowered quickly and the dumpster hit the ground with a loud bang. The outside man unhooked the dumpster and joined his partner in the truck. The kids continued waving and shouting, "Garbage man!" as the driver pulled away, gave a beep of the horn, and steered the truck down the street to the next stop far beyond the sight of the kids" (Corsaro, 2003, pp. 49–50).[b]

Every day the routine was the same, as it was a year later when Corsaro observed a new group of children.

PEER CULTURE IN ITALY. These Italian children are exchanging secrets. Children who spend a lot of time together develop shared understandings and customs.

Themes that regularly guided children's play were those of being scared and finding protection. Children would take turns pretending to be monsters; others would chase or flee from the monsters and find safe haven in a home base. Another concept that pervaded children's play was making friends and protecting fragile friendships. Concerns with loyalty and rivalry were also regularly borne out in interactions among young children.

Finally, children conspired in acts of mischief. For example, children tried to convince teachers that it was acceptable to run inside because they were pretending to be police chasing robbers. Toy weapons were not allowed in school, yet children pretended to shoot one another by pointing and cocking their fingers. A couple of children brought in contraband toys and candy and shared these items with one another out of sight of teachers. Other children regularly shirked their responsibilities at clean-up time by surreptitiously moving from an area that they had messed up to another tidier location in the classroom.

Many aspects of children's peer culture were unknown to the teachers. Although some of children's routines might have been considered objectionable had they been identified, by and large children learned a great deal from their peer culture.

[a]Ethnographies are introduced in Chapter 2.
[b]Excerpts from WE'RE FRIENDS, RIGHT?: INSIDE KIDS' CULTURE by William A. Corsaro. Copyright © 2003 by William A. Corsaro. Reprinted with permission by the National Academy of Sciences, Courtesy of the National Academies Press, Washington, D.C.

OBSERVATION GUIDELINES
Observing the Social Aspects of Young Children's Play

CHARACTERISTIC	LOOK FOR	EXAMPLE	IMPLICATION
Unoccupied Behavior	• *Failure to engage in any activity*, either with or without another individual • *Aimless wandering* • *Quiet sitting and staring*	During free-play time, Donald often retreats to a corner of the play yard, where he sits quietly either running his fingers through the dirt or staring off into space.	Try to engage the child with intriguing toys or other objects, or with a small-group activity. Consult with a specialist if unoccupied behavior is persistent and pervasive despite frequent attempts to engage the child.
Solitary Play	• *Absorption* in one's own playthings • *Apparent lack of awareness* of other children's presence	Although Laura and Erika are sitting next to each other in the sandbox, they are facing in opposite directions. Laura is digging a large hole for her pretend pond, and Erika is making roads with a toy bulldozer for her imaginary city.	Keep in mind that children's independent play has value. On some occasions, present new toys or games that require the participation of two or more children.
Onlooker Behavior	• *Unobtrusive observation* of other children's play activities	As three of his classmates play "store," Jason quietly watches them from the side of the room.	Ask the child if he or she would like to play with the other children. If so, ask the others if the onlooker might join in.
Parallel Play	• *Playing next to another child*, but with little or no interaction • *Similarities in the behaviors of two or more children* who are playing independently near each other	Naticia and Leo are both making "sky-scrapers" with wooden blocks. Sometimes one child looks at what the other is doing, and occasionally one child makes a tower similar to the other's construction	Comment that both children are doing something similar. Gently suggest an enjoyable activity that incorporates what both children are doing, but don't try to force interaction.
Associative Play	• *Some talking and sharing* of objects with another child • *Occasional comments* about what another child is doing	Several children are working at the same table creating different animals from Play-Doh. They occasionally ask for a particular color ("Gimme the red") or make remarks about others' creations ("You made a kitty just like I did").	Keep in mind that associative play is often a productive way for children to get to know one another better. Once children feel comfortable together, you can suggest an activity that would encourage cooperative behaviors.
Cooperative Play	• *Active sharing* of toys and coordination of activities • *Taking on specific roles* related to a common theme	Sheldon sets up a "doctor's office" and Jan comes to visit him with her teddy bear, who has a "sore throat." Sheldon puts a tongue depressor to the bear's mouth and instructs it to "Say 'aahh.'"	Provide a variety of toys and other objects that are best used in group play—balls, props for playing "house" and "store," and so on.

Source: First two columns based on Parten, 1932.

Some developmental trends can be seen in the prevalence of the various kinds of play at different ages. Typically, children become increasingly interactive and cooperative in play activities as they grow older (Gottman, 1983; Howes & Matheson, 1992; Meadows, 2010; Rubin et al., 2006). The imagination and social coordination that characterize cooperative play make it an especially important activity of early childhood.

Yet the other kinds of play also serve important functions for children, especially at the younger ages. Parallel play, though seemingly nonsocial, has a definite social function: Children use it as ways to learn more about peers' interests, initiate conversations, and find common ground for subsequent social interactions (Bakeman & Brownlee, 1980; Gottman, 1983; Rubin et al., 2006).

In one form of cooperative play, *sociodramatic play*, children assume complementary imagined roles and carry out a logical sequence of actions. In the following scenario, we see Eric and Naomi, long-time friends, assuming the roles of husband and wife. Naomi is making plans to go shopping:

N: I'm buying it at a toy store, to buy Eric Fisher a record 'cause he doesn't
      have a. . . .
E: What happened to his old one?

N: It's all broken.

E: How did it get all broken?

N: Ah, a robber stealed it, I think. That's what he said, a robber stealed it.

E: Did he see what the action was? You know my gun is in here, so could you go get my gun? It's right over there, back there, back there, not paper . . . did you get it?

N: Yes, I found the robbers right in the closet.

E: Good, kill 'em.

N: I killed 'em.

E: Already?

N: Yes, so quick they can't believe it. (Gottman, 1986, p. 191)

ARTIFACT 15-2 Our robot. Alex (age 5) and Davis (age 6) shared fantasies that guided them in drawing this picture together. As they worked on the picture, the boys continually listened to one another, built on each other's ideas, and drew from their many past experiences together.

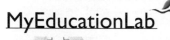

Observe Acadia and Cody coordinating their activities and resolving their differences in the "Physical Activity: Early Childhood" video. (Find Video Examples in Topic 15 of MyEducationLab.)

Sociodramatic play activities contribute in many ways to children's growing social competence. In this kind of play children coordinate their actions and perspectives, share fantasies, take turns, and in other ways consider what a playmate is doing (Meadows, 2010; Rubin et al., 2006). They must agree on individual roles ("I'll be the warrior"; "Okay, I'll be the chief"), props ("The log can be our base"), and rules and guidelines that govern actions ("We'll let Frances play, but she has to be the horse") (Garvey, 1990; Howes & Matheson, 1992).

In the process of playing, children develop skills in assertiveness, negotiation, conflict resolution, and self-regulation (Gioia & Tobin, 2010; Göncü, 1993; Gottman, 1986). Many become increasingly polite in making requests. Whereas a 3-year-old is apt to be a bit bossy ("Give me the red one"; "You hafta . . ."), 5- and 6-year-olds are more likely to use hints and suggestions ("Would you like. . .?" "Let's . . .") (Parkhurst & Gottman, 1986, p. 329). Through negotiating roles and story lines, they discover the advantages of compromise ("I want to be the Mommy, you're the baby"; "No, you were the Mommy last time, so it's *my* turn"; "Okay, but next time I get to be the Mommy"). And children learn how to give one another emotional support, perhaps by voicing approval for one another's actions ("That's pretty") or expressing sympathy for a playmate's distress ("Don't worry about that, it'll come off") (Gottman, 1983, p. 58; Rubin et al., 2006).

In the "Physical Activity: Early Childhood" video in MyEducationLab, you can watch two 4-year-olds, Acadia and Cody, use a variety of strategies to nourish their relationship and prevent any disagreements from escalating. They make explicit reference to their friendship ("Let's go, Cody, my best friend"). They encourage one another to climb ("This is gonna be cool!"). They admit when they're wrong ("Silly me, I forget everything"). And eventually they come to agreement about which slide to go down ("Yeah. Let's do it").

Middle Childhood (6–10 years).   Once children begin elementary school, about 30 percent of their social interactions are with peers (Rubin et al, 2006). As a result of their many social experiences, children become aware that some ways of behaving are acceptable to peers, whereas other ways are not. In the following gossip session, 8-year-old Erica and Mikaila reveal their shared belief that tattling on others is inappropriate:

E: Katie's just a. . . .

M: Tattletale.

E: Yeah, she tells on everything.

M: Yeah. (Gottman & Mettetal, 1986, p. 206; reprinted with permission of Cambridge University Press)

With their growing awareness of other people's opinions, most children become eager to behave in socially acceptable ways. They also become more concerned about equitably resolving conflicts and preserving friendships (Frederickson & Simmonds, 2008; Hartup, 1996; Newcomb & Bagwell, 1995). Not all attempts to resolve conflicts are successful, of course. Most children discover that such strategies as sulking ("I'm going home!"), threatening ("I'm never gonna play with you again!"), and hitting ("Take that!") rarely work. Through experimentation with a variety of strategies and through their growing capacity for social perspective taking, most children become proficient at maintaining amicable relationships with age-mates.

Whereas younger children are apt to get together in groups of two or three and engage in free-flowing fantasy, elementary school children often convene in larger groups and choose games that have established rules. Verbal contests (e.g., "Twenty Questions," "I Spy"), board games, computer games, and team sports are common (Corsaro, 1985; Hartup, 1984; Meadows, 2010). By participating in such activities, children discover how to use rules to their own advantage ("If I put another house on Boardwalk, you have to pay me double the next time you land on it"). They learn how to form alliances with other children ("I'll run behind him, and then you pass me the ball over his head"). And they develop strategies for dealing with ambiguous situations ("It was *in!*" "Are you kidding? It was *out!*" "Okay, we'll say it's out, but next time *I* get to decide!").

Early Adolescence (10–14 years). Once children reach puberty, they increasingly rely on their peers for emotional support as well as recreation (Buchanan & Bowen, 2008; Levitt, Guacci-Franco, & Levitt, 1993; Ryan et al., 1994). Many begin to reveal their innermost thoughts to others, especially to peers during face-to-face conversations and electronically mediated communications (e.g., text-messages and over the Internet) (Basinger et al., 1995; Levitt et al., 1993; Subrahmanyam, Garcia, Harsono, Li, & Lipana, 2009). But even as their tendency for self-disclosure expands, young adolescents become self-conscious about what others might think of them and susceptible to their influence. Age-mates frequently exert **peer pressure** by strongly encouraging adolescents to behave in certain ways and not to behave in others. Youngsters who have poor relationships with their families, live in economically disadvantaged neighborhoods, and base their self-esteem on other people's opinions seem to be especially vulnerable to negative peer pressure (Erwin, 1993; Matjasko, Needham, Grunden, & Farb, 2010; Rudolph et al., 2005). Yet young people obviously make their own choices and may imitate peers' behavior out of their own initiative, as this reflection by a youngster reveals:

> There's all this crap about being accepted into a group and struggling and making an effort to make friends and not being comfortable about your own self-worth as a human being. You're trying very hard to show everyone what a great person you are, and the best way to do that is if everyone else is drinking therefore they think that's the thing to do, then you might do the same thing to prove to them that you have the same values that they do and therefore you're okay. At the same time, the idea of peer pressure is a lot of bunk. What I heard about peer pressure all the way through school is that someone is going to walk up to me and say, "Here, drink this and you'll be cool." It wasn't like that at all. You go somewhere and everyone else would be doing it and you'd think, "Hey, everyone else is doing it and they seem to be having a good time—now why wouldn't I do this?" In that sense, the preparation of the powers that be, the lessons that they tried to drill into me, they were completely off. They had no idea what we are up against. (C. Lightfoot, 1992, p. 240)

Because much of the motivation to conform to peers' standards for behavior comes from within rather than from other people, young people need to gain a firm sense of their own identity and preferences (Hartup, 1983; Owens, 1996). Given the productive and destructive behaviors that many adolescents are exposed to, responding appropriately to temptations from peers is an important social skill for adolescents to learn.

Another challenge that adolescents tackle is finding a comfortable niche within a complex social environment. Young adolescents have a tendency to categorize other people, especially their peers. They are apt to pigeonhole classmates into such groups as "brains," "jocks," "skaters," and "geeks" and to affiliate with the groups they perceive to be a close match with their own interests and values (B. B. Brown & Dietz, 2009; J. R. Harris, 1995; Pipher, 1994). Often, young adolescents divide into racial or ethnic groups, even if they have previously mingled freely with one another in the elementary school grades. To some extent,

ARTIFACT 15-3 **Making peace.** Ten-year-old Jacob drew a child getting into an argument with a friend and then coming to a mutually acceptable solution. In his, artwork Jacob reveals his awareness that arguing with friends can be unpleasant, but that disputes often can be resolved to everyone's satisfaction.

peer pressure
Tactics used to encourage some behaviors and discourage others in age-mates.

such self-imposed segregation reflects youngsters' desires to affiliate with peers who, in their eyes, can better understand and help them deal with the issues they face (B. D. Tatum, 1997).

Late Adolescence (14–18 years).   Older adolescents spend almost a third of their waking hours interacting with peers (Rubin et al., 2006). They now spend little time with adults and very little time *exclusively* with an adult, such as a parent or teacher (Csikszentmihalyi, 1995; Csikszentmihalyi & Larson, 1984). In their efforts to develop a sense of identity, they often use peers as a forum for self-exploration and self-understanding (Gottman & Mettetal, 1986; Meadows, 2010). In the following dialogue, two girls struggle with their beliefs about premarital sexual intercourse as they discuss one girl's recent breakup with her boyfriend Randy:

A: [*joking*] I think you should take Randy to court for statutory rape.
B: I don't. I'm to the point of wondering what "that kind of girl" . . . I don't know about the whole scene.
A: The thing is. . . .
B: It depends on the reasoning. And how long you've been going out with somebody.
A: Yeah, I'm satisfied with my morals.
B: As long as you're satisfied with your morals, that's cool.
A: Yeah, but other people. . . .
B: And I'm pretty, I'm pretty sturdy in mine.
A: Yeah [*giggle*], I know that. Mine tend to bend too easily. (Gottman & Mettetal, 1986, p. 218; reprinted with the permission of Cambridge University Press)

A greater capacity for abstract thought allows older adolescents to think of other people as unique individuals rather than as members of specific groups. Older teens also become increasingly aware of the characteristics they share with people from diverse backgrounds. Perhaps as a result, ties to specific peer groups dissipate, hostilities between groups soften, and youngsters become more flexible about the people with whom they associate (B. B. Brown & Dietz, 2009; Gavin & Furman, 1989; Shrum & Cheek, 1987). One graduate of a racially mixed high school put it this way:

Senior year was wonderful, when the black kids and the white kids got to be friends again, and the graduation parties where everyone mixed. . . . It was so much better. (T. Lewin, 2000, p. 20)

Bioecology of Child Development

Children's personal characteristics, gender, family experience, and culture collectively influence their emerging social skills.

The Bioecology of Social Skills

The particular social skills that children use depend not only on their age but also on their individual characteristics and social experiences. Specifically, children's social skills are affected by their personal characteristics, gender, family experiences, and culture.

Personal Characteristics.   Children's biological predispositions play a part in their peer relationships. Children who are born with a tendency to be impulsive and irritable may become somewhat disruptive and aggressive in peer relationships (Berdan, Keane, & Calkins, 2008). Those who are especially shy and withdrawn may also have trouble because they fail to initiate contact with peers. Of course, with support, virtually all children are capable of forming productive peer relationships.

On average, children and adolescents with high intelligence (e.g., youngsters whom school personnel have identified as gifted) have good social skills. However, a few youngsters with highly advanced intellectual abilities have trouble establishing and maintaining effective interpersonal relationships with age-mates because they are in some ways so *very* different from their peers (A. E. Gottfried, Fleming, & Gottfried, 1994; Keogh & MacMillan, 1996; Winner, 1997).

Many children with disabilities, too, have good interpersonal skills, but some others do not. Children with significant physical disabilities may have few opportunities to interact with their peers. And children who have impaired social cognition—for instance, children with a significant intellectual disability or one of the autism spectrum disorders—often have deficiencies in social skills as well (S. Greenspan & Granfield, 1992; Milch-Reich, Campbell,

Pelham, Connelly, & Geva, 1999; Nicpon, Doobay, & Assouline, 2010).[2] For instance, a child who is autistic may fail to express empathy to peers in distress or may carry on a one-sided conversation or exhibit tantrums when frustrated. Youngsters with chronic emotional and behavioral problems (e.g., conduct disorders) typically have some difficulty making and keeping friends, usually because of poor social problem solving skills (Asher & Coie, 1990; Cartledge & Milburn, 1995; Renk, White, Scott, & Middleton, 2009).

Gender. At the preschool level, boys and girls tend to segregate into same-gender groups (Dunsmore, Noguchi, Garner, Casey, & Bhullar, 2008; Paley, 1984; Parke & Clarke-Stewart, 2011). In sociodramatic play, girls tend to enact scenarios that are relatively calm and sedate (e.g., playing house or school). In contrast, boys often introduce elements of adventure and danger (e.g., playing cops and robbers or fighting intergalactic battles).

As boys grow older they continue to place high priority on physical action. Girls spend much more time simply talking—sharing personal concerns, telling secrets, offering emotional support, and so on (Berndt, 1992; Rose & Smith, 2009; Underwood, 2007). Girls are also more sensitive to the subtle, nonverbal messages (body language) that others communicate (J. H. Block, 1983; Deaux, 1984). On average, girls are slightly more kind and considerate, but in many circumstances boys do show their "softer" sides, displaying affection and sympathy appropriate for the occasion (Eisenberg & Fabes, 1998).

Family and Community Experiences. Many families promote their children's peer relationships by encouraging their children to get together with peers who live close by. Parents commonly coach children in social skills, for example, encouraging them to take turns instead of fighting over toys (Russell & Finnie, 1990). Yet children's contact with peers is influenced by local circumstances. Generally, children in working-class and middle-class neighborhoods have numerous peers who live in nearby homes (Ladd, 2005). Some parents living in economically disadvantaged communities restrict their children's free time with peers due to concerns about safety in the neighborhood. In affluent communities, few families with children are apt to live nearby, and parents may or may not have time to chauffeur children around to social events (Medrich, 1981). Numerous parents from all backgrounds manage to overcome barriers to social contact for their children but certain other parents do not.

Culture. Cultural patterns guide children's involvement with peers. In North America most children come into frequent contact with age-mates from an early age. Parents value the ability of their children to get along with peers, encourage their children's friendships, and may even arrange "play dates," appointments for their children to get together with peers at one house or another. Japanese children have less free time than do U.S. children and often prefer to stay home with parents than affiliate with peers (Rothbaum, Pott, Azuma, Miyake, & Weisz, 2000). To some degree, different cultural groups also model and teach different interpersonal behaviors. Children in China, especially in the rural areas, are encouraged to be shy, whereas those in Israel are encouraged to be assertive (X. Chen, Rubin, & Li, 1995; X. Chen, Wang, & Wang, 2009; Krispin, Sternberg, & Lamb, 1992). And whereas some children emphasize harmony in their interactions with friends, Italian children enjoy heated discussions with friends, not concerned that disagreement might undermine their relationships (Casiglia, LoCoco, & Zappulla, 1998).

Types of Peer Relationships

Children and adolescents affiliate with one another in four distinct ways. First, they select social partners with whom to affiliate informally, often on a short-term basis, for example, choosing whom to sit next to at lunchtime, with the result that some children are regularly accepted as buddies and others are not. Second, young people form friends with whom they regularly share secrets and pastimes. Third, young people form larger social groups and congregate within them, especially during the adolescent years. Finally, they become partners in romance, again principally during the adolescent period.

[2]The autism spectrum disorders are examined in Chapter 12.

Peer Acceptance

Children make many choices everyday as to which age-mates to affiliate with—whom to walk home with after school, to ask for help with homework, and to invite to their birthday parties. Socially skilled children are frequently approached by peers and thereby gain beneficial opportunities for social learning (Blandon, Calkins, Grimm, Keane, & O'Brien, 2010).

Developmental researchers examine peer acceptance by asking children in a classroom or other setting to confidentially nominate individual children with whom they would like to interact and others whom they would prefer to avoid. Researchers then collect these nominations and classify the children into one of five groups: *popular, rejected, neglected, controversial,* and *average* (Coie, Dodge, & Coppotelli, 1982; Rubin et al., 2006; S. Walker, 2009). Researchers subsequently compare the typical social features of children in the five groups.

Children who are well liked by numerous peers are considered **popular**. When researchers ask children to identify classmates they would most like to do something with, the children don't necessarily choose those whom they and their teachers perceive to be the most admired members of the student body (Lafontana & Cillessen, 1998; Parkhurst & Hopmeyer, 1998). When we talk about *popular children* in terms of peer acceptance, we are describing young people who are well liked, kind, and trustworthy, rather than those who hold obvious high-status positions such as head cheerleader or football quarterback. Children who are well accepted by peers typically have good social skills. They know how to initiate and sustain conversations, refrain from talking only about their own needs, show sensitivity to the subtle social cues that others give them, adjust their behaviors to changing circumstances, and act prosocially, often helping, sharing, cooperating, and empathizing with others (Caprara, Barbaranelli, Pastorelli, Bandura, & Zimbardo, 2000; Parke & Clarke-Stewart, 2011; Oortwijn, Boekaerts, Vedder, & Fortuin, 2008).

Children who are frequently selected for exclusion by peers are known as **rejected children**. Rejected children often have poor social skills—for example, they may continually try to draw attention to themselves and may also be impulsive and disruptive in the classroom (Asher & Renshaw, 1981; Pellegrini, Bartini, & Brooks, 1999; Putallaz & Heflin, 1986; Rubin et al., 2006). Some rejected children are aggressive, placing a higher priority on acquiring objects and gaining power over others than on maintaining congenial interpersonal relationships (Dodge, Bates, & Pettit, 1990; Ladd & Burgess, 1999; Parke & Clarke-Stewart, 2011). Other rejected children appear to peers to be immature, insensitive, inattentive, strange, or exceptionally timid (Bierman, 2004; Rubin et al., 2006). Rejected children's tendency to alienate others leaves them few opportunities to develop the social skills they so desperately need, and many consequently feel lonely and unhappy or become targets of other children's bullying behaviors (Bierman, 2004; Bullock, 1993; Coie & Cillessen, 1993; Rubin et al., 2006).

A third group of children consists of **neglected children**, those whom age-mates rarely select as peers they would either most like or least like to do something with (Asher & Renshaw, 1981). Neglected children tend to be quiet and keep to themselves. Some prefer to be alone, others may simply not know how to go about making friends, and still others may be quite content with one or two close friends (Guay et al., 1999; Parke & Clarke-Stewart, 2011; Rubin & Krasnor, 1986). Neglected status is often only a temporary situation; children categorized as neglected at one time are not always so categorized in follow-up assessments (Rubin et al., 2006; S. Walker, 2009).

A fourth category, **controversial children**, includes youngsters who are very well liked by some of their peers and intensely disliked by others. Controversial children are apt to have characteristics of both popular and rejected children. For example, they may be aggressive on some occasions and helpful and cooperative at other times (Coie & Dodge, 1988; D. A. Nelson, Robinson, Hart, Albano, & Marshall, 2010; Rubin et al., 2006). The fifth group consists of children who, for lack of a better term, are known simply as *average:* Some peers like them and others don't, but without the intensity of feelings shown for popular, rejected, or controversial children and also without the invisibility of neglected children.

Because of its important effects on the development of children and adolescents, peer acceptance is an important quality for adults to monitor. In the Observation Guidelines table "Noticing Children's Level of Peer Acceptance," we present common characteristics of

popular children
Children whom many peers like and perceive to be kind and trustworthy.

rejected children
Children whom many peers identify as being unfavorable social partners.

neglected children
Children whom peers rarely select as someone they would either most like or least like to do something with.

controversial children
Children whom some peers really like and other peers strongly dislike.

OBSERVATION GUIDELINES
Noticing Children's Level of Peer Acceptance

CHARACTERISTIC	LOOK FOR	EXAMPLE	IMPLICATION
Popular Children	• *Good communication skills* • *Sensitivity and responsiveness* to others' wishes and needs • *Willingness to assimilate* into ongoing activities • *Signs of leadership potential*	On the playground, 8-year-old Daequan moves easily from one group to another. Before joining a conversation, he listens to what others are saying and adds an appropriate comment. He doesn't draw much attention to himself but is well liked by most of his classmates.	Use popular children as leaders when trying to change other children's behavior. For example, when starting a recycling program, ask a well-regarded youngster to help get the program off the ground.
Rejected Children	• *For some, high rates of aggression; for others, immature, anxious, or impulsive behavior; for still others, unusually shy and withdrawn behavior* • *For some, frequent disruptive behavior* in class • *Unwillingness of other children* to play or work with them • *In some cases, appearance to other children of being strange and annoying*	Most children dislike 10-year-old Terra. She frequently calls other children insulting nicknames, threatens to beat them up, and noisily intrudes into their private conversations.	Help rejected children learn basic social skills, such as how to initiate a conversation. Place them in cooperative groups with children who are likely to be accepting. With aggressive children, give appropriate consequences and teach self-regulatory strategies for controlling impulses. Publicly compliment all youngsters (including rejected children) on things they do well. When rejected children fail to respond to informal interventions, consult counselors.
Neglected Children	• *Tendency to be relatively quiet*; little or no disruptive behavior • *Fewer-than-average interactions* with age-mates but possible friendships with one or two peers • *For some, anxiety about interacting with others* • *Possible temporary nature* of neglected status	Fourteen-year-old Sedna is initially reserved at her new school. Later in the year, however, she seems to be happier and more involved in school activities.	Identify group activities in which neglected children might feel comfortable and be successful. Arrange situations in which shy children with similar interests can get to know one another.
Controversial Children	• *Acceptance by some peers, rejection by others* • *Possible aggression and disruptive behavior in some situations, yet helpfulness, cooperation, and social sensitivity in others*	Thirteen-year-old Marcus is usually charming and cheerful, but occasionally he makes jokes at someone else's expense. His sunny personality impresses many classmates, yet his biting humor offends others.	Let controversial children know in no uncertain terms when their behaviors are inappropriate, but acknowledge their effective social skills as well.
Average Children	• *Tendency to be liked by some peers but disliked by others* • *Average interpersonal skills* (e.g., typical levels of prosocial behavior and aggression) • *Ability to find a comfortable social niche*	Five-year-old Joachim doesn't draw much attention to himself. He's made a few friends in kindergarten and seems to get along fairly well with them, but he sometimes has trouble handling disagreements.	Help average children refine their emerging social skills. Encourage them to be tactful, honest, and kind with peers.

Sources: Bierman, 2004; Coie & Dodge, 1988; Coie & Kupersmidt, 1983; Dodge, 1983; Dodge, Coie, & Brakke, 1982; Dodge, Schlundt, Schocken, & Delugach, 1983; D. A. Nelson et al., 2010; Newcomb & Bukowski, 1984; Newcomb, Bukowski, & Pattee, 1993; Parke & Clarke-Stewart, 2011; Putallaz & Gottman, 1981; Rubin et al., 2006; S. Walker, 2009.

popular, rejected, neglected, controversial, and average children, and we suggest some basic strategies for supporting children at these varying levels of peer acceptance.

Friendships

In addition to wanting to be accepted by peers, children invariably hope to have one or more friends. Some of children's friendships are brief liaisons and others last a lifetime. Some are relatively casual; others are deep and intimate. Some children have many friends;

My best friend is brian and we have had many fun times together with my other friends (anthony and anhuu) too. We have been friends since 1st grade, He has always been in my class those years, so has anhuu and Anthony, We have had sad and happy times/adventures. We sometimes argued. We would play hide and seek and get soda and other things at the Mobile home park, We both enjoyed hamsters as pets, Sometimes he came to my house to play

ARTIFACT 15-4 **My best friend.** Ten-year-old Joseph explains that he has shared many experiences with his friend Brian.

Today Miranda walked me to school and she is going to walk me back. Miranda is my best friend we met egether after lunch. Miranda is teching me lots of things she the best friend any boty cwold have.

ARTIFACT 15-5 **The best friend anybody could have.** Seven-year-old Jessica recognizes the value of a good friend.

Improving Your Observation Skills

Friends or acquaintances? These two adolescent girls are amused at something. Do the girls seem to be friends or acquaintances? Compare your response with the explanation at the end of the chapter.

others invest steadfastly in a few close ones. Despite their varied types, friendships have four common qualities that distinguish them from other kinds of peer relationships:

• *Friendships are voluntary relationships.* Children often spend time with peers through happenstance: Perhaps they ride the same school bus, are members of the same class, or join the same sports team. In contrast, children *choose* their friends. Children make active efforts to affiliate with their friends, and two or more youngsters typically remain friends as long as they continue to enjoy one another's company and can successfully resolve their differences.

• *Friendships are powered by shared routines.* Friends find activities that are mutually meaningful and enjoyable. Over time, friends acquire a common set of experiences that enable them to share certain perspectives on life (McDougall & Hymel, 2007; Suttles, 1970; Troutman & Fletcher, 2010). As a result, they can easily communicate about many topics. Children talk, smile, and laugh more often with friends than with nonfriends; they also engage in more complex fantasy play with friends (J. G. Parker, 1986).

• *Friendships are reciprocal relationships.* In the time they spend together, friends address one another's needs (J. L. Epstein, 1986; Poulin & Chan, 2010; Rubin et al., 2006). Although friends take on slightly different roles in their relationship, generally they are equal partners. One friend may instigate fun activities, and the other friend may be an especially sympathetic listener, with both styles reflecting the children's mutual regard.

• *Friendships ensure ongoing, dependable sources of support.* Friends help each other cope with stressful events by providing emotional support (Berndt & Keefe, 1995; McDougall & Hymel, 2007; Peltonen, Qouta, El Sarraj, & Punamäki, 2010). Because friends have an emotional investment in their relationship, they work hard to look at situations from each other's point of view and resolve disputes that threaten to be divisive. As a result, they develop enhanced perspective taking and conflict resolution skills (Basinger et al., 1995; DeVries, 1997).

The particular benefits that friendships have for children depend somewhat on their developmental abilities. As we look at the nature of friendship across the five developmental periods, we see that friendships begin with mutual enjoyment and gradually reflect such additional characteristics as loyalty, trust, compromise, and intimacy.

Infancy (birth–2 years). Primitive relationships among peers emerge during infancy. In the beginning, social interests are fleeting and exploratory, and infants are as likely to crawl over one another as to initiate social contact. Yet as infants grow, develop some basic cognitive and language skills, and become familiar with one another, they smile, watch one another's faces and actions, and coordinate some aspects of their play (Rubin et al., 2006; S. T. Williams, Mastergeorge, & Ontai, 2010). When Teresa's son Connor was 9 months old, he became friendly with Patrick, another boy of the same age at his child care center. The two boys established familiar play routines, often laughing and chasing one another as they crawled around the room. Although they weren't yet speaking, and they certainly didn't swap secrets, they were clearly attuned to each other's behaviors. Such social interests solidify, and in their second year, toddlers make social overtures more consistently, carry on complex interactions, and display positive emotions with children whom they know and like (Howes, 1988).

Early Childhood (2–6 years). In the preschool years children infuse language, fantasy, and play into social interactions with familiar peers. When 3- and 4-year-olds interact with friends rather than other children who are not friends, they are more likely to offer social greetings, share materials, carry on a conversation, engage in complex play, and exhibit good social skills (Charlesworth & LaFreniere, 1983; Hinde, Titmus, Easton, & Tamplin, 1985; C. Moore, 2009). Of course, early friendships also provide opportunities for disagreements (Hartup & Laursen, 1991). In the process of working through conflicts with friends, children learn to assert themselves while showing their regard for friends.

Middle Childhood (6–10 years). During the elementary school years, children continue to act differently with friends than with peers who are not friends. With friends they are more likely to express their feelings and speculate about one another's emotional states (Newcomb & Bagwell, 1995; Newcomb & Brady, 1982). At this age friends develop a sense of loyalty to one another, and many of them, girls especially, use self-disclosure as a strategy for maintaining a friendship (Diaz & Berndt, 1982; Swenson & Rose, 2009; R. N. Turner, Hewstone, & Voci, 2007). Friendships are more stable in middle childhood than in earlier years, and children are more deliberate in selecting playmates with qualities similar to their own (Berndt & Hoyle, 1985; Rubin, Lynch, Coplan, Rose-Krasnor, & Booth, 1994).

Youngsters typically choose friends of their own gender, perhaps in part because same-gender peers are more likely to share interests and pastimes (Baines & Blatchford, 2009; Gottman, 1986; Maccoby, 1990). However, numerous children of this age do have cross-gender friendships, and such relationships tend to promote social perspective taking and flexible communication skills (McDougall & Hymel, 2007).

Early Adolescence (10–14 years). Differences in relationships between friends and nonfriends intensify during early adolescence (Basinger et al., 1995; J. G. Parker & Gottman, 1989). Many young adolescents let down their guard and reveal their weaknesses and vulnerabilities to close friends, even as they may try to maintain a demeanor of competence and self-confidence in front of other age-mates. Adolescents also confront feelings of possessiveness and jealousy about friends (J. G. Parker, Kruse, & Aikins, 2010). Gradually, young adolescents learn that friendships don't have to be exclusive, and friendship pairs converge into larger groups.

Late Adolescence (14–18 years). Older adolescents tend to be quite selective in their choice of friends (J. L. Epstein, 1986). Gone are the days when they run out of fingers as they count off their "close" friends. Instead, older teenagers tend to nurture relationships with a few friends that they keep for some time, perhaps throughout their lives. They frequently turn to friends for emotional support in times of trouble or confusion, and they are likely to engage in lengthy discussions about personal problems and possible solutions (Asher & Parker, 1989; Buhrmester, 1996; Weeks & Pasupathi, 2010).

ARTIFACT 15-6 Friends. Four-year-old Dana drew a picture of herself and her friend Dina. The two girls met in child care and became close companions. Afterwards, they moved to separate towns but happily renewed their friendship when given the chance at summer camp.

ARTIFACT 15-7 Good buddies. Ten-year-old Andres drew a picture of himself with two of his buddies. Many close friendships in the elementary and middle school years are among children of the same gender.

Social Groups

Another kind of peer relationship occurs as a result of the formation of social groups in middle childhood and adolescence. As a result of their expanding social lives, youngsters come into contact with many peers and begin to form larger social groups that regularly fraternize (Rubin et al., 2006). Initially, these groups are comprised of collections of single-gender friendships, but in adolescence they often include both boys and girls.

Youngsters' social groups vary considerably in size, function, and character. However, many have the following attributes:

Group members develop a common culture. As you have learned, children who choose to affiliate with one another share routines and ways of thinking about their lives. This shared culture gives group members a sense of community, belonging, and identity. Identification with a group also leads young people to notice that they are different from individuals in other groups who have their own distinct appearances and habits.

Group members socialize one another to follow the group's norms. Group members encourage conformity by reinforcing behaviors that are appropriate in the eyes of the group and by discouraging behaviors that are not (Clasen & Brown, 1985; Killeya-Jones et al., 2007; Scull, Kupersmidt, Parker, Elmore, & Benson, 2010). Fortunately, many peer groups embrace productive behaviors, such as honesty, fairness, cooperation, academic achievement, and a sense of humor (Damon, 1988; Kindermann, 1993; Peters, Cillessen, Riksen-Walraven, & Haselager, 2010). Others, however, encourage unproductive behaviors, such as threatening and pushing classmates around; making fun of "brainy" students; and endorsing cheating, cutting class, skipping school, or using drugs (B. B. Brown, 1993; B. C. Kelly, 2007; Matjasko et al., 2010). Of course, young people do not passively become what other group members

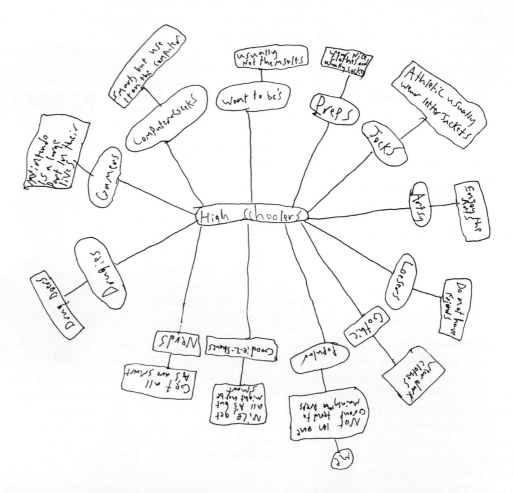

ARTIFACT 15-8 Social networks. Fourteen-year-old Connor diagrammed the complex collection of student groupings he observed during his freshman year in high school. In his inner circle he labeled the different groups (e.g., *preps, jocks, gamers*), and in the outer circle he described each one (e.g., "wear nice clothes and usually cocky," "athletic, usually wear letter jackets," "Nintendo is a large part in their lives").

want them to be. Youngsters generally affiliate with peers who have similar characteristics and then pressure themselves to adopt their group's norms and values (Gottman & Mettetal, 1986; Kwon & Lease, 2009).

Group members influence youngsters more strongly in some areas of life than others. Young people rarely accept a peer's suggestions without question (B. B. Brown, 1990; Padilla-Walker & Carlo, 2007). Instead, they typically evaluate what peers ask them to do and may consider advice they have previously received from people outside the peer group. Peer groups are particularly influential in matters of style—for example, in dress, music, and social activities. In contrast, parents, teachers, and other significant adults continue to be influential in most young people's views about education, morality, religion, and careers (E. C. Cook, Buehler, & Henson, 2009; Hartup, 1983; Sewald, 1986).

Group members have a sense of unity as a group. Once youngsters gel as a group, they prefer other group members to nonmembers, and they develop feelings of loyalty to individuals within the group. In some cases they also feel hostility toward members of other groups and view their competitors as unfriendly and incompetent (Files, Casey, & Oleson, 2010; Sherif, Harvey, White, Hood, & Sherif, 1961). Such feelings toward *out-groups* are particularly intense when two or more groups actively compete for status or resources, as rival athletic teams and adolescent gangs often do.

Dominance hierarchies emerge within the group. When children's groups continue for any length of time, a pecking order, or **dominance hierarchy**, gradually evolves (J. L. Martin, 2009; Strayer, 1991). Some group members rise to the top, leading the way and making decisions for the entire group. Other group members are followers: They look to those around them for guidance about how to behave and assume lesser roles in the group's activities. Sometimes these less dominant individuals find unique niches within the group, perhaps becoming the clown, daredevil, or brain of the group.

Once youngsters reach puberty, social groups become a particularly prominent feature of their social worlds. Developmental researchers have described several kinds of groups that are significant during the adolescent years: cliques and crowds, subcultures, and gangs.

Cliques and Crowds. **Cliques** are moderately stable friendship groups of perhaps three to nine individuals, often of the same gender. Cliques provide the basis for many voluntary social interactions during childhood and adolescence (X. Chen, Chang, & He, 2003; Witvliet, van Lier, Cuijpers, & Koot, 2010). Clique boundaries tend to be fairly rigid and exclusive (some people are in, others are out), and membership in various cliques affects social status and dominance with peers.

Children begin to form cliques as early as first grade, with dyads of friends affiliating with other friends and becoming cliques (Witvliet et al., 2010). These cliques remain moderately stable, with individual children often affiliating with the same group for a year or more but also entering and exiting at will and allowing others to join in occasionally. As children grow, they may become increasingly concerned about being accepted into a particular clique. Young adolescents wonder about their social standing: "Who likes me?" "Will I be popular at my new school?" "Why didn't Sal invite me to his party?" (Gavin & Furman, 1989). When they leave one clique to join another, they are apt to engender feelings of betrayal, hurt, and jealousy in the friends they leave behind (Kanner, Feldman, Weinberger, & Ford, 1987).

Cliques decline in prevalence during the adolescent years and are replaced by **crowds**, larger collections of peers who share certain characteristics and are defined by others according to their reputation (B. B. Brown & Dietz, 2009). Like cliques, crowds provide support to young people and opportunities to practice social skills, although some young people affiliate with crowds that reinforce negative behaviors. Crowds tend to disband during the final two years of high school, when young people feel freer to act as individuals and intermingle more easily with people from different backgrounds.

Subcultures. Some adolescents affiliate with a well-defined **subculture**, a group that resists a powerful dominant culture by adopting a significantly different way of life (J. S. Epstein, 1998; Tanner, Asbridge, & Wortley, 2008). Some subcultures are tightly knit groups, and

dominance hierarchy
Relative standing of group members in terms of such qualities as leadership and social influence.

clique
Moderately stable friendship group of perhaps three to nine members.

crowd
Large collection of adolescents who share certain characteristics, tend to affiliate together, and are defined by others according to their reputations.

subculture
Group that resists the ways of the dominant culture and adopts its own norms for behavior.

others are loosely configured, with members coming and going. Some subcultures are relatively benign; for instance, a middle school skateboarders' subculture may simply espouse a particular mode of dress and a recreational pastime. Other subcultures, such as those that promote drug use, endorse racist and anti-Semitic behaviors (e.g., skinheads), or practice Satanic rituals, are obviously worrisome (B. C. Kelly, 2007; C. C. Clark, 1992; So, 2009).

Adolescents are apt to affiliate with subcultures when they feel alienated from the dominant culture (perhaps that of their school or society more generally), uncomfortable about fitting in with unfamiliar peers, or pessimistic about their future (Bešić & Kerr, 2009; C. C. Clark, 1992; J. S. Epstein, 1998; J. R. Harris, 1998). Some young people feel not only disenfranchised from society but also rejected by their families, heightening their need for intimacy in a new group. For example, "street families" of homeless youth offer one another protection and emotional support. One 16-year-old girl described her street family:

> Well, it's like we all just put what we have together and share. In our family, we all work together to make sure we are all taken care of. It's like someone will panhandle one day and someone else will do it the next. And whatever people get they will bring it back and share with everyone. (H. Smith, 2008, p. 764)

Gangs. A **gang** is a cohesive social group characterized by initiation rites, distinctive colors and symbols, alleged ownership of a specific territory, feuds with one or more rival groups, and criminal activity (A. Campbell, 1984; Gover, Jennings, & Tewksbury, R. 2009; Kodluboy, 2004). Gangs have well-defined dominance hierarchies, strict rules, and stiff penalties for breaking them.

Once confined to a few neighborhoods in inner cities, gangs have now become widespread, especially in lower-income inner-city areas but also in suburbs and rural areas (National Drug Intelligence Center, 2008; Rojek, Petrocelli, & Oberweis, 2010). Young people who join gangs often live in low-income neighborhoods with high rates of community violence and have few opportunities for steady employment (J. S. Hong, 2010). Joining a gang enables young people to demonstrate their loyalty to friends and family, gain recognition for accomplishments, obtain financial rewards (through criminal activities), and receive missing emotional support (A. Campbell, 1984; Kodluboy, 2004; Melde, Taylor, & Esbensen, 2009).

In some instances gang members endorse prosocial behaviors, including caring for one another and encouraging one another's self-expression (Moje, 2000). But generally speaking, gangs do more harm than good. High rates of using and selling drugs, carrying destructive weapons, and intimidating peers make gangs a serious concern for law enforcement officers and community leaders (Parks, 1995). Although many gang members report joining gangs to escape violence in their community, the reality is that they face a greater risk of being victimized if they join a gang. Numerous gang members are targeted inside of the gang during initiation, as a result of punishment for violating a gang rule, or as part of a sexual assault; they also become hurt during conflicts with other gangs, for example, in fights or altercations involving weapons (Melde et al., 2009).

Many educators recognize gangs as a serious problem. Youth in gangs often intimidate classmates, defend the school as their own territory, and recruit new members from among the student body. Ideally, educators try to address children's needs long before children are tempted to join gangs.[3] When youngsters feel cared for by teachers and are confident in their own academic abilities, they are more likely to remain in school, avoid criminal activity, and resist the pressures of gangs (M. M. Jensen, 2005). Valuable *prevention strategies* include early childhood curricula that prepare young children with emergent literacy skills and a healthy self-confidence, and after-school programs that give older children support and productive outlets for their time (e.g., Boys and Girls Clubs of America) (Grekul & Sanderson, 2011; Howell, 2000; D. Peterson & Esbensen, 2004). *Interventions* entice youths to leave gangs by offering job training, adult mentoring, gang mediation, and counseling (Howell, 2000; Winterdyk & Ruddell, 2010). *Suppression programs* try to reduce gang activities through weapon seizures and arrests for gang-related incidents near schools.

gang
Cohesive social group characterized by initiation rites, distinctive colors and symbols, territorial orientation, feuds with rival groups, and criminal activity.

---

[3]Multitiered educational strategies that discourage children from joining gangs and intervene with young people who have already joined gangs are described in Chapter 14.

Romance

Awareness of romantic relationships first develops in early childhood. Many children, especially those living in traditional two-parent families, believe that getting married and having children is a normal, perhaps inevitable, part of growing up. They sometimes act out their fantasies in play, as this episode involving Eric and Naomi illustrates:

E: Hey, Naomi, I know what we can play today.
N: What?
E: How about, um, the marry game. You like that.
N: Marry?
E: How about baker or something? How about this. Marry you? OK, Naomi, you want to pretend that?
N: Yes.
E: OK, Naomi, do you want to marry me?
N: Yeah.
E: Good, just a minute, Naomi, we don't have any marry place.
N: We could pretend this is the marry place.
E: Oh, well, pretend this, ah, there'll have to be a cake.
N: The wedding is here first.
E: OK, but listen to this, we have to have a baby, oh, and a pet.
N: This is our baby. (Gottman, 1986, p. 157)

Consistent with what we have learned about cognitive abilities at this age, young children's understandings of courtship and marriage are simple and concrete. In the preceding scenario, the children focus on having a "marry place" and wedding cake. Such fantasies help young children anticipate their eventual entry into romantic relationships.

Dating. As children grow, they gradually expand on their ideas about what it means to participate in romantic relationships, and many eventually begin to date. Prior to puberty some children practice courtship behaviors, with girls vying for the attention of boys by using cosmetics and choosing clothing and hairstyles that make them look older and (they think) prettier, and with boys flaunting whatever manly airs they can muster (Elkind, 1981b; Giordano, 2003). The early romances of late middle childhood and early adolescence often exist more in youngsters' minds than in reality, as the following conversation between two young teenage girls illustrates:

A: How's Lance [*giggle*]? Has he taken you to a movie yet?
B: No. Saw him today but I don't care.
A: Didn't he say anything to you?
B: Oh . . .
A: Lovers!
B: Shut up!
A: Lovers at first sight! [*Giggle.*]
B: [*Giggle.*] Quit it! (Gottman & Mettetal, 1986, p. 210; reprinted with the permission of Cambridge University Press)

As young people reach adolescence, many form as couples and date. Relationships may become increasingly serious and involve emotional intimacy and self-disclosure (Connolly & McIsaac, 2009; Rubin et al., 2006). In determining how to act in romantic relationships, adolescents turn to familiar people and institutions. Both genders pay close attention to the activities of those around them and absorb the many romantic images they see in the media (Larson, Clore, & Wood, 1999; H. Montgomery, 2009). Adolescents also absorb customs in their own peer culture, perhaps being loyal to one partner, "hooking up" (being intimate on a one-time basis with a stranger), or having a "friendship with benefits" (a casual relationship in which the partners are sexually active but not committed to one another or romantically involved) (Connolly & McIsaac, 2009).

Young people also apply the social skills and understandings that they have gained in close relationships. Adolescents with secure attachments to family members are likely to have

ARTIFACT 15-9 **Wedding day.** Most preschoolers are curious about courtship and marriage. Here Teresa's son Alex (age 5) depicts his image of his parents getting married.

successful dating experiences, probably because they have greater self-confidence, better social skills, and more experience in trusting relationships (S. K. Cheung & McBride-Chang, 2011; W. A. Collins & Sroufe, 1999; Connolly & McIsaac, 2009). Adolescents who are accustomed to a balanced give-and-take style of decision making at home are apt to use this same general method with romantic partners, negotiating what movie to see, which party to attend, and so on. In contrast, teenagers who have seen family violence may hit and push dating partners or, conversely, tolerate partners' aggressive behavior ("He didn't mean it"; "She was drunk"; "He'll outgrow it") (D. A. Wolfe & Wekerle, 1997).

Adolescents' first romantic relationships offer young people definite benefits. Being in a relationship fulfills needs for companionship, affection, and security and may significantly enhance social status with peers (W. A. Collins & Sroufe, 1999; Connolly & McIsaac, 2009; Furman & Simon, 1999). Such relationships also provide opportunities for young people to experiment with new interpersonal behaviors and examine previously unexplored aspects of their own identity.

At the same time, romantic relationships can wreak havoc on adolescents' emotions (W. A. Collins & van Dulmen, 2006; Connolly & McIsaac, 2009). Adolescents can find it exciting and frustrating to enter (and exit) romantic liaisons with one another. In some cases the emotional highs and lows that come with romance—the roller-coaster ride between exhilaration and disappointment—cloud judgment, trigger depression, and distract young people from schoolwork (Davila, 2008; Larson et al., 1999; Rubin et al., 2006).

Sexual Intimacy. Both genders have some capacity for sexual arousal even before puberty (Conn & Kanner, 1940; de Graaf & Rademakers, 2006). Children and preadolescents occasionally look at or touch one another in private places and play games (e.g., strip poker) that have sexual overtones (Dornbusch et al., 1981; Katchadourian, 1990; A. Montgomery, 2009). However, sexual contact before adolescence typically lacks the erotic features present in later development. During adolescence, young people develop both the physical structures and the physiological impetus to become sexually active.

Although sexual maturation is a natural process, it is not a simple matter to address. No one knows how best to handle adolescent sexuality—not parents, not teachers, and certainly not adolescents themselves. Many adults ignore the topic, assuming (or perhaps hoping) it's not yet relevant for the adolescents in their care. Even teenagers who have good relationships with their parents have few chances to talk about sex (Brooks-Gunn & Furstenberg, 1990; Robert & Sonenstein, 2010). And when parents and teachers do broach the topic of sexuality, they often raise it in conjunction with problems, such as irresponsible behavior, substance abuse, disease, and unwanted pregnancy.

Adolescents, meanwhile, must come to terms with their emerging sexuality. They must learn to accept their changing bodies, cope with unanticipated feelings of sexual desire, and try to reconcile the conflicting messages they get from home, peers, religious groups, and the media as to the circumstances in which varying degrees of sexual intimacy are appropriate (Brooks-Gunn & Paikoff, 1993).

For adolescents who become sexually active, there is a developmental sequence to sexual behaviors. Young people often begin with hand-holding and a simple kiss and then add other personal contacts. Typically, adolescents initiate sexual intercourse only after several years of experience with less intimate contacts (Connolly & McIsaac, 2009; DeLamater & MacCorquodale, 1979; Udry, 1988).[4]

For many adolescents sexual intimacy goes hand in hand with, and is a natural outgrowth of, long-term romantic relationships (Connolly & McIsaac, 2009; Graber, Britto, & Brooks-Gunn, 1999; B. C. Miller & Benson, 1999). For others, however, it is something that should be saved for the "right moment," perhaps for marriage. And for a few, sexual intimacy is an activity completely separate from romantic involvement. For these individuals, it may be a means of enhancing social standings with peers, experimenting with a risky activity, exploring sexual orientations, gaining others' attention and affection, or simply experiencing physical pleasure (W. A. Collins & Sroufe, 1999; Peltzer, 2010; Woody, D'Souza, & Russel, 2003).

---

[4]See Chapter 5 for a discussion of adolescents' unsafe sexual behaviors.

Sexual Orientation and Gender Identity. By **sexual orientation**, we mean the particular sex(es) to whom an individual is romantically and sexually attracted. A small but significant percentage of adolescents find themselves sexually attracted to their own gender either instead of or in addition to the opposite gender. Although it has been difficult to establish precise figures, researchers have estimated that 2 to 3 percent of young people report being gay, lesbian, or bisexual, with an additional few percent either having some degree of same-sex attractions while continuing to identify primarily as heterosexual or realizing later in adulthood that they are homosexual or bisexual (Bailey, Dunne, & Martin, 2000; Savin-Williams, 2005).

A few youngsters are transgendered, believing that they have a different *gender identity* than is apparent from their physiological characteristics. Gender identity refers to the commitment a person has of himself or herself as having masculine or feminine characteristics. A young person may identify as male, female, both, neither, or none. Gender identity is *not* the same as sexual orientation. A person who is transgendered may have any sexual orientation.

It has become increasingly clear that sexual orientation and gender identity are at least partly caused by biological factors (Dawood, Bailey, & Martin, 2009; Richmond, Carroll, & Denboske, 2010; Savin-Williams & Diamond, 1997). Some evidence for a genetic component comes from twin studies: Monozygotic (identical) twins are more similar in their sexual orientation and gender identity than are dizygotic (fraternal) twins (Dawood et al., 2009; Gabard, 1999). Other research has revealed variations in hormones circulating in the prenatal environment that initiate a cascade of physiological effects, including subtle changes to brain circuits, which may ultimately influence sexual orientation and gender identity (Bailey & Pillard, 1997; LeVay, 2011; Rahman & Wilson, 2003).

Regardless of the exact blend of factors that determines sexual orientation and gender identity, these important aspects of human development do not appear to be voluntary decisions. Many homosexual, bisexual, and transgendered young people recall feeling "different" from peers since childhood (D. A. Anderson, 1994; Carver, Egan, & Perry, 2004; Rieger,

sexual orientation
Particular genders to which an individual is romantically and sexually attracted.

As long as I can remember, I always felt a little different when it came to having crushes on other people. When I was in elementary school I never had crushes on girls, and when I look back on that time now, I was probably most attracted to my male friends. I participated in some of the typical "boy" activities, like trading baseball cards and playing video games, but I was never very interested in rough sports. I often preferred to play with the girls in more role-playing and cooperative games. Of course, I didn't understand much about sex or gender roles at the time. I just figured I would become more masculine and develop feelings for the opposite sex after going through puberty.

To my dismay, middle school and the onset of puberty only brought more attention to my lack of interest in girls. The first time I thought about being gay was when I was in 6th grade, so I was probably 11 or 12 years old at the time. But in my mind, being gay was not an option and I began to expend an incredible amount of energy repressing my developing homosexual urges. In 7th grade, I had my first experience with major depression. Looking back on it, I am almost positive that being gay was the immediate cause of the depression. . . . When I finally recovered from the episode a few months later, I did my best to move on with my life and forget about my problems with sexuality. I continued to repress my feelings through high school, a task that became more and more difficult as the years went by. I never really dated any girls and my group of friends in high school was highly female. When I was 16, a junior in high school, I had another more severe bout of

depression. . . . I continued to be ashamed of my feelings and refused to even tell my psychologist about concerns over my sexuality. After finally emerging from my depression, I came to somewhat of an agreement with myself. I decided that I would simply put my conflict on hold, hoping it would resolve itself. Unfortunately, I still held on to the hope that it would resolve itself in heterosexuality and I remained distraught by my feelings. I finally came out during my freshman year at [college] with the support of my friends and an extremely accepting social environment.

Having exposure to the homosexual lifestyle in college is what finally made me realize that I could have a normal life and that I would not have to compromise my dreams because of it. Even though my high school was relatively liberal and very supportive of different backgrounds, there was very little discussion about homosexuality, even in health class. We had visibly gay teachers, but it was rarely openly talked about. I think the reason it took me so long to accept my sexuality was simply because I had no exposure to it while growing up. It angers me that people refer to homosexuality as a lifestyle choice because I had no choice over my sexuality. I spent seven years of my life denying my homosexuality, and believe me, if there had ever been a choice between gay or straight during that time, I would have chosen straight in a second. Today I can't imagine my life without being gay and I would never choose to be straight.

Essay used with permission.

ARTIFACT 15-10 This Is Who I Am. After a year of college, 19-year-old Michael wrote this essay.

Linsenmeier, Gygax, & Bailey, 2008). Adolescence can be a particularly confusing time for them, as they struggle to form an identity while feeling different and isolated from peers (Morrow, 1997; Needham & Austin, 2010; C. J. Patterson, 1995). When their attractions to same-gender peers become stronger, they may initially work hard to ignore or discount such sentiments. At an older age, they may begin to accept some aspects of their homosexuality and gender identity, and later still they may "come out" and identify fully and openly with other gay, lesbian, or transgendered individuals. The road to self-acceptance for these adolescents can be a rocky one, and anger and depression occasionally occur along the way (T. S. Davis, Saltzburg, & Locke, 2009; Elia, 1994).

When the topic of homosexuality comes up in the school curriculum, it is usually within the context of acquired immunodeficiency syndrome (AIDS) and other risks (Filax, 2007; Malinsky, 1997). Furthermore, adolescents with a homosexual, bisexual, or transgender orientation are frequently harassed by peers and occasionally become the victims of hate crimes (Elze, 2003; McGuire, Anderson, Toomey, & Russell, 2010; Savin-Williams, 1995). Under such circumstances some gay, lesbian, bisexual, and transgendered youth become "silent, invisible, and fearful" (M. B. Harris, 1997, p. xxi). Feeling that school is not a safe place for them to be, these youth may decide to drop out of school (T. S. Davis et al., 2009; Elia, 1994; Filax, 2007).

Despite these social hardships, most gay, lesbian, and transgendered youths are most certainly psychologically and socially healthy and find the social support they need (Savin-Williams, 1989; Savin-Williams & Ream, 2003). Rates of depression and anxiety are higher than usual in transgendered youth, but some of this adjustment problem is most certainly due to ostracism from peers and family (K. Richmond et al., 2010).

Fostering Productive Peer Relationships

Group environments for children—classrooms, schools, after-school programs, and so forth—are excellent settings for fostering children's social skills, peer acceptance, and friendships. Thoughtful intervention is particularly important for youngsters who are socially isolated or rejected by their peers. We offer the following suggestions:

• **Set up situations in which youngsters can enjoy friendly interactions with one another.** Teachers can arrange structured cooperative learning activities that require all group members to share equal responsibility, and they can provide play equipment such as balls and climbing structures that lend themselves to coordinated interaction (S. S. Martin, Brady, & Williams, 1991; J. W. Schofield, 1995; Slavin, 1990). Adults can also ask youngsters to read to a peer with a visual impairment, sign to a child with hearing loss, provide tutoring to a classmate with a learning disability, or take notes for a child with a physical impairment. In addition, teachers can acknowledge the mutual benefits of children's helpful gestures ("Thanks, Jamie, for helping Branson—he really appreciates your assistance, and you seemed to learn a lot yourself from explaining the assignment to him").

• **Help young children ease into social groups.** Young children who are shy or new to a community can benefit from intercession by teachers and caregivers. In the following anecdote, Mrs. Kusumoto, a Japanese preschool teacher, skillfully models desired behaviors and helps one child, Fumiko, enter a group of peers:

> Mrs. Kusumoto helps Fumiko put a cha-cha-cha tape in the portable cassette player, and calls a second girl to come over and join them on a small stage made of blocks. The two girls and Mrs. Kusumoto stand on the stage, singing and shaking their maracas. Then Mrs. Kusumoto steps down and faces them, singing along and encouraging them to continue. After a few minutes she attempts to melt away. The girls continue singing briefly, but when the song ends the second girl runs off, leaving Fumiko alone and unoccupied. She looks for Mrs. Kusumoto and begins following her around again. Mrs. Kusumoto approaches a small group of girls who are playing house, asking them: "Would you like to invite this girl over for dinner? After giving the concert, she is very hungry." One of the girls nods silently. Fumiko smiles and enters the "house." She stands there uncertainly, saying nothing. Mrs. Kusumoto inquires, "Fumiko-chan. Have you had your dinner? Why don't you join us? Don't you want something to eat? It looks good." Fumiko nods and the girls bring her a couple [of] dishes of clay "food." Mrs. Kusumoto looks on briefly, then moves quietly out of the scene. (Holloway, 2000, pp. 100–101)

As Mrs. Kusumoto's gestures suggest, teachers can sometimes gently nudge children into cooperative play, although children naturally choose their own friends (Hollingsworth & Buysse, 2009).

• **Teach social skills and social problem-solving strategies.** Through frequent interactions with adults and peers, many youngsters acquire effective social behaviors on their own. But many others—perhaps because of limited opportunities to interact with age-mates, poor role models at home, or a cognitive disability—know little about how to initiate conversations, exchange compliments, offer emotional support, or in other ways establish and maintain rewarding interpersonal relationships. Some also lack productive strategies for solving social problems. They may barge into a game without asking if they can participate or respond to any provocation with aggression. Teachers and counselors can coach these children in effective strategies, perhaps advising a child, "To join a conversation, stand for a moment next to the other students who are talking and then watch for a time when you might say something relevant to their topic. You can also offer a compliment or ask the students about their opinion on something."

• **Minimize or eliminate barriers to social interaction.** Children and adolescents are less likely to interact with peers when physical, linguistic, or social barriers stand in the way (Hollingsworth & Buysse, 2009; Matheson, Olsen, & Weisner, 2007). Jeanne recalls a junior high school student who could not negotiate the cafeteria steps with her wheelchair and frequently ended up eating lunch alone. Educators can be on the lookout for such physical impediments to interaction and campaign for their removal. They can also teach groups of youngsters who speak different languages (including American Sign Language) some basic vocabulary and simple phrases in one another's native tongues. Moreover, educators must actively address the prejudices and tensions that sometimes separate diverse ethnic groups.[5]

• **Cultivate children's empathy for peers with special needs.** Some children feel resentment or anger because of their belief that peers with special needs should be able to control inappropriate behaviors (Juvonen, 1991; Juvonen & Weiner, 1993). Consequently, children are less likely to be tolerant of peers with cognitive difficulties or emotional and behavioral disorders than they are of peers with obvious physical disabilities (Madden & Slavin, 1983; Ysseldyke & Algozzine, 1984). Through paired or small-group activities, adults can show nondisabled youngsters that peers with disabilities have many of the same talents, thoughts, feelings, and desires that they have (James & Leyden, 2010; Staub, 1998).

• **Encourage a general feeling of respect for others.** Adults who effectively promote friendships among diverse groups of children are often those who consistently communicate that all members of their community are welcome and respected (Allodi, 2010; Battistich et al., 1995; Osterman, 2000). Fernando Arias, a high school vocational education teacher, put it this way:

> In our school, our philosophy is that we treat everybody the way we'd like to be treated. . . . Our school is a unique situation where we have pregnant young ladies who go to our school. We have special education children. We have the regular kids, and we have the drop-out recovery program . . . we're all equal. We all have an equal chance. And we have members of every gang at our school, and we hardly have any fights, and there are close to about 300 gangs in our city. We all get along. It's one big family unit it seems like. (Turnbull, Pereira, & Blue-Banning, 2000, p. 67)

• **Be a backup system when relationships with peers aren't going well.** Disruptions in peer relationships—perhaps because of interpersonal conflicts or a friend's relocation to a distant city—can trigger emotional distress in youngsters (Wentzel, 2009). Warm, supportive adults can lessen the pain in such circumstances, and ongoing gestures of affection can also bolster the spirits of other children who, for whatever reasons, have no close friends (Guay et al., 1999; Wentzel, 1999). Such sympathetic overtures may be especially important for children who have little support at home and might otherwise turn to deviant peer groups for attention (Parks, 1995).

[5]Children's prejudices are introduced in Chapter 12.

• **Be aware of family factors that affect children's relationships with peers.** Parents' beliefs and practices influence children's interactions with peers (Goudena, 2006). Some parents are quite protective, rarely allowing their children to play with children outside the family, whereas other parents actively arrange for children to affiliate with peers (A. C. Fletcher, Bridges, & Hunter, 2007). Children who have not had much experience with peers at home or in the neighborhood can gain valuable experience in social groups at school, particularly when teachers use subtle strategies for inclusion. For example, a teacher might sit with a group of children at lunch and, when noticing a child eating alone, invite him or her to join them (e.g., "Sasha, would you like to join us? We're talking about our pets, and you can tell us about your new puppy").

• **Provide the specific kinds of support that rejected children need most.** An important first step in helping rejected children is to determine the reasons why other children find them unpleasant to be around (Bierman, 2004; Bierman, & Powers, 2009). As you have learned, some rejected children are aggressive, have limited social skills, and use coercive behaviors to get their way. Other rejected children have trouble asserting their desires and opinions. Once educators understand exactly what is missing from rejected children's repertoires of social skills, they can take steps to help children acquire the missing competencies.

• **Help change the reputations of rejected children.** Unfortunately, bad reputations often live on long after people's behavior has changed for the better. Even after children show dramatic improvements in social behavior, peers may continue to dislike and reject them (Bierman, Miller, & Staub, 1987; Prinstein, Rancourt, Guerry, & Browne, 2009). When encountering formerly aggressive children, many peers assume "once a bully, always a bully." To improve children's reputations, adults can create structured cooperative learning groups and extracurricular activities in which children can use their newly developed social skills. In one way or another, adults must help previously annoying and abrasive children to show peers that they can be good companions.

• **Accept the new preoccupations of adolescents.** When young people reach puberty, they become preoccupied with who harbors secret yearnings for whom, whether the targets of desire reciprocate with affection, and which friends are sexually active. As an educator or other practitioner potentially working with young people, you may find this undercurrent of romantic desire to be a distraction. While endeavoring to keep young people focused on their academic learning, you can nevertheless try to accept that these preoccupations are a natural, healthy part of coming-of-age.

LIFE'S LESSONS. Although adolescents' preoccupation with romance may occasionally distract them from academic learning, romantic interludes are important training grounds for future relationships.

• **Expect diversity in adolescents' romantic relationships.** Some young people attract a series of steady admirers, whereas others may be inexperienced in, possibly even indifferent to, the world of romance. And, as mentioned earlier, a small percentage of adolescents will have yearnings for members of their own gender. Thus, adults should not presume that an adolescent girl wants to have a boyfriend, a boy wants to have a girlfriend, or even that the young person sees dating as a culturally appropriate option.

• **Keep on hand information about human sexuality.** A conventional belief has held that education about human sexuality is the prerogative of parents and has no place in schools. Typically, if sex education is a part of the school curriculum at all, it focuses on the biological aspects of sexual intercourse and offers little information to help teens make sense of their conflicting thoughts and feelings about physical intimacy. Adolescents' participation in a sex education curriculum usually requires parents' approval, and many parents are loath to give it. Less controversial alternatives include making developmentally appropriate literature about a variety of related issues accessible in school libraries and letting adolescents know that school counselors and nurses are always willing to talk with them about matters of health.

• **Be supportive when young people are struggling with the dissolution of a romantic relationships.** To some adults the romantic bonds and breakups of adolescents often seem trivial, but they may cause considerable stress in teenagers. Adolescents may feel deep humiliation after rejection by a desired romantic partner or a profound sense of loss as a long-term relationship ends. In such situations teachers and counselors can help adolescents sort through their feelings and look forward with optimism to brighter days and new relationships (Bannister, Jakubec, & Stein, 2003; Larson et al., 1999).

• **Describe sexual harassment and indicate why it is prohibited.** **Sexual harassment** is any action that a target can reasonably construe as hostile, humiliating, or sexually offensive (Sjostrom & Stein, 1996). It is a form of discrimination and therefore is prohibited by the laws of many nations, including federal U.S. laws. Sexual harassment can be a problem at the late elementary, middle school, and high school levels, when youngsters are maturing and developing an interest in sexual matters. Youngsters must be advised that sexual harassment will not be tolerated. They should be informed that under no circumstances may they degrade one another—by words, gestures, or actions—with regard to physical traits or sexual orientation. An example of a description of sexual harassment, appropriate for students at varying grade levels, appears in Figure 15-1.

• **Protect the human rights of gay, lesbian, bisexual, and transgender youth.** Teachers and other adults may overhear peers teasing students who violate traditional gender roles or speak openly about attraction to same-sex individuals. Unfortunately, many educators tolerate these remarks and contribute to an environment that is hostile to gay, lesbian, bisexual, and transgender youth. As one transgendered adolescent advised, "[teachers] should actually speak up, because I've been in a lot of classrooms where stuff is said, and the teachers don't do [anything]. And if they did, it would stop right there" (McGuire et al., 2010, p. 1183). But, of course, teachers and other practitioners can instead be proactive,

sexual harassment
Form of discrimination in which a target individual perceives another's actions or statements to be hostile, humiliating, or offensive, especially pertaining to physical appearance or sexual matters.

SEXUAL HARASSMENT: IT'S NO JOKE!

■ **Sexual harassment is unwanted and unwelcomed sexual behavior** which interferes with your right to get an education or to participate in school activities. In school, sexual harassment may result from someone's words, gestures or actions (of a sexual nature) that make you feel uncomfortable, embarrassed, offended, demeaned, frightened, helpless or threatened. If you are the target of sexual harassment, it may be very scary to go to school or hard to concentrate on your school work.

■ **Sexual harassment can happen once, several times, or on a daily basis.**

■ **Sexual harassment can happen any time and anywhere** in school—in hallways or in the lunchroom, on the playground or the bus, at dances or on field trips.

■ **Sexual harassment can happen to anyone!** Girls and boys both get sexually harassed by other students in school.

■ **Agreement isn't needed.** The target of sexual harassment and the harasser do not have to agree about what is happening; sexual harassment is defined by the girl or boy who is targeted. The harasser may tell you that he or she is only joking, but if their words, gestures or actions (of a sexual nature) are making you uncomfortable or afraid, then you're

being sexually harassed. You do not have to get others, either your friends, teachers or school officials, to agree with you.

■ **No one has the right to sexually harass another person!** School officials are legally responsible to guarantee that all students, you included, can learn in a safe environment which is free from sexual harassment and sex discrimination. If you are being sexually harassed, your student rights are being violated. Find an adult you trust and tell them what's happening, so that something can be done to stop the harassment.

■ **Examples of sexual harassment in school:**
• touching, pinching, and grabbing body parts
• being cornered
• sending sexual notes or pictures
• writing sexual graffiti on desks, bathroom walls or buildings
• making suggestive or sexual gestures, looks, jokes, or verbal comments (including "mooing," "barking" and other noises)
• spreading sexual rumors or making sexual propositions
• pulling off someone's clothes
• pulling off your own clothes
• being forced to kiss someone or do something sexual
• attempted rape and rape

REMEMBER: SEXUAL HARASSMENT IS SERIOUS AND AGAINST THE LAW!

FIGURE 15-1 It's no joke. Example of how teachers and school counselors might describe sexual harassment in language that children and adolescents understand.
Excerpt from "Stop Sexual Harassment in Schools" by Nan Stein, from USA TODAY, May 18, 1993. Copyright © 1993 by Nan Stein, Ed.D. Used with permission of the author.

establishing a welcome environment for all youth and intervening when they hear young people being teased or harassed.

• **Make appropriate referrals when necessary.** Teachers occasionally learn unexpectedly about aspects of youngsters' personal lives. Students may tell teachers they are pregnant, have a pregnant girlfriend, have been raped or sexually abused, or suspect they've contracted a sexually transmitted infection. Educators need to be prepared to make appropriate referrals to counselors and other officials and to encourage adolescents to talk with family members.

As you have learned, adults can do many things to foster productive peer relationships in children. In the Developmental Trends table "Peer Relationships at Different Age Levels," you can review typical features and variations in peer relationships during the developmental periods and consider their implications for youngsters of various ages.

DEVELOPMENTAL TRENDS
Peer Relationships at Different Age Levels

AGE	WHAT YOU MIGHT OBSERVE	DIVERSITY	IMPLICATIONS
Infancy (Birth–2 Years) 	• Growing interest in other infants in the same child care setting • Beginning attempts to make contact with familiar infants, such as looking at their faces and smiling at them • In second year, side-by-side play and awareness of one another's actions	• Some infants have not had social experiences with siblings or other children in child care; they may need time to adjust to the presence of other children. • Security of attachment to caregivers may affect children's interaction style with peers. • Infants who are temperamentally inclined to be shy, fearful, or inhibited may be wary of other children.	• Place small babies side by side when they are calm and alert. • Talk about what other children are doing (e.g., "Look at Willonda shaking that toy; let's go watch how she makes the beads spin"). • Supervise small children to prevent them from hurting one another. When they accidentally bump into others, redirect them to a different path (e.g., "Come this way, Tammy. Chloe doesn't like it when you bump into her").
Early Childhood (2–6 Years) 	• Increasing frequency and complexity of interactions with familiar peers • Developing preference for play activities with particular peers • Formation of rudimentary friendships based on proximity and easy access (e.g., formation of friendships with neighbors and preschool classmates) • Involved conversations and imaginative fantasies with friends	• Children with prior social experiences may find it easier to make friends in a new preschool or child care center. • Children who have sociable and easygoing temperaments tend to form and keep friends more easily than children who are shy, aggressive, anxious, or high-strung.	• Help shy children gain entry into groups, especially if they have previously had limited social experiences. • When necessary, help children resolve conflicts with friends, but encourage them to identify solutions that benefit everyone, and let them do as much of the negotiation as possible.
Middle Childhood (6–10 Years) 	• Concern about being accepted by peers • Tendency to assemble in larger groups than in early childhood • Less need for adult supervision than in early childhood • Outdoor peer groups structured with games and sports • Increase in gossip as children show concern over friends and enemies • Some social exclusiveness, with friends being reluctant to have others join in their activities • Predominance of same-gender friendships	• Boys tend to play in larger groups than girls do. • Some children are temperamentally cautious and timid; they may stand at the periphery of groups and show little social initiative. • Some children are actively rejected by peers, perhaps because they are perceived as odd or have poor social skills.	• Supervise children's peer relationships from a distance; intervene when needed to defuse an escalating situation. • Tactfully facilitate the entry of isolated and rejected children into ongoing games, cooperative learning groups, and informal lunch groups. • Teach rejected children how to interact appropriately with peers.

DEVELOPMENTAL TRENDS (continued)

AGE	WHAT YOU MIGHT OBSERVE	DIVERSITY	IMPLICATIONS
Early Adolescence (10–14 Years) 	• Variety of contexts (e.g., competitive sports, extracurricular activities, parties) in which interactions with peers take place • Heightened concern about acceptance and popularity among peers • Fads and conformity in dress and communication styles in peer groups • Same-gender cliques, often restricted to members of a single ethnic group • Increasing intimacy, self-disclosure, and loyalty among friends • New interest in members of the opposite gender; for gay and lesbian youths, new kind of interest in same gender • For some, initiation of dating, often within the context of group activities	• Some young adolescents are very socially minded; others are more quiet and reserved. • Gossiping and social exclusion may continue in some groups. • Some young adolescents become involved in gangs or other delinquent social groups. • A few young adolescents are sexually active. • A small percentage of adolescents begin to construct an identity as gay or lesbian individuals.	• Make classrooms, schools, and other settings friendly, affirming places for all adolescents. Create an atmosphere of acceptance and respect for diverse kinds of students. • Do not tolerate name calling, insensitive remarks, or sexual harassment. • Provide appropriate places for adolescents to hang out before and after school. • Identify mechanisms (e.g., cooperative learning groups, public service projects) through which teenagers can work toward academic or prosocial goals. • On some occasions, decide which youngsters will fraternize; on other occasions, let them choose their work partners. • Sponsor after-school activities (e.g., in sports, music, or academic interest areas).
Late Adolescence (14–18 Years) 	• Emerging understanding that relationships with numerous peers do not necessarily threaten close friendships • Increasing dependence on friends for advice and emotional support, with adults remaining important in such matters as educational choices and career goals • Less cliquishness toward the end of high school; greater tendency to affiliate in larger, less exclusive crowds • Increasing amount of time spent in mixed-gender groups • Many social activities unsupervised by adults • Emergence of committed romantic couples, especially in the last 2 years of high school	• Some teenagers have parents who continue to monitor their whereabouts; others have little adult supervision. • Adolescents' choices of friends and social groups affect their leisure activities, risk-taking behaviors, and attitudes about schoolwork. Some adolescents actively seek out risky activities. • Teens who find themselves attracted to same-gender peers face additional challenges in constructing their adult identities, especially if others are not accepting of their sexual orientation.	• In literature and history, assign readings with themes of psychological interest to adolescents (e.g., loyalty among friends, self-disclosure of feelings, and vulnerability). • Encourage adolescents to join extracurricular activities that make them feel an integral part of their school. • Sponsor dances and other supervised social events that give adolescents opportunities to socialize.

SCHOOLS

You have learned in this book that teachers and other practitioners can nurture children and adolescents by providing age-appropriate instruction, adequate physical activity, good nutrition, affectionate care, clear rules, and appropriate discipline. When educators integrate such practices into effectively governed classrooms and schools, youngsters truly stand to gain. Let's consider three institutional characteristics of schools that make them enriching environments for children and adolescents: a sense of community, affirming socialization messages, and sensitivity to developmental transitions.

The School as a Community

Educators foster a **sense of community** in schools when students, teachers, and other school staff have shared goals, support one another's efforts, and believe that everyone makes an important contribution (Hom & Battistich, 1995; D. Kim, Solomon, & Roberts, 1995; F. Rowe & Stewart, 2009). When schools cultivate a sense of community, students are more likely to exhibit prosocial behavior, positive attitudes about school, intrinsic motivation to

sense of community
In a classroom or school, a collection of widely shared beliefs that students, teachers, and other staff have common goals, support one another's efforts, and make important contributions to everyone's success.

MyEducationLab

This poster in a middle school corridor (shown in the "Environments: Early Adolescence" video in the Video Examples section of Topic 15 in MyEducationLab) illustrates one important element of classroom climate: the feeling that one is physically and psychologically safe at school.

Preparing for Your Licensure Examination

Your teaching test might ask about strategies for establishing a productive classroom environment.

learn, and high achievement. Furthermore, a sense of community is associated with lower rates of disruptive classroom behavior, emotional distress, truancy, violence, drug use, and dropping out of school (D. Kim et al., 1995; O'Brennan & Furlong, 2010; Osterman, 2000).

A sense of community is the outgrowth of hard work by teachers, other school staff, families, and students themselves. Successful teachers address three factors: (a) the climate of the classroom, (b) instructional methods, and (c) school traditions.

Classroom Climate

Teachers foster a productive climate when they establish a warm, supportive atmosphere in the classroom, show that they care for children, and express their support for children's learning. Children are apt to thrive personally and academically when their classrooms exhibit the following features:

- Teachers communicate genuine caring, respect, and support for all students.
- Students feel both physically and psychologically safe; for instance, they know that they can make mistakes without being ridiculed by their teacher or classmates and that they can seek help from others when they need it. You can examine a poster that communicates a school is a safe place in the "Environments: Early Adolescence" video in MyEducationLab.
- Teachers adopt an *authoritative* approach to instruction and classroom management, setting clear guidelines for behavior but, in the process, also considering students' needs and involving students in decision making.[6]
- Teachers provide sufficient order and structure to guide classroom assignments while also giving students opportunities to engage in appropriate self-chosen and self-directed activities.[7]
- Teachers encourage children to pursue common goals, giving them the sense that they are a bonded group.
- Teachers implement some fun routines, perhaps arranging for enjoyable games during recess or classroom activities.

Classrooms that reflect these principles are, in general, productive ones: Students are motivated to learn new skills, perceive themselves as being reasonably capable, achieve at high academic levels, and act in a socially competent manner (G. A. Davis & Thomas, 1989; Juvonen, 2006; Scott-Little & Holloway, 1992; Wentzel, 1999; H. K. Wilson, Pianta, & Stuhlman, 2007). When other aspects of children's lives trouble them—for instance, when children have strained family relationships, live in dangerous and economically disadvantaged neighborhoods, or are confronted with a natural disaster—perceived support from teachers is especially important in helping youngsters feel safe, competent, valued, and understood (Loukas, Roalson, & Herrera, 2010; McMahon, Parnes, Keys, & Viola, 2008; E. P. Smith, Boutte, Zigler, & Finn-Stevenson, 2004).

Instructional Methods

Teachers can also promote a sense of community by using instructional methods that are active, engaging, and cooperative. In one instructional model, children form a **community of learners**, a classroom arrangement in which students help one another achieve common learning goals. A community of learners has characteristics such as these:

- All students are active participants in classroom activities.
- Collaboration among two or more students is a common occurrence and plays a key role in learning.
- Diversity in students' interests and rates of progress is expected and respected.
- Students and teacher coordinate their efforts at helping one another learn; no one has exclusive responsibility for teaching others.
- Everyone is a potential resource for the others; different individuals are likely to serve as local experts on different occasions, depending on the topics and tasks at hand.

community of learners
A classroom in which teacher(s) and students actively and collaboratively work to help one another learn.

[6]Authoritative parenting is examined in Chapter 3.
[7]Motivational principles for independent choices are described in Chapter 13.

- The teacher provides some guidance and direction for classroom activities, but students may also contribute to the course of activities.
- Students regularly critique one another's work.
- The process of learning is emphasized as much as, and sometimes more than, the finished product. (Boersma, ten Dam, Volman, & Wardekker, 2010; A. L. Brown & Campione, 1994, 1996; Campione, Shapiro, & Brown, 1995; Given et al., 2010; Rogoff, 1994)

The outcomes of community-of-learners groups are often quite positive, especially when teachers encourage children to abide by age-appropriate rules for interaction. Communities of learners tend to promote fairly complex thinking processes and are highly motivating for students (A. L. Brown & Campione, 1994; Turkanis, 2001). For instance, students in these groups often insist on going to school even when they are ill and are disappointed when summer vacation begins (Rogoff, 1994).

School Traditions

Teachers can also foster a sense of community by encouraging children to participate actively in school activities and day-to-day operations. Schools that operate as true communities encourage everyone to work together as cooperative and productive citizens (Battistich et al., 1995; Battistich, Solomon, Watson, & Schaps, 1997; Cemalcilar, 2010; Rothstein-Fisch & Trumbull, 2008). Several strategies are helpful in creating this positive school spirit:

- Soliciting students' ideas about school activities, such as how Valentine's Day might be observed
- Creating mechanisms through which students can help make the school run smoothly and efficiently (e.g., assigning various helper roles to individual students on a rotating basis)
- Emphasizing prosocial values in school codes of conduct, in newsletters, and on bulletin boards
- Providing public recognition of students' contributions to the overall success of the classroom and school
- Creating schoolwide traditions that are fun for youngsters and their families, such as carnivals and field days (D. Kim et al., 1995; Lickona, 1991; Osterman, 2000)

Improving Your Observation Skills

Sense of community. These children are constructing original pieces of art with encouragement from their teacher. What specifically is the teacher doing to establish a productive sense of community in her classroom? Compare your response with the explanation at the end of the chapter.

Ideally, the various instructional practices and traditions of an educational environment combine to help fulfill children's many needs. Early childhood educator **Robert Pianta** and his colleagues have found that children at the elementary level often have good relationships at school, but do not receive the instructional support they need to make adequate academic progress (Downer, Booren, Lima, Luckner, & Pianta, 2010; Jerome, Hamre, & Pianta, 2009; La Paro et al., 2009). Although children are resilient to a certain number of less-than-optimal conditions in their lives, educators can increase children's chances for flourishing by providing for the full range of needs, including children's desires for warm relationships, effective instruction, and an affectionate school environment.

Socialization in Schools

Teachers extend the work that has begun by parents in socializing children to follow certain behaviors (e.g., showing politeness by saying "please" and "thank you") and avoid others (e.g., hitting other children).[8] They also transmit information about values specific to the school environment and their expectations about children's abilities to achieve in school.

[8]The socialization tactics of parents are outlined in Chapter 3.

School Values

Teachers begin to socialize children the moment that children enter school. Teachers typically expect and encourage behaviors such as these:

- Showing respect for authority figures
- Controlling impulses
- Following instructions
- Completing assigned tasks in a timely manner
- Working independently
- Cooperating with classmates
- Striving for academic excellence

Children seem to cope most effectively in a new classroom when teachers openly communicate such expectations. However, much of the time teachers do not remember to articulate their standards. Teachers' unstated expectations for behavior are sometimes known as the *hidden curriculum* (Anyon, 1988; Langhout & Mitchell, 2008; Solmon & Lee, 2008).

A teacher's hidden curriculum may or may not be consistent with sound developmental principles. A teacher may emphasize the importance of always getting the right answer, doing tasks in a particular way, or, as the following dialogue between a teacher and several students illustrates, getting things done as quickly as possible:

Teacher:	I will put some problems on the board. You are to divide.
Child:	We got to divide?
Teacher:	Yes.
Several children:	[*Groan*] Not again, Mr. B., we done this yesterday.
Child:	Do we put the date?
Teacher:	Yes. I hope we remember we work in silence. You're supposed to do it on white paper. I'll explain it later.
Child:	Somebody broke my pencil. [*Crash*—a child falls out of his chair.]
Child:	[*repeats*] Mr. B., somebody broke my *pencil!*
Child:	Are we going to be here all morning? (Anyon, 1988, p. 367)

In this situation the teacher presents math problems merely as things that need to be done—not as tasks that might actually have some benefit—and the children clearly have little interest in the assignment.

Children may or may not find it easy to live up to teachers' standards for behavior, but they are more likely to be successful in the classroom if they are at least *aware* of these standards. Teachers can do three things:

• **Tell children about expected behavior.** Children come to school with their own styles of acting and do not automatically decipher teachers' expectations for how students are supposed to communicate in groups, ask for help, express their confusion, and so forth. In general, children find it easier to act in acceptable ways when teachers explain their expectations, post important rules of behavior on a bulletin board, or disseminate them in simple handouts (Gettinger & Kohler, 2006; Thornberg, 2008).

• **Ask children about their perceptions of classroom rules.** Children actively interpret classroom events and can offer informative points of view about classroom rules. In one study in Sweden, children viewed teachers as being hypocritical by asking children not to chew gum but then surreptitiously chewing gum themselves (Thornberg, 2008). In one conversation with a researcher, three 11-year-old boys complained about having to go outside during breaks, saying that they did not get headaches when they stayed inside even though this was the reason for outside time given by teachers (Thornberg, 2008). A more thorough discussion between the teachers and children might have led to a mutually respectful understanding and perhaps even a plan that everyone found reasonable.

• **Offer extra help to students who find it difficult to identify expectations at school.** Some youngsters, perhaps due to a cognitive or social-emotional disability, find it particularly challenging to determine which behaviors are appropriate and which are inappropriate in various situations. A particular child with Asperger syndrome, a type of autism spectrum disorder, might need to be told that although squealing on the playground is considered fun, shouting inside the classroom will annoy others (Myles & Simpson, 2001).[9] Strategies that appear effective in making the hidden curriculum transparent for children with disabilities include role playing, asking children to speculate about proper courses of action in various situations, and conducting "social autopsies"—conversations between a child and adult about social mistakes and better courses of action for the future (Myles & Simpson, 2001).

Teachers' Expectations About the Abilities of Students

As we have seen, teachers have expectations for how their students should behave in the classroom. But teachers also form expectations about how individual students are *likely* to perform. In many instances teachers size up their students fairly accurately: They know which ones need help with reading skills, which ones have trouble working together in the same cooperative group, and so on, and they adapt their instruction accordingly (Alber-Morgan, 2010; Goldenberg, 1992; Good & Nichols, 2001).

But teachers occasionally make inaccurate assessments. Teachers often underestimate the abilities of students who

- Are physically unattractive
- Misbehave frequently in class
- Speak in dialects other than Standard English
- Are members of ethnic minority groups
- Are recent immigrants
- Come from low-income backgrounds
- Have a disability (Amatea & West-Olatunji, 2007; R. E. Bennett et al., 1993; Gray, 2010; McKown & Weinstein, 2008; J. Oakes & Guiton, 1995; Ritts, Patterson, & Tubbs, 1992; G. Thompson, 2008)

Teachers with low expectations for certain students offer them few opportunities for speaking in class, ask them easy questions, give little feedback about their responses, and present them with few, if any, challenging assignments (Good & Brophy, 1994; Rosenthal, 1994; Rubie-Davies, 2010). In contrast, teachers with high expectations for students are apt to create a warmer classroom climate, interact with students more frequently, provide more opportunities for students to respond, and give more positive feedback (Rubie-Davies, 2010).

Most children and adolescents are well aware of their teachers' differential treatment of individual students and use it to draw inferences about their own and others' abilities (R. Butler, 1994; Good & Nichols, 2001; Weinstein, 1993). Children who routinely receive low-ability messages from teachers begin to see themselves as their teachers see them. Furthermore, students may exert little effort on academic tasks, or they may frequently misbehave in class (Marachi, Friedel, & Midgley, 2001; Murdock, 1999). In some cases, then, teachers' expectations lead to a **self-fulfilling prophecy**: What teachers expect students to achieve becomes what students actually do achieve.

Communicating High Expectations

A characteristic consistently found in effective schools is high expectations for student performance (M. Phillips, 1997; Roderick & Camburn, 1999). Even if students' initial academic performance is low, educators and other professionals must remember that cognitive abilities and skills can and do change over time, especially when the environment is conducive to growth. We suggest two strategies to help teachers maintain a realistic yet optimistic outlook on what young people can accomplish:

- **Learn more about students' backgrounds.** Adults are most likely to develop low expectations for students' performance when they have rigid stereotypes about students from certain ethnic or socioeconomic groups (Amatea & West-Olatunji, 2007; J. Conner,

self-fulfilling prophecy
Phenomenon in which an adult's expectations for a child's performance bring about that level of performance.

[9]Autism spectrum disorders are examined in Chapter 12.

2010; Reyna, 2000). Such stereotypes are often the result of ignorance about students' home environments and cultures (K. Alexander et al., 1987; L. Wilson, 2007). Education is the key here: Teachers and other school personnel can learn about students' backgrounds and local communities. With a clear picture of students' families, activities, and values, educators are far more likely to think of students as *individuals*—each with a unique set of talents and skills—than as stereotypical members of a particular group.

• **Collaborate with colleagues to maximize academic success on a schoolwide basis.** Educators are more likely to have high expectations for students when they are confident in their own ability to help students achieve academic and social success (Ashton, 1985; L. Wilson, 2007). Consider the case of one inner-city high school. For many years, teachers at the school believed that their low-achieving students were simply unmotivated to learn. Teachers also saw themselves, their colleagues, and school administrators as ineffective in helping these students succeed. To counteract such tendencies, the school faculty began holding regular 2-hour meetings in which they

• Read research related to low-achieving and at-risk students
• Explored various hypotheses about why their students were having difficulty
• Developed, refined, and evaluated innovative strategies for helping students succeed
• Established a collaborative atmosphere in which, working together, they could take positive action

Such meetings helped the teachers form higher expectations for their students' achievement and a better understanding of what they themselves could do to help the students achieve (Weinstein, Madison, & Kuklinski, 1995).

Transitions to New Schools

Entering any new school requires youngsters to adjust to unfamiliar peers and teachers, new academic expectations, and novel activities in a new building. In other respects, however, the experiences in adjusting to particular school environments present distinct challenges to youngsters.

Elementary Schools

In most Western societies, children typically begin elementary school at the age of 5 or 6, when society declares them "ready" for serious learning. Children generally find it easier to adjust to school when they enter with certain academic skills. Children who have been encouraged to listen to stories and use complex language at home adapt without difficulty to a school's literacy curriculum. Likewise, children who have had many constructive experiences with peers are prepared for a classroom's social environment. In addition, children who have participated in preschool tend to make good social adjustments and perform at reasonably high levels in first grade (Consortium of Longitudinal Studies, 1983; Magnuson, Ruhm, & Waldfogel, 2007; Temple, Reynolds, & Arteaga, 2010).

In the process of adjusting to a school's academic challenges, children get used to the regulatory atmosphere of the classroom. Elementary classrooms tend to be more formal and regimented than the cozy settings of family, child care, and preschool. As a result, when children first enter elementary school, one of their challenges is learning the procedures of the "big kids" school (Corsaro & Molinari, 2005). Here's how first grader Sofia described school rules to her mother and an interviewer:

Mother:	Do you know the rules? What are the rules in first grade?
Sofia:	You cannot run in the corridors, you cannot hurt anyone, you have to raise your hand before talking, you cannot lose toys.
Interviewer:	You know all the rules!
Sofia:	Then you cannot walk around, you cannot shout in the bathroom.
Interviewer:	You know everything.
Mother:	And then? Perhaps you must wait your turn.
Sofia:	And then, you have to be silent, write the date. That's all.
	(Corsaro & Molinari, 2005, pp. 74–75)

Of course, there is more to school than restrictions. To help children adjust to new classrooms, teachers generally offer lots of reassurance during those initial weeks and months when children feel uneasy. Many teachers and schools offer orientations and encourage children and families to visit their classrooms before school begins. We authors recall that our children had elementary teachers who invited them to visit their classrooms in the spring or summer when student placements were announced or sent the children friendly letters before the school year began.

The relationships that children develop with their teacher are an important factor in children's adjustment to school. Teachers can help children adjust by reaching out to them individually, getting to know their names, noticing what they do well, and generally encouraging them. In the elementary grades, each child is one of 15 to 30 students whom a teacher gets to know fairly well. Also easing children's adjustment is the teacher's attention to their individual needs. Especially important are efforts to help children who begin the year lacking age-typical intellectual or social skills. Children with delays most certainly *are* ready to learn but may require individualized services.

Secondary Schools

Young people often make two major transitions at the secondary level. First, beginning at grade 5, 6, or 7, many students move from elementary to either middle school or junior high school. Second, at grade 9 or 10, students move from middle or junior high school to high school. And as they progress through these upper grade levels, students attend separate classes, each with its own teacher. The three secondary configurations—middle, junior high, and high school—have distinctive features but share qualities that distinguish them from elementary schools. A typical secondary school is unlike an elementary school in these ways:

- The school is larger and has more students.
- Teacher–student relationships are more superficial and less personal than they were in elementary school.
- There is more whole-class instruction, with less individualized instruction that takes into account each student's particular needs.
- Classes are less socially cohesive; students may not know their classmates well and be reluctant to call on peers for assistance.
- Competition among students (e.g., for popular classes or spots on an athletic team) is more common, especially in high school.
- Students have more independence and responsibility for their own learning; for instance, they sometimes have relatively unstructured assignments to be accomplished over a 2- or 3-week period and must take the initiative to seek help if they are struggling.
- Standards for assigning grades are more rigorous, so students may earn lower grades than they did in elementary school. Grades are often assigned on a comparative basis, with only the highest-achieving students getting As and Bs. (Darling-Hammond & Friedlaender, 2008; A. J. Davidson, Gest, & Welsh, 2010; Eccles & Midgley, 1989; Futrell & Gomez, 2008; Roderick & Camburn, 1999; Schmakel, 2008; Véronneau & Dishion, 2011; Wigfield et al., 1996)

Many educators lament the apparent mismatch between the secondary environment and the needs of adolescents. At a time when adolescents are self-conscious, uncertain, and confronted with tumultuous changes in their bodies and social relationships, their contact with teachers is superficial and sometimes adversarial. To combat potential feelings of anonymity and disengagement, some high schools arrange for every teacher to take responsibility for a small group of students whom the teacher gets to know individually. Advising teachers orient students to the layout and customs of the school and talk regularly with them about how they are doing in classes, what study skills they are using, and how they are relating to peers (Uvaas, 2010).

Fortunately, many schools are finding ways to welcome entering students and personalize learning environments as students settle into classes. The Development and Practice feature "Easing School Transitions" illustrates several strategies for helping youngsters adjust to new schools.

DEVELOPMENT AND PRACTICE
Easing School Transitions

Make contact with children before the beginning of school.

- In April a kindergarten teacher invites prospective students and their parents to come to an orientation in her classroom. The teacher arranges for snacks to be served and reserves time for a brief presentation and independent exploration of the room. (Early Childhood)

- Late in the summer, a high school teacher sends students in his homeroom a letter introducing himself and welcoming them to his room. He talks about the fun things he has done over the summer, including traveling, camping, reading, and volunteering in a community garden. He mentions his academic interests and tells students he looks forward to hearing about their summer. (Late Adolescence)

Provide a means through which every student can feel a part of a small, close-knit group.

- An elementary physical education teacher arranges for students to work on motor skills in small groups. Students stay in the groups for several weeks and learn how to coach one another. During each lesson, students compliment one another on a particular aspect of the skill (e.g., dribbling or throwing a ball) that they are doing well and offer a suggestion on one feature that could be improved. (Middle Childhood)

- In September a middle-school math teacher establishes *base groups* of three or four students, who provide assistance to one another throughout the school year. At the beginning or end of every class period, the teacher gives students in the base groups 5 minutes to help one another with homework assignments. (Early Adolescence)

Find time to meet one on one with every student.

- An elementary teacher holds individual conferences with children twice a year. The teacher looks through representative works that the children have created but also makes a point to ask the children how they feel about school and their relationships with peers. (Middle Childhood)

- Early in the school year, a middle school social studies teacher holds individual meetings with each of his students. In these meetings he searches for common interests that he and his students share and encourages the students to talk with him whenever they need help with academic or personal problems. Throughout the semester he continues to touch base with individual students (often during lunch or before or after school) to see how they are doing. (Early Adolescence)

Give young people the extra support they may need to master subject matter and study skills.

- An after-school program offers a comprehensive array of services to middle school students. Students receive tutoring in core subjects as well as opportunities to participate in leisure activities. Role models from the community routinely visit the group and serve as mentors, and students discuss goals for the future and strategies for resisting negative temptations (T. E. Hanlon, Simon, O'Grady, Carswell, & Callaman, 2009). (Early Adolescence)

- A high school implements a homework hotline staffed by a teacher and a group of honor students, and teachers in the school make a point of encouraging students to keep up with their work (McCarthy & Kuh, 2005). (Late Adolescence)

SOCIETY

As you have learned, youngsters acquire many skills, beliefs, and attitudes during ongoing interactions in the family, at school, and with peers. Children also learn from others in **society**—an enduring group of people who are socially and economically organized into collective institutions and activities. We now examine the effects on children of society's services, the media, and interactive technologies.

Services for Children and Adolescents

Community organizations often look after children when not under the supervision of parents. Child care and after-school activities are especially important outlets for children's time.

Child Care

Many young children are in the care of adults other than their parents for a significant portion of the week. Children are attended to in a variety of settings, from family homes to commercial buildings, and by caregivers who differ in experience, education, and dedication to children. Such variations raise concerns about the degree to which all children are cared for in a manner that is affectionate, safe, and age-appropriate (Brauner, Gordic, & Zigler, 2004; Burchinal, Vandergrift, Pianta, & Mashburn, 2010).

society
Large, enduring group of people that is socially and economically organized and has collective institutions and activities.

Advocates for high standards in child care have two primary ways of defining quality. *Structural measures* include such objective indicators as caregivers' training and experience, child-to-caregiver ratios, staff turnover, and number and complexity of toys and equipment (Ghazvini & Mullis, 2002; Harrist, Thompson, & Norris, 2007; M. E. Lamb & Ahnert, 2006). Early childhood specialists recommend that the child-to-caregiver ratio be no more than three infants or six toddlers for each adult (Bredekamp & Copple, 1997). *Process measures* of quality include adults' sensitive care of children, affectionate child–caregiver relationships, productive child–peer interactions, and developmentally appropriate activities (Bigras et al., 2010; M. E. Lamb & Ahnert, 2006; NICHD Early Child Care Research Network, 2006a). As an indication of high-quality processes, the schedules of activities in a toddler room might be fairly predictable from day to day but also flexible enough to be guided by children's individual and changing needs (Bredekamp & Copple, 1997). Thus, toddlers might be offered two snacks over the span of the morning, even though only a few choose to eat twice.

HIGH-QUALITY CARE. Young children benefit from interacting with well-trained and sensitive caregivers who focus on their individual needs.

In reality, indicators of structure and process are closely related. Low child-to-staff ratios, small group sizes, and advanced levels of caregiver education tend to be associated with responsive interactions with children (e.g., Bigras et al., 2010; Howes, Smith, & Galinsky, 1995; NICHD Early Child Care Research Network, 2002). When caregivers have too many children to care for, their style of interacting with individual children tends to become rushed and mechanical.

In general, research confirms that high-quality child care yields advantages in children. Infants and small children typically enjoy secure attachments to employed caregivers who are warm, sensitive, and consistently involved in the children's care (Barnas & Cummings, 1994; Ebbeck & Yim, 2009; M. E. Lamb & Ahnert, 2006).[10] In addition, children regularly develop cognitive, linguistic, and social skills while in good care, with the greatest benefits occurring in children whose home environments have been inattentive or unstimulating (Sylva, Melhuish, Sammons, Siraj-Blatchford, & Taggart, 2004; Watamura, Phillips, Morrissey, McCartney, & Bub, 2011).[11]

Child care does create some risks, however. Exposure to child care at a young age and for long hours seems to trigger slight increases in children's aggression and noncompliance (Belsky & Eggebeen, 1991; M. E. Lamb & Ahnert, 2006; NICHD Early Child Care Research Network, 2002, 2005). These effects are not always seen and, when they are, they are smaller for high-quality than for low-quality care.

After-School Programs and Extracurricular Activities

Not every parent has access to affordable care for children, and as they grow, youngsters naturally want to care for themselves (Ceglowski, Shears, & Furman, 2010). Children's frequent *self-care* is a concern because children are not always able to anticipate or avoid dangerous situations. They may open the door when a stranger rings the doorbell, forget that they have the stove on, and decide to partake in alcohol and drugs when tempted by friends. Self-care arrangements are generally more effective when parents explain safety procedures, convey clear and firm expectations for behavior, and monitor children's activities by calling them on the telephone or by having another family member, such as a grandparent, check on them (Galambos & Maggs, 1991; Mahoney & Parente, 2009; Steinberg, 1986).

Communities can help by providing safe, fun, and supervised activities. Young people who have productive outlets for their free time—perhaps in clubs, sports leagues, dance and martial arts lessons, scout troops, and so on—are apt to acquire valuable skills and avoid serious trouble. Twelve-year-old Colin gives a sense of his rich learning experiences in the community in the "After School: Early Adolescence" video in MyEducationLab:

Interviewer:	So you play basketball?
Colin:	Yeah. Yeah.

MyEducationLab

Listen to 12-year-old Colin describe what he does outside school in the "After School: Early Adolescence" video. (Find Video Examples in Topic 15 of MyEducationLab.)

[10]The security of attachments is examined in Chapter 11.
[11]Chapter 8 explains that children from economically disadvantaged families who attend high-quality infant and preschool settings are apt to gain significant intellectual advantages and other benefits.

Interviewer:	What other . . . is that your favorite sport?
Colin:	I like basketball and track about the same.
Interviewer:	Do you play any other sports?
Colin:	Yeah. I play, basically, I play football, baseball, hockey. . . .
Interviewer:	Wow. What do you like about sports?
Colin:	Well, they're fun and just something to do.
Interviewer:	What kinds of hobbies do you have?
Colin:	I like coin collecting and . . . I garden and I try to take sign language and really do sign language. Yeah.
Interviewer:	So what kinds of clubs do you belong to?
Colin:	I belong to . . . well, I used to belong to 4-H. And I'm in the chess club, Boy Scouts, and sign language club.

ARTIFACT 15-11 Enrichment. Effective after-school programs typically offer a variety of activities through which young people can pursue their individual interests. Eleven-year-old Brandon draws several of the activities he enjoys in a community program.

A growing body of research indicates that participation in after-school and summer activities fosters children's cognitive and social-emotional development. Academically oriented programs appear to cultivate positive feelings about school, better school attendance, higher grades and achievement test scores, superior classroom behavior, greater conflict resolution skills, and decreased tension with family members (Dryfoos, 1999; Granger, 2008; Téllez & Waxman, 2010; Vandell & Pierce, 1999). Nonacademic programs, too, seem to have benefits. High school students who participate in their school's extracurricular activities are more likely than nonparticipants to achieve at high levels and graduate from high school. They are also less likely to smoke cigarettes, use alcohol or drugs, exhibit anxiety, join gangs, engage in criminal activities, or become teenage parents (Biddle, 1993; H. Cooper, Valentine, Nye, & Lindsay, 1999; Dimech & Seiler, 2010; Donato et al., 1997; Eppright, Sanfacon, Beck, & Bradley, 1998; Gilman, Meyers, & Perez, 2004; Zill, Nord, & Loomis, 1995).

After-school and summer programs vary in their focus and services, yet most espouse a commitment to providing caring adult–child relationships. In addition, effective programs include these general features:

- Breadth of activities, including recreation, academic and cultural enrichment, and opportunities for pursuit of individual interests
- Chances for meaningful participation in authentic activities, such as building a fort, reading to younger children, or registering voters
- Opportunities for success, perhaps in domains in which youngsters have previously unrecognized talents
- Positive interactions with both adults and peers
- Clear limits, with youngsters' actively participating in establishment of rules
  - High regard and respect for young people's diverse cultural beliefs and practices (C. R. Cooper, Denner, & Lopez, 1999; Durlak, Mahoney, Bohnert, & Parente, 2010; Granger, 2008; Kerewsky & Lefstein, 1982; Lefstein & Lipsitz, 1995)

Many adolescents spend their free time in part-time jobs. Adolescents can gain beneficial experiences from getting to work on time, adhering to the requirements of a position, being courteous in a business setting, and managing money. With limited work hours (e.g., 10 to 15 hours per week), adolescents may have adequate time to study and stay involved in school activities (Mortimer et al., 1994; Staff, Messersmith, & Schulenberg, 2009; Steinberg, Brown, Cider, Kaczmarek, & Lazzaro, 1988). However, some adolescents work long hours in tedious jobs that fail to inculcate them with a motivation to work hard. Excessively long work hours put young people at risk for poor school achievement, limited participation in extracurricular activities, and drug and alcohol use (Staff et al., 2009).

BUILDING A FUTURE. After-school activities can foster young people's dispositions to serve their community.

DEVELOPMENT AND PRACTICE
Enhancing Students' Before- and After-School Experiences

Help children navigate transitions between school and out-of-school care.

- After school a kindergarten teacher walks outside to make sure that each child successfully connects with family members or car pool drivers, gets on the appropriate bus or van, or begins walking home. (Early Childhood)
- A teacher in an after-school elementary program asks children to unpack their homework and put it in a special folder as they arrive at the center. After children have eaten, rested, and gotten a chance to play for a half hour or so, the teacher pulls out assignments and helps the children get started with their homework. (Middle Childhood)

Sponsor after-school clubs at your school.

- A middle school offers several clubs for students to participate in after school. Popular options include a Hispanic cultures club, several athletic teams, an honor society, a band, a community service group, and the yearbook staff. (Early Adolescence)
- Most of the teachers in one high school sponsor one or more after-school activities. The school offers many traditional high school clubs, such as band, a theater group, competitive sports, and a debate society, but also invites students to help organize other activities, for example, ultimate Frisbee and a community service organization. (Late Adolescence)

Inform parents and guardians about youth initiatives in their area.

- At a parent–teacher–student conference, a middle school teacher describes clubs and sports programs available at the school, as well as recreational and service opportunities in the local community. (Early Adolescence)
- A high school includes a page on its website with links to various clubs, leisure activities, and extracurricular options at the school and in the community. During an advising session early in the year, teachers invite students to check out the various options they might consider trying. (Late Adolescence)

Establish a team of school personnel and after-school providers to ensure that after-school programs meet children's physical, social-emotional, and academic needs.

- Two teachers, the principal, and the director of an after-school program meet regularly to discuss space, resources, and ways that the after-school program can give children needed rest, relaxation, snacks, and tutoring. (Middle Childhood)
- A middle school principal invites community leaders to offer a brief presentation to parents and staff at the school. The community leaders inform everyone about the various youth centers and leisure activities that are available in the area. (Early Adolescence)

We cannot be definite about the specific effects of extracurricular activities and after-school programs because youngsters who choose to participate in these services may be different from youngsters who decide not to take advantage of them. Nonetheless, because of the potential—and, we suggest, likely—benefits of extracurricular activities and after-school programs, these services merit investment until social scientists can determine their effects with more certainty. The Development and Practice feature "Enhancing Students' Before- and After-School Experiences" suggests strategies for educators and other practitioners to help young people make good use of their nonschool time.

Television and the Interactive Technologies

In the industrialized world, children regularly watch television and use a growing collection of **interactive technologies**—computers, the Internet, video games, talking books, and cell phones (also known as cellular phones or mobile phones). Most noticeable to many teachers are students frequently sending text messages, brief written messages over cell phones. Other regular pastimes for adolescents are watching video clips, playing electronic games, and using *social network services* (websites that permit individuals to communicate with selected individuals, update information about their activities, participate in common interest groups, and share photographs and website links; examples include *Facebook*, *MySpace*, and *Big Tent*). Many students additionally contribute to *blogs* (personalized websites that permit the documentation of ideas, images, and events, as well as comments on these sites from visitors) and *wikis* (interlinked websites that are created and edited with simple programming languages) (F. W. Baker, 2010).

> **Preparing for Your Licensure Examination**
> Your teaching test might ask about using the Internet and other digital tools to enrich the learning environment for students.

interactive technology
Array of electronic, digitally based machines that are operated dynamically by a person whose commands determine emerging program sequences.

Content of Programs

Fortunately, many programs aired on television and built into interactive technologies have educationally worthwhile content. Educational television programs such as *The Magic School Bus, Reading Rainbow, Between the Lions*, and *Bill Nye the Science Guy* teach children vocabulary, word recognition, reading concepts, problem-solving skills, and scientific principles (D. R. Anderson, 2003; Jennings, Hooker, & Linebarger, 2009; Kirkorian, Wartella, & Anderson, 2008; Linebarger & Piotrowski, 2010). Television programs and video games that model prosocial behaviors, for example, *Mister Rogers' Neighborhood, Sesame Street, Saved by the Bell*, and *Smurfs*, teach children valuable social skills (D. R. Anderson, 2003; C. F. Cole, Labin, & del Rocio Galarza, 2008; A. B. Jordan, 2003). Serious educational games, for example *The Great Entomologist Escape*, expose users to worthwhile scientific information and other academic knowledge. In *The Great Entomologist Escape*, created by a high school science teacher, students pretend to be the lead scientist of a research team who must learn about ants to solve various practical problems (Annetta, 2010).

Unfortunately, developmentally counterproductive content coexists with, and potentially overshadows, socially responsible material in the media. Television programs and video games are apt to show ethnic minorities infrequently and to include grossly stereotypical characters—for instance, women as airheads, men as brutes, and people with dark skin as thugs (Eisenberg et al., 1996; Kahlenberg & Hein, 2010; Tynes & Ward, 2009). Such offensive portrayals are ridiculous distortions of reality but may instill impressionable children with misconceptions about particular social groups. Furthermore, when youngsters repeatedly view slender and athletically toned actors, actresses, and rock stars, they may develop a standard of physical attractiveness that is not realistic for their own body frame (Anschutz, Engels, Van Leeuwe, & Van Strien, 2009). In addition, advertisements on television and Internet websites cultivate desires for particular cereals, fast food, clothing, toys, and digital devices—items that may or may not be in children's best interests (Buijzen & Valkenburg, 2003; Calvert, 2008; S. Reese, 1996; D. M. Thomson, 2010).

The excessively violent and gruesomely graphic scenes of many television programs and video games are another concern. In fact, violence can be found in a large percentage of television programs and video games (C. A. Anderson et al., 2003; Comstock & Scharrer, 2006; Holtz & Appel, 2011). Repeated exposure to violent acts on television seems to make children more aggressive and may be particularly harmful to those already predisposed to aggression (Comstock & Scharrer, 2006; Eron, 1980; Holtz & Appel, 2011). Children inclined to solve conflicts in physically aggressive ways are apt to choose programs with violent content and become *more aggressive* after viewing such programs. In addition, heavy viewing of televised violence and excessive use of violent video games may *desensitize* children to acts of violence; that is, children's repeated viewing of televised violence seems to erode their empathic responses to victims of real violent acts (Holtz & Appel, 2011; Lemmens, Valkenburg, & Peter, 2011; B. J. Wilson, 2008).

Viewing Television

On average, television viewing time increases rapidly during early childhood, continues to increase in middle childhood and early adolescence (reaching a peak of almost 3 hours a day), and then declines gradually after about age 14 (D. F. Roberts & Foehr, 2008). Many developmental experts suggest that television is detrimental for infants, whose foremost psychological needs, especially those for close bonds to caregivers and active exploration of the environment, are not met through this medium (Courage & Setliff, 2010). Developmental scholars, health practitioners, and educators are also concerned about the heavy viewing of older children because of their occasionally high exposure to inappropriate content, low levels of physical activity, and diminished time for interactions with peers (e.g., Caroli, Argentieri, Cardone, & Masi, 2004).

Playing Interactive Games

Interactive games played on game consoles, computers, and handheld devices are an especially popular source of entertainment among Western youth, especially among boys in

ARTIFACT 15-12 Game gadget. Gene drew this picture of his video game equipment from memory, showing his familiarity with the apparatus and a game's combat theme.

middle childhood and adolescence (Hamlen, 2011; Kutner et al., 2008; D. F. Roberts & Foehr, 2008). Youngsters with access to video games spend numerous hours clutching controllers as they engage in virtual punching matches, motorcycle races, and explorations of mythical environments. Six-year-old Brent shows his enthusiasm for video games in the "After School: Early Childhood" video in MyEducationLab. He says:

> I usually play video games. There's this army game and snowboard game and . . . and a game called "Smash Brothers." . . . They're cool.

The appeal of video games results largely from their strikingly effective instructional principles. Video games allow children to pursue a tangible goal, implement continually evolving strategies, make steady progress, experience success, use increasingly advanced tools, and obtain personalized feedback at every step (Gentile & Gentile, 2008; Hamlen, 2011). Playing video games can become a habit, however, and overuse is a concern when it leads children to curtail healthful physical activity. Also, as we indicated earlier, youngsters who play video games are likely to select at least some games that contain violent content and inappropriate social stereotypes.

Nonetheless, video games have the potential to exert some positive influences on children. Numerous nonviolent and creative video games are available, and youngsters can improve such cognitive abilities as spatial and visual-attention skills as they play games (e.g., De Lisi & Wolford, 2002; Greenfield, DeWinstanley, Kilpatrick, & Kaye, 1996; Griffiths, 2010). Children themselves report a variety of benefits from playing video games, including having fun, enjoying the challenge, cooperating with peers, making friends, regulating their feelings, expressing creativity, and trying out new identities (Giffiths, 2010; C. K. Olson, 2010). Particular games, such as those with health-promotion themes, can teach children valuable skills in caring for themselves, eating healthfully, and managing their health conditions (Baranowski et al., 2011; D. A. Lieberman, 1997). In addition, such games as Konami's *Dance Dance Revolution* and Nintendo's *Wii Fit* encourage many young people to engage in exercise (Olmsted, 2008).

Using Computers and the Internet

Personal computers and other electronic devices have many applications in the classroom. Through such mechanisms as electronic mail (e-mail), Web-based chat rooms, and electronic bulletin boards, computer technology enables students to communicate with peers and subject matter experts and to analyze data, exchange perspectives, build on one another's ideas, and solve problems (A. L. Brown & Campione, 1996; Fabos & Young, 1999; Hewitt & Scardamalia, 1996; McCombs & Vakili, 2005; Schachter, 2000; M. Scherer, 2011; Winn, 2002). You can observe children using the Internet to learn about worms in the "Internet and Online Video" in MyEducationLab. A class itself can have a website, allowing students to monitor announcements, turn in assignments, and make comments on a shared bulletin board (L. S. Dunn, 2011).

In addition, well-constructed software and interactive systems give students a carefully structured curriculum with personalized lessons and steady feedback. Examples of dynamic, interactive websites include those of the *National Library of Virtual Manipulatives*,[12] *Cells Alive*,[13] *National Geographic Creature Feature*,[14] and *Math in Daily Life*[15] (Coiro & Fogleman, 2011). *Epistemic games*, electronic games that allow users to learn thinking skills of experts in one or more fields, are becoming increasingly popular. In *Sim City 4*, students function as urban planners in designing simulated residential areas, commercial areas of cities, railways, airports, power plants, and other infrastructures for the locality. As they gain experience on the game, students solve complex real-world problems and learn science, technology, and society (Salmani Nodoushan, 2009). Examples of other epistemic games are *Age of Empires*

MyEducationLab

Listen to Brent talk about video games in the "After School: Early Childhood" video. (Find Video Examples in Topic 15 of MyEducationLab.)

MyEducationLab

Observe children using the Internet to learn about worms in the "Internet and Online Learning" video. (Find Video Examples in Topic 15 of MyEducationLab.)

---

[12]http://nlvm.usu.edu/en/nav/vlibrary.html
[13]http://www.cellsalive.com
[14]http://kids.nationalgeographic.com/kids/animals/creaturefeature
[15]http://www.learner.org/interactives/dailymath

(focusing on history), *Microsoft Flight Simulator* (drawing from knowledge of aircraft flight, airports, and climatic conditions), and *Digital Zoo* (using principles of biomechanical engineering and animal physiology) (Salmani Nodoushan, 2009).

Outside the classroom (and sometimes within it), youngsters increasingly use the Internet for their own personal communications. When making the transition from childhood to adolescence, many youngsters supplement or even replace interests in electronic games with social communication in e-mail, social networks, and chat rooms (Greenfield & Subrahmanyam, 2003; Hellenga, 2002). Young people use these social venues to stay connected with friends and explore new personal identities for themselves. A shy teenager who forms relationships with a few individuals through regular e-mail and chat room exchanges may learn to express feelings of anger, fear, and frustration. Other adolescents may find like-minded individuals who support their interests and orientations (e.g., homosexuality). Adolescents experiment with different personalities at a time when they are wrestling with identity issues; for instance, some young people intentionally project older images or accentuate their physical attractiveness (Clemens et al., 2008; Hellenga, 2002).

Some negative consequences are also possible, however. A teenager may withdraw from family and peers in favor of friends known only electronically. And the desire to stay connected electronically may lead to excessively long hours on the computer. Other youngsters develop bad habits, such as *flaming* (i.e., verbally ridiculing someone in a public electronic site), *trolling* (i.e., making an inflammatory remark to provoke an argument), *hacking* into secured sites to disrupt services or spread computer viruses, and plagiarizing the work of other people (Hellenga, 2002). Furthermore, adolescents who are regular users of the Internet may be sexually harassed or solicited (Finkelhor, Mitchell, & Wolak, 2000; Hinduja & Patchin, 2011; Willard, 2007).

Implications of Television and Technology

If utilized properly, electronic media and technologies contribute to the education of children. We offer the following suggestions:

• **Encourage parents to regulate children's television viewing**. At meetings and school events and in newsletters, educators can encourage parents to set specific television-viewing goals for their children. For instance, if parents find their children watching television many hours a day, they might want to set a 2-hour limit. Parents also may find it informative to watch television with their children. In the process they can discover how their children interpret what they watch and can provide a reality check when characters and story lines consistently violate norms for appropriate behavior ("Do you think people should really insult one another like that?").

• **Teach critical viewing skills**. Practitioners can teach youngsters how to watch television with a critical eye (Calvert, 2008). Elementary teachers can help young children understand that television commercials aim to persuade them to buy something, perhaps toys or hamburgers. Teachers can also point out more subtle advertising ploys, such as the use of color, images (e.g., sexual symbols), and endorsements by famous actors and athletes. And with any medium—television, computers, books, magazines, and so on—adults can help young people become more aware of stereotypes and negative portrayals of men and women, different ethnic groups, and various professions.

• **Educate youngsters about the aggression they see on television and in video games**. Educators and social scientists have had some success in persuading children that the glamorous, humorous, and pervasive manner in which violence is shown on television is misleading (Rosenkoetter, Rosenkoetter, Ozretich, & Acock, 2004). Thus, you can point out that, contrary to typical television scenes, violence is usually *not* an effective way to handle disagreements and often creates additional problems. You can also explain to children that violence is an eye-catching and unrealistic theme that television producers use to attract audiences and make money.

Preparing for Your Licensure Examination

Your teaching test might ask about fostering critical thinking in children.

- **Use televised movies and computer programs that build on instructional units.** Some television programs and videos can make print content more concrete and understandable. For instance, when Teresa and a coleader guided a group of sixth and seventh graders in a discussion of George Bernard Shaw's play *Pygmalion*, everyone struggled to make sense of characters' dialects. Afterward, the group watched segments of *My Fair Lady*, a movie based on the play, and found the dialects much easier to understand.

- **Prepare all children in technology.** Although many middle- and upper-income families now have personal computers, some lower-income families cannot afford them. But computer expertise, including Internet use, is increasingly critical for everyone's success. Fortunately, digital technologies are becoming more and more affordable, and school districts can sometimes make available laptops and handheld devices for use in school (Scherer, 2011). Because not all children are equally proficient in technology, educators can offer instruction in basic technology skills and their applications. A preschool teacher might teach children how to play computer games that give practice in emergent literacy skills, and an after-school tutor might show young people how to use the Internet while completing homework.

- **Teach young people to be critical users of the Internet.** Young people need to learn how to navigate through countless electronic sites. Because information on many significant topics is expanding exponentially, youngsters must learn to find, retrieve, organize, and evaluate information they find on the Internet. As young people begin to use the Internet for classroom assignments, teachers can advise students that data provided by government agencies and well-respected nonprofit organizations are fairly reliable, but opinion pieces on someone's personal Web page may not be.

- **Advise parents of dangers on the Internet.** Parents can familiarize themselves with websites their children visit and can consider using Internet filters or blocks. Parents can also talk with their children about who is on their buddy list for instant messaging communications and discourage any meetings with online acquaintances, in order to avoid exploitation by sexual predators. In addition, parents can learn common acronyms in contemporary use—for example, LOL, laugh out loud; PAW, parents are watching; A/S/L, age, sex, and location; and WTGP, want to go private? (National Center for Missing and Exploited Children, 2004).

- **Discourage youngsters from using technologies for aggressive purposes.** Teachers and other adults must advise children and adolescents to refrain from *cyberbullying*, the sending or posting of harmful messages over the Internet or with other interactive technologies (Hinduja & Patchin, 2011; Willard, 2007). Adults should also discourage young people from posting racist messages or profanity in their blogs and from sending unflattering photographs of others or demeaning messages over cell phones. Some young people also need to be reminded to refrain from sending mocking or threatening statements as text messages or instant messages (synchronous communications on cell phones or over the Internet to individuals on buddy lists) (Willard, 2007).

- **Advise students in "reputation management."** Young people may regularly but impulsively post personal messages and video clips onto social networking websites. Teachers can talk with students about the kinds of information that it is appropriate to share and ways people can track their images in tagged photographs (Richardson, 2011, p. 25). Of course, many students also need to be advised about the possible long-term harm that can befall individuals who portray themselves in a negative light.

As you have learned, children grow up in a complex social world. The Basic Developmental issues table "Social Contexts of Child Development" synthesizes the effects of peers, schools, and society on children from the perspective of nature and nurture, universality and diversity, and qualitative and quantitative change.

BASIC DEVELOPMENTAL ISSUES
Social Contexts of Child Development

ISSUE	INFLUENCES OF PEERS, SCHOOL, AND SOCIETY
Nature and Nurture	In ideal circumstances, peers offer children emotional support, a safe forum for polishing social skills, and reassuring perspectives on confusing events. Teachers communicate expectations about children's abilities, implement classroom traditions, organize learning groups, and cultivate children's sense of belonging at school. Society has institutions that care for children, technological systems that enable widespread communication, and media that transmit messages about expected behaviors. *Nature* provides a necessary foundation for children's social development with a biologically based desire to interact with other people. Maturational changes are evident in children's evolving peer relationships— for example, increases in language and the ability to take the perspective of others enhance children's ability to resolve differences with peers. Individual differences that derive partly from genes (e.g., temperaments and some physical disabilities) can affect children's peer relationships and social acceptance.
Universality and Diversity	*Universality* is present in the benefits children experience from being liked by peers, having relationships with caring adults outside the family (e.g., teachers and child care providers), participating in a school setting where they are encouraged to achieve at high levels and feel that they belong, and having safe and interesting options for free time. *Diversity* occurs in the particular social skills children develop, the extent to which peers find them likable social partners, the suitability of children's environments (e.g., the quality of child care centers), and the degree to which young people engage in risky behaviors with peers (e.g., committing crimes with fellow gang members, engaging in unprotected sexual contact).
Qualitative and Quantitative Change	Children undergo several *qualitative* transformations in their social relationships. Children form associations with peers that are fleeting social exchanges during infancy, but these ties change into rich language-based and stable relationships during early and middle childhood and then into close friendships, cliques, and romantic relationships during adolescence. Other qualitative overhauls occur in the onset of sexual feelings for peers of opposite gender (or in some instances, same gender) and in youngsters' uses of particular technologies (e.g., initially preferring television and video games and later choosing e-mail and chat rooms). Children also exhibit more gradual, *quantitative* changes in their peer relationships, styles of behaving in schools, and uses of society's institutions and services. Children gradually refine their skills for interacting with peers, and once they adjust to a new school, slowly learn to follow its rules and expectations.

SUMMARY

Peers

Peers serve important functions in social-emotional development. Not only do they offer companionship, but they also create contexts for practicing social skills, making sense of social experiences, and shaping habits and ideas. Peer relationships change systematically throughout childhood; activities tend to shift from simple gestures and imitation (infancy), to pretend play (early childhood), to structured group games (middle childhood), to social activities within cliques and crowds (early adolescence), and finally to larger, mixed-gender groups (late adolescence). Friendships are especially important peer relationships that provide emotional support and foster motivation to resolve conflicts in mutually satisfying ways.

Although preschoolers and elementary school children have an interest in romantic relationships, young people do not understand the multifaceted nature of romance until they reach adolescence. As they go through puberty, they must come to terms with their changing bodies, sexual drives, and increasing sexual attraction to peers. Romances, either actual or imagined, can delight youngsters but also wreak havoc on their emotions. Some adolescents experiment with sexual intimacy with only limited information about

the potential risks. Others wrestle with sexual feelings for same-gender peers. As adolescents experience confusing new feelings, they appreciate sensitivity on the part of educators.

Schools

Schools are powerful contexts of development for children and adolescents. Schools not only prepare youngsters with essential academic skills but also serve as complex social environments that communicate to youngsters how welcome they are and how likely they are to succeed. Ideally, schools offer children a sense of community, deliver affirming messages about learning in general and individual abilities in particular, and support children as they transition into new academic environments.

Society

Society plays an important role through its provision of services to children. Groups of children spend time in child care settings that vary enormously in quality—from responsive and developmentally appropriate to overcrowded and harsh. Child care has the potential to be a beneficial experience; after-school programs and extracurricular activities can also bolster the development of youngsters, especially through stable, affectionate relationships with adults and peers and options for productive pastimes.

Children and adolescents spend many hours watching television and playing or working on the computer. Televisions, computers, cell phones, and other media have considerable potential to foster children's cognitive development, but their benefits have not yet been fully realized. Violent and stereotypical content in the media is a definite risk factor for young people, although some child consumers are especially vulnerable to harmful effects.

APPLYING CONCEPTS IN CHILD DEVELOPMENT

The exercises in this section will help you build your ability to apply your knowledge of child development in your work with children.

Improving Your Observation Skills

On page 580, you examined a photograph of two girls who were laughing and were asked, "*Do the girls seem to be friends or acquaintances?*" These girls appear to be enjoying their mutual interaction. The fact that they see the humor in what appears to be a private joke suggests that they have developed common understandings. Their relaxed facial expressions further suggest that the girls are familiar social partners, rather than new acquaintances.

On page 595, you examined a photograph of a group of children completing an art project and were asked, "*What specifically is the teacher doing to establish a productive sense of community in her classroom?*" This teacher is doing several things that contribute to a productive sense of community in her classroom. She appears to communicate that she likes and respects the children through her warm and affectionate demeanor. She uses flexible instructional methods that permit children to be actively engaged and to personalize the steps they take in completing projects. Finally, she arranges for the children to sit together such that they can be a resource for one another as they work on their individual projects.

Practicing for Your Licensure Examination

Many teaching tests require students to use what they have learned about child development in responses to brief vignettes and multiple-choice questions. You can practice for your licensure examination by reading about a friendship at one school.

Aaron and Cole

Read the case and then answer the questions that follow it.

Aaron and Cole became friends when they were both students in Mr. Howard's fifth-grade class. Although Aaron was in most respects a typical fifth grader, Cole had significant developmental delays. Special educator Debbie Staub (1998) described Cole's special educational needs and his strengths as follows:

Cole has limited expressive vocabulary and uses one- or two-word sentences. He does not participate in traditional academic tasks, although he is included with his typically developing schoolmates for the entire school day. Cole has a history of behavioral problems that have ranged from mild noncompliance to adult requests to serious aggressive and destructive behavior such as throwing furniture at others. In spite of his occasional outbursts, however, it is hard not to like him. Cole is like an eager toddler who finds wonder in the world around him. The boys he has befriended in Mr. Howard's class bring him great joy. He appreciates their jokes and harmless teasing. Cole would like nothing better than to hang out with his friends all day, but if he had to choose just one friend, it would be Aaron. (D. Staub, 1998, p. 76)[a]

Throughout their fifth- and sixth-grade years, Aaron was both a good friend and a caring mentor to Cole.

Without prompting from adults, Aaron helped Cole with his work, included him in games at recess, and generally watched out for him. Aaron also assumed responsibility for Cole's behavior by explaining to Cole how his actions affected others. The following excerpt from a classroom observation illustrates Aaron's gentle way with Cole:

Cole was taking Nelle's [a classmate's] things out of her bag and throwing them on the floor. As soon as Aaron saw, he walked right over to Cole and started talking to him. He said, "We're making a new rule—no being mean." Then he walked with Cole to the front of the room and told him to tell another boy what the new rule was. Cole tapped the boy's shoulder to tell him but the boy walked away. Cole looked confused. Aaron smiled and put his hand on Cole's shoulder and told him, "It's okay. Just remember the rule." Then he walked Cole back to Nelle's stuff and quietly asked Cole to put everything back. (pp. 77–78)

Aaron, too, benefited from the friendship, as his mother explained: "Our family has recently gone through a tough divorce and there are a lot of hurt feelings out there for everyone. But at least when Aaron is at school he feels good about being there and I think a big reason is because he has Cole and he knows that he is an important person in Cole's life" (pp. 90–91).

Dr. Staub observed that, despite their developmental differences, the boys' relationship was in many respects a normal one:

I asked Mr. Howard once, "Do you think Cole's and Aaron's friendship looks different from others' in your class?" Mr. Howard thought for a moment before responding: "No, I don't think it looks that different. Well, I was going to say one of the differences is that Aaron sometimes tells Cole to be quiet, or 'Hey Cole, I gotta do my work!' But I don't know if that is any different than what he might say to Ben leaning over and interrupting him. I think I would say that Aaron honestly likes Cole and it's not because he's a special-needs kid." (p. 78)

Aaron and Cole remained close until Cole moved 30 miles away at the beginning of seventh grade.

Constructed-Response Question

1. In what ways did the friendship of Aaron and Cole promote each boy's social-emotional development?

Multiple-Choice Questions

2. What did Aaron do that probably helped Cole become more socially competent with other peers?

   a. Aaron helped Cole to be accepted by peers by convincing Cole to join him in some risky behaviors.
   b. Aaron did Cole's homework so that Cole looked more capable in front of peers.
   c. Aaron encouraged Cole to avoid other children and remain his friend exclusively.
   d. Aaron coached Cole in such social skills as controlling his temper and remaining friendly with peers.

3. Aaron's and Cole's teacher, Mr. Howard, seemed to be supportive of the boys' friendship. Considering the perspectives in this chapter, what might Mr. Howard have done if he were committed to establishing an effective classroom climate?

   a. Communicate genuine caring and respect for all students.
   b. Encourage students to pursue common goals.
   c. Implement some fun routines on a regular basis.
   d. All of the above.

Once you have answered these questions, compare your responses with those presented in Appendix A.

Improving Your Ability to Interpret Children's Artifacts and Reflections

Consider what you've learned about schools as environments for child development as you analyze the following artifacts from several children.

Teachers at Work

A group of researchers asked students in elementary and middle schools to draw pictures of their teachers working in the classroom (Haney, Russell, & Bebell, 2004). We've selected five of the students' pictures and have given the artists fictitious names to help you identify them individually in your response. As you examine the pictures below and on the following page, consider these questions:

- What do each of the students seem to be suggesting about how teachers *socialize* children?
- What might the students be communicating about the *hidden curriculum* in their school?

Once you have analyzed the artwork, compare your ideas with those presented in Appendix B. For further practice in analyzing children's artifacts and reflections, go to the Activities and Applications section in Chapter 15 of MyEducationLab.

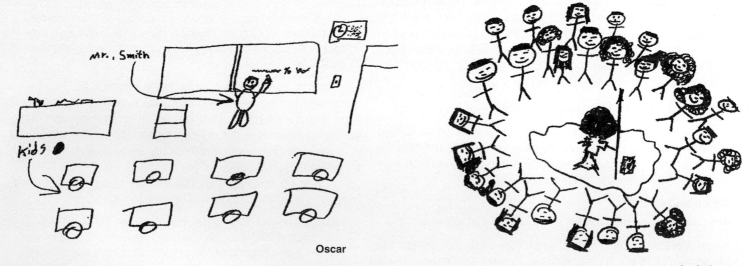

Oscar

Ladarius

"Drawing on Education: Using Drawings to Document Schooling and Support Change" by Walt Haney, Michael Russell, and Damian Bebell, from HARVARD EDUCATIONAL REVIEW, v74:3, Fall 2004. Copyright © 2004 by the President and Fellows of Harvard College. All rights reserved. For more information, please visit www.harvardeducationalreview.org Drawings are taken from pp. 245 (Luis), 248 (Oscar), 250 (Ladarius), and 255 (Evelyn and Jon). Children's names are fictitious.

Evelyn

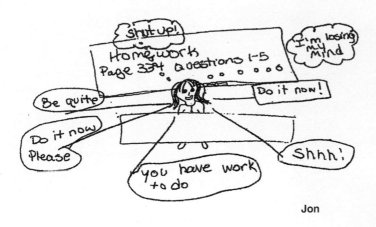

Jon

Luis

Key Concepts

PEARSON
myeducationlab

Now go to www.myeducationlab.com to:

- Take a Quiz to test your mastery of chapter objectives.
- Study chapter content with an individualized Study Plan.
- Deepen your understanding of particular concepts and principles with Review, Remediation, and Enrichment Exercises.
- Apply what you have learned in the chapter to your work with children in Building Teaching Skills and Dispositions exercises.
- Observe children and their unique contexts in Video Examples.

Analyses of End-of-Chapter Case Studies

Chapter 1: Latisha (p. 32)

1. *Your response should contain three or more of the following ideas:*
   - It appears that Latisha's mother offers the loving care and stable home environment Latisha needs to become an optimistic and productive citizen. Her mother also demonstrates a strong work ethic and has exposed Latisha to the healing powers of modern medicine.
   - Two men, Latisha's stepfather and an uncle, appear to take an interest in her welfare.
   - Prevailing dangers in the neighborhood obviously bother Latisha, but her family serves as a safe haven.
   - School seems to be a generally nurturing environment for Latisha; she achieves at sufficiently high levels that she is able to consider becoming a doctor.
   - Latisha seems to have absorbed many of the principles of her culture, such as feeling obligated to help others.

2. *d*—Cognitive-developmental theories, such as the frameworks of Jean Piaget and Lawrence Kohlberg, emphasize children's own initiative and activity. Cognitive-developmental theories also reveal periodic stage-like progressions in children's thinking.

3. *c*—Developmental systems theories, such as Urie Bronfenbrenner's bioecological model, explain children's development in terms of children's own activity and the complex, interacting influences that occur in their social environments.

Chapter 2: The Study Skills Class (p. 64)

1. *Your response should indicate that Deborah observed the students' behavior and collected other information through questionnaires, interviews, and school records of grades and attendance. You may have explained that these methods have the following advantages and disadvantages:*
   - Observations have the advantage of documenting actions that people may not be able or willing to articulate. However, it is not always clear whether actions are typical for a group, nor is it fully apparent what the actions mean. For example, might students be off task if the work is too simple, difficult, tedious, or unrelated to their prior experiences? Furthermore, the presence of observers—in this case Deborah herself—is likely to affect the behaviors of those being observed, and observers' interpretations are often affected by their expectations.
   - Questionnaires allow researchers to collect and analyze a lot of information from a fairly large group of people over a short period of time. However, questionnaires exceed some respondents' reading abilities and do not permit follow-up or probing. In addition, when respondents are not honest or when items are out of sync with respondents' ideas, the data that questionnaires yield can be misleading. It is not apparent from Deborah's report whether she was sufficiently knowledgeable about her students to have been able to present them with meaningful questions and response choices.
   - Interviews have the advantage of permitting respondents to describe their thoughts in depth, but they are time-consuming to conduct and require good rapport between the interviewer and respondents. It is possible that the students were not fully honest with Deborah when answering her questions about school.
   - Records of grades and attendance can be accurate measures of students' academic achievement and enrollment. However, grades are often affected by teachers'

subjective impressions of students, and records of attendance do not reveal *why* students attend or miss school.

2. *a*—Deborah conducted action research. As part of her teaching assignment, she posed questions that arose during her instruction and collected information that helped her answer particular questions.

3. *c*—Deborah's conclusion that her teaching was responsible for the drop in grades is not necessarily justified. A range of factors can affect students' grades, including other events occurring at school and in students' lives outside of school. Even if Deborah's teaching methods were the cause of students' academic decline, it would not be obvious which aspects of her behavior or instruction—such as her grading scheme, instructional methods, or relationships with students—were influential factors. With an experimental design, researchers can be much more certain about causality.

Chapter 3: Four-Year-Old Sons (p. 108)

1. *Both mothers care for their sons but respond to their question-asking differently. Elizabeth interprets Charles's questions as acts of defiance. She believes that Charles is trying to provoke her with his questions. In contrast, Joyce sees Peter's questions as an outgrowth of his natural curiosity. We might expect that Elizabeth discourages Charles's questions and expects his immediate compliance. In contrast, we might expect that Joyce will actually encourage Peter's questioning by responding with elaborate explanations and, in disciplinary situations, with reasons for following a certain course of action.*

2. *d*—A teacher could try each of the strategies mentioned, determining the goals each mother (and father) has for children, advising parents about how children show their curiosity by asking a lot of questions, and using several distinct formats of communication with families.

3. *b*—There is no evidence that Elizabeth is maltreating her son. The description reveals no indications of neglect, physical abuse, sexual abuse, or emotional abuse. Joyce may be using a style that is more likely to be valued in many classrooms, but Elizabeth is most certainly genuinely concerned with her son's well-being.

Chapter 4: Adolescent Childbearing (pp. 145–146)

1. *These young women have some common perspectives as well as some unique experiences in becoming mothers. Karen, Sophie, and Mary similarly expressed reservations about becoming a mother. At the same time, each young woman was becoming invested in some of the tangible responsibilities of parenting. They realized that after birth they will be busy feeding, diapering, comforting, and watching over their infant and doing such chores as laundry. The three young women were likewise apprehensive about their own ability to meet the needs of their newborn babies. The young women appeared not to know what newborn infants are like or how to meet their needs. Two of the young women, Karen and Sophie, mentioned that they will be relying on their own mothers to show them how to care for their infants and to share responsibility for the infants' care.*

    In other respects, the young women had distinct experiences in anticipating parenting. Karen viewed parenting as a general set of responsibilities that she was not well prepared for and that could best be met by her own mother. Sophie liked children, had experience babysitting, and expected to receive some assistance from her mother and her boyfriend. Mary did not like children and viewed parenting as an encompassing and frightening role that would require numerous changes for her personally.

2. *b*—Practitioners can encourage the young women to relax, avoid such potentially damaging substances as cigarettes and alcohol, and obtain medical care. They might also advise them about nutritional programs if they are not aware of these resources and encourage them to talk further about their hopes and concerns and begin to prepare for hands on care of the child.

3. *d*—Practitioners can do all of these things and additionally teach relaxation and breathing techniques and encourage them to find a partner or coach who can assist during labor and delivery.

Chapter 5: Lucy (p. 191)

1. *Lucy had leukemia, a disease that triggers the uncontrolled proliferation of white blood cells and is often treated with chemotherapy and radiation. Lucy's disease and invasive medical treatments delayed her progress through puberty, caused her hair loss, weakened her immune system, and may have impaired the functioning of some of her internal organs, particularly her spleen. The illness also affected Lucy's social development. Lucy would have seemed unusual to peers—she appeared young and frail, had missed many important social events, and savored rather than resisted her family's protective gestures. The effects of the illness on her cognitive development are less clear, but her extended absences from school and her diminished energy may have made it difficult for her to keep up with increasingly challenging academic work.*

2. *a*—Lucy's parents commented that her development was affected by her illness. In some respects (e.g., possibly her understanding of human physiology and her perspective on the meaning of life), Lucy's illness led her to develop more rapidly. In other areas (e.g., her puberty and peer relationships), she was delayed.

3. *d*—Lucy's teacher can try all of these measures to ease Lucy's adjustment during her return to school, close the gap toward academic targets, fortify her peer relationships, and foster her ability to monitor her own health conditions.

Chapter 6: Adolescent Scientists (pp. 237–238)

1. *Mr. Sowell asks several questions that encourage the students to reconsider and revise their findings. He points out that they have simultaneously changed both length and weight and asks, "Why can't you come to a conclusion by looking at the two frequencies?" He guides them toward identifying an error in their reasoning and then asks, "Can you think of a way to redesign your experiments so that you're changing only weight?" In general, he guides them in their thinking but does not specifically tell them the correct answer.*

2. *c*—Students' reasoning is consistent with Piaget's concrete operations stage, in which children can think logically with tangible objects but have difficulty with abstractions and with separating and controlling for variables.

3. *d*—Teachers can give students experiences in separating and controlling variables. Students are apt to exhibit formal operational skills when given opportunities to work with the subject matter and tasks with which they are familiar (response "d"). Children will not necessarily develop formal operations merely by growing older (response "a"). Furthermore, students tend not to develop higher cognitive skills from simply listening to explanations from adults (response "b"). Experiences with transformations to substances that do not alter their volume or number are more likely to help children in transition from preoperational to concrete operations stages, not those in transition from the concrete to the formal operations stage (response "c").

Chapter 7: The Library Project (pp. 282–283)

1. *The intern breaks the large project into several smaller pieces—gathering information at the library, writing rough drafts, and so on—and assigns each group member a particular topic to research. At the school library, the librarian locates appropriate resources, and the intern provides guidance as the students conduct their research. The following day, the intern gives suggestions about how the students might effectively use an index to find the information they need.*

2. *d*—Students' lack of knowledge about the topics they are investigating and the research process they are using creates several challenges for them in completing the assignment.

3. *b*—The intern can help the students by explicitly teaching them such learning strategies as identifying the main point of a passage, paraphrasing the material they read, referring to an index in a book, and keeping notes organized. Students of this age are well able to acquire effective learning strategies but often do not do so without guidance in their use.

Chapter 8: Fresh Vegetables (p. 322)

1. *Although he has been labeled as having an intellectual disability, this diagnosis is suspect. Two characteristics must be present for a diagnosis of an intellectual disability: (a) significantly below-average general intelligence and (b) deficits in adaptive behavior. Although Steven's early IQ scores were low, the case revealed no evidence that he had deficits in adaptive functioning. Furthermore, evidence of his below-average intellectual functioning was transitory. He caught up with the curriculum when gaps in his background knowledge were addressed, and he later earned a high grade point average in regular high school classes.*

2. *c*—As with every child, Steven's skills and limitations derive from a combination of genetic and environmental factors.

3. *a*—Steven missed out on many childhood experiences, and most certainly important academic ones, that are needed to keep up with peers at school. These deficits make it highly unlikely that he could initially succeed in a general education classroom without intensive instruction in areas in which he lags behind his age-mates.

Chapter 9: Boarding School (pp. 366–367)

1. *Joseph probably views his native dialect as an important part of his ethnic identity. He is also proficient in using his dialect to communicate subtle meanings to peers. Furthermore, he undoubtedly knows that his dialect is the preferred way of speaking in his local community; he is most likely to be accepted by peers and others whom he respects when he speaks in his own vernacular.*

2. *d*—The counselor apparently believes that Joseph's dialect was inferior to Standard English and that the dialect was a problem that needed to be corrected.

3. *c*—Ultimately people from diverse ethnic groups are most successful when they can use both their local dialect and Standard English in appropriate settings. One effective instructional strategy would be to require Standard English in most written work and in formal oral presentations but to encourage the local dialect in creative writing and informal class discussions.

Chapter 10: Beating the Odds (pp. 414–415)

1. *To a considerable degree, the students' achievement was the result of nurture: Mr. Escalante provided intensive instruction, to the point that students knew calculus thoroughly and probably had automatized many basic calculus skills. He also communicated high expectations for students' performance. Parents and friends likely played a part in supporting the students' efforts, especially when students were studying hard for the AP test at the end of the year. Nature also would have played a role. All of the students must have had genetic profiles that permitted their brains to develop efficient circuits for processing advanced mathematical concepts.*

2. *c*—Although a skilled and inspirational teacher, Mr. Escalante would not have been able to achieve the same results with preschool children because children of that age would not typically have automatized such essential prerequisite skills as multiplication and would not be able to reason about the abstract mathematical concepts involved in calculus (e.g., functions, derivatives, integrals, and infinite series).

3. *d*—Average gender differences in math ability tend to be fairly small, but there are some distinctions between boys and girls. On average, boys and girls tend to perform at roughly the same levels in mathematics, although boys show more variability in achievement, tend to exhibit more advanced visual-spatial ability, are often more confident in their mathematical abilities, and frequently receive more encouragement in this subject.

Chapter 11: The Girly Shirt (pp. 453–454)

1. *Ms. Fox might, with Tim's help, formulate one or more plans to help him acquire skills for controlling his emotions. Together, they might target Tim's social-emotional skills and specifically focus on his ability to express his emotions productively. The plans might have a few objectives, such as (a) fostering Tim's social sensitivity and friendship skills so that he*

becomes a desirable social partner that other children genuinely care about; (b) helping Tim recognize and label his feelings as they occur (e.g., noticing when he is feeling happy, sad, embarrassed, disappointed, angry, ashamed, and so forth); and (c) asking Tim to use a strategy for coping with unpleasant feelings such as anger (e.g., initially stopping to recognize that he is angered by another child's rude remark, taking a deep breath, and considering several actions and their consequences before responding). Because Tim's explosive anger might, unchecked, jeopardize his social standing among peers, become a detrimental habit, and disrupt the entire class, Ms. Fox will need to monitor his emotional expression. She can praise him when he shows restraint, and she can remove privileges from him (or apply another consequence) when he allows his temper to escalate. Ms. Fox might also ask a school counselor or psychologist for additional strategies she could use with Tim.

2. *a*—Tim is having difficulty dealings with his anger, a component of emotional regulation.

3. *c*—Tim's temperament is probably due to a variety of factors, including his genetic disposition, his family relationships, and his own choices and experiences.

Chapter 12: Joachín's Dilemma (p. 492)

1. *Forming an identity typically involves consideration of one's origins, abilities, convictions, and goals in life. For Joachín, the process of identity formation required him to reconcile society's unfair stereotypes of young African American men with the many assets that he personally had in his life. For 2 years, he followed a torturous quest, responding to the pessimistic views he had absorbed from his friends and the broader community. In the process he found that acting tough gained him respect from others. For a time he withdrew from his family, stumbled in his studies, and set aside the hobbies he had grown to enjoy. Joachín eventually realized that he could choose a different path. He knew that he had the skills he needed to succeed academically, a family that supported him, and good prospects for contributing to society. A likable young man, Joachín probably also made new friends who affirmed his academic, athletic, and musical talents.*

2. *d*—Joachín went through a period of *moratorium*, in which he actively searched for a core sense of beliefs and commitments as to who he was and what he stood for.

3. *d*—Margaret Beale Spencer's model indicates that protective and risk factors and the development of Joachín's coping skills all contribute to Joachín's evolving sense of identity.

Chapter 13: Derrika (p. 530)

1. *A variety of strategies are possible for guiding Derrika. Following are examples:*
   - Tailor assignments to Derrika's current knowledge and skills.
   - Scaffold Derrika's efforts on challenging tasks.
   - Teach Derrika specific self-regulation techniques (e.g., self-reinforcement for completing assignments, self-monitoring of progress, self-evaluating quality of work).
   - Initiate an after-school homework program in which Derrika and other struggling students have a regular time to complete assignments and receive guidance in basic self-regulation skills.

2. *b*—Even though Derrika would like to attend college, she frequently cut class and often didn't get up in time for biology class, suggesting that she is having trouble motivating herself, keeping track of her progress in school, and resisting temptation.

3. *b*—Derrika's elementary teachers seemed to attribute children's performance to hard work and effective strategies, whereas the secondary teachers seemed to attribute students' performance to lack of intelligence.

Chapter 14: Gang Mediation (pp. 564–565)

1. *Possible reasons include the following:*
   - The students were given concrete guidelines about acceptable and unacceptable interpersonal behaviors.
   - Discussions with rival gang members probably promoted a better understanding of why rivals might act as they do and how rivals might interpret one another's

behaviors. These discussions may have elicited empathy for the distress that others felt when faced with intimidation.

- Discussions may have appealed to the adolescents' sense of fairness and justice. Students may have come to appreciate that everyone at school is entitled to walk the school halls without fear of harassment.

- Participation in the meetings may have reminded the students of their personal moral standards, increasing the likelihood that they would act in accordance with these principles.

- When members of rival gangs discussed a source of conflict, they may have acquired more effective social problem-solving skills (e.g., looking at a situation from all sides and trying to find a reasonable compromise that addresses everyone's needs).

- In conducting the mediation sessions, the counselors modeled effective interpersonal behaviors and social problem-solving skills.

- Prior to the peer mediation, school personnel instituted regulations (e.g., dress codes, weapon searches) that the students may have perceived as punishment. In contrast, the peer mediation approach used induction, giving reasons for why certain behaviors are unacceptable. Inductive discipline promotes compliance with rules and fosters empathy.

2. *d*—All of these actions could be effective in fostering good outcomes for children who might be in or at risk for joining gangs. Educators can look carefully at the curriculum, recruit children into interesting after-school activities, and arrange individual counseling for students who have already shown a propensity for violence.

3. *b*—Several specific and interacting factors are typically responsible for excessive levels of aggressive behavior in children.

Chapter 15: Aaron and Cole (pp. 609–610)

1. *Aaron and Cole's friendship gave both boys mutual encouragement and support. Other benefits differed slightly for the two boys. During the time Aaron's parents were getting divorced, Aaron felt sad, confused, and vulnerable. Cole helped Aaron feel needed and appreciated. Aaron also displayed leadership among his classmates by serving as a positive role model who interacted patiently and inclusively with a peer with a disability. Cole benefited from the reassurance, acceptance, and guidance he received from Aaron. Cole also was included in certain social groups because of Aaron's intercession.*

2. *d*—When Cole was disruptive with another student, Aaron reminded him about not being mean. He then tried to ensure that Cole had learned the rule by having him restate it to another student. Cole did not understand the request, but Aaron advised him to remember it and probably reminded him to act appropriately with peers when he later was insensitive or unkind.

3. *d*—To foster an effective classroom climate, Mr. Howard might try all of the listed strategies.

Analyses of End-of-Chapter Artifacts

Chapter 1: James's Changes, Big and Small (p. 33)

- James describes some of the changes as "small," and he seems to see these developments as quantitative improvements. Examples include growing larger physically, gaining athletic skills, becoming better educated, and completing more homework. Some modifications in his environment appear to have caused qualitative changes. James suggests that the opportunity to participate in sports at seventh grade, not possible by school policy the previous year, makes a big difference in life, at least in part because he now must use his time efficiently in order to complete his homework.

  James also writes that his parents have new expectations of him, reflecting their faith in his character, which he enjoys but seems to perceive as a demand for heightened maturity. James also believes that his parents misunderstand him, which is a common perception of young adolescents. James's insight that he is now having conversations with teachers instead of "just talking about school" may reflect a qualitative change in his thinking and behavior. James indicates that he is "a lot more concerned about . . . grades as the years pass," a statement that may indicate that his academic performance is becoming increasingly salient to him or has taken a qualitatively new place in his value system. James's comments about relationships with girls may be addressing both qualitative dynamics (perhaps an entirely new tendency for in-depth conversation) and quantitative changes (possibly more contact).

- The many changes that James is undergoing, both internally and in his social world at school, suggest that James needs reassurance from trusted adults. Hence, his teachers can capitalize on his interest in talking with them by spending relaxed time in conversation about matters of substance. Ideally, James would have an adviser who would keep an eye on him and express interest in his adjustment to middle school. His teachers can also give James and his classmates regular chances to work together in small groups so that they get to know one another better.

Chapter 2: I Went to Davis's House (p. 64)

In Chapter 2, you learned that every piece of data has advantages and disadvantages as an indication of what children truly understand and can do. Possibly you noticed that Alex is inconsistent in his punctuation. He capitalizes the pronoun and one proper noun (*I* and *Alex*) and fails to capitalize the other proper noun *(davis)*. He marks possession properly *(davis's)* and indents his name, as he might in a letter. Thus, there is some evidence that Alex's understanding of punctuation is emerging but incomplete. However, Alex might also be imitating a *style* of informal writing (e.g., as young people do in preparing text messages on cell phones) rather than trying to follow all rules of punctuation. Before designing instruction in punctuation for Alex, you would want to obtain other writing samples and assessments from him.

Chapter 3: In My Neighborhood (p. 109)

The adolescents seem to have benefited from several features of their neighborhoods. A large, quiet, and well-equipped park supported the youngsters' recreation and served as a sanctuary. The adolescents also appeared to have vigilant parents who directed their safe passage through nearby streets. Police officers were present and seen as protectors. On the negative side, adolescents encountered a lot of violence on the streets and viewed some of their neighbors as threatening. The physical surroundings could also be unpleasant, with trash dumped and buildings burning nearby.

Chapter 4: Horses by Nadia (pp. 146–147)

Children who are autistic have trouble expressing their thoughts verbally. Nadia used little language in her daily life and was unable to describe the sophisticated artwork she produced. Nadia's autism, limited language, and tendency to become absorbed by particular topics probably had a genetic basis or been due to exposure to an unknown teratogen during her prenatal development.

Despite her limited verbal abilities and tendency to withdraw from social interaction, Nadia showed extraordinary artistic ability as early as age 3. She adeptly represented the contours of moving animals; gave special attention to faces, legs, and hooves; and realistically captured depth and perspective. It is likely that her artistic talent also had some genetic basis. It seems that her brain allowed her to keep detailed images of horses in mind and impelled her to reproduce these images on paper.

The effects of the environment can be seen in the encouragement that Nadia received to draw. Once it became evident that she had this talent, she was given supplies to foster her artistic self-expression. Nadia's interest in horses was nurtured with exposure to pictures of animals, yet it is not obvious why she chose horses from among other possible themes.

Chapter 5: MyPyramid Worksheet by Alex (p. 192)

The U.S. Department of Agriculture (2008) recommends that children eat a diet that is rich in whole grains, fresh vegetables and fruits, low-fat milk products, and foods that are high in protein, including lean meat, poultry, fish, beans, peas, nuts, and seeds. Alex's worksheet included goals within the main categories of grains, vegetables, fruits, milk, and meat and beans. Alex came closest to achieving dietary goals related to grains, fruits, and meats and beans. He did not achieve goals related to vegetables and milk. Alex exceeded the goal related to physical activity. Alex seemed to have a fairly realistic sense of the value of health-promoting behaviors and may have been able to evaluate his actions sensibly because the form makes it fairly apparent where the successes and gaps are in one's diet.

Chapter 6: Fish in a Boat (p. 238)

The various concepts depicted in the cartoon—fish, boat, oar, leak, bailing water, and so on—are cognitive tools that Brady coordinated as he depicted a humorous situation. Brady's artistic techniques—shading the clouds with diagonal lines; depicting upward motion with short, curved lines below the two fish; putting one fish's comment in a "talk balloon"—are also cognitive tools that Western culture has passed down from previous generations. Furthermore, to the extent that the computer software facilitated Brady's ability to create the cartoon, it, too, may have been a cognitive tool as well as a physical tool.

The situation Brady violates several basic principles of the physical world. For instance, air is lighter than water and so would hardly seep downward into the boat. Furthermore, of course, fish don't talk or row, nor are they even likely to sit in a rowboat. To create the cartoon, then, Brady had to engage in contrary-to-fact reasoning—an ability associated with Piaget's formal operations stage.

Chapter 7: Interview with Aletha (p. 283)

Aletha knows that attention is critical for getting information into memory ("To learn new things you have to pay attention"). She also knows that paying attention involves more than just directing her eyes and ears in a particular direction—that it involves a certain amount of mental effort as well ("It's hard if you're not interested, but that's not how it works. You have to pay attention"). In her own way, she also knows that working memory has a limited capacity ("You can't read a book because it's hard to do both," ". . . it's hard because I had to write while I was listening"). Furthermore, by asking herself questions that she hopes her teacher will answer, she increases the odds that she will keep her attention focused on the lesson and can monitor her ongoing comprehension of it—two signs of self-regulated learning. Aletha's metacognitive development is hardly complete, however: Her view of learning from an educational film is simply to "memorize" her notes.

Chapter 8: Jermaine's Life (pp. 322–323)

Jermaine's story has two qualities that suggest he is exceptionally talented in verbal abilities. First, as a first grader (when he would have been about 6 or 7 years old), Jermaine took the initiative to write a book, with the passage presented here being only one brief excerpt. Second, Jermaine used writing tools that arc advanced for his age: a sophisticated vocabulary (e.g., *triton, saddled, nonsense, toothless*), a vivid and original plot (the outsmarting of fierce dragons), and well-constructed sentences (e.g., "I saddled up my dragon, grabbed my triton, and tried to escape"). For Jermaine's verbal skills to blossom further, he may benefit from continued encouragement at school, the availability of challenging literature, opportunities to discuss literature with teachers and at least a few peers with similar interests, additional outlets to share his inventive stories, and exposure to role models who make their livings as writers or other professionals who rely on strong verbal skills and imaginative abilities. The scholars who first described this case (Hebert & Beardsley, 2001) inform us that Jermaine's being identified as gifted led to him gaining access to appropriate resources for nurturing his extraordinary talents.

Chapter 9: Figure of Speech (p. 367)

Jeff clearly understands the literal meaning of the sentence, because the eyes in his drawing are quite a bit larger than the person's very narrow waistline. In addition, Jeff has mastered the correct spellings of the words in the sentence. The person he has drawn is an unrealistic, somewhat cartoonish one, so perhaps he has an inkling that the sentence is not intended to be taken entirely at face value. However, he misses the meaning that this common figure of speech usually conveys: that a person requests more food than he or she can possibly eat at a single sitting. Jeff's focus on the literal rather than figurative meaning of the sentence is hardly surprising. As you've learned, understanding figurative speech is far more common in adolescence than at younger ages.

Chapter 10: The Pet Who Came to Dinner (p. 415)

- Justin's misspellings reveal a great deal about his phonological awareness. He captures some but not all of the sounds in words—for example:
  - He accurately (although incorrectly) captures all of the sounds in several words, including *done* ("dun"), *there* ("ther"), *water* ("wodr"), *were* ("wr"), and *newspaper* ("nuwspapr")—note that in the last three of these he uses the letter *r* to represent the "er" sound.
  - *Once* is spelled as both "owans" and "ouns," in the first case adding an "a" vowel and in the second case omitting the "w" sound.
  - *Drink* is spelled "briak," omitting the "n" sound (he has probably reversed the letter *d*, making it look like a *b*).
  - *Dessert* is spelled "dasrt," which changes the initial vowel sound from short-*e* to short-*a*; again the *r* probably represents the "er" sound.
  - *Having* is spelled "aving," omitting the *b* sound.
  - *Rushed* is spelled "rust," changing the *sh* sound to an *s* sound.
  - *Started* is spelled "stor did," changing the short-*a* to a long-*o* sound.
  - *Snoring* is spelled "soreing," omitting the *n* sound.

  It appears, then, that Justin's phonological awareness still needs some fine-tuning.

- With the exception of lowercase *d* (which he occasionally reverses so that it looks like a *b*), Justin knows his uppercase and lowercase letters and can form them with reasonable smoothness.
- Justin knows that sentences should begin with a capital letter and end with a period. He knows, too, that possessive nouns require an apostrophe ("mom's" and "dad's"). He hasn't completely mastered capitalization rules: He capitalizes "Came" and "Dinner" in the middle of a sentence, and he neglects to capitalize two proper nouns ("mom's" and "dad's"). He creates two run-on sentences: "Owans ther was a cat who came to

Dinner he eat all the food," and "Owans he was dun he ask for dasrt for dasrt we wr aving cake." He is inconsistent in his use of past-tense verbs (e.g., "Came," "was") versus present-tense verbs (e.g., "eat," "ask") to tell his story. And he has not yet learned that the title of a story should appear in a line by itself, centered at the top of the page. In summary, Justin has mastered some but not all aspects of capitalization, punctuation, grammar, and conventions in written English.

- Justin's narrative is simply a sequence of events strung together, without regard for cause-and-effect relationships and with no attention to characters' mental or emotional states. If this were an *oral* narrative, we would conclude that his story is more typical of a preschooler than of a 7-year-old. However, Justin had to consider writing mechanics as well as the story line as he wrote, possibly stretching his working memory capacity and reducing the complexity of the story he was able to write.

If you were to see many other second graders' written short stories, you would probably conclude that Justin's story is fairly typical for a native English-speaking second grader.

Chapter 11: Paint Me Like I Am (p. 454)

Delia expresses a range of emotions in her poem. She communicates clearly and vividly about happiness, a pleasant emotion she associates with beauty in nature and a sense of freedom. Delia also writes about sadness and pain, emotions that she would prefer to keep to herself. Writing poems may be a therapeutic pastime for Delia because it allows her to reflect on the full range of her feelings and deal with them productively. As she imagines a painter rendering a contented expression on her face, Delia seems to suggesting that her unpleasant feelings need not define who she is, either to herself or to others.

Chapter 12: Two Histories (pp. 492–493)

For Rachel, forming an ethnic identity took considerable work. She had to confront blatantly rude comments from other children (and possibly adults), who themselves found it unsettling that Rachel possessed some features characteristic of people from Jewish backgrounds (e.g., light-colored skin) and other features characteristic of people from African American descent (e.g., broad facial features). Some people made remarks that criticized her for being multiethnic (e.g., "Looks more Latina than half-breed," "But that boy always called me mixed in such an ugly way"). A few responses were vehemently racist (e.g., "Some say, 'Nigga get off the swing'") or pitted one racial heritage against the other (e.g., "Act White," "Won't date Black men," "And I get told it's better to pretend I'm White").

Rachel struggles with being a "compromise," a blend of two heritages. Yet Rachel clearly rejects the ignorant interpretations she has heard over the years, and she enjoys the traditions of both cultural groups (e.g., their meals, styles of dance, and cultural symbols). She realizes she has qualities that are shared by her two heritages and fused within her core: Although Rachel feels tormented, she also believes she has the strength of a warrior.

Chapter 13: Tears of Pearls (p. 531)

Writing an essay of this kind has several potential benefits. First, by knowing why homework was turned in late, the teacher can help Andrea develop a better strategy for future homework assignments (e.g., Andrea might make a point to check her social studies folder as soon as she arrives at class each day). Second, in writing the essay, Andrea must engage in some degree of self-monitoring and self-evaluation. Third, Andrea must describe a future course of action (how she intends to get future assignments in on time) to someone else. By describing her future plans to someone else, Andrea may begin to internalize such future planning and do it more regularly even in the absence of a teacher's direction.

It is clear in Andrea's essay that she does have some ability to regulate her learning and behavior, albeit with assistance from her mother. In particular, she says, "Every night I do my homework and my mom checks it and it goes in my backpack." She also feels *guilt* about not getting her homework in on time, a reaction indicating that she is at least in the introjection phase of internalizing certain guidelines for behavior (look once again at Figure 13-1). Much as guilt is an unpleasant feeling, it can be a powerful motivator in adhering to certain standards for behavior.

Chapter 14: Remembering 9/11 (pp. 565–566)

Antonio appears to interpret the events of September 11th as a moral transgression because he emphasizes the harm caused to American people. The characters in Antonio's drawing are obviously distressed. Antonio aptly portrays grief, disbelief, and possibly anger in the survivors of the September 11th attacks. He communicates such intense emotions by drawing tears, open mouths, bared teeth, tilted heads, and flung-open arms. By placing his characters in front of an American flag (a symbol of the United States), Antonio may be suggesting that the entire nation shared in the anguish and outrage.

Chapter 15: Teachers at Work (pp. 610–611)

The pictures by Oscar, Evelyn, and Jon reveal that school can be a controlling and tedious place. Oscar shows his teacher, Mr. Smith, holding a piece of chalk in front of the board and commanding the attention of the children, who in turn sit at their desks in rows. The children are anonymous, having no faces or individual features, and are socialized to be quiet, still, and attentive. The hidden curriculum is that the teacher is in charge and the children are there to obey him. Evelyn depicts an apparently dull and long-winded teacher who punctuates speeches with demands for children to sit down. Once again, children are socialized to be quiet, still, and attentive. The hidden curriculum conveys that it is children's job to appease an insensitive teacher who is unaware that children are not understanding or even attending to her monologues. Jon shows a teacher sitting at her desk, presumably in the front of the room, uttering a string of directions that vary in tone (e.g., "Do it now, please," "Shut up!" and "I'm losing my mind"). The hidden curriculum suggests that children are to comply with an unstable and didactic teacher.

The pictures by Ladarius and Luis reveal a different spirit in the classroom: Children are happy and engaged in their learning. Ladarius shows a teacher surrounded by smiling, standing children. The hidden curriculum seems to be that children are to be involved participants in interesting lessons. Luis shows a classroom with smiling children carrying out lessons in cooperative groups. The teacher is circulating among the groups and encouraging children in their work ("Good job"). The hidden curriculum seems to be that children are to work together and enjoy themselves in the process.

Glossary

accommodation Process of responding to a new event by either modifying an existing scheme or forming a new one.

acculturation Process of taking on the customs and values of a new culture.

action research Systematic study of an issue or problem by a teacher or other practitioner, with the goal of bringing about more productive outcomes for children.

adaptive behavior Behavior related to daily living skills and appropriate conduct in social situations.

addiction Physical and psychological dependence on a substance, such that increasing quantities must be taken to produce the desired effect and withdrawal produces adverse physiological and psychological effects.

African American English Dialect of some African American communities that includes pronunciations, idioms, and grammatical constructions different from those of Standard English.

aggression Action intentionally taken to hurt another either physically or psychologically.

alleles Genes located at the same point on corresponding (paired) chromosomes and related to the same physical characteristic.

amusia Inability to detect the small changes in pitch that are common in melodics; an extreme form of tone deafness.

anorexia nervosa Eating disorder in which a person eats little or nothing for weeks or months and seriously jeopardizes health.

anxiety Emotional state characterized by worry and apprehension.

anxiety disorder Chronic emotional condition characterized by excessive, debilitating worry.

apprenticeship Mentorship in which a novice works intensively with an expert to learn how to accomplish complex tasks in a particular domain.

appropriation Gradual adoption of (and perhaps also adaptation of) other people's ways of thinking and behaving for one's own purposes.

assessment Task that children complete and researchers use to make judgments of children's understandings and skills.

assimilation Form of acculturation in which a person totally embraces a culture, abandoning a previous culture in the process. Also, in Piaget's theory, process of responding (either physically or mentally) to a new event in a way that is consistent with an existing scheme.

astrocyte Glial cell that regulates blood flow in the brain, brings nutrients to and metabolizes chemicals for neurons, and communicates with other similar cells and with neurons.

attachment An enduring emotional tie uniting one person to another.

attention-deficit hyperactivity disorder (ADHD) Disability characterized by inattention, by hyperactivity and impulsive behavior, or by all of these characteristics.

attribution Belief about the cause of one's own or another person's success or failure.

authentic activity Instructional activity similar to one that a child might eventually encounter in the outside world.

authoritarian parenting style Parenting style characterized by strict expectations for behavior and rigid rules that children are expected to obey without question.

authoritative parenting style Parenting style characterized by emotional warmth, high expectations and standards for behavior, consistent enforcement of rules, explanations regarding the reasons behind these rules, and the inclusion of children in decision making.

autism spectrum disorders Disorders marked by impaired social cognition, social skills, and social interaction, as well as by repetitive behaviors; extreme forms are often associated with significant cognitive and linguistic delays and highly unusual behaviors.

autobiographical self Mental "history" of important events in one's life.

automatization Process of becoming able to respond quickly and efficiently while mentally processing or physically performing certain tasks.

axon Armlike part of a neuron that sends information to other neurons.

babbling Repeating certain consonant-vowel syllables over and over (e.g., "mamamama"); common in the latter half of the first year.

behaviorism Theoretical perspective in which children's behavioral and emotional responses change as a direct result of particular environmental stimuli.

bicultural orientation Form of acculturation in which a person is familiar with two cultures and selectively draws from the values and traditions of one or both cultures depending on the context.

bilingual education Approach to second-language instruction in which students are instructed in academic subject areas in their native language while simultaneously being taught to speak, read, and write in a second language.

bilingualism Knowing and speaking two languages fluently.

biological theory Theoretical perspective that focuses on inherited physiological structures of the body and brain that support survival, growth, and learning.

bulimia Eating disorder in which a person, in an attempt to be thin, eats a large amount of food and then purposefully purges it from the body by vomiting or taking laxatives.

bully Child or adolescent who frequently threatens, harasses, or causes physical or psychological injury to particular peers.

canalization Tight genetic control of a particular aspect of development.

care orientation Focus on nurturance and concern for others in moral decision making.

case study Naturalistic research study in which investigators document a single person's or a small group's experiences in depth over a period of time.

central conceptual structure Integrated network of concepts and cognitive processes that forms the basis for much of one's thinking, reasoning, and learning in a specific content domain.

central executive Component of the human information processing system that oversees the flow of information throughout the system.

cephalocaudal trend Vertical ordering of motor skills and physical development; order is head first to feet last.

child development Study of the persistent, cumulative, and progressive changes in the physical, cognitive, and social-emotional development of children and adolescents.

child maltreatment Adverse treatment of a child in the form of neglect, physical abuse, sexual abuse, or emotional abuse.

chromosome Rodlike structure that resides in the nucleus of every cell of the body and contains genes that guide growth and development; each chromosome is made up of DNA and other biological instructions.

class inclusion Recognition that an object simultaneously belongs to a particular category and to one of its subcategories.

clinical method Procedure in which an adult probes a child's reasoning about a task or problem, tailoring questions in light of what the child has previously said or done in the interview.

clique Moderately stable friendship group of perhaps three to nine members.

co-regulated learning Process through which an adult and child share responsibility for directing various aspects of the child's learning.

codominance Situation in which the two genes of an allele pair, although not identical, both have some influence on a characteristic.

cognitive apprenticeship Mentorship in which an expert and a novice work together on a challenging task and the expert suggests ways to think about the task.

cognitive development Systematic changes in reasoning, concepts, memory, and language.

cognitive process theory Theoretical perspective that focuses on the precise nature of human mental operations.

cognitive strategy Specific mental process that people intentionally use to acquire or manipulate information.

cognitive tool Concept, symbol, strategy, or other culturally constructed mechanism that helps people think more effectively.

cognitive-developmental theory Theoretical perspective that focuses on major transformations to the underlying structures of thinking over the course of development.

collectivistic culture Cultural group that encourages obedience to and dependence on authority figures and being honorable, cooperative, and invested in group accomplishments.

community The neighborhood in which a child and his or her family live and the surrounding vicinity.

community of learners A classroom in which teacher(s) and students actively and collaboratively work to help one another learn.

comprehension monitoring The process of evaluating one's comprehension of oral messages or written material.

conceptual change Revision of one's knowledge and understanding of a topic in response to new information about the topic.

conduct disorder Chronic emotional condition characterized by lack of concern for the rights of others.

conscience An internalized sense of right and wrong for guiding and evaluating one's behavior.

conservation Realization that if nothing is added or taken away, an amount stays the same regardless of any alterations in shape or arrangement.

constructivism Theoretical perspective proposing that learners construct a body of knowledge and beliefs, rather than absorbing information exactly as it is received.

context The broad social environments, including family, schools, neighborhoods, community organizations, culture, ethnicity, and society at large, that influence children's development.

contingent self-worth Overall sense of self that is highly dependent on others' opinions.

control group Group of participants in a research study who do not receive the treatment under investigation; often used in an experimental study.

controversial children Children whom some peers really like and other peers strongly dislike.

conventional morality In Kohlberg's theory, acceptance of society's conventions regarding right and wrong; behaving to please others or to live up to society's expectations for appropriate behavior.

conventional transgression In social domain theory, action that violates society's general guidelines (often unspoken) for socially acceptable behavior.

cooing Making and repeating vowel sounds (e.g., "oooooo"); common in early infancy.

coparents The two (or more) parents who share responsibility for rearing their children.

correlation Extent to which two variables are related to each other, such that when one variable increases, the other either increases or decreases in a somewhat predictable fashion.

correlational study Research study that explores relationships among variables.

cortex Part of the forebrain that enables conscious thinking processes, including executive functions.

cross-sectional study Research study in which the performance of individuals at different ages is compared at a single point in time.

crowd Large collection of adolescents who share certain characteristics, tend to affiliate together, and are defined by others according to their reputations.

crystallized intelligence Knowledge and skills accumulated from one's prior experience, schooling, and culture.

cultural bias Extent to which an assessment offends or unfairly penalizes some individuals because of their ethnicity or cultural background, gender, or socioeconomic status.

culturally responsive teaching A teacher's use of particular instructional strategies based on knowledge of children's cultural backgrounds and individual characteristics.

culture The values, traditions, and symbol systems of a long-standing social group that give purpose and meaning to children's daily activities and interpersonal relationships.

culture shock Sense of confusion that occurs when one encounters an environment with expectations for behavior very different from those in one's home environment.

delay of gratification Forgoing small immediate rewards for larger ones at a future time.

dendrite Branchlike part of a neuron that receives information from other neurons.

depression Emotional condition characterized by significant sadness, discouragement, hopelessness, and, in children, irritability.

developmental systems theory Theoretical perspective that focuses on the multiple factors, including systems inside and outside children, that combine to influence children's development.

developmentally appropriate practice Instruction and other services adapted to the age, characteristics, and developmental progress of individual children.

dialect Form of a language characteristic of a particular geographic region or ethnic group.

differentiation A gradual transition from general possibility to specialized functioning over the course of development.

disequilibrium State of being unable to address new events with existing schemes.

disorganized and disoriented attachment Attachment classification in which children lack a single coherent way of responding to attachment figures.

distributed intelligence Thinking facilitated by physical objects and technology, social support, and concepts and symbols of one's culture.

distributive justice Beliefs about what constitutes people's fair share of a valued commodity.

diversity In a particular aspect of human development, the varied ways in which individuals progress.

dizygotic twins Twins that began as two separate zygotes and so are as genetically similar as two siblings conceived and born at different times.

DNA A spiral-staircase–shaped molecule that guides the production of proteins needed by the body for growth and development; short for *deoxyribonucleic acid*.

dominance hierarchy Relative standing of group members in terms of such qualities as leadership and social influence.

dominant gene Gene that overrides any competing instructions in an allele pair.

dynamic assessment Systematic examination of how a child's knowledge or reasoning may change as a result of learning a specific task or performing it with adult guidance.

dyscalculia Inability to master basic numerical concepts and operations in a developmentally typical time frame despite normal instruction.

dyslexia Inability to master basic reading skills in a developmentally typical time frame despite normal reading instruction.

egocentrism Inability of a child in Piaget's preoperational stage to view situations from another person's perspective.

elaboration Process of using prior knowledge to embellish new information and thereby learn it more effectively.

embryo During prenatal weeks 2 through 8, the developing offspring that is in the process of forming major body structures and organs.

emergent literacy Knowledge and skills that lay a foundation for reading and writing; typically develops in the preschool years from early experiences with written language.

emotion Affective response to an event that is personally relevant to one's needs and goals.

emotional contagion Tendency for infants to cry spontaneously when they hear other infants crying.

emotional regulation Strategies to manage affective states.

empathy Capacity to experience the same feelings as another person, especially when the feeling is pain or distress.

English language learner (ELL) School-age child who is not fully fluent in English because his or her family speaks a language other than English at home.

entity view (of ability) Belief that ability is a "thing" that is relatively permanent and unchangeable.

epistemic belief Belief regarding the nature of knowledge and knowledge acquisition.

equilibration Movement from equilibrium to disequilibrium and back to equilibrium; a process that promotes the development of increasingly complex forms of thought and knowledge.

equilibrium State of being able to address new events using existing schemes.

ethnic identity Awareness of being a member of a particular ethnic or cultural group and willingness to adopt certain values and behaviors characteristic of that group.

ethnicity Membership in a group of people with a common cultural heritage and shared values, beliefs, and behaviors.

ethnography Naturalistic research study in which investigators spend an extensive period of time documenting the cultural patterns of a group of people in the group's everyday settings.

ethological attachment theory Theoretical perspective that emphasizes the benefits to children derived from close bonds with caregivers, particularly protection from harm and a secure base from which to explore the environment.

executive functions Purposeful and goal-directed intellectual processes (e.g., planning, decision making) made possible by higher brain structures.

expansion Repetition of a child's short utterances in more complete and grammatically correct forms.

experimental study Research study in which a researcher manipulates one aspect of the environment (a treatment), controls other aspects of the environment, and assesses the treatment's effects on participants' behavior.

expressive language Ability to communicate effectively through speaking and writing.

extrinsic motivation Motivation provoked by the external consequences that certain behaviors bring.

family Two or more people who live together and are related by such enduring factors as birth, marriage, adoption, or long-term mutual commitment.

family structure In a family with children, the family's makeup; specifically, the children in a family home and the adults who live with and care for the children.

fast mapping Inferring a word's general meaning after a single exposure.

fetus During prenatal week 9 until birth, the developing offspring that is growing in size and weight and in sensory abilities, brain structures, and organs needed for survival.

figurative speech Speech that communicates meaning beyond a literal interpretation of its words.

fine motor skills Small, precise movements of particular parts of the body, especially the hands.

fluid intelligence Ability to acquire knowledge quickly and thereby adapt effectively to new situations.

Flynn effect Gradual increase in intelligence test performance observed in many countries during the past several decades.

forebrain Part of the brain responsible for complex thinking, emotions, and motivation.

foreign language instruction Approach to second-language instruction in which native English speakers receive lessons in a new language for less than an hour once or twice a week or occasionally more often.

functionalism Theoretical perspective of language development that emphasizes the purposes language serves for human beings.

g General factor in intelligence that influences performance in a wide variety of tasks and content domains.

gamete Reproductive cell that, in humans, contains 23 chromosomes rather than the 46 chromosomes present in other cells in the body; a male gamete (sperm) and a female gamete (ovum) join at conception.

gang Cohesive social group characterized by initiation rites, distinctive colors and symbols, territorial orientation, feuds with rival groups, and criminal activity.

gender schema Self-constructed body of beliefs about the traits and behaviors of males or females.

gene Basic unit of heredity in a living cell; genes are made up of DNA and contained on chromosomes.

giftedness Unusually high ability in one or more areas, to the point where children require special educational services to help them meet their full potential.

glial cell Cell in the brain that provides structural or functional support for, and in some cases direction to, one or more neurons.

goal-directed behavior Intentional behavior aimed at bringing about an anticipated outcome.

grammatical word Nonlexical word that affects the meanings of other words or the interrelationships among words in a sentence.

gross motor skills Large movements of the body that permit locomotion through and within the environment.

grounded theory study Naturalistic research study in which investigators develop and elaborate new theories while comparing data (such as interview statements from participants) to the researchers' emerging interpretations.

growth spurt Rapid increase in height and weight during puberty.

guided participation Active engagement in adult activities, initially with considerable direction from an adult or other more advanced individual and subsequently with opportunities for increasing responsibility and independence.

guilt Feeling of discomfort when one inflicts damage or causes someone else pain or distress.

habituation Changes in children's physiological responses to repeated displays of the same stimulus, reflecting loss of interest.

hindbrain Part of the brain controlling the basic physiological processes that sustain survival.

holophrase A single word used to express a complete thought; commonly observed in children's earliest speech.

hostile attributional bias Tendency to interpret others' behaviors as reflecting hostile or aggressive intentions.

identity Self-constructed definition of who one is, what things one finds important, what one believes, and what goals one wants to accomplish in life.

imaginary audience Belief that one is the center of attention in any social situation.

immersion Approach to second-language instruction in which native English speakers hear and speak the second language almost exclusively in the classroom.

inclusion Practice of educating all students, including those with severe and multiple disabilities, in neighborhood schools and general education classrooms.

incremental view (of ability) Belief that ability can and does improve with effort and practice.

individual constructivism Theoretical perspective that focuses on how people independently construct meaning from their experiences.

individualistic culture Cultural group that encourages independence, self-assertion, competition, and expression of personal needs.

induction Act of explaining why a certain behavior is unacceptable, usually with a focus on the pain or distress that someone has caused another.

infant-directed speech Short, simple, high-pitched speech often used when talking to young children.

infantile amnesia General inability to recall events that have occurred in the early years of life.

information processing theories Theoretical perspectives that focus on the specific ways in which people mentally acquire, interpret, and remember information and how such cognitive processes change over the course of development.

inner speech "Talking" to oneself mentally rather than aloud as a way of guiding oneself through a task.

insecure-avoidant attachment Attachment classification in which children appear somewhat indifferent to attachment figures.

insecure-resistant attachment Attachment classification in which children are preoccupied with their attachment figures but gain little comfort from them when distressed.

integration An increasing coordination of body parts over the course of development.

intellectual disability Disability marked by significantly below-average general intelligence and deficits in adaptive behavior.

intelligence Ability to apply past knowledge and experiences flexibly to accomplish challenging new tasks.

intelligence test General measure of current cognitive functioning, used primarily to predict academic achievement over the short run.

intentionality Engagement in an action congruent with one's purpose or goal.

interactive technology Array of electronic, digitally based machines that are operated dynamically by a person whose commands determine emerging program sequences.

internalization In Vygotsky's theory, the gradual evolution of external, social activities into internal, mental activities.

internalized motivation Adoption of behaviors that others value, whether or not one's immediate environment reinforces those behaviors.

intersubjectivity Awareness of shared perceptions and understandings that provide the foundation for social interaction.

interview Data collection technique that obtains self-report data through face-to-face conversation.

intrinsic motivation Motivation resulting from personal characteristics or from factors inherent in the task being performed.

invented spelling A child's early, self-constructed word spelling, which may reflect only some of the word's phonemes.

IQ score Score on an intelligence test, determined by comparing one's performance with the performance of same-age peers.

IRE cycle Adult–child interaction pattern marked by adult *initiation*, child *response*, and adult *evaluation*; in Western cultures, such a pattern is often seen in instructional settings.

joint attention Phenomenon in which two people (e.g., a child and caregiver) simultaneously focus on the same object or event, monitor each other's attention, and coordinate their responses.

justice orientation Focus on individual rights in moral decision making.

knowledge base One's knowledge about specific topics and the world in general.

knowledge telling Writing down ideas in whatever order they come to mind, with little regard for communicating the ideas effectively.

knowledge transforming Writing about ideas in such a way as to intentionally help the reader understand them.

language acquisition device Biologically built-in mechanism hypothesized to facilitate language learning.

language socialization Direct and indirect means through which other people teach children the language and verbal behaviors deemed to be appropriate in their culture.

learned helplessness General belief that one is incapable of accomplishing tasks and has little or no control of the environment.

learning disability Significant deficit in one or more cognitive processes, to the point where special educational services are required.

left hemisphere Left side of the cortex; largely responsible for sequential reasoning and analysis, especially in right-handed people.

lexical word Word that in some way represents an aspect of one's physical, social, or psychological world.

long-term memory Component of memory that holds knowledge and skills for a relatively long period of time.

longitudinal study Research study in which the performance of a single group of people is tracked over a period of time.

mastery goal Desire to acquire additional knowledge or master new skills (also known as a *learning goal*).

mastery orientation General belief that one is capable of accomplishing challenging tasks, accompanied by an intent to master such tasks.

maturation Genetically guided changes that occur over the course of development.

mediated learning experience Discussion between an adult and a child in which the adult helps the child make sense of an event they have mutually experienced.

mediation In Vygotsky's theory, a process through which adults help children make culturally appropriate sense of their experiences, perhaps by attaching labels to objects or explaining the nature of certain phenomena.

meiosis The process of cell division and reproduction by which gametes are formed.

menarche First menstrual period in an adolescent female.

metacognition Knowledge and beliefs about one's own cognitive processes, as well as efforts to regulate those cognitive processes to maximize learning and memory.

metacognitive awareness Extent to which one is able to reflect on the nature of one's own thinking processes.

metalinguistic awareness Extent to which one consciously understands and thinks about the nature and functions of language.

midbrain Part of the brain that coordinates communication between the hindbrain and forebrain.

mirror neuron Specialized cell in the brain that either fires when the person performs a particular act or observes another individual performing the same act.

mitosis The process of cell duplication by which chromosomes are preserved and a human being or other biological organism can grow.

monozygotic twins Twins that began as a single zygote and so share the same genetic makeup.

moral development Advancements in reasoning and behaving in accordance with culturally prescribed or self-constructed standards of right and wrong.

moral dilemma Situation in which there is no clear-cut answer regarding the morally right thing to do.

moral transgression In social domain theory, action that causes damage or harm or in some other way infringes on the needs and rights of others.

motivation State that energizes, directs, and sustains behavior.

multifactorial trait Particular characteristic determined by many separate genes combining in influence with environmental factors.

music literacy Ability to read and understand musical notation.

myelination The growth of a fatty sheath around neurons that allows them to transmit messages more quickly.

narrative Verbal account of a temporal sequence of logically interconnected events; a story.

native language The first language a child learns.

nativism Theoretical perspective proposing that some knowledge is biologically built-in and available at birth or soon thereafter.

nature Inherited characteristics and tendencies that affect development.

need for relatedness Fundamental need to feel socially connected to, and loved and respected by, other people.

neglected children Children whom peers rarely select as someone they would either most like or least like to do something with.

neo-Piagetian theory Theoretical perspective that combines elements of Piaget's theory with more contemporary research findings and suggests that development in specific content domains is often stagelike in nature.

neuron Cell that transmits information to other cells; also called a *nerve cell*.

niche construction A child's active shaping of the environment through behaviors, activities, and choices, often in accordance with personal genetically based tendencies.

niche-picking Tendency to actively seek out environments that match one's inherited abilities.

nurture Environmental conditions that affect development.

obesity Condition in which a person's body mass index, a measure of weight in relation to height, is at or above the 95th percentile for someone of the same age and gender.

object permanence Realization that objects continue to exist even when they are out of sight.

observation Data collection technique whereby a researcher carefully observes and documents the behaviors of participants in a research study.

operation In Piaget's theory, an organized and integrated system of logical thought processes.

organization Process of identifying interrelationships among pieces of information as a way of learning them more effectively.

overextension Overly broad meaning for a word, such that it is used in situations to which it does not apply.

overregularization Use of a syntactic rule in situations where an exception to the rule applies.

parenting style General pattern of behaviors that a parent uses to nurture and discipline his or her children.

peer culture General set of rules, expectations, and interpretations that influence how members of a particular peer group behave.

peer mediation Approach to conflict resolution in which one child or adolescent (the mediator) asks peers in conflict to express their differing viewpoints and then work together to identify an appropriate compromise.

peer pressure Tactics used to encourage some behaviors and discourage others in age-mates.

perception Interpretation of stimuli that the body has sensed.

performance goal Desire to demonstrate high ability and make a good impression.

performance-approach goal Desire to look good and receive favorable judgments from others.

performance-avoidance goal Desire not to look bad or receive unfavorable judgments from others.

permissive parenting style Parenting style characterized by emotional warmth but few expectations or standards for children's behavior.

personal fable Belief held by many adolescents that they are unique beings invulnerable to normal risks and dangers.

personal interest Long-term, relatively stable interest in a particular topic or activity.

personal matter In social domain theory, action that is considered a choice that an individual can make without consulting others.

personal space A child's personally and culturally preferred distance from other people during social interaction.

personality Characteristic way a person behaves, thinks, and feels.

phonemes Smallest units of a spoken language that signify differences in meaning.

phonological awareness Ability to hear the distinct sounds of which spoken words are comprised.

phonology The sound system of a language; how words sound and are produced.

physical aggression Action that can potentially cause bodily injury (for example, hitting or scratching another person).

physical development Systematic changes of the body and brain and age-related changes in motor skills and health behaviors.

physiological measure Direct assessment of physical development or physiological functioning.

playing the dozens Friendly, playful exchange of insults, common in some African American communities; also called *joaning* or *sounding*.

popular children Children whom many peers like and perceive to be kind and trustworthy.

postconventional morality In Kohlberg's theory, behaving in accordance with self-developed abstract principles regarding right and wrong.

pragmatics Conventions and strategies used in effective and socially acceptable verbal interactions.

preconventional morality In Kohlberg's theory, a lack of internalized standards about right and wrong; making decisions based on what is best for oneself, without regard for others' needs and feelings.

prejudice Display of negative attitudes, feelings, and behaviors toward particular individuals because of their membership in a specific group.

premature infant Infant born early (before 37 weeks of prenatal growth) and sometimes with serious medical problems.

prenatal development Growth that takes place between conception and birth.

primary reinforcer Stimulus or event that satisfies a built-in biological need.

proactive aggression Deliberate aggression against another as a means of obtaining a desired goal.

prosocial behavior Action intended to benefit another person (for example, sharing with or helping another person).

proximodistal trend Inside-outside ordering of motor skills and physical development; order is inside first and outside last.

psychodynamic theory Theoretical perspective that focuses on how early experiences and internal conflicts affect social and personality development.

psychosocial stages In Erikson's theory, eight periods of life that involve age-related challenges.

puberty Physiological changes that occur during adolescence and lead to reproductive maturation.

punishment Consequence of a response that leads to a decrease in the frequency of that response.

qualitative change Relatively dramatic developmental change that reflects considerable reorganization or modification of functioning.

quantitative change Developmental change that involves a series of minor, trendlike modifications.

quasi-experimental study Research study in which one or more experimental treatments are administered but in which random assignment to groups is not possible.

questionnaire Data collection technique that obtains self-report data through a paper-and-pencil inventory.

reactive aggression Aggressive response to frustration or provocation.

receptive language Ability to understand the language one hears or reads.

recessive gene Gene that influences growth and development primarily when the other gene in the allele pair is identical to it.

reciprocal teaching Approach to teaching reading comprehension in which students take turns asking teacher-like questions of their classmates.

recursive thinking Thinking about what other people may be thinking about oneself, possibly through multiple iterations.

reflex Automatic motor response to a particular kind of stimulus.

rehearsal Attempt to learn and remember information by repeating it over and over.

reinforcer Consequence of a response that leads to an increase in the frequency of that response.

rejected children Children whom many peers identify as being unfavorable social partners.

rejection Form of acculturation in which a person fails to learn or accept any customs and values from a new cultural environment.

relational aggression Action that can adversely affect interpersonal relationships (for example, calling another person names or socially excluding the person).

reliability Extent to which a data collection technique yields consistent, dependable results—results that are only minimally affected by temporary and irrelevant influences.

resilience Ability of some youngsters (often enhanced with environmental support) to thrive despite adverse environmental conditions.

right hemisphere Right side of the cortex; largely responsible for simultaneous processing and synthesis, especially in right-handed people.

rough-and-tumble play Playful physical "fighting" common in early and middle childhood.

rubric A list of the ideal features of an assessment, often used by students in completing a task and by teachers in evaluating students' performance.

sample The specific participants in a research study; their performance is often assumed to indicate how a larger population of individuals would perform.

scaffolding Support mechanism, provided by a more competent individual, that helps a child successfully perform a task within his or her zone of proximal development.

schema Tightly integrated set of ideas about a specific object or situation.

scheme In Piaget's theory, an organized group of similar actions or thoughts that are used repeatedly in response to the environment.

schizophrenia A psychiatric condition characterized by irrational ideas and disorganized thinking.

scientific method Multistep process of carefully defining and addressing a research question using critical thinking and analysis of the evidence.

scientific reasoning Cognitive processes central to conducting scientific research and interpreting findings appropriately.

script Schema that involves a predictable sequence of events related to a common activity.

secondary reinforcer Stimulus or event that becomes reinforcing over time through its association with one or more other reinforcers.

secure attachment Attachment classification in which children use attachment figures as a source of comfort in times of distress and as a secure base from which to explore.

selective adoption Form of acculturation in which a person assumes some customs of a new culture while also retaining some customs of a previous culture.

self-conscious emotion Affective state that reflects awareness of a community's social standards (e.g., pride, guilt, shame).

self-efficacy Belief that one is capable of executing certain behaviors or reaching certain goals.

self-evaluation Judging one's own performance in accordance with predetermined criteria.

self-fulfilling prophecy Phenomenon in which an adult's expectations for a child's performance bring about that level of performance.

self-handicapping Action that undermines one's own success as a way of protecting self-worth during difficult tasks.

self-instructions Specific directions that one gives oneself while performing a complex behavior; a form of *self-talk*.

self-monitoring Process of observing and recording one's own behavior.

self-motivation Intentionally using certain strategies to keep oneself on task during a dull but important activity.

self-regulated learning Directing and controlling one's own cognitive processes in order to learn successfully.

self-regulation Process of directing and controlling one's personal actions and emotions.

self-reinforcement Self-imposed pleasurable consequence for a desired behavior.

self-report Data collection technique whereby participants are asked to describe their own characteristics and performance.

self-socialization Tendency to integrate personal observations and others' input into self-constructed standards for behavior and to choose actions consistent with those standards.

self-talk Talking to oneself as a way of guiding oneself through a task.

semantic bootstrapping Using knowledge of word meanings to derive knowledge about syntactic categories and structures.

semantics The meanings of words and word combinations.

sensation Physiological detection of stimuli in the environment.

sense of community In a classroom or school, a collection of widely shared beliefs that students, teachers, and other staff have common goals, support one another's efforts, and make important contributions to everyone's success.

sense of self-determination Belief that one has some choice and control regarding the future course of one's life.

sense of self Knowledge, beliefs, judgments, and feelings about oneself as a person.

sensitive period A period in development when certain environmental experiences have a more pronounced influence than is true at other times.

sensory register Component of memory that holds incoming information in an unanalyzed form for a very brief time (2 to 3 seconds or less).

service learning Activity that promotes learning and skill development through volunteerism or community service.

sexual harassment Form of discrimination in which a target individual perceives another's actions or statements to be hostile, humiliating, or offensive, especially pertaining to physical appearance or sexual matters.

sexual orientation Particular genders to which an individual is romantically and sexually attracted.

shame Feeling of embarrassment or humiliation after failing to meet certain standards for moral behavior.

sight vocabulary Words that a child can immediately recognize while reading.

situated motivation Phenomenon in which aspects of the immediate environment enhance motivation to learn particular things or behave in particular ways.

situational interest Interest evoked temporarily by something in the environment.

social cognition Process of thinking about how other people are likely to think, act, and react and choosing one's own interpersonal behaviors accordingly.

social constructivism Theoretical perspective that focuses on people's collective efforts to impose meaning on the world.

social goal Goal related to establishing or maintaining relationships with other people.

social learning theory Theoretical perspective that focuses on how children's beliefs and goals influence their actions and how they often learn by observing others.

social perspective taking Imagining what someone else might be thinking or feeling.

social referencing Looking at someone else (e.g., a caregiver) for clues about how to respond to a particular object or event.

social skills Strategies used to interact effectively with others.

social-cognitive bias Mental shortcut used when thinking about other people or social events.

social-emotional development Systematic changes in emotions, self-concept, motivation, social relationships, and moral reasoning and behavior.

socialization Systematic efforts by other people and institutions to prepare youngsters to act in ways deemed by society to be appropriate and responsible.

society Large, enduring group of people that is socially and economically organized and has collective institutions and activities.

sociocognitive conflict Situation in which one encounters and has to wrestle with ideas and viewpoints different from one's own.

sociocultural theory Theoretical perspective that focuses on children's learning of tools, thinking processes, and communication systems through practice in meaningful tasks with other people.

sociodramatic play Play in which children take on specific roles and act out a scenario of imaginary events.

socioeconomic status (SES) One's general standing in an economically stratified society, encompassing family income, type of job, and education level.

sociolinguistic behaviors Social conventions (often culture specific) that govern appropriate verbal interaction.

specific language impairment Disability characterized by abnormalities in producing or understanding spoken language, to the point where special educational services are required.

spermarche First ejaculation in an adolescent male.

stage theory Theory that describes development as involving a series of qualitatively distinct changes.

stage A period of development characterized by a qualitatively distinct way of behaving or thinking.

Standard English Form of English generally considered acceptable in school (as reflected in textbooks, grammar instruction, etc.) and in other formal institutions by teachers and others.

standards In education, general statements regarding the knowledge and skills that students should gain and the characteristics that accomplishments should reflect.

state of arousal Physiological condition of sleepiness or wakefulness.

stepfamily Family created when one parent–child(ren) group combines with another parent figure and any children in his or her custody.

stereotype Rigid, simplistic, and erroneous characterization of a particular group.

stereotype threat Reduction in performance (often unintentional) as a result of a belief that one's group typically performs poorly.

story schema Knowledge of the typical elements and sequence of a narrative.

stranger anxiety Fear of unfamiliar adults in the latter half of the first year and into the second year of life.

structured English immersion Approach to second-language instruction for English language learners in which the children receive intensive lessons in English for a year or so and are then placed in the regular classroom.

subculture Group that resists the ways of the dominant culture and adopts its own norms for behavior.

submersion Approach to second-language instruction in which English language learners are placed in the regular classroom and expected to acquire the new language simply through exposure.

substance schema General view of all physical phenomena as being either touchable substances or properties of those substances.

subtractive bilingualism Phenomenon in which immersion in a new-language environment leads to deficits in one's native language.

sudden infant death syndrome (SIDS) Death of an infant in the first year of life, typically during sleep, that cannot be explained by a thorough medical examination; the risk of SIDS is highest between 2 and 4 months of age.

symbol Mental entity that represents an external object or event, typically without reflecting its perceptual and behavioral qualities.

symbolic thought Ability to mentally represent and think about external objects and events.

sympathy Feeling of sorrow and concern about another's problems or distress.

synapse Junction between two neurons.

synaptic pruning A process in brain development whereby many previously formed synapses wither away, especially if they have not been used frequently.

synaptogenesis A process in brain development whereby many new synapses appear during the first few years of life.

syntax Rules consistently used to put words together into sentences.

telegraphic speech Short, grammatically incomplete sentences that include lexical (rather than grammatical) words almost exclusively; common in toddlers.

temperament A child's characteristic ways of responding to emotional events, novel stimuli, and personal impulses.

teratogen Potentially harmful substance that can cause damaging effects during prenatal development.

test Instrument designed to assess knowledge, abilities, or skills in a consistent fashion across individuals.

theory Integrated collection of principles and explanations regarding a particular phenomenon.

theory of mind Awareness that people have an inner, psychological life (thoughts, beliefs, feelings, etc.).

theory theory Theoretical perspective proposing that children construct increasingly integrated and complex understandings of physical and mental phenomena.

underextension Overly restricted meaning for a word that excludes some situations to which the word applies.

uninvolved parenting style Parenting style characterized by a lack of emotional support and a lack of standards regarding appropriate behavior.

universality In a particular aspect of human development, the commonalities seen in the way virtually all individuals progress.

validity Extent to which a data collection technique actually assesses what the researcher intends for it to assess.

value Belief that a particular activity has direct or indirect benefits.

vicarious punishment Phenomenon in which a child decreases a certain response after seeing someone else punished for that response.

vicarious reinforcement Phenomenon in which a child increases a certain response after seeing someone else reinforced for that response.

visual-spatial ability Ability to imagine and mentally manipulate two- and three-dimensional figures.

wait time The length of time a teacher pauses, after either asking a question or hearing a student's comment, before saying something.

working memory Component of memory that enables people to actively think about and process a small amount of information.

zone of proximal development (ZPD) Range of tasks that one cannot yet perform independently but can perform with the help and guidance of others.

zygote Cell formed when a male sperm joins with a female ovum; with reasonably healthy genes and nurturing conditions in the uterus, it may develop into a fetus and be born as a live infant.

References

Aalsma, M. C., Lapsley, D. K., & Flannery, D. J. (2006). Personal fables, narcissism, and adolescent adjustment. *Psychology in the Schools, 43,* 481–491.

Abe, J. A. A. (2005). The predictive validity of the five-factor model of personality with preschool age children: A nine year follow-up study. *Journal of Research in Personality, 39,* 423–442.

Abelev, M. S. (2009). Advancing out of poverty: Social class worldview and its relation to resilience. *Journal of Adolescent Research, 24*(1), 114–141.

Abi-Nader, J. (1993). Meeting the needs of multicultural classrooms: Family values and the motivation of minority students. In M. J. O'Hair & S. J. Odell (Eds.), *Diversity and teaching: Teacher education yearbook I.* Fort Worth, TX: Harcourt Brace Jovanovich.

Aboud, F. E. (1988). *Children and prejudice.* New York: Basil Blackwell.

Aboud, F. E. (2005). The development of prejudice in childhood and adolescence. In J. F. Dovidio, P. Glick, & L. A. Rudman (Eds.), *On the nature of prejudice: Fifty years after Allport* (pp. 310–326). Malden, MA: Blackwell.

Aboud, F. E., & Fenwick, V. (1999). Exploring and evaluating school-based interventions to reduce prejudice. *Journal of Social Issues, 55*(4), 767–785. doi:10.1111/0022-4537.00146

Abrams, D., Rutland, A., Cameron, L., & Ferrell, J. (2007). Older but wilier: In-group accountability and the development of subjective group dynamics. *Developmental Psychology, 43,* 134–148.

Ackerman, C. M., & Fifield, A. (2005). *Education policy brief: Gifted and talented education.* Retrieved March 3, 2008, from http://www.rdc.udel.edu/policy_briefs/v19_May.pdf

Ackerman, P. L., & Lohman, D. F. (2006). Individual differences in cognitive functions. In P. A. Alexander & P. H. Winne (Eds.), *Handbook of educational psychology* (2nd ed., pp. 139–161). Mahwah, NJ: Erlbaum.

Acredolo, L. P., & Goodwyn, S. W. (1990). Sign language in babies: The significance of symbolic gesturing for understanding language development. In R. Vasta (Ed.), *Annals of child development: A research annual* (Vol. 7, pp. 1–42). London, England: Jessica Kingsley Publisher.

Adam, E. K. (2004). Beyond quality: Parental and residential stability and children's adjustment. *Current Directions in Psychological Science, 13,* 210–213.

Adam, E. K., Snell, E. K., & Pendry, P. (2007). Sleep timing and quantity in ecological and family context: A nationally representative time-diary study. *Journal of Family Psychology, 21,* 4–19.

Adams, B. (2008). Here comes the sun. *Science and Children, 46*(1), 56–58.

Adams, G. R., Gullotta, T. P., & Markstrom-Adams, C. (1994). *Adolescent life experiences* (3rd ed.). Pacific Grove, CA: Brooks/Cole.

Adamson, L. B., & Bakeman, R. (1991). The development of shared attention during infancy. In R. Vasta (Ed.), *Annals of child development* (Vol. 8, pp. 1–41). London: Kingsley.

Adamson, L. B., & McArthur, D. (1995). Joint attention, affect, and culture. In C. Moore & P. J. Dunham (Eds.), *Joint attention: Its origins and role in development* (pp. 205–221). Hillsdale, NJ: Erlbaum.

Adlof, S. M., Catts, H. W., & Lee, J. (2010). Kindergarten predictors of second versus eighth grade reading comprehension impairments. *Journal of Learning Disabilities, 43*(4), 332–345.

Afflerbach, P., VanSledright, B., & Dromsky, A. (2003, April). *Reading and thinking like historians: Investigating a 4th grade performance assessment.* Paper presented at the annual meeting of the American Educational Research Association, Chicago.

Agency for Toxic Substances and Disease Registry. (1999, June). *ToxFAQs™ for lead.* Retrieved January 19, 2003, from http://www.atsdr.cdc.gov/tfacts13.html

Agirdag, O. (2009). All languages welcomed here. *Educational Leadership, 66*(7), 20–25.

Agostino, A., Johnson, J., & Pascual-Leone, J. (2010). Executive functions underlying multiplicative reasoning: Problem type matters. *Journal of Experimental Child Psychology, 105*(4), 286–305.

Ahamed, Y., Macdonald, H., Reed, K., Naylor, P. J., Liu-Ambrose, T., & McKay, H. (2007). School-based physical activity does not compromise children's academic performance. *Medicine and Science in Sports and Exercise, 39*(2), 371–376.

Ahern, A. L., & Hetherington, M. M. (2006). The thin ideal and body image: An experimental study of implicit attitudes. *Psychology of Addictive Behaviors, 20,* 338–342.

Ahnert, L., Pinquart, M., & Lamb, M. E. (2006). Security of children's relationships with nonparental care providers: A meta-analysis. *Child Development, 74,* 664–679.

Aikins, J. W., Howes, C., & Hamilton, C. (2009). Attachment stability and the emergence of unresolved representations during adolescence. *Attachment & Human Development, 11*(5), 491–512.

Ainsworth, M. D. S. (1963). The development of infant–mother interaction among the Ganda. In B. M. Foss (Ed.), *Determinants of infant behavior* (Vol. 2, pp. 67–104). New York: Wiley.

Ainsworth, M. D. S. (1973). The development of infant–mother attachment. In B. Caldwell & H. Ricciuti (Eds.), *Review of child development research* (Vol. 3, pp. 1–94). Chicago: University of Chicago Press.

Ainsworth, M. D. S., Blehar, M. C., Waters, E., & Wall, S. (1978). *Patterns of attachment.* Hillsdale, NJ: Erlbaum.

Akhtar, N., Jipson, J., & Callanan, M. A. (2001). Learning words through overhearing. *Child Development, 72,* 416–430.

Akiba, D., & García Coll, C. (2003). Effective interventions with children of color and their families: A contextual developmental approach. In T. B. Smith (Ed.), *Practicing multiculturalism: Internalizing and affirming diversity in counseling and psychology* (pp. 148–177). Boston: Allyn & Bacon.

Akiskal, H. S., & McKinney, W. T. (1973). Depressive disorders: Toward a unified hypothesis. *Science, 162,* 20–29.

Alan Guttmacher Institute (2001). *Can more progress be made? Teenage sexual and reproductive behavior in developed countries.* Retrieved February 1, 2008, from http://www.guttmacher.org/pubs/summaries/euroteens_summ.pdf

Alber-Morgan, S. (2010). *Using RTI to teach literacy to diverse learners, K–8: Strategies for the inclusive classroom.* Thousand Oaks, CA: Corwin Press.

Albers, C. A., & Grieve, A. J. (2007). Test review: Bayley, N. (2006). Bayley Scales of Infant and Toddler Development—Third Edition. San Antonio, TX: Harcourt Assessment. *Journal of Psychoeducational Assessment, 25,* 180–198.

Alberts, A., Elkind, D., & Ginsberg, S. (2007). The personal fable and risk-taking in early adolescence. *Journal of Youth and Adolescence, 36,* 71–76.

Alderman, M. K. (1990). Motivation for at-risk students. *Educational Leadership, 48*(1), 27–30.

Aldridge, M. A., Stillman, R. D., & Bower, T. G. R. (2001). Newborn categorization of vowel-like sounds. *Developmental Science, 4,* 220–232.

Alessandri, S. M., & Lewis, M. (1993). Parental evaluation and its relation to shame and pride in young children. *Sex Roles, 29,* 335–343.

Alexander, E. S. (2006, April). *Beyond S.M.A.R.T.? Integrating hopeful thinking into goal setting for adolescents at-risk of dropping out of high school.* Paper presented at the annual meeting of the American Educational Research Association, San Francisco.

Alexander, J. M., Johnson, K. E., Leibham, M. E., & Kelley, K. (2008). The development of conceptual interests in young children. *Cognitive Development, 23,* 324–334.

Alexander, K., Entwisle, D., & Thompson, M. (1987). School performance, status relations, and the structure of sentiment: Bringing the teacher back in. *American Sociological Review, 52,* 665–682.

Alexander, P. A., Graham, S., & Harris, K. R. (1998). A perspective on strategy research: Progress and prospects. *Educational Psychology Review, 10,* 129–154.

Alfassi, M., Weiss, I., & Lifshitz, H. (2009). The efficacy of reciprocal teaching in fostering the reading literacy of students with intellectual disabilities. *European Journal of Special Needs Education, 24*(3), 291–305.

Alland, A. (1983). *Playing with form.* New York: Columbia University Press.

Allison, K. W. (1998). Stress and oppressed social category membership. In J. K. Swim & C. Stangor (Eds.), *Prejudice: The target's perspective* (pp. 149–170). San Diego, CA: Academic Press.

Allodi, M. W. (2010). Goals and values in school: A model developed for describing, evaluating and changing the social climate of learning environments. *Social Psychology of Education, 13*(2), 207–235. doi:10.1007/s11218-009-9110-6

Alloway, T. P., & Alloway, R. G. (2010). Investigating the predictive roles of working memory and IQ in academic attainment. *Journal of Experimental Child Psychology, 106*(1), 20–29.

Altermatt, E. R., & Broady, E. F. (2009). Coping with achievement-related failure: An examination of conversations between friends. *Merrill-Palmer Quarterly 55*(4), 454–487.

Alvermann, D. E., & Moore, D. W. (1991). Secondary school reading. In R. Barr, M. L. Kamil, P. B. Mosenthal, & P. D. Pearson (Eds.), *Handbook of reading research* (Vol. II, pp. 951–983). New York: Longman.

Aman, M. G., McDougle, C. J., Scahill, L., Handen, B., Arnold, L. E. A., Johnson, C., et al. (2009). Medication and parent training in children with pervasive developmental disorders and serious behavior problems: Results from a randomized clinical trial. *Journal of the American Academy of Child & Adolescent Psychiatry, 48*(12), 1143–1154.

Amatea, E. S., & West-Olatunji, C. A. (2007). Joining the conversation about educating our poorest children: Emerging leadership roles for school counselors in high-poverty schools. *Professional School Counseling, 11*(2), 81–89.

Ambrose, D., Allen, J., & Huntley, S. B. (1994). Mentorship of the highly creative. *Roeper Review, 17,* 131–133.

American Academy of Pediatrics Committee on Pediatric AIDS and Committee on Adolescence. (2001). Adolescents and human immunodeficiency virus infection: The role of the pediatrician in prevention and intervention. *Pediatrics, 107,* 188–190.

American Academy of Pediatrics Committee on Pediatric AIDS and Committee on Infectious Diseases. (1999). Issues related to human immunodeficiency virus transmission in schools, child care, medical settings, home, and community. *Pediatrics, 104,* 318–324.

American Academy of Pediatrics Committee on Sports Medicine and Fitness. (2000). Intensive training and sports specialization in young athletes. *Pediatrics, 106,* 154–157.

American Academy of Pediatrics Task Force on Infant Sleep Position and Sudden Infant Death Syndrome. (2000). Changing concepts of sudden infant death syndrome: Implications for infant sleeping environment and sleep position. *Pediatrics, 105,* 650–656.

American Association on Intellectual and Developmental Disabilities. (2008). *Frequently asked questions on intellectual disability and the AAIDD definition.* Retrieved March 4, 2008, from http://www.aamr.org/Policies/faq_mental_retardation.shtml

American Educational Research Association. (2000). AERA position statement on high-stakes testing in pre-K–12 education. Retrieved October 15, 2007, from https://www.aera.net/policyandprograms/?id=378

American Psychiatric Association. (1994). *Diagnostic and statistical manual of mental disorders* (4th ed.). Washington, DC: Author.

American Psychiatric Association. (2000). *Diagnostic and statistical manual of mental disorders* (4th ed., text rev.). Washington, DC: Author.

American Psychological Association. (2002). Ethical principles of psychologists and code of conduct. *American Psychologist, 57,* 1060–1073.

American Speech-Language-Hearing Association (1993). Definitions of communication disorders and variations. *ASHA, 35*(Suppl. 10), 40–41.

Ames, C. (1984). Competitive, cooperative, and individualistic goal structures: A cognitive-motivational analysis. In R. Ames & C. Ames (Eds.), *Research on motivation in education: Vol. 1. Student motivation* (pp. 177–207). San Diego, CA: Academic Press.

Ames, C. (1992). Classrooms: Goals, structures, and student motivation. *Journal of Educational Psychology, 84,* 261–271.

Anastasi, A., & Urbina, S. (1997). *Psychological testing* (7th ed.). Upper Saddle River, NJ: Prentice Hall.

Anderman, E. M., & Maehr, M. L. (1994). Motivation and schooling in the middle grades. *Review of Educational Research, 64,* 287–309.

Anderman, L. H., & Anderman, E. M. (1999). Social predictors of changes in students' achievement goal orientation. *Contemporary Educational Psychology, 25,* 21–37.

Anderman, L. H., Patrick, H., Hruda, L. Z., & Linnenbrink, E. A. (2002). Observing classroom goal structures to clarify and expand goal theory. In C. Midgley (Ed.), *Goals, goal structures, and patterns of adaptive learning* (pp. 243–278). Mahwah, NJ: Erlbaum.

Anderson, C. A., Berkowitz, L., Donnerstein, E., Huesmann, L. R., Johnson, J. D., Linz, D., et al.

(2003). The influence of media violence on youth. *Psychological Science in the Public Interest, 4,* 81–110.

Anderson, C. L., & Brown, C. E. L. (2009). Fetal abnormalities: Antenatal screening and diagnosis. *American Family Physician, 79*(2), 117–123.

Anderson, D. A. (1994). Lesbian and gay adolescents: Social and developmental considerations. *The High School Journal, 77* (1,2), 13–19.

Anderson, D. R. (2003). The Children's Television Act: A public policy that benefits children. *Applied Developmental Psychology, 24,* 337–340.

Anderson, J. C. (1983). *The architecture of cognition.* Cambridge, MA: Harvard University Press.

Anderson, K. E., Lytton, H., & Romney, D. M. (1986). Mothers' interactions with normal and conduct-disordered boys: Who affects whom? *Developmental Psychology, 22,* 604–609.

Anderson, L. W., & Pellicer, L. O. (1998). Toward an understanding of unusually successful programs for economically disadvantaged students. *Journal of Education for Students Placed at Risk, 3,* 237–263.

Anderson, R. C., Nguyen-Jahiel, K., McNurlen, B., Archodidou, A., Kim, S.-Y., Reznitskaya, A., et al. (2001). The snowball phenomenon: Spread of ways of talking and ways of thinking across groups of children. *Cognition and Instruction, 19,* 1–46.

Anderson, R. C., Shirey, L., Wilson, P., & Fielding, L. (1987). Interestingness of children's reading materials. In R. Snow & M. Farr (Eds.), *Aptitude, learning, and instruction: III. Cognitive and affective process analyses* (pp. 287–299). Hillsdale, NJ: Erlbaum.

Andersson, U. (2010). Skill development in different components of arithmetic and basic cognitive functions: Findings from a 3-year longitudinal study of children with different types of learning difficulties. *Journal of Educational Psychology, 102*(1), 115–134.

Andrade, H. L., Wang, X., Du, Y., & Akawi, R. L. (2009). Rubric-referenced self-assessment and self-efficacy for writing. *Journal of Educational Research, 102*(4), 287–301. doi:10.3200/JOER.102.4.287-302

Andrews, G., Halford, G. S., Murphy, K., & Knox, K. (2009). Integration of weight and distance information in young children: The role of relational complexity. *Cognitive Development, 24*(1), 49–60.

Andrews, J. F., & Mason, J. M. (1986). Childhood deafness and the acquisition of print concepts. In D. B. Yaden, Jr., & S. Templeton (Eds.), *Metalinguistic awareness and beginning literacy: Conceptualizing what it means to read and write* (pp. 277–290). Portsmouth, NH: Heinemann.

Andriessen, J. (2006). Arguing to learn. In R. K. Sawyer (Ed.), *The Cambridge handbook of the learning sciences* (pp. 443–459). Cambridge, England: Cambridge University Press.

Androutsopoulos, J., & Georgakopoulou, A. (2010). Youth, discourse, and interpersonal management. In D. Matsumoto (Ed.), *APA handbook of interpersonal communication* (pp. 235–252). Washington, DC: American Psychological Association.

Ang, S., Rodgers, J., & Wänström, L. (2010). The Flynn Effect within subgroups in the U.S.: Gender, race, income, education, and urbanization differences in the NLSY-Children data. *Intelligence, 38*(4), 367–384.

Anglin, J. M. (1977). *Word, object, and conceptual development.* New York: Norton.

Anjum, A., Gait, P., Cullen, K. R., & White, T. (2010). Schizophrenia in adolescents and young adults. In J. E. Grant & M. N. Potenza (Eds.), *Young adult mental health* (pp. 362–378). New York: Oxford University Press.

Annett, R. D. (2004). Asthma. In R. T. Brown (Ed.), *Handbook of pediatric psychology in school settings* (pp. 149–167). Mahwah, NJ: Erlbaum.

Annetta, L. A. (2010). The "I's" have it: A framework for serious educational game design. Review of General Psychology, 14(2), 105–112. doi:10.1037/a0018985

Ansalone, G. (2006). Perceptions of ability and equity in the U.S. and Japan: Understanding the pervasiveness of tracking. *Radical Pedagogy, 8*(1).

Anschutz, D., Engels, R., Van Leeuwe, J., & Van Strien, T. (2009). Watching your weight? The relations between watching soaps and music television and body dissatisfaction and restrained eating in young girls. *Psychology & Health, 24*(9), 1035–1050. doi:10.1080/08870440802192268

Anthony, J. L., & Francis, D. J. (2005). Development of phonological awareness. *Current Directions in Psychological Science, 14,* 255–259.

Anthony, J. L., Lonigan, C. J., & Dyer, S. M. (1996, April). *The development of reading comprehension: Listening comprehension or basic language processes?* Paper presented at the annual meeting of the American Educational Research Association, New York.

Anthos, J. S. (2004). The healing power of art. *School Arts, 103*(10), 46–47.

Anyon, J. (1988). Social class and the hidden curriculum of work. In G. Handel (Ed.), *Childhood socialization* (pp. 357–382). New York: Aldine de Gruyter.

Arbib, M. (Ed.). (2005). *Action to language via the mirror neuron system.* New York: Cambridge University Press.

Archer, J. (1991). The influence of testosterone on human aggression. *British Journal of Psychology, 82,* 1–28.

Arcus, D. M. (1991). *Experiential modification of temperamental bias in inhibited and uninhibited children.* Unpublished doctoral dissertation, Harvard University, Cambridge, MA.

Arcus, D. M. (2001). Inhibited and uninhibited children: Biology in the social context. In T. D. Wachs & G. A. Kohnstamm (Eds.), *Temperament in context* (pp. 43–60). Mahwah, NJ: Erlbaum.

Ardila-Rey, A., & Killen, M. (2001). Middle class Colombian children's evaluations of personal, moral, and social-conventional interactions in the classroom. *International Journal of Behavioral Development, 25*(3), 246–255. doi:10.1080/01650250042000221

Ardila-Rey, A., Killen, M., & Brenick, A. (2009). Moral reasoning in violent contexts: Displaced and non-displaced Colombian children's evaluations of moral transgressions, retaliation, and reconciliation. *Social Development, 18*(1), 181–209. doi:10.1111/j.1467-9507.2008.00483.x

Armstrong, T. (2009). *Multiple intelligences in the classroom.* Alexandria, VA: Association for Supervision and Curriculum Development.

Arndt, T. L., Stodgell, C. J., & Rodier, P. M. (2005). The teratology of autism. *International Journal of Developmental Neuroscience, 23,* 189–199.

Arnett, J. J. (1999). Adolescent storm and stress, reconsidered. *American Psychologist, 54,* 317–326.

Arnold, M. L. (2000). Stage, sequence, and sequels: Changing conceptions of morality, post-Kohlberg. *Educational Psychology Review, 12,* 365–383.

Aronson, S. R., & Huston, A. C. (2004). The mother–infant relationship in single, cohabiting, and married families: A case for marriage? *Journal of Family Psychology, 18,* 5–18.

Arsenio, W. F., & Lemerise, E. A. (2010). Introduction. In W. F. Arsenio & E. A. Lemerise (Eds.), *Emotions, aggression, and morality in children: Bridging development and psychopathology* (pp. 3–9). Washington, DC: American Psychological Association.

Arshavsky, Y. I. (2009). Two functions of early language experience. *Brain Research Reviews, 60*(2), 327–340

Artman, L., & Cahan, S. (1993). Schooling and the development of transitive inference. *Developmental Psychology, 29,* 753–759.

Asai, S. (1993). In search of Asia through music: Guidelines and ideas for teaching Asian music. In T. Perry & J. W. Fraser (Eds.), *Freedom's plow: Teaching in the multicultural classroom.* New York: Routledge.

Ashcraft, M. H. (1982). The development of mental arithmetic: A chronometric approach. *Developmental Review, 2,* 212–236.

Asher, S. R., & Coie, J. D. (Eds.). (1990). *Peer rejection in childhood.* Cambridge, England: Cambridge University Press.

Asher, S. R., & Parker, J. G. (1989). Significance of peer relationship problems in childhood. In B. H. Schneider, G. Attili, J. Nadel, & R. P. Weissberg (Eds.), *Social competence in developmental perspective.* Dordrecht, The Netherlands: Kluwer.

Asher, S. R., & Renshaw, P. D. (1981). Children without friends: Social knowledge and social skill training. In S. R. Asher & J. M. Gottman (Eds.), *The development of children's friendships* (pp. 273–296). Cambridge, England: Cambridge University Press.

Ashiabi, G. S. (2007). Play in the preschool classroom: Its socioemotional significance and the teacher's role in play. *Early Childhood Education Journal, 35*(2), 199–207.

Ashmore, R., & DelBoca, F. (1976). Psychological approaches. In P. A. Katz (Ed.), *Elimination of racism.* New York: Pergamon.

Ashton, P. (1985). Motivation and the teacher's sense of efficacy. In C. Ames & R. Ames (Eds.), *Research on motivation in education: Vol. 2. The classroom milieu.* San Diego, CA: Academic Press.

Aslin, R. N., Saffran, J. R., & Newport, E. L. (1998). Computation of conditional probability statistics by 8-month-old infants. *Psychological Science, 9,* 321–324.

Association for Childhood Education International. (2009). *Preparation of elementary teachers.* ACEI position paper. Retrieved October 25, 2009, from http://www.acei.org/prepel.htm

Assor, A., & Connell, J. P. (1992). The validity of students' self-reports as measures of performance affecting self-appraisals. In D. H. Schunk & J. L. Meece (Eds.), *Student perceptions in the classroom.* Hillsdale, NJ: Erlbaum.

Astington, J. W. (1991). Intention in the child's theory of mind. In C. Moore & D. Frye (Eds.), *Children's theories of mind* (pp. 157–172). Hillsdale, NJ: Erlbaum.

Astington, J. W., & Pelletier, J. (1996). The language of mind: Its role in teaching and learning. In D. R. Olson & N. Torrance (Eds.), *The handbook of education and human development: New models of learning, teaching and schooling* (pp. 593–619). Cambridge, MA: Blackwell.

Atkinson, M. (1992). *Children's syntax: An introduction to principles and parameters theory.* Oxford, England: Blackwell.

Atkinson, R. C., & Shiffrin, R. M. (1968). Human memory: A proposed system and its control processes. In K. Spence & J. Spence (Eds.), *The psychology of learning and motivation* (Vol. 2, pp. 89–195). New York: Academic Press.

Attie, I., Brooks-Gunn, J., & Petersen, A. (1990). A developmental perspective on eating disorders and eating problems. In M. Lewis & S. M. Miller (Eds.), *Handbook of developmental psychopathology* (pp. 409–420). New York: Plenum Press.

Atwater, E. (1996). *Adolescence.* Upper Saddle River, NJ: Prentice Hall.

Au, T. K., & Glusman, M. (1990). The principle of mutual exclusivity in word learning: To honor or not to honor? *Child Development, 61,* 1474–1490.

Au, T. K.-F., Chan, C. K. K., Chan, T.-K., Cheung, M. W. L., Ho, J. Y. S., & Ip, G. W. M. (2008). Folkbiology meets microbiology: A study of conceptual and behavioral change. *Cognitive Psychology, 57,* 1–19.

Austin, S. B., Ziyadeh, N. J., Forman, S., Prokop, L. A., Keliher, A., & Jacobs, D. (2008). Screening high school students for eating disorders: Results of a national initiative. *Preventing Chronic Disease, 5*(4). Retrieved April 1, 2010, from http://www.cdc.gov/pcd/issues/2008/oct/07_0164.htm

Averill, R., Anderson, D., Easton, H., Te Maro, P., Smith, D., & Hynds, A. (2009). Culturally responsive teaching of mathematics: Three models from linked studies. *Journal for Research in Mathematics Education, 40*(2), 157–186.

Ayçiçegi-Dinn, A., & Caldwell-Harris, C. L. (2011). Individualism–collectivism among Americans, Turks and Turkish immigrants to the U.S. *International Journal of Intercultural Relations, 35*(1), 9–16. doi:10.1016/j.ijintrel.2010.11.006

Ayoub, C. C. (2006). Adaptive and maladaptive parenting: Influence on child development. In H. E. Fitzgerald, R. Zucker, & K. Freeark (Eds. in Chief), & N. F. Watt, C. Ayoub, R. H. Bradley, J. E. Puma, & W. A. LeBouef (Vol. Eds.), *The crisis in youth mental health: Critical issues and effective programs: Vol. 1. Early intervention programs and policies* (pp. 121–413). Westport, CT: Praeger.

Azzam, A. M. (2009/2010). Finding our way back to healthy eating: A conversation with David A. Kessler. *Educational Leadership, 67*(4), 6–10.

Baddeley, A. (1981). The concept of working memory: A view of its current state and probable future development. *Cognition, 10*(1–3), 17–23.

Bahrick, L. E., Gogate, L. J., & Ruiz, I. (2002). Attention and memory for faces and actions in infancy: The salience of actions over faces in dynamic events. *Child Development, 73,* 1629–1643.

Bailes, A., & Jackson, M. E. (2000). Shared responsibility in home birth practice: Collaborating with clients. *Journal of Midwifery and Women's Health, 45*(6), 537–543.

Bailey, J. M., Dunne, M. P., & Martin, N. G. (2000). Genetic and environmental influences on sexual orientation and its correlates in an Australian twin sample. *Journal of Personality and Social Psychology, 78,* 524–536.

Bailey, J. M., & Pillard, R. C. (1997). The innateness of homosexuality. In M. R. Walsh (Ed.), *Women, men, and gender: Ongoing debates* (pp. 184–187). New Haven, CT: Yale University Press.

Baillargeon, R. (1994). How do infants learn about the physical world? *Current Directions in Psychological Science, 3,* 133–140.

Baillargeon, R. (2004). Infants' physical worlds. *Current Directions in Psychological Science, 13,* 89–94.

Baillargeon, R. (2008). Innate ideas revisited: For a principle of persistence in infants' physical reasoning. *Perspectives on Psychological Science, 3,* 2–13.

Baines, E., & Blatchford, P. (2009). Sex differences in the structure and stability of children's playground social networks and their overlap with friendship relations. *British Journal of Developmental Psychology, 27*(3), 743–760. doi:10.1348/026151008X371114

Baird, A. A. (2010). The terrible twelves. In P. D. Zelazo, M. Chandler, & E. Crone (Eds.), *Developmental social cognitive neuroscience. The Jean Piaget symposium series* (pp. 191–207). New York: Psychology Press.

Baird, J. A., & Astington, J. W. (2005). The development of the intention concept: From the observable world to the unobservable mind. In R. R. Hassin, J. S. Uleman, & J. A. Bargh (Eds.), *The new unconscious* (pp. 256–276). New York: Oxford University Press.

Bakari, R. (2000). *The development and validation of an instrument to measure preservice teachers' attitudes toward teaching African American students.* Unpublished doctoral dissertation, University of Northern Colorado, Greeley.

Bakeman, R., & Brownlee, J. R. (1980). The strategic use of parallel play: A sequential analysis. *Child Development, 51,* 873–878.

Baker, C. (1993). *Foundations of bilingual education and bilingualism.* Clevedon, England: Multilingual Matters.

Baker, F. W. (2010). Media literacy: 21st century literacy skills. In H. H. Jacobs (Ed.), *Curriculum 21: Essential education for a changing world* (pp. 133–152). Alexandria, VA: Association for Supervision and Curriculum Development.

Baker, L., Scher, D., & Mackler, K. (1997). Home and family influences on motivations for reading. *Educational Psychologist, 32,* 69–82.

Baker, R. K., & White, K. M. (2010). Predicting adolescents' use of social networking sites from an extended theory of planned behaviour perspective. *Computers in Human Behavior, 26*(6), 1591–1597.

Bakermans-Kranenburg, M. J., van IJzendoorn, M. H., & Juffer, F. (2003). Less is more: Meta-analyses of sensitivity and attachment interventions in early childhood. *Psychological Bulletin, 129,* 195–215.

Balcomb, F. K., & Gerken, L. (2008). Three-year-old children can access their own memory to guide responses on a visual matching task. *Developmental Science, 11*(5), 750–760.

Baldwin, D. A. (1993). Early referential understanding: Infants' ability to recognize referential acts for what they are. *Developmental Psychology, 29,* 832–843.

Baldwin, D. A. (2000). Interpersonal understanding fuels knowledge acquisition. *Current Directions in Psychological Science, 9,* 40–45.

Baldwin, M. W., Keelan, J. P. R., Fehr, B., Enns, V., & Koh-Rangarajoo, E. (1996). Social-cognitive conceptualization of attachment working models: Availability and accessibility effects. *Journal of Personality and Social Psychology, 71,* 94–109.

Ball, J. W., Bindler, R. C., & Cowen, K. J. (2010). *Child health nursing: Partnering with children and families* (2nd ed.). Upper Saddle River, NJ: Pearson Education.

Balog, H. (2010). A comparison of maternal and child intonation: Does adult input support child production? *Infant Behavior & Development, 33*(3), 337–345.

Baltes, P. B. (1997). On the incomplete architecture of human ontogeny: Selection, optimization, and compensation as a foundation of developmental theory. *American Psychologist, 52,* 366–380.

Baltes, P. B., Lindenberger, U., & Staudinger, U. M. (2006). Life span theory in developmental psychology. In W. Damon & R. M. Lerner (Eds. in Chief) & R. M. Lerner (Vol. Ed.), *Handbook of child psychology: Vol. 1. Theoretical models of human development* (6th ed., pp. 569–664). Hoboken, NJ: Wiley.

Banaclocha, M. A. M. (2007). Neuromagnetic dialogue between neuronal minicolumns and astroglial network: A new approach for memory and cerebral computation. *Brain Research Bulletin, 73,* 21–27.

Bandura, A. (1965). Influence of models' reinforcement contingencies on the acquisition of imitative responses. *Journal of Personality and Social Psychology, 1,* 589–595.

Bandura, A. (1977). *Social learning theory.* Englewood Cliffs, NJ: Prentice Hall.

Bandura, A. (1986). *Social foundations of thought and action: A social cognitive theory.* Englewood Cliffs, NJ: Prentice-Hall, Inc.

Bandura, A. (1997). *Self-efficacy: The exercise of control.* New York: Freeman.

Bandura, A. (2006). Toward a psychology of human agency. *Perspectives on Psychological Science, 1,* 164–180.

Bandura, A., Barbaranelli, C., Caprara, G. V., & Pastorelli, C. (2001). Self-efficacy beliefs as shapers of children's aspirations and career trajectories. *Child Development, 72,* 187–206.

Bandura, A., & Mischel, W. (1965). Modification of self-imposed delay of reward through exposure to live and symbolic models. *Journal of Personality and Social Psychology, 2,* 698–705.

Banich, M. (2010, April). *The development of executive function during adolescence: Empirical findings and implications for the law.* Paper presented at the annual meeting of the Rocky Mountain Psychological Association, Denver.

Banks, J. A. (1994). *An introduction to multicultural education.* Needham Heights, MA: Allyn & Bacon.

Banks, J. A., & Banks, C. A. M. (Eds.). (1995). *Handbook of research on multicultural education.* New York: Macmillan.

Bannister, E. M., Jakubec, S. L., & Stein, J. A. (2003). "Like, what am I supposed to do?": Adolescents' health concerns in their dating relationships. *Canadian Journal of Nursing Research, 35*(2), 16–33.

Bao, X.-H., & Lam, S.-F. (2008). Who makes the choice? Rethinking the role of autonomy and relatedness in Chinese children's motivation. *Child Development, 79,* 269–283.

Barab, S. A., & Plucker, J. A. (2002). Smart people or smart contexts? Cognition, ability, and talent development in an age of situated approaches to knowing and learning. *Educational Psychologist, 37,* 165–182.

Barakat, L. P., Nicolaou, D. C., O'Hara, E. A., & Allen, S. L. (2009). Sickle cell disease. In W. T. O'Donohue & L. W. Tolle (Eds.), *Behavioral approaches to chronic disease in adolescence: A guide to integrative care* (pp. 253–267). New York: Springer Science + Business Media.

Baraldi, C., & Iervese, V. (2010). Dialogic mediation in conflict resolution education. *Conflict Resolution Quarterly, 27*(4), 423–445. doi:10.1002/crq.20005

Baranowski, T., Baranowski, J., Thompson, D., Buday, R., Jago, R., Griffith, M. J., et al. (2011). Video game play, child diet, and physical activity behavior change: A randomized clinical trial. *American Journal of Preventive Medicine, 40*(1), 33–38. doi:10.1016/j.amepre.2010.09.029

Barber, J. G., & Delfabbro, P. H. (2004). *Children in foster care.* New York: Routledge.

Barchfeld, P., Sodian, B., Thoermer, C., & Bullock, M. (2005, April). *The development of experiment generation abilities from primary school to late adolescence.* Poster presented at the biennial meeting of the Society for Research in Child Development, Atlanta, GA.

Barga, N. K. (1996). Students with learning disabilities in education: Managing a disability. *Journal of Learning Disabilities, 29,* 413–421.

Barkatsas, A., Kasimatis, K., & Gialamas, V. (2009). Learning secondary mathematics with technology: Exploring the complex interrelationship between students' attitudes, engagement, gender and achievement. *Computers & Education, 52*(3), 562–570.

Barker, C. E., Bird, C. E., Pradhan, A., & Shakya, G. (2007). Support to the Safe Motherhood Programme in Nepal: An integrated approach. *Reproductive Health Matters, 15*(30), 1–10.

Barkley, R. A. (1998). *Attention-deficit hyperactivity disorder: A handbook for diagnosis and treatment* (2nd ed.). New York: Guilford Press.

Barlow, K. (2010). Sharing food, sharing values: Mothering and empathy in Murik society. *Ethos, 38*(4), 339–353. doi:10.1111/j.1548-1352.2010.01154.x

Barnas, M. V., & Cummings, E. M. (1994). Caregiver stability and toddlers' attachment-related behaviors towards caregivers in day care. *Infant Behavior and Development, 17,* 141–147.

Barnett, J. E. (2001, April). *Study strategies and preparing for exams: A survey of middle and high school students.* Paper presented at the annual meeting of the American Educational Research Association, Seattle, WA.

Barnett, W. S. (1992). Benefits of compensatory preschool education. *Journal of Human Resources, 27,* 279–312.

Baron-Cohen, S., Tager-Flusberg, H., & Cohen, D. J. (1993). *Understanding other minds: Perspectives from autism.* Oxford, England: Oxford University Press.

Baroody, A. J., Tiilikainen, S. H., & Tai, Y.-C. (2006). The application and development of an addition goal sketch. *Cognition and Instruction, 24,* 123–170.

Barrett, J. G. (2005). Conduct disorders. In C. B. Fisher & R. M. Lerner (Eds.), *Encyclopedia of applied developmental science* (Vol. 1, pp. 294–295). Thousand Oaks, CA: Sage.

Barrett, K. C. (2005). The origins of social emotions and self-regulation in toddlerhood: New evidence. *Cognition and Emotion, 19*(7), 953–979. doi:10.1080/02699930500172515

Barringer, C., & Gholson, B. (1979). Effects of type and combination of feedback upon conceptual learning by children: Implications for research in academic learning. *Review of Educational Research, 49,* 459–478.

Barrouillet, P., Gavens, N., Vergauwe, E., Gaillard, V., & Camos, V. (2009). Working memory span development: A time-based resource-sharing model account. *Developmental Psychology, 45*(2), 477–490.

Barrow, F. H., Armstrong, M. I., Vargo, A., & Boothroyd, R. A. (2007). Understanding the findings of resilience-related research for fostering the development of African American adolescents. *Child and Adolescent Psychiatric Clinics of North America, 16,* 393–413.

Barth, R. P. (2009). Preventing child abuse and neglect with parent training: Evidence and opportunities. *Future of Children, 19*(2), 95–118.

Barton, K. C., & Levstik, L. S. (1996). "Back when God was around and everything": Elementary children's understanding of historical time. *American Educational Research Journal, 33,* 419–454.

Bartoszuk, K., & Pittman, J. F. (2010). Profiles of identity exploration and commitment across domains. *Journal of Child and Family Studies, 19*(4), 444–450.

Bartsch, K., & Wellman, H. M. (1995). *Children talk about the mind.* New York: Oxford University Press.

Basinger, K. S., Gibbs, J. C., & Fuller, D. (1995). Context and the measurement of moral judgment. *International Journal of Behavioral Development, 18,* 537–556.

Basso, K. (1972). To give up on words: Silence in western Apache culture. In P. Giglioli (Ed.), *Language and social context.* New York: Penguin Books.

Basso, K. H. (1984). Stalking with stories: Names, places, and moral narratives among the Western Apache. In E. M. Bruner & S. Plattner (Eds.), *Text, play and story: The construction and reconstruction of self and society* (pp. 19–55). Washington, DC: American Ethnological Society.

Basu, M., Krishnan, A., & Weber-Fox, C. (2010). Brainstem correlates of temporal auditory processing in children with specific language impairment. *Developmental Science, 13*(1), 77–91.

Bates, E., & MacWhinney, B. (1987). Competition, variation, and language learning. In B. MacWhinney (Ed.), *Mechanisms of language acquisition.* Hillsdale, NJ: Erlbaum.

Batshaw, M. L., & Shapiro, B. K. (1997). Mental retardation. In M. L. Batshaw (Ed.), *Children with disabilities* (4th ed.). Baltimore, MD: Paul H. Brookes.

Batson, C. D. (1991). *The altruism question: Toward a social-psychological answer.* Hillsdale, NJ: Erlbaum.

Batson, C. D., & Thompson, E. R. (2001). Why don't moral people act morally? Motivational considerations. *Current Directions in Psychological Science, 10,* 54–57.

Battin-Pearson, S., Newcomb, M. D., Abbott, R. D., Hill, K. G., Catalano, R. F., & Hawkins, J. D. (2000). Predictors of early high school dropout: A test of five theories. *Journal of Educational Psychology, 92,* 568–582.

Battistich, V. (2003). Effects of a school-based program to enhance prosocial development on children's peer relations and social adjustment. *Journal of Research in Character Education, 1*(1), 1–17.

Battistich, V., Solomon, D., Kim, D., Watson, M., & Schaps, E. (1995). Schools as communities, poverty levels of student populations, and students' attitudes, motives, and performance: A multilevel analysis. *American Educational Research Journal, 32,* 627–658.

Battistich, V., Solomon, D., Watson, M., & Schaps, E. (1997). Caring school communities. *Educational Psychologist, 32,* 137–151.

Bauer, P. J. (2006). Event memory. In W. Damon & R. M. Lerner (Series Eds.), & D. Kuhn & R. Siegler (Vol. Eds.), *Handbook of child psychology: Vol. 2. Cognition, perception, and language* (6th ed., pp. 373–425). New York: Wiley.

Bauer, P. J. (2009). Neurodevelopmental changes in infancy and beyond: Implications for learning and memory. In O. A. Barbarin & B. H. Wasik (Eds.), *Handbook of child development and early education* (pp. 78–102). New York: Guilford Press.

Bauer, P. J., DeBoer, T., & Lukowski, A. F. (2007). In the language of multiple memory systems: Defining and describing developments in long-term declarative memory. In L. M. Oakes & P. J. Bauer (Eds.), *Short- and long-term memory in infancy and early childhood: Taking the first steps toward remembering* (pp. 240–270). New York: Oxford University Press.

Bauer, P. J., & Dow, G. A. (1994). Episodic memory in 16- and 20-month-old children: Specifics not generalized, but not forgotten. *Developmental Psychology, 30,* 403–417.

Baughman, F. D., & Cooper, R. P. (2007). Inhibition and young children's performance on the Tower of London. *Cognitive Systems Research, 8*(3), 216–226.

Baum, J. R., & Bird, B. J. (2010). The successful intelligence of high-growth entrepreneurs: Links to new venture growth. *Organization Science, 21*(2), 397–412. doi:10.1287/orsc.1090.0445

Bauman, S. (2011). *Cyberbullying: What counselors need to know.* Alexandria, VA: American Counseling Association.

Baumeister, R. F., Campbell, J. D., Krueger, J. I., & Vohs, K. D. (2003). Does high self-esteem cause better performance, interpersonal success, happiness, or healthier lifestyles? *Psychological Science in the Public Interest, 4*(1), 1–44.

Bauminger, N., & Kimhi-Kind, I. (2008). Social information processing, security of attachment, and emotion regulation in children with learning disabilities. *Journal of Learning Disabilities, 41*(4), 315-332.

Baumrind, D. (1967). Child care practices anteceding three patterns of preschool behavior. *Genetic Psychology Monographs, 75,* 43–88.

Baumrind, D. (1971). Current patterns of parental authority. *Developmental Psychology Monographs, 4*(1, Pt. 2).

Baumrind, D. (1980). New directions in socialization research. *American Psychologist, 35,* 639–652.

Baumrind, D. (1982). An explanatory study of socialization effects on Black children: Some

Black-White comparisons. *Child Development, 43,* 261–267.

Baumrind, D. (1989). Rearing competent children. In W. Damon (Ed.), *Child development today and tomorrow.* San Francisco: Jossey-Bass.

Baumrind, D. (1991). Parenting styles and adolescent development. In R. Lerner, A. C. Petersen, & J. Brooks-Gunn (Eds.), *The encyclopedia of adolescence.* New York: Garland Press.

Baumrind, D., Larzelere, R. E., & Owens, E. B. (2010). Effects of preschool parents' power assertive patterns and practices on adolescent development. *Parenting: Science and Practice, 10*(3), 157–201. doi:10.1080/15295190903290790

Bay-Hinitz, A. K., Peterson, R. F., & Quilitch, H. R. (1994). Cooperative games: A way to modify aggressive and cooperative behaviors in young children. *Journal of Applied Behavior Analysis, 27,* 435–446.

Bayley, N. (2005). *Bayley Scales of Infant Development* (3rd ed.). San Antonio, TX: Psychological Corporation.

Bayley, N. (2006). *Bayley Scales of Infant and Toddler Development—Third edition: Administration manual.* San Antonio, TX: Harcourt Assessment.

Beal, C. R. (1996). The role of comprehension monitoring in children's revision. *Educational Psychology Review, 8,* 219–238.

Bear, D. R., Invernizzi, M., Templeton, S., & Johnston, F. (2008). *Words their way: Word study for phonics, vocabulary, and spelling instruction* (4th ed.). Upper Saddle River, NJ: Pearson Prentice Hall.

Bearison, D., & Levey, L. (1977). Children's comprehension of referential communication: Decoding ambiguous messages. *Child Development, 48,* 716–720.

Bearison, D. J. (1998). Pediatric psychology and children's medical problems. In W. Damon (Series Ed.), & I. E. Sigel & K. A. Renninger (Vol. Eds.), *Handbook of child psychology: Vol. 4. Child psychology in practice* (5th ed., pp. 635–711). New York: Wiley.

Beaty, J. J. (1998). *Observing development of the young child* (4th ed.). Upper Saddle River, NJ: Merrill/Prentice Hall.

Beauchaine, T. P., Klein, D. N., Crowell, S. E., Derbridge, C., & Gatzke-Kopp, L. (2009). Multifinality in the development of personality disorders: A biology X sex X environment interaction model of antisocial and borderline traits. *Development and Psychopathology, 21,* 735–770.

Beaumont, R., & Sofronoff, K. (2008). A multi-component social skills intervention for children with Asperger syndrome: The Junior Detective Training Program. *Journal of Child Psychology and Psychiatry, 49*(7), 743–753.

Beck, S. R., Robinson, E. J., Carroll, D. J., & Apperly, I. A. (2006). Children's thinking about counterfactuals and future hypotheticals as possibilities. *Child Development, 77,* 413–426.

Beckert, T. E., Strom, P. S., Strom, R. D., Darre, K., & Weed, A. (2008). Single mothers of early adolescents: Perceptions of competence. *Adolescence, 43*(170), 275–290.

Beers, S. F., & Nagy, W. E. (2009). Syntactic complexity as a predictor of adolescent writing quality: Which measures? Which genre? *Reading and Writing, 22*(2), 185–200.

Beharelle, A. R., Dick, A. S., Josse, G., Solodkin, A., Huttenlocher, P. R., Levine, S. C., & Small, S. L. (2010). Left hemisphere regions are critical for language in the face of early left focal brain injury. *Brain: A Journal of Neurology, 133*(6), 1707–1716.

Behnke, A. O., Gonzalez, L. M., & Cox, R. B. (2010). Latino students in new arrival states: Factors and services to prevent youth from dropping out. *Hispanic Journal of Behavioral Sciences, 32*(3), 385–409. doi:10.1177/0739986310374025

Bekkhus, M., Rutter, M., Barker, E. D., & Borge, A. I. H. (2011). The role of pre- and postnatal timing of family risk factors on child behavior at 36 months. *Journal of Abnormal Child Psychology, 39*(4), 611–621. doi:10.1007/s10802-010-9477-z

Belenky, M. F., Bond, L. A., & Weinstock, J. S. (1997). *A tradition that has no name: Nurturing the development of people, families, and communities.* New York: Basic Books.

Belenky, M. F., Clinchy, B. M., Goldberger, N. R., & Tarule, J. M. (1986). *Women's ways of knowing: The development of self, voice, and mind.* New York: Basic Books.

Belfiore, P. J., & Hornyak, R. S. (1998). Operant theory and application to self-monitoring in adolescents. In D. H. Schunk and B. J. Zimmerman (Eds.), *Self-regulated learning: From teaching to self-reflective practice.* New York: Guilford Press.

Bell, L. A. (1989). Something's wrong here and it's not me: Challenging the dilemmas that block girls' success. *Journal for the Education of the Gifted, 12,* 118–130.

Bell, P., & Linn, M. C. (2002). Beliefs about science: How does science instruction contribute? In B. K. Hofer & P. R. Pintrich (Eds.), *Personal epistemology: The psychology of beliefs about knowledge and knowing* (pp. 321–346). Mahwah, NJ: Erlbaum.

Bell, R. Q. (1988). Contributions of human infants to caregiving and social interaction. In G. Handel (Ed.), *Childhood socialization* (pp. 103–122). New York: Aldine de Gruyter.

Belsky, J., & Eggebeen, D. (1991). Early and extensive maternal employment and young children's socio-emotional development: Children of the National Longitudinal Survey of Youth. *Journal of Marriage and Family, 53*(4), 1083–1098.

Belsky, J., Gilstrap, B., & Rovine, M. (1984). The Pennsylvania Infant and Family Development Project, I: Stability and change in mother–infant and father–infant interaction in a family setting at one, three, and nine months. *Child Development, 55,* 692–705.

Bem, S. L. (1981). Gender schema theory: A cognitive account of sex typing. *Psychological Review, 88,* 354–364.

Bem, S. L. (1989). Genital knowledge and gender constancy in preschool children. *Child Development, 60,* 649–662.

Bembenutty, H. (2009). The last word: An interview with Lyn Corno—The ingredients for making a self-regulated scholar. *Journal of Advanced Academics, 21*(4), 142–156.

Bembenutty, H., & Karabenick, S. A. (2004). Inherent association between academic delay of gratification, future time perspective, and self-regulated learning. *Educational Psychology Review, 16,* 35–57.

Benbow, C. P., & Lubinski, D. (2009). Extending Sandra Scarr's ideas about development to the longitudinal study of intellectually precocious youth. In K. McCartney, & R. A. Weinberg (Eds.), *Annual meeting of the Association for Psychological Science (APS), 19th, May 2007, Washington, DC, US; This festschrift for Sandra Scarr was organized and presented at the aforementioned conference.* (pp. 231–252). New York: Psychology Press.

Benbow, C. P., Lubinski, D., Shea, D. L., & Eftekhari-Sanjani, H. (2000). Sex differences in mathematical reasoning ability at age 13: Their status 20 years later. *Psychological Science, 11,* 474–480.

Bender, G. (2001). Resisting dominance? The study of a marginalized masculinity and its construction within high school walls. In J. N. Burstyn, G. Bender, R. Casella, H. W. Gordon, D. P. Guerra, K. V. Luschen, et al., *Preventing violence in schools: A challenge to American democracy* (pp. 61–77). Mahwah, NJ: Erlbaum.

Bender, S. S. (2008). Three cases of adolescent childbearing decision-making: The importance of ambivalence. *Adolescence, 43*(172), 861–879.

Benenson, J. F., Maiese, R., Dolenszky, E., Dolensky, N., Sinclair, N., & Simpson, A. (2002). Group size regulates self-assertive versus self-deprecating responses to interpersonal competition. *Child Development, 73,* 1818–1829.

Beneventi, H., Tønnessen, F. E., Ersland, L., & Hugdahl, K. (2010). Working memory deficit in dyslexia: Behavioral and fMRI evidence. *International Journal of Neuroscience, 120*(1), 51–59.

Bennett, A., Bridglall, B. L., Cauce, A. M., Everson, H. T., Gordon, E. W., Lee, C. D., et al. (2007). Task force report on the affirmative development of academic ability: All students reaching the top: Strategies for closing academic achievement gaps. In E. W. Gordon & B. L. Bridglall (Eds.), *Affirmative development: Cultivating academic ability* (pp. 239–275). Lanham, MD: Rowman.

Bennett, G. K., Seashore, H. G., & Wesman, A. G. (1982). *Differential Aptitude Tests.* San Antonio, TX: Psychological Corporation.

Bennett, R. E., Gottesman, R. L., Rock, D. A., & Cerullo, F. (1993). Influence of behavior perceptions and gender on teachers' judgments of students' academic skill. *Journal of Educational Psychology, 85,* 347–356.

Benoit, D., & Parker, K. C. (1994). Stability and transmission of attachment across three generations. *Child Development, 65,* 1444–1456.

Benton, D. (2001). Micro-nutrient supplementation and the intelligence of children. *Neuroscience and Biobehavioral Reviews, 25*(4), 297–309.

Benton, S. L. (1997). Psychological foundations of elementary writing instruction. In G. D. Phye (Ed.), *Handbook of academic learning: Construction of knowledge.* San Diego, CA: Academic Press.

Benware, C., & Deci, E. L. (1984). Quality of learning with an active versus passive motivational set. *American Educational Research Journal, 21,* 755–765.

Berdan, L. E., Keane, S. P., & Calkins, S. D. (2008). Temperament and externalizing behavior: Social preference and perceived acceptance as protective factors. *Developmental Psychology, 44*(4), 957–968. doi:10.1037/0012-1649.44.4.957

Bereiter, C. (1994). Implications of postmodernism for science, or, science as progressive discourse. *Educational Psychologist, 29,* 3–12.

Bereiter, C., & Scardamalia, M. (1987). *The psychology of written composition.* Hillsdale, NJ: Erlbaum.

Bereiter, C., & Scardamalia, M. (2006). Education for the Knowledge Age: Design-centered models of teaching and instruction. In P. A. Alexander & P. H. Winne (Eds.), *Handbook of educational psychology* (2nd ed., pp. 695–713). Mahwah, NJ: Erlbaum.

Berenstain, S., & Berenstain, J. (1990). *The Berenstain bears' trouble with pets.* New York: Random House.

Bergen, D., & Fromberg, D. P. (2009). Play and social interaction in middle childhood. *Phi Delta Kappan, 90*(6), 426–430.

Berger, I., & Felsenthal-Berger, N. (2009). Attention-deficit hyperactivity disorder (ADHD) and birth order. *Journal of Child Neurology, 24*(6), 692–696.

Berger, L. M., Paxson, C., & Waldfogel, J. (2009). Income and child development. *Children and Youth Services Review, 31,* 978–989.

Berger, R. (2000). Remarried families of 2000: Definitions, descriptions, and interventions. In W. C. Nichols, M. A. Pace-Nichols, D. S. Becvar, & A. Y. Napier (Eds.), *Handbook of family development* (pp. 371–390). New York: Wiley.

Bergeron, R., & Floyd, R. G. (2006). Broad cognitive abilities of children with mental retardation: An analysis of group and individual profiles. *American Journal on Mental Retardation, 111,* 417–432.

Bergin, C. A., & Bergin, D. A. (2009/2010). Sleep: The E-zzz intervention. *Educational Leadership, 67*(4), 44–47.

Berk, L. E. (1994). Why children talk to themselves. *Scientific American, 271,* 78–83.

Berkeley, S., Mastropieri, M., & Scruggs, T. (2008, March). *Reading comprehension strategy instruction and attribution retraining for secondary students with disabilities.* Paper presented at the annual meeting of the American Educational Research Association, New York.

Berlin, L. J., Cassidy, J., & Appleyard, K. (2008). The influence of early attachments on other relationships. In J. Cassidy & P. R. Shaver (Eds.), *Handbook of attachment: Theory, research, and clinical applications* (2nd ed., pp. 333–347). New York: Guilford Press.

Berliner, D. (2006). Our impoverished view of educational research. *Teachers College Record, 108,* 949–995.

Berliner, D. (2009). *Poverty and potential: Out-of-school factors and school success.* Boulder, CO, and Tempe, AZ: Education and the Public Interest Center & Education Policy Research. Retrieved January 15, 2010, from http://epicpolicy.org/publication/poverty-and-potential

Berliner, D. C. (2005, April). *Ignoring the forest, blaming the trees: Our impoverished view of educational reform.* Paper presented at the annual meeting of the American Educational Research Association, Montreal, Canada.

Bermejo, V. (1996). Cardinality development and counting. *Developmental Psychology, 32,* 263–268.

Bernard, R. S., Cohen, L. L., & Moffet, K. (2009). A token economy for exercise adherence in pediatric cystic fibrosis: A single-subject analysis. *Journal of Pediatric Psychology, 34*(4), 354–365.

Berndt, T. J. (1992). Friendship and friends' influence in adolescence. *Current Directions in Psychological Science, 1,* 156–159.

Berndt, T. J., & Hoyle, S. G. (1985). Stability and change in childhood and adolescent friendships. *Developmental Psychology, 21,* 1007–1015.

Berndt, T. J., & Keefe, K. (1995). Friends' influence on adolescents' adjustment to school. *Child Development, 66,* 1312–1329.

Berndt, T. J., & Keefe, K. (1996). Friends' influence on school adjustment: A motivational analysis. In J. Juvonen & K. R. Wentzel (Eds.), *Social motivation: Understanding children's school adjustment* (pp. 248–278). Cambridge, England: Cambridge University Press.

Berninger, V. W. (2004). Understanding the graphia in developmental dysgraphia: A developmental neuropsychological perspective for disorders in producing written language. In D. Dewey & D. Tupper (Eds.), *Developmental motor disorders: A neuropsychological perspective* (pp. 189–233). New York: Guilford Press.

Berninger, V. W., Abbott, R. D., Trivedi, P., Olson, E., Gould, L., Hiramatsu, S., et al. (2010). Applying the multiple dimensions of reading fluency to assessment and instruction. *Journal of Psychoeducational Assessment, 28*(1), 3–18.

Berninger, V. W., Fuller, F., & Whitaker, D. (1996). A process model of writing development across the life span. *Educational Psychology Review, 8,* 193–218.

Bertenthal, B. I., Campos, J. J., & Kermoian, R. (1994). An epigenetic perspective on the development of self-produced locomotion and its consequences. *Current Directions in Psychological Science, 3,* 140–145.

Berthold, K., & Renkl, A. (2009). Instructional aids to support a conceptual understanding of multiple representations. *Journal of Educational Psychology, 101*(1), 70–87.

Bešić, N., & Kerr, M. (2009). Punks, goths, and other eye-catching peer crowds: Do they fulfill a function for shy youths? *Journal of Research on Adolescence, 19*(1), 113–121. doi:10.1111/j.1532-7795.2009.00584.x

Bialystok, E. (1994a). Representation and ways of knowing: Three issues in second language acquisition. In N. C. Ellis (Ed.), *Implicit and explicit learning of languages.* London: Academic Press.

Bialystok, E. (1994b). Towards an explanation of second language acquisition. In G. Brown, K. Malmkjær, A. Pollitt, & J. Williams (Eds.), *Language and understanding.* Oxford, England: Oxford University Press.

Bialystok, E. (2001). *Bilingualism in development: Language, literacy, and cognition.* Cambridge, England: Cambridge University Press.

Bialystok, E., & Senman, L. (2004). Executive processes in appearance–reality tasks: The role of inhibition of attention and symbolic representation. *Child Development, 75,* 562–579.

Bialystok, E., & Viswanathan, M. (2009). Components of executive control with advantages for bilingual children in two cultures. *Cognition, 112*(3), 494–500.

Bibace, R., & Walsh, M. E. (1981). Children's conceptions of illness. In R. Bibace & M. E. Walsh (Eds.), *New directions for child development: Children's conceptions of health, illness, and bodily functions* (pp. 31–48). San Francisco: Jossey-Bass.

Bicais, J., & Correia, M. G. (2008). Peer-learning spaces: A staple in English language learners' tool kit for developing language and literacy. *Journal of Research in Childhood Education, 22*(4), 363–375.

Biddle, S. J. (1993). Children, exercise and mental health. *International Journal of Sport Psychology, 24,* 200–216.

Biemiller, A. (1994). Some observations on beginning reading instruction. *Educational Psychologist, 29,* 203–209.

Biemiller, A., Shany, M., Inglis, A., & Meichenbaum, D. (1998). Factors influencing children's acquisition and demonstration of self-regulation on academic tasks. In D. H. Schunk & B. J. Zimmerman (Eds.), *Self-regulated learning: From teaching to self-reflective practice* (pp. 203–224). New York: Guilford Press.

Bierman, K. L. (2004). *Peer rejection: Developmental processes and intervention strategies.* New York: Guilford Press.

Bierman, K. L., Miller, C. L., & Staub, S. D. (1987). Improving the social behavior and peer acceptance of rejected boys: Effect of social skill training with instructions and prohibitions. *Journal of Consulting and Clinical Psychology, 55,* 194–200.

Bierman, K. L., & Powers, C. J. (2009). Social skills training to improve peer relations. In K. H. Rubin, W. M. Bukowski, & B. Laursen (Eds.), *Handbook of peer interactions, relationships, and groups* (pp. 603–621). New York: Guilford Press.

Bigelow, A. E., MacLean, K., Proctor, J., Myatt, T., Gillis, R., & Power, M. (2010). Maternal sensitivity throughout infancy: Continuity and relation to attachment security. *Infant Behavior & Development, 33*(1), 50–60.

Biggs, J. L. (1998). *Inuit morality play: The emotional education of a three-year-old.* New Haven, CT: Yale University Press.

Bigler, R. S., & Liben, L. S. (2007). Developmental intergroup theory: Explaining and reducing children's social stereotyping and prejudice. *Current Directions in Psychological Science, 16,* 162–166.

Bigner, B. J. (2006). *Parent–child relations: An introduction to parenting* (7th ed.). Upper Saddle River, NJ: Pearson Merrill Prentice Hall.

Bigras, N., Bouchard, C., Cantin, G., Brunson, L., Coutu, S., Lemay, L., et al. (2010). A comparative study of structural and process quality in center-based and family-based child care services. *Child & Youth Care Forum, 39*(3), 129–150. doi:10.1007/s10566-009-9088-4

Binder, L. M., Dixon, M. R., & Ghezzi, P. M. (2000). A procedure to teach self-control to children with attention deficit hyperactivity disorder. *Journal of Applied Behavior Analysis, 33,* 233–237.

Bird, R. (2009). *Overcoming difficulties with number: Supporting dyscalculia and students who struggle with maths.* Los Angeles, CA: Sage.

Birkas, E., Horváth, J., Lakatos, K., Nemoda, Z., Sasvari-Szekely, M., Winkler, I., et al. (2006). Association between dopamine D4 receptor (DRD4) gene polymorphisms and novelty-elicited auditory event-related potentials in preschool children. *Brain Research, 1103*(1), 150–158.

Bishop, D. (2010). Specific language impairment. In C. L. Cooper, J. Field, U. Goswami, R. Jenkins, & B. Sahakian (Eds.), *Mental capital and well-being* (pp. 767–773). Ames, IA: Wiley-Blackwell.

Bishop, E. G., Cherny, S. S., Corley, R., Plomin, R., DeFries, J. C., & Hewitt, J. K. (2003). Development genetic analysis of general cognitive ability from 1 to 12 years in a sample of adoptees, biological siblings, and twins. *Intelligence, 31,* 31–49.

Bivens, J. A., & Berk, L. E. (1990). A longitudinal study of the development of elementary school children's private speech. *Merrill-Palmer Quarterly, 36,* 443–463.

Bjorklund, D. F. (1987). How age changes in knowledge base contribute to the development of children's memory: An interpretive review. *Developmental Review, 7,* 93–130.

Bjorklund, D. F. (1997). In search of a metatheory for cognitive development (or, Piaget is dead and I don't feel so good myself). *Child Development, 68,* 144–148.

Bjorklund, D. F. (2003). Evolutionary psychology from a developmental systems perspective: Comment on Lickliter and Honeycutt (2003). *Psychological Bulletin, 129,* 836–841.

Bjorklund, D. F., Dukes, C., & Brown, R. D. (2009). The development of memory strategies. In M. L. Courage & N. Cowan (Eds.), *The development of memory in infancy and childhood* (pp. 145–175). New York: Psychology Press.

Bjorklund, D. F., & Green, B. L. (1992). The adaptive nature of cognitive immaturity. *American Psychologist, 47,* 46–54.

Bjorklund, D. F., Periss, V., & Causey, K. (2009). The benefits of youth. *European Journal of Developmental Psychology, 6*(1), 120–137.

Blachford, S. L. (2002). *The Gale encyclopedia of genetic disorders.* Detroit, MI: Gale Group.

Black, E., Peppé, S., & Gibbon, F. (2008). The relationship between socio-economic status and lexical development. *Clinical Linguistics & Phonetics, 22*(4–5), 259–265.

Black-Gutman, D., & Hickson, F. (1996). The relationship between racial attitudes and social-cognitive development in children: An Australian study. *Developmental Psychology, 32,* 448–456.

Blackson, T. C., Butler, T., Belsky, J., Ammerman, R. T., Shaw, D. S., & Tarter, R. E. (1999). Individual traits and family contexts predict sons' externalizing behavior and preliminary relative risk ratios for conduct disorder and substance use disorder outcomes. *Drug and Alcohol Dependence, 56,* 115–131.

Blackwell, L. S., Trzesniewski, K. H., & Dweck, C. S. (2007). Implicit theories of intelligence predict achievement across an adolescent transition: A longitudinal study and an intervention. *Child Development, 78,* 246–263.

Blades, M., & Spencer, C. (1987). Young children's strategies when using maps with landmarks. *Journal of Environmental Psychology, 7,* 201–217.

Blair, C. (2002). School readiness: Integrating cognition and emotion in a neurobiological conceptualization of children's functioning at school entry. *American Psychologist, 57,* 111–127.

Blair, C., & Razza, R. P. (2007). Relating effortful control, executive function, and false belief understanding to emerging math and literacy ability in kindergarten. *Child Development, 78,* 647–663.

Blakemore, C. (1976). The conditions required for the maintenance of binocularity in the kitten's visual cortex. *Journal of Physiology, 261,* 423–444.

Blakcmore, J. E. O., Berenbaum, S. A., & Liben, L. S. (2009). *Gender development.* New York: Psychology Press.

Blandon, A. Y., Calkins, S. D., Grimm, K. J., Keane, S. P., & O'Brien, M. (2010). Testing a developmental cascade model of emotional and social competence and early peer acceptance. *Development and Psychopathology, 22*(4), 737–748. doi:10.1017/S0954579410000428

Bleeker, M. M., & Jacobs, J. E. (2004). Achievement in math and science: Do mothers' beliefs matter 12 years later? *Journal of Educational Psychology, 96,* 97–109.

Blevins, C. (2010). *Math lesson plan.* Retrieved May 10, 2010, from http://www.athens.edu/vinsobm/lesson_5.html.

Block, C. C., Parris, S. R., Reed, K. L., Whiteley, C. S., & Cleveland, M. D. (2009). Instructional approaches that significantly increase reading comprehension. *Journal of Educational Psychology, 101*(2), 262–281.

Block, J. H. (1983). Differential premises arising from differential socialization of the sexes: Some conjectures. *Child Development, 54,* 1335–1354.

Bloom, B. S. (1964). *Stability and change in human characteristics.* New York: Wiley.

Bloom, K., Russell, A., & Wassenberg, K. (1987). Turn taking affects the quality of infant vocalizations. *Journal of Child Language, 14,* 211–227.

Bloom, L., & Lahey, M. (1978). *Language development and language disorders.* New York: Wiley.

Bloom, L., & Tinker, E. (2001). The intentionality model and language acquisition. *Monographs of the Society for Research in Child Development, 66*(4, Serial No. 267).

Boccia, M., & Campos, J. J. (1989). Maternal emotional signals, social referencing, and infants' reactions to strangers. In N. Eisenberg (Ed.), *New directions for child development* (Vol. 44, pp. 25–49). San Francisco: Jossey-Bass.

Bochenhauer, M. H. (1990, April.) *Connections: Geographic education and the National Geographic Society.* Paper presented at the annual meeting of the American Educational Research Association, Boston.

Bock, J., & Johnson, S. E. (2004). Subsistence ecology and play among the Okavango Delta peoples of Botswana. *Human Nature, 15,* 63–81.

Bodrova, E., & Leong, D. J. (1996). *Tools of the mind: The Vygotskian approach to early childhood education.* Upper Saddle River, NJ: Merrill/Prentice Hall.

Bodrova, E., & Leong, D. J. (2009). Tools of the mind: A Vygotskian-based early childhood curriculum. *Early Childhood Services: An Interdisciplinary Journal of Effectiveness, 3*(3), 245–262.

Bodrow, W., & Magalashvili, V. (2009). Knowledge visualization in IT-based discovery learning. *Communication and Cognition, 42*(1 & 2), 101–112.

Boeckx, C., Fodor, J. D., Gleitman, L., & Rizzi, L. (2009). Round table: Language universals: Yesterday, today, and tomorrow. In M. Piattelli-Palmarini, J. Uriagereka, & P. Salaburu (Eds.), *Of minds and language: A dialogue with Noam Chomsky in the Basque country* (pp. 195–220). New York: Oxford University Press.

Boekaerts, M. (2006). Self-regulation and effort investment. In W. Damon & R. M. Lerner (Eds. in Chief), & K. A. Renninger & I. E. Sigel (Vol. Eds.), *Handbook of child psychology. Vol. 4: Child psychology in practice* (pp. 345–377). New York: Wiley.

Boekaerts, M. (2009). Goal-directed behavior in the classroom. In K. R. Wenzel, & A. Wigfield (Eds.), *Handbook of motivation at school. Educational psychology handbook series* (pp. 105–122). New York: Routledge/Taylor & Francis Group.

Boekaerts, M., de Koning, E., & Vedder, P. (2006). Goal-directed behavior and contextual factors in the classroom: An innovative approach to the study of multiple goals. *Educational Psychologist, 41,* 33–51.

Boersma, A., ten Dam, G., Volman, M., & Wardekker, W. (2010). 'This baby . . . it isn't alive.' Towards a community of learners for vocational orientation. *British Educational Research Journal, 36*(1), 3–25. doi:10.1080/01411920802642355

Bohannon, J. N., MacWhinney, B., & Snow, C. (1990). No negative evidence revisited: Beyond learnability, or who has to prove what to whom. *Developmental Psychology, 26,* 221–226.

Bokhorst, C. L., Westenberg, P. M., Oosterlaan, J., & Heyne, D. A. (2008). Changes in social fears across childhood and adolescence: Age-related differences in the factor structure of the Fear Survey Schedule for Children—Revised. *Journal of Anxiety Disorders, 22,* 135–142.

Boling, C. J., & Evans, W. H. (2008). Reading success in the secondary classroom. *Preventing School Failure, 52*(2), 59–66. doi:10.3200/PSFL.52.2.59-66

Bong, M. (2001). Between- and within-domain relations of academic motivation among middle and high school students: Self-efficacy, task-value, and achievement goals. *Journal of Educational Psychology, 93,* 23–34.

Bong, M. (2009). Age-related differences in achievement goal differentiation. *Journal of Educational Psychology, 101*(4), 879–896. doi:10.1037/a0015945

Bonta, B. D. (1997). Cooperation and competition in peaceful societies. *Psychological Bulletin, 121*(2), 299–320.

Boom, J., Brugman, D., & van der Heijden, P. G. M. (2001). Hierarchical structure of moral stages assessed by a sorting task. *Child Development, 72,* 535–548.

Booth, M. Z., & Sheehan, H. C. (2008). Perceptions of people and place: Young adolescents' interpretation of their schools in the United States and the United Kingdom. *Journal of Adolescent Research, 23*(6), 722–744.

Booth-LaForce, C., & Kerns, K. A. (2009). Child-parent attachment relationships, peer relationships, and peer-group functioning. In K. H. Rubin, W. M. Bukowski, & B. Laursen (Eds.), *Handbook of peer interactions, relationships, and* (pp. 490–507). New York: Guilford Press.

Borelli, J. L., Crowley, M. J., David, D. H., Sbarra, D. A., Anderson, G. M., & Mayes, L. C. (2010). Attachment and emotion in school-aged children. *Emotion, 10*(4), 475–485.

Borkowski, J. G., Bisconti, T., Willard, C. C., Keogh, D. A., Whitman, T. L., & Weed, K. (2002). The adolescent as parent: Influences on children's intellectual, academic, and socioemotional development. In J. G. Borkowski, S. L. Ramey, & M. Bristol-Power (Eds.), *Parenting and the child's world: Influences on academic, intellectual, and social-emotional development* (pp. 161–184). Mahwah, NJ: Erlbaum.

Bornstein, M. H. (2006). Parenting science and practice. In W. Damon & R. M. Lerner (Eds. in Chief) & K. A. Renninger & I. E. Sigel (Vol. Eds.), *Handbook of child psychology: Vol. 4. Child psychology in practice* (6th ed., pp. 893–949). Hoboken, NJ: Wiley.

Bornstein, M. H. (2009). Toward a model of culture↔parent↔child transactions. In A. Sameroff (Ed.), *The transactional model of development: How children and contexts shape each other* (pp. 139–161). Washington, DC: American Psychological Association.

Bornstein, M. H. (2010). (Ed.). *Handbook of cultural developmental science.* New York: Psychology Press.

Bornstein, M. H., & Arterberry, M. E. (2010). The development of object categorization in young children: Hierarchical inclusiveness, age, perceptual attribute, and group versus individual analyses. *Developmental Psychology, 46*(2), 350–365.

Bornstein, M. H., Arterberry, M. E., & Mash, C. (2010). Infant object categorization transcends diverse object–context relations. *Infant Behavior & Development, 33*(1), 7–15.

Bornstein, M. H., & Cote, L. R., with Maital, S., Painter, K., Park, S., Pascual, L., et al. (2004). Cross-linguistic analysis of vocabulary in young children: Spanish, Dutch, French, Hebrew, Italian, Korean, and American English. *Child Development, 75,* 1115–1139.

Bornstein, M. H., Hahn, C., & Haynes, O. M. (2010). Social competence, externalizing, and internalizing behavioral adjustment from early childhood through early adolescence: Developmental cascades. *Development and Psychopathology, 22*(4), 717–735. doi:10.1017/S0954579410000416

Bornstein, M. H., & Lansford, J. E. (2010). Parenting. In M. H. Bornstein (Ed.), *Handbook of cultural developmental science* (pp. 259–277). New York: Psychology Press.

Bornstein, M. H., Toda, S., Azuma, H., Tamis-LeMonda, C. S., & Ogino, M. (1990). Mother and infant activity and interaction in Japan and in the United States: II. A comparative microanalysis of naturalistic exchanges focused on the organisation of infant attention. *International Journal of Behavioral Development, 13*(3), 289–308.

Bortfeld, H., Morgan, J. L., Golinkoff, R. M., & Rathbun, K. (2005). Mommy and me: Familiar names help launch babies into speech-stream segmentation. *Psychological Science, 16,* 298–304.

Bortfeld, H., & Whitehurst, G. J. (2001). Sensitive periods in first language acquisition. In D. B. Bailey, Jr., J. T. Bruer, F. J. Symons, & J. W. Lichtman (Eds.), *Critical thinking about critical periods* (pp. 173–192). Baltimore, MD: Paul H. Brookes.

Bosacki, S. L. (2000). Theory of mind and self-concept in preadolescents: Links with gender and language. *Journal of Educational Psychology, 92,* 709–717.

Boscardin, C. K., Muthén, B., Francis, D. J., & Baker, E. L. (2008). Early identification of reading difficulties using heterogeneous developmental trajectories. *Journal of Educational Psychology, 100,* 192–208.

Boseovski, J. J., & Lee, K. (2006). Children's use of frequency information for trait categorization and behavioral prediction. *Developmental Psychology, 42*(3), 500–513. doi:10.1037/0012-1649.42.3.500

Botvin, G. J., & Scheier, L. M. (1997). Preventing drug abuse and violence. In D. K. Wilson, J. R. Rodrigue, & W. C. Taylor (Eds.), *Health-promoting and health-compromising behaviors among minority adolescents* (pp. 55–86). Washington, DC: American Psychological Association.

Bouchard, C., Bigras, N., Cantin, G., Coutu, S., Blain-Brière, B., Eryasa, J., et al. (2010). Early childhood educators' use of language-support practices with 4-year-old children in child care centers. *Early Childhood Education Journal, 37*(5), 371–379.

Bouchard, C., Trudeau, N., Sutton, A., Boudreault, M., & Deneault, J. (2009). Gender differences in language development in French Canadian children between 8 and 30 months of age. *Applied Psycholinguistics, 30*(4), 685–707.

Bouchard, T. J., Jr. (1997). IQ similarity in twins reared apart: Findings and responses to critics. In R. J. Sternberg & E. L. Grigorenko (Eds.), *Intelligence, heredity, and environment* (pp. 126–160). Cambridge, England: Cambridge University Press.

Bouchard, T. J., & McGue, M. (1981). Familial studies of intelligence: A review. *Science, 212,* 1056.

Bouffard, T., Marcoux, M.-F., Vezeau, C., & Bordeleau, L. (2003). Changes in self-perceptions of competence and intrinsic motivation among elementary schoolchildren. *British Journal of Educational Psychology, 73,* 171–186.

Bourke, L., & Adams, A. (2010). Cognitive constraints and the early learning goals in writing. *Journal of Research in Reading, 33*(1), 94–110.

Boutte, G. S., & McCormick, C. B. (1992). Authentic multicultural activities: Avoiding pseudomulticulturalism. *Childhood Education, 68*(3), 140–144.

Bowlby, J. (1951). *Maternal care and mental health.* Geneva: World Health Organization.

Bowlby, J. (1958). The nature of the child's tie to his mother. *International Journal of Psycho-Analysis, 39,* 350–373.

Bowlby, J. (1969/1982). *Attachment and loss: Vol. 1. Attachment* (2nd ed.). New York: Basic Books.

Bowlby, J. (1973). *Attachment and loss: Vol. 2. Separation: Anxiety and anger.* New York: Basic Books.

Bowlby, J. (1988). *A secure base: Parent–child attachment and healthy human development.* New York: Basic Books.

Bowman, B. T. (1989). Educating language-minority children: Challenges and opportunities. *Phi Delta Kappan, 71,* 118–120.

Bowyer-Crane, C., & Snowling, M. J. (2010). Turning frogs into princes: Can children make inferences from fairy tales? *Reading and Writing, 23*(1), 19–29.

Boyle, B., & Charles, M. (2011). "The three hags and Pocahontas": How collaboration develops early years writing skills. *Literacy, 45*(1), 10–18. doi:10.1111/j.1741-4369.2011.00576.x

Boyer, T. W., Levine, S. C., & Huttenlocher, J. (2008). Development of proportional reasoning: Where young children go wrong. *Developmental Psychology, 44*(5), 1478–1490.

Boykin, A. W. (1994). Harvesting talent and culture: African-American children and educational reform. In R. J. Rossi (Ed.), *Schools and students at risk: Context and framework for positive change.* New York: Teachers College Press.

Braaten, E. B. (2011). *How to find mental health care for your child.* Washington, DC: American Psychological Association.

Brabham, E. G., & Lynch-Brown, C. (2002). Effects of teachers' reading-aloud styles on vocabulary acquisition and comprehension of students in the early elementary grades. *Journal of Educational Psychology, 94,* 465–473.

Bracken, B. A., & McCallum, R. S. (1998). *Universal Nonverbal Intelligence Test.* Itasca, IL: Riverside.

Bracken, B. A., & McCallum, R. S. (2009). Universal Nonverbal Intelligence Test (UNIT). In J. A. Naglieri & S. Goldstein (Eds.), *Practitioner's guide to assessing intelligence and achievement* (pp. 291–313). Hoboken, NJ: Wiley.

Bracken, B. A., McCallum, R. S., & Shaughnessy, M. F. (1999). An interview with Bruce A. Bracken and R. Steve McCallum, authors of the Universal Nonverbal Intelligence Test (UNIT). *North American Journal of Psychology, 1,* 277–288.

Bradley, L., & Bryant, P. (1991). Phonological skills before and after learning to read. In S. A. Brady & D. P. Shankweiler (Eds.), *Phonological processes in literacy.* Hillsdale, NJ: Erlbaum.

Bradley, R. H., & Caldwell, B. M. (1984). The relation of infants' home environments to achievement test performance in first grade: A follow-up study. *Child Development, 55,* 803–809.

Bradley, R. H., Corwyn, R. F., McAdoo, H., & Coll, C. (2001). The home environments of children in the United States: Part I. Variations by age, ethnicity, and poverty status. *Child Development, 72,* 1844–1867.

Bradley-Johnson, S. (2001). Cognitive assessment for the youngest children: A critical review of tests. *Journal of Psychoeducational Assessments, 19,* 19–44.

Braine, L. G., Schauble, L., Kugelmass, S., & Winter, A. (1993). Representation of depth by children:

Spatial strategies and lateral biases. *Developmental Psychology, 29,* 466–479.

Brainerd, C. J. (2003). Jean Piaget, learning research, and American education. In B. J. Zimmerman & D. H. Schunk (Eds.), *Educational psychology: A century of contributions* (pp. 251–287). Mahwah, NJ: Erlbaum.

Branch, C. (1999). Race and human development. In R. H. Sheets & E. R. Hollins (Eds.), *Racial and ethnic identity in school practices: Aspects of human development* (pp. 7–28). Mahwah, NJ: Erlbaum.

Brannon, M. E. (2002). The development of ordinal numerical knowledge in infancy. *Cognition, 83,* 223–240.

Brant, A. M., Haberstick, B. C., Corley, R. P., Wadsworth, S. J., DeFries, J. C., & Hewitt, J. K. (2009). The developmental etiology of high IQ. *Behavior Genetics, 39*(4), 393–405.

Braswell, G. S., & Callanan, M. A. (2003). Learning to draw recognizable graphic representations during mother–child interactions. *Merrill-Palmer Quarterly, 49,* 471–494.

Brauner, J., Gordic, B., & Zigler, E. (2004). Putting the child back into child care: Combining care and education for children ages 3–5. *Social Policy Report, 18.* Ann Arbor, MI: Society for Research in Child Development.

Braungart-Rieker, J. M., Hill-Soderlund, A. L., & Karrass, J. (2010). Fear and anger reactivity trajectories from 4 to 16 months: The roles of temperament, regulation, and maternal sensitivity. *Developmental Psychology, 46*(4), 791–804. doi:10.1037/a0019673

Brayboy, B. M. J., & Castagno, A. (2009). Self-determination through self-education: Culturally responsive schooling for indigenous students in the USA. *Teaching Education, 20*(1), 31–53.

Brazelton, T. B. (2009). The role of the Neonatal Behavioral Assessment Scale: Personal reflections. In J. K. Nugent, B. J. Petrauskas, & T. B. Brazelton (Eds.), *The newborn as a person* (pp. 278–286). Hoboken, NJ: Wiley.

Brazelton, T. B., & Nugent, J. K. (1995). *The Neonatal Behavioral Assessment Scale.* London, England: Mac Keith Press.

Bredekamp, S. (2011). *Effective practices in early childhood education: Building a foundation.* Upper Saddle River, NJ: Pearson Education.

Bredekamp, S., & Copple, C. (Eds.). (1997). *Developmentally appropriate practice in early childhood programs* (3rd ed.). Washington, DC: National Association for the Education of Young Children.

Brendgen, M., Boivin, M., Vitaro, F., Bukowski, W. M., Dionne, G., Tremblay, R. E. et al. (2008). Linkages between children's and their friends' social and physical aggression: Evidence for a gene-environment interaction? *Child Development, 79,* 13–29.

Brendgen, M., Wanner, G., Vitaro, F., Bukowski, W. M., & Tremblay, R. E. (2007). Verbal abuse by the teacher during childhood and academic, behavioral, and emotional adjustment in young adulthood. *Journal of Educational Psychology, 99,* 26–38.

Brenner, E. M., & Salovey, P. (1997). Emotion regulation during childhood: Developmental, interpersonal, and individual considerations. In P. Salovey & D. J. Sluyter (Eds.), *Emotional development and emotional intelligence: Educational implications* (pp. 168–195). New York: Basic Books.

Brenner, L. A., Koehler, D. J., Liberman, V., & Tversky, A. (1996). Overconfidence in probability and frequency judgments: A critical examination. *Organizational Behavior and Human Decision Processes, 65,* 212–219.

Bretherton, I. (1991). Pouring new wine into old bottles: The social self as internal working model. In M. R. Gunnar & L. A. Sroufe (Eds.), *Self*

processes and development: The Minnesota Symposia on Child Development (Vol. 23, pp. 1–42). Hillsdale, NJ: Erlbaum.

Bretherton, I., Fritz, J., Zahn-Waxler, C., & Ridgeway, D. (1986). Learning to talk about emotions: A functionalist perspective. *Child Development, 57,* 529–548.

Brietzke, E., Moreira, C. L. R., Toniolo, R. A., & Lafer, B. (2011). Clinical correlates of eating disorder comorbidity in women with bipolar disorder type I. *Journal of Affective Disorders, 130*(1-2), 162–165. doi:10.1016/j.jad.2010.10.020

Briggs, N. C., Lambert, E. W., Goldzweig, I. A., Levine, R. S., & Warren, R. C. (2008). Driver and passenger seatbelt use among U.S. high school students. *American Journal of Preventive Medicine, 35*(3), 224–229.

Brinton, B., & Fujiki, M. (1984). Development of topic manipulation skills in discourse. *Journal of Speech and Hearing Research, 27,* 350–358.

Britt, M. A., Rouet, J.-F., Georgi, M. C., & Perfetti, C. A. (1994). Learning from history texts: From causal analysis to argument models. In G. Leinhardt, I. L. Beck, & C. Stainton (Eds.), *Teaching and learning in history.* Hillsdale, NJ: Erlbaum.

Brody, G. H., Chen, Y.-F., Murry, V. M., Ge, X., Simons, R. L., Gibbons, F. X., et al. (2006). Perceived discrimination and the adjustment of African American youths: A five-year longitudinal analysis with contextual moderation effects. *Child Development, 77,* 1170–1189.

Brody, G. H., Stoneman, Z., & McCoy, J. K. (1994). Forecasting sibling relationships in early adolescence from child temperament and family processes in middle childhood. *Child Development, 65,* 771–784.

Brody, N. (1992). *Intelligence.* New York: Academic Press.

Brody, N. (1997). Intelligence, schooling, and society. *American Psychologist, 52,* 1046–1050.

Brody, N. (2006). Geocentric theory: A valid interpretation of Gardner's theory of intelligence. In J. A. Schaler (Ed.), *Howard Gardner under fire: The rebel psychologist faces his critics* (pp. 73–94). Chicago: Open Court.

Brodzinsky, D. M. (2006). Family structural openness and communication openness as predictors in the adjustment of adopted children. *Adoption Quarterly, 9*(4), 1–19.

Bronfenbrenner, U. (1979). *The ecology of human development: Experiments by nature and design.* Cambridge, MA: Harvard University Press.

Bronfenbrenner, U. (1999). Is early intervention effective? Some studies of early education in familial and extra-familial settings. In A. Montagu (Ed.), *Race and IQ* (expanded ed., pp. 343–378). New York: Oxford University Press.

Bronfenbrenner, U. (2001). The bioecological theory of human development. In N. J. Smelser & P. B. Baltes (Eds.), *International encyclopedia of the social and behavioral sciences* (Vol. 10, pp. 6963–6970). New York: Elsevier.

Bronfenbrenner, U. (2005). *Making human beings human: Bioecological perspectives on human development.* Thousand Oaks, CA: Sage.

Bronfenbrenner, U., Alvarez, W. F., & Henderson, C. R., Jr. (1984). Working and watching: Maternal employment status and parents' perceptions of their three-year-old children. *Child Development, 55,* 1362–1379.

Bronfenbrenner, U., & Morris, P. A. (2006). The bio-ecological model of human development. In W. Damon & R. M. Lerner (Eds. in Chief) & R. M. Lerner (Vol. Ed.), *Handbook of child psychology: Vol. 1. Theoretical models of human development* (6th ed., pp. 793–828). Hoboken, NJ: Wiley.

Bronson, M. B. (2000). *Self-regulation in early childhood: Nature and nurture.* New York: Guilford Press.

Brook, J., Chenshu, Z., Finch, S., & Brook, D. (2010). Adolescent pathways to adult smoking: Ethnic identity, peer substance use, and antisocial behavior. *American Journal on Addictions, 19*(2), 178–186.

Brooks-Gunn, J. (2003). Do you believe in magic? What we can expect from early childhood intervention programs. *Social Policy Report, 17*(1). Ann Arbor, MI: Society for Research in Child Development.

Brooks-Gunn, J., & Furstenberg, F. F. (1990). Coming of age in the era of AIDS: Puberty, sexuality, and contraception. *Milbrank Quarterly, 68*(Suppl. 1), 59–84.

Brooks-Gunn, J., Klebanov, P. K., & Duncan, G. J. (1996). Ethnic differences in children's intelligence test scores: Role of economic deprivation, home environment, and maternal characteristics. *Child Development, 67,* 396–408.

Brooks-Gunn, J., & Paikoff, R. L. (1992). Changes in self-feelings during the transition toward adolescence. In H. R. McGurk (Ed.), *Childhood social development: Contemporary perspectives* (pp. 63–97). Hillsdale, NJ: Erlbaum.

Brooks-Gunn, J., & Paikoff, R. L. (1993). "Sex is a gamble, kissing is a game": Adolescent sexuality and health promotion. In S. G. Millstein, A. C. Petersen, & E. O. Nightingale (Eds.), *Promoting the health of adolescents: New directions for the twenty-first century* (pp. 180–208). New York: Oxford University Press.

Brophy, J. E. (2004). *Motivating students to learn* (2nd ed.). Mahwah, NJ: Erlbaum.

Brophy, J. E., & Alleman, J. (1996). *Powerful social studies for elementary students.* Fort Worth, TX: Harcourt Brace.

Brophy, J. E., Alleman, J., & Knighton, B. (2009). *Inside the social studies classroom.* New York: Routledge.

Brophy, J. E., & VanSledright, B. (1997). *Teaching and learning history in elementary schools.* New York: Teachers College Press.

Brown, A. L., & Campione, J. C. (1994). Guided discovery in a community of learners. In K. McGilly (Ed.), *Classroom lessons: Integrating cognitive theory and classroom practice.* Cambridge, MA: MIT Press.

Brown, A. L., & Campione, J. C. (1996). Psychological theory and the design of innovative learning environments: On procedures, principles, and systems. In L. Schauble & R. Glaser (Eds.), *Innovations in learning: New environments for education.* Mahwah, NJ: Erlbaum.

Brown, A. L., & Palincsar, A. S. (1987). Reciprocal teaching of comprehension strategies: A natural history of one program for enhancing learning. In J. Borkowski & J. D. Day (Eds.), *Cognition in special education: Comparative approaches to retardation, learning disabilities, and giftedness.* Norwood, NJ: Ablex.

Brown, A. S., Deicken, R. F., Vinogradov, S., Kremen, W. S., Poole, J. H., Penner, J. D., et al. (2009). Prenatal infection and cavum septum pellucidum in adult schizophrenia. *Schizophrenia Research, 108,* 285–287.

Brown, B. B. (1990). Peer groups and peer culture. In S. S. Feldman & G. R. Elliott (Eds.), *At the threshold: The developing adolescent* (pp. 171–196). Cambridge, MA: Harvard University Press.

Brown, B. B. (1993). School culture, social politics, and the academic motivation of U.S. citizens. In T. M. Tomlinson (Ed.), *Motivating students to learn: Overcoming barriers to high achievement.* Berkeley, CA: McCutchan.

Brown, B. B., & Dietz, E. L. (2009). Informal peer groups in middle childhood and adolescence. In K. H. Rubin, W. M. Bukowski, & B. Laursen (Eds.), *Handbook of peer interactions, relationships, and groups* (pp. 361–376). New York: Guilford Press.

Brown, B. B., Eicher, S. A., & Petrie, S. (1986). The importance of peer group ("crowd") affiliation in adolescence. *Journal of Adolescence, 9,* 73–96.

Brown, J. D., & Siegel, J. D. (1988). Exercise as a buffer of life stress: A prospective study of adolescent health. *Health Psychology, 7,* 341–353.

Brown, J. V., Bakeman, R., Coles, C. D., Platzman, K. A., & Lynch, M. E. (2004). Prenatal cocaine exposure: A comparison of 2-year-old children in parental and nonparental care. *Child Development, 75,* 1282–1295.

Brown, K. J. (2009). Placing and pacing beginning readers in texts: The match between texts and children's knowledge of words. In E. H. Hiebert, & M. Sailors (Eds.), *Finding the right texts: What works for beginning and struggling readers. Solving problems in the teaching literacy* (pp. 177–202). New York: Guilford Press.

Brown, L. M., Tappan, M. B., & Gilligan, C. (1995). Listening to different voices. In W. M. Kurtines & J. L. Gewirtz (Eds.), *Moral development: An introduction.* Boston: Allyn & Bacon.

Brown, M. R. (2009). A new multicultural population: Creating effective partnerships with multiracial families. *Intervention in School and Clinic, 45*(2), 124–131.

Brown, R. (1973). *A first language: The early stages.* Cambridge, MA: Harvard University Press.

Brown, R., & Hanlon, C. (1970). Derivational complexity and order of acquisition in child speech. In J. R. Hayes (Ed.), *Cognition and the development of language.* New York: Wiley.

Brownell, M. T., Mellard, D. F., & Deshler, D. D. (1993). Differences in the learning and transfer performance between students with learning disabilities and other low-achieving students on problem-solving tasks. *Learning Disabilities Quarterly, 16,* 138–156.

Brown-Mizuno, C. (1990). Success strategies for learners who are learning disabled as well as gifted. *Teaching Exceptional Children, 23*(1), 10–12.

Bruer, J. T. (1999). *The myth of the first three years: A new understanding of early brain development and lifelong learning.* New York: Free Press.

Brugman, D. (2010). Moral reasoning competence and the moral judgment-action discrepancy in young adolescents. In W. Koops, D. Brugman, T. J. Ferguson & A. F. Sanders (Eds.), *The development and structure of conscience* (pp. 119–133). New York: Psychology Press.

Bruner, J. S. (1966). *Toward a theory of instruction.* Cambridge, MA: Harvard University Press.

Bruner, J. S. (1972). The nature and uses of immaturity. *American Psychologist, 27,* 687–708.

Bruner, J. S. (1983). The acquisition of pragmatic commitments. In R. M. Golinkoff (Ed.), *The transition from prelinguistic to linguistic communication* (pp. 27–42). Hillsdale, NJ: Erlbaum.

Bruner, J. S., & Sherwood, V. (1976). Early rule structure: The case of "peekaboo." In R. Harre (Ed.), *Life sentences* (pp. 55–62). London: Wiley.

Bruni, M. (1998). *Fine-motor skills in children with Down syndrome: A guide for parents and professionals.* Bethesda, MD: Woodbine House.

Bryan, J., & Henry, L. (2008). Strengths-based partnerships: A school-family-community partnership approach to empowering students. *Professional School Counseling, 12*(2), 149–156.

Bryan, J. H., Redfield, J., & Mader, S. (1971). Words and deeds concerning altruism and subsequent reinforcement power of the model. *Child Development, 42,* 1501–1508.

Bryan, T., Burstein, K., & Bryan, J. (2001). Students with learning disabilities: Homework problems and promising practices. *Educational Psychologist, 36,* 167–180.

Bryant, J. B. (2001). Language in social contexts: Communicative competence. In J. B. Gleason (Ed.), *The development of language* (pp. 167–209). Boston: Allyn & Bacon.

Bryant, P., & Nuñes, T. (2011). *Children's understanding of mathematics.* In U. Goswami (Ed.), *The Wiley-Blackwell handbook of childhood cognitive development* (2nd ed., pp. 549–573). Malden, MA: Wiley-Blackwell.

Bryant, P., Nunes, T., & Aidinis, A. (1999). Different morphemes, same spelling problems: Cross-linguistic developmental studies. In M. Harris & G. Hatano (Eds.), *Learning to read and write: A cross-linguistic perspective.* Cambridge, England: Cambridge University Press.

Buchanan, C. M., Eccles, J. S., & Becker, J. B. (1992). Are adolescents the victims of raging hormones: Evidence for activational effects of hormones on moods and behaviors at adolescence. *Psychological Bulletin, 111,* 62–107.

Buchanan, R., & Bowen, G. (2008). In the context of adult support: The influence of peer support on the psychological well-being of middle-school students. *Child & Adolescent Social Work Journal, 25*(5), 397–407. doi:10.1007/s10560-008-0143-z

Buchoff, T. (1990). Attention deficit disorder: Help for the classroom teacher. *Childhood Education, 67*(2), 86–90.

Budd, G. M., & Volpe, S. L. (2006). School-based obesity prevention: Research, challenges, and recommendations. *Journal of School Health, 76,* 485–495.

Buehl, M. M., & Alexander, P. A. (2006). Examining the dual nature of epistemological beliefs. *International Journal of Educational Research, 45,* 28–42.

Bugental, D. (2009). Predicting and preventing child maltreatment: A biocognitive transactional approach. In A. Sameroff (Ed.), *The transactional model of development: How children and contexts shape each other* (pp. 97–115). Washington, DC: American Psychological Association.

Buhrmester, D. (1992). The developmental courses of sibling and peer relationships. In F. Boer & J. Dunn (Eds.), *Children's sibling relationships: Developmental and clinical issues.* Hillsdale, NJ: Erlbaum.

Buhrmester, D. (1996). Need fulfillment, interpersonal competence, and the developmental contexts of friendship. In W. M. Bukowski, A. F. Newcomb, & W. W. Hartup (Eds.), *The company they keep: Friendship during childhood and adolescence* (pp. 158–185). New York: Cambridge University Press.

Buijzen, M., & Valkenburg, P. M. (2003). The effects of television advertising on materialism, parent–child conflict, and unhappiness: A review of research. *Applied Developmental Psychology, 24,* 437–456.

Buka, S. L., Cannon, T. D., Torrey, E. F., Yolken, R. H., and the Collaborative Study Group on the Perinatal Origins of Severe Psychiatric Disorders (2008). Maternal exposure to herpes simplex virus and risk of psychosis among adult offspring. *Biological Psychiatry, 63*(8), 809–815.

Bukstein, O. C., & Deas, D. (2010). Substance abuse and addictions. In M. K. Dulcan (Eds.), *Dulcan's textbook of child and adolescent psychiatry* (pp. 241–258). Arlington, VA: American Psychiatric Publishing.

Bullock, J. R. (1993). Children's loneliness and their relationships with family and peers. *Family Relations, 42,* 46–49.

Bullock, M., & Ziegler, A. (1999). Scientific reasoning: Developmental and individual differences. In F. E. Weinert & W. Schneider (Eds.), *Individual development from 3 to 12: Findings from the Munich longitudinal study.* New York: Cambridge University Press.

Burchinal, M., Vandergrift, N., Pianta, R., & Mashburn, A. (2010). Threshold analysis of association between child care quality and child outcomes for low-income children in pre-kindergarten programs. *Early Childhood Research Quarterly, 25*(2), 166–176. DOI: 10.1016/j.ecresq.2009.10.004.

Burhans, K. K., & Dweck, C. S. (1995). Helplessness in early childhood: The role of contingent worth. *Child Development, 66,* 1719–1738.

Burkam, D. T., Lee, V. E., & Smerdon, B. A. (1997). Gender and science learning early in high school: Subject matter and laboratory experiences. *American Educational Research Journal, 34,* 297–331.

Burnett, P. (2001). Elementary students' preferences for teacher praise. *Journal of Classroom Interaction, 36,* 16–23.

Burns, C. E., Brady, M. A., Dunn, A. M., & Starr, N. B. (2000). *Pediatric primary care: A handbook for nurse practitioners,* (2nd ed.). Philadelphia, PA: Saunders.

Burrous, C. E., Crockenberg, S. C., & Leerkes, E. M. (2009). Developmental history of care and control, depression and anger: Correlates of maternal sensitivity in toddlerhood. *Infant Mental Health Journal, 30*(2), 103–123.

Burstyn, J. N., Bender, G., Casella, R., Gordon, H. W., Guerra, D. P., Luschen, K. V., et al. (2001). *Preventing violence in schools: A challenge to American democracy.* Mahwah, NJ: Erlbaum.

Burstyn, J. N., & Stevens, R. (2001). Involving the whole school in violence prevention. In J. N. Burstyn, G. Bender, R. Casella, H. W. Gordon, D. P. Guerra, K. V. Luschen, et al. (Eds.), *Preventing violence in schools: A challenge to American democracy* (pp. 139–158). Mahwah, NJ: Erlbaum.

Bursuck, B., & Blanks, B. (2010). Evidence-based early reading practices within a response to intervention system. *Psychology in the Schools. Special Issue: Literacy and Disabilities, 47*(5), 421–431.

Burton, S., & Mitchell, P. (2003). Judging who knows best about yourself: Developmental change in citing the self across middle childhood. *Child Development, 74,* 426–443.

Buss, C., Davis, E. P., Muftuler, L. T., Head, K., & Sandman, C. A. (2010). High pregnancy anxiety during mid-gestation is associated with decreased gray matter density in 6–9-year-old children. *Psychoneuroendocrinology, 35,* 141–153.

Bussi, M. G. B., & Boni, M. (2009). The early construction of mathematical meanings: Learning positional representation of numbers. In O. A. Barbarin & B. H. Wasik (Eds.), *Handbook of early child development and early education: Research to practice* (pp. 455–477). New York: Guilford Press.

Butler, D. L., & Winne, P. H. (1995). Feedback and self-regulated learning: A theoretical synthesis. *Review of Educational Research, 65,* 245–281.

Butler, R. (1994). Teacher communication and student interpretations: Effects of teacher responses to failing students on attributional inferences in two age groups. *British Journal of Educational Psychology, 64,* 277–294.

Butler, R. N. (1963). The life review: An interpretation of reminiscence in the aged. *Psychiatry, 26,* 65–76.

Butterfield, E. C., & Ferretti, R. P. (1987). Toward a theoretical integration of cognitive hypotheses about intellectual differences among children. In J. G. Borkowski & J. D. Day (Eds.), *Cognition in special children: Approaches to retardation, learning disabilities, and giftedness.* Norwood, NJ: Ablex.

Button, R. E. (2007). Teachers' anger, frustration, and self-regulation. In P. A. Schutz, & R. Pekrun (Eds.), *Emotion in education. Educational psychology series* (pp. 259–274). San Diego, CA: Elsevier Academic Press.

Byrne, B. M. (2002). Validating the measurement and structure of self-concept: Snapshots of past, present, and future research. *American Psychologist, 57,* 897–909.

Byrne, B. M., & Shavelson, R. J. (1986, April). *On gender differences in the structure of adolescent self concept.* Paper presented at the annual meeting of the American Educational Research Association, San Francisco.

Byrnes, J. P. (1996). *Cognitive development and learning in instructional contexts.* Boston: Allyn & Bacon.

Byrnes, J. P., & Wasik, B. A. (2009). *Language and literacy development: What educators need to know.* New York: Guilford Press.

Cabell, S. Q., Justice, L. M., Konold, T. R., & McGinty, A. S. (2010). Profiles of emergent literacy skills among preschool children who are at risk for academic difficulties. *Early Childhood Research Quarterly, 26*(1), 1-14.

Cain, C. S. (2006). *Attachment disorders: Treatment strategies for traumatized children.* Lantham, MD: Jason Aronson Publishing.

Cain, K., & Oakhill, J. (1998). Comprehension skill and inference-making ability: Issues of causality. In C. Hulme & R. M. Joshi (Eds.), *Reading and spelling: Development and disorders.* Mahwah, NJ: Erlbaum.

Calfee, R. C., & Masuda, W. V. (1997). Classroom assessment as inquiry. In G. D. Phye (Ed.), *Handbook of classroom assessment: Learning, achievement, and adjustment.* San Diego, CA: Academic Press.

Calin-Jageman, R. J., & Ratner, H. H. (2005). The role of encoding in the self-explanation effect. *Cognition and Instruction, 23,* 523–543.

Calkins, S. D., Hungerford, A., & Dedmon, S. E. (2004). Mothers' interactions with temperamentally frustrated infants. *Infant Mental Health Journal, 25,* 219–239.

Calkins, S. D., & Marcovitch, S. (2010). Emotion regulation and executive functioning in early development: Integrated mechanisms of control supporting adaptive functioning. In S. D. Calkins & M. A. Bell (Eds.), *Child development at the intersection of emotion and cognition* (pp. 37–57). Washington, DC: American Psychological Association.

Callaghan, T., Rochat, P., Lillard, A., Claux, M. L., Odden, H., Itakura, S., et al. (2005). Synchrony in the onset of mental-state reasoning. *Psychological Science, 16,* 378–384.

Callanan, M. A., & Oakes, L. M. (1992). Preschoolers' questions and parents' explanations: Causal thinking in everyday activity. *Cognitive Development, 7,* 213–233.

Calvert, S. L. (2008). Children as consumers: Advertising and marketing. *Future of Children, 18*(1), 205–234.

Calvin, C. M., Fernandes, C., Smith, P., Visscher, P. M., & Deary, I. J. (2010). Sex, intelligence and educational achievement in a national cohort of over 175,000 11-year-old schoolchildren in England. *Intelligence, 38,* 424–432.

Cameron, C. A., Hunt, A. K., & Linton, M. J. (1996). Written expression as recontextualization: Children write in social time. *Educational Psychology Review, 8,* 125–150.

Cameron, J. (2001). Negative effects of reward on intrinsic motivation—a limited phenomenon: Comment on Deci, Koestner, and Ryan (2001). *Review of Educational Research, 71,* 29–42.

Campbell, A. (1984). *The girls in the gang: A report from New York City.* New York: Basil Blackwell.

Campbell, D. T., & Stanley, J. C. (1963). Experimental and quasi-experimental designs for research on teaching. In N. L. Gage (Ed.), *Handbook of research on teaching* (pp. 171–246). Chicago: Rand McNally.

Campbell, F. A., Pungello, E. P., Miller-Johnson, S., Burchinal, M., & Ramey, C. T. (2001). The development of cognitive and academic abilities: Growth curves from an early childhood educational experiment. *Developmental Psychology, 37*(2), 231–242.

Campbell, F. A., & Ramey, C. T. (1994). Effects of early intervention on intellectual and academic achievement: A follow-up study of children from low-income families. *Child Development, 65,* 684–698.

Campbell, F. A., & Ramey, C. T. (1995). Cognitive and school outcomes for high-risk African-American students at middle adolescence: Positive effects of early intervention. *American Educational Research Journal, 32*(4), 743–772.

Campbell, F. A., Ramey, C. T., Pungello, E., Sparling, J., & Miller-Johnson, S. (2002). Early childhood education: Young adult outcomes from the Abecedarian Project. *Applied Developmental Science, 6,* 42–57.

Campbell, L., Campbell, B., & Dickinson, D. (1998). *Teaching and learning through multiple intelligences* (2nd ed.). Boston: Allyn & Bacon.

Campbell, T. F., Dollaghan, C. A., Rockette, H. E., Paradise, J. L., Feldman, H. M., Shriberg, L. D., et al. (2003). Risk factors for speech delay of unknown origin in 3-year-old children. *Child Development, 74,* 346–357.

Campione, J. C., Shapiro, A. M., & Brown, A. L. (1995). Forms of transfer in a community of learners: Flexible learning and understanding. In A. McKeough, J. Lupart, & A. Marini (Eds.), *Teaching for transfer: Fostering generalization in learning.* Mahwah, NJ: Erlbaum.

Campos, J. J., Frankel, C. B., & Camras, L. (2004). On the nature of emotion regulation. *Child Development, 75,* 377–394.

Camras, L. A., Malatesta, C., & Izard, C. (1991). The development of facial expressions in infancy. In R. S. Feldman & B. Rime (Eds.), *Fundamentals of nonverbal behavior: Studies in emotion and social interaction* (pp. 73–105). New York: Cambridge University Press.

Camras, L. A., Oster, H., Campos, J., Campos, R., Ujiie, T., Miyake, K., et al. (1998). Production of emotional facial expressions in European American, Japanese, and Chinese infants. *Developmental Psychology, 34*(4), 616–628.

Canfield, R. L., & Smith, E. G. (1996). Number-based expectations and sequential enumeration by 5-month-old infants. *Developmental Psychology, 32,* 269–279.

Capelli, C. A., Nakagawa, N., & Madden, C. M. (1990). How children understand sarcasm: The role of context and intonation. *Child Development, 61,* 1824–1841.

Caplan, M., Vespo, J. E., Pedersen, J., & Hay, D. F. (1991). Conflict over resources in small groups of 1- and 2-year-olds. *Child Development, 62,* 1513–1524.

Caprara, G. V., Barbaranelli, C., Pastorelli, C., Bandura, A., & Zimbardo, P. G. (2000). Prosocial foundations of children's academic achievement. *Psychological Science, 11,* 302–306.

Caprara, G. V., Fagnani, C., Alessandri, G., Steca, P., Gigantesco, A., Cavalli Sforza, L. L., & Stazi, M. A. (2009). Human optimal functioning: The genetics of positive orientation towards self, life, and the future. *Behavior Genetics, 39*(3), 277–284.

Capron, C., & Duyme, M. (1989). Assessment of effects of socio-economic status on IQ in a full cross-fostering study. *Nature, 340*(6234), 552–554.

Cardelle-Elawar, M. (1992). Effects of teaching metacognitive skills to students with low mathematics ability. *Teaching and Teacher Education, 8,* 109–121.

Carey, S. (1978). The child as word learner. In M. Halle, J. Bresnan, & G. Miller (Eds.), *Linguistic theory and psychological reality.* Cambridge, MA: MIT Press.

Carey, S. (1985). *Conceptual change in childhood.* Cambridge, MA: MIT Press.

Carey, S., & Bartlett, E. (1978). Acquiring a single new word. *Papers and Reports on Child Language Development, 15,* 17–29.

Carey, S., Evans, R., Honda, M., Jay, E., & Unger, C. (1989). "An experiment is when you try it and see if it works": A study of grade 7 students' understanding of the construction of scientific knowledge. *International Journal of Science Education, 11*, 514–529.

Carla, B. (2003). Natural birthing lessons from Nepal. *British Journal of Midwifery, 11*(8), 492–495.

Carlo, G., Koller, S., Raffaelli, M., & de Guzman, M. R. T. (2007). Culture-related strengths among Latin American families: A case study of Brazil. *Marriage and Family Review, 41*(3/4), 335–360.

Carlson, E. A., Sampson, M. C., & Sroufe, L. A. (2003). Implications of attachment theory and research for developmental-behavioral pediatrics. *Journal of Developmental and Behavioral Pediatrics, 24,* 364–379.

Carlson, N. R. (2011). *Foundational of behavioral neuroscience* (8th ed.). Boston: Pearson Allyn & Bacon.

Carlson, S. A., Fulton, J. E., Lee, S. M., Maynard, M., Brown, D. R., Kohl, H. W. III, et al.. (2008). Physical education and academic achievement in elementary school: Data from the early childhood longitudinal study. *American Journal of Public Health, 98*(4), 721–727.

Carmona, S., Proal, E., Hoekzema, E. A., Gispert, J., Picado, M., Moreno, I., et al. (2009). Ventro-striatal reductions underpin symptoms of hyperactivity and impulsivity in attention-deficit/hyperactivity disorder. *Biological Psychiatry, 66*(10), 972–977.

Carney, D. R., & Mason, M. F. (2010). Decision making and testosterone: When the ends justify the means. *Journal of Experimental Social Psychology, 46*(4), 668–671. doi:10.1016/j.jesp.2010.02.003

Caroli, M., Argentieri, L., Cardone, M., & Masi, A. (2004). Role of television in childhood obesity prevention. *International Journal of Obesity, 28,* S105–S108.

Carpenter, D. O., & Nevin, R. (2010). Environmental causes of violence. *Physiology & Behavior, 99*(2), 260–268.

Carpenter, M. (2011). Social cognition and social motivations in infancy. In U. Goswami (Ed.), *The Wiley-Blackwell handbook of childhood cognitive development* (2nd ed., pp. 106–128). Malden, MA: Wiley-Blackwell.

Carr, M. (2010). The importance of metacognition for conceptual change and strategy use in mathematics. In H. S. Waters & W. Schneider (Eds.), *Metacognition, strategy use, and instruction* (pp. 176–197). New York: Guilford Press.

Carr, M., & Biddlecomb, B. (1998). Metacognition in mathematics from a constructivist perspective. In D. J. Hacker, J. Dunlosky, & A. C. Graesser (Eds.), *Metacognition in educational theory and practice* (pp. 69–91). Mahwah, NJ: Erlbaum.

Carr, M., & Schneider, W. (1991). Long-term maintenance of organizational strategies in kindergarten children. *Contemporary Educational Psychology, 16,* 61–72.

Carraher, T. N., Carraher, D. W., & Schliemann, A. D. (1985). Mathematics in the streets and in the schools. *British Journal of Developmental Psychology, 3,* 21–29.

Carranza, M. E. (2007). Building resilience and resistance against racism and discrimination among Salvadorian female youth in Canada. *Child and Family Social Work, 12*, 390–398.

Carroll, J. B. (1993). *Human cognitive abilities: A survey of factor-analytic studies.* New York: Cambridge University Press.

Carroll, J. B. (2003). The higher stratum structure of cognitive abilities: Current evidence supports *g* and about ten broad factors. *The scientific study of general intelligence: Tribute to Arthur Jensen* (pp. 5–21). Oxford, England: Elsevier.

Carter, D. E., Detine-Carter, S. L., & Benson, F. W. (1995). Interracial acceptance in the classroom.

In H. C. Foot, A. J. Chapman, & J. R. Smith (Eds.), *Friendship and social relations in children* (pp. 117–143). New Brunswick, NJ: Transaction.

Carter, K., & Doyle, W. (2006). Classroom management in early childhood and elementary classrooms. In C. M. Evertson & C. S. Weinstein (Eds.), *Handbook of classroom management: Research, practice, and contemporary issues* (pp. 373–406). Mahwah, NJ: Erlbaum.

Carter, K. R. (1991). Evaluation of gifted programs. In N. Buchanan & J. Feldhusen (Eds.), *Conducting research and evaluation in gifted education: A handbook of methods and applications.* New York: Teachers College Press.

Carter, K. R., & Ormrod, J. E. (1982). Acquisition of formal operations by intellectually gifted children. *Gifted Child Quarterly, 26,* 110–115.

Carter, R., Jaccard, J., Silverman, W. K., & Pina, A. A. (2009). Pubertal timing and its link to behavioral and emotional problems among 'at risk' African American adolescent girls. *Journal of Adolescence, 32,* 467–481.

Cartledge, G., & Milburn, J. F. (1995). *Teaching social skills to children and youth: Innovative approaches* (3rd ed.). Needham Heights, MA: Allyn & Bacon.

Cartwright, K. B., Galupo, M. P., Tyree, S. D., & Jennings, J. G. (2009). Reliability and validity of the Complex Postformal Thought Questionnaire: Assessing adults' cognitive development. *Journal of Adult Development, 16,* 183–189.

Carver, P. R., Egan, S. K., & Perry, D. G. (2004). Children who question their heterosexuality. *Developmental Psychology, 40*(1), 43–53.

Casanova, M. F. (2008). The significance of minicolumnar size variability in autism: A perspective from comparative anatomy. In A. W. Zimmerman (Ed.), *Autism: Current theories and evidence* (pp. 349–360). Totowa, NJ: Humana Press. doi:10.1007/978-1-60327-489-0_16

Case, R. (1980). Implications of a neo-Piagetian theory for improving the design of instruction. In J. R. Kirby & J. B. Biggs (Eds.), *Cognition, development, and instruction* (pp. 161–186). New York: Academic Press.

Case, R. (1985). *Intellectual development: Birth to adulthood.* Orlando, FL: Academic Press.

Case, R. (1991). *The mind's staircase: Exploring the conceptual underpinnings of children's thought ad knowledge.* Hillsdale, NJ: Erlbaum.

Case, R., & Okamoto, Y., in collaboration with Griffin, S., McKeough, A., Bleiker, C., Henderson, B., & Stephenson, K. M. (1996). The role of central conceptual structures in the development of children's thought. *Monographs of the Society for Research in Child Development, 61*(1–2, Serial No. 246).

Case, R., Okamoto, Y., Henderson, B., & McKeough, A. (1993). Individual variability and consistency in cognitive development: New evidence for the existence of central conceptual structures. In R. Case & W. Edelstein (Eds.), *The new structuralism in cognitive development: Theory and research on individual pathways.* Basel, Switzerland: Karger.

Casella, R. (2001). The cultural foundations of peer mediation: Beyond a behaviorist model of urban school conflict. In J. N. Burstyn, G. Bender, R. Casella, H. W. Gordon, D. P. Guerra, K. V. Luschen, et al. *Preventing violence in schools: A challenge to American democracy* (pp. 159–179). Mahwah, NJ: Erlbaum.

Case-Smith, J. (1996). Fine motor outcomes in preschool children who receive occupational therapy services. *American Journal of Occupational Therapy, 50,* 52–61.

Casey, B. J., Giedd, J. N., & Thomas, K. M. (2000). Structural and functional brain development and its relation to cognitive development. *Biological Psychology, 54,* 241–257.

Casiglia, A. C., LoCoco, A., & Zappulla, C. (1998). Aspects of social reputation and peer relationships in Italian children: A cross-cultural perspective. *Developmental Psychology, 34*(4), 723–730. doi:10.1037/0012-1649.34.4.723

Caspi, A., McClay, J., Moffitt, T. E., Mill, J., Martin, J., Craig, I. W., et al. (2002). Role of genotype in the cycle of violence in maltreated children. *Science, 297,* 851–854.

Caspi, A., Sugden, K., Moffitt, T. E., Taylor, A., Craig, I. W., Harrington, J., et al. (2003). Influence of life stress on depression: Moderation by the polymorphism in the 5-HTT gene. *Science, 30,* 1386–1389.

Cassano, M. C., & Zeman, J. L. (2010). Parental socialization of sadness regulation in middle childhood: The role of expectations and gender. *Developmental Psychology, 46*(5), 1214–1226.

Cassidy, M., & Berlin, L. J. (1994). The insecure/ambivalent pattern of attachment: Theory and research. *Child Development, 65,* 971–991.

Cattell, R. B. (1963). Theory of fluid and crystallized intelligence: A critical experiment. *Journal of Educational Psychology, 54,* 1–22.

Cattell, R. B. (1980). The heritability of fluid, *gf,* and crystallised, *gc,* intelligence, estimated by a least squares use of the MAVA method. *British Journal of Educational Psychology, 50,* 253–265.

Cattell, R. B. (1987). *Intelligence: Its structure, growth, and action.* Amsterdam: North-Holland.

Catts, H. W., Adlof, S. M., Hogan, T. P., & Weismer, S. E. (2005). Are specific language impairments and dyslexia distinct disorders? *Journal of Speech, Language and Hearing Research, 48,* 1378–1396.

Cauffman, E., Shulman, E. P., Steinberg, L., Claus, E., Banich, M. T., Graham, S., et al. (2010). Age differences in affective decision making as indexed by performance on the Iowa Gambling Task. *Developmental Psychology, 46*(1), 193–207.

Cavell, T. A., Hymel, S., Malcolm, K. T., & Seay, A. (2007). Socialization and interventions for antisocial youth. In J. E. Grusec & P. D. Hastings (Eds.), *Handbook of socialization: Theory and research* (pp. 42–67). New York: Guilford Press.

Cazden, C. B. (1968). The acquisition of noun and verb inflections. *Child Development, 39,* 433–448.

Cazden, C. B. (1976). Play with language and metalinguistic awareness: One dimension of language experience. In J. Bruner, A. Jolly, & K. Sylva (Eds.), *Play: Its role in development and evolution.* New York: Basic Books.

Ceci, S. J. (2003). Cast in six ponds and you'll reel in something: Looking back on 25 years of research. *American Psychologist, 58,* 855–864.

Ceci, S. J., & Roazzi, A. (1994). The effects of context on cognition: Postcards from Brazil. In R. J. Sternberg & R. K. Wagner (Eds.), *Mind in context: Interactionist perspectives on human intelligence.* Cambridge, England: Cambridge University Press.

Ceci, S. J., Rosenblum, T. B., & Kumpf, M. (1998). The shrinking gap between high- and low-scoring groups: Current trends and possible causes. In U. Neisser (Ed.), *The rising curve: Long-term gains in IQ and related measures* (pp. 287–302). Washington, DC: American Psychological Association.

Ceci, S. J., & Williams, W. M. (1997). Schooling, intelligence, and income. *American Psychologist, 52,* 1051–1058.

Ceglowski, D., Shears, J., & Furman, R. (2010). "I want child care he's gonna be happy in": A case study of a father's child care experiences. *Early Education and Development, 21*(1), 1–20. doi:10.1080/10409280902783467

Cemalcilar, Z. (2010). Schools as socialisation contexts: Understanding the impact of school climate factors on students' sense of school belonging. *Applied Psychology, 59*(2), 243–272. doi:10.1111/j.1464-0597.2009.00389.x

Center for History and New Media. (2006). Teaching American history: Conflict and consensus. Key moments in U.S. history. Retrieved May 11, 2010, from http://chnm.gmu.edu/mcpstah/lesson-plans/1950-to-present/?planid=26

Centers for Disease Control and Prevention. (2002, Fall). *Planning for physical activity* (a BAM! Body and Mind Teacher's Corner resource). Retrieved January 19, 2003, from http://www.bam.gov/teachers/activities/planning.htm

Centers for Disease Control and Prevention. (2005a). *Nutrition and the health of young people.* Atlanta, GA: Author.

Centers for Disease Control and Prevention. (2005b). QuickStats: Total and primary cesarean rate and vaginal birth after previous cesarean (VBAC) rate—United States, 1989–2003. *Morbidity and Mortality Weekly Report, 54*(2), 46.

Centers for Disease Control and Prevention. (2007). *Autism spectrum disorder fact sheet.* Retrieved January 22, 2008, from http://www.cdc.gov/ncbddd/autism/ActEarly/autism.html

Centers for Disease Control and Prevention. (2008). *Youth risk behavior surveillance—United States, 2007.* Atlanta, GA: Author.

Centers for Disease Control and Prevention. (2009a). Obesity prevalence among low-income, preschool-aged children—United States, 1998-2008. *Morbidity and Mortality Weekly Report, 58*(28), 769–773.

Centers for Disease Control and Prevention. (2009b). *Understanding child maltreatment.* Retrieved January 4, 2010, from http://www.cdc.gov/violenceprevention/pdf/CM-FactSheet-a.pdf

Central Intelligence Agency. (2010, January 15). *The world factbook. South Asia: Nepal.* Retrieved February 6, 2010, from https://www.cia.gov/library/publications/the-world-factbook/geos/np.html

Cermak, L. S., & Craik, F. I. M. (Eds.). (1979). *Levels of processing in human memory.* Hillsdale, NJ: Erlbaum.

Certo, J., Cauley, K. M., & Chafin, C. (2002, April). *Students' perspectives on their high school experience.* Paper presented at the annual meeting of the American Educational Research Association, New Orleans, LA.

Chafel, J. A. (1991). The play of children: Developmental processes and policy implications. *Child & Youth Care Forum, 20,* 115–132.

Chall, J. S. (1996). *Stages of reading development* (2nd ed.) Fort Worth, TX: Harcourt, Brace.

Champagne, F. A. (2009). Beyond nature vs. nurture: Philosophical insights from molecular biology. *Observer, 22*(4), 4, 27–28.

Chan, S. M. (2010). Aggressive behaviour in early elementary school children: Relations to authoritarian parenting, children's negative emotionality and coping strategies. *Early Child Development and Care, 180*(9), 1253–1269. doi:10.1080/03004430902981447

Chandler, M., & Boyes, M. (1982). Social-cognitive development. In B. Wolman (Ed.), *Handbook of developmental psychology.* Upper Saddle River, NJ: Prentice Hall.

Chandler, M., & Moran, T. (1990). Psychopathy and moral development: A comparative study of delinquent and nondelinquent youth. *Development and Psychopathology, 2,* 227–246.

Chandler, M. J. (1987). The Othello effect: Essay on the emergence and eclipse of skeptical doubt. *Human Development, 30,* 137–159.

Chandler, M. J., Hallett, D., & Sokol, B. W. (2002). Competing claims about competing knowledge claims. In B. K. Hofer & P. R. Pintrich (Eds.), *Personal epistemology: The psychology of beliefs about knowledge and knowing* (pp. 145–168). Mahwah, NJ: Erlbaum.

Chant, R. H. (2009). Developing involved and active citizens: The role of personal practical theories and action research in a standards-based social studies classroom. *Teacher Education Quarterly, 36*(1), 181–190.

Chao, R. K. (1994). Beyond parental control and authoritarian parenting style: Understanding Chinese parenting through the cultural notion of training. *Child Development, 65,* 1111–1119.

Chao, R. K. (2000). Cultural explanations for the role of parenting in the school success of Asian-American children. In R. D. Taylor & M. C. Wang (Eds.), *Resilience across contexts: Family, work, culture, and community* (pp. 333–363). Mahwah, NJ: Erlbaum.

Chapman, M. (1988). *Constructive evolution: Origins and development of Piaget's thought.* Cambridge, England: Cambridge University Press.

Charity, A. H., Scarborough, H. S., & Griffin, D. M. (2004). Familiarity with school English in African American children and its relation to early reading achievement. *Child Development, 75,* 1340–1356.

Charles, E. P., & Rivera, S. M. (2009). Object permanence and method of disappearance: Looking measures further contradict reaching measures. *Developmental Science, 12*(6), 991–1006.

Charlesworth, W. R., & LaFreniere, P. (1983). Dominance, friendship, and resource utilization in preschool children's groups. *Ethology and Sociobiology, 4,* 175–186.

Chavous, T. M., Bernat, D. H., Schmeelk-Cone, K., Caldwell, C. H., Kohn-Wood, L., et al. (2003). Racial identity and academic attainment among African American adolescents. *Child Development, 74,* 1076–1090.

Chazan-Cohen, R., Jerald, J., & Stark, D. R. (2001). A commitment to supporting the mental health of our youngest children. *Zero to Three, 22*(1), 4–12.

Chedzoy, S., & Burden, R. (2009). Primary school children's reflections on physical education lessons: An attributional analysis and possible implications for teacher action. *Thinking Skills and Creativity, 4*(3), 185–193. doi:10.1016/j.tsc.2009.09.008

Chelonis, J. J., Johnson, T. A., Ferguson, S. A., Berry, K. J., Kubacak, B., Edwards, M. C., et al. (2011). Effect of methylphenidate on motivation in children with attention-deficit/hyperactivity disorder. *Experimental and Clinical Psychopharmacology, 19*(2), 145–153. doi:10.1037/a0022794

Chen, J. A., & Pajares, F. (2010). Implicit theories of ability of grade 6 science students: Relation to epistemological beliefs and academic motivation and achievement in science. *Contemporary Educational Psychology, 35,* 75–87.

Chen, J.-Q. (2009). China's assimilation of MI theory in education: Accent on the family and harmony. In J.-Q. Chen, S. Moran, H. Gardner (Eds.), *Multiple intelligences around the world* (pp. 29–42). San Francisco: Jossey-Bass.

Chen, L. H., Wu, C., Kee, Y. H., Lin, M., & Shui, S. (2009). Fear of failure, 2×2 achievement goal and self-handicapping: An examination of the hierarchical model of achievement motivation in physical education. *Contemporary Educational Psychology, 34*(4), 298–305.

Chen, L.-L., Su, Y.-C., Su, C.-H., Lin, H.-C., & Kuo, H.-W. (2008). Acupressure and meridian massage: Combined effects on increasing body weight in premature infants. *Journal of Clinical Nursing, 17*(9), 1174–1181.

Chen, M.-J., Gruenewald, P. J., & Remer, L. G. (2009). Does alcohol outlet density affect youth access to alcohol? *Journal of Adolescent Health, 44,* 582–589.

Chen, R., & Simons-Morton, B. (2009). Concurrent changes in conduct problems and depressive symptoms in early adolescents: A developmental person-centered approach. *Development and Psychopathology, 21*(1), 285–307.

Chen, X., Anderson, R. C., Li, W., Hao, M., Wu, X., & Shu, H. (2004). Phonological awareness of bilingual and monolingual Chinese children. *Journal of Educational Psychology, 96,* 142–151.

Chen, X., Chang, L., & He, Y. (2003). The peer group as a context: Mediating and moderating effects on the relations between academic achievement and social functioning in Chinese children. *Child Development, 74,* 710–727.

Chen, X., DeSouza, A. T., Chen, H., & Wang, L. (2006). Reticent behavior and experiences in peer interactions in Chinese and Canadian children. *Developmental Psychology, 42*(4), 656–665.

Chen, X., Hastings, P. D., Rubin, K. H., Chen, H., Cen, G., & Stewart, S. L. (1998). Child-rearing attitudes and behavioral inhibition in Chinese and Canadian toddlers: A cross-cultural study. *Developmental Psychology, 34*(4), 677–686.

Chen, X., Rubin, K. H., & Li, Z. (1995). Social functioning and adjustment in Chinese children. *Developmental Psychology, 31,* 531–539.

Chen, X., Rubin, K. H., Liu, M., Chen, H., Wang, L., Li, D., et al. (2003). Compliance in Chinese and Canadian toddlers: A cross-cultural study. *International Journal of Behavioral Development, 27*(5), 428–436.

Chen, X., & Wang, L. (2010). China. In M. H. Bornstein (Ed.), *Handbook of cultural developmental science* (pp. 429–444). New York: Psychology Press.

Chen, X., Wang, L., & Wang, Z. (2009). Shyness-sensitivity and social, school, and psychological adjustment in rural migrant and urban children in china. *Child Development, 80*(5), 1499–1513. doi:10.1111/j.1467-8624.2009.01347.x

Chen, Z., Sanchez, R. P., & Campbell, T. (1997). From beyond to within their grasp: The rudiments of analogical problem solving in 10- and 13-month-olds. *Developmental Psychology, 33,* pp. 790–801.

Chess, S., & Thomas, A. (1992). Interactions between offspring and parents in development. In B. Tizard & V. P. Varma (Eds.), *Vulnerability and resilience in human development: A festschrift for Ann and Alan Clarke* (pp. 72–87). London, England: Jessica Kingsley Publishers.

Chetland, E., & Fluck, M. (2007). Children's performance on the 'give x' task: A microgenetic analysis of 'counting' and 'grabbing' behavior. *Infant and Child Development. Special Issue: Using the Microgenetic Method to Investigate Cognitive Development, 16*(1), 35–51.

Cheung, H. H.-P. (2009). Multiple intelligences in China: Challenges and hopes. In J.-Q. Chen, S. Moran, H. Gardner (Eds.), *Multiple intelligences around the world* (pp. 43–54). San Francisco: Jossey-Bass.

Cheung, S. K., & McBride-Chang, C. (2011). Relations of gender, gender-related personality characteristics, and dating status to adolescents' cross-sex friendship quality. *Sex Roles, 64*(1–2), 59–69. doi:10.1007/s11199-010-9880-5

Chi, M. T. H. (1978). Knowledge structures and memory development. In R. S. Siegler (Ed.), *Children's thinking: What develops?* Hillsdale, NJ: Erlbaum.

Chipman, S. F. (2005). Research on the women and mathematics issue: A personal case history. In A. M. Gallagher & J. C. Kaufman (Eds.), *Gender differences in mathematics: An integrative psychological approach* (pp. 1–24). Cambridge, England: Cambridge University Press.

Chisholm, K., Carter, M. C., Ames, E. W., & Morison, S. J. (1995). Attachment security and indiscriminately friendly behavior in children adopted from Romanian orphanages. *Development and Psychopathology, 7,* 283–297.

Chiu, M. M. (2007). Families, economies, cultures, and science achievement in 41 countries: Country-, school-, and student-level analyses. *Journal of Family Psychology, 21,* 510–519.

Choi, S., & McDonough, L. (2007). Adapting spatial concepts for different languages: From preverbal event schemas to semantic categories. In J. M. Plumert & J. P. Spencer (Eds.), *The emerging spatial mind* (pp. 142–167). New York: Oxford University Press.

Chomsky, C. S. (1969). *The acquisition of syntax in children from 5 to 10.* Cambridge, MA: MIT Press.

Chomsky, N. (1959). Review of B. F. Skinner's *Verbal Behavior. Language, 35,* 26–58.

Chomsky, N. (1965). *Aspects of the theory of syntax.* Cambridge, MA: MIT Press.

Chomsky, N. (1972). *Language and mind* (enlarged ed.). San Diego, CA: Harcourt Brace Jovanovich.

Chomsky, N. (1976). *Reflections on language.* London: Temple Smith.

Chomsky, N. (2006). *Language and mind* (3rd ed.). Cambridge, England: Cambridge University Press.

Choo, C. M. (2009). *The benefits of peer teaching in the early years: The learning advantage in a Montessori mixed-age preschool.* Retrieved May 7, 2010, from http://earlychildhood.suite101.com/article.cfm/the_benefits_of_peer_teaching_in_the_early_years

Chouinard, M. M. (2007). Children's questions: A mechanism for cognitive development. *Monographs of the Society for Research in Child Development, 72* (1; Serial No. 286).

Christenson, S., Palan, R., & Scullin, S. (2009). Family–school partnerships: An essential component of student achievement. *Principal Leadership, 9*(9), 10–16.

Christenson, S. L., & Thurlow, M. L. (2004). School dropouts: Prevention, considerations, interventions, and challenges. *Current Directions in Psychological Science, 13,* 36–39.

Christie, J. F., & Johnsen, E. P. (1983). The role of play in social-intellectual development. *Review of Educational Research, 53,* 93–115.

Chukovsky, K. (1968). *From two to five* (M. Morton, Trans.). Berkeley: University of California Press.

Chung, K., Reavis, S., Mosconi, M., Drewry, J., Matthews, T., & Tassé. M. J. (2007). Peermediated social skills training program for young children with high-functioning autism. *Research in Developmental Disabilities, 28*(4), 423–436. doi:10.1016/j.ridd.2006.05.002

Ciarrochi, J., & Heaven, P. C. L. (2008). Learned social hopelessness: The role of explanatory style in predicting social support during adolescence. *Journal of Child Psychology and Psychiatry, 49*(12), 1279–1286. doi:10.1111/j.1469-7610.2008.01950.x

Cicchetti, D., Rogosch, F. A., & Toth, S. L. (1997). Ontogenesis, depressotypic organization, and the depressive spectrum. In S. S. Luthar, J. A. Burack, D. Cicchetti, & J. R. Weisz (Eds.), *Developmental psychopathology: Perspectives on adjustment, risk, and disorder* (pp. 273–313). Cambridge, England: Cambridge University Press.

Cimpian, A., Arce, H.-M. C., Markman, E. M., & Dweck, C. S. (2007). Subtle linguistic cues affect children's motivation. *Psychological Science, 18,* 314–316.

Clark, B. (1997). *Growing up gifted* (5th ed.). Upper Saddle River, NJ: Merrill/Prentice Hall.

Clark, C. C. (1992). Deviant adolescent subcultures: Assessment strategies and clinical interventions. *Adolescence, 27*(106), 283–293.

Clark, D. B. (2006). Longitudinal conceptual change in students' understanding of thermal equilibrium: An examination of the process of conceptual restructuring. *Cognition and Instruction, 24,* 467–563.

Clark, K. (2009). The case for structured English immersion. *Educational Leadership, 66*(7), 42–46.

Clark, R. M. (1983). *Family life and school achievement: Why poor Black children succeed or fail.* Chicago: University of Chicago Press.

Clasen, D. R., & Brown, B. B. (1985). The multidimensionality of peer pressure in adolescence. *Journal of Youth and Adolescence, 14,* 451–468.

Clemens, E. V., Shipp, A. E., & Pisarik, C. T. (2008). Myspace as a tool for mental health professionals. *Child and Adolescent Mental Health, 13*(2), 97–98.

Clifford, M. M. (1990). Students need challenge, not easy success. *Educational Leadership, 48*(1), 22–26.

Cochran, M., & Niego, S. (2002). Parenting and social networks. In M. H. Bornstein (Ed.), *Handbook of parenting: Vol. 4. Social conditions and applied parenting* (2nd ed., pp. 123–148). Mahwah, NJ: Erlbaum.

Cochran-Smith, M., & Lytle, S. (1993). *Inside out: Teacher research and knowledge.* New York: Teachers College Press.

Cody, H., & Kamphaus, R. W. (1999). Down syndrome. In S. Goldstein & C. R. Reynolds (Eds.), *Handbook of neurodevelopmental and genetic disorders* (pp. 385–405). New York: Guilford Press.

Cohen, E. G. (1994). Restructuring the classroom: Conditions for productive small groups. *Review of Educational Research, 64,* 1–35.

Cohen, J. R., & Lieberman, M. D. (2010). The common neural basis of exerting self-control in multiple domains. In R. R. Hassin, K. N. Ochsner & Y. Trope (Eds.), *Self control in society, mind, and brain* (pp. 141–160). New York: Oxford University Press. doi:10.1093/acprof:oso/9780195391381.003.0008

Cohen, L. B., & Cashon, C. H. (2006). Infant cognition. In W. Damon & R. M. Lerner (Eds. in Chief) & D. Kuhn & R. S. Siegler (Vol. Eds.), *Handbook of child psychology: Vol. 2. Cognition, perception, and language* (6th ed., pp. 214–251). Hoboken, NJ: Wiley.

Cohen, M. N. (1998, April 17). Culture, not race, explains human diversity. *The Chronicle of Higher Education,* p. B4.

Cohen, M. R. (1997). Individual and sex differences in speed of handwriting among high school students. *Perceptual and Motor Skills, 84*(3, Pt. 2), 1428–1430.

Coie, J. D., & Cillessen, A. H. N. (1993). Peer rejection: Origins and effects on children's development. *Current Directions in Psychological Science, 2,* 89–92.

Coie, J. D., & Dodge, K. A. (1988). Multiple sources of data on social behavior and social status. *Child Development, 59,* 815–829.

Coie, J. D., Dodge, K. A., & Coppotelli, H. (1982). Dimensions and types of social status: A cross-age perspective. *Developmental Psychology, 18,* 557–570.

Coie, J. D., Dodge, K. A., Terry, R., & Wright, V. (1991). The role of aggression in peer relations: An analysis of aggression episodes in boys' play groups. *Child Development, 62,* 812–826.

Coie, J. D., & Kupersmidt, J. (1983). A behavioral analysis of emerging social status in boys' groups. *Child Development, 54,* 1400–1416.

Coiro, J., & Fogleman, J. (2011, February). Using websites wisely. *Educational Leadership, 68*(5), 34–38.

Coker, D. (2007). Writing instruction for young children: Methods targeting the multiple demands that writers face. In S. Graham, C. A. MacArthur, & J. Fitzgerald (Eds.), *Best practices in writing instruction: Solving problems in the teaching of literacy* (pp. 101–118). New York: Guilford.

Coker, T. R., Elliott, M. N., Kanouse, D. E., Grunbaum, J. A., Schwebel, D. C., Gilliland, M. J., et al. (2009). Perceived racial/ethnic discrimination among fifth-grade students and its association with mental health. *American Journal of Public Health, 99*(5), 878–884.

Colby, A., & Kohlberg, L. (1984). Invariant sequence and internal consistency in moral judgment stages. In W. M. Kurtines & J. L. Gewirtz (Eds.), *Morality, moral behavior, and moral development.* New York: Wiley.

Colby, A., Kohlberg, L., Gibbs, J., & Lieberman, M. (1983). A longitudinal study of moral judgment. *Monographs of the Society for Research in Child Development, 48*(1–2, Serial No. 200).

Cole, C., & Winsler, A. (2010). Protecting children from exposure to lead: Old problem, new data, and new policy needs. *Social Policy Report, 24*(1). Ann Arbor, MI: Society for Research in Child Development.

Cole, C. F., Labin, D. B., & del Rocio Galarza, M. (2008). Begin with the children: What research on *Sesame Street's* international coproductions reveals about using media to promote a new more peaceful world. *International Journal of Behavioral Development, 32*(4), 359–365. doi:10.1177/0165025408090977

Cole, D. A., Martin, J. M., Peeke, L. A., Seroczynski, A. D., & Fier, J. (1999). Children's over- and underestimation of academic competence: A longitudinal study of gender differences, depression, and anxiety. *Child Development, 70,* 459–473.

Cole, M. (1990). Cognitive development and formal schooling: The evidence from cross-cultural research. In L. C. Moll (Ed.), *Vygotsky and education* (pp. 89–110). New York: Cambridge University Press.

Cole, M. (2006). Culture and cognitive development in phylogenetic, historical and ontogenetic perspective. In W. Damon & R. M. Lerner (Series Eds.) & D. Kuhn & R. Siegler (Vol. Eds.), *Handbook of child psychology: Vol. 2. Cognition, perception, and language* (6th ed., pp. 636–683). New York: Wiley.

Cole, M., & Cagigas, X. E. (2010). Cognition. In M. H. Bornstein (Ed.), *Handbook of cultural developmental science* (pp. 127–142). New York: Psychology Press.

Cole, M., & Hatano, G. (2007). Cultural-historical activity theory: Integrating phylogeny, cultural history, and ontogenesis in cultural psychology. In S. Kitayama & D. Cohen (Eds.), *Handbook of cultural psychology* (pp. 109–135). New York: Guilford Press.

Cole, M., & Packer, M. (2011). Culture in development. In M. H. Bornstein & M. E. Lamb (Eds.), *Developmental science: An advanced textbook* (6th ed., pp. 51–107). New York: Psychology Press.

Cole, M., & Scribner, S. (1978). Introduction. In L. S. Vygotsky, *Mind in society: The development of higher psychological processes* (M. Cole, V. John-Steiner, S. Scribner, & E. Souberman, Eds.). Cambridge, MA: Harvard University Press.

Cole, P. M., Armstrong, L. M., & Pemberton, C. K. (2010). The role of language in the development of emotion regulation. In S. D. Calkins, & M. A. Bell (Eds.), *Child development at the intersection of emotion and cognition* (pp. 59–77). Washington, DC: American Psychological Association.

Cole, P. M., & Tamang, B. L. (2001). Nepali children's ideas about emotional displays in hypothetical challenges. *Developmental Psychology, 34,* 640–646.

Cole, P. M., & Tan, P. Z. (2007). Emotion socialization from a cultural perspective. In J. E. Grusec & P. D. Hastings (Eds.), *Handbook of socialization: Theory and research* (pp. 516–542). New York: Guilford Press.

Coles, R. L. (2006). *Race and family: A structural approach.* Thousand Oaks, CA: Sage.

Coley, R. L., & Chase-Lansdale, P. L. (1998). Adolescent pregnancy and parenthood. *American Psychologist, 53,* 152–166.

Collier, V. P. (1989). How long? A synthesis of research on academic achievement in a second language. *TESOL Quarterly, 23,* 509–523.

Collier, V. P. (1992). The Canadian bilingual immersion debate: A synthesis of research findings. *Studies in Second Language Acquisition, 14,* 87–97.

Collingwood, T. R. (1997). *Helping at-risk youth through physical fitness programming.* Champaign, IL: Human Kinetics.

Collins, A. (2006). Cognitive apprenticeship. In R. K. Sawyer (Ed.), *The Cambridge handbook of the learning sciences* (pp. 47–60). Cambridge, England: Cambridge University Press.

Collins, A., Brown, J. S., & Newman, S. E. (1989). Cognitive apprenticeship: Teaching the crafts of reading, writing, and mathematics. In L. B. Resnick (Ed.), *Knowing, learning, and instruction: Essays in honor of Robert Glaser.* Hillsdale, NJ: Erlbaum.

Collins, M. F. (2010). ELL preschoolers' English vocabulary acquisition from storybook reading. *Early Childhood Research Quarterly, 25*(1), 84–97.

Collins, W. A. (1990). Parent–child relationships in the transition to adolescence: Continuity and change in interaction, affects, and cognition. In R. Montemayor, G. Adams, & T. Gullota (Eds.), *Advances in adolescent development* (Vol. 2). Beverly Hills, CA: Sage.

Collins, W. A., Maccoby, E. E., Steinberg, L., Hetherington, E. M., & Bornstein, M. H. (2000). Contemporary research on parenting: The case for nature and nurture. *American Psychologist, 55,* 218–232.

Collins, W. A., & Sroufe, L. A. (1999). Capacity for intimate relationships: A developmental construction. In W. Furman, B. B. Brown, & C. Feiring (Eds.), *The development of romantic relationships in adolescence* (pp. 125–147). Cambridge, England: Cambridge University Press.

Collins, W. A., & van Dulmen, M. (2006). "The course of true love(s)?": Origins and pathways in the development of romantic relationships. In A. C. Crouter & A. Booth (Eds.), *Romance and sex in adolescence and emerging adulthood: Risks and opportunities* (pp. 53–86). Mahwah, NJ: Erlbaum.

Colombo, J. (1993). *Infant cognition: Predicting later intellectual functioning.* Newbury Park, CA: Sage.

Colombo, J., & Mitchell, D. W. (2009). Infant visual habituation. *Neurobiology of Learning and Memory, 92,* 225–234.

Colombo, J., Shaddy, D. J., Blaga, O. M., Anderson, C. J., & Kannass, K. N. (2009). High cognitive ability in infancy and early childhood. In F. D. Horowitz, R. F. Subotnik, & D. J. Matthews (Eds.), *The development of giftedness and talent across the life span* (pp. 23–42). Washington, DC: American Psychological Association.

Colorado Department of Education. (2007). *Colorado K–12 academic standards.* Retrieved October 25, 2007, from http://www.cde.state.co.us/cdeassess/documents/olr/k12_standards.html

Comeau, L., Cormier, P., Grandmaison, É., & Lacroix, D. (1999). A longitudinal study of phonological processing skills in children learning to read in a second language. *Journal of Educational Psychology, 91,* 29–43.

Comstock, G., & Scharrer, E. (2006). Media and popular culture. In W. Damon & R. M. Lerner (Series Eds.) & K. A. Renninger & I. E. Sigel (Vol. Eds.), *Handbook of child psychology: Vol. 3. Social, emotional, and personality development* (6th ed., pp. 817–863). New York: Wiley.

Condon, J. C., & Yousef, F. S. (1975). *An introduction to intercultural communication.* Indianapolis, IN: Bobbs-Merrill.

Condry, J. C., & Ross, D. F. (1985). Sex and aggression: The influence of gender label on the perception of aggression in children. *Child Development, 56,* 225–233.

Conduct Problems Prevention Research Group. (2010). The effects of a multiyear universal social–emotional learning program: The role of student and school characteristics. *Journal of Consulting and Clinical Psychology, 78*(2), 156–168. doi:10.1037/a0018607

Conel, J. L. (1939, 1975). *Postnatal development of the human cerebral cortex* (Vols. 1–8). Cambridge, MA: Harvard University Press.

Conn, J., & Kanner, L. (1940). Spontaneous erections in childhood. *Journal of Pediatrics, 16,* 237–240.

Conner, B. T., Hellemann, G. S., Ritchie, T. L., & Noble, E. P. (2010). Genetic, personality, and environmental predictors of drug use in adolescents. *Journal of Substance Abuse Treatment, 38,* 178–190.

Conner, J. (2010). Learning to unlearn: How a service-learning project can help teacher candidates to reframe urban students. *Teaching and Teacher Education, 26*(5), 1170–1177. doi:10.1016/j.tate.2010.02.001

Connolly, J., & Goldberg, A. (1999). Romantic relationships in adolescence: The role of friends and peers in their emergence and development. In W. Furman, B. B. Brown, & C. Feiring (Eds.), *The development of romantic relationships in adolescence* (pp. 266–290). Cambridge, England: Cambridge University Press.

Connolly, J. A., & McIsaac, C. (2009). Romantic relationships in adolescence. In R. M. Lerner, & L. Steinberg (Eds.), *Handbook of adolescent psychology, Vol. 2: Contextual influences on adolescent development* (3rd ed., pp. 104–151). Hoboken, NJ: Wiley.

Connor, P., Bartlett, S., Mendelson, M., Condon, K., Sutcliffe, J., et al. (2010). WIC participant and program characteristics 2008 (WIC-08-PC). Alexandria, VA: Office of Research and Analysis, USDA Food and Nutrition Service. Retrieved February 24, 2010, from http://www.fns.usda.gov/ora/MENU/Published/recentreleases.htm

Connor, P. D., Sampson, P. D., Streissguth, A. P., Bookstein, F. L., & Barr, H. M. (2006). Effects of prenatal alcohol exposure on fine motor coordination and balance: A study of two adult samples. *Neuropsychologia, 44,* 744–751.

Conradt, E., & Ablow, J. (2010). Infant physiological response to the still-face paradigm: Contributions of maternal sensitivity and infants' early regulatory behavior. *Infant Behavior & Development, 33*(3), 251–265.

Consortium of Longitudinal Studies. (Ed.). (1983). *As the twig is bent: Lasting effects of preschool programs.* Mahwah, NJ: Erlbaum.

Cook, E. C., Buehler, C., & Henson, R. (2009). Parents and peers as social influences to deter antisocial behavior. *Journal of Youth and Adolescence, 38*(9), 1240–1252. doi:10.1007/s10964-008-9348-x

Cook, V., & Newson, M. (1996). *Chomsky's universal grammar: An introduction* (2nd ed.). Oxford, England: Blackwell.

Cooney, F. E. (2008). Adolescent self-regulation skills, working portfolios, and explicit instruction: A mixed methods study (ProQuest Information & Learning). *Dissertation Abstracts International Section A: Humanities and Social Sciences, 68.* Retrieved from http://www.csa. (2008-99090-473)

Cooney, J. B., & Ladd, S. F. (1992). The influence of verbal protocol methods on children's mental computation. *Learning and Individual Differences, 4,* 237–257.

Cooney, J. B., Swanson, H. L., & Ladd, S. F. (1988). Acquisition of mental multiplication skill: Evidence for the transition between counting and retrieval strategies. *Cognition and Instruction, 5,* 323–345.

Cooper, C. R., Denner, J., & Lopez, E. M. (1999, Fall). Cultural brokers: Helping Latino children on pathways toward success. *The Future of Children: When School Is Out, 9,* 51–57.

Cooper, C. R., Jackson, J. F., Azmitia, M., Lopez, E., & Dunbar, N. (1995). Bridging students' multiple worlds: African American and Latino youth in academic outreach programs. In R. F. Macias & R. G. Garcia-Ramos (Eds.), *Changing schools for changing students: An anthology of research on language minorities* (pp. 211–234). Santa Barbara: University of California Linguistic Minority Research Institute.

Cooper, H., & Dorr, N. (1995). Race comparisons on need for achievement: A meta-analytic alternative to Graham's narrative review. *Review of Educational Research, 65,* 483–508.

Cooper, H., Robinson, J. C., & Patall, E. A. (2006). Does homework improve academic achievement? A synthesis of research, 1987–2003. *Review of Educational Research, 76,* 1–62.

Cooper, H., Valentine, J. C., Nye, B., & Lindsay, J. J. (1999). Relationships between five after-school activities and academic achievement. *Journal of Educational Psychology, 91,* 369–378.

Cooper, P. M. (2009). *The classrooms all young children need: Lessons in teaching from Vivian Paley.* Chicago: University of Chicago Press.

Cooper, S. M., & Smalls, C. (2010). Culturally distinctive and academic socialization: Direct and interactive relationships with African American adolescents' academic adjustment. *Journal of Youth and Adolescence, 39*(2), 199–212.

Coopersmith, S. (1967). *The antecedents of self-esteem.* San Francisco: Freeman.

Coplan, R. J., & Evans, M. A. (2009). At a loss for words? introduction to the special issue on shyness and language in childhood. *Infant and Child Development, 18*(3), 211–215.

Corbin, J. M., & Strauss, A. (2008). *Basics of qualitative research: Techniques and procedures for developing grounded theory* (3rd ed.). Los Angeles, CA: Sage.

Corkum, P., Humphries, K., Mullane, J. C., & Theriault, F. (2008). Private speech in children with ADHD and their typically developing peers during problem-solving and inhibition tasks. *Contemporary Educational Psychology, 33,* 97–115.

Cornell, D. G., Pelton, G. M., Bassin, L. E., Landrum, M., Ramsay, S. G., Cooley, M. R., et al. (1990). Self-concept and peer status among gifted program youth. *Journal of Educational Psychology, 82,* 456–463.

Cornish, K., Burack, J. A., Rahman, A., Munir, F., Russo, N., & Grant, C. (2005). Theory of mind deficits in children with fragile X syndrome. *Journal of Intellectual Disability Research, 49,* 372–378.

Corno, L., & Mandinach, E. B. (2004). What we have learned about student engagement in the past twenty years. In D. M. McNerney & S. Van Etten (Eds.), *Big theories revisited* (pp. 299–328). Greenwich, CT: Information Age.

Cornoldi, C. (2010). Metacognition, intelligence, and academic performance. In H. S. Waters, & W. Schneider (Eds.), *Metacognition, strategy use, and instruction* (pp. 257–277). New York: Guilford Press.

Corpus, J. H., McClintic-Gilbert, M. S., & Hayenga, A. O. (2006, April). *Understanding intrinsic and extrinsic motivation: Age differences and links to children's beliefs and goals.* Paper presented at the annual meeting of the American Educational Research Association, San Francisco.

Corpus, J., McClintic-Gilbert, M., & Hagenga, A. (2009). Within-year changes in children's intrinsic and extrinsic motivational orientations: Contextual predictors and academic outcomes. *Contemporary Educational Psychology, 34*(2), 154–166. doi:10.1016/j.cedpsych.2009.01.001

Corriveau, K., Pasquini, E., & Goswami, U. (2007). Basic auditory processing skills and specific language impairment: A new look at an old hypothesis. *Journal of Speech, Language, and Hearing Research, 50,* 647–666.

Corriveau, K. H., Goswami, U., & Thomson, J. M. (2010). Auditory processing and early literacy skills in a preschool and kindergarten population. *Journal of Learning Disabilities, 43*(4), 369–382.

Corsaro, W. A. (1985). *Friendship and peer culture in the early years.* Norwood, NJ: Ablex.

Corsaro, W. A. (2003). *We're friends, right? Inside kids' culture.* Washington, DC: Joseph Henry Press.

Corsaro, W. A., & Eder, D. (1990). Children's peer cultures. *Annual Review of Sociology, 16,* 197–220.

Corsaro, W. A., & Molinari, L. (2005). *I compagni: Understanding children's transition from preschool to elementary school.* New York: Teachers College Press.

Cosden, M., Morrison, G., Albanese, A. L., & Macias, S. (2001). When homework is not home work: After-school programs for homework assistance. *Educational Psychologist, 36,* 211–221.

Cossu, G. (1999). The acquisition of Italian orthography. In M. Harris & G. Hatano (Eds.), *Learning to read and write: A cross-linguistic perspective.* Cambridge, England: Cambridge University Press.

Costigan, C. L., Hua, J. M., & Su, T. F. (2010). Living up to expectations: The strengths and challenges experienced by Chinese Canadian students. *Canadian Journal of School Psychology, 25*(3), 223–245.

Côté, J. E. (2005). Erikson's theory. In C. B. Fisher & R. M. Lerner (Eds.), *Encyclopedia of applied developmental science* (Vol. 1, pp. 406–409). Thousand Oaks, CA: Sage.

Cotterell, J. L. (1992). The relation of attachments and supports to adolescent well-being and school adjustment. *Journal of Adolescent Research, 7,* 28–42.

Cotton, S. M., & Richdale, A. L. (2010). Sleep patterns and behavior in typically developing children with autism, Down syndrome, Prader-Willi syndrome and intellectual disability. *Research in Autism Spectrum Disorders, 4,* 490–500.

Council for Exceptional Children. (1995). *Toward a common agenda: Linking gifted education and school reform.* Reston, VA: Author.

Council of National Psychological Associations for the Advancement of Ethnic Minority Interests. (2009). *Psychological education and training from culture-specific and multiracial perspectives: Critical issues and recommendations.* Washington, DC: American Psychological Association.

Courage, M. L., & Adams, R. J. (1990). Visual acuity assessment from birth to three years using the acuity card procedures: Cross-sectional and longitudinal samples. *Optometry and Vision Science, 67,* 713–718.

Courage, M. L., Reynolds, G. D., & Richards, J. E. (2006). Infants' attention to patterned stimuli: Developmental change from 3 to 12 months of age. *Child Development, 77,* 680–695.

Courage, M. L., & Setliff, A. E. (2010). When babies watch television: Attention-getting, attention-holding, and the implications for learning from video material. *Developmental Review, 30*(2), 220–238. doi:10.1016/j.dr.2010.03.003

Covington, M. V. (1987). Achievement motivation, self-attributions, and the exceptional learner. In J. D. Day & J. G. Borkowski (Eds.), *Intelligence and exceptionality.* Norwood, NJ: Ablex.

Covington, M. V. (1992). *Making the grade: A self-worth perspective on motivation and school reform.* Cambridge, England: Cambridge University Press.

Covington, M. V., & Müeller, K. J. (2001). Intrinsic versus extrinsic motivation: An approach/

avoidance reformulation. *Educational Psychology Review, 13,* 157–176.

Cowan, N., & Alloway, T. (2009). Development of working memory in childhood. In M. L. Courage & N. Cowan (Eds.), *The development of memory in infancy and childhood* (pp. 303–342). New York: Psychology Press.

Cowan, N., Morey, C. C., AuBuchon, A. M., Zwilling, C. E., & Gilchrist, A. L. (2010). Seven-year-olds allocate attention like adults unless working memory is overloaded. *Developmental Science, 13*(1), 120–133.

Cowan, W. M. (1979). The development of the brain. *Scientific American, 241,* 106–117.

Cox, C. B. (2000). *Empowering grandparents raising grandchildren.* New York: Springer.

Cox, M. E., Orme, J. G., & Rhoades, K. W. (2003). Willingness to foster children with emotional or behavioral problems. *Journal of Social Service Research, 29,* 23–51.

Craft, M. (1984). Education for diversity. In M. Craft (Ed.), *Educational and cultural pluralism.* London: Falmer Press.

Crago, M. B. (1988). *Cultural context in the communicative interaction of young Inuit children.* Unpublished doctoral dissertation, McGill University, Montreal, Canada.

Crago, M. B., Allen, S. E. M., & Hough-Eyamie, W. P. (1997). Exploring innateness through cultural and linguistic variation. In M. Gopnik (Ed.), *The inheritance and innateness of grammars.* New York: Oxford University Press.

Crago, M. B., Annahatak, B., & Ningiuruvik, L. (1993). Changing patterns of language socialization in Inuit homes. *Anthropology and Education Quarterly, 24,* 205–223.

Craig, L. (2006). Does father care mean fathers share? A comparison of how mothers and fathers in intact families spend time with their children. *Gender & Society, 20,* 259–281.

Crain, W. (2011). *Theories of development: Concepts and applications* (6th ed.). Upper Saddle River, NJ: Pearson Prentice Hall.

Crick, N. R., Casas, J. F., & Nelson, D. A. (2002). Toward a more comprehensive understanding of peer maltreatment: Studies of relational victimization. *Current Directions in Psychological Science, 11,* 98–101.

Crick, N. R., & Dodge, K. A. (1996). Social information-processing mechanisms in reactive and proactive aggression. *Child Development, 67,* 993–1002.

Crick, N. R., Grotpeter, J. K., & Bigbee, M. A. (2002). Relationally and physically aggressive children's intent attributions and feelings of distress for relational and instrumental peer provocation. *Child Development, 73,* 1134–1142..

Criss, M. M., Pettit, G. S., Bates, J. E., Dodge, K. A., & Lapp, A. L. (1992). Family adversity, positive peer relationships, and children's externalizing behavior: A longitudinal perspective on risk and resilience. *Child Development, 73,* 1220–1237.

Critten, S., Pine, K., & Steffler, D. (2007). Spelling development in young children: A case of representational redescription? *Journal of Educational Psychology, 99,* 207–220.

Crohn, H. M. (2006). Five styles of positive stepmothering from the perspective of young adult stepdaughters. *Journal of Divorce and Remarriage, 46*(1/2), 119–134.

Cromer, R. F. (1993). Language growth with experience without feedback. In P. Bloom (Ed.), *Language acquisition: Core readings.* Cambridge, MA: MIT Press.

Cromley, J. G., & Azevedo, R. (2007). Testing and refining the direct and inferential mediation model of reading comprehension. *Journal of Educational Psychology, 99,* 311–325.

Crosnoe, R. (2009). Family–school connections and the transitions of low-income youths and

English language learners from middle school to high school. *Developmental Psychology, 45*(4), 1061–1076.

Crosnoe, R., & Elder, G. H., Jr. (2004). Family dynamics, supportive relationships, and educational resilience during adolescence. *Journal of Family Issues, 25*(5), 571–602.

Crosnoe, R., & Huston, A. C. (2007). Socioeconomic status, schooling, and the developmental trajectories of adolescents. *Developmental Psychology, 43,* 1097–1110.

Cross, S. L., Day, A. G., & Byers, L. G. (2010). American Indian grand families: A qualitative study conducted with grandmothers and grandfathers who provide sole care for their grandchildren. *Journal of Cross-Cultural Gerontology, 25*(4), 371–383. doi:10.1007/s10823-010-9127-5

Crowley, K., & Jacobs, M. (2002). Building islands of expertise in everyday family activity. In G. Leinhardt, K. Crowley, & K. Knutson (Eds.), *Learning conversations in museums* (pp. 333–356). Mahwah, NJ: Erlbaum.

Csikszentmihalyi, M. (1995). Education for the twenty-first century. *Daedalus, 124*(4), 107–114.

Csikszentmihalyi, M., & Larson, R. (1984). *Being adolescent: Conflict and growth in the teenage years.* New York: Basic Books.

Cummings, E. M., & Merrilees, C. E. (2010). Identifying the dynamic processes underlying links between marital conflict and child adjustment. In M. S. Schulz, M. K. Pruett, P. K. Kerig, & R. D. Parke (Eds.), *Strengthening couple relationships for optimal child development: Lessons from research and intervention* (pp. 27–40). Washington, DC: American Psychological Association.

Cummins, J. (1981). Age on arrival and immigrant second language learning in Canada: A reassessment. *Applied Linguistics, 2,* 132–149.

Cummins, J. (2000). *Language, power, and pedagogy: Bilingual children in the crossfire.* Clevedon, England: Multilingual Matters.

Cunningham, C. E., & Cunningham, L. J. (1998). Student-mediated conflict resolution programs. In R. A. Barkley (Ed.), *Attention-deficit hyperactivity disorder: A handbook for diagnosis and treatment* (2nd ed., pp. 491–509). New York: Guilford Press.

Cunningham, C. E., Cunningham, L. J., Ratcliffe, J., & Vaillancourt, T. (2010). A qualitative analysis of the bullying prevention and intervention recommendations of students in grades 5 to 8. *Journal of School Violence, 9*(4), 321–338. doi:10.1080/15388220.2010.507146

Cunningham, T. H., & Graham, C. R. (2000). Increasing native English vocabulary recognition through Spanish immersion: Cognate transfer from foreign to first language. *Journal of Educational Psychology, 92,* 37–49.

Cunningham, W. A., & Zelazo, P. D. (2010). The development of iterative reprocessing: Implications for affect and its regulation. In P. D. Zelazo, M. Chandler, & E. Crone (Eds.), *Developmental social cognitive neuroscience* (pp. 81–98). New York: Psychology Press.

Curtiss, S. (1977). *Genie: A psycholinguistic study of a modern-day "wild child."* New York: Academic Press.

Cushman, P., & Cowan, J. (2010). Enhancing student self-worth in the primary school learning environment: Teachers' views and students' views. *Pastoral Care in Education, 28*(2), 81–95.

Dabrowska, E., Rowland, C., & Theakston, A. (2009). The acquisition of questions with long-distance dependencies. *Cognitive Linguistics, 20*(3), 571–597.

Dahan, A., & McAfee, S. G. (2009). A proposed role for the psychiatrist in the treatment of adolescents with Type I diabetes. *Psychiatric Quarterly, 80*(2), 75-75-85. doi:10.1007/s11126-009-9099-1

Dahl, R. E., & Lewin, D. S. (2002). Pathways to adolescent health: Sleep regulation and behavior. *Journal of Adolescent Health, 31*(6 Suppl.), 175–184.

Dahlgren, S., Sandberg, A., & Larsson, M. (2010). Theory of mind in children with severe speech and physical impairments. *Research in Developmental Disabilities, 31*(2), 617–624. doi:10.1016/j.ridd.2009.12.010

Dahlin, B., & Watkins, D. (2000). The role of repetition in the processes of memorizing and understanding: A comparison of the views of Western and Chinese secondary students in Hong Kong. *British Journal of Educational Psychology, 70,* 65–84.

d'Ailly, H. (2003). Children's autonomy and perceived control in learning: A model of motivation and achievement in Taiwan. *Journal of Educational Psychology, 95,* 84–96.

Daley, T. C., Whaley, S. E., Sigman, M. D., Espinosa, M. P., & Neumann, C. (2003). IQ on the rise: The Flynn effect in rural Kenyan children. *Psychological Science, 14,* 215–219.

Damon, W. (1977). *The social world of the child.* San Francisco: Jossey-Bass.

Damon, W. (1981). Exploring children's social cognitions on two fronts. In J. M. Flavell & L. Ross (Eds.), *Social cognitive development: Frontiers and possible futures* (pp. 154–175). Cambridge, England: Cambridge University Press.

Damon, W. (1984). Peer education: The untapped potential. *Journal of Applied Developmental Psychology, 5,* 331–343.

Damon, W. (1988). *The moral child: Nurturing children's natural moral growth.* New York: Free Press.

Damon, W. (1991). Putting substance into self-esteem: A focus on academic and moral values. *Educational Horizons, 70*(1), 12–18.

Damon, W., & Hart, D. (1988). *Self-understanding in childhood and adolescence.* New York: Cambridge University Press.

DanceSafe. (2000a). *What is LSD?* Retrieved November 1, 2005, from http://www.dancesafe.org/documents/druginfo/lsd.php

DanceSafe. (2000b). *What is speed?* Retrieved November 1, 2005, from http://www.dancesafe.org/documents/druginfo/speed.php

Danckaerts, M., Sonuga-Barke, E. J. S., Banaschewski, T., Buitelaar, J., Döpfner, M., Hollis, C., et al. (2010). The quality of life of children with attention deficit/hyperactivity disorder: A systematic review. *European Child & Adolescent Psychiatry, 19*(2), 83–105.

Daniel, J. (2009). Intentionally thoughtful family engagement in early childhood education. *Young Children, 64*(5), 10–14.

Danner, F. W., & Day, M. C. (1977). Eliciting formal operations. *Child Development, 48,* 1600–1606.

Darling-Hammond, L. (1995). Inequality and access to knowledge. In J. A. Banks & C. A. M. Banks (Eds.), *Handbook of research on multicultural education.* New York: Macmillan.

Darling-Hammond, L., & Bransford, J. (Eds.). (2005). *Preparing teachers for a changing world: What teachers should learn and be able to do.* San Francisco: Jossey-Bass/Wiley.

Darling-Hammond, L., & Friedlaender, D. (2008, May). Creating excellent and equitable schools. *Educational Leadership, 65*(8), 14–21.

Darvin, J. (2009). Make books, not war: Workshops at a summer camp in Bosnia. *Literacy, 43*(1), 50–59.

Daunic, A. P., & Smith, S. W. (2010). Conflict resolution, peer mediation, and bullying prevention. In B. Algozzine, A. P. Daunic, & S. W. Smith (Eds.), *Preventing problem behaviors: Schoolwide programs and classroom practices* (2nd ed., pp. 113–132). Thousand Oaks, CA: Corwin Press

Davenport, E. C., Jr., Davison, M. L., Kuang, H., Ding, S., Kim, S., & Kwak, N. (1998). High school mathematics course-taking by gender and ethnicity. *American Educational Research Journal, 35,* 497–514.

Davidse, N., de Jong, M., Bus, A., Huijbregts, S., & Swaab, H. (2011). Cognitive and environmental predictors of early literacy skills. *Reading and Writing, 24*(4), 395–412. doi:10.1007/s11145-010-9233-3

Davidson, A. J., Gest, S. D., & Welsh, J. A. (2010). Relatedness with teachers and peers during early adolescence: An integrated variable-oriented and person-oriented approach. *Journal of School Psychology, 48*(6), 483–510. doi:10.1016/j.jsp.2010.08.002

Davidson, F. H. (1976). Ability to respect persons compared to ethnic prejudice in childhood. *Journal of Personality and Social Psychology, 34,* 1256–1267.

Davidson, J., Faulkner, R., & McPherson, G. (2009). Motivating musical learning. *The Psychologist, 22*(12), 1026–1029.

Davidson, M. R., London, M. L., & Ladewig, P. A. W. (2008). *Olds' maternal-newborn nursing and women's health across the lifespan.* Upper Saddle River, NJ: Pearson Prentice Hall.

Davidson, P., & Youniss, J. (1995). Moral development and social construction. In W. M. Kurtines & J. L. Gewirtz (Eds.), *Moral development: An introduction.* Boston: Allyn & Bacon.

Davies, C., & Uttal, D. H. (2007). Map use and the development of spatial cognition. In J. M. Plumert & J. P. Spencer (Eds.), *The emerging spatial mind* (pp. 219–247). New York: Oxford University Press.

Davies, P. T., Sturge-Apple, M. L., Woitach, M. J., & Cummings, E. M. (2009). A process analysis of the transmission of distress from interparental conflict to parenting: Adult relationship security as an explanatory mechanism. *Developmental Psychology, 45,* 1761–1773.

Davila, J. (2008). Depressive symptoms and adolescent romance: Theory, research, and implications. *Child Development Perspectives, 2*(1), 26–31.

Davis, A. C., & Jackson, J. W. (1998). *"Yo, little brother . . . ": Basic rules of survival for young African American males.* Chicago: African American Images.

Davis, B. (2001). The restorative power of emotions in Child Protective Services. *Child and Adolescent Social Work Journal, 18,* 437–454.

Davis, E. L., Levine, L. J., Lench, H. C., & Quas, J. A. (2010). Metacognitive emotion regulation: Children's awareness that changing thoughts and goals can alleviate negative emotions. *Emotion, 10*(4), 498–510.

Davis, G. A., & Rimm, S. B. (1998). *Education of the gifted and talented* (4th ed.). Boston: Allyn & Bacon.

Davis, G. A., & Thomas, M. A. (1989). *Effective schools and effective teachers.* Needham Heights, MA: Allyn & Bacon.

Davis, H. A. (2003). Conceptualizing the role and influence of student–teacher relationships on children's social and cognitive development. *Educational Psychologist, 38,* 207–234.

Davis, H. A., Schutz, P. A., & Chambless, C. B. (2001, April). *Uncovering the impact of social relationships in the classroom: Viewing relationships with teachers from different lenses.* Paper presented at the annual meeting of the American Educational Research Association, Seattle, WA.

Davis, J. H. (2008). *Why our schools need the arts.* New York: Teachers College Press.

Davis, T. S., Saltzburg, S., & Locke, C. R. (2009). Supporting the emotional and psychological well being of sexual minority youth: Youth ideas for action. *Children and Youth Services Review, 31*(9), 1030–1041. doi:10.1016/j.childyouth.2009.05.003

Davis-Kean, P. E., & Sandler, H. M. (2001). A meta-analysis of measures of self-esteem for young children: A framework for future measures. *Child Development, 72,* 887–906.

Dawood, K., Bailey, J. M., & Martin, N. G. (2009). Genetic and environmental influences on sexual orientation. In Y. Kim (Ed.), *Handbook of behavior genetics* (pp. 269–279). New York: Springer Science + Business Media. doi:10.1007/978-0-387-76727-7_19

De Brauwer, J., & Fias, W. (2009). A longitudinal study of children's performance on simple multiplication and division problems. *Developmental Psychology, 45*(5), 1480–1496.

de Castro-Manglano, P., Mechelli, A., Soutullo, C., Gimenez-Amaya, J., Ortuño, F., & McGuire, P. (2011). Longitudinal changes in brain structure following the first episode of psychosis. *Psychiatry Research: Neuroimaging, 191*(3), 166–173. doi:10.1016/j.pscychresns.2010.10.010

De Corte, E., Greer, B., & Verschaffel, L. (1996). Mathematics teaching and learning. In D. C. Berliner & R. C. Calfee (Eds.), *Handbook of educational psychology* (pp. 491–549). New York: Macmillan.

De Corte, E., Op't Eynde, P., Depaepe, F., & Verschaffel, L. (2010). The reflexive relation between students' mathematics-related beliefs and the mathematics classroom culture. In L. D. Bendixen & F. C. Feucht (Eds.), *Personal epistemology in the classroom: Theory, research, and implications for practice* (pp. 292–327). New York: Cambridge University Press.

De Corte, E., Op't Eynde, P., & Verschaffel, L. (2002). "Knowing what to believe": The relevance of students' mathematical beliefs for mathematics education. In B. K. Hofer & P. R. Pintrich (Eds.), *Personal epistemology: The psychology of beliefs about knowledge and knowing* (pp. 297–320). Mahwah, NJ: Erlbaum.

de Graaf, H., & Rademakers, J. (2006). Sexual behavior of prepubertal children. *Journal of Psychology and Human Sexuality, 18*(1), 1–21.

de Heering, A., Turati, C., Rossion, B., Bulf, H., Goffaux, V., & Simion, F. (2008). Newborns' face recognition is based on spatial frequencies below 0.5 cycles per degree. *Cognition, 106*(1), 444–454.

de Jong, T., & van Joolingen, W. R. (1998). Scientific discovery learning with computer simulations of conceptual domains. *Review of Educational Research, 68,* 179–201.

De La Paz, S. (2005). Effects of historical reasoning instruction and writing strategy mastery in culturally and academically diverse middle school classrooms. *Journal of Educational Psychology, 97,* 139–156.

De Lisi, R., & Golbeck, S. L. (1999). Implications of Piagetian theory for peer learning. In A. M. O'Donnell & A. King (Eds.), *Cognitive perspectives on peer learning* (pp. 3–37). Mahwah, NJ: Erlbaum.

De Lisi, R., & Wolford, J. I. (2002). Improving children's mental rotation accuracy with computer game playing. *Journal of Genetic Psychology, 16*(3), 272–282.

de Villiers, J. (1995). Empty categories and complex sentences: The case of wh- questions. In P. Fletcher & B. MacWhinney (Eds.), *The handbook of child language* (pp. 508–540). Oxford, England: Blackwell.

Deater-Deckard, K. (2009). Parenting the genotype. In K. McCartney & R. A. Weinberg (Eds.), *Experience and development: A festschrift in honor of Sandra Wood Scarr* (pp. 141–161). New York: Psychology Press.

Deater-Deckard, K., Dodge, K., Bates, J., & Pettit, G. (1996). Physical discipline among African American and European American mothers: Links to children's externalizing behaviors. *Developmental Psychology, 32,* 1065–1072.

Deaux, K. (1984). From individual differences to social categories: Analysis of a decade's research on gender. *American Psychologist, 39,* 105–116.

DeBose, C. E. (2007). The Ebonics phenomenon, language planning, and the hegemony of Standard English. In H. S. Alim & J. Baugh (Eds.), *Talkin Black talk: Language, education, and social change* (pp. 30–42). New York: Teachers College Press.

DeCasper, A. J., & Fifer, W. P. (1980). Of human bonding: Newborns prefer their mothers' voices. *Science, 208,* 1174–1176.

DeCasper, A. J., & Prescott, P. (2009). Lateralized processes constrain auditory reinforcement in human newborns. *Hearing Research, 255*(1–2), 135–141.

Deci, E. L. (1992). The relation of interest to the motivation of behavior: A self-determination theory perspective. In K. A. Renninger, S. Hidi, & A. Krapp (Eds.), *The role of interest in learning and development.* Hillsdale, NJ: Erlbaum.

Deci, E. L., & Ryan, R. M. (1985). *Intrinsic motivation and self-determination in human behavior.* New York: Plenum Press.

Deci, E. L., & Ryan, R. M. (1992). The initiation and regulation of intrinsically motivated learning and achievement. In A. K. Boggiano & T. S. Pittman (Eds.), *Achievement and motivation: A social-developmental perspective.* Cambridge, England: Cambridge University Press.

Deeters, K. M. (2008). *Investigating a computerized scaffolding software for student designed science investigations.* (Doctoral dissertation, University of Nebraska, Lincoln). Available from ProQuest Dissertations and Theses database. (UMI Microform 3352767)

Deitrick, L. M., & Draves, P. R. (2008). Attitudes toward doula support during pregnancy by clients, doulas, and labor-and-delivery nurses: A case study from Tampa, Florida. *Human Organization, 67*(4), 397–406.

Del Giudice, M., Manera, V., & Keysers, C. (2009). Programmed to learn? The ontogeny of mirror neurons. *Developmental Science, 12*(2), 350–363.

DeLamater, J., & MacCorquodale, P. (1979). *Premarital sexuality: Attitudes, relationships, behavior.* Madison: University of Wisconsin Press.

Delaney, K. R. (2006). Following the affect: Learning to observe emotional regulation. *Journal of Child and Adolescent Psychiatric Nursing, 19*(4), 175–181.

Delgado-Gaitan, C. (1994). Socializing young children in Mexican-American families: An intergenerational perspective. In P. M. Greenfield & R. R. Cocking (Eds.), *Cross-cultural roots of minority child development* (pp. 55–86). Hillsdale, NJ: Erlbaum.

DeLisle, J. R. (1984). *Gifted children speak out.* New York: Walker.

DeLoache, J. S. (2011). Early development of the understanding and use of symbolic artifacts In U. Goswami (Ed.), *The Wiley-Blackwell handbook of childhood cognitive development* (2nd ed., pp. 312–336). Malden, MA: Wiley-Blackwell.

DeLoache, J. S., Cassidy, D. J., & Brown, A. L. (1985). Precursors of mnemonic strategies in very young children's memory. *Child Development, 56,* 125–137.

DeLoache, J. S., & Ganea, P. A. (2009). Symbol-based learning in infancy. In A. Woodward & A. Needham (Eds.), *Learning and the infant mind* (pp. 263–285). New York: Oxford University Press.

DeLoache, J. S., Miller, K. F., & Rosengren, K. S. (1997). The credible shrinking room: Very young children's performance with symbolic and nonsymbolic relations. *Psychological Science, 8,* 308–313.

DeLoache, J. S., & Todd, C. M. (1988). Young children's use of spatial categorization as a mnemonic strategy. *Journal of Experimental Child Psychology, 46,* 1–20.

Demarest, R. J., & Charon, R. (1996). *An illustrated guide to human reproduction and fertility control.* New York: Parthenon.

Demetriou, A. (2000). Organization and development of self-understanding and self-regulation. In M. Boekaerts, P. Pintrich, & M. Zeidner (Eds.), *Handbook of self-regulation* (pp. 209–251). Sand Diego, CA: Academic Press.

Demetriou, A., Mouyi, A., & Spanoudis, G. (2008). Modelling the structure and development of g. *Intelligence, 36*(5), 437–454.

Dempster, F. N., & Corkill, A. J. (1999). Interference and inhibition in cognition and behavior: Unifying themes for educational psychology. *Educational Psychology Review, 11,* 1–88.

Denckla, M. B. (2007). Executive function: Binding together the definitions of attention-deficit/hyperactivity disorder and learning disabilities. In L. Meltzer (Ed.), *Executive function in education: From theory to practice* (pp. 5–18). New York: Guilford Press.

Dennis, T. A., Cole, P. M., Wiggins, C. N., Cohen, L. H., & Zalewski, M. (2009). The functional organization of preschool-age children's emotion expressions and actions in challenging situations. *Emotion, 9*(4), 520–530.

Denno, D. M., Carr, V., & Bell, S. H. (2010). *Addressing challenging behaviors in early childhood settings: A teacher's guide.* Baltimore, MD: Paul H. Brookes.

Deshler, D. D. (2005). Adolescents with learning disabilities: Unique challenges and reasons for hope. *Learning Disability Quarterly, 28*(2), 122–124.

Deshler, D. D., & Schumaker, J. B. (1988). An instructional model for teaching students how to learn. In J. L. Graden, J. E. Zins, & M. J. Curtis (Eds.), *Alternative educational delivery systems: Enhancing instructional options for all students.* Washington, DC: National Association of School Psychologists.

Desoete, A. (2009). Metacognitive prediction and evaluation skills and mathematical learning in third-grade students. *Educational Research and Evaluation, 15*(5), 435–446.

Dessel, A. (2010). Prejudice in schools: Promotion of an inclusive culture and climate. *Education and Urban Society, 42*(4), 407–429.

Deutsch, M. (1993). Educating for a peaceful world. *American Psychologist, 48,* 510–517.

Devlin, B., Daniels, M., & Roeder, K. (1997). The heritability of IQ. *Nature, 388*(6641), 468–471.

Devlin, B., Fienberg, S. E., Resnick, D. P., & Roeder, K. (1995). Galton redux: Intelligence, race, and society: A review of "The Bell Curve: Intelligence and Class Structure in American Life." *American Statistician, 90,* 1483–1488.

DeVoe, J. F., Peter, K., Kaufman, P., Ruddy, S. A., Miller, A. K., Planty, M., et al. (2003). *Indicators of school crime and safety: 2002* (NCES 2003-009/NCJ 196753). Washington, DC: U.S. Departments of Education and Justice.

DeVries, R. (1997). Piaget's social theory. *Educational Researcher, 26*(2), 4–17.

DeVries, R., & Zan, B. (1996). A constructivist perspective on the role of the sociomoral atmosphere in promoting children's development. In C. T. Fosnot (Ed.), *Constructivism: Theory, perspectives, and practice.* New York: Teachers College Press.

Deyhle, D., & LeCompte, M. (1999). Cultural differences in child development: Navajo adolescents in middle schools. In R. H. Sheets & E. R. Hollins (Eds.), *Racial and ethnic identity in school practices: Aspects of human development* (pp. 123–139). Mahwah, NJ: Erlbaum.

Di Giunta, L., Pastorelli, C., Eisenberg, N., Gerbino, M., Castellani, V., & Bombi, A. S. (2010). Developmental trajectories of physical aggression: Prediction of overt and covert antisocial behaviors from self- and mothers' reports. *European Child & Adolescent Psychiatry, 19*(12), 873–882. doi:10.1007/s00787-010-0134-4

Diagram Group. (1983). *The human body on file.* New York: Facts on File.

Diamond, A., Barnett, W. S., Thomas, J., & Munro, S. (2007). Preschool program improves cognitive control. *Science, 318*(5855), 1387–1388. doi:10.1126/science.1151148

Diamond, M., & Hopson, J. (1998). *Magic trees of the mind.* New York: Dutton.

Diamond, S. C. (1991). What to do when you can't do anything: Working with disturbed adolescents. *Clearing House, 64,* 232–234.

Diaz, R. M. (1983). Thought and two languages: The impact of bilingualism on cognitive development. In E. W. Gordon (Ed.), *Review of research in education* (Vol. 10). Washington, DC: American Educational Research Association.

Diaz, R. M., & Berndt, T. J. (1982). Children's knowledge of best friend: Fact or fancy? *Developmental Psychology, 18,* 787–794.

Diaz, R. M., & Klingler, C. (1991). Toward an explanatory model of the interaction between bilingualism and cognitive development. In E. Bialystok (Ed.), *Language processing in bilingual children.* Cambridge, England: Cambridge University Press.

Dibbens, L. M., Heron, S. E., & Mulley, J. C. (2007). A polygenic heterogeneity model for common epilepsies with complex genetics. *Genes, Brain & Behavior, 6,* 593–597.

Dichele, A., & Gordon, M. (2007). Literacy in urban education: Problems and promises. In J. L. Kincheloe, K. Hayes, K. Rose, & P. M. Anderson (Eds.), *Urban education: A comprehensive guide for educators, parents, and teachers* (pp. 263–273). Lanham, MD: Rowman & Littlefield Education.

Dickens, W. T., & Flynn, J. R. (2001). Heritability estimates versus large environmental effects: The IQ paradox resolved. *Psychological Review, 108,* 346–369.

Dickinson, D., Wolf, M., & Stotsky, S. (1993). Words move: The interwoven development of oral and written language. In J. B. Gleason (Ed.), *The development of language.* Boston: Allyn & Bacon.

Dick-Read, G. (1944). *Childbirth without fear.* New York: Harper & Brothers.

Dien, T. (1998). Language and literacy in Vietnamese American communities. In B. Pérez (Ed.), *Sociocultural contexts of language and literacy.* Mahwah, NJ: Erlbaum.

Diesendruck, G., & Lindenbaum, T. (2009). Self-protective optimism: Children's biased beliefs about the stability of traits. *Social Development, 18*(4), 946–961.

Dilworth-Bart J. E., & Moore, C. F. (2006). Mercy mercy me: Social injustice and the prevention of environmental pollutant exposures among ethnic minority and poor children. *Child Development, 77*(2), 247–265.

Dimech, A. S., & Seiler, R. (2010). The association between extra-curricular sport participation and social anxiety symptoms in children. *Journal of Clinical Sport Psychology, 4*(3), 191–203.

Dion, E., Brodeur, M., Gosselin, C., Campeau, M., & Fuchs, D. (2010). Implementing research-based instruction to prevent reading problems among low-income students: Is earlier better? *Learning Disabilities Research & Practice, 25*(2), 87–96.

DiPietro, J. A. (2004). The role of prenatal maternal stress in child development. *Current Directions in Psychological Science, 13,* 71–74.

diSessa, A. A. (1996). What do "just plain folk" know about physics? In D. R. Olson & N. Torrance (Eds.), *The handbook of education and human development: New models of learning, teaching, and schooling.* Cambridge, MA: Blackwell.

diSessa, A. A. (2006). A history of conceptual change research. In R. K. Sawyer (Ed.), *The Cambridge handbook of the learning sciences* (pp. 265–281). Cambridge, England: Cambridge University Press.

diSessa, A. A. (2007). An interactional analysis of clinical interviewing. *Cognition and Instruction, 25,* 523–565.

diSessa, A. A., Gillespie, N. M., & Esterly, J. B. (2004). Coherence versus fragmentation in the development in the concept of force. *Cognitive Science, 28,* 843–900.

Dix, T., Stewart, A. D., Gershoff, E. T., & Day, W. H. (2007). Autonomy and children's reactions to being controlled: Evidence that both compliance and defiance may be positive markers in early development. *Child Development, 78,* 1204–1221.

Dixon, J. A., & Kelley, E. (2007). Theory revision and redescription. *Current Directions in Psychological Science, 16,* 111–115.

Dixon, M. L., Zelazo, P. D., & De Rosa, E. (2010). Evidence for intact memory-guided attention in school-aged children. *Developmental Science, 13*(1), 161–169.

Dodge, K. A. (1983). Behavioral antecedents of peer social status. *Child Development, 54,* 1386–1399.

Dodge, K. A., Bates, J. E., & Pettit, G. S. (1990). Mechanisms in the cycle of violence. *Science, 250,* 1678–1683.

Dodge, K. A., Coie, J. D., & Brakke, N. P. (1982). Behavior patterns of socially rejected and neglected preadolescents: The role of social approach and aggression. *Journal of Abnormal Child Psychology, 10,* 389–410.

Dodge, K. A., Coie, J., & Lynam, D. (2006). Aggression and antisocial behavior in youth. In W. Damon & R. M. Lerner (Series Eds.) & N. Eisenberg (Vol. Ed.), *Handbook of child psychology: Vol. 3. Social, emotional, and personality development* (6th ed., pp. 719–788). New York: Wiley.

Dodge, K. A., Lansford, J. E., Burks, V. S., Bates, J. E., Pettit, G. S., Fontaine, R., et al. (2003). Peer rejection and social information-processing factors in the development of aggressive behavior problems in children. *Child Development, 74,* 374–393.

Dodge, K. A., Schlundt, D. G., Schocken, I., & Delugach, J. D. (1983). Social competence and children's social status: The role of peer group entry strategies. *Merrill-Palmer Quarterly, 29,* 309–336.

Doehnert, M., Brandeis, D., Imhof, K., Drechsler, R., & Steinhausen, H. (2010). Mapping attention-deficit/hyperactivity disorder from childhood to adolescence—No neurophysiologic evidence for a developmental lag of attention but some for inhibition. *Biological Psychiatry, 67*(7), 608–616.

Doescher, S. M., & Sugawara, A. I. (1989). Encouraging prosocial behavior in young children. *Childhood Education, 65,* 213–216.

Dohnt, H., & Tiggemann, M. (2006). The contribution of peer and media influences to the development of body satisfaction and self-esteem in young girls: A prospective study. *Developmental Psychology, 42,* 929–936.

Dolan, M. M., Casanueva, C., Smith, K. R., & Bradley, R. H. (2009). Parenting and the home environment provided by grandmothers of children in the child welfare system. *Children and Youth Services Review, 31,* 784–796.

Dolan, S., Biermann, J., & Damus, K. (2007). Genomics for health in preconception and prenatal periods. *Journal of Nursing Scholarship, 39*(1), 4–9.

Dominé, F., Berchtold, A., Akré, C., Michaud, P.-A., & Suris, J.-C. (2009). Disordered eating behaviors: What about boys? *Journal of Adolescent Health, 44,* 111–117.

Domitrovich, C. E., Cortes, R. C., & Greenberg, M. T. (2007). Improving young children's social and emotional competence: A randomized trial of the preschool "PATHS" curriculum. *Journal of Primary Prevention, 28,* 67–91.

Donaldson, M. (1978). *Children's minds.* New York: Norton.

Donaldson, S. K., & Westerman, M. A. (1986). Development of children's understanding of ambivalence and causal theories of emotion. *Developmental Psychology, 22,* 655–662.

Donato, F., Assanelli, D., Chiesa, R., Poeta, M. L., Tomansoni, V., & Turla, C. (1997). Cigarette smoking and sports participation in adolescents: A cross-sectional survey among high school students in Italy. *Substance Use and Misuse, 32,* 1555–1572.

Donovan, C. A. (1999, April). *"Stories have a beginning, a middle, and an end. Information only has a beginning": Elementary school children's genre and writing development.* Paper presented at the annual meeting of the American Educational Research Association, San Diego, CA.

Dornbusch, S. M., Carlsmith, J. M., Gross, R. T., Martin, J. A., Jennings, D., Rosenberg, A., et al. (1981). Sexual development, age, and dating: A comparison of biological and social influences upon one set of behaviors. *Child Development, 52,* 179–185.

Dornbusch, S. M., Ritter, P. L., Leiderman, P. H., Roberts, D. F., & Fraleigh, M. J. (1987). The relation of parenting style to adolescent school performance. *Child Development, 58,* 1244–1257.

Dotson-Blake, K. P., Foster, V. A., & Gressard, C. F. (2009). Ending the silence of Mexican immigrant voice in public education: Creating culturally inclusive family–school–community partnerships. *Professional School Counseling, 12*(3), 230–239.

Dovidio, J. F., & Gaertner, S. L. (1999). Reducing prejudice: Combating intergroup biases. *Current Directions in Psychological Science, 8,* 101–105.

Dowdy, J. K. (2002). Ovuh Dyuh. In L. Delpit & J. K. Dowdy (Eds.), *The skin that we speak: Thoughts on language and culture in the classroom* (pp. 3–13). New York: The New Press.

Downer, J. T., Booren, L. M., Lima, O. K., Luckner, A. E., & Pianta, R. C. (2010). The individualized classroom assessment scoring system (inCLASS): Preliminary reliability and validity of a system for observing preschoolers' competence in classroom interactions. *Early Childhood Research Quarterly, 25*(1), 1–16. doi:10.1016/j.ecresq.2009.08.004

Downey, J. (2000, March). *The role of schools in adolescent resilience: Recommendations from the literature.* Paper presented at the International Association of Adolescent Health, Washington, DC.

Dowson, M., & McInerney, D. M. (2001). Psychological parameters of students' social and work avoidance goals: A qualitative investigation. *Journal of Educational Psychology, 93,* 35–42.

Doyle, A. (1982). Friends, acquaintances, and strangers: The influence of familiarity and ethnolinguistic background on social interaction. In K. H. Rubin & H. S. Ross (Eds.), *Peer relationships and social skills in childhood* (pp. 229–252). New York: Springer-Verlag.

Doyle, P. A., Bird, B. C., Appel, S., Parisi, D., Rogers, P., Glarso, R., et al. (2006). Developing an effective communications campaign to reach pregnant women at high risk of late or no prenatal care. *Social Marketing Quarterly, 12*(4), 35–50.

Doyle, W. (1986). Classroom organization and management. In M. C. Wittrock (Ed.), *Handbook of research on teaching* (3rd ed.). New York: Macmillan.

Dray, A. J., & Selman, R. L., & Schultz, L. H. (2009). Communicating with intent: A study of social awareness and children's writing. *Journal of Applied Developmental Psychology, 30,* 116–128.

Dreweke, J., & Wind, R. (2007, May). *Strong evidence favors comprehensive approach to sex ed.* Guttmacher Institute Media Center. Retrieved February 1, 2008, from http://www.guttmacher.org/media/nr/2007/05/23/index.html

Drugli, M. B., Fossum, S., Larsson, B., & Morch, W. (2010). Characteristics of young children with persistent conduct problems 1 year after treatment with the incredible years program. *European Child & Adolescent Psychiatry, 19*(7), 559–565.

Dryden, M. A., & Jefferson, P. (1994, April). *Use of background knowledge and reading achievement among elementary school students.* Paper presented at the annual meeting of the American Educational Research Association, New Orleans, LA.

Dryfoos, J. G. (1997). The prevalence of problem behaviors: Implications for programs. In R. P. Weissberg, T. P. Gullotta, R. L. Hamptom, B. A. Ryan, & G. R. Adams (Eds.), *Enhancing children's wellness* (Vol. 8, pp. 17–46). Thousand Oaks, CA: Sage.

Dryfoos, J. G. (1999, Fall). The role of the school in children's out-of-school time. *The Future of Children: When School Is Out, 9,* 117–134.

Dube, M., Julien, D., Lebeau, E., & Gagnon, I. (2000). Marital satisfaction of mothers and the quality of daily interaction with their adolescents. *Canadian Journal of Behavioural Science, 32,* 18–28.

Duchesne, S., & Ratelle, C. (2010). Parental behaviors and adolescents' achievement goals at the beginning of middle school: Emotional problems as potential mediators. *Journal of Educational Psychology, 102*(2), 497–507. doi:10.1037/a0019320

Duckworth, A. L., & Seligman, M. E. P. (2005). Self-discipline outdoes IQ in predicting academic performance of adolescents. *Psychological Science, 16,* 939–944.

Duckworth, A. L., & Seligman, M. E. P. (2006). Self-discipline gives girls the edge: Gender in self-discipline, grades, and achievement test scores. *Journal of Educational Psychology, 98,* 198–208.

Duncan, G. J., Dowsett, C. J., Claessens, A., Magnuson, K., Huston, A. C., Klebanov, P., et al. (2007). School readiness and later achievement. *Developmental Psychology, 43,* 1428–1446.

Dunham, P. J., Dunham, F., & Curwin, A. (1993). Joint-attentional states and lexical acquisition at 18 months. *Developmental Psychology, 29,* 827–831.

Dunkel, C. S., & Sefcek, J. A. (2009). Eriksonian lifespan theory and life history theory: An integration using the example of identity formation. *Review of General Psychology, 13*(1), 13–23.

Dunn, J. (1984). *Sisters and brothers.* Cambridge, MA: Harvard University Press.

Dunn, J. (2006). Moral development in early childhood and social interaction in the family. In M. Killen & J. G. Smetana (Eds.), *Handbook of moral development* (pp. 331–350). Mahwah, NJ: Erlbaum.

Dunn, J. (2007). Siblings and socialization. In J. E. Grusec & P. D. Hastings (Eds.), *Handbook of socialization: Theory and research* (pp. 309–327). New York: Guilford Press.

Dunn, J., Brown, J., & Beardsall, L. (1991). Family talk about feeling states and children's later understanding of others' emotions. *Developmental Psychology, 27,* 448–455.

Dunn, J., & Munn, P. (1985). Becoming a family member: Family conflict and the development of social understanding in the second year. *Child Development, 56,* 480–492.

Dunn, L. S. (2011, February). Making the most of your class website. *Educational Leadership, 68*(5), 60–62.

Dunsmore, J. C., Noguchi, R. J. P., Garner, P. W., Casey, E. C., & Bhullar, N. (2008). Gender-specific linkages of affective social competence with peer relations in preschool children. *Early Education and Development, 19*(2), 211–237.

DuPaul, G., & Hoff, K. (1998). Reducing disruptive behavior in general education classrooms: The use of self-management strategies. *School Psychology Review, 27,* 290–304.

Durand, V. M. (1998). *Sleep better: A guide to improving sleep for children with special needs.* Baltimore, MD: Paul H. Brookes.

Durik, A., M., Vida, M., & Eccles, J. S. (2006). Task values and ability beliefs as predictors of high school literacy choices: A developmental analysis. *Journal of Educational Psychology, 98,* 382–393.

Durkin, K., & Conti-Ramsden, G. (2007). Language, social behavior, and the quality of friendships in adolescents with and without a history of specific language impairment. *Child Development, 78,* 1441–1457.

Durlak, J. A., Mahoney, J. L., Bohnert, A. M., & Parente, M. E. (2010). Developing and improving after-school programs to enhance youth's personal growth and adjustment: A special issue of AJCP. *American Journal of Community Psychology, 45*(3–4), 285–293. doi:10.1007/s10464-010-9298-9

Durlak, J. A., Weissberg, R. P., Dymnicki, A. B., Taylor, R. D., & Schellinger, K. B. (2011). The impact of enhancing students' social and emotional learning: A meta-analysis of school-based universal interventions. *Child Development, 82*(1), 405–432. doi:10.1111/j.1467-8624.2010.01564.x

Dwairy, M., Achoui, M., Abouserie, R., Farah, A., Sakhleh, A. A., Fayad, M., et al. (2006). Parenting styles in Arab societies: A first cross-regional research study. *Journal of Cross Cultural Psychology, 37,* 230–247.

Dweck, C. S. (1975). The role of expectations and attributions in the alleviation of learned helplessness. *Journal of Personality and Social Psychology, 31,* 674–685.

Dweck, C. S. (1986). Motivational processes affecting learning. *American Psychologist, 41,* 1040–1048.

Dweck, C. S. (2000). *Self-theories: Their role in motivation, personality, and development.* Philadelphia, PA: Psychology Press.

Dweck, C. S. (2009). Foreword. In F. D. Horowitz, R. F. Subotnik & D. J. Matthews (Eds.), *The development of giftedness and talent across the life span* (pp. xi–xiv). Washington, DC: American Psychological Association.

Dweck, C. S., & Elliott, E. S. (1983). Achievement motivation. In E. M. Hetherington (Ed.), *Handbook of child psychology: Vol. 4. Socialization, personality, and social development* (4th ed.). New York: Wiley.

Dweck, C. S., & Master, A. (2009). Self-theories and motivation: Students' beliefs about intelligence. K. R. Wentzel & A. Wigfield (Eds.), *Handbook of motivation at school* (pp. 123–140). New York: Routledge/Taylor & Francis Group.

Dweck, C. S., Mangels, J. A., & Good, C. (2004). Motivational effects on attention, cognition, and performance. In D. Y. Dai & R. J. Sternberg (Eds.), *Motivation, emotion, and cognition: Integrative perspectives on intellectual functioning and development* (pp. 41–55). Mahwah, NJ: Erlbaum.

Dwyer, K., & Osher, D. (2000). *Safeguarding our children: An action guide.* Washington, DC: U.S. Departments of Education and Justice, American Institutes for Research. Retrieved February 26, 2004, from http://www.ed.gov/pubs/edpubs.html

Dwyer, K., Osher, D., & Warger, C. (1998). *Early warning, timely response: A guide to safe schools.* Washington, DC: U.S. Department of Education. Retrieved February 26, 2004, from http://www.ed.gov/offices/OSERS/OSEP/earlywrn.html

Dykens, E. M., & Cassidy, S. B. (1999). Prader-Willi syndrome. In S. Goldstein & C. R. Reynolds (Eds.), *Handbook of neurodevelopmental and genetic disorders* (pp. 525–554). New York: Guilford Press.

Eagly, A. H. (1987). *Sex differences in social behavior: A social-role interpretation.* Hillsdale, NJ: Erlbaum.

Eamon, M. K., & Mulder, C. (2005). Predicting antisocial behavior among Latino young adolescents: An ecological systems analysis. *American Journal of Orthopsychiatry, 75,* 117–127.

Early, D. M., Maxwell, K. L., Burchinal M., Alva, S., Bender, R. H., Bryant, D., et al. (2007). Teachers' education, classroom quality, and young children's academic skills: Results from seven studies of preschool programs. *Child Development, 78,* 558–580.

Ebbeck, M., & Yim, H. Y. B. (2009). Rethinking attachment: fostering positive relationships between infants, toddlers and their primary caregivers. *Early Child Development & Care, 179*(7), 899–909. doi:10.1080/03004430701567934

Eberhardt, M. (2009). The sociolinguistics of ethnicity in Pittsburgh. *Language and Linguistics Compass, 3*(6), 1443–1454.

Eccles, J. (2010, April). *Race/ethnicity as a context for adolescent development.* Paper presented at the annual meeting of the Rocky Mountain Psychological Association, Denver.

Eccles, J. S. (2007). Families, schools, and developing achievement-related motivations and engagement. In J. E. Grusec & P. D. Hastings (Eds.), *Handbook of socialization: Theory and research* (pp. 665–691). New York: Guilford Press.

Eccles, J. S., Freedman-Doan, C., Frome, P., Jacobs, J., & Yoon, K. S. (2000). Gender-role socialization in the family: A longitudinal approach. In T. Eckes & H. M. Trautner (Eds.), *The developmental social psychology of gender* (pp. 333–360). Mahwah, NH: Erlbaum.

Eccles, J. S., & Midgley, C. (1989). Stage-environment fit: Developmentally appropriate classrooms for young adolescents. In C. Ames & R. Ames (Eds.), *Research on motivation in education: Vol. 3. Goals and cognition.* San Diego, CA: Academic Press.

Eccles, J. S., & Roeser, R. W. (2009). Schools, academic motivation, and stage-environment fit. In R. M. Lerner & L. Steinberg (Eds.), *Handbook of adolescent psychology, Vol. 1: Individual bases of adolescent development* (3rd ed., pp. 404–434). Hoboken, NJ: Wiley.

Eccles, J. S., & Wigfield, A. (1985). Teacher expectations and student motivation. In J. B. Dusek (Ed.), *Teacher expectancies.* Hillsdale, NJ: Erlbaum.

Eccles, J. S., Wigfield, A., & Schiefele, U. (1998). Motivation to succeed. In W. Damon (Series Ed.) & N. Eisenberg (Vol. Ed.), *Handbook of child psychology: Vol 3. Social, emotional, and personality development* (5th ed., pp. 1017–1095). New York: Wiley.

Eccles (Parsons), J. S. (1983). Expectancies, values, and academic behaviors. In J. T. Spence (Ed.), *Achievement and achievement motivation.* San Francisco: Freeman.

Eckerman, C. O. (1979). The human infant in social interaction. In R. Cairns (Ed.), *The analysis of social interactions: Methods, issues, and illustrations* (pp. 163–178). Hillsdale, NJ: Erlbaum.

Edens, K. M., & Potter, E. F. (2001). Promoting conceptual understanding through pictorial representation. *Studies in Art Education, 42,* 214–233.

Edmonds, C. J., & Pring, L. (2006). Generating inferences from written and spoken language: A comparison of children with visual impairment and children with sight. *British Journal of Developmental Psychology, 24*(2), 337–351.

Edmunds, A. L., & Edmunds, G. A. (2005). Sensitivity: A double-edged sword for the pre-adolescent and adolescent gifted child. *Roeper Review, 27*(2), 69–77.

Edwards, O. W., & Taub, G. E. (2009). A conceptual pathways model to promote positive youth development in children raised by their grandparents. *School Psychology Quarterly, 24,* 160–172.

Edwards, P. A., & Garcia, G. E. (1994). The implications of Vygotskian theory for the development of home-school programs: A focus on storybook reading. In V. John-Steiner, C. P. Panofsky, & L. W. Smith (Eds.), *Sociocultural approaches to language and literacy: An interactionist perspective.* Cambridge, England: Cambridge University Press.

Eeds, M., & Wells, D. (1989). Grand conversations: An explanation of meaning construction in literature study groups. *Research in the Teaching of English, 23,* 4–29.

Egan, L. C., Santos, L. R., & Bloom, P. (2007). The origins of cognitive dissonance: Evidence from children and monkeys. *Psychological Science, 18,* 978–983.

Egeland, B. (2009). Taking stock: Childhood emotional maltreatment and developmental psychopathology. *Child Abuse and Neglect, 33,* 22–26.

Egilson, S. T., & Traustadottir, R. (2009). Assistance to pupils with physical disabilities in regular schools: Promoting inclusion or creating dependency? *European Journal of Special Needs Education, 24*(1), 21–36. doi:10.1080/08856250802596766

Ehri, L. C. (1991). Development of the ability to read words. In P. D. Pearson (Ed.), *Handbook of reading research* (Vol. II). New York: Longman.

Ehri, L. C. (1994). Development of the ability to read words: Update. In R. B. Ruddell, M. R. Ruddell, & H. Singer (Eds.), *Theoretical models and processes of reading* (4th ed.). Newark, DE: International Reading Association.

Ehri, L. C., Dreyer, L. G., Flugman, B., & Gross, A. (2007). Reading Rescue: An effective tutoring intervention model for language-minority students who are struggling readers in first grade. *American Educational Research Journal, 44,* 414–448.

Ehri, L. C., & Robbins, C. (1992). Beginners need some decoding skill to read words by analogy. *Reading Research Quarterly, 27,* 12–27.

Ehrler, D. J., Evans, J. G., & McGhee, R. L. (1999). Extending big-five theory into childhood: A preliminary investigation into the relationship between big-five personality traits and behavior problems in children. *Psychology in the Schools, 36,* 451–458.

Ehrlich, S. Z., & Blum-Kulka, S. (2010). Peer talk as a 'double opportunity space': The case of argumentative discourse. *Discourse & Society, 21*(2), 211–233. doi:10.1177/0957926509353847

Eigsti, I.-M., Zayas, V., Mischel, W., Shoda, Y., Ayduk, O., Dadlani, M. B., Davidson, M. C., Aber, J. L., & Casey, B. J. (2006). Predicting cognitive control from preschool to late adolescence and young adulthood. *Psychological Science, 17,* 478–484.

Eilam, B. (2001). Primary strategies for promoting homework performance. *American Educational Research Journal, 38,* 691–725.

Eilers, R. E., & Oller, D. K. (1994). Infant vocalizations and early diagnosis of severe hearing impairment. *Journal of Pediatrics, 124,* 199–203.

Eisenberg, N. (1982). The development of reasoning regarding prosocial behavior. In N. Eisenberg (Ed.), *The development of prosocial behavior.* New York: Academic Press.

Eisenberg, N. (1992). *The caring child.* Cambridge, MA: Harvard University Press.

Eisenberg, N. (1995). Prosocial development: A multifaceted model. In W. M. Kurtines & J. L. Gewirtz (Eds.), *Moral development: An introduction.* Boston: Allyn & Bacon.

Eisenberg, N. (2006). Emotion-related regulation. In H. E. Fitzgerald, B. M. Lester, & B. Zuckerman (Vol. Eds.), & H. E. Fitzgerald, R. Zucker, & K. Freeark (Eds. in Chief), *The crisis in youth mental health: Critical issues and effective programs. Vol. 1:*

Childhood disorders (pp. 133–155). Westport, CT: Praeger.

Eisenberg, N., Carlo, G., Murphy, B., & Van Court, N. (1995). Prosocial development in late adolescence: A longitudinal study. *Child Development, 66,* 1179–1197.

Eisenberg, N., Chang, L., Ma, Y., & Huang, X. (2009). Relations of parenting style to Chinese children's effortful control, ego resilience, and maladjustment. *Development and Psychopathology, 21,* 455–477.

Eisenberg, N., Cumberland, A., & Spinrad, T. L. (1988). Parental socialization of emotion. *Psychological Inquiry, 9,* 241–273.

Eisenberg, N., Eggum, N. D., & Edwards, A. (2010). Empathy-related responding and moral development. In W. F. Arsenio & E. A. Lemerise (Eds.), *Emotions, aggression, and morality in children: Bridging development and psychopathology* (pp. 115–135). Washington, DC: American Psychological Association.

Eisenberg, N., & Fabes, R. A. (1998). Prosocial development. In W. Damon (Series Ed.) & N. Eisenberg (Vol. Ed.), *Handbook of child psychology: Vol. 3. Social, emotional, and personality development* (pp. 701–778). New York: Wiley.

Eisenberg, N., Fabes, R. A., Carlo, G., & Karbon, M. (1992). Emotional responsivity to others: Behavioral correlates and socialization antecedents. In N. Eisenberg & R. A. Fabes (Eds.), *New directions in child development* (No. 55, pp. 57–73). San Francisco: Jossey-Bass.

Eisenberg, N., Fabes, R. A., Schaller, M., Carlo, G., & Miller, P. A. (1991). The relations of parental characteristics and practices to children's vicarious emotional responding. *Child Development, 62,* 1393–1408.

Eisenberg, N., Fabes, R. A., & Spinrad, T. L. (2006). Prosocial development. In W. Damon & R. M. Lerner (Series Eds.) & N. Eisenberg (Vol. Ed.), *Handbook of child psychology: Vol. 3. Social, emotional, and personality development* (6th ed., pp. 646–718). New York: Wiley.

Eisenberg, N., Lennon, R., & Pasternack, J. F. (1986). Altruistic values and moral judgment. In N. Eisenberg (Ed.), *Altruistic emotion, cognition, and behavior.* Hillsdale, NJ: Erlbaum.

Eisenberg, N., Martin, C. L., & Fabes, R. A. (1996). Gender development and gender effects. In D. C. Berliner & R. C. Calfee (Eds.), *Handbook of educational psychology.* New York: Macmillan.

Eisenberg, N., Miller, P. A., Shell, R., McNalley, S., & Shea, C. (1991). Prosocial development in adolescence: A longitudinal study. *Developmental Psychology, 27,* 849–857.

Eisenberg, N., Spinrad, T. L., & Sadovsky, A. (2006). Empathy-related responding in children. In M. Killen & J. G. Smetana (Eds.), *Handbook of moral development* (pp. 517–549). Mahwah, NJ: Erlbaum.

Eisenberg, N., Zhou, Q., & Koller, S. (2001). Brazilian adolescents' prosocial moral judgment and behavior: Relations to sympathy, perspective taking, gender-role orientation, and demographic characteristics. *Child Development, 72,* 518–534.

Eisenberger, R. (1992). Learned industriousness. *Psychological Review, 99,* 248–267.

Ekelin, M., Crang-Svalenius, E., & Dykes, A. K. (2004). A qualitative study of mothers' and fathers' experiences of routine ultrasound examination in Sweden. *Midwifery, 20,* 335–344.

Elbro, C., & Petersen, D. K. (2004). Long-term effects of phoneme awareness and letter sound training: An intervention study with children at risk for dyslexia. *Journal of Educational Psychology, 96,* 660–670.

Elder, A. D. (2002). Characterizing fifth grade students' epistemological beliefs in science. In B. K. Hofer & P. R. Pintrich (Eds.), *Personal epistemology: The psychology of beliefs about knowledge and knowing* (pp. 347–363). Mahwah, NJ: Erlbaum.

El-Dib, M., Massaro, A. N., Glass, P., & Aly, H. (2011). Neurodevelopmental assessment of the newborn: An opportunity for prediction of outcome. *Brain & Development, 33*(2), 95–105. doi:10.1016/j.braindev.2010.04.004

Elia, J. P. (1994). Homophobia in the high school: A problem in need of a resolution. *Journal of Homosexuality, 77*(1), 177–185.

Elias, G., & Broerse, J. (1996). Developmental changes in the incidence and likelihood of simultaneous talk during the first two years: A question of function. *Journal of Child Language, 23,* 201–217.

Elkind, D. (1981a). *Children and adolescents: Interpretive essays on Jean Piaget* (3rd ed.). New York: Oxford University Press.

Elkind, D. (1981b). *The hurried child: Growing up too fast too soon.* Reading, MA: Addison-Wesley.

Elkind, D. (2007). *The power of play: How spontaneous, imaginative activities lead to happier, healthier children.* Cambridge, MA: Da Capo Lifelong Books.

Elliot, A. J., & McGregor, H. A. (2000, April). Approach and avoidance goals and autonomous-controlled regulation: Empirical and conceptual relations. In A. Assor (Chair), *Self-determination theory and achievement goal theory: Convergences, divergences, and educational implications.* Symposium conducted at the annual meeting of the American Educational Research Association, New Orleans, LA.

Elliott, D. J. (1995). *Music matters: A new philosophy of music education.* New York: Oxford University Press.

Elliott, R., & Vasta, R. (1970). The modeling of sharing: Effects associated with vicarious reinforcement, symbolization, age, and generalization. *Journal of Experimental Child Psychology, 10,* 8–15.

Elmore, G. M., & Huebner, E. S. (2010). Adolescents' satisfaction with school experiences: Relationships with demographics, attachment relationships, and school engagement behavior. *Psychology in the Schools, 47*(6), 525–537.

Else-Quest, N. M., Hyde, J. S., & Linn, M. C. (2010). Cross-national patterns of gender differences in mathematics: A meta-analysis. *Psychological Bulletin, 136*(1), 103–127.

Elze, D. E. (2003). Gay, lesbian, and bisexual youths' perceptions of their high school environments and comfort in school. *Children and Schools, 25*(4), 225–239.

Emde, R., Gaensbauer, T., & Harmon, R. (1976). *Emotional expression in infancy: A biobehavioral study* (Psychological Issues, Vol. 10, No. 37). New York: International Universities Press.

Emde, R. N., & Buchsbaum, H. (1990). "Didn't you hear my mommy?" Autonomy with connectedness in moral self-emergence. In D. Cicchetti & M. Beeghly (Eds.), *The self in transition: Infancy to adulthood* (pp. 35–60). Chicago: University of Chicago Press.

Emmer, E. T., Evertson, C. M., & Worsham, M. E. (2000). *Classroom management for secondary teachers* (5th ed.). Boston: Allyn & Bacon.

Empson, S. B. (1999). Equal sharing and shared meaning: The development of fraction concepts in a first-grade classroom. *Cognition and Instruction, 17,* 283–342.

Engel, S., & Randall, K. (2009). How teachers respond to children's inquiry. *American Educational Research Journal, 46*(1), 183–202.

English, D. J. (1998). The extent and consequences of child maltreatment. *The Future of Children: Protecting Children from Abuse and Neglect, 8*(1), 39–53.

Enyedy, N. (2005). Inventing mapping: Creating cultural forms to solve collective problems. *Cognition and Instruction, 23,* 427–466.

Eppig, C., Fincher, C. L., & Thornhill, R. (2010). Parasite prevalence and the worldwide distribution of cognitive ability. *Proceedings of the Royal Society,* 1–8. doi:10.1098/rspb.2010.0973

Eppright, T. D., Sanfacon, J. A., Beck, N. C., & Bradley, S. J. (1998). Sport psychiatry in childhood and adolescence: An overview. *Child Psychiatry and Human Development, 28,* 71–88.

Epstein, J. A., Botvin, G. J., Diaz, T., Toth, V., & Schinke, S. P. (1995). Social and personal factors in marijuana use and intentions to use drugs among inner city minority youth. *Journal of Developmental and Behavioral Pediatrics, 16,* 14–20.

Epstein, J. L. (1986). Friendship selection: Developmental and environmental influences. In E. Mueller & C. Cooper (Eds.), *Process and outcome in peer relationships* (pp. 129–160). New York: Academic Press.

Epstein, J. L. (1996). Perspectives and previews on research and policy for school, family, and community partnerships. In A. Booth & J. F. Dunn (Eds.), *Family–school links: How do they affect educational outcomes?* Mahwah, NJ: Erlbaum.

Epstein, J. S. (1998). Introduction: Generation X, youth culture, and identity. In J. S. Epstein (Ed.), *Youth culture: Identity in a postmodern world* (pp. 1–23). Malden, MA: Blackwell.

Epstein, S., & Morling, B. (1995). Is the self motivated to do more than enhance and/or verify itself? In M. H. Kernis (Ed.), *Efficacy, agency, and self-esteem.* New York: Plenum Press.

Erath, S. A., Flanagan, K. S., Bierman, K. L., & Tu, K. M. (2010). Friendships moderate psychosocial maladjustment in socially anxious early adolescents. *Journal of Applied Developmental Psychology, 31*(1), 15–26. doi:10.1016/j.appdev.2009.05.005

Erickson, J. E., Keil, F. C., & Lockhart, K. L. (2010). Sensing the coherence of biology in contrast to psychology: Young children's use of causal relations to distinguish two foundational domains. *Child Development, 81*(1), 390–409.

Erikson, E. H. (1963). *Childhood and society* (2nd ed.). New York: Norton.

Erikson, E. H. (1972). *Eight ages of man.* In C. S. Lavatelli & F. Stendler (Eds.), *Readings in child behavior and child development.* San Diego, CA: Harcourt Brace Jovanovich.

Ernst, M., & Hardin, M. (2010). Neurodevelopment underlying adolescent behavior. In P. D. Zelazo, M. Chandler, & E. Crone (Eds.), *Developmental social cognitive neuroscience. The Jean Piaget symposium series* (pp. 165–189). New York: Psychology Press.

Eron, L. D. (1980). Prescription for reduction of aggression. *American Psychologist, 35,* 244–252.

Eron, L. D. (1987). The development of aggressive behavior from the perspective of a developing behaviorism. *American Psychologist, 42,* 435–442.

Erwin, P. (1993). *Friendship and peer relations in children.* Chichester, England: Wiley.

Espinosa, L. (2007). English-language learners as they enter school. In R. Pianta, M. Cox, & K. Snow (Eds.), *School readiness and the transition to kindergarten in the era of accountability* (pp. 175–196). Baltimore, MD: Paul H. Brookes.

Espinosa, L. (2008). *Challenging common myths about young English language learners.* FCD Policy Brief: Advancing PK-3 (No. 8). New York: Foundation for Child Development.

Estes, D., Chandler, M., Horvath, K. J., & Backus, D. W. (2003). American and British college students' epistemological beliefs about research on psychological and biological development. *Applied Developmental Psychology, 23,* 625–642.

Estes, K. G., Evans, J. L., Alibali, M. W., & Saffran, J. R. (2007). Can infants map meaning to newly segmented words? Statistical segmentation and word learning. *Psychological Science, 18,* 254–260.

Estrada, V. L., Gómez, L., & Ruiz-Escalante, J. A. (2009). Let's make dual language the norm. *Educational Leadership, 66*(7), 54–58.

Evans, E. M. (2001). Cognitive and contextual factors in the emergence of diverse belief systems: Creation versus evolution. *Cognitive Psychology, 42,* 217–266.

Evans, E. M., Schweingruber, H., & Stevenson, H. W. (2002). Gender differences in interest and knowledge acquisition: The United States, Taiwan, and Japan. *Sex Roles, 47,* 153–167.

Evans, G. W., & Kim, P. (2007). Childhood poverty and health: Cumulative risk exposure and stress dysregulation. *Psychological Science, 18,* 953–957.

Evans, G. W., & Schamberg, M. A. (2009). Childhood poverty, chronic stress, and adult working memory. *PNAS Proceedings of the National Academy of the United States, 106*(16), 6545–6549.

Evans, J. L., Hahn, J. A., Lum, P. J., Stein, E. S., & Page, K. (2009). Predictors of injection drug use cessation and relapse in a prospective cohort of young injection drug users in San Francisco, CA (UFO Study). *Drug and Alcohol Dependence, 101,* 152–157.

Evans, M. A., & Saint-Aubin, J. (2005). What children are looking at during shared storybook reading: Evidence from eye movement monitoring. *Psychological Science, 16,* 913–920.

Evans, R. R., Roy, J., Geiger, B. F., Werner, K. A., & Burnett, D. (2008). Ecological strategies to promote healthy body image among children. *Journal of School Health, 78*(7), 359–367.

Fabes, R. A., Eisenberg, N., Jones, S., Smith, M., Guthrie, I., Poulin, R., et al. (1999). Regulation, emotionality, and preschoolers' socially competent peer interactions. *Child Development, 70,* 432–442.

Fabos, B., & Young, M. D. (1999). Telecommunication in the classroom: Rhetoric versus reality. *Review of Educational Research, 69,* 217–259.

Fadiman, A. (1997). *The spirit catches you and you fall down: The Hmong child, her American doctors, and the collision of two cultures.* New York: Noonday Press/Farrar, Straus and Giroux.

Fagan, J. F., Holland, C. R., & Wheeler, K. (2007). The prediction, from infancy, of adult IQ and achievement. *Intelligence, 35,* 225–231.

Fahrmeier, E. D. (1978). The development of concrete operations among the Hausa. *Journal of Cross-Cultural Psychology, 9,* 23–44.

Fairchild, H. H., & Edwards-Evans, S. (1990). African American dialects and schooling: A review. In A. M. Padilla, H. H. Fairchild, & C. M. Valadez (Eds.), *Bilingual education: Issues and strategies.* Newbury Park, CA: Sage.

Fais, L., Kajikawa, S., Shigeaki, A., & Werker, J. F. (2009). Infant discrimination of a morphologically relevant word-final contrast. *Infancy, 14*(4), 488–499.

Falbo, T. (1992). Social norms and the one-child family: Clinical and policy implications. In F. Boer & J. Dunn (Eds.), *Children's sibling relationships* (pp. 71–82). Hillsdale, NJ: Erlbaum.

Falbo, T., & Polit, D. (1986). A quantitative review of the only child literature: Research evidence and theory development. *Psychological Bulletin, 100,* 176–189.

Fan, Y., Decety, J., Yang, C., Liu, J., & Cheng, Y. (2010). Unbroken mirror neurons in autism spectrum disorders. *Journal of Child Psychology and Psychiatry, 51*(9), 981–988. doi:10.1111/j.1469-7610.2010.02269.x

Fanti, K. A., & Henrich, C. C. (2010). Trajectories of pure and co-occurring internalizing and externalizing problems from age 2 to age 12: Findings from the National Institute of Child Health and Human Development Study of Early Child Care. *Developmental Psychology, 46*(5), 1159–1175.

Fantini, A. E. (1985). *Language acquisition of a bilingual child: A sociolinguistic perspective.* Clevedon, England: Multilingual Matters. (Available from the SIT Bookstore, School for International Training, Kipling Road, Brattleboro, VT 05302)

Fantino, A. M., & Colak, A. (2001). Refugee children in Canada: Searching for identity. *Child Welfare, 80,* 587–596.

Farber, B., Mindel, C. H., & Lazerwitz, B. (1988). The Jewish American family. In C. H. Mindel, R. W. Habenstein, & R. Wright (Eds.), *Ethnic families in America: Patterns and variations.* New York: Elsevier.

Farran, D. C. (2001). Critical periods and early intervention. In D. B. Bailey, Jr., J. T. Bruer, F. J. Symons, & J. W. Lichtman (Eds.), *Critical thinking about critical periods* (pp. 233–266). Baltimore, MD: Paul H. Brookes.

Farrell, A. D., Erwin, E. H., Bettencourt, A., Mays, S., Vulin-Reynolds, M., Sullivan, T., et al. (2008). Individual factors influencing effective nonviolent behavior and fighting in peer situations: A qualitative study with urban African American adolescents. *Journal of Clinical Child and Adolescent Psychology, 37*(2), 397–411.

Farrell, M. M., & Phelps, L. (2000). A comparison of the Leiter-R and the Universal Nonverbal Intelligence Test (UNIT) with children classified as language impaired. *Journal of Psychoeducational Assessment, 18,* 268–274.

Farrington-Flint, L., & Wood, C. (2007). The role of lexical analogies in beginning reading: Insights from children's self-reports. *Journal of Educational Psychology, 99,* 326–338.

Farver, J. A. M., & Branstetter, W. H. (1994). Preschoolers' prosocial responses to their peers' distress. *Developmental Psychology, 30,* 334–341.

Farver, J. M., & Shin, Y. L. (1997). Social pretend play in Korean- and Anglo-American pre-schoolers. *Child Development, 68*(3), 544–556.

Fausel, D. F. (1986). Loss after divorce: Helping children grieve. *Journal of Independent Social Work, 1*(1), 39–47.

Federal Interagency Forum on Child and Family Statistics. (2009). *America's children: Key national indicators of well-being, 2009.* Washington, DC: U.S. Government Printing Office.

Federal Interagency Forum on Child and Family Statistics. (2010). *America's children in brief: Key national indicators of well-being, 2010.* Washington, DC: U.S. Government Printing Office.

Fegley, S. G., Spencer, M. B., Goss, T. N., Harpalani, V., & Charles, N. (2008). Colorism embodied: Skin tone and psychological well-being in adolescence. In W. F. Overton, U. Müller, J. L. Newman (Eds.), *Developmental perspectives on embodiment and consciousness* (pp. 281–311). New York: Lawrence Erlbaum.

Feigenberg, L., King, M., Barr, D., & Selman, R. (2008). Belonging to and exclusion from the peer group in schools: influences on adolescents' moral choices. *Journal of Moral Education, 37*(2), 165–184. doi:10.1080/03057240802009306

Feinberg, M. E., Kan, M. L., & Goslin, M. C. (2009). Enhancing coparenting, parenting, and child self-regulation: Effects of family foundations 1 year after birth. *Prevention Science, 10*(3), 276–285.

Feinberg, M. E., Kan, M. L., & Hetherington, E. M. (2007). The longitudinal influence of coparenting conflict on parental negativity and adolescent adjustment. *Journal of Marriage and Family, 69,* 687–702.

Feinman, S. (1992). *Social referencing and the social construction of reality in infancy.* New York: Plenum Press.

Feldhusen, J. F. (1989). Synthesis of research on gifted youth. *Educational Leadership, 26*(1), 6–11.

Feldhusen, J. F., Van Winkle, L., & Ehle, D. A. (1996). Is it acceleration or simply appropriate instruction for precocious youth? *Teaching Exceptional Children, 28*(3), 48–51.

Feldman, D. H. (2004). Piaget's stages: The unfinished symphony of cognitive development. *New Ideas in Psychology, 22,* 175–231.

Feldman, S. S., & Wood, D. N. (1994). Parents' expectations for preadolescent sons' behavioral autonomy: A longitudinal study of correlates and outcomes. *Journal of Research on Adolescence, 4,* 45–70.

Felton, R. H. (1998). The development of reading skills in poor readers: Educational implications. In C. Hulme & R. M. Joshi (Eds.), *Reading and spelling: Development and disorders.* Mahwah, NJ: Erlbaum.

Fennell, C. T., Byers-Heinlein, K., & Werker, J. F. (2007). Using speech sounds to guide word learning: The case of bilingual infants. *Child Development, 78,* 1510–1525.

Fenson, L., Dale, P., Reznick, J., Bates, E., Thal, D., & Pethick, S. (1994). Variability in early communicative development. *Monographs of the Society for Research in Child Development, 59*(5, Serial No. 242), 1–173.

Ferla, J., Valcke, M., & Cai, Y. (2009). Academic self-efficacy and academic self-concept: Reconsidering structural relationships. *Learning & Individual Differences, 19*(4), 499–505.

Fernald, A. (1992). Human maternal vocalizations to infants as biologically relevant signals: An evolutionary perspective. In J. Barkow, L. Cosmides, & J. Tooby (Eds.), *Evolutionary psychology and the generation of culture.* New York: Oxford University Press.

Fernald, A., Swingley, D., & Pinto, J. P. (2001). When half a word is enough: Infants can recognize spoken words using partial phonetic information. *Child Development, 72,* 1003–1015.

Fetro, J. V., Givens, C., & Carroll, K. (2009/2010). Coordinated school health: Getting it all together. *Educational Leadership, 67*(4), 32–37.

Feuerstein, R. (1979). *The dynamic assessment of retarded performers: The Learning Potential Assessment Device, theory, instruments, and techniques.* Baltimore, MD: University Park Press.

Feuerstein, R. (1990). The theory of structural cognitive modifiability. In B. Z. Presseisen (Ed.), *Learning and thinking styles: Classroom interaction.* Washington, DC: National Education Association.

Feuerstein, R., Feuerstein, R., & Gross, S. (1997). The Learning Potential Assessment Device. In D. P. Flanagan, J. L. Genshaft, & P. L. Harrison (Eds.), *Contemporary intellectual assessment: Theories, tests, and issues* (pp. 297–313). New York: Guilford Press.

Fewell, R. R., & Sandall, S. R. (1983). Curricula adaptations for young children: Visually impaired, hearing impaired, and physically impaired. *Curricula in Early Childhood Special Education, 2*(4), 51–66.

Fiedler, E. D., Lange, R. E., & Winebrenner, S. (1993). In search of reality: Unraveling the myths about tracking, ability grouping and the gifted. *Roeper Review, 16*(1), 4–7.

Field, D. (1987). A review of preschool conservation training: An analysis of analyses. *Developmental Review, 7,* 210–251.

Field, S. L., Labbo, L. D., & Ash, G. E. (1999, April). *Investigating young children's construction of social studies concepts and the intersection of literacy learning.* Paper presented at the annual meeting of the American Educational Research Association, Montreal, Canada.

Field, T. (2001). Massage therapy facilitates weight gain in preterm infants. *Current Directions in Psychological Science, 10,* 51–54.

Field, T., Woodson, R., Greenberg, R., & Cohen, D. (1982). Discrimination and imitation of facial expressions by neonates. *Science, 218,* 179–81.

Fields, R. D. (2009). *The other brain: From dementia to schizophrenia, how new discoveries are revolutionizing medicine and science.* New York: Simon & Schuster.

Fifer, W. P., & Moon, C. M. (1995). The effects of fetal experience with sound. In J. P. Lecanuet, W. P. Fifer, N. A. Krasnegor, & W. P. Smotherman (Eds.), *Fetal development: A psychobiological perspective.* Hillsdale, NJ: Erlbaum.

Filax, G. (2007). Queer in/visibility: The case of Ellen, Michel, and Oscar. In S. Books (Ed.), *Invisible children in the society and its schools* (3rd ed., pp. 213–234). Mahwah, NJ: Erlbaum.

Files, J. S., Casey, C. M., & Oleson, K. C. (2010). Intergroup bias in children: Development and persistence. *European Journal of Social Psychology. Special Issue: Origins of Intergroup Bias: Developmental and Social Cognitive Research on Intergroup Attitudes, 40*(4), 671–678. doi:10.1002/ejsp.734

Finders, M., & Lewis, C. (1994). Why some parents don't come to school. *Educational Leadership, 51*(8), 50–54.

Finger, B., Hans, S. L., Bernstein, V. J., & Cox, S. M. (2009). Parent relationship quality and infant–mother attachment. *Attachment and Human Development, 11*(3), 285–306.

Finkelhor, D., Ormrod, R., Turner, H., & Hamby, S. L. (2005). The victimization of children and youth: A comprehensive, national study. *Child Maltreatment, 10*(1), 5–25.

Finkelhor, D., Mitchell, K. J., & Wolak, J. (2000). *Online victimization: A report on the nation's youth.* Durham, NH: Crimes Against Children Research Center. Retrieved March 7, 2003, from http://www.unh.edu/ccrc/pdf/Victimization_Online_Survey.pdf

Fiorello, C. A., & Primerano, D. (2005). Research into practice: Cattell-Horn-Carroll cognitive assessment in practice: Eligibility and program development issues. *Psychology in the Schools, 42*(5), 525–536.

Fireman, G. D., & Kose, G. (2010). Perspective taking. In E. H. Sandberg, & B. L. Spritz (Eds.), *A clinician's guide to normal cognitive development in childhood* (pp. 85–100). New York: Routledge/Taylor & Francis Group.

Fischer, K. (2005, April). Dynamic skill development and integration of motivation, emotion, and cognition. In D. Y. Dai (Chair), *Beyond cognitivism: Where are we now?* Symposium presented at the annual meeting of the American Educational Research Association, Montreal, Canada.

Fischer, K. W. (2008). Dynamic cycles of cognitive and brain development: Measuring growth in mind, brain, and education. In A. M. Battro, K. W. Fischer, & P. J. Lena (Eds.), *The educated brain* (pp. 127–150). New York: Cambridge University Press.

Fischer, K. W., & Bidell, T. (1991). Constraining nativist inferences about cognitive capacities. In S. Carey & R. Gelman (Eds.), *The epigenesis of mind: Essays on biology and cognition.* Hillsdale, NJ: Erlbaum.

Fischer, K. W., & Bidell, T. R. (2006). Dynamic development of action and thought. In W. Damon & R. M. Lerner (Eds. in Chief) & R. M. Lerner (Vol. Ed.), *Handbook of child psychology: Vol. 1. Theoretical models of human development* (6th ed., pp. 313–399). Hoboken, NJ: Wiley.

Fischer, K. W., & Daley, S. G. (2007). Connecting cognitive science and neuroscience to education: Potentials and pitfalls in inferring executive processes. In L. Meltzer (Ed.), *Executive function in education: From theory to practice* (pp. 55–72). New York: Guilford Press.

Fischer, K. W., & Immordino-Yang, M. H. (2002). Cognitive development and education: From dynamic general structure to specific learning and teaching. In E. Lagemann (Ed.), *Traditions of scholarship in education* (pp. 1–55). Chicago: Spencer Foundation.

Fischer, K. W., Stein, Z., & Heikkinen, K. (2009). Narrow assessments misrepresent development and misguide policy: Comment on Steinberg, Cauffman, Woolard, Graham, and Banich (2009). *American Psychologist, 64*(7), 595–600.

Fish, T., Rabidoux, P., Ober, J., & Graff, V. L. W. (2009). *Next chapter book club: A model community literacy program for people with intellectual disabilities.* Bethesda, MD: Woodbine House.

Fishbein, D. H., Hyde, C., Eldreth, D., Paschall, M. J., Hubal, R., Das, A., et al. (2006). Neurocognitive skills moderate urban male adolescents' responses to preventive intervention materials. *Drug and Alcohol Dependence, 82*(1), 47–60.

Fisher, C. B., Jackson, J. F., & Villarruel, F. A. (1998). The study of African American and Latin American children and youth. In W. Damon (Series Ed.) & R. M. Lerner (Vol. Ed.), *Handbook of child psychology: Vol. 1. Theoretical models of human development* (5th ed., pp. 1145–1207). New York: Wiley.

Fisher, D., & Frey, N. (2007). *Checking for understanding: Formative assessment techniques for your classroom.* Alexandria, VA: Association for Super-vision and Curriculum Development.

Fisher, P. A., Kim, H. K., & Pears, K. C. (2009). Effects of Multidimensional Treatment Foster Care for Preschoolers (MTFC-P) on reducing permanent placement failures among children with placement instability. *Children and Youth Services Review, 31,* 541–546.

Fite, P. J., Vitulano, M., Wynn, P., Wimsatt, A., Gaertner, A., & Rathert, J. (2010). Influence of perceived neighborhood safety on proactive and reactive aggression. *Journal of Community Psychology, 38*(6), 757–768. doi:10.1002/jcop.20393

Fitzgerald, J. (1987). Research on revision in writing. *Review of Educational Research, 57,* 481–506.

Fivush, R. (1994). Constructing narrative, emotion, and self in parent-child conversations about the past. In U. Neisser & R. Fivush (Eds.), *The remembering self: Construction and accuracy in the self-narrative* (pp. 136–157). Cambridge, England: Cambridge University Press.

Fivush, R. (2009). Sociocultural perspectives on autobiographical memory. In M. L. Courage & N. Cowan (Eds.), *The development of memory in infancy and childhood* (pp. 283–301). New York: Psychology Press.

Fivush, R., & Buckner, J. P. (2003). Creating gender and identity through autobiographical narratives. In R. Fivush & C. A. Haden (Eds.), *Autobiographical memory and the construction of a narrative self* (pp. 149–167). Mahwah, NJ: Erlbaum.

Fivush, R., Haden, C., & Adam, S. (1995). Structure and coherence of preschoolers' personal narratives over time: Implications for childhood amnesia. *Journal of Experimental Child Psychology, 60,* 32–56.

Fivush, R., Haden, C. A., & Reese, E. (2006). Elaborating on elaborations: Role of maternal reminiscing style in cognitive and socioemotional development. *Child Development, 77,* 1568–1588.

Fivush, R., & Nelson, K. (2004). Culture and language in the emergence of autobiographical memory. *Psychological Science, 15,* 573–577.

Flanagan, C. A., & Faison, N. (2001). Youth civic development: Implications of research for social policy and programs. *Social Policy Report, 15*(1), 1–14. Ann Arbor, MI: Society for Research in Child Development.

Flanagan, C. A., & Tucker, C. J. (1999). Adolescents' explanations for political issues: Concordance with their views of self and society. *Developmental Psychology, 35,* 1198–1209.

Flanders, J. L., Simard, M., Paquette, D., Parent, S., Vitaro, F., Pihl, R. O., et al. (2010). Rough-and-tumble play and the development of physical aggression and emotion regulation: A five-year follow-up study. *Journal of Family Violence, 25*(4), 357–367. doi:10.1007/s10896-009-9297-5

Flannery-Schroeder, E., & Lamb, A. N. (2009). Cognitive behavior therapy. In J. L. Matson, F. Andrasik & M. L. Matson (Eds.), *Treating childhood psychopathology and developmental disabilities* (pp. 55–78). New York: Springer Science + Business Media. doi:10.1007/978-0-387-09530-1_3

Flavell, J. H. (1994). Cognitive development: Past, present, and future. In R. D. Parke, P. A. Ornstein, J. J. Rieser, & C. Zahn-Waxler (Eds.), *A century of developmental psychology* (pp. 569–587). Washington, DC: American Psychological Association.

Flavell, J. H. (2000). Development of children's knowledge about the mental world. *International Journal of Behavioral Development, 24*(1), 15–23.

Flavell, J. H., Flavell, E. R., & Green, F. L. (2001). Development of children's understanding of connections between thinking and feeling. *Psychological Science, 12,* 430–432.

Flavell, J. H., Friedrichs, A. G., & Hoyt, J. D. (1970). Developmental changes in memorization processes. *Cognitive Psychology, 1,* 324–340.

Flavell, J. H., Green, F. L., & Flavell, E. R. (1995). Young children's knowledge about thinking. *Monographs of the Society for Research in Child Development, 60*(1, Serial No. 243).

Flavell, J. H., Green, F. L., & Flavell, E. R. (2000). Development of children's awareness of their own thoughts. *Journal of Cognitive Development, 1,* 97–112.

Flavell, J. H., & Miller, P. H. (1998). Social cognition. In W. Damon (Series Ed.), & D. Kuhn & R. S. Siegler (Vol. Eds.), *Handbook of child psychology: Vol. 2. Cognition, perception, and language* (5th ed.). New York: Wiley.

Flavell, J. H., Miller, P. H., & Miller, S. A. (2002). *Cognitive development* (4th ed.). Upper Saddle River, NJ: Prentice Hall.

Flay, B. R., & Allred, C. G. (2003). Long-term effects of the Positive Action program. *American Journal of Health Behavior, 27*(1), 6–21.

Flege, J. E., Munro, M. J., & MacKay, I. R. A. (1995). Effects of age of second-language learning on the production of English consonants. *Speech Communication, 16,* 1–26.

Fleming, D. (2002). *Alphabet under construction.* New York: Henry Holt.

Fletcher, A. C., Bridges, T. H., & Hunter, A. G. (2007). Managing children's friendships through interparental relationships: Roles of ethnicity and friendship context. *Journal of Marriage and Family, 69,* 1135–1149.

Fletcher, A. C., Hunter, A. G., & Eanes, A. Y. (2006). Links between social network closure and child well-being: The organizing role of friendship context. *Developmental Psychology, 42,* 1057–1068.

Fletcher, J. M., Lyon, G. R., Fuchs, L. S., & Barnes, M. A. (2007). *Learning disabilities: From identification to intervention.* New York: Guilford Press.

Fletcher, K. L., & Bray, N. W. (1996). External memory strategy use in preschool children. *Merrill-Palmer Quarterly, 42,* 379–396.

Fletcher, R. (2006). *Boy writers.* Portland, ME: Stenhouse.

Flieller, A. (1999). Comparison of the development of formal thought in adolescent cohorts aged 10 to 15 years (1967–1996 and 1972–1993). *Developmental Psychology, 35,* 1048–1058.

Florit, E., Roch, M., Altoè, G., & Levorato, M. C. (2009). Listening comprehension in preschoolers: The role of memory. *British Journal of Developmental Psychology, 27*(4), 935–951.

Floyd, R. G., Bergeron, R., & Alfonso, V. C. (2006). Cattell-Horn-Carroll cognitive ability profiles of poor comprehenders. *Reading and Writing, 19,* 427–456.

Floyd, R. G., McGrew, K. S., Barry, A., Rafael, F., & Rogers, J. (2009). General and specific effects on Cattell-Horn-Carroll broad ability composites: Analysis of the Woodcock-Johnson III normative update Cattell-Horn-Carroll factor clusters across development. *School Psychology Review, 38*(2), 249–265.

Flum, H., & Kaplan, A. (2006). Exploratory orientation as an educational goal. *Educational Psychologist, 41,* 99–110.

Flynn, J. R. (1987). Massive IQ gains in 14 nations: What IQ tests really measure. *Psychological Bulletin, 101,* 171–191.

Flynn, J. R. (2003). Movies about intelligence: The limitations of *g*. *Current Directions in Psychological Science, 12,* 95–99.

Flynn, J. R. (2007). *What is intelligence? Beyond the Flynn effect.* New York: Cambridge University Press.

Folmer, A., Cole, D., Sigal, A., Benbow, L., Satterwhite, L., Swygert, K., et al. (2008). Age-related changes in children's understanding of effort and ability: Implications for attribution theory and motivation. *Journal of Experimental Child Psychology, 99*(2), 114–134. doi:10.1016/j.jecp.2007.09.003.

Fontaine, K. L. (2011). *Complementary and alternative therapies for nursing practice* (3rd ed.). Upper Saddle River, NJ: Pearson Education.

Forbes, M. L., Ormrod, J. E., Bernardi, J. D., Taylor, S. L., & Jackson, D. L. (1999, April). *Children's conceptions of space, as reflected in maps of their hometown.* Paper presented at the annual meeting of the American Educational Research Association, Montreal, Canada.

Ford, D. Y. (1996). *Reversing underachievement among gifted Black students.* New York: Teachers College Press.

Ford, L., & Dahinten, V. S. (2005). Use of intelligence tests in the assessment of preschoolers. In D. P. Flanagan & P. L. Harrison (Eds.), *Contemporary intellectual assessment: Theories, tests, and issues* (2nd ed., pp. 487–503). New York: Guilford Press.

Ford, M. E. (1996). Motivational opportunities and obstacles associated with social responsibility and caring behavior in school contexts. In J. Juvonen & K. R. Wentzel (Eds.), *Social motivation: Understanding children's school adjustment* (pp. 126–153). Cambridge, England: Cambridge University Press.

Ford, M. E., & Smith, P. R. (2007). Thriving with social purpose: An integrative approach to the development of optimal human functioning. *Educational Psychologist, 42,* 153–171.

Ford, M. E., & Smith, P. R. (2009). Commentary: Building on a strong foundation: Five pathways to the next level of motivational theorizing. K. R. Wentzel & A. Wigfield (Eds.), *Handbook of motivation at school* (pp. 265–275). New York: Routledge/Taylor & Francis Group.

Forthun, L. F., Montgomery, M. J., & Bell, N. J. (2006). Identity formation in a relational context: A person-centered analysis of troubled youth. *Identity, 6*(2), 141–167.

Fowler, J. W., & Peterson, P. L. (1981). Increasing reading persistence and altering attributional style of learned helpless children. *Journal of Educational Psychology, 73,* 251–260.

Fox, E. (2009). The role of reader characteristics in processing and learning from informational text. *Review of Educational Research, 79*(1), 197–261.

Fox, N. A., Henderson, H. A., Rubin, K. H., Calkins, S. D., & Schmidt, L. A. (2001). Continuity and discontinuity of behavioral inhibition and exuberance: Psychophysiological and behavioral influences across the first 4 years of life. *Child Development, 72*(1), 1–21.

Francis, M., & McCutchen, D. (1994, April). *Strategy differences in revising between skilled and less skilled writers.* Paper presented at the annual meeting of the American Educational Research Association, New Orleans, LA.

Frank, A. (1967). *The diary of a young girl* (B. M. Mooyaart, Trans.). New York: Doubleday.

Frank, C. (1999). *Ethnographic eyes: A teacher's guide to classroom observation.* Portsmouth, NH: Heinemann.

Frank, H., Harvey, O. J., & Verdun, K. (2000). American responses to five categories of shame in chinese culture: A preliminary cross-cultural construct validation. *Personality and Individual Differences, 28*(5), 887–896.

Frazier, B. N., Gelman, S. A., & Wellman, H. M. (2009). Preschoolers' search for explanatory information within adult-child conversation. *Child Development, 80*(6), 1592–1611.

Frederickson, N. L., & Simmonds, E. A. (2008). Special needs, relationship type and distributive justice norms in early and later years of middle childhood. *Social Development, 17*(4), 1056–1073. doi:10.1111/j.1467-9507.2008.00477.x

Frederiksen, N. (1984). Implications of cognitive theory for instruction in problem-solving. *Review of Educational Research, 54,* 363–407.

Fredricks, J. A., Blumenfeld, P. C., & Paris, A. H. (2004). School engagement: Potential of the concept, state of the evidence. *Review of Educational Research, 74,* 59–109.

Freeark, K. (2006). Adoption and youth: Critical issues and strengths-based programming to address them. In K. Freeark & W. S. Davidson (Eds.), *The crisis in youth mental health: Critical issues and effective programs: Vol. 3. Issues for families, schools, and communities* (pp. 121–146). Westport, CT: Praeger/Greenwood.

Freedenthal, S., & Stiffman, A. R. (2007). "They might think I was crazy": Young American Indians' reasons for not seeking help when suicidal. *Journal of Adolescent Research, 22,* 58–77.

Freedman, B. A. (2003, April). *Boys and literacy: Why boys? Which boys? Why now?.* Paper presented at the annual meeting of the American Educational Research Association, Chicago.

The Freedom Writers (with Gruwell, E.) (1999). *The Freedom Writers diary: How a teacher and 150 teens used writing to change themselves and the world around them.* New York: Broadway Books.

Freeman, H., Newland, L. A., & Coyl, D. D. (2010). New directions in father attachment. *Early Child Development and Care, 180*(1&2), 1–8.

Freitag, C. M. (2007). The genetics of autistic disorders and its clinical relevance: A review of the literature. *Molecular Psychiatry, 12,* 2–22.

French, L., & Brown, A. (1977). Comprehension of "before" and "after" in logical and arbitrary sequences. *Journal of Child Language, 4,* 247–256.

French, S. E., Seidman, E., Allen, L., & Aber, J. L. (2006). The development of ethnic identity during adolescence. *Developmental Psychology, 42,* 1–10.

Frensch, P. A., & Rünger, D. (2003). Implicit learning. *Current Directions in Psychological Science, 12,* 13–18.

Freud, S. (1905). *Three contributions to the theory of sex. The basic writings of Sigmund Freud* (A. A. Brill, Trans.). New York: The Modern Library.

Freud, S. (1910). *The origin and development of psychoanalysis.* New York: Henry Regnery (Gateway Editions), 1965.

Freud, S. (1923). *The ego and the id* (J. Riviere, Trans.). New York: Norton, 1960.

Freund, L. (1990). Maternal regulation of children's problem solving behavior and its impact on children's performance. *Child Development, 61,* 113–126.

Frick, P. J., Barry, C. T., & Kamphaus, R. W. (2010). *Clinical assessment of child and adolescent personality and behavior* (3rd ed.). New York: Springer Science + Business Media.

Friedman, C. K., Leaper, C., & Bigler, R. S. (2007). Do mothers' gender-related attitudes or comments predict young children's gender beliefs? *Parenting: Science and Practice, 7,* 357–366.

Friedman, L. (1994, April). *The role of spatial skill in gender differences in mathematics: Meta-analytic evidence.* Paper presented at the annual meeting of the American Educational Research Association, New Orleans, LA.

Frosch, C. A., Mangelsdorf, S. C., & McHale, J. L. (2000). Marital behavior and the security of preschooler-parent attachment relationships. *Journal of Family Psychology, 14,* 144–161.

Frost, J. L., Shin, D., & Jacobs, P. J. (1998). Physical environments and children's play. In O. N. Saracho & B. Spodek (Eds.), *Multiple perspectives on play in early childhood education.* Albany: State University of New York Press.

Fruchter, N. (2007). *Urban schools, public will: Making education work for all our children.* New York: Teachers College Press.

Fry, A. F., & Hale, S. (1996). Processing speed, working memory, and fluid intelligence. *Psychological Science, 7,* 237–241.

Fuchs, D., Fuchs, L. S., Mathes, P. G., & Simmons, D. C. (1997). Peer-assisted learning strategies: Making classrooms more responsive to diversity. *American Educational Research Journal, 34,* 174–206.

Fuchs, L., Powell, S., Seethaler, P., Cirino, P., Fletcher, J., Fuchs, D., et al. (2010). The effects of strategic counting instruction, with and without deliberate practice, on number combination skill among students with mathematics difficulties. *Learning and Individual Differences, 20*(2), 89–100.

Fuchs, L. S., Fuchs, D., Prentice, K., Burch, M., Hamlett, C. L., Owen, R., et al. (2003). Enhancing third-grade students' mathematical problem solving with self-regulated learning strategies. *Journal of Educational Psychology, 95,* 306–315.

Fujimura, N. (2001). Facilitating children's proportional reasoning: A model of reasoning processes and effects of intervention on strategy change. *Journal of Educational Psychology, 93,* 589–603.

Fujioka, T., Mourad, N., & Trainor, L. J. (2011). Development of auditory-specific brain rhythm in infants. *European Journal of Neuroscience, 33*(3), 521–529. doi:10.1111/j.1460-9568.2010.07544.x

Fukkink, R. G., & de Glopper, K. (1998). Effects of instruction in deriving word meanings from context: A meta-analysis. *Review of Educational Research, 68,* 450–469.

Fuller, M. L. (2001). Multicultural concerns and classroom management. In C. A. Grant & M. L. Gomez, *Campus and classroom: Making schooling multicultural* (pp. 109–134). Upper Saddle River, NJ: Merrill/Prentice Hall.

Fuller, R. G., Campbell, T. C., Dykstra, D. I. Jr., & Stevens, S. M. (2009). The learning cycle: College teaching and the development of reasoning. In R. G. Fuller, T. C. Campbell, D. I. Dykstra Jr., & S. M. Stevens (Eds.) *College teaching and the development of reasoning: Science and engineering education sources* (pp. 115–133). Charlotte, NC: Information Age Publishing.

Fung, H., & Smith, B. (2010). Learning morality. In D. F. Lancy, J. Bock & S. Gaskins (Eds.), *The anthropology of learning in childhood* (pp. 261–285). Walnut Creek, CA: AltaMira Press.

Furman, W., & Simon, V. A. (1999). Cognitive representations of adolescent romantic relationships. In W. Furman, B. B. Brown, & C. Feiring (Eds.), *The development of romantic relationships in adolescence* (pp. 75–98). Cambridge, England: Cambridge University Press.

Fusaro, M., & Nelson, C. A. III. (2009). Developmental cognitive neuroscience and education practice. In O. A. Barbarin & B. H. Wasik (Eds.), *Handbook of child development and early education: Research to practice* (pp. 57–77). New York: Guilford Press.

Fuson, K. C., & Briars, D. J. (1990). Using a base-ten blocks learning/teaching approach for first- and second-grade place-value and multidigit addition and subtraction. *Journal for Research in Mathematics Education, 21*, 180–206.

Fuson, K. C., & Hall, J. W. (1983). The acquisition of early word meanings: A conceptual analysis and review. In H. P. Ginsburg (Ed.), *Children's mathematical thinking*. New York: Academic Press.

Fuson, K. C., & Kwon, Y. (1992). Korean children's understanding of multidigit addition and subtraction. *Child Development, 63*, 491–506.

Futrell, M. H., & Gomez, J. (2008, May). How tracking creates a poverty of learning. *Educational Leadership, 65*(8), 74–28.

Futterman, D., Chabon, B., & Hoffman, N. D. (2000). HIV and AIDS in adolescents. *Pediatric Clinics of North America, 47*, 171–188.

Gabard, D. L. (1999). Homosexuality and the Human Genome Project: Private and public choices. *Journal of Homosexuality, 37*, 25–51.

Gabrysch, S., Lema, C., Bedriñana, E., Bautista, M. A., Malca, R., Campbell, O. M. R., & Miranda, J. J. (2009). Cultural adaptation of birthing services in rural Ayacucho, Peru. *Bulletin of the World Health Organization, 87*, 724–729.

Gaffan, E. A., Martins, C., Healy, S., & Murray, L. (2010). Early social experience and individual differences in infants' joint attention. *Social Development, 19*(2), 369–393.

Gagnon, S. G., Huelsman, T. J., Kidder-Ashley, P., & Ballard, M. (2009). Student–teacher relationships matter: Moderating influences between temperament and preschool social competence. *Psychology in the Schools, 46*(6), 553–567.

Gainotti, G. (2007). Face familiarity feelings, the right temporal lobe and the possible underlying neural mechanisms. *Brain Research Reviews, 56*(1), 214–235.

Galaburda, A. M., & Rosen, G. D. (2001). Neural plasticity in dyslexia: A window to mechanisms of learning disabilities. In J. L. McClelland & R. S. Siegler (Eds.), *Mechanisms of cognitive development: Behavioral and neural perspectives* (pp. 307–323). Mahwah, NJ: Erlbaum.

Galambos, N. L., Almeida, D. M., & Petersen, A. C. (1990). Masculinity, femininity, and sex role attitudes in early adolescence: Exploring gender intensification. *Child Development, 61*, 1905–1914.

Galambos, N. L., & Maggs, J. L. (1991). Children in self-care: Figures, facts and fiction. In J. V. Verner & N. L. Galambos (Eds.), *Employed mothers and their children* (pp. 131–157). New York: Garland Press.

Gallagher, A. M., & Kaufman, J. C. (Eds.) (2005). *Gender differences in mathematics: An integrative psychological approach*. Cambridge, England: Cambridge University Press.

Gallagher, J. J. (1991). Personal patterns of underachievement. *Journal for the Education of the Gifted, 14*, 221–233.

Gallahue, D. L., & Ozmun, J. C. (1998). *Understanding motor development: Infants, children, adolescents, adults*. Boston: McGraw-Hill.

Galliger, C., Tisak, M., & Tisak, J. (2009). When the wheels on the bus go round: Social interactions on the school bus. *Social Psychology of Education, 12*(1), 43–62. doi:10.1007/s11218-008-9072-0

Gallimore, R., & Goldenberg, C. (2001). Analyzing cultural models and settings to connect minority achievement and school improvement research. *Educational Psychologist, 36*, 45–56.

Gallimore, R., & Tharp, R. (1990). Teaching mind in society: Teaching, schooling, and literate discourse. In L. C. Moll (Ed.), *Vygotsky and education: Instructional implications and applications of sociohistorical psychology*. Cambridge, England: Cambridge University Press.

Gallistel, C. R., Brown, A. L., Carey, S., Gelman, R., & Keil, F. C. (1991). In S. Carey & R. Gelman (Eds.), *Epigenesis of mind: Essays on biology and cognition*. Hillsdale, NJ: Erlbaum.

Gallistel, C. R., & Gelman, R. (1992). Preverbal and verbal counting and computation. *Cognition, 44*, 43–74.

Gallo, A. M., Hadley, E. K., Angst, D. B., Knafl, K. A., & Smith, C. A. M. (2008). Parents' concerns about issues related to their children's genetic conditions. *Journal for Specialists in Pediatric Nursing, 13*(1), 4–14.

Galotti, K. M., Komatsu, L. K., & Voelz, S. (1997). Children's differential performance on deductive and inductive syllogisms. *Developmental Psychology, 33*, 70–78.

Gambrell, L. B., & Bales, R. J. (1986). Mental imagery and the comprehension-monitoring performance of fourth- and fifth-grade poor readers. *Reading Research Quarterly, 21*, 454–464.

Ganiban, J. M., Ulbricht, J., Saudino, K. J., Reiss, D., & Neiderhiser, J. M. (2011). Understanding child-based effects on parenting: Temperament as a moderator of genetic and environmental contributions to parenting. *Developmental Psychology, 47*(3), 676–692. doi:10.1037/a0021812

Garbarino, J., & Abramowitz, R. H. (1992). Sociocultural risk and opportunity. In J. Garbarino (Ed.), *Children and families in the social environment* (pp. 35–70). New York: Aldine de Gruyter.

Garbarino, J., Bradshaw, C. P., & Vorrasi, J. A. (2002). Mitigating the effects of gun violence on children and youth. *The Future of Children, 12*(2), 73–85.

Garces, E., Thomas, D., & Currie, J. (2002). Longer-term effects of Head Start. *American Economic Review, 92*(4), 999–1012.

García, E., Arias, M., Murri, N., & Serna, C. (2010). Developing responsive teachers: A challenge for a demographic reality. *Journal of Teacher Education, 61*(1/2), 132–142.

García, E. E. (1994). *Understanding and meeting the challenge of student cultural diversity*. Boston: Houghton Mifflin.

García, E. E. (1995). Educating Mexican American students: Past treatment and recent developments in theory, research, policy, and practice. In J. A. Banks & C. A. M. Banks (Eds.), *Handbook of research on multicultural education*. New York: Macmillan.

García, E. E., & Jensen, B. (2007). Helping young Hispanic learners. *Educational Leadership, 64*(6), 34–39.

García, E. E., Jensen, B. T., & Scribner, K. P. (2009). The demographic imperative. *Educational Leadership, 66*(7), 8–13.

García Coll, C., Lamberty, G., Jenkins, R., McAdoo, H. P., Crnic, K., Wasik, B. H., et al. (1996). An integrative model for the study of developmental competencies in minority children. *Child Development, 67*, 1891–1914.

García Coll, C. G., & Marks, A. K. (2009). *Immigrant stories: Ethnicity and academics in middle childhood*. New York: Oxford University Press.

Gardiner, H. W., & Kosmitzki, C. (2008). *Lives across cultures: Cross-cultural human development* (4th ed.). Boston: Pearson Allyn & Bacon.

Gardner, H. (1983). *Frames of mind: The theory of multiple intelligences*. New York: Basic Books.

Gardner, H. (1993). *Multiple intelligences: The theory in practice*. New York: Basic Books.

Gardner, H. (1995). Reflections on multiple intelligences: Myths and messages. *Phi Delta Kappan, 77*, 200–209.

Gardner, H. (1999). *Intelligence reframed: Multiple intelligences for the 21st century*. New York: Basic Books.

Gardner, H. (2000). A case against spiritual intelligence. *International Journal of the Psychology of Religion, 10*(1), 27–34.

Gardner, H. (2003). *Multiple intelligences after twenty years*. Paper presented at the annual meeting of the American Educational Research Association, Chicago, IL. Retrieved February 25, 2008, from http://www.pz.harvard.edu/PIs/HG_MI_after_20_years.pdf

Gardner, H. (2006). Replies to my critics. In J. A. Schaler (Ed.), *Howard Gardner under fire: The rebel psychologist faces his critics* (pp. 277–344). Chicago: Open Court.

Gardner, H. (2008). *The 25th anniversary of the publication of Howard Gardner's* Frames of mind: The theory of multiple intelligences. Retrieved June 30, 2010, from http://www.howardgardner.com

Gardner, H. (2009). Birth and the spreading of a "meme." In J.-Q. Chen, S. Moran, & H. Gardner, (Eds.), *Multiple intelligences around the world* (pp. 3–16). San Francisco: Jossey-Bass.

Gardner, H., & Hatch, T. (1990). Multiple intelligences go to school: Educational implications of the theory of multiple intelligences. *Educational Researcher, 18*(8), 4–10.

Gardner, H., & Moran, S. (2006). The science of multiple intelligences theory: A response to Lynn Waterhouse. *Educational Psychologist, 41*(4), 227–232.

Gardner, H., Torff, B., & Hatch, T. (1996). The age of innocence reconsidered: Preserving the best of the progressive traditions in psychology and education. In D. R. Olson & N. Torrance (Eds.), *The handbook of education and human development: New models of learning, teaching and schooling* (pp. 28–55). Cambridge, MA: Blackwell.

Garland, A., Augustyn, M., & Stein, M. T. (2007). Disruptive and oppositional behavior in an 11-year-old boy. *Journal of Developmental and Behavioral Pediatrics, 28*, 406–408.

Garner, R. (1987). Strategies for reading and studying expository texts. *Educational Psychologist, 22*, 299–312.

Garner, R. (1998). Epilogue: Choosing to learn or not-learn in school. *Educational Psychology Review, 10*, 227–237.

Garrison, L. (1989). Programming for the gifted American Indian student. In C. J. Maker & S. W. Schiever (Eds.), *Critical issues in gifted education: Vol. 2. Defensible programs for cultural and ethnic minorities*. Austin, TX: Pro-Ed.

Garvey, C. (1990). *Play*. Cambridge, MA: Harvard University Press.

Garvey, C., & Berninger, G. (1981). Timing and turn taking in children's conversations. *Discourse Processes, 4*, 27–59.

Garvey, C., & Hogan, R. (1973). Social speech and social interaction: Egocentrism revisited. *Child Development, 44*(3), 562–568. doi:10.2307/1128013

Gaskins, I. W., Satlow, E., & Pressley, M. (2007). Executive control of reading comprehension in the elementary school. In L. Meltzer (Ed.), *Executive function in education: From theory to practice* (pp. 194–215). New York: Guilford Press.

Gaskins, S. (1999). Children's daily lives in a Mayan village: A case study of culturally constructed roles and activities. In A. Göncü (Ed.), *Children's engagement in the world: Sociocultural perspectives* (pp. 25–61). Cambridge, England: Cambridge University Press.

Gates, G., & Ost, J. (2004). *The gay and lesbian atlas*. Washington, DC: The Urban Institute.

Gatzke-Kopp, L. M., & Beauchaine, T. P. (2007). Central nervous system substrates of impulsivity: Implications for the development of attention-deficit/

hyperactivity disorder and conduct disorder. In D. Coch, G. Dawson, & K. W. Fischer (Eds.), *Human behavior, learning, and the developing brain: Atypical development* (pp. 239–263). New York: Guilford Press.

Gaunt, K. D. (2006). *The games Black girls play: Learning the ropes from double-dutch to hip-hop.* New York: New York University Press.

Gauvain, M. (2001). *The social context of cognitive development.* New York: Guilford Press.

Gauvain, M. (2009). Social and cultural transactions in cognitive development: A cross-generational view. In A. Sameroff (Ed.), *The transactional model of development: How children and contexts shape each other* (pp. 163–182). Washington, DC: American Psychological Association.

Gauvain, M., & Munroe, R. L. (2009). Contributions of societal modernity to cognitive development: A comparison of four cultures. *Child Development, 80*(6), 1628–1642.

Gauvain, M., & Parke, R. D. (2010). Socialization. In M. H. Bornstein (Ed.), *Handbook of cultural developmental science* (pp. 239–258). New York: Psychology Press.

Gauvain, M., & Perez, S. M. (2005). Parent–child participation in planning children's activities outside of school in European American and Latino families. *Child Development, 76,* 371–383.

Gavin, L. A., & Fuhrman, W. (1989). Age differences in adolescents' perceptions of their peer groups. *Developmental Psychology, 25,* 827–834.

Gay, G. (2006). Connections between classroom management and culturally responsive teaching. In C. M. Evertson & C. S. Weinstein (Eds.), *Handbook of classroom management: Research, practice, and contemporary issues* (pp. 343–370). Mahwah, NJ: Erlbaum.

Geary, D. C. (1994). *Children's mathematical development: Research and practical applications.* Washington, DC: American Psychological Association.

Geary, D. C. (2005). Folk knowledge and academic learning. In B. J. Ellis & D. F. Bjorklund (Eds.), *Origins of the social mind: Evolutionary psychology and child development* (pp. 493–519). New York: Guilford Press.

Geary, D. C. (2006). Development of mathematical understanding. In W. Damon & R. M. Lerner (Series Eds.), & D. Kuhn & R. Siegler (Vol. Eds.), *Handbook of child psychology: Vol. 1. Cognition, perception, and language* (6th ed.). New York: Wiley.

Geary, D. C. (2010). Mathematical disabilities: Reflections on cognitive, neuropsychological, and genetic components. *Learning and Individual Differences, 20*(2), 130–133.

Gelhorn, H., Hartman, C., Sakai, J., Mikulich-Gilbertson, S., Stallings, M., Young, S., et al. (2009). An item response theory analysis of conduct disorder. *Journal of the American Academy of Child & Adolescent Psychiatry, 48*(1), 42–50.

Gelman, R., & Baillargeon, R. (1983). A review of some Piagetian concepts. In J. H. Flavell & E. M. Markman (Eds.), *Handbook of child psychology: Vol. 3. Cognitive development.* New York: Wiley.

Gelman, S. A. (2003). *The essential child: Origins of essentialism in everyday thought.* New York: Oxford University Press.

Gelman, S. A., & Kalish, C. W. (2006). Conceptual development. In W. Damon & R. M. Lerner (Series Eds.), & D. Kuhn & R. Siegler (Vol. Eds.), *Handbook of child psychology: Vol. 1. Cognition, perception, and language* (6th ed.). New York: Wiley.

Gelman, S. A., & Markman, E. M. (1986). Categories and induction in young children. *Cognition, 23,* 183–209.

Gelman, S. A., & Raman, L. (2003). Preschool children use linguistic form class and pragmatic cues to interpret generics. *Child Development, 74,* 308–325.

Gelman, S. A., & Taylor, M. (1984). How two-year-old children interpret proper and common names for unfamiliar objects. *Child Development, 55,* 1535–1540.

Genesee, F. (1985). Second language learning through immersion: A review of U.S. programs. *Review of Educational Research, 55,* 541–561.

Genesoni, L., & Tallandini, M. A. (2009). Men's psychological transition to fatherhood: An analysis of the literature, 1989–2008. *Birth, 36*(4), 305–317.

Gentile, D. A., & Gentile, J. R. (2008). Violent video games as exemplary teachers: A conceptual analysis. *Journal of Youth and Adolescence, 37,* 127–141.

Gentner, D. (2006). Why verbs are hard to learn. In K. Hirsh-Pasek, & R. M. Golinkoff (Eds.), *Action meets word: How children learn verbs* (pp. 544–564). New York: Oxford University Press.

Gentry, R. (1982). An analysis of the developmental spellings in *Gnys at Wrk. The Reading Teacher, 36,* 192–200.

Genzuk, M. (1999). Tapping into community funds of knowledge. In *Effective strategies for English language acquisition: Curriculum guide for the professional development of teachers grades kindergarten through eight* (pp. 9–21). Los Angeles, CA: Los Angeles Annenberg Metropolitan Project, ARCO Foundation.

George, L. (2005). Lack of preparedness: Experiences of first-time mothers. *American Journal of Maternal/Child Nursing, 30*(4), 251–255.

Georgiou, S., Demetriou, A., & Stavrinides, P. (2008). Attachment style and mentoring relationships in adolescence. *Educational Psychology, 28*(6), 603–614.

Geraci, A. (2009/2010). Good food in the city. *Educational Leadership, 67*(4), 12–16.

Gerken, L. (1994). Child phonology: Past research, present questions, future directions. In M. A. Gernsbacher (Ed.), *Handbook of psycholinguistics* (pp. 781–820). San Diego, CA: Academic Press.

Gernsbacher, M. A., Stevenson, J. L., Khandakar, S., & Goldsmith, H. H. (2008). Why does joint attention look atypical in autism. *Child Development Perspectives, 2*(1), 38–45.

Gershoff, E. T., Aber, J. L., & Raver, C. C. (2005). Child poverty in the United States: An evidence-based conceptual framework for programs and policies. In R. M. Lerner, F. Jacobs, & D. Wertlieb (Eds.), *Applied developmental science: An advanced textbook* (pp. 269–324). Thousand Oaks, CA: Sage.

Gertner, Y., Fisher, C., & Eisengart, J. (2006). Learning words and rules: Abstract knowledge of word order in early sentence comprehension. *Psychological Science, 17,* 684–691.

Gervai, J. (2009). Environmental and genetic influences on early attachment. *Child and Adolescent Psychiatry and Mental Health, 3*(Sep 4).

Gervain, J., Macagno, F., Cogoi, S., Peña, M., & Mehler, J. (2008). The neonate brain detects speech structure. *Proceedings of the National Academy of Sciences of the United States of America, 105*(37), 14222–14227.

Gervain, J., & Mehler, J. (2010). Speech perception and language acquisition in the first year of life. *Annual Review of Psychology, 61,* 191–218.

Gesell, A. (1928). *Infancy and human growth.* New York: Macmillan.

Gettinger, M., & Kohler, K. M. (2006). Process-outcome approaches to classroom management and effective teaching. In C. M. Evertson & C. S. Weinstein (Eds.), *Handbook of classroom management: Research, practice, and contemporary issues* (pp. 73–95). Mahwah, NJ: Erlbaum.

Ghazvini, A., & Mullis, R. L. (2002). Center-based care for young children: Examining predictors of quality. *Journal of Genetic Psychology, 163,* 112–125.

Gibson, E. J., & Walk, R. D. (1960). The "visual cliff." *Scientific American, 202*(4), 64–71.

Gibson, J. J. (1979). *The ecological approach to visual perception.* Boston: Houghton-Mifflin.

Gibson, M. A., & Lawson, D. W. (2011). "Modernization" increases parental investment and sibling resource competition: Evidence from a rural development initiative in Ethiopia. *Evolution and Human Behavior, 32*(2), 97–105. doi:10.1016/j.evolhumbehav.2010.10.002

Gillam, R. B., & Johnston, J. R. (1992). Spoken and written language relationships in language/learning-impaired and normal achieving school-age children. *Journal of Speech and Hearing Research, 35,* 1303–1315.

Gillham, J. E., Reivich, K. J., Jaycox, L. H., & Seligman, M. E. P. (1995). Prevention of depressive symptoms in schoolchildren: Two-year follow-up. *Psychological Science, 6,* 343–351.

Gilligan, C. (1982). *In a different voice: Psychological theory and women's development.* Cambridge, MA: Harvard University Press.

Gilligan, C. F. (1985, March). *Keynote address at the Conference on Women and Moral Theory,* Stony Brook, NY.

Gilligan, C. F. (1987). Moral orientation and moral development. In E. F. Kittay & D. T. Meyers (Eds.), *Women and moral theory.* Totowa, NJ: Rowman & Littlefield.

Gilligan, C. F., & Attanucci, J. (1988). Two moral orientations. In C. F. Gilligan, J. V. Ward, & J. M. Taylor (Eds.), *Mapping the moral domain: A contribution of women's thinking to psychological theory and education.* Cambridge, MA: Center for the Study of Gender, Education, and Human Development (distributed by Harvard University Press).

Gilliland, H. (1988). Discovering and emphasizing the positive aspects of the culture. In H. Gilliland & J. Reyhner (Eds.), *Teaching the Native American.* Dubuque, IA: Kendall/Hunt.

Gilman, R., Meyers, J., & Perez, L. (2004). Structured extracurricular activities among adolescents: Findings and implications for school psychologists. *Psychology in the Schools, 41,* 31–41.

Ginsburg, H. P. (2009). The challenge of formative assessment in mathematics education: Children's minds, teachers' minds. *Human Development, 52,* 109–128.

Ginsburg, H. P., Cannon, J., Eisenband, J., & Pappas, S. (2006). Mathematical thinking and learning. In K. McCartney & D. Phillips (Eds.), *Blackwell handbook of early childhood development* (pp. 208–229). Malden, MA: Blackwell.

Ginsburg, H. P., Lee, J. S., & Boyd, J. S. (2008). Mathematics education for young children: What it is and how to promote it. *Social Policy Report, 22*(1). Ann Arbor, MI: Society for Research in Child Development.

Gioia, K. A., & Tobin, R. M. (2010). Role of sociodramatic play in promoting self-regulation. In C. E. Schaefer (Ed.), Play therapy for preschool children (pp. 181–198). Washington, DC: American Psychological Association. doi:10.1037/12060-009

Giordano, P. C. (2003). Relationships in adolescence. *Annual Review of Sociology, 29,* 257–281.

Giorgio, A., Watkins, K. E., Chadwick, M., James, S., Winmill, L., Douaud, G., et al. (2010). Longitudinal changes in grey and white matter during adolescence. *NeuroImage, 49,* 94–103.

Given, H., Kuh, L., LeeKeenan, D., Mardell, B., Redditt, S., & Twombly, S. (2010). Changing School Culture: Using documentation to support collaborative inquiry. *Theory into Practice, 49*(1), 36–46. doi:10.1080/00405840903435733

Glahn, D. C., & Burdick, K. E. (2011). Clinical endophenotypes for bipolar disorder. In H. K. Manji & C. A. Zarate Jr. (Eds.), *Behavioral neurobiology of bipolar disorder and its treatment* (pp. 51–67). New York: Springer Science.

Gläscher, J., Rudrauf, D., Colom, R., Paul, L. K., Tranel, D., Damasio, H., & Adolphs, R. (2010). Distributed neural system for general intelligence revealed by lesion mapping. *Proceedings of the National Academy of Sciences of the United States of America, 107*(10), 4705–4709.

Glaser, C., & Brunstein, J. C. (2007). Improving fourth-grade students' composition skills: Effects of strategy instruction and self-regulation procedures. *Journal of Educational Psychology, 99,* 297–310.

Glasgow, J. N. (1994). Action research changes cultural attitudes. *Teaching Education, 6,* 41–48.

Gleitman, L. R., Cassidy, K., Nappa, R., Papafragou, A., & Trueswell, J. C. (2005). Hard words. *Language Learning and Development, 1*(1), 23–64.

Glenwright, M., & Pexman, P. M. (2010). Development of children's ability to distinguish sarcasm and verbal irony. *Journal of Child Language, 37*(2), 429–451.

Glick, J. (1975). Cognitive development in cross-cultural perspective. In F. Horowitz (Ed.), *Review of child development research* (Vol. 4). Chicago: University of Chicago Press.

Glick, J. E., & Bates, L. (2010). Diversity in academic achievement: Children of immigrants in US schools. In E. L. Grigorenko & R. Takanishi (Eds.), *Immigration, diversity, and education* (pp. 112–129). New York: Routledge.

Glucksberg, S., & Krauss, R. M. (1967). What do people say after they have learned to talk? Studies of the development of referential communication. *Merrill-Palmer Quarterly, 13,* 309–316.

Gluszek, A., & Dovidio, J. F. (2010). The way they speak: A social psychological perspective on the stigma of nonnative accents in communication. *Personality and Social Psychology Review, 14*(2), 214–237.

Glynn, S. M., Yeany, R. H., & Britton, B. K. (1991a). A constructive view of learning science. In S. M. Glynn, R. H. Yeany, & B. K. Britton (Eds.), *The psychology of learning science* (pp. 3–19). Mahwah, NJ: Erlbaum.

Glynn, S. M., Yeany, R. H., & Britton, B. K. (Eds.) (1991b). *The psychology of learning science.* Hillsdale, NJ: Erlbaum.

Gnepp, J. (1989). Children's use of personal information to understand other people's feelings. In C. Saarni & P. L. Harris (Eds.), *Children's understanding of emotion.* Cambridge, England: Cambridge University Press.

Goghari, V. M., Sponheim, S. R., & MacDonald, A. W. III. (2010). The functional neuroanatomy of symptom dimensions in schizophrenia: A qualitative and quantitative review of a persistent question. *Neuroscience and Behavioral Reviews, 34,* 468–486.

Gogtay, N., & Thompson, P. M. (2010). Mapping gray matter development: Implications for typical development and vulnerability to psychopathology. *Brain and Cognition, 72,* 6–15.

Golay, P., & Lecerf, T. (2011). Orthogonal higher order structure and confirmatory factor analysis of the French Wechsler Adult Intelligence Scale (WAIS-III). *Psychological Assessment, 23*(1), 143–152. doi:10.1037/a0021230

Gold, J. M. (2009). Stepparents and the law: Knowledge for counselors, guidelines for family members. *The Family Journal, 17*(3), 272–276.

Goldberg, A. E. (2010). *Lesbian and gay parents and their children: Research on the family life cycle.* Washington, DC: American Psychological Association.

Goldenberg, C. (1992). The limits of expectations: A case for case knowledge about teacher expectancy effects. *American Educational Research Journal, 29,* 517–544.

Goldin-Meadow, S. (1997). When gestures and words speak differently. *Current Directions in Psychological Science, 6,* 138–143.

Goldin-Meadow, S. (2006). Talking and thinking with our hands. *Current Directions in Psychological Science, 15,* 34–39.

Goldin-Meadow, S., & Mylander, C. (1993). Beyond the input given: The child's role in the acquisition of language. In P. Bloom (Ed.), *Language acquisition: Core readings.* Cambridge, MA: MIT Press.

Goldin-Meadow, S., Nusbaum, H., Kelly, S. D., & Wagner, S. (2001). Explaining math: Gesturing lightens the load. *Psychological Science, 12,* 516–522.

Goldstein, M. H., & Schwade, J. A. (2008). Social feedback to infants' babbling facilitates rapid phonological learning. *Psychological Science, 19,* 515–523.

Goldstein, S., & Brooks, R. B. (Eds.) (2006). *Handbook of resilience in children.* New York: Springer.

Goldstein, S., & Rider, R. (2006). Resilience and the disruptive disorders of childhood. In S. Goldstein & R. B. Brooks (Eds.), *Handbook of resilience in children* (pp. 203–222). New York: Springer.

Goleman, D. (1995). *Emotional intelligence.* New York: Bantam Books.

Golinkoff, R. M., & Hirsh-Pasek, K. (2006). Baby wordsmith: From associationistic to social sophisticate. *Current Directions in Psychological Science, 15,* 30–33.

Golinkoff, R. M., & Hirsh-Pasek, K. (2008). How toddlers begin to learn verbs. *Trends in Cognitive Sciences, 12*(10), 397–403.

Golinkoff, R. M., Hirsh-Pasek, K., Bailey, L., & Wenger, N. (1992). Young children and adults use lexical principles to learn new nouns. *Developmental Psychology, 28,* 99–108.

Gollnick, D. M., & Chinn, P. C. (2002). *Multicultural education in a pluralistic society* (6th ed.). Upper Saddle River, NJ: Merrill/Prentice Hall.

Golomb, C. (2004). *The child's creation of a pictorial world* (2nd ed.). Mahwah, NJ: Erlbaum.

Gomby, D. S., Culross, P. L., & Behrman, R. E. (1999). Home visiting: Recent program evaluations—Analysis and recommendations. *The Future of Children. Home Visiting: Recent Program Evaluations, 9*(1), 4–26.

Gomez, M. L., Schieble, M., Curwood, J. S., & Hassett, D. (2010). Technology, learning and instruction: Distributed cognition in the secondary English classroom. *Literacy, 44*(1), 20–27.

Göncü, A. (1993). Development of intersubjectivity in the dyadic play of preschoolers. *Early Childhood Research Quarterly, 8,* 99–116.

Góngora, X., & Farkas, C. (2009). Infant sign language program effects on synchronic mother-infant interactions. *Infant Behavior & Development, 32*(2), 216–225.

Gonzalez, A.-L., & Wolters, C. A. (2006). The relation between perceived parenting practices and achievement motivation in mathematics. *Journal of Research in Childhood Education, 21,* 203–217.

González, N., Moll, L. C., & Amanti, C. (2005). Introduction: Theorizing practices. *Funds of knowledge: Theorizing practices in households, communities, and classrooms* (pp. 1–24). Mahwah, NJ: Erlbaum.

Gonzalez-Mena, J. (2002). *The child in the family and the community* (3rd ed.). Upper Saddle River, NJ: Merrill/Prentice Hall.

Gonzalez-Mena, J. (2010). Compassionate roots begin with babies. *Exchange, 32*(3), 46–49.

Good, T. L., & Brophy, J. E. (1994). *Looking in classrooms* (6th ed.). New York: HarperCollins.

Good, T. L., McCaslin, M. M., & Reys, B. J. (1992). Investigating work groups to promote problem solving in mathematics. In J. Brophy (Ed.), *Advances in research on teaching: Vol. 3. Planning and managing learning tasks and activities.* Greenwich, CT: JAI Press.

Good, T. L., & Nichols, S. L. (2001). Expectancy effects in the classroom: A special focus on improving the reading performance of minority students in first-grade classrooms. *Educational Psychologist, 36,* 113–126.

Goodman, K. (2008). Making reading curriculum by professional consensus and by legislative mandate. *Journal of Reading Education, 34*(1), 5–15.

Goodman, K. S. (1989). Whole-language research: Foundations and development. *Elementary School Journal, 90,* 207–221.

Goodnow, J. J. (2010). Culture. In M. H. Bornstein (Ed.), *Handbook of cultural developmental science* (pp. 3–19). New York: Psychology Press.

Goodwin, M. H. (2006). *The hidden life of girls: Games of stance, status, and exclusion.* Malden, MA: Blackwell.

Goodwyn, S. W., & Acredolo, L. P. (1998). Encouraging symbolic gestures: A new perspective on the relationship between gesture and speech. In J. M. Iverson & S. Goldin-Meadow (Eds.), *Nature and functions of gesture in children's communication.* San Francisco: Jossey-Bass.

Goodwyn, S. W., Acredolo, L. P., & Brown, C. A. (2000). Impact of symbolic gesturing on early language development. *Journal of Nonverbal Behavior, 24,* 81–103.

Gopnik, A. (2009a, August 1). Babies rule! *New Scientist, 203*(2719).

Gopnik, A. (2009b). Rational constructivism: A new way to bridge rationalism and empiricism. *Behavioral and Brain Sciences, 32*(2), 208–209.

Gopnik, A. (2009c, August 16). Your baby is smarter than you think. *New York Times.*

Gopnik, M. (Ed.) (1997). *The inheritance and innateness of grammars.* New York: Oxford University Press.

Gordon, P. (2004). Numerical cognition without words: Evidence from Amazonia. *Science, 306,* 496–499.

Goswami, U. (1999). The relationship between phonological awareness and orthographic representation in different orthographies. In M. Harris & G. Hatano (Eds.), *Learning to read and write: A cross-linguistic perspective.* Cambridge, England: Cambridge University Press.

Goswami, U. (2007). Typical reading development and developmental dyslexia across languages. In D. Coch, G. Dawson, & K. W. Fischer (Eds.), *Human behavior, learning, and the developing brain: Atypical development* (pp. 145–167). New York: Guilford Press.

Goswami, U. (2011). *Inductive and deductive reasoning.* In U. Goswami (Ed.), *The Wiley-Blackwell handbook of childhood cognitive development* (2nd ed., pp. pp. 399–419). Malden, MA: Wiley-Blackwell.

Gottfredson, L. (2003). Dissecting practical intelligence theory: Its claims and evidence. *Intelligence, 31,* 343–397.

Gottfried, A. E., Fleming, J. S., & Gottfried, A. W. (1994). Role of parental motivational practices in children's academic intrinsic motivation and achievement. *Journal of Educational Psychology, 86,* 104–113.

Gottfried, A. E., Fleming, J. S., & Gottfried, A. W. (2001). Continuity of academic intrinsic motivation from childhood through late adolescence: A longitudinal study. *Journal of Educational Psychology, 93,* 3–13.

Gottfried, A. E., Marcoulides, G. A., Gottfried, A. W., & Oliver, P. H. (2009). A latent curve model of parental motivational practices and developmental decline in math and science academic intrinsic motivation. *Journal of Educational Psychology, 101*(3), 729–739. doi:10.1037/a0015084

Gottfried, A. W., Gottfried, A. E., Bathurst, K., & Guerin, D. W. (1994). *Gifted IQ: Early developmental aspects.* New York: Plenum Press.

Gottfried, A. W., Gottfried, A. E., & Guerin, D. W. (2009). Issues in early prediction and identification of intellectual giftedness. In F. D. Horowitz, R. F. Subotnik, & D. J. Matthews (Eds.),

The development of giftedness and talent across the life span (pp. 43–56). Washington, DC: American Psychological Association.

Gottlieb, G. (1991). Experiential canalization of behavioral development: Theory. *Developmental Psychology, 27,* 4–13.

Gottlieb, G. (1992). *Individual development and evolution: The genesis of novel behavior.* New York: Oxford University Press.

Gottlieb, G., Wahlsten, D., & Lickliter, R. (2006). The significance of biology for human development: A developmental psychobiological systems view. In W. Damon & R. M. Lerner (Eds. in Chief) & R. M. Lerner (Vol. Ed.), *Handbook of child psychology: Vol. 1. Theoretical models of human development* (6th ed., pp. 210–257). Hoboken, NJ: Wiley.

Gottman, J. M. (1983). How children become friends. *Monographs of the Society for Research in Child Development, 48*(3, Serial No. 201).

Gottman, J. M. (1986). The world of coordinated play: Same- and cross-sex friendship in young children. In J. M. Gottman & J. G. Parker (Eds.), *Conversations of friends: Speculations on affective development* (pp. 139–191). Cambridge, England: Cambridge University Press.

Gottman, J. M., & Mettetal, G. (1986). Speculations about social and affective development: Friendship and acquaintanceship through adolescence. In J. M. Gottman & J. G. Parker (Eds.), *Conversations of friends: Speculations on affective development* (pp. 192–237). Cambridge, England: Cambridge University Press.

Goudena, P. (2006). Real and symbolic entry of children in the social world of peers and parent-child interactions. In X. Chen, D. C. French, & B. H. Schneider (Eds.), *Peer relationships in cultural context* (pp. 247–263). New York: Cambridge University Press.

Goulven, J., Ferath, K., Guillaume, F., Seghier, M. L., & Price, C. J. (1995). Predicting language lateralization from gray matter. *Journal of Neuroscience, 29*(43), 13516–13523.

Gover, A. R., Jennings, W. G., & Tewksbury, R. (2009). Adolescent male and female gang members' experiences with violent victimization, dating violence, and sexual assault. *American Journal of Criminal Justice, 34*(1–2), 103–115. doi:10.1007/s12103-008-9053-z

Graber, J. A., Britto, P. R., & Brooks-Gunn, J. (1999). What's love got to do with it? Adolescents' and young adults' beliefs about sexual and romantic relationships. In W. Furman, B. B. Brown, & C. Feiring (Eds.), *The development of romantic relationships in adolescence* (pp. 364–395). Cambridge, England: Cambridge University Press.

Graesch, A. P. (2009). Material indicators of family busyness. *Social Indicators Research, 93,* 85–94.

Graesser, A., Golding, J. M., & Long, D. L. (1991). Narrative representation and comprehension. In R. Barr, M. L. Kamil, P. Mosenthal, & P. D. Pearson (Eds.), *Handbook of reading research* (Vol. II). New York: Longman.

Graham, S. (1989). Motivation in Afro-Americans. In G. L. Berry & J. K. Asamen (Eds.), *Black students: Psychosocial issues and academic achievement.* Newbury Park, CA: Sage.

Graham, S. (1997). Using attribution theory to understand social and academic motivation in African American youth. *Educational Psychologist, 32,* 21–34.

Graham, S. (2006). Writing. In P. A. Alexander & P. H. Winne (Eds.), *Handbook of educational psychology* (2nd ed., pp. 457–478). Mahwah, NJ: Erlbaum.

Graham, S. (2009). Giftedness in adolescence: African American gifted youth and their challenges from a motivational perspective. In F. D. Horowitz, R. F. Subotnik, & D. J. Matthews (Eds.), *The development of giftedness and talent across the*

life span (pp. 109–129). Washington, DC: American Psychological Association.

Graham, S., Harris, K. R., & Fink, B. (2000). Is handwriting causally related to learning to write? Treatment of handwriting problems in beginning writers. *Journal of Educational Psychology, 92,* 620–633.

Graham, S., Harris, K. R., & Olinghouse, N. (2007). Addressing executive function problems in writing: An example from the self-regulated strategy development model. In L. Meltzer (Ed.), *Executive function in education: From theory to practice* (pp. 216–236). New York: Guilford Press.

Graham, S., & Perin, D. (2007). A meta-analysis of writing instruction for adolescent students. *Journal of Educational Psychology, 99,* 445–476.

Graham, S., Schwartz, S. S., & MacArthur, C. A. (1993). Knowledge of writing and the composing process, attitude toward writing, and self-efficacy for students with and without learning disabilities. *Journal of Learning Disabilities, 26,* 237–249.

Graham, S., & Weintraub, N. (1996). A review of handwriting research: Progress and prospects from 1980 to 1994. *Educational Psychology Review, 8,* 7–87.

Graham, S., & Williams, C. (2009). An attributional approach to motivation in school. In K. R. Wentzel & A. Wigfield (Eds.), *Handbook of motivation at school* (pp. 11–33). New York: Routledge.

Gralinski, J. H., & Kopp, C. B. (1993). Everyday rules for behavior: Mothers' requests to young children. *Developmental Psychology, 29*(3), 573–584. doi:10.1037/0012-1649.29.3.573

Grammer, J. K., Purtell, K. M., Coffman, J. L., & Ornstein, P. A. (2011). Relations between children's metamemory and strategic performance: Time-varying covariates in early elementary school. *Journal of Experimental Child Psychology, 108*(1), 139–155. doi:10.1016/j.jecp.2010.08.001

Grandin, T. (1995). *Thinking in pictures and other reports of my life with autism.* New York: Random House.

Granger, R. C. (2008). After-school programs and academics: Implications for policy, practice, and research. *Social Policy Report, 22*(2). Ann Arbor, MI: Society for Research in Child Development.

Granrud, C. E. (2006). Size constancy in infants: 4-month-olds' responses to physical versus retinal image size. *Journal of Experimental Psychology: Human Perception and Performance, 32,* 1398–1404.

Grant, C. A., & Gomez, M. L. (2001). *Campus and classroom: Making schooling multicultural* (2nd ed.). Upper Saddle River, NJ: Merrill/Prentice Hall.

Grant, H., & Dweck, C. (2001). Cross-cultural response to failure: Considering outcome attributions with different goals. In F. Salili & C. Chiu (Eds.), *Student motivation: The culture and context of learning* (pp. 203–219). Dordrecht, The Netherlands: Kluwer Academic.

Graue, M. E., & Walsh, D. J. (1998). *Studying children in context.* Thousand Oaks, CA: Sage.

Gray, C. (2010). Visual impairment: The educational experiences of young people in Northern Ireland. *Educational and Child Psychology, 27*(2), 68–78.

Gredler, M. E., & Shields, C. C. (2008). *Vygotsky's legacy: A foundation for research and practice.* New York: Guilford Press.

Green, L., Fry, A. F., & Myerson, J. (1994). Discounting of delayed rewards: A life-span comparison. *Psychological Science, 5,* 33–36.

Greenberg, B. S., & Mastro, D. E. (2008). Children, race, ethnicity, and media. In S. L. Calvert, & B. J. Wilson (Eds.), *The handbook of children, media, and development. Handbooks in communication and media* (pp. 74–97). Malden, MA: Blackwell Publishing. doi:10.1002/9781444302752.ch4

Greenberg, M. T. (1999). Attachment and psychopathology in childhood. In J. Cassidy & P. R. Shaver (Eds.), *Handbook of attachment: Theory, research, and clinical applications* (pp. 469–496). New York: Guilford Press.

Greenberg, M. T., Weissberg, R. P., O'Brien, M. U., Zins, J. E., Fredericks, L., Resnik, H., et al. (2003). Enhancing school-based prevention and youth development through coordinated social, emotional, and academic learning. *American Psychologist, 58,* 466–474.

Greene, J. P., & Forster, G. (2004). *Sex, drugs, and delinquency in urban and suburban public schools* (Education Working Paper). Manhattan Institute for Policy Research. Retrieved August 12, 2008, from www.manhattan-institute.org/html/ewp_04.htm

Greenfield, P. M. (1998). The cultural evolution of IQ. In U. Neisser (Ed.), *The rising curve: Long-term gains in IQ and related measures* (pp. 81–123). Washington, DC: American Psychological Association.

Greenfield, P. M., DeWinstanley, P., Kilpatrick, H., & Kaye, D. (1996). Action video games and informal education: Effects on strategies for dividing visual attention. In P. M. Greenfield & R. R. Cocking (Eds.), *Advances in applied developmental psychology: Vol. 11. Interacting with video* (pp. 187–205). Westport, CT: Ablex.

Greenfield, P. M., & Subrahmanyam, K. (2003). Online discourse in a teen chatroom: New codes and new modes of coherence in a visual medium. *Applied Developmental Psychology, 24,* 713–738.

Greenfield, P. M., Trumbull, E., Keller, H., Rothstein-Fisch, C., Suzuki, L. K., & Quiroz, B. (2006). Cultural conceptions of learning and development. In P. A. Alexander & P. H. Winne (Eds.), *Handbook of educational psychology* (2nd ed., pp. 675–692). Mahwah, NJ: Erlbaum.

Greeno, J. G. (2007). Toward the development of intellective character. In E. W. Gordon & B. L. Bridglall (Eds.), *Affirmative development: Cultivating academic ability* (pp. 17–47). Lanham, MD: Rowman.

Greeno, J. G., Collins, A. M., & Resnick, L. B. (1996). Cognition and learning. In D. C. Berliner & R. C. Calfee (Eds.), *Handbook of educational psychology.* New York: Macmillan.

Greenough, W. T., & Black, J. E. (1992). Induction of brain structure by experience: Substrates for cognitive development. In M. R. Gunnar & C. A. Nelson (Eds.), *Developmental behavioral neuroscience. The Minnesota Symposium on Child Psychology* (Vol. 24, pp. 155–200). Mahwah, NJ: Erlbaum.

Greenough, W. T., Black, J. E., & Wallace, C. S. (1987). Experience and brain development. *Child Development, 58,* 539–559.

Greenspan, D. A., Solomon, B., & Gardner, H. (2004). The development of talent in different domains. In L. V. Shavinina & M. Ferrari (Eds.), *Beyond knowledge: Extracognitive aspects of developing high ability* (pp. 119–135). Mahwah, NJ: Erlbaum.

Greenspan, S., & Granfield, J. M. (1992). Reconsidering the construct of mental retardation: Implications of a model of social competence. *American Journal of Mental Retardation, 96,* 442–453.

Greenspan, S. I., & Meisels, S. (1996). Toward a new vision for the developmental assessment of infants and young children. In S. J. Meisels & E. Fenichel (Eds.), *New visions for the developmental assessment of infants and young children.* Washington, DC: Zero to Three.

Gregg, M., & Leinhardt, G. (1994a, April). *Constructing geography.* Paper presented at the annual meeting of the American Educational Research Association, New Orleans, LA.

Gregg, M., & Leinhardt, G. (1994b). Mapping out geography: An example of epistemology and education. *Review of Educational Research, 64,* 311–361.

Gregory, A., Cornell, D., Fan, X., Sheras, P., Shih, T., & Huang, F. (2010). Authoritative school discipline: High school practices associated with lower bullying and victimization. *Journal of Educational Psychology, 102*(2), 483–496. doi:10.1037/a0018562

Greif, M. L., Kemler Nelson, D. G., Keil, F. C., & Gutierrez, F. (2006). What do children want to know about artifacts? Domain-specific requests for information. *Psychological Science, 17,* 455–459.

Grekul, J., & Sanderson, K. (2011). "I thought people would be mean and shout." introducing the Hobbema Community Cadet Corps: A response to youth gang involvement? *Journal of Youth Studies, 14*(1), 41–57. doi:10.1080/13676261.2010.489602

Griedler, M. E., & Shields, C. C. (2008). *Vygotsky's legacy: A foundation for research and practice.* New York: Guilford Press.

Griffin, S. (2009). Learning sequences in the acquisition of mathematical knowledge: Using cognitive developmental theory to inform curriculum design for pre-K–6 mathematics education. *Mind, Brain, and Education, 3*(2), 96–107.

Griffin, S., Case, R., & Capodilupo, A. (1995). Teaching for understanding: The importance of the central conceptual structures in the elementary mathematics curriculum. In A. McKeough, J. Lupart, & A. Marini (Eds.), *Teaching for transfer: Fostering generalization in learning.* Mahwah, NJ: Erlbaum.

Griffin, S. A., Case, R., & Siegler, R. S. (1994). Rightstart: Providing the central conceptual prerequisites for first formal learning of arithmetic to students at risk for school failure. In K. McGilly (Ed.), *Classroom lessons: Integrating cognitive theory and classroom practice.* Cambridge, MA: MIT Press.

Griffiths, M. (2010). Online video gaming: What should educational psychologists know? *Educational Psychology in Practice, 26*(1), 35–40. doi:10.1080/02667360903522769

Grigorenko, E, L., & Takanishi, R. (2010). (Eds.) *Immigration, diversity, and education.* New York: Routledge.

Griswold, K. S., & Pessar, L. F. (2000). Management of bipolar disorder. *American Family Physician, 62,* 1343–1356.

Grolnick, W. S., & Pomerantz, E. M. (2009). Issues and challenges in studying parental control: Toward a new conceptualization. *Child Development Perspectives, 3*(3), 165–170.

Gromko, J. E. (1994). Children's invented notations as measures of musical understanding. *Psychology of Music, 22,* 136–147.

Gromko, J. E. (1996, April). *Theorizing symbolic development in music: Interpretive interactions with preschool children.* Paper presented at the Music Educators National Conference, Kansas City, MO.

Gromko, J. E. (1998). Young children's symbol use: Common principles and cognitive processes. *Update: Applications of Research in Music Education, 16*(2), 3–7.

Gromko, J. E. (2004). Predictors of music sight-reading ability in high school wind players. *Journal of Research in Music Education, 52,* 6–15.

Gromko, J. E., & Poorman, A. S. (1998). Developmental trends and relationships in children's aural perception and symbol use. *Journal of Research in Music Education, 46,* 16–23.

Gronlund, N. E., & Brookhart, S. M. (2009). *Gronlund's writing instructional objectives* (8th ed.). Upper Saddle River, NJ: Pearson Education.

Gross, D., Garvey, C., Julion, W., Fogg, L., Tucker, S., & Mokros, H. (2009). Efficacy of the Chicago Parent Program with low-income African American and Latino parents of young children. *Prevention Science, 10,* 54–65.

Gross, R. H. (2004). Sports medicine in youth athletes. *Southern Medical Journal, 97,* 880.

Gross, T. (2010). Service learning builds bonds to school for young learners. *Phi Delta Kappan, 91*(5), 24–26.

Grossman, H. L. (1994). *Classroom behavior management in a diverse society.* Mountain View, CA: Mayfield.

Grossmann, K. E., Grossmann, K., Huber, F., & Wartner, U. (1981). German children's behavior toward their mothers at 12 months and their fathers at 18 months in Ainsworth's Strange Situation. *International Journal of Behavioral Development, 4,* 157–181.

Grusec, J. (2006). The development of moral behavior and conscience from a socialization perspective. In M. Killen & J. G. Smetana (Eds.), *Handbook of moral development* (pp. 243–265). Mahwah, NJ: Erlbaum.

Grusec, J. E., & Davidov, M. (2007). Socialization in the family: The roles of parents. In J. E. Grusec & P. D. Hastings (Eds.), *Handbook of socialization: Theory and research* (pp. 284–308). New York: Guilford Press.

Grusec, J. E., & Redler, E. (1980). Attribution, reinforcement, and altruism. *Developmental Psychology, 16,* 525–534.

Guay, F., Boivin, M., & Hodges, E. V. E. (1999). Social comparison processes and academic achievement: The dependence of the development of self-evaluations on friends' performance. *Journal of Educational Psychology, 91,* 564–568.

Guberman, S. R., Rahm, J., & Menk, D. W. (1998). Transforming cultural practices: Illustrations from children's game play. *Anthropology and Education Quarterly, 29,* 419–445.

Gummerum, M., Keller, M., Takezawa, M., & Mata, J. (2008). To give or not to give: Children's and adolescents' sharing and moral negotiations in economic decision situations. *Child Development, 79,* 562–576.

Gupta, A. (2009). Vygotskian perspectives on using dramatic play to enhance children's development and balance creativity with structure in the early childhood classroom. *Early Child Development and Care, 179*(8), 1041–1054.

Guthrie, J. T. (2008). Growing motivation: How students develop. In J. T. Guthrie (Ed.), *Engaging adolescents in reading* (pp. 99–113). Thousand Oaks, CA: Corwin Press.

Guthrie, J. T., Cox, K. E., Anderson, E., Harris, K., Mazzoni, S., & Rach, L. (1998). Principles of integrated instruction for engagement in reading. *Educational Psychology Review, 10,* 177–199.

Gutiérrez, K. D., & Rogoff, B. (2003). Cultural ways of learning: Individual traits or repertoires of practice. *Educational Researcher, 32*(5), 19–25.

Guyll, M., Madon, S., Prieto, L., & Scherr, K. C. (2010). The potential roles of self-fulfilling prophecies, stigma consciousness, and stereotype threat in linking Latino a ethnicity and educational outcomes. *Journal of Social Issues, 66*(1), 113–130.

Habgood, M. P. J., & Ainsworth, S. E. (2011). Motivating children to learn effectively: Exploring the value of intrinsic integration in educational games. *Journal of the Learning Sciences, 20*(2), 169–206. doi:10.1080/10508406.2010.508029

Hacker, D. J. (1995, April). *Comprehension monitoring of written discourse across early-to-middle adolescence.* Paper presented at the annual meeting of the American Educational Research Association, San Francisco.

Haenan, J. (1996). Piotr Gal'perin's criticism and extension of Lev Vygotsky's work. *Journal of Russian and East European Psychology, 34*(2), 54–60.

Haenen, J., Schrijnemakers, H., & Stufkens, J. (2003). Sociocultural theory and the practice of teaching historical concepts. In A. Kozulin, B. Gindis, V. S. Ageyev, & S. M. Miller (Eds.), *Vygotsky's educational theory in cultural context* (pp. 246–266). Cambridge, England: Cambridge University Press.

Haerens, L., Deforche, B., Maes, L., Cardon, G., Stevens, V., & De Bourdeaudhuij, I. (2006). Evaluation of a 2-year physical activity and healthy eating intervention in middle school children. *Health Education Research, 21,* 911–921.

Hagen, J. W., & Stanovich, K. G. (1977). Memory: Strategies of acquisition. In R. V. Kail, Jr., & J. W. Hagen (Eds.), *Perspectives on the development of memory and cognition.* Hillsdale, NJ: Erlbaum.

Hagerman, R. J., & Lampe, M. E. (1999). Fragile X syndrome. In S. Goldstein & C. R. Reynolds (Eds.), *Handbook of neurodevelopmental and genetic disorders* (pp. 298–316). New York: Guilford Press.

Hagger, M. S., Chatzisarantis, N. L. D., Barkoukis, V., Wang, C. K. J., & Baranowski, J. (2005). Perceived autonomy support in physical education and leisure-time physical activity: A cross-cultural evaluation of the trans-contextual model. *Journal of Educational Psychology, 97,* 376–390.

Hahn, N., Jansen, P., & Heil, M. (2010). Preschoolers' mental rotation: Sex differences in hemispheric asymmetry. *Journal of Cognitive Neuroscience, 22*(6), 1244–1250.

Hahn-Holbrook, J., Holbrook, C., & Bering, J. (2010). Snakes, spiders, strangers: How the evolved fear of strangers may misdirect efforts to protect children from harm. In J. M. Lampinen & K. Sexton-Radek (Eds.), *Protecting children from violence: Evidence-based interventions* (pp. 263–289). New York: Psychology Press.

Haider-Markel, D. P., & Joslyn, M. R. (2008). Pulpits versus ivory towers: Socializing agents and evolution attitudes. *Social Science Quarterly, 89*(3), 665–683.

Haidt, J. (2008). Morality. *Perspectives on Psychological Science, 3*(1), 65–72.

Haight, B. K. (1992). Long-term effects of a structured life review process. *Journal of Gerontology: Psychological Sciences, 47,* 312–315.

Haight, W. L. (1999). The pragmatics of caregiver–child pretending at home: Understanding culturally specific socialization practices. In A. Göncü (Ed.), *Children's engagement in the world: Sociocultural perspectives* (pp. 128–147). Cambridge, England: Cambridge University Press.

Haight, W. L., Wang, X., Fung, H. H., Williams, K., & Mintz, J. (1999). Universal, developmental, and variable aspects of young children's play: A cross-cultural comparison of pretending at home. *Child Development, 70,* 1477–1488.

Hains, A. A., & Hains, A. H. (1988). Cognitive-behavioral training of problem-solving and impulse-control with delinquent adolescents. *Journal of Offender Counseling, Services & Rehabilitation, 12*(2), 95–113.

Haith, M. M. (1990). Perceptual and sensory processes in early infancy. *Merrill-Palmer Quarterly, 36,* 1–26.

Haith, M. M., Hazan, C., & Goodman, G. S. (1988). Expectation and anticipation of dynamic visual events by 3.5-month-old babies. *Child Development, 59,* 467–479.

Hale-Benson, J. E. (1986). *Black children: Their roots, culture, and learning styles.* Baltimore, MD: Johns Hopkins University Press.

Halford, G. S., & Andrews, G. (2006). Reasoning and problem solving. In W. Damon & R. M. Lerner (Series Eds.), & D. Kuhn & R. Siegler (Vol. Eds.), *Handbook of child psychology: Vol. 2. Cognition, perception, and language* (6th ed.). New York: Wiley.

Halgunseth, L. (2009). Family engagement, diverse families, and early childhood education programs: An integrated review of the literature. *Young Children, 64*(5), 56–58.

Hall, W. A., Hauck, Y. L., Carty, E. M., Hutton, E. K., Fenwick, J., & Stoll, K. (2009). Childbirth fear, anxiety, fatigue, and sleep deprivation in pregnant women. *Journal of Obstetric, Gynecologic, and Neonatal Nursing, 38*, 567–576.

Hallenbeck, M. J. (1996). The cognitive strategy in writing: Welcome relief for adolescents with learning disabilities. *Learning Disabilities Research and Practice, 11*, 107–119.

Halpern, D. F. (1992). *Sex differences in cognitive abilities* (2nd ed.). Hillsdale, NJ:

Halpern, D. F. (1998). Teaching critical thinking for transfer across domains. *American Psychologist, 53*, 449–455.

Halpern, D. F. (2004). A cognitive-process taxonomy for sex differences in cognitive abilities. *Current Directions in Psychological Science, 13*, 135–139.

Halpern, D. F. (2006). Assessing gender gaps in learning and academic achievement. In P. A. Alexander & P. H. Winne (Eds.), *Handbook of educational psychology* (2nd ed., pp. 635–653). Mahwah, NJ: Erlbaum.

Halpern, D. F., Bendow, C. P., Geary, D. C., Gur, R. C., Hyde, J. S., & Gernsbacher, M. A. (2007). The science of sex differences in science and mathematics. *Psychological Science in the Public Interest, 8*(1), 1–51.

Halpern, D. F., & LaMay, M. L. (2000). The smarter sex: A critical review of sex differences in intelligence. *Educational Psychology Review, 12*, 229–246.

Hamers, J. H. M., & Ruijssenaars, A. J. J. M. (1997). Assessing classroom learning potential. In G. D. Phye (Ed.), *Handbook of academic learning: Construction of knowledge*. San Diego, CA: Academic Press.

Hamill, P. V., Drizd, T. A., Johnson, C. L., Reed, R. B., Roche, A. F., & Moore, W. M. (1979). Physical growth: National Center for Health Statistics percentiles. *American Journal of Clinical Nutrition, 32*, 607–629.

Hamlen, K. R. (2011). Children's choices and strategies in video games. *Computers in Human Behavior, 27*(1), 532–539. doi:10.1016/j.chb.2010.10.001

Hammerman, E. (2008). Science for real life. *Principal Leadership (Middle School Ed.), 8*(9), 34–39.

Hammond, L. (2001). Notes from California: An anthropological approach to urban science education for language minority families. *Journal of Research in Science Teaching, 38*(9), 983–999.

Hamre, B. K., & Pianta, R. C. (2005). Can instructional and emotional support in the first-grade classroom make a difference for children at risk for school failure? *Child Development, 76*, 949–967.

Haney, W., Russell, M., & Bebell, D. (2004). Drawing on education: Using drawings to document schooling and support change. *Harvard Educational Review, 74*, 241–272.

Hankin, B. L., Oppenheimer, C., Jenness, J., Barrocas, A., Shapero, B. G., & Goldband, J. (2009). Developmental origins of cognitive vulnerabilities to depression: Review of processes contributing to stability and change across time. *Journal of Clinical Psychology, 65*(12), 1327–1338.

Hanlon, T. E., Simon, B. D., O'Grady, K. E., Carswell, S. B., & Callaman, J. M. (2009). The effectiveness of an after-school program targeting urban African American youth. *Education and Urban Society, 42*(1), 96–118. doi:10.1177/0013124509343144

Hannon, E. E., & Trehub, S. E. (2005). Metrical categories in infancy and adulthood. *Psychological Science, 16*, 48–55.

Hansen, J., & Kissel, B. (2009). Writing instruction for adolescent learners. In K. D. Wood & W. E. Blanton (Eds.), *Literacy instruction for adolescents: Research-based practice* (pp. 392–419). New York: Guilford Press.

Hansen, M., & Markman, E. (2009). Children's use of mutual exclusivity to learn labels for parts of objects. *Developmental Psychology, 45*(2), 592–596.

Harach, L., & Kuczynski, L. (2005). Construction and maintenance of parent–child relationships: Bidirectional contributions from the perspectives of parents. *Infant and Child Development, 14*, 327–343.

Harackiewicz, J. M., Barron, K. E., Pintrich, P. R., Elliot, A. J., & Thrash, T. M. (2002). Revision of achievement goal theory: Necessary and illuminating. *Journal of Educational Psychology, 94*, 638–645.

Hardy, I., Jonen, A., Möller, K., & Stern, E. (2006). Effects of instructional support within constructivist learning environments for elementary school students' understanding of "floating and sinking." *Journal of Educational Psychology, 98*, 307–326.

Hareli, S., & Weiner, B. (2002). Social emotions and personality inferences: A scaffold for a new direction in the study of achievement motivation. *Educational Psychologist, 37*, 183–193.

Harlow, H. F., & Zimmerman, R. R. (1959). Affectional responses in the infant monkey. *Science, 130*, 421–432.

Harris, C. R. (1991). Identifying and serving the gifted new immigrants. *Teaching Exceptional Children, 23*(4), 26–30.

Harris, J. R. (1995). Where is the child's environment? A group socialization theory of development. *Psychological Review, 102*, 458–489.

Harris, J. R. (1998). *The nurture assumption: Why children turn out the way they do*. New York: Free Press.

Harris, K. R., & Graham, S. (1992). Self regulated strategy development: A part of the writing process. In M. Pressley, K. R. Harris, & J. T. Guthrie (Eds.), *Promoting academic competence and literacy in school*. San Diego, CA: Academic Press.

Harris, K. R., Santangelo, T., & Graham, S. (2010). Metacognition and strategies instruction in writing. In H. S. Waters & W. Schneider (Eds.), *Metacognition, strategy use, and instruction* (pp. 226–256). New York: Guilford Press.

Harris, M. (1992). *Language experience and early language development: From input to uptake*. Hove, England: Erlbaum.

Harris, M., & Giannouli, V. (1999). Learning to read and spell in Greek: The importance of letter knowledge and morphological awareness. In M. Harris & G. Hatano (Eds.), *Learning to read and write: A cross-linguistic perspective*. Cambridge, England: Cambridge University Press.

Harris, M., & Hatano, G. (Eds.). (1999). *Learning to read and write: A cross-linguistic perspective*. Cambridge, England: Cambridge University Press.

Harris, M. B. (1997). Preface: Images of the invisible minority. In M. B. Harris (Ed.), *School experiences of gay and lesbian youth: The invisible minority* (pp. xiv–xxii). Binghamton, NY: Harrington Park Press.

Harris, M. J., & Rosenthal, R. (1985). Mediation of interpersonal expectancy effects: 31 meta-analyses. *Psychological Bulletin, 97*, 363–386.

Harris, P. L. (1989). *Children and emotion: The development of psychological understanding*. Oxford, England: Basil Blackwell.

Harris, P. L. (2006). Social cognition. In W. Damon & R. M. Lerner (Series Eds.), & D. Kuhn & R. Siegler (Vol. Eds.), *Handbook of child psychology: Vol. 2. Cognition, perception, and language* (6th ed., pp. 811–858). New York: Wiley.

Harris, Y. R., & Graham, J. A. (2007). *The African American child: Development and challenges*. New York: Springer.

Harrison, A. O., Wilson, M. N., Pine, C. J., Chan, S. Q., & Buriel, R. (1990). Family ecologies of ethnic minority children. *Child Development, 61*, 347–362.

Harrison, C. (2004). Giftedness in early childhood: The search for complexity and connection. *Roeper Review, 26*(2), 78–84.

Harrison, K., & Hefner, V. (2008). Media, body image, and eating disorders. In S. L. Calvert & B. J. Wilson (Eds.), *The handbook of children, media, and development* (pp. 381–431). Malden, MA: Blackwell.

Harrison, P. L. (2009). Preschool assessment. In T. B. Gutkin & C. R. Reynolds (Eds.), *The handbook of school psychology* (4th ed., pp. 247–268). Hoboken, NJ: Wiley.

Harrist, A. W., Thompson, S. D., & Norris, D. J. (2007). Defining quality child care: Multiple stakeholder perspectives. *Early Education and Development, 18*(2), 305–336.

Hart, B., & Risley, T. R. (1995). *Meaningful differences in the everyday experiences of young American children*. Baltimore, MD: Paul H. Brookes.

Hart, B., & Risley, T. R. (1999). *The social world of children learning to talk*. Baltimore, MD: Paul H. Brookes.

Hart, D. (1988). The adolescent self-concept in social context. In D. K. Lapsley & F. C. Power (Eds.), *Self, ego, and identity: Integrative approaches* (pp. 71–90). New York: Springer-Verlag.

Hart, D., Atkins, R., & Donnelly, T. M. (2006). Community service and moral development. In M. Killen & J. G. Smetana (Eds.), *Handbook of moral development* (pp. 633–656). Mahwah, NJ: Erlbaum.

Hart, D., & Fegley, S. (1995). Prosocial behavior and caring in adolescence: Relations to self-understanding and social judgment. *Child Development, 66*, 1346–1359.

Hart, E. L., Lahey, B. B., Loeber, R., Applegate, B., & Frick, P. J. (1995). Developmental changes in attention-deficit hyperactivity disorder in boys: A four-year longitudinal study. *Journal of Abnormal Child Psychology, 23*, 729–750.

Hart, S. (2011). *The impact of attachment*. New York: Norton.

Harter, S. (1992). The relationship between perceived competence, affect, and motivational orientation within the classroom: Processes and patterns of change. In A. K. Boggiano & T. S. Pittman (Eds.), *Achievement and motivation: A social-developmental perspective*. Cambridge, England: Cambridge University Press.

Harter, S. (1996). Teacher and classmate influences on scholastic motivation, self-esteem, and level of voice in adolescents. In J. Juvonen & K. Wentzel (Eds.), *Social motivation: Understanding children's school adjustment*. New York: Cambridge University Press.

Harter, S. (1999). *The construction of the self*. New York: Guilford Press.

Harter, S. (2006). The self. In W. Damon & R. M. Lerner (Eds. in Chief) & N. Eisenberg (Vol. Ed.), *Handbook of child psychology, Vol. 3. Social, emotional, and personality development* (6th ed., pp. 505–570). Hoboken, NJ: Wiley.

Harter, S., Stocker, C., & Robinson, N. S. (1996). The perceived directionality of the link between approval and self-worth: The liabilities of a looking glass self-orientation among young adolescents. *Journal of Research on Adolescence, 6*, 285–308.

Harter, S., & Whitesell, N. R. (1989). Developmental changes in children's understanding of single, multiple, and blended emotion concepts. In C. Saarni & P. Harris (Eds.), *Children's understanding of emotion* (pp. 81–116). Cambridge, England: Cambridge University Press.

Harter, S., Whitesell, N. R., & Junkin, L. J. (1998). Similarities and differences in domain-specific and global self-evaluations of learning-disabled, behaviorally disordered, and normally achieving adolescents. *American Educational Research Journal, 35*, 653–680.

Hartup, W. W. (1983). Peer relations. In P. H. Mussen (Ed.), *Handbook of child psychology: Vol. IV. Socialization* (4th ed.). New York: Wiley.

Hartup, W. W. (1984). The peer context in middle childhood. In A. Collins (Ed.), *Development during middle childhood: The years from six to twelve.* Washington, DC: National Academy Press.

Hartup, W. W. (1996). The company they keep: Friendships and their developmental significance. *Child Development, 67,* 1–13.

Hartup, W. W. (2009). Critical issues and theoretical viewpoints. In K. H. Rubin, W. M. Bukowski, & B. Laursen (Eds.) *Handbook of peer interactions, relationships, and groups* (pp. 3–19). New York: Guilford Press.

Hartup, W. W., & Laursen, B. (1991). Relationships as developmental contexts. In R. Cohen & W. A. Siegel (Eds.), *Context and development* (pp. 253–279). Hillsdale, NJ: Erlbaum.

Harwood, R. L., Miller, J. G., & Irizarry, N. L. (1995). *Culture and attachment: Perceptions of the child in context.* New York: Guilford Press.

Haskill, A. M., & Corts, D. P. (2010). Acquiring language. In E. H. Sandberg & B. L. Spritz (Eds.), *A clinician's guide to normal cognitive development in childhood* (pp. 23–41). New York: Routledge/Taylor & Francis.

Hatano, G., & Inagaki, K. (1996). Cognitive and cultural factors in the acquisition of intuitive biology. In D. R. Olson & N. Torrance (Eds.), *The handbook of education and human development: New models of learning, teaching, and schooling.* Cambridge, MA: Blackwell.

Hatfield, E., Cacioppo, J. T., & Rapson, R. L. (1994). *Emotional contagion.* Cambridge, England: Cambridge University Press.

Haviland, J. M., & Lelwica, M. (1987). The induced affect response: 10-week-old infants' responses to three emotional expressions. *Developmental Psychology, 23,* 97–104.

Hawkins, F. P. L. (1997). *Journey with children: The autobiography of a teacher.* Niwot: University Press of Colorado.

Hawley, C. A. (2005). Saint or sinner? Teacher perceptions of a child with traumatic brain injury. *Pediatric Rehabilitation, 8,* 117–129.

Hay, D. F., Perra, O., Hudson, K., Waters, C. S., Mundy, L., Phillips, R., et al. (2010). Identifying early signs of aggression: Psychometric properties of the Cardiff Infant Contentiousness Scale. *Aggressive Behavior, 36*(6), 351–357. doi:10.1002/ab.20363

Hayashi, A., Karasawa, M., & Tobin, J. (2009). The Japanese preschool's pedagogy of feeling: Cultural strategies for supporting young children's emotional development. *Journal of the Society for Psychological Anthropology, 37*(1), 32–49.

Hayden, A., Bhatt, R. S., Kangas, A., & Zieber, N. (2011). Parts, cavities, and object representation in infancy. *Journal of Experimental Psychology: Human Perception and Performance, 37*(1), 314–317. doi:10.1037/a0020987

Hayes, D. P., & Grether, J. (1983). The school year and vacations: When do students learn? *Cornell Journal of Social Relations, 17*(1), 56–71.

Hayes, R. A., & Slater, A. (2008). Three-month-olds' detection of alliteration in syllables. *Infant Behavior and Development, 31,* 153–156.

Hayne, H. (2007). Infant memory development: New questions, new answers. In L. M. Oakes & P. J. Bauer (Eds.), *Short- and long-term memory in infancy and early childhood: Taking the first steps toward remembering* (pp. 209–239). New York: Oxford University Press.

Hayne, H., & Simcock, G. (2009). Memory development in toddlers. In M. L. Courage & N. Cowan (Eds.), *The development of memory in infancy and childhood* (pp. 43–68). New York: Psychology Press.

Hayslip, B., Jr. (1994). Stability of intelligence. In R. J. Sternberg (Ed.), *Encyclopedia of human intelligence* (Vol. 2). New York: Macmillan.

Haywood, H. C., & Lidz, C. S. (2007). *Dynamic assessment in practice: Clinical and educational applications.* Cambridge, England: Cambridge University Press.

Hazlett, H. C., Gaspar De Alba, M., & Hooper, S. R. (2011). Klinefelter syndrome. In S. Goldstein & C. R. Reynolds (Eds.), *Handbook of neurodevelopmental and genetic disorders in children* (2nd ed., pp. 382–397). New York: Guilford Press.

Heath, S. B. (1980). Questioning at home and at school: A comparative study. In G. Spindler (Ed.), *The ethnography of schooling: Educational anthropology in action.* New York: Holt, Rinehart & Winston.

Heath, S. B. (1983). *Ways with words: Language, life, and work in communities and classrooms.* Cambridge, England: Cambridge University Press.

Heath, S. B. (1989). Oral and literate traditions among Black Americans living in poverty. *American Psychologist, 44,* 367–373.

Hébert, T., & Pagnani, A. (2010). Engaging gifted boys in new literacies. *Gifted Child Today, 33*(3), 36–45.

Hébert, T. P., & Beardsley, T. M. (2001). Jermaine: A critical case study of a gifted black child living in rural poverty. *Gifted Child Quarterly, 45,* 85–103.

Hecht, S. A., Close, L., & Santisi, M. (2003). Sources of individual differences in fraction skills. *Journal of Experimental Child Psychology, 86,* 277–302.

Heckhausen, H. (1984). Emergent achievement behavior: Some early developments. In J. Nicholls (Ed.), *Advances in achievement motivation.* Greenwich, CT: JAI Press.

Heckhausen, H. (1987). Emotional components of action: Their ontogeny as reflected in achievement behavior. In D. Girlitz & J. F. Wohlwill (Eds.), *Curiosity, imagination, and play.* Hillsdale, NJ: Erlbaum.

Hedges, L. V., & Nowell, A. (1995). Sex differences in mental test scores, variability, and numbers of high-scoring individuals. *Science, 269,* 41–45.

Hegarty, M., & Kozhevnikov, M. (1999). Types of visual-spatial representations and mathematical problem solving. *Journal of Educational Psychology, 91,* 684–689.

Heineman, K. R., Middelburg, K. J., & Hadders-Algra, M. (2010). Development of adaptive motor behaviour in typically developing infants. *Acta Paediatrica, 99*(4), 618–624.

Hellenga, K. (2002). Social space, the final frontier: Adolescents on the Internet. In J. T. Mortimer & R. W. Larson (Eds.), *The changing adolescent experience: Societal trends and the transition to adulthood* (pp. 208–249). Cambridge, England: Cambridge University Press.

Helwig, C. C., & Jasiobedzka, U. (2001). The relation between law and morality: Children's reasoning about socially beneficial and unjust laws. *Child Development, 72,* 1382–1393.

Helwig, C. C., Zelazo, P. D., & Wilson, M. (2001). Children's judgments of psychological harm in normal and noncanonical situations. *Child Development, 72,* 66–81.

Hemphill, L., & Snow, C. (1996). Language and literacy development: Discontinuities and differences. In D. R. Olson & N. Torrance (Eds.), *The handbook of education and human development: New models of learning, teaching, and schooling.* Cambridge, MA: Blackwell.

Henderson, J. (2009). Paying for performance: Giving students cash incentives for learning. *Education Update, 51*(3), 1, 6–7.

Henderson, N. D. (1982). Human behavior genetics. *Annual Review of Psychology, 33,* 403–440.

Hendriksen, R. C., Jr., & Paladino, D. A. (2009). Identity development in a multiple heritage world. In R.C. Hendriksen & D. A. Paladino (Eds.), *Counseling multiple heritage individuals, couples, and families.* Alexandria, VA: American Counseling Association.

Hennessey, B. A. (1995). Social, environmental, and developmental issues and creativity. *Educational Psychology Review, 7,* 163–183.

Hennessey, M. G. (2003). Metacognitive aspects of students' reflective discourse: Implications for intentional conceptual change teaching and learning. In G. M. Sinatra & P. R. Pintrich (Eds.), *Intentional conceptual change* (pp. 103–132). Mahwah, NJ: Erlbaum.

Henry, L., & Winfield, J. (2010). Working memory and educational achievement in children with intellectual disabilities. *Journal of Intellectual Disability Research, 54*(4), 354–365.

Hermans, H. J. M., & Dimaggio, G. (2007). Self, identity, and globalization in times of uncertainty: A dialogical analysis. *Review of General Psychology, 11*(1), 31–61.

Hernandez, D. J. (2010). Internationally comparable indicators for children of immigrants. *Child Indicators Research, 3,* 409–411.

Hernandez, D. J., Denton, N. A., & Macartney, S. E. (2010). Children of immigrants and the future of America. In E. L. Grigorenko & R. Takanishi (Eds.), *Immigration, diversity, and education* (pp. 7–25). New York: Routledge.

Herrell, A., & Jordan, M. (2004). *Fifty strategies for teaching English language learners* (2nd ed.). Upper Saddle River, NJ: Merrill/Prentice Hall.

Hersh, C. A., Stone, B. J., & Ford, L. (1996). Learning disabilities and learned helplessness: A heuristic approach. *International Journal of Neuroscience, 84,* 103–113.

Hespos, S. J., Saylor, M. M., & Grossman, S. R. (2009). Infants' ability to parse continuous actions. *Developmental Psychology, 45,* 575–585.

Hess, R. D., & Azuma, M. (1991). Cultural support for learning: Contrasts between Japan and the United States. *Educational Researcher, 29*(9), 2–8.

Hess, R. D., & Holloway, S. D. (1984). Family and school as educational institutions. In R. D. Parke, R. N. Emde, H. P. McAdoo, & G. P. Sackett (Eds.), *Review of child development research: Vol. 7. The family* (pp. 179–222). Chicago: University of Chicago Press.

Hetherington, E. M., Bridges, M., & Insabella, G. M. (1998). What matters? What does not? Five perspectives on the association between marital transitions and children's adjustment. *American Psychologist, 53,* 167–184.

Hetherington, E. M., & Clingempeel, W. G. (1992). Coping with marital transitions: A family systems perspective. *Monographs of the Society for Research in Child Development, 57*(2–3, Serial No. 227).

Hetherington, E. M., Cox, M., & Cox, R. (1978). The aftermath of divorce. In J. H. Stevens, Jr., & M. Matthews (Eds.), *Mother–child, father–child relations* (pp. 110–155). Washington, DC: National Association for the Education of Young Children.

Hettinger, H. R., & Knapp, N. F. (2001). Potential, performance, and paradox: A case study of J.P., a verbally gifted, struggling reader. *Journal for the Education of the Gifted, 24,* 248–289.

Hewitt, J., & Scardamalia, M. (1996, April). *Design principles for the support of distributed processes.* Paper presented at the annual meeting of the American Educational Research Association, San Francisco.

Hickey, D. T. (1997). Motivation and contemporary socio-constructivist instructional perspectives. *Educational Psychologist, 32,* 175–193.

Hickey, D. T., & Granade, J. B. (2004). The influence of sociocultural theory on our theories of engagement and motivation. In D. M. McInerney & S. Van

Etten (Eds.), *Big theories revisited* (pp. 223–247). Greenwich, CT: Information Age.

Hickey, T. L., & Peduzzi, J. D. (1987). Structure and development of the visual system. In P. Salapatek & L. Cohen (Eds.), *Handbook of infant perception: Vol. 1. From sensation to perception*. New York: Academic Press.

Hicks, L. (1997). Academic motivation and peer relationships—How do they mix in an adolescent world? *Middle School Journal, 28*, 18–22.

Hidalgo, N. M., Siu, S., Bright, J. A., Swap, S. M., & Epstein, J. L. (1995). Research on families, schools, and communities: A multicultural perspective. In J. A. Banks & C. A. M. Banks (Eds.), *Handbook of research on multicultural education*. New York: Macmillan.

Hidi, S., & Harackiewicz, J. M. (2000). Motivating the academically unmotivated: A critical issue for the 21st century. *Review of Educational Research, 70*, 151–179.

Hidi, S., & Renninger, K. A. (2006). The four-phase model of interest development. *Educational Psychologist, 41*, 111–127.

Hidi, S., Renninger, K. A., & Krapp, A. (2004). Interest, a motivational variable that combines affecting and cognitive functioning. In D. Y. Dai & R. J. Sternberg (Eds.), *Motivation, emotion, and cognition: Integrative perspectives on intellectual functioning and development* (pp. 89–115). Mahwah, NJ: Erlbaum.

Hiebert, E. H., & Fisher, C. W. (1992). The tasks of school literacy: Trends and issues. In J. Brophy (Ed.), *Advances in research on teaching: Vol. 3. Planning and managing learning tasks and activities*. Greenwich, CT: JAI Press.

Hiebert, E. H., & Raphael, T. E. (1996). Psychological perspectives on literacy and extensions to educational practice. In D. C. Berliner & R. C. Calfee (Eds.), *Handbook of educational psychology*. New York: Macmillan.

Hiebert, J., Carpenter, T. P., Fennema, E., Fuson, K. C., Wearne, D., Murray, H., et al. (1997). *Making sense: Teaching and learning mathematics with understanding*. Portsmouth, NH: Heinemann.

Higgins, A. (1995). Educating for justice and community: Lawrence Kohlberg's vision of moral education. In W. M. Kurtines & J. L. Gewirtz (Eds.), *Moral development: An introduction*. Boston: Allyn & Bacon.

Hill, P. L., & Lapsley, D. K. (2011). Adaptive and maladaptive narcissism in adolescent development. In C. T. Barry, P. K. Kerig, K. K. Stellwagen, & T. D. Barry (Eds.), *Narcissism and Machiavellianism in youth: Implications for the development of adaptive and maladaptive behavior* (pp. 89–105). Washington, DC: American Psychological Association.

Hill, P. R., Hogben, J. H., & Bishop, D. V. M. (2005). Auditory frequency discrimination in children with specific language impairment: A longitudinal study. *Journal of Speech, Language and Hearing Research, 48*, 1136–1146.

Hilliard, A., & Vaughn-Scott, M. (1982). The quest for the minority child. In S. G. Moore & C. R. Cooper (Eds.), *The young child: Reviews of research* (Vol. 3). Washington, DC: National Association for the Education of Young Children.

Hillier, D. (2003). *Childbirth in the global village: Implications for midwifery education and practice*. New York: Routledge.

Hilt, L. M., Cha, C. B., & Nolen-Hoeksema, S. (2008). Nonsuicidal self-injury in young adolescent girls: Moderators of the distress-function relationship. *Journal of Consulting and Clinical Psychology, 76*(1), 63–71.

Hilt, L. M., & Nolen-Hoeksema, S. (2009). The emergence of gender differences in depression in adolescence. In S. Nolen-Hoeksema & L. M. Hilt (Eds.), *Handbook of depression in adolescents* (pp. 111–135). New York: Routledge.

Hinde, R. A., Titmus, G., Easton, D., & Tamplin, A. (1985). Incidence of "friendship" and behavior with strong associates versus non-associates in preschoolers. *Child Development, 56*, 234–245.

Hinduja, S., & Patchin, J. W. (2011, February). High-tech cruelty. *Educational Leadership, 68*(5), 48–52.

Hinkley, J. W., McInerney, D. M., & Marsh, H. W. (2001, April). *The multi-faceted structure of school achievement motivation: A case for social goals*. Paper presented at the annual meeting of the American Educational Research Association, Seattle, WA.

Hirschfield, P. (2009). Another way out: The impact of juvenile arrests on high school dropout. *Sociology of Education, 82*(4), 368–393. doi:10.1177/003804070908200404

Hirsh-Pasek, K., & Golinkoff, R. M. (1996). *The origins of grammar: Evidence from early language comprehension*. Cambridge, MA: MIT Press.

Hirsh-Pasek, K., Golinkoff, R. M., Berk, L. E., & Singer, D. G. (2009). *A mandate for playful learning in preschool: Presenting the evidence*. New York: Oxford University Press.

Ho, C. S., & Fuson, K. C. (1998). Children's knowledge of teen quantities as tens and ones: Comparisons of Chinese, British, and American kindergartners. *Journal of Educational Psychology, 90*, 536–544.

Ho, D. Y. F. (1994). Cognitive socialization in Confucian heritage cultures. In P. M. Greenfield & R. R. Cocking (Eds.), *Cross-cultural roots of minority child development*. Hillsdale, NJ: Erlbaum.

Hobson, P. (2004). *The cradle of thought: Exploring the origins of thinking*. Oxford, England: Oxford University Press.

Hobson, P. R., Chidambi, G., Lee, A., & Meyer, J. (2006). Foundations for self-awareness: An exploration through autism. *Monographs of the Society for Research in Child Development, Serial No. 84, 71*(2), 1–166.

Hoekstra, R. A., Bartels, M., & Boomsma, D. I. (2007). Longitudinal genetic study of verbal and nonverbal IQ from early childhood to young adulthood. *Learning and Individual Differences, 17*, 97–114.

Hoerger, M. L., & Mace, F. C. (2006). A computerized test of self-control predicts classroom behavior. *Journal of Applied Behavior Analysis, 39*, 147–159.

Hoerr, T. R. (2003). Distributed intelligence and why schools need to foster it. *Independent School, 63*, 76–83.

Hofer, B. K. (2000). Dimensionality and disciplinary differences in personal epistemology. *Contemporary Educational Psychology, 25*, 378–405.

Hofer, B. K., & Pintrich, P. R. (1997). The development of epistemological theories: Beliefs about knowledge and knowing and their relation to learning. *Review of Educational Research, 67*, 88–140.

Hofer, B. K., & Pintrich, P. R. (Eds.). (2002). *Personal epistemology: The psychology of beliefs about knowledge and knowing*. Mahwah, NJ: Erlbaum.

Hofer, B. K., & Sinatra, G. M. (2010). Epistemology, metacognition, and self-regulation: Musings on an emerging field. *Metacognition Learning, 5*, 113–120.

Hofer, M. A. (2006). Psychobiological roots of early attachment. *Current Directions in Psychological Science, 15*(2), 84–87.

Hoff, E. (2001). *Language development* (2nd ed.). Belmont, CA: Wadsworth/Thomson Learning.

Hoff, E. (2003). The specificity of environmental influence: Socioeconomic status affects early vocabulary development via maternal speech. *Child Development, 74*, 1368–1378.

Hoff, E., & Naigles, L. (2002). How children use input to acquire a lexicon. *Child Development, 73*, 418–433.

Hoffman, M. L. (1975). Altruistic behavior and the parent–child relationship. *Journal of Personality and Social Psychology, 31*, 937–943.

Hoffman, M. L. (1979). Development of moral thought, feeling, and behavior. *American Psychologist, 34*(10), 958–966. doi:10.1037/0003-066X.34.10.958

Hoffman, M. L. (1981). Is altruism part of human nature? *Journal of Personality and Social Psychology, 40*, 121–137.

Hoffman, M. L. (1988). Moral development. In M. H. Bornstein & M. E. Lamb (Eds.), *Developmental psychology: An advanced textbook* (2nd ed.). Hillsdale, NJ: Erlbaum.

Hoffman, M. L. (1991). Empathy, social cognition, and moral action. In W. M. Kurtines & J. L. Gewirtz (Eds.), *Moral behavior and development: Vol. 1. Theory*. Hillsdale, NJ: Erlbaum.

Hoffman, M. L. (1994). Discipline and internalization. *Developmental Psychology, 30*, 26–28.

Hoffman, M. L. (2000). *Empathy and moral development: Implications for caring and justice*. New York: Cambridge University Press.

Hogdon, L. A. (1995). *Visual strategies for improving communication: Vol. 1: Practical supports for school and home*. Troy, MI: Quirk Roberts.

Hohenberger, A., & Peltzer-Karpf, A. (2009). Language learning from the perspective of nonlinear dynamic systems. *Linguistics, 47*, 481–511.

Hohmann, M., & Weikart, D. P. (2002). *Educating young children: Active learning practices for preschool and child care programs*. Ypsilanti, MI: High/Scope Press.

Hokoda, A., & Fincham, F. D. (1995). Origins of children's helplessness and mastery achievement patterns in the family. *Journal of Educational Psychology, 87*, 375–385.

Holler, K. A., & Greene, S. M. (2010). Developmental changes in children's executive functioning. In E. J. Sandberg & B. L. Spritz (Eds.), *A clinician's guide to normal cognitive development in childhood* (pp. 215–238). New York: Routledge.

Hollingsworth, H. L., & Buysse, V. (2009). Establishing friendships in early childhood inclusive settings: What roles do parents and teachers play? *Journal of Early Intervention, 31*(4), 287–307. doi:10.1177/1053815109352659

Holloway, S. D. (2000). *Contested childhood: Diversity and change in Japanese preschools*. New York: Routledge.

Holm, A., Farrier, F., & Dodd, B. (2007). Phonological awareness, reading accuracy and spelling ability of children with inconsistent phonological disorder. *International Journal of Language and Communication Disorders, 43*, 300–322.

Holm, S. M., Forbes, E. E., Ryan, N. D., Phillips, M. L., Tarr, J. A., & Dahl, R. E. (2009). Reward-related brain function and sleep in pre/early pubertal and mid/late pubertal adolescents. *Journal of Adolescent Health, 45*, 326–334.

Holmes, J., Gathercole, S. E., Place, M., Alloway, T. P., Elliott, J. G., & Hilton, K. A. (2010). The diagnostic utility of executive function assessments in the identification of ADHD in children. *Child and Adolescent Mental Health, 15*(1), 37–43.

Holt, N. L., Tink, L. N., Mandigo, J. L., & Fox, K. R. (2008). Do youth learn life skills through their involvement in high school sport? A case study. *Canadian Journal of Education, 31*(2), 281–304.

Holtz, P., & Appel, M. (2011). Internet use and video gaming predict problem behavior in early adolescence. *Journal of Adolescence, 34*(1), 49–58. doi:10.1016/j.adolescence.2010.02.004

Hom, A., & Battistich, V. (1995, April). *Students' sense of school community as a factor in reducing drug use and delinquency*. Paper presented at the annual meeting of the American Educational Research Association, San Francisco.

Homer, S. L. (2005). Categories of environmental print: All logos are not created equal. *Early Childhood Education Journal, 33*(2), 113–119.

Hong, J. S. (2010). Understanding Vietnamese youth gangs in America: An ecological systems analysis. *Aggression and Violent Behavior, 15*(4), 253–260. doi:10.1016/j.avb.2010.01.003

Hong, Y., Chiu, C., & Dweck, C. S. (1995). Implicit theories of intelligence: Reconsidering the role of confidence in achievement motivation. In M. H. Kernis (Ed.), *Efficacy, agency, and self-esteem*. New York: Plenum Press.

Honig, A. S. (2009). Understanding and working with non-compliant and aggressive young children. *Early Child Development and Care, 179*(8), 1007–1023. doi:10.1080/03004430701726217

Hoover-Dempsey, K. V., & Sandler, H. M. (1997). Why do parents become involved in their children's education? *Review of Educational Research, 67,* 3–42.

Horn, J. L. (2008). Spearman, *g*, expertise, and the nature of human cognitive capability. In P. C. Kyllonen, R. D. Roberts, L. Stankov (Eds.), *Extending intelligence: Enhancement and new constructs* (pp. 185–230). New York: Erlbaum/Taylor & Francis.

Horn, J. L., & Noll, J. (1997). Human cognitive capabilities: Gf-Gc theory. In D. P. Flanagan, J. L. Genshaft, & P. L. Harrison (Eds.), *Contemporary intellectual assessment: Theories, tests, and issues* (pp. 53–91). New York: Guilford Press.

Horn, J. M., & Loehlin, J. C. (2010). *Heredity and environment in 300 adoptive families: The Texas adoption project*. New Brunswick, NJ: AldineTransaction.

Horne, P. J., Erjavec, M., & Lovett, V. E. (2009). The effects of modelling, local stimulus enhancement, and affordance demonstration on the production of object-directed actions in 6-month-old infants. *British Journal of Developmental Psychology, 27*(2), 269–281.

Horowitz, F. D., Darling-Hammond, L., & Bransford, J. (with Comer, J., Rosebrock, K., Austin, K., & Rust, F.) (2005). Educating teachers for developmentally appropriate practice. In L. Darling-Hammond & J. Bransford (Eds.), *Preparing teachers for a changing world: What teachers should learn and be able to do* (pp. 88–125). San Francisco: Jossey-Bass/Wiley.

Horst, J. S., Oakes, L. M., & Madole, K. L. (2005). What does it look like and what can it do? Category structure influences how infants categorize. *Child Development, 76,* 614–631.

Hoskyn, M. (2010). Working memory in infancy and early childhood: What develops? In B. W. Sokol, U. Müller, J. I. M. Carpendale, A. R. Young, & G. Iarocci (Eds.), *Self and social regulation: Social interaction and the development of social understanding and executive functions* (pp. 155–184). New York: Oxford University Press.

Hoskyn, M., & Tzoneva, I. (2008). Relations between working memory and emergent writing among preschool-aged children. *Exceptionality Education Canada, 18*(1), 33–58.

Howard, G. R. (2007). As diversity grows, so must we. *Educational Leadership, 64*(6), 16–22.

Howe, C. (2009). Collaborative group work in middle childhood. *Human Development, 52,* 215–239.

Howe, C. (2010). *Peer groups and children's development*. Malden, MA: Wiley-Blackwell.

Howe, D. (2006). Disabled children, parent–child interaction and attachment. *Child and Family Social Work, 11,* 95–106.

Howe, M. L. (2003). Memories from the cradle. *Current Directions in Psychological Science, 12,* 62–65.

Howe, M. L., Courage, M. L., & Rooksby, M. (2009). The genesis and development of autobiographical

memory. In M. L. Courage & N. Cowan (Eds.), *The development of memory in infancy and childhood* (pp. 177–196). New York: Psychology Press. Howell, J. C. (2000, August). *Youth gang programs and strategies*. Washington, DC: U.S. Department of Justice, Office of Juvenile Justice and Delinquency Prevention.

Howell, J. C., & Lynch, J. P. (2000, August). Youth gangs in schools. *Juvenile Justice Bulletin* (OJJDP Publication NCJ-183015). Washington, DC: U.S. Department of Justice, Office of Juvenile Justice and Delinquency Prevention.

Howes, C. (1988). The peer interactions of young children. *Monographs of the Society for Research in Child Development, 53*(1, Serial No. 217).

Howes, C. (1999). Attachment relationships in the context of multiple caregivers. In J. Cassidy & P. R. Shaver (Eds.), *Handbook of attachment: Theory, research, and clinical applications* (pp. 671–687). New York: Guilford Press.

Howes, C., & Matheson, C. C. (1992). Sequences in the development of competent play with peers: Social and social-pretend play. *Developmental Psychology, 28,* 961–974.

Howes, C., & Ritchie, S. (1998). Changes in child–teacher relationships in a therapeutic preschool program. *Early Education and Development, 9,* 411–422.

Howes, C., & Ritchie, S. (2002). *A matter of trust: Connecting teachers and learners in the early childhood classroom*. New York: Teachers College Press.

Howes, C., Smith, E., & Galinsky, E. (1995). *The Florida child care quality improvement study*. New York: Families and Work Institute.

Howie, J. D. (2002, April). *Effects of audience, gender, and achievement level on adolescent students' communicated attributions and affect in response to academic success and failure*. Paper presented at the annual meeting of the American Educational Research Association, New Orleans, LA.

Hrabok, M., & Kerns, K. A. (2010). The development of self-regulation: A neuropsychological perspective. In B. W. Sokol, U. Müeller, J. I. M. Carpendale, A. R. Young, & G. Iarocci (Eds.), *Self and social regulation: Social interaction and the development of social understanding and executive functions* (pp. 129–154). New York: Oxford University Press.

Hromek, R., & Roffey, S. (2009). Promoting social and emotional learning with games: "It's fun and we learn things." *Simulation and Gaming, 40*(5), 626–644.

Hubbard, J. A., Morrow, M. T., Romano, L. J., & McAuliffe, M. D. (2010). The role of anger in children's reactive versus proactive aggression: Review of findings, issues of measurement, and implications for intervention. In W. F. Arsenio & E. A. Lemerise (Eds.), *Emotions, aggression, and morality in children: Bridging development and psychopathology* (pp. 201–217). Washington, DC: American Psychological Association. doi:10.1037/12129-01

Hubel, D., & Wiesel, T. (1965). Binocular interaction in striate cortex of kittens reared with artificial squint. *Journal of Neurophysiology, 28,* 1041–1059.

Hudley, A. H. C. (2009). African American English. In H. A. Neville, B. M. Tynes, & S. O. Utsey (Eds.), *Handbook of African American Psychology* (pp. 199–210).Thousand Oaks, CA: Sage.

Hudson, J. A., & Mayhew, E. M. Y. (2009). The development of memory for recurring events. In M. L. Courage & N. Cowan (Eds.), *The development of memory in infancy and childhood* (pp. 69–91). New York: Psychology Press.

Huebner, C. E., & Payne, K. (2010). Home support for emergent literacy: Follow-up of a community-based

implementation of dialogic reading. *Journal of Applied Developmental Psychology, 31*(3), 195–201.

Huennekens, M. E., & Xu, Y. (2010). Effects of a cross-linguistic storybook intervention on the second language development of two preschool English language learners. *Early Childhood Education Journal, 38*(1), 19–26.

Huesmann, L. R., Dubow, E. F., & Boxer, P. (2011). The transmission of aggressiveness across generations: Biological, contextual, and social learning processes. In P. R. Shaver & M. Mikulincer (Eds.), *Human aggression and violence: Causes, manifestations, and consequences. Herzilya series on personality and social psychology* (pp. 123–142). Washington, DC: American Psychological Association. doi:10.1037/12346-007

Hufton, N., Elliott, J., & Illushin, L. (2002). Achievement motivation across cultures: Some puzzles and their implications for future research. *New Directions for Child and Adolescent Development, 96,* 65–85.

Hughes, C., & Dunn, J. (2007). Children's relationships with other children. In C. A. Brownell & C. B. Kopp (Eds.), *Socioemotional development in the toddler years: Transitions and transformations* (pp. 177–200). New York: Guilford Press.

Hughes, D. (2003). Correlates of African American and Latino parents' messages to children about ethnicity and race: A comparative study of racial socialization. *American Journal of Community Psychology, 31,* 15–33.

Hughes, F. P. (1998). Play in special populations. In O. N. Saracho & B. Spodek (Eds.), *Multiple perspectives on play in early childhood education* (pp. 171–193). Albany: State University of New York Press.

Hughes, F. P. (2010). *Children, play, and development* (4th ed.). Los Angeles, CA: Sage.

Hughes, J., & Kwok, O. (2007). Influence of student–teacher and parent–teacher relationships on lower achieving readers' engagement and achievement in the primary grades. *Journal of Educational Psychology, 99,* 39–51.

Huizink, A. C., Mulder, E. J. H., & Buitelaar, J. K. (2004). Prenatal stress and risk for psychopathology: Special effects or induction of general susceptibility? *Psychological Bulletin, 130,* 115–142.

Hulit, L. M., & Howard, M. R. (2006). *Born to talk* (4th ed.). Boston: Allyn & Bacon.

Hulme, C., & Joshi, R. M. (Eds.). (1998). *Reading and spelling: Development and disorders*. Mahwah, NJ: Erlbaum.

Humphreys, A. P., & Smith, P. K. (1987). Rough-and-tumble play, friendship, and dominance in school children: Evidence for continuity and change with age. *Child Development, 58,* 201–212.

Humphreys, C., Lowe, P., & Williams, S. (2008). Sleep disruption and domestic violence: Exploring the interconnections between mothers and children. *Child and Family Social Work, 14,* 6–14.

Humphreys, L. G. (1992). What both critics and users of ability tests need to know. *Psychological Science, 3,* 271–274.

Hunninus, S., & Bekkering, H. (2010). The early development of object knowledge: A study of infants' visual anticipations during action observation. *Developmental Psychology, 46*(2), 446–454.

Hunt, E. (1997). Nature vs. nurture: The feeling of *vujà dé*. In R. J. Sternberg & E. L. Grigorenko (Eds.), *Intelligence, heredity, and environment* (pp. 531–551). Cambridge, England: Cambridge University Press.

Hursh, D. (2007). Assessing No Child Left Behind and the rise of neoliberal education policies. *American Educational Research Journal, 44,* 493–518.

Husman, J., & Freeman, B. (1999, April). *The effect of perceptions of instrumentality on intrinsic motivation*. Paper presented at the annual meeting of the American Educational Research Association, Montreal, Canada.

Hussong, A., Chassin, L., & Hicks, R. (1999, April). *The elusive relation between negative affect and adolescent substance use: Does it exist?* Paper presented at the biennial meeting of the Society for Research in Child Development, Albuquerque, NM.

Huston, A. C., Donnerstein, E., Fairchild, H., Feshbach, N. D., Katz, P. A., Murray, J. P., et al. (1992). *Big world, small screen: The role of television in American society.* Lincoln: University of Nebraska Press.

Hutman, T., & Dapretto, M. (2009). The emergence of empathy during infancy. *Cognition, Brain, Behavior, 13*(4), 367–390.

Huttenlocher, J., Jordan, N. C., & Levine, S. C. (1994). A mental model for early arithmetic. *Journal of Experimental Psychology: General, 123*, 284–296.

Huttenlocher, J., Newcombe, N., & Vasilyeva, M. (1999). Spatial scaling in young children. *Psychological Science, 10*, 393–398.

Huttenlocher, P. R. (1990). Morphometric study of human cerebral cortex development. *Neuropsychologia, 28*, 517–527.

Hwang, W.-C. (2006). Acculturative family distancing: Theory, research, and clinical practice. *Psychotherapy: Theory, Research, Practice, Training, 43*, 397–409.

Hyde, C., & Wilson, P. H. (2011). Dissecting online control in developmental coordination disorder: A kinematic analysis of double-step reaching. *Brain and Cognition, 75*(3), 232–241. doi:10.1016/j.bandc.2010.12.004

Hyde, J. S., Mezulis, A. H., & Abramson, L. Y. (2008). The ABCs of depression: Integrating affective, biological, and cognitive models to explain the emergence of the gender difference in depression. *Psychological Review, 115*(2), 291–313.

Hyde, K. L., & Peretz, I. (2004). Brains that are out of tune but in time. *Psychological Science, 15*, 356–360.

Hyman, I., Kay, B., Tabori, A., Weber, M., Mahon, M., & Cohen, I. (2006). Bullying: Theory, research, and interventions. In C. M. Evertson & C. S. Weinstein (Eds.), *Handbook of classroom management: Research, practice, and contemporary issues* (pp. 855–884). Mahwah, NJ: Erlbaum.

Hynd, C. (1998). Conceptual change in a high school physics class. In B. Guzzetti & C. Hynd (Eds.), *Perspectives on conceptual change: Multiple ways to understand knowing and learning in a complex world* (pp. 27–36). Mahwah, NJ: Erlbaum.

Hyson, M. C., Hirsh-Pasek, K., Rescorla, L., Cone, J., & Martell-Boinske, L. (1991). Ingredients of parental "pressure" in early childhood. *Journal of Applied Developmental Psychology, 12*(3), 347–365.

Hyvönen, P., & Kangas, M. (2007). From bogey mountains to funny houses: Children's desires for play environment. *Australian Journal of Early Childhood, 32*(3), 39–47.

Iacoboni, M., & Woods, R. P. (1999). Cortical mechanisms of human imitation. *Science, 286*, 2526–2528.

Igoa, C. (1995). *The inner world of the immigrant child.* Mahwah, NJ: Erlbaum.

Imhof, M. (2001, March). *In the eye of the beholder: Children's perception of good and poor listening behavior.* Paper presented at the annual meeting of the International Listening Association, Chicago.

Immordino-Yang, M. H., & Damasio, A. (2007). We feel, therefore we learn: The relevance of affective and social neuroscience to education. *Mind, Brain, and Education, 1*, 3–10.

Inglis, A., & Biemiller, A. (1997, March). *Fostering self-direction in mathematics: A cross-age tutoring program that enhances math problem solving.* Paper presented at the annual meeting of the American Educational Research Association, Chicago.

Inhelder, B., & Piaget, J. (1958). *The growth of logical thinking from childhood to adolescence* (A. Parsons & S. Milgram, Trans.). New York: Basic Books.

Institute of Education Sciences. (2006). *Character education.* Retrieved October 9, 2007, from http://ies.ed.gov/ncee/wwc/reports/character_education/index.asp

Intrator, S. M., & Siegel, D. (2008). Project Coach: Youth development and academic achievement through sport. *Journal of Physical Education, Recreation, and Dance, 79*(7), 17–23.

Irujo, S. (1988). An introduction to intercultural differences and similarities in nonverbal communication. In J. S. Wurzel (Ed.), *Toward multiculturalism: A reader in multicultural education.* Yarmouth, ME: Intercultural Press.

Isabella, R. A., & Belsky, J. (1991). Interactional synchrony and the origins of infant-mother attachment: A replication study. *Child Development, 62*, 373–384.

Iusitini, L., Gao, W., Sundborn, G., & Paterson, J. (2011). Parenting practices among fathers of a cohort of pacific infants in New Zealand. *Journal of Cross-Cultural Psychology, 42*(1), 39–55. doi:10.1177/0022022110361778

Iyengar, S. S., & Lepper, M. R. (1999). Rethinking the value of choice: A cultural perspective on intrinsic motivation. *Journal of Personality and Social Psychology, 76*, 349–366.

Jacklin, C. N. (1989). Female and male: Issues of gender. *American Psychologist, 44*, 127–133.

Jacob, B. A. (2007). The challenges of staffing urban schools with effective teachers. *Future of Children, 17*(1), 129–153.

Jacobs, J. E., Davis-Kean, P., Bleeker, M., Eccles, J. S., & Malanchuk, O. (2005). "I can, but I don't want to": The impact of parents, interests, and activities on gender differences in math. In A. M. Gallagher & J. C. Kaufman (Eds.), *Gender differences in mathematics: An integrative psychological approach* (pp. 246–263). Cambridge, England: Cambridge University Press.

Jacobs, J. E., Lanza, S., Osgood, D. W., Eccles, J. S., & Wigfield, A. (2002). Changes in children's self-competence and values: Gender and domain differences across grades one through twelve. *Child Development, 73*, 509–527.

Jacobsen, B., Lowery, B., & DuCette, J. (1986). Attributions of learning disabled children. *Journal of Educational Psychology, 78*, 59–64.

Jadcherla, S. R., Gupta, A., Stoner, E., Fernandez, S., & Shaker, R. (2007). Pharyngeal swallowing: Defining pharyngeal and supper esophageal sphincter relationships in human neonates. *Journal of Pediatrics, 151*, 597–603.

Jaddoe, V. W. V. (2009). Antenatal education programmes: Do they work? *Lancet, 374* (9693), 863–864.

Jalongo, M. R. (2008). *Learning to listen, listening to learn: Building essential skills in young children.* Washington, DC: National Association for the Education of Young Children Press.

Jalongo, M. R., Isenberg, J. P., & Gerbracht, G. (1995). *Teachers' stories: From personal narrative to professional insight.* San Francisco: Jossey-Bass.

James, A., & Leyden, G. (2010). Putting the circle back into circle of friends: A grounded theory study. *Educational and Child Psychology. Special Issue: In-School Relationships and their Outcomes, 27*(1), 52–63.

Janssen, P. A., Saxell, L., Page, L. A., Klein, M. C., Liston, R. M., & Shoo, K. L. (2009). Outcomes of planned home birth with registered midwife versus planned hospital birth with midwife or physician. *Canadian Medical Association Journal, 181*(6–7), 377–383.

Jaswal, V. K., & Dodson, C. S. (2009). Metamemory development: Understanding the role of similarity in false memories. *Child Development, 80*(3), 629–635.

Jaswal, V. K., & Markman, E. M. (2001). Learning proper and common names in inferential versus ostensive contexts. *Child Development, 72*, 768–786.

Jeffrey, R. (2009/2010). First steps to a healthier school. *Educational Leadership, 67*(4), 82–83.

Jelalian, E., Wember, Y. M., Bungeroth, H., & Birmaher, V. (2007). Practitioner review: Bridging the gap between research and clinical practice in pediatric obesity. *Journal of Child Psychology and Psychiatry, 48*, 115–127.

Jeltova, I., Birney, D., Fredine, N., Jarvine, L., Sternberg, R. J., & Grigorenko. E. L. (2007). Dynamic assessment as a process-oriented assessment in educational settings. *Advances in Speech-Language Pathology, 9*(4), 273–285.

Jenkins, J. M., Turrell, S. L., Kogushi, Y., Lollis, S., & Ross, H. S. (2003). A longitudinal investigation of the dynamics of mental state talk in families. *Child Development, 74*, 905–920.

Jenkins, S., Bax, M., & Hart, H. (1980). Behavior problems in preschool children. *Journal of Child Psychology and Psychiatry, 21*, 5–18.

Jenlink, C. L. (1994, April). *Music: A lifeline for the self-esteem of at-risk students.* Paper presented at the annual meeting of the American Educational Research Association, New Orleans, LA.

Jennings, N. A., Hooker, S. D., & Linebarger, D. L. (2009). Educational television as mediated literacy environments for preschoolers. *Learning, Media and Technology, 34*(3), 229–242. doi:10.1080/17439880903141513

Jensen, A. R. (2007). Book review: *Howard Gardner under fire: The Rebel psychologist faces his critics. Intelligence, 36*, 96–97.

Jensen, M. M. (2005). *Introduction to emotional and behavioral disorders: Recognizing and managing problems in the classroom.* Upper Saddle River, NJ: Merrill Prentice Hall.

Jeong, Y., Levine, S. C., & Huttenlocher, J. (2007). The development of proportional reasoning: Effect of continuous versus discrete quantities. *Journal of Cognition and Development, 8*(2), 237–256.

Jerome, E. M., Hamre, B. K., & Pianta, R. C. (2009). Teacher–child relationships from kindergarten to sixth grade: Early childhood predictors of teacher-perceived conflict and closeness. *Social Development, 18*(4), 915–945. doi:10.1111/sode.2009.18.issue-410.1111/j.1467-9507.2008.00508.x

Jessor, R., & Jessor, S. L. (1977). *Problem behavior and psychosocial development: A longitudinal study of youth.* San Diego, CA: Academic Press.

Ji, C. S., & Koblinsky, S. A. (2009). Parent involvement in children's education: An exploratory study of urban, Chinese immigrant families. *Urban Education, 44*(6), 687–709.

Jimerson, S., Egeland, B., & Teo, A. (1999). A longitudinal study of achievement trajectories: Factors associated with change. *Journal of Educational Psychology, 91*, 116–126.

Jipson, J. L., & Callanan, M. A. (2003). Mother-child conversation and children's understanding of biological and nonbiological changes in size. *Child Development, 74*, 629–644.

Joanisse, M. F. (2007). Phonological deficits and developmental language impairments: Evidence from connectionist models. In D. Mareschal, S. Sirois, G. Westermann, & M. H. Johnson (Eds.), *Neuro-constructivism: Vol. 2. Perspectives and prospects* (pp. 205–229). Oxford, England: Oxford University Press.

Johanning, D. I., D'Agostino, J. V., Steele, D. F., & Shumow, L. (1999, April). *Student writing, post-writing group collaboration, and learning in pre-algebra*. Paper presented at the annual meeting of the American Educational Research Association, Montreal, Canada.

John, O. P., Caspi, A., Robins, R. W., Moffitt, T. E., & Stouthamer-Loeber, M. (1994). The "Little Five": Exploring the five-factor model of personality in adolescent boys. *Child Development, 65,* 160–178.

Johnson, D. W., & Johnson, R. T. (1996). Conflict resolution and peer mediation programs in elementary and secondary schools: A review of the research. *Review of Educational Research, 66,* 459–506.

Johnson, D. W., Johnson, R., Dudley, B., Ward, M., & Magnuson, D. (1995). The impact of peer mediation training on the management of school and home conflicts. *American Educational Research Journal, 32,* 829–844.

Johnson, J. S., & Newport, E. L. (1989). Critical period effects in second language learning: The influence of maturational state on acquisition of English as a second language. *Cognitive Psychology, 21,* 60–99.

Johnson, K. E., Alexander, J. M., Spencer, S., Leibham, M. E., & Neitzel, C. (2004). Factors associated with the early emergence of intense interests within conceptual domains. *Cognitive Development, 19,* 325–343.

Johnson, M. H. (2009). The human social brain: An "evo-devo" perspective. In L. Tommasi, M. A. Peterson & L. Nadel (Eds.), *Cognitive biology: Evolutionary and developmental perspectives on mind, brain, and behavior* (pp. 309–319). Cambridge, MA: MIT Press.

Johnson, S. C., Dweck, C. S., Chen, F. S., Stern, H. L., Ok, S., & Barth, M. (2010). At the intersection of social and cognitive development: Internal working models of attachment in infancy. *Cognitive Science, 34*(5), 807–825.

Johnson, W., Bouchard, T. J., Jr., McGue, M., Segal, N. L., Tellegen, A., Keyes, M., et al. (2007). Genetic and environmental influences on the Verbal-Perceptual-Image Rotation (VPR) model of the structure of mental abilities in the Minnesota study of twins reared apart. *Intelligence, 35,* 542–562.

Johnson, W., Deary, I. J., & Iacono, W. G. (2009). Genetic and environmental transactions underlying educational attainment. *Intelligence, 37,* 466–478.

Johnston, J. R. (1997). Specific language impairment, cognition and the biological basis of language. In M. Gopnik (Ed.), *The inheritance and innateness of grammars.* New York: Oxford University Press.

Johnston, L. D., O'Malley, P. M., Bachman, J. G., & Schulenberg, J. E. (2007). *Monitoring the Future national results on adolescent drug use: Overview of key findings, 2006* (NIH Publication No. 07-6202). Bethesda, MD: National Institute on Drug Abuse.

Johnston, M. V. (2008). Neonatal encephalopathy. In P. J. Accardo (Ed.), *Capute and Accardo's neurodevelopmental disabilities in infancy and childhood. Vol. 1: Neurodevelopmental diagnosis and treatment* (3rd ed., pp. 147–154). Baltimore, MD: Paul H. Brookes.

Johnston, P., & Afflerbach, P. (1985). The process of constructing main ideas from text. *Cognition and Instruction, 2,* 207–232.

Johnston, T. D., & Edwards, L. (2002). Genes, interactions, and the development of behavior. *Psychological Review, 109,* 26–34.

Jones, C. R. G., Happé, F., Golden, H., Marsden, A. J. S., Tregay, J., Simonoff, E., et al. (2009). Reading and arithmetic in adolescents with autism spectrum disorders: Peaks and dips in attainment. *Neuropsychology, 23*(6), 718–728. doi:10.1037/a0016360

Jordan, A. B. (2003). Children remember prosocial program lessons but how much are they learning? *Applied Developmental Psychology, 24,* 341–345.

Jordan, A. B. (2005). Learning to use books and television. *American Behavioral Scientist, 48*(5), 523–538.

Jordan, A. H., & Lovett, B. J. (2007). Stereotype threat and test performance: A primer for school psychologists. *Journal of School Psychology, 45,* 45–59.

Jordan, J.-A., Mulhern, G., & Wylie, J. (2009). Individual differences in trajectories of arithmetical development in typically achieving 5- to 7-year-olds. *Journal of Experimental Child Psychology, 103*(4), 455–468.

Jordan, N. C., Glutting, J., & Ramineni, C. (2010). The importance of number sense to mathematics achievement in first and third grades. *Learning and Individual Differences, 20*(2), 82–88.

Jordan, N. C., Hanich, L. B., & Kaplan, D. (2003). A longitudinal study of mathematical competencies in children with specific mathematics difficulties versus children with comorbid mathematics and reading difficulties. *Child Development, 74,* 834–850.

Jorde, L. B., Carey, J. C., & Bamshad, M. J. (2010). *Medical genetics* (4th ed.). Philadelphia, PA: Mosby Elsevier.

Joseph, N. (2010). Metacognition needed: Teaching middle and high school students to develop strategic learning skills. *Preventing School Failure, 54*(2), 99–103.

Josselson, R. (1988). The embedded self: I and Thou revisited. In D. K. Lapsley & F. C. Power (Eds.), *Self, ego, and identity: Integrative approaches* (pp. 91–106). New York: Springer-Verlag.

Jovanovic, J., & King, S. S. (1998). Boys and girls in the performance-based science classroom: Who's doing the performing? *American Educational Research Journal, 35,* 477–496.

Juel, C. (1991). Beginning reading. In R. Barr, M. Kamii, P. Mosenthal, & P. D. Pearson (Eds.), *Handbook of reading research* (Vol. II). New York: Longman.

Juel, C. (1998). What kind of one-on-one tutoring helps a poor reader? In C. Hulme & R. M. Joshi (Eds.), *Reading and spelling: Development and disorders.* Mahwah, NJ: Erlbaum.

Jusczyk, P. W. (1995). Language acquisition: Speech sounds and phonological development. In J. L. Miller & P. D. Eimas (Eds.), *Handbook of perception and cognition: Vol. 11. Speech, language, and communication.* Orlando, FL: Academic Press.

Jusczyk, P. W. (1997). Finding and remembering words: Some beginnings by English-learning infants. *Current Directions in Psychological Science, 6,* 170–174.

Jusczyk, P. W. (2002). How infants adapt speech-processing capacities to native-language structure. *Current Directions in Psychological Science, 11,* 15–18.

Jusczyk, P. W., & Aslin, R. N. (1995). Infants' detection of the sound patterns of words in fluent speech. *Cognitive Psychology, 29,* 1–23.

Juster, N. (1961). *The phantom tollbooth.* New York: Random House.

Justice, J. (1984). Can socio-cultural information improve health planning? A case study of Nepal's assistant nurse-midwife. *Social Science and Medicine, 19*(3), 193–198.

Jutta, K., Jutta, E., & Karbach, J. (2008). Verbal self-instructions in task switching: A compensatory tool for action-control deficits in childhood and old age? *Developmental Science, 11,* 223–236.

Juvonen, J. (1991). Deviance, perceived responsibility, and negative peer reactions. *Developmental Psychology, 27,* 672–681.

Juvonen, J. (2000). The social functions of attributional face-saving tactics among early adolescents. *Educational Psychology Review, 12,* 15–32.

Juvonen, J. (2006). Sense of belonging, social bonds, and school functioning. In P. A. Alexander &

P. H. Winne (Eds.), *Handbook of educational psychology* (2nd ed., pp. 655–674). Mahwah, NJ: Erlbaum.

Juvonen, J., Nishina, A., & Graham, S. (2000). Peer harassment, psychological adjustment, and school functioning in early adolescence. *Journal of Educational Psychology, 92,* 349–359.

Juvonen, J., & Weiner, B. (1993). An attributional analysis of students' interactions: The social consequences of perceived responsibility. *Educational Psychology Review, 5,* 325–345.

Kagan, J. (1981). *The second year: The emergence of self-awareness.* Cambridge, MA: Harvard University Press.

Kagan, J. (1984). *The nature of the child.* New York: Basic Books.

Kagan, J. (2010). Emotions and temperament. In M. H. Bornstein (Ed.), *Handbook of cultural developmental science* (pp. 175–194). New York: Psychology Press.

Kagan, J., Snidman, N., Vahn, V., & Towsley, S. (2007). The preservation of two infant temperaments into adolescence. *Monographs of the Society for Research in Child Development, 72,* 1–80.

Kagan, J. K., & Fox, N. A. (2006). Biology, culture, and temperamental biases. In W. Damon & R. M. Lerner (Eds. in Chief) & N. Eisenberg (Vol. Ed.), *Handbook of child psychology, Vol. 3. Social, emotional, and personality development* (6th ed., pp. 167–225). Hoboken, NJ: Wiley.

Kağitçibaşi, Ç. (2007). *Family, self, and human development across cultures: Theory and applications* (2nd ed.). Mahwah, NJ: Erlbaum.

Kahl, B., & Woloshyn, V. E. (1994). Using elaborative interrogation to facilitate acquisition of factual information in cooperative learning settings: One good strategy deserves another. *Applied Cognitive Psychology, 8,* 465–478.

Kahlenberg, S. G., & Hein, M. M. (2010). Progression on Nickelodeon? Gender-role stereotypes in toy commercials. *Sex Roles, 62*(11–12), 830–847. doi:10.1007/s11199-009-9653-1

Kail, R. (1990). *The development of memory in children* (3rd ed.). New York: Freeman.

Kail, R. V. (1998). *Children and their development.* Upper Saddle River, NJ: Prentice Hall.

Kail, R. V., & Ferrer, E. (2007). Processing speed in childhood and adolescence: Longitudinal models for examining developmental change. *Child Development, 78,* 1760–1770.

Kaler, S. R., & Kopp, C. B. (1990). Compliance and comprehension in very young toddlers. *Child Development, 61,* 1997–2003.

Kanner, A. D., Feldman, S. S., Weinberger, D. A., & Ford, M. E. (1987). Uplifts, hassles, and adaptational outcomes in early adolescents. *Journal of Early Adolescence, 7,* 371–394.

Kaplan, A., Middleton, M. J., Urdan, T., & Midgley, C. (2002). Achievement goals and goal structures. In C. Midgley (Ed.), *Goals, goal structures, and patterns of adaptive learning* (pp. 21–53). Mahwah, NJ: Erlbaum.

Kaplan, A., & Midgley, C. (1997). The effect of achievement goals: Does level of perceived academic competence make a difference? *Contemporary Educational Psychology, 22,* 415–435.

Kapp-Simon, K., & Simon, D. J. (1991). Meeting the challenge: Social skills training for teens with special needs. *Connections: The Newsletter of the National Center for Youth and Disabilities, 2*(2), 1–5.

Karabenick, S. A., & Sharma, R. (1994). Seeking academic assistance as a strategic learning resource. In P. R. Pintrich, D. R. Brown, & C. E. Weinstein (Eds.), *Student motivation, cognition, and learning: Essays in honor of Wilbert J. McKeachie.* Hillsdale, NJ: Erlbaum.

Karafantis, D. M., & Levy, S. R. (2004). The role of children's lay theories about the malleability of human attributes in beliefs about and volunteering for disadvantaged groups. *Child Development, 75,* 236–250.

Karcher, M. (2009). Increases in academic connectedness and self-esteem among high-school students who serve as cross-age peer mentors. *Professional School Counseling, 12*(4), 292–299.

Kardash, C. A. M., & Howell, K. L. (1996, April). *Effects of epistemological beliefs on strategies employed to comprehend dual-positional text.* Paper presented at the annual meeting of the American Educational Research Association, New York.

Karemaker, A., Pitchford, N. J., & O'Malley, C. (2010). Enhanced recognition of written words and enjoyment of reading in struggling beginner readers through whole-word multimedia software. *Computers & Education, 54*(1), 199–208.

Karmiloff-Smith, A. (1979). Language development after five. In P. Fletcher & M. Garman (Eds.), *Language acquisition: Studies in first language development.* Cambridge, England: Cambridge University Press.

Karniol, R. (2010). *Social development as preference management: How infants, children, and parents get what they want from one another.* New York: Cambridge University Press.

Karpov, Y. V. (2003). Development through the lifespan. In A. Kozulin, B. Gindis, V. S. Ageyev, & S. M. Miller (Eds.), *Vygotsky's educational theory in cultural context* (pp. 138–155). Cambridge, England: Cambridge University Press.

Karpov, Y. V., & Haywood, H. C. (1998). Two ways to elaborate Vygotsky's concept of mediation: Implications for instruction. *American Psychologist, 53,* 27–36.

Kärtner, J., Keller, H., & Chaudhary, N. (2010). Cognitive and social influences on early prosocial behavior in two sociocultural contexts. *Developmental Psychology, 46*(4), 905–914. doi:10.1037/a0019718

Kasanen, K., Räty, H., & Eklund, A. (2009). Elementary school pupils' evaluations of the malleability of their academic abilities. *Educational Research, 51*(1), 27–38.

Kaslow, F. W. (2000). Families experiencing divorce. In W. C. Nichols, M. A. Pace-Nichols, D. S. Becvar, & Y. A. Napier (Eds.), *Handbook of family development and intervention* (pp. 341–368). New York: Wiley.

Katchadourian, H. (1990). Sexuality. In S. S. Feldman & G. R. Elliott (Eds.), *At the threshold: The developing adolescent* (pp. 330–351). Cambridge, MA: Harvard University Press.

Katkovsky, W., Crandall, V. C., & Good, S. (1967). Parental antecedents of children's beliefs in internal-external control of reinforcements in intellectual achievement situations. *Child Development, 38,* 765–776.

Katz, E. W., & Brent, S. B. (1968). Understanding connectives. *Journal of Verbal Learning and Verbal Behavior, 7,* 501–509.

Katz, L. F., & Gottman, J. M. (1991). Marital discord and child outcomes: A social psychophysiological approach. In J. Garber & K. A. Dodge (Eds.), *The development of emotion regulation and dysregulation.* Cambridge, England: Cambridge University Press.

Katz, S. L., Selman, R. L., & Mason, J. R. (2008). A study of teasing in the real world through the eyes of a practice-inspired researcher. *Educational Action Research, 16*(4), 469–480.

Kauffman, J., & Sasso, G. (2006). Toward ending cultural and cognitive relativism in special education. *Exceptionality, 14*(2), 65–90.

Kaufman, J., & Needham, A. (2010). The role of surface discontinuity and shape in 4-month-old infants' object segregation. *Visual Cognition, 18*(5), 751–766.

Kaufmann, L. (2008). Discalculia: Neuroscience and education. *Educational Research, 50*(2), 163–175.

Kawabata, Y., Crick, N. R., & Hamaguchi, Y. (2010). The role of culture in relational aggression: Associations with social-psychological adjustment problems in japanese and US school-aged children. *International Journal of Behavioral Development, 34*(4), 354–362. doi:10.1177/0165025409339151

Kazdin, A. E. (1997). Conduct disorder across the lifespan. In S. S. Luthar, J. A. Burack, D. Cicchetti, & J. R. Weisz (Eds.), *Developmental psychopathology: Perspectives on adjustment, risk, and disorder* (pp. 248–272). Cambridge, England: Cambridge University Press.

Kearins, J. M. (1981). Visual spatial memory in Australian Aboriginal children of desert regions. *Cognitive Psychology, 13,* 434–460.

Keen, R. (2009). A view from the lab. In K. J. Nugent, B. J. Petrauskas, & T. B. Brazelton (Eds.), *The newborn as an infant: Enabling health infant development worldwide* (pp. 237–242). Hoboken, NJ: Wiley.

Keil, F. C. (1989). *Concepts, kinds, and cognitive development.* Cambridge, MA: MIT Press.

Keil, F. C. (1994). The birth and nurturance of concepts by domains: The origins of concepts of living things. In L. A. Hirschfeld & S. A. Gelman (Eds.), *Mapping the mind: Domain specificity in cognition and culture.* New York: Cambridge University Press.

Keil, F. C. (2010). The feasibility of folk science. *Cognitive Science, 34*(5), 826–862. doi:10.1111/j.1551-6709.2010.01108.x

Keil, F. C., & Silberstein, C. S. (1996). Schooling and the acquisition of theoretical knowledge. In D. R. Olson & N. Torrance (Eds.), *The handbook of education and human development: New models of learning, teaching, and schooling.* Cambridge, MA: Blackwell.

Kelemen, D. (1999). Why are rocks pointy? Children's preference for teleological explanations of the natural world. *Developmental Psychology, 35,* 1440–1452.

Kelemen, D. (2004). Are children "intuitive theists"?: Reasoning about purpose and design in nature. *Psychological Science, 15,* 295–301.

Keller, H. (2003). Socialization for competence: Cultural models of infancy. *Human Development, 46,* 288–311.

Keller, T. A., & Just, M. A. (2009). Altering cortical connectivity: Remediation-induced changes in the white matter of poor readers. *Neuron, 64*(5), 624–631.

Kellogg, R. (1967). *The psychology of children's art.* New York: CRM-Random House.

Kelly, B. C. (2007). Club drug use and risk management among "Bridge and Tunnel" youth. *Journal of Drug Issues, 37*(2), 425–444.

Kelly, J. A., Murphy, D. A., Sikkema, K. J., & Kalichman, S. C. (1993). Psychological interventions to prevent HIV infection are urgently needed. *American Psychologist, 48,* 1023–1034.

Kelly, J. B. (2007). Children's living arrangements following separation and divorce: Insights from empirical and clinical research. *Family Process, 46,* 35–52.

Kelly, J. B., & Lamb, M. E. (2000). Using child development research to make appropriate custody and access decisions for young children. *Family and Conciliation Courts Review, 38*(3), 297–311.

Kemler Nelson, D. G., Egan, L. C., & Holt, M. B. (2004). When children ask, "What is it?" what do they want to know about artifacts? *Psychological Science, 15,* 384–389.

Kemper, S. (1984). The development of narrative skills: Explanations and entertainments. In S. Kuczaj (Ed.), *Discourse development: Progress in cognitive development research.* New York: Springer-Verlag.

Kendig, S. M., & Bianchi, S. M. (2008). Single, cohabitating, and married mothers' time with children. *Journal of Marriage and Family, 70,* 1228–1240.

Kennedy Root, A. K., & Denham, S. A. (2010). The role of gender in the socialization of emotion: Key concepts and critical issues. In A. Kennedy Root & S. A. Denham (Eds.), *The role of gender in the socialization of emotion: Key concepts and critical issues. New Directions for Child and Adolescent Development, 128,* 1–9. San Francisco: Jossey-Bass.

Keogh, B. K. (2003). *Temperament in the classroom: Understanding individual differences.* Baltimore, MD: Paul H. Brookes.

Keogh, B. K., & MacMillan, D. L. (1996). Exceptionality. In D. C. Berliner & R. C. Calfee (Eds.), *Handbook of educational psychology.* New York: Macmillan.

Keramati, M. (2010). Effect of cooperative learning on academic achievement of physics course. *Journal of Computers in Mathematics and Science Teaching, 29*(2), 155–173.

Kerewsky, W., & Lefstein, L. M. (1982). Young adolescents and their community: A shared responsibility. In L. M. Lefstein et al. (Eds.), *3:00 to 6:00 p.m.: Young adolescents at home and in the community.* Carrboro, NC: Center for Early Adolescence.

Kerns, K. A., Brumariu, L. E., & Abraham, M. M. (2008). Homesickness at summer camp: Associations with the mother–child relationship, social self-concept, and peer relationships in middle childhood. *Merrill-Palmer Quarterly: Journal of Developmental Psychology, 54*(4), 473–498.

Kerns, L. L., & Lieberman, A. B. (1993). *Helping your depressed child.* Rocklin, CA: Prima.

Kersey, K. C., & Masterson, M. L. (2009). Teachers connecting with families: In the best interest of children. *Young Children, 64*(5), 34–38.

Khalid, T. (2010). An integrated inquiry activity in an elementary teaching methods classroom. *Science Activities, 47*(1), 29–34.

Kiang, L., & Fuligni, A. J. (2010). Meaning in life as a mediator of ethnic identity and adjustment among adolescents from Latin, Asian, and European American backgrounds. *Journal of Youth and Adolescence, 39*(11), 1253–1264.

Kienbaum, J., & Wilkening, F. (2009). Children's and adolescents' intuitive judgements about distributive justice: Integrating need, effort, and luck. *European Journal of Developmental Psychology, 6*(4), 481–498.

Killen, M., Margie, N. G., & Sinno, S. (2006). Morality in the context of intergroup relationships. In M. Killen & J. G. Smetana (Eds.), *Handbook of moral development* (pp. 155–183). Mahwah, NJ: Erlbaum.

Killen, M., & Nucci, L. P. (1995). Morality, autonomy, and social conflict. In M. Killen & D. Hart (Eds.), *Morality in everyday life: Developmental perspectives* (pp. 52–86). Cambridge, England: Cambridge University Press.

Killen, M., & Smetana, J. G. (2010). Future directions: Social development in the context of social justice. *Social Development, 19*(3), 642–657. doi:10.1111/j.1467-9507.2009.00548.x

Killeya-Jones, L. A., Costanzo, P. R., Malone, P., Quinlan, N. P., & Miller-Johnson, S. (2007). Norm-narrowing and self- and other-perceived aggression in early-adolescent same-sex and mixed-sex cliques. *Journal of School Psychology, 45,* 549–565.

Killip, S., Bennett, J. M., & Chambers, M. D. (2007). Iron deficiency anemia. *American Family Physician, 75,* 671–678.

Kim, D., Solomon, D., & Roberts, W. (1995, April). *Classroom practices that enhance students' sense of community.* Paper presented at the annual meeting of the American Educational Research Association, San Francisco.

Kim, G., Walden, T. A., & Knieps, L. J. (2010). Impact and characteristics of positive and fearful emotional messages during infant social referencing. *Infant Behavior & Development, 33*(2), 189–195.

Kim, J., & Cicchetti, D. (2009). Mean-level change and intraindividual variability in self-esteem and depression among high-risk children. *International Journal of Behavioral Development, 33*(3), 202–214.

Kim, J., Schallert, D. L., & Kim, M. (2010). An integrative cultural view of achievement motivation: Parental and classroom predictors of children's goal orientations when learning mathematics in Korea. *Journal of Educational Psychology, 102*(2), 418–437. doi:10.1037/a0018676

Kim, K. H., Relkin, N. R., Lee, K. M., & Hirsch, J. (1997). Distinct cortical areas associated with native and second languages. *Nature, 388,* 171–174.

Kim, S., Kim, S., & Kamphaus, R. W. (2010). Is aggression the same for boys and girls? assessing measurement invariance with confirmatory factor analysis and item response theory. *School Psychology Quarterly, 25*(1), 45–61. doi:10.1037/a0018768

Kim, Y. (2010). Componential skills in early spelling development in Korean. *Scientific Studies of Reading, 14*(2), 137–158.

Kim, Y., Petscher, Y., Schatschneider, C., & Foorman, B. (2010). Does growth rate in oral reading fluency matter in predicting reading comprehension achievement? *Journal of Educational Psychology, 102*(3), 652–667.

Kim-Cohen, J., Moffitt, T. E., Caspi, A., & Taylor A. (2004). Genetic and environmental processes in young children's resilience and vulnerability to socioeconomic deprivation. *Child Development, 75,* 651–668.

Kindermann, T. A. (1993). Natural peer groups as contexts for individual development: The case of children's motivation in school. *Developmental Psychology, 29,* 970–977.

King, A. (1999). Discourse patterns for mediating peer learning. In A. M. O'Donnell & A. King

King, P. E., & Benson, P. L. (2006). Spiritual development and adolescent well-being and thriving. In E. C. Roehlkepartain, P. E. King, L. Wagener, & P. L. Benson (Eds.), *The handbook of spiritual development in childhood and adolescence* (pp. 384–398). Thousand Oaks, CA: Sage.

Kingery, J. N., Erdley, C. A., Marshall, K. C., Whitaker, K. G., & Reuter, T. R. (2010). Peer experiences of anxious and socially withdrawn youth: An integrative review of the developmental and clinical literature. *Clinical Child and Family Psychology Review, 13*(1), 91–128.

Kingstone, A., Smilek, D., Ristic, J., Friesen, C. K., & Eastwood, J. D. (2003). Attention, researchers! It is time to take a look at the real world. *Current Directions in Psychological Science, 12,* 176–180.

Kinnally, E. L., Huang, Y.-Y., Haverly, R., Burke, A. K., Galfalvy, H., Brent, D. P., et al. (2009). Parental care moderates the influence of MAOA-uVNTR genotype and childhood stressors on trait impulsivity and aggression in adult women. *Psychiatric Genetics, 19*(3), 126–133.

Kinney, H. C. (2009). Brainstem mechanisms underlying the sudden infant death syndrome: Evidence from human pathologic studies. *Developmental Psychobiology, 51*(3), 223–233.

Kirby, A., Edwards, L., & Hughes, A. (2008). Parents' concerns about children with specific learning difficulties: Insights gained from an online message centre. *Support for Learning, 23*(4), 193–200.

Kirby, D., & Laris, B. A. (2009). Effective curriculum-based sex and STD/HIV education programs for adolescents. *Child Development Perspectives, 3*(1), 21–29.

Kirby, J. R., Parrila, R. K., & Pfeiffer, S. L. (2003). Naming speed and phonological awareness as

predictors of reading development. *Journal of Educational Psychology, 95,* 453–464.

Kirkorian, H. L., Wartella, E. A., & Anderson, D. R. (2008). Media and young children's learning. *Future of Children, 18*(1), 39–61.

Kirschenbaum, R. J. (1989). Identification of the gifted and talented American Indian student. In C. J. Maker & S. W. Schiever (Eds.), *Critical issues in gifted education: Vol. 2. Defensible programs for cultural and ethnic minorities.* Austin, TX: Pro-Ed.

Kirschner, P. A., Sweller, J., & Clark, R. E. (2006). Why minimal guidance during instruction does not work: An analysis of the failure of constructivist, discovery, problem-based, experiential, and inquiry-based teaching. *Educational Psychologist, 41,* 75–86.

Kirshner, B. (2008). Guided participation in three youth activism organizations: Facilitation, apprenticeship, and joint work. *Journal of the Learning Sciences, 17,* 60–101.

Kisilevsky, B. S., Hains, S. M. J., Brown, C. A., Lee, C. T., Cowperthwaite, B., Stutzman, S. S., et al. (2009). Fetal sensitivity to properties of maternal speech and language. *Infant Behavior and Development, 32*(1), 59–71.

Kitamura, T., Shikai, N., Uji, M., Hiramura, H., Tanaka, N., & Shono, M. (2009). Intergenerational transmission of parenting style and personality: Direct influence or mediation? *Journal of Child and Family Studies, 18*(5), 541–556.

Kitayama, S., Duffy, S., & Uchida, Y. (2007). Self as cultural mode of being. In S. Kitayama & D. Cohen (Eds.), *Handbook of cultural psychology* (pp. 136–174). New York: Guilford Press.

Klaczynski, P. (2000). Motivated scientific reasoning biases, epistemological beliefs, and theory polarization: A two-process approach to adolescent cognition. *Child Development, 71,* 1347–1366.

Klaczynski, P. A. (2001). Analytic and heuristic processing influences on adolescent reasoning and decision-making. *Child Development, 72,* 844–861.

Klahr, D. (1982). Non-monotone assessment of monotone development: An information processing analysis. In S. Strauss & R. Stavy (Eds.), *U-shaped behavioral growth* (pp. 63–86). New York: Academic Press.

Klahr, D., & Robinson, M. (1981). Formal assessment of problem solving and planning processes in children. *Cognitive Psychology, 13,* 113–148.

Klassen, T. P., MacKay, J. M., Moher, D., Walker, A., & Jones, A. L. (2000). Community-based injury prevention interventions. *The Future of Children, 10*(1), 83–110.

Klausi, J. F., & Owen, M. T. (2009). Stable maternal cohabitation, couple relationship quality, and characteristics of the home environment in the child's first two years. *Journal of Family Psychology, 23*(1), 103–106.

Klein, P. D. (2006). The challenges of scientific literacy: From the viewpoint of second-generation cognitive science. *International Journal of Science Education, 28*(2–3), 143–178.

Klibanoff, R. S., Levine, S. C., Huttenlocher, J., Vasilyeva, M., & Hedges, L. V. (2006). Preschool children's mathematical knowledge: The effect of teacher "math talk." *Developmental Psychology, 42,* 59–69.

Klinnert, M. D. (1984). The regulation of infant behavior by maternal facial expression. *Infant Behavior and Development, 7,* 447–465.

Klinnert, M. D., Emde, R. N., Butterfield, P., & Campos, J. J. (1986). Social referencing: The infant's use of emotional signals from a friendly adult with mother present. *Developmental Psychology, 22,* 427–434.

Kluger, A. N., & DeNisi, A. (1998). Feedback interventions: Toward the understanding of a

double-edged sword. *Current Directions in Psychological Science, 7,* 67–72.

Knafo, A., Iervolino, A. C., & Plomin, R. (2005). Masculine girls and feminine boys: Genetic and environmental contributions to atypical gender development in early childhood. *Journal of Personality and Social Psychology, 88*(2), 400–412. doi:10.1037/0022-3514.88.2.400

Knafo, A., & Plomin, R. (2006). Prosocial behavior from early to middle childhood: Genetic and environmental influences on stability and change. *Developmental Psychology, 42,* 771–786.

Knafo, A., Zahn-Waxler, C., Van Hulle, C., Robinson, J. L., & Rhee, S. H. (2008). The developmental origins of a disposition toward empathy: Genetic and environmental contributions. *Emotion, 8*(6), 737–752. doi:10.1037/a0014179

Knapp, M. S., Turnbull, B. J., & Shields, P. M. (1990). New directions for educating the children of poverty. *Educational Leadership, 48*(1), 4–9.

Knapp, N. F. (2002). Tom and Joshua: Perceptions, conceptions and progress in meaning-based reading instruction. *Journal of Literacy Research, 34,* 59–98.

Knauss, C., Paxton, S. J., & Alsaker, F. D. (2007). Relationships among body dissatisfaction, internalisation of the media body ideal and perceived pressure from media in adolescent girls and boys. *Body Image, 4,* 353–360.

Knickmeyer, R. C., & Baron-Cohen, S. (2006). Fetal testosterone and sex differences. *Early Human Development, 82,* 755–760.

Knisel, E., Opitz, S., Wossmann, M., & Ketelhut, K. (2009). Sport motivation and physical activity of students in three European schools. *International Journal of Physical Education, 46*(2), 40–53.

Knudson, R. E. (1992). The development of written argumentation: An analysis and comparison of argumentative writing at four grade levels. *Child Study Journal, 22,* 167–181.

Kochanska, G. (1993). Toward a synthesis of parental socialization and child temperament in early development of conscience. *Child Development, 64,* 325–347.

Kochanska, G., & Aksan, N. (2006). Children's conscience and self-regulation. *Journal of Personality, 74,* 1587–1618.

Kochanska, G., Casey, R. J., & Fukumoto, A. (1995). Toddlers' sensitivity to standard violations. *Child Development, 66,* 643–656.

Kochanska, G., Coy, K. C., & Murray, K. T. (2001). The development of self-regulation in the first four years of life. *Child Development, 72,* 1091–1111.

Kochanska, G., Gross, J. N., Lin, M.-H., & Nichols, K. E. (2002). Guilt in young children: Development, determinants, and relations with a broader system of standards. *Child Development, 73,* 461–482.

Kochanska, G., Koenig, J. L., Barry, R. A., Kim, S., & Yoon, J. E. (2010). Children's conscience during toddler and preschool years, moral self, and a competent, adaptive developmental trajectory. *Developmental Psychology, 46*(5), 1320–1332. doi:10.1037/a0020381

Kodluboy, D. W. (2004). Gang-oriented interventions. In J. C. Conoley & A. P. Goldstein (Eds.), *School violence intervention* (2nd ed., pp. 194–232). New York: Guilford Press.

Koegel, L. K. (1995). Communication and language intervention. In R. L. Koegel & L. K. Koegel (Eds.), *Strategies for initiating positive interactions and improving learning opportunities.* Baltimore, MD: Paul H. Brookes.

Koekoek, J., Knoppers, A., & Stegeman, H. (2009). How do children think they learn skills in physical education? *Journal of Teaching in Physical Education, 28,* 310–332.

Koelch, M., Singer, H., Prestel, A, Burkert, J., Schulze, U., & Fegert, J. M. (2009). ". . . because

I am something special" or "I think I will be something like a guinea pig": Information and assent of legal minors in clinical trials—Assessment of understanding, appreciation, and reasoning. *Child and Adolescent Psychiatry and Mental Health, 3,* 2. doi:10.1186/1753-2000-3-2

Koenig, M. A., Clément, F., & Harris, P. L. (2004). Trust in testimony: Children's use of true and false statements. *Psychological Science, 15,* 694–698.

Koenig, M. A., & Woodward, A. L. (2010). Sensitivity of 24-month-olds to the prior inaccuracy of the source: Possible mechanisms. *Developmental Psychology, 46*(4), 815–826.

Koeppel, J., & Mulrooney, M. (1992). The Sister Schools Program: A way for children to learn about cultural diversity—When there isn't any in their school. *Young Children, 48*(1), 44–47.

Kohlberg, L. (1963). Moral development and identification. In H. Stevenson (Ed.), *Child psychology: The sixty-second yearbook of the National Society for the Study of Education* (pp. 277–332). Chicago: University of Chicago Press.

Kohlberg, L. (1964). Development of moral character and moral ideology. In M. L. Hoffman & L. W. Hoffman (Eds.), *Review of child development research: Vol. 1* (pp. 383–432). New York: Russell Sage Foundation.

Kohlberg, L. (1966). A cognitive developmental analysis of children's sex-role concepts and attitudes. In E. E. Maccoby (Ed.), *The development of sex differences* (pp. 82–173). Stanford, CA: Stanford University Press.

Kohlberg, L. (1969). Stage and sequence: The cognitive-developmental approach to socialization. In D. A. Goslin (Ed.), *Handbook of socialization theory and research* (pp. 347–480). Chicago: Rand McNally.

Kohlberg, L. (1975). The cognitive-developmental approach to moral education. *Phi Delta Kappan, 57,* 670–677.

Kohlberg, L. (1976). Moral stages and moralization: The cognitive-developmental approach. In T. Lickona (Ed.), *Moral development and behavior: Theory, research, and social issues.* New York: Holt, Rinehart & Winston.

Kohlberg, L. (1981). *The philosophy of moral development: Moral stages and the idea of justice.* San Francisco: Harper & Row.

Kohlberg, L. (1984). *The psychology of moral development: The nature and validity of moral stages.* San Francisco: Harper & Row.

Kohlberg, L. (1986). A current statement on some theoretical issues. In S. Modgil & C. Modgil (Eds.), *Lawrence Kohlberg: Consensus and controversy.* Philadelphia, PA: Falmer Press.

Kohlberg, L., & Candee, D. (1984). The relationship of moral judgment to moral action. In W. M. Kurtines & J. L. Gewirtz (Eds.), *Morality, moral behavior, and moral development.* New York: Wiley.

Kohlberg, L., & Fein, G. G. (1987). Play and constructive work as contributors to development. In L. Kohlberg (Ed.), *Child psychology and childhood education: A cognitive-developmental view* (pp. 392–440). New York: Longman.

Kohlberg, L., & Kramer, R. (1969). Continuities and discontinuities in childhood and adult moral development. *Human Development, 12,* 93–120.

Kohlberg, L., Levine, C., & Hewer, A. (1983). Moral stages: A current formulation and a response to critics. *Contributions to Human Development, 10,* 1–174.

Kohlberg, L., & Mayer, R. (1972). Development as the aim of education. *Harvard Educational Review, 42,* 449–496.

Kohler, F. W., Greteman, C., Raschke, D., & Highnam, C. (2007). Using a buddy skills package to increase the social interactions between a preschooler with autism and her peers. *Topics in Early Childhood Education, 27,* 155–163.

Kohn, A. (2008). Why self-discipline is overrated: The (troubling) theory and practice of control from within. *Phi Delta Kappan, 90*(3), 168–176.

Kohn, M. L. (1977). *Class and conformity* (2nd ed.). Chicago: University of Chicago Press.

Koinis-Mitchell, D., McQuaid, E. L., Seifer, R., Kopel, S. J., Nassau, J. H., Klein, R. B., et al. (2009). Symptom perception in children with asthma: Cognitive and psychological factors. *Health Psychology, 28*(2), 226–237.

Kolb, B., Gibb, R., & Robinson, T. E. (2003). Brain plasticity and behavior. *Current Directions in Psychological Science, 12,* 1–5.

Koob, A. (2009). *The root of thought: Unlocking glia—The brain cell that will help us sharpen our wits, heal injury, and treat brain disease.* Upper Saddle River, NJ: Pearson Education.

Koole, S. L. (2009). The psychology or emotion regulation: An integrative review. *Cognition and Emotion, 23*(1), 4–41.

Koops, L. H. (2010). "Deñuy Jàngal seen bopp" (They teach themselves): Children's music learning in The Gambia. *Journal of Research in Music Education, 58*(1), 18–36

Kopp, C. B. (1982). Antecedents of self-regulation: A developmental perspective. *Developmental Psychology, 18,* 199–214.

Koren-Karie, N., Oppenheim, D., Dolev, S., Sher, E., & Etzion-Carasso, A. (2002). Mothers' insightfulness regarding their infants' internal experience: Relations with maternal sensitivity and infant attachment. *Developmental Psychology, 38*(4), 534–542.

Koskinen, P. S., Blum, I. H., Bisson, S. A., Phillips, S. M., Creamer, T. S., & Baker, T. K. (2000). Book access, shared reading, and audio models. The effects of supporting the literacy learning of linguistically diverse students in school and at home. *Journal of Educational Psychology, 92,* 23–36.

Kotilahti, K., Nissilä, l., Näsi, T., Lipiäinen, L., Noponen, T., Meriläinen, P., et al. (2010). Hemodynamic responses to speech and music in newborn infants. *Human Brain Mapping, 31*(4), 595–603.

Kovack-Lesh, K. A., Horst, J. S., & Oakes, L. M. (2008). The cat is out of the bag: The joint influence of previous experience and looking behavior on infant categorization. *Infancy, 13*(4), 285–307.

Kovas, Y., Haworth, C. M. A., Dale, P. S., & Plomin, R. (2007). The genetic and environmental origins of learning abilities and disabilities in the early school years. *Monographs of the Society for Research in Child Development, 72*(3, Serial No. 288), 1–160.

Kozulin, A. (1986). Vygotsky in context. In A. S. Vygotsky, *Thought and language* (rev. ed.; A. Kozulin, Ed. and Trans.). Cambridge, MA: MIT Press.

Kozulin, A., Lebeer, J., Madella-Noja, A., Gonzalez, F., Jeffrey, I., Rosenthal, N., et al. (2010). Cognitive modifiability of children with developmental disabilities: A multicentre study using Feuerstein's Instrumental Enrichment—Basic program. *Research in Developmental Disabilities, 31,* 551–559.

Krampen, G. (1987). Differential effects of teacher comments. *Journal of Educational Psychology, 79,* 137–146.

Krasa, N., & Shunkwiler, S. (2009). *Number sense and number nonsense: Understanding the challenges of learning math.* Baltimore, MD: Paul H. Brookes.

Krashen, S. D. (1996). *Under attack: The case against bilingual education.* Culver City, CA: Language Education Associates.

Krebs, D. L., & Van Hesteren, F. (1994). The development of altruism: Toward an integrative model. *Developmental Review, 14,* 103–158.

Krebs, P. L. (1995). Mental retardation. In J. P. Winnick (Ed.), *Adapted physical education and sport*

(2nd ed., pp. 93–109). Champaign, IL: Human Kinetics.

Kreider, R. M., & Fields, J. (2005, July). *Living arrangements of children: 2001* (Current Population Reports, P70–104). Washington, DC: U.S. Department of Commerce, U.S. Census Bureau.

Kreutzer, M. A., Leonard, C., & Flavell, J. H. (1975). An interview study of children's knowledge about memory. *Monographs of the Society for Research in Child Development, 40*(1, Serial No. 159).

Krispin, O., Sternberg, K. J., & Lamb, M. E. (1992). The dimensions of peer evaluation in Israel: A cross-cultural perspective. *International Journal of Behavioral Development, 15,* 299–314.

Kristjánsson, Á., Sigfúsdóttir, I. D., & Allegrante, J. P. (2010). Health behavior and academic achievement among adolescents: The relative contribution of dietary habits, physical activity, body mass index, and self-esteem. *Health Education and Behavior, 37*(1), 51–64.

Krivitski, E. C., McIntosh, D. E., Rothlisberg, B., & Finch, H. (2004). Profile analysis of deaf children using the Universal Nonverbal Intelligence Test. *Journal of Psychoeducational Assessment, 22,* 338–350.

Kroger, J. (2003). What transits in an identity status transition? *Identity: An International Journal of Theory and Research, 3,* 197–220.

Kroger, J. (2004). Identity in formation. In K. Hoover (Ed.), *The future of identity: Centennial reflections on the legacy of Erik Erikson* (pp. 61–76). Lanham, MD: Lexington Books.

Kroger, S. M., Schettler, T., & Weiss, B. (2005). Environmental toxicants and developmental disabilities. *American Psychologist, 60*(3), 243–255.

Kufeldt, K., Simard, M., & Vachon, J. (2003). Improving outcomes for children in care: Giving youth a voice. *Adoptions and Fostering, 27,* 8–19.

Kugiumutzakis, G. (1999). Genesis and development of early infant mimesis to facial and vocal models. In J. Nadel & G. Butterworth (Eds.), *Imitation in infancy* (pp. 36–59). New York: Cambridge University Press.

Kuhl, P. K. (2004). Early language acquisition: Cracking the speech code. *Nature Reviews Neuroscience, 5,* 831–843.

Kuhl, P. K. (2007). Is speech learning "gated" by the social brain? *Developmental Science, 10,* 110–120.

Kuhl, P. K., Conboy, B. T., Padden, D., Nelson, T., & Pruitt, J. (2005). Early speech perception and later language development: Implications for the "critical period." *Language Learning and Development, 1,* 237–264.

Kuhl, P. K., & Meltzoff, A. N. (1997). Evolution, nativism and learning in the development of language and speech. In M. Gopnik (Ed.), *The inheritance and innateness of grammars.* New York: Oxford University Press.

Kuhlmeier, V., Wynn, K., & Bloom, P. (2003). Attribution of dispositional states by 12-month-olds. *Psychological Science, 14,* 402–408.

Kuhn, D. (1993). Connecting scientific and informal reasoning. *Merrill-Palmer Quarterly, 39,* 74–103.

Kuhn, D. (1997). Constraints or guideposts? Developmental psychology and science education. *Review of Educational Research, 67,* 141–150.

Kuhn, D. (2001a). How do people know? *Psychological Science, 12,* 1–8.

Kuhn, D. (2001b). Why development does (and does not) occur: Evidence from the domain of inductive reasoning. In J. L. McClelland & R. S. Siegler (Eds.), *Mechanisms of cognitive development: Behavioral and neural perspectives* (pp. 221–249). Mahwah, NJ: Erlbaum.

Kuhn, D. (2006). Do cognitive changes accompany developments in the adolescent brain? *Perspectives on Psychological Science, 1,* 59–67.

Kuhn, D. (2007). Is direct instruction an answer to the right question? *Educational Psychologist, 42,* 109–113.

Kuhn, D. (2008). Formal operations from a twenty-first century perspective. *Human Development, 51,* 48–55.

Kuhn, D. (2009). Adolescent thinking. In R. M. Lerner, & L. Steinberg (Eds.), *Handbook of adolescent psychology, Vol. 1: Individual bases of adolescent development* (3rd ed., pp. 152–186). Hoboken, NJ: John Wiley & Sons Inc.

Kuhn, D., Amsel, E., & O'Loughlin, M. (1988). *The development of scientific thinking skills.* San Diego, CA: Academic Press.

Kuhn, D., Daniels, S., & Krishnan, A. (2003, April). *Epistemology and intellectual values as core metacognitive constructs.* Paper presented at the annual meeting of the American Educational Research Association, Chicago.

Kuhn, D., & Dean, D., Jr. (2005). Is developing scientific thinking all about learning to control variables? *Psychological Science, 16,* 866–870.

Kuhn, D., & Franklin, S. (2006). The second decade: What develops (and how)? In W. Damon & R. M. Lerner (Series Eds.), & D. Kuhn & R. Siegler (Vol. Eds.), *Handbook of child psychology: Vol. 1. Cognition, perception, and language* (6th ed.). New York: Wiley.

Kuhn, D., Garcia-Mila, M., Zohar, A., & Andersen, C. (1995). Strategies of knowledge acquisition. *Monographs of the Society for Research in Child Development, 60*(4, Whole No. 245).

Kuhn, D., & Park, S.-H. (2005). Epistemological understanding and the development of intellectual values. *International Journal of Educational Research, 43,* 111–124.

Kuhn, D., & Pearsall, S. (2000). Developmental origins of scientific thinking. *Journal of Cognition and Development, 1,* 113–129.

Kuhn, D., & Pease, M. (2010). The dual components of developing strategy use: Production and inhibition. In H. S. Waters & W. Schneider (Eds.), *Metacognition, strategy use, and instruction* (pp. 135–159). New York: Guilford Press.

Kuhn, D., Pease, M., & Wirkala, C. (2009). Coordinating the effects of multiple variables: A skill fundamental to scientific thinking. *Journal of Experimental Child Psychology, 103*(3), 268–284.

Kuhn, D., Shaw, V., & Felton, M. (1997). Effects of dyadic interaction on argumentative reasoning. *Cognition and Instruction, 15,* 287–315.

Kuhn, D., & Udell, W. (2003). The development of argument skills. *Child Development, 74,* 1245–1260.

Kuhn, D., & Weinstock, M. (2002). What is epistemological thinking and why does it matter? In B. K. Hofer & P. R. Pintrich (Eds.), *Personal epistemology: The psychology of beliefs about knowledge and knowing* (pp. 121–144). Mahwah, NJ: Erlbaum.

Kulberg, A. (1986). Substance abuse: Clinical identification and management. *Pediatrics Clinics of North America, 33,* 325–361.

Kulik, J. A., & Kulik, C. C. (1997). Ability grouping. In N. Colangelo & G. Davis (Eds.), *Handbook of gifted education* (2nd ed., pp. 230–242). Boston: Allyn & Bacon.

Kulkarni, B., Christian, P., LeClerq, S. C., & Khatry, S. K. (2009). Determinants of compliance to antenatal micronutrient supplementation and women's perceptions of supplement use in rural Nepal. *Public Health Nutrition, 13*(1), 82–90.

Kunjufu, J. (2006). *An African centered response to Ruby Payne's poverty theory.* Chicago: African American Images.

Kunnen, E. S. (2009). Qualitative and quantitative aspects of commitment development in psychology students. *Journal of Adolescence, 32*(3), 567–584.

Kunzinger, E. L., III (1985). A short-term longitudinal study of memorial development during early grade school. *Developmental Psychology, 21,* 642–646.

Kuo, L., & Anderson, R. C. (2006). Morphological awareness and learning to read: A cross-language perspective. *Educational Psychologist, 41,* 161–180.

Kurtines, W. M., Berman, S. L., Ittel, A., & Williamson, S. (1995). Moral development: A co-constructivist perspective. In W. M. Kurtines & J. L. Gewirtz (Eds.), *Moral development: An introduction.* Boston: Allyn & Bacon.

Kurtines, W. M., & Gewirtz, J. L. (Eds.). (1991). *Moral behavior and development: Vol. 2. Research.* Hillsdale, NJ: Erlbaum.

Kushner, M. A. (2009). A review of the empirical literature about child development and adjustment postseparation. *Journal of Divorce and Remarriage, 50,* 496–516.

Kutner, L. A., Olson, C. K., Warner, D. E., & Hertzog, S. M. (2008). Parents' and sons' perspectives on video game play: A qualitative study. *Journal of Adolescent Research, 23*(1), 76–96.

Kutnick, P., & Berdondini, L. (2009). Can the enhancement of group working in classrooms provide a basis for effective communication in support of school-based cognitive achievement in classrooms of young learners? *Cambridge Journal of Education, 39*(1), 71–94.

Kwisthout, J., Vogt, P., Haselager, P., & Dijkstra, T. (2008). Joint attention and language evolution. *Connection Science, 20*(2–3), 155–171.

Kwok, O.-M., Hughes, J. N., & Luo, W. (2007). Role of resilient personality on lower achieving first grade students' current and future achievement. *Journal of School Psychology, 45,* 61–82.

Kwon, K., & Lease, A. M. (2009). Children's social identification with a friendship group: A moderating effect on intent to conform to norms. *Small Group Research, 40*(6), 694–719. doi:10.1177/1046496409346578

Kwong, T. E., & Varnhagen, C. K. (2005). Strategy development and learning to spell new words: Generalization of a process. *Developmental Psychology, 41*(1), 148–159.

Kyle, F. E., & Harris, M. (2010). Predictors of reading development in deaf children: A 3-year longitudinal study. *Journal of Experimental Child Psychology, 107*(3), 229–243.

Kyza, E. A. (2009). Middle-school students' reasoning about alternative hypotheses in a scaffolded, software-based inquiry investigation. *Cognition and Instruction, 27*(4), 277–311.

La Guardia, J. G., Ryan, R. M., Couchman, C. E., & Deci, E. L. (2000). Within-person variation in security of attachment: A self-determination theory perspective on attachment, need fulfillment, and well-being. *Journal of Personality and Social Psychology, 79,* 367–384.

La Paro, K. M., Hamre, B. K., Locasale-Crouch, J., Pianta, R. C., Bryant, D., Early, D., et al. (2009). Quality in kindergarten classrooms: Observational evidence for the need to increase children's learning opportunities in early education classrooms. *Early Education and Development, 20*(4), 657–692. doi:10.1080/10409280802541965

La Paro, K. M., & Pianta, R. C. (2000). Predicting children's competence in the early school years: A meta-analytic review. *Review of Educational Research, 70,* 443–484.

LaBlance, G. R., Steckol, K. F., & Smith, V. L. (1994). Stuttering: The role of the classroom teacher. *Teaching Exceptional Children, 26*(2), 10–12.

Laboratory of Comparative Human Cognition. (1982). Culture and intelligence. In R. J. Sternberg (Ed.), *Handbook of human intelligence.* Cambridge, England: Cambridge University Press.

Ladd, G. W. (2005). *Children's peer relations and social competence: A century of progress.* New Haven, CT: Yale University Press.

Ladd, G. W., & Burgess, K. B. (1999). Charting the relationship trajectories of aggressive, withdrawn, and aggressive/withdrawn children during early grade school. *Child Development, 70,* 910–929.

Ladd, G. W., Herald-Brown, S. L., & Kochel, K. P. (2009). Peers and motivation. In K. R. Wentzel & A. Wigfield (Eds.), *Handbook of motivation at school* (pp. 323–348). New York: Routledge.

Ladson-Billings, G. (1994). *The dreamkeepers: Successful teachers of African American children.* San Francisco: Jossey-Bass.

Ladson-Billings, G. (1995). But that's just good teaching! The case for culturally relevant pedagogy. *Theory Into Practice, 34*(3), 159–165.

Lafontana, K. M., & Cillessen, A. H. N. (1998). The nature of children's stereotypes of popularity. *Social Development, 7,* 301–320.

LaGrange, B., Cole, D. A., Dallaire, D. H., Ciesla, J. A., Pineda, A. Q., Truss, A. E., et al. (2008). Developmental changes in depressive cognitions: A longitudinal evaluation of the cognitive triad inventory for children. *Psychological Assessment, 20*(3), 217–226.

Lahman, M. K. E. (2008). Always othered: Ethical research with children. *Early Childhood Research, 6*(3), 281–300.

Laible, D., & Thompson, R. A. (2007). Early socialization: A relationship perspective. In J. E. Grusec & P. D. Hastings (Eds.), *Handbook of socialization: Theory and research* (pp. 181–207). New York: Guilford Press.

Laible, D. J. (2004). Mother–child discourse surrounding a child's past behavior at 30 months: Links to emotional understanding and early conscience development at 36 months. *Merrill-Palmer Quarterly: Journal of Developmental Psychology, 50*(2), 159–180. doi:10.1353/mpq.2004.0013

Laible, D. J., & Thompson, R. A. (2000). Mother–child discourse, attachment security, shared positive affect, and early conscience development. *Child Development, 71*(5), 1424–1440. doi:10.1111/1467-8624.00237

Lajoie, S. P., & Derry, S. J. (Eds.). (1993). *Computers as cognitive tools.* Mahwah, NJ: Erlbaum.

Lakatos, K., Birkas, E., Nemoda, Z., & Gervai, J. (2007, March). *Genetic influence on the ability to delay gratification in childhood.* Paper presented at the biennial meeting of the Society for Research in Child Development, Boston.

Laland, K., Odling-Smee, J., & Feldman, M. (2000). Niche construction, biological evolution, and cultural change. *Behavioral and Brain Sciences, 23,* 131–175.

Lalor, J., Begley, C., & Galavan, E. (2009). Recasting hope: A process of adaptation following fetal anomaly diagnosis. *Social Science and Medicine, 68,* 462–472.

Lamaze, F. (1958). *Painless childbirth.* London: Burke.

Lamb, M. E., & Ahnert, L. (2006). Nonparental child care: Context, concepts, correlates, and consequences. In W. Damon & R. M. Lerner (Series Eds.) & K. A. Renninger & I. E. Sigel (Vol. Eds.), *Handbook of child psychology: Vol. 3. Social, emotional, and personality development* (6th ed., pp. 950–1016). New York: Wiley.

Lamb, M. E., Chuang, S. S., & Cabrera, N. (2005). Promoting child adjustment by fostering positive paternal involvement. In R. M. Lerner, F. Jacobs, & D. Wertlieb (Eds.), *Applied developmental science: An advanced textbook* (pp. 179–200). Thousand Oaks, CA: Sage.

Lamb, M. E., Frodi, A. M., Hwang, C. P., Frodi, M., & Steinberg, J. (1982). Mother– and father–infant interactions involving play and holding in traditional and non-traditional Swedish families. *Developmental Psychology, 18,* 215–221.

Lamb, M. E., & Lewis, C. (2004). The development and significance of father–child relationships in two-parent families. In M. E. Lamb (Ed.), *The role of the father in child development* (4th ed., pp. 272–306). Hoboken, NJ: John Wiley.

Lamb, S., & Feeny, N. C. (1995). Early moral sense and socialization. In W. M. Kurtines & J. L. Gewirtz

(Eds.), *Moral development: An introduction.* Boston: Allyn & Bacon.

Lamborn, S. D., Mounts, N. S., Steinberg, L., & Dornbusch, S. M. (1991). Patterns of competence and adjustment among adolescents from authoritative, authoritarian, indulgent, and neglectful families. *Child Development, 62,* 1049–1065.

Lancy, D. F. (2008). *The anthropology of childhood: Cherubs, chattel, and changelings.* Cambridge, England: Cambridge University Press.

Landrum, T. J., & Kauffman, J. M. (2006). Behavioral approaches to classroom management. In C. M. Evertson & C. S. Weinstein (Eds.), *Handbook of classroom management: Research, practice, and contemporary issues* (pp. 47–71). Mahwah, NJ: Erlbaum.

Landry, S. H., & Smith, K. E. (2010). Early social and cognitive precursors and parental support for self-regulation and executive function: Relations from early childhood into adolescence. In B. W. Sokol, U. Müeller, J. I. M. Carpendale, A. R. Young, & G. Iarocci (Eds.), *Self and social regulation: Social interaction and the development of social understanding and executive functions* (pp. 386–417). New York: Oxford University Press.

Langacker, R. (1986). An introduction to cognitive grammar. *Cognitive Science, 10,* 1–40.

Langdon, P. E., Clare, I. C. H., & Murphy, G. H. (2010). Developing an understanding of the literature relating to the moral development of people with intellectual disabilities. *Developmental Review, 30*(3), 273–293. doi:10.1016/j.dr.2010.01.001

Lange, G., & Pierce, S. H. (1992). Memory-strategy learning and maintenance in preschool children. *Developmental Psychology, 28,* 453 462.

Langhaug, L. F., Cheung, Y. B., Pascoe, S., Hayes, R., Cowan, F. M. (2009). Differences in prevalence of common mental disorders as measured during four questionnaire delivery methods among young people in rural Zimbabwe. *Journal of Affective Disorders, 118,* 220–223.

Langhout, R. D., & Mitchell, C. A. (2008). Engaging contexts: Drawing the link between student and teacher experiences of the hidden curriculum. *Journal of Community & Applied Social Psychology, 18*(6), 593–614. doi:10.1002/casp.974

Lansford, J. E. (2009). Parental divorce and children's adjustment. *Perspectives on Psychological Science, 4*(2), 140–152.

Lapan, R. T., Tucker, B., Kim, S.-K., & Kosciulek, J. F. (2003). Preparing rural adolescents for post-high school transitions. *Journal of Counseling and Development, 81,* 329–342.

Lapsley, D. K. (1993). Toward an integrated theory of adolescent ego development: The "new look" at adolescent egocentrism. *American Journal of Orthopsychiatry, 63,* 562–571.

Lareau, A. (2003). *Unequal childhoods: Class, race, and family life.* Berkeley: University of California Press.

Larner, M. B., Stevenson, C. S., & Behrman, R. E. (1998). Protecting children from abuse and neglect: Analysis and recommendations. *The Future of Children: Protecting Children from Abuse and Neglect, 8*(1), 4–22.

Larson, R., & Richards, M. H. (1994). *Divergent realities: The emotional lives of mothers, fathers, and adolescents.* New York: Basic Books.

Larson, R. W. (2000). Toward a psychology of positive youth development. *American Psychologist, 55,* 170–183.

Larson, R. W., Clore, G. L., & Wood, G. A (1999). The emotions of romantic relationships: Do they wreak havoc on adolescents? In W. Furman, B. B. Brown, & C. Feiring (Eds.), *The development of romantic relationships in adolescence* (pp. 19–49). Cambridge, England: Cambridge University Press.

Last, C. G., Hersen, M., Kazdin, A. E., Francis, G., & Grubb, H. J. (1987). Psychiatric illness in the mothers of anxious children. *American Journal of Psychiatry, 144,* 1580–1583.

Lau, P. W. C., Cheung, M. W. L., & Ransdell, L. B. (2008). A structural equation model of the relationship between body perception and self-esteem: Global physical self-concept as the mediator. *Psychology of Sport and Exercise, 9,* 493–509.

Laundra, K., & Sutton, T. (2008). You think you know ghetto? Contemporizing the Dove "Black IQ Test." *Teaching Sociology, 36*(4), 366–377.

Laupa, M., & Turiel, E. (1995). Social domain theory. In W. M. Kurtines & J. L. Gewirtz (Eds.), *Moral development: An introduction.* Boston: Allyn & Bacon.

Lave, J., & Wenger, E. (1991). *Situated learning: Legitimate peripheral participation.* Cambridge, England: Cambridge University Press.

Lawrence, B. K. (2009). Rural gifted education: A comprehensive literature review. *Journal for the Education of the Gifted, 32*(4), 461–494.

Lawrence, J. S., & Crocker, J. (2009). Academic contingencies of self-worth impair positively- and negatively-stereotyped students' performance in performance-goal settings. *Journal of Research in Personality, 43*(5), 868–874.

Leaper, C., & Friedman, C. K. (2007). The socialization of gender. In J. E. Grusec & P. D. Hastings (Eds.), *Handbook of socialization: Theory and research* (pp. 561–587). New York: Guilford Press.

Leaper, C., & Smith, T. E. (2004). A meta-analytic review of gender variations in children's language use: Talkativeness, affiliative speech, and assertive speech. *Developmental Psychology, 40*(6), 993–1027. doi:10.1037/0012-1649.40.6.993

Learning First Alliance. (2001). *Every child learning: Safe and supportive schools.* Washington, DC: Learning First Alliance and Association for Supervision and Curriculum Development.

Lebrun, M. (2009). *Books, blackboards, and bullets: School shootings and violence in America.* Lanham, MD: Rowman & Littlefield Education.

Lee, C., & Chen, M. (2010). Taiwanese junior high school students' mathematics attitudes and perceptions towards virtual manipulatives. *British Journal of Educational Technology, 41*(2), E17–E21.

Lee, C. D., & Slaughter-Defoe, D. T. (1995). Historical and sociocultural influences on African and American education. In J. A. Banks & C. A. M. Banks (Eds.), *Handbook of research on multicultural education.* New York: Macmillan.

Lee, E. J., & Lee, S. H. (2009). Effects of instructional rubrics on class engagement behaviors and the achievement of lesson objectives by students with mild mental retardation and their typical peers. *Education and Training in Developmental Disabilities, 44*(3), 396–408.

Lee, J. (2009). Escaping embarrassment: Face-work in the rap cipher. *Social Psychology Quarterly, 72*(4), 306–324.

Lee, K., Cameron, C. A., Doucette, J., & Talwar, V. (2002). Phantoms and fabrications: Young children's detection of implausible lies. *Child Development, 73,* 1688–1702.

Lee, M. H., & Hanuscin, D. L. (2008). A (mis)understanding of astronomical proportions. *Science and Children, 46*(1), 60–61.

Lee, O. (1999). Science knowledge, world views, and information sources in social and cultural contexts: Making sense after a natural disaster. *American Educational Research Journal, 36,* 187–219.

Lee, S. (1985). Children's acquisition of conditional logic structure: Teachable? *Contemporary Educational Psychology, 10,* 14–27.

Lee, V. E., & Burkam, D. T. (2003). Dropping out of high school: The role of school organization and structure. *American Educational Research Journal, 40,* 353–393.

Lee-Pearce, M. L., Plowman, T. S., & Touchstone, D. (1998). Starbase-Atlantis, a school without walls: A comparative study of an innovative science program for at-risk urban elementary students. *Journal of Education for Students Placed at Risk, 3,* 223–235.

Lefever, J. B., Nicholson, J. S., & Noria, C. W. (2007). Children's uncertain futures: Problems in school. In J. G. Borkowski, J. R. Farris, T. L. Whitman, S. S. Carothers, K. Weed, & D. A. Keogh (Eds.), *Risk and resilience: Adolescent mothers and their children grow up* (pp. 259–278). Mahwah, NJ: Erlbaum.

LeFevre, J.-A., Shwarchuk, S.-L., Smith-Chant, B. L., Fast, L., Kamawar, D., & Bisanz, J. (2009). Home numeracy experiences and children's math performance in the early school years. *Canadian Journal of Behavioural Sciences, 41*(2), 55–66.

Leflot, G., Onghena, P., & Colpin, H. (2010). Teacher–child interactions: Relations with children's self-concept in second grade. *Infant and Child Development, 19*(4), 385–405.

Lefstein, L. M., & Lipsitz, J. (1995). *3:00 to 6:00 p.m.: Programs for young adolescents.* Minneapolis, MN: Search Institute.

Legare, C. H., & Gelman, S. A. (2007, March). *Bewitchment, biology, or both: The co-existence of natural and supernatural explanatory frameworks across development.* Paper presented at the biennial meeting of the Society for Research in Child Development, Boston.

Legaspi, B., & Straits, W. (2011). Living or nonliving? *Science and Children, 48*(8), 27–31.

Lehman, D. R., & Nisbett, R. E. (1990). A longitudinal study of the effects of undergraduate training on reasoning. *Developmental Psychology, 26,* 952–960.

Lehmann, M., & Hasselhorn, M. (2007). Variable memory strategy use in children's adaptive intra-task learning behavior: Developmental changes and working memory influences in free recall. *Child Development, 78,* 1068–1082.

Leichtentritt, J., & Shechtman, Z.. (2010). Children with and without learning disabilities: A comparison of processes and outcomes following group counseling. *Journal of Learning Disabilities, 43*(2), 169–179.

Leichtman, M. D., & Ceci, S. J. (1995). The effects of stereotypes and suggestions on preschoolers' reports. *Developmental Psychology, 31,* 568–578.

Leichtman, M. D., Pillemer, D. B., Wang, Q., Koreishi, A., & Han, J. J. (2000). When Baby Maisy came to school: Mothers' interview styles and preschoolers' event memories. *Cognitive Development, 15,* 99–114.

Lein, L. (1975). Black American immigrant children: Their speech at home and school. *Council on Anthropology and Education Quarterly, 6,* 1–11.

Leinhardt, G. (1994). History: A time to be mindful. In G. Leinhardt, I. L. Beck, & C. Stainton (Eds.), *Teaching and learning in history.* Hillsdale, NJ: Erlbaum.

Leinhardt, G., Crowley, K., & Knutson, K. (2002). *Learning conversations in museums.* New York: Routledge.

Leman, P. J., & Björnberg, M. (2010). Conversation, development, and gender: A study of changes in children's concepts of punishment. *Child Development, 81*(3), 958–971. doi:10.1111/j.1467-8624.2010.01445.x

Lemanek, K. L. (2004). Adherence. In R. T. Brown (Ed.), *Handbook of pediatric psychology in school settings* (pp. 129–148). Mahwah, NJ: Erlbaum.

Leming, J. S. (2000). Tell me a story: An evaluation of a literature-based character education programme. *Journal of Moral Education, 29,* 413–427.

Lemmens, J. S., Valkenburg, P. M., & Peter, J. (2011). The effects of pathological gaming on aggressive behavior. *Journal of Youth and Adolescence, 40*(1), 38–47. doi:10.1007/s10964-010-9558-x

Lennox, C., & Siegel, L. S. (1998). Phonological and orthographic processes in good and poor spellers. In C. Hulme & R. M. Joshi (Eds.), *Reading and spelling: Development and disorders.* Mahwah, NJ: Erlbaum.

Lens, W. (2001). How to combine intrinsic task motivation with the motivational effects of the instrumentality of present tasks for future goals. In Efklides, A., Kuhl, J., & Sorrentino, R. (Eds.), *Trends and prospects in motivation research* (pp. 37–52). Dordrecht, The Netherlands: Kluwer.

Lenzi, D., Trentini, C., Pantano, P., Macaluso, E., Iacoboni, M., Lenzi, G. L., et al. (2009). Neural basis of maternal communication and emotional expression processing during infant preverbal stage. *Cerebral Cortex, 19*(5), 1124–1133.

Leonard, L. B. (2009). Some reflections on the study of children with specific language impairment. *Child Language Teaching and Therapy, 25*(2), 169–171.

Lepper, M. R., Corpus, J. H., & Iyengar, S. S. (2005). Intrinsic and extrinsic motivational orientations in the classroom: Age differences and academic correlates. *Journal of Educational Psychology, 97,* 184–196.

Lerner, R. M. (2002). *Concepts and theories of human development* (3rd ed.). Mahwah, NJ: Erlbaum.

Lessard, A., Fortin, L., Marcotte, D., Potvin, P., & Royer, É. (2009). Why did they not drop out? Narratives from resilient students. *The Prevention Researcher, 16*(3), 21–24.

Letiecq, B. L., Bailey, S. J., & Dahlen, P. (2008). Ambivalence and coping among custodial grandparents. In B. Hayslip & P. L. Kaminski (Eds.), *Parenting the custodial grandchild* (pp. 3–16). New York: Springer.

Letourneau, E. J., Ellis, D. A., Naar-King, S., Cunningham, P. B., & Fowler, S. L. (2009). Case study: Multisystemic therapy for adolescents who engage in HIV transmission behaviors. *Journal of Pediatric Psychology, 35*(2), 120–127.

LeVay, S. (2011). *Gay, straight, and the reason why: The science of sexual orientation.* New York: Oxford University Press.

Leventhal, T., Dupéré, V., & Brooks-Gunn, J. (2009). Neighborhood influences on adolescent development. In R. M. Lerner & L. Steinberg (Eds.) *Handbook of adolescent psychology, Vol 2: Contextual influences on adolescent development* (3rd ed, pp. 411–443). Hoboken, NJ: Wiley.

Leventhal, T., Xue, Y., & Brooks-Gunn, J. (2006). Immigrant differences in school-age children's verbal trajectories: A look at four racial/ethnic groups. *Child Development, 77,* 1359–1374.

Levine, E. (2010). The rigors and rewards of internships. *Educational Leadership, 68*(1), 44–48.

Levine, L. (1983). Mine: Self-definition in 2-year-old boys. *Developmental Psychology, 19,* 544–549.

Levine, M. (2006). The price of privilege: How parental pressure and material advantage are creating a generation of disconnected and unhappy kids. New York: HarperCollins.

LeVine, R. A. (2004). Challenging expert knowledge: Findings from an African study of infant care and development. In U. P. Gielen & J. P. Roopnarine (Eds.), *Childhood and adolescence: Cross-cultural perspectives and applications* (pp. 149–165). Westport, CT: Praeger.

LeVine, R. A., & Norman, K. (2008). Attachment in anthropological perspective. In R. A. LeVine & R. S. New (Eds.), *Anthropology and child development: A cross-cultural reader* (pp. 127–142). Malden, MA: Blackwell Publishing.

Levitt, M. J., Guacci-Franco, N., & Levitt, J. L. (1993). Convoys of social support in childhood and early adolescence: Structure and function. *Developmental Psychology, 29,* 811–818.

Levpušček, M. P., & Zupančič, M. (2009). Math achievement in early adolescence: The role of parental involvement, teachers' behavior, and students' motivational beliefs about math. *Journal of Early Adolescence, 29*(4), 541–570.

Levstik, L. S. (2008). Building a sense of history in a first-grade classroom. In L. S. Levstik & K. C. Barton (Eds.), *Researching history education: Theory, method, and context* (pp. 30–60). New York: Routledge.

Lewandowski, L. J., & Rieger, B. (2009). The role of a school psychologist in concussion. *Journal of Applied School Psychology, 25*(1), 95–110.

Lewin, T. (2000, June 25). Growing up, growing apart: Fast friends try to resist the pressure to divide by race. *The New York Times,* pp. 1, 18–20.

Lewis, M. (1993). Self-conscious emotions: Embarrassment, pride, shame, and guilt. In M. Lewis & J. Haviland (Eds.), *The handbook of emotions* (pp. 563–573). New York: Guilford Press.

Lewis, M. (1995). Embarrassment: The emotion of self-exposure and evaluation. In J. Tangney & K. Fischer (Eds.), *Self-conscious emotions: The psychology of shame, guilt, embarrassment and pride* (pp. 198–218). New York: Guilford Press.

Lewis, M. (2000). The emergence of human emotions. In M. Lewis & J. M. Haviland-Jones (Eds.), *Handbook of emotions* (2nd ed., pp. 265–280). New York: Guilford Press.

Lewis, M. (2005). The child and its family: The social network model. *Human Development, 48,* 8–27.

Lewis, M., & Brooks-Gunn, J. (1979). *Social cognition and the acquisition of self.* New York: Plenum.

Lewis, M., & Carmody, D. P. (2008). Self-representation and brain development. *Developmental Psychology, 44,* 1329–1334.

Lewis, M., Feiring, C., & Rosenthal, S. (2000). Attachment over time. *Child Development, 71,* 707–720.

Lewis, P., Abbeduto, L., Murphy, M., Richmond, E., Giles, N., Bruno, L., et al. (2006). Cognitive, language and social-cognitive skills of individuals with fragile X with and without autism. *Journal of Intellectual Disability Research, 50,* 532–545.

Li, G. (2010). Race, class, and schooling: Multicultural families doing the hard work of home literacy in America's inner city. *Reading & Writing Quarterly: Overcoming Learning Difficulties, 26*(2), 140–165.

Li, J. (2004). High abilities and excellence: A cultural perspective. In L. V. Shavinina & M. Ferrari (Eds.), *Beyond knowledge: Extracognitive aspects of developing high ability* (pp. 187–208). Mahwah, NJ: Erlbaum.

Li, J. (2006). Self in learning: Chinese adolescents' goals and sense of agency. *Child Development, 77,* 482–501.

Li, J., & Fischer, K. W. (2004). Thought and affect in American and Chinese learners' beliefs about learning. In D. Y. Dai & R. J. Sternberg (Eds.), *Motivation, emotion, and cognition: Integrative perspectives on intellectual functioning and development* (pp. 385–418). Mahwah, NJ: Erlbaum.

Li, S., Jin, X., Yan, C., Wu, S., Jiang, F., & Shen, X. (2009). Factors associated with bed and room sharing in Chinese school-age children. *Child: Care, Health, and Development, 35*(2), 171–177.

Li, S.-C. (2007). Biocultural co-construction of developmental plasticity across the lifespan. In S. Kitayama & D. Cohen (Eds.), *Handbook of cultural psychology* (pp. 528–544). New York: Guilford Press.

Liben, L. S. (2009). The road to understanding maps. *Current Directions in Psychological Science, 18*(6), 310–315.

Liben, L. S., & Downs, R. M. (1989a). Educating with maps: Part I, the place of maps. *Teaching Thinking and Problem Solving, 11*(1), 6–9.

Liben, L. S., & Downs, R. M. (1989b). Understanding maps as symbols: The development of map concepts in children. In H. W. Reese (Ed.), *Advances in child development and behavior* (Vol. 22). San Diego, CA: Harcourt Brace Jovanovich.

Liben, L. S., Kastens, K. A., & Stevenson, L. M. (2002). Real-world knowledge through real-world maps: A developmental guide for navigating the educational terrain. *Developmental Review, 22,* 267–322.

Liben, L. S., & Myers, L. J. (2007). Developmental changes in children's understanding of maps: What, when, and how? In J. M. Plumert & J. P. Spencer (Eds.), *The emerging spatial mind* (pp. 193–218). New York: Oxford University Press.

Lichtenberger, E. O., & Kaufman, A. S. (2003). *Essentials of WPPSI-III assessment.* New York: Wiley.

Lickona, T. (1991). Moral development in the elementary school classroom. In W. M. Kurtines & J. L. Gewirtz (Eds.), *Moral behavior and development: Vol. 3. Application.* Hillsdale, NJ: Erlbaum.

Lidz, C. S. (1991). Issues in the assessment of preschool children. In B. A. Bracken (Ed.), *The psychoeducational assessment of preschool children* (2nd ed., pp. 18–31). Boston: Allyn & Bacon.

Lidz, C. S., & Gindis, B. (2003). Dynamic assessment of the evolving cognitive functions in children. In A. Kozulin, B. Gindis, V. S. Ageyev, & S. M. Miller (Eds.), *Vygotsky's educational theory in cultural context* (pp. 99–116). Cambridge, England: Cambridge University Press.

Lieberman, A. (1993). *The emotional life of the toddler.* New York: Free Press.

Lieberman, D. A. (1997). Interactive video games for health promotion: Effects on knowledge, self-efficacy, social support, and health. In R. L. Street, Jr., W. R. Gold, & T. R. Manning (Eds.), *Health promotion and interactive technology: Theoretical applications and future directions* (pp. 103–120). Mahwah, NJ: Erlbaum.

Lieven, E., & Stoll, S. (2010). Language. In M. H. Bornstein (Ed.), *Handbook of cultural developmental science* (pp. 143–160). New York: Psychology Press.

Light, P., & Butterworth, G. (Eds.). (1993). *Context and cognition: Ways of learning and knowing.* Hillsdale, NJ: Erlbaum.

Light, S. N., Coan, J. A., Zahn-Waxler, C., Frye, C., Goldsmith, H. H., & Davidson, R. J. (2009). Empathy is associated with dynamic change in prefrontal brain electrical activity during positive emotion in children. *Child Development, 80*(4), 1210–1231. doi:10.1111/j.1467-8624.2009.01326.x

Lightfoot, C. (1992). Constructing self and peer culture: A narrative perspective on adolescent risk taking. In L. T. Winegar & J. Valsiner (Eds.), *Children's development within social context: Vol. 2. Research and methodology* (pp. 229–245). Hillsdale, NJ: Erlbaum.

Lightfoot, D. (1999). *The development of language: Acquisition, change, and evolution.* Malden, MA: Blackwell.

Lillard, A. S. (1993). Pretend play skills and the child's theory of mind. *Child Development, 64,* 348–371.

Lillard, A. S. (1997). Other folks' theories of mind and behavior. *Psychological Science, 8,* 268–274.

Lillard, A. S. (1998). Playing with a theory of mind. In O. N. Saracho & B. Spodek (Eds.), *Multiple perspectives on play in early childhood education.* Albany: State University of New York Press.

Lillard, A. S. (1999). Developing a cultural theory of mind: The CIAO approach. *Current Directions in Psychological Science, 8,* 57–61.

Lillemyr, O. F., Søbstad, F., Marder, K., & Flowerday, T. (2011). A multicultural perspective on play and learning in primary school. *International Journal of Early Childhood, 43*(1), 43–65. doi:10.1007/s13158-010-0021-7

Lin, Z. (2010). Interactive dynamic assessment with children learning EFL in kindergarten. *Early Childhood Education Journal, 37,* 279–287.

Linder, J. R., & Gentile, D. A. (2009). Is the television rating system valid? Indirect, verbal, and physical aggression in programs viewed by fifth grade girls and associations with behavior. *Journal of Applied Developmental Psychology, 30,* 286–297.

Linder, T. W. (1993). *Transdisciplinary play-based assessment: A functional approach to working with young children.* Baltimore, MD: Paul H. Brookes.

Lindfors, K., Elovainio, M., Wickman, S., Vuorinen, R., Sinkkonen, J., Dunkel, L., et al. (2007). Brief report: The role of ego development in psychosocial adjustment among boys with delayed puberty. *Journal of Research on Adolescence, 17*(4), 601–612.

Lindsey, E. W., & Caldera, Y. M. (2005). Interparental agreement on the use of control in childrearing and infants' compliance to mother's control strategies. *Infant Behavior & Development, 28*(2), 165–178. doi:10.1016/j.infbeh.2005.02.004

Linebarger, D. L., & Piotrowski, J. (2010). Structure and strategies in children's educational television: The roles of program type and learning strategies in children's learning. *Child Development, 81*(5), 1582–1597. doi:10.1111/j.1467-8624.2010.01493.x

Linn, M. C., Clement, C., Pulos, S., & Sullivan, P. (1989). Scientific reasoning during adolescence: The influence of instruction in science knowledge and reasoning strategies. *Journal of Research in Science Teaching, 26,* 171–187.

Linn, M. C., & Muilenburg, L. (1996). Creating lifelong science learners: What models form a life foundation? *Educational Researcher, 25*(5), 18–24.

Linn, M. C., Songer, N. B., & Eylon, B. (1996). Shifts and convergences in science learning and instruction. In D. C. Berliner & R. C. Calfee (Eds.), *Handbook of educational psychology.* New York: Macmillan.

Linn, R. L., & Miller, M.D. (2005). *Measurement and assessment in teaching* (9th ed.). Upper Saddle River, NJ: Merrill/Prentice Hall.

Linnenbrink, E. A. (2005). The dilemma of performance-approach goals: The use of multiple goal contexts to promote students' motivation and learning. *Journal of Educational Psychology, 97,* 197–213.

Linnenbrink, E. A., & Pintrich, P. R. (2004). Role of affect in cognitive processing in academic contexts. In D. Y. Dia & R. J. Sternberg (Eds.), *Motivation, emotion, and cognition: Integrative perspectives on intellectual functioning and development* (pp. 57–87). Mahwah, NJ: Erlbaum.

Linver, M. R., Brooks-Gunn, J., & Kohen, D. E. (2002). Family processes as pathways from income to young children's development. *Developmental Psychology, 38,* 719–734.

Lippa, R. A. (2002). *Gender, nature, and nurture.* Mahwah, NJ: Erlbaum.

Lipson, M. Y. (1983). The influence of religious affiliation on children's memory for text information. *Reading Research Quarterly, 18,* 448–457.

Lipton, J. S., & Spelke, E. S. (2005). Preschool children's mapping of number words to nonsymbolic numerosities. *Child Development, 76,* 978–988.

Little, L. (2001). Peer victimization of children with Asperger-spectrum disorders. *Journal of the American Academy of Child and Adolescent Psychiatry, 40*(9), 995–996.

Little, T. D., Oettingen, G., Stetsenko, A., & Baltes, P. B. (1995). Children's action-control beliefs about school performance: How do American children compare with German and Russian children? *Journal of Personality and Social Psychology, 69,* 686–700.

Liu, D., Wellman, H. M., Tardif, T., & Sabbagh, M. A. (2008). Theory of mind development in Chinese children: A meta-analysis of false-belief understanding across cultures and languages. *Developmental Psychology, 44,* 523–531.

Lloyd, M. E., & Newcombe, N. S. (2009). Implicit memory in childhood: Reassessing developmental invariance. In M. L. Courage & N. Cowan (Eds.), *The development of memory in infancy and childhood* (pp. 93–113). New York: Psychology Press.

Lobel, A. (1979). *Frog and Toad are friends.* New York: HarperCollins.

Lochman, J. E., & Dodge, K. A. (1994). Social-cognitive processes of severely violent, moderately aggressive, and nonaggressive boys. *Journal of Consulting and Clinical Psychology, 62,* 366–374.

Lochman, J. E., Wayland, K. K., & White, K. J. (1993). Social goals: Relationship to adolescent adjustment and to social problem solving. *Journal of Abnormal Child Psychology, 21,* 1993.

Locke, J. L. (1993). *The child's path to spoken language.* Cambridge, MA: Harvard University Press.

Locke, E. A., & Latham, G. P. (2006). New directions in goal-setting theory. *Current Directions in Psychological Science, 15,* 265–268.

Lockhart, K. L., Chang, B., & Story, T. (2002). Young children's beliefs about the stability of traits: Protective optimism? *Child Development, 73,* 1408–1430.

Lodewyk, K. R., & Winne, P. H. (2005). Relations among the structure of learning tasks, achievement, and changes in self-efficacy in secondary students. *Journal of Educational Psychology, 97,* 3–12.

Loeb, S., Fuller, B., Kagan, S. L., & Carrol, B. (2004). Child care in poor communities: Early learning effects of type, quality, and stability. *Child Development, 75,* 47–65.

Logan, K. R., Alberto, P. A., Kana, T. G., & Waylor-Bowen, T. (1994). Curriculum development and instructional design for students with profound disabilities. In L. Sternberg (Ed.), *Individuals with profound disabilities: Instructional and assistive strategies* (3rd ed.). Austin, TX: Pro-Ed.

Logsdon, B. J., Alleman, L. M., Straits, S. A., Belka, D. E., & Clark, D. (1997). *Physical education unit plans for grades 5–6* (2nd ed.). Champaign, IL: Human Kinetics.

London, M. L., Ladewig, P. W., Ball, J. W., & Bindler, R. C. (2007). *Maternal and child nursing care* (2nd ed.). Upper Saddle River, NJ: Pearson Prentice Hall.

London, M. L., Ladewig, P. A. W., Ball, J. W., Bindler, R. C., & Cowen, K. J. (2011). *Maternal and child nursing care* (3rd ed.). Upper Saddle River, NJ: Pearson.

Long, M. (1995). The role of the linguistic environment in second language acquisition. In W. C. Ritchie & T. K. Bhatia (Eds.), *Handbook of language acquisition: Vol. 2. Second language acquisition.* San Diego, CA: Academic Press.

Longhi, E. (2009). "Songese": Maternal structuring of musical interaction with infants. *Psychology of Music, 37*(2), 195–213.

Lonigan, C. J., Burgess, S. R., Anthony, J. L., & Barker, T. A. (1998). Development of phonological sensitivity in 2- to 5-year-old children. *Journal of Educational Psychology, 90,* 294–311.

Lonigan, C. J., Farver, J. M., Phillips, B. M., & Clancy-Menchetti, J. (2011). Promoting the development of preschool children's emergent literacy skills: A randomized evaluation of a literacy-focused curriculum and two professional development models. *Reading and Writing, 24*(3), 305–337. doi:10.1007/s11145-009-9214-6

Lopez, A. M. (2003). Mixed-race school-age children: A summary of census 2000 data. *Educational Researcher, 32*(6), 25–37.

Lopez, E. C. (1997). The cognitive assessment of limited English proficient and bilingual children. In D. P. Flanagan, J. L. Genshaft, & P. L. Harrison (Eds.), *Contemporary intellectual assessment: Theories, tests, and issues* (pp. 503–516). New York: Guilford Press.

López, G. R., Scribner, J. D., & Mahitivanichcha, K. (2001). Redefining parental involvement: Lessons from high-performing migrant-impacted schools. *American Educational Research Journal, 38,* 253–288.

Lopez, V. A., & Emmer, E. T. (2002). Influences of beliefs and values on male adolescents' decision to commit violent offenses. *Psychology of Men and Masculinity, 3,* 28–40.

Lord, C., & Bishop, S. L. (2010). Autism spectrum disorders: Diagnosis, prevalence, and services for children and families. *Social Policy Report, 24*(2). Ann Arbor, MI: Society for Research in Child Development.

Losey, K. M. (1995). Mexican American students and classroom interaction: An overview and critique. *Review of Educational Research, 65,* 283–318.

Lotan, R. A. (2006). Managing groupwork in the heterogeneous classroom. In C. M. Evertson & C. S. Weinstein (Eds.), *Handbook of classroom management: Research, practice, and contemporary issues* (pp. 525–539). Mahwah, NJ: Erlbaum.

Lou, Y., Abrami, P. C., Spence, J. C., Poulsen, C., Chambers, B., & d'Apollonia, S. (1996). Within-class grouping: A meta-analysis. *Review of Educational Research, 66,* 423–458.

Loukas, A., Roalson, L. A., & Herrera, D. E. (2010). School connectedness buffers the effects of negative family relations and poor effortful control on early adolescent conduct problems. *Journal of Research on Adolescence, 20*(1), 13–22. doi:10.1111/j.1532-7795.2009.00632.x

Lovett, S. B., & Flavell, J. H. (1990). Understanding and remembering: Children's knowledge about the differential effects of strategy and task variables on comprehension and memorization. *Child Development, 61,* 1842–1858.

Lubinski, D., & Bleske-Rechek, A. (2008). Enhancing development in intellectually talented populations. In P. C. Kyllonen, R. D. Roberts, & L. Stankov (Eds.), *Extending intelligence: Enhancement and new constructs* (pp. 109–132). New York: Erlbaum/Taylor & Francis.

Luby, J., Belden, A., Sullivan, J., Hayen, R., McCadney, A., & Spitznagel, E. (2009). Shame and guilt in preschool depression: Evidence for elevations in self-conscious emotions in depression as early as age 3. *Journal of Child Psychology and Psychiatry, 50*(9), 1156–1166. doi:10.1111/j.1469-7610.2009.02077.x

Luby, J. L. (2010). Preschool depression: The importance of identification of depression early in development. *Current Directions in Psychological Science, 19*(2), 91–95.

Lucariello, J., Kyratzis, A., & Nelson, K. (1992). Taxonomic knowledge: What kind and when? *Child Development, 63,* 978–998.

Lucas-Thompson, R., & Clarke-Stewart, K. A. (2007). Forecasting friendship: How marital quality, maternal mood, and attachment security are linked to children's peer relationships. *Journal of Applied Developmental Psychology, 28,* 499–514.

Luckasson, R., Borthwick-Duffy, S., Buntinx, W. H. E., Coulter, D. L., Craig, E. M., Reeve, A., et al. (Eds.). (2002). *Mental retardation: Definition, classification, and systems of supports* (10th ed.). Washington, DC: American Association on Mental Retardation.

Luders, E., Narr, K. L., Thompson, P. M., & Toga, A. W. (2009). Neuroanatomical correlates of intelligence. *Intelligence, 37*(2), 156–163.

Ludwig, J., & Miller, D. L. (2007). Does Head Start improve children's life chances? Evidence from a regression discontinuity design. *Quarterly Journal of Economics, 122,* 159–208.

Luehrman, M., & Unrath, K. (2006). Making theories of children's artistic development meaningful for preservice teachers. *Art Education, 59*(3), 6–12.

Lueptow, L. B. (1984). *Adolescent sex roles and social change.* New York: Columbia University Press.

Lugo-Gil, J., & Tamis-LeMonda, C. S. (2008). Family resources and parenting quality: Links to children's cognitive development across the first 3 years. *Child Development, 79*(4), 1065–1085.

Luijk, M. P. C. M., Saridjan, N., Tharner, A., van IJzendoorn, M. H., Bakermans-Kranenburg, M. J., Jaddoe, V. W. V., et al. (2010). Attachment, depression, and cortisol: Deviant patterns in insecure-resistant and disorganized infants. *Developmental Psychobiology, 52*(5), 441–452.

Luiselli, J. K. (2009). Aggression and noncompliance. In J. L. Matson (Ed.), *Applied behavior analysis for children with autism spectrum disorders* (pp. 175–187). New York: Springer Science + Business Media. doi:10.1007/978-1-4419-0088-3_10

Lumeng, J. (2006). Childhood obesity prevention: Responsibilities of the family, schools, and community. In K. Freeark & W. S. Davidson II (Vol. Eds.), & H. E. Fitzgerald, R. Zucker, & K. Freeark (Eds. in Chief), *The crisis in mental health: Critical issues and effective programs. Vol. 3: Issues for families, schools, and communities* (pp. 55–77). Westport, CT: Praeger.

Luna, B. (2009). The maturation of cognitive control and the adolescent brain. In F. Aboitiz & D. Cosmelli (Eds.), *From attention to goal-directed behavior: Neurodynamical, methodological, clinical trends* (pp. 249–274). Berlin, Germany: Springer.

Luo, Y., Kaufman, L., & Baillargeon, R. (2009). Young infants' reasoning about physical events involving inert and self-propelled objects. *Cognitive Psychology, 58*, 441–486.

Lupart, J. L. (1995). Exceptional learners and teaching for transfer. In A. McKeough, J. Lupart, & A. Marini (Eds.), *Teaching for transfer: Fostering generalization in learning*. Mahwah, NJ: Erlbaum.

Luster, L. (1992). *Schooling, survival, and struggle: Black women and the GED*. Unpublished doctoral dissertation, Stanford University, School of Education, Stanford, CA.

Luthar, S. S., & Goldstein, A. S. (2008). Substance use and related behaviors among suburban late adolescents: The importance of perceived parent containment. *Development and Psychopathology, 20*, 591–614.

Luthar, S. S., & Latendresse, S. J. (2005). Children of the affluent: Challenges to well-being. *Current Directions in Psychological Science, 14*, 49–53.

Lutke, J. (1997). Spider web walking: Hope for children with FAS through understanding. In A. Streissguth & J. Kanter (Eds.), *The challenge of fetal alcohol syndrome: Overcoming secondary disabilities* (pp. 181–188). Seattle: University of Washington Press.

Luyckx, K., Goossens, L., & Soenens, B. (2006). A developmental contextual perspective on identity construction in emerging adulthood: Change dynamics in commitment formation and commitment evaluation. *Developmental Psychology, 42*, 366–380.

Luykx, A., Lee, O., Mahotiere, M., Lester, B., Hart, J., & Deaktor, R. (2007). Cultural and home influences on children's responses to science assessments. *Teachers College Record, 109*, 897–926.

Lyman, E. T. (1981). The responsive classroom discussion: The inclusion of all students. In A. Anderson (Ed.), *Mainstreaming digest* (pp. 109–113). College Park: University of Maryland Press.

Lynn, R. (2009). Fluid intelligence but not vocabulary has increased in Britain, 1979–2008. *Intelligence, 37*(3), 249–255.

Lyon, T. D., & Flavell, J. H. (1994). Young children's understanding of "remember" and "forget." *Child Development, 65*, 1357–1371.

Määttä, S., Nurmi, J., & Stattin, H. (2007). Achievement orientations, school adjustment, and well-being: A longitudinal study. *Journal of Research on Adolescence, 17*(4), 789–812.

MacArthur, C., & Graham, S. (1987). Learning disabled students' composing with three methods: Handwriting, dictation, and word processing. *Journal of Special Education, 21*, 22–42.

Maccoby, E. E. (1984). Middle childhood in the context of the family. In W. A. Collins (Ed.), *Development during middle childhood* (pp. 184–239). Washington, DC: National Academy Press.

Maccoby, E. E. (1990). Gender and relationships: A developmental account. *American Psychologist, 45*, 513–520.

Maccoby, E. E. (2007). Historical overview of socialization research and theory. In J. E. Grusec & P. D. Hastings (Eds.), *Handbook of socialization: Theory and research* (pp. 13–41). New York: Guilford.

Maccoby, E. E., & Hagen, J. W. (1965). Effects of distraction upon central versus incidental recall: Developmental trends. *Journal of Experimental Child Psychology, 2*, 280–289.

Maccoby, E. E., & Jacklin, C. N. (1974). *The psychology of sex differences*. Stanford, CA: Stanford University Press.

MacDermott, S. T., Gullone, E., Allen, J. S., King, N. J., & Tonge, B. (2010). The emotion regulation index for children and adolescents (ERICA): A psychometric investigation. *Journal of Psychopathology and Behavioral Assessment, 32*(3), 301–314. doi:10.1007/s10862-009-9154-0

MacDonald, S., Uesiliana, K., & Hayne, H. (2000). Cross-cultural and gender differences in childhood amnesia. *Memory, 8*, 365–376.

Mackey, W. C. (2001). Support for the existence of an independent man-to-child affiliative bond: Fatherhood as a biocultural invention. *Psychology of Men and Masculinity, 2*, 51–66.

Macklem, G. L. (2008). *Practitioner's guide to emotion regulation in school-aged children*. New York: Springer Science + Business Media.

MacMaster, K., Donovan, L. A., & MacIntyre, P. D. (2002). The effects of being diagnosed with a learning disability on children's self-esteem. *Child Study Journal, 32*, 101–108.

MacWhinney, B. (2010). Computational models of child language learning: An introduction. *Journal of Child Language, 37*(3), 477–485.

MacWhinney, B., & Chang, F. (1995). Connectionism and language learning. In C. Nelson (Ed.), *Basic and applied perspectives on learning, cognition, and development: The Minnesota Symposia on Child Psychology* (Vol. 28). Mahwah, NJ: Erlbaum.

Madden, N. A., & Slavin, R. E. (1983). Mainstreaming students with mild handicaps: Academic and social outcomes. *Review of Educational Research, 53*, 519–569.

Maehr, M. L., & Zusho, A. (2009). Achievement goal theory: The past, present, and future. In K. R. Wenzel & A. Wigfield (Eds.), *Handbook of motivation at school. Educational psychology handbook series* (pp. 77–104). New York: Routledge/Taylor & Francis Group.

Magnuson, K., & Berger, L. M. (2009). Family structure states and transitions: Associations with children's well-being during middle childhood. *Journal of Marriage and Family, 71*, 575–591.

Magnuson, K. A., Meyers, M. K., Ruhm, C. J., & Waldfogel, J. (2004). Inequality in preschool education and school readiness. *American Educational Research Journal, 41*, 115–157.

Magnuson, K. A., Ruhm, C., & Waldfogel, J. (2007). The persistence of preschool effects: Do subsequent classroom experiences matter? *Early Childhood Research Quarterly, 22*, 18–38.

Mahaffy, K. A., & Ward, S. K. (2002). The gendering of adolescents' childbearing and educational plans: Reciprocal effects and the influence of social context. *Sex Roles, 46*, 403–417.

Maher, J. K., Herbst, K. C., Childs, N. M., & Finn, S. (2008). Racial stereotypes in children's commercials. *Journal of Advertising Research, 48*(1), 80–93.

Mahoney J. L., & Parente, M. E. (2009). Should we care about adolescents who care for themselves? What we have learned and what we need to know about youth in self-care. *Child Development Perspectives, 3*(3), 189–195.

Maier, M. A., Bernier, A., Pekrun, R., Zimmermann, P., & Grossmann, K. E. (2004). Attachment working models as unconscious structures: An experimental test. *International Journal of Behavioral Development, 28*(2), 180–189.

Main, M., & Cassidy, J. (1988). Categories of response to reunion with the parent at age 6: Predictable from infant attachment classification and stable over a 1-month period. *Developmental Psychology, 24*, 415–426.

Main, M., Kaplan, N., & Cassidy, J. (1985). Security in infancy, childhood, and adulthood: A move to the level of representation. *Monographs of the Society for Research in Child Development, 50*, 66–104.

Main, M., & Solomon, J. (1986). Discovery of an insecure-disorganized/disoriented attachment pattern. In T. B. Brazelton & M. W. Yogman (Eds.), *Affective development in infancy* (pp. 95–124). Norwood, NJ: Ablex.

Main, M., & Solomon, J. (1990). Procedures for identifying infants as disorganized/disoriented during the Ainsworth Strange Situation. In M. T. Greenberg, D. Cicchetti, & E. M. Cummings (Eds.), *Attachment in the preschool years* (pp. 121–160). Chicago: University of Chicago Press.

Maker, C. J. (1993). Creativity, intelligence, and problem solving: A definition and design for cross-cultural research and measurement related to giftedness. *Gifted Education International, 9*(2), 68–77.

Maker, C. J., & Schiever, S. W. (Eds.). (1989). *Critical issues in gifted education: Vol. 2. Defensible programs for cultural and ethnic minorities*. Austin, TX: Pro-Ed.

Malatesta, C. Z., & Haviland, J. M. (1982). Learning display rules: The socialization of emotion expression in infancy. *Child Development, 53*, 991–1003.

Maldonado-Molina, M. M., Reingle, J. M., Tobler, A. L., Jennings, W. G., & Komro, K. A. (2010). Trajectories of physical aggression among Hispanic urban adolescents and young adults: An application of latent trajectory modeling from ages 12 to 18. *American Journal of Criminal Justice, 35*(3), 121–133. doi:10.1007/s12103-010-9074-2

Malinsky, K. P. (1997). Learning to be invisible: Female sexual minority students in America's public high schools. In M. B. Harris (Ed.), *School experiences of gay and lesbian youth: The invisible minority* (pp. 35–50). Binghamton, NY: Harrington Park Press.

Maller, S. J. (2000). Item invariance of four subtests of the Universal Nonverbal Intelligence Test across groups of deaf and hearing children. *Journal of Psychoeducational Assessment, 18*, 240–254.

Mallick, S. K., & McCandless, B. R. (1966). A study of catharsis of aggression. *Journal of Personality and Social Psychology, 4*, 591–596.

Malmberg, L.-E., Stein, A., West, A., Simon, L., Barnes, J., Leach, P., et al. (2007). Parent–infant interaction: A growth model approach. *Infant Behavior and Development, 30*, 615–630.

Malone, D. M., Stoneham, Z., & Langone, J. (1995). Contextual variation of correspondences among measures of play and developmental level of preschool children. *Journal of Early Intervention, 18*, 199–215.

Malti, T., Gasser, L., & Gutzwiller-Helfenfinger, E. (2010). Children's interpretive understanding, moral judgments, and emotion attributions: Relations to social behaviour. *British Journal of Developmental Psychology, 28*(2), 275–292. doi:10.1348/026151009X403838

Malykh, S. B., Gindina, E. D., & Nadyseva, V. V. (2009). Genetic and environmental influences on temperament in adolescence. *Psychology in Russia: State of the Art, 2,* 361–384.

Mana, A., Orr, E., & Mana, Y. (2009). An integrated acculturation model of immigrants' social identity. *Journal of Social Psychology, 149*(4), 450–473.

Mancilla-Martinez, J., Kieffer, M. J., Biancarosa, G., Christodoulou, J. A., & Snow, C. E. (2011). Investigating English reading comprehension growth in adolescent language minority learners: Some insights from the simple view. *Reading and Writing, 24*(3), 339–354. doi:10.1007/s11145-009-9215-5

Mandel, D. R., Jusczyk, P. W., & Pisoni, D. B. (1995). Infants' recognition of the sound patterns of their own names. *Psychological Science, 6,* 314–317.

Mandler, J. M. (2007a). The conceptual foundations of animals and artifacts. In E. Margolis & S. Laurence (Eds.), *Creations of the mind: Theories of artifacts and their representation* (pp. 191–211). New York: Oxford University Press.

Mandler, J. M. (2007b). On the origins of the conceptual system. *American Psychologist, 62,* 741–751.

Mandler, J. M., Fivush, R., & Reznick, J. S. (1987). The development of contextual categories. *Cognitive Development, 2,* 339–354.

Mangelsdorf, S. C., Shapiro, J. R., & Marzolf, D. (1995). Developmental and temperamental differences in emotion regulation in infancy. *Child Development, 66,* 1817–1828.

Manis, F. R. (1996). Current trends in dyslexia research. In B. J. Cratty & R. L. Goldman (Eds.), *Learning disabilities: Contemporary viewpoints.* Amsterdam: Harwood Academic.

Mann, W., Marshall, C. R., Mason, K., & Morgan, G. (2010). The acquisition of sign language: The impact of phonetic complexity on phonology. *Language Learning and Development, 6*(1), 60–86.

Manolitsis, G., Georgiou, G. K., & Parrila, R. (2011). Revisiting the home literacy model of reading development in an orthographically consistent language. *Learning & Instruction,* 21(4), 496–505. doi:10.1016/j.learninstruc.2010.06.005

Mar, R. A., & Oatley, K. (2008). The function of fiction is the abstraction and simulation of social experience. *Perspectives on Psychological Science, 3,* 173–192.

Marachi, R., Friedel, J., & Midgley, C. (2001, April). "*I sometimes annoy my teacher during math": Relations between student perceptions of the teacher and disruptive behavior in the classroom.* Paper presented at the annual meeting of the American Educational Research Association, Seattle, WA.

Maraj, B. K. V., & Bonertz, C. M. (2007). Verbal-motor learning in children with Down syndrome. *Journal of Sport and Exercise Psychology, 29* (Supplement), 108.

March of Dimes. (2010). *Chromosomal abnormalities.* Retrieved February 10, 2010, from http://www.marchofdimes.com/professionals/14332_1209.asp

Marchand, G., & Skinner, E. A. (2007). Motivational dynamics of children's help-seeking and concealment. *Journal of Educational Psychology, 99*(1), 65–82.

Marcia, J. (1991). Identity and self-development. In R. M. Lerner, A. C. Petersen, & J. Brooks-Gunn (Eds.), *Encyclopedia of adolescence* (Vol. 1, pp. 529–533). New York: Garland.

Marcia, J. E. (1980). Identity in adolescence. In J. Adelson (Ed.), *Handbook of adolescent psychology.* New York: Wiley.

Marcia, J. E. (1988). Common processes underlying ego identity, cognitive/moral development, and individuation. In D. K. Lapsley & F. C. Power (Eds.), *Self, ego, and identity: Integrative approaches* (pp. 211–225). New York: Springer-Verlag.

Marcovitch, S., Goldberg, S., Gold, A., Washington, J., Wasson, C., Krekewich, K., et al. (1997). Determinants of behavioral problems in Romanian children adopted in Ontario. *International Journal of Behavioral Development, 20,* 17–31.

Marcus, G. F. (1996). Why do children say "breaked"? *Current Directions in Psychological Science, 5,* 81–85.

Marcus, G. F., Vijayan, S., Bandi Rao, S., & Vishton, P. M. (1999). Rule learning by seven-month-old infants. *Science, 283,* 77–80.

Mares, M., Palmer, E., & Sullivan, T. (2008). Prosocial effects of media exposure. In S. L. Calvert, & B. J. Wilson (Eds.), *The handbook of children, media, and development. Handbooks in communication and media* (pp. 268–289). Malden, MA: Blackwell Publishing. doi:10.1002/9781444302752.ch12

Mares, S. H. W., de Leeuw, R. N. H., Scholte, R. H. J., & Engels, R. C. M. E. (2010). Facial attractiveness and self-esteem in adolescence. *Journal of Clinical Child and Adolescent Psychology, 39*(5), 627–637.

Mareschal, D., Johnson, M. H., Sirois, S., Spratling, M. W., Thomas, M. S. C., & Westermann, G. (2007). *Neuroconstructivism: Vol. 1. How the brain constructs cognition.* Oxford, England: Oxford University Press.

Marinak, B. A., & Gambrell, L. B. (2010). Reading motivation: Exploring the elementary gender gap. *Literacy Research and Instruction, 49*(2), 129–141.

Markman, E. M. (1979). Realizing that you don't understand: Elementary school children's awareness of inconsistencies. *Child Development, 50*(3), 643–655.

Markman, E. M. (1989). *Categorization and naming in children: Problems of induction.* Cambridge, MA: MIT Press.

Marks, D. F. (2011). IQ variations across time, race, and nationality: An artifact of differences in literacy skills. *Counselor Education and Supervision, 50*(3), 643–664.

Markstrom, C. A., Huey, E., Stiles, B. M., & Krause, A. L. (2010). Frameworks of caring and helping in adolescence: Are empathy, religiosity, and spirituality related constructs? *Youth & Society, 42*(1), 59–80. doi:10.1177/0044118X09333644

Markus, H. R., & Hamedani, M. G. (2007). Sociocultural psychology: The dynamic interdependence among self systems and social systems. In S. Kitayama & D. Cohen (Eds.), *Handbook of cultural psychology* (pp. 3–39). New York: Guilford Press.

Markus, H. R., & Kitayama, S. (1991). Culture and the self: Implications for cognition, emotion, and motivation. *Psychological Review, 98,* 224–253.

Marques, S. C. F., Oliveira, C. R., Pereira, C. M. F., & Outeiro, T. F. (2011). Epigenetics in neurodegeneration: A new layer of complexity. *Progress in Neuro-Psychopharmacology & Biological Psychiatry, 35*(2), 348–355. doi:10.1016/j.pnpbp.2010.08.008

Marsh, H. W. (1990a). Causal ordering of academic self-concept and academic achievement: A multiwave, longitudinal panel analysis. *Journal of Educational Psychology, 82,* 646–656.

Marsh, H. W. (1990b). A multidimensional, hierarchical model of self-concept: Theoretical and empirical justification. *Educational Psychology Review, 2,* 77–172.

Marsh, H. W., & Craven, R. (1997). Academic self-concept: Beyond the dustbowl. In G. D. Phye (Ed.), *Handbook of classroom assessment: Learning, achievement, and adjustment.* San Diego, CA: Academic Press.

Marsh, H. W., & Hau, K.-T. (2003). Big-fish–little-pond effect on academic self-concept: A cross-cultural (26-country) test of the negative effects of academically selective schools. *American Psychologist, 58,* 364–376.

Marsh, H. W., Parada, R. H., Yeung, A. S., & Healey, J. (2001). Aggressive school troublemakers and victims: A longitudinal model examining the pivotal role of self-concept. *Journal of Educational Psychology, 93,* 411–419.

Marsh, H. W., Trautwein, U., Lüdtke, O., Köller, O., & Baumert, J. (2005). Academic self-concept, interest, grades, and standardize test scores: Reciprocal effects models of causal ordering. *Child Development, 76,* 397–416.

Marshall, N. L. (2004). The quality of early child care and children's development. *Current Directions in Psychological Science, 13,* 165–168.

Martens, R., de Brabander, C., Rozendaal, J., Boekaerts, M., & van der Leeden, R. (2010). Inducing mind sets in self-regulated learning with motivational information. *Educational Studies, 36*(3), 311–327. doi:10.1080/03055690903424915

Martin, C. L. (2000). Cognitive theories of gender development. In T. Eckes & H. Trautner (Eds.), *The developmental social psychology of gender* (pp. 91–121). Mahwah, NJ: Erlbaum.

Martin, C. L., & Ruble, D. N. (2010). Patterns of gender development. *Annual Review of Psychology, 61,* 353–381. doi:10.1146/annurev.psych.093008.100511

Martin, C. L., Ruble, D. N., & Szkrybalo, J. (2002). Cognitive theories of early gender development. *Psychological Bulletin, 128,* 903–933.

Martin, J. L. (2009). Formation and stabilization of vertical hierarchies among adolescents: Towards a quantitative ethology of dominance among humans. *Social Psychology Quarterly, 72*(3), 241–264. doi:10.1177/019027250907200307

Martin, S. S., Brady, M. P., & Williams, R. E. (1991). Effects of toys on the social behavior of preschool children in integrated and nonintegrated groups: Investigation of a setting event. *Journal of Early Intervention, 15,* 153–161.

Martinez, C. R., & Forgatch, M. S. (2001). Preventing problems with boys' noncompliance: Effects of a parent-training intervention for divorcing mothers. *Journal of Consulting and Clinical Psychology, 69,* 416–428.

Martinez, M. E. (2010). *Learning and cognition: The design of the mind.* Upper Saddle River, NJ: Pearson Merrill.

Martino, S. C., Ellickson, P. L., Klein, D. J., McCaffrey, D., & Edelen, M. O. (2008). Multiple trajectories of physical aggression among adolescent boys and girls. *Aggressive Behavior, 34,* 61–75.

Masataka, N. (1992). Pitch characteristics of Japanese maternal speech to infants. *Journal of Child Language, 19,* 213–224.

Maschinot, B. (2008). *The changing face of the United States: The influence of culture on early child development.* Washington, DC: Zero to Three.

Mason, L. (2003). Personal epistemologies and intentional conceptual change. In G. M. Sinatra & P. R. Pintrich (Eds.), *Intentional conceptual change* (pp. 199–236). Mahwah, NJ: Erlbaum.

Mason, L., Boldrin, A., & Ariasi, N. (2010). Epistemic metacognition in context: Evaluating and learning online information. *Metacognition Learning, 5,* 67–90.

Massey, C. M., & Gelman, R. (1988). Preschoolers' ability to decide whether a photographed unfamiliar object can move itself. *Developmental Psychology, 24,* 307–317.

Massey, D. S., & Denton, N. A. (1993). *American apartheid: Segregation and the making of the underclass.* Cambridge, MA: Cambridge University Press.

Massimini, K. (2000). *Genetic disorders sourcebook* (2nd ed.). Detroit, MI: Omnigraphics.

Masten, A. S., Cutuli, J. J., Herbers, J. E., & Reed, M.-G. J. (2009). Resilience in development. In S. J. Lopez & C. R. Snyder (Eds.), *Oxford handbook of positive psychology* (2nd ed., pp. 117–131). New York: Oxford University Press.

Masur, E. F., McIntyre, C. W., & Flavell, J. H. (1973). Developmental changes in apportionment of study time among items in a multitrial free recall task. *Journal of Experimental Child Psychology, 15,* 237–246.

Mather, N. (2009). The intelligent testing of children with specific learning disabilities. In J. C. Kaufman (Ed.), *Intelligent testing: Integrating psychological theory and clinical practice* (pp. 30–52). New York: Cambridge University Press.

Matheson, C., Olsen, R. J., & Weisner, T. (2007). A good friend is hard to find: Friendship among adolescents with disabilities. *American Journal on Mental Retardation, 112*(5), 319–329.

Mathews, J. (1988). *Escalante: The best teacher in America.* New York: Henry Holt.

Mathieson, K., & Banerjee, R. (2010). Pre-school peer play: The beginnings of social competence. *Educational and Child Psychology. Special Issue: In-School Relationships and their Outcomes, 27*(1), 9–20.

Matjasko, J. L., Needham, B. L., Grunden, L. N., & Farb, A. F. (2010). Violent victimization and perpetration during adolescence: Developmental stage dependent ecological models. *Journal of Youth and Adolescence, 39*(9), 1053–1066. doi:10.1007/s10964-010-9508-7

Matson, J. L., & Fodstad, J. C. (2010). Teaching social skills to developmentally delayed preschoolers. In C. E. Schaefer (Ed.), *Play therapy for preschool children* (pp. 301–322). Washington, DC: American Psychological Association

Matsuyama, A., & Moji, K. (2008). Perception of bleeding as a danger sign during pregnancy, delivery, and the postpartum period in rural Nepal. *Qualitative Health Research, 18*(2), 196–208.

Matthews, D., Lieven, E., & Tomasello, M. (2007). How toddlers and preschoolers learn to uniquely identify referents for others: A training study. *Child Development, 78,* 1744–1759.

Matthews, D. J. (2009). Developmental transitions in giftedness and talent: Childhood into adolescence. In F. D. Horowitz, R. F. Subotnik & D. J. Matthews (Eds.), *The development of giftedness and talent across the life span* (pp. 89–107). Washington, DC: American Psychological Association.

Matthews, J. (2010). Scribble: The development of children's mark-making. In B. Wagoner (Ed.), *Symbolic transformation: The mind in movement through culture and society. Cultural dynamics of social representation* (pp. 209–231). New York: Routledge/Taylor & Francis Group.

Mayer, D. L., & Dobson, V. (1982). Visual acuity development in infants and young children, as assessed by operant preferential looking. *Vision Research, 22,* 1141–1151.

Mayer, R. E. (2004). Should there be a three-strikes rule against pure discovery learning? *American Psychologist, 59,* 14–19.

Mayer, R. E. (2010). Fostering scientific reasoning with multimedia instruction. In H. S. Waters & W. Schneider (Eds.), *Metacognition, strategy use, and instruction* (pp. 160–175). New York: Guilford Press.

Mayes, L. C., & Bornstein, M. H. (1997). The development of children exposed to cocaine. In S. S. Luthar, J. A. Burack, D. Cicchetti, & J. R. Weisz (Eds.), *Developmental psychopathology: Perspectives on adjustment, risk, and disorder* (pp. 166–188). Cambridge, England: Cambridge University Press.

Mayes, S. D., Calhoun, S. L., Bixler, E. O., & Zimmerman, D. N. (2009). IQ and neuropsychological predictors of academic achievement. *Learning and Individual Differences, 19*(2), 238–241.

Maynard, A. E. (2002). Cultural teaching: The development of teaching skills in Maya sibling interactions. *Child Development, 73,* 969–982.

Maynard, A. E. (2008). What we thought we knew and how we came to know it: Four decades of cross-cultural research from a Piagetian point of view. *Human Development, 51,* 56–65.

Mayor, J., & Plunkett, K. (2010). A neurocomputational account of taxonomic responding and fast mapping in early word learning. *Developmental Review, 117*(1), 1–31.

Mayseless, O. (2005). Ontogeny of attachment in middle childhood: Conceptualization of normative changes. In K. A. Kerns & R. A. Richardson (Eds.), *Attachment in middle childhood* (pp. 1–23). New York: Guilford Press.

McAdoo, H. P., & Martin, A. (2005). Families and ethnicity. In R. M. Lerner, F. Jacobs, & D. Wertlieb (Eds.), *Applied developmental science: An advanced textbook* (pp. 141–154). Thousand Oaks, CA: Sage.

McAlpine, L., & Taylor, D. M. (1993). Instructional preferences of Cree, Inuit, and Mohawk teachers. *Journal of American Indian Education, 33*(1), 1–20.

McArdle, S. (2009). Exploring the development of perfectionistic cognitions and self-beliefs. *Cognitive Therapy and Research, 33*(6), 597–614.

McAuliff, B. D., Kovera, M. B., & Nunez, G. (2009). Can jurors recognize missing control groups, confounds, and experimenter bias in psychological science? *Law and Human Behavior, 33*(3), 247–257.

McBride-Chang, C., & Treiman, R. (2003). Hong Kong Chinese kindergartners learn to read English analytically. *Psychological Science, 14,* 138–143.

McBrien, J. L. (2005a). *Discrimination and academic motivation in adolescent refugee girls.* Unpublished doctoral dissertation, Emory University, Atlanta, GA. *Dissertation Abstracts International Section A: Humanities and Social Sciences, 66*(5-A), 2055, pp. 1602.

McBrien, J. L. (2005b). Educational needs and barriers for refugee students in the United States: A review of the literature. *Review of Educational Research, 75,* 329–364.

McCafferty, S. G. (2008). Mimesis and second language acquisition: A sociocultural perspective. *Studies in Second Language Acquisition, 30*(2), 147–167.

McCall, R. B. (1993). Developmental functions for general mental performance. In D. K. Detterman (Ed.), *Current topics in human intelligence* (Vol. 3). Norwood, NJ: Ablex.

McCall, R. B., Kennedy, C. B., & Applebaum, M. I. (1977). Magnitude of discrepancy and the distribution of attention in infants. *Child Development, 48,* 772–786.

McCallum, R. S. (1991). The assessment of preschool children with the Stanford-Binet Intelligence Scale: Fourth Edition. In B. A. Bracken (Ed.), *The psycho-educational assessment of preschool children* (2nd ed., pp. 107–132). Boston: Allyn & Bacon.

McCallum, R. S. (1999). A "baker's dozen" criteria for evaluating fairness in nonverbal testing. *The School Psychologist, 53,* 41–60.

McCallum, R. S., & Bracken, B. A. (1997). The Universal Nonverbal Intelligence Test. In D. P. Flanagan, J. L. Genshaft, & P. L. Harrison (Eds.), *Contemporary intellectual assessment: Theories, tests, and issues* (pp. 268–280). New York: Guilford Press.

McCallum, R. S., & Bracken, B. A. (2005). The Universal Nonverbal Intelligence Test: A multidimensional measure of intelligence. In D. P. Flanagan & P. L. Harrison (Eds.), *Contemporary intellectual assessment: Theories, tests, and issues* (2nd ed., pp. 425–440). New York: Guilford Press.

McCann, T. M. (1989). Student argumentative writing knowledge and ability at three grade levels. *Research in the Teaching of English, 23,* 62–72.

McCarthy, M., & Kuh, G. D. (2005, September 9). Student engagement: A missing link in improving high schools. *Teachers College Record, 87*(9), 664–669.

McCarty, T. (2009). The impact of high-stakes accountability policies on Native American learners: evidence from research. *Teaching Education, 20*(1), 7–29.

McCarty, T. L., & Watahomigie, L. J. (1998). Language and literacy in American Indian and Alaska Native communities. In B. Pérez (Ed.), *Sociocultural contexts of language and literacy.* Mahwah, NJ: Erlbaum.

McCaslin, M., & Good, T. L. (1996). The informal curriculum. In D. C. Berliner & R. C. Calfee (Eds.), *Handbook of educational psychology.* New York: Macmillan.

McClelland, J. L. (2001). Failures to learn and their remediation: A Hebbian account. In J. L. McClelland & R. S. Siegler (Eds.), *Mechanisms of cognitive development: Behavioral and neural perspectives* (pp. 97–121). Mahwah, NJ: Erlbaum.

McClelland, J. L., Fiez, J. A., & McCandliss, B. D. (2002). Teaching the /r/–/l/ discrimination to Japanese adults: Behavioral and neural aspects. *Physiology and Behavior, 77,* 657–662.

McCloskey, M. (1983). Naïve theories of motion. In D. Genter & A. L. Stevens (Eds.), *Mental models* (pp. 299–324). Hillsdale, NJ: Erlbaum.

McCloskey, R. (1948). *Blueberries for Sal.* New York: Viking Press.

McCombs, B. L., & Vakili, D. (2005). A learner-centered framework for e-learning. *Teachers College Record, 107*(8), 1582–1600.

McCourt, F. (2005). *Teacher man: A memoir.* New York: Scribner.

McCoy, K. (1994). *Understanding your teenager's depression.* New York: Perigee.

McCrae, R. R., Costa, P. T., Jr., & Busch, C. M. (1986). Evaluating comprehensiveness in personality systems: The California Q-Set and the five-factor model. *Journal of Personality, 54,* 430–446.

McCreary, M. L., Slavin, L. A., & Berry, E. J. (1996). Predicting problem behavior and self-esteem among African-American adolescents. *Journal of Adolescent Research, 11,* 216–234.

McCrink, K., & Wynn, K. (2004). Large-number addition and subtraction by 9-month-old infants. *Psychological Science, 15,* 776–781.

McCrink, K., & Wynn, K. (2007). Ratio abstraction by 6-month-old infants. *Psychological Science, 18,* 740–745.

McCrink, K., & Wynn, K. (2009). Operational momentum in large-number addition and subtraction by 9-month-olds. *Journal of Experimental Child Psychology, 103*(4), 400–408.

McCullough, M. E., Kurzban, R., & Tabak, B. A. (2011). Evolved mechanisms for revenge and forgiveness. In P. R. Shaver & M. Mikulincer (Eds.), *Human aggression and violence: Causes, manifestations, and consequences. Herzilya series on personality and social psychology* (pp. 221–239). Washington, DC: American Psychological Association. doi:10.1037/12346-012

McCutchen, D. (1987). Children's discourse skill: Form and modality requirements of schooled writing. *Discourse Processes, 10,* 267–286.

McDermott, S., Durkin, M. S., Schupf, N., & Stein, Z. A. (2007). Epidemiology and etiology of mental retardation. In J. W. Jacobson, J. A. Mulick, & J. Rojahn (Eds.), *Handbook of intellectual and developmental disabilities* (pp. 3–40). New York: Springer.

McDevitt, M. (2005). The partisan child: Developmental provocation as a model of political socialization. *International Journal of Public Opinion, 18*(1), 67–88.

McDevitt, M., & Kiousis, S. (2007, August). *Political socialization upside down: The adolescent's contribution to civic parenting.* Paper presented at annual meeting of the Association for Education in Journalism and Mass Communication, Washington, DC.

McDevitt, M., & Ostrowski, A. (2009). The adolescent unbound: Unintentional influence of curricula on ideological conflict seeking. *Political Communication, 26,* 11–29.

McDevitt, M. J., & Caton-Rosser, M. S. (2009). Deliberative Barbarians: Reconciling the civic and the agonistic in democratic education. *Inter-Actions, 5*(2).

McDevitt, T. M. (1990). Encouraging young children's listening skills. *Academic Therapy, 25,* 569–577.

McDevitt, T. M., & Ford, M. E. (1987). Processes in young children's communicative functioning and development. In M. E. Ford & D. H. Ford (Eds.), *Humans as self-constructing systems: Putting the framework to work.* (pp. 145–175). Hillsdale, NJ: Erlbaum.

McDevitt, T. M., Jobes, R. D., Sheehan, E. P., & Cochran, K. (2010). Is it nature of nurture? Beliefs about child development held by students in psychology courses. *College Student Journal, 44*(2), 533–550.

McDevitt, T. M., Sheehan, E. P., Sinco, S. R., Cochran, L. S., Lauer, D., & Starr, N. L. (2008). These are my goals: Academic self-regulation in reading by middle-school students. *Reading Improvement, 45*(3), 115–138.

McDevitt, T. M., Spivey, N., Sheehan, E. P., Lennon, R., & Story, R. (1990). Children's beliefs about listening: Is it enough to be still and quiet? *Child Development, 61,* 713–721.

McDougall, P., & Hymel, S. (2007). Same-gender versus cross-gender friendship conceptions. *Merrill-Palmer Quarterly, 53,* 347–380.

McGlothlin, H., & Killen, M. (2005). Children's perceptions of intergroup and intragroup similarity and the role of social experience. *Applied Developmental Psychology, 26,* 680–698.

McGowan, D. (2007). *Parenting beyond belief: On raising ethical, caring kids without religion.* New York: AMACOM.

McGregor, K. K., Rohlfing, K. J., Bean, A., & Marschner, E. (2009). Gesture as a support for word learning: The case of *under. Journal of Child Language, 36*(4), 807–828.

McGrew, K. S. (2005). The Cattell-Horn-Carroll theory of cognitive abilities: Past, present, and future. In D. P. Flanagan & P. L. Harrison (Eds.), *Contemporary intellectual assessment: Theories, tests, and issues* (2nd ed., pp. 136–181). New York: Guilford Press.

McGue, M., Bouchard, T. J., Jr., Iacono, W. G., & Lykken, D. T. (1993). Behavioral genetics of cognitive ability: A life-span perspective. In R. Plomin & G. E. McClearn (Eds.), *Nature, nurture, and psychology.* Washington, DC: American Psychological Association.

McGuire, J. K., Anderson, C. R., Toomey, R. B., & Russell, S. T. (2010). School climate for transgender youth: A mixed method investigation of student experiences and school responses. *Journal of Youth and Adolescence, 39*(10), 1175–1188. doi:10.1007/s10964-010-9540-7

McHale, J. P., & Rasmussen, J. L. (1998). Coparental and family group-level dynamics during infancy: Early family precursors of child and family functioning during preschool. *Development and Psychopathology, 10,* 39–59.

McHale, S. M., & Crouter, A. C. (1996). The family context of children's sibling relationships. In G. Brody (Ed.), *Sibling relationships: Their causes and consequences* (pp. 173–195). Norwood, NJ: Ablex.

McKenzie, J. K. (1993). Adoption of children with special needs. *The Future of Children, 3*(1), 26–42.

McKeough, A. (1995). Teaching narrative knowledge for transfer in the early school years. In A. McKeough, J. Lupart, & A. Marini (Eds.), *Teaching for transfer: Fostering generalization in learning.* Mahwah, NJ: Erlbaum.

McKinlay, A., Grace, R. C., Horwood, L. J., Fergusson, D. M., Ridder, E. M., & MacFarlane, M. R. (2008). Prevalence of traumatic brain injury among children, adolescents and young adults: Prospective evidence from a birth cohort. *Brain Injury, 22*(2), 175–181.

McKown, C., & Weinstein, R. S. (2008). Teacher expectations, classroom context, and the achievement gap. *Journal of School Psychology, 46,* 235–261.

McLane, J. B., & McNamee, G. D. (1990). *Early literacy.* Cambridge, MA: Harvard University Press.

McLoyd, V. C. (1998a). Children in poverty: Development, public policy, and practice. In W. Damon (Series Ed.), & I. E. Sigel, & K. A. Renninger (Vol. Eds.), *Handbook of child psychology: Vol. 4. Child psychology in practice* (5th ed., pp. 135–208). New York: Wiley.

McLoyd, V. C. (1998b). Socioeconomic disadvantage and child development. *American Psychologist, 53,* 185–204.

McLoyd, V. C., Aikens, N. L., & Burton, L. M. (2006). Childhood poverty, policy, and practice. In W. Damon & R. M. Lerner (Eds. in Chief) & K. A. Renninger & I. E. Sigel (Vol. Ed.), *Handbook of child psychology, Vol. 4. Child psychology in practice* (6th ed., pp. 700–775). Hoboken, NJ: Wiley.

McLoyd, V. C., Kaplan, R., Purtell, K. M., Bagley, E., Hardaway, C. R., & Smalls, C. (2009). Poverty and socioeconomic disadvantage in adolescence. In R. M. Lerner & L. Steinberg (Eds.), *Handbook of adolescent psychology. Vol. 2. Contextual influences on adolescent development* (3rd ed., pp. 444–491). Hoboken, NJ: Wiley.

McMahon, S. (1992). Book club: A case study of a group of fifth graders as they participate in a literature-based reading program. *Reading Research Quarterly, 27,* 292–294.

McMahon, S. D., Parnes, A. L., Keys, C. B., & Viola, J. J. (2008). School belonging among low-income urban youth with disabilities: Testing a theoretical model. *Psychology in the Schools, 45*(5), 387–401.

McNeill, D. (1966). Developmental psycholinguistics. In F. Smith & G. A. Miller (Eds.), *The genesis of language.* Cambridge, MA: MIT Press.

McNeill, D. (1970). *The acquisition of language: The study of developmental psycholinguistics.* New York: Harper & Row.

McVey, G. L., Kirsh, G., Maker, D., Walker, K. S., Mullane, J., Laliberte, M., et al. (2010). Promoting positive body image among university students: A collaborative pilot study. *Body Image, 7*(3), 200–204.

McWayne, C. M., Owsianik, M., Green, L. E., & Fantuzzo, J. W. (2008). Parenting behaviors and preschool children's social and emotional skills: A question of consequential validity of traditional parenting constructs for low-income African Americans. *Early Childhood Research Quarterly, 23,* 173–192.

Meadows, S. (2010). *The child as a social person.* London, England: Routledge.

Medrich, E. A. (1981). *The serious business of growing up: A study of children's lives outside the school.* Berkeley: University of California Press.

Meece, J. L., & Holt, K. (1993). A pattern analysis of students' achievement goals. *Journal of Educational Psychology, 85,* 582–590.

Meehan, B. T., Hughes, J. N., & Cavell, T. A. (2003). Teacher–student relationships as compensatory resources for aggressive children. *Child Development, 74,* 1145–1157.

Megalakaki, O. (2008). Pupils' conceptions of force in inanimates and animates. *European Journal of Psychology of Education, 23*(3), 339–353.

Mehan, H. (1979). *Social organization in the classroom.* Cambridge, MA: Harvard University Press.

Mehler, J., Jusczyk, P., Lambertz, G., Halsted, N., Bertoncini, J., & Amiel-Tison, C. (1988). A precursor of language acquisition in young infants. *Cognition, 29*(2), 143–178.

Mehta, C. M., & Strough, J. (2009). Sex segregation in friendships and normative contexts across the life span. *Developmental Review, 29*(3), 201–220.

Mehta, P. H., & Beer, J. (2010). Neural mechanisms of the testosterone-aggression relation: The role of orbitofrontal cortex. *Journal of Cognitive Neuroscience, 22*(10), 2357–2368. doi:10.1162/jocn.2009.21389

Meichenbaum, D. (1977). *Cognitive-behavior modification: An integrative approach.* New York: Plenum Press.

Meichenbaum, D. (1985). Teaching thinking: A cognitive-behavioral perspective. In S. F. Chipman, J. W. Segal, & R. Glaser (Eds.), *Thinking and learning skills: Vol. 2. Research and open questions.* Hillsdale, NJ: Erlbaum.

Meichenbaum, D., & Goodman, J. (1971). Training impulsive children to talk to themselves: A means of developing self-control. *Journal of Abnormal Psychology, 77,* 115–126.

Meins, E., Fernyhough, C., Wainwright, R., Clark-Carter, D., Gupta, M. D., Fradley, E., et al. (2003). Pathways to understanding mind: Construct validity and predictive validity of maternal mind-mindedness. *Child Development, 74,* 1194–1211.

Meisels, S. J., Wen, X., & Beachy-Quick, K. (2010). Authentic assessment for infants and toddlers: Exploring the reliability and validity of the ounce scale. *Applied Developmental Science, 14*(2), 55–71. doi:10.1080/10888691003697911

Melde, C., Taylor, T. J., & Esbensen, F. (2009). "I got your back": An examination of the protective function of gang membership in adolescence. *Criminology: An Interdisciplinary Journal, 47*(2), 565–594. doi:10.1111/j.1745-9125.2009.00148.x

Meltzer, L. (Ed.). (2007). *Executive function in education: From theory to practice.* New York: Guilford Press.

Meltzer, L. (2010). *Promoting executive function in the classroom.* New York: Guilford Press.

Meltzer, L., & Krishnan, K. (2007). Executive function difficulties and learning disabilities: Understandings and misunderstandings. In L. Meltzer (Ed.), *Executive function in education: From theory to practice* (pp. 77–105). New York: Guilford Press.

Meltzer, L., Pollica, L. S., & Barzillai, M. (2007). Executive function in the classroom: Embedding strategy instruction into daily teaching practices. In L. Meltzer (Ed.), *Executive function in education: From theory to practice* (pp. 165–193). New York: Guilford Press.

Meltzoff, A. N. (1990). Foundations for developing a concept of self: The role of imitation in relating self to other and the value of social mirroring, social modeling, and self practice in infancy. In D. Cicchetti & M. Beeghly (Eds.), *The self in transition: Infancy to childhood* (pp. 139–164). Chicago: University of Chicago Press.

Meltzoff, A. N. (2007). "Like me": A foundation for social cognition. *Developmental Science, 10*(1), 126–134.

Meltzoff, A. N., & Moore, M. K. (1977). Imitation of facial and manual gestures by human neonates. *Science, 198,* 74–78.

Mena, J. G., & Eyer, D. W. (2007). *Infants, toddlers, and caregivers: A curriculum of respectful, responsive care and education* (7th ed.). Boston: McGraw-Hill.

Mendes, D., Seidl-de-Moura, M., & Siqueira, J. (2009). The ontogenesis of smiling and its association with mothers' affective behaviors: A longitudinal study. *Infant Behavior & Development, 32*(4), 445–453.

Menéndez, R. (Director). (1988). *Stand and deliver* [Motion picture]. United States: Warner Studios.

Menghini, D., Finzi, A., Benassi, M., Bolzani, R., Facoetti, A., Giovagnoli, S., et al. (2010). Different underlying neurocognitive deficits in developmental dyslexia: A comparative study. *Neuropsychologia, 48*(4), 863–872.

Mennella, J. A., Jagnow, C. P., & Beauchamp, G. K. (2001). Prenatal and postnatal flavor learning by human infants. *Pediatrics, 107,* 88.

Menyuk, P., & Menyuk, D. (1988). Communicative competence: A historical and cultural perspective. In J. S. Wurzel (Ed.), *Toward multiculturalism: A reader in multicultural education.* Yarmouth, ME: Intercultural Press.

Mercer, J. (2006). *Understanding attachment: Parenting, child care, and emotional development.* Westport, CT: Praeger.

Mestre, M. V., Samper, P., Frías, M. D., & Tur, A. M. (2009). Are women more empathetic than men? A longitudinal study in adolescence. *The Spanish Journal of Psychology, 12*(1), 76–83.

Meteyer, K. B., & Perry-Jenkins, M. (2009). Dyadic parenting and children's externalizing symptoms. *Family Relations, 58,* 289–302.

Metz, K. E. (1995). Reassessment of developmental constraints on children's science instruction. *Review of Educational Research, 65,* 93–127.

Metz, K. E. (2004). Children's understanding of scientific inquiry: Their conceptualizations of uncertainty in investigations of their own design. *Cognition and Instruction, 22,* 219–290.

Meyer, D., Madden, D., & McGrath, D. J. (2005). English language learner students in U.S. public schools: 1994 and 2000. *Education Statistics Quarterly, 6*(3). Retrieved April 7, 2008, from http://nces.ed.gov/programs/quarterly/vol_6/6_3/3_4.asp

Meyer, D. K., Turner, J. C., & Spencer, C. A. (1994, April). *Academic risk taking and motivation in an elementary mathematics classroom.* Paper presented at the annual meeting of the American Educational Research Association, New Orleans, LA.

Meyer, D. K., Turner, J. C., & Spencer, C. A. (1997). Challenge in a mathematics classroom: Students' motivation and strategies in project-based learning. *Elementary School Journal, 97,* 501–521.

Meyers, D. T. (1987). The socialized individual and individual autonomy: An intersection between philosophy and psychology. In E. F. Kittay and D. T. Meyers (Eds.), *Women and moral theory.* Totowa, NJ: Rowman & Littlefield.

Meyerstein, I. (2001). A systemic approach to fetal loss following genetic testing. *Contemporary Family Therapy, 23,* 385–402.

Miao, X., & Wang, W. (2003). A century of Chinese developmental psychology. *International Journal of Psychology, 38*(5), 258–273.

Michel, C. (1989). Radiation embryology. *Experientia, 45,* 69–77.

Micheli, L. J. (1995). Sports injuries in children and adolescents: Questions and controversies. *Clinics in Sports Medicine, 14,* 727–745.

Midgley, C. (Ed.). (2002). *Goals, goal structures, and patterns of adaptive learning.* Mahwah, NJ: Erlbaum.

Midgley, C., Feldlaufer, H., & Eccles, J. S. (1989). Change in teacher efficacy and student self- and task-related beliefs in mathematics during the transition to junior high school. *Journal of Educational Psychology, 81,* 247–258.

Midgley, C., Kaplan, A., & Middleton, M. (2001). Performance-approach goals: Good for what, for whom, under what circumstances, and at what cost? *Journal of Educational Psychology, 93,* 77–86.

Mikulincer, M., & Shaver, P. R. (2007). *Attachment in adulthood: Structure, dynamics, and change.* New York: Guilford Press.

Milch-Reich, S., Campbell, S. B., Pelham, W. E., Jr., Connelly, L. M., & Geva, D. (1999). Developmental and individual differences in children's on-line representations of dynamic social events. *Child Development, 70,* 413–431.

Miller, B. C., & Benson, B. (1999). Romantic and sexual relationship development during adolescence. In W. Furman, B. B. Brown, & C. Feiring (Eds.), *The development of romantic relationships in adolescence* (pp. 99–121). Cambridge, England: Cambridge University Press.

Miller, G. A., & Gildea, P. M. (1987). How children learn words. *Scientific American, 257,* 94–99.

Miller, J. G. (1987). Cultural influences on the development of conceptual differentiation in person description. *British Journal of Developmental Psychology, 5,* 309–319.

Miller, J. G. (1997). A cultural-psychology perspective on intelligence. In R. J. Sternberg & E. L. Grigorenko (Eds.), *Intelligence, heredity, and environment* (pp. 269–302). Cambridge, England: Cambridge University Press.

Miller, J. G. (2007). Cultural psychology of moral development. In S. Kitayama & D. Cohen (Eds.), *Handbook of cultural psychology* (pp. 477–499). New York: Guilford Press.

Miller, K. (1989). Measurement as a tool for thought: The role of measuring procedures in children's understanding of quantitative invariance. *Developmental Psychology, 25,* 589–600.

Miller, K. F., Smith, C. M., Zhu, J., & Zhang, H. (1995). Preschool origins of cross-national differences in mathematical competence: The role of number-naming systems. *Psychological Science, 6,* 56–60.

Miller, L. S. (1995). *An American imperative: Accelerating minority educational advancement.* New Haven, CT: Yale University Press.

Miller, N., & Maruyama, G. (1976). Ordinal position and peer popularity. *Journal of Personality and Social Psychology, 33,* 123–131.

Miller, P., & Seier, W. (1994). Strategy utilization deficiencies in children: when, where, and why. In H. Reese (Ed.), *Advances in child development and behavior* (Vol. 25). New York: Academic Press.

Miller, P. J., & Goodnow, J. J. (1995). Cultural practices: Toward an integration of culture and development. In J. J. Goodnow & P. J. Miller (Eds.), *Cultural practices as contexts for development* (New Directions for Child Development, No. 67; pp. 5–16). San Francisco: Jossey-Bass.

Miller, P. M., Danaher, D. L., & Forbes, D. (1986). Sex-related strategies of coping with interpersonal conflict in children aged four to seven. *Developmental Psychology, 22,* 543–548.

Miller, R. B., & Brickman, S. J. (2004). A model of future-oriented motivation and self-regulation. *Educational Psychology Review, 16,* 9–33.

Miller, S. D., Heafner, T., Massey, D., & Strahan, D. B. (2003, April). *Students' reactions to teachers' attempts to create the necessary conditions to promote the acquisition of self-regulation skills.* Paper presented at the annual meeting of the American Educational Research Association, Chicago.

Mills, G. E. (2007). *Action research: A guide for the teacher researcher* (3rd ed.). Upper Saddle River, NJ: Pearson Merrill/Prentice Hall.

Mills, R. S. L., Arbeau, K. A., Lall, D. I. K., & De Jaeger, A. E. (2010). Parenting and child characteristics in the prediction of shame in early and middle childhood. *Merrill-Palmer Quarterly, 56*(4), 500–528.

Mills, R. S. L., & Grusec, J. E. (1989). Cognitive, affective, and behavioral consequences of praising altruism. *Merrill-Palmer Quarterly, 35,* 299–326.

Milne, E., White, S., Campbell, R., Swettenham, J., Jansen, P., & Ramas, F. (2006). Motion and form coherence detection in autistic spectrum disorder: Relationship to motor control and 2:4 digit ratio. *Journal of Autism and Developmental Disorders, 36,* 225–237.

Milner, H. R. (2006). Classroom management in urban classrooms. In C. M. Evertson & C. S. Weinstein (Eds.), *Handbook of classroom management: Research, practice, and contemporary issues* (pp. 491–522). Mahwah, NJ: Erlbaum.

Milner, H. R., & Ford, D. Y. (2007). Cultural considerations of culturally diverse elementary students in gifted education. *Roeper Review, 29*(3), 166–173.

Mingroni, M. A. (2007). Resolving the IQ paradox: Heterosis as a cause of the Flynn effect and other trends. *Psychological Review, 114,* 806–829.

Minshawi, N. F., Ashby, I., & Swiezy, N. (2009). Adaptive and self-help skills. In J. L. Matson (Ed.), *Applied behavior analysis for children with autism spectrum disorders* (pp. 189–206). New York: Springer Science + Business Media. doi:10.1007/978-1-4419-0088-3_11

Minshew, N. J., & Williams, D. L. (2007). The new neurobiology of autism: Cortex, connectivity, and neuronal organization. *Archives of Neurology, 64*(7), 945–950. doi:10.1001/archneur.64.7.945

Minskoff, E. H. (1980). Teaching approach for developing nonverbal communication skills in students with social perception deficits: II. Proxemic, vocalic, and artifactual cues. *Journal of Learning Disabilities, 13,* 203–208.

Minstrell, J., & Stimpson, V. (1996). A classroom environment for learning: Guiding students' reconstruction of understanding and reasoning. In L. Schauble & R. Glaser (Eds.), *Innovations in learning: New environments for education.* Mahwah, NJ: Erlbaum.

Mischel, W. (1974). Processes in delay of gratification. In L. Berkowitz (Ed.), *Advances in experimental social psychology* (Vol. 7, pp. 249–292). New York: Academic Press.

Mischel, W., & Ebbesen, E. (1970). Attention in delay of gratification. *Journal of Personality and Social Psychology, 16,* 329–337.

Mitchell, E. A. (2009). What is the mechanism of SIDS? Clues from epidemiology. *Developmental Psychobiology, 51*(3), 216–222.

Mitchell, S., Foulger, T. S., & Wetzel, K. (2009). Ten tips for involving families through internet-based communication. *Young Children, 64*(5), 46–49.

Mithaug, D. K., & Mithaug, D. E. (2003). Effects of teacher-directed versus student-directed instruction on self-management of young children with disabilities. *Journal of Applied Behavior Analysis, 36,* 133–136.

Mitru, G., Millrood, D., & Mateika, J. H. (2002). The impact of sleep on learning and behavior of adolescents. *Teachers College Record, 104,* 704–726.

Miura, I. T., Okamoto, Y., Vlahovic-Stetic, V., Kim, C. C., & Han, J. H. (1999). Language supports for children's understanding of numerical fractions: Cross-national comparisons. *Journal of Experimental Child Psychology, 74,* 356–365.

Miyake, K., Campos, J., Kagan, J., & Bradshaw, D. (1986). Issues in socioemotional development in Japan. In H. Azuma, K. Hakuta, & H. Stevenson (Eds.), *Kodomo: Child development and education in Japan* (pp. 238–261). San Francisco: Freeman.

Miyake, K., Chen, S.-J., & Campos, J. J. (1985). Infant temperament, mother's mode of interaction, and attachment in Japan: An interim report. In I. Bretherton & E. Waters (Eds.), Growing points of attachment theory and research. *Monographs of the Society for Research in Child Development, 50*(1–2, Serial No. 209), 276–297.

Modestou, M., & Gagatsis, A. (2010). Cognitive and Metacognitive Aspects of Proportional Reasoning. *Mathematical Thinking and Learning, 12*(1), 36–53.

Moely, B. E., Santulli, K. A., & Obach, M. S. (1995). Strategy instruction, metacognition, and motivation in the elementary school classroom. In F. E. Weinert & W. Schneider (Eds.), *Memory performance and competencies: Issues in growth and development* (pp. 301–321). Hillsdale, NJ: Erlbaum.

Mohatt, G., & Erickson, F. (1981). Cultural differences in teaching styles in an Odawa school: A sociolinguistic approach. In H. T. Trueba, G. P. Guthrie, & K. H. Au (Eds.), *Culture and the bilingual classroom: Studies in classroom ethnography.* Rowley, MA: Newbury House.

Mohr, N. (1979). *Felita.* New York: Bantam Doubleday Dell.

Moje, E. B. (2000). "To be part of the story": The literacy practices of gangsta adolescents. *Teachers College Record, 102*(3), 651–690.

Moksnes, U. K., Moljord, I. E. O., Espnes, G. A., & Byrne, D. G. (2010). The association between stress and emotional states in adolescents: The role of gender and self-esteem. *Personality and Individual Differences, 49*(5), 430–435.

Moll, L., Amanti, C., Neff, D., & González, N. (2005). Funds of knowledge for teaching: Using a qualitative approach to connect homes and classrooms. In N. González, L. C. Moll, & C. Amanti (Eds.), *Funds of knowledge: Theorizing practices in households, communities, and classrooms* (pp. 71–87). Mahwah, NJ: Erlbaum.

Moller, A. C., Deci, E. L., & Elliot, A. J. (2010). Person-level relatedness and the incremental value of relating. *Personality and Social Psychology Bulletin, 36*(6), 754–767.

Montagu, A. (1999). Introduction. In A. Montagu (Ed.), *Race and IQ* (expanded ed., pp. 1–18). New York: Oxford University Press.

Montague, D. P. F., & Walker-Andrews, A. S. (2001). Peekaboo: A new look at infants' perceptions of emotion expressions. *Developmental Psychology, 37,* 826–838.

Montemayor, R. (1982). The relationship between parent–adolescent conflict and the amount of time adolescents spend with parents, peers, and alone. *Child Development, 53,* 1512–1519.

Montessori, M. (1936). *The secret of childhood* (M. J. Costelloe, Trans.). New York: Ballantine Books, 1966.

Montessori, M. (1949). *The absorbent mind* (M. J. Costelloe, Trans.). New York: Holt, Rinehart & Winston.

Montgomery, H. (2009). *An introduction to childhood: Anthropological perspectives on children's lives.* Chichester, United Kingdom: Wiley.

Montgomery, K. S., Mackey, J., Thuett, K., Ginestra, S., Bizon, J. L., & Abbott, L. C. (2008). Chronic, low-dose prenatal exposure to methylmercury impairs motor and mnemonic function in adult C57/B6 mice. *Behavioural Brain Research, 191,* 55–61.

Moon, C., Cooper, R. P., & Fifer, W. P. (1993). Two-day-olds prefer their native language. *Infant Behavior & Development, 16*(4), 495–500.

Moon, S. M., Feldhusen, J. F., & Dillon, D. R. (1994). Long term effects of an enrichment program based on the Purdue three-stage model. *Gifted Child Quarterly, 38,* 38–47.

Moore, C. (2009). Fairness in children's resource allocation depends on the recipient. *Psychological Science, 20*(8), 944–948. doi:10.1111/j.1467-9280.2009.02378.x

Moore, C. (2010). The development of future-oriented decision-making. In B. W. Sokol, U. Müeller, J. I. M. Carpendale, A. R. Young, & G. Iarocci (Eds.), *Self and social regulation: Social interaction and the development of social understanding and executive functions* (pp. 270–286). New York: Oxford University Press.

Moore, C., & Barresi, J. (2010). The construction of commonsense psychology in infancy. In P. D. Zelazo, M. Chandler, & E. Crone (Eds.), *Developmental social cognitive neuroscience* (pp. 43–62). New York: Psychology Press.

Moore, G. A., Cohn, J. F., & Campbell, S. B. (2001). Infant affective responses to mother's still face at 6 months differentially predict externalizing and internalizing behaviors at 18 months. *Developmental Psychology, 37,* 706–714.

Moore, K. L., & Persaud, T. V. N. (2008). *Before we are born: Essentials of embryology and birth defects* (7th ed.). Philadelphia, PA: Saunders/Elsevier.

Moore, K. L., Persaud, T. V. N., & Shiota, K. (2000). *Color atlas of clinical embryology* (2nd ed.). Philadelphia, PA: Saunders.

Moore, L. C. (2006). Learning by heart in Qur'anic and public schools in northern Cameroon. *Social Analysis, 50*(3), 109–126.

Moore, L. C. (2010). Learning in schools. In D. F. Lancy, J. Bock, & S. Gaskins (Eds.), *The anthropology of learning in childhood* (pp. 207–232). Lanham, MD: AltaMira Press/Rowman & Littlefield.

Moore, P. S., Whaley, S. E., & Sigman, M. (2004). Interactions between mothers and children: Impacts of maternal and child anxiety. *Journal of Abnormal Psychology, 113*(3), 471–476.

Moore-Brown, B., Huerta, M., Uranga-Hernandez, Y., & Peña, E. D. (2006). Using dynamic assessment to evaluate children with suspected learning disabilities. *Intervention in School and Clinic, 41*(4), 209–217.

Mora, J. K. (2009). From the ballot box to the classroom. *Educational Leadership, 66*(7), 14–19.

Moran, C. E., & Hakuta, K. (1995). Bilingual education: Broadening research perspectives. In J. A. Banks & C. A. M. Banks (Eds.), *Handbook of research on multicultural education.* New York: Macmillan.

Moran, S., & Gardner, H. (2006). Extraordinary achievements: A developmental and systems analysis. In W. Damon & R. M. Lerner (Series Eds.), & D. Kuhn & R. Siegler (Vol. Eds.), *Handbook of child psychology: Vol. 2. Cognition, perception, and language* (6th ed.). New York: Wiley.

Morelli, G. A., & Rothbaum, F. (2007). Situating the child in context: Attachment relationships and self-regulation in different cultures. In S. Kitayama & D. Cohen (Eds.), *Handbook of cultural psychology* (pp. 500–527). New York: Guilford Press.

Morgan, K. E., Rothlisberg, B. A., McIntosh, D. E., & Hunt, M. S. (2009). Confirmatory factor analysis of the KABC-II in preschool children. *Psychology in the Schools, 46*(6), 515–526.

Morgan, M. (1985). Self-monitoring of attained subgoals in private study. *Journal of Educational Psychology, 77,* 623–630.

Morra, S., & Camba, R. (2009). Vocabulary learning in primary school children: Working memory and long-term memory components. *Journal of Experimental Child Psychology, 104,* 156–178.

Morra, S., Gobbo, C., Marini, Z., & Sheese, R. (2008). *Cognitive development: Neo-Piagetian perspectives.* New York: Erlbaum.

Morris, D. (1977). *Manwatching: A field guide to human behaviour.* New York: Harry N. Abrams.

Morrison, G. M., Furlong, M. J., D'Incau, B., & Morrison, R. L. (2004). The safe school: Integrating the school reform agenda to prevent disruption and violence at school. In J. C. Conoley & A. P. Goldstein (Ed.), *School violence intervention* (2nd ed., pp. 256–296). New York: Guilford Press.

Morrongiello, B. A., Fenwick, K. D., Hillier, L., & Chance, G. (1994). Sound localization in newborn human infants. *Developmental Psychobiology, 27,* 519–538.

Morrow, S. L. (1997). Career development of lesbian and gay youth: Effects of sexual orientation, coming out, and homophobia. In M. B. Harris (Ed.), *School experiences of gay and lesbian youth: The invisible minority* (pp. 1–15). Binghamton, NY: Harrington Park Press.

Mortimer, J. T., Shanahan, M., & Ryu, S. (1994). The effects of adolescent employment on school-related orientation and behavior. In R. K. Silbereisen & E. Todt (Eds.), *Adolescence in context: The interplay of family, school, peers and work in adjustment.* New York: Springer-Verlag.

Moschner, B., Anschuetz, A., Wernke, S., & Wagener, U. (2008). Measurement of epistemological beliefs and learning strategies of elementary school children. In M. S. Khine (Ed.), *Knowing, knowledge and beliefs: Epistemological studies across diverse cultures* (pp. 113–133). New York: Springer Science + Business Media.

Mueller, E., & Silverman, N. (1989). Peer relations in maltreated children. In D. Cicchetti & V. Carlson (Eds.), *Child maltreatment: Theory and research on the causes and consequences of child abuse and neglect* (pp. 529–579). New York: Cambridge University Press 7.

Müeller, U., & Overton, W. F. (2010). Thinking about thinking—Thinking about measurement: A Rasch analysis of recursive thinking. *Journal of Applied Measurement, 11*(1), 78–90.

Muennig, P., Schweinhart, L., Montie, J., & Neidell, M. (2009). Effect of a prekindergarten educational intervention on adult health: 37-year follow-up results of a randomized control trial. *American Journal of Public Health, 99*(5), 1431–1437.

Muis, K. R. (2004). Personal epistemology and mathematics: A critical review and synthesis of research. *Review of Educational Research, 74,* 317–377.

Muis, K. R. (2007). The role of epistemic beliefs in self-regulated learning. *Educational Psychologist, 42,* 173–190.

Muis, K. R., Bendixen, L. D., & Haerle, F. C. (2006). Domain-generality and domain-specificity in personal epistemology research: Philosophical and empirical reflections in the development of a theoretical framework. *Educational Psychology Review, 18,* 3–54.

Mulcahey, C. (2009, July). Providing rich art activities for young children. *Young Children, 64*(4), 107–112.

Mullins, D., & Tisak, M. S. (2006). Moral, conventional, and personal rules: The perspective of foster youth. *Journal of Applied Developmental Psychology, 27,* 310–325.

Mullis, R. L., Graf, S. C., & Mullis, A. K. (2009). Parental relationships, autonomy, and identity processes of high school students. *The Journal of Genetic Psychology: Research and Theory on Human Development, 170*(4), 326–338.

Mulvaney, M. K., & Mebert, C. J. (2010). Stress appraisal and attitudes towards corporal punishment as intervening processes between corporal punishment and subsequent mental health. *Journal of Family Violence, 25*(4), 401–412.

Mundy, E., & Gilmore, C. K. (2009). Children's mapping between symbolic and nonsymbolic representations of number. *Journal of Experimental Child Psychology, 103,* 490–502.

Mundy, P., & Newell, L. (2007). Attention, joint attention, and social cognition. *Current Directions in Psychological Science, 16,* 269–274.

Munroe, R. L., & Munroe, P. J. (1992). Fathers in children's environments: A four culture study. In B. S. Hewlett (Ed.), *Father–child relations: Cultural and biosocial contexts* (pp. 213–230). New York: Aldine de Gruyter.

Muramoto, Y., Yamaguchi, S., & Kim, U. (2009). Perception of achievement attribution in individual and group contexts: Comparative analysis of Japanese, Korean, and Asian-American results. *Asian Journal of Social Psychology, 12*(3), 199–210. doi:10.1111/j.1467-839X.2009.01285.x

Murdock, T. B. (1999). The social context of risk: Status and motivational predictors of alienation in middle school. *Journal of Educational Psychology, 91,* 62–75.

Murdock, T. B. (2009). Achievement motivation in racial and ethnic context. In K. R. Wentzel & A. Wigfield (Eds.), *Handbook of motivation at school* (pp. 433–461). New York: Routledge.

Muris, P., Meesters, C., & Rompelberg, L. (2006). Attention control in middle childhood: Relations to psychopathological symptoms and threat perception distortions. *Behaviour Research and Therapy, 45,* 997–1010.

Murnane, R. J. (2007, Fall). Improving the education of children living in poverty. *The Future of Children, 17*(2), 161–182.

Murphy, P. K. (2007). The eye of the beholder: The interplay of social and cognitive components in change. *Educational Psychologist, 42,* 41–53.

Murphy, P. K., & Alexander, P. A. (2008). Examining the influence of knowledge, beliefs, and motivation in conceptual change. In S. Vosniadou (Ed.), *International handbook of research on conceptual change* (pp. 583–616). New York: Taylor & Francis.

Murphy, P. K., & Mason, L. (2006). Changing knowledge and beliefs. In P. A. Alexander & P. H. Winne (Eds.), *Handbook of educational psychology* (2nd ed., pp. 305–324). Mahwah, NJ: Erlbaum.

Mussolin, C., Mejias, S., & Noël, M. (2010). Symbolic and nonsymbolic number comparison in children with and without dyscalculia. *Cognition, 115*(1), 10–25.

Mustanski, B. S., Viken, R. J., Kaprio, J., Pulkkinen, L., & Rose, R. (2004). Genetic and environmental influences on pubertal influences on pubertal development: Longitudinal data from Finnish twins at ages 11 and 14. *Developmental Psychology, 40,* 1188–1198.

Muter, V. (1998). Phonological awareness: Its nature and its influence over early literacy development. In C. Hulme & R. M. Joshi (Eds.), *Reading and spelling: Development and disorders.* Mahwah, NJ: Erlbaum.

Myant, K. A., & Williams, J. M. (2008). What do children learn about biology from factual information? A comparison of interventions to improve understanding of contagious illnesses. *British Journal of Educational Psychology, 78,* 223–244.

Myles, B. M., & Simpson, R. L. (2001). Understanding the hidden curriculum: An essential social skill for children and youth with Asperger syndrome. *Intervention in School and Clinic, 36*(5), 279–286.

Myrberg, E., & Rosén, M. (2009). Direct and indirect effects of parents' education on reading achievement among third graders in Sweden. *British Journal of Educational Psychology, 79*(4), 695–711.

Nabors, L. A., Little, S. G., Akin-Little, A., & Iobst, E. A. (2008). Teacher knowledge of and confidence in meeting the needs of children with chronic medical conditions: Pediatric psychology's contribution to education. *Psychology in the Schools, 45*(3), 217–226.

Nader-Grosbois, N., Normandeau, S., Ricard-Cossette, M., & Quintal, G. (2008). Mother's, father's regulation and child's self-regulation in a computer-mediated learning situation. *European Journal of Psychology of Education, 23*(1), 95–115.

Naegele, J. R., & Lombroso, P. J. (2001). Genetics of central nervous system developmental disorders. *Child and Adolescent Psychiatric Clinics of North America, 10,* 225–239.

Naglieri, J. A., & Conway, C. (2009). The Cognitive Assessment System. In J. A. Naglieri & S. Goldstein (Eds.), *Practitioner's guide to assessing intelligence and achievement* (pp. 27–59). Hoboken, NJ: Wiley.

Naglieri, J. A., De Lauder, B. Y., Goldstein, S., & Schwebech, A. (2006). WISC-III and CAS: Which correlates higher with achievement for a clinical sample? *School Psychology Quarterly, 21*(1), 62–76.

Nagy, E. (2008). Innate intersubjectivity: Newborns' sensitivity to communication disturbance. *Developmental Psychology, 44*(6), 1779–1784.

Nagy, G., Watt, H. M. G., Eccles, J. S., Trautwein, U., Lüdtke, O., & Baumert, J. (2010). The development of students' mathematics self-concept in relation to gender: Different countries, different trajectories? *Journal of Research on Adolescence, 20*(2), 482–506.

Nagy, W. E., Berninger, V., Abbott, R., Vaughan, K., & Vermeulen, K. (2003). Relationship of morphology and other language skills to literacy skills in at-risk second-grade readers and at-risk fourth-grade writers. *Journal of Educational Psychology, 95,* 730–742.

Nagy, W. E., Herman, P. A., & Anderson, R. C. (1985). Learning words from context. *Reading Research Quarterly, 20,* 233–253.

Nakata, N., & Trehub, S. E. (2004). Infants' responsiveness to maternal speech and singing. *Infant Behavior and Development, 27,* 455–464.

Nakazawa, C., Takahira, S., Muramatsu, Y., Kawano, G., Fujiwara, C., Takahashi, M., et al. (2001, April). *Gender issues in mathematics, science and technology.* Paper presented at the annual meeting of the American Educational Research Association, Seattle, WA.

Nalkur, P. G. (2009). A cultural comparison of Tanzanian street children, former street children, and school-going children. *Journal of Cross-Cultural Psychology, 40*(6), 1012–1027. doi:10.1177/0022022109346954

Narayanan, U., & Warren, S. T. (2006). Neurobiology of related disorders: Fragile X syndrome. In S. O. Moldin & J. L. R. Rubenstein (Eds.), *Understanding autism: From basic neuroscience to treatment* (pp. 113–131). Boca Raton, FL: CRC Press.

Narváez, D. (1998). The influence of moral schemas on the reconstruction of moral narratives in eighth graders and college students. *Journal of Educational Psychology, 90,* 13–24.

Narváez, D., & Rest, J. (1995). The four components of acting morally. In W. M. Kurtines & J. L. Gewirtz (Eds.), *Moral development: An introduction.* Boston: Allyn & Bacon.

Nation, K., & Hulme, C. (1998). The role of analogy in early spelling development. In C. Hulme & R. M. Joshi (Eds.), *Reading and spelling: Development and disorders.* Mahwah, NJ: Erlbaum.

National Association for the Education of Young Children. (1997). *Developmentally appropriate practice in early childhood programs serving children from birth through age 8.* Washington, DC: Author.

National Association for the Education of Young Children (2009). *Developmentally appropriate practice in early childhood programs serving children birth through age 8.* Retrieved October 13, 2009, from http://208.118.177.216/about/positions/pdf/PSDAP.pdf

National Association of Bilingual Education. (1993). Census reports sharp increase in number of non-English speaking Americans. *NABE News, 16*(6), 1, 25.

National Association of Secondary School Principals. (2004). *Breaking ranks II: Strategies for leading high school reform.* Reston, VA: Author.

National Board for Professional Teaching Standards (2001). *NBTS Middle childhood generalist standards* (2nd ed.), Retrieved October 25, 2009, from http://www.nbpts.org/the_standards/standards_by_cert?ID=27&x=57&y=9

National Center for Education Statistics. (2003). *Percentage of high school completers ages 16–24 who were enrolled in college the October after completing high school, by type of institution, family income, and race/ethnicity: October 1972–96.* Washington, DC: Author. Retrieved February 24, 2003, from http://nces.ed.gov/quicktables/Detail.asp?Key5147

National Center for Education Statistics. (2007). *Digest of education statistics. Table 183. Graduation rates and postsecondary attendance rates of recent high school students, by selected high school characteristics: 1999–2000.* National Center for Education Statistics, Institute of Education Sciences, U.S. Department of Education. Retrieved December 6, 2007, from http://nces.ed.gov/programs/digest/d05/tables/dt05_183.asp

National Center for Health Statistics. (2005). *NCHS Data on Adolescent Health.* Retrieved February 1, 2008, from http://www.cdc.gov/nchs/data/factsheets/adolescenthlth.pdf

National Center for Missing and Exploited Children. (2004). *HDOP: Help delete online predators.* Retrieved November 20, 2005, from http://www.missingkids.com/adcouncil

National Clearinghouse for English Language Acquisition. (2006). *Resources about secondary English language learners.* Retrieved December 3, 2007, from http://www.ncela.gwu.edu/resabout/ells/intro

National Council for the Social Studies. (2010). *About National Council for the Social Studies.* Retrieved August 30, 2010, from http://www.socialstudies.org/about

National Drug Intelligence Center. (2008). *Attorney General's report to Congress on the growth of violent street gangs in suburban areas.* Retrieved June 10, 2008, from http://www.usdoj.gov/ndic/pubs27/27612/estimate.htm

National Institute of Child Health and Human Development Early Child Care Research Network. (2008). Mothers' and fathers' support for child autonomy and early school achievement. *Developmental Psychology, 44,* 895–907.

National Institute of Mental Health. (2008a). *Autism spectrum disorders (Pervasive developmental disorders).* Retrieved January 22, 2008, from http://www.nimh.nih.gov/health/publications/autism/summary.shtml

National Institute of Mental Health. (2008b). *Suicide in the U.S.: Statistics and prevention.* Retrieved April 28, 2008, from http://www.nimh.nih.gov/health/publications/suicide-in-the-us-statistics-and-prevention.shtml#races

National Institute on Drug Abuse. (2003). *Preventing drug use among children and adolescents: A research-based guide for parents, educators, and community leaders.* Bethesda, MD: U.S. Department of Health and Human Services, National Institutes of Health, National Institute on Drug Abuse.

National Institute on Drug Abuse. (2009). *Principles of drug addiction treatment: A research-based guide* (2nd ed.). Retrieved April 6, 2010, from http://www.drugabuse.gov/PODAT/PODATIndex.html

National Institute on Drug Abuse. (2010a). *Alcohol.* Retrieved April 6, 2010, from http://www.drugabuse.gov/drugpages/alcohol.html

National Institute on Drug Abuse. (2010b). *Cocaine.* Retrieved April 6, 2010, from http://www.drugabuse.gov/drugpages/cocaine.html

National Institute on Drug Abuse. (2010c). *Inhalants.* Retrieved April 6, 2010, from http://www.drugabuse.gov/drugpages/inhalants.html.

National Institute on Drug Abuse. (2010d). *Marijuana.* Retrieved April 6, 2010, from http://www.drugabuse.gov/drugpages/marijuana.html

National Institute on Drug Abuse. (2010e). *MDMA (Ecstasy).* Retrieved April 6, 2010, from http://www.drugabuse.gov/drugpages/mdma.html

National Institute on Drug Abuse. (2010f). *Methamphetamines.* Retrieved April 6, 2010, from http://www.drugabuse.gov/drugpages/methamphetamine.html

National Institute on Drug Abuse. (2010g). *Prescription drugs.* Retrieved April 6, 2010, from http://www.drugabuse.gov/drugpages/prescription.html

National Institute on Drug Abuse. (2010h). *Steroids (anabolic).* Retrieved April 6, 2010, from http://www.drugabuse.gov/drugpages/steroids.html

National Joint Committee on Learning Disabilities. (1994). Learning disabilities: Issues on definition, a position paper of the National Joint Committee on Learning Disabilities. In *Collective perspectives on issues affecting learning disabilities: Position papers and statements.* Austin, TX: Pro-Ed.

National Middle School Association. (2003). *This we believe: Successful schools for young adolescents.* Columbus, OH: Author.

National Research Council. (1999). *How people learn: Brain, mind, experience, and school.* Washington, DC: Author.

National Science Foundation. (2007). *Women, minorities, and persons with disabilities in science and engineering: 2007.* Retrieved July 12, 2007, from http://www.nsf.gov/statistics/wmpd

Natsuaki, M. N. Ge, X., Reiss, D., & Neiderhiser, J. M. (2009). Aggressive behavior between siblings and the development of externalizing problems: Evidence from a genetically sensitive study. *Developmental Psychology, 45*(4), 1009–1018.

Navarro, J., & Mora, J. (2011). Analysis of the implementation of a dynamic assessment device of processes involved in reading with learning-disabled children. *Learning and Individual Differences, 21*(2), 168–175. doi:10.1016/j.lindif.2010.11.008

Nayak, A., & Kehily, M. J. (2008). *Gender, youth and culture: Young masculinities and femininities.* Houndmills, Basingstoke, Hampshire, England: Palgrave Macmillan.

NCSS Task Force on Ethnic Studies Curriculum Guidelines. (1992). Curriculum guidelines for multicultural education. *Social Education, 56,* 274–294.

Needham, B. L., & Austin, E. L. (2010). Sexual orientation, parental support, and health during the transition to young adulthood. *Journal of Youth and Adolescence, 39*(10), 1189–1198. doi:10.1007/s10964-010-9533-6

Neinstein, L. S. (2004). *Substance abuse—Stimulants/inhalants/opioids/anabolic steroids/designer and club drugs. Adolescent health curriculum.* Retrieved February 1, 2008, from http://www.usc.edu/student-affairs/Health_Center/adolhealth/content/b8subs3.html

Neisser, U. (1976). *Cognition and reality.* San Francisco: Freeman.

Neisser, U. (1998a). Introduction: Rising test scores and what they mean. In U. Neisser (Ed.), *The rising curve: Long-term gains in IQ and related measures* (pp. 3–22). Washington, DC: American Psychological Association.

Neisser, U. (Ed.). (1998b). *The rising curve: Long-term gains in IQ and related measures.* Washington, DC: American Psychological Association.

Neisser, U., Boodoo, G., Bouchard, T. J., Boykin, A. W., Brody, N., Ceci, S. J., et al. (1996). Intelligence: Knowns and unknowns. *American Psychologist, 51,* 77–101.

Nelson, C. A. (2005, April). *Brain development and plasticity: Examples from the study of early institutional rearing.* Invited address at the Developmental Science Teaching Institute at the biennial meeting of the Society for Research in Child Development, Atlanta.

Nelson, C. A., & Fivush, R. (2004). The emergence of autobiographical memory: A social cultural developmental theory. *Psychological Review, 111,* 486–511.

Nelson, C. A., III, Thomas, K. M., & de Haan, M. (2006). Neural bases of cognitive development. In D. Kuhn & R. Siegler (Vol. Eds.), & W. Damon & R. M. Lerner (Series Eds.), *Handbook of child psychology. Vol. 2: Cognition, perception, and language* (6th ed., pp. 3–57). New York: Wiley.

Nelson, D. A., Robinson, C. C., Hart, C. H., Albano, A. D., & Marshall, S. J. (2010). Italian preschoolers' peer-status linkages with sociability and subtypes of aggression and victimization. *Social Development, 19*(4), 698–720. doi:10.1111/j.1467-9507.2009.00551.x

Nelson, K. (1973). Structure and strategy in learning to talk. *Monographs of the Society for Research in Child Development, 38*(1–2, Serial No. 149).

Nelson, K. (1996a). *Language in cognitive development: The emergence of the mediated mind.* Cambridge, England: Cambridge University Press.

Nelson, K. (1996b). Memory development from 4 to 7 years. In A. J. Sameroff & M. M. Haith (Eds.), *The 5 to 7 shift* (pp. 141–160). Chicago: University of Chicago Press.

Nelson, K. (1997). Event representations then, now, and next. In P. van den Broek, P. J. Bauer, & T. Bourg (Eds.), *Developmental spans in event representation and comprehension: Bridging fictional and actual events* (pp. 1–26). Mahwah, NJ: Erlbaum.

Nelson, K. (2005). Evolution and development of human memory systems. In B. J. Ellis & D. F. Bjorklund (Eds.), *Origins of the social mind: Evolutionary psychology and child development* (pp. 354–382). New York: Guilford Press.

Nelson, L. J., Hart, C. H., & Evans, C. A. (2008). Solitary-functional play and solitary-pretend play: Another look at the construct of solitary-active behavior using playground observations. *Social Development, 17*(4), 812–831.

Nelson, S. W., & Guerra, P. L. (2009). For diverse families, parent involvement takes on a new meaning. *Journal of Staff Development, 30*(4), 65–66.

Nesteruk, O., Marks, L., & Garrison, M. E. B. (2009). Immigrant parents' concerns regarding their children's education in the United States. *Family and Consumer Sciences Research Journal, 37*(4), 422–441.

Nettelbeck, T., & Wilson, C. (2005). Intelligence and IQ: What teachers should know. *Educational Psychology, 25*(6), 609–630.

Nevels, R. M., Dehon, E. E., Alexander, K., & Gontkovsky, S. T. (2010). Psychopharmacology of aggression in children and adolescents with primary neuropsychiatric disorders: A review of current and potentially promising treatment options. *Experimental and Clinical Psychopharmacology, 18*(2), 184–201.

Nevid, J. S., Rathus, S. A., & Greene, B. (2006). *Abnormal psychology in a changing world* (6th ed.). Upper Saddle River, NJ: Pearson Prentice Hall.

Neville, H. J., & Bavelier, D. (2001). Variability of developmental plasticity. In J. L. McClelland & R. S. Siegler (Eds.), *Mechanisms of cognitive development: Behavioral and neural perspectives* (pp. 271–287). Mahwah, NJ: Erlbaum.

Newcomb, A. F., & Bagwell, C. L. (1995). Children's friendship relations: A meta-analysis review. *Psychological Bulletin, 117,* 306–347.

Newcomb, A. F., & Brady, J. E. (1982). Mutuality in boys' friendship relations. *Child Development, 53,* 392–395.

Newcomb, A. F., & Bukowski, W. M. (1984). A longitudinal study of the utility of social preference and social impact sociometric classification schemes. *Child Development, 55,* 1434–1447.

Newcomb, A. F., Bukowski, W. M., & Pattee, L. (1993). Children's peer relations: A meta-analytic review of popular, rejected, controversial, and average sociometric status. *Psychological Bulletin, 113,* 99–128.

Newcombe, N. S., Sluzenski, J., & Huttenlocher, J. (2005). Preexisting knowledge versus on-line learning: What do young infants really know about spatial location? *Psychological Science, 16,* 222–227.

Newell, G. E., Koukis, S., & Boster, S. (2007). Best practices in developing a writing across the curriculum program in the secondary school. In S. Graham, C. A. MacArthur, & J. Fitzgerald (Eds.), *Best practices in writing instruction: Solving problems in the teaching of literacy* (pp. 74–98). New York: Guilford.

Newkirk, T. (2002). *Misreading masculinity: Boys, literacy, and popular culture.* Portsmouth, NH: Heinemann.

Newman, A. J., Supalla, T., Hauser, P. C., Newport, E. L., & Bavelier, D. (2010). Prosodic and narrative processing in American Sign Language: An fMRI study. *NeuroImage, 52*(2), 669–676.

Newman, L. S. (1990). Intentional and unintentional memory in young children: Remembering vs. playing. *Journal of Experimental Child Psychology, 50,* 243–258.

Newman, R. S., & Schwager, M. T. (1992). Student perceptions and academic help seeking. In D. Schunk & J. Meece (Eds.), *Student perceptions in the classroom.* Hillsdale, NJ: Erlbaum.

Newman, S. (2001). *Parenting and only child: The joys and challenges of raising your one and only.* New York: Broadway Books.

Newport, E. L. (1990). Maturational constraints on language learning. *Cognitive Science, 14,* 11–28.

Newson, J., & Newson, E. (1975). Intersubjectivity and the transmission of culture: On the origins of symbolic functioning. *Bulletin of the British Psychological Society, 28,* 437–446.

Nguyen, P. V. (2008). Perceptions of Vietnamese fathers' acculturation levels, parenting styles, and mental health outcomes in Vietnamese American adolescent immigrants. *Social Work, 53*(4), 337–346.

Ni, Y., & Zhou, Y.-D. (2005). Teaching and learning fraction and rational numbers: The origins and implications of whole number bias. *Educational Psychologist, 40,* 27–52.

NICHD Early Child Care Research Network. (1997). The effects of infant child care on infant–mother attachment security: Results of the NICHD study of early child care. *Child Development, 68,* 860–879.

NICHD Early Child Care Research Network. (2002). Early child care and children's development prior to school entry: Results from the NICHD study of early child care. *American Educational Research Journal, 39*(1), 133–164.

NICHD Early Child Care Research Network. (2005). Early child care and children's development in the primary grades: Follow-up results from the NICHD study of early child care. *American Educational Research Journal, 42*(3), 537–570.

NICHD Early Child Care Research Network. (2006a). Child-care effect sizes for the NICHD Study of Early Child Care and Youth Development. *American Psychologist, 61,* 99–116.

NICHD Early Child Care Research Network. (2006b). Infant–mother attachment classification: Risk and protection in relation to changing maternal caregiving quality. *Developmental Psychology, 42,* 38–58.

Nicholls, J. G. (1984). Conceptions of ability and achievement motivation. In R. Ames & C. Ames (Eds.), *Research on motivation in education: Vol. 1. Student motivation.* San Diego, CA: Academic Press.

Nicholls, J. G. (1990). What is ability and why are we mindful of it? A developmental perspective. In R. J. Sternberg & J. Kolligian (Eds.), *Competence considered.* New Haven, CT: Yale University Press.

Nicholls, J. G., Cobb, P., Yackel, E., Wood, T., & Wheatley, G. (1990). Students' theories of mathematics and their mathematical knowledge: Multiple dimensions of assessment. In G. Kulm (Ed.), *Assessing higher order thinking in mathematics.* Washington, DC: American Association for the Advancement of Science.

Nichols, M. L., & Ganschow, L. (1992). Has there been a paradigm shift in gifted education? In N. Coangelo, S. G. Assouline, & D. L. Ambroson (Eds.), *Talent development: Proceedings from the 1991 Henry B. and Jocelyn Wallace National Research Symposium on Talent Development.* New York: Trillium.

Nichter, M., Nichter, M., Muramoto, M., Adrian, S., Goldade, K., Tesler, L., et al. (2007). Smoking among low-income pregnant women: An ethnographic analysis. *Health Education and Behavior, 34*(5), 748–764.

Nickerson, A. B., & Nagle, R. J. (2005). Parent and peer attachment in late childhood and early adolescence. *Journal of Early Adolescence, 25,* 223–249.

Nickerson, R. S. (2010). *Mathematical reasoning: Patterns, problems, conjectures, and proofs.* New York: Psychology Press.

Nicolopoulou, A., & Richner, E. S. (2007). From actors to agents to persons: The development of character representation in young children's narratives. *Child Development, 78,* 412–429.

Nicolson, S., & Shipstead, S. G. (2002). *Through the looking glass: Observations in the early childhood classroom* (3rd ed.). Upper Saddle River, NJ: Merrill/Prentice Hall.

Nicpon, M. F., Doobay, A. F., & Assouline, S. G. (2010). Parent, teacher, and self perceptions of psychosocial functioning in intellectually gifted children and adolescents with autism spectrum disorder. *Journal of Autism and Developmental Disorders, 40*(8), 1028–1038. doi:10.1007/s10803-010-0952-8

Nieto, S. (1995). *Affirming diversity* (2nd ed.). White Plains, NY: Longman.

Nievar, M. A., & Becker, B. J. (2008). Sensitivity as a privileged predictor of attachment: A second perspective on De Wolff and van IJzendoorn's meta-analysis. *Social Development, 17,* 102–114.

Nigg, J. T., Nikolas, M., Knottnerus, G. M., Cavanagh, K., & Friderici, K. (2010). Confirmation and extension of association of blood lead with attention-deficit/hyperactivity disorder (ADHD) and ADHD symptom domains at population-typical exposure levels. *Journal of Child Psychology and Psychiatry, 51*(1), 58–65.

Nilsson, D. E., & Bradford, L. W. (1999). Neurofibromatosis. In S. Goldstein & C. R. Reynolds (Eds.), *Handbook of neurodevelopmental and genetic disorders* (pp. 350–367). New York: Guilford Press.

Nippold, M. A. (1988). The literate lexicon. In M. A. Nippold (Ed.), *Later language development: Ages nine through nineteen.* Boston: Little, Brown.

Nippold, M. A., & Taylor, C. L. (1995). Idiom understanding in youth: Further examination of familiarity and transparency. *Journal of Speech and Hearing Research, 38,* 426–433.

Nippold, M. A., Ward-Lonergan, J. M., & Fanning, J. L. (2005). Persuasive writing in children, adolescents, and adults: A study of syntactic, semantic, and pragmatic development. *Language, Speech, and Hearing Services in Schools, 36*(2), 125–138.

Nisbett, R. E. (2005). Heredity, environment, and race: Differences in IQ: A commentary on Rushton and Jensen. *Psychology, Public Policy, and Law, 11,* 302–310.

Nisbett, R. E. (2009). *Intelligence and how to get it: Why schools and cultures count.* New York: W. W. Norton.

Noffke, S. (1997). Professional, personal, and political dimensions of action research. *Review of Research in Education, 22,* 305–343.

Noguera, P. A. (2003). "Joachín's dilemma": Understanding the link between racial identity and school-related behaviors. In M. Sadowski (Eds.), *Adolescents at school: Perspectives on youth, identity, and education* (pp. 19–30). Cambridge, MA: Harvard Education Press.

Nokes, J. D., Dole, J. A., & Hacker, D. J. (2007). Teaching high school students to use heuristics while reading historical texts. *Journal of Educational Psychology, 99,* 492–504.

Nolen-Hoeksema, S., Morrow, J., & Fredrickson, B. L. (1993). Response styles and the duration of episodes of depressed moods. *Journal of Abnormal Psychology, 102,* 20–28.

Nomura, Y., Fifer, W., & Brooks-Gunn, J. (2005). *The role of perinatal factors for risk of co-occurring psychiatric and medical disorders in adulthood.* Paper presented at the biennial meeting of the Society for Research in Child Development, Atlanta, GA.

Norenzayan, A., Choi, I., & Peng, K. (2007). Perception and cognition. In S. Kitayama & D. Cohen (Eds.), *Handbook of cultural psychology* (pp. 569–594). New York: Guilford Press.

North Central Regional Educational Laboratory. (2008). Implementing the No Child Left Behind Act: Implications for rural schools and districts. Retrieved August 12, 2008, from http://www.ncrel .org/policy/pubs/html/implicate/challenge.htm

Nucci, L. P. (2001). *Education in the moral domain.* Cambridge, England: Cambridge University Press.

Nucci, L. P. (2006). Education for moral development. In M. Killen & J. G. Smetana (Eds.), *Handbook of moral development* (pp. 657–681). Mahwah, NJ: Erlbaum.

Nucci, L. P. (2009). *Nice is not enough: Facilitating moral development.* Upper Saddle River, NJ: Pearson Education.

Nucci, L. P., & Weber, E. K. (1991). The domain approach to values education: From theory to practice. In W. M. Kurtines & J. L. Gewirtz (Eds.), *Handbook of moral behavior and development: Vol. 3. Application* (pp. 251–266). Hillsdale, NJ: Erlbaum.

Nucci, L. P., & Weber, E. K. (1995). Social interactions in the home and the development of young children's conceptions of the personal. *Child Development, 66,* 1438–1452.

Nuijens, K. L., Teglasi, H., & Hancock, G. R. (2009). Self-perceptions, discrepancies between self- and other-perceptions, and children's self-reported emotions. *Journal of Psychoeducational Assessment, 27*(6), 477–493.

Nunner-Winkler, G. (1984). Two moralities? A critical discussion of an ethic of care and responsibility versus an ethic of rights and justice. In W. M. Kurtines & J. L. Gewirtz (Eds.), *Morality, moral behavior, and moral development.* New York: Wiley.

Nunner-Winkler, G. (2007). Development of moral motivation from childhood to early adulthood. *Journal of Moral Education, 36*(4), 399–414. doi:10.1080/03057240701687970

Nuttall, R. L., Casey, M. B., & Pezaris, E. (2005). Spatial ability as mediator of gender differences on mathematics tests. In A. M. Gallagher & J. C. Kaufman (Eds.), *Gender differences in mathematics: An integrative psychological approach* (pp. 121–142). Cambridge, England: Cambridge University Press.

Oakes, J., & Guiton, G. (1995). Matchmaking: The dynamics of high school tracking decisions. *American Educational Research Journal, 32,* 3–33.

Oakes, L. M., & Rakison, D. H. (2003). Issues in the early development of concepts and categories: An introduction. In D. H. Rakison & L. M. Oakes (Eds.), *Early category and concept development: Making sense of the blooming, buzzing confusion* (pp. 3–23). Oxford, England: Oxford University Press.

Oberheim, N. A., Takano, T., Han, X., He, W., Lin, J. H. C., Wang, F., et al. (2009). Uniquely hominid features of adult human astrocytes. *Journal of Neuroscience, 29*(10), 3276–3287.

Obradović, J., Long, J. D., Cutuli, J. J., Chan, C., Hinz, E., Heistad, D., et al. (2009). Academic achievement of homeless and highly mobile children in an urban school district: Longitudinal evidence on risk, growth, and resilience. *Development and Psychopathology, 21*(2), 493–518.

O'Brennan, L. M., & Furlong, M. J. (2010). Relations between students' perceptions of school connectedness and peer victimization. *Journal of School Violence, 9*(4), 375–391. doi:10.1080/15388220 .2010.509009

Ochs, E. (2002). Becoming a speaker of culture. In C. Kramsch (Ed.), *Language acquisition and language socialization* (pp. 99–120). London: Continuum.

Ochs, E., & Schieffelin, B. (1995). The impact of language socialization on grammatical development. In P. Fletcher & B. MacWhinney (Eds.), *The handbook of child language.* Cambridge, MA: Blackwell.

O'Connell, D. C., & Kowal, S. (2008). *Communicating with one another: Toward a psychology of spontaneous spoken discourse.* New York: Springer Science + Business Media.

O'Connor, E., & McCartney, K. (2006). Testing associations between young children's relationships with mothers and teachers. *Journal of Educational Psychology, 98,* 87–98.

O'Connor, T. G., & Hirsch, N. (1999). Intra-individual differences and relationship-specificity of mentalising in early adolescence. *Social Development, 8*(2), 256–274. doi:10.1111/1467-9507.00094

Odendaal, W., van Niekerk, A., Jordaan, E., & Seedat, M. (2009). The impact of a home visitation programme on household hazards associated with unintentional childhood injuries: A randomised controlled trial. *Accident Analysis and Prevention, 41,* 183–190.

O'Donnell, L. (2009). The Wechsler Intelligence Scale for Children-Fourth Edition. In J. A. Naglieri & S. Goldstein (Eds.), *Practitioner's guide to assessing intelligence and achievement* (pp. 153–190). Hoboken, NJ: Wiley.

Office for Human Research Protections. (2008). *Special protections for children as research subjects.* Retrieved November 17, 2009, from http://www .hhs.gov/ohrp/children

Ogbu, J. U. (1994). From cultural differences to differences in cultural frames of reference. In P. M. Greenfield & R. R. Cocking (Eds.), *Cross-cultural roots of minority child development* (pp. 365–391). Hillsdale, NJ: Erlbaum.

Ogbu, J. U. (1999). Beyond language: Ebonics, proper English, and identity in a Black-American speech community. *American Educational Research Journal, 36,* 147–184.

Ogbu, J. U. (2003). *Black American students in an affluent suburb: A study of academic disengagement.* Mahwah, NJ: Erlbaum.

Ogden, C. L., Carroll, M. D., Curtin, L. R., Lamb, M. M., & Flegal, K. M. (2010). Prevalence of high body mass index in U.S. children and adolescents, 2007–2008. *Journal of the American Medical Association, 303*(3), 242–249.

Ogden, E. H., & Germinario, V. (1988). *The at-risk student: Answers for educators.* Lancaster, PA: Technomic.

Ogliari, A., Spatola, C. A., Pesenti-Gritti, P., Medda, E., Penna, L., Stazi, M. A., Battaglia, M., & Fagnani, C. (2010). The role of genes and environment in shaping co-occurrence of DSM-IV defined anxiety dimensions among Italian twins aged 8–17. *Journal of Anxiety Disorders, 24*(4), 433–439.

O'Grady, W. (1997). *Syntactic development.* Chicago: University of Chicago Press.

Oguntoyinbo, L. (2009). Disappearing act. *Diverse Issues in Higher Education, 26*(16), 14–15.

Ohgi, S., Akiyama, T., & Fukuda, M. (2005). Neurobehavioural profile of low-birthweight infants with cystic periventricular leukomalacia. *Developmental Medicine and Child Neurology, 47,* 221–228.

Okagaki, L. (2001). Triarchic model of minority children's school achievement. *Educational Psychologist, 36,* 9–20.

Okagaki, L. (2006). Ethnicity and learning. In P. A. Alexander & P. H. Winne (Eds.), *Handbook of educational psychology* (2nd ed., pp. 615–634). Mahwah, NJ: Erlbaum.

Oldfather, P., & West, J. (1999). *Learning through children's eyes: Social constructivism and the desire to learn.* Washington, DC: American Psychological Association.

O'Leary, K. D., & O'Leary, S. G. (Eds.). (1972). *Classroom management: The successful use of behavior modification.* New York: Pergamon Press.

O'Leary, S. G., & Vidair, H. B. (2005). Marital adjustment, child-rearing disagreements, and overreactive parenting: Predicting child behavior problems. *Journal of Family Psychology, 19,* 208–216.

Olive, T., Favart, M., Beauvais, C., & Beauvais, L. (2009). Children's cognitive effort and fluency in writing: Effects of genre and of handwriting automatisation. *Learning and Instruction, 19*(4), 299–308.

Ollendick, T. H., Costa, N. M., & Benoit, K. E. (2010). Interpersonal processes and the anxiety disorders of childhood. In J. G. Beck (Ed.), *Interpersonal processes in the anxiety disorders: Implications for understanding psychopathology and treatment* (pp. 71–95). Washington, DC: American Psychological Association.

Olmedo, I. M. (2009). Blending borders of language and culture: Schooling in La Villita. *Journal of Latinos and Education, 8*(1), 22–37.

Olmsted, B. J. (2008). *The effects of interactive video (DDR) on heart rate, perceived exertion, step count, self-efficacy, and enjoyment in elementary school children. Dissertation Abstracts International Section A: Humanities and Social Sciences, 68*(8-A).

Olshansky, B. (1995). Picture this: An arts-based literacy program. *Educational Leadership, 53*(1), 44–47.

Olshansky, B., O'Connor, S., & O'Byrne, S. (2006, April). *Picture writing: Fostering literacy through art—diverse perspectives.* Paper presented at the annual meeting of the American Educational Research Association, San Francisco, CA.

Olson, C. K. (2010). Children's motivations for video game play in the context of normal development. *Review of General Psychology, 14*(2), 180–187. doi:10.1037/a0018984

Olson, L., Evans, J., & Keckler, W. (2006). Precocious Readers: Past, Present, and Future. *Journal for the Education of the Gifted, 30*(2), 205–235.

Olson, R. K. (2008). Genetic and environmental influences on word-reading skills. In E. L. Grigorenko & A. J. Naples (Eds.), *Single-word reading: Behavioral and biological perspectives. New directions in communication disorders research: Integrative approaches* (pp. 233–253). Mahwah, NJ: Erlbaum.

Olthof, T. (2010). Conscience in the classroom: Early adolescents' moral emotions, moral judgments, and moral identity as predictors of their interpersonal behaviour. In W. Koops, D. Brugman, T. J. Ferguson & A. F. Sanders (Eds.), *The development and structure of conscience* (pp. 327–341). New York: Psychology Press.

Oltmanns, T. F., & Emery, R. E. (2007). *Abnormal psychology* (5th ed.). Upper Saddle River, NJ: Pearson Prentice Hall.

O'Malley, P. M., & Bachman, J. G. (1983). Self-esteem: Change and stability between ages 13 and 23. *Developmental Psychology, 19,* 257–268.

Oortwijn, M. B., Boekaerts, M., Vedder, P., & Fortuin, J. (2008). The impact of a cooperative learning experience on pupils' popularity, non-cooperativeness, and interethnic bias in multiethnic elementary schools. *Educational Psychology, 28*(2), 211–221.

Oppenheim, D., Koren-Karie, N., Dolev, S., & Yirmiya, N. (2008). Secure attachment in children with autism spectrum disorders. *Zero to Three, 28*(4), 25–30.

O'Reilly, A. W. (1995). Using representations: Comprehension and production of actions with imagined objects. *Child Development, 66,* 999–1010.

Orme, J. G., & Buehler, C. (2001). Foster family characteristics and behavioral and emotional problems of foster children: A narrative review. *Family Relations, 50,* 3–15.

Ormrod, J. E. (2008). *Human learning* (5th ed.). Upper Saddle River, NJ: Merrill/Prentice Hall.

Ormrod, J. E. (2011). *Educational psychology: Developing learners* (7th ed.). Boston: Pearson/Allyn & Bacon.

Ormrod, J. E., Jackson, D. L., Kirby, B., Davis, J., & Benson, C. (1999, April). *Cognitive development as reflected in children's conceptions of early American history.* Paper presented at the annual meeting of the American Educational Research Association, Montreal, Canada.

Ormrod, J. E., & McGuire, D. J. (2007). *Case studies: Applying educational psychology* (2nd ed.). Upper Saddle River, NJ: Merrill/Prentice Hall.

Ornstein, P. A., & Haden, C. A. (2009). Developments in the study of the development of memory. In M. L. Courage & N. Cowan (Eds.), *The development of memory in infancy and childhood* (2nd ed., pp. 367–385). New York: Psychology Press.

Ornstein, P. A., Coffman, J. L., & Grammer, J. K. (2009). Learning to remember. In O. A. Barbarin & B. H. Wasik (Eds.), *Handbook of child development and early education: Research to practice* (pp. 103–122). New York: Guilford Press.

Ornstein, P. A., Grammer, J. K., & Coffman, J. L. (2010). Teachers' "mnemonic style" and the development of skilled memory. In H. S. Waters, & W. Schneider (Eds.), *Metacognition, strategy use, and instruction.* (pp. 23–53). New York: Guilford Press

Ornstein, R. (1997). *The right mind: Making sense of the hemispheres.* San Diego, CA: Harcourt Brace.

Ortony, A., Turner, T. J., & Larson-Shapiro, N. (1985). Cultural and instructional influences on figurative comprehension by inner city children. *Research in the Teaching of English, 19*(1), 25–36.

Oskamp, S. (Ed.). (2000). *Reducing prejudice and discrimination.* Mahwah, NJ: Erlbaum.

Ostad, S. A., & Askeland, M. (2008). Sound-based number facts training in a private speech internalization perspective: Evidence for effectiveness of an intervention in grade 3. *Journal of Research in Childhood Education, 23*(1), 109–124.

Osterman, K. F. (2000). Students' need for belonging in the school community. *Review of Educational Research, 70,* 323–367.

Ostrov, J. M., & Godleski, S. A. (2010). Toward an integrated gender-linked model of aggression subtypes in early and middle childhood. *Psychological Review, 117*(1), 233–242. doi:10.1037/a0018070

O'Sullivan-Lago, R., & de Abreu, G. (2010). The dialogical self in a cultural contact zone: Exploring the perceived 'cultural correction' function of schooling. *Journal of Community and Applied Social Psychology, 20,* 275–287.

Otis, N., Grouzet, F. M. E., & Pelletier, L. G. (2005). Latent motivational change in an academic setting: A 3-year longitudinal study. *Journal of Educational Psychology, 97,* 170–183.

O'Toole, M. E. (2000). *The school shooter: A threat assessment perspective.* Quantico, VA: Federal Bureau of Investigation. Retrieved February 26, 2004, from http://www.fbi.gov/publications/school/school2.pdf

Otto, B. (2010). *Language development in early childhood* (3rd ed.). Upper Saddle River, NJ: Merrill Pearson.

Owens, R. E., Jr. (1996). *Language development* (4th ed.). Boston: Allyn & Bacon.

Owens, R. E., Jr. (2008). *Language development* (7th ed.). Boston: Allyn & Bacon.

Oyserman, D., & Lee, S. W.-S. (2007). Priming "culture": Culture as situated cognition. In S. Kitayama & D. Cohen (Eds.), *Handbook of cultural psychology* (pp. 255–279). New York: Guilford Press.

Oyserman, D., & Markus, H. R. (1993). The sociocultural self. In J. Suls (Ed.), *Psychological perspectives on the self* (Vol. 7, pp. 187–220). Mahwah, NJ: Erlbaum.

Ozdemir, A. (2008). Shopping malls: Measuring interpersonal distance under changing conditions and across cultures. *Field Methods, 20*(3), 226–248.

Ozdemir, M. (2010). *Predictors and outcomes of adolescent self-efficacy beliefs: An analysis of individual, peer, family, and neighborhood level variables* (ProQuest Information & Learning). *Dissertation Abstracts International: Section B: The Sciences and Engineering, 70.* Retrieved from http://www.csa.com. (2010-99040-476)

Ozechowski, T. J., & Waldron, H. B. (2010). Assertive outreach strategies for narrowing the adolescence substance abuse treatment gap: Implications for research, practice, and policy. *Journal of Behavioral Health Services and Research, 37*(1), 40–63.

Ozonoff, S. (2010). Autism spectrum disorders. In K. O. Yeates, M. D. Ris, H. G. Taylor, & B. F. Pennington (Eds.), *Pediatric neuropsychology: Research, theory, and practice* (pp. 418–446). New York: Guilford Press.

Padilla, A. M. (2006). Second language learning: Issues in research and teaching. In P. A. Alexander & P. H. Winne (Eds.), *Handbook of educational psychology* (2nd ed., pp. 571–591). Mahwah, NJ: Erlbaum.

Padilla, M. J. (1991). Science activities, process skills, and thinking. In S. M. Glynn, R. H. Yeany, & B. K. Britton (Eds.), *The psychology of learning science.* Hillsdale, NJ: Erlbaum.

Padilla-Walker, L. M., & Carlo, G. (2007). Personal values as a mediator between parent and peer expectations and adolescent behaviors. *Journal of Family Psychology, 21,* 538–541.

Paget, K. F., Kritt, D., & Bergemann, L. (1984). Understanding strategic interactions in television commercials: A developmental study. *Journal of Applied Developmental Psychology, 5,* 145–161.

Page-Voth, V., & Graham, S. (1999). Effects of goal setting and strategy use on the writing performance and self-efficacy of students with writing and learning problems. *Journal of Educational Psychology, 91,* 230–240.

Pahl, K., & Way, N. (2006). Longitudinal trajectories of ethnic identity among urban Black and Latino adolescents. *Child Development, 77,* 1403–1415.

Paikoff, R. L., & Brooks-Gunn, J. (1991). Do parent–child relationships change during puberty? *Psychological Bulletin, 110,* 47–66.

Pajares, F. (2005). Gender differences in mathematics self-efficacy beliefs. In A. M. Gallagher & J. C. Kaufman (Eds.), *Gender differences in mathematics: An integrative psychological approach* (pp. 294–315). Cambridge, England: Cambridge University Press.

Pajares, F., & Valiante, G. (1999). *Writing self-efficacy of middle school students: Relation to motivation constructs, achievement, gender, and gender orientation.* Paper presented at the annual meeting of the American Educational Research Association, Montreal, Canada.

Palacios, J., & Sánchez-Sandoval, Y. (2005). Beyond adopted/nonadopted comparisons. In D. M. Brodzinsky & J. Palacios (Eds.), *Psychological issues in adoption: Research and practice* (pp. 117–144). Westport, CT: Praeger/Greenwood.

Palermo, D. S. (1974). Still more about the comprehension of "less." *Developmental Psychology, 10,* 827–829.

Paley, V. G. (1984). *Boys and girls: Superheroes in the doll corner.* Chicago: University of Chicago Press.

Paley, V. G. (2007). Goldilocks and her sister: An anecdotal guide to the doll corner. *Harvard Educational Review, 77*(2), 144–151.

Palincsar, A. S., & Brown, A. L. (1984). Reciprocal teaching of comprehension-fostering and comprehension-monitoring activities. *Cognition and Instruction, 1,* 117–175.

Palincsar, A. S., & Brown, A. L. (1989). Classroom dialogues to promote self-regulated comprehension. In J. Brophy (Ed.), *Advances in research on teaching* (Vol. 1). Greenwich, CT: JAI Press.

Palincsar, A. S., & Herrenkohl, L. R. (1999). Designing collaborative contexts: Lessons from three research programs. In A. M. O'Donnell & A. King (Eds.), *Cognitive perspectives on peer learning* (pp. 151–177). Mahwah, NJ: Erlbaum.

Pallotta, J., & Masiello, R. (Illustrator). (1992). *The icky bug counting book*. Watertown, MA: Charlesbridge.

Pallotta, J., & Mazzola, F., Jr. (Illustrator). (1986). *The ocean alphabet book*. Watertown, MA: Charlesbridge.

Palmer, E. L. (1965). Accelerating the child's cognitive attainments through the inducement of cognitive conflict: An interpretation of the Piagetian position. *Journal of Research in Science Teaching, 3*, 324.

Pan, B. A., Rowe, M. L., Singer, J. D., & Snow, C. E. (2005). Maternal correlates of growth in toddler vocabulary production in low-income families. *Child Development, 76*, 763–782.

Pang, V. O. (1995). Asian Pacific American students: A diverse and complex population. In J. A. Banks & C. A. M. Banks (Eds.), *Handbook of research on multicultural education*. New York: Macmillan.

Pangrazi, R. P., & Beighle, A. (2010). *Dynamic physical education for elementary school children* (16th ed.). San Francisco: Pearson Benjamin Cummings.

Panksepp, J. (1986). The psychobiology of prosocial behaviors: Separation distress, play, and altruism. In C. Zahn-Waxler, E. M. Cummings, & R. Iannotti (Eds.), *Altruism and aggression: Biological and social origins* (pp. 19–57). Cambridge, England: Cambridge University Press.

Panksepp, J. (1998). Attention deficit hyperactivity disorders, psychostimulants, and intolerance of childhood playfulness: A tragedy in the making? *Current Directions in Psychological Science, 7*, 91–98.

Panofsky, C. P. (1994). Developing the representational functions of language: The role of parent–child book-reading activity. In V. John-Steiner, C. P. Panofsky, & L. W. Smith (Eds.), *Sociocultural approaches to language and literacy: An interactionist perspective*. Cambridge, England: Cambridge University Press.

Pan-Skadden, J., Wilder, D. A., Sparling, J., Severtson, E., Donaldson, J., Postma, N., et al. (2009). The use of behavioral skills training and in-situ training to teach children to solicit help when lost: A Preliminary investigation. *Education and Treatment of Children, 32*(3), 359–370.

Paradise, R., & Rogoff, B. (2009). Side by side: Learning by observing and pitching in. *Ethos, 37*(1), 102–138.

Paris, D. (2009). "They're in my culture, they speak the same way": African American language in multiethnic high schools. *Harvard Educational Review, 79*(3), 428–447.

Paris, S. G., & Ayres, L. R. (1994). *Becoming reflective students and teachers with portfolios and authentic assessment*. Washington, DC: American Psychological Association.

Paris, S. G., & Byrnes, J. P. (1989). The constructivist approach to self-regulation and learning in the classroom. In B. J. Zimmerman & D. H. Schunk (Eds.), *Self-regulated learning and academic achievement: Theory, research, and practice*. New York: Springer-Verlag.

Paris, S. G., & Cunningham, A. E. (1996). Children becoming students. In D. C. Berliner & R. C. Calfee (Eds.), *Handbook of educational psychology*. New York: Macmillan.

Paris, S. G., Morrison, F. J., & Miller, K. F. (2006). Academic pathways from preschool through elementary school. In P. A. Alexander & P. H. Winne (Eds.), *Handbook of educational psychology* (2nd ed., pp. 61–85). Mahwah, NJ: Erlbaum.

Paris, S. G., & Turner, J. C. (1994). Situated motivation. In P. R. Pintrich, D. R. Brown, & C. E. Weinstein (Eds.), *Student motivation, cognition, and learning: Essays in honor of Wilbert J. McKeachie*. Mahwah, NJ: Erlbaum.

Paris, S. G., & Upton, L. R. (1976). Children's memory for inferential relationships in prose. *Child Development, 47*, 660–668.

Parish, P., & Sweat, L. (2003). *Amelia Bedelia goes camping*. New York: HarperCollins.

Park, L. E., Crocker, J., & Vohs, K. D. (2006). Contingencies of self-worth and self-validation goals: Implications for close relationships. In K. D. Vohs & E. J. Finkel (Eds.), *Self and relationships: Connecting intrapersonal and interpersonal processes* (pp. 84–103). New York: Guilford Press.

Parke, R. D., & Buriel, R. (2006). Socialization in the family: Ethnic and ecological perspectives. In W. Damon & R. M. Lerner (Eds. in Chief) & N. Eisenberg (Vol. Ed.), *Handbook of child psychology: Vol. 3. Social, emotional, and personality development* (6th ed., pp. 429–504). Hoboken, NJ: Wiley.

Parke, R. D., & Clarke-Stewart, A. (2011). *Social development*. Hoboken, NJ: Wiley.

Parke, R. D., Ornstein, P. A., Rieser, J. J., & Zahn-Waxler, C. (1994). The past as prologue: An overview of a century of developmental psychology. In R. D. Parke, P. A. Ornstein, J. J. Rieser, & C. Zahn-Waxler (Eds.), *A century of developmental psychology* (pp. 1–70). Washington, DC: American Psychological Association.

Parker, A. K. (2009). Elementary organizational structures and young adolescents' self-concept and classroom environment perceptions across the transition to middle school. *Journal of Research in Childhood Education, 23*(3), 325–339.

Parker, J. G. (1986). Becoming friends: Conversational skills for friendship formation in young children. In J. M. Gottman & J. G. Parker (Eds.), *Conversations of friends: Speculations on affective development* (pp. 103–138). Cambridge, England: Cambridge University Press.

Parker, J. G., & Gottman, J. M. (1989). Social and emotional development in a relational context: Friendship interaction from early childhood to adolescence. In T. J. Berndt & G. W. Ladd (Eds.), *Peer relations in child development* (pp. 95–131). New York: Wiley.

Parker, J. G., Kruse, S. A., & Aikins, J. W. (2010). When friends have other friends: Friendship jealousy in childhood and early adolescence. In S. L. Hart & M. Legerstee (Eds.), *Handbook of jealousy: Theory, research, and multidisciplinary approaches* (pp. 516–546). Chichester, UK/Malden, MA: Wiley-Blackwell. doi:10.1002/9781444323542.ch22

Parker, J. G., Low, C. M., Walker, A. R., & Gamm, B. K. (2005). Friendship jealousy in young adolescents: Individual differences and links to sex, self-esteem, aggression, and social adjustment. *Developmental Psychology, 41*, 235–250.

Parker, W. D. (1997). An empirical typology of perfectionism in academically talented children. *American Educational Research Journal, 34*, 545–562.

Parkhurst, J., & Gottman, J. M. (1986). How young children get what they want. In J. M. Gottman & J. G. Parker (Eds.), *Conversations of friends: Speculations on affective development* (pp. 315–345). Cambridge, England: Cambridge University Press.

Parkhurst, J. T., & Hopmeyer, A. (1998). Socio-metric popularity and peer-perceived popularity: Two distinct dimensions of peer status. *Journal of Early Adolescence, 18*, 125–144.

Parks, C. P. (1995). Gang behavior in the schools: Reality or myth? *Educational Psychology Review, 7*, 41–68.

Parten, M. B. (1932). Social participation among preschool children. *Journal of Abnormal and Social Psychology, 27*, 243–269.

Parton, B. S., & Hancock, R. (2008, September/October). When physical and digital worlds collide: A tool for early childhood learners. *TechTrends, 52*(5), 22–25.

Pascarella, E. T., & Terenzini, P. T. (1991). *How college affects students: Findings and insights from twenty years of research*. San Francisco: Jossey-Bass.

Pascual-Leone, J. (1970). A mathematical model for the transition rule in Piaget's developmental stages. *Acta Psychologica, 32*, 301–345.

Patall, E. A., Cooper, H., & Wynn, S. (2008, March). *The importance of providing choices in the classroom*. Paper presented at the annual meeting of the American Educational Research Association, New York.

Pate, R. R., Long, B. J., & Heath, G. (1994). Descriptive epidemiology of physical activity in adolescents. *Pediatric Exercise Science, 6*, 434–447.

Patrick, H., Mantzicopoulos, Y., & Samarapungavan, A. (2008, March). *Sex differences in young children's motivation for science*. Poster presented at the annual meeting of the American Educational Research Association, New York.

Patterson, C. J. (1995). Sexual orientation and human development: An overview. *Developmental Psychology, 31*, 3–11.

Patterson, C. J. (2009). Children of lesbian and gay parents: Psychology, law, and policy. *American Psychologist, 64*(8), 727–736.

Patterson, C. J., & Hastings, P. D. (2007). Socialization in the context of family diversity. In J. E. Grusec & P. D. Hastings (Eds.), *Handbook of socialization: Theory and research* (pp. 328–351). New York: Guilford.

Patterson, G. R., DeBaryshe, B. D., & Ramsey, E. (1989). A developmental perspective on antisocial behavior. *American Psychologist, 44*, 329–335.

Patterson, G. R., & Reid, J. B. (1970). Reciprocity and coercion: Two facets of social systems. In C. Neuringer & J. Michael (Eds.), *Behavior modification in clinical psychology*. New York: Appleton-Century-Crofts.

Patton, J. R., Blackbourn, J. M., & Fad, K. (1996). *Exceptional individuals in focus* (6th ed.). Upper Saddle River, NJ: Merrill/Prentice Hall.

Paul, R. (1990). Comprehension strategies: Interactions between world knowledge and the development of sentence comprehension. *Topics in Language Disorders, 10*(3), 63–75.

Paus, T. (2005). Brain mapping. In C. B. Fisher & R. M. Lerner (Eds.). *Encyclopedia of applied developmental science* (Vol. 1, pp. 178–181). Thousand Oaks, CA: Sage.

Pavey, L., Greitemeyer, T., & Sparks, P. (2011). Highlighting Relatedness Promotes Prosocial Motives and Behavior. *Personality and Social Psychology Bulletin, 37*(7), 905–917. doi:10.1177/014616721405994

Pawlas, G. E. (1994). Homeless students at the school door. *Educational Leadership, 51*(8), 79–82.

Payne, R. K., DeVol, P., & Smith, R. D. (2006). *Bridges out of poverty: Strategies for professionals and communities*. Highlands, TX: aha! Process.

PE 4 Life (n.d.). *The First Choice physical fitness program*. Retrieved September 26, 2008, from http://www.pe4life.org/UserFiles/File/FirstChoice.pdf

Pea, R. D. (1993). Practices of distributed intelligence and designs for education. In G. Salomon (Ed.), *Distributed cognitions: Psychological and educational considerations*. Cambridge, England: Cambridge University Press.

Peak, L. (1993). Academic effort in international perspective. In T. M. Tomlinson (Ed.), *Motivating students to learn: Overcoming barriers to high achievement*. Berkeley, CA: McCutchan.

Peak, L. (2001). Learning to become part of the group: The Japanese child's transition to preschool. In H. Shimizu & R. A. Levine (Eds.), *Japanese frames of mind: Cultural perspectives on human development* (pp. 143–169). New York: Cambridge University Press.

Pearson, B. Z., Velleman, S. L., Bryant, T. J., & Charko, T. (2009). Phonological milestones for African American English-speaking children learning Mainstream American English as a second dialect. *Language, Speech, and Hearing Services in Schools, 40*(3), 229–244.

Pearson, P. D., Hansen, J., & Gordon, C. (1979). The effect of background knowledge on young children's comprehension of explicit and implicit information. *Journal of Reading Behavior, 11,* 201–209.

Pederson, D. R., Rook-Green, A., & Elder, J. L. (1981). The role of action in the development of pretend play in young children. *Developmental Psychology, 17,* 756–759.

Pedro-Carroll, J. L. (2005). Fostering resilience in the aftermath of divorce: The role of evidence-based programs for children. *Family Court Review, 43,* 52–64.

Pellegrini, A. D. (1996). *Observing children in their natural worlds: A methodological primer.* Mahwah, NJ: Erlbaum.

Pellegrini, A. D. (2002). Bullying, victimization, and sexual harassment during the transition to middle school. *Educational Psychologist, 37,* 151–163.

Pellegrini, A. D. (2006). The development and function of rough-and-tumble play in childhood and adolescence: A sexual selection theory perspective. In A. Göncü & S. Gaskins (Eds.), *Play and development: Evolutionary, sociocultural, and functional perspectives* (pp. 77–98) Mahwah, NJ: Erlbaum.

Pellegrini, A. D., Bartini, M., & Brooks, F. (1999). School bullies, victims, and aggressive victims: Factors relating to group affiliation and victimization in early adolescence. *Journal of Educational Psychology, 91,* 216–224.

Pellegrini, A. D., & Bjorklund, D. F. (1997). The role of recess in children's cognitive performance. *Educational Psychologist, 32,* 35–40.

Pellegrini, A. D., & Bohn, C. M. (2005). The role of recess in children's cognitive performance and school adjustment. *Educational Researcher, 34*(1), 13–19.

Pellegrini, A. D., & Horvat, M. (1995). A developmental contextualist critique of attention deficit hyperactivity disorder. *Educational Researcher, 24*(1), 13–19.

Pellicano, E. (2010). The development of core cognitive skills in autism: A 3-year prospective study. *Child Development, 81*(5), 1400–1416.

Peltonen, K., Qouta, S., El Sarraj, E., & Punamäki, R. (2010). Military trauma and social development: The moderating and mediating roles of peer and sibling relations in mental health. *International Journal of Behavioral Development, 34*(6), 554–563.

Peltzer, K. (2010). Early sexual debut and associated factors among in-school adolescents in eight African countries. *Acta Paediatrica, 99*(8), 1242–1247. doi:10.1111/j.1651-2227.2010.01874. xdoi:10.1177/0165025410368943

Pence, K. L., & Justice, L. M. (2008). *Language development from theory to practice.* Upper Saddle River, NJ: Merrill/Prentice Hall.

Penner, A. M. (2003). International gender X item difficulty interactions in mathematics and science achievement tests. *Journal of Educational Psychology, 95,* 650–655.

Pennington, B. F., & Bennetto, L. (1993). Main effects of transactions in the neuropsychology of conduct disorder. Commentary on "The neuropsychology of conduct disorder." *Development and Psychopathology, 5,* 153–164.

Pentimonti, J. M., & Justice, L. M. (2010). Teachers' use of scaffolding strategies during read alouds in the preschool classroom. *Early Childhood Education, 37,* 241–248.

Peralta, O. A., & Maita, M. D. R. (2007, March). *Teaching very young children the symbolic function of a map.* Paper presented at the biennial meeting of the Society for Research in Child Development, Boston.

Peregoy, S. F., & Boyle, O. F. (2008). *Reading, writing, and learning in ESL: A resource book for teaching K–12 English learners.* Boston: Pearson Education/Allyn & Bacon.

Perels, F., Merget-Kullmann, M., Wende, M., Schmitz, B., & Buchbinder, C. (2009). Improving self-regulated learning of preschool children: Evaluation of training for kindergarten teachers. *British Journal of Educational Psychology, 79*(2), 311–327.

Pérez, B. (Ed.). (1998). *Sociocultural contexts of language and literacy.* Mahwah, NJ: Erlbaum.

Perez, S. M., & Gauvain, M. (2009). Mother-child planning, child emotional functioning, and children's transition to first grade. *Child Development, 80*(3), 776–791.

Pérez-Edgar, K., McDermott, J. N. M., Korelitz, K., Degnan, K. A., Curby, T. W., Pine, D. S., & Fox, N. A. (2010). Patterns of sustained attention in infancy shape the developmental trajectory of social behavior from toddlerhood through adolescence. *Developmental Psychology, 46*(6), 1723–1730. doi:10.1037/a0021064

Perfetti, C. A. (1985). Reading ability. In R. J. Sternberg (Ed.), *Human abilities: An information-processing approach.* New York: Freeman.

Perfetti, C. A., & McCutchen, D. (1987). Schooled language competence: Linguistic abilities in reading and writing. In S. Rosenberg (Ed.), *Advances in applied psycholinguistics.* Cambridge, England: Cambridge University Press.

Perkins, D., & Ritchhart, R. (2004). When is good thinking? In D. Y. Dai & R. J. Sternberg (Eds.), *Motivation, emotion, and cognition: Integrative perspectives on intellectual functioning and development* (pp. 351–384). Mahwah, NJ: Erlbaum.

Perkins, D. N. (1992). *Smart schools: From training memories to educating minds.* New York: Free Press/Macmillan.

Perkins, D. N. (1995). *Outsmarting IQ: The emerging science of learnable intelligence.* New York: Free Press.

Perner, J., & Wimmer, H. (1985). "John *thinks* that Mary *thinks* that??" Attribution of second-order beliefs by 5- to 10-year-old children. *Journal of Experimental Child Psychology, 39,* 437–471.

Perry, N. E. (1998). Young children's self-regulated learning and contexts that support it. *Journal of Educational Psychology, 90,* 715–729.

Perry, N. E., Turner, J. C., & Meyer, D. K. (2006). Classrooms as contexts for motivating learning. In P. A. Alexander & P. H. Winne (Eds.), *Handbook of educational psychology* (2nd ed., pp. 327–348). Mahwah, NJ: Erlbaum.

Perry, N. E., VandeKamp, K. O., Mercer, L. K., & Nordby, C. J. (2002). Investigating teacher–student interactions that foster self-regulated learning. *Educational Psychologist, 37,* 5–15.

Perry, N. E., & Winne, P. H. (2004). Motivational messages from home and school: How do they influence young children's engagement in learning? In D. M. McNerney & S. Van Etten (Eds.), *Big theories revisited* (pp. 199–222). Greenwich, CT: Information Age.

Persellin, D., & Bateman, L. (2009). A comparative study on the effectiveness of two song-teaching methods: Holistic vs. phrase-by-phrase. *Early Child Development and Care, 179*(6), 799–806.

Peters, A. M. (1983). *The units of language acquisition.* New York: Cambridge University Press.

Peters, E., Cillessen, A. H. N., Riksen-Walraven, J. M., & Haselager, G. J. T. (2010). Best friends' preference and popularity: Associations with aggression and prosocial behavior. *International Journal of Behavioral Development, 34*(5), 398–405. doi:10.1177/0165025409343709

Petersen, S., & Wittmer, D. (2008). Relationship-based infant care: Responsive, on demand, and predictable. *Young Children, 63*(3), 40–42.

Peterson, B. E., & Stewart, A. J. (1996). The antecedents and contexts of generativity motivation at midlife. *Psychology and Aging, 11*(1), 21–33.

Peterson, C. (1990). Explanatory style in the classroom and on the playing field. In S. Graham &

V. S. Folkes (Eds.), *Attribution theory: Applications to achievement, mental health, and interpersonal conflict.* Hillsdale, NJ: Erlbaum.

Peterson, C., Maier, S. F., & Seligman, M. E. P. (1993). *Learned helplessness: A theory for the age of personal control.* New York: Oxford University Press.

Peterson, C. C. (2002). Drawing insight from pictures: The development of concepts of false drawing and false belief in children with deafness, normal hearing, and autism. *Child Development, 73,* 1442–1459.

Peterson, D., & Esbensen, F. A. (2004). The outlook is G.R.E.A.T.: What educators say about school-based prevention and the Gang Resistance Education and Training (G.R.E.A.T.) Program. *Evaluation Review, 28*(3), 218–245.

Peterson, K. A., Paulson, S. E., & Williams, K. K. (2007). Relations of eating disorder symptomology with perceptions of pressures from mother, peers, and media in adolescent girls and boys. *Sex Roles, 57,* 629–639.

Peterson, L. (1980). Developmental changes in verbal and behavioral sensitivity to cues of social norms of altruism. *Child Development, 51,* 830–838.

Peterson, R. L., & Pennington, B. F. (2010). Reading disability. In K. O. Yeates, M. D. Ris, H. G. Taylor & B. F. Pennington (Eds.), *Pediatric neuropsychology: Research, theory, and practice* (2nd ed., pp. 324–362). New York: Guilford Press.

Petitto, A. L. (1985). Division of labor: Procedural learning in teacher-led small groups. *Cognition and Instruction, 2,* 233–270.

Petitto, L. (2009). New discoveries from the bilingual brain and mind across the life span: Implications for education. *Mind, Brain, and Education, 3*(4), 185–197.

Petitto, L. A. (1997). In the beginning: On the genetic and environmental factors that make early language acquisition possible. In M. Gopnik (Ed.), *The inheritance and innateness of grammars.* New York: Oxford University Press.

Petrill, S. A., Lipton, P. A., Hewitt, J. K., Plomin, R., Cherny, S. S., Corley, R., et al. (2004). Genetic and environmental contributions to general cognitive ability through the first 16 years of life. *Developmental Psychology, 40,* 805–812.

Petrill, S. A., & Wilkerson, B. (2000). Intelligence and achievement: A behavioral genetic perspective. *Educational Psychology Review, 12,* 185–199.

Pfefferbaum, B., Pfefferbaum, R. L., & Norris, F. H. (2010). Community resilience and wellness for the children exposed to Hurricane Katrina. In R. P. Kilmer, V. Gil-Rivas, R. G. Tedeschi, & L. G. Calhoun (Eds.), *Helping families and communities recover from disaster: Lessons learned from Hurricane Katrina and its aftermath* (pp. 265–285). Washington, DC: American Psychological Association.

Pfeifer, J. H., Brown, C. S., & Juvonen, J. (2007). Prejudice reduction in schools. Teaching tolerance in schools: Lessons learned since *Brown v. Board of Education* about the development and reduction of children's prejudice. *Social Policy Report, 21*(2), 1, 3–13, 20–23. Ann Arbor, MI: Society for Research in Child Development.

Pfeifer, M., Goldsmith, H. H., Davidson, R. J., & Rickman, M. (2002). Continuity and change in inhibited and uninhibited children. *Child Development, 73,* 1474–1485.

Phalet, K., Andriessen, I., & Lens, W. (2004). How future goals enhance motivation and learning in multicultural classrooms. *Educational Psychology Review, 16,* 59–89.

Phares, V., Fields, S., & Kamboukos, D. (2009). Fathers' and mothers' involvement with their adolescents. *Journal of Child and Family Studies, 28,* 1–9.

Phasha, T. N. (2008). The role of the teacher in helping learners overcome the negative impact of child sexual abuse. *School Psychology International, 29*(3), 303–327.

Phelan, P., Yu, H. C., & Davidson, A. L. (1994). Navigating the psychosocial pressures of adolescence: The voices and experiences of high school youth. *American Educational Research Journal, 31,* 415–447.

Phillips, D., & Zimmerman, M. (1990). The developmental course of perceived competence and incompetence among competent children. In R. Sternberg & J. Kolligian (Eds.), *Competence considered* (pp. 41–66). New Haven, CT: Yale University Press.

Phillips, M. (1997). What makes schools effective? A comparison of the relationships of communitarian climate and academic climate to mathematics achievement and attendance during middle school. *American Educational Research Journal, 34,* 633–662.

Phinney, J. S. (1989). Stages of ethnic identity development in minority group adolescents. *Journal of Early Adolescence, 9,* 34–49.

Phinney, J. S. (1990). Ethnic identity in adolescents and adults: Review of research. *Psychological Bulletin, 108,* 499–514.

Phinney, J. S., Cantu, C. L., & Kurtz, D. A. (1997). Ethnic and American identity as predictors of self-esteem among African American, Latino, and White adolescents. *Journal of Youth and Adolescence, 26,* 165–185.

Phinney, J. S., & Tarver, S. (1988). Ethnic identity search and commitment in Black and White eighth graders. *Journal of Early Adolescence, 8,* 265–277.

Piaget, J. (1928). *Judgment and reasoning in the child* (M. Warden, Trans.). New York: Harcourt, Brace.

Piaget, J. (1929). *The child's conception of the world.* New York: Harcourt, Brace.

Piaget, J. (1940). Le mécanisme du développement mental et les lois du groupement des opérations. *Archives de Psychologie, 28,* 215–285.

Piaget, J. (1950). *Introduction à l'épistémologie génétique.* Paris: Presses Universitaires de France.

Piaget, J. (1952a). *The child's conception of number* (C. Gattegno & F. M. Hodgson, Trans.). London: Routledge & Kegan Paul.

Piaget, J. (1952b). *The origins of intelligence in children.* New York: International Universities Press.

Piaget, J. (1954). *The construction of reality in the child.* New York: Basic Books.

Piaget, J. (1959). *The language and thought of the child* (3rd ed.; M. Gabain, Trans.). London: Routledge & Kegan Paul.

Piaget, J. (1960a). *The child's conception of physical causality* (M. Gabain, Trans.). Paterson, NJ: Littlefield, Adams.

Piaget, J. (1960b). The definition of stages of development. In J. M. Tanner & B. Inhelder (Eds.), *Discussions on child development: A consideration of the biological, psychological and cultural approaches to the understanding of human development and behavior: Vol. 4. The proceedings of the fourth meeting of the World Health Organization Study Group on the Psychobiological Development of the Child, Geneva, 1956* (pp. 116–135). New York: International Universities Press.

Piaget, J. (1960c). *The moral judgment of the child* (M. Gabain, Trans.). Glencoe, IL: Free Press. (Original work published 1932)

Piaget, J. (1962). *Play, dreams, and imitation in childhood.* New York: W. W. Norton.

Piaget, J. (1971). The theory of stages in cognitive development. In D. R. Green (Ed.), *Measurement and Piaget* (pp. 1–11). New York: McGraw-Hill.

Piaget, J. (1972). Intellectual evolution from adolescence to adulthood. *Human Development, 15,* 1–12.

Piaget, J. (1985). *The equilibration of cognitive structures: The central problem of intellectual development.* Chicago: University of Chicago Press.

Pianta, R. C. (1999). *Enhancing relationships between children and teachers.* Washington, DC: American Psychological Association.

Pianta, R. C. (2006). Classroom management and relationships between children and teachers: Implications for research and practice. In C. M. Evertson & C. S. Weinstein (Eds.), *Handbook of classroom management: Research, practice, and contemporary issues* (pp. 685–709). Mahwah, NJ: Erlbaum.

Pianta, R. C., Belsky, J., Houts, R., & Morrison, F. (2007). Opportunities to learn in America's elementary classrooms. *Science, 315*(5820), 1795–1796.

Pianta, R. C., Hamre, B., & Stuhlman, M. (2003). Relationships between teachers and children. In W. M. Reynolds & G. E. Miller (Eds.), *Handbook of psychology: Educational psychology* (Vol. 7, pp. 199–234). New York: Wiley.

Pianta, R. C., & Steinberg, M. (1992). Teacher–child relationships and the process of adjusting to school. In R. C. Pianta (Ed.), *Beyond the parent: The role of other adults in children's lives* (pp. 61–80). San Francisco: Jossey-Bass.

Piasta, S. B., & Wagner, R. K. (2010). Learning letter names and sounds: Effects of instruction, letter type, and phonological processing skill. *Journal of Experimental Child Psychology, 105*(4), 324–344.

Piirto, J. (1999). *Talented children and adults: Their development and education* (2nd ed.). Upper Saddle River, NJ: Merrill/Prentice Hall.

Pillow, B. H. (2002). Children's and adults' evaluation of the certainty of deductive inferences, inductive inferences, and guesses. *Child Development, 73,* 779–792.

Pilonieta, P., & Medina, A. L. (2009). Reciprocal teaching for the primary grades: "We can do it, too!" *The Reading Teacher, 63*(2), 120–129.

Pine, K. J., Lufkin, N., Kirk, E., & Messer, D. (2007). A microgenetic analysis of the relationship between speech and gesture in children: Evidence for semantic and temporal asynchrony. *Language and Cognitive Processes, 22*(2), 234–246.

Pinel, P., & Dehaene, S. (2009). Beyond hemispheric dominance: Brain regions underlying the joint lateralization of language and arithmetic to the left hemisphere. *Journal of Cognitive Neuroscience, 22*(1), 48–66.

Pinker, S. (1982). A theory of the acquisition of lexical interpretive grammars. In J. Bresnan (Ed.), *The mental representation of grammatical notions.* Cambridge, MA: MIT Press.

Pinker, S. (1984). *Language learnability and language development.* Cambridge, MA: Harvard University Press.

Pinker, S. (1987). The bootstrapping problem in language acquisition. In B. MacWhinney (Ed.), *Mechanisms of language acquisition* (pp. 399–441). Hillsdale, NJ: Erlbaum.

Pintrich, P. R., & Schunk, D. H. (2002). *Motivation in education: Theory, research, and applications* (2nd ed.). Upper Saddle River, NJ: Merrill/Prentice Hall.

Pipe, M.-E., & Salmon, K. (2009). Memory development and the forensic context. In M. L. Courage & N. Cowan (Eds.), *The development of memory in infancy and childhood* (pp. 241–282). New York: Psychology Press.

Pipher, M. (1994). *Reviving Ophelia: Saving the selves of adolescent girls.* New York: Putnam.

Plomin, R., Fulker, D. W., Corley, R., & DeFries, J. C. (1997). Nature, nurture, and cognitive development from 1 to 16 years: A parent–offspring adoption study. *Psychological Science, 8,* 442–447.

Plomin, R., Owen, M. J., & McGuffin, P. (1994). The genetic basis of complex human behaviors. *Science, 24,* 1733–1739.

Plomin, R., & Petrill, S. A. (1997). Genetics and intelligence: What's new? *Intelligence, 24,* 53–77.

Plomin, R., & Spinath, F. M. (2004). Intelligence: Genetics, genes, and genomics. *Journal of Personality and Social Psychology, 86,* 112–129.

Poel, E. W. (2007). Enhancing what students can do. *Educational Leadership, 64,* 64–66.

Pollack, W. (1998). *Real boys: Rescuing our sons from the myths of boyhood.* New York: Henry Holt.

Pollitt, E., & Oh, S. (1994). Early supplemental feeding, child development and health policy. *Food & Nutrition Bulletin, 15,* 208–214.

Pomerantz, E. M., Altermatt, E. R., & Saxon, J. L. (2002). Making the grade but feeling distressed: Gender differences in academic performance and internal distress. *Journal of Educational Psychology, 94,* 396–404.

Pomerantz, E. M., Moorman, E. A., & Litwack, S. D. (2007). The how, whom, and why of parents' involvement in children's academic lives: More is not always better. *Review of Educational Research, 77,* 373–410.

Pomerantz, E. M., & Wang, Q. (2009). The role of parental control in children's development in Western and East Asian Countries. *Current Directions in Psychological Science, 18*(5), 285–289.

Ponder, J., Vander Veldt, M., & Lewis-Ferrell, G. (2011). Lessons from the journey: Exploring citizenship through active civic involvement. In B. D. Schultz (Ed.), *Listening to and learning from students: Possibilities for teaching, learning, and curriculum* (pp. 115–130). Greenwich, CT: IAP Information Age Publishing.

Poresky, R. H., Daniels, A. M., Mukerjee, J., & Gunnell, K. (1999, April). *Community and family influences on adolescents' use of alcohol and other drugs: An exploratory ecological analysis.* Paper presented at the biennial meeting of the Society for Research in Child Development, Albuquerque, NM.

Portes, P. R. (1996). Ethnicity and culture in educational psychology. In D. C. Berliner & R. C. Calfee (Eds.), *Handbook of educational psychology.* New York: Macmillan.

Posner, M. I. (Ed.). (2004). *Cognitive neuroscience of attention.* New York: Guilford Press.

Posner, M. I., & Rothbart, M. K. (2007). *Educating the human brain.* Washington, DC: American Psychological Association.

Poulin, F., & Boivin, M. (1999). Proactive and reactive aggression and boys' friendship quality in mainstream classrooms. *Journal of Emotional and Behavioral Disorders, 7,* 168–177.

Poulin, F., & Chan, A. (2010). Friendship stability and change in childhood and adolescence. *Developmental Review, 30*(3), 257–272. doi:10.1016/j.dr.2009.01.001

Poulin-Dubois, D., Frenkiel-Fishman, S., Nayer, S., & Johnson, S. (2006). Infants' inductive generalization of bodily, motion, and sensory properties to animals and people. *Journal of Cognition and Development, 7*(4), 431–453.

Powell, M. P., & Schulte, T. (1999). Turner syndrome. In S. Goldstein & C. R. Reynolds (Eds.), *Handbook of neurodevelopmental and genetic disorders* (pp. 277–297). New York: Guilford Press.

Power, F. C., Higgins, A., & Kohlberg, L. (1989). *Lawrence Kohlberg's approach to moral education.* New York: Columbia University Press.

Powers, N., & Trevarthen, C. (2009). Voices of shared emotion and meaning: Young infants and their mothers in Scotland and Japan. In S. Malloch & C. Trevarthen (Eds.), *Communicative musicality: Exploring the basis of human companionship* (pp. 209–240). New York: Oxford University Press.

Preedy, P. (1999). Meeting the educational needs of pre-school and primary aged twins and higher multiples. In A. C. Sandbank (Ed.), *Twin and triplet psychology: A professional guide to working with multiples* (pp. 70–99). London: Routledge.

Pressley, M. (1982). Elaboration and memory development. *Child Development, 53,* 296–309.

Pressley, M., Almasi, J., Schuder, T., Bergman, J., Hite, S., El-Dinary, P. B., et al. (1994). Transactional instruction of comprehension strategies: The Montgomery County Maryland SAIL program. *Reading and Writing Quarterly, 10,* 5–19.

Pressley, M., Borkowski, J. G., & Schneider, W. (1987). Cognitive strategies: Good strategy users coordinate metacognition and knowledge. In R. Vasta (Ed.), *Annals of child development* (Vol. 4). Greenwich, CT: JAI Press.

Pressley, M., El-Dinary, P. B., Marks, M. B., Brown, R., & Stein, S. (1992). Good strategy instruction is motivating and interesting. In K. A. Renninger, S. Hidi, & A. Krapp (Eds.), *The role of interest in learning and development.* Hillsdale, NJ: Erlbaum.

Pressley, M., & Hilden, K. (2006). Cognitive strategies: Production deficiencies and successful strategy instruction everywhere. In W. Damon & R. M. Lerner (Series Eds.), & D. Kuhn & R. Siegler (Vol. Eds.), *Handbook of child psychology: Vol. 2. Cognition, perception, and language* (6th ed.). New York: Wiley.

Pribilsky, J. (2001). Nervios and 'modern childhood': Migration and shifting contexts of child life in the Ecuadorian Andes. *Childhood, 8*(2), 251–273.

Price, J. R., Roberts, J. E., & Jackson, S. C. (2006). Structural development of the fictional narratives of African American preschoolers. *Language, Speech, and Hearing Services in Schools, 37,* 178–190.

Price, S., Noseworthy, J., & Thornton, J. (2007). Women's experience with social presence during childbirth. *MCN: The American Journal of Maternal/Child Nursing, 32*(3), 184 191.

Price-Williams, D. R., Gordon, W., & Ramirez, M. (1969). Skill and conservation. *Developmental Psychology, 1,* 769.

Prinstein, M. J., Rancourt, D., Guerry, J. D., & Browne, C. B. (2009). Peer reputations and psychological adjustment. In K. H. Rubin, W. M. Bukowski, & B. Laursen (Eds.), *Handbook of peer interactions, relationships, and groups* (pp. 548–567). New York: Guilford Press.

Proctor, C. P., August, D., Carlo, M. S., & Snow, C. (2006). The intriguing role of Spanish language vocabulary knowledge in predicting English reading comprehension. *Journal of Educational Psychology, 98,* 159–169.

Proctor, R. W., & Dutta, A. (1995). *Skill acquisition and human performance.* Thousand Oaks, CA: Sage.

Provasnik, S., KewalRamani, A., Coleman, M. M., Gilbertson, L., Herring, W., & Xie, Q. (2007). *Status of education in rural America* (NCES 2007-040). Washington, DC: National Center for Education Statistics, Institute of Education Sciences, U.S. Department of Education.

Provost, B., Lopez, B. R., & Heimerl, S. (2007). A comparison of motor delays in young children: Autism spectrum disorder, developmental delay, and developmental concerns. *Journal of Autism and Developmental Disorders, 37*(2), 321–328.

Pruden, S. M., Hirsh-Pasek, K., Golinkoff, R. M., & Hennon, E. A. (2006). The birth of words: Ten-month-olds learn words through perceptual salience. *Child Development, 77,* 266–280.

Pruett, K., & Pruett, M. K. (2009). *Partnership parenting: How men and women parent differently—Why it helps your kids and can strengthen your marriage.* Cambridge, MA: Da Capo Press.

Pugh, K. J. (2011). Transformative experience: An integrative construct in the spirit of Deweyan pragmatism. *Educational Psychologist, 46*(2), 107–121. doi:10.1080/00461520.2011.558817

Pulkkinen, L. (1982). Self-control and continuity from childhood to adolescence. In P. B. Baltes & O. G. Brim (Eds.), *Life-span development and behavior* (Vol. 4). Orlando, FL: Academic Press.

Pulos, S. (1997). Adolescents' implicit theories of physical phenomena: A matter of gravity. *International Journal of Behavioral Development, 20,* 493–507.

Pulos, S., & Linn, M. C. (1981). Generality of the controlling variables scheme in early adolescence. *Journal of Early Adolescence, 1,* 26–37.

Puntambekar, S., & Hübscher, R. (2005). Tools for scaffolding students in a complex learning environment: What have we gained and what have we missed? *Educational Psychologist, 40,* 1–12.

Purcell-Gates, V. (1995). *Other people's words: The cycle of low literacy.* Cambridge, MA: Harvard University Press.

Purcell-Gates, V., McIntyre, E., & Freppon, P. A. (1995). Learning written storybook language in school: A comparison of low-SES children in skills-based and whole language classrooms. *American Educational Research Journal, 32,* 659–685.

Purdie, N., & Hattie, J. (1996). Cultural differences in the use of strategies for self-regulated learning. *American Educational Research Journal, 33,* 845–871.

Purdie, N., Hattie, J., & Douglas, G. (1996). Student conceptions of learning and their use of self-regulated learning strategies: A cross-cultural comparison. *Journal of Educational Psychology, 88,* 87–100.

Putallaz, M., & Gottman, J. M. (1981). Social skills and group acceptance. In S. R. Asher & J. M. Gottman (Eds.), *The development of children's friendships* (pp. 116–149). New York: Cambridge University Press.

Putallaz, M., & Heflin, A. H. (1986). Toward a model of peer acceptance. In J. M. Gottman & J. G. Parker (Eds.), *Conversations of friends: Speculations on affective development* (pp. 292–314). Cambridge, England: Cambridge University Press.

Puustinen, M., Lyyra, A., Metsäpelto, R., & Pulkkinen, L. (2008). Children's help seeking: The role of parenting. *Learning and Instruction, 18*(2), 160–171.

Qian, G., & Pan, J. (2002). A comparison of epistemological beliefs and learning from science text between American and Chinese high school students. In B. K. Hofer & P. R. Pintrich (Eds.), *Personal epistemology: The psychology of beliefs about knowledge and knowing* (pp. 365–385). Mahwah, NJ: Erlbaum.

Quill, K. A. (1995). Visually cued instruction for children with autism and pervasive developmental disorders. *Focus on Autistic Behavior, 10*(3), 10–20.

Quinn, P. C. (2002). Category representation in young infants. *Current Directions in Psychological Science, 11,* 66–70.

Quinn, P. C. (2007). On the infant's prelinguistic conception of spatial relations: Three developmental trends and their implications for spatial language learning. In J. M. Plumert & J. P. Spencer (Eds.), *The emerging spatial mind* (pp. 117–141). New York: Oxford University Press.

Quittner, A. L., Modi, A. C., & Roux, A. L. (2004). Psychosocial challenges and clinical interventions for children and adolescents with cystic fibrosis: A developmental approach. In R. T. Brown (Ed.), *Handbook of pediatric psychology in school settings* (pp. 333–361). Mahwah, NJ: Erlbaum.

Raevuori, A., Dick, D. M., Keski-Rahkonen, A., Pulkkinen, L., Rose, R. J., Rissanen, A., et al. (2007). Genetic and environmental factors affecting self-esteem from age 14 to 17: A longitudinal study of Finnish twins. *Psychological Medicine, 37,* 1625–1633.

Rahman, Q., & Wilson, G. D. (2003). Sexual orientation and the 2nd to 4th finger length ratio: Evidence for organising effects of sex hormones or developmental instability? *Psychoneuroendocrinology, 28,* 288–303.

Raikes, H., Pan, B. A., Luze, G., Tamis-LeMonda, C. S., Brooks-Gunn, J., Constantine, J., et al. (2006). Mother–child book reading in low-income families: Correlates and outcomes during the first three years of life. *Child Development, 77,* 924–953.

Raine, A., & Scerbo, A. (1991). Biological theories of violence. In J. S. Milner (Ed.), *Neuropsychology of aggression* (pp. 1–25). Boston: Kluwer Academic Press.

Rakes, C, R., Valentine, J. C., McGatha, M. B., & Ronau, R. N. (2010). Methods of instructional improvement in algebra: A systematic review and meta-analysis. *Review of Educational Research, 80*(3), 372–400.

Rakic, P. (1995). Corticogenesis in human and nonhuman primates. In M. S. Gazzaniga (Ed.), *The cognitive neurosciences* (pp. 127–145). Cambridge, MA: MIT Press.

Rakison, D. H. (2005). Infant perception and cognition: An evolutionary perspective on early learning. In B. J. Ellis & D. F. Bjorklund (Eds.), *Origins of the social mind: Evolutionary psychology and child development* (pp. 317–353). New York: Guilford Press.

Ramani, G. B., & Siegler, R. S. (2008). Promoting broad and stable improvements in low-income children's numerical knowledge through playing number board games. *Child Development, 79,* 375–394.

Ramaswamy, V., & Bergin, C. (2009). Do reinforcement and induction increase prosocial behavior? Results of a teacher-based intervention in preschools. *Journal of Research in Childhood Education, 23*(4), 527–538.

Ramey, C. T., Campbell, F. A., Burchinal, M., Skinner, M. L., Gardner, D. M., & Ramey, S. L. (2000). Persistent effects of early childhood education on high-risk children and their mothers. *Applied Developmental Science, 4*(1), 2–14.

Ramey, S. L., & Ramey, C. T. (1999). Early experience and early intervention for children "at risk" for developmental delay and mental retardation. *Mental Retardation and Developmental Disabilities Research Reviews, 5*(1), 1–10.

Ramirez, A. Y. F., & Soto-Hinman, I. (2009). A place for all families. *Educational Leadership, 66*(7), 79–82.

Randell, A. C., & Peterson, C. C. (2009). Affective qualities of sibling disputes, mothers' conflict attitudes, and children's theory of mind development. *Social Development, 18*(4), 857–874.

Rasmussen, S. (2009). Opening up perspectives on autonomy and relatedness in parent–children dynamics: Anthropological insights. *Culture & Psychology, 15*(4), 433–449.

Rassin, M., Klug, E., Nathanzon, H., Kan, A., & Silner, D. (2009). Cultural differences in child delivery: Comparisons between Jewish and Arab women. *International Nursing Review, 56,* 123–130.

Ratner, H. H. (1984). Memory demands and the development of young children's memory. *Child Development, 55,* 2173–2191.

Ravid, D., & Geiger, V. (2009). Promoting morphological awareness in Hebrew-speaking grade-schoolers: An intervention study using linguistic humor. *First Language, 29*(1), 81–112.

Ravid, D., & Zilberbuch, S. (2003). Morphosyntactic constructs in the development of spoken and written Hebrew text production. *Journal of Child Language, 30,* 395–418.

Ray, J. A., Prewitt-Kinder, J., & George, S. (2009). Partnering with families of children with special needs. *Young Children, 64*(5), 16–22.

Rayner, K., Foorman, B. R., Perfetti, C. A., Pesetsky, D., & Seidenberg, M. S. (2001). How psychological science informs the teaching of reading. *Psychological Science in the Public Interest, 2,* 31–74.

Reardon, L. E., Leen-Feldner, E. W., & Hayward, C. (2009). A critical review of the empirical literature on the relation between anxiety and puberty. *Clinical Psychology Review, 29,* 1–23.

Recchia, H. E., & Howe, N. (2009). Associations between social understanding, sibling relationship quality, and siblings' conflict strategies and outcomes. *Child Development, 80*(5), 1564–1578.

Recker, N., Clark, L., & Foote, R. A. (2008, June). About my families and me. *Journal of Extension, 46*(3).

Rees, S., Harding, R., & Inder, T. (2006). The developmental environment and the origins of neurological disorders. In P. Gluckman & M. Hanson (Ed.), *Developmental origins of health and disease* (pp. 379–391). New York: Cambridge University Press.

Reese, E., Hayne, H., & MacDonald, S. (2008). Looking back to the future: Māori and Pakeha mother–child birth stories. *Child Development, 79*(1), 114–125.

Reese, E., Sparks, A., & Leyva, D. (2010). A review of parent interventions for preschool children's language and emergent literacy. *Journal of Early Childhood Literacy, 10*(1), 97–117.

Reese, E., Yan, C., Fiona, J., & Hayne, H. (2010). Emerging identities: Narrative and self from early childhood to early adolescence. In K. C. McLean & M. Pasupathi (Eds.), *Narrative development in adolescence: Creating the storied self* (pp. 23–43). New York: Springer Science + Business Media.

Reese, E., Yan, C., Jack, F., & Hayne, H. (2010). Emerging identities: Narrative and self from early childhood to early adolescence. In K. C. McLean, & M. Pasupathi (Eds.), *Narrative development in adolescence: Creating the storied self. Advancing responsible adolescent development* (pp. 23–43). New York: Springer Science + Business Media.

Reese, L., Garnier, H., Gallimore, R., & Goldenberg, C. (2000). Longitudinal analysis of the antecedents of emergent Spanish literacy and middle-school English reading achievement of Spanish-speaking students. *American Educational Research Journal, 37,* 633–662.

Reese, S. (1996). KIDMONEY: Children as big business. *Technos Quarterly, 5*(4), 1–7. Retrieved November 21, 2005, at http://www.ait.net/technos/tq_05/4reesephp

Reeve, J. (2006). Extrinsic rewards and inner motivation. In C. M. Evertson & C. S. Weinstein (Eds.), *Handbook of classroom management: Research, practice, and contemporary issues* (pp. 645–664.). Mahwah, NJ: Erlbaum.

Reeve, J., Bolt, E., & Cai, Y. (1999). Autonomy-supportive teachers: How they teach and motivate students. *Journal of Educational Psychology, 91,* 537–548.

Reeve, J., Deci, E. L., & Ryan, R. M. (2004). Self-determination theory: A dialectical framework for understanding sociocultural influences on student motivation. In D. M. McInerney & S. Van Etten (Eds.), *Big theories revisited* (pp. 31–60). Greenwich, CT: Information Age.

Regmi, K., & Madison, J. (2009). Contemporary childbirth practices in Nepal: Improving outcomes. *British Journal of Midwifery, 17*(6), 382–387.

Reich, P. A. (1986). *Language development.* Englewood Cliffs, NJ: Prentice Hall.

Reid, N. (1989). Contemporary Polynesian conceptions of giftedness. *Gifted Education International, 6*(1), 30–38.

Reid, R., Gonzalez, J. E., Nordness, P. D., Trout, A., & Epstein, M. H. (2004). A meta-analysis of the academic status of students with emotional/behavioral disturbance. *The Journal of Special Education, 38,* 130–143.

Reimer, J., Paolitto, D. P., & Hersh, R. H. (1983). *Promoting moral growth: From Piaget to Kohlberg* (2nd ed.). White Plains, NY: Longman.

Reiner, M., Slotta, J. D., Chi, M. T. H., & Resnick, L. B. (2000). Naïve physics reasoning: A commitment to substance-based conceptions. *Cognition and Instruction, 18,* 1–34.

Reis, S. M. (2011). Self-regulated learning and academically talented students. In J. L. Jolly, D. J. Treffinger, T. F. Inman, & J. F. Smutny, (Eds.), *Parenting gifted children: The authoritative guide from the National Association for Gifted Children* (pp. 42–52). Waco, TX: Prufrock Press.

Reiss, D. (2005). The interplay between genotypes and family relationships: Reframing concepts of development and prevention. *Current Directions in Psychological Science, 14,* 139–143.

Reissland, N. (2006). Teaching a baby the language of emotions: A father's experience. *Zero to Three, 27*(1), 42–47.

Renk, K., White, R. W., Scott, S., & Middleton, M. (2009). Evidence-based methods of dealing with social deficits in conduct disorder. In J. L. Matson (Ed.), *Social behavior and skills in children* (pp. 187–218). New York: Springer Science + Business Media.

Repacholi, B. M., & Gopnik, A. (1997). Early reasoning about desires: Evidence from 14- and 18-month-olds. *Developmental Psychology, 33,* 12–21.

Repetti, R., & Wang, S.-W. (2010). Parent employment and chaos in the family. In G. W. Evans & T. D. Wachs (Eds.), *Chaos and its influence on children's development: An ecological perspective* (pp. 191–208). Washington, DC: American Psychological Association.

Rest, J. R., Narváez, D., Bebeau, M., & Thoma, S. (1999). A neo-Kohlbergian approach: The DIT and schema theory. *Educational Psychology Review, 11,* 291–324.

Reston, J. (2007). Reflecting on admission criteria. In G. E. Mills, *Action research: A guide for the teacher researcher* (3rd ed., pp. 141–142). Upper Saddle River, NJ: Pearson Merrill/Prentice Hall.

Reyes, I., & Azuara, P. (2008). Emergent biliteracy in young Mexican immigrant children. *Reading Research Quarterly, 43*(4), 374–398.

Reyna, C. (2000). Lazy, dumb, or industrious: When stereotypes convey attribution information in the classroom. *Educational Psychology Review, 12,* 85–110.

Reyna, V. F., & Farley, F. (2006). Risk and rationality in adolescent decision making: Implications for theory, practice, and public policy. *Psychological Science in the Public Interest, 7,* 1–44.

Reynolds, M. R., Keith, T. Z., Ridley, K. P., & Patel, P. G. (2008). Sex differences in latent general and broad cognitive abilities for children and youth: Evidence from higher-order MG-MACS and MIMIC models. *Intelligence, 36*(3), 236–260.

Reznick, J. S. (2009). Working memory in infants and toddlers. In M. L. Courage & N. Cowan (Eds.), *The development of memory in infancy and childhood* (pp. 343–365). New York: Psychology Press.

Reznick, J. S., & Goldfield, B. A. (1992). Rapid change in lexical development in comprehension and production. *Developmental Psychology, 28,* 408–414.

Rhoads, D. (1956). *The corn grows ripe.* Illustrated by Jean Charlot. New York: Viking Press.

Rhodes, J. E., & Lowe, S. R. (2009). Mentoring in adolescence. In R. M. Lerner & L. Steinberg (Eds.), *Handbook of adolescent psychology. Vol. 2. Contextual influences on adolescent development* (3rd ed., pp. 152–190). Hoboken, NJ: Wiley.

Ricci, D., Romeo, D. M. M., Serrao, F., Cesarini, L., Gallini, F., Cota, F., et al. (2008). Application of a neonatal assessment of visual function in a population of low risk full-term newborn. *Early Human Development, 84,* 277–280.

Ricciuti, H. N. (1993). Nutrition and mental development. *Current Directions in Psychological Science, 2,* 43–46.

Ricco, R., Pierce, S. S., & Medinilla, C. (2010). Epistemic beliefs and achievement motivation in early adolescence. *Journal of Early Adolescence, 30*(2), 305–340.

Rice, M., Hadley, P. A., & Alexander, A. L. (1993). Social biases toward children with speech and language impairments: A correlative causal model of language limitations. *Applied Psycholinguistics, 14,* 445–471.

Richard, J. F., & Schneider, B. H. (2005). Assessing friendship motivation during preadolescence and early adolescence. *Journal of Early Adolescence, 25*(3), 367–385.

Richards, J. E., & Turner, E. D. (2001). Extended visual fixation and distractibility in children from six to twenty-four months of age. *Child Development, 72,* 963–972.

Richardson, W. (2011, February). Publishers, participants all. *Educational Leadership, 68*(5), 22–26.

Richman, G., Hope, T., & Mihalas, S. (2010). Assessment and treatment of self-esteem in adolescents with ADHD. In M. H. Guindon (Ed.), *Self-esteem across the lifespan: Issues and interventions* (pp. 111–123). New York: Routledge/Taylor & Francis Group.

Richmond, K., Carroll, K., & Denboske, K. (2010). Gender identity disorder: Concerns and controversies. In J. C. Chrisler & D. R. McCreary (Eds.), *Handbook of gender research in psychology, Vol. 2: Gender research in social and applied psychology* (pp. 111–131). New York: Springer Science + Business Media. doi:10.1007/978-1-4419-1467-5_6

Ricketts, H., & Anderson, P. (2008). The impact of poverty and stress on the interaction of Jamaican caregivers with young children. *International Journal of Early Years Education, 16*(1), 61–74.

Ridenour, T. A., Clark, D. B., & Cottler, L. B. (2009). The illustration-based assessment of liability and exposure to substance use and antisocial behavior for children. *The American Journal of Drug and Alcohol Abuse, 35*(4), 242–252.

Rief, S. F., & Heimburge, J. A. (2007). *How to reach and teach all children through balanced literacy: User-friendly strategies, tools, activities, and ready-to-use materials (grades 3–8).* San Francisco: Jossey-Bass.

Rieger, G., Linsenmeier, J. A. W., Gygax, L., & Bailey, J. M. (2008). Sexual orientation and childhood gender nonconformity: Evidence from home videos. *Developmental Psychology, 44*(1), 46–58. doi:10.1037/0012-1649.44.1.46

Riemer, F. J., & Blasi, M. (2008). Rethinking relationships, reconfiguring teacher research: Teachers as ethnographers of culture, childhood, and classrooms. *Action in Teacher Education, 29*(4), 53–65.

Rihtman, T., Tekuzener, E., Parush, S., Tenenbaum, A., Bachrach, S. J., & Ornoy, A. (2010). Are the cognitive functions of children with Down syndrome related to their participation? *Developmental Medicine & Child Neurology, 52*(1), 72–78.

Riley, D., San Juan, R. R., Klinkner, J., & Ramminger, A. (2008). *Social and emotional development: Connecting science and practice in early childhood settings.* St. Paul, MN: Redleaf Press.

Rimm-Kaufman, S. E., Early, D. M., Cox, M. J., Saluja, G., Pianta, R. C., Bradley, R. H., et al. (2002). Early behavioral attributes and teachers' sensitivity as predictors of competent behavior in the kindergarten classroom. *Journal of Applied Developmental Psychology, 23*(4), 451–470.

Rinehart, S. D., Stahl, S. A., & Erickson, L. G. (1986). Some effects of summarization training on reading and studying. *Reading Research Quarterly, 21,* 422–438.

Ringdahl, J. E., Kopelman, T., & Falcomata, T. S. (2009). Applied behavior analysis and its application to autism and autism related disorders.

In J. L. Matson (Ed.), *Applied behavior analysis for children with autism spectrum disorders* (pp. 15–32). New York: Springer Science + Business Media. doi:10.1007/978-1-4419-0088-3_2

Riojas-Cortez, M., Huerta, M. E., Florcs, B. B., Perez, B., & Clark, E. R. (2008). Using cultural tools to develop scientific literacy of young Mexican American preschoolers. *Early Child Development and Care, 178*(5), 527–536.

Rios-Aguilar, C. González-Canche, M., Moll, L. C. (2010). *The study of Arizona's teachers of English Language learners*. Retrieved August 9, 2010, from http://http://civilrightsproject.ucla.edu/research/k-12-education/language-minority-students/a-study-of-arizonas-teachers-of-english-language-learners.

Rittle-Johnson, B. (2006). Promoting transfer: Effects of self-explanation and direct instruction. *Child Development, 77*, 1–15.

Rittle-Johnson, B., & Koedinger, K. R. (2005). Designing knowledge scaffolds to support mathematical problem solving. *Cognition and Instruction, 23*, 313–349.

Rittle-Johnson, B., & Siegler, R. S. (1999). Learning to spell: Variability, choice, and change in children's strategy use. *Child Development, 70*, 332–348.

Ritts, V., Patterson, M. L., & Tubbs, M. E. (1992). Expectations, impressions, and judgments of physically attractive students: A review. *Review of Educational Research, 62*, 413–426.

Rivas-Drake, D., Hughes, D., & Way, N. (2009). A preliminary analysis of associations among ethnic racial socialization, ethnic discrimination, and ethnic identity among urban sixth graders. *Journal of Research on Adolescence, 19*(3), 558–584.

Rizzo, V. (2009). The Howard Gardner School for Discovery. In J.-Q. Chen, S. Moran, & H. Gardner, H. (Eds.), *Multiple intelligences around the world* (pp. 3–16). San Francisco: Jossey-Bass.

Rizzolatti, G., & Fabbri-Destro, M. (2010). Mirror neurons: From discovery to autism. *Experimental Brain Research, 200*(3–4), 223–237. doi:10.1007/s00221-009-2002-3

Robbers, M. L. P. (2008). The caring equation: An intervention program for teenage mothers and thcir male partners. *Children and Schools, 30*(1), 37–47.

Robbins, V., Dollard, N., Armstrong, B. J., Kutash, K., & Vergon, K. S. (2008). Mental health needs of poor suburban and rural children and their families. *Journal of Loss and Trauma, 13*, 94–122.

Robbins, W. J., Brody, S., Hogan, A. G., Jackson, C. M., & Green, C. W. (Eds.). (1928). *Growth*. New Haven, CT: Yale University Press.

Robert, A. C., & Sonenstein, F. L. (2010). Adolescents' reports of communication with their parents about sexually transmitted diseases and birth control: 1988, 1995, and 2002. *Journal of Adolescent Health, 46*(6), 532–537.

Roberts, A. R. (2008). School-based, adolescent suicidality: Lethality assessments and crisis intervention protocols. In C. Franklin, M. B. Harris & P. Allen-Meares (Eds.), *The school practitioner's concise companion to mental health. The school practitioner's concise companions* (pp. 163–177). New York: Oxford University Press.

Roberts, D. F., Christenson, P., Gibson, W. A., Mooser, L., & Goldberg, M. E. (1980). Developing discriminating consumers. *Journal of Communication, 30*, 94–105.

Roberts, D. F., & Foehr, U. G. (2008). Trends in media use. *Future of Children, 18*(1), 11–37.

Roberts, M. C., Brown, K. J., Boles, R. E., & Mashunkashey, J. O. (2004). Prevention of injuries: Concepts and interventions for pediatric psychology in the schools. In R. T. Brown (Ed.), *Handbook of pediatric psychology in school settings* (pp. 65–80). Mahwah, NJ: Erlbaum.

Roberts, T. A. (2005). Articulation accuracy and vocabulary size contributions to phonemic awareness and word reading in English language learners. *Journal of Educational Psychology, 97*, 601–616.

Roberts, T. A., & Meiring, A. (2006). Teaching phonics in the context of children's literature or spelling: Influences on first-grade reading, spelling, and writing and fifth-grade comprehension. *Journal of Educational Psychology, 98*, 690–713.

Robertson, J. S. (2000). Is attribution training a worthwhile classroom intervention for K–12 students with learning difficulties? *Educational Psychology Review, 12*, 111–134.

Robin, D. J., Berthier, N. E., & Clifton, R. K. (1996). Infants' predictive reaching for moving objects in the dark. *Developmental Psychology, 32*, 824–835.

Robins, R. W., & Trzesniewski, K. H. (2005). Self-esteem development across the lifespan. *Current Directions in Psychological Science, 14*, 158–162.

Rochat, P., & Bullinger, A. (1994). Posture and functional action in infancy. In A. Vyt, H. Bloch, & M. H. Bornstein (Eds.), *Early child development in the French tradition: Contributions from current research*. Hillsdale, NJ: Erlbaum.

Rochat, P., & Goubet, N. (1995). Development of sitting and reaching in 5- to 6-month-old infants. *Infant behavior and development, 18*, 53–68.

Roderick, M., & Camburn, E. (1999). Risk and recovery from course failure in the early years of high school. *American Educational Research Journal, 36*, 303–343.

Rodríguez-García, J., & Wagner, U. (2009). Learning to be prejudiced: A test of unidirectional and bidirectional models of parent–offspring socialization. *International Journal of Intercultural Relations, 33*(6), 516–523. doi.10.1016/j.ijintrel.2009.08.001

Roeser, R. W., Eccles, J. S., & Sameroff, A. J. (2000). School as a context of early adolescents' academic social-emotional development: A summary of research findings. *The Elementary School Journal, 100*, 443–471.

Roeser, R. W., Midgley, C., & Urdan, T. C. (1996). Perceptions of school psychological environment and early adolescents' psychological and behavioral functioning in school: The mediating role of goals and belonging. *Journal of Educational Psychology, 88*, 408–422.

Roffwarg, H. P., Muzio, J. N., & Dement, W. C. (1966). Ontogenetic development of the human sleep-dream cycle. *Science, 152*, 604–619.

Rogers, K. B. (2002). *Re-forming gifted education*. Scottsdale, AZ: Great Potential Press.

Rogoff, B. (1990). *Apprenticeship in thinking: Cognitive development in social context*. New York: Oxford University Press.

Rogoff, B. (1991). Social interaction as apprenticeship in thinking: Guidance and participation in spatial planning. In L. B. Resnick, J. M. Levine, & S. D. Teasley (Eds.), *Perspectives on socially shared cognition*. Washington, DC: American Psychological Association.

Rogoff, B. (1994, April). *Developing understanding of the idea of communities of learners*. Paper presented at the annual meeting of the American Educational Research Association, New Orleans, LA.

Rogoff, B. (1995). Observing sociocultural activity on three planes: Participatory appropriation, guided participation, and apprenticeship. In J. V. Wertsch, P. del Rio, & A. Alvarez (Eds.), *Sociocultural studies of mind*. Cambridge, England: Cambridge University Press.

Rogoff, B. (2003). *The cultural nature of human development*. New York: Oxford University Press.

Rogoff, B., Mistry, J., Göncü, A., & Mosier, C. (1993). Guided participation in cultural activity by toddlers and caregivers. *Monographs of the Society for Research in Child Development, 58*(8, Serial No. 236).

Rogoff, B., Moore, L., Najafi, B., Dexter, A., Correa-Chávez, M., & Solís, J. (2007). Children's development of cultural repertoires through participation in everyday routines and practices. In J. E. Grusec & P. D. Hastings (Eds.), *Handbook of socialization: Theory and research* (pp. 490–515). New York: Guilford Press.

Rogoff, B., & Morelli, G. (1989). Perspectives on children's development from cultural psychology. *American Psychologist, 44*, 343–348.

Rogoff, B., Morelli, G. A., & Chavajay, P. (2010). Children's integration in communities and segregation from people of differing ages. *Perspectives on Psychological Science, 5*(4), 431–440.

Rohner, R. P., & Rohner, E. C. (1981). Parental acceptance-rejection and parental control: Cross-cultural codes. *Ethnology, 20*, 245–260.

Rohr, L. E. (2006). Gender-specific movement strategies using a computer-pointing task. *Journal of Motor Behavior, 38*(6), 431–437.

Roid, G. (2003). *Stanford-Binet Intelligence Scales* (5th ed.). Itasca, IL: Riverside.

Roid, G. H., & Tippin, S. M. (2009). Assessment of intellectual strengths and weaknesses with the Stanford-Binet Intelligence Scales–Fifth Edition (SB5). In J. A. Naglieri & S. Goldstein (Eds.), *Practitioner's guide to assessing intelligence and achievement* (pp. 127-). Hoboken, NJ: Wiley.

Rojek, J., Petrocelli, M., & Oberweis, T. (2010). Recent patterns in gang prevalence: A two state comparison. *Journal of Gang Research, 18*(1), 1–18.

Rolls, C., & Chamberlain, M. (2004). From east to west: Nepalese women's experiences. *International Council of Nurses, 51*, 176–184.

Romero, A. J., & Roberts, R. E. (2003). The impact of multiple dimensions of ethnic identity on discrimination and adolescents' self-esteem. *Journal of Applied Social Psychology, 33*, 2288–2305.

Rondan, C., & Deruelle, C. (2007). Global and configural visual processing in adults with autism and Asperger syndrome. *Research in Developmental Disabilities, 28*, 197–206.

Rönnau-Böse, M., & Fröhlich-Gildhoff, K. (2009). The promotion of resilience: A person-centered perspective of prevention in early childhood institutions. *Person-Centered and Experiential Psychotherapies, 8*(4), 299–318.

Roosa, M. W., Weaver, S. R., White, R. M. B., Tein, J.-Y., Knight, G. P., Gonzales, N., & Saenz, D. (2009). Family and neighborhood fit or misfit and the adaptation of Mexican Americans. *American Journal of Community Psychology, 44*, 15–27.

Roscigno, V. J., Karafin, D. L., & Tester, G. (2009). The complexities and processes of racial housing discrimination. *Social Problems, 56*(1), 49–69.

Rose, A. J., & Smith, R. L. (2009). Sex differences in peer relationships. In K. H. Rubin, W. M. Bukowski, & B. Laursen (Eds.), *Handbook of peer interactions, relationships, and groups* (pp. 379–393). New York: Guilford Press.

Roseboom, T., de Rooij, S., & Painter, R. (2006). The Dutch famine and its long-term consequences for adult health. *Early Human Development, 82*(8), 485–491.

Rosenberg, M. (1986). Self-concept from middle childhood through adolescence. In S. Suls & A. Greenwald (Eds.), *Psychological perspectives on the self* (Vol. 3, pp. 107–135). Hillsdale, NJ: Erlbaum.

Rosenkoetter, L. I., Rosenkoetter, S. E., Ozretich, R. A., & Acock, A. C. (2004). Mitigating the harmful effects of violent television. *Applied Developmental Psychology, 25*, 25–47.

Rosenshine, B., & Meister, C. (1992). The use of scaffolds for teaching higher-level cognitive strategies. *Educational Leadership, 49*(7), 26–33.

Rosenshine, B., & Meister, C. (1994). Reciprocal teaching: A review of the research. *Review of Educational Research, 64*, 479–530.

Rosenshine, B., Meister, C., & Chapman, S. (1996). Teaching students to generate questions: A review of the intervention studies. *Review of Educational Research, 66,* 181–221.

Rosenthal, R. (1994). Interpersonal expectancy effects: A 30-year perspective. *Current Directions in Psychological Science, 3,* 176–179.

Rotenberg, K. J., & Mayer, E. V. (1990). Delay of gratification in Native and White children: A cross-cultural comparison. *International Journal of Behavioral Development, 13,* 23–30.

Rothbart, M. K. (2007). Temperament, development, and personality. *Current Directions in Psychological Science, 16,* 207–212.

Rothbart, M. K., & Bates, J. E. (2006). Temperament. In W. Damon & R. M. Lerner (Eds. in Chief) & N. Eisenberg (Vol. Ed.), *Handbook of child psychology, Vol. 3. Social, emotional, and personality development* (6th ed., pp. 99–225). Hoboken, NJ: Wiley.

Rothbart, M. K., Hanley, D., & Albert, M. (1986). Gender differences in moral reasoning. *Sex Roles, 15,* 645–653.

Rothbart, M. K., Posner, M. I., & Kieras, J. (2006). Temperament, attention, and the development of self-regulation. In K. McCartney & D. Phillips (Eds.), *Blackwell handbook of early childhood development* (pp. 338–357). Malden, MA: Blackwell.

Rothbart, M. K., Sheese, B. E., & Conradt, E. D. (2009). Childhood temperament. In P. J. Corr, & G. Matthews (Eds.), The Cambridge handbook of personality psychology (pp. 177–190). New York: Cambridge University Press.

Rothbaum, F., Nagaoka, R., & Ponte, I. C. (2006). Caregiver sensitivity in cultural context: Japanese and U.S. teachers' beliefs about anticipating and responding to children's needs. *Journal of Research in Childhood Education, 21*(1), 23–40.

Rothbaum, F., Pott, M., Azuma, H., Miyake, K., & Weisz, J. (2000). The development of close relationships in Japan and the United States: Paths of symbiotic harmony and generative tension. *Child Development, 71*(5), 1121–1142. doi:10.1111/1467-8624.00214

Rothenberg, C., & Fisher, D. (2007). *Teaching English language learners: A differentiated approach.* Upper Saddle River, NJ: Pearson Merrill.

Rothrauff, T. C., Cooney, T. M., & An, J. S. (2009). Remembered parenting styles and adjustment in middle and late adulthood. *Journal of Gerontology, 64B*(1), 137–146.

Rothstein-Fisch, C. & Trumbull, E. (2008). *Managing diverse classrooms: How to build on students' strengths.* Alexandria, VA: Association for Supervision and Curriculum Development.

Rothstein-Fisch, C., Trumbull, E., & Garcia, S. G. (2009). Making the implicit explicit: Supporting teachers to bridge cultures. *Early Childhood Research Quarterly, 24,* 474–486. doi:10.1016/j.ecresq.2009.08.006

Rovee-Collier, C. (1999). The development of infant memory. *Current Directions in Psychological Science, 8,* 80–85.

Rovee-Collier, C., & Cuevas, K. (2009). Multiple memory systems are unnecessary to account for infant memory development: An ecological model. *Developmental Psychology, 45*(1), 160–174. doi:10.1037/a0014538

Rowe, D. C., Almeida, D. M., & Jacobson, K. C. (1999). School context and genetic influences on aggression in adolescence. *Psychological Science, 10,* 277–280.

Rowe, D. C., Jacobson, K. C., & Van den Oord, E. J. C. G. (1999). Genetic and environmental influences on Vocabulary IQ: Parental education level as moderator. *Child Development, 70,* 1151–1162.

Rowe, D. W., & Harste, J. C. (1986). Metalinguistic awareness in writing and reading: The young child as curricular informant. In D. B. Yaden, Jr., & S. Templeton (Eds.), *Metalinguistic awareness and beginning literacy: Conceptualizing what it means to read and write.* Portsmouth, NH: Heinemann.

Rowe, F., & Stewart, D. (2009). Promoting connectedness through whole-school approaches: A qualitative study. *Health Education, 109*(5), 396–413. doi:10.1108/09654280910984816

Rowe, M. B. (1974). Wait-time and rewards as instructional variables, their influence on language, logic, and fate control: Part one—wait time. *Journal of Research in Science Teaching, 11,* 81–94.

Rowe, M. B. (1978). *Teaching science as continuous inquiry.* New York: McGraw-Hill.

Rowe, M. B. (1987). Wait-time: Slowing down may be a way of speeding up. *American Educator, 11,* 38–43, 47.

Rowland, T. W. (1990). *Exercise and children's health.* Champaign, IL: Human Kinetics.

Rowley, S. J., Cooper, S. M., & Clinton, Y. C. (2006). Family and school support for healthy racial identity development in African American youth. In K. Freeark & W. S. Davidson II (Vol. Eds.), & H. E. Fitzgerald, R. Zucker, & K. Freeark (Eds. in Chief), *The crisis in youth mental health. Vol. 3: Critical issues and effective programs* (pp. 79–98). Westport, CT: Praeger.

Rozalski, M. E., & Yell, M. L. (2004). Law and school safety. In: J. C. Conoley & A. P. Goldstein (Eds.), *School violence intervention* (2nd ed., pp. 507–523). New York: Guilford Press.

Rozendaal, M., & Baker, A. (2010). The acquisition of reference: Pragmatic aspects and the influence of language input. *Journal of Pragmatics, 42*(7), 1866–1879. doi:10.1016/j.pragma.2009.05.013

Rubie-Davies, C. M. (2007). Classroom interactions: Exploring the practices of high- and low- expectation teachers. *British Journal of Educational Psychology, 77,* 289–306.

Rubin, K., Fein, G., & Vandenberg, B. (1983). Play. In E. M. Hetherington (Ed.), *Handbook of child psychology: Vol. 4. Socialization, personality, and social development* (pp. 693–774). New York: Wiley.

Rubin, K. H., Bowker, J. C., & Kennedy, A. E. (2009). Avoiding and withdrawing from the peer group. In K. H. Rubin, W. M. Bukowski, & B. Laursen (Eds.), *Handbook of peer interactions, relationships, and groups* (pp. 303–321). New York: Guilford Press.

Rubin, K. H., Bukowski, W. M., & Parker, J. G. (2006). Peer interactions, relationships, and groups. In W. Damon & R. M. Lerner (Series Eds.) & N. Eisenberg (Vol. Ed.), *Handbook of child psychology: Vol. 3. Social, emotional, and personality development* (6th ed., pp. 571–645). New York: Wiley.

Rubin, K. H., & Krasnor, L. R. (1986). Social-cognitive and social behavioral perspectives on problem solving. In M. Perlmutter (Ed.), *Minnesota symposia on child psychology: Vol. 19. Cognitive perspectives on children's social and behavioral development.* Hillsdale, NJ: Erlbaum.

Rubin, K. H., Lynch, D., Coplan, R., Rose-Krasnor, L., & Booth, C. L. (1994). "Birds of a feather": Behavioral concordances and preferential personal attraction in children. *Child Development, 65,* 1778–1785.

Ruble, D. N., Martin, C. L., & Berenbaum, S. A. (2006). Gender development. In W. Damon & R. M. Lerner (Eds. in Chief) & N. Eisenberg (Vol. Ed.), *Handbook of child psychology, Vol. 3. Social, emotional, and personality development* (6th ed., pp. 858–932). Hoboken, NJ: Wiley.

Ruble, D. N., Taylor, L. J., Cyphers, L., Greulich, F. K., Lurye, L. E., & Shrout, P. E. (2007). The role of gender constancy in early gender development. *Child Development, 78,* 1121–1136.

Ruby, P., & Decety, J. (2001). Effect of subjective perspective taking during simulation of action: A PET investigation of agency. *Nature and Neuroscience, 4,* 546–550.

Rudasill, K. M., Gallagher, K. C., & White, J. M. (2010). Temperamental attention and activity, classroom emotional support, and academic achievement in third grade. *Journal of School Psychology, 48*(2), 113–134.

Rudlin, C. R. (1993). Growth and sexual development: What is normal, and what is not? *Journal of the American Academy of Physician Assistants, 6,* 25–35.

Rudolph, K. D., Caldwell, M. S., & Conley, C. S. (2005). Need for approval and children's well-being. *Child Development, 76,* 309–323.

Rudy, D., & Grusec, J. E. (2006). Authoritarian parenting in individualistic and collectivist groups: Associations with maternal emotion and cognition and children's self-esteem. *Journal of Family Psychology, 20,* 68–78.

Ruff, H. A., & Lawson, K. R. (1990). Development of sustained, focused attention in young children during free play. *Developmental Psychology, 26,* 85–93.

Ruff, H. A., & Rothbart, M. K. (1996). *Attention in early development: Themes and variations.* New York: Oxford University Press.

Rule, A. C. (2007). Mystery boxes: Helping children improve their reasoning. *Early Childhood Education Journal, 35*(1), 13–18.

Rumberger, R. W. (1995). Dropping out of middle school: A multilevel analysis of students and schools. *American Educational Research Journal, 32,* 583–625.

Rumelhart, D. E., & McClelland, J. L. (1987). Learning the past tenses of English verbs: Implicit rules or parallel distributed processing? In B. MacWhinney (Ed.), *Mechanisms of language acquisition* (pp. 195–248). Hillsdale, NJ: Erlbaum.

Rushton, J. P. (1980). *Altruism, socialization, and society.* Upper Saddle River, NJ: Prentice Hall.

Rushton, J. P., Fulkner, D. W., Neal, M. C., Nias, D. K. B., & Eysenck, H. J. (1986). Altruism and aggression: The heritability of individual differences. *Journal of Personality and Social Psychology, 50,* 1192–1198.

Russell, A., & Finnie, V. (1990). Preschool children's social status and maternal instructions to assist group entry. *Developmental Psychology, 26*(4), 603–611. doi:10.1037/0012-1649.26.4.603

Rutland, A., Killen, M., & Abrams, D. (2010). A new social-cognitive developmental perspective on prejudice: The interplay between morality and group identity. *Perspectives on Psychological Science, 5*(3), 279–291. doi:10.1177/1745691610369468

Rutter, M. (2005). Adverse preadoption experiences and psychological outcomes. In D. M. Brodzinsky & J. Palacios (Eds.), *Psychological issues in adoption: Research and practice* (pp. 67–92). Westport, CT: Praeger/Greenwood.

Rutter, M. L. (1997). Nature–nurture integration: The example of antisocial behavior. *American Psychologist, 52,* 390–398.

Ryan, A. M. (2000). Peer groups as a context for the socialization of adolescents' motivation, engagement, and achievement in school. *Educational Psychologist, 35,* 101–111.

Ryan, A. M., & Patrick, H. (2001). The classroom social environment and changes in adolescents' motivation and engagement during middle school. *American Educational Research Journal, 38,* 437–460.

Ryan, R. (2005, April). *Legislating competence: High stakes testing, school reform, and motivation from a self-determination theory viewpoint.* Paper presented at the annual meeting of the American Educational Research Association, Montreal.

Ryan, R. M., Connell, J. P., & Grolnick, W. S. (1992). When achievement is *not* intrinsically motivated: A theory of internalization and self-regulation in school. In A. K. Boggiano & T. S. Pittman

(Eds.), *Achievement and motivation: A social-developmental perspective*. Cambridge, England: Cambridge University Press.

Ryan, R. M., & Deci, E. L. (2000). Self-determination theory and the facilitation of intrinsic motivation, social development, and well-being. *American Psychologist, 55*, 68–78.

Ryan, R. M., & Deci, E. L. (2009). Promoting self-determined school engagement. In K. R. Wentzel & A. Wigfield (Eds.), *Handbook of motivation at school* (pp. 171–195). New York: Routledge.

Ryan, R. M., & Kuczkowski, R. (1994). The imaginary audience, self-consciousness, and public individuation in adolescence. *Journal of Personality, 62*, 219–237.

Ryan, R. M., & Lynch, J. H. (1989). Emotional autonomy versus detachment: Revisiting the vicissitudes of adolescence and young adulthood. *Child Development, 60*, 340–356.

Ryan, R. M., Stiller, J. D., & Lynch, J. H. (1994). Representations of relationships to teachers, parents, and friends as predictors of academic motivation and self-esteem. *Journal of Early Adolescence, 14*, 226–249.

Rycus, J. S., Freundlich, M., Hughes, R. C., Keefer, B., & Oakes, E. J. (2006). Confronting barriers to adoption success. *Family Court Review, 44*, 210–230.

Ryder, J. F., Tunmer, W. E., & Greaney, K. T. (2008). Explicit instruction in phonemic awareness and phonemically based decoding skills as an intervention strategy for struggling readers in whole language classrooms. *Reading and Writing, 21*(4), 349–369.

Saarni, C., Campos, J. J., Camras, L. A., & Witherington, D. (2006). Emotional development: Action, communication, and understanding. In W. Damon & R. M. Lerner (Eds. in Chief) & N. Eisenberg (Vol. Ed.), *Handbook of child psychology, Vol. 3. Social, emotional, and personality development* (6th ed., pp. 226–299). Hoboken, NJ: Wiley.

Sabbagh, M. A., Xu, F., Carlson, S. M., Moses, L. J., & Lee, K. (2006). The development of executive functioning and theory of mind: A comparison of Chinese and U.S. preschoolers. *Psychological Science, 17*, 74–81.

Sacks, C. H., & Mergendoller, J. R. (1997). The relationship between teachers' theoretical orientation toward reading and student outcomes in kindergarten children with different initial reading abilities. *American Educational Research Journal, 34*, 721–739.

Sadeh, A., Gruber, R., & Raviv, A. (2002). Sleep, neurobehavioral functioning, and behavior problems in school-age children. *Child Development, 73*, 405–417.

Sadler, T. W. (2010). *Langman's medical embryology* (11th ed.). Baltimore, MD: Lippincott Williams & Wilkins.

Safe Motherhood Network Federation. (2010). *Safe motherhood in Nepal.* Retrieved February 6, 2010, from http://www.safemotherhood.org.np/index.php.

Saffran, J. R. (2003). Statistical language learning: Mechanisms and constraints. *Current Directions in Psychological Science, 12*, 110–114.

Saffran, J. R., Aslin, R. N., & Newport, E. L. (1996). Statistical learning by 8-month-old infants. *Science, 274*, 1926–1928.

Saffran, J. R., & Griepentrog, G. J. (2001). Absolute pitch in infant auditory learning: Evidence for developmental reorganization. *Developmental Psychology, 37*, 74–85.

Salend, S. J., & Taylor, L. (1993). Working with families: A cross-cultural perspective. *Remedial and Special Education, 14*, 25–32, 39.

Salley, C. G., Vannatta, K., Gerhardt, C. A., & Noll, R. B. (2010). Social self-perception accuracy: Variations as a function of child age and gender. *Self and Identity, 9*(2), 209–223.

Salmani Nodoushan, M. (2009). The Shaffer-Gee perspective: Can epistemic games serve education?. *Teaching and Teacher Education, 25*(6), 897–901. doi:10.1016/j.tate.2009.01.013

Saltz, E. (1971). *The cognitive bases of human learning.* Homewood, IL: Dorsey.

Sameroff, A. (2009). The transactional model. In A. Sameroff (Ed.), *The transactional model of development: How children and contexts shape each other* (pp. 3–21). Washington, DC: American Psychological Association.

Samuels, G. M. (2009a). Ambiguous loss of home: The experience of familial (im)permanence among young adults with foster care backgrounds. *Children and Youth Services Review, 31*, 1229–1239.

Samuels, G. M. (2009b). "Being raised by White people": Navigating racial difference among adopted multiracial adults. *Journal of Marriage and Family, 71*, 80–94.

Sanchez, F., & Anderson, M. L. (1990). Gang mediation: A process that works. *Principal, 69*(4), 54–56.

Sandamas, G., Foreman, N., & Coulson, M. (2009). Interface familiarity restores active advantage in a virtual exploration and reconstruction task in children. *Spatial Cognition and Computation, 9*(2), 96–108.

Sanders, W. H. (2010). Walking alongside children as they form compassion. *Exchange, 32*(3), 50–53.

Sands, D. J., & Wehmeyer, M. L. (Eds.). (1996). *Self-determination across the life span: Independence and choice for people with disabilities.* Baltimore, MD: Paul H. Brookes.

Sann, C., & Streri, A. (2008). The limits of newborn's grasping to detect texture in a cross-modal transfer task. *Infant Behavior & Development, 31*(3), 523–531.

Santamaria, L. J. (2009). Culturally responsive differentiated instruction: Narrowing gaps between best pedagogical practices benefiting all learners. *Teachers College Record, 111*(1), 214–247.

Santelli, J. S., Orr, M., Lindberg, L. D., & Diaz, D. C. (2009). Changing behavioral risk for pregnancy among high school students in the united states, 1991–2007. *Journal of Adolescent Health, 45*(1), 25–32.

Sarrazin, J., & Cyr, F. (2007). Parental conflicts and their damaging effects on children. *Journal of Divorce and Remarriage, 47*, 77–93.

Satcher, D. (2010). Taking charge of school wellness. *Educational Leadership, 67*(4), 38–43.

Sattler, J. M. (2001). *Assessment of children: Cognitive applications* (4th ed.). San Diego, CA: Author.

Savage, R. S., Abrami, P., Hipps, G., & Deault, L. (2009). A randomized controlled trial study of the ABRACADABRA reading intervention program in grade 1. *Journal of Educational Psychology, 101*(3), 590–604.

Savin-Williams, R. C. (1989). Gay and lesbian adolescents. *Marriage and Family Review, 14*(3–4), 197–216.

Savin-Williams, R. C. (1995). Lesbian, gay male, and bisexual adolescents. In R. D'Augelli & C. J. Patterson (Eds.), *Lesbian, gay, and bisexual identities over the lifespan: Psychological perspectives* (pp. 165–189). New York: Oxford University Press.

Savin-Williams, R. C. (2005). *The new gay teenager.* Cambridge, MA: Harvard University Press.

Savin-Williams, R. C., & Diamond, L. M. (1997). Sexual orientation as a developmental context for lesbians, gays, and bisexuals: Biological perspectives. In N. L. Segal, G. E. Weisfeld, & C. C. Weisfeld (Eds.), *Uniting psychology and biology: Integrative perspectives on human development* (pp. 217–238). Washington, DC: American Psychological Association.

Savin-Williams, R. C., & Ream, G. L. (2003). Suicide attempts among sexual-minority male youth.

Journal of Clinical Child and Adolescent Psychology, 32(4), 509–522.

Sawyer, M. G., Pfeiffer, S., Spence, S. H., Bond, L., Graetz, B., Kay, D., Patton, G., & Sheffield, J. (2010). School-based prevention of depression: A randomised controlled study of the *beyondblue* schools research initiative. *Journal of Child Psychology and Psychiatry, 51*(2), 199–209.

Sawyer, R. J., Graham, S., & Harris, K. R. (1992). Direct teaching, strategy instruction, and strategy instruction with explicit self-regulation: Effects on the composition skills and self-efficacy of students with learning disabilities. *Journal of Educational Psychology, 84*, 340–352.

Saxe, G. B. (1988). The mathematics of child street vendors. *Child Development, 59*(5), 1415–1425.

Scarborough, H. (2001). Connecting early language and literacy to later reading (dis)abilities: Evidence, theory, and practice. In S. Neuman & D. Dickinson (Eds.), *Handbook of early literacy research* (pp. 97–110). New York: Guilford.

Scardamalia, M., & Bereiter, C. (1986). Research on written composition. In M. C. Wittrock (Ed.), *Handbook of research on teaching* (3rd ed.). New York: Macmillan.

Scarr, S. (1992). Developmental theories for the 1990s: Development and individual differences. *Child Development, 63*, 1–19.

Scarr, S., & McCartney, K. (1983). How people make their own environments: A theory of genotype environment effects. *Child Development, 54*, 424–435.

Scarr, S., & Weinberg, R. A. (1976). IQ test performance of Black children adopted by White families. *American Psychologist, 31*, 726–739.

Schachter, J. (2000). Does individual tutoring produce optimal learning? *American Educational Research Journal, 37*, 801–829.

Schaefer-McDaniel, N. (2007). "They be doing illegal things": Early adolescents talk about their inner-city neighborhoods. *Journal of Adolescent Research, 22*, 413–436.

Schaffer, H. R. (1996). *Social development.* Cambridge, MA: Blackwell.

Schaie, K. W., & Willis, S. L. (2000). A stage theory model of adult cognitive development revisited. In R. L. Rubinstein, M. Moss, & M. H. Klebans (Eds.), *The many dimensions of aging* (pp. 175–193). New York: Springer.

Schauble, L. (1990). Belief revision in children: The role of prior knowledge and strategies for generating evidence. *Journal of Experimental Child Psychology, 49*, 31–57.

Schellenberg, E. G. (2006). Long-term positive associations between music lessons and IQ. *Journal of Educational Psychology, 98*, 457–468.

Scherer, M. (2011, February). Transforming education with technology. *Educational Leadership, 68*(5), 17–21.

Scherer, N., & Olswang, L. (1984). Role of mothers' expansions in stimulating children's language production. *Journal of Speech and Hearing Research, 27*, 387–396.

Schiefele, U. (2009). Situational and individual interest. In K. R. Wentzel & A. Wigfield (Eds.), *Handbook of motivation at school* (pp. 197–222). New York: Routledge.

Schieffelin, B. B. (1985). The acquisition of Kaluli. In D. I Slobin (Ed.), *The crosslinguistic study of language acquisition* (pp. 525–593). Hillsdale, NJ: Erlbaum.

Schieffelin, B. B. (1990). *The give and take of everyday life: Language socialization of Kaluli children.* New York: Cambridge University Press.

Schilling, T. A. (2008). An examination of resilience processes in context: The case of Tasha. *Urban Review, 40*, 296–316.

Schimmoeller, M. A. (1998, April). *Influence of private speech on the writing behaviors of young children: Four case studies*. Paper presented at the annual meeting of the American Educational Research Association, San Diego, CA.

Schinke, S. P., Moncher, M. S., & Singer, B. R. (1994). Native American youths and cancer risk prevention. *Journal of Adolescent Health, 15,* 105–110.

Schlaefli, A., Rest, J. R., & Thoma, S. J. (1985). Does moral education improve moral judgment? A meta-analysis of intervention studies using the defining issues test. *Review of Educational Research, 55,* 319–352.

Schlegel, A., & Barry, H. L., III. (1980). The evolutionary significance of adolescent initiation ceremonies. *American Ethnologist, 7*(4), 696–715.

Schleppenbach, M., Perry, M., Miller, K. F., Sims, L., & Fang, G. (2007). The answer is only the beginning: Extended discourse in Chinese and U.S. mathematics classrooms. *Journal of Educational Psychology, 99,* 380–396.

Schlotz, W., & Phillips, D. I. W. (2009). Fetal origins of mental health: Evidence and mechanisms. *Brain, Behavior, and Immunity, 23,* 905–916.

Schmakel, P. O. (2008). Early adolescents' perspectives on motivation and achievement in academics. *Urban Education, 43*(6), 723–749. doi:10.1177/0042085907311831

Schmidt, L. A., Fox, N. A., Perez-Edgar, K., & Hamer, D. H. (2009). Linking gene, brain, and behavior: DRD4, frontal asymmetry, and temperament. *Psychological Science, 20*(7), 831–837.

Schmidt, M. E., Pempek, T. A., Kirkorian, H. L., Lund, A. F., & Anderson, D. R. (2008). The effects of background television on the toy play behavior of very young children. *Child Development, 79*(4), 1137–1151.

Schmidt, W. H. (2008, Spring). What's missing from math standards? *American Educator.* Retrieved March 3, 2008, from http://www.aft.org/pubs-reports/american_educator/issues/spring2008/schmidt.htm

Schneider, W., Korkel, J., & Weinert, F. E. (1989). Domain-specific knowledge and memory performance: A comparison of high- and low-aptitude children. *Journal of Educational Psychology, 81,* 306–312.

Schneider, W., & Lockl, K. (2002). The development of metacognitive knowledge in children and adolescents. In T. J. Perfect & B. L. Schwartz (Eds.), *Applied metacognition* (pp. 224–257). Cambridge, England: Cambridge University Press.

Schneider, W., & Pressley, M. (1989). *Memory development between 2 and 20.* New York: Springer-Verlag.

Schneider, W., Roth, E., & Ennemoser, M. (2000). Training phonological skills and letter knowledge in children at risk for dyslexia: A comparison of three kindergarten intervention programs. *Journal of Educational Psychology, 92,* 284–295.

Schneider, W., & Shiffrin, R. M. (1977). Controlled and automatic human information processing: I. Detection, search, and attention. *Psychological Review, 84,* 1–66.

Schoenfeld, A. H. (1988). When good teaching leads to bad results: The disasters of "well-taught" mathematics courses. *Educational Psychologist, 23,* 145–166.

Schoenfeld, A. H. (1992). Learning to think mathematically: Problem solving, metacognition, and sense making in mathematics. In D. A. Grouws (Ed.), *Handbook of research on mathematics teaching and learning.* New York: Macmillan.

Schofield, G., & Beek, M. (2009). Growing up in foster care: Providing a secure base through adolescence. *Child and Family Social Work, 14,* 255–266.

Schofield, J. W. (1995). Improving intergroup relations among students. In J. A. Banks & C. A. M. Banks (Eds.), *Handbook of research on multicultural education.* New York: Macmillan.

Schommer, M. (1994a). An emerging conceptualization of epistemological beliefs and their role in learning. In R. Garner & P. A. Alexander (Eds.), *Beliefs about text and instruction with text.* Hillsdale, NJ: Erlbaum.

Schommer, M. (1994b). Synthesizing epistemological belief research: Tentative understandings and provocative confusions. *Educational Psychology Review, 6,* 293–319.

Schommer, M., Calvert, C., Gariglietti, G., & Bajaj, A. (1997). The development of epistemological beliefs among secondary students: A longitudinal study. *Journal of Educational Psychology, 89,* 37–40.

Schonert-Reichl, K. A. (1993). Empathy and social relationships in adolescents with behavioral disorders. *Behavioral Disorders, 18,* 189–204.

Schraw, G. (2006). Knowledge: Structures and processes. In P. A. Alexander & P. H. Winne (Eds.), *Handbook of educational psychology* (2nd ed., pp. 245–263). Mahwah, NJ: Erlbaum.

Schraw, G., Flowerday, T., & Lehman, S. (2001). Increasing situational interest in the classroom. *Educational Psychology Review, 13,* 211–224.

Schraw, G., Potenza, M. T., & Nebelsick-Gullet, L. (1993). Constraints on the calibration of performance. *Contemporary Educational Psychology, 18,* 455–463.

Schreibman, L. (2008). Treatment controversies in autism. *Zero to Three, 28*(4), 38–45.

Schuchardt, K., Gebhardt, M., & Mäehler, C. (2010). Working memory functions in children with different degrees of intellectual disability. *Journal of Intellectual Disability Research, 54*(4), 346–353.

Schultz, E. (2009). Resolving the anti-evolutionism dilemma: A brief for relational evolutionary thinking in anthropology. *American Anthropologist, 111*(2), 224–237.

Schultz, G. F., & Switzky, H. N. (1990). The development of intrinsic motivation in students with learning problems: Suggestions for more effective instructional practice. *Preventing School Failure, 34*(2), 14–20.

Schulz, L. E., Goodman, N. D., Tenenbaum, J. B., & Jenkins, A. C. (2008). Going beyond the evidence: Abstract laws and preschoolers' responses to anomalous data. *Cognition, 109,* 211–223.

Schunk, D. H. (1990, April). *Socialization and the development of self-regulated learning: The role of attributions.* Paper presented at the annual meeting of the American Educational Research Association, Boston.

Schunk, D. H. (1996). Goal and self-evaluative influences during children's cognitive skill learning. *American Educational Research Journal, 33,* 359–382.

Schunk, D. H., & Hanson, A. R. (1985). Peer models: Influence on children's self-efficacy and achievement. *Journal of Educational Psychology, 77,* 313–322.

Schunk, D. H., & Pajares, F. (2004). Self-efficacy in education revisited: Empirical and applied evidence. In D. M. McNerney & S. Van Etten (Eds.), *Big theories revisited* (pp. 115–138). Greenwich, CT: Information Age.

Schunk, D. H., & Pajares, F. (2009). Self-efficacy theory. In K. R. Wentzel & A. Wigfield (Eds.), *Handbook of motivation at school* (pp. 35–53). New York: Routledge.

Schunk, D. H., & Rice, J. (1989). Learning goals and children's reading comprehension. *Journal of Reading Behavior, 21,* 279–293.

Schutz, P. A. (1994). Goals as the transactive point between motivation and cognition. In P. R. Pintrich, D. R. Brown, & C. E. Weinstein (Eds.), *Student motivation, cognition, and learning: Essays in honor of Wilbert J. McKeachie.* Hillsdale, NJ: Erlbaum.

Schwartz, B. L., & Perfect, T. J. (2002). Introduction: Toward an applied metacognition. In T. J. Perfect & B. L. Schwartz (Eds.), *Applied metacognition* (pp. 1–11). Cambridge, England: Cambridge University Press.

Schwartz, D., Gorman, A. H., Duong, M. T., & Nakamoto, J. (2008). Peer relationships and academic achievement as interacting predictors of depressive symptoms during middle childhood. *Journal of Abnormal Psychology, 117*(2), 289–299.

Schwartz, G. M., Izard, C. E., & Ansul, S. E. (1985). The 5-month-old's ability to discriminate facial expressions of emotion. *Infant Behavior and Development, 8*(1), 65–67.

Schwartz, J. L., Yarushalmy, M., & Wilson, B. (Eds.) (1993). *The geometric supposer: What is it a case of?* Hillsdale, NJ: Erlbaum.

Schwartz, M., S. Sadler, P. M., Sonnert, G., & Tai, R. H. (2009). Depth versus breadth: How content coverage in high school science courses relates to later success in college science coursework. *Science Education, 93*(5), 798–826.

Schwartz, P. D., Maynard, A. M., & Uzelac, S. M. (2008). Adolescent egocentrism: A contemporary view. *Adolescence, 43*(171), 441–448.

Schwarz, C. V., & White, B. Y. (2005). Metamodeling knowledge: Developing students' understanding of scientific modeling. *Cognition and Instruction, 23,* 165–205.

Schweinhart, L. J., & Weikart, D. P. (1993, November). Success by empowerment: The High/Scope Perry Preschool Study through age 27. *Young Children, 48,* 54–58.

Scott-Little, M., & Holloway, S. (1992). Child care providers' reasoning about misbehaviors: Relation to classroom control strategies and professional training. *Early Childhood Research Quarterly, 7,* 595–606.

Scull, T. M., Kupersmidt, J. B., Parker, A. E., Elmore, K. C., & Benson, J. W. (2010). Adolescents' media-related cognitions and substance use in the context of parental and peer influences. *Journal of Youth and Adolescence, 39*(9), 981–998. doi:10.1007/s10964-009-9455-3

Sear, R., & Mace, R. (2008). Who keeps children alive? A review of the effects of kin on child survival. *Evolution and Human Behavior, 29,* 1–18.

Segal, N. L. (2000). Virtual twins: New findings on within-family environmental influences on intelligence. *Journal of Educational Psychology, 92,* 442–448.

Segal, N. L., & Hur, Y. (2008). Reared apart Korean female twins: Genetic and cultural influences on life histories, physical and health-related measures, and behavioral traits. *International Journal of Behavioral Development, 32*(6), 542–548.

Segal, N. L., & Russell, J. M. (1992). Twins in the classroom: School policy issues and recommendations. *Journal of Educational and Psychological Consultation, 3,* 69–84.

Seibert, A. C., & Kerns, K. A. (2009). Attachment figures in middle childhood. *International Journal of Behavioral Development, 33*(4), 347–355.

Sejnost, R. L., & Thiese, S. M. (2010). *Building content literacy: Strategies for the adolescent learner.* Thousand Oaks, CA: Corwin Press.

Selfe, L. (1977). *Nadia: A case of extraordinary drawing ability in an autistic child.* London: Academic Press.

Selfe, L. (1995). Nadia reconsidered. In C. Golomb (Ed.), *The development of artistically gifted children: Selected case studies* (pp. 197–236). Hillsdale, NJ: Erlbaum.

Seligman, M. E. P. (1975). *Helplessness: On depression, development, and death.* San Francisco: Freeman.

Seligman, M. E. P. (1991). *Learned optimism.* New York: Knopf.

Selman, R. L. (1980). *The growth of interpersonal understanding: Developmental and clinical analysis.* New York: Academic Press.

Selman, R. L. (2003). *The promotion of social awareness: Powerful lessons from the partnership of developmental theory and classroom practice.* New York: Russell Sage Foundation.

Selman, R. L., & Byrne, D. F. (1974). A structural-developmental analysis of levels of role taking in middle childhood. *Child Development, 45,* 803–806.

Selman, R. L., & Schultz, L. J. (1990). *Making a friend in youth: Developmental theory and pair therapy.* Chicago: University of Chicago Press.

Seltzer, V. C. (1982). *Adolescent social development: Dynamic functional interaction.* Lexington, MA: Heath.

Semb, G. B., Ellis, J. A., & Araujo, J. (1993). Long-term memory for knowledge learned in school. *Journal of Educational Psychology, 85,* 305–316.

Sénéchal, M., & LeFevre, J.-A. (2002). Parental involvement in the development of children's reading skill: A five-year longitudinal study. *Child Development, 73,* 445–460.

Sénéchal, M., Thomas, E., & Monker, J. (1995). Individual differences in 4-year-old children's acquisition of vocabulary during storybook reading. *Journal of Educational Psychology, 87,* 218–229.

Senghas, A., & Coppola, M. (2001). Children creating language: How Nicaraguan Sign Language acquired a spatial grammar. *Psychological Science, 12,* 323–328.

Serpell, R., Baker, L., & Sonnenschein, S. (2005). *Becoming literate in the city: The Baltimore Early Childhood Project.* Cambridge, England: Cambridge University Press.

Seuss, Dr. (1968). *The foot book.* New York, New York: Random House.

Sewald, H. (1986). Adolescents' shifting orientation toward parents and peers: A curvilinear trend over recent decades. *Journal of Marriage and the Family, 48,* 5–13.

Shahinfar, A., Kupersmidt, J. B., & Matza, L. S. (2001). The relation between exposure to violence and social information processing among incarcerated adolescents. *Journal of Abnormal Psychology, 110,* 136–141.

Shanahan, L., McHale, S. M., Osgood, W., & Crouter, A. C. (2007). Conflict frequency with mothers and fathers from middle childhood to late adolescence: Within- and between-families comparisons. *Developmental Psychology, 43*(3), 539–550.

Shanahan, T., & Tierney, R. J. (1990). Reading-writing connection: The relations among three perspectives. In J. Zutell & S. McCormick (Eds.), *Literacy theory and research: Analyses from multiple paradigms. Thirty-ninth yearbook of the National Reading Conference.* Chicago: National Reading Conference.

Shapiro, E. S., & Manz, P. H. (2004). Collaborating with schools in the provision of pediatric psychological services. In R. T. Brown (Ed.), *Handbook of pediatric psychology in school settings* (pp. 49–64). Mahwah, NJ: Erlbaum.

Share, D. L., & Gur, T. (1999). How reading begins: A study of preschoolers' print identification strategies. *Cognition and Instruction, 17,* 177–213.

Sharkey, J. D., Shekhtmeyster, Z., Chavez-Lopez, L., Norris, E., & Sass, L. (2010). The protective influence of gangs: Can schools compensate? *Aggression and Violent Behavior,* doi:10.1016/j.avb.2010.11.001

Shatz, M., & Gelman, R. (1973). The development of communication skills: Modifications in the speech of young children as a function of the listener. *Monographs of the Society for Research in Child Development, 38* (5, Serial No. 152).

Shavinina, L. V., & Ferrari, M. (2004). Extracognitive facets of developing high ability: Introduction to some important issues. In L. V. Shavinina & M. Ferrari (Eds.), *Beyond knowledge: Extracognitive aspects of developing high ability* (pp. 3–13). Mahwah, NJ: Erlbaum.

Shayer, M., & Ginsburg, D. (2009). Thirty years on—A large anti-Flynn effect? (II): 13- and 14-year-olds. Piagetian tests of formal operations norms 1976-2006/7. *British Journal of Educational Psychology, 79,* 409–418.

Shaywitz, S. E. (2004). *Overcoming dyslexia.* New York: Knopf.

Shaywitz, S. E., Mody, M., & Shaywitz, B. A. (2006). Neural mechanisms in dyslexia. *Current Directions in Psychological Science, 15,* 278–281.

Shechtman, Z., & Ifargan, M. (2009). School-based integrated and segregated interventions to reduce aggression. *Aggressive Behavior, 35,* 342–356.

Sheehan, E. P., & Smith, H. V. (1986). Cerebral lateralization and handedness and their effects on verbal and spatial reasoning. *Neuropsychologia, 24,* 531–540.

Sheets, R. H. (1999). Human development and ethnic identity. In R. H. Sheets & E. R. Hollins (Eds.), *Racial and ethnic identity in school practices: Aspects of human development* (pp. 91–101). Mahwah, NJ: Erlbaum.

Sheets, R. H., & Hollins, E. R. (Eds.). (1999). *Racial and ethnic identity in school practices: Aspects of human development.* Mahwah, NJ: Erlbaum.

Sheffield, E., Stromswold, K., & Molnar, D. (2005, April). *Do prematurely born infants catch up?* Paper presented at the biennial meeting of the Society for Research in Child Development, Atlanta, GA.

Sheldon, J., Arbreton, A., Hopkins, L., & Grossman, J. B. (2010). Investing in success: Key strategies for building quality in after-school programs. *American Journal of Community Psychology, 45*(3–4), 394–404.

Shellenberg, E. G., & Trehub, S. E. (2003). Good pitch memory is widespread. *Psychological Science, 14,* 262–266.

Shen, Z. (2009). Multiple intelligences theory on the mainland of China. In J.-Q. Chen, S. Moran, H. Gardner (Eds.), *Multiple intelligences around the world* (pp. 55–65). San Francisco: Jossey-Bass.

Shenfield, T., Trehub, S. E., & Nakata, T. (2003). Maternal singing modulates infant arousal. *Psychology of Music, 31,* 365–375.

Shenkin, S. D., Starr, J. M., & Deary, I. J. (2004). Birth weight and cognitive ability in childhood: A systematic review. *Psychological Bulletin, 130,* 989–1013.

Shepard, R. N., & Metzler, J. (1971). Mental rotation of three-dimensional objects. *Science, 171,* 701–703.

Sheridan, M. D. (1975). *Children's developmental progress from birth to five years: The Stycar Sequences.* Windsor, England: NFER.

Sherif, M., Harvey, O. J., White, B. J., Hood, W. R., & Sherif, C. (1961). *Inter-group conflict and cooperation: The Robbers Cave experiment.* Norman: University of Oklahoma Press.

Sherwen, L. N., Scoloveno, M. A., & Weingarten, C. T. (1999). *Maternity nursing: Care of the childbearing family* (3rd ed.). Stamford, CT: Appleton & Lange.

Shevell, M. (2009). The tripartite origins of the tonic neck reflex. *Neurology, 72,* 850–853.

Shi, R., & Werker, J. F. (2001). Six-month-old infants' preference for lexical words. *Psychological Science, 12,* 70–75.

Shields, M. K., & Behrman, R. E. (2004). Children of immigrant families: Analysis and recommendations. *The Future of Children, 14*(2), 4–15.

Shih, S. (2009). An examination of factors related to Taiwanese adolescents' reports of avoidance strategies. *Journal of Educational Research (Washington, D.C.), 102*(5), 377–388.

Shin, J. C. (2011). The development of temporal coordination in children. *Brain and Cognition, 76*(1), 106–114. doi:10.1016/j.bandc.2011.02.011

Shinskey, J. L., & Munakata, Y. (2010). Something old, something new: A developmental transition from familiarity to novelty preferences with hidden objects. *Developmental Science, 13*(2), 378–384.

Shonkoff, J. P. & Phillips, D. A. (Eds.). (2000). *From neurons to neighborhoods: The science of early childhood development.* Washington, DC: National Academy of Sciences.

Short, E. J., & Ryan, E. B. (1984). Metacognitive differences between skilled and less skilled readers: Remediating deficits through story grammar and attribution training. *Journal of Educational Psychology, 76,* 225–235.

Short, E. J., Schatschneider, C. W., & Friebert, S. E. (1993). Relationship between memory and metamemory performance: A comparison of specific and general strategy knowledge. *Journal of Educational Psychology, 85,* 412–423.

Shreyar, S., Zolkower, B., & Pérez, S. (2010). Thinking aloud together: A teacher's semiotic mediation of a whole-class conversation about percents. *Educational Studies in Mathematics, 73,* 21–53.

Shrum, W., & Cheek, N. H. (1987). Social structure during the school years: Onset of the degrouping process. *American Sociological Review, 52,* 218–223.

Shultz, T. R. (1974). Development of the appreciation of riddles. *Child Development, 45,* 100–105.

Shultz, T. R., & Horibe, F. (1974). Development of the appreciation of verbal jokes. *Developmental Psychology, 10,* 13–20.

Shweder, R. A., Goodnow, J., Hatano, G., LeVine, R. A., Markus, H., & Miller, P. (1998). The cultural psychology of development: One mind, many mentalities. In W. Damon (Series Ed.) & R. M. Lerner (Vol. Ed.), *Handbook of child psychology: Vol. 1. Theoretical models of human development* (5th ed., pp. 865–937). New York: Wiley.

Shweder, R. A., Mahapatra, M., & Miller, J. G. (1987). Culture and moral development. In J. Kagan & S. Lamb (Eds.), *The emergence of morality in young children* (pp. 1–83). Chicago: University of Chicago Press.

Sidel, R. (1996). *Keeping women and children last: America's war on the poor.* New York: Penguin Books.

Siegel, D. J. (1999). *The developing mind: How relationships and the brain interact to shape who we are.* New York: Guilford Press.

Siegel, D. J. (2001). Toward an interpersonal neurobiology of the developing mind: Attachment relationships, "mindsight," and neural integration. *Infant Mental Health Journal, 22,* 67–94.

Sieger, K., & Renk, K. (2007). Pregnant and parenting adolescents: A study of ethnic identity, emotional and behavioral functioning, child characteristics, and social support. *Journal of Youth and Adolescence, 36*(4), 567–581.

Siegler, R. S. (1976). Three aspects of cognitive development. *Cognitive Psychology, 8,* 481–520.

Siegler, R. S. (1978). The origins of scientific reasoning. In R. S. Siegler (Ed.), *Children's thinking: What develops?* Hillsdale, NJ: Erlbaum.

Siegler, R. S. (1989). Mechanisms of cognitive growth. *Annual Review of Psychology, 40,* 353–379.

Siegler, R. S. (1994). Cognitive variability: A key to understanding cognitive development. *Current Directions in Psychological Science, 3,* 1–5.

Siegler, R. S. (1996). *Emerging minds: The process of change in children's thinking.* New York: Oxford University Press.

Siegler, R. S. (2006). Microgenetic analyses of learning. In W. Damon & R. M. Lerner (Eds. in Chief) & D. Kuhn & R. S. Siegler (Vol. Eds.), *Handbook of child psychology: Vol. 2. Cognition, perception, and language* (6th ed., pp. 464–510). Hoboken, NJ: Wiley.

Siegler, R. S., & Alibali, M. W. (2005). *Children's thinking* (4th ed.). Upper Saddle River, NJ: Prentice Hall.

Siegler, R. S., & Jenkins, E. (1989). *How children discover new strategies.* Hillsdale, NJ: Erlbaum.

Siegler, R. S., & Robinson, M. (1982). The development of numerical understandings. In H. W. Reese & L. P. Lipsitt (Eds.), *Advances in child development and behavior* (Vol. 16). New York: Academic Press.

Siegler, R. S., & Svetina, M. (2006). What leads children to adopt new strategies? A microgenetic/cross-sectional study of class inclusion. *Child Development, 77,* 997–1015.

Siever, L., & Davis, K. (1985). Overview: Toward a dysregulation hypothesis of depression. *American Journal of Psychiatry, 142,* 1017–1031.

Sigman, M., & Whaley, S. E. (1998). The role of nutrition in the development of intelligence. In U. Neisser (Ed.), *The rising curve: Long-term gains in IQ and related measures* (pp. 155–182). Washington, DC: American Psychological Association.

Sijtsema, J. J., Veenstra, R., Lindenberg, S., & Salmivalli, C. (2009). Empirical test of bullies' status goals: Assessing direct goals, aggression, and prestige. *Aggressive Behavior, 35*(1), 57–67. doi:10.1002/ab.20282

Silver, E. A., & Kenney, P. A. (1995). Sources of assessment information for instructional guidance in mathematics. In T. Romberg (Ed.), *Reform in school mathematics and authentic assessment.* Albany: State University of New York Press.

Silverman, L. K. (1994). The moral sensitivity of gifted children and the evolution of society. *Roeper Review, 17*(2), 110–116.

Simons, R. L., Robertson, J. F., & Downs, W. R. (1989). The nature of the association between parental rejection and delinquent behavior. *Journal of Youth and Adolescence, 18,* 297–310.

Simons, R. L., Whitbeck, L. B., Conger, R. D., & Conger, K. J. (1991). Parenting factors, social skills, and value commitments as precursors to school failure, involvement with deviant peers, and delinquent behavior. *Journal of Youth and Adolescence, 20,* 645–664.

Simons-Morton, B., & Chen, R. (2009). Peer and parent influences on school engagement among early adolescents. *Youth and Society, 41(1),* 3–25.

Simonton, D. K. (2001). Talent development as a multidimensional, multiplicative, and dynamic process. *Current Directions in Psychological Science, 10,* 39–42.

Simos, P. G., Fletcher, J. M., Sarkari, S., Billingsley, R. L., Denton, C., & Papanicolaou, A. C. (2007). Altering the brain circuits for reading through intervention: A magnetic source imaging study. *Neuropsychology, 21,* 485–496.

Simpson, J. S., & Parsons, E. C. (2009). African American perspectives and informal science educational experiences. *Science Education, 93*(2), 293–321.

Sims, M. (1993). How my question keeps evolving. In M. Cochran-Smith & S. L. Lytle (Eds.), *Inside/outside: Teacher research and knowledge* (pp. 283–289). New York: Teachers College Press.

Singer, E., & Doornenbal, J. (2006). Learning morality in peer conflict: A study of schoolchildren's narratives about being betrayed by a friend. *Childhood, 13*(2), 225–245.

Singer, J., Marx, R. W., Krajcik, J., & Chambers, J. C. (2000). Constructing extended inquiry projects: Curriculum materials for science education reform. *Educational Psychologist, 35,* 165–178.

Sinkus, M. L., Lee, M. J., Gault, J., Logel, J., Short, M., Freedman, R., et al. (2009). A 2-base pair deletion polymorphism in the partial duplication of the α7 nicotinic acetylcholine gene (*CHRFAM7A*) on chromosome 15q14 is associated with schizophrenia. *Brain Research, 1291,* 1–11.

Sinnott, J. D. (2009). Cognitive development as the dance of adaptive transformation: Neo-Piagetian perspectives on adult cognitive development. In M. C. Smith & N. DeFrates-Densch (Eds.), *Handbook of research on adult*

learning and development (pp. 103–134). New York: Routledge/Taylor & Francis.

Sipe, R. B. (2006). Grammar matters. *English Journal, 95,* 15–17.

Sirois, S., Buckingham, D., & Shultz, T. R. (2000). Artificial grammar learning by infants: An auto-associator perspective. *Developmental Science, 3,* 442–456.

Sirota, K. G. (2010). Fun morality reconsidered: Mothering and the relational contours of maternal-child play in U.S. working family life. *Ethos, 38*(4), 388–405. doi:10.1111/j.1548-1352.2010.01157.x

Sitko, B. M. (1998). Knowing how to write: Metacognition and writing instruction. In D. J. Hacker, J. Dunlosky, & A. C. Graesser (Eds.), *Metacognition in educational theory and practice* (pp. 93–115). Mahwah, NJ: Erlbaum.

Sjostrom, L., & Stein, N. (1996). *Bully proof: A teacher's guide on teasing and bullying for use with fourth and fifth grade students.* Wellesley, MA: Wellesley College Center for Women.

Skarakis-Doyle, E., & Dempsey, L. (2008). The detection and monitoring of comprehension errors by preschool children with and without language impairment. *Journal of Speech, Language, and Hearing Research, 51*(5), 1227–1243.

Skelley, S. L., & Crnic, K. A. (2010). Communicating about internal states. In E. H. Sandberg, & B. L. Spritz (Eds.), *A clinician's guide to normal cognitive development in childhood* (pp. 43–61). New York: Routledge/Taylor & Francis Group.

Skinner, B. F. (1953). *Science and human behavior.* New York: Macmillan.

Skinner, B. F. (1957). *Verbal behavior.* New York: Appleton-Century-Crofts.

Skinner, B. F. (1968). *The technology of teaching.* New York: Appleton-Century-Crofts.

Slater, A. (2000). Visual perception in the young infant: Early organization and rapid learning. In D. Muir & A. Slater (Eds.), *Infant development: The essential readings.* (pp. 95–116). Malden: Blackwell Publishing.

Slater, A. M., Mattock, A., & Brown, E. (1990). Size constancy at birth: Newborn infants' responses to retinal and real size. *Journal of Experimental Child Psychology, 49,* 314–322.

Slavin, R., Lake, C., & Groff, C. (2009). Effective programs in middle and high school mathematics: A best-evidence synthesis. *Review of Educational Research, 79*(2), 839–911. doi:10.3102/0034654308330968

Slavin, R. E. (1990). *Cooperative learning: Theory, research, and practice.* Upper Saddle River, NJ: Prentice Hall.

Slavin, R. E., & Cheung, A. (2005). A synthesis of research on language of reading instruction for English language learners. *Review of Educational Research, 75,* 247–284.

Sleeter, C. E., & Grant, C. A. (1999). *Making choices for multicultural education: Five approaches to race, class, and gender* (3rd ed.). Upper Saddle River, NJ: Merrill/Prentice Hall.

Slobin, D. I. (1985). *Crosslinguistic evidence for the language-making capacity.* Hillsdale, NJ: Erlbaum.

Slotkin, T. A. (2008). If nicotine is a developmental neurotoxicant in animal studies, dare we recommend nicotine replacement therapy in pregnant women and adolescents? *Neurotoxicology and Teratology, 20,* 1–19.

Smart, C., Neale, B., & Wade, A. (2001). *The changing experience of childhood: Families and divorce.* Cambridge, England: Polity.

Smetana, J. G. (1981). Preschool children's conceptions of moral and social rules. *Child Development, 52,* 1333–1336.

Smetana, J. G. (2006). Social-cognitive domain theory: Consistencies and variations in children's moral and social judgments. In M. Killen & J. G.

Smetana (Eds.), *Handbook of moral development* (pp. 119–153). Mahwah, NJ: Lawrence.

Smetana, J. G., & Braeges, J. L. (1990). The development of toddlers' moral and conventional judgments. *Merrill-Palmer Quarterly, 36,* 329–346.

Smetana, J. G., & Killen, M. (2008). Moral cognitions, emotions, and neuroscience: An integrative developmental view. *European Journal of Developmental Science, 2*(3), 324–339.

Smetana, J. G., Killen, M., & Turiel, E. (1991). Children's reasoning about interpersonal and moral conflicts. *Child Development, 62,* 629–644.

Smetana, J. G., Metzger, A., Gettman, D. C., & Campione-Barr, N. (2006). Disclosure and secrecy in adolescent–parent relationships. *Child Development, 77,* 201–217.

Smetana, J. G., & Villalobos, M. (2009). Social cognitive development in adolescence. In R. M. Lerner & L. Steinberg (Eds.), *Handbook of adolescent psychology. Vol. 1: Individual bases of adolescent development* (3rd ed., pp. 187–228). Hoboken, NJ: Wiley.

Smilansky, S. (1968). *The effects of sociodramatic play on disadvantaged preschool children.* Oxford, England: Wiley.

Smith, C. B., Battin, M. P., Francis, L. P., & Jacobson, J. A. (2007). Should rapid tests for HIV infection now be mandatory during pregnancy? Global differences in scarcity and a dilemma of technological advance. *Developing World Bioethics, 7*(2), 86–103.

Smith, C. E., Fischer, K. W., & Watson, M. W. (2009). Toward a refined view of aggressive fantasy as a risk factor for aggression: Interaction effects involving cognitive and situational variables. *Aggressive Behavior, 35*(4), 313–323.

Smith, C. L. (2007). Bootstrapping processes in the development of students' commonsense matter theories: Using analogical mappings, thought experiments, and learning to measure to promote conceptual restructuring. *Cognition and Instruction, 25,* 337–398.

Smith, C. L., Maclin, D., Houghton, C., & Hennessey, M. G. (2000). Sixth-grade students' epistemologies of science: The impact of school science experiences on epistemological development. *Cognition and Instruction, 18,* 349–422.

Smith, E. P., Boutte, G. S., Zigler, E., & Finn-Stevenson, M. (2004). Opportunities for schools to promote resilience in children and youth. In K. I. Maton, C. J. Schellenbach, B. J. Leadbeater, & A. L. Solarz (Eds.), *Investing in children, youth, families, and communities: Strengths-based research and policy* (pp. 213–231). Washington, DC: American Psychological Association.

Smith, H. (2008). Searching for kinship: The creation of street families among homeless youth. *American Behavioral Scientist, 51*(6), 756–771.

Smith, H. L. (1998). Literacy and instruction in African American communities: Shall we overcome? In B. Pérez (Ed.), *Sociocultural contexts of language and literacy.* Mahwah, NJ: Erlbaum.

Smith, J. T. (1999). Sickle cell disease. In S. Goldstein & C. R. Reynolds (Eds.), *Handbook of neurodevelopmental and genetic disorders* (pp. 368–384). New York: Guilford Press.

Smith, L. (1994, February 16). Bad habits: Testament to the downward spiral of drugs and teen angst. *Los Angeles Times,* p. 1.

Smith, M. J., & Perkins, K. (2008). Attending to the voice of adolescents who are overweight to promote mental health. *Archives of Psychiatric Nursing, 22*(6), 391–393.

Smith, N. R., Cicchetti, L., Clark, M. C., Fucigna, C., Gordon-O'Connor, B., Halley, B. A., et al. (1998). *Observation drawing with children: A framework for teachers.* New York: Teachers College Press.

Smith, R. A., Martin, S. C., & Wolters, P. L. (2004). Pediatric and adolescent HIV/AIDS. In R. T. Brown

(Ed.), *Handbook of pediatric psychology in school settings* (pp. 195–220). Mahwah, NJ: Erlbaum.

Smith, R. E., & Smoll, F. L. (1997). Coaching the coaches: Youth sports as a scientific and applied behavioral setting. *Current Directions in Psychological Science, 6,* 16–21.

Smitherman, G. (1994). "The blacker the berry the sweeter the juice": African American student writers. In A. H. Dyson & C. Genishi (Eds.), *The need for story: Cultural diversity in classroom and community.* Urbana, IL: National Council of Teachers of English.

Smitherman, G. (2007). The power of the rap: The Black idiom and the new Black poetry. In H. S. Alim & J. Baugh (Eds.), *Talkin Black talk: Language, education, and social change* (pp. 77–91). New York: Teachers College Press.

Smithsonian National Museum of Natural History. (2010). Volcanoes and hot sports. Retrieved May 11, 2010, from http://www.mnh.si.edu/earth/main_frames.html

Smutny, J. F., & von Fremd, S. E. (2009). *Igniting creativity in gifted learners, K–6: Strategies for every teacher.* Thousand Oaks, CA: Corwin Press.

Smutny, J. F., von Fremd, S. E., & Artabasy, J. (2009). Creativity: A gift for the gifted. In J. F. Smutny, & S. E. von Fremd (Eds.), *Igniting creativity in gifted learners, K–6: Strategies for every teacher* (pp. 5–17). Thousand Oaks, CA: Corwin Press.

Smyke, A. T., Zeanah, C. H., Jr., Fox, N. A., & Nelson, C. A., III. (2009). A new model of foster care for young children: The Bucharest Early Intervention Project. *Child and Adolescent Psychiatric Clinics of North America, 18*(3), 721–734.

Snedeker, J., Geren, J., & Shafto, C. L. (2007). Starting over: International adoption as a natural experiment in language development. *Psychological Science, 18,* 79–87.

Snow, C. E., & Van Hemel, S. B. (Eds.) (2008). *Early childhood assessment: Why, what, and how/Committee on Developmental Outcomes and Assessment of Young Children.* Washington, DC: National Research Council.

Snow, C. W., & McGaha, C. G. (2003). *Infant development* (3rd ed.). Upper Saddle River, NJ: Prentice Hall.

Snyder, K. A. (2007). Neural mechanisms of attention and memory in preferential looking tasks. In L. M. Oakes & P. J. Bauer (Eds.), *Short- and long-term memory in infancy and early childhood: Taking the first steps toward remembering* (pp. 179–208). New York: Oxford University Press.

Snyder, L., & Caccamise, D. (2010). Comprehension processes for expository text: Building meaning and making sense. In M. A. Nippold & C. M. Scott (Eds.), *Expository discourse in children, adolescents, and adults: Development and disorders. New directions in communication disorders research: Integrative approaches* (pp. 13–39). New York: Psychology Press.

So, E. C. K. (2009). Changes in drug subculture and drug trafficking among young people. *Journal of Youth Studies, 12,* 171–176.

Sobel, D. M. (2009). Enabling conditions and children's understanding of pretense. *Cognition, 113,* 177–188.

Society for Research in Child Development. (2007). *Ethical standards for research with children.* First published in the 1990–91 Directory and Fall 1991 Newsletter. Retrieved October 3, 2007, from http://www.srcd.org/ethicalstandards.html

Soenens, B., & Vansteenkiste, M. (2010). A theoretical upgrade of the concept of parental psychological control: Proposing new insights on the basis of self-determination theory. *Developmental Review, 30*(1), 74–99. doi:10.1016/j.dr.2009.11.001

Soet, J. E., Brack, G. A., & Dilorio, C. (2003). Prevalence and predictors of women's experience of psychological trauma during childbirth. *Birth, 30* (1), 36–46.

Solity, J., & Vousden, J. (2009). Real books vs reading schemes: A new perspective from instructional psychology. *Educational Psychology, 29*(4), 469–511.

Solmon, M. A., & Lee, A. M. (2008). Research on social issues in elementary school physical education. *Elementary School Journal, 108*(3), 229–239.

Solomon, D., Watson, M., Battistich, E., Schaps, E., & Delucchi, K. (1992). Creating a caring community: Educational practices that promote children's prosocial development. In F. K. Oser, A. Dick, & J. L. Patry (Eds.), *Effective and responsible teaching: The new synthesis.* San Francisco: Jossey-Bass.

Solomon, D., Watson, M. S., Delucchi, K. L., Schaps, E., & Battistich, V. (1988). Enhancing children's prosocial behavior in the classroom. *American Educational Research Journal, 25,* 527–554.

Somerville, L. H., Jones, R. M., & Casey, B. J. (2010). A time of change: Behavioral and neural correlates of adolescent sensitivity to appetitive and aversive environmental cues. *Brain and Cognition, 72,* 124–133.

Son, J., & Wilson, J. (2010). Genetic variation in volunteerism. *The Sociological Quarterly, 51*(1), 46–64. doi:10.1111/j.1533-8525.2009.01167.x

Sonnenschein, S. (1988). The development of referential communication: Speaking to different listeners. *Child Development, 59,* 694–702.

Sophian, C. (2008). Precursors to number: Equivalence relations, less-than and greater-than relations, and units. *Behavioral and Brain Sciences, 31*(6), 670–671.

Sophian, C., & Vong, K. I. (1995). The parts and wholes of arithmetic story problems: Developing knowledge in the preschool years. *Cognition and Instruction, 13,* 469–477.

Sorkhabi, N. (2005). Applicability of Baumrind's parent typology to collective cultures: Analysis of cultural explanations of parent socialization effects. *International Journal of Behavioral Development, 29,* 552–563.

Sousa, D. A. (2009). *How the gifted brain works* (2nd ed.). Thousand Oaks, CA: Corwin.

South, D. (2007). What motivates unmotivated students? In G. E. Mills, *Action research: A guide for the teacher researcher* (3rd ed., pp. 1–2). Upper Saddle River, NJ: Pearson Merrill/Prentice Hall.

Southerland, S. A., & Sinatra, G. M. (2003). Learning about biological evolution: A special case of intentional conceptual change. In G. M. Sinatra & P. R. Pintrich (Eds.), *Intentional conceptual change* (pp. 317–345). Mahwah, NJ: Erlbaum.

Sowell, E. R., Delis, D., Stiles, J., & Jernigan, T. L. (2001). Improved memory functioning and frontal lobe maturation between childhood and adolescence: A structural MRI study. *Journal of the International Neuropsychological Society, 7,* 312–322.

Sowell, E. R., Thompson, P. M., Rex, D., Kornsand, D., Tessner, K. D., Jernigan, T. L., et al. (2002). Mapping sulcal pattern asymmetry and local cortical surface gray matter distribution *in vivo*: Maturation in the perisylvian cortices. *Cerebral Cortex, 12,* 17–26.

Spear, L. P. (2007). Brain development and adolescent behavior. In D. Coch, K. W. Fischer, & G. Dawson (Eds.), *Human behavior, learning, and the developing brain: Typical development* (pp. 362–396). New York: Guilford Press.

Spearman, C. (1904). General intelligence, objectively determined and measured. *American Journal of Psychology, 15,* 201–293.

Spearman, C. (1927). *The abilities of man: Their nature and measurement.* New York: Macmillan.

Spector, R. E. (2004). *Cultural diversity in health and illness* (6th ed.). Upper Saddle River, NJ: Prentice Hall.

Spelke, E. S. (1994). Initial knowledge: Six suggestions. *Cognition, 50,* 431–445.

Spelke, E. S. (2000). Core knowledge. *American Psychologist, 55,* pp. 1233–1243.

Spelke, E. S. (2005). Sex differences in intrinsic aptitude for mathematics and science? A critical review. *American Psychologist, 60,* 950–958.

Spelke, E. S., & Kinzler, K. D. (2007). Core knowledge. *Developmental Science, 10*(1), 89–96.

Spencer, J. P., Blumberg, M. S., McMurray, B., Robinson, S. R., Samuelson, L. K., & Tomblin, J. B. (2009). Short arms and talking eggs: Why we should no longer abide the nativist-empiricist debate. *Child Development Perspectives, 3*(2), 79–87.

Spencer, M. B. (2006). Phenomenology and ecological systems theory: Development of diverse groups. In W. Damon & R. M. Lerner (Eds. in Chief) & R. M. Lerner (Vol. Ed.), *Handbook of child psychology, Vol. 1. Theoretical models of human development* (6th ed., pp. 829–893). Hoboken, NJ: Wiley.

Spencer, M. B., & Markstrom-Adams, C. (1990). Identity processes among racial and ethnic minority children in America. *Child Development, 61,* 290–310.

Spencer, M. B., Noll, E., Stoltzfus, J., & Harpalani, V. (2001). Identity and school adjustment: Revisiting the "acting White" assumption. *Educational Psychologist, 36,* 21–30.

Spera, C. (2005). A review of the relationship among parenting practices, parenting styles, and adolescent school achievement. *Educational Psychology Review, 17,* 125–146.

Sperling, M. (1996). Revisiting the writing-speaking connection: Challenges for research on writing and writing instruction. *Review of Educational Research, 66,* 53–86.

Spicker, H. H. (1992). Identifying and enriching: Rural gifted children. *Educational Horizons, 70*(2), 60–65.

Spiegel, C., & Halberda, J. (2011). Rapid fast-mapping abilities in 2-year-olds. *Journal of Experimental Child Psychology, 109*(1), 132–140. doi:10.1016/j.jecp.2010.10.013

Spilt, J. L., Koomen, H. M. Y., Thijs, J. T., Stoel, R. D., & van der Leij, A. (2010). Teachers' assessment of antisocial behavior in kindergarten: Physical aggression and measurement bias across gender. *Journal of Psychoeducational Assessment, 28*(2), 129–138. doi:10.1177/0734282909340236

Spinath, B., & Steinmayr, R. (2008). Longitudinal analysis of intrinsic motivation and competence beliefs: Is there a relation over time? *Child Development, 79*(5), 1555–1569. doi:10.1111/j.1467-8624.2008.01205.x

Spinath, F. M., Price, T. S., Dale, P. S., & Plomin, R. (2004). The genetic and environmental origins of language disability and ability. *Child Development, 75,* 445–454.

Spirito, A., Valeri, S., Boergers, J., & Donaldson, D. (2003). Predictors of continued suicidal behaviors in adolescents following a suicide attempt. *Journal of Clinical Child and Adolescent Psychology, 32,* 284–289.

Spivey, N. N. (1997). *The constructivist metaphor: Reading, writing, and the making of meaning.* San Diego, CA: Academic Press.

Sprafkin, C., Serbin, L. A., Denier, C., & Connor, J. M. (1983). Sex-differentiated play: Cognitive consequences and early interventions. In M. B. Liss (Ed.), *Social and cognitive skills: Sex roles and children's play.* San Diego, CA: Academic Press.

Spritz, B. L., Fergusson, A. S., & Bankoff, S. M. (2010). False beliefs and the development of deception. In E. H. Sandberg & B. L. Spritz (Eds.), *A clinician's guide to normal cognitive development in childhood* (pp. 101–120). New York: Routledge/Taylor & Francis.

Sroufe, L. A. (1983). Infant-caregiver attachment and patterns of adaptation in preschool: The roots of maladaptation and competence. In M. Perlmutter (Ed.), Development and policy concerning children with special needs. *Minnesota Symposium on Child Psychology, 16,* 41–83. Hillsdale, NJ: Erlbaum.

Sroufe, L. A., Egeland, B., Carlson, E., & Collins, W. (2005). *Minnesota study of risk and adaptation from birth to maturity: The development of the person.* New York: Guilford Press.

St. James-Roberts, I., & Plewis, I. (1996). Individual differences, daily fluctuations, and developmental changes in amounts of infant waking, fussiness, crying, feeding, and sleeping. *Child Development, 67,* 2527–2540.

Staff, J., Messersmith, E. E., & Schulenberg, J. E. (2009). Adolescents and the world of work. In R. M. Lerner & L. Steinberg (Eds.), *Handbook of adolescent psychology, Vol 2: Contextual influences on adolescent development* (pp. 270–313). Hoboken, NJ: Wiley.

Stahl, S. A., & Miller, P. D. (1989). Whole language and language experience approaches for beginning reading: A quantitative research synthesis. *Review of Educational Research, 59,* 87–116.

Stainthorp, R., Stuart, M., Powell, D., Quinlan, P., & Garwood, H. (2010). Visual processing deficits in children with slow RAN performance. *Scientific Studies of Reading, 14*(3), 266–292.

Stanley, J. C. (1980). On educating the gifted. *Educational Researcher, 9*(3), 8–12.

Stanovich, K. E. (1999). The sociopsychometrics of learning disabilities. *Journal of Learning Disabilities, 32,* 350–361.

Stanovich, K. E. (2000). *Progress in understanding reading: Scientific foundations and new frontiers.* New York: Guilford Press.

Staples, M. (2007). Supporting whole-class collaborative inquiry in a secondary mathematics classroom. *Cognition and Instruction, 25,* 161–217.

Starke, M., Wikland, K. A., & Möller, A. (2003). Parents' descriptions of development and problems associated with infants with Turner syndrome: A retrospective study. *Journal of Paediatrics and Child Health, 39,* 293–298.

Staub, D. (1998). *Delicate threads: Friendships between children with and without special needs in inclusive settings.* Bethesda, MD: Woodbine House.

Staudt, M. M. (2001). Use of services prior to and following intensive family preservation services. *Journal of Child and Family Studies, 10,* 101–114.

Steele, C. M. (1997). A threat in the air: How stereotypes shape intellectual identity and performance. *American Psychologist, 52,* 613–629.

Stein, J. A., & Krishnan, K. (2007). Nonverbal learning disabilities and executive function: The challenges of effective assessment and teaching. In L. Meltzer (Ed.), *Executive function in education: From theory to practice* (pp. 106–132). New York: Guilford Press.

Stein, N. (1993, May). Stop sexual harassment in schools. *USA Today.*

Stein, N., Trabasso, T., & Liwag, M. (2000). A goal appraisal theory of emotional understanding: Implications for development and learning. In M. Lewis & J. Haviland (Eds.), *Handbook of emotions* (2nd ed., pp. 436–457). New York: Guilford Press.

Stein, N. L. (1982). What's in a story: Interpreting the interpretations of story grammars. *Discourse Processes, 5,* 319–335.

Steinberg, L. (1986). Latchkey children and susceptibility to peer pressure: An ecological analysis. *Developmental Psychology, 22,* 433–439.

Steinberg, L. (2007). Risk taking in adolescence: New perspectives from brain and behavioral science. *Current Directions in Psychological Science, 16,* 55–59.

Steinberg, L., Blinde, P. L., & Chan, K. S. (1984). Dropping out among language minority youth. *Review of Educational Research, 54,* 113–132.

Steinberg, L., Brown, B. B., Cider, M., Kaczmarek, N., & Lazzaro, C. (1988). *Noninstructional influences on high school student achievement: The contributions of parents, peers, extracurricular activities, and part-time work.* Madison, WI: National Center on Effective Secondary Schools. (ERIC Document Reproduction Service No. ED 307 509)

Steinberg, L., Elmen, J., & Mounts, N. (1989). Authoritative parenting, psychosocial maturity, and academic success among adolescents. *Child Development, 60,* 1424–1436.

Steinberg, L., Lamborn, S., Darling, N., Mounts, S., & Dornbusch, S. (1994). Over time change in adjustment and competence among adolescents from authoritative, authoritarian, indulgent, and neglectful families. *Child Development, 65,* 754–770.

Steiner, H. H., & Carr, M. (2003). Cognitive development in gifted children: Toward a more precise understanding of emerging differences in intelligence. *Educational Psychology Review, 15,* 215–246.

Steinmayr, R., & Spinath, B. (2009). What explains boys' stronger confidence in their intelligence? *Sex Roles, 61*(9–10), 736–749.

Stenberg, C. R., & Campos, J. J. (1990). The development of anger expressions in infancy. In N. L. Stein, B. Leventhal, & T. Trabasso (Eds.), *Psychological and biological approaches to emotion* (pp. 247–282). Hillsdale, NJ: Erlbaum.

Stenberg, G. (2009). Selectivity in infant social referencing. *Infancy, 14*(4), 457–473.

Stephan, K. E., Fink, G. R., & Marshall, J. C. (2007). Mechanisms of hemispheric specialization: Insights from analyses of connectivity. *Neuropsychologia, 45,* 209–228.

Stephenson, J. (2010). Book reading as an intervention context for children beginning to use graphic symbols for communication. *Journal of Developmental and Physical Disabilities, 22*(3), 257–271.

Stern, D. N. (1977). *The first relationship: Mother and infant.* Cambridge, MA: Harvard University Press.

Stern, W. (1912). *Die psychologischen Methoden der Intelligenzprufung.* Leipzig, Germany: Barth.

Sternberg, R. J. (1985). *Beyond IQ: A triarchic theory of human intelligence.* Cambridge, England: Cambridge University Press.

Sternberg, R. J. (1996). Myths, countermyths, and truths about intelligence. *Educational Researcher, 25*(2), 11–16.

Sternberg, R. J. (1997). The concept of intelligence and its role in lifelong learning and success. *American Psychologist, 52,* 1030–1037.

Sternberg, R. J. (2002). Raising the achievement of all students: Teaching for successful intelligence. *Educational Psychology Review, 14,* 383–393.

Sternberg, R. J. (2003a). "My house is a very very very fine house"—But it is not the only house. In H. Nyborg (Ed.), *The scientific study of general intelligence: Tribute to Arthur Jensen* (pp. 373–395). Oxford, England: Elsevier.

Sternberg, R. J. (2003b). *Wisdom, intelligence, and creativity synthesized.* Cambridge, England: Cambridge University Press.

Sternberg, R. J. (2005). The triarchic theory of successful intelligence. In D. P. Flanagan & P. L. Harrison (Eds.), *Contemporary intellectual assessment: Theories, tests, and issues* (2nd ed., pp. 103–119). New York: Guilford Press.

Sternberg, R. J. (2007). Who are the bright children? The cultural context of being and acting intelligent. *Educational Researcher, 36,* 148–155.

Sternberg, R. J. (2009). The theory of successful intelligence as a basis for new forms of ability testing at the high school, college, and graduate school levels. In J. C. Kaufman (Ed.), *Intelligent testing: Integrating psychological theory and clinical practice* (pp. 113–147). New York: Cambridge University Press.

Sternberg, R. J., Forsythe, G. B., Hedlund, J., Horvath, J. A., Wagner, R. K., Williams, W. M., et al. (2000). *Practical intelligence in everyday life.* Cambridge, England: Cambridge University Press.

Sternberg, R. J., & Grigorenko, E. L. (2000). Theme-park psychology: A case study regarding human intelligence and its implications for education. *Educational Psychology Review, 12,* 247–268.

Sternberg, R. J., Grigorenko, E. L., & Bridglall, B. L. (2007). Intelligence as a socialized phenomenon. In E. W. Gordon & B. L. Bridglall (Eds.), *Affirmative development: Cultivating academic ability* (pp. 49–72). Lanham, MD: Rowman.

Sternberg, R. J., Jarvin, L., & Grigorenko, E. L. (2009). *Teaching for wisdom, intelligence, creativity, and success.* Thousand Oaks, CA: Corwin.

Sternberg, R. J., Jarvin, L., & Grigorenko, E. L. (2011). *Explorations in giftedness.* New York: Cambridge University Press.

Sternberg, R. J., Torff, B., & Grigorenko, E. L. (1998). Teaching for successful intelligence raises school achievement. *Phi Delta Kappa, 79,* 667–669.

Sternberg, R. J., & Zhang, L. (1995). What do we mean by giftedness? A pentagonal implicit theory. *Gifted Child Quarterly, 39,* 88–94.

Sterponi, L. (2010). Learning communicative competence. In D. F. Lancy, J. Bock, & S. Gaskins (Eds.), *The anthropology of learning in childhood* (pp. 235–259). Lanham, MD: AltaMira Press/ Rowman & Littlefield

Sterzer, P., & Stadler, C. (2009, October). Neuroimaging of aggressive and violent behaviour in children and adolescents. *Frontiers in Behavioral Neuroscience, 3.* doi:10.3389/neuro.08.035.2009

Stevens, R. J., & Slavin, R. E. (1995). The cooperative elementary school: Effects of students' achievement, attitudes, and social relations. *American Educational Research Journal, 32,* 321–351.

Stevenson, H. W., Chen, C., & Uttal, D. H. (1990). Beliefs and achievement: A study of Black, White, and Hispanic children. *Child Development, 61,* 508–523.

Stevick, R. A. (2007). *Growing up Amish: The teenage years.* Baltimore, MD: Johns Hopkins University Press.

Stewart, L., & Pascual-Leone, J. (1992). Mental capacity constraints and the development of moral reasoning. *Journal of Experimental Child Psychology, 54,* 251–287.

Stiggins, R. (2007). Assessment through students' eyes. *Educational Leadership, 64*(8), 22–26.

Stiles, J. (2008). *The fundamentals of brain development: Integrating nature and nurture.* Cambridge, MA: Harvard University Press.

Stiles, J., & Thal, D. (1993). Linguistic and spatial cognitive development following early focal brain injury: Patterns of deficit and recovery. In M. Johnson (Ed.), *Brain development and cognition.* Oxford, England: Blackwell.

Stipek, D. (2002). At what age should children enter kindergarten? A question for policy makers and parents. *Social Policy Report, 16,* 1, 3–16. Ann Arbor, MI: Society for Research in Child Development.

Stipek, D. J. (1993). *Motivation to learn: From theory to practice* (2nd ed.). Needham Heights, MA: Allyn & Bacon.

Stipek, D. J. (1996). Motivation and instruction. In D. C. Berliner & R. C. Calfee (Eds.), *Handbook of educational psychology.* New York: Macmillan.

Stipek, D. J., & Kowalski, P. S. (1989). Learned helplessness in task-orienting versus performance-orienting testing conditions. *Journal of Educational Psychology, 81,* 384–391.

Stipek, D. J., Recchia, S., & McClintic, S. M. (1992). Self-evaluation in young children. *Monographs of the Society for Research in Child Development, 57*(2, Serial No. 226).

Stock, P., Desoete, A., & Roeyers, H. (2009). Mastery of the counting principles in toddlers: A crucial step in the development of budding arithmetic abilities? *Learning and Individual Differences, 19*(4), 419–422.

Stormont, M. (2001). Social outcomes of children with AD/HD: Contributing factors and implications for practice. *Psychology in the Schools, 38,* 521–531.

Stormont, M., Stebbins, M. S., & Holliday, G. (2001). Characteristics and educational support needs of underrepresented gifted adolescents. *Psychology in the Schools, 38*(5), 413–423.

Strand-Cary, M., & Klahr, D. (2008). Developing elementary science skills: Instructional effectiveness and path independence. *Cognitive Development, 23,* 488–511.

Strapp, C. M., & Federico, A. (2000). Imitations and repetitions: What do children say following recasts? *First Language, 20,* 273–290.

Strauch, B. (2003). *The primal teen: What the new discoveries about the teenage brain tells us about our kids.* New York: Doubleday.

Straus, M. A. (2000). The benefits of never spanking: New and more definitive evidence. In M. A. Straus, *Beating the devil out of them: Corporal punishment by American families and its effects on children.* New Brunswick, NJ: Transaction Publications.

Strayer, F. F. (1991). The development of agonistic and affiliative structures in preschool play groups. In J. Silverberg & P. Gray (Eds.), *To fight or not to fight: Violence and peacefulness in humans and other primates.* Oxford, England: Oxford University Press.

Streissguth, A. P., Barr, H. M., Sampson, P. D., & Bookstein, F. L. (1994). Prenatal alcohol and offspring development: The first fourteen years. *Drug and Alcohol Dependence, 36,* 89–99.

Stricklin, K. (2011). Hands-on reciprocal teaching: A comprehension technique. *The Reading Teacher, 64*(8), 620–625. doi:10.1598/RT.64.8.8

Stright, A. D., Neitzel, C., Sears, K. G., & Hoke-Sinex, L. (2001). Instruction begins in the home: Relations between parental instruction and children's self-regulation in the classroom. *Journal of Educational Psychology, 93,* 456–466.

Strike, K. A., & Posner, G. J. (1992). A revisionist theory of conceptual change. In R. A. Duschl & R. J. Hamilton (Eds.), *Philosophy of science, cognitive psychology, and educational theory and practice.* Albany: State University of New York Press.

Stroink, M., & Lalonde, R. (2009). Bicultural identity conflict in second-generation Asian Canadians. *The Journal of Social Psychology, 149*(1), 44–65.

Strozer, J. R. (1994). *Language acquisition after puberty.* Washington, DC: Georgetown University Press.

Styne, D. M. (2003). The regulation of pubertal growth. *Hormone Research, 60*(Suppl.1), 22–26.

Su, W., Mrug, S., & Windle, M. (2010). Social cognitive and emotional mediators link violence exposure and parental nurturance to adolescent aggression. *Journal of Clinical Child and Adolescent Psychology, 39*(6), 814–824. doi:10.1080/15374416.2010.517163

Suárez-Orozco, C., Suárez-Orozco, M. M., & Todorova, I. (2008). *Learning a new land: Immigrant students in American society.* Cambridge, MA: Belknap Press.

Subrahmanyam, K., Garcia, E. C. M., Harsono, L. S., Li, J. S., & Lipana, L. (2009). In their words: Connecting on-line weblogs to developmental processes. *British Journal of Developmental Psychology. Special Issue: Young People and the Media, 27*(1), 219–245. doi:10.1348/026151008X345979

Sudhalter, V., & Braine, M. D. (1985). How does comprehension of passives develop? A comparison of actional and experiential verbs. *Journal of Child Language, 12,* 455–470.

Suh, S., Suh, J., & Houston, I. (2007). Predictors of categorical at-risk high school dropouts. *Journal of Counseling & Development, 85,* 196–203.

Suhr, D. D. (1999). *An investigation of mathematics and reading achievement of 5- through 14-year-olds using latent growth curve methodology.* Unpublished doctoral dissertation, University of Northern Colorado, Greeley.

Suina, J. H., & Smolkin, L. B. (1994). From natal culture to school culture to dominant society culture: Supporting transitions for Pueblo Indian students. In P. M. Greenfield & R. R. Cocking (Eds.), *Cross-cultural roots of minority child development.* Mahwah, NJ: Erlbaum.

Suizzo, M., Robinson, C., & Pahlke, E. (2008). African American mothers' socialization beliefs and goals with young children: Themes of history, education, and collective independence. *Journal of Family Issues, 29*(3), 287–316. doi:10.1177/0192513X07308368

Sullivan, F. M., & Barlow, S. M. (2001). Review of risk factors for sudden infant death syndrome. *Paediatric and Perinatal Epidemiology, 15,* 144–200.

Sullivan, H. S. (1953). *The interpersonal theory of psychiatry.* New York: Norton.

Sullivan, J. R., & Conoley, J. C. (2004). Academic and instructional interventions with aggressive students. In J. C. Conoley & A. P. Goldstein (Eds.), *School violence intervention* (2nd ed., pp. 235–255). New York: Guilford Press.

Sullivan, M. W., & Lewis, M. (2003). Contextual determinants of anger and other negative expressions in young infants. *Developmental Psychology, 39,* 693–705.

Sullivan, R. C. (1994). Autism: Definitions past and present. *Journal of Vocational Rehabilitation, 4,* 4–9.

Sullivan-DeCarlo, C., DeFalco, K., & Roberts, V. (1998). Helping students avoid risky behavior. *Educational Leadership, 56*(1), 80–82.

Sulzby, E. (1985). Children's emergent reading of favorite storybooks: A developmental study. *Reading Research Quarterly, 20,* 458–481.

Sulzby, E. (1986). Children's elicitation and use of metalinguistic knowledge about *word* during literacy interactions. In D. B. Yaden, Jr., & S. Templeton (Eds.), *Metalinguistic awareness and beginning literacy: Conceptualizing what it means to read and write.* Portsmouth, NH: Heinemann.

Suskind, R. (1998). *A hope in the unseen: An American odyssey from the inner city to the Ivy League.* New York: Broadway Books.

Susman, E. J., Inoff-Germain, G., Nottelmann, E. D., Loriaux, D. L., Cutler, J., Gordon, B., et al. (1987). Hormones, emotional dispositions, and aggressive attributes in young adolescents. *Child Development, 58,* 1114–1134.

Suttles, G. D. (1970). Friendship as a social institution. In G. J. McCall, M. McCall, N. K. Denzin, G. D. Scuttles, & S. Kurth (Eds.), *Social relationships* (pp. 95–135). Chicago: Aldine de Gruyter.

Sutton-Smith, B. (Ed.). (1979). *Play and learning.* New York: Gardner Press.

Sutton-Smith, B. (1986). The development of fictional narrative performances. *Topics in Language Disorders, 7*(1), 1–10.

Svanberg, P. O., Mennet, L., & Spieker, S. (2010). Promoting a secure attachment: A primary prevention practice model. *Clinical Child Psychology and Psychiatry, 15*(3), 363–378.

Svirsky, M. A., Robbins, A. M., Kirk, K. I., Pisoni, D. B., & Miyamoto, R. T. (2000). Language development in profoundly deaf children with cochlear implants. *Psychological Science, 11,* 153–158.

Swanborn, M. S. L., & de Glopper, K. (1999). Incidental word learning while reading: A meta-analysis. *Review of Educational Research, 69,* 261–285.

Swann, W. B., Jr. (1997). The trouble with change: Self-verification and allegiance to the self. *Psychological Science, 8,* 177–180.

Swanson, D. P., Cunningham, M., Youngblood, J. II, & Spencer, M. B. (2009). Racial identity development during childhood. In H. A. Neville, B. M. Tynes, S. O. Utsey (Eds.), *Handbook of African American psychology* (pp. 269–281). Thousand Oaks, CA: Sage Publications.

Swanson, H. L., & Jerman, O. (2006). Math disabilities: A selective meta-analysis of the literature. *Review of Educational Research, 76,* 249–274.

Swanson, H. L., Jerman, O., & Zheng, X. (2008). Growth in working memory and mathematical problem solving in children at risk and not at risk for serious math difficulties. *Journal of Educational Psychology, 100,* 343–379.

Swanson, H. L., & Lussier, C. M. (2001). A selective synthesis of the experimental literature on dynamic assessment. *Review of Educational Research, 71,* 321–363.

Swanson, H. L., Mink, J., & Bocian, K. M. (1999). Cognitive processing deficits in poor readers with symptoms of reading disabilities and ADHD: More alike than different? *Journal of Educational Psychology, 91,* 321–333.

Swenson, L. P., & Rose, A. J. (2009). Friends' knowledge of youth internalizing and externalizing adjustment: Accuracy, bias, and the influences of gender, grade, positive friendship quality, and self-disclosure. *Journal of Abnormal Child Psychology, 37*(6), 887–901. doi:10.1007/s10802-009-9319-z

Swim, J. K., & Stangor, C. (Eds.). (1998). *Prejudice: The target's perspective* (pp. 220–241). San Diego, CA: Academic Press.

Sylva, K., Melhuish, E., Sammons, P., Siraj-Blatchford, I., & Taggart, B. (2004). *Effective pre-school education.* London: Institute of Education, University of London.

Symon, A., Winter, C., Inkster, M. & Donnan, P. T. (2009). Outcomes for births booked under and independent midwife and births in NHS maternity units: Matched comparison study. *British Medical Journal, 338,* 1–9.

Szynal-Brown, C., & Morgan, R. R. (1983). The effects of reward on tutor's behaviors in a cross-age tutoring context. *Journal of Experimental Child Psychology, 36,* 196–208.

Tabak, I., & Weinstock, M. (2008). A sociocultural exploration of epistemological beliefs. In M. S. Khine (Ed.), *Knowing, knowledge and beliefs: Epistemological studies across diverse cultures* (pp. 177–195). New York: Springer Science + Business Media.

Tager-Flusberg, H., & Skwerer, D. P. (2007). Williams syndrome: A model developmental syndrome for exploring brain-behavior relationships. In D. Coch, G. Dawson, & K. W. Fischer (Eds.), *Human behavior, learning, and the developing brain: Atypical development* (pp. 87–116). New York: Guilford Press.

Takahashi, K. (1990). Are the key assumptions of the "Strange Situation" procedure universal? A view from Japanese research. *Human Development, 33,* 23–30.

Takeuchi, A. H., & Hulse, S. H. (1993). Absolute pitch. *Psychological Bulletin, 113,* 345–361.

Tallal, P. (2003). Language learning disabilities: Integrating research approaches. *Current Directions in Psychological Science, 12,* 206–211.

Tamburrini, J. (1982). Some educational implications of Piaget's theory. In S. Modgil & C. Modgil (Eds.), *Jean Piaget: Consensus and controversy.* New York: Praeger.

Tan, E. T., & Goldberg, W. A. (2009). Parental school involvement in relation to children's grades and adaptation to school. *Journal of Applied Developmental Psychology, 30,* 442–453.

Tan, T. X. (2009). School-age adopted Chinese girls' behavioral adjustment, academic performance, and social skills: Longitudinal results. *American Journal of Orthopsychiatry, 79,* 244–251.

Tangney, J. P., & Dearing, R. L. (2002). *Shame and guilt*. New York: Guilford Press.

Tannen, D. (1990). *You just don't understand: Talk between the sexes*. New York: Ballantine.

Tanner, J., Asbridge, M., & Wortley, S. (2008). Our favorite melodies: Musical consumption and teenage lifestyles. *British Journal of Sociology, 59*(1), 117–144.

Tanner, J. M. (1990). *Foetus into man: Physical growth from conception to maturity* (Rev. ed.). Cambridge, MA: Harvard University Press.

Tarullo, A., Obradovic, J., & Gunnar, M. (2009). Self-control and the developing brain. *Zero to Three, 29*(3), 31–37.

Tattersall, I. (2006). How we came to be human. *Scientific American, 16*(2), 66–73.

Tatum, A. W. (2008). Toward a more anatomically complete model of literacy instruction: A focus on African American male adolescents and teens. *Harvard Educational Review, 78*(1), 155–180.

Tatum, B. D. (1997). *Why are all the Black kids sitting together in the cafeteria? and other conversations about race*. New York: Basic Books.

Taumoepeau, M., & Ruffman, T. (2008). Stepping stones to others' minds: Maternal talk relates to child mental state language and emotion understandings at 15, 24, and 33 months. *Child Development, 79*, 284–302.

Taylor, D., & Lorimer, M. (2002–2003). Helping boys succeed. *Educational Leadership, 60*(4), 68–70.

Taylor, J. M. (1994). *MDMA frequently asked questions list*. Retrieved from http://ibbserver.ibb.uu.nl/jboschma/ecstasy/xtc01

Taylor, M., Esbensen, B. M., & Bennett, R. T. (1994). Children's understanding of knowledge acquisition: The tendency for children to report that they have always known what they have just learned. *Child Development, 65*, 1581–1604.

Taylor, R. D., Casten, R., Flickinger, S. M., Roberts, D., & Fulmore, C. D. (1994). Explaining the school performance of African American adolescents. *Journal of Research on Adolescence, 4*, 21–44.

Taylor, W. C., Beech, B. M., & Cummings, S. S. (1998). Increasing physical activity levels among youth: A public health challenge. In D. K. Wilson, J. R. Rodrigue, & W. C. Taylor (Eds.), *Health-promoting and health-compromising behaviors among minority adolescents* (pp. 107–128). Washington, DC: American Psychological Association.

Tehrani, J. J., & Riede, F. (2008). Towards an archaeology of pedagogy: Learning, teaching and the generation of material culture traditions. *World Archaeology, 40*(3), 316–331.

Tellegren, A., Lykken, D. T., Bouchard, T. J., & Wilcox, K. J. (1988). Personality similarity in twins reared apart and together. *Journal of Personality and Social Psychology, 54*, 1031–1039.

Téllez, K., & Waxman, H. (2010). A review of research on effective community programs for English Language Learners. *School Community Journal, 20*(1), 103–119.

Temple, J., Reynolds, A., & Arteaga, I. (2010). Low birth weight, preschool education, and school remediation. *Education and Urban Society, 42*(6), 705–729. doi:10.1177/0013124510330946

Tennenbaum, H. R., & Leaper, C. (2002). Are parents' gender schemas related to their children's gender-related cognitions? A meta-analysis. *Developmental Psychology, 38*, 615–630.

Tennyson, R. D., & Cocchiarella, M. J. (1986). An empirically based instructional design theory for teaching concepts. *Review of Educational Research, 56*, 40–71.

Terman, L. M. (1916). *The measurement of intelligence*. Boston: Houghton Mifflin.

Terman, L. M., & Merrill, M. A. (1972). *Stanford-Binet Intelligence Scale* (3rd ed.). Boston: Houghton Mifflin.

Terry, A. W. (2000). An early glimpse: Service learning from an adolescent perspective. *Journal of Secondary Gifted Education, 11*(3), 115–134.

Terry, A. W. (2001). *A case study of community action service learning on young, gifted adolescents and their community* (Doctoral dissertation, University of Georgia, 2000). *Dissertation Abstracts International, 61*(08), 3058.

Terry, A. W. (2003). Effects of service learning on young, gifted adolescents and their community. *Gifted Child Quarterly, 47*(4), 295–308.

Terry, A. W. (2008). Student voices, global echoes: Service-learning and the gifted. *Roeper Review, 30*, 45–51.

Terry, A., & Panter, T. (2010). Students make sure the Cherokees are not removed . . . again: A study of service-learning and artful learning in teaching history. *Journal for the Education of the Gifted, 34*(1), 156–176.

Teti, D. M., Gelfand, D., Messinger, D. S., & Isabella, R. (1995). Maternal depression and the quality of early attachment: An examination of infants, preschoolers and their mothers. *Developmental Psychology, 31*, 364–376.

Tharp, R. G. (1989). Psychocultural variables and constants: Effects on teaching and learning in schools. *American Psychologist, 44*, 349–359.

Tharp, R. G. (1994). Intergroup differences among Native Americans in socialization and child cognition: An ethnogenetic analysis. In P. M. Greenfield & R. R. Cocking (Eds.), *Cross-cultural roots of minority child development* (pp. 87–105). Hillsdale, NJ: Erlbaum.

Thatch, L. V. L. (2008). *A case study of an elementary science teacher's efforts to transform students' scientific communication from "informal science talk" to "formal science talk."* Ph.D. dissertation, The University of Texas at Austin, United States–Texas. Retrieved August 30, 2010, from Dissertations & Theses: A&I. (Publication No. AAT 3315081)

Thatcher, K. L. (2010). The development of phonological awareness with specific language-impaired and typical children. *Psychology in the Schools, 47*(5), 467–480.

Thelen, E., & Smith, L. B. (2006). Dynamic systems theories. In W. Damon & R. M. Lerner (Eds. in Chief) & R. M. Lerner (Vol. Ed.), *Handbook of child psychology: Vol. 1. Theoretical models of human development* (6th ed., pp. 258–312). Hoboken, NJ: Wiley.

Theodore, R. M., Demuth, K., & Shattuck-Hufnagel, S. (2011). Acoustic evidence for positional and complexity effects on children's production of plural --s. *Journal of Speech, Language & Hearing Research, 54*(2), 539–548. doi:10.1044/1092-4388(2010/10-0035)

Thomas, A., & Chess, S. (1977). *Temperament and development*. New York: Brunner/Mazel.

Thomas, H. (2006). Obesity prevention programs for children and youth: Why are their results so modest? *Health Education Research, 21*, 783–795.

Thomas, J. W. (1993). Promoting independent learning in the middle grades: The role of instructional support practices. *Elementary School Journal, 93*, 575–591.

Thomas, R. M. (2005). *High-stakes testing: Coping with collateral damage*. Mahwah, NJ: Erlbaum.

Thomas, S., & Oldfather, P. (1997). Intrinsic motivations, literacy, and assessment practices: "That's my grade. That's me." *Educational Psychologist, 32*, 107–123.

Thompson, G. (2008, March). Beneath the apathy. *Educational Leadership, 65*(6), 50–54.

Thompson, H., & Carr, M. (1995, April). *Brief metacognitive intervention and interest as predictors of memory for text*. Paper presented at the annual meeting of the American Educational Research Association, San Francisco.

Thompson, M., & Grace, C. O. (with L. J. Cohen) (2001). *Best friends, worst enemies: Understanding the social lives of children*. New York: Ballantine.

Thompson, R. A. (1994a). Emotion regulation: A theme in search of a definition. *Monographs of the Society for Research in Child Development, 59*(2–3, Serial No. 240), 25–52.

Thompson, R. A. (1994b). The role of the father after divorce. *The Future of Children: Children and Divorce, 4*(1), 210–235.

Thompson, R. A. (2006). The development of the person: Social understanding, relationships, conscience, self. In W. Damon & R. M. Lerner (Eds. in Chief) & N. Eisenberg (Vol. Ed.), *Handbook of child psychology, Vol. 3. Social, emotional, and personality development* (6th ed., pp. 24–98). Hoboken, NJ: Wiley.

Thompson, R. A., Easterbrooks, M. A., & Padilla-Walker, L. M. (2003). Social and emotional development in infancy. In R. M. Lerner, M. A. Easterbrooks, & J. Mistry (Vol. Eds.), & I. B. Weiner (Editor-in-Chief), *Handbook of psychology. Vol. 6: Developmental psychology* (pp. 91–112). Hoboken, NJ: John Wiley & Sons.

Thompson, R. A., & Newton, E. K. (2010). Emotions in early conscience. In W. F. Arsenio & E. A. Lemerise (Eds.), *Emotions, aggression, and morality in children: Bridging development and psychopathology* (pp. 13–31). Washington, DC: American Psychological Association.

Thompson, R. A., & Virmani, E. A. (2010). Self and personality. In M. H. Bornstein (Ed.), *Handbook of cultural developmental science* (pp. 195–207). New York: Psychology Press.

Thompson, R. H., Cotnoir-Bichelman, N. M., McKerchar, P. M., Tate, T. L., & Dancho, K. A. (2007). Enhancing early communication through infant sign training. *Journal of Applied Behavior Analysis, 40*, 15–23.

Thompson, R. H., McKerchar, P. M., & Dancho, K. A. (2004). The effects of delayed physical prompts and reinforcement on infant sign language acquisition. *Journal of Applied Behavior Analysis, 37*, 379–383.

Thompson-Schill, S. L., Ramscar, M., & Chrysikou, E. G. (2009). Cognition without control: When a little frontal lobe goes a long way. *Current Directions in Psychological Science, 18*(5), 259–263.

Thomson, D. M. (2010). Marshmallow power and frooty treasures: Disciplining the child consumer through online cereal advergaming. *Critical Studies in Media Communication, 27*(5), 438–454. doi:10.1080/15295030903583648

Thomson, J. M., & Goswami, U. (2010). Learning novel phonological representations in developmental dyslexia: Associations with basic auditory processing of rise time and phonological awareness. *Reading and Writing, 23*(5), 453–473.

Thorkildsen, T. A. (1995). Conceptions of social justice. In W. M. Kurtines & J. L. Gewirtz (Eds.), *Moral development: An introduction*. Boston: Allyn & Bacon.

Thornberg, R. (2008). 'It's not fair!'—Voicing pupils' criticisms of school rules. *Children & Society, 22*(6), 418–428. doi:10.1111/j.1099-0860.2007.00121.x

Thornberg, R. (2010). A study of children's conceptions of school rules by investigating their judgements of transgressions in the absence of rules. *Educational Psychology, 30*(5), 583–603. doi:10.1080/01443410.2010.492348

Thorndike, R., Hagen, E., & Sattler, J. (1986). *Stanford-Binet Intelligence Scale* (4th ed.). Chicago: Riverside.

Tiedemann, J. (2000). Parents' gender stereotypes and teachers' beliefs as predictors of children's concept of their mathematical ability in elementary school. *Journal of Educational Psychology, 92*, 144–151.

Tierney, A. L., & Nelson, C. A. III. (2009). Brain development and the role of experience in the early years. *Zero to Three, 30*(2), 9–13.

Tiggemann, M. (2003). Media exposure, body dissatisfaction, and disordered eating: Television and magazines are not the same! *European Eating Disorders Review, 11,* 418–430.

Timler, G. R., Olswang, L. B., & Coggins, L. E. (2005). "Do I know what I need to do?" A social communication intervention for children with complex clinical profiles. *Language, Speech, and Hearing Services in Schools, 36,* 73–85.

Tincoff, R., & Jusczyk, P. W. (1999). Some beginnings of word comprehension in 6-month-olds. *Psychological Science, 10,* 172–175.

Tinglof, C. B. (2007). *Parenting school-age twins and multiples.* New York: McGraw-Hill.

Tisak, M. S. (1993). Preschool children's judgments of moral and personal events involving physical harm and property damage. *Merrill-Palmer Quarterly: Journal of Developmental Psychology, 39*(3), 375–390.

Tisak, M. S., & Turiel, E. (1984). Children's conceptions of moral and prudential rules. *Child Development, 55*(3), 1030–1039. doi:10.2307/1130154

Tobias, S. (1977). A model for research on the effect of anxiety on instruction. In J. E. Sieber, H. F. O'Neil, Jr., & S. Tobias (Eds.), *Anxiety, learning, and instruction.* Hillsdale, NJ: Erlbaum.

Tobin, D. D., Menon, M., Menon, M., Spatta, B. C., Hodges, E. V. E., & Perry, D. G. (2010). The intrapsychics of gender: A model of self-socialization. *Psychological Review, 117*(2), 601–622.

Toga, A. W., & Thompson, P. M. (2003). Mapping brain asymmetry. *Nature Review Neuroscience, 4,* 37–48.

Tolani, N., & Brooks-Gunn, J. (2006). Are there socioeconomic disparities in children's mental health? In H. E. Fitzgerald, B. M. Lester, & B. Zuckerman (Vol. Eds.), & H. E. Fitzgerald, R. Zucker, & K. Freeark (Eds. in Chief), *The crisis in youth mental health: Critical issues and effective programs* (Vol. 1, pp. 277–303). Westport, CT: Praeger.

Tolmie, A. K., Topping, K. J., Christie, D., Donaldson, C., Howe, C., Jessiman, E., Livingston, K., & Thurston, A. (2010). Social effects of collaborative learning in primary schools. *Learning and Instruction, 20*(3), 177–191. doi:10.1016/j.learninstruc.2009.01.005

Tomasello, M. (1999). *The cultural origins of human cognition.* Cambridge, MA: Harvard University Press.

Tomasello, M., Carpenter, M., & Liszkowski, U. (2007). A new look at infant pointing. *Child Development, 78,* 705–722.

Tompkins, G. E., & McGee, L. M. (1986). Visually impaired and sighted children's emerging concepts about written language. In D. B. Yaden, Jr., & S. Templeton (Eds.), *Metalinguistic awareness and beginning literacy: Conceptualizing what it means to read and write.* Portsmouth, NH: Heinemann.

Tong, S., Baghurst, P., Vimpani, G., & McMichael, A. (2007). Socioeconomic position, maternal IQ, home environment, and cognitive development. *Journal of Pediatrics, 151*(3), 284–288.e1.

Torges, C., Stewart, A., & Duncan, L. (2009). Appreciating life's complexities: Assessing narrative ego integrity in late midlife. *Journal of Research in Personality, 43*(1), 66–74.

Torquati, J. C. (2002). Personal and social resources as predictors of parenting in homeless families. *Journal of Family Issues, 23,* 463–485.

Torrance, E. P. (1995). Insights about creativity: Questioned, rejected, ridiculed, ignored. *Educational Psychology Review, 7,* 313–322.

Torres-Guzmán, M. E. (1998). Language, culture, and literacy in Puerto Rican communities. In B. Pérez (Ed.), *Sociocultural contexts of language and literacy.* Mahwah, NJ: Erlbaum.

Torres-Guzmán, M. E. (2011). Methodologies and teacher stances: How do they interact in classrooms? *International Journal of Bilingual Education and Bilingualism, 14*(2), 225–241. doi:10.1080/13670050.2010.539675

Tourniaire, F., & Pulos, S. (1985). Proportional reasoning: A review of the literature. *Educational Studies in Mathematics, 16,* 181–204.

Touwen, B. C. L. (1974). The neurological development of the infant. In J. A. Davis & J. Dobbing (Eds.), *Scientific foundations of pediatrics.* Philadelphia, PA: Saunders.

Towne, J. (2009). A Dropout's guide to education reform. *Education Week, 29*(8), 25.

Tracy, B., Reid, R., & Graham, S. (2009). Teaching young students strategies for planning and drafting stories: The impact of self-regulated strategy development. *Journal of Educational Research, 102*(5), 323–331.

Trainor, L. J., Austin, C. M., & Desjardins, R. N. (2000). Is infant-directed speech prosody a result of the vocal expression of emotion? *Psychological Science, 11,* 188–195.

Trainor, L. J., & Trehub, S. E. (1992). A comparison of infants' and adults' sensitivity to Western tonal structure. *Journal of Experimental Psychology: Human Perception and Performance, 19,* 615–626.

Trautner, H. M. (1992). The development of sex-typing in children: A longitudinal analysis. *German Journal of Psychology, 16,* 183–199.

Trawick-Smith, J. (2003). *Early childhood development: A multicultural perspective* (3rd ed.). Upper Saddle River, NJ: Merrill/Prentice Hall.

Trawick-Smith, J (2010). *Early childhood development: A multicultural perspective* (5th ed.). Upper Saddle River, NJ: Merrill/Pearson.

Treffert, D. A., & Wallace, G. L. (2002). Islands of genius. *Scientific American, 286*(6), 76–85.

Treiman, R. (1998). Beginning to spell in English. In C. Hulme & R. M. Joshi (Eds.), *Reading and spelling: Development and disorders.* Mahwah, NJ: Erlbaum.

Treiman, R., Cohen, J., Mulqueeny, K., Kessler, B., & Schechtman, S. (2007). Young children's knowledge about printed names. *Child Development, 78,* 1458–1471.

Trelease, J. (1982). *The read-aloud handbook.* New York: Penguin Books.

Tremarche, P., Robinson, E., & Graham, L. (2007). Physical education and its effects on elementary testing results. *Physical Educator, 64*(2), 58–64.

Tremblay, R. E. (2010). Developmental origins of disruptive behaviour problems: The original sin hypothesis, epigenetics and their consequences for prevention. *Journal of Child Psychology and Psychiatry, 51*(4), 341–367. doi:10.1111/j.1469-7610.2010.02211.x

Tremblay, R. E., Nagin, D. S, Seguin, J. R., Zoccolillo, M., Zelazo, P. D., Boivin, M., Perusse, D., & Japel, C. (2004). Physical aggression during early childhood: Trajectories and predictors. *Pediatrics, 114,* E43–E50.

Trevarthen, C., & Hubley, P. (1978). Secondary intersubjectivity: Confidence, confiding and acts of meaning in the first year. In A. Lock (Ed.), *Action, gesture, and symbol: The emergence of language.* London: Academic Press.

Trezise, K. L., Gray, K. M., & Sheppard, D. M. (2008). Attention and vigilance in children with down syndrome. *Journal of Applied Research in Intellectual Disabilities, 21*(6), 502–508.

Triandis, H. C. (1995). *Individualism and collectivism.* Boulder, CO: Westview Press.

Triandis, H. C. (2007). Culture and psychology: A history of the study of their relationship. In S. Kitayama & D. Cohen (Eds.), *Handbook of cultural psychology* (pp. 59–76). New York: Guilford Press.

Tronick, E. Z., Als, H., Adamson, L., Wise, S., & Brazelton, B. (1978). The infants' response to entrapment between contradictory messages in face-to-face interaction. *American Academy of Child Psychiatry, 1,* 1–13.

Tronick, E. Z., Cohn, J., & Shea, E. (1986). The transfer of affect between mother and infant. In T. B. Brazelton & M. W. Yogman (Eds.), *Affective development in infancy* (pp. 11–25). Norwood, NJ: Ablex.

Trost, S. G., & van der Mars, H. (2009/2010). Why we should not cut P.E. *Educational Leadership, 67*(4), 60–65.

Trout, J. D. (2003). Biological specializations for speech: What can the animals tell us? *Current Directions in Psychological Science, 12,* 155–159.

Troutman, D. R., & Fletcher, A. C. (2010). Context and companionship in children's short-term versus long-term friendships. *Journal of Social and Personal Relationships, 27*(8), 1060–1074. doi:10.1177/0265407510381253

Tsai, Y.-M., Kunter, M., Lüdtke, O., Trautwein, U., & Ryan, R. M. (2008). What makes lessons interesting? The role of situational and individual factors in three school subjects. *Journal of Educational Psychology, 100,* 460–472.

Tse, L. (2001). *Why don't they learn English: Separating fact from fallacy in the U.S. language debate.* New York: Teachers College Press.

Tsui, J. M., & Mazzocco, M. M. M. (2007). Effects of math anxiety and perfectionism on timed versus untimed math testing in mathematically gifted sixth graders. *Roeper Review, 29*(2), 132–139.

Tucker, J. S., Ellickson, P. L., & Klein, D. J. (2008). Growing up in a permissive household: What deters at-risk adolescents from heavy drinking. *Journal of Studies on Alcohol and Drugs, 69*(4), 528-528-534.

Tunmer, W. E., Pratt, C., & Herriman, M. L. (Eds.). (1984). *Metalinguistic awareness in children: Theory, research, and implications.* Berlin, Germany: Springer-Verlag.

Turiel, E. (1983). *The development of social knowledge: Morality and convention.* Cambridge, England: Cambridge University Press.

Turiel, E. (1998). The development of morality. In W. Damon (Series Ed.) & N. Eisenberg (Vol. Ed.), *Handbook of child psychology: Vol. 3. Social, emotional, and personality development* (pp. 863–932). New York: Wiley.

Turiel, E. (2002). *The culture of morality: Social development, context, and conflict.* Cambridge, England: Cambridge University Press.

Turiel, E. (2006a). The development of morality. In W. Damon & R. M. Lerner (Eds. in Chief) & N. Eisenberg (Vol. Ed.), *Handbook of child psychology, Vol. 3. Social, emotional, and personality development* (6th ed., pp. 789–857). Hoboken, NJ: Wiley.

Turiel, E. (2006b). Thought, emotions, and social interactional processes in moral development. In M. Killen & J. G. Smetana (Eds.), *Handbook of moral development* (pp. 7–35). Mahwah, NJ: Erlbaum.

Turiel, E. (2008a). The development of children's orientations toward moral, social, and personal orders: More than a sequence in development. *Human Development, 51,* 21–39.

Turiel, E. (2008b). Thought about actions in social domains: Morality, social conventions, and social interactions. *Cognitive Development, 23*(1), 136–154. doi:10.1016/j.cogdev.2007.04.001

Turiel, E., & Killen, M. (2010). Taking emotions seriously: The role of emotions in moral development. In W. F. Arsenio & E. A. Lemerise (Eds.), *Emotions, aggression, and morality in children: Bridging development and psychopathology* (pp. 33–52). Washington, DC: American Psychological Association.

Turiel, E., Killen, M., & Helwig, C. C. (1987). Morality: Its structure, function, and vagaries. In J. Kagan & S. Lamb (Eds.), *The emergence of morality in young children* (pp. 155–243). Chicago: University of Chicago Press.

Turiel, E., Smetana, J. G., & Killen, M. (1991). Social contexts in social cognitive development. In W. M. Kurtines & J. L. Gewirtz (Eds.), *Moral behavior and development: Vol. 2. Research.* Hillsdale, NJ: Erlbaum.

Turkanis, C. G. (2001). Creating curriculum with children. In B. Rogoff, C. G. Turkanis, & L. Bartlett (Eds.), *Learning together: Children and adults in a school community* (pp. 91–102). New York: Oxford University Press.

Turkheimer, E. (2000). Three laws of behavior genetics and what they mean. *Current Directions in Psychological Science, 9,* 160–164.

Turkheimer, E., Haley, A., Waldron, M., D'Onofrio, B., & Gottesman, I. I. (2003). Socioeconomic status modifies heritability of IQ in young children. *Psychological Science, 14,* 623–628.

Turnbull, A. P., Pereira, L., & Blue-Banning, M. (2000). Teachers as friendship facilitators: Respeto and personalismo. *Teaching Exceptional Children, 32*(5), 66–70.

Turnbull, A. P., Turnbull, R., & Wehmeyer, M. L. (2007). *Exceptional lives: Special education in today's schools* (5th ed.). Upper Saddle River, NJ: Merrill/Prentice Hall.

Turnbull, A. P., Turnbull, R., & Wehmeyer, M. L. (2010). *Exceptional lives: Special education in today's schools* (6th ed.). Upper Saddle River, NJ: Merrill Pearson.

Turner, J. C. (1995). The influence of classroom contexts on young children's motivation for literacy. *Reading Research Quarterly, 30,* 410–441.

Turner, J. C., Meyer, D. K., Cox, K. E., Logan, C., DiCintio, M., & Thomas, C. T. (1998). Creating contexts for involvement in mathematics. *Journal of Educational Psychology, 90,* 730–745.

Turner, K. L., & Brown, C. S. (2007). The centrality of gender and ethnic identities across individuals and contexts. *Social Development, 16,* 700–719.

Turner, R. N., Hewstone, M., & Voci, A. (2007). Reducing explicit and implicit outgroup prejudice via direct and extended contact: The mediating role or self-disclosure and intergroup anxiety. *Journal of Personality and Social Psychology, 94,* 369–388.

Turner, S. L., & Conkel, J. L. (2010). Evaluation of a career development skills intervention with adolescents living in an inner city. *Journal of Counseling and Development, 88,* 457–465.

Tusing, M. E., & Ford, L. (2004). Examining preschool cognitive abilities using a CHC framework. *International Journal of Testing, 4,* 91–114.

Tversky, A., & Kahneman, D. (1990). Judgment under uncertainty: Heuristics and biases. In P. K. Moser (Ed.), *Rationality in action: Contemporary approaches* (pp. 171–188). New York: Cambridge University Press.

Tynes, B. M. (2007). Role taking in online "classrooms": What adolescents are learning about race and ethnicity. *Developmental Psychology, 43*(6), 1312–1320.

Tynes, B. M., & Ward, L. M. (2009). The role of media use and portrayals in African Americans' psychosocial development. In H. A. Neville, B. M. Tynes, & S. O. Utsey (Eds.), *Handbook of African American Psychology* (pp. 143–158). Thousand Oaks, CA: Sage.

Tzuriel, D. (2000). Dynamic assessment of young children: Educational and intervention perspectives. *Educational Psychology Review, 12,* 385–435.

Udall, A. J. (1989). Curriculum for gifted Hispanic students. In C. J. Maker & S. W. Schiever (Eds.), *Critical issues in gifted education: Vol. 2. Defensible programs for cultural and ethnic minorities.* Austin, TX: Pro-Ed.

Udry, J. R. (1988). Biological predispositions and social control in adolescent sexual behavior. *American Sociological Review, 53*(5), 709–722.

Uekermann, J., Kraemer, M., Abdel-Hamid, M., Schimmelmann, B. G., Hebebrand, J., Daum, I., Wiltfang, J., & Kis, B. (2010). Social cognition in attention-deficit hyperactivity disorder (ADHD). *Neuroscience and Biobehavioral Reviews, 34*(5), 734–743. doi:10.1016/j.neubiorev.2009.10.009

Ullman, E. (2010a, March). Closing the STEM gender gap. *Education Update, 52*(3), 1, 6–7.

Ullman, E. (2010b). Providing professional development to educators in rural areas. *Education Update, 52*(1), 1, 4–5.

Ullrich-French, S., & Smith, A. L. (2006). Perceptions of relationships with parents and peers in youth sport: Independent and combined prediction of motivational outcome. *Psychology of Sport and Exercise, 7,* 193–214.

Umaña-Taylor, A. J., & Alfaro, E. C. (2006). Ethnic identity among U.S. Latino adolescents: Theory, measurement, and implications for well-being. In K. Freeark & W. S. Davidson II (Vol. Eds.), & H. E. Fitzgerald, R. Zucker, & K. Freeark (Eds. in Chief), *The crisis in youth mental health: Vol. 3: Critical issues and effective programs* (pp. 195–211). Westport, CT: Praeger.

Underwood, M. K. (2007). Do girls' and boys' friendships constitute different peer cultures, and what are the trade-offs for development? *Merrill-Palmer Quarterly, 53,* 319–324.

Urban, J., Carlson, E., Egeland, B., & Sroufe, L. A. (1991). Patterns of individual adaptation across childhood. *Development and Psychopathology, 3,* 445–460.

Urdan, T. (1997). Achievement goal theory: Past results, future directions. In M. L. Maehr & P. R. Pintrich (Eds.), *Advances in motivation and achievement* (Vol. 10). Greenwich, CT: JAI Press.

Urdan, T. (2004). Predicators of academic self-handicapping and achievement: Examining achievement goals, classroom goal structures, and culture. *Journal of Educational Psychology, 96,* 251–264.

Urdan, T., Ryan, A. M., Anderman, E. M., & Gheen, M. H. (2002). Goals, goal structures, and avoidance behaviors. In C. Midgley (Ed.), *Goals, goal structures, and patterns of adaptive learning* (pp. 55–83). Mahwah, NJ: Erlbaum.

U.S. Census Bureau. (2004, September). National adoption month. Facts for features (CB04-FFSE.12). Retrieved November 16, 2007, from http://www.census.gov/Press-Release/www/releases/archives/facts_for_features_special_editions/002683.html

U.S. Census Bureau. (2009a). *American families and living arrangements: 2008. Table C3. Living arrangements of children under 18 years/1 and marital status of parents, by age, gender, race, and Hispanic origin/2 and selected characteristics of the child for all children: 2008.* Retrieved December 27, 2009, from http://www.census.gov/population/www/socdemo/hh-fam/cps2008.html

U.S. Census Bureau. (2009b). *American families and living arrangements: 2008. Table C4. Children/1 with grandparents by presence of parents, sex, race, and Hispanic origin/2 for selected characteristics: 2008.* Retrieved December 27, 2009, from http://www.census.gov/population/www/socdemo/hh-fam/cps2008.html

U.S. Department of Agriculture (2005a). *My Pyramid print materials: Poster, advanced version.* Retrieved March 31, 2010, at http://teamnutrition.usda.gov/Resources/mpk_poster2.pdf

U.S. Department of Agriculture (2005b). *My Pyramid print materials: Poster, simplified version.* Retrieved March 31, 2010, at http://teamnutrition.usda.gov/Resources/mpk_poster.pdf

U.S. Department of Agriculture. (2008). *MyPyramid Plan.* Retrieved January 16, 2008, from http://wwww.mypyramid.gov

U.S. Department of Agriculture (2010). *MyPyramid.gov: Steps to a healthier you.* Retrieved March 31, 2010 from http://www.mypyramid.gov

U.S. Department of Education. (1993). *National excellence: A case for developing America's talent.* Washington, DC: Office of Educational Research and Improvement.

U.S. Department of Energy Office of Science (2008). *Genomics and its impact on science and society.* Retrieved February8, 2010, from http://www.ornl.gov/sci/techresources/Human_Genome/publicat/primer/

U.S. Department of Health and Human Services. (2000). *Eating disorders.* Retrieved January 31, 2008, from http://4women.gov/owh/pub/factsheets/eatingdis.htm

U.S. Department of Health and Human Services. (2007). *The AFCARS Report: Preliminary FY 2005 estimates as of September 2006.* Retrieved November 19, 2007, from http://www.acf.hhs.gov/programs/cb/stats_research/afcars/tar/report13.htm

U.S. Department of Health and Human Services. (2009). *Communities that care community planning system.* Retrieved November 19, 2010, from http://www.preventionplatform.samhsa.gov

U.S. Drug Enforcement Administration. (2002). *Team up: A drug prevention manual for high school athletic coaches.* Washington, DC: U.S. Department of Justice Drug Enforcement Administration

U.S. Secret Service National Threat Assessment Center, in collaboration with the U.S. Department of Education (2000, October). *Safe school initiative: An interim report on the prevention of targeted violence in schools.* Retrieved from January 4, 2011, from http://cecp.air.org/download/ntac_ssi_report.pdf

Usinger, J., & Smith, M. (2010). Career development in the context of self-construction during adolescence. *Journal of Vocational Behavior, 76*(3), 580–591. doi:10.1016/j.jvb.2010.01.010

Uttal, D. H., Liu, L. L., & DeLoache, J. S. (2006). Concreteness and symbolic development. In L. Balter & C. S. Tamis-LeMonda (Eds.), *Child psychology: A handbook of contemporary issues* (2nd ed., pp. 167–184). New York: Psychology Press.

Uvaas, T. (2010). *Improving transitions to high school: Examining the effectiveness of a school connectedness program* (ProQuest Information & Learning). Retrieved from http://www.csa.com.(2010-99041-034)

Valdés, G., Bunch, G., Snow, C., & Lee, C. (with Matos, L.). (2005). Enhancing the development of students' language(s). In L. Darling-Hammond & J. Bransford (Eds.), *Preparing teachers for a changing world: What teachers should learn and be able to do* (pp. 126–168). San Francisco: Jossey-Bass/Wiley.

Valentine, J. C., Cooper, H., Bettencourt, B. A., & DuBois, D. L. (2002). Out-of-school activities and academic achievement: The mediating role of self-beliefs. *Educational Psychologist, 37,* 245–256.

Valiente, C., Lemery-Chalfant, K., Swanson, J., & Reiser, M. (2008). Prediction of children's academic competence from their effortful control, relationships, and classroom participation. *Journal of Educational Psychology, 100*(1), 67–77.

Valli, L., & Buese, D. (2007). The changing roles of teachers in an era of high-stakes accountability. *American Educational Research Journal, 44,* 519–558.

van de Weijer-Bergsma, E., Wijnroks, L., & Jongmans, M. J. (2008). Attention development in infants and preschool children born preterm: A review. *Infant Behavior and Development, 31,* 333–351.

van den Broek, P., Bauer, P. J., & Bourg, T. (Eds.). (1997). *Developmental spans in event comprehension and representation: Bridging fictional and actual events.* Mahwah, NJ: Erlbaum.

van den Broek, P., Lynch, J. S., Naslund, J., Ievers-Landis, C. E., & Verduin, K. (2003). The development of comprehension of main ideas in narratives: Evidence from the selection of titles. *Journal of Educational Psychology, 95,* 707–718.

van den Heuvel, M. P., Stam, C. J., Kahn, R. S., & Hulshoff Pol, H. E. (2009). Efficiency of functional brain networks and intellectual performance. *Journal of Neuroscience, 29*(23), 7619–7624.

Van Dooren, W., De Bock, D., Hessels, A., Janssens, D., & Verschaffel, L. (2005). Not everything is proportional: Effects of age and problem type on propensities for overgeneralization. *Cognition and Instruction, 23,* 57–86.

van Hof-van Duin, J., & Mohn, G. (1986). The development of visual acuity in normal full-term and preterm infants. *Vision Research, 26,* 909–916.

Van Hoorn, J., Nourot, P. M., Scales, B., & Alward, K. R. (1999). *Play at the center of the curriculum* (2nd ed.). Upper Saddle River, NJ: Merrill/Prentice Hall.

Van Hulle, C. A., Goldsmith, H. H., & Lemery, K. S. (2004). Genetic, environmental, and gender effects on individual differences in toddler expressive language. *Journal of Speech, Language, and Hearing Research, 47,* 904–912.

van IJzendoorn, M. H., Bakermans-Kranenburg, M. J., Pannebakker, F., & Out, D. (2010). In defence of situational morality: Genetic, dispositional and situational determinants of children's donating to charity. *Journal of Moral Education, 39*(1), 1–20. doi:10.1080/03057240903528535

van IJzendoorn, M. H., Goldberg, S., Kroonenberg, P. M., & Frenkel, O. J. (1992). The relative effects of maternal and child problems on the quality of attachment: A meta-analysis of attachment in clinical samples. *Child Development, 63,* 840–858.

Van Kleeck, A. (2008). Providing preschool foundations for later reading comprehension: The importance of and ideas for targeting inferencing in storybook-sharing interventions. *Psychology in the Schools. Special Issue: Communication Disorders, 45*(7), 627–643

van Kraayenoord, C. E., & Paris, S. G. (1997). Children's self-appraisal of their work samples and academic progress. *Elementary School Journal, 97,* 523–537.

van Laar, C. (2000). The paradox of low academic achievement but high self-esteem in African American students: An attributional account. *Educational Psychology Review, 12,* 33–61.

Van Leijenhorst, L., & Crone, E. A. (2010). Paradoxes in adolescent risk taking. In P. D. Zelazo, M. Chandler, & E. Crone (Eds.), *Developmental social cognitive neuroscience. The Jean Piaget symposium series* (pp. 209–225). New York: Psychology Press.

Vandell, D. L., & Pierce, K. M. (1999, April). *Can after-school programs benefit children who live in high-crime neighborhoods?* Paper presented at the biennial meeting of the Society for Research in Child Development, Albuquerque, NM.

Vandermaas-Peeler, M., Nelson, J., Bumpass, C., & Sassine, B. (2009). Social contexts of development: Parent-child interactions during reading and play. *Journal of Early Childhood Literacy, 9*(3), 295–317.

VanSledright, B., & Limón, M. (2006). Learning and teaching social studies: A review of cognitive research in history and geography. In P. A. Alexander & P. H. Winne (Eds.), *Handbook of educational psychology* (2nd ed., pp. 545–570). Mahwah, NJ: Erlbaum.

Vansteenkiste, M., Lens, W., & Deci, E. L. (2006). Intrinsic versus extrinsic goal contents in self-determination theory: Another look at the quality of academic motivation. *Educational Psychologist, 41,* 19–31.

Vansteenkiste, M., Zhou, M., Lens, W., & Soenens, B. (2005). Experiences of autonomy and control among Chinese learners: Vitalizing or immobilizing? *Journal of Educational Psychology, 97,* 468–483.

Varela, R. E., Vernberg, E. M., Sanchez-Sosa, J. J., Riveros, A., Mitchell, M., & Mashunkashey, J. (2004). Parenting style of Mexican, Mexican American, and Caucasian-non-Hispanic families: Social context and cultural influences. *Journal of Family Psychology, 18,* 651–657.

Vasquez, J. A. (1990). Teaching to the distinctive traits of minority students. *Clearing House, 63,* 299–304.

Vaughn, B. E., Egeland, B., Sroufe, L. A., & Waters, E. (1979). Individual differences in infant-mother attachment at twelve and eighteen months: Stability and change in families under stress. *Child Development, 50,* 971–975.

Vaughn, B. E., Kopp, C. B., & Krakow, J. B. (1984). The emergence and consolidation of self-control from eighteen to thirty months of age: Normative trends and individual differences. *Child Development, 55,* 990–1004.

Vaughn, B. E., Shin, N., Kim, M., Coppola, G., Krzysik, L., Santos, A. J., et al. (2009). Hierarchical models of social competence in preschool children: A multisite, multinational study. *Child Development, 80*(6), 1775–1796. doi:10.1111/j.1467-8624.2009.01367.x

Vavra, E. (1987). Grammar and syntax: The student's perspective. *English Journal, 76,* 42–48.

Vedamurthy, I., Suttle, C. M., Alexander, J., & Asper, L. J. (2008). A psychophysical study of human binocular interactions in normal and amblyopic visual systems. *Vision Research, 48*(14), 1522–1531.

Venter, J. C., et al. (2001). The sequence of the human genome. *Science, 291,* 1304–1351.

Veríssimo, M., Santos, A. J., Vaughn, B. E., Torres, N., Monteiro, L., & Santos, O. (2011). Quality of attachment to father and mother and number of reciprocal friends. *Early Child Development and Care, 181*(1), 27–38. doi:10.1080/03004430903211208

Vermeer, H. J., Boekaerts, M., & Seegers, G. (2000). Motivational and gender differences: Sixth-grade students' mathematical problem-solving behavior. *Journal of Educational Psychology, 92,* 308–315.

Véronneau, M., & Dishion, T. J. (2011). Middle school friendships and academic achievement in early adolescence: A longitudinal analysis. *The Journal of Early Adolescence, 31*(1), 99–124. doi:10.1177/0272431610384485

Vieillevoye, S., & Nader-Grosbois, N. (2008). Self-regulation during pretend play in children with intellectual disability and in normally developing children. *Research in Developmental Disabilities, 29*(3), 256–272. doi:10.1016/j.ridd.2007.05.003

Villegas, A. M., & Lucas, T. (2007). The culturally responsive teacher. *Educational Leadership, 64*(6), 28–33.

Vogel, G. (1997). Cocaine wreaks subtle damage on developing brains. *Science, 278,* 38–39.

Volker, M. A., Lopata, C., & Cook-Cottone, C. (2006). Assessment of children with intellectual giftedness and reading disabilities. *Psychology in the Schools, 43,* 855–869.

Volling, B. L. (2001). Early attachment relationships as predictors of preschool children's emotion regulation with a distressed sibling. *Early Education and Development, 12*(2), 185–207.

Volling, B. L., Mahoney, A., & Rauer, A. J. (2009). Sanctification of parenting, moral socialization, and young children's conscience development. *Psychology of Religion and Spirituality, 1*(1), 53–68. doi:10.1037/a0014958

Vollmer, T. R., & Hackenberg, T. D. (2001). Reinforcement contingencies and social reinforcement: Some reciprocal relations between basic and applied research. *Journal of Applied Behavior Analysis, 34,* 241–253.

Volterra, V., Caselli, M. C., Capirci, O., & Pizzuto, E. (2005). Gesture and the emergence and development of language. In M. Tomasello & D. I. Slobin (Eds.), *Beyond nature–nurture: Essays in honor of Elizabeth Bates* (pp. 3–40). Mahwah, NH: Erlbaum.

Vorrath, H. (1985). *Positive peer culture.* New York: Aldine de Gruyter.

Vosniadou, S. (1991). Conceptual development in astronomy. In S. M. Glynn, R. H. Yeany, & B. K. Britton (Eds.), *The psychology of learning science.* Hillsdale, NJ: Erlbaum.

Vosniadou, S. (2003). Exploring the relationships between conceptual change and intentional learning. In G. M. Sinatra & P. R. Pintrich (Eds.), *Intentional conceptual change* (pp. 377–406). Mahwah, NJ: Erlbaum.

Vosniadou, S. (2009). Science education for young children: A conceptual-change point of view. In O. A. Barbarin & B. H. Wasik (Eds.), *Handbook of child development and early education: Research to practice* (pp. 544–557). New York: Guilford Press.

Vygotsky, L. S. (1934/1986). *Thought and language* (rev. ed.; A. Kozulin, Ed. and Trans.). Cambridge, MA: MIT Press. (Original work published 1934)

Vygotsky, L. S. (1962). *Thought and language* (E. Haufmann & G. Vakar, Eds. and Trans.). Cambridge, MA: MIT Press.

Vygotsky, L. S. (1966). [Imaginary] play and its role in the mental development of the child. *Soviet Psychology, 5*(3), 6–18. (Original work published 1931)

Vygotsky, L. S. (1978). *Mind in society: The development of higher psychological processes* (M. Cole, V. John-Steiner, S. Scribner, & E. Souberman, Eds.). Cambridge, MA: Harvard University Press.

Vygotsky, L. S. (1987). The problem and the method of investigation. In R. W. Rieber & A. S. Carton (Eds.), *Collected works of L. S. Vygotsky: Vol. 1. Problems of general psychology* (pp. 167–241). New York: Plenum Press.

Vygotsky, L. S. (1997a). Analysis of higher mental functions. In R. W. Rieber (Ed.), *Collected works of L. S. Vygotsky: Vol. 4. The history of the development of higher mental functions* (pp. 65–82). New York: Plenum Press.

Vygotsky, L. S. (1997b). *Educational psychology.* Boca Raton, FL: St. Lucie Press.

Vygotsky, L. S. (1997c). The development of mnemonic and mnemotechnical functions. In R. W. Rieber (Ed.), *Collected works of L. S. Vygotsky: Vol. 4. The history of the development of higher mental functions* (pp. 179–190). New York: Plenum (Originally published 1982–1984).

Vygotsky, L. S. (1997d). The historical meaning of the crisis in psychology: A methodological investigation. In R. W. Rieber & J. Wollock (Eds.), *Collected works of L. S. Vygotsky: Vol. 3. Problem of the theory and history of psychology* (pp. 233–343). New York: Plenum Press.

Vygotsky, L. S. (1997e). Research method. In R. W. Rieber (Ed.), *Collected works of L. S. Vygotsky: Vol. 4. The history of the development of higher mental functions* (pp. 27–63). New York: Plenum. (Originally published 1982–1984)

Waddington, C. H. (1957). *The strategy of the genes.* London: Allyn & Bacon.

Wagley, C. (1977). *Welcome of tears: The Tapirapé Indians of central Brazil.* New York: Oxford University Press.

Wagner, B. M. (2009). *Suicidal behavior in children and adolescents.* New Haven, CT: Yale University Press.

Wagner, M. M. (1995). *The contributions of poverty and ethnic background to the participation of secondary school students in special education.* Washington, DC: U.S. Department of Education.

Wahlsten, D., & Gottlieb, G. (1997). The invalid separation of effects of nature and nurture: Lessons from animal experimentation. In R. J. Sternberg & E. L. Grigorenko (Eds.), *Intelligence, heredity, and environment* (pp. 163–192). Cambridge, England: Cambridge University Press.

Wahlstrom, K., Davison, M., Choi, J., & Ross, J. (2001). *Minneapolis Public Schools start time study.* Center for Applied Research and Educational Improvement. Retrieved April 3, 2010, from http://www.cehd.umn.edu/carei/Reports/docs/SST-2001ES.pdf

Wainryb, C. (2006). Moral development in culture: Diversity, tolerance, and justice. In M. Killen & J. G. Smetana (Eds.), *Handbook of moral development* (pp. 211–240). Mahwah, NJ: Erlbaum.

Waisbren, S. E. (1999). Phenylketonuria. In S. Goldstein & C. R. Reynolds (Eds.), *Handbook of neurodevelopmental and genetic disorders* (pp. 433–458). New York: Guilford Press.

Walczyk, J. J., Marsiglia, C. S., Johns, A. K., & Bryan, K. S. (2004). Children's compensations for poorly automated reading skills. *Discourse Processes, 37*(1), 47–66.

Walker, E., & Tessner, K. (2008). Schizophrenia. *Perspectives on Psychological Science, 3,* 30–37.

Walker, H. M., Horner, R. H., Sugai, G., Bullis, M., Sprague, J. R., Bicker, D., & Kaufman, M. J. (1996). Integrated approaches to preventing antisocial behavior patterns among school-age children and youth. *Journal of Emotional and Behavioral Disorders, 4,* 194–209.

Walker, L. J. (1991). Sex differences in moral reasoning. In W. M. Kurtines & J. L. Gewirtz (Eds.), *Handbook of moral behavior and development: Vol. 2. Research* (pp. 333–364). Hillsdale, NJ: Erlbaum.

Walker, L. J. (1995). Sexism in Kohlberg's moral psychology? In W. M. Kurtines & J. L. Gewirtz (Eds.), *Moral development: An introduction.* Boston: Allyn & Bacon.

Walker, L. J. (2006). Gender and morality. In M. Killen & J. G. Smetana (Eds.), *Handbook of moral development* (pp. 93–115). Mahwah, NJ: Erlbaum.

Walker, L. J., & Reimer, K. S. (2006). The relationship between moral and spiritual development. In E. C. Roehlkepartain, P. E. King, L. Wagener, & P. L. Benson (Eds.), *The handbook of spiritual development in childhood and adolescence* (pp. 224–238). Thousand Oaks, CA: Sage.

Walker, S. (2009). Sociometric stability and the behavioral correlates of peer acceptance in early childhood. *The Journal of Genetic Psychology: Research and Theory on Human Development, 170*(4), 339–358. doi:10.1080/00221320903218364

Walker, S. P., Wachs, T. D., Gardner, J. M., Lozoff, B., Wasserman, G. A., Pollitt, et al. (2007). Child development: Risks factors for adverse outcomes in developing countries. *Lancet, 369*(9556), 145–157.

Wallander, J. L., Eggert, K. M., & Gilbert, K. K. (2004). Adolescent health-related issues. In R. T. Brown (Ed.), *Handbook of pediatric psychology in school settings* (pp. 503–520). Mahwah, NJ: Erlbaum.

Wallerstein, J., & Lewis, J. M. (2007). Sibling outcomes and disparate parenting and stepparenting after divorce: Report from a 10-year longitudinal study. *Psychoanalytic Psychology, 24*(3), 445–458.

Wallerstein, J. S. (1984). Children of divorce: The psychological tasks of the child. In S. Chess (Ed.), *Annual Progress in Child Psychiatry and Child Development* (pp. 263–280). Philadelphia, PA: Brunner-Routledge.

Wallerstein, J. S., & Kelly, J. B. (1980). *Surviving the break-up: How children and parents cope with divorce.* New York: Basic Books.

Wallerstein, J. S., Lewis, J. M., & Blakeslee, S. (2001). *The unexpected legacy of divorce: A twenty-five year landmark study.* New York: Hyperion Press.

Walls, D. (2009). Herbs and natural therapies for pregnancy, birth and breastfeeding. *International Journal of Childbirth Education, 24*(2), 29–37.

Walls, T. A., & Little, T. D. (2005). Relations among personal agency, motivation, and school

adjustment in early adolescence. *Journal of Educational Psychology, 97,* 23–31.

Walters, G. C., & Grusec, J. E. (1977). *Punishment.* San Francisco: Freeman.

Wang, H., & Olson, N. (2009). *A journey to unlearn and learn in multicultural education.* New York: Peter Lang.

Wang, J., & Lin, E. (2005). Comparative studies on U.S. and Chinese mathematics learning and the implications for standards-based mathematics teaching reform. *Educational Researcher, 34*(5), 3–13.

Wang, P. P., & Baron, M. A. (1997). Language and communication: Development and disorders. In M. L. Batshaw (Ed.), *Children with disabilities* (4th ed.). Baltimore, MD: Paul H. Brookes.

Wang, Q. (2006). Culture and the development of self-knowledge. *Current Directions in Psychological Science, 15,* 182–187.

Wang, Q., & Pomerantz, E. M. (2009). The motivational landscape of early adolescence in the United States and China: A longitudinal investigation. *Child Development, 80*(4), 1272–1287.

Wang, Q., & Ross, M. (2007). Culture and memory. In S. Kitayama & D. Cohen (Eds.), *Handbook of cultural psychology* (pp. 645–667). New York: Guilford Press.

Wang, T.-H. (2010). Web-based dynamic assessment: Taking assessment as teaching and learning strategy for improving students' e-learning effectiveness. *Computers and Education, 5,* 1157–1166.

Want, S. C., & Harris, P. L. (2001). Learning from other people's mistakes: Causal understanding in learning to use a tool. *Child Development, 72,* 431–443.

Ward, R. A., & Spitze, G. (1998). Sandwiched marriages: The implications of child and parent relations for marital quality in midlife. *Social Forces, 77,* 647–666.

Ward, T., & Durrant, R. (2011). Evolutionary psychology and the rehabilitation of offenders: Constraints and consequences. *Aggression and Violent Behavior,* doi:10.1016/j.avb.2011.02.011

Warming, H. (2011). Getting under their skins? Accessing young children's perspectives through ethnographic fieldwork. *Childhood: A Global Journal of Child Research, 18*(1), 39–53. doi:10.1177/0907568210364666

Warnick, B., Johnson, B., & Rocha, S. (2010). Tragedy and the Meaning of School Shootings. *Educational Theory, 60*(3), 371–390.

Warren-Leubecker, A., & Bohannon, J. N. (1989). Pragmatics: Language in social contexts. In J. Berko-Gleason (Ed.), *The development of language* (2nd ed.). Upper Saddle River, NJ: Merrill/Prentice Hall.

Warton, P. M., & Goodnow, J. J. (1991). The nature of responsibility: Children's understanding of "Your Job." *Child Development, 62,* 156–165.

Waschbusch, D. A., Craig, R., Pelham, W. E., Jr., & King, S. (2007). Self-handicapping prior to academic-oriented tasks in children with Attention Deficit/Hyperactivity Disorder (ADHD): Medication effects and comparisons with controls. *Journal of Abnormal and Child Psychology, 35,* 275–286.

Wasik, B. A., & Bond, M. A. (2001). Beyond the pages of a book: Interactive book reading and language development in preschool classrooms. *Journal of Educational Psychology, 93,* 243–250.

Wasik, B. A., Karweit, N., Burns, L., & Brodsky, E. (1998, April). *Once upon a time: The role of rereading and retelling in storybook reading.* Paper presented at the annual meeting of the American Educational Research Association, San Diego, CA.

Waszak, F., Li, S.-C., & Hommel, B. (2010). The development of attentional networks: Cross-sectional findings from a life span sample. *Developmental Psychology, 46*(2), 337–349.

Watamura, S., Phillips, D. A., Morrissey, T. W., McCartney, K., & Bub, K. (2011). Double jeopardy:

Poorer social-emotional outcomes for children in the NICHD SECCYD experiencing home and child-care environments that confer risk. *Child Development, 82*(1), 48–65. doi:10.1111/j.1467-8624.2010.01540.x

Water Educational Training Science Project. (2010). *Wet science lesson #6: There is acid in my rain!* Retrieved May 11, 2010, from http://www.cloudnet.com/~edrbsass/edsci.htm#wetlands

Waters, E., Merrick, S., Treboux, D., Crowell, J., & Albersheim, L. (2000). Attachment security in infancy and early adulthood: A twenty-year longitudinal study. *Child Development, 71,* 684–689.

Waters, H. S. (1982). Memory development in adolescence: Relationships between metamemory, strategy use, and performance. *Journal of Experimental Child Psychology, 33,* 183–195.

Waters, S. F., Virmani, E. A., Thompson, R. A., Meyer, S., Raikes, H. A., & Jochem, R. (2010). Emotion regulation and attachment: Unpacking two constructs and their association. *Journal of Psychopathology and Behavioral Assessment, 32*(1), 37–47.

Watson, M., & Battistich, V. (2006). Building and sustaining caring communities. In C. M. Evertson & C. S. Weinstein (Eds.), *Handbook of classroom management: Research, practice, and contemporary issues* (pp. 253–279). Mahwah, NJ: Erlbaum.

Way, N. (1998). *Everyday courage: The lives and stories of urban teenagers.* New York: New York University Press.

Weaver, C. (1990). *Understanding whole language: From principles to practice.* Portsmouth, NH: Heinemann.

Weaver-Hightower, M. (2003). The "boy turn" in research on gender and education. *Review of Educational Research, 73,* 471–498.

Webb, N. M., & Farivar, S. (1994). Promoting helping behavior in cooperative small groups in middle school mathematics. *American Educational Research Journal, 31,* 369–395.

Webb, N. M., & Palincsar, A. S. (1996). Group processes in the classroom. In D. C. Berliner & R. C. Calfee (Eds.), *Handbook of educational psychology.* New York: Macmillan.

Webber, J., Scheuermann, B., McCall, C., & Coleman, M. (1993). Research on self-monitoring as a behavior management technique in special education classrooms: A descriptive review. *Remedial and Special Education, 14*(2), 38–56.

Wechsler, D. (2002). *Wechsler Preschool and Primary Scale of Intelligence–Third Edition.* San Antonio, TX: Psychological Corporation.

Wechsler, D. (2003). *Wechsler Intelligence Scale for Children* (4th ed.). San Antonio, TX: Psychological Corporation.

Weeks, T. L., & Pasupathi, M. (2010). Autonomy, identity, and narrative construction with parents and friends. In K. C. McLean, & M. Pasupathi (Eds.), *Narrative development in adolescence: Creating the storied self. Advancing responsible adolescent development* (pp. 65–91). New York: Springer Science + Business Media. doi:10.1007/978-0-387-89825-4_4

Weinberg, R. A. (1989). Intelligence and IQ: Landmark issues and great debates. *American Psychologist, 44,* 98–104.

Weiner, B. (1984). Principles for a theory of student motivation and their application within an attributional framework. In R. Ames & C. Ames (Eds.), *Research on motivation in education: Vol. 1. Student motivation.* San Diego, CA: Academic Press.

Weiner, B. (1986). *An attributional theory of motivation and emotion.* New York: Springer-Verlag.

Weiner, B. (2000). Intrapersonal and interpersonal theories of motivation from an attributional perspective. *Educational Psychology Review, 12,* 1–14.

Weiner, B. (2004). Attribution theory revisited: Transforming cultural plurality into theoretical unity. In D. M. McNerney & S. Van Etten (Eds.), *Big theories revisited* (pp. 13–29). Greenwich, CT: Information Age.

Weinert, S. (2009). Implicit and explicit modes of learning: Similarities and differences from a developmental perspective. *Linguistics, 47*(2), 241–271.

Weinstein, R. S. (1993). Children's knowledge of differential treatment in school: Implications for motivation. In T. M. Tomlinson (Ed.), *Motivating students to learn: Overcoming barriers to high achievement.* Berkeley, CA: McCutchan.

Weinstein, R. S., Madison, S. M., & Kuklinski, M. R. (1995). Raising expectations in schooling: Obstacles and opportunities for change. *American Educational Research Journal, 32,* 121–159.

Weisgram, E. S., Bigler, R. S., & Liben, L. S. (2010). Gender, values, and occupational interests among children, adolescents, and adults. *Child Development, 81*(3), 778–796. doi:10.1111/j.1467-8624.2010.01433.x

Weisner, T. S., & Gallimore, R. (1977). My brother's keeper: Child and sibling caregiving. *Current Anthropology, 18,* 169–190.

Weiss, M. J., & Hagen, R. (1988). A key to literacy: Kindergartners' awareness of the functions of print. *The Reading Teacher, 41,* 574–578.

Wellman, H. M. (1990). *The child's theory of mind.* Cambridge, MA: MIT Press.

Wellman, H. M., & Estes, D. (1986). Early understanding of mental entities: A reexamination of childhood realism. *Child Development, 57,* 910–923.

Wellman, H. M., Cross, D., & Watson, J. (2001). Meta-analysis of theory-of-mind development: The truth about false belief. *Child Development, 72,* 655–684.

Wellman, H. M., Fang, F., Liu, D., Zhu, L., & Zhu, G. (2006). Scaling of theory-of-mind understandings in Chinese children. *Psychological Science, 17,* 1075–1081.

Wellman, H. M., & Gelman, S. A. (1998). Knowledge acquisition in foundational domains. In W. Damon (Series Ed.), & D. Kuhn & R. S. Siegler (Vol. Eds.), *Handbook of child psychology: Vol. 2. Cognition, perception, and language* (5th ed., pp. 523–573). New York: Wiley.

Wellman, H. M., & Hickling, A. K. (1994). The mind's "I": Children's conception of the mind as an active agent. *Child Development, 65,* 1564–1580.

Wellman, H. M., Phillips, A. T., & Rodriguez, T. (2000). Young children's understanding of perception, desire, and emotion. *Child Development, 71,* 895–912.

Welsh, M. C. (1991). Rule-guided behavior and self-monitoring on the tower of Hanoi disk-transfer task. *Cognitive Development, 4,* 59–76. *Journal of Educational Psychology, 91,* 76–97.

Wen, M. (2008). Family structure and children's health and behavior. *Journal of Family Issues, 29*(11), 1492–1519.

Wentzel, K. R. (1999). Social-motivational processes and interpersonal relationships: Implications for understanding motivation at school. *Journal of Educational Psychology, 91,* 76–97.

Wentzel, K. R. (2000). What is it that I'm trying to achieve? Classroom goals from a content perspective. *Contemporary Educational Psychology, 25,* 105–115.

Wentzel, K. R. (2009). Peers and academic functioning at school. In K. H. Rubin, W. M. Bukowski, & B. Laursen (Eds.), *Handbook of peer interactions, relationships, and groups. Social, emotional, and personality development in context* (pp. 531–547). New York: Guilford Press.

Wentzel, K. R., & Asher, S. R. (1995). The academic lives of neglected, rejected, popular, and controversial children. *Child Development, 66,* 754–763.

Wentzel, K. R., & Wigfield, A. (1998). Academic and social motivational influences on students' academic performance. *Educational Psychology Review, 10,* 155–175.

Werbner, P. (2009). The hidden lion: Tswapong girls' puberty rituals and the problem of history. *American Ethnologist, 36*(3), 441–458.

Werker, J. F., & Lalonde, C. E. (1988). Cross-language speech perception: Initial capabilities and developmental change. *Developmental Psychology, 24,* 672–683.

Werker, J. F., Maurer, D. M., & Yoshida, K. A. (2010). Perception. In M. H. Bornstein (Ed.), *Handbook of cultural developmental science.* (pp. 89–125). New York: Psychology Press.

Werker, J. F., & Tees, R. C. (1999). Influences on infant speech processing: Toward a new synthesis. *Annual Review of Psychology, 50,* 509–535.

Werner, E. E., & Smith, R. S. (2001). *Journeys from childhood to midlife: Risk, resilience, and recovery.* Ithaca, NY: Cornell University Press.

Wertsch, J. V. (1984). The zone of proximal development: Some conceptual issues. *Children's learning in the zone of proximal development: New directions for child development* (No. 23). San Francisco: Jossey-Bass.

Whalen, C. K., Jamner, L. D., Henker, B., Delfino, R. J., & Lozano, J. M. (2002). The ADHD spectrum and everyday life: Experience sampling of adolescent moods, activities, smoking, and drinking. *Child Development, 73,* 209–227.

Whipple, N., Bernier, A., & Mageau, G. (2011). A dimensional approach to maternal attachment state of mind: Relations to maternal sensitivity and maternal autonomy support. *Developmental Psychology, 47*(2), 396–403. doi:10.1037/a0021310

White, B. Y., & Frederiksen, J. (2005). A theoretical framework and approach for fostering metacognitive development. *Educational Psychologist, 40,* 211–223.

White, B. Y., & Frederiksen, J. R. (1998). Inquiry, modeling, and metacognition: Making science accessible to all students. *Cognition and Instruction, 16,* 3–118.

White, J. J., & Rumsey, S. (1994). Teaching for understanding in a third-grade geography lesson. In J. Brophy (Ed.), *Advances in research on teaching: Vol. 4. Case studies of teaching and learning in social studies* (pp. 33–69). Greenwich, CT: JAI Press.

White, M. (1993). *The material child: Coming of age of Japan and America.* New York: Free Press.

White, R. (1959). Motivation reconsidered: The concept of competence. *Psychological Review, 66,* 297–333.

Whitehurst, G. J., Arnold, D. S., Epstein, J. N., Angell, A. L., Smith, M., & Fischel, J. E. (1994). A picture book reading intervention in day care and home for children from low-income families. *Developmental Psychology, 30,* 679–689.

Whiting, B. B., & Edwards, C. P. (1988). *Children of different worlds.* Cambridge, MA: Harvard University Press.

Whiting, B. B., & Whiting, J. W. M. (1975). *Children of six cultures: A psycho-cultural analysis.* Cambridge, MA: Harvard University Press.

Whitley, B. E., Jr., & Frieze, I. H. (1985). Children's causal attributions for success and failure in achievement settings: A meta-analysis. *Journal of Educational Psychology, 77,* 608–616.

Wieder, S., Greenspan, S., & Kalmanson, B. (2008). Autism assessment and intervention: The developmental individual-difference, relationship-based DIR®/Floortime™ model. *Zero to Three, 28*(4), 31–37.

Wigfield, A. (1994). Expectancy-value theory of achievement motivation: A developmental perspective. *Educational Psychology Review, 6,* 49–78.

Wigfield, A., Byrnes, J. P., & Eccles, J. S. (2006). Development during early and middle adolescence. In P. A. Alexander & P. H. Winne (Eds.), *Handbook of educational psychology* (2nd ed., pp. 87–113). Mahwah, NJ: Erlbaum.

Wigfield, A., & Eccles, J. (2000). Expectancy-value theory of achievement motivation. *Contemporary Educational Psychology, 25,* 68–81.

Wigfield, A., & Eccles, J. S. (1994). Children's competence beliefs, achievement values, and general self-esteem: Change across elementary and middle school. *Journal of Early Adolescence, 14,* 107–138.

Wigfield, A., Eccles, J., Mac Iver, D., Reuman, D., & Midgley, C. (1991). Transitions at early adolescence: Changes in children's domain-specific self-perceptions and general self-esteem across the transition to junior high school. *Developmental Psychology, 27,* 552–565.

Wigfield, A., Eccles, J. S., & Pintrich, P. R. (1996). Development between the ages of 11 and 25. In D. C. Berliner & R. C. Calfee (Eds.), *Handbook of educational psychology.* New York: Macmillan.

Wigfield, A., Tonks, S., & Eccles, J. S. (2004). Expectancy value theory in cross-cultural perspective. In D. M. McInerney & S. Van Etten (Eds.), *Big theories revisited* (pp. 165–198). Greenwich, CT: Information Age.

Wigfield, A., Tonks, S., & Klauda, S. L. (2009). Expectancy-value theory. In K. R. Wentzel & A. Wigfield (Eds.), *Handbook of motivation at school* (pp. 55–75). New York: Routledge.

Wiig, E. H., Gilbert, M. F., & Christian, S. H. (1978). Developmental sequences in perception and interpretation of ambiguous sentences. *Perceptual and Motor Skills, 46,* 959–969.

Wilcox, S. (1994). Struggling for a voice: An interactionist view of language and literacy in Deaf education. In V. John-Steiner, C. P. Panofsky, & L. W. Smith (Eds.), *Sociocultural approaches to language and literacy: An interactionist perspective.* Cambridge, England: Cambridge University Press.

Wilgenbusch, T., & Merrell, K. W. (1999). Gender differences in self-concept among children and adolescents: A meta-analysis of multidimensional studies. *School Psychology Quarterly, 14*(2), 101–120.

Willard, N. E. (2007). *Cyberbullying and cyberthreats: Responding to the challenge of online social aggression, threats, and distress.* Champaign, IL: Research Press.

Willats, J. (1995). An information-processing approach to drawing development. In C. Lange-Kuttner & G. V. Thomas (Eds.), *Drawing and looking: Theoretical approaches to pictorial representation in children* (pp. 27–43). New York: Harvester Wheatsheaf.

Willatts, P. (1990). Development of problem solving strategies in infancy. In D. F. Bjorklund (Ed.), *Children's strategies* (pp. 23–66). Hillsdale, NJ: Erlbaum.

Williams, D. (1996). *Autism: An inside-outside approach.* London: Kingsley.

Williams, D. L. (2008). What neuroscience has taught us about autism. *Zero to Three, 28*(4), 38–45.

Williams, H. L., & Conway, M. A. (2009). Networks of autobiographical memories. In P. Boyer & J. V. Wertsch (Eds.), *Memory in mind and culture* (pp. 33–61). New York: Cambridge University Press.

Williams, J. (2004). Seizure disorders. In R. T. Brown (Ed.), *Handbook of pediatric psychology in school settings* (pp. 221–239). Mahwah, NJ: Erlbaum.

Williams, J., & Williamson, K. (1992). "I wouldn't want to shoot nobody": The out-of-school curriculum as described by urban students. *Action in Teacher Education, 14*(2), 9–15.

Williams, K. M. (2001). What derails peer mediation? In J. N. Burstyn, G. Bender, R. Casella, H. W. Gordon, D. P. Guerra, K. V. Luschen, et al. *Preventing violence in schools: A challenge to American democracy* (pp. 199–208). Mahwah, NJ: Erlbaum.

Williams, P. E., Weiss, L. G., & Rolfhus, E. L. (2003). *WISC-IV technical report #2: Psycho metric properties.* San Antonio, TX: Harcourt Assessment. Retrieved September 6, 2005, from http://www.harcourtassessment.com

Williams, R. W., & Herrup, K. (1998). The control of neuron number. *Annual Review of Neuroscience, 11,* 423–453.

Williams, S. T., Mastergeorge, A. M., & Ontai, L. L. (2010). Caregiver involvement in infant peer interactions: Scaffolding in a social context. *Early Childhood Research Quarterly, 25*(2), 251–266. doi:10.1016/j.ecresq.2009.11.004

Williams, S. T., Ontai, L. L., & Mastergeorge, A. M. (2010). The development of peer interaction in infancy: Exploring the dyadic processes. *Social Development, 19*(2), 348–368. doi:10.1111/j.1467-9507.2009.00542.x

Wilson, A. J., & Dehaene, S. (2007). Number sense and developmental dyscalculia. In D. Coch, G. Dawson, & K. W. Fischer (Eds.), *Human behavior, learning, and the developing brain: Atypical development* (pp. 212–238). New York: Guilford Press.

Wilson, B. (1997). Types of child art and alternative developmental accounts: Interpreting the interpreters. *Human Development, 40*, 155–168.

Wilson, B. J. (2008). Media and children's aggression, fear, and altruism. *Future of Children, 18*(1), 87–118.

Wilson, B. L., & Corbett, H. D. (2001). *Listening to urban kids: School reform and the teachers they want.* Albany, NY: State University of New York Press.

Wilson, D. K., Nicholson, S. C., & Krishnamoorthy, J. S. (1998). The role of diet in minority adolescent health promotion. In D. K. Wilson, J. R. Rodrigue, & W. C. Taylor (Eds.), *Health-promoting and health-compromising behaviors among minority adolescents* (pp. 129–151). Washington, DC: American Psychological Association.

Wilson, H. K., Pianta, R. C., & Stuhlman, M. (2007). Typical classroom experiences in first grade: The role of classroom climate and functional risk in the development of social competencies. *Elementary School Journal, 108*(2), 81–96.

Wilson, L. (2007). Great American schools: The power of culture and passion. *Educational Horizons, 86*(1), 33–44.

Wilson, S. A. (2010). *Exploring avenues toward activism: Using a phenomenological variant of ecological systems theory (PVEST) to examine the perceptions of black youth engaged in community-focused, media skills training* (ProQuest Information & Learning). *Dissertation Abstracts International Section A: Humanities and Social Sciences, 70.* Retrieved from http://www.csa .com. (2010-99071-081)

Wimmer, H., & Perner, J. (1983). Beliefs about beliefs: Representation and constraining function of wrong beliefs in young children's understanding of deception. *Cognition, 13*, 103–128.

Wimmer, H., Mayringer, H., & Landerl, K. (2000). The double-deficit hypothesis and difficulties in learning to read a regular orthography. *Journal of Educational Psychology, 92*, 668–680.

Wimmer, M. C., & Howe, M. L. (2009). The development of automatic associative processes and children's false memories. *Journal of Experimental Child Psychology, 104*, 447–465.

Winberg, J. (2005). Mother and newborn baby: Mutual regulation of physiology and behavior—A selective review. *Developmental Psychobiology, 47*, 219–229.

Wineburg, S. S. (1994). The cognitive representation of historical texts. In G. Leinhardt, I. L. Beck, & C. Stainton (Eds.), *Teaching and learning in history.* Hillsdale, NJ: Erlbaum.

Winn, W. (2002). Current trends in educational technology research: The study of learning environments. *Educational Psychology Review, 14*, 331–351.

Winne, P. H. (1995a). Inherent details in self-regulated learning. *Educational Psychologist, 30*, 173–187.

Winne, P. H. (1995b). Self-regulation is ubiquitous but its forms vary with knowledge. *Educational Psychologist, 30*, 223–228.

Winner, E. (1988). *The point of words.* Cambridge, MA: Harvard University Press.

Winner, E. (1997). Exceptionally high intelligence and schooling. *American Psychologist, 52*, 1070–1081.

Winner, E. (2000). The origins and ends of giftedness. *American Psychologist, 55*, 159–169.

Winner, E. (2006). Development in the arts: Drawing and music. In W. Damon & R. M. Lerner (Series Eds.), & D. Kuhn & R. Siegler (Vol. Eds.), *Handbook of child psychology: Vol. 2. Cognition, perception, and language* (6th ed.). New York: Wiley.

Winsler, A., Díaz, R. M., Espinosa, L., & Rodriguez, J. L. (1999). When learning a second language does not mean losing the first: Bilingual language development in low-income, Spanish-speaking children attending bilingual preschool. *Child Development, 70*, 349–362.

Winsler, A., & Naglieri, J. (2003). Overt and covert verbal problem-solving strategies: Developmental trends in use, awareness, and relations with task performance in children aged 5 to 17. *Child Development, 74*, 659–678.

Winston, P. (1973). Learning to identify toy block structures. In R. L. Solso (Ed.), *Contemporary issues in cognitive psychology: The Loyola Symposium.* Washington, DC: V. H. Winston.

Winterdyk, J., & Ruddell, R. (2010). Managing prison gangs: Results from a survey of U.S. prison systems. *Journal of Criminal Justice, 38*(4), 730–736. doi:10.1016/j.jcrimjus.2010.04.047

Witherington, D. C., Campos, J. J., Anderson, D. I., Lejeune, L., & Seah, E. (2005). Avoidance of heights on the visual cliff in newly walking infants. *Infancy, 7*(3), 285–298

Witkow, M. R., & Fuligni, A. J. (2007). Achievement goals and daily school experiences among adolescents with Asian, Latino, and European American backgrounds. *Journal of Educational Psychology, 99*, 584–596.

Wittmer, D. S., & Honig, A. S. (1994). Encouraging positive social development in young children. *Young Children, 49*(5), 4–12.

Witvliet, M., van Lier, P. A. C., Cuijpers, P., & Koot, H. M. (2010). Change and stability in childhood clique membership, isolation from cliques, and associated child characteristics. *Journal of Clinical Child and Adolescent Psychology, 39*(1), 12–24. doi:10.1080/15374410903401161

Wodrich, D. L., Tarbox, J., Balles, J., & Gorin, J. (2010). Medical diagnostic consultation concerning mental retardation: An analogue study of school psychologists' attitudes. *Psychology in the Schools, 47*(3), 246–256.

Wolcott, H. F. (1999). *Ethnography: A way of seeing.* Walnut Creek, CA: AltMira.

Wolf, M., & Bowers, P. G. (1999). The double-deficit hypothesis for the developmental dyslexias. *Journal of Educational Psychology, 91*, 415–438.

Wolfe, D. A., & Wekerle, C. (1997). Pathways to violence in teen dating relationships. In D. Cicchetti & S. L. Toth (Eds.), Developmental perspectives on trauma: Theory, research, and intervention. *Rochester Symposium on Developmental Psychology, 8*, 315–341. Rochester, NY: University of Rochester Press.

Wolfe, M. B. W., & Goldman, S. R. (2005). Relations between adolescents' text processing and reasoning. *Cognition and Instruction, 23*, 467–502.

Wolff, P. G. (1966). The causes, controls, and organization of behavior in the neonate. *Psychological Issues, 5*(1, Serial No. 17).

Wolfson, A. R., & Carskadon, M. A. (2005). A survey of factors influencing high school start times. *NASSP Bulletin, 89*(642), 47–66.

Wolock, I., Sherman, P., Feldman, L. H., & Metzger, B. (2001). Child abuse and neglect referral patterns: A longitudinal study. *Children and Youth Services Review, 23*, 21–47.

Wolters, C. A. (2003). Regulation of motivation: Evaluating an underemphasized aspect of self-regulated learning. *Educational Psychologist, 38*, 189–205.

Wong, M. S., Mangelsdorf, S. C., Brown, G. L., Neff, C., & Schoppe-Sullivan, S. J. (2009). Parental beliefs, infant temperament, and marital quality: Associations with infant-mother and infant-father attachment. *Journal of Family Psychology, 23*(6), 828–838.

Wong, S. C. (1993). Promises, pitfalls, and principles of text selection in curricular diversification: The Asian-American case. In T. Perry & J. W. Fraser (Eds.), *Freedom's plow: Teaching in the multicultural classroom.* New York: Routledge.

Wood, A., & Wood, B. (2001). *Alphabet adventure.* New York: Scholastic Books.

Wood, A. C., Saudino, K. J., Rogers, H., Asherson, P., & Kuntsi, J. (2007). Genetic influences on mechanically-assessed activity level in children. *Journal of Child Psychology and Psychiatry, 48*, 695–702.

Wood, D., Bruner, J. S., & Ross, G. (1976). The role of tutoring in problem-solving. *Journal of Child Psychology and Psychiatry, 17*, 89–100.

Wood, E., Willoughby, T., McDermott, C., Motz, M., Kaspar, V., & Ducharme, M. J. (1999). Developmental differences in study behavior. *Journal of Educational Psychology, 91*, 527–536.

Wood, J. W. (1998). *Adapting instruction to accommodate students in inclusive settings* (3rd ed.). Upper Saddle River, NJ: Merrill/Prentice Hall.

Woods, S. A., & Hampson, S. E. (2010). Predicting adult occupational environments from gender and childhood personality traits. *Journal of Applied Psychology.*

Woodward, A. L., Markman, E. M., & Fitzsimmons, C. M. (1994). Rapid word learning in 13- and 18-month-olds. *Developmental Psychology, 30*, 553–566.

Woody, J. D., D'Souza, H. J., & Russel, R. (2003). Emotions and motivations in first adolescent intercourse: An exploratory study based on object relations theory. *Canadian Journal of Human Sexuality, 12*(1), 35–51.

Woolley, J. D. (1995). The fictional mind: Young children's understanding of pretense, imagination, and dreams. *Developmental Review, 15*, 172–211.

World Health Organization. (2000). *Obesity: Preventing and managing the global epidemic* (WHO Report No. 894). Geneva: Author.

Wright, R. (2009). Methods for improving test scores: The good, the bad, and the ugly. *Kappa Delta Pi Record, 45*(3), 116–121.

WritersCorps. (2003). *Paint me like I am: Teen poems from WritersCorps.* New York: HarperTempest.

Wu, P., Liu, X., & Fan, B. (2010). Factors associated with initiation of ecstasy use among US adolescents: Findings from a national survey. *Drug and Alcohol Dependence, 106*(2–3), 193–198.

Wu, P.-L., & Chiou, W.-B. (2008). Postformal thinking and creativity among late adolescents: A post-Piagetian approach. *Adolescence, 43*(170), 237–251.

Wu, R., Gopnik, A., Richardson, D. C., & Kirkham, N. Z. (2011). Infants learn about objects from statistics and people. *Developmental Psychology.* doi:10.1037/a0024023

Wu, W., West, S. G., & Hughes, J. N. (2010). Effect of grade retention in first grade on psychosocial outcomes. *Journal of Educational Psychology, 102*(1), 135–152.

Wulczyn, F. (2009). Epidemiological perspectives on maltreatment prevention. *Future of Children, 19*(2), 39–66.

Wynbrandt, J., & Ludman, M. D. (2000). *The encyclopedia of genetic disorders and birth defects* (2nd ed.). New York: Facts on File.

Wynn, K. (1990). Children's understanding of counting. *Cognition, 36*, 155–193.

Wynn, K. (1992). Addition and subtraction by human infants. *Nature, 358*, 749–750.

Wynn, K. (1995). Infants possess a system of numerical knowledge. *Current Directions in Psychological Science, 4*, 172–177.

Xu, F., & Spelke, E. S. (2000). Large number discrimination in 6-month-old infants. *Cognition, 74*, B1–B11.

Xu, J. (2008). Sibship size and educational achievement: The role of welfare regimes cross-nationally. *Comparative Education Review, 52*(3), 413–436.

Xu, M.-Q., Sun, W.-S., Liu, B. X., Feng, G.-Y., Yu, L., Yang, L., et al. (2009). Prenatal malnutrition and adult schizophrenia: Further evidence from the 1959–1961 Chinese famine. *Schizophrenia Bulletin, 35*(3), 568–576.

Xu, Y., Farver, J. A. M., Chang, L., Zhang, Z., & Yu, L. (2007). Moving away or fitting in? understanding shyness in Chinese children. *Merrill-Palmer Quarterly: Journal of Developmental Psychology, 53*(4), 527–556.

Yaden, D. B., Jr., & Templeton, S. (Eds.). (1986). *Metalinguistic awareness and beginning literacy: Conceptualizing what it means to read and write.* Portsmouth, NH: Heinemann.

Yakovlev, P. I., & Lecours, A. R. (1967). The myelogenetic cycles of regional maturation of the brain. In A. Minkowski (Ed.), *Regional development of the brain in early life* (pp. 3–70). Oxford, England: Blackwell Scientific.

Yang, F., & Tsai, C. (2010). Reasoning about science-related uncertain issues and epistemological perspectives among children. *Instructional Science, 38*(4), 325–354.

Yarrow, M. R., Scott, P. M., & Waxler, C. Z. (1973). Learning concern for others. *Developmental Psychology, 8,* 240–260.

Yates, M., & Youniss, J. (1996). A developmental perspective on community service in adolescence. *Social Development, 5,* 85–111.

Yau, J., & Smetana, J. G. (2003). Conceptions of moral, social-conventional, and personal events among Chinese preschoolers in Hong Kong. *Child Development, 74,* 647–658.

Yeager, E. A., Foster, S. J., Maley, S. D., Anderson, T., Morris, J. W., III, & Davis, O. L., Jr. (1997, March). *The role of empathy in the development of historical understanding.* Paper presented at the annual meeting of the American Educational Research Association, Chicago.

Ying, Y.-W., & Han, M. (2007). The longitudinal effect of intergenerational gap in acculturation on conflict and mental health in Southeast Asian American adolescents. *American Journal of Orthopsychiatry, 77,* 61–66.

Yip, T., & Fuligni, A. J. (2002). Daily variation in ethnic identity, ethnic behaviors, and psychological well-being among American adolescents of Chinese descent. *Child Development, 73,* 1557–1572.

Yoon, C. (2009). Self-regulated learning and instructional factors in the scientific inquiry of scientifically gifted Korean middle school students. *Gifted Child Quarterly, 53*(3), 203–216.

Young, E. L., & Assing, R. (2000). Review of The Universal Nonverbal Intelligence Test. *Journal of Psychoeducational Assessment, 18,* 280–288.

Young, J. M., Howell, A. N., & Hauser-Cram, P. (2005, April). *Predictors of mastery motivation in children with disabilities born prematurely.* Paper presented at the biennial meeting of the Society for Research in Child Development, Atlanta, GA.

Young, S., & Amarasinghe, J. M. (2010). Practitioner review: Non-pharmacological treatments for ADHD: A lifespan approach. *Journal of Child Psychology and Psychiatry, 51*(2), 116–133.

Youngblood, J., II, & Spencer, M. B. (2002). Integrating normative identity processes and academic support requirements for special needs adolescents: The application of an identity-focused cultural ecological (ICE) perspective. *Applied Developmental Science, 6,* 95–108.

Young-Hyman, D. (2004). Diabetes and the school-age child and adolescent: Facilitating good glycemic control and quality of life. In R. T. Brown (Ed.), *Handbook of pediatric psychology in school settings* (pp. 169–193). Mahwah, NJ: Erlbaum.

Youniss, J. (1983). Social construction of adolescence by adolescents and their parents. In H. D. Grotevant & C. R. Cooper (Eds.), *Adolescent development in the family: New directions for child development* (No. 22). San Francisco: Jossey-Bass.

Youniss, J., & Yates, M. (1999). Youth service and moral-civic identity: A case of everyday morality. *Educational Psychology Review, 11,* 361–376.

Ysseldyke, J. E., & Algozzine, B. (1984). *Introduction to special education.* Boston: Houghton Mifflin.

Yuill, N. (2009). The relation between ambiguity understanding and metalinguistic discussion of joking riddles in good and poor comprehenders: Potential for intervention and possible processes of change. *First Language, 29*(1), 65–79.

Zahn-Waxler, C., Friedman, R. J., Cole, P., Mizuta, I., & Hiruma, N. (1996). Japanese and United States preschool children's responses to conflict and distress. *Child Development, 67,* 2462–2477.

Zahn-Waxler, C., & Kochanska, G. (1990). The origins of guilt. In R. A. Dientsbier (Series Ed.), & R. A. Thompson (Vol. Ed.), *The 36th Annual Nebraska Symposium on Motivation: Socioemotional development. Current theory and research in motivation* (Vol. 36, pp. 183–258). Lincoln: University of Nebraska Press.

Zahn-Waxler, C., Radke-Yarrow, M., Wagner, E., & Chapman, M. (1992). Development of concern for others. *Developmental Psychology, 28,* 126–136.

Zahn-Waxler, C., & Robinson, J. (1995). Empathy and guilt: Early origins of feelings of responsibility. In J. P. Tangney & K. W. Fischer (Eds.), *Self-conscious emotions: The psychology of shame, guilt, embarrassment, and pride* (pp. 143–173). New York: Guilford Press.

Zajonc, R. B., & Mullally, P. R. (1997). Birth order: Reconciling conflicting effects. *American Psychologist, 52,* 685–699.

Zamarian, L., Ischebeck, A., & Delazer, M. (2009). Neuroscience of learning arithmetic—Evidence from brain imaging studies. *Neuroscience and Biobehavioral Reviews, 33*(6), 909–925.

Zambo, D. (2003, April). *Thinking about reading: Talking to children with learning disabilities.* Paper presented at the annual meeting of the American Educational Research Association, Chicago.

Zambo, D., & Brem, S. K. (2004). Emotion and cognition in students who struggle to read: New insights and ideas. *Reading Psychology, 25,* 1–16.

Zeanah, C. H. (2000). Disturbances of attachment in young children adopted from institutions. *Journal of Developmental and Behavioral Pediatrics, 21,* 230–236.

Zeece, P. D., & Wallace, B. M. (2009). Books and good stuff: A strategy for building school to home literacy connections. *Early Childhood Education, 37,* 35–42.

Zehr, J. L., Culbert, K. M., Sisk, C. L., & Klump, K. L. (2007). An association of early puberty with disordered eating and anxiety in a population of undergraduate women and men. *Hormones and Behavior, 52,* 427–435.

Zeisel, S. H. (2009). Is maternal diet supplementation beneficial? Optimal development of infant depends on mother's diet. *American Journal of Clinical Nutrition, 89*(2), 685S–687S.

Zelazo, P. D., Müller, U., Frye, D., & Marcovitch, S. (2003). The development of executive function in early childhood. *Monographs of the Society for Research in Child Development, 68*(3, Serial No. 274).

Zentner, M., & Eerola, T. (2010). Rhythmic engagement with music in infancy. *Proceedings of the National Academy of Sciences of the United States of America, 107*(13), 5768–5773.

Zero to Three: National Center for Infants, Toddlers, and Families. (2002). *Temperament.* Retrieved January 16, 2003, from http://www.zerotothree.org/Archive/TEMPERAM.HTM

Zero to Three: National Center for Infants, Toddlers, and Families. (2010). *It's too mushy! It's too spicy! The peas are touching the chicken! (Or, how to handle your picky eater).* Retrieved April 8, 2010, from http://www.zerotothree.org/site/PageServer?pagename=ter_key_health_picky

Zervigon-Hakes, A. (1984). Materials mastery and symbolic development in construction play: Stages of development. *Early Child Development and Care, 17,* 37–47.

Zhang, L., Li, X., Kaljee, L., Fang, X., Lin, X., Zhao, G., et al. (2009). "I felt I have grown up as an adult":

Caregiving experience of children affected by HIV/AIDS in China. *Child: Care, Health, and Development, 35*(4), 542–550.

Zhou, Q., Eisenberg, N., Losoya, S. H., Fabes, R. A., Reiser, M., Guthrie, I. K., et al. (2002). The relations of parental warmth and positive expressiveness to children's empathy-related responding and social functioning: A longitudinal study. *Child Development, 73,* 893–915.

Ziegert, D. I., Kistner, J. A., Castro, R., & Robertson, B. (2001). Longitudinal study of young children's responses to challenging achievement situations. *Child Development, 72,* 609–624.

Ziegert, J. C., & Hanges, P. J. (2005). Employment discrimination: The role of implicit attitudes, motivation, and a climate or racial bias. *Journal of Applied Psychology, 90,* 553–562.

Ziegler, S. G. (1987). Effects of stimulus cueing on the acquisition of groundstrokes by beginning tennis players. *Journal of Applied Behavior Analysis, 20,* 405–411.

Zigler, E. (2003). Forty years of believing in magic is enough. *Social Policy Report, 17*(1), 10. Ann Arbor, MI: Society for Research in Child Development.

Zigler, E., & Styfco, S. J. (2010). *The hidden history of Head Start.* New York: Oxford University Press.

Zigler, E. F., & Finn-Stevenson, M. (1992). Applied developmental psychology. In M. H. Bornstein & M. E. Lamb (Eds.), *Developmental psychology: An advanced textbook.* Hillsdale, NJ: Erlbaum.

Zigmond, N., Kloo, A., & Volonino, V. (2009). What, where, and how? Special education in the climate of full inclusion. *Exceptionality, 17,* 189–204.

Zilberstein, K., & Messer, E. A. (2010). Building a secure base: Treatment of a child with disorganized attachment. *Clinical Social Work Journal, 38*(1), 85–97.

Zill, N., Nord, C., & Loomis, L. (1995, September). *Adolescent time use, risky behavior, and outcomes: An analysis of national data.* Rockville, MD: Westat.

Zimmerman, B. J. (2004). Sociocultural influence and students' development of academic self-regulation: A social-cognitive perspective. In D. M. McInerney & S. Van Etten (Eds.), *Big theories revisited* (pp. 139–164). Greenwich, CT: Information Age.

Zimmerman, B. J., & Cleary, T. J. (2009). Motives to self-regulate learning. In K. R. Wentzel & A. Wigfield (Eds.), *Handbook of motivation at school* (pp. 247–264). New York: Routledge.

Zimmerman, B. J., & Risemberg, R. (1997). Self-regulatory dimensions of academic learning and motivation. In G. D. Phye (Ed.), *Handbook of academic learning: Construction of knowledge.* San Diego, CA: Academic Press.

Zimmerman, B. J., & Schunk, D. H. (2004). Self-regulating intellectual processes and outcomes; A social cognitive perspective. In D. Y. Dai & R. J. Sternberg (Eds.), *Motivation, emotion, and cognition: Integrative perspectives on intellectual functioning and development* (pp. 323–349). Mahwah, NJ: Erlbaum.

Zimmerman, C. (2007). The development of scientific thinking skills in elementary and middle school. *Developmental Review, 27,* 172–223.

Zosuls, K. M., Ruble, D. N., Tamis-LeMonda, C. S., Shrout, P. E., Bornstein, M. H., & Greulich, F. K. (2009). The acquisition of gender labels in infancy: Implications for gender-typed play. *Developmental Psychology, 45*(3), 688–701.

Zuckerman, G. A. (1994). A pilot study of a ten-day course in cooperative learning for beginning Russian first graders. *Elementary School Journal, 94,* 405–420.

Zuckerman, M. U. (2007). *Sensation seeking and risky behavior.* Washington, DC: American Psychological Association.

Subject Index

Abecedarian Program, 308
Absolute pitch, 409
Abstract thought
  brain development and, 160, 162, 167
  cognitive-developmental theories and, 15
  formal operations stage and, 203, 205
  language development and, 335
  mathematics and, 390
  observations of, 212
  science and, 399, 402
  social skills and, 576
Academic achievement
  attention-deficit hyperactivity disorder and, 279–280
  culture and, 69, 351
  elaboration and, 258
  ethnic identity and, 472
  family involvement and, 81
  family structure and, 72, 77
  gender and, 510–511
  intelligence tests and, 294, 299
  IQ scores and, 304
  learning disabilities and, 279
  motivation and, 519–520, 521
  parenting styles and, 79, 80
  part-time employment and, 602
  peer relationships and, 570
  physical activity and, 175
  rest and sleep, 179
  school readiness tests and, 302
  second language development and, 355
  self-regulated learning and, 268
  sense of community and, 594
  sense of self and, 461
  socialization in schools and, 598
  social skills and, 571
Academic domains. See also Mathematics; Reading; Science; Writing
  art, 407–408, 409, 410, 411
  case studies, 369
  cognitive tools and, 226
  developmental issues and, 410
  development in, 403–409
  discovery learning and, 211
  epistemic beliefs and, 264
  gender and, 510, 511
  intrinsic motivation and, 501–503
  music, 408–409, 410, 411
  neo-Piagetian theories and, 209
  social studies, 404–407, 410, 411
  standards in, 411–412
Accommodation
  definition of, 197
  Piaget's cognitive development theory and, 197–198, 246
Acculturation, 95
Achievement goals, 504–505

Action research
  definition of, 59
  ethical conduct and, 60, 62–63
  professional practice and, 59–60, 62
Activity level, and temperament, 443, 445–446
Actual developmental level, 218, 300
Acupuncture, 136
Adaptation, 197–198, 285, 292
Adaptive behavior, 319
Addiction, 182, 184
Adolescence. See also Early adolescence; Late adolescence
  art and, 408
  attachment and, 424, 429, 432
  brain development and, 159–160, 182
  cortex and, 159, 167
  depression and, 450
  eating disorders and, 173
  egocentrism and, 202n
  emotional development and, 436–437, 438
  epistemic beliefs and, 263–264
  Erikson's psychosocial stages and, 419
  handwriting and, 383
  idealism and, 202n, 205
  identity versus role confusion and, 419, 420
  initiation ceremonies, 161
  language development and, 339, 346
  learned helplessness and, 509
  long-term goals and, 516
  mathematics and, 390
  metacognitive awareness and, 261–262
  peer relationships and, 424, 571, 576
  physical activity and, 175–176
  physical needs of, 168
  reading development and, 374, 379
  rest and sleep, 178–179
  science and, 399
  self-regulation and, 525–526
  sense of self and, 460, 461
  theory theory and, 275
  thinking/reasoning skills and, 252
  writing and, 382–384
Adolescent parents, 77
Adoption, 76, 78
Adoption studies, 305–306, 307, 309
Adult activities, participation in, 224–225
Adults and adulthood
  attributions and, 510
  children's interacting with, 349, 350
  Erikson's psychosocial stages and, 419
  long-term memory and, 249
  postformal stage and, 205–206
  sense of self and, 460
  social construction of meaning and, 222

social perspective taking and, 484
  Vygotsky's cognitive development theory and, 214, 215, 216–217, 219, 234
advisers, 24
Affective states, 434. See also Emotions
African American English, 361, 361n
African Americans
  confidence-building strategies of, 98
  dialects and, 361, 361n
  ethnic identity and, 470
  IQ scores and, 311
  motivation and, 511
  narratives and, 346
  playing the dozens, 346
  reading and, 378–379
  sense of self and, 468
  sociolinguistic behaviors and, 349, 350, 351
Afterbirth, 137
After-school programs, 104, 106, 584, 601–603
Age of Empires, 605–606
Aggression
  bioecology of, 552, 554–557
  child care and, 601
  conduct disorder and, 451
  correlational studies and, 47
  curbing aggressive impulses, 557–560
  definition of, 548
  developmental issues of, 557
  development of, 549–552
  documentation of, 559
  emotional development and, 424, 439
  experimental studies and, 46
  gangs and, 563
  gender and, 469, 552
  longitudinal studies of, 48
  naturalistic studies and, 49
  parenting styles and, 80
  psychodynamic theories and, 14
  reactive aggression, 551, 554, 559–560
  rejected children and, 578, 590
  relational aggression, 549, 551, 555, 556, 559, 561
  rest and sleep, 179
  shame and, 540
  television and, 47, 604, 606
Agreeableness, 444, 447
AIDS/HIV, 128, 129, 131, 182, 184, 512, 588
Alcohol
  brain development and, 156
  fetal alcohol syndrome, 129, 162, 306–307, 319
  health-compromising behavior and, 181–182
  self-handicapping and, 459
  as teratogen, 128, 129, 132
Alice's Adventures in Wonderland (Carroll), 354
Alleles, 117
Alphabet Adventure (Wood & Wood), 372
Alternative therapies, 136

Altruism, 543, 552
Amelia Bedelia Goes Camping (Parish), 353–354
American Alliance for Health, Physical Education, Recreation and Dance, 189
American Athletic Association for the Deaf, 189
American Sign Language, 347, 356, 364, 377, 589
Amish, 159–160, 538
Amniocentesis, 130–131
Amusia, 409
Analgesics, 138–139
Analysis, and left hemisphere, 155
Analytical intelligence, 292, 293
Anecdotal records, 57, 58
Anesthetics, 139
Angelman syndrome, 118
Anger, 424, 430, 434, 436, 438, 441
Anorexia nervosa, 173
Anxiety
  birth and, 134
  definition of, 441
  emotional development and, 435, 441
  emotional problems and, 452
  prenatal development and, 129
  puberty and, 168
  stranger anxiety, 423, 436
Anxiety disorders, 450
Apgar Scale, 301
Apprenticeships, 224–225
Appropriation, 218
Arab Americans, 349–350
Arousal system, 246
Art, 407–408, 409, 410, 411
Articulation, 362
Asian Americans
  attachments and, 428
  birth and, 139
  culture and, 69
  IQ scores and, 311
  mathematics and, 394
  metacognition and, 265
  motivation and, 511
  parenting styles and, 80, 88
  self-regulation and, 524–525
  sociolinguistic behaviors and, 350
Asperger's syndrome, 486
Assessment of learning potential, 300
Assessments. See also Observations
  cultural bias in, 54
  as data collection technique, 41–42
  definition of, 42
  developmental assessments, 300–302
  dynamic assessment, 299–300
  interpretation of, 53–54
Assimilation (cognitive)
  definition of, 95n, 197, 197n
  Piaget's cognitive development theory and, 197–198, 246n
Assimilation (culture), definition of, 95, 95n, 96, 197n

Associations, and research design, 47
Associative play, 573
Astrocytes, 154, 156n, 157
Athletics. See Organized sports
Attachment-in-the-making, 422
Attachments
  attachment security and later development, 429–430
  bioecology of, 425–428
  definition of, 421
  developmental course of, 422–423
  developmental issues and, 442
  emotional development and, 421–433
  individual differences in, 424–425
  multiple attachments, 428–429, 432–433
  research implications, 430–433
  sense of self and, 467
Attention
  developmentally appropriate practice and, 254
  distractions and, 246–247, 252–253
  information processing theories and, 244, 246–247, 270
  joint attention, 270, 330, 463
  language development and, 328–329
  learning disabilities and, 279
  observation of, 278
  purposeful nature of, 247
  stimuli and, 246, 246n, 252, 253
Attention-deficit hyperactivity disorder (ADHD), 279–280, 317, 486, 510
Attribution retraining, 519
Attributions
  culture and, 512
  definition of, 507
  development of, 507–510
  gender and, 511
  motivation and, 507–510, 517, 519
  origins of, 509–510
Audience
  composition skills and, 384
  imaginary audience, 465, 482
Auditory processing, 288
Australia, 488
Authentic activities
  definition of, 228
  science and, 402–403
  sociocultural theories and, 16
  writing and, 228, 230, 387
Authoritarian parenting style
  aggression and, 554
  definition of, 80
Authoritative parenting style
  definition of, 80
  prosocial behavior and, 554, 556
Authority figures, behavior towards, 101
Autism
  giftedness and, 317
  language development and, 362
  motor skills and, 164